Langenscheidt
Pocket Dictionary

Korean

Korean – English
English – Korean

Langenscheidt

Compiled by LEXUS Ltd.

Neither the presence nor the absence of a designation indicating that any entered word constitutes a trademark should be regarded as affecting the legal status thereof.

1. Auflage 2022 (1,01 - 2022)
© PONS GmbH, Stöckachstraße 11, 70190 Stuttgart 2022
All Rights Reserved.

www.langenscheidt.com

Print: Druckerei C. H. Beck Nördlingen
Printed in Germany

ISBN 978-3-12-514459-0

Preface

Here is a new dictionary of English and Korean, a tool with some 40,000 references for those who work with the English and Korean languages at beginner's or intermediate level.

Focusing on modern usage, the dictionary offers coverage of everyday language, including vocabulary from areas such as computers and business.

The Korean in this dictionary is written both in Korean script and in a romanized pronunciation system - a specially modified version of McCune-Reischauer.

The two sides of this dictionary, the English-Korean and the Korean-English, are quite different in structure and purpose. The English-Korean is designed for productive usage, for self-expression in Korean. The Korean-English is a decoding dictionary, a dictionary to enable the native speaker of English to understand Korean.

Clarity of presentation has been a major objective. The editors have provided the means to enable you, the user of the dictionary, to get straight to the translation that fits a particular context of use. Is the *mouse* you need for your computer, for example, the same in Korean as the *mouse* you don't want in the house? Is *flimsy* referring to furniture the same in Korean as *flimsy* referring to an excuse? The English-Korean dictionary is rich in sense distinctions like this – and in translation options tied to specific, identified senses.

Grammatical or function words are treated in some detail, on both the English-Korean and the Korean-English sides. And a large number of idiomatic phrases are given to show how the two languages correspond in context.

All in all, this is a book full of information, which will, we hope, become a valuable part of your language toolkit.

Contents

How to use the dictionary 5

Korean personal pronouns 12

The pronunciation of Korean 15

Abbreviations 20

Korean-English 21

English-Korean 291

Numbers 671

How to use the dictionary

To get the most out of your dictionary you should understand how and where to find the information you need. Whether you are yourself writing a text in Korean or wanting to understand a text in Korean, the following pages should help.

1. How and where do I find a word?

1.1 English headwords. The English word list is arranged in alphabetical order.

Sometimes you might want to look up terms made up of two separate words, for example **antivirus program**, or hyphenated words, for example **absent-minded**. These words are treated as though they were a single word and their alphabetical ordering reflects this. Compound words like **bookseller**, **bookstall**, **bookstore** are also listed in alphabetical order.

The only exception to this strict alphabetical ordering is made for English phrasal verbs - words like ♦**go off**, ♦**go out**, ♦**go up**. These are positioned directly after their main verb (in this case **go**), rather than being scattered around in alphabetical positions.

1.2 Korean headwords. The Korean word list is arranged in English alphabetical order by being sorted on the romanization system. The Hangul romanization chart on pages 15-19 will help with this.

You will need to remember the following special points about the alphabetical ordering of the Hangul romanization system:

i) ŏ and ŭ are each treated as separate vowels and are listed before o and u respectively

ii) words starting with ch' are listed after words starting with ch

iii) words starting with k' are listed after words starting with k

iv) words starting with p' are listed after words starting with p

v) words starting with t' are listed after words starting with t

vi) when an apostrophe occurs within a word it is handled as coming after z, so, for example, a typical sequence is:

choripsshigŭi 조립식의 prefabricated
chorip tanwi 조립 단위 module
chorip'ada 조립하다 assemble, set up

vii) romanization can change according to the position of a Korean letter in a word. So, for example, the *p* in

ip 입 mouth

will become a *b* in

ibŭl tamulda 입을 다물다 clam up, keep silent

This means that some phrases in an entry may have a romanization that differs from the main headword. And some compound words may be listed at some distance from the headword.

The chart on pages 15-19 shows which letters are liable to these changes.

viii) Some commonly used phrases or expressions are entered in their alphabetical position rather than under the main term from which they are derived. For example:

majayo! 맞아요! that's it!, that's right!

will be found under maj... and not under

mat-tta 맞다 be right

ix) Some roman letters (including: b, d, g, j, r,) are not used to start words in the romanization system used in this dictionary. However, important suffixes or infixes may begin with some of these letters. These suffixes and infixes have been listed in a block at the end of the preceding letter of the roman alphabet. For example:

...dŏrado ...더라도 even though

is listed in a block at the end of letter C (since there is no letter D).

1.3 Running heads. If you are looking for an English or a Korean word you can use the **running heads** printed in bold in the top corner of each page. The running head on the left tells you the *first* headword on the left-hand page and the one on the right tells you the *last* headword on the right-hand page.

2. Swung dashes

2.1 A swung dash (~) replaces the entire headword when the
headword is repeated within an entry:

> **sly** kyohwarhan 교활한; **on the** ~ nam mollae saltchak
> 남 몰래 살짝

Here **on the** ~ means **on the sly**.

2.2 When a headword changes form in an entry, for example if
it is put in the past tense or in the plural, then the past tense
or plural ending is added to the swung dash - but only if the
rest of the word doesn't change:

> **fluster** *v/t* tanghwanghage hada 당황하게 하다; **get ~ed**
> tanghwanghada 당황하다

But:

> **horrify**: *I was horrified* ch'unggyŏktchŏgiŏssŏyo
> 충격적이었어요

> ◆**come back** toraoda 돌아오다; *it came back to me*
> tashi saenggangnassŏ 다시 생각났어

2.3 Headwords made up of two, or sometimes three, words are
replaced by a single swung dash:

> ◆**hold on** *v/i* (*wait*) kidarida 기다리다; TELEC
> kkŭntchiank'o it-tta 끊지않고 있다; *now ~ a minute!*
> chamkkanman kidaryŏ poseyo! 잠깐만 기다려 보세요!

> ◆**come in on**: ~ *a deal* kŏraee ch'amgahada 거래에
> 참가하다

3. What do the different typefaces mean?

3.1 All Korean and English headwords and the Arabic numerals differentiating English parts of speech appear in **bold**:

> **alcoholic 1** *n* alk'o-ol chungdoktcha 알코올 중독자
> **2** *adj* alk'o-olssŏng-ŭi 알코올성의

3.2 *italics* are used for:

a) abbreviated grammatical labels: *adj, adv, v/i, v/t* etc

b) all the indicating words which are the signposts pointing
to the correct translation for your needs

> **mailbox** (*in street*) uch'et'ong 우체통; (*of house*)
> up'yŏnham 우편함; COMPUT meilbakssŭ 메일박스

Thai 1 *adj* T'aegugŭi 태국의 **2** *n* (*person*) T'aegugin
태국인; (*language*) T'aegugŏ 태국어

serve 1 *n* (*in tennis*) sŏbŭ 서브 **2** *v/t food, meal* naeda
내다; *person, guests* shijungdŭlda 시중들다; *customer in
shop* moshida 모시다; *one's country, the people*
pongsahada 봉사하다

hwamulsshil 화물실 hold (*on ship, plane*)

yŏbo 여보 honey (*form of address to husband*)

3.3 All phrases (examples and idioms) are given in ***secondary
bold italics***:

ch'aegim 책임 responsibility; accountability; ***...e
ch'aegimi it-tta*** ...에 책임이 있다 be responsible for

knowledge chishik 지식; ***to the best of my ~*** naega algo
itkkironŭn 내가 알고 있기로는; ***have a good ~ of*** ...e
chŏngt'onghada ...에 정통하다

3.4 Normal typeface is used for the translations.

3.5 If a translation is given in italics, and not in the normal
typeface, this means that the translation is more of an
explanation in the other language and that an explanation
has to be given because there is no real equivalent:

walk-up *n* ellibeit'ŏga ŏmnŭn ap'at'ŭ 엘리베이터가 없는
아파트

kkakttugi 깍두기 *spicy, pickled white radish*

4. What do the various symbols and abbreviations tell you?

4.1 A solid black lozenge is used to indicate a phrasal verb:

♦**auction off** kyŏngmaehada 경매하다

4.2 A white lozenge ◊ is used to divide up longer entries into
more easily digested chunks of related bits of text:

a, an ◊ (*no equivalent in Korean*): ***a book about Korea***
Han-guge kwanhan ch'aek 한국에 관한 책; ***he bought
a car*** kŭnŭn ch'arŭl sassŏyo 그는 차를 샀어요 ◊ (*with
a measure word*) hanaŭi 하나의, han 한; ***a cup of coffee***
k'ŏp'i han chan 커피 한 잔; ***five men and a woman***
tasŏt namjawa han yŏja 다섯 남자와 한 여자 ◊ (*per*)
han 한; ***$50 a ride*** han pŏne 50tallŏ 한 번에 50달러;
$15 a head han saram tang 15tallŏ 한 사람 당 15달러

It is also used, in the Korean-English dictionary, to split translations within an entry when the part of speech of each translation is different:

kŭndae 근대 modern times ◊ modern

kŏmsa 검사 examination (*of patient*); prosecutor ◊ exploratory

4.3 The abbreviation F tells you that the word or phrase is used colloquially rather than in formal contexts. The abbreviation V warns you that a word or phrase is vulgar or taboo. Be careful how you use these words. The abbreviation H means that the word is used to make yourself humble before the person you are speaking to.

4.4 A colon before an English or Korean word or phrase means that usage is restricted to this specific example (at least as far as this dictionary's choice of vocabulary is concerned):

accord: *of one's own* ~ chabaltchŏguro 자발적으로

shisok 시속: *shisok 150mairŭi sokttoro* 시속 150마일의 속도로 at a speed of 150 mph

4.5 The letters X and Y are used to indicate insertion points for other words if you are building a complete sentence in Korean, for example:

glue 1 *n* p'ul 풀 **2** *v/t* p'ullo puch'ida 풀로 붙이다; ~ *X to Y* Xŭl / rŭl Ye p'ullo puch'ida X을 / 를 Y에 풀로 붙이다

Suspension points (...) are used in a similar way:

♦ **major in** ...ŭl/rŭl chŏn-gonghada ...을 / 를 전공하다

5. Does the dictionary deal with grammar too?

5.1 All English headwords are given a part of speech label, unless, in normal modern English, the headword is only used as one part of speech and so no confusion or ambiguity is possible. In these cases no part of speech label is needed.

abolish p'yejihada 폐지하다

lastly majimagŭro 마지막으로

But:

glory *n* yŏnggwang 영광 (*n* given because 'glory' could be a verb)

own[1] *v/t* soyuhada 소유하다 (*v/t* given because 'own' is also an adjective)

5.2 Korean headwords are not given part of speech labels. Where their English translations are of more than one part of speech, these are separated by a white lozenge. For example:

Sŏyang 서양 the West ◊ Western

5.3 Where a Korean word has a grammatical function, this is illustrated:

...nŭn ...는 (*forms adjectives*): **nurŏputtchiannŭn** 눌어붙지 않는 nonstick

...rŭl ...를 *object particle*

...get... ...겠... shall (*indicates future tense, intention, or supposition*)

5.4 Particles

Particles such as **...rŭl** ...를, **...ŭl** ...을 or **...e** ...에 are included with translations in the English-Korean half of the dictionary:

correspond ... ~ *to* ...e haedanghada ...에 해당하다

♦**count on** ...ege kidaeda ...에게 기대다

infer: ~ *X from Y* Yesŏ Xŭl / rŭl ch'uronhada Y에서 X을 / 를 추론하다

This shows you the ending that is needed when you are building a sentence in Korean.

Some particle endings have more than one version. For example, **ŭl** is used after consonants and **rŭl** after vowels.

These particles are mostly omitted on the Korean-English side of the dictionary.

6. hada 하다

In the English-Korean dictionary an appropriate form of the verb **hada** 하다 'to do' is used to mark the insertion point for any verb that would be used in a real sentence. For example:

when... 2 *conj* ...hal ttae ...할 때

about ... *be* ~ *to* ... mak ...haryŏgo hada 막 ...하려고 하다

can[1] ◊ (*ability*) ...hal su it-tta ...할 수 있다

These forms are used to show a general structure, which, in a particular example, may become, say:

> *can you hear me?* nae marŭl tŭrŭl su issŏyo? 내 말을 들을 수 있어요?

In the Korean-English part of the dictionary, the verb **hada** is removed in such cases and only the element which would be common to any verbal insertion is left:

> **ttae** ... *-l ttae* -ㄹ 때 when

> **su** 수: *...l su it-tta* ...ㄹ 수 있다 can; *...l su ŏptta* ...ㄹ 수 없다 cannot

7. English adjectives and Korean descriptive verbs

In general the English-Korean dictionary will give an adjectival form that corresponds to an English adjective. For example:

> **pretty** yeppŭn 예쁜

In Korean these adjectives are formed from "descriptive verbs". The form of the descriptive verb that corresponds to an English adjective is made by adding **n** ㄴ to the verb stem:

> **yeppŭ** 예쁘 + ㄴ = 예쁜 pretty

Where in English "is pretty" is formed from the verb "be" + the adjective "pretty", in Korean it is formed by the single descriptive verb **yeppŭda** 예쁘다 be pretty.

> **that little girl is wearing a very pretty hat**
> chŏ chagŭn yŏja aiga aju yeppŭn mojarŭl ssŏssŏyo
> 저 작은 여자 아이가 아주 예쁜 모자를 썼어요

> **those flowers are really pretty**
> 저꽃이 참 예뻐요
> chŏ kkoch'i ch'am yeppŏyo

Korean personal pronouns

As a result of Confucian cultural influence on Korean society and language, personal pronouns and the way in which they are used in Korean reflect a concern for relative seniority and status. There is a large variety of forms of pronouns. The following table provides a basic outline (but is not exhaustive).

	I	you	she / he
plain	na / nae 나 / 내	nŏ / ne 너 / 네	i / kŭ / chŏ saram 이 / 그 / 저 사람
humble	chŏ / che 저 / 제		
honorific		sŏnsaeng(nim); 선생(님); tangshin 당신	i- / kŭ- / chŏ-bun 이 / 그 / 저분

	we	you	they
plain	uri 우리	nŏhŭi(dŭl) 너희(들)	i / kŭ / chŏ saramdŭl 이 / 그 / 저 사람들
humble	chŏhŭi(dŭl) 저희(들)		
honorific		sŏnsaeng(nim)dŭl 선생(님)들	i- / kŭ- / chŏ-bundŭl 이 / 그 / 저분들

I

When referring to oneself before equals and juniors the plain form **na** 나 may be used (**nae** 내 with the subject particle **ka** 가). When speaking to an older person or someone in seniority, the humble term **chŏ** 저 is used (**che** 제 with the subject particle **ka** 가).

You (singular)

The term **nŏ** 너 (**ne** 네 with the subject particle **ka** 가) may only be used by adults to young children, by older siblings to younger siblings or between intimate friends.

Although **tangshin** 당신 is considered a respectful form of *you*, its use is somewhat restricted and it should definitely not be used when speaking to older people. Koreans generally avoid using *you* when speaking to people with whom they are not familiar and address each other with appropriate titles such as **sŏnsaengnim** 선생님 (sir, a polite form), **ajŏsshi** 아저씨 (used to address men), **ajumma** 아줌마 (used to address women), **samonim** 사모님 (madam, a polite form), and so on. Actual job titles can also be used as a form of address together with the honorific ending **nim** 님. For instance you could address someone as 'doctor, taxi-driver, professor, manager etc'.

She / he

These forms are not really simple pronouns but a combination of the demonstrative forms **i** 이 (this), **kŭ** 그 (that), and **chŏ** 저 (that over there) and the words **saram** 사람 (person) and **pun** 분 (*respectful* person). The terms **i** 이, **kŭ** 그, and **chŏ** 저 may also be used with other words such as **yŏja** 여자 (woman), **agasshi** 아가씨 (young lady), **ajŏsshi** 아저씨 (uncle) and so on to form alternative equivalents to *she/he* in English. They may also be used with the word **kŏt** 것 (thing) to form the demonstrative pronouns *this*, *that*, and *that over there*. The terms **kŭnŭn** 그는 and **kŭnyŏnŭn** 그녀는 are also used in written Korean to indicate *he* and *she* respectively.

We

Korean also uses **uri** 우리 and derivatives where English uses *I* or *my* etc:

uri abŏji 우리 아버지 my father (literally: our father)

This reflects the tendency for Koreans to emphasize the group over the individual.

You (plural)

The same as *you* (singular) with the addition of the plural suffix **-dŭl** 들. The same restrictions on usage also apply.

They

The same as *she/he* with the addition of the plural suffix **-dul** 들.

Finally, it is important to remember that, in Korean, the subject of a sentence is often omitted, providing that context removes any ambiguity.

Here are some examples of the use and omission of personal pronouns in Korean:

ŏdi kaseyo?
어디가세요
where are you going? (*you* omitted)

hak-kkyo-e kassŏyo
학교에 갔어요
I / he / she / we / they went to school (subject omitted)

ajŏsshi, naeil Sŏure kaseyo?
아저씨, 내일 서울에 가세요?
are you going to Seoul tomorrow? (ajŏsshi used in place of *you*)

nega haenni?
네가 했니?
did you do it? (adult to a child; *it* omitted)

kŭbuni osyŏssŏyo
그분이 오셨어요
he came (use of the honorific form, showing respect)

kwajangnim, k'ŏp'i han chan hashigessŏyo?
과장님, 커피 한 잔 하시겠어요?
would you like a cup of coffee? (kwajangnim is a common title for a department manager)

The pronunciation of Korean

Vowels

ㅏ	a	as in c*a*t
		longer as in f*a*ther when coming at the end of a word or when coming before a syllable that starts with a vowel or a *y* (eg: **ch'uk'ayŏn** 축하연)
ㅓ	ŏ	a short *o* sound as in fa*u*lt or the British pronunciation of n*o*t
ㅗ	o	a longer *o* sound as in *o*we
ㅜ	u	as in d*o*
ㅡ	ŭ	a short sound as in heav*e*n
ㅣ	i	a short *i* as in t*i*n
		longer as in s*ee* when coming at the end of a word or when coming before a syllable starting with a vowel or a *y* (eg: **p'iano** 피아노)
ㅐ	ae	as in b*ea*r or h*ai*ry but without any *r* sound
ㅔ	e	as in *e*delweiss
ㅑ	ya	as in *ya*m
		as in *ya*rd but without the *r* sound when it comes at the end of a word or before a vowel or before the letter *h*
ㅕ	yŏ	as in *Yo*rk but without the *r* sound
ㅛ	yo	as in *yo*del
ㅠ	yu	as in *you*
ㅒ	yae	as in *yea*h
ㅖ	ye	as in *Ya*le
ㅘ	wa	as in abatt*oir*
ㅙ	wae	as in *whe*re

ᅬ	oe	as in *way* but sometimes shorter as in *whe*n
ᅯ	wŏ	as in *wa*sh
ᅰ	we	as in *way*
ᅱ	wi	as in *wi*nd
		longer as in *wee* when coming at the end of a word or when coming before a syllable that starts with a vowel or a *y* (eg: **kwiyŏun** 귀여운)
ᅴ	ŭi	officially pronounced uh-ee; but Koreans often say this as in Y*a*le

Consonants

ᄀ	at the start and the end of a word	k	강 kang 시작 shijak	between a *k* and a *g*
	vowel + ᄀ + vowel	g	가구 kagu	
	ㄴ,ㄹ,ㅁ,ㅇ + ᄀ + vowel	g	설계도 sŏlgyedo	
ㄴ		n	나 na	
ㄷ	at the start and the end of a word	t	달 tal 곧 kot	between a *t* and a *d*
	vowel + ㄷ + vowel	d	바둑 paduk	
	ㄴ, ㄹ, ㅁ, ㅇ + ㄷ + vowel	d	날다 nalda	
ㄹ	at the start of a word	l	라디오 ladio	for loan words, it is between an *l* and an *r*; we have used an *l*
	at the end of a word	l	달 tal	
	vowel + ㄹ + vowel	r	사랑 sarang	
	ㄹ + consonant	l	물건 mulgŏn	
ㅁ		m	밤 pam	

→

ㅂ	at the start and the end of a word	p	보리 pori 밥 pap	between a *p* and a *b*
	vowel + ㅂ + vowel	b	아버지 abŏji	
	ㄴ, ㄹ, ㅁ, ㅇ + ㅂ + vowel	b	담배 tambae	
ㅅ		s	상표 sangp'yo	as in *s*aint
	ㅅ + ㅣ, ㅒ, ㅑ, ㅕ, ㅛ, ㅠ, ㅖ, ㅟ	sh	신 shin 섀시 shyaeshi 쉬다 shwida	
	at the end of a word	t	것 kŏt	
ㅇ	at the start of a word	silent	아버지 abŏji	a filler letter
	at the end of a word	ng	자랑 charang	as in you*ng*
ㅈ	at the start of a word	ch	자유 chayu	as in *j*ade but between a *ch* and a *j*
	at the end of a word	t	낮 nat	
	vowel + ㅈ + vowel	j	자주 chaju	
	ㄴ, ㄹ, ㅁ, ㅇ + ㅈ + vowel	j	반지 panji	
ㅊ		ch'	차 ch'a	as in *ch*urch but pronounced more strongly
	at the end of a word	t	닻 tat	
ㅋ		k'	코 k'o	as in *k*ing, but pronounced more strongly
	at the end of a word	k	부엌 puŏk	as in coo*k*

→

ㅌ		t'	타다 t'ada	as in *t*errace, but pronounced more strongly
	at the end of a word	t	논밭 nonbat	as in fla*t*
ㅍ		p'	파란 p'aran	as in *p*opstar, but pronounced more strongly
	at the end of a word	p	입 ip	as in hi*p*
ㅎ	at the start of a word	h	하늘 hanŭl	as in *h*ello

The four consonants ch', k', t' and p' (known as aspirated consonants) are pronounced with a stronger puff of breath than their basic equivalents (ch, k, t and p). If you hold your palm in front of your face when speaking these consonants you should be able to feel your breath.

Double consonants

These are also known as 'tense consonants'. They are pronounced with more force than their single equivalents.

ㄲ	kk	깨다 kkaeda	as in book *k*eeper
ㄸ	tt	때 ttae	as in hit *t*en
ㅃ	pp	빠른 (pparŭn)	as in top *p*eople
ㅆ	ss	쌀 (ssal)	as in those *s*ongs
ㅉ	tch	짜르다 (tcharŭda)	as in that *j*udge

General notes on the pronunciation system

Double vowels are each given their full value. So, for example, **p'yeam** is pronounced 'p'yay-am' and **uul** is pronounced 'oo-ool'.

g is always as in *g*ive, not as in *g*in
s is always as in loo*s*e, not as in lo*s*e

There is no stress in Korean, so give equal weight to all syllables.

What is written and what is said

There are many combinations of Korean consonants or of

vowels plus consonants that, taken together, create a sound that is not reflected in the actual Korean script. So, for example, in:

관점 **kwantchŏm** point of view
the letter ㅈ (ch/j) is actually pronounced ㅉ (tch)

맞다 **mat-tta** be right
the letter ㄷ (t) is actually pronounced ㄸ (tt)

고압선용 철탑 **koapssŏnnyong ch'ŏlt'ap** electricity pylon
the letter 용 (yong) is actually pronounced 뇽 (nyong)

학교 **hak-kkyo** school
the letter ㄱ (k/g) is actually pronounced ㄲ (kk)

괴롭히다 **koerop'ida** trouble
the letter ㅂ (p/b) is actually pronounced ㅍ (p')

괜찮다 **kwaench'ant'a** be OK, be alright
the letters 찮 (ch'an) and 다 (ta) are actually pronounced ch'ant'a

The romanization system used in this dictionary reflects this feature of Korean pronunciation.

Abbreviations

adj	adjective	MIL	military
adv	adverb	MOT	motoring
ANAT	anatomy	MUS	music
BIO	biology	*n*	noun
BOT	botany	NAUT	nautical
Br	British English	*pej*	pejorative
CHEM	chemistry	PHOT	photography
COM	commerce, business	PHYS	physics
		POL	politics
COMPUT	computers, IT term	*prep*	preposition
conj	conjunction	*pron*	pronoun
EDU	education	PSYCH	psychology
ELEC	electricity, electronics	RAD	radio
		RAIL	railroad
euph	euphemistic	REL	religion
F	familiar, colloquial	s.o.	someone
fig	figurative	SP	sports
FIN	financial	sth	something
fml	formal usage	TECH	technology
GRAM	grammar	TELEC	telecommunications
H	humble, showing humility to the listener	THEA	theater
		TV	television
		V	vulgar
hum	humorous	*v/i*	intransitive verb
interj	interjection	*v/t*	transitive verb
LAW	law	→	see
MATH	mathematics	®	registered trademark
MED	medicine		

A

aak 아악 court music
aboji 아버지 father
ach'i 아치 arch
ach'im 아침 morning; breakfast;
ach'ime 아침에 in the morning;
ach'imŭl mŏkta 아침을 먹다 have
breakfast
ach'ŏm 아첨 flattery
ach'ŏmhada 아첨하다 flatter, butter
up
ach'ŏmhanŭn 아첨하는 flattering
ach'ŏmkkun 아첨꾼 flatterer;
yesman
adamhan 아담한 compact; small
adongbok 아동복 children's clothes
adŭl 아들 son; boy
aech'ŏroun 애처로운 pathetic;
touching
aedo 애도 condolences
aeguk-kka 애국가 national anthem
aeguksshim 애국심 patriotism
aeguktcha 애국자 patriot
aeguktchŏgin 애국적인 patriotic
aehoga 애호가 fan; devotee;
connoisseur; *ch'a aehoga* 차
애호가 avid tea drinker
aehohada 애호하다 be fond of
aein 애인 lover; sweetheart;
boyfriend; girlfriend
aejijungjihada 애지중지하다 pamper
aejŏng 애정 affection, fondness
aejŏng-i innŭn 애정이 있는 loving
aek 액 fluid
aekch'e 액체 liquid
aekkŭlk'e hanŭn 애끓게 하는
heartbreaking
aekssellŏreit'ŏ 액셀러레이터 gas,
accelerator
aekssellŏreit'ŏ p'edal 액셀러레이터
페달 gas pedal, accelerator
aektchŏng p'yoshi changch'i 액정
표시 장치 LCD, liquid crystal
display
aelbŏm 앨범 (photograph) album

aemaehan 애매한 evasive
aemaemohohan 애매모호한
ambiguous; noncommittal
aemp'ŭ 앰프 amplifier
aemu 애무 caress
aemuhada 애무하다 caress; kiss; pet
aengk'ŏ 앵커 anchor man
aengmusae 앵무새 parrot
aengmyŏnkka 액면가 face value
aengmyŏn kŭmaek 액면 금액
denomination FIN
aenimeishyŏn 애니메이션 animation
aep'ŭt'ŏ shyeibŭ loshyŏn 애프터
세이브 로션 aftershave
aep'ŭt'ŏ sŏbisŭ 애프터 서비스 after
sales service
aerosahang 애로사항 bottleneck;
logjam
aesŏk'ada 애석하다 be regrettable;
...dani aesŏk'agunyo ...다니
애석하군요 it's a pity that ...
aessŭda 애쓰다 make an effort;
*kŭnyŏnŭn ihaeharyŏgo aessŏt-
tta* 그녀는 이해하려고 애썼다 she
was struggling to understand; *...gi
wihae mopsshi aessŭda* ...기 위해
몹시 애쓰다 take great pains to ...
aet'age parada 애타게 바라다 long
for; *muŏt hanŭn kŏsŭl aet'age
parada* 무엇 하는 것을 애타게
바라다 be longing to do sth
aet'ajŏgin 애타적인 altruistic
aet'onghan 애통한 tragic *voice*
aewandongmul 애완동물 pet
(*animal*)
aeyong 애용 patronage, custom
agami 아가미 gill
agasshi 아가씨 ma'am; miss
(*unmarried woman*)
agi 아기 baby
agŏ 악어 alligator; crocodile
agŭi 악의 ill will; malice
agŭiga ŏmnŭn 악의가 없는
inoffensive

agüi innŭn 악의 있는 malevolent; malicious

agüi-ŏmnŭn kŏjinmal 악의없는 거짓말 white lie

agun 악운 bad luck; devil's own luck

agyong 악용 abuse

ahop 아홉 nine

ahop pŏntchaeŭi 아홉 번째의 ninth

ahŭn 아흔 ninety

ahŭn pŏntchaeŭi 아흔 번째의 nintieth

ai 아이 child, kid

aiemep'ŭ 아이엠에프 IMF

aik'on 아이콘 icon COMPUT

aik'yu 아이큐 IQ

Aillaendŭ 아일랜드 Ireland ◊ Irish

airainŏ 아이라이너 eyeliner

airisŭ 아이리스 iris BOT

airŏni 아이러니 irony

aishyaedou 아이섀도우 eyeshadow

aishyop'inghada 아이쇼핑하다 go window-shopping

aisŭ hak'i 아이스 하키 (ice) hockey

aisŭ k'eik'ŭ 아이스 케이크 Popsicle®, ice lolly

aisŭ k'ŏp'i 아이스 커피 iced coffee

aisŭ k'ŭrim 아이스 크림 ice cream

aisŭ k'ŭrim kage 아이스 크림 가게 ice-cream parlor

aisŭ pakssŭ 아이스 박스 icebox, refrigerator

ajaeng 아쟁 (seven-stringed) zither

ajaeng-ajang kŏt-tta 아장아장 걷다 toddle

...ajida ...아지다 become ..., get ...

ajik 아직 yet, so far; *kŭ saramŭn yŏgi wassŏyo? – ajik* 그 사람은 여기 왔어요? – 아직 is he here yet? – not yet

ajikto 아직도 still, even now

ajirang-i 아지랑이 haze

ajŏsshi 아저씨 uncle (*friendly form of address for men who are not actually related*)

aju 아주 extremely, very; completely

aju chohŭn 아주 좋은 amazing, excellent

aju manŭn 아주 많은 a huge amount of

ajumma 아줌마 aunt (*friendly form of address for women who are not actually related*)

ajumoni 아주머니 *polite form of ajumma*

ak 악 evil; vice

akch'wi 악취 stench

akdan 악단 band, group

akkaptta 아깝다 be regrettable

akkida 아끼다 stint on, be mean with; hold dear; *noryŏgŭl akkiji ant'a* 노력을 아끼지 않다 be unstinting in one's efforts

ak-kki 악기 (musical) instrument

ak-kkiŭi ŭmŭl match'uda 악기의 음을 맞추다 tune up

akkyŏ ssŭda 아껴 쓰다 stretch, eke out

akppo 악보 sheet music, score

akssent'ŭ 악센트 accent, stress

akssŏng-ŭi 악성의 malignant *tumor*

akssu 악수 handshake

akssuhada 악수하다 shake hands

aktchang 악장 movement MUS

aktchŏn kot'u 악전 고투 struggle, hard time

akttang 악당 villain, scoundrel

ak'ada 악하다 be evil; be immoral

ak'wa 악화 decline, worsening

ak'wadoeda 악화되다 deteriorate; decline, get worse (*of health*)

ak'washik'ida 악화시키다 aggravate

al 알 egg

alda 알다 know; understand, see; appreciate, acknowledge; be aware of; *naega algo itkkironŭn* 내가 알고 있기로는 to the best of my knowledge; *naega al pa anida* 내가 알 바 아니다 for all I care; *naega alkke mwŏya!* 내가 알게 뭐야! I don't give a damn!; *naega anŭn han* 내가 아는 한 as far as I know; *naega anŭn paronŭn* 내가 아는 바로는 for all I know

algaeng-i 알갱이 grain (*of rice*); *chagŭn algaeng-i* 작은 알갱이 granule

algi shwiun 알기 쉬운 clear, lucid

alk'o-ol 알코올 alcohol

alk'o-ol chungdoktcha 알코올 중독자 alcoholic

alk'o-olssŏng-ŭi 알코올성의 alcoholic

alk'oori ŏmnŭn 알코올이 없는 nonalcoholic

allak 안락 comfort

allak'an 안락한 comfortable

allakssa 안락사 euthanasia

allakssa shik'ida 안락사 시키다 put away, put down *animal*

allak üija 안락 의자 armchair

allanggŏrinŭn 알랑거리는 slimy, smarmy

allerŭgi 알레르기 allergy; *...e allerŭgi panŭng-i it-tta* ...에 알레르기 반응이 있다 be allergic to

allibai 알리바이 alibi

allida 알리다 inform

allim 알림 announcement

alluminyum 알루미늄 aluminum

allyak 알약 tablet

allyŏjida 알려지다 break, become known

allyŏjin 알려진 noted

allyŏjuda 알려주다 inform; *Xege Yrŭl allyŏjuda* X에게 Y를 알려주다 inform X of Y

allyŏjum 알려줌 hint

almajŭn 알맞은 proper, fitting

almat-tta 알맞다 be proper, be fitting

almomŭi 알몸의 nude

alp'abesŭi 알파벳의 alphabetical

alp'abet 알파벳 alphabet

am 암 cancer

ama 아마 probably; perhaps

amach'uŏ 아마추어 layman; amateur

amado 아마도 perhaps, maybe; probably; presumably

amch'o 암초 reef

amdamhan 암담한 dark, grim

Amerik'a 아메리카 America ◊ American

Amerik'a Haptchungguk 아메리카 합중국 United States (of America)

Amerik'ain 아메리카인 American

amgihada 암기하다 memorize

amho 암호 password

amhŭk 암흑 darkness, blackness

amhŭk-kka 암흑가 underworld (*criminal*)

Amit'abul 아미타불 Amitabha Buddha

amk'ae 암캐 bitch (*dog*)

amk'ŏt 암컷 female (*animal, plant*)

ammal 암말 mare

ammŏri 앞머리 fringe (*hair*)

ammun 앞문 front door

amnae 암내 body odor

amnyang 암양 ewe

amnyŏgŭl kahada 압력을 가하다 pressure, force

amnyŏk 압력 pressure

amnyŏk tanch'e 압력 단체 pressure group, lobby

amnyu 압류 seizure, impounding

amnyuhada 압류하다 seize, impound

amnyuri 앞유리: (*chadongch'a*) *amnyuri* (자동차) 앞유리 windshield

amondŭ 아몬드 almond

amp'yosang 암표상 scalper

amsae 암새 hen (*of bird*)

amsal 암살 assassination

amsalbŏm 암살범 assassin

amsalttan 암살단 hit squad

amsan 암산 mental arithmetic

amsarhada 암살하다 assassinate

amshi 암시 pointer; hint

amshihada 암시하다 imply; point to; indicate

amshijang 암시장 black market

amso 암소 cow

amssasŭm 암사슴 doe

amt'ak 암탉 hen (*of chicken*)

amt'waeji 암퇘지 sow

amu 아무 any; none; anyone; so-and-so; *amu ch'yok'ollitto* 아무 쵸콜릿도 (+ *negative verb*) none of the chocolate; *amu kŏktchŏng ŏmnŭn* 아무 걱정 없는 carefree

amudo 아무도 (+ *negative verb*) nobody

amu ...do 아무 ...도 (+ *negative verb*) any ...at all; *amu saenggaktto ŏpsshi* 아무 생각도 없이 without any thought at all; *kŭnŭn amu yŏngojado ŏptta* 그는 아무 연고자도 없다 he doesn't have any family

amugae 아무개 so-and-so; any person

amugaemunja 아무개문자 wildcard character COMPUT

amu kŏt 아무 것 (+ *negative verb*) nothing, not any

amu kot 아무 곳 anywhere

amuri 아무리: *amuri k'ŭda* / *puyuhada hadŏrado* 아무리 크다/부유하다 하더라도 however big/rich they are

amurŏk'e 아무렇게 in whatever way

amurŏk'ena hanŭn 아무렇게나 하는 offhand

amurŏn 아무런 any; *amurŏn chuŭirŭl haji ant'a* 아무런 주의를 하지 않다 not take any notice of

amu ttae 아무 때 any time; *chŏnŭn amu ttaerado chossŭmnida* 저는 아무 때라도 좋습니다 any time is alright with me

amut'ŭn 아무튼 anyway

an 안 inside; ...(*ŭ*)*ro anŭl taeda* ...(으)로 안을 대다 line with; insulate with

an... 안 ... (*negating particle*): *wae hak-kkyoe anwassŏyo?* 왜 학교에 안왔어요? why didn't you come to school?

anae 아내 wife

anaewŏn 안내원 tour operator

anallogŭ 아날로그 analog

ana ollida 안아 올리다 scoop up

anaunsŏ 아나운서 announcer

anbu 안부 (kind) regards; *Minaege anbu chŏnhae chuseyo* 민아에게 안부 전해주세요 give my regards to Mina

ando 안도 relief; *andoŭi hansumŭl shwida* 안도의 한숨을 쉬다 heave a sigh of relief

andwaetkkunyo! 안됐군요! what a pity!; *kŭ yŏjaga andwaetkkunyo* 그 여자가 안됐군요 I feel sorry for her

...ane ...안에 in; *tu shigan ane* 두 시간 안에 in two hours (from now)

anemone 아네모네 snowdrop

...anesŏ ...안에(서) in

an-gae 안개 fog

an-gae kkin 안개 낀 foggy; misty

anggap'ŭmŭl hada 앙갚음을 하다 pay back, get even with

angk'orŭ 앙코르 encore

angma 악마 devil, demon

angmong 악몽 nightmare

angmulda 악물다 clench

angmyŏng nop'ŭn 악명 높은

infamous, notorious

an-gwa ŭisa 안과 의사 ophthalmologist

an-gyŏng 안경 glasses

an-gyŏngsang 안경상 optician

anida 아니다 be not; no; *igŏshi anira chŏgŏt* 이것이 아니라 저것 not this one, that one; *usŭl iri anida* 웃을 일이 아니다 it's not funny

anihage nak-kkwanjŏgin saeng-gak 안이하게 낙관적인 생각 wishful thinking

anikkoun saram 아니꼬운 사람 creep, jerk

anin 아닌 no

anio 아니오 no

anjang 안장 saddle

anjŏlbujŏl mot'ada 안절부절 못하다 be in a flap; get the jitters; fidget

anjŏlbujŏl mot'anŭn 안절부절 못하는 jittery; uptight

anjŏn 안전 safety

anjŏnbelt'ŭ 안전벨트 safety belt

anjŏngdoeda 안정되다 stabilize, steady, become stable

anjŏngdoen 안정된 stable, balanced

anjŏngshik'ida 안정시키다 stabilize, steady, make stable

anjŏngssŏng 안정성 stability

anjŏn-gun 안전군 security forces

anjŏng yoppŏp 안정 요법 rest cure

anjŏnhada 안전하다 be safe; be secure

anjŏnhage 안전하게 safely

anjŏnhage hada 안전하게 하다 secure, make safe

anjŏnhaji anŭn 안전하지 않은 unsafe

anjŏnhan 안전한 safe, secure

anjŏn helmet 안전 헬멧 crash helmet

anjŏnp'in 안전핀 safety pin

anjŏnssŏng 안전성 safety, security

anjŏnŭl saenggak'anŭn 안전을 생각하는 safety-conscious

anjŏn usŏn 안전 우선 safety first

ankkam 안감 lining

anma 안마 massage

anmadang 안마당 courtyard

anmahada 안마하다 massage

anmasa 안마사 masseur; masseuse

anmogi nop'ŭn 안목이 높은

anmu 안무 choreography

anmuga 안무가 choreographer

annae 안내 directions, guidance

annaech'aektcha 안내책자 handbook

annaehada 안내하다 direct, guide

annaeja 안내자 guide; usher

annaesŏ 안내서 guide(book)

annae tesŭk'ŭ 안내 데스크 reception desk

annaewŏn 안내원 courier

annyŏng 안녕 hello, hi; goodbye, so long

annyŏnghaseyo 안녕하세요 good morning; good afternoon; good evening

annyŏnghi chumushipsshiyo 안녕히 주무십시요 good night

annyŏnghi chumusyŏssŏyo 안녕히 주무셨어요 good morning (*on waking up*)

annyŏnghi kaseyo 안녕히 가세요 goodbye (*polite, to person leaving*)

annyŏnghi kyeseyo 안녕히 계세요 goodbye (*polite, to person staying*)

anppang 안방 master bedroom; living room

ansaek 안색 coloring, complexion

anshikch'ŏ 안식처 haven

anshim 안심 peace of mind; relief

anshimhada 안심하다 feel easy; feel safe

anshimhanŭn 안심하는 secure

anshimshik'ida 안심시키다 reassure

anshingnyŏn 안식년 sabbatical

ansŏng match'umŭi 안성 맞춤의 tailor-made *fig*

antchŏgŭro 안쪽으로 inward

antchoge(sŏ) 안쪽에(서) in back, out the back

antchok 안쪽 inside, nearside

antchok kil 안쪽 길 inside lane

antchuin 안주인 hostess

antchumŏni 안주머니 inside pocket

antta 안다 hug

antta 앉다 sit, sit down; settle, alight

anttŭl 안뜰 courtyard, quadrangle

ant'a 않다 be not; do not; *...e ikssuk'aji ant'a* ...에 익숙하지 않다 not be familiar with

ant'ena 안테나 antenna

anŭi 안의 internal

anŭk'an 아늑한 cozy, snug

anŭn ch'e hanŭn saram 아는 체 하는 사람 know-it-all

anŭro 안으로 inside, indoors ◊ into

ap 앞 front

apch'ukttoen 압축된 compact

apch'uk'ada 압축하다 compress; condense

appa 아빠 dad, pop

appak'ada 압박하다 oppress

appubun 앞부분 opening, beginning

app'in 압핀 thumbtack

ap sŏn 앞 선 advanced

apssŏ kada 앞서 가다 lead the way, lead

apssŭng 압승 landslide victory

apssuhada 압수하다 confiscate

aptchang sŏda 앞장 서다 lead on, go ahead

aptchehada 압제하다 tyrannize

aptchŏng 압정 tack

...aptchoge(sŏ) ...앞쪽에(서) before; in front of, at the front of

aptchogŭi 앞쪽의 front

aptchul 앞줄 front row

aptchwasŏk sŭnggaek 앞좌석 승객 front seat passenger

apttodanghada 압도당하다 dazzle; overwhelm

apttohada 압도하다 dominate; overwhelm

apttohanŭn 압도하는 devastating

apttwiro 앞뒤로 back and forth, to and fro

ap'ahada 아파하다 be in pain; *ap'asŏ momŭl kuburida* 아파서 몸을 구부리다 double up in pain; *ap'ayo?* is it sore?; *momi ap'ayo?* 몸이 아파요? are you ill?

ap'at'ŭ 아파트 apartment

ap'at'ŭ tanji 아파트 단지 apartment block

ap'e 앞에 be ahead of

ap'e(sŏ) 앞에(서) in front; at the front

ap'i poiji annŭn 앞이 보이지 않는 blind *corner*

ap'ŭda 아프다 ache, hurt

Ap'ŭganisŭt'an 아프가니스탄 Afghanistan ◊ Afghan

ap'ŭi 앞의 preceding

ap'ŭm 아픔 ache, pain; discomfort

ap'ŭn 아픈 sick; painful, sore

Ap'ŭrik'a 아프리카 Africa ◊ African

Ap'ŭrik'a saram 아프리카 사람 African

ap'ŭro 앞으로 forward; onward

arabia suttcha 아라비아 숫자 digit; Arabic numbers

Arabin 아랍인 Arab

Arabŏ 아랍어 Arabic (*language*)

araboda 알아보다 check; check out; recognize, identify

arabol su innŭn 알아볼 수 있는 recognizable; discernible

arach'aeda 알아채다 notice; take note of; detect; sense; spot

arach'arida 알아차리다 perceive; become aware of; interpret

arae 아래 the lower part ◊ under, below

araech'ŭng-ŭi 아래층의 downstairs

araech'ung-e(sŏ) 아래층에(서) downstairs

...araee(sŏ) ...아래에(서) below, under; lower than

araetchogŭro 아래쪽으로 down, downward

araet saram 아랫 사람 subordinate

araet-tchoge(sŏ) 아랫쪽에(서) below

arae-ŭi 아래의 subordinate

aranaeda 알아내다 find out; identify

ara nuwŏ it-tta 앓아 누워 있다 be confined to one's bed

ara tŭt-tta 알아 듣다 catch, hear

Arŭhent'ina 아르헨티나 Argentina ◊ Argentinian

arŭmdaptta 아름답다 be beautiful

arŭmdaum 아름다움 beauty

arŭmdaun 아름다운 beautiful, lovely; fond *memories*

arŭn-gŏrida 아른거리다 shimmer

aryak 알약 pill

Ashia 아시아 Asia ◊ Asian

Ashiain 아시아인 Asian

asŭp'alt'ŭ 아스팔트 asphalt, pavement

asŭp'aragŏsŭ 아스파라거스 asparagus

asŭp'irin 아스피린 aspirin

asurajang 아수라장 pandemonium

ausŏng 아우성 outcry

...aya handa ...아야 한다 have to, must; be bound to

...ayaman hada ...아야만 하다 have (got) to; should, must

ayŏn 아연 zinc

CH

cha 자 ruler
chaa 자아 self; ego
chabach'aeda 잡아채다 snatch; pull away
chabadangginŭn kori 잡아당기는 고리 ring-pull
chabaek 자백 confession
chabaek'ada 자백하다 confess
chabaltchŏgin 자발적인 spontaneous; voluntary
chabaltchŏguro 자발적으로 of one's own accord
chabamŏktta 잡아먹다 prey on, feed on; absorb
chabang 자방 ovary (of plant, flower)
chaba ppoptta 잡아 뽑다 pull up plant
chaba tanggida 잡아 당기다 pull; tug, haul
chaba t'ada 잡아 타다 catch bus etc
chabi 자비 mercy
chabiroun 자비로운 merciful
chabon 자본 capital, money
chabon chŭngga 자본 증가 capital growth
chabon-ga 자본가 capitalist
chabonjuŭi 자본주의 capitalism
chabonjuŭija 자본주의자 capitalist, believer in capitalism
chabonjuŭijŏk 자본주의적 capitalist
chabushim 자부심 ego, self-esteem
chach'aek 자책 remorse
chach'i 자치 autonomy
chach'wi 자취 mark, trace
chach'wi-rŭl kamch'uda 자취를 감추다 disappear, run away
chada 자다 sleep; drop (of wind)
chadong 자동 automatic movement; intransitivity ◊ automatic
chadong chŏmmyŏl changch'i 자동 점멸 장치 flasher, direction indicator
chadong chojong changch'i 자동

조종 장치 autopilot
chadongch'a 자동차 automobile; motor vehicle
chadongch'a haengnyŏl 자동차 행렬 motorcade
chadongch'a sanŏp 자동차 산업 automobile industry
chadongch'a suriso 자동차 수리소 garage (for repairs)
chadonghwa 자동화 automation
chadonghwahada 자동화하다 automate
chadongkigye 자동기계 automatic
chadong ondo chojŏl changch'i 자동 온도 조절 장치 thermostat
chadong p'anmaegi 자동 판매기 vending machine
chadongsa 자동사 intransitive verb
chadong sohwa changch'i 자동 소화 장치 sprinkler
chadong taech'e 자동 대체 banker's order
chadong-ŭngdapkki 자동응답기 answerphone
chadong-ŭro 자동으로 automatically
chadu 자두 plum
chae 재 ash; ashes
chaebaech'ihada 재배치하다 relocate
chaebaeyŏrhada 재배열하다 rearrange
chaebal 재발 relapse
chaebangmun 재방문 follow-up visit
chaebangsong 재방송 repeat, rerun
chaebarhada 재발하다 recur
chaebarhanŭn 재발하는 recurrent
chaebŏl 재벌 conglomerate
chaebongsa 재봉사 tailor
chaebongt'ŭl 재봉틀 sewing machine
chaebongt'ŭllo paktta 재봉틀로 박다 machine
chaech'aegi 재채기 sneeze
chaech'aegihada 재채기하다 sneeze

chaech'ep'ohada 재체포하다 recapture

chaech'i 재치 tact; wit; witticism

chaech'i innŭn 재치 있는 tactful; quickwitted; witty

chaech'i innŭn mal 재치 있는 말 quip

chaech'i ŏmnŭn 재치 없는 tactless

chaech'ŏng 재청 encore

chaech'ok'ada 재촉하다 hurry up

chaeda 재다 take *temperature*

chaedan 재단 foundation, organization

chaegae 재개 renewal

chaegaebarhada 재개발하다 redevelop

chaegaehada 재개하다 renew, resume

chaegaejanghada 재개장하다 reopen

chaegal 재갈 gag; *chaegarŭl mullida* 재갈을 물리다 gag

chaegŏmt'o 재검토 review (*of situation*)

chaegŏmt'ohada 재검토하다 review *situation*

chaegŏnhada 재건하다 reconstruct

chaegŏrae 재거래 repeat business

chaego chŏngni seil 재고 정리 세일 clearance sale

chaegohada 재고하다 reconsider

chaego josa 재고 조사 stocktaking

chaegŭro mirŏ ollida 잭으로 밀어 올리다 jack up

chaegyoyuk kwajŏng 재교육 과정 refresher course

chaehae 재해 disaster

chaehae chiyŏk 재해 지역 disaster area

Chaehŏnjŏl 재헌절 Constitution Day

chaehoe 재회 reunion

chaehoehada 재회하다 reunite

chaehonhada 재혼하다 remarry

chaehyŏnhada 재현하다 reproduce; reconstruct *crime*; return (*of doubts etc*)

chaeil kyop'o 재일 교포 Korean resident in Japan

chaemi kyop'o 재미 교포 Korean resident in the USA

chaejalgŏrida 재잘거리다 yap

chaejin 재진 follow-up visit

chaejŏng 재정 finance ◊ financial

chaejŏngga 재정가 financier

chaejŏngnihada 재정리하다 readjust; reschedule; rearrange

chaejŏgŭnghada 재적응하다 readjust (*to conditions*)

chaeju 재즈 jazz

chaeju nŏmkki 재주 넘기 somersault

chaeju nŏmtta 재주 넘다 somersault

chaejurŭl purida 재주를 부리다 juggle; deal with

chaek 잭 jack (*for car, in cards*)

chaek'it 재킷 jacket

chaem 잼 conserve; jelly

chaemi 재미 fun, amusement

chaemiinnŭn 재미있는 amusing, entertaining; interesting

chaemiinnŭn saram 재미있는 사람 clown, joker

chaemi ŏmnŭn 재미없는 uninteresting

chaemiro 재미로 for fun, for kicks

chaemok 재목 lumber

Chaemubu 재무부 Ministry of Finance

Chaemujanggwan 재무장관 Secretary of the Treasury

chaemujanghada 재무장하다 rearm

chaemul 재물 worldly goods

Chaemusŏng 재무성 Treasury Department

chaengban 쟁반 tray

chaenggi 쟁기 plow

chaengtchŏm 쟁점 issue, matter

chaeng-ŭi 쟁의 dispute

chaenŭng 재능 flair, talent

chaenŭng-innŭn 재능있는 talented

chaeŏjida 재어지다 measure

chaeppalli 재빨리 quickly, swiftly

chaepparŭge tolda 재빠르게 돌다 spin around

chaepparŭn 재빠른 agile, nimble

chaepssage umjigida 잽싸게 움직이다 move quickly, zap along

chaep'an 재판 judgment LAW; reprint; *Xŭl/rŭl chaep'ane kŏlda* X을/를 재판에 걸다 take X to court

chaep'anhada 재판하다 judge; try LAW; reprint

chaep'ojanghada 재포장하다
resurface

chaep'yŏnsŏng 재편성
reorganization

chaep'yŏnsŏnghada 재편성하다
reorganize

chaeryang 재량 discretion; *tangshinŭi chaeryang-ŭro* 당신의 재량으로 at your discretion

chaeryo 재료 ingredient; material

chaesaeng 재생 replay, playback; reproduction

chaesaeng iyong 재생 이용
recycling

chaesaeng iyonghada 재생 이용하다 recycle

chaesaengshik 재생식
reproduction; breeding

chaesaengshik'ada 재생식하다
reproduce; breed

chaesaengshik'anŭn 재생식하는
reproductive

chaesan 재산 means; possessions; assets

chaesangyŏnghada 재상영하다
rerun

chaesan kwalli sangt'aee noyŏ itta 재산 관리 상태에 놓여 있다 be in receivership

chaesayonghada 재사용하다 reuse

chaesayong-i kanŭnghan 재사용이 가능한 reusable

chaeshihap 재시합 replay

chaeshihap'ada 재시합하다 replay

chaesuŏmnŭn saram 재수없는 사람 jinx (*person*)

chaesuŏpkkun! 재수없군! hard luck!

chaettŏri 재떨이 ashtray

chaet'onghap'ada 재통합하다
reunite

chaet'ujahada 재투자하다 reinvest, plow back

chaewŏjuda 재워주다 put up

chaewŏn 재원 financial resources

chaga chejak yŏnghwa 자가 제작 영화 home movie

chagae 자개 mother-of-pearl

chagae changshik 자개 장식
mother-of-pearl inlay

chagajida 작아지다 grow smaller; *chŏmjŏm chagajida* 점점 작아지다

dwindle

chagal 자갈 gravel; shingle; pebble; gravestone

chagayong unjŏnsa 자가용 운전사
chauffeur

chagi 자기 china (*pottery*); honey, darling; magnetism ◊ magnetic

chagi chabon 자기 자본 equity capital

chagi chashin 자기 자신 oneself

chagi chungshimŭi 자기 중심의
egocentric

chagi kŭrŭt 자기 그릇 china (*material*)

chagi manjok 자기 만족
complacency

chagi manjoktchŏgin 자기 만족적인
complacent

chagi maŭmdaerohada 자기 마음대로 하다 have one's (own) way

chagi pang-ŏ 자기 방어 self-defense

chagi ponwiŭi 자기 본위의 self-centered

chagi pulsshin 자기 불신 self-doubt

chagi sŏnjŏn-ga 자기 선전가
exhibitionist

chagi suyang 자기 수양 self-discipline

chagiya! 자기야! darling!

chagŏp inbu 작업 인부 workman

chagŏp kongjŏngdo 작업 공정도
flowchart

chagŏpsshil 작업실 studio

chagŏptchang 작업장 workshop

chagŏpttae 작업대 work bench

chagŏp yŏn-gu 작업 연구 work study

chagŭk 자극 spur, incentive

chagŭk'ada 자극하다 rouse, stimulate; spur on; arouse

chagŭk'anŭn 자극하는 provocative; controversial; pungent

chagŭktchŏgin 자극적인 electric *atmosphere*; stimulating; provocative, alluring; sharp *taste*

chagŭm 자금 fund

chagŭmahan 자그마한 diminutive; insignificant

chagŭm chiwŏnŭl hada 자금 지원을 하다 finance

chagŭm pujogŭro pullihan 자금 부족으로 불리한 underfunded

chagŭmsŏng 자금성 forbidden city

chagŭmŭl taeda 자금을 대다 bankroll

chagŭn 작은 little, small; low

chaguk 자국 mark, trace; one's own country; *chagugŭl naeda* 자국을 내다 mark, stain; *nullŏ tchigŭn chaguk* 눌러 찍은 자국 imprint

chagŭmnong 자급농 subsistence farmer

chagung 자궁 uterus, womb

chagung chŏkch'ulssul 자궁 적출술 hysterectomy

chagungam kŏmsa 자궁암 검사 cervical smear

chagungnada 자국나다 mark, become stained

chagyŏgi innŭn 자격이 있는 eligible

chagyŏgi ŏmnŭn 자격이 없는 ineligible; unqualified

chagyŏgŭl chuda 자격을 주다 entitle, qualify

chagyŏgŭl ŏt-tta 자격을 얻다 qualify

chagyŏk 자격 qualification; *...l chagyŏgi it-tta* ...ㄹ 자격이 있다 be qualified to ...; *tongdŭnghan / tarŭn chagyŏgida* 동등한 / 다른 자격이다 be on the same / a different footing

chagyŏktchŭng 자격증 certificate

chagyŏktchŭng-i innŭn 자격증이 있는 qualified

chagyong 작용 action; operation; function

chahoesa 자회사 subsidiary; wholly owned subsidiary

chainhada 자인하다 acknowledge, admit; *choerŭl chainhada* 죄를 자인하다 incriminate oneself

chainhanŭn 자인하는 self-confessed

chajangga 자장가 lullaby

chaje 자제 self-control

chajehada 자제하다 control oneself, restrain oneself

chajehanŭn 자제하는 lowkey

chajilgurehan changshin-gu 자질구레한 장신구 knick-knacks; trinket

chajinhaesŏ hada 자진해서 하다 volunteer

chajŏng 자정 midnight; *chajŏng-e* 자정에 at midnight

chajŏn-gŏ 자전거 bicycle

chajŏn-gŏ haendŭl 자전거 핸들 handlebars

chajŏn-gŏrŭl t'ada 자전거를 타다 bike; pedal

chajonshim 자존심 pride, self-respect

chajŭn 잦은 frequent

chaju 자주 often

chaju ch'at-tta 자주 찾다 frequent, visit

chaju onŭn 자주 오는 frequent

chajuppich'ŭi 자주빛의 purple

chak-kka 작가 writer; scriptwriter; author

chak-kkak'ada 착각하다 mistake, confuse

chak-kkok 작곡 composition

chak-kkok-kka 작곡가 composer

chak-kkok'ada 작곡하다 compose

chakppyŏl insa 작별 인사 parting greeting; *nuguege chakppyŏl insarŭl hada* 누구에게 작별 인사를 하다 say goodbye to s.o.

chakp'um 작품 work (*literary, artistic*)

chakssa chak-kkok-kka 작사 작곡가 songwriter

chakssaga 작사가 lyricist

chakssal 작살 harpoon

chakssihada 작시하다 rhyme

chakssŏnghada 작성하다 draw up, write; *ch'ogorŭl chakssŏnghada* 초고를 작성하다 draft

chaktchŏnghada 작정하다 decide, determine; *muŏsŭl haryŏgo chaktchŏnghada* 무엇을 하려고 작정하다 be intent on doing sth; *X hanŭn kŏsŭl chaktchŏnghada* X 하는 것을 작정하다 set out to do X

chaktchŏng-ida 작정이다 intend; *muŏsŭl hal chaktchŏng-ida* 무엇을 할 작정이다 intend to do sth

chaktchŏn kiji 작전 기지 base MIL

chaktta 작다 be small, be little

chakttonghada 작동하다 go, function; perform; engage, kick in

chakttong pullyang 작동 불량 malfunction

chakŭktche 자극제 stimulant

chak'uji 자쿠지 jacuzzi, whirlpool

chal 잘 well; nicely

chal allyŏjin 잘 알려진 well-known

chal anŭn 잘 아는 familiar

chal arajunŭn 잘 알아주는 sympathetic, understanding

chal cha 잘 자 good night (*informal*)

chal hada 잘 하다 do well; *na-ege marŭl chal haet-tta* 내게 말을 잘 했다 good thing you told me

chal igŭn 잘 익은 well-done *food*

chal ihaehada 잘 이해하다 sympathize with

chal ijŏbŏrinŭn 잘 잊어버리는 forgetful

chal it-tta 잘 있다 be well

chaljalmot 잘잘못 right and wrong

chal kakkuŏjin 잘 가꾸어진 in good condition

chal kŏnjodoen 잘 건조된 seasoned *wood*

challabŏrida 잘라버리다 slash

challanaeda 잘라내다 cut off ◊

challan ch'ŏk'anŭn 잘난 척하는 pretentious

challanoŭn ppang 잘라놓은 빵 sliced bread

chal mandŭrŏjin 잘 만들어진 well-made

chal minnŭn 잘 믿는 credulous

chalmot 잘못 error; wrong ◊ wrongly; badly; *nŏŭi / naŭi chalmoshida* 너의/나의 잘못이다 it's your/my fault

chalmot chidodoen 잘못 지도된 misguided

chalmot chun 잘못 준 misplaced

chalmot ch'ŏltchahada 잘못 철자하다 misspell

chalmot haesŏk'ada 잘못 해석하다 misinterpret, misconstrue

chalmot iltta 잘못 읽다 misread

chalmot köllin chŏnhwa 잘못 걸린 전화 wrong number

chalmot kyesanhada 잘못 계산하다 miscalculate

chalmot match'uda 잘못 맞추다 mismatch

chalmot p'andanhada 잘못 판단하다 misjudge

chalmot saenggak'ada 잘못 생각하다 be under a misapprehension

chalmot sayonghada 잘못 사용하다 misuse

chalmot taruda 잘못 다루다 mishandle

chalmot-ttoeda 잘못되다 go wrong; *mwŏga chalmot twaennayo?* 뭐가 잘못 됐나요? is something wrong?

chalmot-ttoen 잘못된 wrong; unfortunate

chalmot-ttoen haesŏk 잘못된 해석 misinterpretation

chalmot-ttoen inswae 잘못된 인쇄 misprint

chalmot-ttoen unyŏng 잘못된 운영 mismanagement

chalmot unyŏnghada 잘못 운영하다 mismanage

chal nan ch'ehanŭn 잘 난 체하는 smug

chal padadŭrida 잘 받아들이다 be receptive to

chal saenggin 잘 생긴 good-looking

chal sagwida 잘 사귀다 cultivate *person*

chal salp'yŏboda 잘 살펴보다 study, examine

chal songnŭn 잘 속는 gullible

chal sonjildoen 잘 손질된 well groomed

chal tadŭmŏjin 잘 다듬어진 polished, accomplished

chal toeda 잘 되다 work, succeed; work out, be successful

chal tolbonŭn 잘 돌보는 caring

chal tolbwajunŭn 잘 돌봐주는 obliging

chal tolda 잘 돌다 negotiate

chal towajunŭn 잘 도와주는 supportive

chal ttaragada 잘 따라가다 stick to

cham 잠 sleep

chamae toshi 자매 도시 twin town

chamagŭl talda 자막을 달다 subtitle

chamak 자막 subtitle

chaman 자만 conceit

chamanhanŭn 자만하는 conceited

chamanshim 자만심 vanity

chambok'ada 잠복하다 lurk

chamdŭlda 잠들다 fall asleep

chamgida 잠기다 fasten

chamgŭda 잠그다 fasten; lock; turn off *faucet*

chamhaengssŏng-ŭi 잠행성의 insidious

chami kkaeda 잠이 깨다 wake (up)

chami tŭlda 잠이 들다 drop off; go to sleep

chamjaehada 잠재하다 lurk

chamjaejŏgin 잠재적인 potential, possible

chamjaejŏgŭro 잠재적으로 potentially

chamjaeryŏk 잠재력 potential, possibilities

chamjarie tŭlda 잠자리에 들다 go to bed

chamkkan 잠깐 a bit, a while

chamkkanmanyo 잠깐만요 just a second

chamkkan tong-anŭi 잠깐 동안의 fleeting

cham mot irunŭn 잠 못 이루는 sleepless

chamot 잠옷 pajamas; nightshirt; nightdress

chamot paji 잠옷 바지 pajama pants

chamot wit-ttori 잠옷 윗도리 pajama jacket

chamshi antta 잠시 앉다 perch, sit

chamshi chungdandoem 잠시 중단됨 lull, break

chamshidong-an 잠시동안 briefly

chamshi hu 잠시 후 a little later; *nanŭn chamshi hue kŏgi toch'ak'al kŏmnida* 나는 잠시 후에 거기 도착할 겁니다 I'll be there in a bit

chamshi mŏmum 잠시 머뭄 stopover

chamshi mŏmurŭda 잠시 머무르다 stop over

chamshinham 참신함 novelty

chamshi tong-an 잠시 동안 for a while, for a moment

chamsu 잠수 dive (*underwater*)

chamsubu 잠수부 diver, frogman

chamsuhada 잠수하다 dive, submerge; go diving

chamsuham 잠수함 submarine

chamulssoe 자물쇠 bolt; lock

chamulssoe chejogong 자물쇠 제조공 locksmith

chamulssoeŭi pŏnho 자물쇠의 번호 combination (*of safe*)

chamyŏnghan 자명한 self-evident

chamyŏngjong shigye 자명종 시계 alarm clock

chan 잔 cup; tumbler; *... han chan* ...한 잔 a drink of; a glass of; a cup of

chanaegŭl ch'ogwahanŭn inch'ul 잔액을 초과하는 인출 overdraft

chanaekppoda tŏ inch'urhada 잔액보다 더 인출하다 have an overdraft; *...esŏ chanaekppoda tŏ inch'ulshik'ida* ...에서 잔액보다 더 인출시키다 overdraw

chanch'itssang 잔칫상 spread, meal

chandi 잔디 lawn; (piece of) turf

chandibat 잔디밭 turf, grass

chandi kkangnŭn kigye 잔디 깎는 기계 lawn mower

chandon 잔돈 change, loose change

chang 장 chief, head; sheet (*of paper*); chapter; scene (*in theater*); exposure (*on film*); copy; ice rink ◊ *countword for paper and thin flat objects*

chang-ae 장애 problem; disorder MED; hitch; hindrance; obstacle; burden

chang-aemul 장애물 stumbling-block; blockage; hurdle SP

chang-aemul kyŏnggi 장애물 경기 steeplechase (*athletics*)

chang-aemul kyŏngju 장애물 경주 hurdles

chang-aemul kyŏngjuja 장애물 경주자 hurdler

chang-aemul kyŏngjuma 장애물 경주마 jumper (*horse*)

chang-aemul ttwiŏnŏmkki 장애물 뛰어넘기 show jumping

chang-aeŏpssi 장애없이 without a hitch

chang-ak'ada 장악하다 take over; *muŏsŭl chang-ak'ada* 무엇을 장악하다 tighten one's grip on sth changbi 장비 equipment, plant; kit

changboda 장보다 do one's shopping

changbu 장부 accounts book; (real) man; *changburŭl sogida* 장부를 속이다 fiddle the accounts

changch'i 장치 apparatus, equipment; device; system

changgap 장갑 glove

changgapch'a 장갑차 armored vehicle

changgi 장기 Korean chess

changgijŏgin 장기적인 long-range; *changgijŏgŭro* 장기적으로 in the long term

changgiŭi 장기의 long-term

changgŏriŭi 장거리의 long-distance

changgo 장고 hourglass drum

changgun 장군 general MIL; checkmate

changgunp'ul 장군풀 rhubarb

changgwan 장관 minister, secretary; spectacle

changgwan-ŭi 장관의 ministerial

changgyo 장교 officer MIL

changhak-kkŭm 장학금 grant, scholarship

changhwa 장화 boot

chang-in 장인 craftsman; father-in-law

chang-in ŏrŭn 장인 어른 father-in-law

changjŏng 장정 binding; epic journey

changjŏngbon 장정본 hardback (*book*)

changjŏnhada 장전하다 load *gun*

changjo 장조 major MUS

changjogŭi paltchŏnŭl hada 장족의 발전을 하다 make great strides

changk'waehan 장쾌한 stirring

changma 장마 the rains

changmach'ŏl 장마철 rainy season

changmi 장미 rose

changmun 작문 composition, essay

changmyŏn 장면 scene

changnaesŏng ŏmnŭn chigŏp 장래성 없는 직업 dead-end job

changnaeŭi hŭimang 장래의 희망 expectations

changnan 장난 prank; *nuguege*

changnanjirŭl hada 누구에게 장난질을 하다 play a trick on s.o.; *chitkkujŭn changnan* 짓궂은 장난 practical joke

changnanch'ida 장난치다 fool around

changnankkam 장난감 toy

changnankkurŏgi 장난꾸러기 little rascal, cheeky child

Changno Kyohoe 장로 교회 Presbyterian Church

changnong 장롱 chest, box

changnyeshik 장례식 funeral

changnyŏhan 장려한 magnificent

changnyŏn ŏnjen-ga 작년 언젠가 sometime last year

chang-ŏ 장어 eel

chan-go 잔고 balance

chan-go chohoe 잔고 조회 bank statement

chan-goran 잔고란 debit

chan-gorane kiip'ada 잔고란에 기입하다 debit

chang pon mulgŏn 장 본 물건 shopping, purchases

changp'a 장파 long wave

changp'yŏn yŏnghwa 장편 영화 movie; feature

changsahada 장사하다 trade, do business

changshik 장식 decoration, decor

changshik-kka 장식가 painter

changshiktchang 장식장 cabinet

changshik'ada 장식하다 embellish, adorn

changshingnyong-ŭi 장식용의 ornamental

changshin-gu 장신구 accessory

changso 장소 place, spot; site; venue; room, space; *...ŭl/rŭl wihan changsoga ŏptta* ...을/를 위한 장소가 없다 there's no room for

changsshik 장식 décor

changsshikp'um 장식품 ornament

changsshik'ada 장식하다 decorate

changtchŏm 장점 merit, strength

changttae nop'i ttwigi 장대 높이 뛰기 polevault

changt'ip'usŭ 장티푸스 typhoid

chang-ŭisa 장의사 mortician

chanhae 잔해 wreck, wreckage

chaninhada 잔인하다 be cruel

chaninhage 잔인하게 brutally

chaninham 잔인함 cruelty; brutality; ferocity

chanmorae 잔모래 grit (for roads)

chansorihada 잔소리하다 go on at, nag

chansorihanǔn 잔소리하는 nagging

chanttǔk mǒktta 잔뜩 먹다 eat one's fill

chanyǒgǔm 잔여금 balance, remainder

chanyǒmul 잔여물 residue

chaoesǒn 자외선 ultraviolet rays

chapch'o 잡초 weed

chapkki 잡기 catch

chap-ppi 잡비 incidental expenses

chapssǒk 잡석 rubble

chaptchi 잡지 magazine, journal

chaptchong 잡종 hybrid

chaptchonggyǒn 잡종견 mongrel

chaptta 잡다 catch; seize; hold

chapttahan kǒttǔl 잡다한 것들 odds and ends, little jobs

chapttam 잡담 chat, small talk

chapttamhada 잡담하다 chat, gossip

chapttongsani 잡동사니 odds and ends; paraphernalia

chap'an 자판 dial, face

chap'an-gi 자판기 vending machine

chap'ojagishig-ǔi haengdong 자포자기식의 행동 an act of desperation

chap'yetchǔng-ǔi 자폐증의 autistic

charada 자라다 grow; chal charada 잘 자라다 flourish

charak 자락 patch (of fog)

charanada 자라나다 grow up

charang 자랑 pride

charanghada 자랑하다 boast

charang kǒri 자랑 거리 boast

charangsǔrǒpkke 자랑스럽게 proudly

charangsǔrǒptta 자랑스럽다 be proud

charangsǔrǒun 자랑스러운 proud

charhada 잘하다 be good at

charhan hǔngjǒng 잘한 흥정 bargain, good deal

chari 자리 place, seat; floor mat

charijaptta 자리잡다 settle down, calm down (in lifestyle)

charirǔl mandǔlda 자리를 만들다 move up, make room

charǒ kada 자러 가다 go to bed

charǔda 자르다 carve; cut

charǔgi 자르기 cut; carve meat

charu 자루 hilt; shaft ◊ countword for pencils, brushes, pens, chalk, scissors, rifles etc

charyo 자료 materials; data

chasal 자살 suicide

chasan 자산 asset

chasan sodǔksse 자산 소득세 capital gains tax

chasarhada 자살하다 commit suicide

chase 자세 position, posture

chasehada 자세하다 be detailed

chasehage 자세하게 in detail

chasehan chosa 철저한 조사 investigation, probe

chasehan naeyong 자세한 내용 detail

chasehi chosahada 자세히 조사하다 scrutinize, probe

chasehi poda 자세히 보다 peer; study, pore over

chashik 자식 offspring

chashin 자신 self-confidence; chashinǔl ǒktchehal su ǒpkke toeda 자신을 억제할 수 없게 되다 lose control of oneself, get angry, get upset

chashin innǔn 자신 있는 self-confident, self-assured

chashini nǒmch'yǒboinǔn 자신이 넘쳐보이는 flamboyant

chasǒjǒn 자서전 autobiography

chasǒk 자석 magnet

chasǒn 자선 charity; philanthropy

chasǒn-ga 자선가 philanthropist

chasǒnshimi manǔn 자선심이 많은 charitable

chasǒn tanch'e 자선 단체 charity (organization)

chasǒnǔi 자선의 charitable

chason 자손 descendant

chasonida 자손이다 be descended from

chasu 자수 embroidery

chasusǒnggahan saram 자수성가한 사람 self-made man

chattchip 찻집 tearoom
chattchujŏnja 찻주전자 teapot
chat'aek kŭnmu 자택 근무 work from home
chaŭishigi kanghan 자의식이 강한 self-conscious
chaŭm 자음 consonant
chawihada 자위하다 masturbate
chawŏn 자원 resource
chawŏn ipttaehada 자원 입대하다 enlist
chawŏnja 자원자 volunteer
chawŏn kogal 자원 고갈 a drain on resources
chawŏn pohoronja 자원 보호론자 conservationist
chayŏn 자연 nature
chayŏng-ŭi 자영의 self-employed
chayŏn kwahak 자연 과학 natural science
chayŏn kwahaktcha 자연 과학자 natural scientist
chayŏn pohogu 자연 보호구 nature reserve
chayŏnsa 자연사 natural death
chayŏn shikp'um 자연 식품 whole food
chayŏnsŭrŏpkke 자연스럽게 naturally
chayŏntchŏgin 자연적인 natural *death*
chayŏnŭi 자연의 natural *resources etc*
chayu 자유 freedom, liberty
chayujuŭiŭi 자유주의의 liberal
chayu kyeyagŭi 자유 계약의 freelance
chayuro 자유로 at liberty
chayurowajin 자유로와진 emancipated, liberated
chayu shijang kyŏngje 자유 시장 경제 free market economy
chayuŭi 자유의 free, at liberty
chayuŭi yŏshinsang 자유의 여신상 Statue of Liberty
che 제 my; **kŭ sŭt'eik'ŭnŭn che kŏshimnida** 그 스테이크는 제 것입니다 the steak is for me
chean 제안 approach, arrival; motion, proposal; suggestion
cheanhada 제안하다 advance,

propose, suggest; hold out, offer
cheap'ada 제압하다 restrain
chebal 제발 please, kindly
chebang 제방 river bank
chebi 제비 swallow
chebikkot 제비꽃 violet
chebinghada 제빙하다 de-ice
chebingje 제빙제 de-icer
chebi ppopkki 제비 뽑기 raffle, draw
chebirŭl ppoptta 제비를 뽑다 draw
chebok 제복 uniform
chebyŏng 제병 wafer
chech'oje 제초제 weedkiller
chech'uran 제출안 submission
chech'urhada 제출하다 bring in, introduce; hand in; send in; submit, lodge; **chŭnggŏrŭl chech'urhada** 증거를 제출하다 produce evidence
chedae 제대 discharge (*from the army*)
chedaero 제대로 properly
chedan 제단 altar
chedop'an 제도판 drawing board
chegihada 제기하다 raise, bring up *question*
chegirŏl 제기랄! damn!
chegŏ 제거 removal, elimination
chegŏhada 제거하다 eliminate, root out
chegong 제공 offer
chegonghada 제공하다 offer, provide; **chinael kosŭl chegonghada** 지낼 곳을 제공하다 accommodate
chegop 제곱 square MATH
chegopkkŭn 제곱근 square root
chegugŭi 제국의 imperial
cheguk 제국 empire
cheguryŏk 제구력 control
chehada 제하다 allow; calculate
chehan 제한 restriction; qualification
chehandoen 제한된 confined *space*; qualified, limited
chehan-guyŏk 제한구역 restricted area
chehanhada 제한하다 confine, restrict; qualify
chehan pŏmwi 제한 범위 parameter

chehan shigan 제한 시간 time limit

che himŭro kkuryŏnagada 제힘으로 꾸려나가다 fend for oneself

che himŭro ŏdŭn 제 힘으로 얻은 well-earned

cheil 제일 best

cheil choahanŭn 제일 좋아하는 favorite

cheja 제자 disciple

chejae 제재 sanction, penalty

chejak 제작 production

chejaktcha 제작자 producer

chejak'ada 제작하다 produce

chejarie tollyŏnot'a 제자리에 돌려놓다 put back, replace

chejŏnghada 제정하다 enact *law*; legislate

chejŏngshin 제정신 sanity

chejŏngshinŭi 제정신의 sane, lucid

chejŏngshinŭl ilt'a 제정신을 잃다 go insane; be beside oneself

chejohada 제조하다 manufacture

chejoŏp 제조업 manufacture; manufacturing

chejoŏptcha 제조업자 manufacturer

chel 젤 gel

chemŏt-ttaeroin 제멋대로인 wanton; wayward

chemok 제목 title, name; *...(i)ranŭn chemogŭi* ...(이)라는 제목의 entitled, called; *chagŭn chemok* 작은 제목 subheading

chemot-ttaero nolda 제멋대로 놀다 run wild

chemoyongp'um 제모용품 hair remover

chemul 제물 sacrifice

chemyŏngshik'ida 제명시키다 drop

chenjang! 젠장! damn it!

cheŏ 제어 control

cheŏban 제어반 control panel

cheŏhada 제어하다 bring under control

cheoehada 제외하다 eliminate, rule out; exclude, leave out

cheoehago 제외하고 aside from, except for; excluding

cheoeshik'ida 제외시키다 leave out; *chŏnŭn i iresŏ cheoeshik'yŏ chushipsshio* 저는 이 일에서 제외시켜 주십시오 leave me out of

this

cheppang-ŏptcha 제빵업자 baker

chep'um 제품 product; goods; wares

chero sŏngjang 제로 성장 zero growth

chesa 제사 ancestral rite

Chesam Segye 제3 세계 Third World

cheshigane 제시간에 promptly, on time; *cheshigan ane hada* 제시간 안에 하다 make it, get there on time

cheshihada 제시하다 put in *request*

chesŏlgi 제설기 snowplow

chet'ŭ enjin 제트 엔진 jet engine

chet'ŭgi 제트기 jet

cheŭi 제의 proposition

cheŭihada 제의하다 make overtures to

chewang chŏlgae 제왕 절개 Cesarean section

cheyagŭi 제약의 pharmaceutical

cheyak 제약 pharmaceuticals

chiap 지압 acupressure massage

chibae 지배 control; domination

chibaehada 지배하다 control, be in control of; dominate

chibaehanŭn 지배하는 ruling

chibaein 지배인 manager

chibaejŏgin 지배적인 domineering

chibaejŏk ikkwŏn 지배적 이권 controlling interest

chibang 지방 region; province; fat *(on meat)* ◊ regional; local

chibang chach'i 지방 자치 local government

chibang-i manŭn 지방이 많은 fatty

chibang kŏmsa 지방 검사 DA, district attorney

chibang punkkwŏnhwa hada 지방 분권화 하다 decentralize

chibang saram 지방 사람 local; inhabitant

chibang t'ŭkssanmul 지방 특산물 local produce

chiban il 집안 일 chore; housework

chibe 집에 home, at home

chibesŏ mandŭn 집에서 만든 homemade

chibŏdŭlda 집어들다 hold

chibŏmnŭn 집없는 homeless

chibŏ nŏt'a 집어 넣다 get in; store;

fit in
chibŏ tŭlda 집어 들다 pick up
chibu 지부 branch, chapter
chibul 지불 payment, settlement
chibul nŭngnyŏgi innŭn 지불 능력이 있는 solvent
chibul ponggŭp ch'ongaek 지불 봉급 총액 payroll
chibul pullŭng-ŭi 지불 불능의 insolvent
chibung 지붕 roof
chibung kkokttaegi 지붕 꼭대기 ridge (*of roof*)
chiburhada 지불하다 pay, pay up, settle
chiburin 지불인 payer
chibyohan 집요한 persistent
chich'e 지체 delay, holdup
chich'ehada 지체하다 delay, wait
chich'eshik'ida 지체시키다 detain, delay
chich'ida 지치다 tire, flag
chich'ige hada 지치게 하다 tire, wear out, exhaust
chich'ige hanŭn 지치게 하는 tiring, exhausting
chich'il chul morŭnŭn 지칠 줄 모르는 tireless, inexhaustible
chich'im 지침 pointer; guidelines
chich'in 지친 run-down, worn out, pooped
chich'ul 지출 expenditure
chida 지다 lose; get a beating; go down (*of sun*); be out (*of sun, flower*)
chidae 지대 zone
chido 지도 map; leadership
chidoch'aek 지도책 atlas
chidoja 지도자 leader; mastermind
chidoja sŏn-gŏ hoeŭi 지도자 선거 회의 leadership contest
chidok'ada 지독하다 be vicious; be terrible; be tough
chidok'age 지독하게 terribly, atrociously; viciously
chidoryŏk 지도력 leadership skills
chigagi innŭn 지각이 있는 conscious, aware
chigak 지각 awareness; insight
chigak'ada 지각하다 be delayed
chigap 지갑 billfold, pocketbook

chigech'a 지게차 forklift truck
chigŏbtchŏgin 직업적인 professional
chigŏp 직업 employment; job; profession; trade
chigŏp annaeso 직업 안내소 employment agency
chigŏp manjoktto 직업 만족도 job satisfaction
chigŏpssang-ŭi 직업상의 vocational
chigohan 지고한 lofty, high
chigo it-tta 지고 있다 be behind
chigüjaegŭhyŏng 지그재그형 zigzag
chigüjaegŭro umjigida 지그재그로 움직이다 zigzag
chigüjaegŭshigüi 지그재그식의 erratic
chigülgŏrida 지글거리다 sizzle
chigŭm 지금 now, currently, at present; *paro chigŭm* 바로 지금 right now
chigŭmbut'ŏ 지금부터 from now on
chigŭmkkaji 지금까지 ever; yet; so far
chigŭmtchŭm 지금쯤 by now
chigŭmŭi 지금의 current
chigŭmŭn 지금은 at the moment
chigŭp'ada 지급하다 issue
chigu 지구 earth; globe
chigubon 지구본 globe
chiguin 지구인 inhabitant of earth
chiguryŏk 지구력 endurance
chigwŏn 직원 attendant; staff; personnel
chigyŏng 지경 boundary; verge; ...ㄹ 지경이다 *...l chigyŏng-ida* be on the verge of
chigyŏwŏhada 지겨워하다 loathe
chiha 지하 underground
chiha ch'anggo 지하 창고 vault, cellar
chihach'ŏl 지하철 subway RAIL
chihach'ŭng 지하층 basement
chihado 지하도 underpass
chihaesŏ 지하에서 underground
chihashil 지하실 cellar, basement
chihasumyŏn 지하 수면 waterline
chiha undong 지하 운동 underground activities
chihwihada 지휘하다 conduct MUS
chihwija 지휘자 conductor
chihye 지혜 wisdom

chihyŏng 지형 terrain

chijang-ŭl pat-tta 지장을 받다 suffer

chiji 지지 support, backing

chijida 지지다 fry

chijihada 지지하다 support; endorse; confirm, stand by

chijija 지지자 supporter, follower; following

chijil 지질 geology (of area) ◊ geological

chijin 지진 earthquake

chijinhak 지진학 seismology

chijirhak 지질학 geology (subject)

chijirhaktcha 지질학자 geologist

chijirhaktchŏk 지질학적 geological

chijŏbunhada 지저분하다 be messy; be filthy

chijŏbunham 지저분함 disorder, untidiness

chijŏgwida 지저귀다 chirp; twitter

chijŏk'ada 지적하다 point out

chijŏm 지점 branch

chijŏmjang 지점장 branch manager; *ŭnhaeng chijŏmjang* 은행 지점장 bank manager

chijŏnghada 지정하다 designate

chiju 지주 land owner

chik kangha 직 강하 plummet

chik-kkaguro 직각으로 at right-angles to

chik-kkak 직각 right-angle

chik-kkwan 직관 intuition

chik-kkyŏng 직경 diameter

chikssagak'yŏng 직사각형 rectangle

chikssa kŏrieso 직사 거리에서 at point-blank range

chiktchang-e it-tta 직장에 있다 be at work

chiktchŏp 직접 in person, personally

chiktchŏptchŏgin 직접적인 direct

chiktchŏptchŏguro 직접적으로 firsthand ◊ at first hand

chik'aeng pihaenggi 직행 비행기 through flight

chik'aeng-ŭi 직행의 direct, nonstop

chik'aeng-uro 직행으로 nonstop

chik'aeng yŏlch'a 직행 열차 through train

chik'am 직함 title, form of address

chik'ang 직황 direct flight

chik'ida 지키다 defend; keep to; guard; keep *promise*

chik'yŏboda 지켜보다 watch; monitor; keep an eye on, look after

chil 질 vagina

chilbyŏng 질병 disease

chilch'aek'ada 질책하다 rebuke

chilch'ŏk'an 질척한 slimey

chilgin 질긴 stout; tough

chilgŏp'age hada 질겁하게 하다 appall

chiljil kkŭlda 질질 끌다 drag on

chillajŭn 질낮은 mediocre

chillida 질리다 be fed up with

chillin 질린 fed up

chillo 진로 path

chillyobi 진료비 fee

chillyo kwajŏng 진료 과정 course of treatment

chillyoso 진료소 clinic; infirmary

chilmŏjida 짊어지다 hump; shoulder *burden*

chilmun 질문 question

chilmunhada 질문하다 ask; question

chilmunsŏ 질문서 questionnaire

chilso 질소 nitrogen

chilsshik 질식 suffocation

chilsshik shik'ida 질식 시키다 smother; suffocate

chiltchu 질주 sprint

chiltchuhada 질주하다 race, sprint; tear; gallop

chilt'u 질투 jealousy

chilt'uhada 질투하다 be jealous; be jealous of

chilt'uhanŭn 질투하는 jealous

chilt'ushim 질투심 jealousy

chim 짐 load, burden; belongings; *chim kkurida* 짐 꾸리다 pack

chimjak'ada 짐작하다 suspect

chimmach'a 짐마차 cart

chimsŭng 짐승 beast

chimun 지문 fingerprint

chimyŏng subaedoen 지명 수배된 wanted

chin 진 gin; resin

chinach'ida 지나치다 exceed, overdo

chinach'ige 지나치게 overly; unduly

chinach'ige pohohada 지나치게 보호하다 overprotect

chinach'ige sŏlch'inŭn 지나치게 설치는 hyperactive

chinach'in 지나친 drastic, excessive, undue

chinach'yŏ kada 지나쳐 가다 turn away

chinaeda 지내다 celebrate; get along, progress; *yojŭm musŭn irŭl hamyŏ chinaeshimnikka?* 요즘 무슨 일을 하며 지내십니까? what are you up to these days?

chinagada 지나가다 pass; pass by, go by; get on; *ttwiŏsŏ / kŏrŏsŏ chinagada* 뛰어서 / 걸어서 지나가다 run / walk past

chinan myŏch'il 지난 며칠 the past few days

chinan pŏne 지난 번에 last time

chinap 진압 repression

chinap'ada 진압하다 suppress, put down

chinasŏ 지나서 beyond; past, by

chinbo 진보 advance

chinbohada 진보하다 advance, progress

chinbojŏgin 진보적인 progressive

chinbuhan 진부한 trite; corny; stale *news*; ready-made *solution*

chinch'arhada 진찰하다 examine

chinch'ŏkttoeda 진척되다 get on, make progress

chinch'ul 진출 penetration

chinch'urhada 진출하다 penetrate; *uri t'imŭn chun-gyŏlssŭngjŏne chinch'urhaet-tta* 우리 팀은 준결승전에 진출했다 our team has gotten through to the semi-final

chinch'wijŏgin 진취적인 enterprising, dynamic, go-ahead

chinch'wijŏk kisang 진취적 기상 enterprise, initiative

chindansŏ 진단서 medical certificate

chindo 진도 rate

chindoga nagada 진도가 나가다 progress

chindong 진동 vibration

chindonghada 진동하다 pulsate; rock

ching 징 gong

chingbyŏng 징병 draft MIL

chingbyŏnghada 징병하다 draft MIL

chingbyŏng kip'ija 징병 기피자 draft dodger

chinggyehada 징계하다 discipline

chinggyeŭi 징계의 disciplinary

chin-gihan 진기한 rare

chingjip-ppyŏng 징집병 draftee

chingmul 직물 fabric, textile; texture

chingmu naeyong sŏlmyŏngsŏ 직무 내용 설명서 job description

chingmurŏp 직물업 textile business; textiles

chingmyŏnhada 직면하다 face

chingnŭng 직능 function

chingnyu 직류 direct current

chin-gong 진공 vacuum

chin-gong ch'ŏngsogi 진공 청소기 vacuum cleaner

chin-gonggwan 진공관 vacuum flask

chin-gongp'ojang-ŭi 진공포장의 vacuum-packed

chingse 징세 taxation

chingsuhada 징수하다 levy

chinhaeng 진행 progress

chinhaeng chung-ida 진행 중이다 be under way

chinhaengdoeda 진행되다 proceed; progress; come along

chinhaenghada 진행하다 advance, go on; front TV

chinhaenghanŭn 진행하는 progressive

chinhan 진한 dark; deep *color*; strong *tea etc*

chinhongsaegŭi 진홍색의 crimson

chinhŭk 진흙 clay; mud

chinhŭkt'usŏng-iŭi 진흙투성이의 muddy

chinhwa 진화 evolution

chinhwahada 진화하다 evolve

chinida 지니다 assume

chinigo tanida 지니고 다니다 carry around

chinimno 진입로 access road

chinji 진지 position

chinjihage 진지하게 in earnest; *nugurŭl chinjihage saenggak'ada* 누구를 진지하게 생각하다 take s.o. seriously

chinjihan 진지한 earnest, serious

chinjŏlmŏri nanŭn 진절머리 나는 disgusting, repulsive

chinjŏng 진정 lull

chinjŏngdoeda 진정되다 quieten down

chinjŏngje 진정제 sedative, tranquilizer

chinjŏngshik'ida 진정시키다 control; pacify; soothe; defuse; keep down *costs*

chinjŏngŭro 진정으로 seriously

chinjŏ p'iŏ 진저 비어 gingerbeer

chinju 진주 pearl

chinmi 진미 delicacy

chinp'um 진품 rarity

chinshil 진실 truth

chinshillo 진실로 truly; sincerely

chinshimiya 진심이야 I'm serious

chinshimŭi 진심의 whole-hearted

chinshimŭro 진심으로 sincerely

chinshirhada 진실하다 be truthful, be sincere

chinshirŭl iptchŭnghada 진실을 입증하다 vindicate

chinsu 진수 launch

chinsuhada 진수하다 launch

chinsul 진술 statement

chinsushik 진수식 launch ceremony

chinsusŏn 진수선 launch

chintcha 진짜 the real thing ◊ authentic, genuine; original; real; truthful

chint'ang surŭl mashida 진탕 술을 마시다 go on a bender

chint'oeyangnan 진퇴양난 dilemma; deadlock

chint'ongje 진통제 painkiller

chint'onik 진토닉 gin and tonic

chinŭng 지능 intelligence, brains

chinŭrŏmi 지느러미 fin

chinwŏnji 진원지 epicenter

chinyŏl 진열 display; *chinyŏldoen* 진열된 in the window

chinyŏltchang 진열장 display cabinet

chinyŏlttae 진열대 stall

chinyŏrhada 진열하다 display, lay out

chiŏnaen iyagi 지어낸 이야기 story

chiok 지옥 hell

chip 집 home; house; collection (*of writings*); straw

chipch'ak'ada 집착하다 cling to

chipkke 집게 tongs

chipkkebal 집게발 pincers

chipkke sonkkarak 집게 손가락 forefinger, index finger

chipkkwŏnhanŭn 집권하는 in power

chipkkyŏltchi 집결지 rendez-vous

chipp'iltcha 집필자 author

chipsaram 집사람 wife

chiptchŏk hoero 집적 회로 integrated circuit

chiptchung 집중 concentration

chiptchunghada 집중하다 concentrate

chiptchungjŏgin 집중적인 intensive

chiptchung kangjwa 집중 강좌 crash course

chiptchung kyŏrŭihada 집중 결의하다 centralize

chiptchung k'osŭ 집중 코스 intensive course

chiptchung sagyŏk 집중 사격 burst

chiptchungshik'ida 집중시키다 concentrate

chiptchuso 집주소 home address

chipttan 집단 circle, set, group

chipttanjŏgin 집단적인 collective

chipttan p'ok'aeng-ŭl kahada 집단 폭행을 가하다 lynch

chipttŭri 집들이 housewarming

chip'aeng yuye 집행 유예 probation; reprieve

chip'ang-i 지팡이 walking stick

chip'ap 집합 set MATH

chip'atchang 집하장 terminal

chip'apch'e 집합체 complex

chip'ŏ 지퍼 zipper

chip'ŏrŭl chamgŭda 지퍼를 잠그다 zip up

chip'ŏrŭl yŏlda 지퍼를 열다 unzip

chip'oe 집회 congregation REL

chip'uch'a 지프차 jeep

chip'ye 지폐 (bank) bill

chip'yŏngsŏn 지평선 horizon

chip'yo 지표 barometer *fig*

chirado 지라도: *...I chirado* ...ㄹ 지라도 while; although; even though

chire 지레 lever

chirhwan 질환 condition MED

chiri 지리 geography

chirijŏk 지리적 geographical

chirimyŏllŏrhan 지리멸렬한 scrappy

chiroe 지뢰 mine

chiroepat 지뢰밭 minefield

chiroe t'amsaekssŏn 지뢰 탐색선 minesweeper

chirŭi 질의 vaginal

chirŭmkkil 지름길 short cut

chiruhada 지루하다 be tedious; drag

chiruhaejida 지루해지다 be bored

chiruhaesŏ mich'ilkkŏt kat'ŭn 지루해서 미칠것 같은 deadly, boring

chiruhan 지루한 boring, dull

chiryu 지류 tributary

chisa 지사 governor

chisang 지상 the ground ◊ ground; earthly, terrestrial

chisang kŭnmuwŏn 지상 근무원 ground crew; ground staff

chisang kwanje 지상 관제 ground control

chishigi innŭn 지식이 있는 knowledgeable

chishigin 지식인 intellectual

chishiginŭi 지식인의 intellectual, highbrow

chishihada 지시하다 instruct

chishi sahang 지시 사항 instruction

chisŏng 지성 intellect

chisŏng-in 지성인 intellectual

chisok 지속 persistence

chisok kigan 지속 기간 duration

chisoktchŏgin 지속적인 enduring; persistent

chisokttoeda 지속되다 last

chisok'ada 지속하다 persist; maintain; sustain

chitchŏgin 지적인 intellectual

chitchŏgŭro 지적으로 mentally

chitkkujŭn 짓궂은 mischievous

chit-tta 짖다 bark

chit'aenghada 지탱하다 bear, hold, support

chit'ŭm 질음 depth

chit'ŭn 질은 thick

chiuda 지우다 erase, delete; scrap; remove; blot out *memory*

chiugae 지우개 eraser

chiwi 지위 position; status, standing

chiwŏn 지원 application; backup

chiwŏnhada 지원하다 apply for

chiwŏnsŏ 지원서 application form

chiyŏgŭi 지역의 regional

chiyŏk 지역 area; region; district; quarter

chiyŏk pŏnho 지역 번호 area code

chiyŏnshik'ida 지연시키다 stall

chŏ 저 ㅐ I; me; mine; that

chŏ araee 저 아래에 down there

chŏbŏduda 접어두다 put aside; *chinan irŭn kŭnyang chŏbŏduja* 지난 일은 그냥 접어두자 let bygones be bygones

chŏbŏ nŏt'a 접어 넣다 tuck in

chŏbŭn chari 접은 자리 fold

chŏch'eontchŭng 저체온증 hypothermia

chŏch'uk ŭnhaeng 저축 은행 savings bank

chŏch'uk'ada 저축하다 save

chŏdang 저당 mortgage

chŏdang chap'ida 저당 잡히다 mortgage; pawn

chŏgiap 저기압 depression, low

chŏgiap chidae 저기압 지대 low-pressure area

chŏgi araetchoge 저기 아래쪽에 down there

chŏgŏdo 적어도 at least

chŏgŏduda 적어두다 note down

chŏgŏsŭn muŏshimnikka? 저것은 무엇입니까? what is that?

chŏgŏt 저것 that one

chŏgoesŏnŭi 적외선의 infra-red

chŏgori 저고리 short jacket

chŏgŭmhada 저금하다 put aside, save

chŏgŭn 적은 small; slight; a small number of

chŏgŭnghada 적응하다 adapt, acclimatize

chŏgŭngnyŏgi innŭn 적응력이 있는 adaptable

chŏgŭngshik'igi 적응시키기 conditioning

chŏgŭng-ŭl mot'anŭn 적응을 못하는 maladjusted

chŏgyŏkppyŏng 저격병 sniper

chŏgyongdoeda 적용되다 apply; apply to

chŏgyonghada 적용하다 apply

chŏhadoeda 저하되다 slip, decline

chŏhang 저항 resistance
chŏhanghada 저항하다 resist
chŏhangnyŏgi innŭn 저항력이 있는 resistant
chŏjak-kkwŏn 저작권 copyright
chŏjang 저장 store, stock
chŏjanghada 저장하다 store; preserve; save COMPUT
chŏjangshikp'um 저장식품 preserves
chŏjang t'aengk'ŭ 저장 탱크 tank
chŏjangt'ong 저장통 bin
chŏji 저지 jersey; lowlands
chŏjibang-ŭi 저지방의 low-fat
chŏjihada 저지하다 save
chŏjil 저질 mediocrity
chŏjŏllo 저절로 by itself
chŏjo 저조 low
chŏjul tchada 젖을 짜다 milk
chŏjul tteda 젖을 떼다 wean
chŏjŭn 젖은 soggy
chŏju 저주 curse
chŏjuhada 저주하다 curse
chŏk 적 enemy; adversary
chŏkch'urŭi 적출의 legitimate
chŏk-kkŭktchŏgin 적극적인 positive
chŏkkŭk p'anmae 적극 판매 hardsell
chŏkppŏbŭi 적법의 legitimate
chŏkssshida 적시다 soak
Chŏksshiptcha 적십자 Red Cross
chŏksshiŭi 적시의 timely
chŏkssŏng 적성 aptitude
chŏktaeshim 적대심 antagonism
chŏktcha 적자 deficit
chŏktchaehada 적재하다 load; carry
chŏktchaehan 적재한 laden
chŏktchaga nada 적자가 나다 in the red
chŏktcha saengjon 적자 생존 survival of the fittest
chŏktchŏrhan 적절한 appropriate; right; pertinent
chŏktta 적다 take notes
chŏkttaejŏgin 적대적인 hostile
chŏkttaeshim 적대심 hostility
chŏkttanghada 적당하다 be suitable; be adequate
chŏkttanghage 적당하게 moderately; in moderation
chŏkttanghan 적당한 adequate;

moderate; reasonable; decent; suitable
chŏkttanghi hada 적당히 하다 moderate
chŏktto 적도 equator
chŏk'alloriŭi 저칼로리의 low-calorie
chŏk'ap'ada 적합하다 be suited for, be cut out for
chŏk'ap'age 적합하게 properly
chŏk'ap'an 적합한 morally fit
chŏk'apssŏng 적합성 compatibility
chŏl 절 clause; passage; verse; bow, obeisance; Buddhist temple
chŏlbak'an 절박한 imminent
chŏlbyŏk 절벽 cliff
chŏlch'a 절차 procedure
chŏlch'wisŏn 절취선 perforations
chŏlgae 절개 incision
chŏlgyohada 절교하다 drop
chŏllŭmbariŭi 절름발이의 lame
chŏllŭmgŏrida 절름거리다 hobble
chŏllyak 전략 strategy
chŏllyaktchŏgin 전략적인 strategic
chŏllye ŏmnŭn 전례 없는 unheard-of, unprecedented
chŏllyŏm 전념 commitment
chŏllyu 전류 current ELEC
chŏlmang 절망 despair
chŏlmanghada 절망하다 despair; *chŏlmanghayŏ* 절망하여 in despair
chŏlmangjŏgin 절망적인 desperate
chŏlmtta 젊다 be young
chŏlmŭn 젊은 young, youthful
chŏlmŭni 젊은이 youth, youngster, young man
chŏlmyohan 절묘한 exquisite
chŏlp'andoen 절판된 out of print
chŏlsshirhan 절실한 pressing
chŏltchŏng 절정 climax; high point; summit; height
chŏltchŏng-e tarhada 절정에 달하다 culminate in
chŏlttae 절대 absolutely; *chŏlttae ando-emnida!* 절대 안됩니다! absolutely not!
chŏlttaejŏgin 절대적인 absolute; *chŏlttaero amuegedo iyagi-haesŏnŭn andoemnida* 절대로 아무에게도 이야기해서는 안됩니다 on no account must you tell anybody

chŏlttanhada 절단하다 sever; amputate

chŏlttotchoe 절도죄 larceny

chŏlttuk-kkŏrim 절뚝거림 limp

chŏm 점 dot; spot; mole; *mŏnji han chŏm ŏmnŭn* 먼지 한 점 없는 spotless

chŏmaek 점액 mucus

chŏmanje 점안제 drops

chŏmch'ajŏgin 점차적인 gradual

chŏmch'ajŏgŭro 점차적으로 gradually

chŏmch'ajŏgŭro ŏpssŏjida 점차적으로 없어지다 peter out

chŏmgŏm 점검 inspection

chŏmgŏmhada 점검하다 check; inspect; vet

chŏmho 점호 roll call

chŏmhwa changch'i 점화 장치 ignition

chŏmhwahada 점화하다 set off *explosion*

chŏmhwajŏn 점화전 spark plug

chŏmhwa p'ullŏgŭ 점화 플러그 (spark) plug

chŏmida 저미다 mince

chŏmjaeng-i 점쟁이 fortune-teller

chŏmjanch'i mot'an 점잖지 못한 indecent

chŏmjanŭn 점잖은 gentle

chŏmjŏk 점적 drip

chŏmjŏm 점점 by degrees, gradually; *chŏmjŏm tŏ manŭn hakssaengdŭl / shigan* 점점 더 많은 학생들 / 시간 more and more students / time; *chŏmjŏm ch'uwŏjida / tŏwŏjida* 점점 추워지다 / 더워지다 be getting colder / warmer; *chŏmjŏm sarajida* 점점 사라지다 die away; fade away; slowly disappear

chŏm kŭlkkol 점 글꼴 bitmap font

chŏmnŭn 접는 folding

chŏmnyŏng 점령 capture; occupation

chŏmnyŏnghada 점령하다 capture; occupy

chŏmp'o 점퍼 jumper COMPUT

chŏmp'o 점포 booth

chŏmshim 점심 lunch

chŏmshimshigan 점심시간 lunch

break, lunchtime

chŏmsŏn 점선 dotted line

chŏmsŏngga 점성가 astrologer

chŏmsŏng komu 점성 고무 gum

chŏmsŏngsul 점성술 astrology; horoscope

chŏmsŏni tchik'in 점선이 찍힌 perforated

chŏmsu 점수 point

chŏmtcha 점자 braille

chŏmwŏn 점원 assistant; clerk

chŏmyŏnghan 저명한 distinguished, eminent

chŏn 전 pancake (*Korean-style*)

chŏn(ŭi) 전(의) preceding; front; former ◊ before; ago

chŏnaegŭl naeda 전액을 내다 pay in full

chŏnap 전압 voltage

chŏnbanjŏgin 전반적인 overall

chŏnbŏnŭi 전번의 last

chŏnbo 전보 telegram

chŏnbok 전복 overthrow

chŏnbokshik'ida 전복시키다 bring down, topple

chŏnbok'ada 전복하다 overthrow, overturn

chŏnbu 전부 in all; all of it; altogether

chŏnbuin 전부인 ex-wife

chŏnbuŭi 전부의 complete

chŏn chong-ŏbwŏn 전 종업원 workforce

chŏnch'a 전차 streetcar

chŏnch'ae 전채 appetizer, hors d'oeuvre

chŏnch'e 전체 whole; *Miguk chŏnch'e* 미국 전체 the whole of the United States

chŏnch'ejŏgin 전체적인 general

chŏnch'ejŏgŭro 전체적으로 throughout

chŏnch'ejuŭi 전체주의 totalitarianism

chŏnch'ejuŭiŭi 전체주의의 totalitarian

chŏnch'eŭi 전체의 entire; overall; total

chŏnch'isa 전치사 preposition

chŏndaehada 전대하다 sublet

chŏndal sudan 전달 수단 vehicle

(for information)
chŏndan 전단 leaflet
chŏndangp'o 전당포 pawnshop
chŏndangp'o chuin 전당포 주인 pawnbroker
chŏndarhada 전달하다 communicate; deliver
chŏndoga ch'angch'anghan 전도가 창창한 promising
chŏndohada 전도하다 conduct ELEC; evangelize
chŏndŭnggat 전등갓 lampshade
...chŏne ...전에 before ◊ previously; *3il chŏne* 3일 전에 3 days ago; *...gi chŏne* ...기 전에 before ...ing
chŏn-gaehada 전개하다 develop, pan out
chŏng-aek 정액 semen, sperm
chŏngbaksshik'ida 정박시키다 moor
chŏngbaktchang 정박장 berth, moorings
chŏngbandaeŭi 정반대의 diametrically opposed
chŏngbidoeda 정비되다 be in good order
chŏngbigong 정비공 fitter
chŏngbiwŏn 정비원 ground staff
chŏngbo 정보 information, data, intelligence
chŏngbo chegongja 정보 제공자 informant, source
chŏngboga manŭn 정보가 많은 informative
chŏngbok 정복 conquest; mastery
chŏngbo kigwan 정보 기관 intelligence service
chŏngbo kisul 정보 기술 IT, information technology
chŏngboktcha 정복자 conqueror
chŏngbo kwahak 정보 과학 information science
chŏngbo kwahaktcha 정보 과학자 information scientist
chŏngbok'ada 정복하다 conquer
chŏngbu 정부 government; mistress; *chŏngbu kyugyŏge ttarŭda* 정부 규격에 따르다 conform to government standards
chŏngch'aek 정책 policy
chŏngch'ahada 정차하다 call at

chŏngch'ak'ada 정착하다 settle; settle down
chŏngch'al 정찰 reconnaissance
chŏngch'i 정치 politics
chŏngch'iga 정치가 politician, statesman
chŏngch'i hŏn-gŭm 정치 헌금 political donation
chŏngch'ijŏgin 정치적인 political
chŏngch'ijŏk mangmyŏng-ŭl shinch'ŏnghada 정치적 망명을 신청하다 seek political asylum
chŏngch'ŏ 정처 fixed place; *chŏngch'ŏŏpsshi pangnanghada* 정처없이 방랑하다 drift
chŏngdang 정당 party
chŏngdanghage 정당하게 justifiably; justly
chŏngdanghan 정당한 legitimate; above board
chŏngdanghwa 정당화 justification
chŏngdanghwahada 정당화하다 justify
chŏngdanghwa hal su innŭn 정당화할 수 있는 justifiable
chŏngdang kangnyŏng 정당 강령 party platform
chŏngdo 정도 degree; *50 chŏngdo* 50정도 50 or so, about 50; *i chŏngdoro k'ŭda/noptta* 이 정도로 크다/높다 this big/high; *i chŏngdo sokttomyŏn* 이 정도 속도면 at this rate
chŏngdondoen 정돈된 straight, tidy
chŏngdonhada 정돈하다 clear up, tidy
chŏngdorŭl ttŏrŏttŭrida 정도를 떨어뜨리다 downgrade
chŏnggage 정각에 on time
chŏnggak tu shie 정각 두 시에 at two o'clock prompt
chŏnggang-i 정강이 shin
chŏnggi hanggonog'yŏn 정기 항공편 scheduled flight
chŏnggi iptchangkkwŏn 정기 입장권 season ticket
chŏnggijŏgŭro 정기적으로 periodically
chŏnggijŏn 정기전 fixture
chŏnggi kanhaengmul 정기 간행물 periodical

chŏnggi kudok 정기 구독
subscription

chŏnggi kudoktcha 정기 구독자
subscriber

chŏnggi kudok'ada 정기 구독하다
subscribe to

chŏnggisŏn 정기선 liner

chŏnggi süngch'akkwŏn 정기
승차권 season ticket

chŏnggŏjang 정거장 depot RAIL

chŏnggwansa 정관사 definite article

chŏnggyohage hada 정교하게 하다
refine

chŏnggyohan 정교한 sophisticated;
fine *print*

chŏnggyosujik 정교수직 chair

chŏnggyuŭi wich'ie 정규의 위치에
onside

chŏnghada 정하다 set, fix

chŏnghaptchŏgin 정합적인
coherent

chŏnghwahada 정화하다 purify

chŏnghwak 정확 accuracy, precision

chŏnghwak'ada 정확하다 be right

chŏnghwak'age 정확하게 precisely

chŏnghwak'an 정확한 accurate;
definite; exact

chŏnghwak'i 정확히 exactly;
punctually, on the dot

chŏnghwak'i aranaeda 정확히
알아내다 pinpoint

chŏnghyŏng oekkwaŭi 정형 외과의
orthopedic

chŏn-gi 전기 electricity, power;
biography

chŏn-gi ch'ŏngsogi 전기 청소기
hoover

chŏn-giga t'onghago innŭn 전기가
통하고 있는 live *wire*

chŏn-gi kisa 전기 기사 electrician

chŏn-gi papssot 전기 밥솥
(electric) rice cooker

chŏn-girŭl t'onghage hada 전기를
통하게 하다 electrify

chŏn-gisŏn 전기선 power line

chŏn-gisŏnyong komut'eip'ŭ
전기선용 고무테이프 friction tape

chŏn-gi somoga chŏgŭn shiganŭi
전기 소모가 적은 시간의 off-peak
electricity

chŏn-gi tamnyo 전기 담요 electric

blanket

chŏngit-tchul 전깃줄 wire

chŏn-giŭi 전기의 electric, electrical

chŏn-gi ŭija 전기 의자 electric chair

chŏngja 정자 sperm

chŏngja ŭnhaeng 정자 은행 sperm
bank

chŏngje 정제 tablet

chŏngjehada 정제하다 refine

chŏngje sŏlt'ang 정제 설탕
confectioners' sugar

chŏngjeso 정제소 refinery

chŏngji 정지 halt; suspension

chŏngjihan 정지한 stationary

chŏngjik 정직 honesty, integrity

chŏngjik'ada 정직하다 be on the
level

chŏngjik'an 정직한 honest

chŏngji pŏt'ŭn 정지 버튼 off switch

chŏngjishik'ida 정지시키다 suspend;
chiburŭl chŏngjishik'ida 지불을
정지시키다 stop a check

chŏngjŏn 정전 power cut, power
outage

chŏngjŏn-gi 정전기 static ELEC

chŏngjong 정종 distilled rice wine

chŏngjunghage 정중하게
respectfully

chŏngjunghan 정중한 courteous;
deferential; gallant

chŏngkka 정가 net COM

chŏngkkwŏn 정권 regime

chŏngk'ŭ p'udŭ 정크 푸드 junk food

chŏngmaek 정맥 vein

chŏngmaeng-naeŭi 정맥내의
intravenous

chŏngmal 정말 truth; fact ◊ truly,
really; quite; very

chŏngmallo 정말로 actually; really;
sure enough

chŏngmil chosahada 정밀 조사하다
investigate in detail

chŏngmil kŏmsahada 정밀 검사하다
overhaul

chŏngmil kŏmt'ohada 정밀
검토하다 overhaul

chŏngmun 정문 front entrance

chŏngmyŏn 정면 façade

chŏngmyŏnch'ungdorŭi 정면충돌의
head-on

chŏngnarahan 적나라한 naked *truth*,

aggression; stark

chŏngnyŏgŭl tahada 정력을 다하다
burn oneself out

chŏngnyŏltchŏgin 정열적인
passionate

chŏngnyŏn 정년 retirement age

chŏngnyujang 정류장 (bus) depot;
(bus) shelter; (bus) stop

chŏngnyu ktchŏm 정육점 butcher's

chŏngnyuktchŏm chuin 정육점 주인
butcher

chŏng-ŏri 정어리 sardine

chŏng-o 정오 midday

chŏn-gongdae 천공대 drilling rig

chŏn-gonghada 전공하다 specialize;
specialize in; major in

chŏngsa 정사 love affair

chŏngsang 정상 norm; peak;
summit; tip; pinnacle ◊ normal;
chŏngsang-e orŭda 정상에 오르다
get to the top

chŏngsanghwahada 정상화하다
normalize

chŏngsang sangt'ae 정상 상태
normality

chŏngsang-ŭro 정상으로 normally

chŏngshigŭi 정식의 proper, real

chŏngshik 정식 set meal

chŏngshin 정신 mind; soul; spirit ◊
psycho-, mental; *chŏngshini
mŏnghada* 정신이 멍하다 my
mind's a blank

chŏngshinbunsŏk 정신분석
psychoanalysis

chŏngshin chang-aega innŭn 정신
장애가 있는 mentally handicapped

chŏngshin ch'angnane köllin 정신
착란에 걸린 demented

chŏngshin ch'angnanŭi 정신 착란의
delirious

chŏngshin ch'arige hada 정신
차리게 하다 bring around

chŏngshini mŏnghan 정신이 멍한
dazed

chŏngshini nagada 정신이 나가다
be out of one's mind

chŏngshin isang 정신 이상 insanity

chŏngshin isang-ŭi 정신 이상의
disturbed

chŏngshin kamŭng 정신 감응
telepathy

chŏngshin kamŭng-ŭi 정신 감응의
telepathic

chŏngshinkkwaŭi 정신과의
psychiatric

chŏngshinkkwa ŭisa 정신과 의사
psychiatrist

chŏngshinŏpsshi chikkŏrida
정신없이 지껄이다 rave on
mindlessly

chŏngshin pagyaktcha 정신박약자
imbecile

chŏngshinppyŏng 정신병 mental
illness

chŏngshinppyŏng-i innŭn 정신병이
있는 mentally ill

chŏngshinppyŏngja 정신병자
psychopath

chŏngshinppyŏng-ŭi 정신병의
mental, crazy

chŏngshinppyŏng-wŏn 정신병원
asylum, mental hospital

chŏngshin punsŏk 정신 분석
psychoanalysis

chŏngshin punsŏk haktcha 정신
분석 학자 psychoanalyst

chŏngshin punsŏk'ada 정신
분석하다 psychoanalyse

chŏngshin punyŏltchŭng 정신
분열증 schizophrenia

chŏngshin punyŏltchŭng hwanja
정신 분열증 환자 schizophrenic
patient

chŏngshin punyŏltchŭng-ŭi 정신
분열증의 schizophrenic

chŏngshin sangt'ae 정신 상태
mental state

chŏngshintchŏgin 정신적인
spiritual; platonic

chŏngshintchŏk chang-aega innŭn
정신적 장애가 있는 mentally
handicapped

chŏngshintchŏk hakttae 정신적
학대 mental cruelty

chŏngshinŭi 정신의 mental

chŏngshinŭihak 정신의학 psychiatry

chŏngsŏnhan 정선한 select,
exclusive

chŏngt'ong 정통 familiarity

chŏngt'onghada 정통하다 know;
have a good knowledge of; master;
be a master of

chŏng-ŭi 정의 justice; definition

chŏng-ŭirŭl naerida 정의를 내리다 define

chŏn-gŭk 전극 electrode

chŏn-gu 전구 light bulb

chŏn-gun 전군 the forces MIL

chŏng-wŏn 정원 garden

chŏng-wŏnnyong kawi 정원용 가위 clippers

chŏng-wŏnsa 정원사 gardener

chŏng-ye 정예 elite

chŏng-yeŭi 정예의 elite

chŏn-gyŏng 전경 foreground

chŏnhaeda 전하다 pass on, relay

chŏnhaejuda 전해주다 pass, hand

chŏnhanŭn mal 전하는 말 message

chŏnhuŭi 전후의 postwar

chŏnhwa 전화 telephone; phone call; *chŏnhwarŭl ssŏdo toemnikka?* 전화를 써도 됩니까 can I use the phone?

chŏnhwabŏnhobu 전화번호부 phone book

chŏnhwahada 전화하다 phone, call

chŏnhwa kŏlda 전화 걸다 phone

chŏnhwa kyohwan-guk 전화 교환국 telephone exchange

chŏnhwan 전환 change; changeover; conversion

chŏnhwanjŏm 전환점 turning point

chŏnhwa pŏnho 전화 번호 telephone number

chŏnhwa pŏnhobu 전화 번호부 telephone directory

chŏnhwa p'anmae 전화 판매 telesales

chŏnhwarŭl hada 전화를 하다 make a telephone call

chŏnhwarŭl kkŭnt'a 전화를 끊다 hang up

chŏnhwarŭl kŏlda 전화를 걸다 call; telephone; dial

chŏnhwarŭl pat-tta 전화를 받다 answer the telephone

chŏnhyang 전향 convert

chŏnhyangshik'ida 전향시키다 convert *person*

chŏnhyŏ 전혀 entirely, completely, utterly; *chŏnhyŏ ...ji ant'a* 전혀 ...지 않다 be anything but; do anything but; *chŏnhyŏ kwanshimi*

ŏpssŏ 전혀 관심이 없어 I couldn't care less

chŏnhyŏng 전형 stereotype

chŏnhyŏngjŏgin 전형적인 typical

chŏnimja 전임자 predecessor

chŏnja 전자 the former; electron ◊ electronic

chŏnja chep'um 전자 제품 electrical appliance

chŏnja chŏngbo ch'ŏri 전자 정보 처리 EDP, electronic data processing

chŏnjaeng 전쟁 war; warfare

chŏnjaeng chŏnŭi 전쟁 전의 prewar

chŏnjaeng p'oro 전쟁 포로 prisoner of war

chŏnjaengt'ŏ 전쟁터 battlefield, battleground

chŏnjaeng-ŭi ch'amsa 전쟁의 참사 horrors of war

chŏnja keship'an 전자 게시판 bulletin board

chŏnja konghak 전자 공학 electronics

chŏnja k'adŭ 전자 카드 smart card

chŏnja orak 전자 오락 electronic game

chŏnjarenji 전자렌지 microwave

chŏnja sanŏp 전자 산업 electronics industry

chŏnja up'yŏn 전자 우편 electronic mail

chŏnje chŏngch'i 전제 정치 tyranny

chŏnjejokkŏn 전제조건 prerequisite

chŏnji 전지 battery

chŏnjin 전진 advance

chŏnjinhada 전진하다 advance; move on

chŏnjip 전집 collected works

chŏnjugok 전주곡 prelude

chŏnkkwa 전과 criminal record

chŏnmang 전망 prospects

chŏnmang-i chŏun chijŏm 전망이 좋은 지점 vantage point

chŏnmŏgi twaeji 젖먹이 돼지 sucking pig

chŏnmun 전문 specialty

chŏnmun chishik 전문 지식 expertise

chŏnmun-ga 전문가 expert, specialist

chŏnmun-gaŭi ch'unggo 전문가의 충고 expert advice

chŏnmunindaptchi anŭn 전문인답지 않은 unprofessional

chŏnmunjik chongsaja 전문직 종사자 professional

chŏnmunjŏgin 전문적인 professional

chŏnmunjŏguro 전문적으로 professionally

chŏnmun kisul 전문 기술 expertise

chŏnmunsŏng 전문성 technicality, technical nature

chŏnmunŭi 전문의 technical

chŏnmunŭro hada 전문으로 하다 specialize in; specialize

chŏnmun yong-ŏ 전문 용어 terminology, jargon

chŏnmyŏlshik'ida 전멸시키다 exterminate, wipe out

chŏnmyŏnjŏgin 전면적인 sweeping

chŏnnamp'yŏn 전남편 ex-husband

chŏnnamu 전나무 fir

Chŏnnŭngja 전능자 the Almighty

chŏnnŭn pae 젓는 배 rowboat

chŏnnyŏm 전념 dedication

chŏnnyŏmhada 전념하다 dedicate oneself to; keep one's mind on; concentrate

chŏnnyŏmhanŭn 전념하는 single-minded, dedicated

chŏnsa 전사 warrior, fighter

chŏnsanhwahada 전산화하다 computerize

chŏnsegi 전세기 charter flight

chŏnsegŭm 전세금 deposit money for a lease on an apartment

chŏnsegyeŭi 전세계의 global

chŏnse naeda 전세 내다 charter

chŏnse not'a 전세 놓다 lease an apartment on a deposit basis

chŏnshi 전시 display; exhibition; wartime

chŏnshiganjero 전시간제로 full time

chŏnshiganjeŭi 전시간제의 full-time

chŏnshihada 전시하다 display, show, exhibit

chŏnshindaeŭi 전신대의 full-length

chŏnshinju 전신주 telegraph pole

chŏnshin mach'wi 전신 마취 general anesthetic

chŏnship'um 전시품 exhibit

chŏnsŏl 전설 legend

chŏnsŏljŏgin 전설적인 legendary

chŏnsŏn 전선 front MIL, (of weather); cord; cable

chŏnsŏnggi 전성기 heyday

chŏnsonghada 전송하다 export COMPUT

chŏnsongnyŏguro hada 전속력으로 하다 flat out

chŏnsul 전술 tactics

chŏnsultchŏgin 전술적인 tactical

chŏntchŏk 전적 complete, whole; *chŏntchŏguro matsŭmnida* 전적으로 맞습니다 that's absolutely right

chŏnt'ong 전통 tradition

chŏnt'ongjŏgin 전통적인 traditional, conventional

chŏnt'ongjŏguro 전통적으로 traditionally

chŏnt'u 전투 battle; combat; hostilities

chŏnt'ugi 전투기 fighter (airplane)

chŏnŭi 전의 former

chŏnŭnghan 저능한 retarded

chŏnya 전야 eve

chŏnyŏge 저녁에 in the evening

chŏnyŏk 전역 evening; all parts; *Hanguk chŏnyŏgŭl yŏhaenghada* 한국 전역을 여행하다 travel all over Korea

chŏnyŏk shikssa 저녁 식사 supper

chŏnyŏm 전염 transmission

chŏnyŏmdoenŭn 전염되는 contagious

chŏnyŏmppyŏng 전염병 plague

chŏnyŏmshik'ida 전염시키다 transmit *disease*

chŏnyŏmssŏng-ŭi 전염성의 infectious

chŏnyul 전율 thrill

chŏŏgada 저어가다 row

chŏpch'aktche 접착제 adhesive

chŏpch'ak'ada 접착하다 bond, stick

chŏpch'ok 접촉 contact; touch

chŏpch'ok yŏng-yŏk 접촉 영역 interface

chŏpch'ok'ada 접촉하다 approach, contact; touch

chŏpkkŭn 접근 access

chŏpkkŭnhada 접근하다 access

chŏpkkŭn pangbŏp 접근 방법 approach

chŏppuchi'gi 접붙이기 graft BOT

chŏpssi 접시 plate

chŏpssosogŭl kkŭnt'a 접속서글 끊다 go off-line

chŏpssoksssa 접속사 conjunction GRAM

chŏpssoksshik'ida 접속시키다 connect

chŏpssu kyewŏn 접수 계원 desk clerk

chŏpssok'ada 접속하다 interface; connect with; go on-line to

chŏpssuwŏn 접수원 receptionist

chŏptchi 접지 ground ELEC

chŏptchihada 접지하다 ground ELEC

chŏptta 접다 fold; fold up; turn down

chŏpttusa 접두사 prefix

chŏp'ae it-tta 접해 있다 border

chŏp'ida 접히다 fold up

chŏp'yŏnŭro 저편으로 beyond

chŏrhoehada 철회하다 retrograde

chŏrida 절이다 marinate; pickle

chŏrim 저림 pins and needles

chŏrŏn! 저런! good heavens!

chŏryak 절약 economy; saving

chŏryakpun 절약분 saving

chŏryak undong 절약 운동 economy drive

chŏryak'ada 절약하다 economize; economize on, save

chŏryak'anŭn 절약하는 economical, thrifty

chŏryak'yŏng 절약형 economy size

chŏryŏn 절연 insulation

chŏryŏnhada 절연하다 insulate; sever

chŏsok'an 저속한 vulgar

chŏsŭng 저승 underworld

chŏsuji 저수지 reservoir

chŏtkkarak 젓가락 chopsticks

chŏtkkasŭm 젖가슴 bosom, breast

chŏtkkoktchi 젖꼭지 nipple; teat

chŏt-tta 젖다 get wet

chŏt-tta 젓다 paddle

chŏt'aek 저택 mansion

chŏüi 저의 ㅂ my

chŏŭm poepkkessŭmnida 처음 뵙겠습니다 how do you do (formal greeting used on first meeting)

chŏŭmüi 저음의 deep; bass

chŏul 저울 scales

chŏ wie 저 위에 over there

cho 조 trillion; millet; article, clause; dynasty; tune; air

choahada 좋아하다 like, be fond of; *muŏt hanŭn kŏsŭl choahada* 무엇 하는 것을 좋아하다 like to do sth; *Xŭl / rŭl Ypoda tŏ choahada* X을 / 를 Y보다 더 좋아하다 prefer X to Y

choajida 좋아지다 pick up, improve; *nŏn uni choassŏ* 넌 운이 좋았어 you were lucky

choayo 좋아요 right, OK

chobashimhada 조바심하다 be on tenterhooks

chobŭn 좁은 narrow

chobŭn kil 좁은 길 lane

chobumo 조부모 grandparents

choch'a 조차 even, into the bargain; *choch'a ant'a* 조차 않다 not even

choch'ado 조차도 even; *naŭi abŏji choch'ado* 나의 아버지 조차도 even my father

choch'i 조치 step, measure

choch'wirŭl ch'wihada 조치를 취하다 take action

choe 죄 sin; guilt, responsibility

choe chit-tta 죄 짓다 sin

choe chiŭn 죄 지은 guilty

choech'aek-kkam 죄책감 guilt; *...e taehae choech'aek-kkamŭl nŭkkida* ...에 대해 죄책감을 느끼다 feel bad about, feel guilty about

choein 죄인 sinner

choemsoe 죔쇠 clamp

choemsoero choeda 죔쇠로 죄다 clamp

choeoehada 제외하다 rule out

choerŭl ssŭiuda 죄를 씌우다 incriminate

choesonghamnida 죄송합니다 excuse me; I beg your pardon

choesu 죄수 prisoner

choesu hosongch'a 죄수 호송차 patrol wagon

chogaek 조객 mourner

chogak 조각 bit; piece; slice; fragment; shred; lump; carving, sculpture; *p'ai / ppang han chogak*

파이/빵 한 조각 a piece of pie/bread

chogak-kka 조각가 sculptor

chogak kŭrim match'ugi 조각 그림 맞추기 jigsaw (puzzle)

chogak naeda 조각 내다 shred

chogakp'um 조각품 sculpture

chogamdok 조감독 assistant director

chogangnada 조강나다 splinter

choging 조깅 jog; jogging

chogingbok 조깅복 jogging suit

chogingbada 조깅하다 go for a run, jog

choging shyujyu 조깅 슈즈 jogger

chogok 조곡 suite MUS

chogŭm 조금 a bit, a little; a bit of; just a couple ◊ any ◊ some; slightly; **ppang/p'odoju chogŭm** 빵/포도주 조금 a little bread/wine

chogŭmaham 조그마함 modesty

chogŭmahan 조그마한 tiny; modest

chogŭmdo 조금도 (not) at all, in the least, in the slightest; **chogŭmdo animnida** 조금도 아닙니다 not in the slightest

chogŭmsshik 조금씩 little by little

chogŭmsshik tonŭl naeda 조금씩 돈을 내다 chip in

chogŭmŭi 조금의 a few

chogŭmŭn 조금은 little

chohabe kaip'aji anŭn 조합에 가입하지 않은 non-union

chohang 조항 article, clause, section; provision

chohap 조합 association; union; partnership

chohoe 조회 reference

chohoehada 조회하다 refer to

chohwa 조화 harmony; reconciliation

chohwadoen 조화된 harmonious

chohwashik'ida 조화시키다 harmonize; reconcile

chohyŏngjŏgin 조형적인 figurative

choida 조이다 tie

chojak 조작 mockery; fabrication

chojak'ada 조작하다 manufacture; fix; manipulate

chojanghada 조장하다 further *cause*

chojap'an 조잡한 crude

chojeshil 조제실 dispensary

chojik 조직 organization; system; organ ANAT; tissue

chojiktcha 조직자 organizer

chojiktchŏgin 조직적인 systematic

chojik'ada 조직하다 organize

chojŏng chohwa 조정 조화 coordination

chojŏng chohwashik'ida 조정 조화시키다 coordinate

chojŏnghada 조정하다 set, adjust

chojŏrhada 조절하다 tune up

chojong 조종 operation; manipulation; aviation

chojong changch'i 조종 장치 controls

chojonghada 조종하다 operate; manipulate; steer; pilot

chojonghanŭn 조종하는 manipulative

chojongsa 조종사 pilot

chojongshil 조종실 cockpit; flight deck

chokki 조끼 vest

chokkŏn 조건 condition, requirement; **...ranŭn chokkŏnŭro** ...라는 조건으로 on condition that

chokkŏnbuŭi 조건부의 conditional

chokkŏnppŏp 조건법 conditional

chokppo 족보 genealogy book

choktchang 족장 chief

choktchebi 족제비 weasel

choktchipkke 족집게 tweezers

chok'a 조카 nephew

chok'attal 조카딸 niece

chok'ŏ 조커 joker

chol 졸 pawn

cholda 졸다 doze, snooze

cholgi 졸기 doze, snooze

chollamaeda 졸라매다 fasten tightly; **hŏrit tirŭl chollamaeda** 허리띠를 졸라매다 tighten one's belt *fig*

chollida 졸리다 be sleepy

chollin 졸린 sleepy

choltchak 졸작 trash

chom 좀 some; something; **chom hashigessŏyo?** 좀 하시겠어요? would you like some?

chomajomahage hanŭn 조마조마하게 하는 nerve-racking

choman-gan 조만간 sooner or later

chomirhada 조밀하다 be dense; **in-**

guga chomirhan 인구가 조밀한 densely populated

chomiryo 조미료 seasoning; flavoring

chommŏgŭm 좀먹음 erosion *fig*

chommŏktta 좀먹다 erode *fig*

chomttoduktchil 좀도둑질 pilfering

Chomultchu 조물주 the Creator

chomyŏng 조명 lighting

chomyŏnghada 조명하다 illuminate, light

chomyŏngt'an 조명탄 flare

chonan 조난 disaster; accident

chonan sangt'aeŭi 조난 상태의 in distress

chonan shinho 조난 신호 distress signal

chong 종 species; bell

chong-ari 종아리 calf

chongbŏm 종범 accessory LAW

chongdalssae 종달새 lark

chonggi 종기 boil

chonggyo 종교 religion

chonggyojŏgin 종교적인 religious; sacred

chonghap pohŏm 종합 보험 comprehensive insurance

chong-i 종이 paper; *chong-i han chang* 종이 한 장 a piece of paper

chong-i kabang 종이 가방 paper bag

chong-ik'ŏp 종이컵 paper cup

chong-i mukkŭm 종이 묶음 pad

chong-ip'yojiŭi yŏmkkap'an ch'aek 종이표지의 염가판 책 paperback

chong-iro mandŭn 종이로 만든 (made of) paper

chong-i ullida 종이 울리다 chime

chongma 종마 stallion

chongnyang 종양 growth, tumor

chongnyohada 종료하다 log off; shut down

chongnyonaeda 종료내다 shut down

chongnyu 종류 kind, sort; *chŏgŏsŭn ŏttŏn chongnyuŭi kaeimnikka?* 저것은 어떤 종류의 개입니까? what kind of dog is that?; *oman chongnyuŭi saram* 오만 종류의 사람 all kinds of people

chongŏbwŏn 종업원 worker

chongŏbwŏn ch'ongsu 종업원 총수 payroll

chongp'a 종파 denomination

chongsahada 종사하다 practice

chongtchŏm 종점 terminus

chong-ŭl ch'yŏsŏ pullŏjuseyo 종을 쳐서 불러주세요 please ring for attention

chon-gyŏng 존경 respect

chon-gyŏnghada 존경하다 respect, have a great regard for

chon-gyŏnghanŭn sŏnsaengnim-kke 존경하는 선생님께 Dear Sir

chonham 존함 name

chonjae 존재 being, existence

chonjaehada 존재하다 exist

chonjaerŭl mit-tta 존재를 믿다 believe in

chonjunghada 존중하다 respect

chonŏm 존엄 dignity

choŏn 조언 advice; hint; pointer; *nuguŭi choŏnŭl padadŭrida* 누구의 조언을 받아들이다 take s.o.'s advice

choŏnhada 조언하다 advise

choŏp tanch'uk'ada 조업 단축하다 be on short time

chopch'ok'aji ank'o chinaeda 접촉하지 않고 지내다 be out of touch

choptta 좁다 be narrow

chop'ap pubun 접합 부분 joint

chorangmal 조랑말 pony

choribnyongp'um 조립용품 kit

choribŏp 조립법 recipe

choribŭi 조립의 modular

choriga sŏnŭn 조리가 서는 coherent

chorip 조립 assembly

chorip kongjang 조립 공장 assembly plant

choripsshigŭi 조립식의 prefabricated

chorip tanwi 조립 단위 module

chorip'ada 조립하다 assemble, set up

chorŏp 졸업 graduation

chorŏpssaeng 졸업생 graduate

chorŏp'ada 졸업하다 graduate

chorong 조롱 mockery; taunt

choronghada 조롱하다 ridicule; *hyungnaenaemyŏ choronghada* 흉내내며 조롱하다 mock

chorŭda 조르다 press for; badger; pester

choryŏktcha 조력자 mentor

choryu 조류 current; tide; birds, fowls

choryu poho kuyŏk 조류 보호 구역 bird sanctuary

choryuŭi naejang 조류의 내장 giblets

chosa 조사 investigation; scrutiny; survey

chosadan 조사단 panel

chosahada 조사하다 examine, investigate; survey

chosang 조상 ancestor; ancestry

chosang sungbae 조상 숭배 ancestral worship

chosanwŏn 조산원 midwife

chose 조세 tax; taxes; taxation

choseŭi 조세의 fiscal

choshim 조심 caution

choshimhada 조심하다 take care; guard against; beware of; *kyedanŭl choshimhaseyo!* 계단을 조심하세요! mind the step!

choshimsŏng innŭn 조심성 있는 guarded, careful

choshimsŏng ŏmnŭn 조심성 없는 careless

choshimsŭrŏpke 조심스럽게 carefully

choshimsŭrŏun 조심스러운 cautious

chosŏkp'a 조석파 tidal wave

Chosŏn Minjujuŭi Inmin Konghwaguk 조선 민주주의 인민 공화국 Democratic People's Republic of Korea, DPRK

chosŏnso 조선소 dockyard

choso 조소 ridicule

chosu 조수 assistant; tide

chosuga 조숙아 premature baby

chosuk'an 조숙한 precocious

chot 좃 ∨ prick

chot'a 좋다 be good; *...do chot'a* ...해도 좋다 may

choŭn 좋은 good; *choŭn shiganŭl ponaeda* 좋은 시간을 보내다 have a good time

choyak 조약 treaty

choyonghada 조용하다 be quiet

choyonghaejida 조용해지다 quieten down, settle down

choyonghage 조용하게 in silence

choyonghage hada 조용하게 하다 quieten down

choyongham 조용함 hush

choyonghan 조용한 quiet; silent

choyonghi! 조용히! hush!, silence!

choyonghi hada 조용히 하다 be quiet, shut up; *chom choyonghi hae!* 좀 조용히 해! just be quiet!

choyurhada 조율하다 tune

chŭbi manŭn 즙이 많은 juicy

chŭk 즉 namely

chŭk-kkaktchŏgin 즉각적인 speedy; prompt; instant

chŭksshi 즉시 instantly; on the spot; straight away

chŭksshiro 즉시로 immediately

chŭksshiŭi 즉시의 immediate

chŭkssŏgesŏ chit-tta 즉석에서 짓다 improvise, wing it

chŭkssŏgesŏ mandŭlda 즉석에서 만들다 improvise

chŭkssŏgŭi 즉석의 off the cuff

chŭkssŏk shikp'um 즉석 식품 fast food

chŭk'ŭ 즈크 canvas

chŭk'ŭng-ŭro hada 즉흥으로 하다 improvise

chŭlgida 즐기다 enjoy; relish

chŭlgŏpke chinaeda 즐겁게 지내다 enjoy oneself

chŭlgŏpke hada 즐겁게 하다 entertain; *urinŭn chŏngmal chŭlgŏpke ponaessŏyo* 우리는 정말 즐겁게 보냈어요 we had a lovely time

chŭlgŏpta 즐겁다 be delightful, be pleasant

chŭlgŏum 즐거움 enjoyment; amusement

chŭlgŏun 즐거운 enjoyable; pleasing; *chŭlgŏun Sŏngt'ani toegirŭl paramnida!* 즐거운 성탄이 되기를 바랍니다! Merry Christmas!

chŭngbalshik'ida 증발시키다 vaporize

chŭngbarhada 증발하다 evaporate

chŭngga 증가 increase

chŭnggahada 증가하다 increase

chŭnggahanŭn 증가하는 increasing

chŭnggashik'ida 증가시키다 increase, step up

chŭnggi 증기 vapor

chŭnggŏ 증거 evidence, proof

chŭnggŏrŭl taeda 증거를 대다 substantiate

chŭnghu 증후 symptom; ...*ŭi chŭnghurŭl poida* ...의 증후를 보이다 be symptomatic of

chŭng-in 증인 witness

chŭng-insŏk 증인석 witness stand

chŭng-inŭro sŏmyŏnghada 증인으로 서명하다 witness

chŭng-inŭro sŏmyŏngham 증인으로 서명함

chŭng-inŭro sŏnsŏhada 증인으로 선서하다 swear in as a witness

chŭngjŏnghada 증정하다 present

chŭngjobu 증조부 great-grandfather

chŭngjomo 증조모 great-grandmother

chŭngkkwŏn kŏraeso 증권 거래소 stock exchange

chŭngkkwŏn shijang 증권 시장 stock market

chŭngkkwŏn shijang punggoe 증권 시장 붕괴 stockmarket crash

chŭngmyŏnghada 증명하다 prove; validate, verify

chŭngmyŏngsŏ 증명서 certificate; ID

chŭng-ŏn 증언 evidence

chŭng-ŏnhada 증언하다 testify, give evidence

chŭng-o 증오 hatred, animosity

chŭngp'ok'ada 증폭하다 amplify

chŭngsangŭl poida 증상을 보이다 be sickening for

chŭngsŏ 증서 diploma

chŭngson 증손 great-grandchild

chŭng-wŏn-gun 증원군 reinforcements

chu 주 note; province, state; week; Lord

chubang 주방 kitchen

chubangjang 주방장 chef

chubangyong seje 주방용 세제 dishwashing liquid

chubu 주부 housewife

chubyŏn 주변 perimeter

chubyŏn changch'i 주변 장치

peripheral COMPUT

chuch'a 주차 parking

chuch'a changso 주차 장소 parking place

chuch'adae 주차대 rack

chuch'agŭmji 주차금지 no parking

chuch'ahada 주차하다 park

chuch'ajang 주차장 parking lot

chuch'a wiban tansogwŏn 주차 위반 단속원 traffic warden

chuch'a wiban ttaktchi 주차 위반 딱지 parking ticket

chuch'a yogŭmgi 주차 요금기 parking meter

chuch'eŭishik 주체의식 sense of independence and sovereignty; *kungmin chuch'eŭishik* 국민 주체의식 sense of national identity

chuch'iŭi 주치의 family doctor

chuda 주다 give; assign; allow; give away

chudang 주당 weekly rate

chudo 주도 initiative

chudoen 주된 main

chudohada 주도하다 lead the way

chudojŏgin 주도적인 leading

chudokkwŏn 주도권 supremacy

chudoro 주도로 main road

chudung-i 주둥이 muzzle, snout; spout

chudun-gun 주둔군 garrison

chugan 주간 weekly

chugan kongnyŏn 주간 공연 matinée (*of play*)

chugan kosok toro 주간 고속 도로 interstate

chugan sangnyŏng 주간 상영 matinée (*of movie*)

chuga toeŏ it-tta 주가 되어 있다 predominate

chugida 죽이다 kill; deaden

chugijŏgin 주기적인 periodic

chugŏganŭn 죽어가는 dying

chugŏŭi 주거의 residential

chugŭl unmyŏng 죽을 운명 mortality

chugŭm 죽음 death

chugŭn 죽은 dead

chugŭndŭshi choyonghan 죽은듯이 조용한 deadly quiet

chugŭnkkae 주근깨 freckle

chugŭn saram 죽은 사람 the deceased

chugŭp 주급 weekly payment

chugwanjŏgin 주관적인 subjective

chugyŏ ŏpssaeda 죽여 없애다 eliminate, kill

chugyo 주교 bishop

chuhaeng 주행 run, drive

chuhaeng anjŏngssŏng 주행 안정성 road holding

chuhaeng kŏrigye 주행 거리계 odometer

Chuhan Migun 주한 미군 American Military Forces in Korea

chuhongsaek 주홍색 scarlet

chuhwangsaek 주황색 orange (color)

chuhyŏng 주형 cast, mold

chuin 주인 host; landlord; owner, master; mistress

chuin ŏmnŭn 주인 없는 stray (dog)

chuip 주입 injection; transfusion

chuip'ada 주입하다 infuse; instil; indoctrinate; pump; *konggirŭl chuip'ada* 공기를 주입하다 inflate; pump up

chujang 주장 case, argument; claim, assertion; allegation; team captain

chujanghada 주장하다 argue; claim, insist, maintain; *chagirŭl chujang-hada* 자기를 주장하다 assert oneself

chujangdoen 주장된 alleged

chuje 주제 motif; topic

chujega 주제가 theme song

chujenŏmwŏn 주제넘은 uncalled-for

chujŏhada 주저하다 waver

chujŏhanŭn 주저하는 tentative

chujŏnja 주전자 kettle; jug; teapot; coffee pot

chujohada 주조하다 cast metal

chuju kongjang 주조 공장 foundry

chuju 주주 shareholder, stockholder

chujung-e 주중에 midweek

Chu Kidomun 주 기도문 Lord's Prayer

chuktta 죽다 die; *algo ship'ŏ chuk-kket-tta* 알고 싶어 죽겠다 I'm dying to know; *amŭro chuktta* 암으로 죽다 die of cancer

chuk'ŭ pakssŭ 주크 박스 jukebox

chul 줄 column, line; file; strap; string; *chul chiŏ* 줄 지어 in single file; *han churŭi kyedan* 한 줄의 계단 flight (of stairs); *churŭl ch'ida* 줄을 치다 rope off; *churŭl sŏda* 줄을 서다 stand in line

chulda 줄다 decrease, diminish

chuldambaerŭl p'iuda 줄담배를 피우다 chain smoke

chuldambaerŭl p'iunŭn saram 줄담배를 피우는 사람 chain smoker

chulgi 줄기 stalk, stem; trunk; wisp

chulgot 줄곧 all the time; *chulgot irhayŏ* 줄곧 일하여 on the go

chulja 줄자 tape measure

chuljabŭn 줄잡은 conservative

chullŏmkki chul 줄넘기 줄 skipping rope

chullŏmkkihada 줄넘기하다 skip

chulmunŭi 줄무늬 stripe

chulmunŭi ŏlluk 줄무늬 얼룩 streak

chulmunŭi-ŭi 줄무늬의 striped

chul sŏda 줄 서다 line up

chult'agi chul 줄타기 줄 high wire

chumal 주말 weekend; *chumare* 주말에 on the weekend

chumnenjŭ 줌렌즈 zoom lens

chumnenjŭro match'uda 줌렌즈로 맞추다 zoom in on

chumŏk 주먹 fist

chumŏk k'oŭi 주먹코의 snub-nosed

chumŏktchil 주먹질 punch, thump

chumŏni 주머니 pouch, bag; pocket

chumŏnik'al 주머니칼 pocketknife

chumoja 주모자 ringleader

chumok 주목 attention, notice; *mut saramŭi chumogŭl pat-tta* 뭇 사람의 주목을 받다 be in the limelight

chumok'ada 주목하다 pay attention

chumok'ae chushipssshio 주목해 주십시오 your attention please

chumok'al manhan 주목할 만한 remarkable; notable; noticeable

chumun 주문 order; magic spell; *chumune match'uda* 주문에 맞추다 fill an order

chumunhada 주문하다 order

chunbi 준비 preparation

chunbidoen 준비된 ready; *muŏsŭl hal chunbiga toeŏ it-tta* 무엇을 할

준비가 되어 있다 be prepared to do sth, be willing to do sth

chunbihada 준비하다 arrange, fix; prepare; get ready

chunbihaesŏ 준비해서 in preparation for

chunbihanŭn tan-gye-esŏ 준비하는 단계에서 at the planning stage

chunbi undong-ŭl hada 준비 운동을 하다 warmup

chung 중 Buddhist monk; middle ◊ among; out of; in ◊ while; *yŏl kae chung han kae* 열 개 중 한 개 one in ten; *...ŭi chung-ang-esŏ* ...의 중앙에서 in the middle of; *...chunge* ...중에 in the middle of

chung-ang 중앙 center ◊ central

chung-ang anjŏn changch'i 중앙 안전 장치 central locking

chung-ang chamgŭm changch'i 중앙 잠금 장치 central heating

chung-ang ch'ŏri changch'i 중앙 처리 장치 CPU, central processing unit

chung-ang pullidae 중앙 분리대 median strip

chung-ang ŭnhaeng-ŭi kibon kŭmni 중앙 은행의 기본 금리 base rate

chungbokdoeda 중복되다 overlap

chungch'ŭnghyŏng-ŭi ap'at'ŭ 중층형의 아파트 duplex (apartment)

chungch'ujŏgin 중추적인 spinal

chungdaehada 중대하다 be important; *...ranŭn kŏsŭn kŭk'i chungdaehamnida* ...라는 것은 극히 중대합니다 it is vital that

chungdaehan 중대한 significant, momentous; great; grave

chungdan 중단 disruption, interruption; pause

chungdanhada 중단하다 interrupt; cease; pause; cut out; *chamshi chungdanhada* 잠시 중단하다 take a break

chungdan ŏmnŭn 중단 없는 nonstop

chungdan ŏpsshi 중단 없이 nonstop

chungdanshik'ida 중단시키다 cease; pause; disrupt, interrupt; disconnect

chungdo-e 중도에 midway

chungdogida 중독이다 be addicted to

chungdok 중독 addiction

chungdokssŏng-ida 중독성이다 be addictive

chungdoktcha 중독자 addict

Chungdong 중동 Middle East ◊ Middle Eastern

chungdop'a 중도파 center group, center party

chungdŭng kyoyuk 중등 교육 secondary education

chunggae 중개 mediation; *...saiŭi chunggae yŏk'arŭl hada* ...사이의 중개 역할을 하다 bridge *fig*

chunggaehada 중개하다 mediate

chunggaeja 중개자 go-between

chunggaeŏp 중개업 agency

chunggaeŏptcha 중개업자 broker

chunggan chijŏmŭi 중간 지점의 halfway

chunggane 중간에 halfway

chunggan hyushik 중간 휴식 half time

chunggan irŭm 중간 이름 middle name

chunggankkŭp 중간급 middleweight

chunggan k'ŭgi 중간 크기 medium size

chunggansaegŭi 중간색의 neutral *color*

chunggan sang-in 중간 상인 middleman

chungganŭi 중간의 middle; medium; intermediate

chunggoro 중고로 secondhand

chunggoŭi 중고의 secondhand

Chunggug-ŏ 중국어 Chinese *(language)*

Chungguk 중국 China ◊ Chinese

Chungguk pont'o 중국 본토 mainland China

Chungguk pukkyŏngŏ 중국 북경어 Mandarin *(language)*

Chungguk saram 중국 사람 Chinese *(person)*

chunggyehada 중계하다 relay

chunggyein 중계인 contact

chunghan 중한 heavy

chunghon 중혼 bigamy

chunghwahada 중화하다 counteract

chunghwanjashil 중환자실 intensive care (unit)

chung-ida 중이다: *kŭgŏsŭn kŏmt'o / chosa chung-ida* 그것은 검토/조사 중이다 it is under review/investigation

chungjae 중재 intervention; mediation; arbitration

chungjaehada 중재하다 intervene; intercede; arbitrate, mediate

chungjaein 중재인 mediator, intermediary

chungji 중지 cessation

chungjihada 중지하다 discontinue; abort

chungjishik'ida 중지시키다 break up

chungjoe 중죄 felony

chungmae kyŏrhon 중매 결혼 arranged marriage

chungnibŭi 중립의 neutral

chungnip 중립 neutrality; *chung-nibe* 중립에 in neutral

chungnipssŏng 중립성 neutrality

chungniptchŏgin 중립적인 nonaligned

chungnip wich'i 중립 위치 neutral

chungnyang ch'ogwaŭi 중량 초과의 overweight

chungnyŏk 중력 gravity

chungnyŏn 중년 middle age ◊ middle-aged

chungnyohada 중요하다 matter, be important

chungnyohan 중요한 important

chungnyong 중용 moderation

chungnyosŏng 중요성 importance

chung-ŏlgŏrida 중얼거리다 mumble, mutter

chungp'a 중파 medium wave

chungsa 중사 sergeant

chungsanch'ŭng 중산층 middle classes

chungsang 중상 slander

chungsanghada 중상하다 slander

chungsang moryak 중상 모략 smear campaign

chungsanmo 중산모 top hat

Chungse 중세 Middle Ages ◊ medieval

chungshimbue innŭn 중심부에 있는 central

chungshimdae 중심대 crossbar

chungshimga 중심가 main street

chungshimji 중심지 center (region)

chungshimjŏk 중심적 central; *mu-ŏse chungshimjŏgida* 무엇에 중심적이다 be central to sth

chungshimŭi 중심의 central

chungshimŭl tuda 중심을 두다 center on

chungso kiŏp 중소 기업 small and medium industry

chungt'ae 중태 serious condition MED

chungt'ae-esŏ pŏsŏnan 중태에서 벗어난 out of danger MED

chungt'oehada 중퇴하다 drop out

chungt'oeja 중퇴자 dropout

chung-wi 중위 (first) lieutenant

chun-gyŏlssŭng 준결승 semifinal

chung-yohada 중요하다 be important

chung-yohan 중요한 important, crucial

chung-yo insa 중요 인사 very important person

chung-yo shinch'e kigwan 중요 신체 기관 vital organs

chunim 주님 Lord (Jesus)

chunjun-gyŏlssŭng 준준결승 quarter-final

chunjun-gyŏlssŭng chinch'ultcha 준준결승 진출자 quarter-finalist

chun kunsajŏgin 준 군사적인 paramilitary

chun kunsayowŏn 준 군사요원 paramilitary

chunŏmhan 준엄한 austere

chunsŏrhada 준설하다 dredge

chunsuja 준수자 conformist

chun ŭiryo hwalttong chongsaja 준 의료 활동 종사자 paramedic

chuŏ 주어 subject GRAM

chup'asu 주파수 frequency

chu(rib)ŭi 주(립)의 state, provincial

churi chida 줄이 지다 be streaked with

churida 줄이다 reduce; turn down *volume, heating*; cut down, cut down on; cut short; shorten; narrow

churin irŭm 줄인 이름 diminutive

churŏdŭlda 줄어들다 go down; die down; shrink

churŏdŭrŏ it-tta 줄어들어 있다 be down (of numbers, amount)

churo 주로 mainly

churŭm 주름 pleat; crease; wrinkle

churŭm changshik 주름 장식 ruffle

churŭm chegŏsul 주름 제거술 facelift

churŭmjida 주름지다 wrinkle

churŭmjige hada 주름지게 하다 wrinkle

churyehada 주례하다 marry

churyŏssŭda 줄여쓰다 abbreviate

churyu p'anmaejŏm 주류 판매점 liquor store

chusa 주사 injection

chusagi 주사기 syringe

chusahada 주사하다 inject

chusa panŭl 주사 바늘 hypodermic needle

chusawi 주사위 dice

chushik 주식 stock, share

chushik chungmae-in 주식 중매인 stockbroker

chushik hoesa 주식 회사 stock company

chushik shijang 주식 시장 (stock) market

chusŏk 주석 gloss, explanation; tin

chuso 주소 address

chusorok 주소록 address book; mailing list

chusorŭl ssŭda 주소를 쓰다 address letter

chuso sŏngmyŏngnok 주소 성명록 directory

chut'aek 주택 housing

chut'aek sajŏng 주택 사정 housing conditions

chut'aek tanji 주택 단지 housing project

chuŭi 주의 attention; warning; notice

chuŭi chuda 주의 주다 tick off

chuŭigip'ŭn 주의깊은 attentive, watchful

chuŭihada 주의하다 pay attention, take notice of

chuŭi kipkke saenggak'ada 주의 깊게 생각하다 mull over

chuŭirŭl kiurida 주의를 기울이다 pay attention

chuŭirŭl kkŭlda 주의를 끌다 draw attention

chuŭirŭl tollida 주의를 돌리다 sidetrack

chuŭishik'ida 주의시키다 caution

chuwi 주위 perimeter, periphery ◊ around; *chuwie* 주위에 around, in the area

chuwiŭi 주위의 surrounding

chuwŏ moŭda 주워 모으다 gather up

chuwŏ ollida 주워 올리다 pick up

chuya p'yŏngbunshi 주야 평분시 equinox

chuyŏnhada 주연하다 star

chuyŏnŭro hada 주연으로 하다 feature; star

chuyohan 주요한 main, major; predominant

chuyo shikp'um 주요 식품 staple food

chuyoshikttan 주요식단 staple diet

chuyu p'ŏmp'ŭ 주유 펌프 gas pump

chuyuso 주유소 gas station

chwach'ŭk haendŭl unjŏn 좌측 핸들 운전 left-hand drive

chwach'ugŭi 좌측의 port; left-hand

chwadamhoe 좌담회 talk show

chwagol shin-gyŏngt'ong 좌골 신경통 sciatica

chwaigŭi 좌익의 left-wing

chwaik 좌익 left wing ◊ left-wing

chwajŏl 좌절 frustration; setback; discouragement

chwajŏlsshik'ida 좌절시키다 frustrate; defeat; foil, thwart

chwajŏrhada 좌절하다 collapse; go to pieces; get discouraged

chwaumyŏng 좌우명 motto

chwayak 좌약 suppository

chwi 쥐 mouse; rat

chwikkori 쥐꼬리 rat tail

chwikkorimanhan 쥐꼬리만한 derisory, paltry

chyusŭ 쥬스 juice

CH'

ch'a 차 vehicle; car; tea; **ch'aro teryŏjuda** 차로 데려다주다 drive, take by car; **ch'arŭl t'ago kabŏrida** 차를 타고 가버리다 drive away

ch'abŏrida 차버리다 ditch, jilt

ch'abunhan 차분한 placid, serene; imperturbable

ch'abyŏl 차별 discrimination

ch'abyŏrhada 차별하다 differentiate between; discriminate against

ch'ach'a 차차 by degrees

ch'ach'ang 차창 car window; bus window; train window

ch'ach'e 차체 bodywork

ch'ach'e kongjang 차체 공장 body shop

ch'ach'uk 차축 axle

ch'ada 차다 be filled, be packed; be satisfied; expire; kick; reject

ch'adanhada 차단하다 block out; exclude

ch'ado 차도 driveway

ch'adorŭl poida 차도를 보이다 make progress (in health)

ch'ado tchogŭi 차도 쪽의 offside MOT

ch'ae 채 bat ◊ countword for buildings

ch'aegim 책임 responsibility; accountability; **...e ch'aegimi it-tta** ...에 책임이 있다 be responsible for; **ch'aegimŭl chida** 책임을 지다 be held accountable for, answer for; **ch'aegimŭl chŏn-gahada** 책임을 전가하다 pass the buck

ch'aegimi innŭn 책임이 있는 responsible

ch'aegimi mugŏun 책임이 무거운 responsible job

ch'aegimja 책임자 person in charge; **ch'aegimjarŭl mannal su issŭlkkayo?** 책임자를 만날 수 있을까요? can I see the manager?

ch'aegim pohŏm 책임 보험 liability insurance

ch'aegurhada 채굴하다 mine for

ch'aegwangch'ang 채광창 skylight

ch'aegwŏnja 채권자 creditor

ch'aek 책 book

ch'aek-kkabang 책가방 school bag

ch'aekkwŏn 책권 bond

ch'aekssang 책상 desk

ch'aektchang 책장 bookcase

ch'aek k'ŏbŏ 책 커버 dust jacket

ch'aemp'iŏn 챔피언 champion

ch'aemuja 채무자 debtor

ch'aeng 챙 visor

ch'aenggyŏduda 챙겨두다 set aside

ch'aengnyak 책략 maneuver

ch'aenŏl 채널 channel

ch'aeshigŭi 채식의 vegetarian

ch'aeshiktchuŭija 채식주의자 vegetarian

ch'aesŏktchang 채석장 quarry

ch'aetchiktchil 채찍질 beating; whip

ch'aetchiktchirhada 채찍질하다 whip, beat

ch'aet'aek 채택 choice, selection; adoption

ch'aet'aek'hada 채택하다 select, choose; adopt

ch'aeuda 채우다 complete, fill out; do up, fasten; fill; chill

ch'aewŏ nŏt'a 채워 넣다 stuff

ch'agaptta 차갑다 be cold; be coldhearted

ch'agaun 차가운 cold; cool

ch'age hada 차게 하다 chill

ch'agi 차기 kick

ch'ago 차고 (parking) garage

ch'agwandan 차관단 consortium

ch'agyonghada 착용하다 put on; wear; **anjŏnbelt'ŭrŭl ch'agyonghashio** 안전벨트를 착용하시오 fasten your seatbelt

ch'ai 차이 difference; **amurŏn ch'aiga ŏptta** 아무런 차이가 없다 it

doesn't make any difference

ch'ajaboda 찾아보다 look; look up; look out for

ch'ajabogi 찾아보기 index

ch'ajagada 찾아가다 pay a visit to

ch'ajanaeda 찾아내다 dig out; dig up

ch'ajang 차장 conductor (*on train*)

ch'aja tanida 찾아 다니다 scour, search

ch'ajihada 차지하다 occupy, take up

ch'ajŭngnanŭn kŏt 짜증나는 것 irritation

ch'akch'wi 착취 exploitation

ch'akch'wihada 착취하다 exploit; *tonŭl ch'akch'wihada* 돈을 착취하다 bleed, drain *fig*

ch'ak-kkak 착각 delusion

ch'ak-kkakhada 착각하다 mistake; *nŏn sŭsŭro ch'ak-kkak'ago innŭn kŏya* 넌 스스로 착각하고 있는 거야 you're deluding yourself

ch'akssaek 착색 stain (*for wood*)

ch'akssaek'ada 착색하다 stain *wood*

ch'aksshi 착시 optical illusion

ch'aksshirhan saenghwarŭl hada 착실한 생활을 하다 go straight

ch'akssŏk'ayŏ chushipssio 착석하여 주십시오 please take a seat

ch'akssuhada 착수하다 start, commence; mount; launch; *chinjihage ch'akssuhada* 진지하게 착수하다 start in earnest; knuckle down

ch'aktchap'an 착잡한 complex; *nanŭn kŭege ch'aktchap'an shimjŏng-ŭl kajigo it-tta* 나는 그에게 착잡한 심정을 가지고 있다 I have mixed feelings about him

ch'ak'an ch'ŏk'anŭn saram 착한 척하는 사람 goody-goody

ch'algwasang 찰과상 graze

ch'alk'ak'anŭn soriga nada 찰칵하는 소리가 나다 click

ch'alssak ch'ida 찰싹 치다 swat

ch'alssak ttaerida 찰싹 때리다 slap, cuff

ch'alssak ttaerim 찰싹 때림 blow, cuff

ch'am 참 truth ◊ true ◊ truly; what!

ch'amara! 참아라! just be patient!

ch'amch'i 참치 tuna

ch'amga 참가 participation

ch'amgahada 참가하다 enter; participate; play in; *kŏraee ch'amgahada* 거래에 참가하다 come in on a deal

ch'amgaja 참가자 entrant, participant; entry

ch'amgashik'ida 참가시키다 enter

ch'amgohada 참고하다 consult

ch'amgo tosŏ 참고 도서 reference book

ch'am-gyŏn chal hanŭn saram 참견 잘 하는 사람 busybody

ch'amgyŏnhada 참견하다 poke one's nose into

ch'amgyŏnhagi choahanŭn 참견하기 좋아하는 nosy

ch'amho 참호 trench

ch'a mŏlmi 차 멀미 car sickness

ch'amp'ae 참패 thrashing, massacre SP

ch'amp'aeshik'ida 참패시키다 thrash SP

ch'amsae 참새 sparrow

ch'amshinhan 참신한 refreshing; gratifying

ch'amsŏk 참석 attendance

ch'amsŏktcha 참석자 turnout

ch'amsŏk'ada 참석하다 attend, be present; *chamkkan ch'amsŏk'ada* 잠깐 참석하다 put in an appearance

ch'amsŏn 참선 meditation (*Buddhism*)

ch'amsŏnhada 참선하다 meditate (*Buddhism*)

ch'amtta 참다 contain, repress; contain oneself; stand, tolerate; stomach

ch'amŭlssŏng 참을성 patience

ch'amŭlssŏng innŭn 참을성 있는 patient

ch'amŭlssŏng itkke 참을성 있게 patiently

ch'amŭlssŏng ŏmnŭn 참을성 없는 impatient

ch'amŭl su innŭn 참을 수 있는 tolerable

ch'amŭl su ŏmnŭn 참을 수 없는 intolerable

ch'amŭro 참으로 vitally

ch'amyŏhada 참여하다 take part in

ch'anban yangnon 찬반 양론 the pros and cons

ch'angbaek 창백 pallor

ch'angbaek'an 창백한 pale, pasty

ch'anggo 창고 depot, warehouse; storehouse; stockroom; *...*
ch'anggo-e nö-ö pogwanhada ... 창고에 넣어 보관하다 put in storage

ch'anggu 창구 wicket, window

ch'angja 창자 bowels, gut

ch'angjaktcha 창작자 author

ch'angjo 창조 creation

ch'angjohada 창조하다 create

ch'angjoja 창조자 creator

ch'angjojögin 창조적인 creative

ch'angjomul 창조물 creation, work

ch'angmun 창문 window

ch'angmunŭl yörö chushi-gessŭmnikka? 창문을 열어 주시겠습니까? would you mind opening the window?

ch'angnyö 창녀 prostitute, hooker

ch'angnyuk 착륙 landing, touchdown

ch'angnyuk changch'i 착륙 장치 undercarriage, landing gear

ch'angnyukshik'ida 착륙시키다 land

ch'angnyuk'ada 착륙하다 land, touch down

ch'angshija 창시자 originator

ch'angsöltcha 창설자 creator, founder

ch'angt'ök 창턱 windowsill

ch'ang-üijögin 창의적인 inventive

ch'ang-yuri 창유리 pane, windowpane

ch'anmija 찬미자 admirer

ch'annip 찻잎 tea leaf

ch'ansa 찬사 compliment

ch'ansahada 찬사하다 compliment, pay a compliment

ch'ansahanŭn 찬사하는 complimentary

ch'ansönghada 찬성하다 approve; approve of; be in favor of

ch'ansongga 찬송가 hymn

ch'antchang 찬장 cupboard (*in kitchen*); sideboard

ch'a pongji 차 봉지 teabag

ch'apssal 찹쌀 glutinous rice, sticky rice

ch'ap'okttŭng 차폭등 sidelight

ch'arida 차리다 prepare *meal*; set up *shop*; dress up; keep; collect *one's senses*; take care; preserve; *ch'arin kön optchiman mani tŭseyo* 차린 건 없지만 많이 드세요 please help yourself

ch'aryang 차량 railroad car, carriage

ch'aryang kujo hoesa 차량 구조 회사 wrecking company

ch'aryang kyöninso 차량 견인소 pound (*for cars*)

ch'aryang tŭngnok pönho 차량 등록 번호 license plate number

ch'arye 차례 turn, act; *nöŭi ch'arye* 너의 차례 over to you; *ch'arye ch'aryero* 차례 차례로 in turns; *che ch'aryeimnida* 제 차례입니다 it's my turn; *tangshin ch'aryeyeyo* 당신 차례예요 it's your turn

ch'aryö iptta 차려 입다 dress up; *möttchige ch'aryö iptta* 멋지게 차려 입다 get dolled up

ch'aryönaeda 차려내다 serve up

ch'a sech'ök 차 세척 car wash

ch'asön 차선 (*traffic*) lane

ch'atchan 찻잔 teacup

ch'atkki himdŭn 찾기 힘든 elusive

ch'atssutkkarak 찻숟가락 teaspoon

ch'atchan set'ŭ 찻잔 세트 tea service, tea set

ch'attchömja 차점자 runner-up

ch'at-tta 찾다 find; look for; search for *place*

ch'ayang 차양 awning

ch'ayongja 차용자 tenant

ch'e 체 sieve, strainer; pretense

ch'ege 체계 system

ch'egejögŭro 체계적으로 systematically

ch'egyök 체격 physique, build

ch'ehada 체하다 pretend

ch'ehöm 체험 experience

ch'ehyöng 체형 corporal punishment

ch'ein 체인 chain

ch'einjom 체인점 chain (*of stores*)

ch'eisö 체이서 chaser

ch'ejil 체질 constitution

ch'ejo 체조 gymnastics

ch'ejobok 체조복 leotard

ch'ejung kwadaŭi 체중 과다의 overweight

ch'ejung midarŭi 체중 미달의 underweight

ch'ejung-ŭl nŭrida 체중을 늘이다 put on weight

Ch'ek'o 체코 Czech

Ch'ek'o konghwaguk 체코 공화국 Czech Republic

Ch'ek'oŏ 체코어 Czech (language)

Ch'ek'o saram 체코 사람 Czech (person)

ch'ek'ŭaut'ada 체크아웃하다 check out

ch'ek'ŭinhada 체크인하다 check in

ch'ek'ŭ munŭi 체크 무늬 check pattern

ch'ek'ŭ munŭiŭi 체크 무늬의 checked

ch'ek'ŭp'oint'ŭ 체크포인트 checkpoint

ch'ello 첼로 cello

ch'emyŏnŭl ch'arinŭn 체면을 차리는 image-conscious

ch'emyŏnŭl ilt'a 체면을 잃다 lose face; be in the doghouse

ch'emyŏnŭl sonsangshik'ida 체면을 손상시키다 degrade; chagiŭi ch'emyŏnŭl sonsangshik'ida 자기의 체면을 손상시키다 compromise oneself

ch'emyŏnŭl sonsangshik'inŭn 체면을 손상시키는 degrading

ch'enae 체내 inside the body; ch'enaee(sŏ) 체내에(서) internally; ch'enae pangsanŭng punp'o sajin 체내 방사능 분포 사진 scan MED

ch'enap 체납 delinquency

ch'enyŏmhanŭn 체념하는 resigned

ch'eŏ lip'ŭt'ŭ 체어 리프트 chair lift

ch'ep'o 체포 arrest

ch'ep'ohada 체포하다 arrest, pick up

ch'ero ch'ida 체로 치다 sift

ch'eryŏginnŭn 체력있는 athletic

ch'eryŏk 체력 stamina

ch'eryu 체류 residence, stay

ch'esŭ 체스 chess

ch'esŭp'an 체스판 chessboard

ch'eyuk 체육 gym, gymnastics

ch'eyuk-kkwan 체육관 gym, gymnasium

ch'eyuk kyosa 체육 교사 gymnast

ch'ia 치아 teeth ◊ dental

ch'ia kŏmsa 치아 검사 dental checkup

ch'ida 치다 hit, knock; buffet; count, include; strike (of clock); crash (of thunder); draw curtain; pitch tent; take exam

ch'igi 치기 slap, blow

ch'igwan 치관 crown

ch'ijanghada 치장하다 preen oneself

ch'ijil 치질 piles

ch'ijŭ 치즈 cheese

ch'ijŭbŏgŏ 치즈버거 cheeseburger

ch'ijŭk'eik 치즈케익 cheesecake

ch'ikkwa 치과 dental clinic

ch'ikkwa ŭisa 치과 의사 dentist

ch'ik'yŏ ollagan 치켜 올라간 slanting

ch'il 칠 seven; paint; varnish; laquer; ch'il chu-ŭi 칠 주의 wet paint

ch'ilgi 칠기 lacquerware

ch'ilmyŏnjo 칠면조 turkey

ch'ilp'an 칠판 blackboard

ch'ilsship 칠십 seventy

ch'im 침 saliva; acupuncture

ch'ima 치마 skirt

ch'imbŏm 침범 invasion; intrusion

ch'imbŏmhada 침범하다 invade; intrude

ch'imch'ak 침착 calm, composure; poise

ch'imch'ak'ada 침착하다 keep one's cool

ch'imch'ak'age hae! 침착하게 해! steady on!

ch'imch'ak'age it-tta 침착하게 있다 keep calm; keep one's wits about one

ch'imch'ak'am 침착함 presence of mind

ch'imch'ak'an 침착한 calm, composed; poised; unflappable

ch'imch'ehada 침체하다 stagnate

ch'imch'ehan 침체한 stagnant

ch'imdae 침대 bed

ch'imdaebo 침대보 bedspread

ch'imdaech'a 침대차 sleeping car

ch'imdaech'atkkan 침대찻간

couchette

ch'imdaek'an 침대칸 berth

ch'imdaeppo 침대보 cover, blanket

ch'imgu 침구 bedclothes

ch'imha 침하 subsidence

ch'imhaehada 침해하다 encroach on *rights*

ch'imip 침입 break-in, raid

ch'imiptcha 침입자 intruder, raider

ch'imip'ada 침입하다 encroach on; trepass; infiltrate; break in; raid

ch'imjŏnmul 침전물 sediment

ch'immugŭl chik'ida 침묵을 지키다 stay silent

ch'immuk 침묵 silence

ch'immukshik'ida 침묵시키다 silence

ch'imnyak 침략 invasion

ch'imnyak'ada 침략하다 invade

ch'imnyŏpssu 침엽수 conifer

ch'imp'anji 침판지 chimpanzee

ch'imshik 침식 erosion

ch'imshik'ada 침식하다 erode

ch'imshil 침실 bedroom

ch'imsul 침술 acupuncture

ch'imt'u 침투 penetration

ch'imŭl hŭllida 침을 흘리다 dribble

ch'imŭl paet-tta 침을 뱉다 spit

ch'imurhae it-tta 침울해 있다 be gloomy, feel down

ch'imurhage nŭkkida 침울하게 느끼다 be feeling low

ch'imurhan 침울한 melancholy; dismal; sullen; somber

ch'imyŏngjŏgin 치명적인 fatal, lethal; devastating, shattering

ch'imyŏngsang-ŭi 치명상의 fatally injured

ch'inaehanŭn 친애하는 dear

ch'inbumo 친부모 biological parents

ch'inch'ŏgi toenŭn 친척이 되는 related

ch'inch'ŏk 친척 relative, relation

ch'ingch'an 칭찬 praise

ch'ingch'anhada 칭찬하다 praise; pay a compliment

ch'ingch'anhal manhan 칭찬할 만한 creditable; praiseworthy

ch'ingho 칭호 form of address

ch'ing-ŏlgŏrida 칭얼거리다 whine, complain

ch'ingsong 칭송 applause, praise

ch'ingsonghada 칭송하다 applaud, praise

ch'in-gŭnhan 친근한 familiar, friendly

ch'in-gu 친구 friend, buddy

ch'in-guga toeda 친구가 되다 make friends

ch'in-gyo moim 친교 모임 get-together

ch'inhada 친하다 be close; *Xwa/kwa ch'inhage toeda* X와/과 친하게 되다 be friendly with X, be friends with X

ch'inhan 친한 friendly; close

ch'inhwan-gyŏngjŏgin 친환경적인 environmentally friendly

ch'inhwan-gyŏng sech'ŏktche 친환경 세척제 biological detergent

ch'injŏl 친절 kindness

ch'injŏrhada 친절하다 be kind

ch'injŏrhage 친절하게 kindly; *nuguege ch'injŏrhage hada* 누구에게 친절하게 하다 do s.o. a good turn

ch'injŏrhan 친절한 kind

ch'inmogŭi 친목의 social

ch'insuk'am 친숙함 intimacy

ch'insuk'an 친숙한 intimate

ch'iŏ nŏmŏttŭrida 치어 넘어뜨리다 knock over; run over

ch'iŏridŏ 치어리더 cheerleader

ch'ip 칩 chip

ch'irhada 칠하다 paint

ch'irhŭk 칠흑 pitch black

ch'irŭda 치르다 pay; take *examination*; undergo; hold *ceremony*

ch'irwŏl 칠월 July

ch'iryo 치료 cure; treatment; therapy

ch'iryo chŏnmun-ga 치료 전문가 therapist

ch'iryohada 치료하다 treat; cure

ch'iryoŭi 치료의 therapeutic

ch'isŏk 치석 plaque

ch'isot-tta 치솟다 rocket, soar, shoot up

ch'issu 치수 size; measurements

ch'issurŭl chaeda 치수를 재다 measure

ch'itssol 칫솔 toothbrush

ch'it'ong 치통 toothache

ch'iuda 치우다 brush; clear; remove; put away

ch'iyak 치약 toothpaste

ch'iyŏl kyojŏnggi 치열 교정기 brace

ch'iyŏrhan 치열한 cut-throat

ch'iyok 치욕 a disgrace; *ch'iyoktchŏgin iriyeyo* 치욕적인 일이예요 it's a disgrace

ch'iyokssŭrŏpkke 불명예스럽게 disgracefully, shamefully

ch'ŏbanghada 처방하다 prescribe

ch'ŏbangjŏn 처방전 prescription

ch'ŏbŏl 처벌 punishment; penalty

ch'ŏbŏrhada 처벌하다 punish; penalize

ch'ŏbun 처분 disposal

ch'ŏbunhada 처분하다 dispose of; part with

ch'ŏhada 처하다 run into

ch'ŏhyŏng 처형 sister-in-law (*wife's elder sister*)

ch'ŏje 처제 sister-in-law (*wife's younger sister*)

ch'ŏjida 처지다 hang down; *ch'uk ch'ŏjida* 축 처지다 sag (*of ceiling, rope*)

ch'ŏk 척 countword for boats

ch'ŏkch'u 척추 spine

ch'ŏkch'u chiapssa 척추 지압사 chiropractor

ch'ŏkch'udongmul 척추동물 vertebrate

ch'ŏkch'ugol 척추골 vertebra

ch'ŏkch'uŭi 척추의 spinal

ch'ŏktto 척도 yardstick, criterion

ch'ŏk'ada 척하다 pretend, play-act

ch'ŏl 철 season, period

ch'ŏlgap sang-ŏ aljŏt 철갑 상어 알젓 caviar

ch'ŏlgongso 철공소 ironworks

ch'ŏlgŭn k'onk'ŭrit'ŭ 철근 콘크리트 reinforced concrete

ch'ŏlk'ŏdŏnghanŭn sori 철커덩하는 소리 clang

ch'ŏlk'ŏdŏnghanŭn soriga nada 철커덩하는 소리가 나다 clang

ch'ŏlmang 철망 wire netting

ch'ŏlmul 철물 hardware

ch'ŏlmultchŏm 철물점 hardware store

ch'ŏlssa 철사 wire

ch'ŏlssŏk ttaerida 철썩 때리다 whack

ch'ŏlssu 철수 withdrawal

ch'ŏlssuhada 철수하다 withdraw (*of troops*)

ch'ŏlssushik'ida 철수시키다 withdraw *troops*

ch'ŏltcha 철자 spelling

ch'ŏltchahada 철자하다 spell

ch'ŏltcha hwagin 철자 확인 spellcheck

ch'ŏltcha hwagin togu 철자 확인 도구 spellchecker

ch'ŏltchŏhage 철저하게 thoroughly

ch'ŏltchŏhan 철저한 thorough; exhaustive

ch'ŏltchŏhi chosahada 철저히 조사하다 look through

ch'ŏltto 철도 rail; railroad; track

ch'ŏma 처마 eaves

ch'ŏmbusŏ 첨부서 covering letter

ch'ŏmdan kisul 첨단 기술 high technology, high tech

ch'ŏmdanŭi 첨단의 leading-edge

ch'ŏmgaje 첨가제 (food) additive

ch'ŏn 천 cloth; thousand

ch'ŏ-nam 처남 brother-in-law (*wife's younger brother*)

ch'ŏnbak'an 천박한 shallow, superficial; small-minded

ch'ŏnch'amanbyŏrijiyo 천차만별이지요 it varies

ch'ŏnch'ŏnhi 천천히 slowly

ch'ŏnch'ung 촌충 tapeworm

ch'ŏndung 천둥 thunder

ch'ŏngbaji 청바지 jeans

ch'ŏngbu sarinja 청부 살인자 hitman

ch'ŏngch'ŏnbyŏngnyŏk-kkwa kach'i 청천벽력과 같이 like a bolt from the blue

ch'ŏngch'un-gi 청춘기 youth (*age*)

ch'ŏngch'wihada 청취하다 tune in to

ch'ŏngch'wija 청취자 listener; audience (*of radio program*)

ch'ŏngdong 청동 bronze

ch'ŏngdongsaek 청동색 bronze

ch'ŏnggak chang-ae 청각 장애 deafness

ch'ŏngganghada 청강하다 audit

ch'ŏnggangsaeng 청강생 auditor

ch'ŏnggu 청구 claim

ch'ŏngguhada 청구하다 charge; claim

ch'ŏnggusŏ 청구서 bill

ch'ŏnggyŏl 청결 purity

ch'ŏnggyodo 청교도 puritan

ch'ŏnghada 청하다 request

ch'ŏnghon 청혼 proposal

ch'ŏnghonhada 청혼하다 propose

ch'ŏngja 청자 celadon ware

ch'ŏngjin-gii 청진기 stethoscope

ch'ŏngjinhada 청진하다 sound

ch'ŏngjung 청중 audience

ch'ŏngnokssaek 청록색 turquoise

ch'ŏngnyang ŭmnyo 청량 음료 soft drink

ch'ŏngnyŏk 청력 hearing

ch'ŏng-ŏ 청어 herring

ch'ŏn-gonggi 천공기 drill

ch'ŏngsajin 청사진 blueprint

ch'ŏngsan 청산 settlement; liquidation

ch'ŏngsanhada 청산하다 go into liquidation; settle; write off

ch'ŏngsobu 청소부 cleaner

ch'ŏngsohada 청소하다 clean; clean up; rub down; *kkaekkŭt'age ch'ŏngsohada* 깨끗하게 청소하다 clean out *room, closet*

ch'ŏngsohanŭn ajumma 청소하는 아줌마 cleaning woman

ch'ŏngsokkwa 청소과 sanitation department

ch'ŏngsonyŏn 청소년 adolescents, juveniles ◊ juvenile, adolescent

ch'ŏngsonyŏn pihaeng 청소년 비행 youthful misdemeanors

ch'ŏnguk 천국 heaven

Ch'ŏng-wadae 청와대 The Blue House (*South Korean President's residence*)

ch'ŏng-wŏnsŏ 청원서 petition

ch'ŏnhamujŏgŭi 천하무적의 unbeaten

ch'ŏnhan 천한 humble, menial

ch'ŏnjae 천재 genius

ch'ŏnjaejibyŏn 천재지변 catastrophe, disaster

ch'ŏnjang 천장 ceiling

ch'ŏnjang-ŭi nop'i 천장의 높이 headroom

Ch'ŏnji ch'angjo 천지 창조 Creation REL

ch'ŏnjinhan 천진한 childlike; disarming

Ch'ŏnjugyo 천주교 Roman Catholicism

Ch'ŏnjugyo shinja 천주교 신자 Catholic

Ch'ŏnjugyoŭi 천주교의 Catholic

ch'ŏnmagŭl ch'ida 천막을 치다 camp

ch'ŏnmak 천막 tent

ch'ŏnmaneyo 천만에요 you're welcome

ch'ŏnmunhak 천문학 astronomy

ch'ŏnmunhaktcha 천문학자 astronomer

ch'ŏnmunhaktchŏgin 천문학적인 astronomical

ch'ŏnnyŏn 천년 millennium

ch'ŏn pŏntchaeŭi 천 번째의 thousandth

ch'ŏn pŏnŭi 천 번의 thousandth

ch'ŏnshik 천식 asthma

ch'ŏnsŏng 천성 nature, disposition

ch'ŏntchogak 천조각 pad, wad

ch'ŏnyŏ 처녀 virgin (*female*)

ch'ŏnyŏ hanghae 처녀 항해 maiden voyage

ch'ŏnyŏndu 천연두 smallpox

ch'ŏnyŏn kassŭ 천연 가스 natural gas

ch'ŏrhada 철하다 file

ch'ŏrhak 철학 philosophy

ch'ŏrhaktcha 철학자 philosopher

ch'ŏrhatchŏgin 철학적인 philosophical

ch'ŏrhoehada 철회하다 pull out; withdraw; backpedal; dispense with, waive

ch'ŏrihada 처리하다 take care of, deal with; cope with; cope; process; transact

ch'ŏrŏm 처럼 as, like

ch'ŏryak'ada 절약하다 economize

ch'ŏshinhada 처신하다 conduct oneself

ch'ŏt 첫 first; *...ŭi ch'ŏtchaenare* ...의 첫째날에 on the 1st of ...

ch'ŏt-tchaero 첫째로 in the first place

ch'ŏtwŏlgŭp 첫 월급 starting salary

ch'ŏŭm 처음 start

ch'ŏŭmbut'ŏ 처음부터 initially; from the start

ch'ŏŭmbut'ŏ shijak'ada 처음부터 시작하다 start from scratch

ch'ŏŭmenŭn 처음에는 originally, at first

ch'ŏŭmŭi 처음의 first

ch'ŏŭmŭro 처음으로 first; the first time

ch'o 초 candle; excerpt; second; draft; vinegar; beginning, early part ◊ ultra-; *yuwŏl ch'oe* 유월 초에 in early June

ch'oboja 초보자 beginner

ch'och'im 초침 second hand (*on clock*)

ch'odae 초대 invitation

ch'odaehada 초대하다 invite

ch'odŭnghak-kkyo 초등학교 elementary school, infant school

ch'odŭnghak-kkyo kyosa 초등학교 교사 elementary teacher

ch'oe-agŭi sangt'ae-enŭn 최악의 상태에는 if the worst comes to worst

ch'oe-ak 최악 the worst

ch'oech'ŏmdan 최첨단 frontier

ch'oech'ŏmdanŭi 최첨단의 state-of-the-art

ch'oech'oŭi 최초의 original; initial

ch'oedae 최대 maximum; *...ŭl ch'oedaehan hwaryonghayŏ kkŭrŏnaeda* ...을 최대한 활용하여 끌어내다 make the most of

ch'oedaehanŭi 최대한의 utmost

ch'oedaehanŭro 최대한으로 at the outside

ch'oedaehanŭro iyonghada 최대한으로 이용하다 make the best of

ch'oedaehwahada 최대화하다 maximize

ch'oedae saengsannyŏk 최대 생산력 capacity

ch'oedae sobiryang 최대 소비량 peak consumption

ch'oedaeŭi 최대의 maximum

ch'oego 최고 the best

ch'oegoch'i 최고치 peak

ch'oegoch'ie tarhada 최고치에 달하다 peak

ch'oegogŭbŭi 최고급의 first-rate

ch'oego hando 최고 한도 ceiling, limit

ch'oego kyŏngnyŏngja 최고 경영자 CEO, Chief Executive Officer

ch'oego p'umjil pojŭng kigan 최고 품질 보증 기간 best before date

ch'oego saryŏnggwan 최고 사령관 commander-in-chief

ch'oego suwi 최고 수위 high water

ch'oegoŭi 최고의 best; top; terrific

ch'oegoŭmbuŭi 최고음부의 treble

ch'oegowiŭi 최고위의 supreme

ch'oegŭn 최근 newly

ch'oegŭne 최근에 recently; lately

ch'oegŭnŭi 최근의 recent; latest

ch'oehu t'ongch'ŏp 최후 통첩 ultimatum

ch'oehuŭi kyŏng-ŭi 최후의 경의 last respects; *nuguege ch'oehuŭi kyŏng-ŭirŭl p'yohada* 누구에게 최후의 경의를 표하다 pay one's last respects to s.o.

ch'oejŏgŭi 최적의 optimum

ch'oejŏk 최적 optimum

ch'oejong-ŭi 최종의 final

ch'oejŏ ponggŭp 최저 봉급 minimum wage

ch'oejŏ saenghwal sujun 최저 생활 수준 subsistence level

ch'oejŏŭi 최저의 rock-bottom

ch'oejong 최종 the last; the end ◊ final

ch'oejong kyŏlkwa 최종 결과 end result

ch'oejong myŏngdan 최종 명단 shortlist

ch'oejong sayongja 최종 사용자 end-user

ch'oejongsuro 최종수로 at the last count

ch'oemyŏnsul 최면술 hypnosis

ch'oemyŏnsurŭl kŏlda 최면술을 걸다 hypnotize

ch'oemyŏn yoppŏp 최면 요법 hypnotherapy

ch'oerugasŭ 최루가스 tear gas

ch'oesang-ŭi 최상의 top, best; ultimate

ch'oeshin chŏngborŭl chuda 최신 정보를 주다 update

ch'oeshinŭi 최신의 latest; up-to-date

ch'oeshin yuhaeng-ŭi 최신 유행의 trendy

ch'oesŏnŭl tahada 최선을 다하다 do one's best

ch'oeso 최소 minimum

ch'oesohanŭi 최소한의 minimum

ch'oesohwahada 최소화하다 minimize

ch'oesoryang 최소량 least

ch'oesoŭi 최소의 minimal

ch'oeusŏn sahang 최우선 사항 priority

ch'ogangdaeguk 초강대국 superpower

ch'ogi 초기 infancy

ch'ogiŭi 초기의 early, first

ch'ogo 초고 draft

ch'ogosok yŏlch'a 초고속 열차 bullet train

ch'ogwahada 초과하다 exceed; overrun time

ch'ogwahanŭn 초과하는 in excess of

ch'ogwa kŭnmu 초과 근무 overtime

ch'ogwa suhamul 초과 수하물 excess baggage

ch'ogwa yogŭm 초과 요금 excess fare

ch'ohyŏndaejŏgin 초현대적인 futuristic

ch'o ilkki 초 읽기 countdown

ch'oinjŏgin 초인적인 enormous

ch'oinjong 초인종 doorbell

ch'ojayŏnjŏgin 초자연적인 supernatural

ch'ojŏnyŏge 초저녁에 at nightfall

ch'ojohaehada 초조해하다 panic, flap

ch'ojohan 초조한 edgy

ch'ok-kkam 촉감 (sense of) touch

ch'okppak'an 촉박한 tight (of time)

ch'okssu 촉수 tentacle

ch'oktchin 촉진 boost

ch'oktchinhada 촉진하다 promote, foster

ch'oktchinje 촉진제 catalyst

ch'oktchinshik'ida 촉진시키다 boost

ch'ok'ollit 초콜릿 chocolate

ch'ok'ollit k'eik 초콜릿 케익 chocolate cake, brownie

ch'ok'ŭ 초크 choke

ch'ong 총 gun

ch'ong-aek 총액 total amount of money

ch'ong-al 총알 bullet; shotgun pellet

ch'ongbiyong 총비용 capital expenditure

ch'ongch'e 총체 the whole, all

ch'ongch'ong kŏrŭmŭro kada 총총 걸음으로 가다 trot

ch'onggak 총각 bachelor

ch'onggak p'at'i 총각 파티 stag party

ch'onggi hyudaeja 총기 휴대자 gunman

ch'onggye 총계 total; sum; gross

ch'onghoe 총회 general meeting

ch'ongkyŏlssan 총결산 bottom line

ch'ongmae k'ŏnbŏt'ŏ 촉매 컨버터 catalytic converter

ch'ongmyŏngham 총명함 intelligence, brightness

ch'ongmyŏnghan 총명한 intelligent, bright

ch'ongsang 총상 gunshot wound

ch'ongsarhada 총살하다 shoot dead

ch'ongsŏn-gŏ 총선거 general election

ch'ongssori 총소리 gunshot

ch'ongŭk 촌극 sketch THEA

ch'onssŭrŏun 촌스러운 provincial, parochial

ch'onsŭrŏpkke hwaryŏhan 촌스럽게 화려한 gaudy

ch'onsŭrŏun 촌스러운 dowdy

ch'oraehada 초래하다 bring, create; incur

ch'orahan 초라한 humble

ch'osanghwa 초상화 portrait

ch'oshimja 초심자 novice

ch'osohyŏng 초소형 miniature, midget

ch'ossŭngttal 초승달 new moon

ch'otchŏm 초점 focus; *ch'otchŏmi mat-tta/mat-tchi ant'a* 초점이 맞다/맞지 않다 be in focus/out of focus; *ch'otchŏmŭl match'uda* 초점을 맞추다 focus on ch'ot-ttae 촛대 candlestick

ch'oŭmp'a 초음파 ultrasound

ch'oŭmsok 초음속 supersonic speed ◊ supersonic

ch'owŏltchŏgin 초월적인 transcendental

ch'owŏn 초원 meadow

ch'oyŏn 초연 première

ch'oyŏnhan 초연한 aloof, remote

ch'ŭktchŏng 측정 measurement, reading

ch'ŭktchŏnghada 측정하다 gauge

ch'ŭktchŏngppŏp 측정법 system (of measurement)

ch'ŭng 층 layer; floor; tier; deck

ch'ŭnggye 층계 the stairs

ch'ŭnggyech'am 층계참 landing

ch'ubang 추방 exile; expulsion

ch'ubanghada 추방하다 exile; *t'up'yoe ŭihae ch'ubanghada* 투표에 의해 추방하다 vote out

ch'ubangja 추방자 exile

ch'ubun 추분 the autumnal equinox

ch'uch'ŏn 추천 recommendation, endorsement

ch'uch'ŏnhada 추천하다 recommend, endorse

ch'uch'ŏnsŏ 추천서 reference

ch'uch'ŏntchang 추천장 testimonial

ch'uch'ŭk 추측 guess; conjecture; speculation

ch'uch'ŭk'ada 추측하다 expect; gather; speculate; guess

ch'uch'ul 추출 extraction

ch'udohada 추도하다 mourn

ch'uga 추가 addition, supplement ◊ additional, extra

ch'uga-aek 추가액 supplement FIN

ch'ugahada 추가하다 add

ch'uga hangmok 추가 항목 add-on

ch'uganp'an 추간판 slipped disc

ch'ugaro 추가로 in addition

ch'uga yogŭm 추가 요금 extra charge

ch'ugu 추구 search; pursuit

ch'uguhada 추구하다 pursue; search for; seek

ch'ugyŏk 추격 chase

ch'uhu t'ongjiga issŭl ttaekkaji 추후 통지가 있을 때까지 until further notice

ch'ujap'an 추잡판 lewd

ch'ujinhada 추진하다 propel, drive; go ahead with; set things in motion

ch'ujinnyŏk 추진력 driving force

ch'ujŏk 추적 pursuit

ch'ujŏktcha 추적자 pursuer

ch'ujŏk'ada 추적하다 pursue; stalk; trace

ch'ujŏng 추정 presumption

ch'ujŏngdoeda 추정되다 be presumed; *muŏshi ...ttaemunŭro ch'ujŏngdoeda* 무엇이 ...때문으로 추정되다 attribute sth to ...

ch'ujŏnghada 추정하다 presume

ch'ukch'ŏk 축척 scale

ch'ukch'ŏk tomyŏn 축척 도면 scale drawing

ch'ukch'uk'age hada 축축하게 하다 dampen, moisten

ch'ukch'uk'an 축축한 damp, moist

ch'uk-kka 축가 carol

ch'uk-kku 축구 soccer

ch'uk-kku sŏnsu 축구 선수 soccer player

ch'uk-kkugong 축구공 football, ball

ch'ukppok'ada 축복하다 bless

ch'ukssohada 축소하다 cut back

ch'uktche 축제 carnival; festival; feast

ch'uktcheŭi 축제의 festive

ch'uk'a 축하 congratulations

ch'uk'ahada 축하하다 celebrate; congratulate

ch'uk'a haengsa 축하 행사 festivities

ch'uk'ahamnida 축하합니다 congratulations on

ch'uk'ayŏn 축하연 celebration

ch'ulbal 출발 departure; starting; start; *chohŭn* / *nappŭn ch'ulbarŭl hada* 좋은/나쁜 출발을 하다 get off to a good / bad start; *sae ch'ulbal* 새 출발 a new departure

ch'ulbal shigak 출발 시각 departure time

ch'ulbal shigan 출발 시간 flight time

ch'ulbaltchŏm 출발점 starting point; threshold

ch'ulbarhada 출발하다 leave, go; depart; set off

ch'ulgŭnhada 출근하다 go to work

ch'ulgu 출구 exit

ch'ullabwŏn 출납원 cashier

ch'ullyŏk 출력 output

ch'ullyŏk'ada 출력하다 output

ch'ulmahada 출마하다 run, stand; **taet'ongnyŏnge ch'ulmahada** 대통령에 출마하다 run for President

ch'ulp'an 출판 publication

ch'ulp'andoeda 출판되다 be published, be out

ch'ulp'anhada 출판하다 publish

ch'ulp'anŏp 출판업 publishing

ch'ulp'anŏptcha 출판업자 publisher (*person*)

ch'ulp'ansa 출판사 publisher (*company*)

ch'ulsan hyuga 출산 휴가 maternity leave

ch'ulssaeng chŏnŭi 출생 전의 prenatal

ch'ulssaeng chŭngmyŏngsŏ 출생 증명서 birth certificate

ch'ulssaengguk 출생국 native country

ch'ulssaengji 출생지 birthplace

ch'ulssaengnyul 출생률 birthrate

ch'ulssaeng-ŭi 출생의 native

ch'ulssan 출산 birth

ch'ulssan chŏnŭi 출산 전의 antenatal

ch'ulssanhada 출산하다 bear *child*

ch'ulsshihada 출시하다 appear, come out; bring out; release

ch'ulsshinida 출신이다 originate, come from

ch'ulsshin sŏngbun 출신 성분 background

ch'ulssŏk 출석 attendance

ch'ultchang 출장 business trip

ch'ultchŏnhada 출전하다 compete; go in for, enter

ch'ulttu 출두 appearance (*in court*)

ch'ulttuhada 출두하다 appear (*in court*); report

ch'ult'oegŭn shigan 출퇴근 시간 rush hour

ch'ult'oegŭn shigan kirok-kkye 출퇴근 시간 기록계 time clock

ch'um 춤 dance

ch'umch'uda 춤추다 dance

ch'unbun 춘분 the spring equinox

ch'ungbunhada 충분하다 be sufficient; be satisfactory; **kŭgŏllo ch'ungbunhamnida** 그걸로 충분합니다 that should be enough

ch'ungbunhage 충분하게 sufficiently

ch'ungbunhan 충분한 enough

ch'ungbunhan yang 충분한 양 enough

ch'ungbunhi 충분히 duly; enough

ch'ungch'i 충치 cavity

ch'ungch'iga saenggida 충치가 생기다 decay (*of teeth*)

ch'ungdol 충돌 collision; crash; conflict; impact

ch'ungdolshik'ida 충돌시키다 crash

ch'ungdong 충동 urge; impulse; **ch'ungdongjŏgŭro muŏsŭl hada** 충동적으로 무엇을 하다 do sth on an impulse

ch'ungdongjŏgin 충동적인 impulsive

ch'ungdong kumae 충동 구매 impulse buy

ch'ungdongtchŏgŭro 충동적으로 on the spur of the moment

ch'ungdorhada 충돌하다 crash; collide with, hit; clash; be at odds with

ch'unggo 중고 used, secondhand; advice; warning

ch'unggohada 충고하다 advise caution etc

ch'unggo han madi 충고 한 마디 piece of advice

ch'unggyŏgesŏ pŏsŏnaji mot'ada 충격에서 벗어나지 못하다 be in shock

ch'unggyŏgŭl pat-tta 충격을 받다 be shocked; be flabbergasted

ch'unggyŏk 충격 blow, shock

ch'unggyŏktchŏgin 충격적인 shocking, horrifying

ch'unghyŏldoen 충혈된 bloodshot

ch'ungjŏnhada 충전하다 charge battery

ch'ungjokshik'ida 충족시키다 meet, satisfy

ch'ungmanhada 충만하다 be full, be

filled; **hwalgiga ch'ungmanhan**
활기가 충만한 exuberant

ch'ungmyŏn 측면 side

ch'ungnongtchŭng 축농증 sinusitis

ch'ungshil 충실 fidelity, faithfulness

ch'ungshimŭro 충심으로 heartily,
cordially

ch'ungshirhada 충실하다 stick by;
be faithful, be loyal; **sangdaeege
ch'ungshirhada** 상대에게 충실하다
be faithful to one's partner

ch'ungshirhan 충실한 faithful,
staunch

ch'ungsŏngshim 충성심 sense of
loyalty; **kiŏbe taehan
ch'ungsŏngshim** 기업에 대한
충성심 sense of corporate loyalty

ch'ungsŏngsŭrŏun 충성스러운 loyal

ch'ungsu 충수 appendix

ch'ungsuyŏm 충수염 appendicitis

ch'uŏk 추억 memory

ch'up'a 추파 leer

ch'urak 추락 crash, fall

ch'urak'ada 추락하다 crash

ch'urhanghada 출항하다 sail, depart

ch'urhyŏl 출혈 bleeding; hemorrhage

ch'urhyŏn 출현 arrival, appearance

ch'urhyŏrhada 출혈하다 bleed;
hemorrhage

ch'urimmun 출입문 door; entrance;
exit

ch'urimul 추리물 whodunnit

ch'urip 출입 access

ch'uripkku 출입구 doorway

ch'urip kŭmji 출입 금지 off limits; no
trespassing

Ch'urip Kwalliguk 출입 관리국
Immigration Bureau

ch'urip'ang kŭmji 출입항 금지 ban,
embargo

ch'uron 추론 deduction, conclusion;
line of reasoning

ch'uronhada 추론하다 deduce; infer

ch'uryŏn 출연 appearance (*on TV
etc*)

ch'uryŏnaeda 추려내다 remove,
weed out

ch'uryŏnhada 출연하다 appear (*on
TV etc*)

ch'uryŏnjin 출연진 cast (*of play*)

ch'usangjŏgin 추상적인 abstract

ch'ushin 추신 PS, postscript

Ch'usŏk 추석 Harvest Festival

ch'usu 추수 harvest

Ch'usu Kamsajŏl 추수 감사절
Thanksgiving (Day)

ch'uun 추운 cold; freezing

ch'uwi 추위 cold; **chŏnŭn mopsshi
ch'uwŏyo** 저는 몹시 추워요 I'm
freezing cold

ch'uwŏrhada 추월하다 pass MOT

ch'waryŏng 촬영 photography

ch'waryŏnghada 촬영하다 film,
shoot

ch'waryŏngjangso 촬영장소 set (*for
movie*)

ch'waryŏng kisa 촬영 기사
cameraman

ch'wich'im shigan 취침 시간
bedtime

ch'widŭk'ada 취득하다 take

ch'wigŭp 취급 treatment

ch'wigŭp chuŭi 취급 주의 handle
with care!

ch'wihada 취하다 get drunk

ch'wihan 취한 high, loaded, stoned

ch'wihyang 취향 taste

ch'wiimshigŭl kŏhaenghada
취임식을 거행하다 inaugurate

ch'wiji akttan 취주 악단 brass
band

ch'wijung-ŭi 취중의 drunken

ch'wimi 취미 pastime, hobby

ch'wiso 취소 cancellation;
withdrawal

ch'wisohada 취소하다 cancel;
withdraw; tear up

ch'yat'ŭ 차트 chart, map

...dago hani ...다고 하니 that

...dani ...다니 that

...dŏrado ...더라도 even though

...do ...도 as well, also

...do ŏptta ...도 없다 without any ...
at all

...dorok ...도록 so that, in order to;
till; as ... as possible

...dŭshi ...듯이 like, as; as if

E

...e ...에 in; at; on; for; ...e ch'aegimi it-tta ...에 책임이 있다 be responsible for
...eda(ga) ...에다(가) at; in; on
...ege ...에게 to (*a person*)
...egeső ...에게서 from (*a person*)
Eijŭ 에이즈 Aids
Eijŭ yangsŏng panŭng 에이즈 양성 반응 HIV-positive
eksŭsedae 엑스세대 (X-세대) generation X (*Korea's contemporary youth without the same values and sense of purpose as their parents*)
ellibeit'ŏ 엘리베이터 elevator
emt'i 엠티 MT, Membership Training (*for college freshmen*)
en 엔 yen FIN
enamel 에나멜 enamel
enamel kajuk 에나멜 가죽 patent leather
enjin 엔진 engine, motor
enjin ttukkŏng 엔진 뚜껑 hood MOT
enŏji 에너지 energy, power

enŏjirŭl chŏryak'anŭn 에너지를 절약하는 energy-saving
ensedae 엔세대 (N-세대) networking generation (*via internet and cell phone*)
ent'ŏ k'i 엔터 키 enter key
eŏk'on 에어콘 air-conditioning
eŏrobik 에어로빅 aerobics
ep'isodŭ 에피소드 episode
ep'it'aijyŏ 에피타이져 appetizer, starter
erŏ 에러 error COMPUT
erŏ mesiji 에러 메시지 error message
...esŏ ...에서 in; at; on; from
...esŏbut'ŏ ...에서부터 from ... onward
esŭk'ŏlleitŏ 에스칼레이터 escalator
ewŏssada 에워싸다 encircle

...ga ...가 *subject particle* → ...ka ...가
...get... ...겠... shall (*indicates future tense, intention or supposition*)
...gi ...기 위해 in order to
...go ...고 and

H

habanshin mabihwanja 하반신 마비환자 paraplegic
habŭideon 합의된 concerted
habŭihada 합의하다 agree, agree on
habu chojik 하부 조직 infrastructure
habu kujo 하부 구조 infrastructure (*of organisation*)
hach'anŭn 하찮은 insignificant
hach'ŏnghada 하청하다 subcontract
hach'ŏng-ŏptcha 하청업자 subcontractor
hada 하다 ◊ do; make; play; put on ◊ (*makes nouns into verbs*): **sarang-hada** 사랑하다 love ◊ **...ge hada** ...게 하다 make; let; **nugurŭl haengbok'age hada** 누구를 행복하게 하다 make s.o. happy
hadan 하단 bottom, lower part; **hwamyŏnŭi hadane** 화면의 하단에 at the bottom of the screen
hadŭ k'ap'i 하드 카피 hard copy
hadŭ tisŭk'ŭ 하드 디스크 hard disk
hadŭweŏ 하드웨어 hardware
hae 해 harm; **haerŭl ip'ida** ...에 해를 입히다 be to the detriment of
haeansŏn 해안선 coastline; waterline
haebalgodo 해발고도 altitude
haebang 해방 emancipation, liberation
haebanghada 해방하다 emancipate, liberate
haeboda 해보다 try
haebuhak 해부학 anatomy
haebyŏn 해변 beach; **haebyŏne** 해변에 at the seaside
Haebyŏngdae 해병대 Marine Corps
haebyŏnkka 해변가 seaside
haebyŏn lijot'ŭ 해변 리조트 seaside resort
haech'ehada 해체하다 break up; take down
haech'ibaek 해치백 hatchback
haech'ida 해치다 harm, impair
haech'iuda 해치우다 finish off *task*;

kill, do away with
haech'o 해초 seaweed
haech'ung 해충 vermin
haedanghada 해당하다 correspond to
haedap 해답 answer, solution
haedo 해도 chart
haedoktche 해독제 antidote
haedok'ada 해독하다 decode
haego 해고 dismissal
haegohada 해고하다 fire; lay off
haegol 해골 skeleton; skull
haegoshik'ida 해고시키다 dismiss
haegŭi 핵의 nuclear
haegŭm 해금 two-stringed fiddle
haegun 해군 navy; marine
haegun taejang 해군 대장 admiral
haegun kiji 해군 기지 naval base
haegyŏl 해결 fix, solution; resolution (*of problem*)
haegyŏltch'aek 해결책 solution
haegyŏrhada 해결하다 settle, sort out, clear up; work out, crack, solve
haegyŏrhal su innŭn 해결할 수 있는 solvable
haegyŏri kollanhan 해결이 곤란한 difficult, knotty *problem*
haehak 해학 humor
haehyŏp 해협 strait
haejil muryŏp 해질 무렵 sunset, dusk; **haejin hue** 해진 후에 after sunset
haejŏkp'an 해적판 pirated version
haek 핵 nucleus ◊ nuclear
haek enŏji 핵 에너지 nuclear energy
haek konggyŏk'ada 핵 공격하다 make a nuclear strike
haek mugi 핵 무기 nuclear weapons
haek mullihak 핵 물리학 nuclear physics
haek punnyŏl 핵 분열 nuclear fission
haek p'yegimul 핵 폐기물 nuclear waste

haeksshim 핵심 core; heart, nub

haeksshimbu 핵심부 heart, center

haeksshimch'ŭng 핵심층 hard core

haeksshimjŏgin 핵심적인 essential, key

haekssüregi 핵쓰레기 atomic waste

haek'ŏ 해커 hacker

haelssuk'an 핼쑥한 ghastly

haem 행 ham

haema 해마 walrus

haembögö 햄버거 hamburger

haemsütŏ 햄스터 hamster

haemyŏnghada 해명하다 explain, shed light on

haenaeda 해내다 beat; argue down; succeed; accomplish; *chal hae-naeda* 잘 해내다 do well

haenagada 해나가다 carry on

haendübaek 핸드백 purse, pocket book, *Br* handbag

haendŭl 핸들 (steering) wheel

haendŭp'on 핸드폰 cell phone

haeng 행 for, bound for; *Sŏurhaeng pihaenggi* 서울행 비행기 a plane bound for Seoul

haengbok 행복 happiness, well-being

haengbok'ada 행복하다 be happy

haengbok'age 행복하게 happily

haengbok'an 행복한 happy

haengdong 행동 act, deed; behavior

haengdonghada 행동하다 act, behave

haengdong pangch'im 행동 방침 course of action

haenggüllaidŏ 행글라이더 hang glider

haenghada 행하다 render

haengjin 행진 march, procession

haengjinhada 행진하다 march, parade

haengjŏng 행정 administration

haengjŏnggwan 행정관 administrator

haengjŏng kuyŏk 행정 구역 precinct, district

haengjŏng samu 행정 사무 civil service

haengju 행주 dishcloth

haengnakkaek 행락객 vacationist

haengno 행로 course

haengnyŏl 행렬 procession

haengsa 행사 event; function; events; observance

haengsa wiwŏn 행사 위원 marshal

haengsŏng 행성 planet

haeng-un 행운 good fortune; *haeng-uni itkkirŭl!* 행운이 있기를! all the best!

haeng-unŭl kajyŏonŭn 행운을 가져오는 lucky

haeng-unŭl pilda 행운을 빌다 wish good luck

haeng-wi 행위 conduct; deed

haeoe 해외 abroad

haeoe kyop'o 해외 교포 overseas Koreans

haep'ari 해파리 jellyfish

haeri 해리 nautical mile

haeroun 해로운 harmful, damaging

haesam 해삼 sea cucumber, sea slug

haesan 해산 childbirth; confinement

haesangdo 해상도 resolution (*of monitor*)

haesang kyot'ong 해상 교통 shipping

haesanhada 해산하다 give birth; disperse *crowd*; dissolve *assembly*

haesanmul 해산물 seafood

haeshigye 해시계 sundial

haesŏk 해석 interpretation

haesŏk'ada 해석하다 interpret

haesŏl 해설 commentary

haesŏltcha 해설자 commentator

haetppit 햇빛 sunshine

haetppyŏch'e t'ada 햇볕에 타다 tan, go brown

haetppyŏch'e t'aeuda 햇볕에 태우다 get a suntan

haetppyŏch'ŭl tchoeda 햇볕을 쬐다 sunbathe

haetppyŏt'e(sŏ) 햇볕에(서) in the sun

haeunhoesa 해운회사 shipping company

haeyang 해양 ocean, sea

hagang 하강 fall, descent

haganghada 하강하다 descend

hagŭp 하급 low class

hagu 하구 estuary

hagwi 학위 degree

hagwirŭl ttada 학위를 따다

graduate, get one's degree
hagwŏn 학원 academy; institute
hahyang shiseŭi shijang 하향 시세의 시장 bear market
haip'ai 하이파이 hi-fi
haip'ŏt'eksssŭt'ŭ 하이퍼텍스트 hypertext
hairait'ŭ 하이라이트 highlight
hak 학 crane (*bird*)
hak-kki 학기 semester
hak-kkŭp 학급 class
hak-kkwa 학과 department
hak-kkyo 학교 school
hak-kkyo sŏnsaengnim 학교 선생님 schoolteacher
hak-kkujŏgin 학구적인 academic
hakppi 학비 tuition fee
hakppu 학부 faculty
hakssaeng 학생 pupil, student
hakssaeng kunsa kyoryŏndan 학생 군사 교련단 cadet corps
hakssaeng undong 학생 운동 student movement
hakssal 학살 slaughter
hakssaltcha 학살자 killer, murderer
hakssarhada 학살하다 slaughter
hakssŭp 학습 learning
hakssŭp koksssŏn 학습 곡선 learning curve
haktcha 학자 scholar
haktchang 학장 dean
hakttae 학대 abuse; maltreatment
hakttaehada 학대하다 abuse; maltreat
hakttong 학동 schoolchildren
hak'oe 학회 institute
hal il ŏmnŭn 할 일 없는 unoccupied
halkkamalkka saenggak'ada 할까말까 생각하다 think about doing
halkki 핥기 lick
halk'wida 할퀴다 claw; scratch
halk'wigi 할퀴기 scratch
hal marŭl irŭn 할 말을 잃은 speechless
halmŏni 할머니 grandmother, granny
hal su ŏpsshi ... 할 수 없이 ... have to ..., be compelled to ...
haltta 핥다 lick
halttanghada 할당하다 assign; commit

halt'amŏktta 핥아먹다 lap up, drink
hama 하마 hippopotamus
hamburo manjida 함부로 만지다 tamper with
hamburo taruda 함부로 다루다 mishandle
hamch'uk 함축 implication
hamch'uktchŏgin 함축적인 implicit
hamdae 함대 fleet
hamjŏng 함정 pitfall; trap; *nugurŭl hamjŏng-e ppattŭrida* 누구를 함정에 빠뜨리다 set a trap for s.o.; *hamjŏng-e ppajida* 함정에 빠지다 be trapped
hamkke 함께 with, along with ◊ together
hamkke hada 함께 하다 share *feelings*
hamkke nanuda 함께 나누다 share; *hamkke ssŭda* 함께 쓰다 share *room etc*
hamnihwahada 합리화하다 rationalize
hamnijŏgin 합리적인 rational
hamnisŏng 합리성 rationality
hamnyuhada 합류하다 join
hamonik'a 하모니카 harmonica, mouthorgan
hamppak chŏt-tta 함빡 젖다 be wet through
han 한 limit; *...nŭn han* ...는 한 so long as
hana 하나 one; single; *hananŭn ..., namŏjinŭn ...* 하나는 ..., 나머지는 ... one ..., the others ...
hanaga toen 하나가 된 united
hanasshik 하나씩 one by one
hanbam chung-e 한밤 중에 in the middle of the night
hanbŏn 한번 one time, once
hanbŏn tŏ 한번 더 once more
hanbok 한복 Korean costume
hanch'ang ttaeida 한창 때이다 be in one's prime
hando 한도 limit; *muŏsŭl handoro chŏnghada* 무엇을 한도로 정하다 draw the line at sth
handoga ŏmnŭn 한도가 없는 open-ended
...handokkajinŭn ...한도까지는 to such an extent that

hangahan ttaee 한가한 때에 in an idle moment

hang-ari 항아리 storage jar

han-gaunde 한가운데 center, middle

han-gaundero tuda 한가운데로 두다 center, put in the center

hangbok 항복 surrender

hangbok'ada 항복하다 surrender, capitulate, give in

hangbyŏnhada 항변하다 plead; *yujoe/mujoerŭl hangbyŏnhada* 유죄/무죄를 항변하다 plead guilty/not guilty

hangch'e 항체 antibody

hanggong 항공 aviation, flight

hanggongbonghamnyŏpssŏ 항공봉함엽서 air letter

hanggonggi 항공기 aircraft

hanggonghak 항공학 aeronautics

hanggong kyot'ong 항공 교통 air traffic

hanggong kyot'ong kwanje 항공 교통 관제 air-traffic control

hanggong kyot'ong kwanjewŏn 항공 교통 관제원 air-traffic controller

hanggongmoham 항공모함 aircraft carrier

hanggongp'yŏn 항공편 flight

hanggongp'yŏn pŏnho 항공편 번호 flight number

hanggongp'yŏnŭro 항공편으로 by air

hanggongsa 항공사 airline

hanggongsajin 항공사진 aerial photograph

hanggong-ujugonghak 항공우주공학 aerospace industry

hanggong unsonghada 항공 운송하다 fly; send by air

hanggong-up'yŏnŭro 항공우편으로 by airmail

hanggu 항구 harbor; port

hanggudoshi 항구도시 seaport

hanghae 항해 voyage, sea journey

hanghaehada 항해하다 navigate; sail

hanghaesa 항해사 navigator; mate

hanghaesul 항해술 navigation

han-gi 한기 chill

han-gil 한길 mainroad

hangmok 항목 item

hangmokppyŏl kwanggo 항목별 광고 classified advertisement

Hangmu 학무 Crane Dance

hangmun 학문 scholarship

hangnoesŏ pŏsŏnada 항로에서 벗어나다 stray off course

hangnyŏn 학년 academic year; form, class

han-gŏrŭm naedidida 한걸음 내디디다 take a step

hangsaeng multchil 항생 물질 antibiotic

hangsang 항상 always; *tangshinŭn/kŭnŭn hangsang kŭrŏch'ana!* 당신은/그는 항상 그럴잖아! that's typical of you/him!

hangso 항소 appeal LAW

hangsohada 항소하다 appeal LAW

hangssok kŏri 항속 거리 range

hang-ŭi 항의 protest; uproar

hang-ŭihada 항의하다 protest

han-gŭl 한글 hangul, Korean script

Han-gugŏ 한국어 Korean (*language*)

Han-guk 한국 (South) Korea ◊ (South) Korean

Han-guk-kkye 한국계 Korean descent

Han-guk Pangsong Kongsa 한국 방송 공사 Korean Broadcasting System, KBS

Han-guk saram 한국 사람 (South) Korean

Han-gukssan 한국산 made in Korea

han-gye 한계 limit, limitation; *han-gyee irŭda* 한계에 이르다 reach one's limit

han-gyerŭl chŏnghada 한계를 정하다 delimit

hangyŏul 한겨울 midwinter

hanjŏngdoen 한정된 restricted

hanjŏnghada 한정하다 limit

hankkŏbone 한꺼번에 in one, at once

han kyŏure 한 겨울에 in the depths of winter

han myŏng kŏnnŏ 한 명 건너 every other person

hannaeng chŏnsŏn 한랭 전선 cold front

hannyŏrŭm 한여름 midsummer

hanŏmnŭn 한없는 unlimited

han pamtchung-e 한 밤중에 in the middle of the night

han p'an taegyŏl 한 판 대결 showdown

hanp'yŏnŭronŭn ..., tarŭn hanp'yŏnŭronŭn 한편으로는..., 다른 한편으로는 on the one hand ..., on the other hand

hansanhan ttae 한산한 때 offpeak

hanshi 한시 hanshi (*poem in Chinese characters*)

hanshimhan 한심한 pitiful

hansum 한숨 sigh

hansum chada 한숨 자다 take a nap

hansum chit-tta 한숨 짓다 sigh

hantcha 한자 Chinese character

hantchogŭro kiurŏjin 한쪽으로 기울어진 lop-sided

hanttae(e) 한때(에) once, formerly; *hanttae nanŭn kŭrŭl choahaessŏt-tta / arassŏt-tta* 한때 나는 그를 좋아했었다 / 알았었다 I used to like / know him

hant'anhada 한탄하다 deplore

hant'anhal 한탄할 deplorable

hant'ŏk naeda 한턱 내다 pick up the tab; treat

hanŭisa 한의사 Chinese herbal medicine practitioner

hanŭiwŏn 한의원 Chinese medicine clinic

hanŭl 하늘 sky; *hanŭl wie* 하늘 위에 up in the sky; *hanŭl nopkke* 하늘 높게 high in the sky

Hanŭnim 하느님 God

hanyak 한약 Chinese herbal medicine

hanyakppang 한약방 Chinese herbal pharmacy

Hanyang 한양 Hanyang (*Choson name for Seoul*)

hanyŏ 하녀 maid (*servant*)

hapch'ang 합창 chorus, refrain

hapch'angdan 합창단 choir, chorus

hapch'ida 합치다 combine; merge

hapch'yŏjida 합쳐지다 join, meet

Hapkkido 합기도 Hapkkido (*martial art*)

hapkkŭm 합금 alloy

hapkkye 합계 total

hapkkyehada 합계하다 add up

hapkkyŏktchŏm 합격점 pass mark

hapkkyŏk'ada 합격하다 pass *examination*

hap-ppŏp 합법 legality

hap-ppŏp t'ujaeng 합법 투쟁 work-to-rule

hap-ppŏptchŏgin 합법적인 lawful, legal

hap-ppŏp'wahada 합법화하다 legalize

hap-ppyŏng 합병 merger

hap-ppyŏnghada 합병하다 amalgamate, merge; annex; unite

hap-ppyŏngtchŭng 합병증 complications MED

happ'an 합판 plywood

hapssŏng 합성 synthesis; composition

hapssŏngmul 합성물 compound

haptcha hoesa 합자 회사 joint-stock company

haptchak t'uja 합작 투자 joint venture

hapttanghada 합당하다 be appropriate; *kŭnŭn hapttanghan taerŭl padat-tta* 그는 합당한 대우를 받았다 he got what he deserved

hap'ŭ 하프 harp

hap'um 하품 yawn

hap'umhada 하품하다 yawn

haraböji 할아버지 grandfather, grandad

harak 하락 fall, drop

harak'ada 하락하다 fall, drop

harin 할인 discount

harinhada 할인하다 discount; *ishibul harinhayŏ* 20불 할인하여 $20 discount

harinkka(gyŏk) 할인가(격) bargain price

harinkkwŏn 할인권 discount voucher

harin p'anmae 할인 판매 sale

harirŏmnŭn 하릴없는 unavoidable

haru 하루 day; *harue sebŏnŭi hanggongp'yŏn* 하루에 세번의 항공편 three flights a day

haru chong-il 하루 종일 all day

haru könnŏ 하루 건너 every other day

haruppamŭl chinaeda 하룻밤을 지내다 stay overnight

haru shwida 하루 쉬다 take a day off

haryŏgo momburimch'ida 하려고 몸부림치다 struggle to do

haryŏgo noryŏk'ada 하려고 노력하다 strive to do

hasan 하산 descent

hasu 하수 sewage

hasu ch'ŏrijang 하수 처리장 sewage plant

hasugin 하숙인 lodger

hasugu 하수구 drain

hasugwan 하수관 sewer

hasuk 하숙 board and lodging

hasukssaeng 하숙생 boarder

hasuktchip 하숙집 boarding house

hasuk'ada 하숙하다 board with

hat ch'ok'ollit 핫 초콜릿 hot chocolate

hattogŭ 핫도그 hot dog

hat'ŭ 하트 hearts

hawi 하위 low rank

Hawŏn 하원 House of Representatives

hayan 하얀 white

hayan saek 하얀 색 white

hayat'a 하얗다 be white

hayŏt'ŭn 하여튼 anyhow

hearil su ŏmnŭn 헤아릴 수 없는 impenetrable; inestimable

hebikkŭp 헤비급 heavyweight

hech'yŏnagada 헤쳐나가다 wriggle out of

heding 헤딩 header (*in soccer*)

hedŭp'on 헤드폰 earphones

hedŭrait'ŭ 헤드라이트 headlamp, headlight

hellik'opt'ŏ 헬리콥터 helicopter, chopper

hellik'opt'ŏ nalgae 헬리콥터 날개 rotor blade

helmet 헬멧 helmet

helssŭ k'ŭllŏp 헬스 클럽 fitness center, health club

hemaeda 헤매다 stray

hengguda 헹구다 rinse

heŏdŭraiŏ 헤어드라이어 hairdryer

heŏjida 헤어지다 break up, part

heŏsŭp'ŭrei 헤어스프레이 (hair) lacquer

heroin 헤로인 heroin

hiashinsŭ 히아신스 hyacinth

hiiing! 히이잉! neigh!

him 힘 energy; might; power; strength; impetus

himch'an 힘찬 forceful

himdŭlda 힘들다 be difficult; be arduous

himdŭn 힘든 difficult; strenuous

himdŭnŭn 힘드는 painstaking, laborious

himgyŏun 힘겨운 heavy, profuse

himinnŭn 힘있는 mighty; firm

himŏmnŭn 힘없는 weak, feeble

himssen 힘센 strong

himtchul 힘줄 tendon

himŭl ppaeda 힘을 빼다 relax

hinghinggŏrida 힝힝거리다 neigh

hint'ŭ 힌트 hint

hisŭt'eri 히스테리 hysteria, hysterics

hisŭt'erisŏng-ŭi 히스테리성의 hysterical

hit'ŭ 히트 hit MUS

hit'ŭgok sunwi 히트곡 순위 the charts

hŏbihada 허비하다 fritter away, waste

hŏbŭ 허브 herb

hŏbŭ ch'a 허브 차 herbal tea

hŏga 허가 permission, approval

hŏgabat-tta 허가받다 receive permission

hŏgahada 허가하다 clear, authorize; grant; *ipkkugŭl hŏgahada* 입국을 허가하다 admit to a country; *tŭrŏonŭn kŏsŭl hŏgahada* 들어오는 것을 허가하다 admit, allow in

hŏga pat-tta 허가 받다 be licensed; be authorized

hŏgasŏ 허가서 permit

hŏgatchŭng 허가증 license, permit

hŏgu 허구 fabrication; fiction; lie

hŏhwangdoen iyagi 허황된 이야기 farfetched story

hŏksshin-ga 혁신가 innovator

hŏlda 헐다 demolish

hŏlgöpkke 헐겁게 loosely

hŏlgŏun 헐거운 loose

hŏlkkap 헐값 dirt-cheap price

höllanshik'ida 혼란시키다 confuse
höllönghan 헐렁한 baggy; roomy;
  floppy
hölttögida 헐떡이다 be winded
hölttök-kkörida 헐떡거리다 gasp,
  puff
hölttünnün 헐뜯는 disparaging
hölttüt-tta 헐뜯다 slander; malign
hömak'an 험악한 forbidding;
  inclement; unsavory
hömdam 험담 gossip
hömhan pawi 험한 바위 crag
hömulda 허물다 pull down
hömurŏjida 허물어지다 disintegrate
hömurŏjin 허물어진 dilapidated
hömurŏmnŭn 허물없는 candid,
  frank; familiar
hönbyŏng 헌병 MP, military police
Hönggari 헝가리 Hungary ◊
  Hungarian
hönggŏp(tchogak) 헝겊(조각) patch
hönggŏp'ŭl taeda 헝겊을 대다 patch
höngk'ŭrŏjige hada 헝클어지게 하다
  ruffle
höngk'ŭrŏjin 헝클어진 disheveled
hönhyŏltcha 헌혈자 blood donor
hönppŏp 헌법 constitution
hönppŏpssang-ŭi 헌법상의
  constitutional
hönshiltchŏgŭro 현실적으로 in
  practice
hönshin 헌신 commitment, devotion;
  donation
hönshinjŏgida 헌신적이다 be
  devoted to
hönshinjŏgin 헌신적인 devoted
höp'ung 허풍 tall story; hot air
höp'ungjang-i 허풍잡이 show-off
höp'ung-ŭl ttölda 허풍을 떨다
  exaggerate; boast, brag, talk big
hörak 허락 permission
hörak'ada 허락하다 allow, permit
höri 허리 waist
hörirŭl p'yŏda 허리를 펴다
  straighten up
hörisŏn 허리선 waistline
höritti 허리띠 belt
hörŏppajin 헐어빠진 dilapidated
hörŭmhan 허름한 run-down
höse 허세 bravado
höshigŏmnŭn 허식없는

unpretentious
höshik 허식 affectation
höshim t'anhoe 허심 탄회 candor
höshimt'anhoehada 허심탄회하다
  be open-minded
hösuabi 허수아비 scarecrow
hösuk'ihan 허스키한 husky voice
hötchŏm 허점 blind spot; loophole
hötkkallida 헷갈리다 mix up, confuse
hötkkan 헛간 barn
hötkkich'imhada 헛기침하다 clear
  one's throat
hötppae purŭm 헛배 부름 wind,
  flatulence; gas
hötssomunŭl p'ŏttŭrinŭn saram
  헛소문을 퍼뜨리는 사람
  scaremonger
hötssorihada 헛소리하다 rave;
  ramble
hötssugo 헛수고 vain effort;
  kŭdŭrŭi noryŏgŭn hötssugoro
  torakat-tta 그들의 노력은
  헛수고로 돌아갔다 their efforts were
  in vain
höt-ttidida 헛디디다 lose one's
  footing, stumble
höt-ttoege 헛되게 in vain
höt-ttoen 헛된 vain
höt'ŭn sori 허튼 소리 nonsense,
  hokum
höyak 허약 infirmity
höyak'ada 허약하다 be frail
höyak'an 허약한 infirm; delicate;
  puny
höyŏngshim 허영심 vanity; höyŏng-
  shimi manŭn 허영심이 많은 vain
höyongdoel su innŭn 허용될 수
  있는 permissible
höyong pŏmwi 허용 범위 latitude
ho 호 issue, edition
hobak 호박 pumpkin; amber
hobŏk'ŭrap'ŭt'ŭ 호버크라프트
  hovercraft
hoch'ik'isŭ 호치키스 stapler
hoch'ik'isŭ al 호치키스 알 staple
hoch'ik'isŭro tchiktta 호치키스로
  찍다 staple
hoch'ulgi 호출기 pager, bleeper
hoch'ul shigan 호출 시간 access
  time
hoch'urhada 호출하다 summon;

page, bleep

hodoege kkujit-tta 호되게 꾸짖다 scold severely, chew out

hodohada 호도하다 gloss over, whitewash

hodu 호두 walnut

hodu kkanŭn kigu 호두 까는 기구 nutcracker

hoe 회 round, heat; raw fish

hoebanjugŭl parŭda 회반죽을 바르다 plaster

hoebanjuk 회반죽 plaster; mortar

hoebi 회비 fee

hoebok 회복 recovery

hoebok-kki 회복기 convalescence

hoeboktoeda 회복되다 revive, recover

hoebok'ada 회복하다 rebuild; recover; *kŭŭi hoebogŭn sunjorowat-tta* 그의 회복은 순조로왔다 he has made a good recovery; *kŏn-gang-ŭl hoebok'ada* 건강을 회복하다 convalesce

hoebok'al su ŏmnŭn 회복할 수 없는 incurable

hoegohae pomyŏn 회고해 보면 in retrospect

hoegojŏn 회고전 retrospective

hoegorok 회고록 memoirs

hoegwisŏn 회귀선 tropics

hoegye 회계 accounts

hoegyejangbu 회계장부 accounts book; *hoegyejangburŭl chŏngnihada* 회계장부를 정리하다 do the books; *hoegye kyŏlssanhada* 회계 결산하다 balance the books

hoegyesa 회계사 accountant

hoegye tamdangja 회계 담당자 treasurer

hoegye yŏndo 회계 연도 fiscal year, financial year

hoehwa 회화 conversation; picture

hoehwa chakp'um 회화 작품 painting

hoejin 회진 round

hoejŏn 회전 revolution, rotation, turn, rev

hoejŏnhada 회전하다 turn, rotate, swivel

hoejŏn mongma 회전 목마 carousel

hoejŏnmun 회전문 revolving door

hoejŏnshik kŏnjogi 회전식 건조기 tumble-dryer

hoejŏnshik'ida 회전시키다 spin; swing, turn

hoejung chŏndŭng 회중 전등 flashlight

hoek 획 stroke (*in writing*)

hoekch'aek'ada 획책하다 plot

hoek-kkijögin 획기적인 epoch-making

hoekttŭk'ada 획득하다 acquire, obtain

hoengdan 횡단 crossing

hoengdan podo 횡단 보도 crosswalk

hoenggyŏngmak 횡격막 diaphragm ANAT

hoengjae 횡재 windfall

hoengnyŏng 횡령 embezzlement

hoengnyŏnghada 횡령하다 embezzle

hoengp'orŭl purinŭn 횡포를 부리는 dictatorial

hoengsŏlsusŏl 횡설수설 gibberish; rambling

hoe-oribaram 회오리바람 whirlwind, tornado

hoep'i 회피 evasion

hoep'ihada 회피하다 evade

hoero 회로 circuit

hoero ch'adan-gi 회로 차단기 circuit breaker

hoero kyegip'an 회로 계기판 circuit board

hoesa 회사 business, company, firm; *hoesa piyong-ŭro* 회사 비용으로 at the company's expense

hoesa chibunŭl sadŭrida 회사 지분을 사들이다 buy out *company*

hoesa ch'a 회사 차 company car

hoesaek 회색 gray

hoesang 회상 reminiscence

hoesanghada 회상하다 recollect

hoesapŏp 회사법 company law

hoesonghada 회송하다 forward *letter*

hoessu 횟수 frequency

hoeŭi 회의 meeting, conference; assembly; council; *kŭnŭn hoeŭi chung-ida* 그는 회의 중이다 he's in a meeting hoeŭijŏgin 회의적인 skeptical

hoeŭiron 회의론 skepticism

hoeŭironja 회의론자 skeptic

hoeŭishil 회의실 conference room

hoewŏn 회원 member; membership

hoewŏn su 회원 수 membership, number of members

hoewŏntchŭng 회원증 membership card

hoeyujŏgin 회유적인 conciliatory

hogak 호각 whistle

hogami kanŭn 호감이 가는 likable, amiable

hogamŭl kajida 호감을 가지다 be well disposed toward

hogishim 호기심 curiosity; *hogishimesŏ* 호기심에서 out of curiosity

hogishim manŭn 호기심 많은 curious, inquisitive

hogishimŭl chagŭk'anŭn 호기심을 자극하는 intriguing

hogŭn 혹은 or

hohŭp 호흡 breathing

hohŭp kollan 호흡 곤란 breathlessness

hohwandoeji annŭn 호환되지 않는 incompatible

hohwanhal su innŭn 호환할 수 있는 compatible

hohwan pulganŭng 호환 불가능 incompatibility

hohwansŏng 호환성 compatibility

hohwaroptta 호화롭다 be luxurious

hohwaroun 호화로운 de luxe

hoil 호일 foil

hojŏ 호저 porcupine

hojŏk 호적 census registration; census register

hojŏksurŭl mannada 호적수를 만나다 meet one's match

hojŏn 호전 improvement, upturn

hojŏnjŏgin 호전적인 belligerent

hojŏnshik'ida 호전시키다 turn around

Hoju 호주 Australia ◊ Australian

Hojuin 호주인 Australian

hojumŏni 호주머니 pocket

hok 혹 bump, lump; hump

hokp'yŏnghada 혹평하다 criticize severely

hoksshi 혹시: *hokcshi kŭga ttŏnassŭltchi morŭgessŭmnida* 혹시 그가 떠났을지 모르겠습니다 I don't know whether he has left

hokttok'an 혹독한 brutal

hol 홀 hall

hollan 혼란 confusion, muddle; unrest; turmoil

hollanhada 혼란하다 be confused; be chaotic

hollanshik'ida 혼란시키다 confuse

hollansŭrŏptta 혼란스럽다 be topsy-turvy

hollansŭrŏun 혼란스러운 shaken; topsy-turvy

hollansŭrŏwŏ hada 혼란스러워 하다 be mixed up

hollo 홀로 by itself

hollograem 홀로그램 hologram

hollye 혼례 marriage

holssu 홀수 odd number

holssusŏn 홀수선 waterline

holtchak-kkŏrida 홀짝거리다 sip

holtchuk'an 홀쭉한 sunken

holttak panhada 홀딱 반하다 be infatuated with, have a crush on

holttak pŏsŭn 홀딱 벗은 stark naked

holttak ppajida 홀딱 빠지다 dote on

hom 홈 rut

homil 호밀 rye

homil ppang 호밀 빵 rye bread

hom kyŏnggi 홈 경기 home match

hom kyŏnggijang-esŏ 홈 경기장에서 at home SP

homo 호모 fag pej

homp'eiji 홈페이지 home page

homt'ong 홈통 gutter (*on roof*)

hondonghada 혼동하다 confuse

hongbo 홍보 PR, public relations

hongch'a 홍차 black tea

hongch'ae 홍채 iris (*of eye*)

hongdŭngga 홍등가 red light district

honghap 홍합 mussel

hong-igin-gan 홍익인간 devotion to the welfare of mankind

hongjo 홍조 blush

hongjorŭl ttin 홍조를 띤 rosy

Hong Kilttong 홍 길동 Hong Kil-tong (*Korean Robin Hood*)

Hongk'ong 홍콩 Hong Kong

hongnyŏk 홍역 measles

hongsu

hongsu 홍수 flood

hon-gyo 혼교 promiscuity

honhammul 혼합물 concoction, mixture

honhap 혼합 blend, mixture; hybrid; solution

honhap'ada 혼합하다 blend

honja 혼자 alone; on my/her etc own

honjap 혼잡 congestion

honjap'ada 혼잡하다 be congested; be disordered

honjasŏ 혼자서 single-handedly; by oneself; *honjasŏ ŏtchŏl su ŏmnŭn* 혼자서 어쩔 수 없는 alone and helpless

honjŏn(ŭi) 혼전(의) premarital

honsŏn 혼선 interference

honsu sangt'ae 혼수 상태 coma; trance; *honsu sangt'aee ppajida* 혼수 상태에 빠지다 go into a trance; lapse into a coma

hop 홉 hop BOT

horabi 홀아비 widower

horanggashinamu 호랑가시나무 holly

horang-i 호랑이 tiger

horihorihan 호리호리한 lanky

horŭmon 호르몬 hormone

hosohada 호소하다 appeal for; complain of

hosonghada 호송하다 convoy

hosŭ 호스 hose

hosŭt'essŭ 호스테스 hostess, escort

hosu 호수 lake

hot'el 호텔 hotel; *hot'ere muktta* 호텔에 묵다 stay in a hotel

hot'el chong-ŏbwŏn 호텔 종업원 maid

hot'ong-ŭl ch'ida 호통을 치다 bawl out

hoŭi 호의 favor; goodwill; *nuguege hoŭirŭl pep'ulda* 누구에게 호의를 베풀다 do s.o. a favor

hoŭijŏgin 호의적인 favorable

hoŭng 호응 response

howihada 호위하다 escort, convoy

hŭbip 흡입 suction

hŭbipkki 흡입기 inhaler

hŭbip'ada 흡입하다 inhale

hŭbyŏn 흡연 smoking

hŭbyŏnja 흡연자 smoker

hŭbyŏnshil 흡연실 smoking compartment

hŭgin 흑인 black, negro

hŭibak'an 희박한 thin, rare; sparse; *in-guga hŭibak'an* 인구가 희박한 sparsely populated

hŭida 희다 white ◊ be white

hŭigok 희곡 drama

hŭigŭk 희극 comedy

hŭimang 희망 hope

hŭimang-e ch'an 희망에 찬 hopeful

hŭimanghada 희망하다 hope

hŭimang-ŭl irŭn 희망을 잃은 hopeless

hŭimihaejida 희미해지다 fade

hŭimihan 희미한 faint

hŭimihan pit 희미한 빛 glimmer

hŭisa 희사 donation

hŭisaeng 희생 cost; sacrifice; death toll; victim

hŭisaenghada 희생하다 make sacrifices; sacrifice

hŭisaengja 희생자 victim

hŭisaengshikida 희생시키다 victimize

hŭisaengnyang 희생양 scapegoat

hŭisahada 희사하다 donate

hŭi-yŏmŏlgŏn 희여멀건 wishy-washy

hŭk 흙 soil, earth

hŭktcharo 흑자로 in the black FIN

hŭlkkŭt poda 흘끗 보다 catch sight of, catch a glimpse of

hŭllida 흘리다 shed *blood, sweat, tears*; spill *water*

hŭm 흠 blemish, flaw; blot; groove; nick, cut

hŭmjabŭlde ŏmnŭn 흠잡을데 없는 faultless

hŭmjaptta 흠잡다 find fault with

hŭmnaeda 흠내다 blemish

hŭmŏmnŭn 흠없는 flawless

hŭmppŏk chŏjŭn 흠뻑 젖은 dripping, soaking wet

hŭmppŏk chŏksshida 흠뻑 적시다 drench

hŭmppŏk chŏt-tta 흠뻑 젖다 get drenched

hŭmtchibŏmnŭn 흠집없는 unscathed

hŭndŭlda 흔들다 shake; swing; wave; wiggle; undermine; *Xŭl/rŭl toege* *hŭndŭlda* x을/를 되게 흔들다 give X a good shake

hŭndŭlgŏrida 흔들거리다 rock; roll; sway; swing; wag

hŭndŭlgŏrinŭn 흔들거리는 shaky

hŭndŭllida 흔들리다 shake; vibrate; tremble

hŭndŭl ŭija 흔들 의자 rocking chair

hŭngbun 흥분 excitement, kick, thrill; stimulation

hŭngbundoeda 흥분되다 be excited

hŭngbunhada 흥분하다 get excited; *nŏmu hŭngbunhaji maseyo!* 너무 흥분하지 마세요! don't get excited!, take it easy!

hŭngbunshik'ida 흥분시키다 excite

hŭngbunshik'inŭn 흥분시키는 exciting

hŭngch'ŏngmangch'ŏng shyop'ing-ŭl hada 흥청망청 쇼핑을 하다 go on a shopping spree

hŭngjŏnghada 흥정하다 bargain

hŭngmijinjinhan 흥미진진한 very interesting

hŭngmi kkŭlda 흥미 끌다 intrigue

hŭngmirŭl irŭk'ige hada 흥미를 일으키게 하다 interest; arouse interest

hŭngmirŭl kajida 흥미를 가지다 take an interest in

hŭngmirŭl todunŭn 흥미를 돋우는 compelling

hŭnhaji anŭn 흔하지 않은 uncommon

hŭnjŏk 흔적 trace; trail; vestige

hŭnŭjŏk-kkŏrinŭn 흐느적거리는 limping

hŭnŭkkim 흐느낌 sob

hŭnŭkkyŏ ulda 흐느껴 울다 sob

hŭpssuhada 흡수하다 absorb

hŭpssussŏng-ŭi 흡수성의 absorbent

hŭrida 흐리다 be cloudy

hŭrige hada 흐리게 하다 blur; dim

hŭrim 흐림 blur

hŭrin 흐린 cloudy; misty; overcast

hŭrit'aejida 흐릿해지다 blur

hŭrit'an 흐릿한 dim; fuzzy; vague; glazed

hŭrŭda 흐르다 run, flow; stream

hŭrŭm 흐름 current; flow

hŭrŭnŭn 흐르는 flowing; runny

hŭryŏjida 흐려지다 mist over

hŭryŏjin 흐려진 misty; *ont'ong hŭryŏjida* 온통 흐려지다 cloud over

hŭt'ŏjida 흩어지다 disperse, scatter

hŭt'ŏjin 흩어진 scattered

hŭt'ŭrŏjin 흐트러진 disheveled

huban 후반 second half

hubida 후비다 dig up; grub; *k'orŭl hubida* 코를 후비다 pick one's nose

hubo 후보 nominee

huboja 후보자 candidate

hubo sŏnsu 후보 선수 reserve *SP*

hubul 후불 deferred payment; *nanŭn hubullo chigŭppannŭnda* 나는 후불로 지급받는다 I'm paid in arrears

huch'ŏnssŏng myŏnnyŏk kyŏlp'iptchŭng 후천성 면역 결핍증 Aids, acquired immune deficiency syndrome

huch'u 후추 pepper

hudae 후대 posterity

hudu 후두 larynx

hududuk ttŏrŏjida 후두둑 떨어지다 patter

hududuk'anŭn sori 후두둑하는 소리 patter, pattering sound

huduyŏm 후두염 laryngitis

hue 후에: *...n(ŭn) hue* ...ㄴ(은) 후에 since; after

hugak 후각 sense of smell

hugi 후기 epilog

hugyŏnin 후견인 guardian

huhoe 후회 penitence

huhoehada 후회하다 regret; repent

huhoesŭrŏpkkedo 후회스럽게도 regretfully, sadly

huim(ja) 후임(자) successor

huimjaga toeda 후임자가 되다 succeed *person*

huja 후자 the latter

hujin 후진 reverse (gear)

hujinhada 후진하다 reverse, back

hujinshik'ida 후진시키다 reverse, back

huk p'unggim 훅 풍김 whiff

hullyŏn 훈련 drill, exercise; training

hullyŏnhada 훈련하다 practice, drill; train

hullyŏn kyehoek 훈련 계획 training scheme

hullyŏnsa 훈련사 trainer

hullyŏnshik'ida 훈련시키다 train

hullyunghada 훌륭하다 be magnificent; be worthy; admirable; be noble; be great

hullyunghage 훌륭하게 wonderfully, beautifully

hullyunghan 훌륭한 brilliant, fine; masterly; respectable

hultchŏk-kkŏrida 훌쩍거리다 sniffling, snivelling

hultchŏk ttwida 훌쩍 뛰다 leap

hultta 훑다 thresh; strip; remove

hult'ŏboda 훑어보다 skim through *book*; look over *person*

humch'ida 훔치다 steal

humi 후미 inlet

humijin kot 후미진 곳 cove

hunjang-ŭl suyŏhada 훈장을 수여하다 decorate, award a medal

hunjehada 훈제하다 smoke *ham etc*

hunje soegogi 훈제 쇠고기 pastrami

huraip'aen 후라이팬 frying pan

Hurench'ihurai 후렌치후라이 French fries

huryŏch'ida 후려치다 punch

huryŏm 후렴 refrain MUS

hushik 후식 dessert

hut'ŏptchigŭnhada 후텁지근하다 be sultry (*of weather*)

hut'oe 후퇴 setback; retreat

hut'oehada 후퇴하다 retreat; pull out

huwi 후위 back SP

huwŏn 후원 sponsorship, patronage

huwŏnhada 후원하다 back (up), support; sponsor

huwŏnja 후원자 supporter; sponsor; backer; patron

hwanada 화나다 get angry

hwa 화 anger, annoyance

hwabun 화분 pollen; flowerpot

hwabunnyang 화분량 pollen count

hwabyŏng 화병 vase; hypochondria

hwach'a 화차 wagon

hwach'anghada 화창하다 be bright, be sunny

hwach'anghan nalssi 화창한 날씨 Indian summer

hwadan 화단 flowerbed

hwadŏk 화덕 furnace

hwaek sugŭrida 홱 수그리다 duck

hwaek tanggida 홱 당기다 yank, jerk

hwaetppul 횃불 torch (*with flame*)

hwaet-ttae 횃대 perch

hwaet-ttae antta 횃대에앉다 perch

hwaga 화가 painter, drawer

hwaga ch'isot-tta 화가 치솟다 flareup

hwaga nada 화가 나다 get angry, ge worked up

hwaga nan 화가 난 angry, sore

hwagang-am 화강암 granite

hwagin 확인 inspection; confirmation; identification; OK COMPUT

hwaginhada 확인하다 check; confirm; identify; check for; query

hwaginhae tuda 확인해 두다 keep a check on

hwahae 화해 reconciliation; settlement

hwahaehada 화해하다 make up; be reconciled

hwahaeshik'ida 화해시키다 reconcile

hwahak 화학 chemistry

hwahak chep'um 화학 제품 chemical

hwahaktcha 화학자 chemist

hwahaktchŏn 화학전 chemical warfare

hwahak yoppŏp 화학 요법 chemotherapy

hwahwan 화환 garland, wreath

hwail 화일 file COMPUT

hwail maenijŏ 화일 매니저 file manager

hwajae 화재 fire, blaze

hwajae kyŏngbogi 화재 경보기 fire alarm

hwajae p'inan changch'i 화재 피난 장치 fire escape

hwajang 화장 cremation; make-up; beauty care

hwajangdae 화장대 dressing table

hwajanghada 화장하다 cremate; put on make-up

hwajangjang 화장장 crematorium

hwajangji 화장지 tissue; toilet paper

hwajangp'um 화장품 make-up;

cosmetics

hwajangshil 화장실 restroom, bathroom; toilet

hwaje 화제 topic

hwajerŭl pakkŭda 화제를 바꾸다 change the subject

hwak ch'isosŭm 확 치솟음 blaze

hwak-kkohan 확고한 strong, definite, determined, firm

hwakkobudonghan 확고부동한 unswerving

hwaksshilssŏng 확실성 certainty; inevitability

hwaksshin 확신 certainty; confidence

hwaksshine ch'an 확신에 찬 assured

hwaksshinhada 확신하다 be positive; firmly believe; *Xŭl/rŭl hwaksshinhaji mot'ada* X을/를 확신하지 못하다 be uncertain about X

hwaksshinhanŭn 확신하는 certain, sure

hwaksshinshik'ida 확신시키다 convince

hwaksshirhada 확실하다 be certain, be definite

hwaksshirhage 확실하게 reliably

hwaksshirhan 확실한 marked, definite

hwaksshirhi 확실히 certainly definitely; decidedly; doubtless

hwaksssŏnggi 확성기 loudspeaker

hwaktae 확대 zoom in

hwaktchang 확장 expansion; extension

hwaktchanghada 확장하다 expand; diversify

hwaktchang k'adŭ 확장카드 expansion card COMPUT

hwaktchŏngdoeda 확정되다 be finalized

hwaktchŏng kŭmaek 확정 금액 sum insured

hwaktchŭng 확증 confirmation

hwaktchŭnghada 확증하다 confirm

hwakttae chŏgyonghada 확대 적용하다 stretch *rules*

hwaktaehada 확대하다 blow up, enlarge; magnify; escalate

hwak t'ŭin 확 트인 panoramic

hwal 활 bow MUS

hwalbarhada 활발하다 be lively, be brisk

hwalgangno 활강로 chute

hwalgang sŭk'i 활강 스키 downhill skiing

hwalgi 활기 vigor, energy

hwalgi ch'an 활기 찬 lively

hwalgirŭl purhŏnŏt'a 활기를 불어넣다 enliven

hwalgonghada 활공하다 glide

hwallyŏk 활력 drive, energy; vitality

hwalsŏng 활성 active COMPUT

hwaltcha 활자 moveable type

hwaltchak p'in 활짝 핀 in full bloom

hwaltchak ut-tta 활짝 웃다 beam, smile

hwaltchuro 활주로 runway, tarmac

hwalttong 활동 activity, action

hwalttongga 활동가 activist

hwalttong hoewŏn 활동 회원 active member

hwalttongjŏgin 활동적인 active; energetic, dynamic

hwamul 화물 freight; shipment, consignment

hwamulch'a 화물차 freight car; truck

hwamul pihaenggi 화물 비행기 freight plane

hwamulsŏn 화물선 freighter

hwamulsshil 화물실 hold (*on ship, plane*)

hwamul unbanttae 화물 운반대 pallet

hwamul unsongnyo 화물 운송료 freight (costs)

hwamul yŏlch'a 화물 열차 freight train

hwamyŏn 화면 screen; *hwamyŏn-sang-e* 화면상에 on screen

hwamyŏne p'yoshihada 화면에 표시하다 display

hwamyŏn pohogi 화면 보호기 screen saver

hwanada 화나다 be annoyed; get annoyed, blow up

hwanaege hada 화내게 하다 anger

hwanan 화난 exasperated

hwanbul 환불 refund, rebate

hwanbul pulgaŭi 환불 불가의

nonreturnable *deposit*

hwanburhada 환불하다 refund

hwandae 환대 hospitality

hwandaehanŭn 환대하는 hospitable

hwandŭnggi p'illŭm k'arusel 환등기 필름 카루셀 carousel (*for slides*)

hwan-gap 환갑 sixtieth birthday (*61st birthday in the West, since Koreans are one year old at birth*)

hwangdal 황달 jaundice

hwangdodae 황도대 zodiac

hwangdodaeŭi shibi kung 황도대의 십이 궁 12 signs of the zodiac

hwanggalssaek 황갈색 buff (*color*)

hwanggŭmshiganttae 황금시간대 prime time

hwanggŭp'i 황급히 in double-quick time

Hwangha 황하 Yellow River

Hwanghae 황해 Yellow Sea

hwanghol 황홀 ecstasy

hwanghorhan 황홀한 ecstatic

hwan-gich'ang 환기창 vent, ventilation window

hwan-gi changch'i 환기 장치 ventilator; ventilation

hwan-gigaeng 환기갱 ventilation shaft

hwan-gihada 환기하다 ventilate

hwan-gishik'ida 환기시키다 air *room*; challenge; evoke

hwangje 황제 emperor

hwangmuji 황무지 desert; wilderness

hwangnyanghan 황량한 bleak, desolate; godforsaken

hwangp'ye chiyŏk 황폐 지역 wasteland

hwangp'yehaejida 황폐해지다 ravaged by war

hwangp'yehan 황폐한 desolate, inhospitable

hwangsae 황새 stork

hwangsaek shinho-e 황색 신호에 at amber (*of traffic light*)

hwangso 황소 bull, ox

hwangsonghada 황송하다 be indebted, be obliged; *kŭnŭn hwangsonghagedo na-ege marŭl kŏrŏssŏ* 그가 황송하게도 내게 말을 걸었어 he condescended to speak to me

hwan-gyŏng 환경 conditions; surroundings; environment

hwan-gyŏngboho 환경보호 environmental protection

hwan-gyŏngbohoronja 환경보호론자 environmentalist

Hwan-gyŏngch'ŏng 환경처 Department of the Interior

hwan-gyŏng-oyŏm 환경오염 environmental pollution

hwanhada 환하다 be bright; be open

hwanhage 환하게 brightly

hwanhan 환한 bright, broad *smile*

hwanhi pinnanŭn 환히 빛나는 radiant

hwanho 환호 cheer; cheering; jubilation

hwanhohada 환호하다 cheer

hwanhohanŭn 환호하는 jubilant

hwanhoŭi sori 환호의 소리 hurray

hwanhŭi 환희 joy, delight; rapture

hwanja 환자 patient

hwanjŏnhada 환전하다 exchange

hwanmyŏl 환멸 disillusionment

hwannyul 환율 exchange rate

hwanŏŭm 환어음 bill of exchange

hwanp'unggi 환풍기 ventilation fan

hwansaeng 환생 reincarnation

hwansan 환산 conversion

hwansang 환상 fantasy

hwansangjŏgin 환상적인 fantastic

hwansanhada 환산하다 convert

hwansanp'yo 환산표 conversion table

hwanyŏng 환영 reception, welcome; vision; illusion

hwanyŏnghada 환영하다 welcome

hwanyŏng pannŭn 환영 받는 welcome

Hwaŏmgyŏng 화엄경 Flower Garland Sutra

hwap'urihada 화풀이하다 take it out on

hwarang 화랑 gallery

Hwarangdo 화랑도 Youth Corps

hwarŭl ch'amtta 화를 참다 keep one's temper

hwarŭl naeda 화를 내다 lose one's temper; vent one's anger

hwaryŏhada 화려하다 be sumptuous

hwaryŏhage changshik'an 화려하게

장식한 ornate
hwaryŏham 화려함 splendor
hwaryonghada 활용하다 put to practical use, utilize
hwaryongshik'ida 활용시키다 conjugate
hwasal 화살 arrow
hwasalp'yo kŭlsoe 화살표 글쇠 arrow key COMPUT
hwasan 화산 volcano
hwasang 화상 burn (*injury*)
hwasang hoeŭi 화상 회의 video conference
hwashin 화신 embodiment
hwasŏk 화석 fossil
hwasŏng 화성 harmony
Hwasshi 화씨 Fahrenheit
hwayak 화약 gunpowder
hwayoil 화요일 Tuesday
hwesonhada 훼손하다 mutilate; defame
hwibaryu 휘발유 gasoline, gas
hwich'ŏnggŏrida 휘청거리다 stagger
hwida 휘다 bend, warp
hwidurŭda 휘두르다 brandish; wield; flick
hwigalgyŏ ssŭda 휘갈겨 쓰다 scrawl
hwigehada 휘게하다 warp
hwigi shwiun 휘기 쉬운 pliable
hwijang 휘장 drapery
hwijŏnnŭn kigu 휘젓는 기구 whisk
hwijŏt-tta 휘젓다 stir; whisk
hwik kkŭjibŏnaeda 휙 끄집어내다 pull out, whip out
hwilch'ŏ 휠체어 wheelchair
hwin 휜 bent
hwip'aram 휘파람 whistle
hwip'aramŭl pulda 휘파람을 불다 whistle
hwŏlsshin kŭ chŏne 훨씬 그 전에 long before then
hwŏnhada 훤하다 be broad; be extensive; be well versed in; ...*ŭl* / *rŭl hwŏnhi alda* ...을 / 를 훤히 알다 have at one's fingertips
hwŏnhi t'ŭin 훤히 트인 open and bright
hyŏmnyŏktcha 협력자 co-worker, collaborator (*on a project*)
hyŏng 형 elder brother
hyŏnshiljŏgin 현실적인 realistic

hyang 향 incense
hyanggi 향기 aroma, scent; bouquet
hyangginanŭn 향기나는 fragrant
hyanghada 향하다 face
hyanghayŏ 향하여 to; toward; facing
hyangsang 향상 improvement
hyangsangdoeda 향상되다 get better
hyangsanghada 향상하다 improve, progress
hyangsangshik'ida 향상시키다 improve, upgrade
hyangsu 향수 perfume; nostalgia
hyangsuppyŏng-ul alt'a 향수병을 앓다 be homesick
hyang-yŏn 향연 banquet, dinner
hyesŏng 혜성 comet
hyet'aekpat-tchi mot'an 혜택받지 못한 underprivileged
hyŏ 혀 tongue
hyŏbŭihada 협의하다 confer
hyŏksshin 혁신 innovation
hyŏksshinhanŭn hoesa 혁신하는 회사 innovative company
hyŏksshinjŏgin 혁신적인 innovative
hyŏlgi 혈기 blood
hyŏlgu 혈구 corpuscle
hyŏlgwan 혈관 blood vessel
hyŏlgwan ishik 혈관 이식 bypass MED
hyŏllyu 혈류 bloodstream
hyŏlssaegi anjohŭn 혈색이 안좋은 sickly
hyŏltchŏntchŭng 혈전증 thrombosis
hyŏlt'ong 혈통 blood; pedigree
hyŏlt'ong-i punmyŏnghan 혈통이 분명한 pedigree
hyŏmnyŏk kwan-gye 협력 관계 partnership
hyŏmnyŏktcha 협력자 collaborator (*on a project*)
hyŏmnyŏktchŏgin 협력적인 cooperative
hyŏmnyŏk 협력 cooperation
hyŏmnyŏk'ada 협력하다 cooperate; collaborate; ... *wa* / *kwa hyŏmnyŏk'ayŏ* ...와 / 과 협력하여 in association with
hyŏmo 혐오 disgust
hyŏmogamŭl irŭk'ida 혐오감을 일으키다 disgust

hyŏmohada 혐오하다 detest

hyŏmosŭrŏun 혐오스러운 disgusting

hyŏmŭi 혐의 charge LAW

hyŏmŭija 혐의자 suspect

hyŏmŭiriŭl pannŭn 혐의를 받는 suspected

hyŏn 현 chord

hyŏnak-kki 현악기 stringed instrument

hyŏnak-kki yŏnjuja 현악기 연주자 string player; strings

hyŏnch'ang 현창 porthole

Hyŏnch'ung-il 현충일 Memorial Day

hyŏndae 현대 modern times ◊ modern

hyŏndaehwa 현대화 modernization

hyŏndaehwahada 현대화하다 modernize

hyŏndaejŏgin 현대적인 modern

hyŏndaejŏgŭro pakkuda 현대적으로 바꾸다 modernize

hyŏndaeŭi 현대의 contemporary

hyŏngbu 형부 brother-in-law (*woman's elder sister's husband*)

hyŏnggwang 형광 fluorescence

hyŏnggwangp'en 형광펜 highlighter

hyŏnggwang-ŭi 형광의 fluorescent

hyŏn-gitchŭng 현기증 giddiness; vertigo

hyŏn-gitchŭng-i nada 현기증이 나다 feel dizzy

hyŏngje chamae 형제 자매 brothers and sisters

hyŏngmyŏng 혁명 revolution

hyŏngmyŏngga 혁명가 revolutionary

hyŏngmyŏngjŏgin 혁명적인 revolutionary *ideas*

hyŏngmyŏng-ŭi 혁명의 revolutionary *spirit*

hyŏngmyŏng-ŭl irŭk'ida 혁명을 일으키다 revolutionize

hyŏng-ŏnhal su ŏmnŭn 형언할 수 없는 indescribable

hyŏngp'yŏnŏmnŭn 형편없는 wretched, pathetic; useless; disreputable

hyŏngp'yŏnŏpsshi 형편없이 dreadfully; poorly

hyŏngsa 형사 detective; criminal case

hyŏngsang 형상 figure

hyŏngsasang-ŭi 형사상의 criminal

hyŏngshik 형식 format, make-up; formality

hyŏngshiktchŏgin 형식적인 formal; perfunctory

hyŏngshiktchŏgŭro 형식적으로 formally

hyŏngsŏng 형성 formation

hyŏngsŏnghanŭn 형성하는 formative

hyŏngsŏngshik'ida 형성시키다 mold

hyŏngsu 형수 sister-in-law (*elder brother's wife*)

hyŏngt'ae 형태 form

hyŏn-gŭm 현금 cash; *kŭ chariesŏ hyŏn-gŭmŭro* 그 자리에서 현금으로 cash down

hyŏn-gŭm harin 현금 할인 cash discount

hyŏn-gŭm inch'ulgi 현금 인출기 cash machine, ATM

hyŏn-gŭmŭro naeda 현금으로 내다 pay (in) cash

hyŏn-gŭmŭro pakkuda 현금으로 바꾸다 cash *check*

hyŏn-gŭm yuch'urip 현금 유출입 cash flow

hyŏn-gwan 현관 entrance, porch

hyŏng-yongsa 형용사 adjective

hyŏnhaengbŏmŭro 현행범으로 in the very act

hyŏnhaktchŏgin 현학적인 pedantic

hyŏnjae 현재 the present

hyŏnjaehyŏng 현재형 present GRAM

hyŏnjaeronŭn 현재로는 presently, at the moment

hyŏnjaeŭi 현재의 current, present; going

hyŏnjang 현장 scene; *hyŏnjang-e(sŏ)* 현장에(서) on the scene; on the spot; on site

hyŏnji shigan 현지 시간 local time

hyŏnjŏhan 현저한 remarkable, striking

hyŏnjonhanŭn 현존하는 existing

hyŏnmigyŏng 현미경 microscope

hyŏnmyŏnghada 현명하다 be wise

hyŏnmyŏng-hage 현명하게 wisely

hyŏnmyŏnghan 현명한 clever; sensible; wise; advisable

hyŏnsang 현상 phenomenon; development (*of film*)

hyŏnsanghada 현상하다 develop *film*

hyŏnshil 현실 reality

hyŏnshiltchŏgin 현실적인 realistic

hyŏnshiltchuŭi 현실주의 realism

hyŏnshiltchuŭija 현실주의자 realist

hyŏnsugyo 현수교 suspension bridge

hyŏpkkok 협곡 gorge

hyŏp-ppak 협박 threat, intimidation

hyŏp-ppak p'yŏnji 협박 편지 threatening letter

hyŏp-ppak'ada 협박하다 intimidate, threaten

hyŏpssang 협상 negotiation

hyŏpssangga 협상가 negotiator

hyŏpssanghada 협상하다 negotiate

hyŏpsshimtchŭng 협심증 angina

hyŏptchugok 협주곡 concerto

hyŏpttong 협동 collaboration, cooperation

hyŏpttong chagŏp 협동 작업 teamwork

hyŏpttong chohap 협동 조합 cooperative COM

hyŏpttonghada 협동하다 pull together

hyŏraek kŏmsa 혈액 검사 blood test

hyŏraek saemp'ŭl 혈액 샘플 blood sample

hyŏraek ŭnhaeng 혈액 은행 blood bank

hyŏraek'yŏng 혈액형 blood group

hyŏrap 혈압 blood pressure

hyo 효 filial piety (*Confucian*)

hyokkwaga ŏmnŭn 효과가 없는 ineffective

hyokkwajŏgin 효과적인 effective

hyokkwarŭl churida 효과를 줄이다 counter the effect of

hyomo 효모 yeast

hyoryŏgi innŭn 효력이 있는 effective

hyoryŏgŭl nat'anaeda 효력을 나타내다 take effect

hyoyul 효율 efficiency

hyoyultchŏgin 효율적인 efficient

hyoyurhwa 효율화 rationalization

hyoyurhwahada 효율화하다 rationalize

hyudaep'um pogwanso 휴대품 보관소 checkroom

hyudaeyong-(ŭi) 휴대용(의) portable

hyudaeyong ŭija 휴대용 의자 deckchair

hyuga 휴가 vacation; leave

hyugarŭl kat-tta 휴가를 갖다 take a holiday

hyuga yŏhaenggaek 휴가 여행객 vacationer

hyuge shigan 휴게 시간 intermission, interval

hyugeshil 휴게실 lobby

hyugeso 휴게소 service area

hyuhoe 휴회 recess

hyuhwasan 휴화산 dormant volcano

hyuil 휴일 holiday

hyuji 휴지 toilet paper; waste paper

hyujit'ong 휴지통 wastepaper basket

hyujŏn 휴전 cease-fire; truce; armistice

hyujŏngdoeda 휴정되다 adjourn

hyujŏnsŏn 휴전선 ceasefire line

hyung-ak 흉악 atrocity

hyung-akppŏm 흉악범 thug

hyung-akssŏng 흉악성 enormity

hyung-ak'an 흉악한 hideous

hyunghada 흉하다 be hideous; be unlucky

hyunghan 흉한 ugly

hyungmul 흉물 monstrosity

hyungnae 흉내 impersonation take-off

hyungnaenaeda 흉내내다 imitate, take off, mimic; simulate

hyungnaenaegi 흉내내기 impression, take off

hyungp'ohan 흉포한 ferocious

hyungt'ŏ 흉터 scar; *hyungt'ŏrŭl namgida* 흉터를 남기다 leave a scar

hyushik 휴식 rest, respite; *kabyŏun hyushik shigan* 가벼운 휴식 시간 coffee break

hyushikch'ŏ 휴식처 resting place; lounge

hyushik-kki 휴식기 break

hyuyangji 휴양지 resort

I

...i ...이 (*subject particle*): *...i it-tta*
...이 있다 there is/are
i 이 two ◊ tooth; louse; profit; interest
FIN; reason; person ◊ this
ibalssa 이발사 barber
ibanja 입안자 draftsman
ibe taego punŭn pubun 입에 대고
부는 부분 mouthpiece
ibi ttak pŏröjin 입이 딱 벌어진
open-mouthed; wide-mouthed
ibŏboda 입어보다 try on
ibŭl tamulda 입을 다물다 clam up,
keep silent
ibŭl ttak pŏlligo paraboda 입을 딱
벌리고 바라보다 gape
ibul 이불 coverlet
ibunppŏp 이분법 dichotomy
ibwŏnhada 입원하다 go into hospital
ibwŏn hwanja 입원 환자 in-patient
ibyang 입양 adoption
ibyang-a 입양아 foster child
ibyanghada 입양하다 adopt
ibyŏl 이별 farewell; parting
ich'ajŏgŭro chung-yohan
이차적으로 중요한 of secondary
importance
ich'ie matkke 이치에 맞게
reasonably
ich'ŭng ch'imdae 이층 침대 bunk
beds
ich'yŏjida 잊혀지다 fall into oblivion
ida 이다 be; *nanŭn hakssaeng-
iyeyo* 나는 학생이에요 I am a
student
idan kiŏ 이단 기어 second gear
ideollogi 이데올로기 ideology
idojŏdo anin kyŏng-u 이도저도 아닌
경우 a borderline case
idong 이동 shift; transfer; mobility
idong chŏnhwa 이동 전화 cell
phone
idonghada 이동하다 travel around;
change direction
idong-i kanŭnghan 이동이 가능한

mobile
idong musŏn chŏnhwa 이동 무선
전화 cellular phone
idongssŏng 이동성 mobility
idŭgi toeda 이득이 되다 be profitable,
pay off
idŭngsŏgŭi 이등석의 second class
Idu 이두 (*Silla-Choson writing
system*)
iga ŏmnŭn 이가 없는 toothless
iga ppajida 이가 빠지다 be chipped
igida 이기다 win; beat; win out; mix
igijŏgin 이기적인 selfish
igŏt 이것 this ◊ this one
igŏttŭl 이것들 these
igŭllu 이글루 igloo
igŭn 익은 ripe
igŭnishyŏn k'i 이그니션 키 ignition
key
iguktchŏgin 이국적인 exotic
igyŏn 이견 different opinion;
difference (of opinion)
igyŏnaeda 이겨내다 get over,
overcome, surmount
igyodo 이교도 heathen
iha 이하 not exceeding, less than;
under, below; the following; *...iharo*
...이하로 below
ihae 이해 understanding
ihaeganŭn 이해가는 meaningful
ihaehada 이해하다 understand
ihaengjŏng ssaik'ŭrŭi 이행정
싸이클의 two-stroke
ihaeryŏk 이해력 understanding,
comprehension
ihaeshik'ida 이해시키다 make
understand; get through
ihaeshimnŭnŭn 이해심있는
understanding *person*
ihangnyŏn 이학년 sophomore
ihasŏnnyŏm 이하선염 mumps
ihon 이혼 divorce
ihonhada 이혼하다 divorce, get
divorced

ihonhan 이혼한 divorced

ihonnam 이혼남 divorcee (*man*)

ihonnyŏ 이혼녀 divorcee (*woman*)

ihuro 이후로 since; *chinan chu ihuro* 지난 주 이후로 since last week

iigi andoenŭn 이익이 안되는 uneconomic

iigi ŏmnŭn 이익이 없는 unprofitable

iigi toeda 이익이 되다 benefit

iigŭl naeda 이익을 내다 yield a profit

iigŭl ŏt-tta 이익을 얻다 get a profit; benefit

iigŭl poda 이익을 보다 make a profit

ik 이익 benefit; profit, return

iinyong pang 이인용 방 double room

ija 이자 interest

ijayul 이자율 interest rate

ije 이제 now; no longer, not any more; *ije kŭmanhae!* 이제 그만해! I've had enough!, stop!

ijel 이젤 easel

iiltchŏgin 이질적인 alien

ijinppŏp 이진법 binary system

ijipt'ŭ 이집트 Egypt ◊ Egyptian

ijŏbŏrida 잊어버리다 forget, lose sight of; lose

ijŏbŏrigo tŭgo kada 잊어버리고 두고 가다 leave behind, forget

ijŏk haeng-wija 이적 행위자 collaborator *pej*

ijŏk'ada 이적하다 transfer

ijŏne 이전에 before; formerly

ijŏngp'yo 이정표 milestone

ijŏnhada 이전하다 relocate

ijŏnŭi 이전의 ex-; previous, prior

ijŭl su ŏmnŭn 잊을 수 없는 unforgettable

iju 이주 migration; emigration; immigration

ijuhada 이주하다 migrate; immigrate

ijuja 이주자 settler, immigrant

ijung chuch'ashik'ida 이중 주차시키다 double park

ijungch'ang 이중창 duo

ijung in-gyŏkja 이중 인격자 two-faced person

ijung inkkyŏk 이중 인격 split personality

ijungju 이중주 duet

ijung kuktchŏk 이중 국적을 dual nationality

ijungt'ŏk 이중턱 double chin

ijung-ŭi 이중의 dual

ijung yuri 이중 유리 double glazing

iju nodongja 이주 노동자 migrant worker

ikki 이끼 moss

ikki kkin 이끼 낀 mossy

ikkŭlda 이끌다 head, lead; steer

ikkŭlgo kada 이끌고 가다 lead up to

ikssahada 익사하다 be drowned

ikssalburida 익살부리다 joke

ikssashik'ida 익사시키다 drown

ikssuk'aejida 익숙해지다 familiarize oneself with, get used to

ikssuk'aji anŭn 익숙하지 않은 unfamiliar; *...e ikssuk'aji ant'a* ...에 익숙하지 않다 be unfamiliar with, be unaccustomed to

iktta 익다 get used to; get cooked; ripen

ikttŏn kot 읽던 곳 place (*in a book*)

ik'ida 익히다 familiarize; cook

il 일 affair; business; job; pursuit; work; things; *ne irina haera!* 네 일이나 해라! mind your own business!

ilbangjŏgin 일방적인 one-sided, unilateral

ilbang t'onghaengno 일방 통행로 one-way street

ilbanhwa 일반화 generalization

ilbanhwahada 일반화하다 generalize

ilbanin 일반인 civilian

ilbanjŏgin 일반적인 general

ilbanjŏgŭro 일반적으로 generally, in general

ilban sabyŏng 일반 사병 the ranks

ilbŏlle 일벌레 workaholic

ilbo 일보 a step; *ilbo chiktchŏne it-tta* 일보 직전에 있다 be on the verge of

Ilbon 일본 Japan ◊ Japanese

Ilbonŏ 일본어 Japanese (*language*)

Ilbon saram 일본 사람 Japanese

ilbubun 일부분 one part, a portion

ilburŏ 일부러 deliberately

ilbu saramdŭl 일부 사람들 some people

ilch'erŭl p'ohamhayŏ 일체를

포함하여 all inclusive

ilch'i 일치 agreement, consensus; match, correspondence

ilch'ihada 일치하다 agree, match, correspond; agree with

ilch'ihanŭn 일치하는 corresponding, matching; coinciding

ilch'ishik'ida 일치시키다 agree; reconcile

ilch'ŭng 일층 first floor

ilch'ul 일출 sunrise

ilda 일다 brew, get up

ilgan shinmun 일간 신문 daily paper

ilgi 일기 diary

ilgido 일기도 weather chart

ilgi yebo 일기 예보 weather forecast

ilgop 일곱 seven

ilgop pŏntchaeŭi 일곱번째의 seventh

ilgŭl kŏri 읽을 거리 reading matter

ilgŭl su innŭn 읽을 수 있는 readable

ilgwa 일과 routine

ilgwal 일괄 package

ilgwaljŏgŭro ch'wigŭp'ada 일괄적으로 취급하다 lump together

ilgwangnyogŭl hada 일광욕을 하다 sunbathe

ilgwanjagŏp yŏl 일관작업 열 assembly line

ilgwansŏng 일관성 consistency

ilgwansŏng innŭn 일관성 있는 consistent

il hoebun 일 회분 installment, episode

iljikssŏnŭro 일직선으로 in a straight line

ilkkaewŏjuda 일깨워주다 remind

ilke hada 잃게 하다 cost; cause the loss of

ilkki ŏryŏun 읽기 어려운 illegible; unreadable; *ilkki shwiun* 읽기 쉬운 easy to read

illanssŏng ssangdung-i 일란성 쌍둥이 identical twins

illyŏk 인력 manpower

illyŏnbŏnho 일련번호 serial number

illyŏne 일년에 in a year, per annum

illyŏne han ponŭi 일년에 한 번의 annual

illyu 인류 human race; humanity; man

illyunch'a 일륜차 wheelbarrow;

monocycle

illyuŭi 일류의 first-rate

ilmol 일몰 sunset

ilmyŏn 일면 front page

ilmyŏn kisa 일면 기사 front page news

ilsangjŏgin 일상적인 everyday

ilshijŏk yŏn-gi 일시적 연기 reprieve

ilssang 일상 everyday

ilssangbok 일상복 clothes for everyday wear

ilssangjŏgin 일상적인 routine

ilssangjŏgŭro 일상적으로 as a matter of routine, routinely

ilssang-yong-ŏ 일상용어 vernacular

ilssanhwat'anso 일산화탄소 carbon monoxide

ilssappyŏng 일사병 sunstroke

ilsshibul 일시불 lump sum

ilsshijŏgin 일시적인 temporary, casual

ilsshijŏgŭro 일시적으로 temporarily

ilsshijŏk chŭngga 일시적 증가 temporary increase, bulge

ilsshijŏk pyŏndong 일시적 변동 temporary fluctuation, blip

ilsshijŏk taeyuhaeng 일시적 대유행 passing fad, craze

ilsshik 일식 eclipse of the sun

ilsshirŭl chŏnghada 일시를 정하다 fix a time

ilssohada 일소하다 clean up

ilsson 일손 hand, worker

iltchesagyŏk 일제 사격 volley

iltchi 일지 diary; logbook

...iltchido morŭnda ...일지도 모른다 may, might

iltchigin 일찍인 early

iltchik 일찍 early

iltchŏne 일전에 the other day

iltchŏng 일정 agenda; schedule

iltchŏng-aek 일정액 flat rate

iltchŏngch'i anŭn 일정치 않은 unsettled

iltchŏnghada 일정하다 be regular

iltchŏnghaji anŭn 일정하지 않은 erratic

iltchŏnghan 일정한 particular, specific; regular, uniform

iltchŏng-i kkwak ch'ada 일정이 꽉 차다 booked up

iltchŏng kigan 일정 기간 stint

iltchŏngsang 일정상 on the agenda

iltta 읽다 read

ilttŭngshil 일등실 first class cabin / compartment

ilt'a 잃다 lose

ima 이마 forehead, brow

imbak'an 임박한 pending, impending

imdae 임대 lease

imdae chadongch'a 임대 자동차 rental car

imdaehada 임대하다 lease, rent

imdae kyeyaksŏ 임대 계약서 rental agreement

imdaeryo 임대료 rent

imdaeyong 임대용 for rent

imeil 이메일 e-mail

imeil chuso 이메일 주소 e-mail address

imeillo ponaeda 이메일로 보내다 e-mail, send by email

imeirŭl ponaeda 이메일을 보내다 e-mail, send an e-mail to

imgŭm tonggyŏl 임금 동결 wage freeze

imhak 임학 forestry

imi 이미 already

imiji 이미지 image

imin 이민 emigrant

Imin-guk 이민국 Immigration

iminhada 이민하다 emigrate

imjaga pakkwida 임자가 바뀌다 change hands

immagae 입마개 muzzle

immasŭl tashida 입맛을 다시다 lick one's lips

immu 임무 task, brief; assignment; duty

immyŏng 임명 appointment; posting

immyŏnghada 임명하다 appoint, nominate

immyŏngja 임명자 appointee

imnyŏk 입력 input; enter, return

imnyŏkshik'ida 입력시키다 enter COMPUT: *k'ŏmp'yut'ŏe im-nyŏksshik'yŏ not'a* 컴퓨터에 입력시켜 놓다 put sth on computer

imnyŏk tanja 입력 단자 input port

imnyŏk'ada 입력하다 enter, key in

imo 이모 aunt (*mother's sister*)

imobu 이모부 uncle (*mother's sister's husband*)

imsanbok 임산복 maternity dress

imsang-ŭi 임상의 clinical

imshi chigwŏn 임시 직원 temporary employee, temp

imshi chŏjangso 임시 저장소 buffer COMPUT

imshijigŭro irhada 임시직으로 일하다 work on a temporary basis, temp

imshijŏgin 임시적인 temporary, provisional

imshin 임신 conception; pregnancy

imshinbu 임신부 expectant mother

imshinhada 임신하다 conceive; be pregnant

imshinhan 임신한 pregnant

imshinjung-ida 임신 중이다 be expecting

imshi pyŏnt'ong 임시 변통 stopgap

imshi sudan 임시 수단 makeshift

imshiŭi 임시의 temporary, acting

imun 이문 margin

...inae-e ...이내에 within

inboisŭ 인보이스 invoice

inbun 인분 (human) feces; portion

Inch'e Myŏnyŏk Kyŏlp'ip Pairŏsŭ 인체 면역 결핍 바이러스 HIV

inch'i 인치 inch

inch'ing taemyŏngsa 인칭 대명사 personal pronoun

inch'ŏk 인척 in-laws

inch'ul 인출 withdrawal

inch'urhada 인출하다 withdraw

indae 인대 ligament

Indian 인디안 (American) Indian

indo 인도 footpath, sidewalk; surrender; India ◊ India

Indoch'aina 인도차이나 Indochina ◊ Indochinese

indohada 인도하다 lead, take; extradite; usher in

Indoin 인도인 Indian (*person*)

indojuŭi 인도주의 humanism; humanitarianism

Indoneshia 인도네시아 Indonesia ◊ Indonesian

Indoneshiain 인도네시아인 Indonesian (*person*)

in-gan 인간 human (being)

in-ganjŏgin 인간적인 human,

humane

in-ganssŏng 인간성 humanity, humaneness

in-gan ssŭregi 인간 쓰레기 lowlife

in-girŭl ŏt-tta 인기를 얻다 catch on

ingkko 잉꼬 budgerigar

ingk'ŭ 잉크 ink

ingk'ŭ chet p'ŭrint'ŏ 잉크 젯 프린터 inkjet (printer)

ingmyŏng tong-ŏptcha 익명 동업자 silent partner

ingmyŏng-ŭi 익명의 anonymous

in-gong 인공 man-made

in-gong hohŭpkki 인공 호흡기 respirator

in-gongjinŭng 인공지능 artificial intelligence

in-gongjŏgin 인공적인 artificial

in-gong-wisŏng 인공위성 satellite

in-gong-wisŏng chŏpsshi 인공위성 접시 satellite dish

in-gu 인구 population

in-gu miltto 인구 밀도 population density

ing-yŏ 잉여 surplus

inhaesŏ 인해서: *kŭgŏsŭ(ro) inhaesŏ* 그것으로 인해서 so, for that reason

inhwa 인화 print

inhwassŏng(-ŭi) 인화성(의) inflammable

inhyŏng 인형 doll

inishyŏl 이니셜 initial

inishyŏllo ssŭda 이니셜로 쓰다 initial

injae sŭk'aut'ŭ tamdangja 인재 스카우트 담당자 headhunter *fig*

inji 인지 perception

...inji ...인지 if; whether; *...inji anidŭnji kane* ...인지 아니든지 간에 whether or not; *...inji ...inji* ...인지 ...인지 whether ... or ...

injil 인질 hostage

injilbŏm 인질범 hostage taker

injillo chap'ida 인질로 잡히다 be taken hostage

injŏgi kkŭnk'in 인적이 끊긴 deserted

injŏng 인정 acknowledgment

injŏnghada 인정하다 admit; approve of

injŏng-i manŭn 인정이 많은

philanthropic; benevolent

injŏng-innŭn 인정있는 humane

injŏng ŏmnŭn 인정 없는 inhuman

injŏp'an 인접한 adjacent

injong 인종 race

injong ch'abyŏl p'yeji 인종 차별 폐지 abolish racial discrimination, desegregate

injong ch'abyŏltchŏgin 인종 차별적인 racist

injong ch'abyŏltchuŭi 인종 차별주의 racism

injong ch'abyŏltchuŭija 인종 차별주의자 racist

injong p'yŏngdŭng 인종 평등 racial equality

injoŭi 인조의 artificial

inkki 인기 popularity

inkkiinnŭn 인기있는 fashionable, popular

inkki-it-tta 인기있다 be popular

inkkiŏmnŭn 인기없는 unpopular

inkkirŭl ŏt-tta 인기를 얻다 become popular, take off

ink'yubeit'ŏ 인큐베이터 incubator

inmom 잇몸 gum (*in mouth*)

inmul 인물 character

inp'ŭlle(ishyŏn) 인플레(이션) inflation

inp'ŭlleishyŏnŭl yubarhanŭn 인플레이션을 유발하는 inflationary

inp'yŏnŭro 인편으로 by hand

insa 인사 greeting, bow

insaek'ada 인색하다 be miserly

insaek'an 인색한 mean, stingy; miserly; grudging

insaeng 인생 life

insaeng-ŭl chŭlgida 인생을 즐기다 enjoy life

insahada 인사하다 greet; bow

insakkwa 인사과 personnel; human resources

insam 인삼 ginseng

insang 인상 raise, rise; image, reputation; impression; *nuguege chot'ŭn/nappŭn insangŭl chuda* 누구에게 좋은/나쁜 인상을 주다 make a good/bad impression on s.o.; *...(ŭ)n insangŭl pat-tta* ...(으)ㄴ 인상을 받다 I get the impression that

insangjŏgin 인상적인 impressive; imposing, striking

insa pulssŏng 인사 불성 stupor

insa tamdang pujang 인사 담당 부장 personnel manager

inshik 인식 awareness

inshim chot'a 인심 좋다 be generous

inshim chŏun 인심 좋은 generous, good-hearted

inshyullin 인슐린 insulin

insŭt'ŏnt'ŭ k'ŏp'i 인스턴트 커피 instant coffee

insŭt'ŏnt'ŭ shikp'um 인스턴트 식품 convenience food

insu 인수 takeover; factor MATH

insuhada 인수하다 take over

inswae 인쇄 print

inswaegi 인쇄기 printing press

inswaehada 인쇄하다 printout

inswaemul 인쇄물 printed matter

inswaeŏptcha 인쇄업자 printer (*person*)

int'elli 인텔리 egghead; the intelligentsia

int'eriŏ tijain 인테리어 디자인 interior design

int'eriŏ tijainŏ 인테리어 디자이너 interior designer

int'ŏbyu 인터뷰 interview

int'ŏbyuhada 인터뷰하다 interview

int'ŏbyuhanŭn saram 인터뷰하는 사람 interviewer

int'ŏch'einji 인터체인지 interchange

int'ŏk'ŏm 인터컴 intercom

Int'ŏnesŭl tullŏboda 인터넷을 둘러보다 surf the Net

Int'ŏnet 인터넷 Internet; *Int'ŏnet sangesŏ* 인터넷 상에서 on the Internet

int'ŏpeisŭ 인터페이스 interface

inwijŏgin 인위적인 artificial, insincere

inyŏmjŏgin 이념적인 ideological

inyong 인용 quotation; extract

inyonghada 인용하다 quote; *chakkaŭi kŭrŭl inyonghada* 작가의 글을 인용하다 quote from an author

inyongmun 인용문 quote (*from author*)

inyong puho 인용 부호 quotation marks

iŏp'on 이어폰 earphones

...iŏsŏ ...이어서 next to

...ioe-e ...이외에 besides, except for

ip 잎 leaf; blade; foliage

ip 입 mouth; *han ip* 한 입 a bite, a mouthful; *nanŭn surŭl ibe taeji anssŭmnida* 나는 술을 입에 대지 않습니다 I never touch alcohol, I don't drink

ipch'al 입찰 tender; bid

ipch'arhada 입찰하다 bid

ipch'ullyŏk k'odŭ 입출력 코드 access code

ipch'ullyŏk'ada 입출력하다 access

ipkkimŭl pulda 입김을 불다 blow

ipkku 입구 entrance, entry

ipkkuk 입국 arrivals (*at airport*); entry (*to country*)

ipkkuk hŏga 입국 허가 admission (*to country*)

ipkkukpija 입국비자 entry visa

ip ppakkŭro naeda 입 밖으로 내다 let out *gasp, scream etc*

ip-ppangch'e 입방체 cube

ip-ppang-ŭi 입방의 cubic

ip-ppang yongjŏk 입방 용적 cubic volume

ip-ppang yongnyang 입방 용량 cubic capacity

ip-ppŏp 입법 legislation

ip-ppŏp-ppu 입법부 legislature

ippsahada 입사하다 join

ipssanghan 입상한 prizewinning

ipsshim chŏun 입심 좋은 glib, voluble

ipssŏk 입석 standing room

ipssuhada 입수하다 pick up

ipssul 입술 lip

iptchang 입장 entrance; stance; situation

iptchang hŏga 입장 허가 admission

iptchang kŭmji 입장 금지 no admittance

iptchangnyo 입장료 entrance fee

iptchŭng 입증 verification

iptchŭnghada 입증하다 establish, prove

iptta 입다 wear; put on

ipttaehada 입대하다 enlist

ip'agŭl hŏgahada 입학을 허가하다 admit to school

ip'akkŭm 입학금 fee

ip'ak tŭngnogŭl hada 입학 등록을 하다 register (*for school, university*)

ip'ak tŭngnok 입학 등록 registration (*at school, university*)

ip'ak wŏnsŏ 입학 원서 application form (*for school, university*)

ip'oehada 입회하다 join

ip'oe hŏga 입회 허가 admission

ip'oein 입회인 observer

ip'oerŭl hŏgahada 입회를 허가하다 admit to an organization

ip'ubo 입후보 candidacy

iraero 이래로 since

Irak'ŭ 이라크 Iraq ◊ Iraqi

Iran 이란 Iran ◊ Iranian

irhada 일하다 work

irhoe 일회 one time, once

irhoe pogyongnyang 일회 복용량 a dose

irhoeyong 일회용 disposable, throw-away

irhŭn 일흔 seventy

irhŭn pŏntchaeŭi 일흔 번째의 seventieth

irijŏri kŏnilda 이리저리 거닐다 stroll around

iri kkŭnnada 일이 끝나다 get off (work)

irŏbŏrin 잃어버린 missing

irŏktchŏrŏk 이럭저럭 somehow or other; *irŏktchŏrŏk ...haenaeda* 이럭저럭 ...해내다 manage to ... one way or another; *irŏktchŏrŏk saenghwarhada* 이럭저럭 생활하다 scrape a living, get by somehow

irŏk'e 이렇게 this way

irŏn 이런 like this; *irŏn shigŭro irŏnat-tta* 이런 식으로 일어났다 it happened like this; *irŏn, irŏn!* 이런, 이런! well, well!; *irŏn, sesang!* 이런, 세상에! (oh) dear!, dear me!

irŏna antta 일어나 앉다 sit up

irŏnada 일어나다 happen; come about; get up, rise

irŏnal kŏt katchi anŭn 일어날 것 같지 않은 improbable; dim *prospects*

irŏsŏda 일어서다 stand (up), rise

iron 이론 theory

iron mullihak 이론 물리학 theoretical physics

ironsang-ŭro 이론상으로 in theory

irŭda 이르다 come to; reach; carry (*of sound*); range; *chŏgŏsŭn ch'ilman wŏne irŭnda* 저것은 70000원에 이른다 that comes to 70,000 won

irŭge 이르게 early

irŭk'ida 일으키다 cause; generate, stir up; cast *doubt*

irŭl shik'ida 일을 시키다 make work

irŭm 이름 name; first name

irŭmppunin 이름뿐인 nominal

irŭmp'yo 이름표 nametag

irŭmŭl chit-tta 이름을 짓다 name; *Yŭi irŭmŭl ttasŏ Xŭi irŭmŭl chit-tta* Y의 이름을 따서 X의 이름을 짓다 name X for Y

irŭn 이른 early

irŭn 잃은 lost

iruŏjida 이루어지다 be formed; *iruŏjyŏ it-tta* 이루어져 있다 consist of

irwŏl 일월 January

irwŏn 일원 member

irwŏnida 일원이다 belong to, be a member of

irye 이례 exception

iryejŏgin 이례적인 exceptional

iryejŏgŭro 이례적으로 exceptionally

iryŏks-sŏ 이력서 résumé

iryoil 일요일 Sunday

iryongp'um 일용품 daily necessity; daily necessities

iryu 이류 inferiority

iryuk 이륙 takeoff, liftoff

iryuk'ada 이륙하다 take off (*of airplane*)

iryu(ŭi) 이류(의) second-rate; inferior

isa 이사 director; move

isa chŏnmun ŏptch'e 이사 전문 업체 movers

isahada 이사하다 move house, move away

isahoe 이사회 board (of directors)

isa hoeŭi 이사 회의 board meeting

isa hoeŭishil 이사 회의실 board room

isahŭl 이사흘 couple of days

isak 이삭 ear (*of grain*)

isanagada 이사나가다 move out
isang 이상 not less than, more than ◊ ideal ◊ strangeness; *10,000 isang-ŭro* 10,000 이상으로 upward of 10,000; *ch'a-e muŏshin-ga isang-i it-tta* 차에 무엇인가 이상이 있다 there is something wrong with the car
isanghada 이상하다 be strange
isanghage 이상하게 curiously, strangely
isanghagedo 이상하게도 curiously enough
isangjŏgin 이상적인 ideal
isangjuŭijŏgin 이상주의적인 idealistic
isanhwat'anso 이산화탄소 greenhouse gas
isaoda 이사오다 move in
isatchim unsong-ŏptcha 이삿짐 운송업자 movers
isattchim t'ŭrŏk 이삿짐 트럭 movers' van
ishik chojik 이식 조직 graft
ishik susul 이식 수술 transplant
ishik'ada 이식하다 transplant
iship 이십 twenty
isŏ 이서 endorsement
isŏhada 이서하다 endorse
isŏng 이성 the opposite sex; reason
isŏng-aeŭi 이성애의 heterosexual
issŭl su ŏmnŭn 있을 수 없는 unacceptable
issŭm 있음 presence
issushigae 이쑤시개 toothpick
isŭk'eip'ŭ 이스케이프 escape COMPUT
isŭl 이슬 dew
isŭlbi 이슬비 drizzle
isŭlbiga naerida 이슬비가 내리다 drizzle
Isŭllamgyo 이슬람교 Islam (*religion*)
Isŭllam kuk-kka 이슬람 국가 Islam, Islamic world
Isŭllam minjok 이슬람 민족 Islam (*people*)
Isŭrael 이스라엘 Israel ◊ Israeli
Isŭraerin 이스라엘인 Israeli
itchŏm 이점 advantage; perk; plus

itchoguro 이쪽으로 this way
itta 잇다 join; inherit; knit together; preserve
it-tta 있다 be; exist; stay; be located; have, possess; *...i ga issŭmnikka?* ...이/가 있습니까? do you have ...?; *... it-tta* ...있다 there is/are ◊ (*forms continuous present of action verbs*): *...go it-tta* ...고 있다 ...ing; *nŏnŭn irŭl chinach'ige hago it-tta* 너는 일을 지나치게 하고 있다 you're overdoing things
it-tta 잊다 forget; get over
it-ttarŭda 잇따르다 follow one after another; *...ŭl/rŭl it-ttara* ...을/를 잇따라 one after another
it-ttarŭn 잇따른 successive
it'ajŏgin 이타적인 altruistic
it'al 이탈 departure
It'allia 이탈리아 Italy ◊ Italian
It'alliain 이탈리아인 Italian
It'alliaŏ 이탈리아어 Italian (*language*)
it'ŭlmada 이틀마다 every other day
iŭirŭl chegihada 이의를 제기하다 raise an objection, object
iŭirŭl shinch'ŏnghada 이의를 신청하다 take exception, object
iŭmp'yo 이음표 hyphen
iŭn chari 이은 자리 join
iut 이웃 neighborhood; neighbor
iut saram 이웃 사람 neighbor
iut'ada 이웃하다 border on
iwŏl 이월 February
iyagi 이야기 story, tale
iyagihada 이야기하다 tell, narrate
iyagihagi 이야기하기 narration
iyagishigŭi 이야기식의 narrative
iyong 이용 use
iyonghada 이용하다 use, draw on; take advantage of; manipulate
iyu 이유 cause; reason; *amu iyu ŏpsshi* 아무 이유 없이 for nothing, for no reason

-ja -자 (*suffix for persons*): *tokch'angja* 독창자 soloist; *tong-ŏptcha* 동업자 partner
...jamaja ...자 마자 as soon as

K

...ka ...가 (*subject particle*): **kŭ che-ŭiga maŭme tŭmnikka?** 그 제의가 마음에 드니까 does that offer interest you?

kaap'ada 가압하다 push, pressure

kabal 가발 wig

kabang 가방 bag

kabŏrida 가버리다 go off, leave

kabyŏn 가변 variableness ◊ variable

kabyŏpkke 가볍게 lightly

kabyŏpkke hada 가볍게 하다 lighten

kabyŏpta 가볍다 be light; be slight; be frivolous

kabyŏum 가벼움 lightness

kabyŏun 가벼운 light; airy; dismissive

kach'aŏmnŭn 가치없는 ruthless

kach'i 가치 value, worth, merit

kach'i anŭn 같지 않은 unlike

kach'i chada 같이 자다 sleep with; have sex with

kach'iga it-tta 가치가 있다 be worth; merit; count, be important

kach'iga ŏmnŭn 가치가 없는 worthless

kach'iga orŭda 가치가 오르다 rise in value

kach'iga ttŏrŏjida 가치가 떨어지다 fall in value; depreciate

kach'i hada 같이 하다 join in

kach'i harak 가치 하락 depreciation

kach'i itkke yŏgida 가치 있게 여기다 value, prize

kach'iŏmnŭn 가치없는 worthless

kach'i oda 같이 오다 come along, come too

kach'i put'ŏit-tta 같이 붙어있다 stuck together

kach'irŭl ttŏrŏttŭrida 가치를 떨어뜨리다 detract from; run down

kach'ŏbun sodŭk 가처분 소득 disposable income

kach'uk 가축 domestic animal; livestock

kach'uk uri 가축 우리 corral

kada 가다 go (*toward listener*); come; get along (*come to party etc*); proceed (*of people*); **yŏgŭro kanŭn kire issŏyo** 역으로 가는 길에 있어요 it's on the way to the station

kadak 가닥 strip, strand

kadonghaji mot'age hada 가동하지 못하게 하다 immobilize

kadŭk ch'ada 가득 차다 fill up (*of place*) ◊ full up

kadŭk ch'aeuda 가득 채우다 fill up, top up

kadŭk ch'ait-tta 가득 차있다 be bristling with; be crammed with

kadŭk ch'an 가득 찬 full

kadŭk'an 가득한 full of

kaduda 가두다 lock in

kae 개 dog ◊ *general countword*

kaeam 개암 hazelnut

kaeamnamu 개암나무 hazel (tree)

kaebal 개발 development

kaebaldosangguk 개발도상국 developing country

kaebaltcha 개발자 developer

kaebangdoen 개방된 open *market, society*

kaebarhada 개발하다 develop

kaebarhayŏ iyonghada 개발하여 이용하다 exploit, make use of

kaebyŏltchŏgŭro 개별적으로 individually

kae chul 개 줄 leash

kaech'arhada 개찰하다 punch *ticket*

kaech'ŏk'ada 개척하다 pioneer

Kaech'ŏnjŏl 개천절 National Foundation Day

kaech'uk'ada 개축하다 rebuild

kaeda 개다 clear, clear up (*of weather*); fold

kaegae 개개 individually, one by one

kaegaeŭi 개개의 individual, separate

kaegŭ 개그 gag, joke

kaegulgaegul ulda 개굴개굴 울다 croak (of frog)

kaeguri 개구리 frog

kaegwanhada 개관하다 inaugurate

kaehoeshik 개회식 opening ceremony

kaehwahada 개화하다 civilize

kaehyŏk 개혁 reform

kaehyŏk undong 개혁 운동 crusade (for reform)

kaehyŏk'ada 개혁하다 reform

kaein 개인 individual ◊ individual, personal

kaeinbisŏ 개인 비서 PA, personal assistant

kaein hwagin pŏnho 개인 확인 번호 PIN, personal identification number

kaeinjuŭi 개인주의 individualism

kaeinjuŭija 개인주의자 individualist

kaein kyosa 개인 교사 (private) tutor

kaein kyosŭp 개인 교습 (private) tuition

kaeintchŏgin 개인적인 personal, private

kaeinŭi 개인의 individual; personal

kaeinyong k'ŏmp'yut'ŏ 개인용 컴퓨터 PC, personal computer

kaeinyong sŭt'ereo 개인용 스테레오 personal stereo

kaejip 개집 kennel

kaejŏng 개정 sitting (of court); reform

kaejŏng chungim 개정 중임 session (of parliament)

kaejo 개조 conversion; renovation

kaejohada 개조하다 convert; renovate

kaekch'a 객차 car (of a train)

kaekkwanjŏgin 객관적인 objective

kaeksshil 객실 cabin

kaeksshil tamdangja 객실 담당자 room clerk

kaekwan 개관 survey

kaek'owŏnsung-i 개코원숭이 baboon

kaemi 개미 ant

kae mok-kkŏri 개 목걸이 (dog) collar

kaemyŏnghada 개명하다 rename

kaenbŏsŭ 캔버스 canvas (for painting)

kaeng 갱 gang; pit, coal mine

kaengshin 갱신 renewal

kaengshinhada 갱신하다 renew

kaenyŏm 개념 concept

kaeŏp'ada 개업하다 set up (in business)

kaesaekki ∨ 개새끼 son of a bitch, bastard

kaeshi 개시 initiation

kaeshihada 개시하다 initiate

Kaeshin-gyo 개신교 Protestantism

kaeŭich'i ank'o 개의치 않고 regardless of

kaeul 개울 stream

kaeyo 개요 outline; syllabus

kage 가게 store

kage chuin 가게 주인 storekeeper

kagi shwiun 가기 쉬운 accessible

kagonghada 가공하다 process food, raw materials

kagonghaji anŭn 가공하지 않은 raw sugar, iron

kagu 가구 furniture

kagu han chŏm 가구 한 점 a piece of furniture

kagurŭl tŭryŏ not'a 가구를 들여 놓다 furnish

kagyanggakssaek 각양각색 medley, mixture, assortment

kagye 가계 descent, ancestry; housekeeping (money)

kagyebu 가계부 housekeeping book

kagyŏgi orŭda 가격이 오르다 appreciate, increase in value

kagyŏgi pissan 가격이 비싼 expensive

kagyŏgŭl maegida 가격을 매기다 price

kagyŏgŭl naerida 가격을 내리다 mark down, reduce the price of

kagyŏgŭl ollida 가격을 올리다 mark up price

kagyŏk 가격 cost; price

kagyŏk harin kyŏngjaeng 가격 할인 경쟁 price war

kagyŏk insang 가격 인상 price rise; mark-up

kahada 가하다 inflict

kahok 가혹 severity

kahok'an 가혹한 harsh; oppressive

kaijrŏ oda 가지러 오다 come for; collect

kaip'ada 가입하다 join, become a member

kajami 가자미 turbot

kajang 가장 most, very ◊ wage earner; masquerade

kajang chal naganŭn sangp'yo 가장 잘 나가는 상표 brand leader

kajang chari 가장 자리 edge

kajanghada 가장하다 act; put on; pretend

kajangjari 가장자리 edge; rim; brim; brink; verge

kajang mudobok 가장 무도복 fancy dress

kajang mudohoe 가장 무도회 fancy-dress party

kaji 가지 branch; twig; eggplant

kajida 가지다 own, have; hold; *iriro kŭgŏsŭl kajyŏda chullaeyo?* 이리로 그것을 가져다 줄래요? bring it here, will you?

kajigakssaegŭi 가지각색의 miscellaneous

kajigakssaek 가지각색 assortment

kajigo it-tta 가지고 있다 have got

kajigo kada 가지고 가다 take, remove

kajigo nolda 가지고 놀다 toy with

kajirŏ kada 가지러 가다 collect, call for

kajirŏnhi kkot-tta 가지런히 꽂다 put neatly; fix neatly; arrange

kajirŭl ch'ida (가지를) 치다 prune *branch*

kajŏng 가정 assumption; home

kajŏngnyong k'ŏmp'yut'ŏ 가정용 컴퓨터 home computer

kajŏng kyosa 가정 교사 home tutor

kajŏng kyoyuk 가정 교육 upbringing; home education

kajŏngbu 가정부 housekeeper

kajŏnghada 가정하다 assume, suppose

kajŏngjŏgin 가정적인 homeloving, homely

kajŏngnyong-i anin 가정용이 아닌 not designed for use in the home

kajŏnjep'um 가전제품 (household) appliance

kajok 가족 family; household

kajok kyehoek 가족 계획 family planning

kajoktchŏgin 가족적인 paternalistic

kajoktchuŭi 가족주의 paternalism

kajuk 가죽 hide, skin (*of animal*); leather

kajuk kkŭn 가죽 끈 lead, leash; (leather) strap

kajyŏoda 가져오다 bring; get, fetch; earn

kak 각 each, every, all; angle

kakkai 가까이 near ◊ about, approximately

kakkaie 가까이에 at hand, to hand ◊ near; *ŭnhaeng kakkaie* 은행 가까이에 near the bank

kakkaie(sŏ) 가까이에(서) locally

kakkai hagi shwiun 가까이 하기 쉬운 approachable

kakkai kaji mot'age hada 가까이 가지 못하게 하다 prevent from going near, keep away

kakkai tagagada 가까이 다가가다 approach, draw near

kakkai tagaoda 가까이 다가오다 draw near (*of time*)

kakkaihagi ŏryŏun 가까이하기 어려운 unapproachable

kakkapkke 가깝게 close, near

kakkaptta 가깝다 be close, be near

kakkasŭro 가까스로 scarcely, barely; hardly

kakkasŭro ppajyŏnagada 가까스로 빠져나가다 have a narrow escape (*from arrest*)

kakkasŭro saranamtta 가까스로 살아남다 have a narrow escape (*from death*)

kakkaun 가까운 close, near

kak-kkage 각각에 each

kak-kkagŭi 각각의 each, respective

kak-kkak 각각 each

kak-kki 각기 respectively

kak-kkwang 각광 footlights

kakkŭm 가끔 occasionally, sometimes

kakppon 각본 screenplay

kakssaek 각색 adaptation

kaktcha 각자 each other

kaktchu 각주 footnote

kalbi 갈비 spare ribs, barbecued ribs

kalbippyŏ 갈비뼈 rib

kalbitchim 갈비찜 steamed (beef) ribs

kalbi t'ang 갈비탕 beef rib soup

kalda 갈다 change, replace; grind; sharpen; plow

kalga mŏkta 갉아 먹다 nibble

kalgigalgi tchit-tta 갈기갈기 찢다 tear up

kalgo tadŭmtta 갈고 다듬다 polish up

kalgori 갈고리 hook

kalgyŏ ssŭda 갈겨 쓰다 scribble

kalgyŏ ssŭgi 갈겨 쓰기 scribble

kal kiri mŏlda 갈 길이 멀다 it's a long way off

kalk'wi 갈퀴 rake

kallajida 갈라지다 branch off; diverge

kallajin t'ŭm 갈라진 틈 crevice

kallyak 간략 simplicity; brevity; *kallyak'i p'yŏnjirŭl ssŭda* 간략히 편지를 쓰다 drop a line

kallyakhada 간략하다 be simple; be brief

kalmaegi 갈매기 gull; seagull

kalmang 갈망 craving, longing

kalmanghada 갈망하다 crave, long for

kalp'i 갈피 point, sense; *nae maŭmi kalp'irŭl mot-tchamnŭnda* 내 마음이 갈피를 못잡는다 my mind is in a whirl

kalsaek 갈색 brown

kalssurok tŏ 갈수록 더 increasingly

kaltchŭng 갈증 thirst

kaltta 갉다 gnaw

kalttae 갈대 reed

kama 가마 kiln

kamang 가망 chance, possibility

kamang-innŭn 가망있는 hopeful, promising

kamang ŏmnŭn 가망 없는 hopeless, useless

kamangsŏng 가망성 probability

kamanhaejuda 감안해주다 make allowances

kamanhi 가만히 still; *kamanhi issŏ* 가만히 있어! keep still!

kamanittchi mot'anŭn 가만있지 못하는 restless

kambang 감방 cell (*for prisoner*)

kamchwŏjin 감춰진 hidden

kamch'altcha 감찰사 inspector (*in factory*)

kamch'o 감초 licorice

kamch'ok 감촉 feeling; touch; *shilk'ŭwa / myŏn-gwa kat'ŭn kamch'ogida* 실크와 / 면과 같은 감촉이다 it feels like silk / cotton

kamch'uda 감추다 conceal, cover up; withhold

kamdanghada 감당하다 control

kamdanghal su innŭn / ŏmnŭn 감당할 수 있는 / 없는 controllable / uncontrollable

kamdok 감독 director (*of movie*); direction (*of movie*)

kamdoktcha 감독자 supervisor

kamdok'ada 감독하다 direct *movie*; supervise

kamdongjŏgin 감동적인 emotional, poignant

kamdongshik'ida 감동시키다 move, touch (*emotionally*)

kamdongshik'inŭn 감동시키는 touching

kamgaginnŭn 감각있는 tasteful

kamgagŏmnŭn 감각없는 numb

kamgak 감각 sensation; sense (*sight, touch, smell etc*)

kamgaktchŏgin 감각적인 sensuous

kamgi 감기 cold, chill (*illness*)

kamgida 감기다 close; wind round

kamgie kŏllida 감기에 걸리다 catch a cold

kamgin 감긴 closed

kamgŭm 감금 captivity, confinement; detention

kamgŭmhada 감금하다 confine, imprison

kamgyŏk'ada 감격하다 be thrilled

kamgyŏk'age hanŭn 감격하게 하는 thrilling

kamhaenghae popsshida 감행해 봅시다 let's risk it

kamhi 감히 daringly; *nega kamhi ŏttŏk'e!* 네가 감히 어떻게! how dare you!

kamhihada 감히 하다 dare; *kŭnŭn kamhi hal su ŏpssŏssŏyo* 그는

kamhyŏnghada

감히 할 수 없었어요 he didn't dare

kamhyŏnghada 감형하다 commute
death sentence

kamja 감자 potato

kamja ch'ip 감자 칩 potato chip

kamja t'wigim 감자 튀김 French
fries; fried potatoes

kamji 감지 perception (*through
senses*)

kamjihada 감지하다 perceive (*with
senses*)

kamjilnage hanŭn 감질나게 하는
tantalizing

kamjŏng 감정 emotion; valuation

kamjŏngga 감정가 connoisseur

kamjŏng-i sanghagi shwiun 감정이
상하기 쉬운 sensitive

kamjŏngjŏgin 감정적인 emotional

kamjŏng-ŭi p'okppal 감정의 폭발
outburst of emotion

kamjŏng-ŭl ŏngnurŭji mot'ada
감정을 억누르지 못하다 be unable
to control one's emotions, be
overcome by emotion

kamjŏnsashik'ida 감전사시키다
electrocute

kammiroun 감미로운 mellow

kammiryo 감미료 sweetener (*for
drink*)

kammyŏng 감명 deep impression;
*nuguege / muŏse kammyŏng pat-
tta* 누구에게/무엇에 감명 받다 be
impressed by s.o. / sth

kammyŏng chuda 감명 주다 make
an impression

Kamni Kyohoe 감리 교회 Methodist
Church

kamok 감옥 prison

kamsa 감사 gratitude; thanks; audit

kamsagwan 감사관 auditor

kamsahada 감사하다 be grateful for;
thank; audit

kamsahagedo 감사하게도 thankfully

kamsahal chul morŭnŭn 감사할 줄
모르는 ungrateful

kamsahamnida 감사합니다 thank
you (*polite*)

kamsahanŭn 감사하는 thankful

kamsang 감상 sentimentality,
sentiment

kamsangjŏgin 감상적인 sentimental

kamshihada 감시하다 monitor,
watch; spy on; picket

kamso 감소 decrease, decline

kamsohada 감소하다 decline,
decrease

kamsok'ada 감속하다 decelerate,
slow down

kamsuhada 감수하다 reconcile
oneself

kamsusŏng-i kanghan 감수성이
강한 susceptible

kamsusŏng-i yeminhan 감수성이
예민한 impressionable

kamtta 감다 wind, wind up *clock*;
close

kamt'an 감탄 admiration

kamt'anhada 감탄하다 admire

kamum 가뭄 drought

kamwŏn 감원 lay-off, staff cut

kamwŏndoeda 감원되다 be laid off

kamwŏnhada 감원하다 lay off

kamwŏnshik'ida 감원시키다 lay off

kamyŏm 감염 infection

kamyŏmdoeda 감염되다 become
infected

kamyŏmdoen 감염된 infected

kamyŏmshik'ida 감염시키다 infect

kamyŏn 가면 mask

ka-myŏng 가명 pseudonym

kan 간 liver (*food*)

kanan 가난 poverty

kananhada 가난하다 be poor

kananhan 가난한 poor, deprived

kanbu 간부 executive

kanch'ŏk'ada 간척하다 reclaim

kanch'ŏnghada 간청하다 implore,
plead with

kanch'ŏp 간첩 secret agent, spy

kang 강 river

kang-aji 강아지 puppy, pup; whelp

kangbak kwannyŏm 강박 관념
obsession; compulsion

kangbak kwannyŏme sarojap'in
강박 관념에 사로잡힌 obsessive;
compulsive

Kangbuk 강북 Kangbuk (*Seoul,
north of the Han river*)

kangbyŏn 강변 riverside

kangch'ŏl 강철 steel

kangdo 강도 intensity; burglar;
burglary

kangdojil 강도질 robbery

kangdojirhada 강도질하다 burglarize

kangdo(rŭl) tanghada 강도(를) 당하다 be robbed

kangdŭngshik'ida 강등시키다 downgrade

kanggan 강간 rape

kangganbŏm 강간범 rapist

kangganhada 강간하다 rape

kanggŏnhan 강건한 virile

kanggyŏnghan 강경한 strong, firm

kanggyŏngnonja 강경론자 hardliner, hawk *fig*

kanghada 강하다 be strong

kanghaejida 강해지다 strengthen; harden (*of attitude*); intensify

kanghage 강하게 strongly

kangham 강함 strength, intensity

kanghan 강한 intense, strong, high

Kanghwado 강화도 Kanghwa Island

kanghwahada 강화하다 reinforce; tighten *control, security*

kangjangje 강장제 tonic

kangje 강제 force

kangjejŏgin 강제적인 forced

kangjero 강제로 by force; *Xŭl/rŭl kangjero Yhadorok mandŭlda* X을/를 강제로 Y하도록 만들다 force X to do Y

kangjo 강조 emphasis, accent

kangjohada 강조하다 emphasize; highlight

Kangnam 강남 Kangnam (*Seoul, south of the Han river*)

kangnyŏk shilsshihada 강력 실시하다 forcibly carry out, enforce

kangnyŏk'ada 강력하다 be powerful

kangnyŏk'age 강력하게 violently, very strongly

kangnyŏk'an 강력한 powerful, strong; intense

kangnyŏk'i 강력히 strongly

kangnyŏn 강연 talk, lecture

kangnyŏrham 강렬함 violence (*of gale*)

kangnyŏrhan 강렬한 strong, violent

kang-ŏgwi 강 어귀 river mouth

kangppadak 강바닥 riverbed

kangp'an 강판 grater

kangp'ung 강풍 gale

kangsa 강사 lecturer; instructor

kangse 강세 strength; stress, emphasis; *tallŏ kangse* 달러 강세 a run on the dollar

kangse chusik shijang 강세 주식 시장 bull market

kangtchŏm 강점 strong point

kangt'a 강타 blow, punch

kangt'ahada 강타하다 smash, bang

kangt'al 강탈 extortion

kangt'arhada 강탈하다 rob

kang-ŭi 강의 lecture

kang-ŭihada 강의하다 give a lecture, lecture

kang-ŭishil 강의실 lecture hall

kang-u 강우 rainfall

kan-gyŏk 간격 space

kan-gyŏrhage 간결하게 briefly

kan-gyŏrhan 간결한 brief, succinct

kan-gyŏrhi hada 간결히 하다 shorten, trim

kangyohada 강요하다 coerce, force; press, urge; insist on

kanho 간호 care (*of sick person*)

kanho ŏmmu 간호 업무 nursing

kanhosa 간호사 nurse

kanho shilssŭpssaeng 간호 실습생 student nurse

kani ch'imdae 간이 침대 cot

kani maejŏm 간이 매점 kiosk

kani shikttang 간이 식당 snack bar

kanjang 간장 soy sauce; liver ANAT

kanjilppyŏng 간질병 epilepsy

kanjilppyŏng hwanja 간질병 환자 epileptic (*person*)

kanjirida 간질이다 tickle

kanjirŏp'ida 간지럽히다 tickle

kanjirŭi paltchak 간질의 발작 epileptic fit

kanjŏppi 간접비 overhead FIN

kanjŏptchŏgin 간접적인 indirect

kanjŏptchŏgŭro 간접적으로 indirectly

kanjŏrhada 간절하다 be eager, be earnest

kanjŏrhan 간절한 eager

kanjŏrhi 간절히 eagerly

kan kogi 간 고기 ground meat

kanjuhada 간주하다 deem, consider

kannan 갓난 newborn

kannyŏm 간염 hepatitis

kanp'ahanŭn 간파하는 penetrating

kanp'an 간판 notice; signboard (*outside shop, on building*); front, cover organization

kansahae poinŭn 간사해 보이는 shifty-looking *person*

kansahan 간사한 shifty, deceitful

kanshik 간식 snack

kanshinhi 간신히 barely, only just

kansŏndoro 간선도로 arterial road

kansŏp 간섭 interference

kansŏp'ada 간섭하다 interfere

kansu 간수 guard

kansuhada 간수하다 store, keep

kanttanhada 간단하다 be simple; be brief

kanttanhage 간단하게 simply

kanttanham 간단함 simplicity

kanttanhan 간단한 simple, straightforward

kanttanhi 간단히 plainly, simply

kant'ong 간통 adultery; *kant'ongŭl tanghada* 간통을 당하다 commit adultery

kant'ŏng kwan-gye 간통 관계 adulterous relationship; adultery

kanŭlda 가늘다 be thin

kanŭn 가는 thin; fine

kanŭnghada 가능하다 be possible

kanŭnghage hada 가능하게 하다 allow, enable

kanŭnghan 가능한 possible; *kanŭnghan han ppalli* 가능한 한 빨리 as soon as possible; *kanŭnghan kajang tchalbŭn / pparŭn...* 가능한 가장 짧은 / 빠른... the shortest / quickest possible

kanŭngssŏng 가능성 possibility; likelihood; *kanŭngssŏng-i kŏŭi hŭibak'an* 가능성이 거의 희박한 just remotely possible

kanŭn kire 가는 길에: *...ro kanŭn kire* ...로 가는 길에 on the way

kanŭrŏjida 가늘어지다 get thin

kanyalp'ŭn 가냘픈 slender, slight

kap 갑 pack (*of cigarettes*)

kap 값 price

kapkkangnyu 갑각류 shellfish

kap pissan 값 비싼 expensive

kapp'an 갑판 deck NAUT

kapssangsŏn 갑상선 thyroid (gland)

kapsshi pissan 값이 비싼 expensive

kapsshi ssan 값이 싼 inexpensive, cheap

kapssŭl naerida 값을 내리다 knock down, reduce the price of

kaptchagi 갑자기 suddenly, all of a sudden

kaptchakssŭrŏn 갑작스런 sudden, unexpected; abrupt

kaptta 갚다 repay

kap'arŭn 가파른 steep

karaanch'ida 가라앉히다 calm down, sink

kara-anjŭn 가라앉은 subdued

karaantta 가라앉다 go down; subside, settle; cool (down); sink; go under

karaibŭl ot 가라입을 옷 a change of clothes

karaiptta 가라입다 change *clothes*, get changed

karak 가락 tune; pitch; tone

karaok'e 가라오케 karaoke

karat'ada 갈아타다 change *train etc*

karat'agi 갈아타기 change (*in travel*)

karida 가리다 shade; veil *face, eyes*

karik'ida 가리키다 indicate, point at

karoch'aeda 가로채다 intercept

karodŭng 가로등 streetlight

karo panghyang-ŭro 가로 방향으로 landscape *print*

karŭch'ida 가르치다 teach; instruct; coach

karŭdsa 가르다 mark out, set apart

karŭma 가르마 part (*in hair*)

karŭmarŭl t'ada 가르마를 타다 part one's hair

karu 가루 powder

karubinu 가루 비누 washing powder

karyŏnaeda 가려내다 sort out

karyŏptta 가렵다 itch

karyŏum 가려움 itch

kasa 가사 lyrics; housekeeping

kasang 가상 imagination

kasang hyŏnshil 가상 현실 virtual reality

kasang konggan 가상 공간 cyberspace

kashi 가시 thorn; spine; splinter; fish bone

kashi ch'ŏlssa 가시 철사 barbed wire

kashige hada 가시게 하다 rinse away *taste*

kasŏkppang 가석방 parole

kasŏl 가설 temporary construction; hypothesis

kasŏl hwaltchuro 가설 활주로 temporary landing strip

kasŏrhada 가설하다 build; suppose

kasok 가속 acceleration

kasokshik'ida 가속시키다 accelerate

kasok'ada 가속하다 accelerate

kasoktto 가속도 rate of acceleration

kassŭ t'aengk'ŭ 가스탱크 gasometer; gas works

kasŭ 가스 gas (*for cooking*)

kasŭk'et 가스켓 gasket

kasŭm 가슴 chest, bust

kasŭmari 가슴앓이 heartburn

kasŭmi mani p'ain 가슴이 많이 파인 low-cut

kasŭmi pinyaka'n 가슴이 빈약한 flat-chested

kasŭmŭl tŭrŏnaen 가슴을 드러낸 bare-chested

kasŭpkki 가습기 humidifier

kasu 가수 singer

kat 갓 traditional horsehair hat

katcha 가짜 fake

katch'uda 갖추다 possess; have in stock

katch'i 같이 as, like; together with

katch'uŏ chuda 갖추어 주다 equip

katkko nolda 갖고 놀다 mess around with

kat-tta 같다 be the same; be equal; be like; come to MATH; be on a par with; it appears that; *...kŏt kat-tta* ...것 같다 it seems like

kat'a poida 같아 보이다 seem like

kat'ŏ 가터 garter

kat'ŭn 같은 like, such as ◊ same; equal; identical; *...wa / kwa kat'ŭn kŏt* ...와 / 과 같은 것 something like; *kat'ŭn nop'iŭi* 같은 높이의 flush, level

kaŭl 가을 fall, autumn

kaun 가운 gown

kaunde 가운데 middle ◊ among, amongst

kawi 가위 scissors

kawiro charŭda 가위로 자르다 cut with scissors, clip, trim

Kaya 가야 Kaya (*Ancient Kingdom*)

kayagŭm 가야금 Kaya zither

kayŏnssŏng-ŭi 가연성의 flammable

kayongssŏng-ŭi 가용성의 soluble

ke 게 crab

kedaga 게다가 besides, moreover

kegŏlssŭrŏpkke 게걸스럽게 ravenously

kegŏlssŭrŏptta 게걸스럽다 be ravenous

kegŏlssŭrŏun 게걸스러운 ravenous

keim 게임 game (*in tennis*)

keim sent'ŏ 게임 센터 amusement arcade

kerilla 게릴라 guerrilla

keshi 게시 notice, bulletin

keshihada 게시하다 post, put up *notice*

keship'an 게시판 bulletin board

...ket... 겠... shall (*indicates future tense, intention or supposition*)

keŭllihada 게을리하다 shirk

keŭrŭda 게으르다 be lazy

keŭrŭm 게으름 indolence

keŭrŭmbaeng-i 게으름뱅이 layabout

keŭrŭn 게으른 lazy

keyangdoeda 게양되다 fly (*of flag*)

ki 기 era; flag; energy

kia 기아 starvation

kiapkkye 기압계 barometer

kiban 기반 basis, footing

kibarhan 기발한 extraordinary, striking

kibarhan saenggak 기발한 생각 inspiration

kibok 기복 ups and downs

kibonjŏgin 기본적인 basic, fundamental

kibonjŏgŭro 기본적으로 basically

kibonkap 기본값 default COMPUT

kibonŭi 기본의 rudimentary, basic

kibsŭ 깁스 plaster cast

kibu 기부 contribution; donation

kibugŭm mojip 기부금 모집 collection (*in church*)

kibuhada 기부하다 contribute, donate

kibuja 기부자 contributor, donor

kibun 기분 mood, frame of mind; *kibun chŏnhwan* 기분 전환 diversion, recreation; *kibun chŏnhwanŭro* 기분 전환으로 for a change; *onŭl kibuni ŏttŏseyo?* 오늘 기분이 어떠세요? how are you feeling today?

kibunjoŭn 기분좋은 agreeable, pleasant

kibun p'ulda 기분 풀다 lighten up

kibun sanghagehada 기분 상하게하다 upset, offend

kibun sanghan 기분 상한 upset; *kibuni chot'a/nappŭda* 기분이 좋다/나쁘다 be in a good/bad mood; *kibuni chot'a/p'uri chugŏit-tta* 기분이 좋다/풀이 죽어있다 be in good/poor spirits; *kibuni karaantta* 기분이 가라앉다 weigh down (*with worries*); *kibuni nappŭn* 기분이 나쁜 bad-tempered, moody

kibunŭl todunŭn 기분을 돋우는 exhilarating

kich'a 기차 train

kich'ayŏk 기차역 railroad station

kich'e 기체 gas (*oxygen etc*)

kich'eŭi 기체의 pneumatic

kich'im 기침 cough

kich'imhada 기침하다 cough

kich'im sorirŭl naeda 기침 소리를 내다 cough (*to get attention*)

kich'im shirŏp 기침 시럽 cough syrup

kich'im yak 기침 약 cough medicine

kich'o 기초 basis; foundations (*of building*) ◊ basic, fundamental

kich'obut'ŏ hada 기초부터 하다 get down to basics

kich'o chagŏp 기초 작업 groundwork

kich'ohada 기초하다 rest on, be based on

kich'ojŏgin 기초적인 basic

kich'oŭi 기초의 rudimentary

kida 기다 crawl

kidae 기대 expectation, hope

kidaeda 기대다 count on, rely on; lean; balance; recline, lie back

kidaedoenŭn 기대되는 prospective

kidaehada 기대하다 expect; look

forward to; bank on

kidaeŏ not'a 기대어 놓다 prop; lean

kidarida 기다리다 wait for; wait, hang on

kido 기도 prayer

kidohada 기도하다 pray

Kidok-kkyo 기독교 Christianity ◊ Christian

Kidok-kkyo Ch'ŏngnyŏnhoe 기독교 청년회 YMCA

Kidok-kkyo Pangsong 기독교 방송 Christian Broadcasting System, CBS

Kidok-kkyo shinja 기독교 신자 Christian (*person*)

kidung 기둥 column; pole; stilts; supports

kiga kkŏkkin 기가 꺾인 demoralized

kiga mak'inŭn 기가 막히는 staggering, astonishing

kigabait'ŭ 기가바이트 gigabyte

kigan 기간 period, spell, term

kigan shisŏl 기간 시설 infrastructure (*of society*)

kigo 기고 contribution (*to magazine*)

kigoga 기고가 columnist

kigohada 기고하다 contribute (*to magazine, newspaper*)

kigŭn 기근 famine

kigu 기구 organization; balloon (*for flight*)

kigwan 기관 institution; machinery (*governmental*)

kigwanch'ong 기관총 machine gun

kigwanjiyŏm 기관지염 bronchitis

kigwansa 기관사 driver; engineer (*of train*)

kigwan tanch'ong 기관 단총 submachine gun

kigye 기계 appliance, machine ◊ mechanical

kigye changch'i 기계 장치 mechanism

kigyegong 기계공 mechanic

kigyehwahada 기계화하다 mechanize

kigyejŏgin 기계적인 mechanical

kigyejŏgŭro 기계적으로 mechanically

kigyeryu 기계류 machinery, machines

kigyŏlssu 기결수 convict

kigyo 기교 trick, knack; technique

kihahak 기하학 geometry

kihahaktchŏk 기하학적 geometric(al)

kihan mallyo 기한 만료 expiry

kiho 기호 symbol, character; choice; preference

kihoe 기회 chance, opportunity; *kihoerŭl chuda* 기회를 주다 give a break, give an opportunity; *muŏsŭl hal kihoerŭl kajida* 무엇을 할 기회를 가지다 get to do sth

kihonja 기혼자 married person

kihon namsŏng 기혼 남성 married man

kihon yŏsŏng 기혼 여성 married woman

kihu 기후 climate

kihyŏng 기형 deformity; freak

kiil 기일 term, condition

kiinhada 기인하다 result from

kiip'ada 기입하다 enter, write down; fill in, fill out

kija 기자 reporter, journalist

kijahoegyŏn 기자회견 press conference

kijang 기장 captain (*of aircraft*)

kijil 기질 disposition, nature

kijinmaektchinhan 기진맥진한 dog-tired

kijŏgwi 기저귀 diaper

kijŏk 기적 miracle

kijŏkkach'i 기적같이 miraculously

kijŏktchŏgin 기적적인 miraculous

kijŏlsshik'ida 기절시키다 stun (*with a blow*)

kijŏrhada 기절하다 pass out, faint

kijo yŏnsŏl 기조 연설 keynote speech

kijŭng 기증 donate

kijŭnghada 기증하다 donate

kijun 기준 standard

kijunggi 기중기 crane; hoist

kikkŏi 기꺼이 gladly, willingly, with pleasure; *kikkŏi ...hada* 기꺼이 ...하다 be willing to do

kikkŏi padadŭrida 기꺼이 받아들이다 welcome

kikkwŏn 기권 abstention

kikkwŏnhada 기권하다 abstain

kil 길 route; road; avenue; path;

fathom NAUT; *kirŭl ilt'a* 길을 잃다 stray, wander away; get lost

kil annaerŭl hada 길 안내를 하다 navigate

kilda 길다 be long

kildŭryŏjin 길들여진 tame

kilge 길게 at length

kilge nŭllida 길게 늘리다 lengthen; pad *speech*

kilge pomyŏn 길게 보면 in the long run

kilkka 길가 roadside

kilmot'ung-i 길모퉁이 corner

kiltŭrida 길들이다 domesticate

kim 김 steam; laver, edible seaweed

kimch'i 김치 kimchee (*spicy pickled cabbage*)

kimi 기미 sign, indication; streak, touch

kimil 기밀 secrecy ◊ secret

kimi sŏrida 김이 서리다 mist up, steam up

kimirŭi 기밀의 classified, confidential

kimppajin 김빠진 bland; flat *beer*

kimppap 김밥 rice rolled in edible seaweed

kimyoham 기묘함 peculiarity, strangeness

kimyohan 기묘한 peculiar; quaint

kin 긴 long, lengthy

kinbak-kkam 긴박감 tension

kin-gŭp 긴급 urgency

kinjang 긴장 tension, strain

kinjangdoeda 긴장되다 tense up; be tense

kinjangdoen 긴장된 tense *muscle*; keyed up

kinjangdoenŭn 긴장되는 tense *moment*

kinjanghan 긴장한 tense *voice*, *person*

kinjang-ŭl p'ulda 긴장을 풀다 relax, unwind

kinjang-ŭro ttakttak'aejin 긴장으로 딱딱해진 uptight, inhibited

kinjang wanhwa 긴장 완화 détente

kin kŏt'ot 긴 겉옷 gown

kin somaeŭi 긴 소매의 long-sleeved

kinŭng 기능 craft, trade; function

kinŭngk'i 기능키 function key

COMPUT
kinŭng tanwi 기능 단위 unit
kinŭng-ŭl hada 기능을 하다 function as
kinyŏm 기념 commemoration ◊ memorial
kinyŏmbi 기념비 memorial, monument
kinyŏmhada 기념하다 commemorate, mark
kinyŏmil 기념일 (wedding) anniversary
kinyŏmmul 기념물 memento
kinyŏmp'um 기념품 souvenir
kinyŏm tongsang 기념 동상 monument
kinyŏmŭro 기념으로 in commemoration of
kiŏ 기어 gear
kiŏ chŏnhwan changch'i 기어 전환 장치 gear shift
kiŏk 기억 memory
kiŏk yongnyang 기억 용량 storage capacity
kiŏk'ada 기억하다 remember; store COMPUT; *muŏsŭl kiŏk'ago it-tta* 무엇을 기억하고 있다 bear sth in mind
kiŏngnyŏk 기억력 memory
kiŏp 기업 corporation ◊ business *ethics, style etc*
kiŏpkka 기업가 entrepreneur
kipkke 깊게 deeply
kipkke hada 깊게 하다 deepen
kippŏhada 기뻐하다 be delighted
kippŏhanŭn 기뻐하는 delighted; gleeful
kippŏnalttwida 기뻐날뛰다 exult
kiptta 깊다 be deep
kippŭda 기쁘다 be glad
kippŭge 기쁘게 happily, gladly; pleasantly
kippŭge hada 기쁘게 하다 please
kippŭm 기쁨 joy, delight
kippŭn 기쁜 pleased, glad
kip'i 깊이 depth ◊ deeply, soundly
kip'i chamdŭn 깊이 잠든 fast asleep
kip'ŏgada 깊어가다 draw on, advance
kip'oga saenggida 기포가 생기다 blister (*of paint*)

kip'o sujun-gi 기포 수준기 spirit level
kip'ŭm 깊음 depth
kip'ŭn 깊은 deep, profound
kip'um 기품 nobility; elegance
kip'um innŭn 기품 있는 distinguished, dignified
kip'yoso 기표소 polling booth
kiri 길이 length
kirin 기린 giraffe
kirogŭl kkaenŭn 기록을 깨는 record-breaking
kirok 기록 memo; archives; writing (*script*); *muŏshi kirogŭl namgida* 무엇의 기록을 남기다 keep track of sth
kirok munsŏ 기록 문서 record (*written document*)
kirok poyuja 기록 보유자 record holder
kirŭda 기르다 keep; grow; breed
kirŭl kkŏktta 기를 꺾다 daunt, deter, dishearten
kirŭl kkŏngnŭn 기를 꺾는 demoralizing
kirŭm 기름 oil
kirŭmch'irŭl hada 기름칠을 하다 oil
kirŭmgi kkin 기름기 낀 lank, greasy *hair*
kirŭmkki manŭn 기름기 많은 oily, greasy
kirŭmt'ong 기름통 sump
kiryagi p'ungbuhan 기락이 풍부한 resourceful
kiryak 기락 resources
kisa 기사 article (*in newspaper*); engineer; (machine) operator
kisadojŏgin 기사도적인 chivalrous
kisaek 기색 tinge
kisaeng 기생 kisaeng (*traditional female entertainer*)
kisaengch'unggat'ŭn saram 기생충같은 사람 parasite
kisaeng tongshingmul 기생 동식물 parasite
kisa kŏri 기사 거리 copy (*written material*)
kisang 기상 original idea; weather
kisanghak 기상학 meteorology
kisang yebo 기상 예보 weather forecast

kisang yebowŏn 기상 예보원 weatherman

kisŏngbok 기성복 off the peg, ready-to-wear

kiso 기소 prosecution

kisohada 기소하다 prosecute

kisojach'ŭk 기소자측 prosecution

kisŭk 기슭 slope (*of mountain*)

kisu 기수 rider, jockey

kisuk hak-kkyo 기숙 학교 boarding school

kisukssa 기숙사 dormitory

kisul 기술 skill; technique

kisultcha 기술자 technician

kisultchŏgin 기술적인 technical

kisultchŏguro 기술적으로 technically

kit 깃 collar

kitchŏm 기점 starting point

kitppal 깃발 flag

kit'a 기타 the rest; and so on; guitar

kit'adŭngdŭng 기타 등등 and so on, et cetera

kit'a yŏnjuga 기타 연주가 guitarist

kit'ŏl 깃털 feather; plumage

kit'ong 기통 cylinder (*in engine*)

kiulda 기울다 slant; tilt; swing (*of public opinion*)

kiulgi 기울기 slope (*of handwriting*)

kiun 기운 energy; vigor; vapor

kiuni nada 기운이 나다 cheer up

kiunŭl naege hada 기운을 내게 하다 cheer up

kiurida 기울이다 devote; tilt; **kwi kiurida** 귀 기울이다 prick up one's ears

kiwŏn 기원 origin

kiyŏ 기여 contribution (*to discussion*)

kiyŏhada 기여하다 contribute (*to discussion*)

kkach'ibal 까치발 bracket (*for shelf*)

kkadaroptta 까다롭다 be difficult; be strict; be picky

kkadaroun 까다로운 fussy, picky, tricky

kkaeda 깨다 break *record*; rouse

kkaedarŭm 깨달음 realization; understanding; enlightenment

kkaedat-tta 깨닫다 realize; **Xŭl/rŭl kkaedatchi mot'ada** X을/를 깨닫지 못하다 be unconscious of X

kkaejida 깨지다 break; shatter

kkaejin 깨진 broken

kkaek-kkaek-kkŏrida 깩깩거리다 squeal

kkaekkŭshi 깨끗이 completely, clean

kkaekkŭt'ada 깨끗하다 be clean; be pure; be chaste

kkaekkŭt'age hada 깨끗하게 하다 clean

kkaekkŭt'an 깨끗한 clean; pure; tidy, neat

kkaengkkaenggŏrida 깽깽거리다 yelp

kkaennip 깻잎 (pickled) sesame leaf

kkaeŏinnŭn 깨어있는 awake

kkaeŏjida 깨어지다 break up (*of ice*)

kkaeŏjigi shiun 깨어지기 쉬운 breakable

kkaettŭrida 깨뜨리다 break; break off *relationship*; terminate

kkaeuch'ida 깨우치다 educate; make realize

kkaeuda 깨우다 wake

kkaji 까지 until; by; no later than; to; up to; **1989nyŏnkkaji** 1989년까지 until 1989; **hot'elkkaji** 호 텔까지 as far as the hotel

kkakkabŏrida 깎아버리다 shave off *beard*

kkakkanaeda 깎아내다 shave off *from piece of wood*

kkakka tadŭmtta 깎아다듬다 whittle

kkaktta 깎다 cut; trim; shear; shave; sharpen; peel; cut *price*; haggle

kkakttugi 깍두기 spicy, *pickled white radish*

kkalboda 깔보다 criticize, knock

kkalda 깔다 pave

kkalgae 깔개 rug

kkamagwi 까마귀 crow; raven

kkamppagida 깜박이다 flicker, glimmer

kkamppakkŏrida 깜박거리다 twinkle; blink

kkamtchak nollada 깜짝 놀라다 be astonished; **Xŭl/rŭl kkamtchak nollage hada** X을/를 깜짝 놀라게 하다 give X a fright

kkangch'unggŏrimyŏ ttwiŏdanida 깡충거리며 뛰어다니다 skip around

kkangmarŭn 깡마른 skinny

kkangp'ae 깡패 bully; hoodlum,

gangster

kkangt'ong 깡통 can (*for food*)

kkangt'ong ttagae 깡통 따개 can opener

kkich'ida 끼치다 cause; *namege p'yerŭl kkich'ida* 남에게 폐를 끼치다 make a nuisance of oneself, cause trouble; *kŏktchŏng-ŭl kkich'ida* 걱정을 끼치다 affect; concern

kkida 끼이다 be wedged; be caught between

kkilkkil ut-tta 낄낄 웃다 giggle

kkik'anŭn sori 끽하는 소리 screech

kkingkkangjok 낑깡족 *orenjijok* wannabes

kkingkkinggŏrida 낑낑거리다 whimper, whine

kkiŏ nŏt'a 끼어 넣다 squeeze in

kkiuda 끼우다 slot in

kkiwŏjida 끼워지다 slot in

kkiwŏnŏtki 끼워넣기 open; retrieve COMPUT

kkiwŏ nŏt'a 끼워 넣다 put, insert; tuck

kkŏjida 꺼지다 blow out, go out (*of candle*); collapse; vanish

kkŏjin 꺼진 dead *battery, engine*

kkŏjyŏ it-tta 꺼져 있다 be out (*of light, fire*)

kkŏjyŏ pŏrida 꺼져 버리다 buzz off; go out (*of fire*); *kkŏjyŏ (pŏryŏ)! 꺼져 (버려)!* beat it!, get lost!

kkŏk-kkŏk-kkŏrinŭn sori 꺽꺽거리는 소리 squawk

kkŏkkŏnaeda 꺾어내다 break off *piece of chocolate etc*

kkŏktta 꺾다 destroy; break off; pluck; dash

kkŏm 껌 chewing gum

kkŏnaeda 꺼내다 take out (*from bag, pocket etc*); *...e taehan marŭl kkŏnaeda* ...에 대한 말을 꺼내다 drag in

kkŏptchil 껍질 shell; peel; husk; skin

kkŏrida 꺼리다 shun

kkŏrimch'ik'ada 꺼림칙 하다 feel uncomfortable about

kkobak 꼬박 whole

kkobulgŏrinŭn 꼬불거리는 curly

kkoch'ikkoch'i k'aeda 꼬치꼬치

캐다 poke around

kkoch'i p'ida 꽃이 피다 flower

kkoda 꼬다 twist; *tarirŭl kkoda* 다리를 꼬다 cross one's legs

kkoe 꾀 wile, strategem

kkoeda 꾀다 entice; persuade

kkoehada 꾀하다 engineer, contrive

kkoim 꼬임 kink, twist

kkoji 꽂이 rack

kkojiptta 꼬집다 pinch

kkok 꼭 surely; firmly, tightly; exactly

kkoktchi 꼭지 stem; tap, faucet; nipple; handle

kkokttaegi 꼭대기 top, crest

kkokttugaksshi 꼭두각시 puppet

kkolsanaum 꼴사나움 clumsiness

kkoma 꼬마 the little ones; urchin

kkomkkomhan 꼼꼼한 thorough; scrupulous

kkomtchagank'o innŭn 꼼짝않고 있는 stand stock-still

kkomtchak'ada 꼼짝하다 budge, stir; *kŏgisŏ kkomtchaktto hajima!* 거기서 꼼짝도 하지마! stay right there!

kkongch'o 꽁초 stub

kkonnip 꽃잎 petal

kkori 꼬리 tail; *ne kkori pol manhaguna!* 네 꼴이 볼 만하구나! what a sight you are!

kkorip'yo 꼬리표 tag, label

kkorip'yorŭl puch'ida 꼬리표를 붙이다 label, stick a label on

kkorŭrŭkkŏrida 꼬르륵거리다 rumble

kkoshyŏsŏ ŏdŏnaeda 꼬셔서 얻어내다 wheedle

kkot 꽃 flower; blossom

kkotchangsu 꽃장수 florist

kkot hantabal 꽃 한 다발 a bunch of flowers

kkotkkoji 꽃꽂이 arrangement (*of flowers*)

kkotkkot'an 꼿꼿한 straight (*erect, not bent*)

kkotppyŏng 꽃병 vase

kkot-tta 꽃다 attach; pin

kkot-ttabal 꽃다발 bouquet

kkŭch'ŭl maet-tta 끝을 맺다 wind up, finish

kkŭda 끄다 blow out; switch off; be

off; stall

kkŭdögim 끄덕임 nod

kkŭdömnün 끝없는 endless, never-ending

kkŭjibŏ naeda 끄집어 내다 mention, drag up

kkŭl 끌 chisel

kkŭlda 끌다 pull; haul; tow; drag; move slowly; attract; spin out, prolong; appeal to, be attractive to

kkŭlgi 끌기 tow; drag COMPUT

kkŭllida 끌리다 trail, lag behind; be dragged; be attracted to; *...e(ge) maŭmi kkŭllida* ...에(게) 마음이 끌리다 be attached to; *nuguege maŭmi kkŭllida* 누구에게 마음이 끌리다 be attracted to s.o.

kkŭlt'a 끓다 boil

kkŭmtchigi 끔찍이 terribly; exceedingly; kindly

kkŭmtchik'ada 끔찍하다 be hideous

kkŭmtchik'an 끔찍한 hideous, terrible

kkŭn 끈 band (*material*); lace (*for shoe*); tie, bond; string; strap (*of shoe, dress, bra*)

kkŭndöktchige toep'urihada 끈덕지게 되풀이하다 persist in

kkŭndöktchige toep'urihanŭn 끈덕지게 되풀이하는 persistent

kkŭn-gi 끈기 perseverance, persistence

kkŭnimömnŭn 끊임없는 continuous, incessant

kkŭnimömpsshi 끊임없이 incessantly, forever

kkŭnimömpsshi kyesok'aesŏ 끊임없이 계속해서 on and on, endlessly

kkŭnjiljin 끈질긴 dogged; high-powered *salesman*; nagging *pain*

kkŭnjŏk-kkörinün 끈적거리는 sticky; tacky; gooey

kkŭnjŏk-kkŭnjŏk'an 끈적끈적한 tacky; gooey

kkŭnmach'ida 끝마치다 finish off *drink, meal, work etc*

kkŭnmaejŭm 끝맺음 finish (*of product*)

kkŭnmat 끝맛 aftertaste (*from food, drink*)

kkŭnnada 끝나다 end, finish; result in; *ije ta kkŭnnat-tta* 이제 다 끝났다 it's all over now

kkŭnnaeda 끝내다 finish, conclude; *ta kkŭnnaebŏrida* 다 끝내버리다 finish up

kkŭnnaeji anŭn 끝내지 않은 unfinished

kkŭnŏjida 끊어지다 break; blow *fuse*; break off with; be interrupted; run out

kkŭnŏjin 끊어진 dead

kkŭntchiank'o it-tta 끊지않고 있다 hold on TELEC

kkŭntchimalgo kidariseyo 끊지말고 기다리세요 hold the line

kkŭnt'a 끊다 give up, kick; disconnect, cut off; hang up TELEC

kkŭnŭl maeda 끈을 매다 strap on; put on *watch, holster*; lace up

kkŭnŭm 끊음 withdrawal (*from drugs*)

kkŭrida 끓이다 boil, brew

kkŭrŏ antta 끌어 안다 snuggle up to

kkŭrŏjuda 끌어주다 give a tow

kkŭrŏ nŏmch'ida 끓어 넘치다 boil over

kkŭrŏ ollida 끌어 올리다 boost; push up; connect; hitch up; hoist; pull up

kkŭrŏ tanggida 끌어 당기다 pull; drag; retract *undercarriage*

kkŭrŏ tŭrida 끌어 들이다 drag

kkŭt 끝 end, bottom (*of street*); edge; point; nozzle ◊ exit COMPUT; *yŏnghwarŭl kkŭtkkaji poda* 영화를 끝까지 보다 watch a movie to the end

kkŭttchangnaeda 끝장내다 put an end to, end

kkŭt'ŭro 끝으로 in conclusion

kkubŏk-kkubŏk cholda 꾸벅꾸벅 졸다 doze off

kkubulkkuburhan 꾸불꾸불한 winding *road*

kkujit-tta 꾸짖다 scold

kkujunhada 꾸준하다 be persistent; persevere, plug away

kkujunhan 꾸준한 unrelenting

kkuk ch'amtta 꾹 참다 stifle

kkul 꿀 honey

kkulkkŏk-kkulkkŏk mashida 꿀꺽꿀꺽 마시다 gulp down

kkulkkulgŏrida 꿀꿀거리다 grunt

kkum 꿈 dream; ambition

kkumgat'ŭn 꿈같은 dreamlike, dream

kkumida 꾸미다 embellish; embroider; exaggerate; make up *story*; decorate

kkumijianŭn 꾸미지 않은 unadorned, undecorated, plain; austere

kkumin iyagi 꾸민 이야기 fiction

kkumin kŏt 꾸민 것 make-believe, pretense

kkumkkuda 꿈꾸다 dream

kkumkkyŏlgat'ŭn 꿈결같은 dreamy *voice, look*

kkumt'ŭlgŏrimyŏ naagada 꿈틀거리며 나아가다 wriggle (*along the ground*)

kkumŭl kkuda 꿈을 꾸다 dream

kkumuldaenŭn 꾸물대는 slow

kkumulgŏrida 꾸물거리다 dawdle, move slowly

kkumyŏjin il 꾸며진 일 set-up, frame-up

kkumyŏnaen iyagi 꾸며낸 이야기 yarn, story

kkurida 꾸리다 bundle up

kkurŏmi 꾸러미 bundle

kkurŏmiro ssada 꾸러미로 싸다 parcel up

kkuryŏgada 꾸려가다 manage *money*

kkuryŏnagada 꾸려나가다 manage, get by (*financially*)

kkwae 꽤 quite, fairly

kkwaek-kkwaek ulda 꽥꽥 울다 quack

kkwaenggwari 꽹과리 small gong (*made of brass*)

kkwak 꽉 hard; fast; full; compact; packed

kkwak chaptta 꽉 잡다 grip, clutch

kkwak choenŭn 꽉 죄는 skimpy

kkwak chwida 꽉 쥐다 clasp, squeeze; clench

kkwak ch'ada 꽉 차다 be jam-packed

kkwak ch'ait-tta 꽉 차있다 be jammed (*of roads*)

kkwak ch'an 꽉 찬 completely full

kkwak kkiida 꽉 끼이다 squeeze in

kkwak tŭrŏch'an 꽉 들어찬 chockfull, crowded

kkwemaeda 꿰매다 sew; stitch; darn

kkwemaeŏ talda 꿰매어 달다 sew on

kkyŏantta 껴안다 clasp (*to oneself*)

kŏaegŭi sanggŭm 거액의 상금 jackpot

kŏaegŭi sanggŭmŭl t'ada 거액의 상금을 타다 hit the jackpot

kŏbe chillida 겁에 질리다 be terrified

kŏbe chillin 겁에 질린 panic-stricken

kŏbi manŭn 겁이 많은 easily frightened; spineless; cowardly

kŏbŭl mŏgŭn 겁을 먹은 fearful; cowardly, chicken

kŏbŭl mŏk-kko mullŏsŏda 겁을 먹고 물러서다 chicken out

kŏbuhada 거부하다 veto; reject; refuse

kŏbuk 거북 turtle; tortoise

kŏbukkwŏn 거부권 right of veto

kŏbukssŏn 거북선 turtle ship (*first armored warship*)

kŏbuk'aehada 거북해하다 feel awkward

kŏbuk'an 거북한 awkward, embarrassing

kŏch'ida 걷히다 lift, clear (*of fog*)

kŏch'ilda 거칠다 be rough

kŏch'ilge taehada 거칠게 대하다 manhandle; treat roughly

kŏch'in 거친 rough; coarse; rugged

kŏch'yŏsŏ 거쳐서 by way of, via

kŏdaehada 거대하다 be enormous

kŏdaeham 거대함 enormity

kŏdaehan 거대한 enormous, huge

kŏdŏollida 걷어올리다 roll up *sleeves*

kŏdŭrŭm p'iunŭn 거드름 피우는 pompous

kŏgidaga 거기다가 moreover

kŏin 거인 giant

Kŏjedo 거제도 Koje Island

kŏji 거지 beggar

kŏjinmal 거짓말 lie

kŏjinmarhada 거짓말하다 lie, tell a lie

kŏjit 거짓 pretense

kŏjitmaljaeng-i 거짓말쟁이 liar

kŏjŏ ŏt-tta 거저 얻다 cadge, bum

kŏjŏrhada 거절하다 deny; reject; refuse

kŏju 거즈 gauze

kŏjuhada 거주하다 inhabit; reside

kŏju hŏga 거주 허가 residence permit

kŏjuja 거주자 inhabitant; resident

kŏjuji 거주지 residence (*house etc*)

kŏkkuro 거꾸로 upside down; back to front

kŏkkuro hada 거꾸로 하다 reverse

kŏkkuro toen 거꾸로 된 inverse *order*; reverse

kŏktchŏng 걱정 concern, worry, anxiety

kŏktchŏngdoenŭn 걱정되는 worrying

kŏktchŏnghada 걱정하다 worry; be worried, be concerned

kŏktchŏnghanŭn 걱정하는 concerned, anxious

kŏktchŏngshik'ida 걱정시키다 worry, trouble

kŏktchŏngsŭrŏn 걱정스런 worried

kŏktchŏngsŭrŏptta 걱정스럽다 be worried

kŏlch'ida 걸치다 extend, range; span; throw on *clothes*

kŏlda 걸다 hang; stake; be on (*of brake*)

kŏlle 걸레 cloth; tramp (*woman*)

kŏllejirhada 걸레질하다 mop; swab; wipe

kŏllida 걸리다 catch *illness*; take *time*

kŏllŏnaeda 걸러내다 strain; sift

kŏllyŏ nŏmŏjida 걸려 넘어지다 trip, stumble; trip over, stumble over

kŏllyŏonŭn 걸려오는 incoming *phonecall*

kŏlssang 걸상 stool

kŏlssoe 걸쇠 clasp; latch

kŏlsŭk'aut'ŭ 걸스카우트 girl scout

kŏltchuk'age hada 걸쭉하게 하다 thicken

kŏltchuk'an 걸쭉한 thick

kŏm 검 sword

kŏman 거만 arrogance

kŏmanhada 거만하다 be arrogant

kŏmanhan 거만한 arrogant, stuck-up

kŏmch'algwan 검찰관 public prosecutor

kŏmda 검다 be black; be dark

kŏmgŏ 검거 round-up (*of suspects, criminals*)

kŏmgŏhada 검거하다 round up *suspects, criminals*

kŏmi 거미 spider

kŏmijul 거미줄 cobweb

kŏmjŏngsaek 검정색 black

kŏmmanŭn 겁많은 timid

kŏmmŏgŭn 겁먹은 timid

kŏmmŏktta 겁먹다 be afraid, be scared; get cold feet; be overawed

kŏmmunso 검문소 checkpoint

kŏmnada 겁나다 be frightened; be frightened of

kŏmnage hada 겁나게 하다 terrify

kŏmnage hanŭn 겁나게 하는 terrifying

kŏmnanŭn 겁나는 frightening, unnerving

kŏmnyŏk 검역 quarantine (*for animals*)

kŏmp'yowŏn 검표원 inspector (*on buses*)

kŏmp'yut'ŏ chulp'an 컴퓨터 출판 desktop publishing

k'ŏmp'yut'ŏ ch'ŏriga kanŭnghan 컴퓨터 처리가 가능한 machine-readable

k'ŏmp'yut'ŏŭi sohyŏng ch'ŏrigi 컴퓨터의 소형 처리기 microprocessor

kŏmsa 검사 examination (*of patient*); prosecutor ◊ exploratory

kŏmsaek'ada 검색하다 navigate

kŏmshi 검시 post-mortem

kŏmshigwan 검시관 coroner

kŏmt'ohada 검토하다 go over, check; take stock; consider

kŏmŭn 검은 black

kŏmul 거물 tycoon, big shot

kŏmun-go 거문고 zither

kŏmusŭrehan 거무스레한 swarthy

kŏmusŭrŭmhan 거무스름한 dark, somber

kŏmyŏl chedo 검열 제도 censorship

kŏmyŏrhada 검열하다 censor

kŏnbae 건배! cheers!

kŏnbaehada 건배하다 toast
(*drinking*); **nugurŭl wihae
kŏnbaehajago hada** 누구를 위해
건배하자고 하다 propose a toast to
s.o.

kŏnban 건반 keyboard (*of piano*)

kŏnbangjida 건방지다 be forward, be
impertinent

kŏnbangjige kulda 건방지게 굴다
get smart with, be cheeky with

kŏnbangjin 건방진 forward,
impertinent, insolent

kŏnch'o 건초 hay

kŏnch'oyŏl 건초열 hay fever

kŏnch'ugŏp 건축업 builder
(*company*); building trade

kŏnch'ugŏptcha 건축업자 builder
(*person*)

kŏnch'uk 건축 building

kŏnch'uk'ak 건축학 architecture
(*subject*)

kŏnch'ungmul 건축물 construction,
structure

kŏnch'ungnyangshik 건축양식
architecture (*style*)

kŏndal 건달 rogue, good-for-nothing

kŏndubaktchillo 곤두박질로
headlong

kŏn-gang 건강 health; **tangshinŭi
kŏn-gang-ŭl wihae!** 당신의 건강을
위해! your health!

kŏn-gang chindan 건강 진단 checkup MED

kŏn-gang-e choŭn 건강에 좋은
healthy, wholesome

kŏn-ganghada 건강하다 be healthy

kŏn-ganghan 건강한 fit, healthy

kŏn-gang munje 건강 문제 medical
problem

kŏn-gang sangt'ae 건강 상태
condition, state of health

kŏn-gang shikp'um 건강 식품
health food

kŏn-gang shikp'umjŏm 건강 식품점
health food store

kŏnjanghan 건장한 burly

kŏnjŏnhada 건전하다 be wholesome,
be healthy

kŏnjŏnhan 건전한 wholesome,
healthy; sound

kŏnjogi 건조기 drier; dry season

kŏnjohada 건조하다 be dry, be arid

kŏnjohan 건조한 dry

kŏnmosŭp 겉모습 exterior, façade

kŏnmul 건물 building

kŏnmul chosawŏn 건물 조사원
surveyor

kŏnnejuda 건네주다 hand over, give

kŏnnŏ 건너 over, across

kŏnnŏda 건너다 cross, go across

kŏnnŏgada 건너가다 cross, go across

kŏnnŏ p'yŏn 건너 편 across, on the
other side of

kŏnnŏsŏ 건너서 across

kŏnp'odo 건포도 raisin; currant

kŏnsŏl 건설 construction

kŏnsŏltchŏgin 건설적인 constructive

kŏnsŏrŏp 건설업 construction
industry

kŏptchaeng-i 겁쟁이 chicken,
coward

kŏptchuda 겁주다 frighten

kŏptchuŏ tchoch'anaeda 겁주어
쫓아내다 scare away

kŏp'um 거품 bubble; foam; froth

kŏp'umnanŭn 거품나는 effervescent

kŏrae 거래 deal; dealing; dealings;
business; transaction

kŏraehada 거래하다 deal with; deal
in; bank with

kŏraerŭl maedŭp chit-tta 거래를
맺듭 짓다 clinch a deal

kŏri 거리 distance; street; **kŏrie(sŏ)**
거리에(서) in the street

kŏri 걸이 rack

kŏrikkimŏpsshi marhada
거리낌없이 말하다 speak out

kŏrirŭl tuda 거리를 두다 distance
oneself

kŏrŏdanida 걸어다니다 walk around

kŏrŏgada 걸어가다 walk away

kŏrŏmaeda 걸어매다 hitch (onto)

kŏrŏ nŏmŏttŭrida 걸어 넘어뜨리다
trip up

kŏrŏsŏ 걸어서 on foot

kŏrŏsŏ kada 걸어서 가다 walk, go
on foot

kŏrŏsŏ kŏnnŏda 걸어서 건너다 walk
across

kŏrŭda 거르다 filter

kŏrŭm 걸음 step, pace; **kŏrŭmi
nŭrida / pparŭda** 걸음이

느리다 / 빠르다 be a slow / fast walker

kŏsehada 거세하다 neuter *animal*

kŏsehan hwangso 거세한 황소 steer (*animal*)

kŏshida 것이다: *...l kŏshida* ...ㄹ 것이다 shall, will

kŏshiktchŭng 거식증 anorexia

kŏshiktchŭng-ŭl alt'a 거식증을 앓다 be anorexic

kŏshil 거실 living room

kŏsŭllida 거슬리다 grate; jar on

kŏsŭllinŭn 거슬리는 harsh, abrasive

kŏsŭllŏ ollagada 거슬러 올라가다 go back, date back

kŏt 것 thing ◊ (*forms equivalent of relative clause*): *kŭ sarami naeil olgŏsŭl arayo* 그 사람이 내일 올것을 알아요 I know that he will come tomorrow; *nae ch'in-guga ŏjae pyŏngwŏne ibwŏnhan kŏsŭl tŭŏssŏyo* 내 친구가 어재 병원에 입원한 것을 들었어요 I heard that my friend went into the hospital yesterday; *chibe iltchik kanŭn kŏsi natkkessŏyo* 집에 일찍 가는 것이 낫겠어요 it'd be better to go home early ◊ (*forms equivalent of noun form in ...ing*): *suhagŭl kongbuhanŭn kŏsi shiptchi anayo* 수학을 공부하는 것이 쉽지 않아요 studying math is not easy

kŏtch'ire 걸치레 pose, pretense

kŏtkki 걷기 walking

kŏt-tta 걷다 walk

kŏt'ŭronŭn 겉으로는 outwardly, externally

kŏŭi 거의 almost; *kŏŭi kat-tta* 거의 같다 be almost like, verge on; *kŏŭi ŏptta* 거의 없다 scarcely any; *kŏŭi ta* 거의 다 all but, nearly all

kŏul 거울 mirror

kŏwi 거위 goose

kŏyŏk'ada 거역하다 disobey

..ko ...고 and

koa 고아 orphan

koanhada 고안하다 devise

koanmul 고안물 gimmick

koap 고압 high voltage; high pressure ◊ high-voltage; high-pressure

koap kkassŭ 고압 가스 propellant

koapssŏnnyong ch'ŏlt'ap 고압선용

ch'ŏlt'ap (electricity) pylon

koawŏn 고아원 orphanage

kobaek 고백 confession

kobaek'ada 고백하다 confess

kobal 고발 accusation

kobarhada 고발하다 charge, accuse

koch'arhada 고찰하다 look at, consider

koch'e 고체 solid mass

koch'ida 고치다 correct; repair

koch'ŭng piltting 고층 빌딩 high-rise building

koch'u 고추 red pepper; chilli

koch'ugaru 고추가루 chilli (pepper) powder

koch'ujang 고추장 red pepper paste

kodae 고대 antiquity ◊ ancient

kodaehada 고대하다 be anxious for

kodo 고도 altitude

kodok 고독 solitude

kodok'ada 고독하다 be solitary; be lonely

kodok'an 고독한 solitary

kodong 고동 beat (*of heart*)

kodongch'ida 고동치다 pulsate (*of heart, blood*)

kodo pulp'ohwa multchil 고도 불포화 물질 polyunsaturate

kodŭn 곧은 straight (*not curly*)

kodŭnghak-kkyo 고등학교 high school

kodŭnghakssaeng 고등학생 high school student

Kodŭng Pŏbwŏn 고등 법원 Supreme Court

kodŭrŭm 고드름 icicle

koemul 괴물 monster

koemulgat'ŭn 괴물같은 monstrous, frightening

koengjanghada 굉장하다 be awesome

koengjanghage 굉장하게 very, terrifically

koengjanghan 굉장한 awesome; terrific; tremendous

koengjanghi 굉장히 greatly; beautifully; tremendously

koeng-ŭm 굉음 boom (*noise*)

koeŏ innŭn 괴어 있는 stagnant

koeroe chŏngbu 괴뢰 정부 puppet government

koerop'ida 괴롭히다 trouble; torment

koerop'im 괴롭힘 harassment

koetcha 괴짜 crank, eccentric

kogaek 고객 customer, client

kogaek kwalli 고객 관리 customer relations

kogaerŭl chŏt-tta 고개를 젓다 shake one's head

kogaerŭl kkŭdŏgida 고개를 끄덕이다 nod one's head

kogi 고기 meat

kogiap 고기압 high pressure (weather)

kogohak 고고학 archeology

kogohaktcha 고고학자 archeologist

kogŭl 고글 goggles (for skiing)

kogŭp 고급 high class ◊ high-class

kogŭp chaptchi 고급 잡지 glossy (magazine)

koguk 고국 home; native country; **koguge kada** 고국에 가다 go home

Koguryŏ 고구려 Koguryo (Ancient Kingdom)

kogwihan 고귀한 noble

kogye 곡예 acrobatics

kogyesa 곡예사 acrobat

kogyeyong kŭne 곡예용 그네 trapeze

kogyŏrhan 고결한 virtuous

kohae 고해 confession

kohaehada 고해하다 confess

kohaeshil 고해실 confessional

kohae shinbu 고해 신부 confessor

koham 고함 roar, bellow

koham chirŭda 고함 지르다 yell, cry out

kohamch'ida 고함치다 roar, bellow

kohamch'yŏ purŭda 고함쳐 부르다 yell

kohwan 고환 testicle

kohyang 고향 home; roots

kohyŏrap 고혈압 hypertension

koin 고인 the dead, the deceased; ancient people

koindol 고인돌 dolmen

kojajiljaeng-i 고자질쟁이 telltale

kojajirhada 고자질하다 tell tales, snitch

kojang 고장 breakdown; crash (of computer)

kojang suri 고장 수리 troubleshooting

kojang-i nada 고장이 나다 play up; break down; crash COMPUT

kojang-i ŏmnŭn 고장이 없는 trouble-free

kojangna it-tta 고장나 있다 be down, not be working

kojangnan 고장난 out of order, not working

kojibi ssen 고집이 센 stubborn, obstinate

kojip 고집 obstinacy

kojip'ada 고집하다 be stubborn; stand by, adhere to

kojishik'an 고지식한 conservative; straight

kojŏn 고전 classic

kojŏngdoeda 고정되다 be fixed

kojŏngdoen 고정된 fixed part, exchange rate

kojŏngha다 고정하다 fasten, fix; **umjigiji ank'e kojŏngha다** 움직이지 않게 고정하다 set broken limb

kojŏngshik'ida 고정시키다 fix; attach; stabilize; strap in; **muŏsŭl chejarie kojŏngshik'ida** 무엇을 제자리에 고정시키다 lock sth in position

Kojosŏn 고조선 Old Choson (Ancient Kingdom)

kojup'a 고주파 high-frequency

kokka toro 고가 도로 overpass (for car)

kokkurajida 고꾸라지다 fall head over heels

kokssŏn 곡선 curve

koktcho 곡조 tune

koktchoga arŭmdaun 곡조가 아름다운 melodious

kol 골 goal, target

kolbanppyŏ 골반뼈 pelvis

kolch'i ap'ŭn 골치 아픈 troublesom

kolch'itkkŏri 골칫거리 bother, headache

kolch'o 골초 heavy smoker

kolden 골덴 corduroy

kolden paji 골덴 바지 corduroy pants, cords

kolk'ip'ŏ 골키퍼 goalkeeper

kollan 곤란 hardship; embarrassment
kollanaeda 골라내다 pick on; select
kollanhada 곤란하다 be arduous; be awkward
kolmok 골목 alley
kolmok-kkil 골목길 side street
kolmu 골무 thimble
kolp'anji 골판지 corrugated cardboard
kolp'ŭ 골프 golf
kolp'ŭjang 골프장 golf course; golf club
kolp'ŭ k'ŭllŏp 골프 클럽 golf club (*instrument*)
koltcha 골자 core
koltchagi 골짜기 valley
koltchitkkŏri 골칫거리 pest, nuisance
kolttae 골대 goalpost
kolttongp'um 골동품 antique
kolttongp'um sang-in 골동품 상인 antique dealer
kom 곰 bear (*animal*)
komak 고막 eardrum
komapkkedo 고맙게도 thankfully
komapkke yŏginŭn 고맙게 여기는 grateful
komapssŭmnida 고맙습니다 thank you (*polite*)
komaptta 고맙다 thank
komawŏ 고마워 thanks
kombo chaguk 곰보 자국 spot (*caused by measles etc*)
komgomhi saenggak'ada 곰곰히 생각하다 reflect; brood; ponder
komin 고민 distress
komindoenŭn 고민되는 vexed
kominhada 고민하다 worry, fret
kominhage hada 고민하게 하다 concern, worry
komo 고모 aunt (*own, sister of father*)
komobu 고모부 uncle (*father's sister's husband*)
komp'ang-i 곰팡이 mold, mildew
komp'ang-i p'in 곰팡이 핀 moldy
komp'angnae nanŭn 곰팡내 나는 musty
komtta 곪다 go septic
komu 고무 rubber
komu chŏtkkoktchi 고무 젖꼭지 pacifier (*for baby*)

komujul 고무줄 elastic
komul 고물 junk
komul sujipsso 고물 수집소 junkyard
komun 고문 adviser; torture
komunhada 고문하다 torture
komu paendŭ 고무 밴드 rubber band
komu pot'ŭ 고무 보트 inflatable boat
komyŏng-ŭro changshik'ada 고명으로 장식하다 garnish
konbong 곤봉 club, stick
konch'ung 곤충 insect
kong 공 ball (*tennis, golf etc*); zero
kongbaek 공백 blank; empty space; gap
kongbŏm 공범 accomplice
Kongboch'ŏ 공보처 Ministry of Information
kongbu 공부 study, learning
kongbuhada 공부하다 study, learn
kongch'aek 공책 notebook
kongch'ŏga 공처가 henpecked husband
kongch'ŏn 공천 nomination
kongch'ŏnhada 공천하다 nominate
kongch'ŏnja 공천자 nominee; nomination
kongdan 공단 satin
kongdong 공동 cooperation ◊ joint, common
kongdong chŏja 공동 저자 collaborator (*in writing book etc*)
kongdong chŏngnipkkŭm 공동 적립금 kitty, common fund
kongdongch'e 공동체 community
kongdonggigŭm 공동기금 pool, kitty, common fund
kongdong ikkwŏnŭro hada 공동 이권으로 하다 pool, combine, merge
kongdong kujwa 공동 구좌 joint account
kongdong soyuja 공동 소유자 part owner
kongdong-ŭro chŏjak'ada 공동으로 저작하다 collaborate (*on book etc*)
kongdong-ŭro irhada 공동으로 일하다 collaborate, work together
kongdong yŏn-guhada 공동 연구하다 collaborate (*in research*)

kongdŭrin 공들인 elaborate

konggaehada 공개하다 unveil *plans*

konggaejŏgin 공개적인 public

konggaejŏgŭro 공개적으로 publicly

konggae maeip 공개 매입 takeover bid

konggal 공갈 blackmail

konggal ch'ida 공갈 치다 blackmail

konggal ch'inŭn saram 공갈 치는 사람 blackmailer

konggan 공간 space, room

konggi 공기 air; bowl, dish (*for rice*)

konggiga ant'onghanŭn 공기가 안통하는 airtight

konggiga shinsŏnhan 공기가 신선한 airy *room*

konggi tŭril 공기 드릴 pneumatic drill

konggo 공고 notice, announcement

konggohada 공고하다 notify

konggong 공공 public

konggong kigwan 공공 기관 institute (*special home*)

konggong pumun 공공 부문 public sector

konggŭbwŏn 공급원 supplier

konggŭp 공급 supply, provision

konggŭpkkwa suyo 공급과 수요 supply and demand

konggŭp'um 공급품 supplies

konggŭp'ada 공급하다 supply, provide

konggun 공군 air force

konggun kiji 공군 기지 airbase MIL

konggyŏk 공격 offensive, aggression

konggyŏktchŏgin 공격적인 aggressive

konggyŏk'ada 공격하다 attack, go on the offensive

konghak 공학 engineering

konghang 공항 airport

konghang t'ŏminŏl 공항 터미널 air terminal

konghŏ 공허 vacuum *fig*

konghŏham 공허함 emptiness; vanity (*of hopes*)

konghŏhan 공허한 hollow *words*

konghŏn 공헌 contribution (*of time, effort*)

konghŏnhada 공헌하다 contribute (*with time*)

Konghwadang chijija 공화당 지지자 Republican

Konghwadang-wŏn 공화당원 Republican, member of the Republican party

konghwaguk 공화국 republic

kong-ik saŏp 공익 사업 public utilities

kong-in hoegyesa 공인 회계사 certified public accountant

Kongja 공자 Confucius

kongjakssae 공작새 peacock

kongjang 공장 plant; factory; mill

kongjangjang 공장장 foreman

kongje 공제 deduction (*from salary*)

kongjŏ 공저 collaboration (*on book etc*)

kongjŏnghada 공정하다 be fair, be just

kongjŏnghage 공정하게 fairly, justly

kongjŏnghan 공정한 fair, just

kongjŏnhada 공전하다 idle (*of engine*); orbit

kongjon 공존 coexistence

kongjonhada 공존하다 coexist

kongjŭng 공증 notarization

kongjŭng-in 공증인 notary

kongjung 공중 public; air; midair; **kongjung-esŏ** 공중에서 in midair

kongjung chŏnhwa 공중 전화 pay phone

kongjung chŏnhwa pakssŭ 공중 전화 박스 phone booth

kongjung napch'i 공중 납치 hijack

kongjung napch'ibŏm 공중 납치범 hijacker

kongjung napch'ihada 공중 납치하다 hijack

kongjung pihaenghada 공중 비행하다 fly past (in formation)

kongju 공주 princess

kongmin p'yŏngdŭngkkwŏn 공민 평등권 civil rights

kongmohada 공모하다 conspire with, be in cahoots with

kongmul 곡물 cereal (*grain*)

kongmuwŏn 공무원 civil servant, government official

kongnip hak-kkyo 공립 학교 public school

kongno 공로 credit, honor; *Xe tae-han kongnorŭl injŏngpat-tta* X에 대한 공로를 인정받다 get the credit for X

kongnyŏnhada 공연하다 perform, stage; co-star; be futile

kongnyong 공룡 dinosaur

kong-ŏp 공업 manufacturing

kong-ŏpttanji 공업 단지 industrial estate

kongp'an 공판 trial; *kongp'an chung* 공판 중 on trial

kongp'o 공포 horror, terror

kongp'otchŭng 공포증 phobia

kongp'o yŏnghwa 공포 영화 horror movie

kongp'yŏngham 공평함 detachment, objectivity

kongp'yŏnghan 공평한 detached, objective

kongp'yohada 공표하다 declare, state; issue *warning*

kongsa 공사 construction; public and private affairs; minister; *kongsa chung* 공사 중 under construction

kongsajang 공사장 building site, construction site

kongsajang inbu 공사장 인부 construction worker

Kongsandang 공산당 Communist Party

Kongsandang-ŭi 공산당의 Communist

kongsang-e chamgida 공상에 잠기다 daydream

kongsang kwahak sosŏl 공상 과학 소설 science fiction

kongsang kwahak sosŏl chaptchi 공상 과학 소설 잡지 science fiction fanzine

Kongsanjuŭi 공산주의 Communism ◊ Communist

Kongsanjuŭija 공산주의자 Communist

Kongsanjuŭiŭi 공산주의의 Communist

kongshihada 공시하다 post, show *profits*

kongshik 공식 formula; formality ◊ formal, official

kongshiktchŏgin 공식적인 state, ceremonial

kongshiktchŏguro 공식적으로 officially, strictly speaking; *kongshiktchŏgŭro allida* 공식적으로 알리다 officially announce

kongshik'wadoen 공식화된 official, confirmed

kongsŏgin 공석인 vacant

kongsŏk 공석 vacancy

kongsonhada 공손하다 be polite

kongsonhage 공손하게 politely

kongsonhan 공손한 polite

kongsshik pangmun 공식 방문 state visit

kongtcharo 공짜로 for nothing, for free

kongtchŏgin 공적인 official; *kongtchŏgin changso-e(sŏ)* 공적인 장소에(서) in public

kongtchŏgŭro 공적으로 formally

kongt'eip'ŭ 공테이프 blank tape

kongt'ong 공통 common *language etc*

kongt'onghada 공통하다 be common

kongt'ong-ŭro 공통으로 in common; *muŏsŭl nuguwa kongt'ong-ŭro kajigo it-tta* 무엇을 누구와 공통으로 가지고 있다 have sth in common with s.o.

kong-wŏn 공원 park

kong-ye 공예 craft

kong-yŏn 공연 performance

kon-gyŏng 곤경 impasse; mess; plight

kon-gyŏng-e ch'ŏhada 곤경에 처하다 be in a jam

kon-gyŏng-e ch'ŏhae it-tta 곤경에 처해 있다 be in a fix

kon-gyŏng-esŏ kuhaenaeda 곤경에서 구해내다 bail out *fig*

kong-yŏnhada 공연하다 perform

kong-yŏnja 공연자 performer

koppi 고삐 rein

kopssem 곱셈 multiplication

kopssülgŏrida 곱슬거리다 curl

kopssülgŏrim 곱슬거림 curl

kopssülgŏrinŭn 곱슬거리는 curly; frizzy

kopssülgopssürhan 곱슬곱슬한 fuzzy

koptta 곱다 be fine; be fair; be pretty; be gentle

kop'ada 곱하다 multiply

kop'umkkyŏgŭi 교품격의 upmarket

kora ttŏrŏjida 곯아 떨어지다 crash out, fall asleep

korae 고래 whale

koraegorae sorich'ida 고래고래 소리치다 rant and rave

koraejabi 고래잡이 whaling

korhamsŏk 골함석 corrugated iron

kori 고리 catch (*locking device*); hook; link; loop

korilla 고릴라 gorilla

korip 고립 isolation

koripsshik'ida 고립시키다 cut off, isolate

koripttoen 고립된 lonely, isolated

korŭda 고르다 pick and choose; plump for

korŭge 고르게 evenly, regularly

korŭji ank'e 고르지 않게 unevenly

korŭji anŭn 고르지 않은 uneven

korŭm 고름 pus

korŭn 고른 even, regular

koryŏ 고려 consideration, thoughtfulness, concern; Koryo (*Kingdom*)

koryŏhada 고려하다 allow for; make allowances; take on board; consider

koryŏhaji ank'o 고려하지 않고 with no regard for

koryŏhal sahang 고려할 사항 consideration, factor

kosaeng 고생 hardship; toil

kosaenghada 고생하다 suffer, be in pain

kosang 고상 elegance

kosanghan 고상한 elegant

kosŏngnŭng 고성능 high performance

kosŏngnŭng-ŭi 고성능의 high-powered

kosoguro kamtta 고속으로 감다 fast forward

kosohada 고소하다 sue

kosohaehada 고소해하다 gloat; gloat over

kosok ch'asŏn 고속 차선 fast lane

kosok ellibeit'ŏ 고속 엘리베이터 express elevator

kosok kamkki 고속 감기 fast forward

kosok kiŏ 고속 기어 high (gear)

kosokttoro 고속도로 freeway, highway, expressway

kosok yŏlch'a 고속 열차 high-speed train

kosŭmdoch'i 고슴도치 hedgehog

kosu 고수 drummer

kosuhada 고수하다 hold on to *belief*; stick to *story, opinion*

kot 곧 soon, in a minute

kot 곳 joint; place; patch; *...nŭn kot* ...는 곳 where

kotpparo 곧바로 straight; straight away

kot-tchang 곧장 straight; directly, immediately

kot-tchang tallyŏgada 곧장 달려가다 run directly to; make a beeline for

kot'ong 고통 suffering; distress; agony

kot'ongsŭrŏun 고통스러운 painful; agonizing

koŭiga anin 고의가 아닌 unintentional

koŭijŏgin 고의적인 deliberate

koŭijŏgŭro 고의적으로 deliberately

koŭmŭi 고음의 high-pitched

koun 고운 fine

kowi insa 고위 인사 dignitary

kowi kogwanŭi 고위 고관의 high-level

kowŏn 고원 plateau

koyak'ada 고약하다 be foul; be bad

koyak'an 고약한 ugly; vicious; foul; bad; *koyak'an naemsaega nada* 고약한 냄새가 나다 stink, have a foul smell

koyang-i 고양이 cat

koyo 고요 peace; quietness; silence

koyohada 고요하다 be calm

koyohaejida 고요해지다 calm down

koyohan 고요한 still, calm, quiet

koyongdoeda 고용되다 be employed, be on the payroll

koyongdoen 고용된 in the pay of

koyonghada 고용하다 employ, hire

koyong-in 고용인 employee; servant

koyongju 고용주 employer

kŭ 그 the ◊ he; **kŭ sŭsŭro** 그 스스로 by himself

kŭbakke 그밖에 everyone else

kŭbakkŭi tarŭn kŏsŭn? 그밖의 다른 것은? anything else?

kŭbu 급우 school friend

kŭbyŏ 급여 allowance (*money*)

kŭ chashin 그 자신 himself

kŭ chik'ue 그 직후에 whereupon

kŭ chŏne paro 그 전에 바로 shortly before that

kŭ chŏngdo 그 정도 thereabouts

kŭ chŏngdo-ŭi 그 정도의 such a ◊ to that extent

kŭ chŏnjue 그 전주에 the week before

kŭ chŏnnal 그 전날 the day before

kŭ chŏnnare 그 전날에 the day before

kŭch'ida 그치다 stop

kŭdŭl 그들 them; they; those

kŭdŭl chashin 그들 자신 themselves

kŭdŭl sŭsŭro 그들 스스로 by themselves

kŭdŭrŭi 그들의 their; those

kŭdŭrŭi kŏt 그들의 것 theirs

kŭgŏllo twaessŏyo 그걸로 됐어요 alright, that's enough!

kŭgŏsŭi 그것의 its

kŭgŏsŭl 그것을 it (*as object*)

kŭgŏsŭn 그것은 it (*as subject*)

kŭgŏt chach'e 그것 자체 itself

kŭgŏttŭl 그것들 they; those (*things*)

kŭgŏt tul ta 그것 둘 다 both of them (*things*)

kŭgŏttŭrŭi 그것들의 those

kŭgot malgo 그곳 말고 not there

kŭgup'a 극우파 right-wing extremism

kŭ hu chulgot 그 후 줄곧 ever since

kŭ hue 그 후에 subsequently; later, afterward

kŭ ihue 그 이후에 after that

kŭjŏkke 그저께 the day before yesterday

kŭjŏ kŭrŏn 그저 그런 satisfactory; so so, average

kŭk 극 pole

kŭkch'an'anŭi p'yŏng 극찬의 평 rave review

kŭ kose 그 곳에 there

kŭk'i chagŭn 극히 작은 microscopic, minute

kŭk'i chungdaehan 극히 중대한 vitally important

kŭk'wa 극화 dramatization

kŭk'wahada 극화하다 dramatize

kŭk'yŏng 극형 capital punishment

kŭkppi 극비 top secret

kŭkppiŭi 극비의 classified

kŭkppok'ada 극복하다 conquer, overcome

kŭksshimhan 극심한 acute, extreme

kŭksso chŏnja konghak 극소 전자 공학 microelectronics

kŭkssoryang 극소량 iota, grain

kŭktchak-kka 극작가 dramatist

kŭktchang 극장 theater

kŭktchang annaewŏn 극장 안내원 usherette, attendant

kŭktchi 극지 pole ◊ polar

kŭktchŏgin 극적인 dramatic; rousing

kŭktchŏgin sanghwang 극적인 상황 drama, excitement

kŭktta 긁다 scrape; scratch

kŭkttan 극단 extreme; theater company

kŭkttanjŏgin 극단적인 extreme; immoderate

kŭktto 극도 extreme

Kŭkttong 극동 Far East ◊ Far Eastern

kŭkttoŭi p'iro 극도의 피로 exhaustion

kŭlja 글자 character (*in typography*)

kŭlkki 긁기 scratch

kŭlkkol 글꼴 font

kŭlk'in chaguk 긁힌 자국 scrape; scratch

kŭllaidŏ 글라이더 glider

kŭlsseyo 글쎄요 I'm not sure

kŭlsshi 글씨 handwriting

kŭl ssŭgi 글 쓰기 writing

kŭltcha 글자 letter (*of alphabet*)

kŭltchach'e 글자체 script; font

kŭltcha kŭdaero 글자 그대로 literally, to the letter

kŭltcha match'ugi nori 글자 맞추기 놀이 crossword

kŭm 금 gold; break, fracture

kŭmaek 금액 amount

kŭmanduda 그만두다 stop, quit; drop; drop out

kŭmanhan kach'iga it-tta 그만한 가치가 있다 be good value

kŭmbak 금박 gilt

kŭmbal mŏri yŏja 금발 머리 여자 blonde

kŭmbang 금방 directly, immediately

kŭmbung-ŏ 금붕어 goldfish

kŭmdan hyŏnsang 금단 현상 withdrawal symptoms

kŭmgage hada 금가게 하다 crack, fracture

Kŭmgang 금강 Kum River

Kŭmganggyŏng 금강경 Diamond Sutra

kŭmgi 금기 taboo

kŭmgo 금고 safe

kŭmgoe 금괴 gold ingot

kŭmhada 금하다 bar, forbid, ban

kŭmhonshik 금혼식 golden wedding anniversary

kŭmi kada 금이 가다 crack; split up

kŭmi kan 금이 간 cracked

kŭmji 금지 ban, prohibition; *kŭmnyŏn kŭmji* 금연 금지 no smoking

kŭmjidoeda 금지되다 be forbidden

kŭmjidoen 금지된 forbidden

kŭmjihada 금지하다 forbid, ban

kŭmjiryŏng 금지령 prohibition

kŭmjŏn tŭngnok-kki 금전 등록기 cash register

Kŭmjuppŏp 금주법 Prohibition

kŭmnyoil 금요일 Friday

kŭmnyu 급류 torrent; rapids

kŭmnyung 금융 finance; funding ◊ financial; monetary

kŭmnyung shijang 금융 시장 money market

kŭmsegongsa 금세공사 goldsmith

kŭmshi ch'omunida 금시 초문이다 that's news to me

kŭmshik 금식 fast (*not eating*)

kŭmsok 금속 metal

kŭmsoksŏng-ŭi 금속성의 metallic

kŭmul 그물 mesh, net

kŭmyŏn 금연 no smoking

kŭmyoktchŏgin 금욕적인 austere

kŭnbon 근본 root; source; origin

kŭnbonjŏgin 근본적인 basic, fundamental

kŭnbonjŏgŭro 근본적으로 radically

kŭnch'in 근친 next of kin

kŭnch'insanggan 근친상간 incest

kŭnch'ŏ 근처 vicinity; *...ŭi kŭnch'ŏe(sŏ)* ...의 근처에(서) in the vicinity of; *kŭnch'ŏe it-tta* 근처에 있다 be around

kŭndae 근대 modern times ◊ modern

kŭndaeŭi 근대의 modern

kŭndaehwa 근대화 modernization

kŭne 그네 swing

kŭngjŏngjŏgin 긍정적인 positive

kŭn-gŏ 근거 basis, foundation; ground, reason

kŭn-gŏga toeda 근거가 되다 underlie

kŭn-gŏji 근거지 stronghold

kŭn-gŏjirŭl tugo it-tta ...에 근거지를 두고 있다 be based in

kŭn-gŏ ŏmnŭn 근거 없는 groundless, unfounded

kŭn-gyo 근교 environs; suburbs ◊ suburban

kŭnjŏng tchoktchi 근정 쪽지 compliments slip

kŭnjŏp 근접 proximity

kŭnjŏrhada 근절하다 stamp out, eradicate

kŭnmuhada 근무하다 serve

kŭnmu shigan 근무 시간 work hours; work day

kŭnmyŏnhan 근면한 industrious

kŭnŏmhan 근엄한 grave

kŭnsahan 근사한 gorgeous; neat, terrific

kŭnshian 근시안 myopia

kŭnshianjŏgin 근시안적인 shortsighted *fig*; short-term

kŭnshianŭi 근시안의 shortsighted; myopic

kŭnshimhada 근심하다 worry about, have on one's mind

kŭnŭl 그늘 shade; *kŭnŭre(sŏ)* 그늘에(서) in the shade

kŭnŭljige hada 그늘지게 하다 eclipse *fig*

kŭnŭljin 그늘진 shady

kŭnŭn 그는 he

kŭnwŏn 근원 origin; source; root

kŭnwŏnjŏgin 근원적인 underlying

kŭnyang 그냥 as it is; just; *kŭnyang nongdamiyeyo* 그냥 농담이에요 I was just kidding

kŭnyŏ 그녀 she

kŭnyŏ chashin 그녀 자신 herself

kŭnyŏrŭl 그녀를 her (*object*)

kŭnyŏ sŭsŭro 그녀 스스로 by herself

kŭnyŏŭi 그녀의 her

kŭnyŏŭi kŏt 그녀의 것 hers

kŭnyuk 근육 muscle ◊ muscular

kŭnyuk chŭnggangje 근육 증강제 anabolic steroid

kŭpkkangha 급강하 dive; sudden drop

kŭpkkanghahada 급강하하다 dive; drop suddenly

kŭpssangssŭng 급상승 jump; surge; sudden increase

kŭpssangssŭnghada 급상승하다 jump; increase

kŭpssok naengdong naengjanggo 급속 냉동 냉장고 deep freeze (*with fast freeze capability*)

kŭpssok'ada 급속하다 be rapid, be fast

kŭpssok'i orŭda 급속히 오르다 rise rapidly, spiral

kŭpssŭp 급습 raid

kŭpssŭp'ada 급습하다 raid

kŭpssugwan 급수관 water pipe

kŭptchinjŏgin 급진적인 radical

kŭptchinjuŭi 급진주의 radicalism

kŭptchinjuŭija 급진주의자 radical (*person*)

kŭptchŭng 급증 explosion

kŭp'ada 급하다 be urgent; be impatient; be sudden

kŭp'aeng 급행 express; haste ◊ express; hasty; *kŭp'aeng yŏlch'a/pŏssŭ* 급행 열차/버스 express train/bus

kŭp'an 급한 urgent; hasty, rash

kŭp'i kada 급히 가다 dash; rush; zoom

kŭraedo 그래도 nevertheless, still, even so

kŭraem 그램 gram

kŭraendŭ p'iano 그랜드 피아노 grand piano

kŭraengk'uch'uk 크랭크축 crankshaft

kŭraenyudang 그래뉴당 granulated sugar

kŭraep'ik 그래픽 graphic

kŭraep'ik k'adŭ 그래픽카드 graphics card COMPUT

kŭraep'ikssŭ 그래픽스 graphics

kŭraesŏ 그래서 and; so that; that's why; *kŭraesŏ?* 그래서? so what?

kŭraeyaman hada 그래야만 하다 must do, have to do

kŭraeyo 그래요 indeed, really; yes

kŭreihaundŭ 그레이하운드 grayhound

kŭreip'ŭp'ŭrut'ŭ 그레이프프루트 grapefruit

kŭreip'ŭp'ŭrut'ŭ chusŭ 그레이프프루트 주스 grapefruit juice

kŭri 그리 so ◊ there; that direction; *kŭri manch'i anŭn saram* 그리 많지 않은 사람 not so many people

kŭrida 그리다 draw; paint

kŭrigo 그리고 and

kŭrigo nasŏ 그리고 나서 then, after that

kŭrim 그림 drawing; picture; illustration

kŭrimch'aek 그림책 picture book

kŭrimgwa kat'ŭn 그림과 같은 picturesque

kŭrimja 그림자 shadow

kŭrim kŭrigi 그림 그리기 painting

kŭrim put 그림 붓 paintbrush

kŭrimŭl kŭrida 그림을 그리다 draw

kŭrimyŏpssŏ 그림엽서 (picture) postcard

Kŭrisŭ 그리스 Greece ◊ Greek

Kŭrisŭdo 그리스도 Christ

Kŭrisŭŏ 그리스어 Greek (*language*)

kŭriwŏhada 그리워하다 miss

kŭrŏch'i anŭmyŏn 그렇지 않으면 otherwise

kŭrŏch'i anŭn kŏt kat'ayo 그렇지 않은 것 같아요 I guess not

kŭrŏch'iman 그렇지만 but

kŭrŏgil paramnida 그러길 바랍니다 I hope so

kŭrŏktchŏrŏk hada 그럭저럭 하다 get by, just manage; *yŏrŭi ŏpsshi kŭrŏktchŏrŏk hada* 열의 없이 그럭저럭 하다 plod along, plod on

kŭrŏk'e 그렇게 such; so; *kŭrŏk'e*

haseyo 그렇게 하세요 do it like that; go ahead; *kŭrŏk'e manch'i anŭn* 그렇게 많지 않은 not so much; *kŭrŏk'e mani?* 그렇게 많이? as much as that?; *kŭrŏl kŏyeyo* 그릴 거예요 I expect so

kŭrŏltŭt'an 그럴듯한 probable; plausible; *kŭrŏk'e* 그럭게

kŭrŏmedo pulguhago 그럼에도 불구하고 nevertheless, nonetheless

kŭrŏmŭro 그러므로 therefore

kŭrŏmyŏnsŏdo 그러면서도 at the same time, however

kŭrŏn 그런 such, of that kind; *kŭrŏn kŏt kat'ayo* 그런 것 같아요 it looks that way, I guess so; *kŭrŏn kyŏng-ue* 그런 경우에 in that case; *kŭrŏn sanghwang-esŏnŭn* 그런 상황에서는 under those circumstances; *kŭrŏnŭn kwajŏng-e* 그러는 과정에 in the process

kŭrŏna 그러나 however; whereas; but

kŭrŏnde 그런데 but; and yet; by the way

kŭrŏt'a 그렇다 be that way; be so; be true

kŭrŏt'a hadŏrado 그렇다 하더라도 even so, but then (again)

kŭrŏt'amyŏn 그렇다면 then (*deducing*); if so

kŭrŏt'ŏrado 그렇더라도 though

kŭrol suyŏng 크롤 수영 crawl (*in swimming*)

kŭrosŏ 그로서 as such, in that capacity

kŭrŭl 그를 him

kŭrŭl ssŭda 글을 쓰다 write

kŭrŭrŏnggŏrida 그르렁거리다 purr

kŭrŭt 그릇 bowl, dish ◊ *countword for cooked rice*

kŭrŭttoen 그릇된 false

kŭrup 그룹 group

kŭrut'ŏgi 그루터기 stump

kŭ saie 그 사이에 in the meantime, meanwhile

kŭsŭllida 그슬리다 scorch

kŭsŭllin 그슬린 scorched; charred

kŭ tangshienŭn 그 당시에는 in those days

kŭ taŭmnal 그 다음날 the day after, the next day

kŭ taŭmŭi 그 다음의 following

kŭ ttae 그 때 then, at that time

kŭ ttaeenŭn 그 때에는 by then

kŭt-tta 긋다 strike

kŭŭi 그의 his

kŭŭi kŏt 그의 것 his

kŭŭllida 그을리다 singe

kŭŭrŭm 그을음 soot

kŭ yŏja 그 여자 she

ku 구 nine; sphere; district (*part of a city*)

kuaehada 구애하다 make a pass at

kubich'im 굽이침 swell

kubijida 굽이지다 wind, coil

kubunhada 구분하다 sort

kuburida 구부리다 bend, bend down

kuburigi shwiun 구부리기 쉬운 flexible

kuburŏjida 구부러지다 curve; buckle

kuburŏjin 구부러진 crooked

kubyŏl 구별 distinction; differentiation

kubyŏrhada 구별하다 tell; mark out; differentiate; *olk'o kŭrŭmŭl kubyŏrhada* 옳고 그름을 구별하다 know right from wrong

kuch'ehwadoeda 구체화되다 form, take shape, develop

kuch'ehwahada 구체화하다 embody, crystallize

kuch'ejŏgin 구체적인 concrete; specific; definite

kuch'ida 굳히다 cement; harden

kuch'ŏng 구청 district office

kuch'uk'am 구축함 destroyer NAUT

kuch'urhada 구출하다 extricate; release; free

kudŏbŏrin 굳어버린 confirmed, inveterate

kudŏgi 구더기 maggot

kudŏjida 굳어지다 solidify

kudu 구두 shoe

kudusoe 구두쇠 miser

kudu susŏntchip 구두 수선집 heel bar, shoe repairer

kudutppŏp 구두법 punctuation

kuduttchŏm 구두점 punctuation mark

kuduttchŏmŭl tchiktta 구두점을

찍다 punctuate

kkugae 구개 palate ANAT

kugang 구강 mouth ◊ oral MED

kugida 구기다 crease, crumple

kugimsal 구김살 crease

Kugŏ 국어 Korean language

kugŏrhada 구걸하다 beg; cadge

kugoe ch'ubang 국외 추방 deportation

kugoero ch'ubanghada 국외로 추방하다 deport

kugŭn 구근 bulb BOT

kugŭpch'a 구급차 ambulance

kugŭp sangja 구급 상자 first aid kit

kugyŏjida 구겨지다 crease; ruffle

kugyŏng 구경 sightseeing; aperture; caliber

kugyŏnghada 구경하다 see; watch; see the sights

kugyŏnghwahada 국영화하다 nationalize

kugyŏngkkun 구경꾼 onlooker

kuhada 구하다 save, rescue; find, come by

kuhoek 구획 block, section

kuibi kanŭnghan 구입이 가능한 obtainable

kuiyong yŏnggye 구이용 영계 broiler (chicken)

kujebullŭng-in saram 구제불능인 사람 hopeless case, disaster area

kujech'aek 구제책 remedy

kujik'ada 구직하다 be seeking employment

kujo 구조 set-up; structure; rescue; salvation

kujo chojŏng 구조 조정 structural alteration; shake-up

kujoch'a 구조차 wrecker, recovery vehicle

kujodae 구조대 rescue party

kujohada 구조하다 rescue, salvage

kujowŏn 구조원 lifeguard

kujwa 구좌 account

kujwa pŏnho 구좌 번호 account number

kuk 국 soup

kuk kŭrŭt 국 그릇 soup bowl

kukch'ae 국채 national debt

kukki 국기 (national) flag

kuk-kka 국가 state, nation; national

anthem

Kuk-kka Poanppŏp 국가 보안법 National Security Law

kuk-kkaŭi 국가의 national

kuk-kkyŏng 국경 border

kukko 국고 national treasury

kukkun 국군 armed forces

kukppang 국방 national defense

kukppangbi yesan 국방비 예산 defense budget

Kukppangbu 국방부 Department of Defense

Kukppangbuhanggwan 국방부 장관 Defense Secretary

kukppu mach'wi 국부 마취 local anesthetic

Kukssech'ŏng 국세청 Internal Revenue (Service)

kukssu 국수 noodles

kuktcha 국자 ladle; scoop

kuktche 국제 international

kuktchejŏgin 국제적인 international

kuktchejŏgŭro 국제적으로 internationally

kuktche kyŏrhon 국제 결혼 international marriage, mixed marriage

Kuktche Sabŏp Chaep'anso 국제 사법 재판소 International Court of Justice

kuktche suji 국제 수지 balance of payments

Kuktche T'onghwa Kigŭm 국제 통화 기금 IMF, International Monetary Fund

Kuktche Yŏnhap 국제 연합 United Nations

kuktchŏk 국적 nationality

Kuk'oe 국회 Congress; Parliament; National Assembly

kuk'oeŭi 국회의 congressional

kuk'oe ŭisadang 국회 의사당 parliamentary buildings

kuk'oe ŭiwŏn 국회 의원 member of Congress

kuk'oe wiwŏn 국회 위원 congressman

kuk'wa 국화 chrysanthemum

kul 굴 oyster; tunnel; burrow

kulbok'ada 굴복하다 surrender, give in; knuckle under; succumb

kulch'ak changch'i 굴착 장치 (oil) rig

kulch'ak-kki 굴착기 excavator

kulgok 굴곡 twist, bend

kulgŭn kŭlsshich'e 굵은 글씨체 bold *print*

kulkko t'ak'an mokssori 굵고 탁한 목소리 gruff voice

kullida 굴리다 run

kullim 군림 reign

kullimhada 군림하다 reign

kullŏ ttŏrŏjida 굴러 떨어지다 tumble

kullyŏ nŏmŏttŭrida 굴려 넘어뜨리다 roll over

kulttuk 굴뚝 chimney, smokestack; funnel

kultt'uksae 굴뚝새 wren

kumae 구매 purchase

kumaehada 구매하다 buy, purchase

kumaeja 구매자 buyer

kumaesŏrŭl ponaeda 구매서를 보내다 invoice

kumie mat-tta 구미에 맞다 cater for, meet the needs of

kumjurida 굶주리다 starve

kumŏng 구멍 hole; pit; puncture

kumŏng magae 구멍 마개 stopper

kumŏng naeda 구멍 내다 drill; make a hole

kumŏng ttult'a 구멍 뚫다 puncture; punch a hole in

kumyŏng 구명 lifesaving

kumyŏng chokki 구명 조끼 life jacket

kumyŏngjŏng 구명정 lifeboat

kumyŏng tti 구명 띠 life belt

kun 군 the military, army; county; Mr; Lord

kunae 구내 premises; yard

kunae shikttang 구내 식당 canteen (*on the premises*)

kunbi 군비 arms, weapons

kunbongmuhada 군복무하다 do military service

kun chudunji 군 주둔지 garrison

kunch'im hŭllida 군침 흘리다 slobber, drool

kunch'im tolge hanŭn 군침 돌게 하는 mouthwatering

kundae 군대 troops; the services

kundan 군단 corps

kungdung-i 궁둥이 hip; posterior; buttocks

kunggŭktchŏgin 궁극적인 final

kunggŭktchŏgŭro 궁극적으로 eventually

kunggŭmhada 궁금하다 wonder; be anxious about

kunggwŏl 궁궐 palace

kunggwŏlgat'ŭn 궁궐같은 palatial

kunghada 궁하다 be in want; *toni kunghan* 돈이 궁한 hard up, broke

kun-gi 군기 colors

kungji 궁지 predicament; *kungjie moranŏt'a* 궁지에 몰아넣다 drive into a corner

kungmin 국민 national, citizen; the people

kungmin ch'ongsaengsan 국민 총생산 GNP, gross national product

kungmin t'up'yo 국민 투표 referendum

Kungmubu Changgwan 국무부 장관 Secretary of State

Kungmuch'ongni 국무총리 Prime Minister

kungmul 국물 broth

Kungmusŏng 국무성 State Department

kungnae 국내 domestic

kungnae ch'ongsaengsan 국내 총생산 GDP, gross domestic product

kungnaesŏn pihaenggi 국내선 비행기 domestic flight

kungnaeoeesŏ 국내외에서 at home and abroad

kungnip kong-wŏn 국립 공원 national park

kun-goguma 군고구마 baked sweet potato

kunham 군함 warship

kunin 군인 soldier; serviceman

kunju 군주 monarch

kunjung 군중 crowd, crush

kunppŏp hoeŭi 군법 회의 court martial

kunsa 군사 military affairs ◇ military

kunsal 군살 flab

kunsaryŏk 군사력 military capability

kunsashisŏl 군사시설 military

installation
unyonggi 군용기 warplane
upssülgörinün 급슬거리는 wavy
uptta 굽다 bake; roast; broil
up'il su ömnün 굽힐 수 없는 inflexible
urhaji ank'o haenaeda 굴하지 않고 해내다 carry on undaunted
uri 구리 copper
uröngt'öng-i 구렁텅이 abyss
urüda 구르다 roll
urüm 구름 cloud
urüng 구릉 hill ◊ hilly
uryök 굴욕 humiliation
uryogül chuda 굴욕을 주다 humiliate
uryokkamül katkkehada 굴욕감을 갖게하다 feel humiliated
uryokchögin 굴욕적인 humiliating
uryu chung 구류 중 in custody
uryu chung-ida 구류 중이다 be in custody; be on remand
uryushik'ida 구류시키다 remand in custody
usaek 구색 selection, assortment
usang 구상 framework
Kusegun 구세군 Salvation Army
Kuseju 구세주 Lord of Salvation, Savior
ushik 구식 old-fashioned
uship 구십 ninety
usöge(sö) 구석에(서) in the corner
usöguro molda 구석으로 몰다 corner, drive into a corner
usök 구석 corner
usöng 구성 composition, make-up; plot
usöngdoeda 구성되다 comprise
usöngdoeö it-tta 구성되어 있다 be composed of
usönghada 구성하다 compose, constitute, make up, form
usöng yoso 구성 요소 component, constituent
usok'ada 구속하다 tie down, restrict; intern
usongnyögi innün 구속력이 있는 binding
usül 구슬 beads
usüllida 구슬리다 coax
usülp'ün 구슬픈 plaintive

kusülp'ün sori 구슬픈 소리 wail
kusülp'ün sorirül naeda 구슬픈 소리를 내다 wail
kusul 구술 oral statement ◊ oral *exam*
kusurhada 구술하다 dictate
kut 굿 shaman rite of exorcism
kutkke kyölsshimhada 굳게 결심하다 make a firm decision, put one's foot down, be firm
kut-tta 굳다 harden
kut'a 구타 beating
kut'ahada 구타하다 beat up
kut'o 구토 vomit
kuün 구운 baked; roasted
kuwöjida 구워지다 be roasted
kuwöl 구월 September
kuwön 구원 salvation
kuwönhada 구원하다 redeem
Kuyak Söngsö 구약 성서 Old Testament
kuyök 구역 territory
kuyöktchil nanün 구역질 나는 disgusting, sick
kwa 과 section, department; faculty; lesson ◊ with ◊ and; as, like
kwabansu 과반수 majority
kwabansuida 과반수이다 be in the majority
kwabu 과부 widow
kwabugat'ün shinse 과부같은 신세 grass widow
kwabuhahada 과부하하다 overload
kwadae p'yöngkkadoen 과대 평가된 overrated
kwadae p'yöngkkahada 과대 평가하다 overestimate
kwadae sönjön 과대 선전 hype
kwadahage chibuldoen 과다하게 지불된 overpaid
kwadahan 과다한 excessive
kwadogi 과도기 transitional period
kwadojögin 과도적인 transitional
kwaench'ant'a 괜찮다 be OK, be alright; *kwaench'anayo* 괜찮아요 it's not bad; that's alright; *anio, kwaench'ansümnida* 아니오, 괜찮습니다 no, I don't mind; *tambaerül p'iwödo kwaench'ank'essümnikka?* 담배를

피워도 괜찮겠습니까? do you mind
if I smoke?
kwaench'anŭn 괜찮은 acceptable
kwaench'anŭn chŏngdoŭi 괜찮을
정도의 decent, acceptable
kwagamhan 과감한 drastic
kwagamhi haeboda 과감히 해보다
venture boldly
kwagŏ 과거 past; civil service
examination (*formerly*)
kwagŏe 과거에 in the past
kwagŏ punsa 과거 분사 past
participle
kwagŏ shije 과거 시제 past tense
kwagyŏngnonja 과격론자 extremist
kwahak 과학 science
kwahak kisul 과학 기술 technology
kwahak kisul kongp'otchŭng 과학
기술 공포증 technophobia
kwahak kisulsang-ŭi 과학 기술상의
technological
Kwahak-kkisulch'ŏ 과학기술처
Ministry of Science and Technology
kwahaktcha 과학자 scientist
kwahaktchŏgin 과학적인 scientific
kwail 과일 fruit
kwail chyussŭ 과일 쥬스 fruit juice
kwail saellŏdŭ 과일 샐러드 fruit
salad
kwaing pogyong 과잉 복용
overdose
kwaing pohohada 과잉 보호하다
overprotect
kwajang 과장 exaggeration;
department manager
kwajangdoeda 과장되다 be over the
top, be exaggerated
kwajangdoen 과장된 exaggerated;
melodramatic, theatrical
kwajanghada 과장하다 exaggerate
kwajanghan sŏnjŏn 과장한 선전
hype
kwajanghayŏ p'yohyŏnhada
과장하여 표현하다 dramatize,
exaggerate
kwajaryu 과자류 confectionery
kwaje 과제 project
kwajŏng 과정 process
kwajunghan 과중한 stiff
kwak 곽 carton; holder; tub
kwallamgaek 관람객 visitor (*at*

exhibition)
kwallamsŏk 관람석 stand; booth (*at
exhibition*)
kwalli 관리 administration;
management; mandarin
kwalliin 관리인 administrator;
manager; caretaker
kwallija 관리자 administrator;
manager
kwalliŭi 관리의 managerial
kwallyŏn 관련 connection, link;
involvement; *...wa / kwa kwallyŏnhayŏ* ...와 / 과 관련하여 in
connection with
kwallyŏndoeda 관련되다 be
connected with, be involved in; be
relevant; be related
kwallyŏndoen 관련된 related;
relevant
kwallyŏni innŭn 관련이 있는 related
kwallyŏni it-tta 관련이 있다 be
related to; be relevant to
kwallyŏni ŏmnŭn 관련이 없는
irrelevant
kwallyŏnshik'ida 관련시키다 bring
in, involve; connect, link
kwallyŏnssŏng 관련성 relevance
kwallyo 관료 bureaucrat
kwallyoje 관료제 bureaucracy
kwallyojŏgin 관료적인 bureaucratic
kwallyojuŭi 관료주의 bureaucracy,
red tape
kwalmok'al manhan 괄목할 만한
spectacular
kwaminhan 과민한 hypersensitive
kwamok 과목 subject (*branch of
learning*)
kwan 관 casket, coffin; pipe; tube;
crown; mansion
kwanak-kki 관악기 wind instrument
kwanch'al 관찰 observation
kwanch'allyŏgi yerihan 관찰력이
예리한 observant
kwanch'altcha 관찰자 observer
kwanch'arhada 관찰하다 observe
kwanch'ŏng 관청 office, position
kwanch'ŭksso 관측소 observatory
kwandaehada 관대하다 be generous
kwandaehan 관대한 generous;
broadminded; lenient; soft;
permissive

-kwang -광 enthusiast, fan; craze, mania; *yŏnghwagwang / chaejŭgwang* 영화광/재즈광 movie/jazz freak

kwan-gae 관개 irrigation

kwan-gaehada 관개하다 irrigate

kwan-gaek 관객 spectator

kwan-gaeyong suro 관개용 수로 irrigation canal

kwangbŏmwihan 광범위한 extensive, wide

Kwangboktchŏl 광복절 Liberation Day

kwangbu 광부 miner

kwangch'ŏnsu 광천수 mineral water

kwangch'ŭng 광층 seam (*of ore*)

kwangdaeppyŏ 광대뼈 cheekbone

kwanggagŭi 광각의 wide-angle

kwanggo 광고 advertisement, advert, commercial; advertising

kwanggohada 광고하다 advertise; publicize

kwanggoju 광고주 advertiser

kwanggo munan 광고 문안 advertising copy, text

kwanggo-ŏp 광고업 advertising

kwanggo pangsong 광고 방송 commercial break

kwanggop'an 광고판 billboard

kwanggo p'osŭt'ŏ 광고 포스터 bill, poster

kwanggo taehaengsa 광고 대행사 advertising agency

kwanggyŏng 광경 sight, spectacle

kwanggyŏnppyŏng 광견병 rabies

kwanghwarhan 광활한 vast

kwangjang 광장 square, plaza

kwangkki 광기 madness, insanity

kwangmul 광물 mineral

kwangnaeda 광내다 polish

kwangnŭng 관능 sensuality

kwangnŭngtchŏgin 관능적인 sensual

kwangnyŏn 광년 light year

kwang-ŏp 광업 mining

kwangp'ok'aejida 광폭해지다 go berserk

kwangsan 광산 mine

kwangshinja 광신자 fanatic

kwangshinjŏgin 광신적인 fanatical

kwangsŏk 광석 ore

kwangsŏmnyu 광섬유 fiber optics

kwangsŏmnyuŭi 광섬유의 fiber optic

kwangt'aegi ŏmnŭn 광택이 없는 matt

kwangt'aek nanŭn 광택 나는 glossy

kwangt'aek p'eint'ŭ 광택 페인트 gloss paint

kwangt'aektche 광택제 polish

kwan-gwang 관광 tour; sightseeing

kwan-gwang annaeso 관광 안내소 tourist (information) office

kwan-gwanggaek 관광객 visitor, tourist

kwan-gwanghada 관광하다 tour; go sightseeing

kwan-gwang-ŏp 관광업 tourism

kwan-gwang-ŏptcha 관광업자 tour operator

kwan-gwang yŏhaeng 관광 여행 sightseeing tour

kwan-gye 관계 connection, relationship

kwan-gyedoeda 관계되다 get involved with

kwan-gyedoenŭn 관계되는 concerned, involved

kwan-gyega kkŭnnada 관계가 끝나다 be through, be finished

kwan-gyehada 관계하다 involve, concern; get mixed up with

kwan-gyeŏmnŭn 관계없는 unrelated

kwan-gyeŏpsshi 관계없이 irrespective of

kwan-gyerŭl kkŭnt'a 관계를 끊다 dissociate oneself from

kwanhada 관하다 be related to; *...e kwanhaesŏ* ...에 관해서 with regard to; *i chŏme kwanhaesŏnŭn* 이 점에 관해서는 in this regard; *...e kwanhan* ...에 관한 about, concerning; *...e kwanhayŏ* ...에 관하여 concerning; *muŏse kwanhan kŏshimnikka?* 무엇에 관한 것입니까? what's it about?

kwanhae tŭt-tta 관해 듣다 hear about

kwanjanori 관자놀이 temple ANAT

kwanjet'ap 관제탑 control tower

kwanjŏl 관절 joint ANAT

kwanjŏllyŏm 관절염 arthritis

kwanjung 관중 crowd, audience

kwanjungsŏk 관중석 auditorium

kwanmok 관목 bush, shrub; shrubbery

kwanmun 관문 gateway

kwannŭngjŏgin 관능적인 erotic; tasty; sexy; sultry

kwannŭngjuŭi 관능주의 eroticism

kwannyong 관용 forgiveness; clemency

kwansa 관사 article

kwanse 관세 customs; duty, tariff

Kwanseguk 관세국 Customs and Tariff Bureau

kwanshim 관심 interest

kwanshimi innŭn 관심이 있는 interested

kwanshimsa 관심사 concern, business

kwanshimŭl kajida 관심을 가지다 care; care about; have an interest in

kwansŭp 관습 custom, convention; institution

kwansŭppŏp 관습법 unwritten law

kwansŭptchŏgin 관습적인 customary; unwritten

kwantchŏm 관점 position, point of view; **chŏrŏhan kwantchŏmesŏ** 저러한 관점에서 from that point of view, in that respect

kwant'onghada 관통하다 pierce, penetrate

kwanŭro ponaeda 관으로 보내다 pipe

kwanyŏgŭi hanbokp'an 과녁의 한복판 bull's-eye

kwanyŏgŭl match'uda 과녁을 맞추다 hit the bull's-eye

kwanyŏhada 관여하다 concern oneself with

kwanyŏk 과녁 target

kwanyong 관용 tolerance

kwanyong innŭn 관용 있는 tolerant

kwanyongjŏgin 관용적인 idiomatic

kwanyong-ŏ 관용어 idiom

kwarho 괄호 bracket; parenthesis

kwaro 과로 overwork

kwarohada 과로하다 overwork

kwaroshik'ida 과로시키다 overwork s.o.

kwase 과세 taxation

kwashi 과시 demonstration, display

kwashihada 과시하다 parade, flaunt, show off

kwashihanŭn 과시하는 ostentatious

kwashil 과실 malpractice

kwasok 과속 speeding

kwasok pŏlgŭm 과속 벌금 speeding fine

kwasok'ada 과속하다 speed, drive too quickly

kwaso p'yŏngkkahada 과소 평가하다 minimize; undervalue; underestimate

kwasuwŏn 과수원 orchard

kwayuk 과육 pulp

kwedo 궤도 orbit

kweyang 궤양 ulcer

kwi 귀 ear

kwiari 귀앓이 earache

kwich'ank'e hada 귀찮게 하다 bother, disturb

kwich'ank'e kulda 귀찮게 굴다 pester

kwich'ant'a 귀찮다 be a nuisance; **irŏk'e kwich'anŭl suga!** 이렇게 귀찮을 수가! what a nuisance!

kwich'anŭn 귀찮은 tiresome, annoying

kwich'ŏng-i ttŏrŏjil ttŭt'an 귀청이 떨어질 듯한 deafening, ear-piercing

kwie kŏsŭllinŭn 귀에 거슬리는 grating; strident; harsh

kwiga 귀가 homecoming

kwigahada 귀가하다 return home

kwiga kire 귀가 길에 homeward (*to own country*)

kwiga mŏn 귀가 먼 hard of hearing

kwigori 귀고리 earring

kwiguk kire 귀국 길에 homeward (*to own country*)

kwihwahada 귀화하다 become naturalized

kwihwan 귀환 return

kwiji 귀지 earwax

kwijok 귀족 aristocrat; nobility

kwijunghada 귀중하다 be precious

kwijunghan 귀중한 precious, valuable

kwijungp'um 귀중품 valuables

kwimŏgŭn 귀먹은 deaf

kwimŏk-kke hada 귀먹게 하다

deafen

wiri 귀리 oats

wirŭl tchonggŭt seuda 귀를 쫑긋 세우다 prick up one's ears

wishin 귀신 ghost

wishin-gat'ŭn 귀신같은 ghostly

witturami 귀뚜라미 cricket (*insect*)

wiyŏptta 귀엽다 be cute, be lovable

wiyŏun 귀여운 cute, pretty

wŏlli 권리 right, claim; title

wŏllyŏk 권력 power, authority

wŏllyŏk chipttan 권력 집단 the Establishment

wŏn 권 bloc ◊ countword for books

wŏnch'ong 권총 pistol, revolver

wŏnch'ongjip 권총집 holster

wŏnhada 권하다 offer

wŏnhan puyŏ 권한 부여 mandate, authority

wŏnhanŭl chuda 권한을 주다 authorize

wŏnjwa-esŏ ttŏrŏjida 권좌에서 떨어지다 fall from power

wŏnt'ae 권태 boredom

wŏnt'u 권투 boxing

wŏnt'uhada 권투하다 box SP

wŏnt'u shihap 권투 시합 boxing match

wŏnt'u sŏnsu 권투 선수 boxer

wŏnwi 권위 authority

wŏnwiinnŭn 권위있는 authoritative, definitive

wŏnwijaida 권위자이다 be an authority

wŏnyanggi 권양기 winch, windlass

wŏnyuhada 권유하다 canvass; drum up

kye -계: *chaejŭgye* / *mayak-kkye* 재즈계 / 마약계 jazz scene / drugs scene; *k'ŏmpyut'ŏgye* / *yŏngŭk-kkye* 컴퓨터계 / 연극계 the world of computers / the world of the theater

kye 계 credit union; loan club

kyebu 계부 stepfather

kyedan 계단 stair, step

kyedanshik pat 계단식 밭 terraced field

kyeganŭro 계간으로 quarterly

kyegi 계기 gauge

kyegip'an 계기판 dashboard

kyegŏlssŭre mŏktta 게걸스레 먹다

wolf (down)

kyegŭp 계급 class, rank; stripe

kyegŭp chojik 계급 조직 hierarchy

kyegŭp t'ujaeng 계급 투쟁 class warfare

kyehoek 계획 plan; project; strategy

kyehoektchŏgin 계획적인 premeditated

kyehoektchŏgin p'agoe 계획적인 파괴 sabotage

kyehoektchŏgŭro 계획적으로 systematically

kyehoektchŏgŭro p'agoehada 계획적으로 파괴하다 sabotage

kyehoek'ada 계획하다 plan, propose

kyejibae 계집애 little girl; chick, babe

kyejip 계집 female *pej*

kyejŏl 계절 season

kyeju kyŏnggi 계주 경기 relay

kyemo 계모 stepmother

kyemongdoen 계몽된 enlightened, liberal

kyemonghada 계몽하다 enlighten

kyeŏmnyŏng 계엄령 martial law

kyep'i 계피 cinnamon

kyeran 계란 egg

kyeran hurai 계란 후라이 fried egg

kyeryak 계략 plot, conspiracy

kyeryanggi 계량기 meter

kyesan 계산 sum; calculation

kyesandae 계산대 checkout; counter; cash desk

kyesan-gi 계산기 calculator

kyesanhada 계산하다 count, calculate

kyesanjŏgin 계산적인 calculating

kyesansŏ 계산서 bill, check

kyesansŏro ch'ŏngguhada 계산서로 청구하다 bill, invoice

kyesanŭl hal su innŭn 계산을 할 수 있는 numerate

kyesok irŏn sangt'aeramyŏn 계속 이런 상태라면 at this rate; if things go on like this

kyesok ... it-tta 계속 ... 있다 remain, stay

kyesok kajigo it-tta 계속 가지고 있다 hold on to, keep

kyesok myŏt shigan tong-an 계속 몇 시간 동안 for hours on end

kyesok namait-tta 계속 남아있다

hold out

kyesok noryŏk'ada 계속 노력하다 keep (on) trying

kyesok panbok'aesŏ 계속 반복해서 over and over again

kyesok panghaehada 계속 방해하다 keep (on) interrupting

kyesok salda 계속 살다 live on

kyesok seda 계속 세다 keep count of

kyesok shich'ŏnghada 계속 시청하다 follow *TV series, news*

kyesoktchŏgin 계속적인 continual

kyesok ttŏdŭrŏdaeda 계속 떠들어대다 go on about

kyesokttoeda 계속되다 continue

kyesokttoenŭn 계속되는 constant, continuous

kyesok yŏllak'ada 계속 연락하다 keep up with, stay in touch with

kyesok yujihada 계속 유지하다 retain

kyesok'ada 계속하다 continue, carry on; pursue; *kyesok köt-tta / iyagi hada* 계속 걷다 / 이야기 하다 walk / talk on; *kyesok ibwŏnhae itkke hada* 계속 입원해 있게 하다 keep in the hospital

kyesok'aesŏ 계속해서 in succession; perpetually; persistently; continually

kyesok'aesŏ hada 계속해서 하다 persevere

kyesok'aesŏ irŏnada 계속해서 일어나다 follow, dog

kyesŭng 계승 succession (*to the throne*)

kyesŭnghada 계승하다 succeed (*to the throne*)

kyesu 계수 sister-in-law (*younger brother's wife*)

kyeyak 계약 contract, agreement; deal

kyeyak-kkŭm 계약금 down payment, deposit

kyeyakssang-ŭi 계약상의 contractual

kyeyaktcha 계약자 contractor

kyeyak wiban 계약 위반 breach of contract

kyŏdŭrang-i 겨드랑이 armpit

kyŏgillo 격일로 on alternate days

kyŏja 겨자 mustard

kyŏk'an 격한 heated

kyŏkppyŏn 격변 upheaval; revulsion

kyŏkp'ahada 격파하다 whip, defeat

kyŏksshimhan 격심한 vigorous

kyŏktcha 격자 grid

kyŏktta 겪다 go through, experience

kyŏkt'oehada 격퇴하다 repel

kyŏl 결 texture

kyŏlbaek 결백 innocence; purity

kyŏlbaek'an 결백한 innocent; pure

kyŏlbyŏl 결별 separation

kyŏlgŭn 결근 absence

kyŏlgŭnhan 결근한 absent

kyŏlguk 결국 after all, in the end; *kyŏlguk pyŏng-wŏn shinserŭl chida* 결국 병원 신세를 지다 wind up in the hospital

kyŏlkkwa 결과 consequence, result; outcome

kyŏlk'o 결코 surely, assuredly

kyŏllon 결론 conclusion; decision; *kyŏllone irŭda* 결론에 이르다 come to a decision

kyŏllonŭl naerida 결론을 내리다 conclude, deduce

kyŏlmal 결말 ending; conclusion; upshot

kyŏlmangnyŏm 결막염 conjunctivitis

kyŏlmarŭl chit-tta 결말을 짓다 wind up; tie up the loose ends

kyŏlp'ip 결핍 lack, deficiency

kyŏlp'ipttoeda 결핍되다 be deficient in

kyŏlssandoeda 결산되다 balance

kyŏlsshim 결심 determination, resolution

kyŏlsshimhada 결심하다 decide

kyŏlsshimhan 결심한 determined

kyŏlssŏk 결석 absence

kyŏlssŏk'ada 결석하다 be absent

kyŏlssŏk'an 결석한 absent

kyŏlssok 결속 solidarity

kyŏlssŭng 결승 final

kyŏlssŭngjŏm 결승점 winning post, finish

kyŏlssŭngjŏn 결승전 finals; decider SP

kyŏlssŭngjŏn ch'ultchŏn sŏnsu 결승전 출전 선수 finalist

kyŏlssŭngsŏn 결승선 finishing line

yŏltchang 결장 colon ANAT

yŏltchŏm 결점 defect, shortcoming

yŏltchŏm innŭn 결점 있는 faulty

yŏltchŏmi innŭn 결점이 있는 defective, faulty

yŏltchŏng 결정 decision; *kyŏltchŏng-ŭl hada* 결정을 하다 make a decision; *kyŏltchŏng-ŭl naerida* 결정을 내리다 decide, settle

yŏltchŏngdoeji anŭn 결정되지 않은 unsettled, undecided

yŏltchŏnghada 결정하다 decide, determine

yŏltchŏnghaji mot'ada 결정하지 못하다 be undecided about; be unable to decide

yŏltchŏngjŏgin 결정적인 conclusive; critical, crucial; definitive

yŏltchŏngjŏgin kŏmt'o 결정적인 검토 acid test

yŏltchŏngjŏk shigi 결정적 시기 decisive moment

yŏlttanssŏng-i ŏmnŭn 결단성이 없는 indecisive

yŏmja 겸자 forceps

yŏmson 겸손 humility, modesty

yŏmsonhada 겸손하다 be humble, be modest

yŏmsonhan 겸손한 modest, unassuming

yŏnbon 견본 sample, specimen

yŏndida 견디다 endure, wear, last; cope; do without; resist

yŏndil su innŭn 견딜 수 있는 bearable

yŏndil su ŏmnŭn 견딜 수 없는 unbearable

yŏndiŏnaeda 견디어내다 withstand

..kyŏng ...경 around, about; *idal malgyŏng* 이달 말경 around the end of this month

yŏngapkkol 견갑골 shoulder blade

yŏngbi 경비 expenses

yŏngbirŭl chŏlgamhanŭn 경비를 절감하는 cost-conscious

yŏngbiwŏn 경비원 security guard; bouncer

yŏngbŏmtchoe 경범죄 misdemeanor

kyŏngbogi 경보기 alarm

kyŏngboŭm 경보음 alert; signal

kyŏngch'al 경찰 police; cop; *kyŏngch'are ch'asuhada* 경찰에 자수하다 give oneself up to the police

kyŏngch'algwan 경찰관 policeman; marshal

kyŏngch'al kuk-kka 경찰 국가 police state

kyŏngch'al kuktchang 경찰 국장 superintendent

kyŏngch'al sarin chŏndam pusŏ 경찰 살인 전담 부서 homicide (department)

kyŏngch'alsŏ 경찰서 police station

kyŏngch'i 경치 landscape; view

kyŏngch'ŏp 경첩 hinge

kyŏngdo 경도 longitude

kyŏnggam sayu 경감 사유 mitigating circumstances

kyŏnggi 경기 game; meet; fight; play; business; things; times

kyŏnggi ch'amgaja 경기 참가자 participant, entrant SP

kyŏnggi ch'imch'e 경기 침체 (economic) downturn

kyŏnggiga p'okttŭnghada 경기가 폭등하다 boom COM

kyŏnggija 경기자 player

kyŏnggijang 경기장 playing field; stadium

kyŏnggi kirok 경기 기록 record SP

kyŏnggi p'okttŭng 경기 폭등 boom

kyŏnggŏnhan 경건한 pious, devout

kyŏnggo 경고 alarm, warning

kyŏnggohada 경고하다 warn, alert; raise the alarm

kyŏnggwa 경과 passage (of time)

kyŏnggwahada 경과하다 elapse

kyŏnggwan 경관 officer; sights

kyŏnggye 경계 boundary, limit

kyŏnggyehada 경계하다 be on one's guard against, look out for

kyŏnggyehanŭn 경계하는 alert

kyŏnggyesŏn 경계선 boundary, border

kyŏnghŏm 경험 experience

kyŏnghŏmminnŭn 경험있는 experienced

kyŏnghŏmi ŏmnŭn 경험이 없는

inexperienced

kyŏnghŏmŭl ssahŭn 경험을 쌓은 seasoned *traveler etc*

kyŏnghohada 경호하다 escort, act as bodyguard to

kyŏnghowŏn 경호원 bodyguard

kyŏnghyang 경향 tendency; trend

kyŏnghyang-i it-tta 경향이 있다 tend toward; *...nŭn kyŏnghyang-i it-tta* ...는 경향이 있다 be liable to

kyŏngjaeng 경쟁 contest; rivalry; competition

kyŏngjaenghada 경쟁하다 compete; rival

kyŏngjaengja 경쟁자 competitor, rival; competitors; the competition

kyŏngjaengjŏgin 경쟁적인 competitive *person*

kyŏngjaengnyŏk innŭn 경쟁력 있는 competitive *bid*

kyŏngjaeng sangdae 경쟁 상대 competitor

kyŏngjak 경작 cultivation

kyŏngjak'ada 경작하다 plow, till; cultivate

kyŏngje 경제 economy

kyŏngje chaptchi 경제 잡지 financial magazine

kyŏngje chejae 경제 제재 economic sanctions

kyŏngjehak 경제학 economics

kyŏngjehaktcha 경제학자 economist

kyŏngjejŏgin 경제적인 economical, cheap

kyŏngjejŏgŭro 경제적으로 economically

kyŏngjejŏk ch'ŭngmyŏn 경제적 측면 economics; financial aspects

kyŏngjeŭi 경제의 economic

kyŏngjŏgŭl ullida 경적을 울리다 hoot, sound one's horn

kyŏngjŏk 경적 horn

kyŏngjŏn 경전 holy scriptures, holy book

kyŏngju 경주 race; racing

kyŏngjuch'a 경주차 racing car

kyŏngjuhada 경주하다 race, run

kyŏngjuja 경주자 runner, athlete; racing driver

kyŏngjujang 경주장 racetrack

kyŏngju k'osŭ 경주 코스 racecourse

kyŏngjuma 경주마 racehorse

kyŏngma 경마 horse race; the races

kyŏngmae 경매 auction

kyŏngmaehada 경매하다 auction

kyŏngmyŏl 경멸 contempt, scorn

kyŏngmyŏrhada 경멸하다 despise; scorn

kyŏngmyŏrhal manhan 경멸할 만한 contemptible

kyŏngmyŏrhanŭn 경멸하는 derogatory; scornful

kyŏngmyŏrŏ 경멸어 pejorative

kyŏngnapko 격납고 hangar

kyŏngnihayŏ 격리 하여 in isolation

kyŏngni pyŏngdong 격리 병동 isolation ward

kyŏngnishik'ida 격리시키다 isolate

kyŏngno 격노 rage, fury

kyŏngnohada 격노하다 rage, be in a rage

kyŏngnohanŭn 격노하는 furious

kyŏngno shik'ida 격노 시키다 infuriate

kyŏngnye 경례 salute; bow

kyŏngnyehada 경례하다 salute; bow

kyŏngnyerŭl pat-tta 경례를 받다 take the salute

kyŏngnyŏ 격려 boost, encouragement

kyŏngnyŏhada 격려하다 encourage, incite

kyŏngnyŏk 경력 career, profession; experience

kyŏngnyŏl 격렬 intensity

kyŏngnyŏn 경련 convulsion; twitch

kyŏngnyŏng 경영 management (*of big company*)

kyŏngnyŏnghada 경영하다 manage *big company*

kyŏngnyŏnghak 경영학 business studies; management studies

kyŏngnyŏnghak sŏktcha 경영학 석사 Master's in Business Administration, MBA

kyŏngnyŏng-in 경영인 manager, executive; proprietor

kyŏngnyŏngja 경영자 manager (*of company*)

kyŏngnyŏngjin 경영진 management managers

kyŏngnyŏngju 경영주 manager

(*owner*)

yŏngnyŏngkkwŏn maemae 경영권 매매 management buyout

yŏngnyŏng sangdamja 경영 상담자 management consultant

yŏngnyŏng taehagwŏn 경영 대학원 business school

yŏngnyŏngt'im 경영팀 management team

yŏngnyŏni ilda 경련이 일다 twitch; jerk

yŏng-nyŏnŭi 격년의 biennial

yŏngnyŏrhada 격렬하다 be violent

yŏngnyŏrhaejida 격렬해지다 intensify

yŏngnyŏrhage 격렬하게 furiously, violently; with a vengeance

yŏngnyŏrham 격렬함 violence

yŏngnyŏrhan 격렬한 drastic *change*; stormy, turbulent; violent

yŏngnyŏ yŏnsŏl 격려 연설 pep talk

yŏngnyuhayŏ 경유하여 via

yŏngŏnhan 경건한 reverent

yŏn-gohan 견고한 solid, strong

yŏngsa 경사 slant; slope

yŏngsado 경사도 gradient

yŏngsajida 경사지다 slope; descend

yŏngsa-myŏn 경사면 side (*of mountain*)

yŏngshihada 경시하다 downplay

yŏngŭirŭl p'yohada 경의를 표하다 show respect to

yŏng-u 경우 case, instance

yŏng-wi 경위 inspector

yŏngyŏng kwalli 경영 관리 running (*of business*)

yŏnhae 견해 view, opinion

yŏninhada 견인하다 tow away

yŏninnyong patchul 견인용 밧줄 towrope

yŏnje 견제 restraint, brake

yŏnjŏk 견적 estimate; quotation

yŏnjŏk'ada 견적하다 quote

yŏnnunjil 곁눈질 leer

yŏnnunjirhada 곁눈질하다 look away; sneak a glance at

yŏnsonhan 검손한 humble

yŏnsŭp 견습 probation

yŏnsŭp kigan 견습 기간 trial

period, probation period

kyŏnsŭp kwajŏng 견습 과정 training course

kyŏnsŭpsaeng 견습생 apprentice; trainee

kyŏnuda 겨누다 point

kyŏnyang 겨냥 aim

kyŏnyanghada 겨냥하다 aim (at); measure

kyŏpch'ida 겹치다 clash

kyŏrhaek 결핵 tuberculosis

kyŏrhamŭl koch'ida 결함을 고치다 debug

kyŏrhap 결합 combination

kyŏrhap'ada 결합하다 combine, unite

kyŏrhon 결혼 marriage (*institution*)

kyŏrhon chŭngmyŏngsŏ 결혼 증명서 marriage certificate

kyŏrhon kinyŏmil 결혼 기념일 wedding anniversary

kyŏrhon panji 결혼 반지 wedding ring

kyŏrhon saenghwal 결혼 생활 married life; marriage

kyŏrhon sangdamwŏn 결혼 상담원 marriage counselor

kyŏrhon yego 결혼 예고 banns

kyŏrhonhada 결혼하다 marry, get married

kyŏrhonhan 결혼한 married

kyŏrhonshik 결혼식 marriage, wedding

kyŏrhonshingnal 결혼식날 wedding day

kyŏrhonŭi 결혼의 marital

kyŏron chŏnŭi 결혼 전의 prenuptial

kyŏruda 겨루다 play *opponent*; fight, contest

kyŏryŏnham 결연함 resolution, determination

kyŏtssoe 곁쇠 skeleton key

kyŏt'e(sŏ) 곁에(서) beside, next to

kyŏu 겨우 barely, only just

kyŏul 겨울 winter

kyŏul kat'ŭn 겨울같은 wintry

kyŏul sŭp'och'ŭ 겨울 스포츠 winter sports

kyobok 교복 uniform

kyobok sang-ŭi 교복 상의 tunic

kyoch'a 교차 intersection

kyoch'ahada 교차하다 intersect, cross

kyoch'ajŏm 교차점 junction

kyoch'ak sangt'ae 교착 상태 deadlock

kyoch'aro 교차로 cross street

kyoch'ehada 교체하다 alternate

kyodae 교대 shift; turn; *kyodaero hada* 교대로 하다 take turns in doing, do in rotation; *ch'arŭl kyodaero unjŏnhada* 차를 교대로 운전하다 take turns at the wheel

kyodaehada 교대하다 relieve, take over from

kyodae kŭnmu 교대 근무 shift work

kyodogwan 교도관 guard

kyodoso 교도소 jail, penitentiary

kyodosojang 교도소장 prison warden

kyogu mokssa 교구 목사 vicar

kyogu mokssagwan 교구 목사관 vicarage

kyohoe 교회 church

kyohun 교훈 moral, message; school motto

kyohwan 교환 exchange, flow

kyohwang 교황 pope

kyohwanhada 교환하다 exchange, trade; *muŏtkkwa muŏsŭl kyohwanhada* 무엇과 무엇을 교환하다 trade sth for sth

kyohwan kanŭng t'onghwa 교환 가능 통화 hard currency

kyohwansu 교환수 operator TELEC

kyohwanŭro 교환으로 in exchange; in exchange for

kyohwarham 교활함 cunning

kyohwarhan 교활한 crafty, cunning, sly; devious

kyohyanggok 교향곡 symphony

kyojang 교장 principal (*of school*)

kyoje 교제 contact

kyojehada 교제하다 associate with; keep company

kyojigwŏn 교직원 faculty, teaching staff

kyojik 교직 teaching (*profession*)

kyojŏn 교전 battle; war; hostilities

kyojŏn chung-ida 교전 중이다 be at war

kyojŏng 교정 manipulation

kyojŏnghada 교정하다 manipulate; 교정하다 correct *proofs*

kyojŏngswae 교정쇄 proof (*of book*)

kyokkwa kwajŏng 교과 과정 course (*series of lessons*); curriculum

kyokkwasŏ 교과서 textbook

kyomushil 교무실 staffroom

kyomyohada 교묘하다 be crafty; be clever; *kyomyohage shiganŭl kkŭlda* 교묘하게 시간을 끌다 stall, play for time

kyomyohan 교묘한 sneaky, crafty

kyomyohi hoep'ihada 교묘히 회피하다 evade, dodge *responsibility*

kyomyohi umjigida 교묘히 움직이다 maneuver

kyo-oe 교외 suburb

kyop'yŏn 교편 pointer

kyori 교리 dogma

kyoryu 교류 alternating current

kyosa 교사 teacher; academic; teachers; staff

kyosaeng 교생 student teacher

kyosa hullyŏn 교사 훈련 teacher training

kyosarhada 교살하다 strangle

kyoshil 교실 classroom

kyoshin 교신 contact

kyoshinhada 교신하다 contact

kyosŏp 교섭 approach; advance; proposal

kyosu 교수 professor

kyosudae 교수대 gallows

kyosuhyŏng-e ch'ŏhada 교수형에 처하다 string up, hang

kyot'ong 교통 traffic

Kyot'ongbu 교통부 Department of Transportation

kyot'ong ch'ejŭng 교통 체증 traffic jam

kyot'ong honjap 교통 혼잡 jam; traffic congestion

kyot'ongmang chŏngch'e 교통망 정체 gridlock

kyot'ong p'yojip'an 교통 표지판 signpost

Kyot'ong Pŏpkkyu 교통 법규 Highway Code, rules of the road

kyot'ong shinho 교통 신호 traffic sign

yot'ong sudan 교통 수단 means of transportation

yot'ong sun-gyŏng 교통 순경 traffic cop; traffic police

yoyang-i ŏmnŭn 교양이 없는 lowbrow

yoyuge kwanhan 교육에 관한 educational

yoyuk 교육 education; training

yoyukpat-tta 교육받다 be educated; receive one's training

yoyukpadŭn 교육받은 educated

yoyukpat-tchi mot'an 교육받지 못한 uneducated

yoyukppu 교육부 Department of Education

yoyuk shilssŭpssaeng 교육 실습생 student teacher

yoyuktchŏgin 교육적인 educational, instructive, informative

yoyuk'ada 교육하다 educate

yuch'igŭl ttarŭda 규칙을 따르다 follow the rules, toe the line

yuch'ik 규칙 rule, regulation

kyuch'iktchŏgin 규칙적인 regular

kyugyŏk'wahada 규격화하다 standardize

kyujehada 규제하다 regulate

kyuje yangmul 규제 약물 controlled substance

kyujŏng 규정 stipulation, condition

kyujŏnghada 규정하다 stipulate, provide for

kyul 귤 mandarin orange

kyumo 규모 size, scale

kyumoga chulda 규모가 줄다 downsize

kyumorŭl churida 규모를 줄이다 downsize

kyundŭnghage 균등하게 equally; *kyundŭnghage nanuda* 균등하게 나누다 share out equally

kyunhyŏng 균형 balance, equilibrium; *kyunhyŏng-ŭl chaptta* 균형을 잡다 balance

kyunhyŏng chap'in 균형 잡힌 balanced, well-balanced

kyunyŏl 균열 rift

kyuyul 규율 discipline

K'

k'adŭ 카드 card
k'adŭk'i 카드키 cardkey
k'adŭshik saegin 카드식 색인 card index
k'aeda 캐다 nose about
k'aedi 캐디 caddie
k'aemp'ing 캠핑 camping
k'aemp'ŭ 캠프 camp
K'aenada 캐나다 Canada ◊ Canadian
k'aengk'aeng chit-tta 캥캥 짖다 yap
k'aep 캡 cap
k'aepsshyul 캡슐 capsule
k'ajino 카지노 casino
k'akt'eil 칵테일 cocktail
k'al 칼 knife
k'allal 칼날 blade
k'alla sajin 칼라 사진 color photograph
k'alla t'ellebijŏn 칼라 텔레비전 color TV
k'allaro toen 칼라로 된 (in) color
k'allori 칼로리 calorie
k'alshyum 칼슘 calcium
k'alchip 칼집 sheath (for knife)
K'ambodia 캄보디아 Cambodia ◊ Cambodian
k'amera 카메라 camera
k'an 칸 compartment; panel; section
k'aneishyŏn 카네이션 carnation
k'anmagi 칸막이 partition
k'anmagirŭl hada 칸막이를 하다 partition off
k'ap'e 카페 café
k'ap'ein 카페인 caffeine
k'ap'eini chegŏdoen 카페인이 제거된 decaffeinated
k'ap'irait'ŏ 카피라이터 copy-writer
k'arat'e 카라테 karate
k'aset'ŭ p'ŭlleiŏ 카셋트 플레이어 tape deck
k'auboi 카우보이 cowboy
k'aunt'ŏ 카운터 counter (in café etc)
k'aunt'ŭ 카운트 count (in baseball, boxing)

k'ech'ŏp 케첩 catsup, ketchup
k'eibŭlk'a 케이블카 cable car
k'eik'ŭ 케이크 cake
k'eisŭ 케이스 case, container
k'i 키 height; key (on keyboard); helm
k'ibodŭ 키보드 keyboard
k'iga chagŭn 키가 작은 short
k'iga k'ŭn 키가 큰 tall
k'ikk'ik-kkŏrida 킥킥거리다 titter
k'ik'op'ŭ 킥오프 kickoff
k'ilk'il ut-tta 킬킬 웃다 chuckle
k'illo 킬로 kilo
k'illobait'ŭ 킬로바이트 kilobyte
k'illogŭraem 킬로그램 kilogram
k'illomit'ŏ 킬로미터 kilometer
k'ing saijŭ 킹 사이즈 king-size(d)
k'irŭl ch'ida 키를 치다 key, key in COMPUT
k'isŭ 키스 kiss
k'isŭhada 키스하다 kiss
k'iuda 키우다 raise, bring up children
k'ŏbŏ 커버 cover, jacket (of book)
k'ŏjida 커지다 grow (of number, amount)
k'ŏmp'ŏsŭ 컴퍼스 (pair of) compasses
k'ŏmp'yut'ŏ 컴퓨터 computer
k'ŏmp'yut'ŏ ch'ulp'an 컴퓨터 출판 DTP, desk-top publishing
k'ŏmp'yut'ŏ keim 컴퓨터 게임 computer game
k'ŏmp'yut'ŏ kwahak 컴퓨터 과학 computer science
k'ŏmp'yut'ŏ kwahaktcha 컴퓨터 과학자 computer scientist
k'ŏmp'yut'ŏ sayong 컴퓨터 사용 computing
k'ŏmp'yut'ŏro t'ongjedoenŭn 컴퓨터로 통제되는 computer-controlled
k'ŏnbeiŏ pelt'ŭ 컨베이어 벨트 conveyor belt

ŏnbenshyŏn sent'ŏ 컨벤션 센터 convention center

ŏndishyŏn 컨디션 condition, shape

ŏnssŏlt'ŏnt'ŭ 컨설턴트 consultant, adviser

ŏnssŏlt'ŏnt'ŭŏp 컨설턴트업 consultancy (company)

ŏnt'einŏ 컨테이너 container

ŏnt'ŭri myujik 컨트리 뮤직 country and western (music)

ŏnyŏng 커녕 to say nothing of; ...kinŭn k'ŏnyŏng ...기는 커녕 let alone

ŏp 컵 cup; glass

ŏp'i 커피 coffee

ŏp'i meik'ŏ 커피 메이커 coffee maker

ŏp'i p'ot'ŭ 커피 포트 coffee pot

ŏp'i shyop 커피 숍 coffee shop

ŏsŏ 커서 cursor

ŏt'ŭn 커튼 drapes, curtains

o 코 nose; trunk; stitch

och'i 코치 coach SP

odŭ 코드 code

okkiri 코끼리 elephant

o kolda 코 골다 snore

ok'ain 코카인 cocaine

ok'oa 코코아 cocoa

ollesŭt'erol 콜레스테롤 cholesterol

ol t'aeksshi 콜 택시 radio taxi

omidiŏn 코미디언 comedian

omp'aekt'ŭ tisŭk'ŭ 콤팩트 디스크 CD, compact disc

omp'ŭllekssŭ 콤플렉스 complex PSYCH

ondishyŏnŏ 콘디셔너 conditioner

ondo 콘도 condo

ondom 콘돔 condom, sheath

ondominium 콘도미니움 condominium

ong 콩 bean; soy bean

ongp'at 콩팥 soy and red beans; kidney ANAT

onk'ŭrit'ŭ 콘크리트 concrete

onmul 콧물 mucus

onnoraero purŭda 콧노래로 부르다 hum

onŏk'ik 코너킥 corner kick

ont'aekt'ŭrenjŭ 콘택트렌즈 contact lens

onyak 코냑 cognac

k'op'i 코피 nosebleed; copy; nanŭn k'op'iga nanda 나는 코피가 난다 my nose is bleeding

k'orŭk'ŭ 코르크 cork (material)

k'orŭk'ŭ magae 코르크 마개 cork (in bottle)

k'osŭ 코스 course, track

k'otkkumŏng 콧구멍 nostril

k'otppanggwi kkwida 콧방귀 뀌다 snort (disdainfully)

k'otppulsso 코뿔소 rhinoceros

k'otssori 콧소리 twang

k'otssuyŏm 콧수염 mustache

k'ot'inghan 코팅한 laminated

k'ot'ŭ 코트 court SP

k'ŭda 크다 be big

k'ŭge 크게 large ◊ very, highly; greatly; loudly; k'ŭge ttŭn 크게 뜬 wide-open; k'ŭge ut-tta 크게 웃다 roar with laughter

k'ŭge hada 크게 하다 enlarge

k'ŭgi 크기 size

k'ŭllaeshik 클래식 classical

k'ŭllarinet 클라리넷 clarinet

k'ŭllenjŏ 클렌저 cleanser

k'ŭllik 클릭 click

k'ŭllik'ada 클릭하다 click on

k'ŭllip 클립 clip; fastener

k'ŭllip-ppodŭ 클립보드 clipboard

k'ŭllŏch'i 클러치 clutch MOT

k'ŭllŏch'irŭl p'ulda 클러치를 풀다 declutch

k'ŭllojŭŏp 클로즈업 close-up

k'ŭn 큰 big, large

k'ŭngk'ŭnggŏrida 킁킁거리다 sniff

k'ŭn haengbok-kkam 큰 행복감 euphoria

k'ŭn saejang 큰 새장 aviary

k'ŭn ton 큰 돈 fortune; big money

k'ŭraek'ŏ 크래커 cracker

k'ŭreyong 크레용 crayon

k'ŭrim 크림 cream

k'ŭrim ch'ijŭ 크림 치즈 cream cheese

k'ŭrisŭmasŭ 크리스마스 Christmas

k'udet'a 쿠데타 coup

k'uk tchirŭda 쿡 찌르다 jab, poke

k'uk'i 쿠키 cookie

k'ŭllŏp 클럽 club

k'unghanŭn sori 쿵하는 소리 thud, thump

k'ungk'ung kŏt-tta 쿵쿵 걷다 tramp;

trudge

k'up'on 쿠폰 coupon

k'urisŭt'ŏl 크리스털 crystal (*glass*)

k'ushyŏn 쿠션 cushion

k'waehwalhada 쾌활하다 be lively, be vivacious

k'waejŏk'an 쾌적한 delightful

k'waesoktchŏng 쾌속정 speedboat

k'walk'wal hŭllŏnaoda 콸콸 흘러나오다 gush out

k'wang! 꽝! bang!; *munŭl k'wangk'wang tudŭrida* 문을 꽝꽝 두드리다 hammer at the door

k'wang pudich'ida 꽝 부딪히다 bang, hit

k'wang tach'ida 꽝 닫히다 bang, be slammed shut

k'wang tat-tta 꽝 닫다 bang, slam shut

k'wijŭ 퀴즈 quiz

k'wijŭ p'ŭro 퀴즈 프로 quiz program

k'wik'wihan 퀴퀴한 moldy, musty

k'yabare 카바레 cabaret

k'yŏda 켜다 switch on *machine*

k'yŏit-tta 켜있다 be on (*of device*)

k'yŏjida 켜지다 be turned on (*of device*)

k'yŏlle 켤레 pair ◊ *countword for shoes and socks*

k'yŏn ch'aero tuda 켠 채로 두다 leave on *machine*

k'yu 큐 cue

k'yureit'ŏ 큐레이터 curator

L

.l ...ㄹ future particle
abendŏ 라벤더 lavender
adiet'ŏ 라디에이터 radiator
adio 라디오 radio
adio pangsongguk 라디오 방송국
  radio station
aelli 랠리 rally
aem 램 RAM, random access
  memory
aep 랩 rap MUS
aept'ap 랩탑 laptop
agŏ piŏ 라거 비어 lager
ago hanŭn kŏsŭn 라고 하는 것은
  so-called
aillak 라일락 lilac
aim 라임 lime (fruit, tree)
aim nokssaek 라임 녹색 limegreen
aining 라이닝 lining
ait'ŏ 라이터 lighter
ait'ŭkkŭp sŏnsu 라이트급 선수
  lightweight
ait'ŭ p'en 라이트 펜 light pen
ak 락 rock (music)
akk'ŭllol 락큰롤 rock'n'roll
aksŭt'a 락스타 rock star
ak'et 라켓 racket
angdebu 랑데부 rendez-vous
anjeri 란제리 lingerie
aundŭ 라운드 round
aunji 라운지 lounge
.aosŭ 라오스 Laos ◊ Laotian
eiausŭl hada 레이아웃을 하다 lay
  out
eida 레이다 radar
eida yŏngsang 레이더 영상 blip
eijyŏ 레이저 laser
eijyŏ kwangsŏn 레이저 광선 laser
  beam
eijyŏ p'urint'ŏ 레이저 프린터 laser
  printer
eisŭ 레이스 lace
ejŏ sent'ŏ 레저 센터 leisure center
ejŭbiŏn 레즈비언 lesbian
ek'odŭ 레코드 record

lemon 레몬 lemon
lemon chussŭ 레몬 주스 lemon juice
lemonch'a 레몬차 lemon tea
lemoneidŭ 레모네이드 lemonade
lench'i 렌치 wrench
lenjŭ 렌즈 lens
lenjŭ k'ong 렌즈 콩 lentil
lenjŭ k'ong sŭp'ŭ 렌즈 콩 스프
  lentil soup
lenjŭ ttukkŏng 렌즈뚜껑 lens cover
lep'ot'ŭ 레포트 essay
lesŭlling 레슬링 wrestling
lesŭlling kyŏnggi 레슬링 경기
  wrestling bout
lesŭlling sŏnsu 레슬링 선수 wrestler
Libia 리비아 Libya ◊ Libyan
libon 리본 ribbon
libon maedŭp 리본 매듭 bow, knot
lidŭm 리듬 rhythm
lihŏsŏl 리허설 practice; rehearsal
lihŏsŏrhada 리허설하다 rehearse
lik'odŏ 리코더 recorder
lik'yurŭ 리큐르 liqueur
lil 릴 reel
limp'ŭsaem 림프샘 lymph gland
limujin 리무진 limo, limousine
linen 리넨 linen
ling 링 ring
linssŭhada 린스하다 rinse
lipssŭt'ik 립스틱 lipstick
lisait'ŭl 리사이틀 recital
lisepsshyŏn p'at'i 리셉션 파티
  reception
lishibŏ 리시버 receiver (in tennis)
lit'ŏ 리터 liter
lit'ŭribŏ 리트리버 retriever (dog)
lŏm 럼 rum
lŏmp'ŭ sŭt'eik'ŭ 럼프 스테이크
  rumpsteak
Lŏndŏn 런던 London
lŏning shyŏch'ŭ 러닝 셔츠
  undershirt
lŏp'ŭ 러프 rough (in golf)
Lŏshia 러시아 Russia ◊ Russian

Lŏshiain 러시아인 Russian (*person*)

Lŏshiaŏ 러시아어 Russian (*language*)

lobi 로비 lobby

lobot 로봇 robot

lodŭhada 로드하다 load

logo 로고 logo

lok'et 로켓 (space) rocket

lok'ŏ 로커 locker

lol 롤 roll (*of film*)

lollŏ k'osŭt'ŏ 롤러 코스터 roller coaster

lollŏ p̆ulleidŭ 롤러 블레이드 roller blade

lollŏ sŭk'eit'ŭ 롤러 스케이트 roller skate

loippang 롤빵 (bread) roll

lom 롬 ROM, read only memory

lomaensŭ 로맨스 romance; affair

lomaent'ik'ada 로맨틱하다 be romantic

lomaent'ik'an 로맨틱한 romantic

Loma K'at'ollik 로마 카톨릭 Roman Catholic

Loma K'at'ollik-kkyoŭi 로마 카톨릭교의 Roman Catholic

loshyŏn 로션 lotion

lot'ŏri 로터리 traffic circle

loyŏlt'i 로열티 royalty (*on book, recording*)

lubi 루비 ruby

lullet 룰렛 roulette

lum meit'ŭ 룸 메이트 room mate

lum ssŏbissŭ 룸 서비스 room service

lyumat'ijŭm 류마티즘 rheumatism

M

na 마 jinx, bad luck
nabi 마비 paralysis
nabishik'ida 마비시키다 paralyze
nabõbe köllin 마법에 걸린 spellbound, enraptured
nabõbüi 마법의 occult
nabõp 마법 the occult; witchcraft
nabõpsa 마법사 wizard
nabu 마부 groom (for horse)
nach'al 마찰 friction
nach'i ...ch'õrõm 마치 ...처럼 as though
nach'ida 마치다 end, finish
nach'im 마침 just, exactly
nach'imnae 마침내 finally, at last
nach'imp'yo 마침표 period (punctuation mark)
nach'õllu 마천루 skyscraper
nach'wihada 마취하다 drug
nach'wije 마취제 anesthetic
nach'wisa 마취사 anesthetist
nadi 마디 joint; word; phrase; ...wa/kwa handu madi marhada ...와/과 한두 마디 말하다 have a word with
nadit'usõng-iin 마디투성이인 gnarled
nadõbodü 마더보드 motherboard
nae 매 hawk
nae- 매 each, every
naeaehago ulda 매애하고 울다 bleat
naebok 매복 ambush
naech'e 매체 medium, vehicle
naech'un 매춘 prostitution
naech'unbu 매춘부 prostitute
naech'un-gul 매춘굴 brothel
naeda 매다 knot; tether, tie up
naedalda 매달다 suspend, hang; mok maedalda 목 매달다 hang person
naedallida 매달리다 cling to
naedalmada 매달마다 monthly
naedarüi 매달의 monthly

maedogyõn 맹도견 seeing-eye dog
maedok 매독 syphilis
maedüp 매듭 knot; decorative tassle
maegagin 매각인 vendor
maehok 매혹 charm; magnetism
maehoksshik'ida 매혹시키다 fascinate
maehoktchõgin 매혹적인 charming; ravishing; fascinating
maehokttoeda 매혹되다 be fascinated by
maehok'ada 매혹하다 charm
maehyõng 매형 brother-in-law (man's elder sister's husband)
maeil 매일 every day
maeil maeil kyesok'aesõ 매일 매일 계속해서 day in, day out
maeil pame 매일 밤에 nightly
maeiptcha 매입자 purchaser
maeirüi 매일의 daily
maejang 매장 department (of store); outlet; burial
maejangmul 매장물 deposit
maejil 매질 beating, hiding
maejindoen 매진된 out of stock
maejõk'ijüm 매저키즘 masochism
maejõk'isüt'ü 매저키스트 masochist
maejõm 매점 bookstall
maejõmhada 매점하다 buy up
maejõnghan 매정한 heartless, pitiless
maeju 매주 every week
maejumada 매주마다 weekly
maeju-üi 매주의 weekly
makttaehada 막대하다 be huge
maekkürõptta 매끄럽다 be smooth
maekppak 맥박 throb, pulse
maekppak chojõnggi 맥박 조정기 pacemaker
maektchu 맥주 beer
maek'üro 매크로 macro
maemae 매매 marketing ◊ for sale
maemae changso 매매 장소 market-place

maemaeshijang 매매시장 market
maemdom 맴돔 curl
maen araetchok 맨 아래쪽 bottom
maenbarida 맨바리다 be barefoot
maeng-in 맹인 the blind
Maengja 맹자 Mencius
maengjang 맹장 appendix
maengjangnyŏm 맹장염 appendicitis
maengnyŏrhan sokttoro 맹렬한 속도로 at a furious pace
maengnyŏrhi pinanhada 맹렬히 비난하다 hit out at, criticize
maengsehada 맹세하다 swear, promise
maengtchŏm 맹점 blind spot
maenik'yuŏ 매니큐어 manicure; nail polish
maenik'yuŏ chiunŭn yak 매니큐어 지우는 약 nail polish remover
maen katchok 맨 가쪽 bottom
maenmaru 맨마루 bare floor
maen mitppadagŭi 맨 밑바닥의 bottom; lowest
maen twittchogŭi 맨 뒷쪽의 rearmost
maenwiŭi 맨위의 top
maenyŏn 매년 yearly
maenyŏnŭi 매년의 yearly
maenyuŏl 매뉴얼 manual
maepok'ayŏ sŭpkkyŏk'ada 매복하여 습격하다 ambush
maepsshi innŭn 맵시있는 spruce, neat
maeptta 맵다 be hot, be spicy
maep'yogyewŏn 매표계원 booking clerk
maep'yoso 매표소 box office, ticket office
maeryŏginnŭn 매력있는 attractive
maeryŏgi nŏmch'inŭn 매력이 넘치는 glamorous
maeryŏk 매력 appeal, attraction
maeryŏktchŏgin 매력적인 engaging; seductive; cute
maeryodoen 매료된 entranced
maeryohada 매료하다 enchant
maesanggo 매상고 turnover, takings
maesang-ŭl ollida 매상을 올리다 turn over FIN
maeshit'ŭ p'ot'eit'o 매시트 포테이토

mashed potatoes
maesŏun 매서운 severe, strict; piercing
maesŭk'ŏm 매스컴 the media
maesŭk'ŏmŭi kwajang 매스컴의 과장 media hype
maesuhada 매수하다 bribe; corrupt
maet-tta 맺다 form, establish
maet'ŭ 매트 mat
maet'ŭrisŭ 매트리스 mattress
maeu 매우 most, tremendously
maeun 매운 hot, spicy
maeunt'ang 매운탕 spicy fish soup
maewŏl 매월 every month
maeyŏn 매연 fumes
magae 마개 plug
magaerŭl ppoptta 마개를 뽑다 uncork
magaerŭl yŏlda 마개를 열다 unscrew
magamil 마감일 deadline (*day*)
magamshigan 마감시간 deadline (*hour*)
maganaeda 막아내다 keep away, ward off
magarin 마가린 margarine
magi 막이 screen, shield
magu charada 마구 자라다 run wild
magu chitppalp'ida 마구 짓밟히다 be trampled underfoot
magujabiŭi 마구잡이의 haphazard
magutkkan 마구간 stable
magu toradanida 마구 돌아다니다 travel; wander
magu ttaerida 마구 때리다 thrash
magu tudŭlgyŏ p'aeda 마구 두들겨 패다 beat, knock around
magu tudŭrida 마구 두드리다 pound on, hammer on
magwŏnŏptcha 마권업자 bookmaker
magyŏnhan 막연한 indefinable
mahŭn 마흔 forty
mahŭn pŏntchaeŭi 마흔 번째의 fortieth
maik'ŭroch'ip 마이크로칩 microchip
maik'ŭrop'illŭm 마이크로필름 microfilm
maik'ŭrop'ŭrosesŏ 마이크로프로세서 microprocessor

naik'ŭ 마이크 mike, microphone

nail 마일 mile

nail su 마일 수 mileage

najak 마작 mah-jong

najayo! 맞아요! that's it!, that's right!

naji 맏이 the eldest

najihada 맞이하다 meet with

najijak-kkŏrida 만지작거리다 fiddle (around) with

najimagesŏ tu pŏntchae 마지막에서 두 번째 second to last, penultimate

najimagŭi 마지막의 final, last

najimagŭro 마지막으로 finally, lastly

najimak 마지막 last

najimak sudanŭro 마지막 수단으로 as a last resort

najimak sun-gane 마지막 순간에 at the last moment, at the eleventh hour

naji mot'ae 마지 못해 reluctantly

najiro t'aeŏnan 맏이로 태어난 first-born, eldest

najok'ago innŭn 만족하고 있는 contented

najul li ŏpssŏ 맞을 리 없어 that can't be right

najuboda 마주보다 face

najuch'ida 마주치다 meet

najuhada 마주하다 confront, face

najungnagada 마중나가다 collect, meet

najung naoda 마중 나오다 pick up, collect

nak 막 membrane; slick; curtain; act

nak haryŏgo hada 막 하려고 하다 be on the point of; *nanŭn mak ttŏnaryŏdŏn ch'amiŏssŏyo* 나는 막 떠나려던 참이었어요 I was just about to leave

nak-kkan 막간 interlude

nak-kkŏlli 막걸리 rice wine

nakkwŏnŏptcha 마권업자 bookie

nakssa 막사 barracks

nakssangmak'ae irŭda 막상막하에 이르다 draw level

nakshimhan 막심한 heavy

naktta 막다 block; contain; hold back; prevent

nakttae 막대 rod, stick

makttaegi 막대기 bar, stick

makttaegi sat'ang 막대기 사탕 lollipop

makttaehan 막대한 huge, incalculable

makttarŭda 막다르다 be closed off

makttarŭn kil 막다른 길 cul-de-sac

makttarŭn kolmok 막다른 골목 blind alley

mak'ida 막히다 clog up

mak'ige hada 막히게 하다 clog up

mak'im 막힘 congestion

mak'yŏ innŭn kŏt 막혀있는 것 blockage

mal 말 horse; piece (*in board game*); end; word; *idal mare* 이달 말에 at the end of this month; *ch'irwŏl mal* 칠월 말 at the end of July

malbŏl 말벌 wasp; hornet

malch'amgyŏnhada 말참견하다 chip in, interrupt

malda 말다 stop; *kŭnŭn kŭgose salge toego marat-tta* 그는 그곳에 살게 되고 말았다 he finished up living there; *hwanaeji mallagu* 화내지 말라구 don't get angry

maldaekkuhada 말대꾸하다 answer back

maldat'um 말다툼 disagreement, squabble

maldat'umhada 말다툼하다 argue, squabble, bicker

maldŏdŭm 말더듬 stammer

maldo andoenda! 말도 안된다! that's out of the question!

maldo an toenŭn sori 말도 안 되는 소리 nonsense

malgajida 맑아지다 settle; brighten up

malgŭm 맑음 brightness; clearness

malgŭn 맑은 clear; pure; fine

malgup 말굽 horseshoe

malgwallyang-i 말괄량이 tomboy

malkkŭmhan 말끔한 trim, neat

malktta 맑다 be clear; be clean; be honest

Malleiŏ 말레이어 Malay (*language*)

Malleishia 말레이시아 Malaysia ◊ Malaysian

Malleishia saram 말레이시아 사람 Malay (*person*)

mallida 말리다 dry; dissuade; break up *fight*

mallin 말린 dried *fruit etc*

mallin chadu 말린 자두 prune

mallo wihyŏp'ada 말로 위협하다 browbeat

malssong 말썽 disturbance, trouble; *malssŏng-ŭl purida* 말썽을 부리다 cause trouble, make a fuss

malssŏng-i nada 말썽이 나다 get into trouble

malssŏngkkun 말썽꾼 troublemaker

malsso 말소 deletion

malssuga chŏgŭn 말수가 적은 reserved

malssuk'aejida 말쑥해지다 clean up, wash

malssuk'age hada 말쑥하게 하다 smarten up

malttugŭro chijihada 말뚝으로 지지하다 stake, support

malttuk 말뚝 stake, peg

malttuk ult'ari 말뚝 울타리 picket fence

malt'u 말투 speech, way of speaking

Malŭk'ŭsŭjuŭi 마르크스주의 Marxism

mamalleidŭ 마마레이드 marmalade

mamurihada 마무리하다 finalize, round off

man 만 bay, inlet; gulf; ten thousand ◊ after ◊ only, just

manaya 많아야 at (the) most

manbarhada 만발하다 come into full bloom

manch'an 만찬 dinner; feast

manch'an sonnim 만찬 손님 dinner guest

manch'wihan 만취한 drunken

mandŭlda 만들다 ◊ establish, create, form, make ◊ (*causative*): *...ge mandŭlda* ...게 만들다 make

mandu 만두 stuffed dumpling

manek'ing 마네킹 mannequin (*for clothes*)

mang-aji 망아지 colt

mangboda 망보다 keep watch

mangbogi 망보기 lookout

mangch'i 망치 hammer

mangch'ida 망치다 destroy; ruin; spoil

mangch'ijirhada 망치질하다 hammer

mangch'yŏnot'a 망쳐놓다 mess up, spoil; *sŏt'urŭge haesŏ mangch'yŏbŏrida* 서투르게 해서 망쳐버리다 botch, bungle

manggattŭrida 망가뜨리다 ruin

manghada 망하다 fail, fold

man-gi 만기 termination

man-gidoeda 만기되다 expire

man-giga toeda 만기가 되다 mature; run out

mangmyŏng 망명 exile, asylum

mangmyŏngja 망명자 exile (*person*)

mangnani 망나니 bum (*person*)

man-gok 만곡 bend, sweep

mangsa k'ŏt'ŭn 망사 커튼 net curtain

mangsang 망상 myth

mangshinshik'ida 망신시키다 shame, bring dishonor on

mangsŏrida 망설이다 hesitate; *tu taean saiesŏ mangsŏrida* 두 대안 사이에서 망설이다 be torn between two alternatives

mangsŏrim 망설임 hesitation

mang-wŏn-gyŏng 망원경 telescope

mang-wŏn lenjŭ 망원 렌즈 telephoto lens

manhada 만하다 be worth; deserve to; *ilgŭl/pol manhada* 읽을/볼 만하다 be worth reading/seeing; *chumŏngmanhan tol* 주먹만한 돌 a rock the size of your fist

manhwa 만화 cartoon

manhwa chaptchi 만화 잡지 comic (book)

manhwa ch'aek 만화 책 comic book

manhwaran 만화란 comics; comic strip

manhwa yŏnghwa 만화 영화 cartoon

mani 많이 a lot, lots, a good deal; much; *aju mani* 아주 많이 very much; *mani tŭseyo* 많이 드세요 please help yourself; enjoy

manjang-ilch'ihada 만장일치하다 be unanimous on

manjang-ilch'iro 만장일치로 unanimously

manjang-ilch'iŭi 만장일치의

unanimous

anjida 만지다 touch, feel

anjijak-kkŏrida 만지작거리다 meddle with, tinker with

anjo 만조 high tide

anjok 만족 satisfaction, contentment; pleasure; *muŏsesŏ manjogŭl nŭkkida* 무엇에서 만족을 느끼다 get satisfaction out of sth

anjok-kkam 만족감 feeling of satisfaction, fulfillment

anjokssshik'ida 만족시키다 satisfy, gratify

anjokssshik'igi 만족시키기 gratification

anjokssŭrŏun 만족스러운 adequate; fulfilling

anjok'ada 만족하다 be satisfied; content oneself with; feel fulfilled; *...ŭro manjok'ada* ...으로 만족하다 make do with

anjok'an 만족한 satisfactory; pleased

anjok'anŭn 만족하는 content

ank'ŭm 만큼 as; *...mank'ŭm chal hada* ...만큼 잘 하다 be as good as; measure up to; *...mank'ŭm mani* ...만큼 많이 as much as ...

annanda 만나다 meet, meet with; join

annaeda 맛내다 flavor

annal kwŏllirŭl kat-tta 만날 권리를 갖다 have access to *one's children*

annam 만남 meeting

annasŏ pan-gapssŭmnida 만나서 반갑습니다 pleased to meet you; glad to see you

annŭn 맞는 correct, right; *kŭgŏsŭn uriŭi kyehoege tŭrŏ mannŭnda* 그것은 우리의 계획에 들어 맞는다 it fits in well with our plans

annŭng 만능 versatility

annŭng-ŭi 만능의 versatile, all-round

annŭn saenghwarŭl hada 맞는 생활을 하다 live up to

mannyŏnp'il 만년필 (fountain) pen

mansa 만사 everything

mansa p'yŏnanhan 만사 편안한

hunky-dory

manse! 만세! hurray!

mansŏng-ŭi 만성의 chronic

mant'a 많다 be many

manŭl 마늘 garlic

manŭn 많은 many, a lot of, lots of; much; plenty of; heavy

manŭn chŏngdo 많은 정도 number, quantity

manŭn shigani kŏllinŭn 많은 시간이 걸리는 time-consuming

manura 마누라 wife

manyak ...myŏn 만약 ...면 if; on condition that; *manyak tarŭn hal iri ŏpttamyŏn* 만약 다른 할 일이 없다면 if you've got nothing else to do

manyŏ 마녀 witch

manyŏn 만연 spread; diffusion

manyŏn chashil 망연 자실 stupor

manyŏndoen 만연된 widespread

manyŏnhada 만연하다 spread

Map'ia chojik 마피아 조직 the Mafia

marat'on 마라톤 marathon

marhada 말하다 talk; speak; say; tell; *hago ship'ŭn marŭl hada* 하고 싶은 말을 하다 have one's say

marhagi choahanŭn 말하기 좋아하는 talkative; communicative

marhanŭn nŭngnyŏk 말하는 능력 speech (*ability to speak*)

marharyŏhada 말하려하다 get at; imply; mean

mari 마리 countword for animals

mari andwaeyo 말이 안돼요 not make sense

marihwana 마리화나 marijuana

mari manŭn 말이 많은 talkative

mari nan-gime 말이 난김에 incidentally

maronie yŏlmae 마로니에 열매 horse chestnut

marŭda 마르다 dry; waste away; run out (*of money*)

Marŭk'ŭsŭjuŭija 마르크스주의자 Marxist (*person*)

Marŭk'ŭsŭjuŭiŭi 마르크스주의의 Marxist

marŭl kkŏnaeda 말을 꺼내다 bring up, broach

marŭl kollasŏ ssŭda 말을 골라서 쓰다 put into words, formulate

marŭl ttokttok'i mot'anŭn 말을 똑똑히 못하는 inarticulate

marŭl tŭt-tchi annŭn 말을 듣지 않는 disobedient

marŭl t'ago 말을 타고 on horseback

marŭmjil 마름질 cut

marŭmmokkol 마름모꼴 lozenge

marŭn 마른 dry; thin

marŭn haengju 마른 행주 tea cloth, dishcloth

maru 마루 brow

maru kŏlle 마루 걸레 floor cloth

marutppadak 마룻바닥 floor

maryŏk 마력 horsepower

maryŏnhada 마련하다 lay on, provide

masaji 마사지 massage

mashi chinhan 맛이 진한 rich

mashida 마시다 drink

mashil su innŭn 마실 수 있는 drinkable

mashimaello 마시맬로 marshmallow

mashinnŭn 맛있는 tasty, delicious

mashinŭn mul 마시는 물 drinking water

mashitkke tŭseyo! 맛있게 드세요! enjoy!

mashyŏbŏrida 마셔버리다 consume, drink

masŭk'ara 마스카라 mascara

masŭk'ot'ŭ 마스코트 mascot

masul 마술 magic; conjuring tricks

masuljŏgin 마술적인 magical

masulssa 마술사 magician, conjurer

masurŭi 마술의 magic

mat 맛 flavor, taste; *ammu mat ŏmnŭn* 아무 맛 없는 tasteless *food*

match'uda 맞추다 adjust; fit together; be fitting; be appropriate; *ch'aenŏrŭl match'uda* 채널을 맞추다 tune in; *kŭe match'uŏ* 그에 맞추어 accordingly, appropriately

match'ugi 맞추기 justify *text*

match'umbŏp kŏmsagi 맞춤법 검사기 spell checker

match'um k'ap'et 맞춤 카펫 wall-to-wall carpet

match'um puŏk 맞춤 부엌 fitted kitchen

match'umŭi 맞춤의 custom-made, tailor-made

match'uŏ not'a 맞추어 놓다 set; adjust

matkkida 맡기다 entrust

matpakkuda 맞바꾸다 exchange

matppadach'igi 맞받아치기 tit for tat

matpparam 맞바람 headwind

matppoda 맛보다 taste, sample

matpput'ŏ ssauda 맞붙어 싸우다 grapple with

matssŏda 맞서다 meet, confront, stand up to; retaliate

mattakttŭrida 맞닥뜨리다 meet with

mattanghage 마땅하게 justly, deservedly

mattanghan 마땅한 due, proper

mattanghan shillangkkam 마땅한 신랑감 eligible bachelor

mat-tchi ant'a 맞지 않다 be alien to

mat-tta 맞다 be right; fit, go in; take on *job*; suit; match; strike, hit; meet be exposed to; encounter; be struck by; get, have; *mat-tchiyo?* 맞지요? that's right, isn't it?; *chal mat-tta* 잘 맞다 it's a good fit

mat-ttakttŭrida 맞닥뜨리다 encounter

maŭl 마을 village

maŭl saram 마을 사람 villager

maŭm 마음 heart; mind; spirit; *kŭgŏshi maŭme kŏllyŏssŏyo* 그것이 마음에 걸렸어요 it has been on my conscience; *maŭmi t'onghaetkkunyo!* 마음이 통했군요 you must be telepathic!; *hyŏmnyŏktchŏgin maŭmŭro* 협력적인 마음으로 in a spirit of cooperation; *maŭm p'yŏnhage saenggak'ae!* 마음 편하게 생각해! relax!

maŭmdaero 마음대로: *nuguŭi maŭmdaero toeda* 누구의 마음대로 되다 be at s.o.'s mercy; *muŏsŭl maŭmdaero hada* 무엇을 마음대로 하다 be at liberty to do sth; *maŭmdaero haseyo!* 마음대로 하세요! do what you like!, suit yourself!; *Xŭl / rŭl Yŭi maŭmdaero ssŭge hada* X을/를 Y의 마음대로

쓰게 하다 put X at Y's disposal
naŭme mannŭn 마음에 맞는 congenial, pleasant
naŭme p'umtta 마음에 품다 harbor grudge
naŭme tŭlda 마음에 들다 be to s.o.'s liking
naŭme tuda 마음에 두다 mind, heed
naŭmi chobŭn 마음이 좁은 narrow-minded
naŭmi mŏrŏjida 마음이 멀어지다 drift apart (emotionally)
naŭmi naek'iji annŭn 마음이 내키지 않는 half-hearted; disinclined; listless
naŭmi nŏlbŭn 마음이 넓은 liberal, broad-minded
naŭmi nugŭrŏjida 마음이 누그러지다 relent
naŭmi ŏjirŏun 마음이 어지러운 disturbed, concerned, worried
naŭm kabyŏun 마음 가벼운 light-hearted
naŭmkkŏt tŭlda 마음껏 들다 help oneself
naŭm soge ttŏollida 마음 속에 떠올리다 visualize
naŭmsogŭro 마음속으로 inwardly; privately; mentally
naŭmsshi koun 마음씨 고운 kind-hearted
naŭmŭi 마음의 mental
naŭmŭi sangch'ŏrŭl ibŭn 마음의 상처를 입은 broken-hearted
naŭmŭl chŏnghada 마음을 정하다 make up one's mind
naŭmŭl karaanch'ida 마음을 가라앉히다 pull oneself together, compose oneself
naŭmŭl ŏjirŏp'ida 마음을 어지럽히다 disturb, upset
naŭmŭl ŏjirŏp'inŭn 마음을 어지럽히는 disturbing, upsetting
naŭmŭl pakkuda 마음을 바꾸다 change one's mind
naŭmŭl pakkuge hada 마음을 바꾸게 하다 cause to change his/her mind
naŭmŭl p'yŏnhi noch'i mot'ada 마음을 편히 놓지 못하다 feel ill at

ease
maŭmŭl sanghage hada 마음을 상하게 하다 hurt feelings
maŭmŭl sarojaptta 마음을 사로잡다 captivate, enthrall
maŭmŭl t'ŏnot'a 마음을 터놓다 come out of one's shell
maundŭ 마운드 mound (in baseball)
mausŭ 마우스 mouse COMPUT
mausŭ maet'ŭ 마우스 매트 mouse mat
mayagŭl hada 마약을 하다 be on drugs
mayak 마약 narcotic, drug; dope
mayak kŏrae 마약 거래 drug trafficking
mayak milmaehada 마약 밀매하다 push drugs
mayak milmaeja 마약 밀매자 pusher (of drugs)
mayak p'anmaeja 마약 판매자 drug dealer
mayak sang-yongja 마약 상용자 drug addict
mayak tansokppan 마약 단속반 narcotics agent
mayak tillŏ 마약 딜러 (drug) dealer
mayonejŭ 마요네즈 mayo, mayonnaise
meari 메아리 echo
medal 메달 medal
medŭlli 메들리 medley
megabait'ŭ 메가바이트 megabyte
meilbakssŭ 메일박스 mailbox
meilmŏji 메일머지 mail merge
meinbodŭ 메인보드 mainboard
Meksshik'o 멕시코 Mexico ◊ Mexican
melodi 멜로디 melody
melodŭramagat'ŭn 멜로드라마같은 melodramatic
melon 멜론 melon
melppang 멜빵 suspenders (for pants)
melppang paji 멜빵 바지 dungarees
memo 메모 note; memo
memojich'ŏp 메모지첩 notepad
memori 메모리 memory COMPUT
menyu 메뉴 menu also COMPUT
Meri K'ŭrisŭmasŭ 메리 크리스마스! Merry Christmas!

mesiji 메시지 message
mesŭkkŏun 메스꺼운 repulsive
mettugi 메뚜기 grasshopper; locust
meuda 메우다 fill in
mianhae 미안해 (I'm) sorry
mianhamnida 미안합니다 *fml* (I'm) sorry
mibongjŏgŭro koch'ida 미봉적으로 고치다 patch up
mibul 미불 nonpayment
miburŭi 미불의 outstanding *payment*
mich'ida 미치다 become insane; be crazy; reach; happen; match
mich'idŭshi choahada 미치듯이 좋아하다 be mad about, be enthusiastic about
mich'igwang-i 미치광이 lunatic, madman
mich'il tŭshi hwanage hada 미칠 듯이 화나게 하다 madden, infuriate, drive crazy
mich'il tŭshi hwanan 미칠 듯이 화난 mad, angry
mich'il tŭt'an 미칠 듯한 distraught
mich'in 미친 insane, mad, crazy
mich'in tŭshi 미친 듯이 madly, like mad
mich'in tŭt'an 미친 듯한 wild, crazy, frantic
mich'ŏribun 미처리분 backlog
mich'yŏgada 미쳐가다 become insane, go mad
midaji mun 미닫이 문 sliding door
midiŏ 미디어 media
midŏjiji annŭn 믿어지지 않는 incredible, amazing, very good
midŭl manhan 믿을 만한 credible, believable
midŭl su ŏmnŭn 믿을 수 없는 unbelievable; unreliable
midŭm 믿음 belief
midŭng 미등 tail light
migaein 미개인 savage
migaeji 미개지 the wilds
migak 미각 taste (*sense*); palate
Migugin 미국인 American (*person*)
Miguk 미국 USA, America ◊ American
Miguk chung-ang chŏngbobu 미국 중앙 정보부 CIA, Central Intelligence Agency

Miguk kukppangssŏng 미국 국방성 the Pentagon
Miguk nŏguri 미국 너구리 raccoon
Miguk saram 미국 사람 American (*person*)
migyŏltcheŭi 미결제의 unsettled, unpaid
mihaenghada 미행하다 follow, dog
Mihaptchungguk 미합중국 United States of America
mihonŭi 미혼의 unmarried
mijigŭnhan 미지근한 lukewarm, tepid
mijiroŭi yŏhaeng 미지로의 여행 journey into the unknown
mikki 미끼 bait
mikkirŭl mulda 미끼를 물다 bite (*of fish*); get a bite
mikkŭrŏjida 미끄러지다 slip, slither, skid
mikkŭrŏjiji annŭn 미끄러지지 않는 nonslip, nonskid
mikkŭrŏjida 미끄러지다 slip
mikkŭrŏm 미끄럼 skid
mikkŭrŏmt'ŭl 미끄럼틀 slide
mikkŭrŏpkke hada 미끄럽게 하다 lubricate
mikkŭrŏptta 미끄럽다 be smooth; be slippery, be slick
mikkŭrŏun 미끄러운 slippery
mikkŭrŏjida 미끄러지다 slide, glide
mikssŏ 믹서 food mixer
mikssŏgi 믹서기 blender
mil 밀 wheat
milbong 밀봉 seal
milbonghada 밀봉하다 seal
milda 밀다 push, shove
milgam 밀감 tangerine
milgi 밀기 pushing
milgoja 밀고자 informer
milgo kada 밀고 가다 push along
milkkaru 밀가루 flour
milkkaru panjuk 밀가루 반죽 dough, pastry; batter
milk'ŭ chyok'ollit 밀크 쵸콜릿 milk chocolate
milk'ŭ shweik'ŭ 밀크 쉐이크 milk shake
milligŭraem 밀리그램 milligram
millim 밀림 jungle
millimit'ŏ 밀리미터 millimeter

millyŏdŭnŭn p'ado 밀려드는 파도 surf

millyŏ it-tta 밀려있다 be behind with; be backed up

millyŏnagada 밀려나가다 surge forward

millyŏp'ada 밀렵하다 poach *rabbits etc*

milmul 밀물 incoming tide

milmurida 밀물이다 the tide is out

milsshil kongp'otchŭng 밀실 공포증 claustrophobia

milssu 밀수 smuggling

milssuhada 밀수하다 smuggle; traffic in

milssuŏptcha 밀수업자 smuggler

miltchip 밀짚 straw (*of wheat etc*)

miltchip chiyŏk 밀집 지역 crowded area

miltchip'an 밀집한 dense

miman 미만 under, below; less than

mimang-ini toen 미망인이 된 widowed

mimyohan 미묘한 subtle, delicate

mimyoham 미묘함 delicacy

minapkkŭm 미납금 arrears

minap'ada 미납하다 be in arrears

minbak 민박 vacation home

minbang-wi 민방위 civil defense

minch'ŏp'an 민첩한 snappy

mindalp'aeng-i 민달팽이 slug

min-gamhada 민감하다 be sensitive

min-gamham 민감함 sensitivity

min-gane ŭihae 민간에 의해 privately

min-ganin 민간인 civilian

min-gan pangsong 민간 방송 commercial television

min-gan pumun 민간 부문 private sector

min-ganŭi 민간의 civil

min-ganyoppŏp 민간 요법 folk medicine

mingk'ŭ 밍크 mink (*fur*)

mingk'ŭ k'ot'ŭ 밍크 코트 mink (coat)

minhwa 민화 folk painting

mini sŭk'ot'ŭ 미니 스커트 miniskirt

minjogŭi 민족의 ethnic

minjok 민족 people; race; tribe

minjokchipttan 민족집단 ethnic group

minjoktchuŭi 민족주의 nationalism

Minju Chayudang 민주 자유당 Democratic Liberal Party

Minjudang 민주당 Democratic Party

minjudang chijija 민주당 지지자 democrat

Minjudang-wŏn 민주당원 Democrat

minjujuŭi 민주주의 democracy

minjujuŭija 민주주의자 democrat

minjujuŭiŭi 민주주의의 democratic

minjung shinhak 민중 신학 people's theology

minmurŭi 민물의 freshwater

minsok ch'um 민속 춤 folk dance

minsok ŭmak 민속 음악 folk music

mint'ŭ 민트 mint

mint'ŭ chyok'ollit 민트 쵸콜릿 mint

minyo 민요 folk song

minyo kasu 민요 가수 folk singer

mirae 미래 future; *miraeŭi kyehoek / saenggak* 미래에의 계획 / 생각 plan / think ahead

miraehyŏngŭi 미래형의 futuristic

mirhanghada 밀항하다 stow away

mirhangja 밀항자 stowaway

miri 미리 beforehand, in advance

miribogi 미리보기 print preview COMPUT

miri haenghaejida 미리 행해지다 precede

miri mandŭrŏjyŏ innŭn 미리 만들어져 있는 ready-made

miri naeda 미리 내다 advance

miri sŏltchŏngdoen 미리 설정된 default (setting)

mirŏ chech'ida 밀어 제치다 push away

mirŏdakch'yŏ it-tta 밀어닥쳐 있다 be swamped with

mirŏnaeda 밀어내다 shove off, push off; pump

mirŏnŏt'a 밀어넣다 slide; cram

mirŏ puch'ida 밀어 붙이다 squeeze up

mirŏ umjigida 밀어 움직이다 wheel

miro 미로 maze

Mirŭkppul 미륵불 Maitreya Buddha

miruda 미루다 wait

misa 미사 mass

misaegŭi
150

misaegŭi 미색의 off-white
misaengmure ŭihae punhaega toenŭn 미생물에 의해 분해가 되는 biodegradable
misail 미사일 missile
misayŏguŭi 미사여구의 flowery
misehan 미세한 fine
Mishik ch'uk-kku 미식 축구 (American) football
Mishik ch'uk-kku kyŏnggijang 미식 축구 경기장 gridiron
Mishik ch'uk-kku sŏnsu 미식 축구 선수 (American) football player
mishin 미신 superstition
mishinŭl minnŭn 미신을 믿는 superstitious
misŏngnyŏnja 미성년자 minor (child)
misŏngnyŏnjaida 미성년자이다 be underage
misŏngnyŏnŭi 미성년의 underage
misŏngsugŭi 미성숙의 immature
miso 미소 smile
misojit-tta 미소짓다 smile; smile at
misshik-kka 미식가 gourmet
misuga 미숙아 premature baby
misuk'an 미숙한 immature, juvenile; unskilled
misulga 미술가 artist, painter
misulgwan 미술관 art gallery
misungnyŏn nodongja 미숙련 노동자 unskilled labor
mit 밑 base, bottom
mitchul kŭt-tta 밑줄 긋다 underline
mitkkŭrim 밑그림 design
mitppadagŭro ttŏrŏjida 밑바닥으로 떨어지다 reach rock bottom
mitppadak 밑바닥 bottom, underside
mit-tta 믿다 believe
mit'e 밑에 underneath; chang-ŭi/ŏndŏgŭi mit'e 장의/언덕의 밑에 at the foot of the page/hill
mit'ing 미팅 meeting, session; blind date
mit'ŏ 미터 meter
mit'ŏppŏbŭi 미터법의 metric
mit'ŭ 미트 mitt
mit'ŭro tŏnjyŏ 밑으로 던져 underarm throwing
mium 미움 hate
miwallyo 미완료 imperfect

miwŏhada 미워하다 hate
miyak'an 미약한 feeble
miyak'an chinghu 미약한 징후 hint
miyongsa 미용사 beautician; hairdresser
miyongshil 미용실 beauty parlor
mŏdŏmnŭn 멋없는 tasteless
mŏgi 먹이 prey
mŏgida 먹이다 feed
mŏgirŭl chuda 먹이를 주다 feed
mŏgŏbŏrida 먹어버리다 consume, eat up
mŏgŏboda 먹어보다 try food
mŏgŏ ch'iuda 먹어 치우다 eat up
mŏgŭjan 머그잔 mug
mŏgŭl su innŭn 먹을 수 있는 edible
mŏgŭl su ŏmnŭn 먹을 수 없는 uneatable
mŏk-kkie chot'a 먹기에 좋다 nice to eat
mŏk-kko salda 먹고 살다 live on food
mŏktta 먹다 eat, have
mŏlda 멀다 be distant, be remote; be unskilled
mŏlli 멀리 far, far away ◊ remotely
mŏlli ttŏrŏjim 멀리 떨어짐 seclusion
mŏlli ttŏrŏjin 멀리 떨어진 far away, remote
mŏlli ttŏrŏjyŏ hanjŏk'an 멀리 떨어져 한적한 secluded
mŏlli ttŏrŏjyŏ it-tta 멀리 떨어져 있다 it's a long way off
mŏlli ttwigi 멀리 뛰기 broad jump, long jump
mŏlmiga chal nanŭn 멀미가 잘 나는 squeamish
mŏlt'imidiŏ 멀티미디어 multimedia
mŏmch'uda 멈추다 stop; stall; seize up; put a stop to
mŏmch'uge hada 멈추게 하다 stop, halt, bring to a standstill
mŏmch'ul su ŏmnŭn 멈출 수 없는 remorseless, relentless
mŏmch'um chŏngji 멈춤 정지 no stopping
mŏmch'um shinho 멈춤 신호 stop sign
mŏmch'un 멈춘 be at a standstill
mŏmullŏ it-tta 머물러 있다 stick around

nŏmurŭda 머무르다 stay

nŏn 먼 distant, remote

nŏng 멍 bruise

nŏngch'ŏng-i 멍청이 idiot, dope, jerk

nŏngdŭlda 멍들다 bruise

nŏngdŭlge hada 멍들게 하다 bruise

nŏngdŭn nun 멍든 눈 black eye

nŏng-e 멍에 yoke (for oxen)

nŏnghage hada 멍하게 하다 stupefy

nŏnghan 멍한 vacant, blank, absent-minded

nŏngk'i sŭp'aenŏ 멍키 스패너 monkey wrench

nŏngmŏng-i 멍멍이 doggie

nŏngnŭn p'iimyak 먹는 피임약 the (contraceptive) pill

nŏnji 먼지 dirt; grit; dust

nŏnji magi tŏpkkae 먼지 막이 덮개 dust cover

nŏnjirŭl t'ŏlda 먼지를 털다 dust

nŏnji tangnŭn hŏnggŏp 먼지 닦는 헝겊 duster

nŏnjit'usŏng-iŭi 먼지투성이의 dusty

nŏnjŏ 먼저 first

nŏnjŏtppŏnŭi 먼젓번의 past, former

nŏn kose(sŏ) 먼 곳에(서) in the distance

nŏp'in 머핀 muffin

nŏri 머리 head; hair; **mŏrirŭl tchada** 머리를 짜다 rack one's brains

mŏriga nappŭn 머리가 나쁜 not clever

mŏriga pŏtkkyŏjinŭn 머리가 벗겨지는 balding

mŏriga saltchak ton 머리가 살짝 돈 be slightly crazy

mŏrihyŏng 머리형 hairstyle, hairdo

mŏri indu 머리 인두 tongs

mŏri kamtta 머리 감다 shampoo

mŏrikkŭch'i tchuppyŏt'aejinŭn 머리끝이 쭈뼛해지는 hair-raising

mŏrik'arak 머리카락 hair

mŏri manŭn lol 머리 마는 롤 roller (for hair)

mŏrinmal 머릿말 header (in text)

mŏri patch'im 머리 받침 headrest

mŏrip'in 머리핀 hairpin

mŏriro pat-tta 머리로 받다 head ball; head-butt; bump one's head

mŏrirŭl charŭda 머리를 자르다 have a haircut, get one's hair cut

mŏrirŭl handae mat-tta 머리를 한대 맞다 get a bump on the head

mŏrirŭl sonjirhada 머리를 손질하다 have one's hair done

mŏri sŭk'ap'ŭ 머리 스카프 headscarf

mŏritkkajuk 머리가죽 scalp

mŏritkkisa 머릿기사 headline

mŏritkkisaro k'ŭge ch'wigŭpttoeda 머릿기사로 크게 취급되다 make the headlines

mŏshinnŭn 멋있는 stylish

mŏsŭl chal naenŭn 멋을 잘 내는 fashionable

mŏtchida 멋지다 be stylish

mŏtchige 멋지게 impeccably

mŏtchin 멋진 smart, elegant; stylish; nice, lovely

mŏt-tta 멎다 let up; stop

mo 모 countword for tofu

moanot'a 모아놓다 collect

mobang 모방 imitation, copying; copy

mobanghada 모방하다 imitate, copy

mobang pŏmjoe 모방 범죄 copycat crime

mobil 모빌 cell phone, Br mobile

mobŏmjŏgin 모범적인 exemplary

mobŏmŭi 모범의 model, perfect

modakppul 모닥불 camp fire

model 모델 model

modem 모뎀 modem

moderida 모델이다 be a model, model

moderŭl hada 모델을 하다 model clothes

modok 모독 violation

modok'ada 모독하다 violate; blaspheme

modŭ 모드 mode COMPUT

modŭn 모든 all; whole; every

modŭn kwanshimŭl ssot-tta 모든 관심을 쏟다 make a fuss of

modu 모두 everyone; all

mogi 모기 mosquito

mogihyang 모기향 mosquito coil

mogijang 모기장 mosquito net

mogi maeida 목이 매이다 choke

mogi marŭda 목이 마르다 be thirsty

mogi t'ada 목이 타다 be parched

mogong 모공 pore
mogŭl charŭda 목을 자르다 decapitate
mogŭl chorŭda 목을 조르다 choke
mogŭl kilge ppaeda 목을 길게 빼다 crane one's neck
mogŭl kkolttak-kkŏrida 목을 꼴딱거리다 gurgle
mogŭl ppida 목을 빼다 have a crick in the neck
mogugŏ 모국어 native language, mother tongue
moguk 모국 native country
mogyeŭi 모계의 maternal
mogyoil 목요일 Thursday
mogyok 목욕 bath
mogyok kaun 목욕 가운 bathrobe
mogyok sugŏn 목욕 수건 bath towel
mogyokt'ang 목욕탕 public bathhouse
mogyokt'ang kkalgae 목욕탕 깔개 bath mat
mogyok'ada 목욕하다 have a bath, bathe
mohŏm 모험 venture; adventure
mohŏmjŏk 모험적 adventurous
mohŏmŭl chŭlginŭn 모험을 즐기는 adventurous person
mohŏmŭl hada 모험을 하다 venture; take the plunge
mohoesa 모회사 parent company, holding company
mohohage 모호하게 vaguely
mohohan 모호한 vague
mohyŏng 모형 model, miniature; mock-up
mohyŏng-ŭi 모형의 model
moida 모이다 meet; congregate; accumulate
moim 모임 gathering
moirŭl tchoda 모이를 쪼다 pick at one's food
moisch'yŏraijŏ 모이스처라이저 moisturizer
moja 모자 hat
mojaik'ŭ 모자이크 mosaic
mojarada 모자라다 be short of, be wanting in; be stupid
mojaran 모자란 useless
mojaranŭn 모자라는 scarce; chigwŏni mojaranŭn 직원이

모자라는 short-staffed
mojik 모직 woolen
mojim 모짐 severity
mojin 모진 severe
mojingmul 모직물 woolen fabric
mojohada 모조하다 forge
mojo posŏngnyu 모조 보석류 costume jewelry
mojop'um 모조품 imitation
mojori 모조리 without exception; completely
mok 목 neck; throat
mok 몫 share, quota
mokch'oji 목초지 field
mokch'ugŏptcha 목축업자 stockbreeder
mok-kkŏri 목걸이 necklace, pendant
mok-kkŏrijul 목걸이줄 chain (jewelry)
mok-kkong 목공 woodwork
mok-kkwanak-kki 목관악기 woodwind
mok-kkyŏktcha 목격자 (eye)witness
mok-kkyŏk'ada 목격하다 witness
mokkumŏng 목구멍 throat
mokp'yo 목표 objective, goal, target
mokp'yo kŭrup 목표 그룹 target group
mokp'yo magamil 목표 마감일 target date
mokp'yoro hada 목표로 하다 target
mokp'yoro samtta 목표로 삼다 aim at; aim to
mok sat'ang 목 사탕 throat lozenges
mokssa 목사 priest
moksshwin 목쉰 hoarse
mokssŏn 목선 neckline
mokssori 목소리 voice, tone of voice k'ŭn mokssoriro 큰 목소리로 in a loud voice
mokssu 목수 joiner, carpenter
moktchae 목재 timber
moktchang 목장 ranch
moktchangju 목장주 rancher
moktchŏgŏ 목적어 object GRAM
moktchŏk 목적 objective, aim; ...l moktchŏgŭro ...ㄹ 목적으로 with a view to
moktchŏktchi 목적지 destination
moktcho pubun 목조 부분 woodwork, wooden part

moktchorŭda 목조르다 throttle
mokttari 목다리 crutch
mokttŏlmi 목덜미 nape of the neck
mokttori 목도리 scarf, muffler
mokt'an 목탄 charcoal
molda 몰다 drive
molgo tanida 몰고 다니다 kick around
mollae 몰래 secretly, privately; furtively
mollae hanŭn 몰래 하는 stealthy
mollae pekkida 몰래 베끼다 (secretly) copy
mollak 몰락 comedown; downfall
molmon-gyo 몰몬교 Mormonism
molttudoen 몰두된 engrossed in
molttuhada 몰두하다 immerse oneself in; *ire molttuhada* 일에 몰두하다 bury oneself in work
molttuhan 몰두한 preoccupied, absorbed
mom 몸 body; *onmomi ssushida* 온몸이 쑤시다 it hurts all over
momburimch'ida 몸부림치다 writhe, thrash about; struggle
mome kkok mannŭn 몸에 꼭 맞는 skin-tight
momi choch'i anŭn 몸이 좋지 않은 unwell, poorly
momi chot'a 몸이 좋다 feel well
momi pulp'yŏnhan 몸이 불편한 indisposed, unwell
momi tchibudŭdŭhada 몸이 찌부드드하다 be feeling under the weather
momjorishik'ida 몸조리시키다 take good care of
momkkap 몸값 ransom
mommae 몸매 figure, physique
mommae ch'itssu 몸매 치수 vital statistics
momsŏrich'ida 몸서리치다 shudder
momsusaek'ada 몸수색하다 frisk
momtchibi chagŭn 몸집이 작은 petite
momtchit ŏnŏ 몸짓 언어 body language
momttung-i 몸뚱이 trunk
momŭi 몸의 bodily
momŭl kuburida 몸을 구부리다 slouch; crouch

momŭl umsshirhada 몸을 움찔하다 cringe
momŭro 몸으로 bodily
momyŏnhada 모면하다 escape; avoid, evade
monaegi 모내기 rice planting
Monggo 몽고 Mongolia ◊ Mongolian
mongmarŭda 목마르다 be thirsty
mongmarŭn 목마른 thirsty
mongnoge ollida 목록에 올리다 list, put on a list
mongnok 목록 list, roll, inventory
mongnyuppyŏngja 몽유병자 sleep walker
mongsangga 몽상가 (day)dreamer
mongsanghada 몽상하다 (day)dream
mongttang chŏjŏt-tta 몽땅 젖었다 wet through
moning k'ol 모닝 콜 wake-up call
monit'ŏ 모니터 monitor COMPUT
monmŏri 못머리 head
monsun 몬순 monsoon
monsun kyejŏl 몬순 계절 monsoon season
mopsshi 몹시 very, terribly
morae 모래 sand
morae chumŏni 모래 주머니 sandbag
morae ŏndŏk 모래 언덕 sand dune
moraep'an 모래판 sandpit
moraesaegŭi 모래색의 sandy *color*
moranaeda 몰아내다 repel
more 모레 the day after tomorrow
mori 몰이 round-up
morinjŏnghan 몰인정한 inhuman
morŭda 모르다 not know; be ignorant of; not appreciate; ignore; *morŭgessŭmnida* 모르겠습니다 I don't know; *naega kŏŭi morŭnŭn kŏt* 내가 거의 모르는 것 the little I know ◊ *...Itchido morŭnda* ...ㄹ지도 모른다 ...may, might; *kŭ yŏjaga kaltchido morŭnda* 그 여자가 갈지도 모른다 I don't know whether she'll go, she may go
morŭmot'ŭ 모르모트 guinea pig
morŭnŭn 모르는 strange, unknown; ignorant
morŭp'in 모르핀 morphine

moshida 모시다 attend to, serve; accompany, escort

moshinnŭn mŏtjinŭn 멋있는 good-looking *man*

mosŏng 모성 motherhood

mosŏri 모서리 edge

mossaenggida 못생기다 be ugly

mosshi 모씨: *Pak mosshi* 박 모씨 a certain Mr Park

mosun 모순 contradiction; discrepancy

mosundoen 모순된 contradictory

mosundoenŭn 모순되는 inconsistent

mot 못 nail; peg

mot... 못... cannot; *...ji mot'ada* ...지 못하다 be unable to, cannot

motppoda 못보다 overlook

mot salge kulda 못 살게 굴다 bully

motssaenggin 못생긴 plain, homely

mot-ttoen 못된 nasty; *mot-ttoen chisŭl hada* 못된 짓을 하다 be up to something (bad)

mot'age hada 못하게 하다 discourage; stop, prevent

mot'el 모텔 motel

mot'ŏ 모터 motor

mot'ŏbot'ŭ 모터보트 motorboat

mot'o 모토 motto

mot'ung-i 모퉁이 turning, turn, corner

mot'ung-irŭl tolda 모퉁이를 돌다 turn a corner; corner (*of vehicle*)

moŭda 모으다 collect; gather; accumulate; save; *chogagŭl moŭda* 조각을 모으다 piece together

moŭi 모의 scheme

moŭihada 모의하다 scheme

moŭiŭi 모의의 mock

moŭm 모음 vowel

moŭn 모은 collected

moyang 모양 appearance, look; shape

moyŏ it-tta 모여 있다 be gathered together; be crowded

moyok 모욕 insult

moyok'ada 모욕하다 insult

moyurŭl mŏgida 모유를 먹이다 breastfeed

mu 무 nil

mu... 무... non...

mu 무 radish

muak 무악 shamanistic music

mubangbiŭi 무방비의 defenseless, unprotected

mubŏbŭi 무법의 disorderly; lawless

mubunbyŏl 무분별 indiscretion

mubunbyŏrhan 무분별한 indiscreet

much'abyŏrŭi 무차별의 indiscriminate

much'aegimhan 무책임한 irresponsible

much'ŏk 무척 extremely; *much'ŏk ttokttok'an* 무척 똑똑한 brilliant, very intelligent

much'ŏkch'u tongmul 무척추 동물 invertebrate

mudae 무대 stage

mudae paegyŏng 무대 배경 scenery, scenes

mudang 무당 shaman (*female*)

mudangbŏlle 무당벌레 ladybug

mudan hwoengdan 무단 횡단 jaywalking

mudan kŏjuhada 무단 거주하다 squat (*in building*)

mudan kŏjuja 무단 거주자 squatter

mudan kyŏlssŏk'ada 무단 결석하다 play truant

mudin 무딘 blunt

mudŏm 무덤 grave, tomb

mudŏmdŏmhan 무덤덤한 impervious to

mudŭktchŏm 무득점 love (*in tennis*)

mudujirhada 무두질하다 tan *leather*

muga 무가 shaman song

mugamgak 무감각 insensitivity

mugamgak'an 무감각한 callous, insensitive; numb

muge 무게 weight

mugega nagada 무게가 나가다 weigh

mugero nullyŏjida 무게로 눌려지다 be weighed down with

mugerŭl talda 무게를 달다 weigh

mugi 무기 weapon

mugihanŭro 무기한으로 indefinitely

muginhada 묵인하다 tolerate

mugirŭl ppaeat-tta 무기를 빼앗다 disarm

mugiŭi 무기의 inorganic

mugŏptta 무겁다 be heavy; be important

nugŏun 무거운 heavy

nugŏun 무거운 weighty, hefty

nugonghaeŭi 무공해의 nonpolluting

nugŭbŭi 무급의 unpaid

Mugunghwa 무궁화 Rose of Sharon

nugunghwa nesŭi 무궁화 넷의 four-star

nugwanhada 무관하다 be unrelated; be irrelevant

nugwanshim 무관심 indifference

nugwanshimhan 무관심한 offhand, indifferent

muhaehan 무해한 harmless; inoffensive

muhan 무한 infinity

muhanhan 무한한 infinite

muhanjŏnghan 무한정한 indefinite

muhanŭi 무한의 boundless

muhŏgaŭi 무허가의 unauthorized

muhwagwa 무화과 fig

muhyŏrŭi 무혈의 bloodless

muhyohwahada 무효화하다 invalidate; overrule

muhyorohada 무효로 하다 annul, revoke

muhyoŭi 무효의 invalid, null and void

muilp'unŭi 무일푼의 penniless

muinŭi 무인의 unmanned

mujabihan 무자비한 merciless, remorseless

mujagwi ch'uch'ul kŏmsa 무작위 추출 검사 spot check

mujagwihan 무작위한 arbitrary

mujagwiro 무작위로 at random, willy-nilly; *mujagwiro kŏmsahada* 무작위로 검사하다 carry out a spot check

mujagwi saemp'ŭl 무작위 샘플 random sample

mujagwiŭi 무작위의 random

mujang haeje 무장 해제 disarmament

mujang haejeshik'ida 무장 해제시키다 disarm

mujanghan 무장한 armed

mujang kangdo 무장 강도 armed robbery; gunman

mujangshik'ida 무장시키다 arm

mujang-ŭl haejehada 무장을 해제하다 disarm

muji 무지 ignorance

mujigae 무지개 rainbow

mujilssŏ 무질서 lawlessness; confusion; disorder

mujilssŏhan 무질서한 disorganized

mujinjanghan 무진장한 inexhaustible

mujiŭi 무지의 plain

mujŏgŭi 무적의 invincible

mujŏltchehan 무절제한 immoderate

mujŏngbu sangt'ae 무정부 상태 anarchy

mujŏnghan 무정한 unfeeling

mujŏn-gi 무전기 walkie-talkie

mujŏnŭro 무전으로 by radio

mujoeimŭl sŏnŏnhada 무죄임을 선언하다 acquit

mujoero hada 무죄로 하다 acquit, clear

mujoerŭl chŭngmyŏnghada 무죄를 증명하다 exonerate, clear

mujokkŏnŭi 무조건의 unconditional

mujungnyŏgŭi 무중력의 weightless

mujungnyŏk 무중력 weightlessness

mujut'aektcha 무주택자 the homeless

mukke hada 묵게 하다 take in, put up, give accommodation

muk-kke hada 묽게 하다 dilute

mukkŏ not'a 묶어 놓다 tie down

mukkŭm 묶음 packet; *han mukkŭm* 한 묶음 batch

mukssang 묵상 meditation

mukssanghada 묵상하다 meditate

muktta 묶다 tie, tie up

mukwanshimhan 무관심한 apathetic

mul 물 water

mulbang-ul p'ojang 물방울 포장 blister pack

mulbinu 물비누 gel, liquid soap

mulbora 물보라 spray

mulch'e 물체 object

mulda 물다 bite

muldŭrida 물들이다 infect

mulgalk'wi 물갈퀴 flipper

mulgalk'wiga tallin 물갈퀴가 달린 webbed

mulgi 물기 nip, bite

mulgŏn 물건 stuff, things

mulgŭn 묽은 thin, watery

mulgŭn sup'ŭ 묽은 수프 broth, soup

mulkka 물가 shore, waterside

mulkkae 물개 seal

mulkkam 물감 paint

mulkkawa yŏndongshik'in 물가와 연동시킨 index-linked

mulkkiga marŭda 물기가 마르다 drain

mulkkirŭl ppaeda 물기를 빼다 drain

mulkkirŭl tudŭryŏ chiuda 물기를 두드려 지우다 blot (dry)

mulkkogi 물고기 fish

mulkkoktchi 물꼭지 faucet

mulkkyŏl 물결 ripple; stream

mulli ch'iryo 물리 치료 physiotherapy

mulli ch'iryosa 물리 치료사 physiotherapist

mullihak 물리학 physics

mullihaktcha 물리학자 physicist

mullŏnada 물러나다 stand down; back away; ...(ŭ)robut'ŏ mullŏna it-tta ...(으)로부터 물러나 있다 keep away from

mullon 물론 certainly, of course, sure; mullŏn andwaeji! 물론 안돼지! no way!; mullon anijyo! 물론 아니죠! of course not!

mulloniji 물론이지 no problem

mullonimnida 물론입니다 please do, by all means

mullyŏjuda 물려주다 hand down; make over

mulmangch'o 물망초 forget-me-not

mulmul kyohwan 물물 교환 barter

mulmul kyohwanhada 물물 교환하다 barter

mulnaeng-i 물냉이 watercress

mulppang-ul munŭi 물방울 무늬 spot (in pattern)

mulppurigae 물뿌리개 watering can

multchangnanŭl ch'ida 물장난을 치다 paddle

multchibi saenggida 물집이 생기다 blister

multchil 물질 matter

multchip 물집 blister

multchirŭi 물질의 material

mul t'aengk'ŭ 물 탱크 cistern

mul t'winŭn sori 물 튀는 소리 splash

mulyak 물약 mixture; medicine

mumohan 무모한 reckless

mumyŏng-ŭi 무명의 obscure; anonymous

mun 문 door; mune 문에 at the door; kagega munŭl tadat-tta 가게가 문을 닫았다 the store was shut

munbanggu 문방구 stationery

munbanggujŏm 문방구점 stationer

munch'e 문체 style (literary)

mundan 문단 paragraph

mungch'i 뭉치 bundle, wad

mungch'ida 뭉치다 unite together

mungttuk'an 뭉뚝한 stubby

munhagŭi 문학의 literary

munhak 문학 literature

munhak sŏkssa 문학 석사 Master Arts

munhakssa 문학사 arts degree

munhŏn mongnok 문헌 목록 bibliography

munhwa 문화 culture

Munhwach'eyukppu 문화체육부 Ministry of Culture and Sports

munhwajŏgin 문화적인 cultural

munhwajŏk ch'unggyŏk 문화적 충격 culture shock

Munhwa Pangsong 문화 방송 Munhwa Broadcasting Corporation MBC

munhwayesul 문화예술 the arts

munjabi 문잡이 doorknob

munjang 문장 sentence

munjangnon 문장론 syntax

munjap'yo 문자표 character set

munje 문제 problem; trouble; question; tonŭi munjeida 돈의 문제이다 it's a question of money

munje haegyŏl 문제 해결 troubleshooting, problem solving

munje haegyŏlssa 문제 해결사 troubleshooter

munjeŏpsshi 문제없이 without any problems; safely

munjeŭi 문제의 in question

munjillŏ ŏpssaeda 문질러 없애다 rub off

munjillŏ taktta 문질러 닦다 scour

munjirŭda 문지르다 rub, scrub

munkku 문구 phrase

munmaek 문맥 context; Xŭl munmaege match'wŏ /

munmaegŭl pŏsŏna poda ×을/를 문맥에 맞춰/문맥을 벗어나 보다 look at X in context / out of context

nunmaeng-ŭi 문맹의 illiterate

nunmyŏng 문명 civilization

nunŏ 문어 octopus

nunŏjida 무너지다 fall down, collapse, give way

nunŏjilttŭt'an 무너질 듯한 tumbledown

nunŏjim 무너짐 crash

nunŏttŭrida 무너뜨리다 flatten, knock out

nunppŏp 문법 grammar

nunppŏpssang-ŭi 문법상의 grammatical

nunshin 문신 tattoo

nunsŏ 문서 document

nunsŏe ŭihan myŏng-ye hweson 문서에 의한 명예 훼손 libel

nunsŏ ŏmmu 문서 업무 paperwork

nuntcha 문자 character, letter

nuntchibang 문지방 doorstep, threshold

nun tudŭrinŭn sori 문 두드리는 소리 knock

nunŭi 문의 inquiry

nunŭi 무늬 pattern, design

nunŭihada 문의하다 inquire

nunŭi innŭn 무늬 있는 patterned

nunŭng 무능 inability

nunŭnghada 무능하다 be incompetent; *muŏsŭl hanŭn kŏse munŭnghada* 무엇을 하는 것에 무능하다 be incapable of doing sth

nunŭnghage hada 무능하게 하다 incapacitate; cripple

nunŭngnyŏk 무능력 incompetence

nunŭngnyŏktcha 무능력자 incompetent, no-hoper

nunŭngnyŏk'an 무능력한 incompetent

nuŏnŭi 무언의 mute, silent; tacit

nuŏshidŭn 무엇이든 whatever; *...nŭn kosŭn muŏshidŭnji* ...는 것은 무엇이든지 whatever

nuŏshin-ga 무엇인가 something

nuŏt 무엇 something; anything; what

nuŏtppodado 무엇보다도 above all

nuran-gyŏng 물안경 goggles

nure chamgin 물에 잠긴 waterlogged

muri 무리 group; strain; form a group

muri chit-tta 무리 짓다 congregate, form a group

muri choŭn 물이 좋은 freshwater

murie ŏullida 무리에 어울리다 fit in *(with a group)*

murihada 무리하다 be unreasonable

murihage ssŭda 무리하게 쓰다 overuse *machine etc*

murihanŭn 무리하는 compulsive

murihan yogu 무리한 요구 excessive demand, tall order

murijit-tta 무리짓다 group

murirŭl hada 무리를 하다 strain; injure

muri tŭlda 물이 들다 dye; be stained; become infected

murŏboda 물어보다 question, quiz

murŏttŭtda 물어뜯다 bite off

murŭda 무르다 take back; be soft

murŭiktta 무르익다 ripen

murŭl chuda 물을 주다 water *plants, animals*

murŭl naerida 물을 내리다 flush *water*

murŭl t'ada 물을 타다 water down *liquor etc*

murŭl t'wigida 물을 튀기다 splash

murŭmp'yo 물음표 question mark

murŭp 무릎 knee; lap; *murŭp'ŭl kkulk'o* 무릎을 꿇고 down on one's knees

murŭp kkult'a 무릎 꿇다 kneel

murye 무례 rudeness, disrespect

muryehada 무례하다 be rude

muryehan 무례한 rude, disrespectful

muryŏkk'ehada 무력게하다 paralyze

muryŏk'age hada 무력하게 하다 neutralize; overpower

muryŏk'an 무력한 impotent, powerless, helpless

muryoŭi 무료의 free *(no cost)*

muryo iptchang 무료 입장 admission free

muryo kyŏnbon 무료 견본 free sample

muryoro 무료로 free of charge, for free

muryo t'onghwa 무료 통화 toll-free

muryoŭi 무료의 complimentary, free

musaengmurŭi 무생물의 inanimate
musahada 무사하다 be in safety
musahan 무사한 unharmed
musahi 무사히 safely
musahi chinagada 무사히 지나가다 blow over (of crisis)
mushi 무시 disregard
mushihada 무시하다 ignore; dismiss
mushihago 무시하고 in defiance of
mushillonja 무신론자 atheist
mushimushihan 무시무시한 dreadful; lurid; scary
mushin-gyŏnghan 무신경한 insensitive; callous
musŏn chŏnhwagi 무선 전화기 cordless phone; radio telephone
musŏnghan 무성한 overgrown
musŏng-ŭi 무성의 insincerity ◊ silent *movie*
musŏng-ŭihan 무성의한 insincere
musŏnŭi 무선의 wireless
musŏptta 무섭다 be appalling; be frightening
musŏwŏhada 무서워하다 be afraid of, be scared of
musoe 무쇠 cast iron
musoero mandŭn 무쇠로 만든 cast-iron
Musok Shinang 무속 신앙 Shamanism
musŭn 무슨 any; some; what kind of ◊ what; **musŭn il issŏyo?** 무슨 일 있어요? what's up?; **musŭn soriya?** 무슨 소리야? what are you saying?
musŭngbu 무승부 dead heat
musuhan 무수한 innumerable
musul 무술 martial arts
mut-tta 묻다 ask; **..ŭi kŭnhwang-ŭl mut-tta** ...의 근황을 묻다 ask after
muttukttuk'an 무뚝뚝한 surly; brusque
mut'e 뭍에 ashore
mut'e orŭda 뭍에 오르다 go ashore
mut'ong-ŭi 무통의 painless
muŭimi 무의미 nonsense
muŭimihan 무의미한 meaningless, pointless
mu-ŭishik 무의식 the subconscious
muŭishik sangt'aeŭi 무의식 상태의 unconscious
muŭishiktchŏgin 무의식적인

involuntary, unconscious
muyŏk 무역 business, trade
muyŏk chŏnshihoe 무역 전시회 trade fair
muyŏk-kkwan 무역관 trade mission
muyŏk pangnamhoe 무역 박람회 fair, trade show
muyŏk suji 무역 수지 balance of trade
muyŏn hwibaryu 무연 휘발유 unleaded gasoline
muyŏnŭi 무연의 lead-free
muyong 무용 dancing
muyongga 무용가 dancer
mwŏrago? 뭐라고? what?
mwŏragoyo? 뭐라고요? excuse me?
mwŏraguyo? 뭐라구요? pardon me
myŏlch'i 멸치 anchovies
myŏltchong 멸종 extinction
myŏltchongdoen 멸종된 extinct
myŏltchongshik'ida 멸종시키다 exterminate
myŏltchong wigiŭi p'umjong 멸종 위기의 품종 endangered species
myŏn 면 cotton; aspect; township
myŏndo 면도 shave
myŏndogi 면도기 shaver
myŏndohada 면도하다 shave, have a shave
myŏndohaji anŭn 면도하지 않은 unshaven
myŏndok'al 면도칼 razor
myŏndonal 면도날 razor blade
myŏndoyong pinu 면도용 비누 shaving soap
myŏndoyong sol 면도용 솔 shaving brush
myŏng 명 *countword for people*
myŏngbaek'ada 명백하다 be clear
myŏngbaek'age 명백하게 obviously
myŏngbaek'age hada 명백하게 하다 make plain, make clear
myŏngbaek'i 명백히 evidently, apparently; explicitly
myŏngdanŭi ch'ŏnmŏrie 명단의 첫머리에 at the head of the list
myŏnggihada 명기하다 specify
myŏngham 명함 business card, visiting card
myŏnghwak'age hada 명확하게 하다 clarify

nyŏnghwak'am 명확함 clarity
nyŏnghwak'an 명확한 definite; articulate
nyŏnghwak'i 명확히 expressly, explicitly; *myŏnghwak'i p'yohyŏnhada* 명확히 표현하다 express clearly
nyŏngjak 명작 masterpiece
nyŏngminhan 명민한 intelligent, sharp
nyŏngnanghada 명랑하다 be bright; be cheerful
nyŏngnyŏng 명령 command, order
nyŏngnyŏnghada 명령하다 order, command, instruct
nyŏngnyŏngjŏgin 명령적인 dictatorial
nyŏngnyŏngppŏp 명령법 imperative GRAM
nyŏngsa 명사 noun
nyŏngsang 명상 meditation
nyŏngsanghada 명상하다 meditate
nyŏngserŭl palk'ida 명세를 밝히다 itemize
nyŏngsesŏ 명세서 specifications
-nyŏnsŏ 면서 (*indicates two parallel actions*): *mashimyŏnsŏ iyagihapsshida* 마시면서 이야기합시다 let's talk over a drink
nyŏngsŏk'an 명석한 clear
nyŏngsŏng 명성 fame; standing; prestige
nyŏngsŏng-i nainnŭn 명성이 나있는 prestigious
nyŏng-ye 명예 honor
nyŏng-ye hwesonhada 명예 훼손하다 libel
nyŏng-ye t'oejiksshik'ida 명예 퇴직시키다 pension off
nyŏnhada 면하다 look onto
nyŏnhŏ pat-tta 면허 받다 be licensed
nyŏnhŏtchŭng 면허증 license
nyŏnhoe shigan 면회 시간 visiting hours
nyŏnje 면제 immunity
myŏnjedoeda 면제되다 be exempt from
myŏnjedoen 면제된 immune;

exempt
myŏnjehae chuda 면제해 주다 exempt from, excuse from
myŏnjŏk 면적 area
myŏnjŏnesŏ 면전에서 in the presence of
myŏnjŏp 면접 interview
myŏnjŏpkkwan 면접관 interviewer
myŏnjŏp'ada 면접하다 interview
myŏnmirhada 면밀하다 be detailed, be meticulous
myŏnmirhan 면밀한 rigorous
myŏnmirhi 면밀히 meticulously
myŏnmyŏch'ŭi 몇몇의 several
myŏn samuso 면사무소 township office
myŏnsejŏm 면세점 duty-free shop
myŏnsep'um 면세품 duty-free (*goods*)
myŏnseŭi 면세의 duty-free, tax-free
myŏnŭnim 며느님 (*polite*) daughter-in-law
myŏnŭri 며느리 daughter-in-law
myŏnŭro mandŭn 면으로 만든 cotton
myŏnyŏgŭi 면역의 immune
myŏnyŏk 면역 immunity
myŏnyŏk ch'egye 면역 체계 immune system
myŏt 몇 how many; how much; *onŭl myŏch'irijyo?* 오늘 몇일이죠? what's the date today?
myŏt kae 몇 개 several
myŏt pŏnina kyesok 몇 번이나 계속 time and again
myŏt pun ch'airo 몇 분 차이로 by a couple of minutes
myŏt shiimnikka? 몇 시입니까? what's the time?, what time is it?
myoan 묘안 brainwave
myohage tamtta 묘하게 닮다 have an uncanny resemblance to
myohan 묘한 uncanny
myoji 묘지 cemetery, graveyard
myojong 묘종 seedling (*of plant*)
myomok 묘목 seedling (*of tree*)
myosa 묘사 description
myosahada 묘사하다 describe
myujik'ŏl 뮤지컬 musical (*drama*)
myul 물 mule, slipper

na 나 I ◊ me ◊ mine
nabang 나방 moth
nabi 나비 butterfly
nabi nekt'ai 나비 넥타이 bow tie
nabip 납입 payment
nabip chabon 납입자본 equity capital
na chashin 나 자신 myself
nach'ehwa 나체화 nude
nach'ejuŭija 나체주의자 nudist
nach'ero 나체로 in the nude
nach'imban 나침반 compass
nach'uda 낮추다 turn down; belittle
nada 나다 it's me ◊ flare up
nadal 낟알 grain
nae 내 my
naebaet-tta 내뱉다 spit out
naebŏrida 내버리다 throw out, dump
naebŏryŏduda 내버려두다 leave alone; leave unattended
naebŏryŏdun 내버려둔 unattended
naebu 내부 inside
naebu chŏngbo 내부 정보 inside information
naebue(sŏ) 내부에(서) inside
naebu innŭn 내부에 있는 inside
naebu haeksshim chipttan 내부 핵심 집단 in-crowd
naebuin 내부인 insider
naebujŏgŭro 내부적으로 internally
naebuŭi 내부의 inner, internal
naeda 내다 provide; serve; spare; give off
naedaboda 내다보다 look out (of)
naedŏnjida 내던지다 fling, throw
naegak 내각 cabinet
naegi 내기 bet, wager; *...e naegirŭl kŏlda* ...에 내기를 걸다 bet
naegusŏng-i innŭn 내구성이 있는 durable
naegusŏng-i kanghan 내구성이 강한 resilient
naehyangjŏgin 내향적인 retiring
naeil 내일 tomorrow; *naeil ach'im*

내일 아침 in the morning, tomorrow morning; *naeil i shigankkaji* 내일 이 시간까지 by this time tomorrow
naejangdoeŏ innŭn 내장되어 있는 built-in
naejangdoeŏ it-tta 내장되어 있다 be supplied with
naejŏn 내전 civil war
naekkwa ŭisa 내과 의사 physician
nae kŏt 내 것 mine
naek'iji annŭn 내키지 않는 reluctant
naeda 내다 pay; *naega naenda* 내가 낸다 I'm paying, this is on me
naekkwa chŏnmun ŭisa 내과 전문 의사 internist
naembi 냄비 pot, saucepan
naemilda 내밀다 extend, stretch
naemirhage 내밀하게 in private, privately
naemsae 냄새 smell; odor; scent
naemsaega nada 냄새가 나다 smell; reek
naemsae nanŭn 냄새 나는 smelly
naemsaerŭl mat-tta 냄새를 맡다 smell, sniff
Naemubu 내무부 Department of the Interior
naenae 내내 all the time, all along; *wŏryoilbut'ŏ kŭmnyoil tong-an naenae* 월요일부터 금요일 동안 내내 Monday through Friday
naengbang 냉방 air-conditioning
naengbangjung 냉방중 air-conditioned
naengdae 냉대 snub
naengdaehada 냉대하다 snub
naengdam 냉담 reserve, aloofness
naengdamhan 냉담한 unfriendly
naengdong 냉동 freezing
naengdong shikp'um 냉동 식품 frozen food
naengdongshil 냉동실 freezer; freezing compartment
naenghok'age 냉혹하게 in cold

blood

naenghok'an 냉혹한 grim

naenghyŏrhage 냉혈하게 in cold blood

naenghyŏrhan 냉혈한 cold-blooded *fig*

naenghyŏrŭi 냉혈의 cold-blooded

naengjanggo 냉장고 fridge, freezer

naengjŏnghada 냉정하다 be cool, be calm

naengjŏnghan 냉정한 dispassionate, objective; calm, impassive; hardheaded

naengmyŏn 냉면 chilled noodles

naeng-ŏmhan 냉엄한 brutal

naengso 냉소 cynicism

naengsojŏgin 냉소적인 cynical

naeng-yuk 냉육 cold cuts

naenot'a 내놓다 set out; *p'allyŏgo naenot'a* 팔려고 내놓다 put up for sale

naepk'in 냅킨 napkin

naeppumtta 내뿜다 blow *smoke*; snort

naep'aenggaech'ida 내팽개치다 throw; toss away

naep'ip 내핍 austerity

naeribeda 내리베다 slash

naerida 내리다 get out (*of car etc*); get off, disembark; come down (*of rain*); lower; wind down; unload; bring in *verdict*; percolate; filter; *araero naerida* 아래로 내리다 scroll down

naerige hada 내리게 하다 bring down

naerimak-kkiri toeda 내리막길이 되다 go downhill, decline

naeri tŏpch'ida 내리 덮치다 swoop; swoop down on

naeryŏant'a 내려앉다 subside; descend

naeryŏ chuda 내려 주다 let off (*from car*)

naeryŏdaboda 내려다보다 overlook; look down

naeryŏgada 내려가다 go down, descend, get down

naeryŏga it-tta 내려가 있다 be down

naeryŏjuda 내려주다 drop; *ch'a-esŏ naeryŏjuda* 차에서 내려주다 drop

off (*from car*)

naeryŏk 내력 personal history, career

naeryŏoda 내려오다 come down

naeryugŭi 내륙의 inland

naeryuk 내륙 interior

naesaek'aji ant'a 내색하지 않다 disguise one's emotions

naeshwida 내쉬다 exhale

naesŏn 내선 extension

naesŏngjŏgin 내성적인 withdrawn; introspective

naetchŏgin 내적인 inner

naetchot-tta 내쫓다 throw out, oust

naeŭi 내의 underwear

naeyŏlssŏng-ŭi 내열성의 heatproof, heat-resistant

naeyŏn-gigwan 내연기관 internal combustion engine

naeyŏnŭi ch'ŏ 내연의 처 common law wife

naeyong 내용 content; contents

nagada 나가다 go out; *chigŭm chŏng-wŏne nagait-tta* 그는 지금 정원에 나가있다 he's out in the garden; *nagaseyo!* 나가세요! (get) out! *nagayo!* 나가요! get out!

nagage hada 나가게 하다 let out

naga ttŏrŏjige hada 나가 떨어지게 하다 knock out

nagoja 낙오자 dropout

nagwŏn 낙원 paradise

nagwŏn-gat'ŭn 낙원같은 idyllic

nai 나이 age

nai chigŭt'an 나이 지긋한 elderly

naidŭrŏ kada 나이들어 가다 get on, become old

nai kappssŭl hae! 나이 값을 해! grow up!

naillon 나일론 nylon

naillonŭi 나일론의 nylon

nai tŭlda 나이 들다 age

nait'inggeil 나이팅게일 nightingale

nait'ŭ k'ŭllŏp 나이트클럽 nightclub, nightspot

naje 낮에 by day, in the daytime

najŭn 낮은 low

najŭn kubŭi 낮은 굽의 flat

najŭn tchoguro 낮은 쪽으로 down

najŭn ŭmjarip'yo 낮은 음자리표 bass clef

najung-e 나중에 later, later on, afterward; **najung-e poja!** 나중에 보자! see you later!

najung-e tashi chŏnwahada 나중에 다시 전화하다 call back TELEC

nakch'ŏnjŏgin 낙천적인 optimistic, happy-go-lucky

nakch'ŏnjuŭi 낙천주의 optimism

nakch'ŏnjuŭija 낙천주의자 optimist

nakka ch'aeda 낚아 채다 nab

nakkda 낚다 fish, angle; lure, entice; **nakkŭn kŏt** 낚은 것 catch *fish*

nakkwanjŏgin 낙관적인 optimistic

naksshi 낚시 fishing

naksshihada 낚시하다 fish

naksshippanŭl 낚시바늘 fish-hook

naksshitchul 낚싯줄 fishing line

naksshit-ttae 낚싯대 fishing rod

nakssŏ 낙서 graffiti

nakssŏndoen 낙선된 unsuccessful

nakssŭng 낙승 walkover

naktcherŭl pat-tta 낙제를 받다 flunk

naktchi 낙지 octopus

nakttam 낙담 dismay, disappointment

nakttamhan 낙담한 despondent, dejected; disheartened

nakttamshik'ida 낙담시키다 discourage; dishearten

nakt'ae 낙태 abortion

nakt'aehada 낙태하다 have an abortion

nakt'aeshik'ida 낙태시키다 terminate a pregnancy

nak'asan 낙하산 parachute

nak'asanbyŏng 낙하산병 paratrooper

nak'asanŭro naeryŏoda 낙하산으로 내려오다 parachute down

nak'asanŭro t'alch'urhada 낙하산으로 탈출하다 bail out (*of airplane*)

nak'asanŭro t'uhahada 낙하산으로 투하하다 parachute

nal 날 day; edge (*of knife*); blade

nalda 날다 fly

nalgae 날개 wing

nalgi 날기 flight; flying

nalgŭn 낡은 old; shabby; outmoded

nalkkŏsŭi 날것의 raw

nalktta 낡다 be old; be old-fashione◄

nalk'aroptta 날카롭다 be sharp; be incisive; be cutting

nalk'aroun 날카로운 sharp; incisive, penetrating; pointed; searching

nallibŏpssŏk 난리법석 fuss

nallibŏpssŏk ttŏlda 난리법석 떨다 make a fuss

nallich'ida 난리치다 make a fuss; complain

nallida 날리다 spend, blow

nalsshi 날씨 weather

nalsshinhada 날씬하다 be slim

nalsshinhan 날씬한 slim

naltcha 날짜 date

naltchaga chinan 날짜가 지난 out ◄ date

naltcharŭl chŏktta 날짜를 적다 date *document*, put a date on

nalttwimyŏ toradanida 날뛰며 돌아다니다 rampage, go on the rampage

nama it-tta 남아 있다 linger

Namap'ŭrik'a 남아프리카 South Africa ◊ South African

Namap'ŭrik'ain 남아프리카인 South African

Namap'ŭrik'aŭi 남아프리카의 South African

nambi 남비 pan

nambuŭi 남부의 southern

namch'ang 남창 male prostitute

namdongsaeng 남동생 (younger) brother

namdongtchoguŭi 남동쪽의 southeast, southeastern

namdongtchoguro 남동쪽으로 southeast

namdongtchok 남동쪽 southeast

namgida 남기다 leave; **kŭga namgin tu ttal** 그가 남긴 두 딸 his two surviving daughters

Namgŭk-kkwŏn 남극권 Antarctic

namgyŏjida 남겨지다 remain

namgyŏ tuda 남겨 두다 leave

Namhae 남해 South Sea, Korean Strait

Namhaedo 남해도 Namhae Island

namhakssaeng 남학생 schoolboy

Namhan 남한 South Korea ◊ South

Korean

namhanin 남한인 South Korean
namhyang-ŭi 남향의 southerly
namja 남자 man, male
namja ch'in-gu 남자 친구 boyfriend
namjadaum 남자다움 manhood
namjadaun 남자다운 manly; macho; virile
namja hwajangshil 남자 화장실 men's room
namja kanhosa 남자 간호사 male nurse
namja paeu 남자 배우 actor
namja suyŏngbok 남자 수영복 swimsuit
namja undongga 남자 운동가 sportsman
namjit 남짓 more than
Nammi 남미 South America ◊ South American
Nammiin 남미인 South American
Nammiŭi 남미의 South American
nam mollae saltchak 남 몰래 살짝 on the sly
nam morŭge 남 모르게 behind the scenes
namnŭn shigan 남는 시간 spare time
namnuhan 남루한 ragged
namnyŏ konghagŭi 남녀 공학의 coeducational
namŏji 나머지 the rest, remainder
namŏji kŏt 나머지 것 the others
namŏjiŭi 나머지의 surplus
namp'yŏn 남편 husband
namsaek 남색 navy blue
namsŏngdaum 남성다움 virility
namsŏngjŏgin 남성적인 masculine
namsŏngmi 남성미 masculinity
namsŏng-ŭi 남성의 male, masculine
namsŏng uwŏltchuŭija 남성 우월주의자 male chauvinist (pig)
namsŏtchogŭi 남서쪽의 southwest, southwestern
namsŏtchogŭro 남서쪽으로 southwest
namsŏtchok 남서쪽 southwest
namtchoge 남쪽에 to the south of
namtchogŭi 남쪽의 south
namtchogŭro 남쪽으로 south, southward

namtchok 남쪽 south
namtchok chibang 남쪽 지방 south
namtta 남다 be left, remain; *namŭn kŏshi ŏptta 남은 것이 없다 there isn't/aren't any left
namŭn kŏt nŭn 남은 것 left-overs
namu 나무 tree; wood
Namu Amit'abul 나무 아미타불 Namu Amit'abul (*Buddhist chant*)
namuga manŭn 나무가 많은 woody
namuga ugŏjin 나무가 우거진 wooded
namu kkŏptchil 나무 껍질 bark
namukkun 나무꾼 woodcutter
namurada 나무라다 reprimand, give a piece of one's mind
namural te ŏmnŭn 나무랄 데 없는 impeccable, irreproachable
namural te ŏpsshi 나무랄 데 없이 impeccably
namuro toen 나무로 된 wooden
namu sangja 나무 상자 crate
namutkkyŏl 나뭇결 grain
namuttalgi 나무딸기 raspberry
namyong 남용 abuse
nan 난 column
nanari 나날이 day by day
nanbang 난방 heating
nanbang changch'i 난방 장치 heating; heater
nanbanggi 난방기 radiator
nanch'ŏhage hada 난처하게 하다 stump, baffle
nanch'ŏhan 난처한 messy, unpleasant
nanch'ŏng chiyŏgesŏ 난청 지역에서 out of earshot
nanch'o 난초 orchid
nan-gan 난간 handrail
nangbi 낭비 waste
nangbibyŏgi shimhan 낭비벽이 심한 spendthrift
nangbiga shimhan 낭비가 심한 wasteful
nangbihada 낭비하다 waste, squander; *shigan nangbiyeyo 시간 낭비예요 it's a waste of time
nan-giryu 난기류 turbulence
nangnongjang 낙농장 dairy
nangsonghada 낭송하다 recite
nanhaehan 난해한 obscure

nanjaeng-i 난쟁이 dwarf
nanjangp'an 난장판 madhouse
nanjap'an 난잡한 promiscuous
nanmin 난민 refugee
nanp'a 난파 shipwreck
nanp'adoeda 난파되다 be shipwecked
nanp'ashik'ida 난파시키다 shipwreck
nanp'ok'age 난폭하게 violently
nanp'ok'age milda 난폭하게 밀다 jostle
nanp'ok unjŏnja 난폭 운전자 road hog
nanp'ok'an 난폭한 rough, rowdy
nanso 난소 ovary
nant'u 난투 scuffle
nanŭn 나는 I
nanuda 나누다 divide, distribute
nanul su innŭn 나눌 수 있는 divisible
nanuŏ chuda 나누어 주다 hand out, deal out
nanutssem 나눗셈 division
naoda 나오다 come out, get out; add up to
naogehada 나오게 하다 flush out
nap 납 lead (metal)
napch'i 납치 kidnapping
napch'ibŏm 납치범 kidnapper
napch'ihada 납치하다 abduct, kidnap
nappajida 나빠지다 deteriorate, suffer
nap-ppuhada 납부하다 pay
nappŭda 나쁘다 be wrong, be bad (morally)
nappŭge 나쁘게 badly
nappŭge haengdonghada 나쁘게 행동하다 misbehave
nappŭn 나쁜 bad
nappŭn haengdong 나쁜 행동 misbehavior
nappŭn nyŏn ∨나쁜 년 bitch pej
napsseja 납세자 tax payer
napsse shin-gosŏ 납세 신고서 tax return
napttŭk 납득 understanding
nap'al 나팔 brass trumpet
nara 나라 nation, country
naragada 날아가다 fly away, fly off; fly out

naranhi 나란히 side by side
naraŭi 나라의 national
narŭda 나르다 carry
narŭnhan 나른한 drowsy; weak
naruttppae 나룻배 ferry
nasamot 나사못 screw; *muŏsŭl muŏse nasamosŭro kojŏngshik'ida* 무엇을 무엇에 나사못으로 고정시키다 screw sth to sth
nasarŭl p'ulda 나사를 풀다 unscrew
nasasan 나사산 thread (of screw)
nasŏda 나서다 come out, appear
nasŏnhyŏng kyedan 나선형 계단 winding staircase
nasŏnhyŏng-ŭi 나선형의 spiral
nasŏnhyŏng-ŭi ch'ŭnggye 나선형의 층계 spiral staircase
nat 낮 daylight
nat 낫 scythe
natch'uda 낮추다 lower; keep down
natch'un 낮춘 subdued
natch'uŏ poda 낮추어 보다 look down on
natkke hada 낫게 하다 heal
natssŏn saram 낯선 사람 stranger
nattcham 낮잠 nap
nattchamŭl chada 낮잠을 자다 have a nap
nat-tta 낳다 generate, create; *airŭl nat-tta* 아이를 낳다 give birth
nat-tta 낫다 heal, clear up
nat-tta 낮다 be low
nat'a 낳다 bear, give birth to; lay; spawn
nat'aehan 나태한 indolent, idle
nat'anada 나타나다 appear, turn up; manifest itself; haunt
nat'anaeda 나타내다 show, constitute
naŭi 나의 my
ne chashin 네 자신 yourself
Nedŏllandŭin 네덜란드인 the Dutch
Nedŏllandŭŏ 네덜란드어 Dutch (language)
Nedŏllandŭŭi 네덜란드의 Dutch
nekt'ai 넥타이 tie, necktie
neon ssain 네온 싸인 neon light
ne paero hada 네 배로 하다 quadruple

e pal chimsŭng 네 발 짐승 quadruped

e pŏn 네 번 four times

e pŏntchaeŭi 네 번째의 fourth

ep'al 네팔 Nepal ◊ Nepalese

e ssangdung-i 네 쌍둥이 quadruplets

et 넷 four

et'ŭ 네트 net (for tennis)

et'ŭwŏk'ŭ 네트워크 network

nik'el 니켈 nickel

nisŭ 니스 varnish

nisŭrŭl ch'irhada 니스를 칠하다 varnish

nit'ŭ weŏ 니트 웨어 knitwear

...nji ...ㄴ지 → ...inji ...인지

nŏ 너 (informal) you

nŏdobamnamu 너도밤나무 beech

nŏgŭroun 너그러운 decent

nŏhŭidŭl chashin 너희들 자신 yourselves

nŏhŭidŭl sŭsŭro 너희들 스스로 by yourselves

nŏkssŭl ilk'e hada 넋을 잃게 하다 devastate

nŏkssŭl ilt'a 넋을 잃다 get carried away

nŏlbi ttwigi 넓이 뛰기 long jump, broad jump

nŏlbŏjida 넓어지다 broaden, widen

nŏlbŭn 넓은 roomy, wide

nŏlbŭn kang-ŏgwi 넓은 강어귀 estuary

nŏlkke 넓게 widely; nŏlkke pyŏlch'yŏjin 넓게 펼쳐진 a vast expanse of; nŏlkke yŏllin 넓게 열린 wide-open

nŏlli p'ŏjyŏ innŭn 널리 퍼져 있는 pervasive

nŏlppanji 널빤지 plank

nŏlptta 넓다 be wide, be broad

nŏlp'ida 넓히다 broaden, widen; expand; dilate

nŏmch'ida 넘치다 exceed; overflow; kaemidŭllo nŏmch'ida 개미들로 넘치다 be teeming with ants; ...esŏ nŏmch'yŏ hŭrŭda ...에서 넘쳐 흐르다 stream out of; kangttugi nŏmch'ida 강둑이 넘치다 flood its banks; kamjŏng-i nŏmch'inŭn 감정이 넘치는 effusive

nŏmgida 넘기다 turn; ...ege kyŏltchŏng-ŭl / mun-jerŭl nŏmgida ...에게 결정을 / 문제를 넘기다 refer a decision / problem to

nŏmgyŏjuda 넘겨주다 hand over, surrender

nŏmŏ 넘어 past (in time)

nŏmŏjida 넘어지다 fall, trip up; stumble

nŏmŏjim 넘어짐 fall; stumble

nŏmŏsŏ 넘어서 beyond

nŏmŏttŭrida 넘어뜨리다 knock over; hŏrŏ nŏmŏttŭrida 헐어 넘어뜨리다 knock down

nŏmtta 넘어서다 exceed; be past; go over mountain; ilgop shiga nŏmŏssŏyo 일곱 시가 넘었어요 it's past 7 o'clock

nŏmu 너무 too; far; unbanhagie nŏmu mugŏp-tta 운반하기에 너무 무겁다 too heavy to carry; nŏmu andwaessŏyo 너무 안됐어요 that's really too bad; nega nŏmu chi-nach'yŏt-tta 네가 너무 지나쳤다 you've gone too far; kŭdŭlŭn iri nŏmu millyŏ issŏyo 그들은 일이 너무 밀려 있어요 they are way behind with their work

nŏmu honjap'an 너무 혼잡한 overcrowded

nŏmu ik'ida 너무 익히다 overdo

nŏmu mani 너무 많이 too much

nŏmu pissan 너무 비싼 too expensive, overpriced

nŏmu ttabunhan irida 너무 따분한 일이다 it's such a bore

nŏngnŏk'an 넉넉한 plentiful

nŏnjishi pich'ida 넌지시 비치다 insinuate, imply

nŏnjishi pich'uda 넌지시 비추다 make out, imply

nŏnŭn 너는 you (informal); as for you

nŏptchŏkttari 넓적다리 thigh

nŏrŏsŏ mallida 널어서 말리다 dripdry

nŏt'a 넣다 put in, inject

nŏt'ŭ 너트 nut

nŏŭi 너의 (informal) your

no 노 oar; paddle

noajuda 놓아주다 disengage

noa pŏrida 놓아 버리다 let go of

noa tuda 놓아 두다 put

nobaldaebarhada 노발대발하다 be furious with

nobaldaebarhan 노발대발한 livid

noch'ida 놓치다 miss (*not hit*); lose one's hold on; pass up *opportunity*

noch'ŏn k'ap'e 노천 카페 sidewalk café

no chŏt-tta 노 젓다 row *boat*

noch'ul 노출 exposure

noch'uldoen 노출된 revealing

noch'ulshik'ida 노출시키다 expose

noch'urhada 노출하다 expose; *chinach'ige noch'urhada* 지나치게 노출하다 overexpose

noch'uri pujok'an 노출이 부족한 underexposed

nodong 노동 labor

nodong chaeng-ŭi haeng-wi 노동 쟁의 행위 industrial action

nodong chohap 노동 조합 labor union

nodong hŏga 노동 허가 work permit

nodong in-gu 노동 인구 workforce

nodongja 노동자 laborer, worker

nodongja kyegŭbŭi 노동자 계급의 working-class

nodongja kyegŭp 노동자 계급 working class

Nodongjŏl 노동절 May Day, Labor Day

nodongjohabŭi chiktchangwiwŏn 노동조합의 직장위원 shop steward

noe chŏnmun oekkwa ŭisa 뇌 전문 외과 의사 brain surgeon

noejint'ang 뇌진탕 concussion

noejol 뇌졸 stroke

noemangnyŏm 뇌막염 meningitis

noemul 뇌물 bribe

noemul susu 뇌물 수수 bribery

noemurŭl chuda 뇌물을 주다 pay off, bribe

noerirŭl ttŏnaji annŭn 뇌리를 떠나지 않는 haunting

noeu 뇌우 thunderstorm

nogaut'ŭ 녹아웃 knockout

nogida 녹이다 melt; dissolve; defrost

nogi sŭlji annŭn 녹이 슬지 않는 rust-proof

nogi sŭn 녹이 슨 rusty

nogo 노고 toil

nogoltchŏgin 노골적인 direct; point blank; obvious

nogoltchŏgin p'orŭno 노골적인 포르노 hardcore porn

nogoltchŏgŭro 노골적으로 pointblank

nogonhan 노곤한 lethargic

nogŭm 녹음 recording

nogŭmdoen 녹음된 canned

nogŭmgi 녹음기 cassette player; record player

nogŭmhada 녹음하다 tape

nogŭmshil 녹음실 recording studio

nogŭm t'eip'ŭ 녹음 테이프 cassette

nogŭn 녹은 molten

nohau 노하우 knowhow, expertise

noin 노인 geriatric

noinppyŏng-ŭi 노인병의 geriatric

nojang chŏngmaek 노장 정맥 varicose vein

nojo 노조 (labor) union

nok 녹 rust

nok chejŏje 녹 제거제 rust remover

nokch'a 녹차 green tea

nokch'oga toen 녹초가 된 exhausted

nokch'oga toeŏ 녹초가 되어 dead beat, dead tired

nokch'oro mandŭlda 녹초로 만들다 exhaust

nokch'oro mandŭnŭn 녹초로 만드는 grueling

nokkŭn 노끈 cord, string

nokssaegŭi 녹색의 green

nokssŭlda 녹슬다 rust

noktta 녹다 thaw; dissolve; melt

nok'ŭhada 노크하다 knock; *munŭl nok'ŭhada* 문을 노크하다 knock at the door

nok'wahada 녹화하다 tape, record

nok'washil 녹화실 recording studio

nolda 놀다 play

nolgo chinaeda 놀고 지내다 loaf around

nolgo innŭn 놀고 있는 idle

nollada 놀라다 marvel at; be surprised

nollage hada 놀라게 하다 surprise; shock; rock

nollapk'e 놀랍게 suprisingly

nolla poida 놀라 보이다 look surprised

nollaptta 놀랍다 be surprising

nollaŭn kŏt 놀라운 것 marvel

nollaun 놀라운 surprising; wonderful; **...ranŭn kŏsŭn nollaun irida** ...라는 것은 놀라운 일이다 it's a wonder that ...

nolli 논리 reasoning, argument, logic

nollida 놀리다 make fun of, tease; play a joke on; send up; scoff; quip

nollijŏgin 논리적인 logical

non 논 rice field, rice paddy

nonbat 논밭 rice fields and dry fields

nong-ak 농악 farmer's music

nong-akttae 농악대 traditional farmers' band

nong-aŭi 농아의 deaf-and-dumb

nongbu 농부 farmer

nongch'ukttoen 농축된 concentrated

nongdam 농담 joke

nongdamhada 농담하다 joke, jest

nongdam kŭmanhago 농담 그만하고 joking apart

nongdamŭi p'yojŏk 농담의 표적 butt (of joke)

nongdamŭro 농담으로 in jest, jokingly

nongdo 농도 consistency, texture

nongga 농가 farmhouse

nonggu 농구 basketball

nonggyŏng-e almajŭn 농경에 알맞은 arable

nongjang 농장 farm

nongjangmul 농작물 crop

nongjang-ŭi ilkkun 농장의 일꾼 farmworker

nongmal 녹말 cornstarch

nongmin 농민 peasant

nong-ŏbŭi 농업의 agricultural

nong-ŏp 농업 agriculture

nongsa 농사 agriculture, farming; **nongsa chitkko salda** 농사 짓고 살다 make a living from farming

nongsanmul 농산물 produce

nong-yang 농양 abscess

nonhada 논하다 argue, reason

nonjaeng 논쟁 argument; debate; controversy

nonjaenghada 논쟁하다 debate

nonjaengjŏgin 논쟁적인 provocative

nonjaeng-ŭi yŏjiga innŭn 논쟁의 여지가 있는 debatable

nonjaeng-ŭl irŭk'inŭn 논쟁을 일으키는 controversial

nonmun 논문 thesis, academic paper

nonp'iksshyŏn 논픽션 nonfiction

nonp'yŏnghada 논평하다 review

nontchŏm 논점 issue, topic

nonŭi 논의 discussion; **nonŭi sahang** 논의 사항 the point at issue

nonŭihada 논의하다 discuss

nonŭiŭi yŏjiga ŏmnŭn 논의의 여지가 없는 indisputable

nonyŏn 노년 old age

nopkke 높게 high

noptta 높다 be high

nop'i 높이 height; elevation; altitude; **nugurŭl nop'i p'yŏngkkahada** 누구를 높이 평가하다 have a high opinion of s.o.

nop'ida 높이다 increase, turn up; elevate

nop'i ttwigi 높이 뛰기 high jump

nop'ŭn 높은 high

nop'ŭn ponggŭbŭl pat-tta 높은 봉급을 받다 be highly paid

nop'ŭn kubŭi 높은 굽의 high-heeled

nop'ŭn sujun 높은 수준 high (in statistics)

norae 노래 song; chant

noraebang 노래방 karaoke room

noraehada 노래하다 sing; chant

noran 노란 yellow

norang 노랑 yellow

noransaegŭro 노란색으로 in yellow

norat'a 노랗다 be yellow

nori 놀이 play ◊ game

norich'in-gu 놀이친구 playmate

norit'ŏ 놀이터 playground

norŭnja 노른자 yolk

norŭnnorŭt'age kuptta 노릇노릇하게굽다 brown (in cooking)

norŭnnorŭt'age toeda 노릇노릇하게되다 brown (in cooking)

Norŭwei 노르웨이 Norway ◊ Norwegian

Norŭweiin 노르웨이인 Norwegian

Norŭweiŏ 노르웨이어 Norwegian (language)

Norŭweiŭi 노르웨이의 Norwegian

noryŏboda

noryŏboda 노려보다 glare at

noryŏk 노력 effort, attempt

noryŏk'ada 노력하다 try, exert oneself; *tangshinŭn tŏ yŏlshimhi noryŏk'aeya hamnida* 당신은 더 열심히 노력해야 합니다 you must try harder

nosae 노새 mule

nosaganŭi purhwa 노사간의 불화 industrial dispute

nosahyŏbŭihwoe 노사협의회 works council

nosang kangdo 노상 강도 mugger

nosang kangdo haeng-wi 노상 강도 행위 mugging

nosang kangdojirŭl hada 노상 강도질을 하다 mug, rob on the street

nosoe 노쇠 senility

nosoehan 노쇠한 senile

nosuk'ada 노숙하다 sleep rough

notssoe 놋쇠 brass

not'a 놓다 put; put down

not'ŭbuk 노트북 notebook COMPUT

noŭl 노을 twilight

noye 노예 slave

noyŏum 노여움 anger

nŭgŭt'age 느긋하게 in a leisurely way

nŭgŭt'an 느긋한 easy-going, laidback; leisurely

nŭjŏjida 늦어지다 lose

nŭjŏjinda 늦어진다 it's getting late

nŭjŭn 늦은 late, overdue

nŭkkida 느끼다 feel, experience

nŭkkim 느낌 feeling; impression

nŭkkimp'yo 느낌표 exclamation point

nŭkttae 늑대 wolf

nŭl 늘 always, all the time; *nŭl hanŭn kŏsŭro chushipsshio* 늘 하는 것으로 주십시오 the usual, please

nŭlda 늘다 expand; mount up; *op'aundŭga nŭlda* 5파운드가 늘다 gain 5 pounds

nŭlgŏjida 늙어지다 grow old

nŭlgŭn 늙은 old

nŭlgŭnina chŏlmŭnina ttokkach'i 늙은이나 젊은이나 똑같이 old and young alike

nŭlktta 늙다 grow old

nŭllida 늘리다 extend, roll over; raise; lengthen; let out

nŭlsshinhan 늘씬한 trim

...nŭn ... 는 ◊ *(contrast particle, also used to introduce a topic)*: **nŏnŭn** 너는 you; as for you; *...nŭn cheohago* ... 는 제외하고 excluding *(relative)* which; who; whose; *naega kongbuhanŭn kwamok* 내가 공부하는 과목 the subject which I'm studying ◊ *(forms adjectives)*: **nurŏputtchi annŭn** 눌어붙지 않는 nonstick

nŭngdongt'aeŭi 능동태의 active

nŭnggahada 능가하다 surpass, exceed

nŭnggŭlmajŭn usŭm 능글맞은 웃음 smirk

nŭnggŭlmatkke ut-tta 능글맞게 웃다 smirk

nŭngnyŏginnŭn 능력있는 able, skillful

nŭngnyŏgi ŏmnŭn 능력이 없는 incapable; inept

nŭngnyŏgŭl shihŏmhaebonŭn 능력을 시험해보는 challenging

nŭngnyŏk 능력 capability, ability; competence; faculty; *...l nŭngnyŏgi it-tta* ...ㄹ 능력이 있다 be capable of ...ing

nŭngnyŏk innŭn 능력 있는 capable, competent

nŭngnyŏng 능력 capacity, ability

nŭngnyul 능률 efficiency

nŭngnyultchŏgin 능률적인 efficient; streamlined

nŭngnyultchŏgŭro 능률적으로 efficiently

nŭngsuk 능숙 proficiency

nŭngsuk'ada 능숙하다 be skilled; *muŏse nŭngsuk'ada* 무엇에 능숙하다 be good at sth

nŭngsuk'an 능숙한 skillful, proficient

...nŭn kŏt ...는 것 ◊ *(creates a noun form)* ...ing; *kongbu hanŭn kŏt* 공부 하는 것 studying ◊ what; *kŭgŏshi chega choahanŭn kŏshiyeyo* 그것이 제가 좋아하는 것이에요 that's what I like

ŭp 늪 swamp

ŭp kat'ŭn 늪 같은 swampy

ŭrida 늘이다 extend, stretch; take down

ŭrida 느리다 be slow; be loose

ŭrige hada 느리게 하다 slow down

ŭrin 느린 slow, sluggish

ŭrin malt'u 느린 말투 drawl

ŭrinnŭrit kada 느릿느릿 가다 crawl

ŭrinnŭrit'age 느릿느릿하게 at a crawl

ŭrin tongjagŭro 느린 동작으로 in slow motion

ŭrŏjida 늘어지다 stretch; sag, hang; **ch'uk nŭrŏjida** 축 늘어지다 droop, sag

ŭrŏjin 늘어진 flabby

ŭrŏnada 늘어나다 stretch, give

ŭrŏnot'a 늘어놓다 draw up

ŭrŭmnamu 느릅나무 elm

ŭryŏjida 느려지다 slow down

ŭsŭnhage hada 느슨하게 하다 loosen, slacken

ŭsŭnhan 느슨한 loose, slack; lax

ŭtch'uda 늦추다 slacken

ŭtch'uŏjida 늦추어지다 slacken off

ŭtkkim 느낌 sense, feeling

ŭttcham chada 늦잠 자다 sleep late; oversleep

ŭt-tta 늦다 be late

nubida 누비다 weave; move

nubi ibul 누비 이불 quilt

nubi chaek'it 누비 재킷 quilted jacket

nuch'uham 누추함 squalor

nuch'uhan chip 누추한 집 hovel

nuch'ul 누출 escape, leak

nuch'uldoeda 누출되다 escape

nudŏgiga toeŏ 누더기가 되어 in tatters

nuga 누가 nougat; who; Luke

nugŭrŏjida 누그러지다 ease off

nugu 누구 who; *igŏsŭn nuguegesŏ on kŏshinji palk'yŏittchi ant'a* 이것은 누구에게서 온 것인지 밝혀있지 않다 it doesn't say who it's from

nugudo 누구도 any; *hakssaengdŭl chung kŭ nugudo* 학생들 중 그 누구도 (+ *negative verb*) none of the students; *... nugudŭnji ...* 누구든지 whoever

nuguna 누구나 everybody, everyone

nugun-ga 누군가 somebody; anybody

nugurŭl 누구를 who; somebody

nugurŭl chemŏt-ttaero hage nae-bŏryŏduda 누구를 제멋대로 하게 내버려두다 leave s.o. to his own devices

nuguseyo 누구세요 hello

nuguŭi 누구의 whose; *igŏsŭn nuguŭi kŏshimnikka?* 이것은 누구의 것입니까? whose is this?

nuguŭi kŏt 누구의 것 whose

numyŏng ssŭiuda 누명 씌우다 frame *person*

nun 눈 eye; snow

nunal 눈알 eyeball

nunbora 눈보라 snowstorm

nunbushida 눈부시다 be dazzling; be spectacular

nunbushige hada 눈부시게 하다 dazzle

nunbushige pinnada 눈부시게 빛나다 glare

nunbushin 눈부신 dazzling, spectacular

nunbushinŭn pit 눈부시는 빛 glare

nunch'ich'aeda 눈치채다 observe, notice

nunch'i ŏmnŭn 눈치 없는 clumsy, tactless

nundŏmi 눈더미 drift

nune hwak ttŭinŭn 눈에 확 띄는 glaring

nune kashi 눈에 가시 undesirable element

nune katch'in 눈에 갇힌 snowbound

nune saenggirŭl ilt'a 눈에 생기를 잃다 glaze over (of eyes)

nune ttŭida 눈에 띄다 stick out, stand out

nune ttŭige 눈에 띄게 visibly

nune ttŭinŭn 눈에 띄는 visible; *nŏmu nune ttŭinŭn* 너무 눈에 띄는 showy

nun-gama chuda 눈감아 주다 overlook

nun-gŭmp'an 눈금판 dial

nuni ch'imch'imhan 눈이 침침한

bleary-eyed
nuni mŏl chŏngdoŭi 눈이 멀 정도의
blinding
nuni naerida 눈이 내리다 snow
nuni onŭn 눈이 오는 snowy *day*
nuni ssain 눈이 쌓인 snowy *field*
nun karigae 눈 가리개 blindfold
nun kkamtchak'al saie 눈 깜짝할
사이에 in a flash
nunkkŏp'ul 눈꺼풀 eyelid
nunkkŭm 눈금 scale
nun maja taranada 눈 맞아 달아나다
elope
nun mŏlge hada 눈 멀게 하다 blind
nun mŏn 눈 먼 blind
nunmul 눈물 tear
nunmulnage komapkkunyo
눈물나게 고맙군요 thanks a bunch
nunmul ŏrin 눈물 어린 tearful
nunmul pang-ul 눈물 방울 teardrop
nunmul tchage hanŭn kŏt 눈물 짜게
하는 것 slush *pej*
nunmuri nada 눈물이 나다 water (*of*
eyes)
nunmurŭl hŭllida 눈물을 흘리다 be
in tears
nunmurŭl taktta 눈물을 닦다 dry
one's eyes
nun pushige hanŭn 눈 부시게 하는
blinding
nunsat'ae 눈사태 avalanche
nunsong-i 눈송이 snowflake
nunssaram 눈사람 snowman

nunssŏp 눈썹 eyebrow
nunttŏng-i 눈덩이 snowball
nunttongja 눈동자 pupil (*in eye*)
nunŭi kashi 눈의 가시 pain in the
neck (*person*)
nunŭi p'iro 눈의 피로 eye strain
nunŭl karida 눈을 가리다 blindfold
nuptta 눕다 lie, lie down
nurŏputtchi annŭn 눌어붙지 않는
nonstick
nurŭda 누르다 push, press; click
COMPUT
nurŭgi 누르기 push COMPUT
nurŭm tanch'ushigŭi 누름 단추식의
push button
nusŏl 누설 disclosure
nusŏldoeda 누설되다 leak out
nusŏrhada 누설하다 divulge
nwiuch'inŭn 뉘우치는 penitent,
remorseful
nyŏn 년 year; woman *pej*
Nyujillaendŭ 뉴질랜드 New Zealand
Nyujillaendŭin 뉴질랜드인 New
Zealander
nyusŭ 뉴스 news; development;
event
nyusŭ pangsonghanŭn saram 뉴스
방송하는 사람 newsreader
nyusŭ pangsong-ŭl hada 뉴스
방송을 하다 newscast
nyusŭ podo 뉴스 보도 news
report
Nyuyok 뉴욕 New York

ŏ

ŏbŏinal 어버이날 Parents' Day
ŏbu 어부 fisherman
ŏch'i 어치 worth; *samch'ŏn wŏnŏch'i* 삼천 원어치 three thousand wons' worth
ŏch'ŏgŭniŏmnŭn 어처구니없는 absurd
ŏdaept'ŏ 어댑터 adapter ELEC
ŏdi 어디 where; *ŏdie noŭlkkayo?* 어디에 놓을까요? where shall I put this?; *ŏdiesŏ wassŭmnikka?* 어디에서 왔습니까? where are you from?; *ŏdiro kamnikka?* 어디로 갑니까? where are you going?; *ŏdi tarŭn kosŭro kapsshida* 어디 다른 곳으로 갑시다 let's go somewhere else; *ŏdirŭl kadŏrado* 어디를 가더라도 wherever you go; *kŭgŏsŭn Hanguk ŏdiena it-tta* 그것은 한국 어디에나 있다 you find them all over Korea
ŏdidŭnji 어디든지 everywhere, wherever
ŏdin-gae 어딘가에 somewhere
ŏditchŭme(sŏ) 어디쯤에(서) whereabouts, where
ŏdŭl su innŭn 얻을 수 있는 obtainable
ŏdŭl su ŏmnŭn 얻을 수 없는 unobtainable
ŏdŭryŏgo noryŏk'ada 얻으려고 노력하다 strive for
ŏduk'ŏmk'ŏmhan 어두컴컴한 gloomy
ŏdum 어둠 darkness
ŏdumch'imch'imhan 어둠침침한 dim
ŏduptta 어둡다 be dark; be in the dark; be weak
ŏduun 어두운 dark; gloomy
ŏduun pitkkarŭi 어두운 빛깔의 dark-colored
ŏduwŏjida 어두워지다 get dark
ŏgan 어간 stem (*of word*)

ŏgaptchŏgin 억압적인 repressive
ŏgap'ada 억압하다 repress
ŏgŭmni 어금니 molar
ŏgwi 어귀 mouth (*of river*)
ŏgyang 어양 inflection
ŏhagŭi 어학의 linguistic
ŏhoengnyang 어획량 haul (*of fish*)
ŏhwi 어휘 vocabulary
ŏje 어제 yesterday
ŏjetppam 어젯밤 last night
...ŏjida ...어 지다 become ..., get ...
ŏjillŏ noŭn 어질러 놓은 disorderly
ŏjirŏptta 어지럽다 feel faint; be dizzy; be chaotic
ŏjirŏun 어지러운 giddy, faint; messy
ŏjirŭda 어지르다 mess up
ŏjo 어조 tone
ŏkkae 어깨 shoulder; *ŏkkaerŭl ŭssŭk-kkŏrida* 어깨를 으쓱거리다 shrug one's shoulders
ŏkssen 억센 strong, tough, robust
ŏkssen sanai 억센 사나이 tough guy
ŏkssugat'ŭn 억수같은 driving, torrential *rain*; (*piga*) *ŏkssugach'i p'ŏbunnŭnda* (비가) 억수같이 퍼붓는다 it's pouring (with rain)
ŏktche 억제 constraint, curb, inhibition; restraint
ŏktchedoen 억제된 inhibited
ŏktchedoen p'yohyŏn 억제된 표현 understatement
ŏktchehada 억제하다 check, restrain; control; inhibit; stifle
ŏktchehal su ŏmnŭn 억제할 수 없는 irresistible
ŏktchi 억지 obstinacy
ŏktchiro ppaeda 억지로 빼다 wrench; pull
ŏktchiro ...shik'ida 억지로 ...시키다 compel
ŏlbŏmurida 얼버무리다 manipulate; stall
ŏlda 얼다 freeze
ŏlgul 얼굴 face

ŏlgurŭl pulk'ida

ŏlgurŭl pulk'ida 얼굴을 붉히다 blush, go red in the face

ŏlgurŭl tchip'urida 얼굴을 찌푸리다 wince

ŏlk'ida 얽히다 become entangled in

ŏlk'ŭnhage ch'wihan 얼큰하게 취한 tipsy

ŏllida 얼리다 freeze

ŏllon 언론 journalism; the press

ŏllon-gye 언론계 journalism

ŏllonŭi chayu 언론의 자유 free speech

ŏllugi saenggida 얼룩이 생기다 stain

ŏlluk 얼룩 mark; stain; smear; smudge

ŏlluk chegŏje 얼룩 제거제 stain remover

ŏlluktchin 얼룩진 streaky

ŏllungmal 얼룩말 zebra

ŏlma 얼마 how much; how long; how many; how far; *ŏlma andoenŭn* 얼마 안되는 not much; *...ŭn/nŭn ŏlmaimnikka?* ...은/는 얼마입니까? how much is/are ...?

ŏlmana ...? 얼마나 ...? how much?

ŏlmana chaju? 얼마나 자주? how often?

ŏlmana chŏne? 얼마나 전에? how long ago?

ŏlmana kŏllimnikka? 얼마나 걸립니까? how long does it take?

ŏlmana mani? 얼마나 많이? how many?

ŏlp'it poda 얼핏 보다 catch a fleeting glimpse of

ŏmaŏmahan 어마어마한 huge

ŏmch'ŏng manŭn 엄청 많은 an awful lot

ŏmch'ŏngnada 엄청나다 be preposterous

ŏmch'ŏngnage 엄청나게 very, extraordinarily

ŏmch'ŏngnan 엄청난 extraordinary, amazing; preposterous

ŏmhage 엄하게 severely

ŏmhage hada 엄하게 하다 tighten up

ŏmhage tasŭrida 엄하게 다스리다 crack down on

ŏmhan 엄한 grim; strict, tough

ŏmi 어미 ending GRAM

ŏmji sonkkarak 엄지 손가락 thumb

ŏmjunghan 엄중한 stringent

ŏmkkyŏk 엄격 severity; rigor

ŏmkkyŏk'ada 엄격하다 be strict

ŏmkkyŏk'age 엄격하게 strictly; *kŭgŏsŭn ŏmkkyŏk'age kŭmjidoeŏ it-tta* 그것은 엄격하게 금지되어 있다 it is strictly forbidden

ŏmkkyŏk'an 엄격한 strict, stern; straitlaced

ŏmma 엄마 mom

ŏmmang-in sangt'ae 엄망인 상태 muddle, mess

ŏmmirhi 엄밀히 strictly, closely

ŏmmu 업무 affair, business

ŏmmuryang 업무량 workload

ŏmmu shigan 업무 시간 office hours

ŏmmu suhaeng 업무 수행 performance

ŏmni 엄니 fang; tusk

ŏmnŭn 없는 no; *...i/ga ŏmnŭn* ...이/가 없는 without; *toni hanp'undo ŏmnŭn* 돈이 한푼도 없는 penniless

ŏmŏni 어머니 mother

ŏmŏnigat'ŭn 어머니같은 motherly

ŏmŏninal 어머니날 Mother's Day

ŏmŏniŭi 어머니의 maternal

ŏmp'o 엄포 bluff; deception

ŏmp'orŭl not'a 엄포를 놓다 bluff

ŏmssuk'ada 엄숙하다 be solemn

ŏmssuk'an 엄숙한 solemn

ŏndŏk 언덕 hill

ŏndŏk kkokttaegi 언덕 꼭대기 hilltop

ŏngdŏng-i 엉덩이 bottom, butt; buttocks

ŏnggida 엉기다 clot, coagulate

ŏngk'ida 엉키다 get tangled up

ŏngmang 엉망 mess

ŏngmangjinch'ang 엉망진창 havoc

ŏngmang-ŭro mandŭlda 엉망으로 만들다 wreck, mess up

ŏngmang-ŭro p'agoehada 엉망으로 파괴하다 wreck

ŏngnullin 억눌린 repressed, pent-up

ŏngnurŭda 억누르다 repress

ŏngnurŭl su ŏmnŭn 억누를 수 없는 irrepressible

ŏngnyuja 억류자 detainee

ngttunghada 엉뚱하다 be extraordinary

ngttunghan shigane 엉뚱한 시간에 at this unearthly hour

ngt'ŏri 엉터리 broken *Korean etc*

n-gŭp 언급 comment, remark; mention; reference

n-gŭp'ada 언급하다 comment, remark; mention; refer to

nje 언제 when; *...l ttaenŭn ŏnjedŭnji* ...ㄹ 때는 언제든지 whenever; *ŏnjedŭn malman haseyo* 언제든 말만 하세요 I am at your disposal

njekkajina 언제까지나 forever

njena 언제나 always, for ever

njen-ga 언젠가 ever, someday

nŏ 언어 language

nŏ chang-ae 언어 장애 language barrier; speech defect

nŏ ch'iryo chŏnmun-ga 언어 치료 전문가 speech therapist

nŏhaktcha 언어학자 linguist

ntchanahada 언짢아하다 mind, object to

nttŭt poda 언뜻 보다 catch sight of

nŭ 어느 what; which; *ŏnŭ chŏngdo* 어느 정도 some, a measure of; *ŏnŭ chŏngdokkaji* 어느 정도까지 to a certain extent

nŭ han tchogŭi 어느 한 쪽의 either; *Xna Y chung ŏnŭ ha-narado* X나 Y 중 어느 하나라도 either X or Y

nŭ kŏt 어느 것 which; *... ŏnŭ kŏshidŭn(ji)* ... 어느 것이든(지) whichever

nŭ kot 어느 곳 anywhere

nŭnal 어느날 one day

nŭ tchogina 어느 쪽이나 either

pkkŭreidŭ 업그레이드 upgrade

pkkŭreidŭhada 업그레이드하다 upgrade

ppŏp 어법 usage

praitʼŭ p'iano 업라이트 피아노 upright piano

prodŭhada 업로드하다 upload

pssaeda 없애다 remove, get rid of

..ŏpsshi ...없이 without; *...ŏpsshi chinaeda* ...없이 지내다 do without, go without; *...ŏpsshi hada* ...없이

하다 dispense with; *...ŏpsshi sara-gada* ...없이 살아가다 go without

ŏpssŏjida 없어지다 go; disappear; be missing

ŏpssŏsŏ 없어서 for want of

ŏptchillŏjida 엎질러지다 spill

ŏptchirŭda 엎지르다 spill

ŏptchŏk 업적 achievement

ŏptchongbyŏl chŏnhwa pŏnhobu 업종별 전화 번호부 yellow pages

ŏptta 없다 there is no; not have; lack; be out, not be at home; *k'ŏp'i/ch'aga ŏptta* 커피/차가 없다 there's no coffee/tea; *nanŭn ŏnŏe sojiri ŏptta* 나는 언어에 소질이 없다 I'm no linguist

ŏpttŭrida 엎드리다 get down, duck

ŏp'asŭt'ŭrop'i 어퍼스트로피 apostrophe

ŏribŏngbŏnghage hada 어리벙벙하게 하다 stun

ŏrida 어리다 be very young

ŏridungjŏrhaejin 어리둥절해진 dazed

ŏrimdo ŏpssŏ! 어림도 없어! no way!

ŏrimjimjak 어림짐작 guesswork

Ŏrininal 어린이날 Children's Day

ŏriniyong chwasŏk 어린이용 좌석 child's seat, car seat

ŏrin nom 어린 놈 monkey, young rascal

ŏrinshijŏl 어린시절 childhood

ŏrisŏgŭn 어리석은 stupid, dumb; foolish

ŏrisŏgŭn chit 어리석은 짓 folly

ŏrisŏktta 어리석다 be foolish

ŏritkkwangdae 어릿광대 clown

ŏrŭm 얼음 ice; *ŏrŭmŭl kyŏt-ttŭryŏ* 얼음을 곁들여 on the rocks, with ice; *ŏrŭmŭl nŏhŭn* 얼음을 넣은 iced

ŏrŭmi ŏrŭn 얼음이 얼은 icy

ŏrŭn 어른 adult, grown-up

ŏrŭn 얼은 frozen

ŏrŭnsŭrŏun 어른스러운 grown-up

ŏryŏmp'ushi nat'anada 어렴풋이 나타나다 loom up

ŏryŏmp'utʼan 어렴풋한 vague

ŏryŏpkke 어렵게 with difficulty

ŏryŏptta 어렵다 be hard, be difficult

ŏryŏum 어려움 difficulty

ŏryŏun 어려운 difficult

ŏsaek'an 어색한 labored

ŏsŏlp'ŭn 어설픈 rough, careless; lame *excuse*

ŏsŏn 어선 fishing boat

ŏsŭllŏnggŏrida 어슬렁거리다 hang about; saunter; prowl

ŏsŭrehage pich'ida 어스레하게 비치다 gleam

ŏsŭrehan pit 어스레한 빛 gleam

ŏsusŏnhada 행동이 어수선다 be in disorder; *haengdong-i ŏsusŏnhan* 행동이 어수선한 clumsy

ŏtchaet-ttŭn 어쨋든 regardless; in any case; anyhow; *ŏtchaet-ttŭn chossŭmnida* 어쨋든 좋습니다 very well, alright then

ŏtchidoen iriya? 어찌된 일이야? how come?

ŏtchihal parŭl morŭda 어찌할 바를 모르다 be at a loss

ŏtchŏl chul morŭda 어쩔 줄 모르다 be overwhelmed by

ŏtchŏl su ŏmnŭn 어쩔 수 없는 unavoidable

ŏtchŏl su ŏpssŏyo 어쩔 수 없어요 it can't be helped

ŏtchŏnji 어쩐지 somehow, for some unknown reason

ŏtkkallida 엇갈리다 miss (*not meet*)

ŏtkkoja hanŭn 얻고자 하는 acquisitive

ŏttaeyo 것은 how; how about; *k'ŏp'i han chan ŏttaeyo?* 커피 한 잔 어때요? how about a cup of coffee?; *yojŭm ŏttaeyo* 요즘 어때요? how are things?

ŏttŏk'e 어떻게 how; *ŏttŏk'e chinaeseyo? – chal issŭmnida* 어떻게 지내세요? – 잘 있습니다 how are you? – fine; *ŏttŏk'e saeng-gak'aseyo?* 어떻게 생각하세요? what do you think?

ŏttŏk'edŭnji 어떻게든지 somehow

ŏttŏn 어떤 any; some; which; what; what kind of; *ŏttŏn myŏnesŏnŭn* 어떤 면에서는 in a way, in certain respects; *ŏttŏn ŭimiesŏnŭn* 어떤 의미에서는 in a sense; *ŏttŏn ...(i)rado* 어떤 ...(이)라도 whatever; any; *ŏttŏn chongnyuŭi ...?* 어떤 종류의 ...? what kind of ...?

ŏttŏn kŏt 어떤 것 something; *ŏttŏn kŏt?* 어떤 것? which one?; what kind of thing?

ŏttŏn tarŭn kosesŏ 어떤 다른 곳에서 elsewhere, somewhere else; *ŏttŏn tarŭn kosŭro* 어떤 다른 곳으로 elsewhere, somewhere else (*motion toward*)

ŏttŏseyo? 어떠세요? how are you?

ŏt-tta 얻다 get, obtain; earn; gain

ŏullida 어울리다 go with, associate with; mix with; get on with; suit; match

ŏullinŭn 어울리는 matching; suitable

...ŏya handa ...어야 한다 have to, must; be bound to

...ŏyaman hada ...어야만 하다 have (got) to; should, must

O

o 오 five; oh!
oashissŭ 오아시스 oasis
obŏdŭraibŭ 오버드라이브 overdrive
obŭn 오븐 oven
och'an 오찬 lunch
oda 오다 come; fall (of night); ...esŏ oda ...에서 오다 come from
odioŭi 오디오의 audio
odishyŏn 오디션 audition
odogado mot'ada 오도가도 못하다 be stranded, be stuck
odohada 오도하다 mislead
odohanŭn 오도하는 misleading
odumak 오두막 hut
odumaktchip 오두막집 shack
oe 외 outside; except; Sŏul oegwage 서울 외곽에 outside Seoul
oeadŭl 외아들 only son
oebu 외부 outside ◊ external
oebusaram 외부사람 outsider
oech'ida 외치다 cry, exclaim
oech'im 외침 cry, call; scream
oech'yŏ purŭda 외쳐 부르다 cry out
oedongttal 외동딸 only daughter
oegugin 외국인 foreigner
oegugin hyŏmo 외국인 혐오 xenophobia
oegugŏ 외국어 foreign language
oeguk 외국 foreign country ◊ foreign
oeguk'wan 외국환 foreign exchange
oegwan 외관 external appearance
oegwansang-ŭi 외관상의 exterior
oegwanŭl sonsangshik'ida 외관을 손상시키다 disfigure
oegyein 외계인 alien (from space)
oegyo 외교 diplomacy ◊ diplomatic
oegyogwan 외교관 diplomat
oegyomyŏnch'aek 외교면책 diplomatic immunity
oegyosul 외교술 diplomacy, tact
oeharabŏji 외할아버지 maternal grandfather
oehwa 외화 foreign currency
oehyangtchŏgin 외향적인 outgoing

oejin 외진 out of the way
oekkwa ŭisa 외과 의사 surgeon
oekkwayong mesŭ 외과용 메스 scalpel
oemu 외무 foreign affairs ◊ foreign
Oemubu 외무부 Department of State
Oemu changgwan 외무 장관 Secretary of State
oemu chŏngch'aek 외무 정책 foreign policy
oemuŏmmu 외무업무 foreign affairs
oemyŏnhada 외면하다 turn away, look away
oensonjabi 왼손잡이 left-handed
oentchoge(sŏ) 왼쪽에(서) on the left
oentchoguro 왼쪽으로 to the left
oentchok 왼쪽 left
oe pal sŭk'eit'ŭ 외 발 스케이트 scooter (child's)
oep'anwŏn 외판원 commercial traveler
oeroptta 외롭다 be solitary, be lonely
oeroum 외로움 loneliness
oeroun 외로운 lonely
oesamch'on 외삼촌 uncle (mother's brother)
oesang 외상 credit FIN
oesang kŏrae 외상 거래 charge account
oeshik'ada 외식하다 eat out
oesŏltchŏgin 외설적인 pornographic, obscene
oesungmo 외숙모 aunt (mother's brother's wife)
oettan 외딴 isolated, remote
oet'u 외투 overcoat; cloak
oeuda 외우다 memorize
ogap'ada 억압하다 supress
ogoe 옥외 open-air ◊ open air
ohae 오해 misunderstanding, misconception
ohaehada 오해하다 misread, misunderstand

ohiryŏ 오히려 rather, preferably

ohiryŏ naŭn 오히려 나은 preferable

ohu 오후 afternoon; *ohue* 오후에 in the afternoon

oi 오이 cucumber

oil 오일 oil

oji 오지 bush, hinterland

ojik 오직 only, solely

ojing-ŏ 오징어 squid

ojŏn 오전 morning; *ojŏne* 오전에 in the morning

ojon 오존 ozone

ojonch'ŭng 오존층 ozone layer

ojum nuda 오줌 누다 urinate; pee

okp'yŏn 옥편 Chinese character dictionary

oksshin-gaksshinhada 옥신각신하다 argue, squabble

oksusu 옥수수 maize, corn; sweetcorn

ok'esŭt'ŭra 오케스트라 orchestra

ok'ŭ 오크 oak (*wood*)

ok'ŭnamu 오크나무 oak (*tree*)

olbarŭda 올바르다 be straight; be upright; be honest

olbarŭge 올바르게 correctly, right

olbarŭn 올바른 right, proper; just

olch'aeng-i 올챙이 tadpole

olgami 올가미 noose

olk'e 올케 sister-in-law (*woman's brother's wife*)

ollagada 올라가다 go up, climb; *1935nyŏnŭro kŏsŭllŏ ollagasŏ* 1935년으로 거슬러 올라가서 back in 1935

ollain 올라인 on-line

ollain sŏbissŭ 온라인 서비스 on-line service

olla it-tta 올라 있다 be up (*of prices, temperature*)

ollaoda 올라오다 come up

ollibŭ 올리브 olive

ollibŭ kirŭm 올리브 기름 olive oil

ollida 올리다 raise; *p'ŏmp'ŭro p'ŏ ollida* 펌프로 퍼 올리다 pump

ollim 올림 Yours truly, Yours sincerely

Ollimp'ik Keim 올림픽 게임 Olympic Games

olppaemi 올빼미 owl

olt'a 옳다 be right, be correct ◊ OK

omgida 옮기다 move, transfer; carry

omgyŏjigi shwiun 옮겨지기 쉬운 infectious *laughter*

omgyŏt'ada 옮겨타다 transfer

omŭllet 오믈렛 omelet

omŭrida 오므리다 pucker; purse; furl

onch'ŏn 온천 spa

ondo 온도 temperature

ondogye 온도계 thermometer

ondol 온돌 heated floor

ongho 옹호 defense

onghohada 옹호하다 defend

onghoja 옹호자 defender, champion

on-gi 온기 warmth

on-gŏnhan 온건한 moderate

on-gŏnp'a 온건파 moderate party

onhwahan 온화한 mild, gentle; benign

onjŏng 온정 warmth, geniality

onlain 온라인 on-line

onnan chŏnsŏn 온난 전선 warm front

onsang 온상 breeding ground; hotbed

onshil 온실 glasshouse; nursery; conservatory

onshil hyokkwa 온실 효과 greenhouse effect

onsunhan 온순한 gentle, meek

onsu suyŏngjang 온수 수영장 heated swimming pool

ont'ong 온통 entirely

onŭl 오늘 today

onŭl ach'im 오늘 아침 this morning

onŭl chŏnyŏk 오늘 저녁 this evening

onŭllobut'ŏ 오늘로부터 from today on

onŭlnarŭi 오늘날의 present-day

onŭl ohue 오늘 오후에 this afternoon

onŭl pam 오늘 밤 tonight

oppa 오빠 brother (*woman's elder*)

opsshŏn sangp'um 옵션 상품 optional extras

op'era 오페라 opera

op'era haussŭ 오페라 하우스 opera house

op'era kasu 오페라 가수 opera singer

op'era mang-wŏn-gyŏng 오페라 망원경 opera glasses

p'ŏreit'ing shisŭt'em 오퍼레이팅 시스템 operating system

p'ŭnt'ik'et 오픈티켓 open ticket

p'ŭsaidŭ 오프사이드 offside

rae 오래 long, a long while; **orae chŏne** 오래 전에 long ago

raedoen 오래된 old

rae kanŭn 오래 가는 durable

rae kkŭnŭn 오래 끄는 protracted, lengthy

raen 오랜 old

rae sayonghan 오래 사용한 old, veteran

raettong-an 오랫동안 for a long time

rak 오락 entertainment, pleasure

raksshishŏl 오락시설 amenities

ral sseksssŭ 오락 섹스 oral sex

rangmul 오락물 amusements, games

renji 오렌지 orange

renji chyussŭ 오렌지 쥬스 orange juice

renjijok 오렌지족 rich kids (*of Seoul's wealthy elite renowned for their extravagant lifestyle*)

ri 오리 duck

rient'eishyŏn 오리엔테이션 orientation; induction ceremony

rit'ŏl ibul 오리털 이불 eiderdown, quilt

rit'ŏl p'ak'a 오리털 파카 padded jacket

rŭda 오르다 climb; mount; increase

rŭgajŭm 오르가즘 orgasm

rŭgan 오르간 organ MUS

rŭn 옳은 correct

rŭnp'yŏne 오른편에 on the right-hand side

rŭnsonjabiŭi 오른손잡이의 right-handed

rŭntchogŭro 오른쪽으로 right, to the right

orŭntchok 오른쪽 right; **orŭntchoge(sŏ)** 오른쪽에(서) on the right; **orŭntchok panghyang-ŭro** 오른쪽 방향으로 on your right hand

oryŏdugi 오려두기 cut COMPUT

oryŏnaeda 오려내다 cut out

oryŏnaen kŏt 오려낸 것 cutting

osan 오산 miscalculation

Oseania 오세아니아 Oceania ◊ Oceanian

oship 오십 fifty

osolkkil 오솔길 alley

ossak'an 오싹한 eerie

Osŭk'a shisangshik 오스카 시상식 Oscars ceremony

osŭl iptta 옷을 입다 dress, get dressed

osŭl ip'ida 옷을 입히다 dress *person*

osŭl pŏtkkida 옷을 벗기다 undress, strip *person*

osŭl pŏt-tta 옷을 벗다 undress, strip

Osŭt'ŭria 오스트리아 Austria ◊ Austrian

ot 옷 clothes; clothing; **ot hanbŏl** 옷 한벌 an item of clothing

otchŏm 오점 smear (*on character*)

otkkabang 옷가방 suitcase

otkkaji 옷가지 wardrobe (*clothes*)

otkkam 옷감 material, fabric

otkkŏri 옷걸이 clothes hanger

ot-tchang 옷장 closet

ottŏn 어떤 certain, particular

ot-ttan 옷단 hem

ott'ŏri 옷털이 clothes brush

ot'obai 오토바이 motorbike

ot'ŭmil 오트밀 oatmeal

owŏl 오월 May

oyŏm 오염 pollution; contamination

oyŏmmultchil 오염물질 pollutant

oyŏmshik'ida 오염시키다 pollute, contaminate

oyonghada 오용하다 misuse

P

pa 바 way; thing; crossbar; *naega al pa anida* 내가 알 바 아니다 for all I care

pabek'yu 바베큐 barbecue

pabek'yuyong ch'ŏlp'an 바베큐용 철판 barbecue (*equipment*)

pabo 바보 idiot; *pabojisŭl hada* 바보짓을 하다 behave like an idiot

pabosŭrŏun 바보스러운 idiotic

pach'ida 바치다 dedicate, devote; donate; sacrifice

pach'im chŏpsshi 받침 접시 saucer

pada 바다 sea; ocean

pada chŏktta 받아 적다 take down, write down

padadŭrida 받아들이다 assimilate; accept; come to terms with; keep down; *chok'e/nappŭge padadŭryŏjida* 좋게/나쁘게 받아들여지다 go down well/badly

padadŭril su innŭn 받아들일 수 있는 acceptable; admissible

padagŭl pŏsŏnada 바닥을 벗어나다 bottom out

padajŏktta 받아적다 write down

padak 바닥 floor; bottom; sole (*of foot, shoe*)

padassŭgi 받아쓰기 dictation

padatkkajae 바다가재 lobster

padŭl manhada 받을 만하다 deserve

padŭl manhan 받을 만한 be worthy of, deserve

Paduk 바둑 Go

pae 배 stomach, belly; embryo; ship; pear; *han pae saekki* 한 배 새끼 litter (*of animal*); *pae ane* 배 안에 on board

paeban 배반 betrayal, treachery

paebanhada 배반하다 betray, doublecross

paebanhanŭn 배반하는 treacherous

paebanja 배반자 traitor

paebuhada 배부하다 distribute

paeburŭda 배부르다 full up (*with food*)

paech'i 배치 layout; batch (*of data*)

paech'idoeda 배치되다 be stationed at

paech'ihada 배치하다 arrange, position

paech'u 배추 Chinese cabbage

paech'ul 배출 exhaust, fumes

paech'ulgu 배출구 outlet (*of pipe*)

paech'ulshik'ida 배출시키다 drain (off)

paedal 배달 delivery

paedalbu 배달부 messenger, courier

paedalch'a 배달차 delivery van

paedal kuyŏk 배달 구역 round (*of mailman etc*)

paedal naltcha 배달 날짜 delivery date

paedanggŭm 배당금 dividend

paedanghada 배당하다 allot

paedarhada 배달하다 deliver

paedarwŏn 배달원 tradesman

paedŭmint'ŏn 배드민턴 badminton

paedŭmint'ŏn kong 배드민턴 공 shuttlecock

Paegak-kkwan 백악관 White House

paegigwan 배기관 exhaust (pipe); waste pipe

paegi kasŭ 배기 가스 exhaust

paegil 백일 100 day ceremony (*after birth*); one hundred and one

paegilmong 백일몽 daydream

paegin 백인 white (*person*)

paegirhae 백일해 whooping cough

paegŏp 백업 backup

paegŏp tisŭk'ŭ 백업 디스크 backup disk

paegŏp tŭraibŭ 백업 드라이브 backup drive; tape drive

paegŏp'ada 백업하다 back up *file*

paegop'ŭda 배고프다 be hungry

paegop'ŭm 배고픔 hunger

paegop'ŭn 배고픈 hungry; *paega kop'ayo* 배가 고파요 I'm hungry

aegŭböptcha 배급업자 distributor
COM
aegŭmnyang 배급량 ration
aegŭp'ada 배급하다 ration
aegu 배구 volleyball
aegwan 배관 plumbing, pipes
aegwangong 배관공 plumber
aegyŏl chŏn-gu 백열 전구 light
 bulb
aegyŏng 배경 background, setting
aegyŏng ŭmak 배경 음악
 soundtrack
aehu 배후 background; rear
aehu-esŏ chojonghada 배후에서
 조종하다 pull strings
aejehada 배제하다 exclude
aejŏnban 배전반 switchboard
aek 백 hundred; white; back; bag
aek chunyŏn 백 주년 centenary
aek haendŭ 백 핸드 backhand
aek-kkŭm 백금 platinum
aek-kkwa sajŏn 백과 사전
 encyclopedia
aekkop 배꼽 navel
aekppal 백발 white hair; gray hair;
 paekppari toeda 백발이 되다 be
 going gray
aekpparŭi 백발의 gray-haired
aekppunŭi il 백분의 일 hundredth
aek'odoju 백포도주 white wine
aeksshin 백신 vaccine
aekssŭp'eisŭ k'i 백스페이스 키
 backspace (key)
aektcha 백자 white porcelain
 (*Chosŏn*)
aektcho 백조 swan
aek'ap 백합 lily
aek'wajŏm 백화점 department
 store
aelbŭ 밸브 valve
aem 뱀 snake
aemjang-ŏ 뱀장어 eel
aemŏlmi 배멀미 seasickness
aemŏlmiga nan 배멀미가 난
 seasick
aemŏlmihada 배멀미하다 get
 seasick
aenang 배낭 rucksack; *paenang
 maego yŏhaenghada* 배낭 매고
 여행하다 backpack, go backpacking

paenang yŏhaengja 배낭 여행자
 backpacker
paendŭ 밴드 (pop) band
paengman 백만 million
paengman changja 백만 장자
 millionaire
paengmirŏ 백미러 rear-view mirror
paenmŏri 뱃머리 bow, prow
paennori 뱃놀이 sail
paeran ch'oktchinje 배란 촉진제
 fertility drug
paeryŏ 배려 respect; tact;
 consideration
paesang 배상 compensation,
 recompense
paesanghada 배상하다 compensate
paeshimwŏn 배심원 juror
paeshimwŏndan 배심원단 jury
paeshimwŏnjang 배심원장 foreman
 (of the jury)
paesŏhada 배서하다 endorse
paesŏn 배선 wiring
paesok'ada 배속하다 post, transfer,
 send
paesu 배수 drainage; drains
paesugwan 배수관 drainpipe
paesuro 배수로 drain; storm drain
paetchang 배짱 courage, nerve
paetchi 배지 pin, badge
paet'ajŏgin 배타적인 exclusive
paet'al 배탈 upset stomach
paet'alnada 배탈나다 have an upset
 stomach
paet'ŏri 배터리 battery
paeŭi k'i 배의 키 rudder
paeŭnmangdŏk 배은망덕
 ingratitude
paeuda 배우다 learn
paeuga toeda 배우가 되다 become
 an actor/actress
paeuja 배우자 partner; spouse
paeunghada 배웅하다 see off
paeyŏng 배영 backstroke
paeyŏrhada 배열하다 arrange, put in
 order
pagaji kŭltta 바가지 긁다 go on at
pagaji ssŭiuda 바가지 씌우다
 overcharge
paguni 바구니 basket
paindŏ 바인더 binder
paiŏ 바이어 buyer

paiollin 바이올린 violin

paiollin yŏnjuja 바이올린 연주자 violinist

paiosŭ 바이오스 BIOS COMPUT

pairŏsŭ 바이러스 virus COMPUT

pairŏsŭ paeksshin p'ŭrogŭraem 바이러스 백신 프로그램 antivirus program

pait'ŭ 바이트 byte

paji 바지 pants

paji ammun 바지 앞문 fly

pak 박 night (in hotel)

pakk 밖 outside

pakkach'ŭi 바깥의 outside, external

pakkat'e 바깥에 outside

pakkat myŏn 바깥 면 outside

...pakke ...밖에 outside (of); except

pakkŭro 밖으로 outside

pakkuda 바꾸다 change, exchange; swap; vary; move on

pakkul su innŭn 바꿀 수 있는 interchangeable

pakkŭ chuda 바꾸어 주다 change money

pakkŭ iptta 바꾸어 입다 change clothes

pakkuŏjida 바뀌어지다 change

pakkuŏ not'a 바꾸어 놓다 displace, supplant

pakkuŏ t'ada 바꾸어 타다 change trains, planes

pakkwida 바꾸다 switch, change; vary; ...(ŭ)ro pakkwida ...(으)로 바뀌다 give way to, be replaced by

pakkwŏ chuda 바꿔 주다 put through TELEC

pakkwŏt'ada 바꿔타다 transfer

pakkyŏkp'o 박격포 mortar MIL

paksa 박사 PhD, Doctor of Philosophy

pakssae 박새 tit (bird)

pakssa hagwi 박사 학위 doctorate

pakssallaeda 박살내다 write off, wreck

paksshik'an 박식한 erudite

pakssŭ 박스 carton; booth

pakssurŭl ch'ida 박수를 치다 clap, applaud

pakssurŭl ponaeda 박수를 보내다 applaud

paktcha 박자 tempo, beat

paktchwi 박쥐 bat (animal)

paktta 박다 drive in nail

pakt'arhada 박탈하다 deprive; chagyŏgŭl pakt'arhada 자격을 박탈하다 disqualify

pakt'eria 박테리아 bacteria

pak'a 박하 mint (herb)

pak'ae 박해 persecution

pak'aehada 박해하다 persecute, oppress

pak'ahyang 박하향 peppermint (flavoring)

pak'a sat'ang 박하 사탕 mint, peppermint

pak'ida 박히다 lodge (of bullet, ball)

pak'odŭ 바코드 bar code

pak'wi 바퀴 wheel; lap, circuit

pak'wi pŏlle 바퀴 벌레 cockroach

pak'wiŭi chungshimbu 바퀴의 중심부 hub

pal 발 foot; paw

palbal 발발 eruption

palba munggaeda 밟아 뭉개다 trample on

palbarhada 발발하다 erupt

palbyŏnghada 발병하다 affect

palch'we 발췌 clip, extract (from movie)

palgabŏsŭn 발가벗은 naked; bare

palgajida 밝아지다 brighten up, become more cheerful

palgak 발각 detection

palgi 발기 erection (of penis)

palgŭm 밝음 lightness

palgŭn 밝은 bright; light; fair

palgŭp'ada 발급하다 issue, give out

palgul 발굴 excavation

palgurhada 발굴하다 discover; excavate, unearth

palgwang taiodŭ 발광 다이오드 LED, light-emitting diode

palgyŏn 발견 discovery

palgyŏnhada 발견하다 discover, find

palkkarak 발가락 toe

palke hada 밝게 하다 light up, lighten

palkkŏrŭm 발걸음 tread

palktta 밝다 be bright; be keen; be expert; be cheerful; dawn

palkkŭn hwarŭl naeda 발끈 화를 내다 flare up, fly into a rage

alkkŭt pubun 발끝 부분 toe

alkkŭt'ŭro 발끝으로 on tippy-toe

alkkup 발굽 hoof

alk'ida 밝히다 reveal, make known; express

alk'yŏjunŭn 밝혀주는 revealing

alk'yŏnaeda 밝혀내다 find out, uncover

allajida 발라지다 straighten out; spread

allan 반란 mutiny, rebellion

allanaeda 발라내다 shell; clean; take off; debone

allan-gun 반란군 rebel troops

allanŭl irŭk'ida 반란을 이르키다 revolt

alle 발레 ballet

alle muyongga 발레 무용가 ballet dancer

allerina 발레리나 ballerina

allonhada 반론하다 dispute; disagree with

almae 발매 launch; release; sale

almae ch'uk'ayŏn 발매 축하연 launch; release (*event*)

almaehada 발매하다 launch; release; bring out

almok 발목 ankle; *palmogŭl ppida* 발목을 삐다 twist one's ankle

almyŏng 발명 invention

almyŏngga 발명가 inventor

almyŏnghada 발명하다 invent

alp'an 발판 scaffolding; stepping stone

alp'o 발포 gunshot

alppyŏng 발병 bout, attack MED

alppyŏnghada 발병하다 break out (*of disease*)

alp'yŏ chuktta 밟혀 죽다 be trampled to death

alp'yo 발표 release; presentation; statement

alssa 발사 blast-off

alssadae 발사대 launch pad

alssadoeda 발사되다 go off (*of gun*)

alssaeng 발생 happening

alssaengshik'ida 발생시키다 generate, produce

alssahada 발사하다 launch

alssan 발산 emission

palssashik'ida 발사시키다 blast off

palshinŭm 발신음 dial tone

palssong 발송 shipping

palssonghada 발송하다 dispatch, send

palssong-in 발송인 sender

paltchaguk 발자국 footprint

paltchaguk sori 발자국 소리 footstep

paltchak 발작 fit, seizure

paltchaktchŏgin 발작적인 hysterical

paltchin 발진 rash MED

paltchint'ip'usŭ 발진티푸스 typhus

paltchŏn 발전 development; progression

paltchŏn-gi 발전기 dynamo; generator

paltchŏnhada 발전하다 develop; advance, improve

paltchŏnshik'ida 발전시키다 develop, expand

paltchŏnso 발전소 power station

paltta 밟다 tread; tread on; *chandirŭl paltchi mashiyo!* 잔디를 밟지 마시요! keep off the grass!

palttalshik'ida 발달시키다 develop; progress

palttŭng 발등 instep

palt'op 발톱 toenail; claw; talon

pam 밤 night; chestnut; *pame* 밤에 at night-time, in the night-time; *pam saie* 밤 사이에 during the night; *naeil pam* 내일 밤 tomorrow night; *pam nŭjŭn* 밤 늦은 late (at night); *pam yŏhaeng* 밤 여행 travel by night

pambihaenggi 밤비행기 night flight

pamnanu 밤나무 chestnut (tree)

pamsae 밤새 overnight

pan 반 half; *tushi paniyeyo* 두시 반이예요 it's half past two

panana 바나나 banana

panbaji 반바지 shorts

panbak 반박 retort

panbak'ada 반박하다 contradict; protest; retort

panbal 반발 backlash

panbok 반복 repetition

panbok'ada 반복하다 repeat; *muŏsŭl panbok'ada* 무엇을 반복하다 do sth over (again) panch'an 반찬 side dish

panch'anggo 반창고 adhesive tape; Band-Aid®

panch'igŭi 반칙의 irregular

panch'ik 반칙 foul

pandae 반대 opposite; objection; opposition

pandaedoeda 반대되다 run counter to

pandaehada 반대하다 object; object to; oppose, resist; contest; *wae kŭrŭl pandaehanŭn kŏyeyo?* 왜 그를 반대하는 거예요? what do you have against him?

pandaeja 반대자 opponent; dissident

pandaep'yŏn 반대 편 across

pandaero 반대로 on the other hand; conversely; on the contrary; as opposed to; vice versa

pandae shimmunhada 반대 심문하다 cross-examine

pandae tchogŭi 반대 쪽의 opposite

pandaeŭi 반대의 opposite

pandae ŭigyŏn 반대 의견 dissent

pando 반도 peninsula

pandoch'e 반도체 semiconductor

pandongjuŭija 반동주의자 reactionary (*person*)

pandŭshi 반드시 necessarily; certainly

pang 방 room

pan-gam 반감 antipathy

pang-asoe 방아쇠 trigger

pangbŏp 방법 method; style; formula

pangbu ch'ŏrihada 방부 처리하다 embalm

pangbuje 방부제 preservative

pangch'aek 방책 measure, step

pangch'i 방치 neglect

pangch'ŏp 방첩 counterespionage

pangch'ungje 방충제 insect repellent

pangdaehan 방대한 vast, gigantic

Panggŭlladeshi 방글라데시 Bangladesh ◊ Bangladeshi

panggŭm 방금 just now

panggwang 방광 bladder

panggwanhada 방관하다 stand by (and do nothing)

panggwanja 방관자 bystander

panggwi 방귀 fart

panggwi kkwida 방귀 뀌다 fart

panghae 방해 obstacle; disturbance; *panghaerŭl pat-tta* 방해를 받다 suffer a setback

panghaehada 방해하다 disturb; interrupt; disrupt; hinder, impede; jam

panghaehanŭn 방해하는 obstructive

panghaemul 방해물 obstruction; deterrent

panghan 방한 insulation

panghanhada 방한하다 insulate

panghwa 방화 arson

panghwajangch'i 방화장치 incendiary device

panghyang 방향 direction; directions; *panghyang kamgagŭl irŏbŏrin* 방향 감각을 잃어버린 disoriented, confused

panghyang p'yoshidŭng 방향 표시등 turn signal

pangjŏk'ada 방적하다 spin

pangjŏngshik 방정식 equation

pangjonghan 방종한 dissolute, loose

pangmang-i 방망이 bat (*in baseball*)

pangmang-iro ch'ida 방망이로 치다 bat

pangmulgwan 박물관 museum

pangmun 방문 door; visit

pangmunhada 방문하다 visit, call on; look in on; look up

pangmyŏrhada 박멸하다 eradicate

pangnanghada 방랑하다 rove, wander

pangnangja 방랑자 drifter, hobo

pang-ŏ 방어 defense; *pang-ŏhanŭn chasero* 방어하는 자세로 on the defensive

pang-ŏhada 방어하다 defend

pang-ŏjŏgin 방어적인 defensive

pang-ŏyong-ŭi 방어용의 defensive

pan-gongjuŭi 반공주의 anti-Communism

pangp'ae 방패 shield

pangp'aje 방파제 breakwater

pangsanŭng 방사능 radioactivity

pangsanŭng-i innŭn 방사능이 있는 radioactive

pangsanŭng yoppŏp 방사능 요법

radiotherapy

ɔangsasŏn방사선 radiation

ɔangsasong naktchin방사성 낙진 fallout

ɔangshik방식 manner, way; system; method; mode; form; *iltchŏnghan pangshige ttarŭn* 일정한 방식에 따른 methodical

ɔangsong방송 broadcast; broadcasting; *pangsong chung-e* 방송 중에 on the air

ɔangsongguk방송국 station RAD, TV

ɔangsonghada방송하다 broadcast; transmit

ɔangsong-in방송인 broadcaster

ɔangsong p'ŭrogŭraem chaptchi 방송 프로그램 잡지 listings magazine

ɔangsongshil방송실 studio

ɔangsudoenŭn방수되는 waterproof

ɔangsu oet'u방수 외투 mackintosh

ɔangsup'o방수포 tarpaulin

ɔangsuŭi방수의 watertight; showerproof

ɔangt'an chokki방탄 조끼 armor

ɔangt'ang방탕 debauchery

ɔangt'anghan방탕한 debauched, dissolute

ɔang-ŭm방음 soundproofing ◊ soundproof

ɔang-ŭm changch'i방음 장치 muffler MOT

ɔan-gu반구 hemisphere

ɔang-ul방울 drip, drop

ɔang-wi방위 defense

ɔan-gyŏk반격 return

ɔang-yŏnghada방영하다 televise

ɔanhae it-tta반해 있다 be stuck on; have a crush on

ɔanhal manhan반할 만한 adorable

ɔanhang반항 defiance

ɔanhanghada반항하다 defy

ɔanhangjŏgin반항적인 defiant; rebellious

ɔanhayŏ반하여 contrary to

ɔanhwan반환 return

ɔanil kŭnmu반일 근무 part-time job

ɔanilla바닐라 vanilla

ɔanjagyong반작용 reaction

ɔanjagyonghada반작용하다 react

panji반지 ring

panjirŭm반지름 radius

panjŏm반점 spot; blotch

panjŭnghada반증하다 disprove

panju반주 accompaniment; backing

panjudan반주단 backing group

panjuk'ada반죽하다 knead

panjurŭl hada반주를 하다 accompany MUS

pannŭn chŭksshiro받는 즉시로 by return (of mail)

panp'arŭi반팔의 short-sleeved

pansahada반사하다 reflect

pansa shin-gyŏng반사 신경 reflex

pansa undong반사 운동 reflex reaction

pansonghada반송하다 send back

pantchagida반짝이다 shine, gleam; twinkle

pantchak반짝 glint

pantchak-kkŏrida반짝거리다 shine; glisten

pantchak-kkŏrinŭn반짝거리는 shiny

pantchakpantchak pinnada 반짝반짝 빛나다 glitter

pantchak pinnada반짝 빛나다 glint

panŭi반의 half

panŭjil바느질 needlework, sewing

panŭjilkkŏri바느질거리 sewing

panŭjil yongp'um바느질 용품 notions

panŭjirhada바느질하다 sew

panŭl바늘 needle; stitches

panŭlgwi바늘귀 eye (*of needle*)

panŭlttam바늘땀 stitch

panŭm naerimŭi반음 내림의 flat MUS

panŭm nopkke반음 높게 sharp MUS

panŭng반응 reaction

panŭnghada반응하다 react, respond

panŭnghanŭn반응하는 responsive

panŭro chŏptta반으로 접다 fold in half

panŭro hada반으로 하다 halve

panwŏn반원 semicircle

panwŏnhyŏngŭi반원형의 semicircular

panyŏk반역 treason

panyŏktcha반역자 rebel

pap밥 rice

pap kŭrŭt 밥 그릇 rice bowl

pappŭda 바쁘다 be busy; busy oneself with, occupy oneself with; ...*ŭl* / *rŭl hanŭra pappŭda* ...을 / 를 하느라 바쁘다 be busy doing ...

pappŭn 바쁜 busy; full

paraboda 바라보다 view

parada 바라다 hope; wish; hope for; wish for; ...*gŭrŭl parada* ...기를 바라다 may ...; *nanŭn* ...*gŭrŭl paramnida* 나는 ...기를 바랍니다 I wish that ...

paraeda 바래다 fade; take, escort; *munkkaji paraeda chulkkeyo* 문까지 바래다 줄께요 I'll see you to the door

paraedajuda 바래다주다 escort

paraen 바랜 faded

paragŏnde 바라건데 hopefully

param 바람 desire, wish; wind; *parami pulgi shijak'anda* 바람이 불기 시작한다 it's getting windy; *parami shimhan* 바람이 심한 gusty

paramdung-i 바람둥이 womanizer

paramjik'an 바람직한 desirable, advisable

param mach'ida 바람 맞히다 stand up (*on date*)

paramnan 바람난 flirtatious

param punŭn 바람 부는 windy

param p'iuda 바람 피우다 have an affair with; fool around; cheat on one's wife

paramsŏng-ŭi 발암성의 carcinogenic

paramŭl p'iuda 바람을 피우다 have an affair; be unfaithful

parhada 발하다 utter

parhaeng 발행 publication

parhaenghada 발행하다 print; issue

parhaeng pusu 발행 부수 circulation

parhwi 발휘 exhibition (*of skill*)

parhwihada 발휘하다 exert; show off; *chagi nŭngnyŏk isang-ŭl parhwihada* 자기 능력 이상을 발휘하다 excel oneself

parhyo 발효 fermentation

parhyohada 발효하다 ferment

parik'ang 바리캉 hair clippers

parik'eidŭ 바리케이드 barricade; roadblock

parŏnhada 발언하다 speak; state

paro 바로 properly; directly; *paro ap'e* 바로 앞에 straight ahead; *paro chŏne* 바로 전에 recently; *paro kakkaie* 바로 가까이에 close at hand; *paro kyŏt'e* 바로 곁에 close by; *ŭnhaeng paro yŏp'ye* 은행 바로 옆에 right next to the bank; *paro kŭgŏya!* 바로 그거야! that's right!; *paro kŭrŏk'e* 바로 그렇게 just like that, exactly like that; *paro kŭ saenggak* 바로 그 생각 the very thought; *paro kŭ sun-gane* 바로 그 순간에 at the very moment; *paro seuda* 바로 세우다 straighten out; *paro sŏ!* 바로 서! stand up straight!

parŭda 바르다 be straight; be right; stick, paste, plaster; spread; put up *wallpaper*

parŭge hada 바르게 하다 straighten out

parŭl kurŭda 발을 구르다 stamp one's feet

parŭm 발음 pronunciation

parŭmhada 발음하다 pronounce

parŭn 바른 proper, correct; orderly; honest; decent

passak mallida 바싹 말리다 parch

passak marŭda 바싹 마르다 dry up

pasŭk'et 바스켓 basket

pasŭrak-kkŏrida 바스락거리다 rustle

pat 밭 (dry) field

patatkka 바닷가 seaside

patch'imttae 받침대 stand, support, base

pattchul 밧줄 rope

pattchurŭl p'ulda 밧줄을 풀다 cast off

pat-tta 받다 receive, accept; undergo; sustain; butt (*of goat*)

pat'ang 바탕 bout; nature; base; ...*e pat'angŭl tuda* ...에 바탕을 두다 base on

pat'endŏ 바텐더 bartender

pawi 바위 rock

peda 베다 cut

pegae 베개 pillow

pegaennit 베갯잇 pillowcase

pegi 베기 cut, slash

ạeil 베일 veil
ẹisŭ 베이스 bass
ẹkkyŏ ssŭda 베껴 쓰다 copy
ẹlgie 벨기에 Belgium ◊ Belgian
ẹlgiein 벨기에인 Belgian
ẹnch'i 벤치 bench
ẹniŏ happ'an 베니어 합판 veneer
ẹn sangch'ŏ 벤 상처 cut (*injury*)
ẹŏnaeda 베어내다 cut off
ẹŏring 베어링 bearing TECH
ẹranda 베란다 balcony; veranda
ẹsŭt'ŭsellŏ 베스트셀러 best-seller
ẹt'erang 베테랑 veteran
ẹt'ŭnam 베트남 Vietnam ◊
Vietnamese
ẹt'ŭnamin 베트남인 Vietnamese
ẹt'ŭnamŏ 베트남어 Vietnamese
(*language*)
ọi... 비... non..., un...
ị bi 비 rain
ịbang 비방 slur, defamation
ịbanghanŭn 비방하는 defamatory
ịbarame shidallin 비바람에 시달린
weather-beaten
ịbi kkoda 비비 꼬다 squirm (*in
embarrassment*)
ịbimppap 비빔밥 rice mixed with
meat and vegetables
ịbŏnida 비번이다 be off duty
ịch'amhada 비참하다 be miserable
ịch'ida 비치다 flash
ịch'inŭn 비치는 see-through
ịch'ŭl naeda 빛을 내다 glow
ịch'ŭl naenŭn 빛을 내는 luminous
ịch'uda 비추다 shine; flash; reflect;
***...e pich'uŏsŏ** ...에 비추어서 in the
light of
ịch'uk'ada 비축하다 stockpile,
hoard; ***muŏsŭl pich'uk'ada** 무엇을
비축하다 keep sth in reserve
ịda 비다 be empty
ịdan 비단 silk
ịdio 비디오 video
ịdio k'amera 비디오 카메라 video
camera
ịdio k'aset'ŭ 비디오 카세트 video
cassette
ịdio nok'wa 비디오 녹화 video
recording
ịdio nok'wagi 비디오 녹화기 video
recorder

pidioro ch'waryŏnghada 비디오로
촬영하다 video
pidio t'eip'ŭ 비디오 테이프
videotape
pidodŏktchŏgin 비도덕적인
unprincipled
pidŭm 비듬 dandruff
pidulgi 비둘기 dove; pigeon
piga oda 비가 오다 rain
piga onŭn 비가 오는 rainy, wet
pigida 비기다 draw SP
pigŏjuja 비거주자 non-resident
pigŏp 비겁 cowardice
pigŏp'an 비겁한 cowardly
pigongshigŭi 비공식의 informal
pigongshik 비공식 informality
pigongshiktchŏgin 비공식적인
unofficial
pigongshiktchŏgŭro 비공식적으로
unofficially
pigŭk 비극 tragedy
pigŭktchŏgin 비극적인 tragic
pigwanjŏgin 비관적인 pessimistic
pigwanjuŭi 비관주의 pessimism
pigwanjuŭija 비관주의자 pessimist
pigwansŭptchŏgin 비관습적인
unconventional
pigyŏl 비결 tip, piece of advice
pigyo 비교 comparison
pigyodoel su innŭn 비교될 수 있는
comparable
pigyogŭp 비교급 comparative GRAM
pigyohada 비교하다 compare;
***...wa / gwa pigyohaesŏ** ...와 / 과
비교해서 compared with
pigyojŏgin 비교적인 comparative,
relative
pigyojŏgŭro 비교적으로
comparatively
pihaeng 비행 flight; flying; ***pihaeng
chung-ŭi** 비행 중의 in-flight
pihaenggi 비행기 airplane; ***pihaenggiro** 비행기로 by air; ***pihaenggiro toragada** 비행기로
돌아가다 fly back
pihaengjang 비행장 airfield
pihaeng kyŏngno 비행 경로 flight
path
pihal te ŏmnŭn 비할 데 없는
incomparable
pihamnijŏgin 비합리적인

unreasonable

pihŭbyŏnja 비흡연자 non-smoker

pihyŏnshiltchŏgin 비현실적인 impractical, unrealistic

pihyŏptchojŏgin 비협조적인 uncooperative

piin-ganjŏgin 비인간적인 inhuman

pija 비자 visa

pijagŭm 비자금 slush fund

pijŏngsangtchŏgin moyang-ŭi 비정상적인 모양의 misshapen

pijŏngsang-ŭi 비정상의 abnormal

pijobŭn 비좁은 cramped

pijŭnisŭ k'ŭllaesŭ 비즈니스 클래스 business class

pijŭnisŭ mit'ing 비즈니스 미팅 business meeting

pikkoda 비꼬다 twist; give an ironic twist to

pikkonŭn 비꼬는 dry; ironic

pik'ida 비키다 get out of the way; *kirŭl pik'yŏjuda* 길을 비켜주다 make way

pik'ini 비키니 bikini

pilda 빌다 beg; pray; implore

pillida 빌리다 borrow; lend

pillin 빌린 on loan

pillyŏjuda 빌려주다 lend; rent out

pimanhan 비만한 corpulent

pimil 비밀 confidence; secret; *muŏsŭl pimillie hada* 무엇을 비밀리에 하다 do sth in secret; *pimillo* 비밀로 in secret; *nuguege pimirŭl t'ŏrŏnot'a* 누구에게 비밀을 털어놓다 confide in s.o.

pimil chŏngbo kigwan 비밀 정보 기관 secret service

pimil kyŏngch'al 비밀 경찰 secret police

pimillie sumgyŏjin 비밀리에 숨겨진 undercover

pimil pŏnho 비밀 번호 PIN

pimirŭi 비밀의 secret; underground, covert

Pimujang Chidae 비무장 지대 Demilitarized Zone, DMZ

pimun 비문 epitaph

pimyŏng 비명 screech, shriek

pimyŏngŭl chirŭda 비명을 지르다 screech, shriek

pin 빈 empty, free

pinan 비난 blame; accusation; condemnation, reproach

pinanhada 비난하다 accuse; blame; condemn

pinanhanŭn 비난하는 reproachful

pinan padŭlmanhan 비난 받을만한 reprehensible

pinanŭi yŏjiga ŏptta 비난의 여지가 없다 be beyond reproach

pinbŏnhada 빈번하다 be frequent

pindungbindung chinaeda 빈둥빈둥 지내다 while away; bum around, be lazy

pindunggŏrida 빈둥거리다 laze around

pingbing tolda 빙빙 돌다 circle (*of plane*)

pingbing tollida 빙빙 돌리다 twirl

pingha 빙하 glacier

pin-gone tchidŭn 빈곤에 찌든 impoverished

pin-gonhan 빈곤한 destitute

pin-got 빈 곳 gap

pingsan 빙산 iceberg

pingtchŏm 빙점 freezing point

pin-gunghan 빈궁한 needy, poor

pinhyŏltchŭng 빈혈증 anemia

pinil pongji 비닐 봉지 plastic bag

pinjŏngdaeda 빈정대다 get at, criticize

pinjŏngdaenŭn 빈정대는 sarcastic

pin konggan 빈 공간 void

pinmin-ga 빈민가 ghetto, slum

pinnada 빛나다 shine; sparkle, twinkle

pinnagada 빛나가다 swerve; digress; misfire; *yŏp killo pinnagada* 옆 길로 빛나가다 stray

pinnagan 빗나간 stray *bullet*

pinollijŏgin 비논리적인 illogical

pint'ŏlt'ŏri 빈털터리 down-and-out

pint'ŭm ŏmnŭn 빈틈 없는 alert, shrewd, on the ball; scrupulous

pinŭl 비늘 scale (*on fish*)

pinŭngnyultchŏgin 비능률적인 inefficient

pinu 비누 soap; *pinu hanjang* 비누 한 장 a bar of soap

pinyak'an 빈약한 flimsy, skimpy

piŏinnŭn 비어있는 unoccupied

piŏinnŭn shigan 비어있는 시간

(time) slot

iok 비옥 fertility (*of soil*)

iok'an 비옥한 fertile *soil*

ip'anjŏgin 비판적인 critical

ip'anjŏgŭro 비판적으로 critically

ip'anŭl pat-tta 비판을 받다 come in for criticism

ip'ongnyŏgŭi 비폭력의 non-violent

ip'ongnyŏk 비폭력 non-violence

ip'ŭbŏgŏ 비프버거 beefburger

ip'yŏng 비평 criticism, review

ip'yŏngga 비평가 critic

ip'yŏnghada 비평하다 criticize

irömŏgŭl 빌어먹을! blast!

irok ....-ㄹ /-ŭltchirado 비록 ...-ㄹ /-을지라도 although, even if

irot-ttoeda 비롯되다 originate

irot'ada 비롯하다 begin, start

iryehada 비례하다 be proportional to

iryehanŭn 비례하는 proportional, in proportion

iryo 비료 fertilizer, manure

isaengsanjŏgin 비생산적인 unproductive

isagyojŏgin 비사교적인 unsociable

isang 비상 emergency

isang ch'angnyuk 비상 착륙 emergency landing

isangdŭng 비상등 hazard lights

isanggu 비상구 emergency exit

isangnyong hwalgangno 비상용 활강로 escape chute

isangsat'ae 비상사태 state of emergency

isangshi 비상시 time of emergency; *pisangshie* 비상시에 in an emergency

isŏ 비서 secretary

isŏk 비석 tombstone

issada 비싸다 be expensive

issan 비싼 expensive

isŭdŭmhan 비스듬한 slanting

isŭk'et 비스켓 biscuit

isŭt'ada 비슷하다 be alike, be similar

isŭt'an 비슷한 similar

isugi 비수기 low season

pit 빗 comb

pit 빚 debt; *piji it-tta* 빚이 있다 be in debt

pit 빛 light; ray

pitchang 빗장 bar, bolt

pitcharu 빗자루 broom

pitchida 빚지다 owe

pitchirhada 빗질하다 brush

pitkkŭm 빗금 slash, oblique

pitppang-ul 빗방울 raindrop

pit-tta 빗다 comb

pitturŏjida 비뚤어지다 be warped

pitturŏjin 비뚤어진 crooked; warped

pit'amin 비타민 vitamin

pit'an 비탄 lament

pit'ong 비통 grief

pit'onghaehada 비통해하다 grieve

pit'onghan 비통한 heartrending; bitter

pit'ŭ 비트 bit COMPUT

pit'ŭlda 비틀다 contort; wrench

pit'ŭlgŏrida 비틀거리다 lurch, stagger; totter

pit'ŭlgŏrinŭn 비틀거리는 unsteady

pit'ŭmaep 비트맵 bitmap

piuda 비우다 empty; vacate; *chip piuranŭn t'ongjirŭl pat-tta* 집 비우라는 통지를 받다 get one's eviction notice

piunnŭn 비웃는 derisive

piusŭm 비웃음 derision; sneer

piut-tta 비웃다 laugh at, mock, deride; sneer

piwisaengjŏgin 비위생적인 unhygienic

piyŏrhan 비열한 petty; nasty; *piyŏrhan ch'aengnyak* 비열한 책략 dirty trick

piyong 비용 expense; *Xege Yŭi piyong-ŭl kyŏnjŏk'ada* X에게 Y의 비용을 견적하다 give X a quotation for Y; *piyong-i ŏlmana tŭmnikka?* 비용이 얼마나 듭니까? how much does it cost?

piyong myŏngse 비용 명세 expense account

piyong-ŭl kaptta 비용을 갚다 reimburse

piyujŏgin 비유적인 figurative

piyul 비율 proportion; percentage; rate

pŏban 법안 bill POL

pŏbin chojigŭi 법인 조직의 incorporated

pŏbin hoesa 법인 회사 incorporated, inc

pŏbwŏn 법원 courthouse

pŏbwŏn myŏngnyŏng 법원 명령 court order

pŏdŭlgaji 버들가지 wicker

pŏdŭnamu 버드나무 willow

pŏdunggŏrida 버둥거리다 squirm, wriggle

pŏgŭ 버그 bug COMPUT

pŏjŏn 버전 version

pŏk'ŭl 버클 buckle

pŏl 벌 bee; deck, pack; suit; pair; set; plain; punishment ◊ *countword for suit of clothes; pŏrŭl momyŏnhada* 벌을 모면하다 get off scot-free; *pŏrŭl myŏnhada* 벌을 면하다 get off (*not be punished*); *pŏrŭl pattchi ank'o* 벌을 받지 않고 with impunity

pŏlch'unghada 벌충하다 make up for, compensate for

pŏlda 벌다 earn

pŏlgŏbŏsŭn 벌거벗은 naked

pŏlgŭm 벌금 fine; penalty

pŏlk'ŏk sŏngnaeda 벌컥 성내다 fly into a rage

pŏlle 벌레 bug; worm

pŏlle mŏgŭn 벌레 먹은 worm-eaten

pŏllida 벌리다 open

pŏlmok 벌목 woodcut

pŏlssŏ 벌써 already

pŏltchip 벌집 beehive; honeycomb

pŏlttŏk 벌떡 suddenly; *pŏlttŏk irŏnada* 벌떡 일어나다 jump to one's feet

pŏm 범 tiger

Pŏma 버마 Burma ◊ Burmese

pŏmhada 범하다 commit

pŏmin 범인 culprit

pŏmin susaek 범인 수색 manhunt

pŏmjoe 범죄 crime; offense; guilt ◊ criminal

pŏmjoein indo 범죄인 인도 extradition

pŏmjoein indo hyŏptchŏng 범죄인 인도 협정 extradition treaty

pŏmjoeja 범죄자 criminal; offender

pŏmju 범주 category

pŏmnam 범람 flood; flooding

pŏmnamhada 범람하다 flood

pŏmnyŏng 법령 law, statute

pŏmppoptcha 범법자 offender

pŏmp'ŏ 범퍼 bumper

pŏmsŏn 범선 sailing ship

pŏmurida 버무리다 toss

pŏmwi 범위 extent, range; *...ŭi pŏmwirŭl nŏmŏsŏ* ...의 범위를 넘어서 beyond

pŏmyul 법률 legislation

pŏn 번 time, occasion; number; duty; *han pŏn* 한 번 once

pŏnch'ang 번창 prosperity

pŏnch'anghada 번창하다 prosper, flourish

pŏnch'anghanŭn 번창하는 prosperous, flourishing

pŏn-gae 번개 lightning

pŏn-gaech'ŏrŏm tallida 번개처럼 달리다 race; run like the wind; streak

pŏn-gaeppul 번갯불 bolt of lightning

pŏn-gara hanŭn 번갈아 하는 alternate

pŏng-ŏri 벙어리 mute; dumb

pŏng-ŏri changgap 벙어리 장갑 mitten

pŏn-gŏroun 번거로운 complex

pŏnho 번호 number

pŏnhop'an 번호판 license plate

pŏnhorŭl maegida 번호를 매기다 number, put a number on

pŏnhwahan 번화한 busy, lively, bustling

pŏnjida 번지다 run (*of paint, make-up etc*)

pŏnnamu 벚나무 cherry (tree)

pŏnshik 번식 breeding

pŏnshik'ada 번식하다 breed

pŏnshingnyŏgi ŏmnŭn 번식력이 없는 infertile

pŏntchŏk-kkŏrinŭn 번쩍거리는 flashing

pŏnttŭgida 번득이다 glint

pŏnyŏk 번역 translation

pŏnyŏkka 번역가 translator

pŏnyŏk'ada 번역하다 translate

pŏnyŏnghada 번영하다 bloom, flourish

pŏp 법 law; method; *pŏbe ŏgŭnnanŭn* 법에 어긋나는 against

the law

ŏp-ppok 법복 robe (*of judge*)

ŏptchŏgin 법적인 legal

ŏptchŏk choŏnja 법적 조언자 legal adviser

ŏptchŏng 법정 court; courtroom

ŏp'ak 법학 law (*as subject of study*)

ŏrida 버리다 abandon, leave; discard; dump

ŏrida 벌이다 stage *demo*; start *business*

ŏrigo ttŏnada 버리고 떠나다 abandon

ŏrŭdŏpsshi mandŭlda 버릇없이 만들다 spoil *child*

ŏrŭsŭl karŭch'ida 버릇을 가르치다 discipline

ŏrŭt ŏmnŭn 버릇 없는 impolite; spoilt

ŏryŏduda 버려두다 abandon; *naenoŭn ch'ae pŏryŏduda* 내놓은 채 버려두다 leave out, not put away

ŏryŏjin 버려진 derelict, neglected

ŏsŏnada 벗어나다 break away; elude; outgrow; *...esŏ pŏsŏnada* ...에서 벗어나다 depart from; deviate from

ŏsŏt 버섯 mushroom

ŏsŭ 버스 bus *also* COMPUT; *pŏsŭro* 버스로 by bus

ŏsŭ chŏngnyujang 버스 정류장 bus stop

ŏsŭ t'ŏminŏl 버스 터미널 bus terminal, bus station

ŏtkkida 벗기다 remove; rub away; strip; undress; unveil; shell; *kkŏptchirŭl pŏtkkida* 껍질을 벗기다 skin; peel, pare

ŏtkkyŏjida 벗겨지다 come off; peel off (*of paint*)

ŏt-tta 벗다 remove

ŏt'ida 버티다 hold out, survive; resist

ŏt'ŏ 버터 butter

ŏt'ŏrŭl parŭda 버터를 바르다 butter *bread*

ŏt'ŭn 버튼 button

oan 보안 security

oan-gyŏng 보안경 goggles

oan hwagin 보안 확인 security check

poankkwa 보안과 security (*department*)

poan kyŏnggye 보안 경계 security alert

poanŭl chungshihanŭn 보안을 중시하는 security-conscious

pobae 보배 jewel *fig*

pobok 보복 revenge

poboktchŏgin 보복적인 vindictive

pobok'ada 보복하다 take one's revenge

pobyŏng 보병 infantry soldier

pobyŏngdae 보병대 infantry

poch'ŏnggi 보청기 hearing aid

poch'o 보초 sentry

poch'ung 보충 compensation, reward

poch'unghada 보충하다 supplement

poda 보다 look; look at; eye; make out; see; watch ◊ than; *...poda tŏ mani* ...보다 더 많이; *... ŭl/rŭl poji mot'anŭn* ...을/를 보지 못하는 blind to; *shihŏmŭl poda* 시험을 보다 take an exam

poda chagŭn 보다 작은 minor, slight

poda chungnyohada 보다 중요하다 outweigh

...poda natkke ...보다 낮게 beneath (*in status, value*)

poda nat-tta 보다 낫다 be better than

poda naŭn 보다 나은 better

poda orae salda 보다 오래 살다 survive, outlive

podap'ada 보답하다 repay, return

poda suga mant'a 보다 수가 많다 outnumber

poda tŏ 보다 더 more than, over, above

poda tŏ charhada 보다 더 잘하다 outdo

poda tŏ orae salda 보다 더 오래 살다 outlive

poda ttwiŏnan 보다 뛰어난 superior, better

...poda wi ...보다 위 above, higher than

podisut'ŭ 보디수트 body (suit)

podo 보도 report, coverage

podohada 보도하다 report, cover

podŭ keim

podŭ keim 보드 게임 board game
podŭk'a 보드카 vodka
poganghada 보강하다 follow up; reinforce
pogang hoeŭi 보강 회의 follow-up meeting
pogie 보기에 apparently
pogienŭn 보기에는 seemingly; *naega pogienŭn* 내가 보기에는 in my estimation; as far as I'm concerned
pogi hyunghan 보기 흉한 unsightly
pogiwanŭn tarŭn 보기와는 다른 deceptive
pogo 보고 account, report
pogohada 보고하다 report
pogosŏ 보고서 report, account
Pogŭm 복음 the Word REL; Gospels
pogŭm chŏndosa 복음 전도사 evangelist
pogŭmsŏ 복음서 Gospel
pogwan 보관 storage
pogwan changso 보관 장소 storage space
pogwanhada 보관하다 keep, store
pogwanso matkkida 보관소에 맡기다 check (*in checkroom*)
pogwŏnhada 복원하다 reinstate
pogyŏl sŏnsu 보결 선수 substitute
pogyongnyang 복용량 dosage
pogyongppŏp 복용법 directions (*for medicine*)
pogyongshik'ida 복용시키다 administer, give *medicine*
pogyunja 보균자 carrier (*of disease*)
pohaenggi 보행기 walker (*for baby*)
pohaengja 보행자 pedestrian, walker
pohaengja chŏnyong kuyŏk 보행자 전용 구역 pedestrian precinct
pohamhada 포함하다 include, comprise
pohŏm 보험 insurance
pohŏm chŭngsŏ 보험 증서 insurance policy
pohŏme tŭlda 보험에 들다 insure
pohŏm hoesa 보험 회사 insurance company
poho 보호 protection
pohoch'aek 보호책 safeguard
pohohada 보호하다 protect, preserve

pohohanŭn 보호하는 protective
poho kamch'algwan 보호 감찰관 probation officer
poho kuyŏk 보호 구역 (wild animal) sanctuary
poida 보이다 be able to see; be visible; show; seem; *poiji annŭn* 보이지 않는 out of sight
poik'ot 보이콧 boycott
poik'ot'ada 보이콧하다 boycott
poillŏ 보일러 boiler
poinŭn 보이는 visible
poisŭk'aut 보이스카웃 boy scout
pojal kŏt omnŭn 보잘 것 없는 trivial; worthless
pojang 보장 security, guarantee (*for investment*)
pojanghada 보장하다 guarantee, assure
pojogae 보조개 dimple
pojogŭm 보조금 grant, subsidy; *pojogŭmŭl chigŭp'ada* 보조금을 지급하다 subsidize
pojojŏgin 보조적인 auxiliary, supplementary
pojo kyojae 보조 교재 teaching aid
pojon 보존 preservation, maintenance
pojonhada 보존하다 preserve, maintain; conserve
pojoŭi 보조의 auxiliary
pojŭng 보증 guarantee, warranty; assurance; *pojŭng kigan chung-ida* 보증 기간 중이다 be under warranty
pojŭnghada 보증하다 sponsor; guarantee; underwrite; vouch for
pojŭng-in 보증인 guarantor; sponsor
pojŭng kigan 보증 기간 guarantee period
pojŭngsŏ 보증서 letter of guarantee
pok-kku 복구 restoration
pok-kkuhada 복구하다 restore
pok-kkwihada 복귀하다 make a comeback; return; be restored
pokppu 복부 abdomen ◊ abdominal
pokssa 복사 copy
pokssadoen yŏlssoe 복사된 열쇠 duplicate key
pokssagi 복사기 photocopier
pokssahada 복사하다 copy; take a

photocopy of
pokssappyŏ 복사뼈 ankle bone
poksshik 복식 doubles (in tennis)
pokssŭp'ada 복습하다 brush up; review
ookssu 복수 retaliation, reprisal; vengeance
pokssuhada 복수하다 retaliate, take reprisals
pokssuhyŏng 복수형 plural
pokssung-a 복숭아 peach
poktchap'ada 복잡하다 be complicated
poktchap'an 복잡한 complicated; complex
poktche 복제 reproduction
poktchep'um 복제품 replica
poktchi 복지 welfare
poktchiksshik'ida 복직시키다 reinstate
poktchi kuk-kka 복지 국가 welfare state
poktchi saŏp 복지 사업 welfare work
poktchi saŏpkka 복지 사업가 welfare worker
poktchong 복종 obedience; submission
poktta 볶다 stir-fry
poktto 복도 corridor, passage
pokt'ong 복통 stomach-ache
pok'ŏl kŭrup 보컬 그룹 vocal group
pollae 본래 originally; naturally
polling 볼링 bowling
pollinghada 볼링하다 bowl
pollingjang 볼링장 bowling alley
polling kong 볼링 공 bowl
pollingp'in 볼링핀 pin
pol peŏring 볼 베어링 ball bearing
polp'en 볼펜 ballpoint (pen)
polp'umŏmnŭn 볼품없는 unattractive
polt'ŭ 볼트 bolt; volt
polt'ŭro choeda 볼트로 죄다 bolt
pom 봄 look, glance; spring
pomch'ŏl 봄철 springtime
pommaji taech'ŏngso 봄맞이 대청소 spring-cleaning
pomul 보물 treasure

ponaeda 보내다 pass (of time); spend time; send
ponbogi 본보기 model, pattern
ponbu 본부 base, center; headquarters
ponggoch'a 봉고차 van
ponggŭmnal 봉급날 payday
ponggŭp 봉급 pay check
ponggŭp pongt'u 봉급 봉투 pay envelope
ponggŭp sujun 봉급 수준 salary scale
ponghada 봉하다 seal letter
pong-in 봉인 seal
pongji 봉지 packet, sachet; seal
pongni 본리 well-being; compound interest
pongsahada 봉사하다 render a service, serve
pongswae 봉쇄 blockade
pongswaehada 봉쇄하다 blockade; seal off; freeze
pongt'u 봉투 envelope
ponin 본인 oneself; himself; herself; **ponini chiktchŏp** 본인이 직접 in person; **ponin sajin** 본인 사진 a photo of oneself
ponjiltchŏgin 본질적인 fundamental; substantial
ponjiltchŏgŭro 본질적으로 fundamentally, basically, mainly
ponmun 본문 text
ponnŭng 본능 instinct
ponnŭngjŏgin 본능적인 instinctive
ponŏsŭ 보너스 bonus
ponsa 본사 head office
ponttŭda 본뜨다 imitate, emulate
pont'o 본토 mainland
poonbyŏng 보온병 thermos flask
pop'yŏnjŏgin 보편적인 universal, general
pop'yŏnjŏgŭro 보편적으로 universally
porami innŭn 보람이 있는 worthwhile
poram ŏmnŭn 보람 없는 thankless
poratppit 보라빛 violet (color)
pori 보리 barley
porich'a 보리차 roasted barley tea
porŭmttal 보름달 full moon
poryŏnji 볼연지 blusher

poryuhada 보류하다 withhold

Posal 보살 Bodhisattva

posalp'ida 보살피다 look after

posalp'im 보살핌 care

posang 보상 reward; compensation; *posangŭl hada* 보상을 하다 make amends, compensate for

posanghada 보상하다 compensate for

poshint'ang 보신탕 dog meat soup

posŏk 보석 bail; jewel, gem; *posŏgŭl patkke hada* 보석을 받게 하다 bail out

posŏk-kkŭm 보석금 bail (*money*)

posŏksang 보석상 jeweler

posŏngnyu 보석류 jewelry

posŭlbi 보슬비 drizzle

posu 보수 pay; reward, remuneration; conservativeness ◊ conservative

posuga ch'ungbunhan 보수가 충분한 remunerative

posuhada 보수하다 renovate, do up; repair

posujŏgin 보수적인 conservative; conventional

posurŭl chuda 보수를 주다 pay; reward

pot'ong 보통 usual; ordinary ◊ usually

pot'ong chŏngdoŭi 보통 정도의 average, mediocre

pot'ong saram 보통 사람 ordinary person

pot'ongsŏk 보통석 economy class

pot'ong ttaech'ŏrŏm 보통 때처럼 as usual

pot'ong-ŭi 보통의 normal, usual; ordinary; common; standard; mediocre

pot'ong-ŭro 보통으로 normally, usually

pot'ong yegŭm 보통 예금 savings account

pot'ŭ 보트 boat

powanhada 보완하다 complement

powanhanŭn 보완하는 complementary

poyangji 보양지 health resort

poyŏjida 보여지다 appear, seem; show; show up, be visible

poyŏjuda 보여주다 show; expose

poyugŭm 보유금 reserves

poyugwŏn 보육원 kindergarten

poyuja 보유자 holder (*of record*)

ppadŭt'an 빠듯한 full

ppaeat-tta 빼앗다 take by force; *nugurobut'ŏ muŏsŭl ppaeat-tta* 누구로부터 무엇을 빼앗다 take sth away from s.o. (by force), snatch sth from s.o.

ppaeda 빼다 drain off; omit; subtract; *42 ppaegi 18ŭn 24ida* 42 빼기 18은 24이다 42 minus 18 is 24; *...man ppaego* ...만 빼고 all but ..., except ...

ppaedalmŭn mosŭp 빼닮은 모습 image, exact likeness

ppaegi puho 빼기 부호 minus sign

ppaekppaek'age kkwak ch'an 빽빽하게 꽉 찬 jam-packed, crowded

ppaenaeda 빼내다 take out; eject; drain

ppaengsoni sago 뺑소니 사고 hit-and-run accident

ppaengsoni unjŏnsu 뺑소니 운전수 hit-and-run driver

ppajida 빠지다 drain away, ebb; sink in; fall in; fall out; pull out; be hooked on; miss; *sarange ppajida* 사랑에 빠지다 fall in love; *muŏse ppajida* 무엇에 빠지다 indulge in sth; give sth a miss

ppajyŏ nagada 빠져 나가다 slip out, go out; ebb away; *sarami ppajyŏt-tta!* 사람이 빠졌다! man overboard!

ppalda 빨다 wash; suck

ppalgaejida 빨개지다 flush, redden

ppalgan 빨간 red

ppalgan pul 빨간 불 red light

ppalgat'a 빨갛다 be red

ppallae 빨래 washing; *ppallaerŭl hada* 빨래를 하다 do the washing

ppallajida 빨라지다 accelerate

ppalli 빨리 quickly

ppalli chinagada 빨리 지나가다 speed by

ppalli hada 빨리 하다 speed up

ppalli hae! 빨리 해! be quick!

ppalli kada 빨리 가다 speed

ppang 빵 bread

angjip 빵집 bakery

ang karu 빵 가루 breadcrumbs
(or cooking)

ang pusŭrŏgi 빵 부스러기
readcrumbs *(for birds)*

anhi ch'yŏdaboda 빤히 쳐다보다
:are; stare at

aradŭrida 빨아들이다 inhale; suck
1; absorb

ara mŏktta 빨아 먹다 suck

arŭda 빠르다 be fast, be quick

arŭge 빠르게 fast, quickly

arŭn 빠른 fast, quick; speedy

atppat'an 빳빳한 stiff

ida 삐다 sprain

igŏk-kkŏrida 삐걱거리다 creak,
queak

ii hanŭn sori 삐이 하는 소리
:leep

ŏdŏit-tta 뻗어있다 extend

ŏdŏnagago innŭn 뻗어나가고
깄는 sprawling

ŏgŭnhan 빠근한 stiff

ŏnppŏnhada 뻔뻔하다 be
:hameless, be impudent

ŏnppŏnham 뻔뻔함 impudence

ŏnppŏnhan 뻔뻔한 impudent,
resh

ŏnppŏnsŭrŏun 뻔뻔스러운
mpudent, blatant, shameless

ŏtch'ida 뻗치다 stretch, spread

ŏtppŏt'aejida 뻣뻣해지다 stiffen

ŏtppŏt'age hada 뻣뻣하게 하다
stiffen up

ŏtppŏt'an 뻣뻣한 stiff, unyielding

oppo 뽀뽀 peck, kiss

oppohada 뽀뽀하다 give a peck,
kiss

ooptta 뽑다 pull out, extract; pluck;
select

oul 뿔 horn

oult'e an-gyŏng 뿔테 안경 horn-
rimmed spectacles

pumŏjyŏ naoda 뻐어져 나오다
squirt, spurt

pumŏnaeda 뿜어내다 squirt

pun 뿐 nothing but, only; *...I ppun*
... ㄹ 뿐 nothing but; *Xppunman
anira Ydo ttohan* X뿐만 아니라
Y도 또한 not only X but Y also

ppuri 뿌리 root

ppuribak'in 뿌리박힌 entrenched

ppurida 뿌리다 scatter; sprinkle;
slop; spray

ppuri kip'ŭn 뿌리 깊은 deep-rooted

ppurut'unghada 뿌루퉁하다 pout

ppyam 뺨 cheek

ppyŏ 뼈 bone

ppyŏdae 뼈대 frame

ppyojokt'ap 뾰족탑 spire, steeple

ppyojuk'an kkŭt 뾰죽한 끝 spike

pp'im 삠 wrench *(injury)*

pu 부 copy *(of book)*; ministry;
wealth

pu- 부- vice-

püi ai p'i 브이 아이 피이 VIP

püi ssi al 브이 시이 알 VCR

püllaek pakssŭ 블랙 박스 black box,
flight recorder

püllaekrisŭt'üe ollida 블랙리스트에
올리다 blacklist

püllaindŭ 블라인드 blind, shade

püllausŭ 블라우스 blouse

püllogŭ 블로그 blog

püllogŭl ssŭiuda 블록을 씌우다
highlight COMPUT

püllok 블록 block COMPUT

püraendi 브랜디 brandy

Pürajil 브라질 Brazil ◊ Brazilian

Pürajil saram 브라질 사람 Brazilian

püraujŏ 브라우저 browser COMPUT

püreik'ŭ 브레이크 brake

püreik'ŭ lait'ŭ 브레이크 라이트
brake light

püreik'ŭrŭl kŏlda 브레이크를 걸다
brake, put the brake(s) on

pürejiŏ 브레지어 brassière

püroch'i 브로치 brooch

pürogŭraem 프로그램 program

pürogŭraemŏ 프로그래머
programmer

pürogŭraem tchada 프로그램 짜다
program

pürok'olli 브로콜리 broccoli

püroshyŏ 브로셔 brochure

pubu 부부 couple

pubun 부분 part, proportion; portion;
segment; slice

pubuntchŏgin 부분적인 segmented

pubuntchŏgŭro 부분적으로
partially, partly, part

puch'ae 부채 fan

puch'aejirhada 부채질하다 fan oneself

puch'ida 붙이다 attach, stick; pin up

puch'igi 붙이기 paste COMPUT

puch'ŏ 부처 Buddha; department

Puch'ŏnim Oshin Nal 부처님 오신 날 Buddha's Birthday

puch'u 부추 leek

puch'ugida 부추기다 encourage

pudae 부대 unit MIL

pudaep'yo 부대표 deputy leader

pudam 부담 burden; *pudamŭl chuda* 부담을 주다 strain *finances, budget; nuguege pudamŭl chuda* 누구에게 부담을 주다 impose oneself on s.o.

pudamhada 부담하다 bear *costs etc*

pudanghada 부당하다 be unjust

pudanghage 부당하게 wrongly, mistakenly

pudanghan 부당한 wrongful

pudich'ida 부딪히다 bump into; bump; ram

pudodŏk 부도덕 immorality

pudodŏk'an 부도덕한 immoral; unscrupulous

pudong-aek 부동액 antifreeze

pudongsan 부동산 real estate

pudongsan chunggaein 부동산 중개인 realtor

pudŭrŏpkke 부드럽게 softly

pudŭrŏpkke hada 부드럽게 하다 tone down, soften

pudŭrŏptta 부드럽다 be soft; be gentle

pudŭrŏun 부드러운 soft; gentle; mild; smooth

pudŭrŏwŏjida 부드러워지다 soften

pudu 부두 dock; port; wharf; *pudue taeda* 부두에 대다 dock, put in

pudu nodongja 부두 노동자 stevedore

pudut-kka 부둣가 quayside

pugajŏgin 부가적인 supplementary

pugamul 부가물 trappings; frills

puga yogŭm 부가 요금 surcharge

pugi 부기 swelling; book-keeping

pugŏm 부검 autopsy

pugo 부고 obituary

pugŭp'ada 보급하다 spread; disseminate

pugwahada 부과하다 impose; *nuguege ch'aegimŭl pugwaha* 누구에게 책임을 부과하다 set a ta for s.o.

pugyeŭi 부계의 paternal

pugyŏng-yŏng-in 부경영인 assista manager

pugyŏrhada 부결하다 throw out

pugyosu 부교수 associate professo

puha 부하 load ELEC

puhap'ada 부합하다 correspond w

puhwahada 부화하다 hatch out

puhwal 부활 revival; resurrection

Puhwaltchŏl 부활절 Easter

puhwarhada 부활하다 revive

puinhada 부인하다 contradict; den

puja 부자 sage; father and son; rich man

pujae 부재 absence

pujagyong 부작용 side effect

pujang 부장 managing director; assistant director

pujayŏnsŭrŏun 부자연스러운 unnatural

pujibaein 부지배인 assistant mana

pujirŏmnŭn marŭl hada 부질없는 말을 하다 waffle

pujirŏnhan 부지런한 diligent

pujirŏnhi irhada 부지런히 일하다 work hard

pujŏngja 부적응자 misfit

pujŏkkyŏgin 부적격인 (morally) unfit

pujŏktchŏrhan 부적절한 improper

pujŏkttanghada 부적당하다 be unsuitable; be unfit; be inadequat *mŏkkie / mashigie pujŏkttang- hada* 먹기에/마시기에 부적당하다 be unfit to eat / drink

pujŏkttanghan 부적당한 unsuitab inappropriate; inadequate

pujŏng 부정 denial; injustice; infidelity

pujŏng haeng-wi 부정 행위 misconduct

pujŏnghal su ŏmnŭn 부정할 수 없 undeniable

pujŏnghan 부정한 crooked, dishonest; unfaithful

pujŏnghwak'an 부정확한 inaccura

ndeterminate

ijŏngjik 부정직 dishonesty

ijŏngjik'an 부정직한 dishonest

ijŏngjŏgin 부정적인 destructive;
negative

ijŏngsa 부정사 infinitive

ijŏng-ŭi 부정의 negative

ijojongsa 부조종사 copilot

ijok 부족 shortage; shortfall; tribe;

aujok'ami ŏptta 부족함이 없다
want for nothing

ijok'ada 부족하다 be lacking

ijuŭihan 부주의한 inattentive;
slack; sloppy

ik 북 drum; north

ikch'ae 북채 drumstick

ik-kkŭk kom 북극 곰 polar bear

ik-kkyŏng 북경 Beijing

ikkŭk 북극 North Pole

ikkŭkkwŏn 북극권 Arctic

ikkŭröptta 부끄럽다 be ashamed;
be shy; ...**ege pukkŭröpkke yŏgida**
...에게 부끄럽게 여기다 be ashamed
of; **pukkŭröptchido anni!**
부끄럽지도 않니! shame on you!

ikkŭrŏun 부끄러운 shameful

ikppang-e 북방에 north of

ikppet'ŭnam 북베트남 North
Vietnam ◊ North Vietnamese

ikppet'ŭnamin 북베트남인 North
Vietnamese

ikppuŭi 북부의 northern

ikssŏ 북서 northwest

iktchoge 북쪽에 to the north of

iktchogŭro 북쪽으로 northward

iktaesŏyang Choyak Kigu
북대서양 조약 기구 NATO

ikttoduda 북돋우다 bolster

uk'an 북한 North Korea ◊ North
Korean

uk'an saram 북한 사람 North
Korean (person)

uk'yang-ŭi 북향의 northerly

ul 불 fire; dollar; Buddha; France ◊
French; **pul puch'ida** 불 붙이다
light; **pul kat'ŭn** 불 같은 fiery

ul- 불- not; un-; in-; dis-; non-

ulboktchong 불복종 disobedience,
insubordination

ulboktchonghanŭn 불복종하는
disobedient, insubordinate

pulch'ansŏng 불찬성 disapproval

pulch'ansŏnghada 불찬성하다
disapprove of

pulch'injŏrhada 불친절하다 be
unkind

pulch'injŏrhan 불친절한 unfriendly;
unkind; inhospitable

pulch'ippyŏng-ŭi 불치병의
terminally ill

pulch'ungbunhan 불충분한 meager;
insufficient

pulch'ungsshil 불충실 disloyalty

pulch'ungsshirhan 불충실한 disloyal

pulda 불다 blow; inflate

puldoujŏ 불도우저 bulldozer

pulgabunŭi 불가분의 indivisible

pulgamtchŭng-ŭi 불감증의 frigid
MED

pulgansŏp 불간섭 noninterference,
nonintervention

pulganŭng 불가능 impossibility

pulganŭnghada 불가능하다 be
impossible

pulganŭnghan 불가능한 impossible

pulgap'ihada 불가피하다 be
unavoidable

pulgasari 불가사리 starfish

pulgasaŭi 불가사의 mystery

pulgasaŭihan 불가사의한
mysterious, inscrutable

pulgirhae poinŭn 불길해 보이는
sinister

pulgirhan 불길한 ominous

pulgirhan yegam 불길한 예감
foreboding

pulgŏjida 붉어지다 redden, blush

pulgogi 불고기 barbecued beef

pulgongjŏnghan 불공정한 unfair,
unjust; unequal

pulgongp'yŏnghada 불공평하다 be
unfair, be biased

pulgŭn 붉은 ruddy; red

pulguhago 불구하고 in spite of

pulgurŭi 불굴의 indomitable

pulguŭi 불구의 disabled

pulgyŏnggi 불경기 recession, slump

Pulgyo 불교 Buddhism ◊ Buddhist

Pulgyo Shinja 불교 신자 Buddhist

pulgyuch'iktchŏgin 불규칙적인
irregular

pulgyunhyŏng 불균형 disparity

pulgyunhyŏnghan 불균형한 disproportionate

pulkkil 불길 flames

pulkkonnori 불꽃놀이 fireworks

pulkkot 불꽃 flame; spark

pulk'wae 불쾌 displeasure

pulk'waehada 불쾌하다 put off, repel

pulk'waehage hada 불쾌하게 하다 displease

pulk'waehan 불쾌한 nasty, unpleasant; undesirable; offensive, repellent; rotten; sick

pulli 분리 division, separation; segregation

pullihada 분리하다 separate; isolate; segregate; partition; unfix

pullihada 불리하다 be prejudicial to

pullihal su innŭn 분리할 수 있는 detachable

pullihal su ŏmnŭn 분리할 수 없는 inseparable

pullihan 불리한 disadvantageous; *pullihan chokkŏn* 불리한 조건 handicap; *pullihan iptchang-e itta* 불리한 입장에 있다 be at a disadvantage

pullishik'ida 분리시키다 disconnect

pullŏ irŭk'ida 불러 일으키다 arouse; summon up; work up

pullŏogi 불러오기 open COMPUT

pullŏ tŭrida 불러 들이다 call in, summon

pulluk'ada 불룩하다 bulge

pullyangbae 불량배 hooligan

pullyang puch'ae 불량 부채 bad debt

pullyangp'um 불량품 inferior goods; reject

pullyŏnsŏng 불연성 non-combustibility ◊ incombustible; fireproof

pullyu 분류 classification

pullyuhada 분류하다 class; classify; sort; break down; itemize

pullyun 불륜 immorality

pullyunŭi kwan-gye 불륜의 관계 (love) affair

pulman 불만 discontent, dissatisfaction

pulmanida 불만이다 be unhappy with

pulmansŭrŏun 불만스러운 discontented

pulmo 불모 infertility ◊ barren

pulmoji 불모지 unproductive soil

pulmyŏl 불멸 immortality

pulmyŏnghwak'an 불명확한 uncertain

pulmyŏng-ye 불명예 dishonor; disgrace

pulmyŏng-yesŭrŏun 불명예스러운 dishonorable

pulmyŏntchŭng 불면증 insomnia

pulmyŏrŭi 불멸의 immortal

pulppŏp 불법 illegality ◊ illegal

pulppŏp haengwi 불법 행위 unlawful act

pulppŏp koyong 불법 고용 black economy

pul'iryohan 불필요한 unnecessary

pulp'yŏnhage nŭkkida 불편하게 느끼다 feel ill at ease

pulp'yŏn 불편 inconvenience

pulp'yŏng 불평 complaint

pulp'yŏngdŭng 불평등 inequality

pulp'yŏnghada 불평하다 complain; complain about

pulp'yŏngkkŏri 불평거리 complaint; grievance

pulp'yŏng-ŭl nŭrŏnot-tta 불평을 늘어놓다 complain

pulp'yŏnhada 불편하다 be uncomfortable; be inconvenient

pulp'yŏnhan 불편한 uncomfortable; inconvenient

pulshich'ak 불시착 crash landing

pulssanghada 불쌍하다 be piteous, be wretched

pulssanghaejin 불쌍해진 wretched

pulssanghan 불쌍한 piteous, wretched

pulssanghi yŏgida 불쌍히 여기다 take pity on

pulsshie 불시에 unexpectedly, by surprise; *X-ŭl / rŭl pulsshie sŭpkkyŏk'ada* X을/를 불시에 습격하다 catch X unawares

pulsshin 불신 mistrust, doubt

pulsshinhada 불신하다 mistrust

pulssonhan 불손한 insolent, arrogant

ulssuk marhada 불쑥 말하다 blurt
out

ulssuk naoda 불쑥 나오다 stick
out, protrude

ulssuk nat'anada 불쑥 나타나다
pop up, bob up

ulssuk saenggida 불쑥 생기다
shoot up (of new suburb etc)

ulssuk t'wiŏ naoda 불쑥 튀어
나오다 protrude

ulssunhan 불순한 impure

ult'anŭn 불타는 alight, burning

ult'aorŭnŭn 불타오르는 ablaze,
blazing

ult'umyŏnghan 불투명한 opaque

ult'umyŏnghan yuri 불투명한 유리
frosted glass

um 붐 boom

umbida 붐비다 be busy, be crowded

umbinŭn 붐비는 busy, crowded

umo 부모 parent

umok 부목 splint

umo-ŭi 부모의 parental

un 분 face powder; minute;
flowerpot; anger; person (respectful)
◊ countword for people (respectful);
pun tang hoejŏn 분 당 회전 revs
per minute

unbae 분배 distribution

unbaehada 분배하다 share, allocate

unbal 분발 spurt

unbiaek 분비액 secretion

unbihada 분비하다 secrete

unbimul 분비물 secretion (liquid
secreted)

unbyŏl innŭn 분별 있는 sound,
prudent; level-headed; reasonable,
sensible

unch'im 분침 minute hand

unch'ul 분출 torrent

unch'uldoeda 분출되다 spout

unch'ulgi 분출구 jet

unch'urhada 분출하다 erupt (of
volcano)

un-gae 분개 resentment; outrage

un-gaehada 분개하다 resent

un-gaehan 분개한 resentful;
indignant

un-ganhada 분간하다 distinguish

ungdae 붕대 bandage, dressing

ungdaerŭl kamtta 붕대를 감다

bandage, dress

punggoe 붕괴 fall, collapse

punggoedoeda 붕괴되다
disintegrate; crash

pun-gitchŏm 분기점 fork (in road)

Pungmi 북미 North America ◊ North
American

Pungmiin 북미인 North American

Pungmiŭi 북미의 North American

punhaedoeda 분해되다 come apart

punhaehada 분해하다 take to pieces,
dismantle

punhal maeip 분할매입 buying on an
installment plan

punhongsaek 분홍색 pink

punhwa 분화 eruption

punhwagu 분화구 crater (of
volcano)

punja 분자 molecule ◊ molecular

punjae 분재 bonsai

punjaeng 분쟁 dispute

punjaeng chiyŏk 분쟁 지역 hot spot

punjaeng chojŏngja 분쟁 조정자
troubleshooter, mediator

punjangshil 분장실 dressing room

punjuhi irhada 분주히 일하다 bustle
about, be busy

punkkwa wiwŏnhoe 분과 위원회
subcommittee

punman 분만 delivery (of baby);
labor; **punman chung-ida** 분만
중이다 be in labor

punmanhada 분만하다 give birth to

punmang 분망 scramble, rush

punmanshik'ida 분만시키다 deliver
baby

punmanshil 분만실 labor ward

punmugi 분무기 atomizer; spraygun

punmyŏnghada 분명하다 be
obvious; be clear

punmyŏnghage 분명하게 plainly,
clearly

punmyŏnghan 분명한 clear, obvious

punmyŏnghi 분명히 clearly,
evidently; explicitly

punno 분노 wrath

punnŭn 붙는 sticky label

pun parŭda 분 바르다 powder

punp'a 분파 sect; splinter group

punp'il 분필 chalk

punsagirŭl sayonghada 분사기를

사용하다 sandblast
punshilmul sent'ŏ 분실물 센터 lost-and-found
punsŏk 분석 analysis
punsŏk'ada 분석하다 analyze
punsu 분수 fraction; fountain
punsuryŏng 분수령 watershed
punswaegi 분쇄기 mill
punwigi 분위기 atmosphere; mood; tone
punya 분야 area, field
punyŏl 분열 division, split
punyŏlshik'ida 분열시키다 split
punyŏlsshik'inŭn 분열시키는 disruptive
punyŏrhada 분열하다 be divided; be split
puŏk 부엌 kitchen
puŏngbuŏng ulda 부엉부엉 울다 hoot (*of owl*)
puŏ nŏt'a 부어 넣다 add *water, salt etc*
puŏorŭn 부어 오른 puffy, swollen
puŏp 부업 sideline, side job
pup'ae 부패 decay
pup'aehada 부패하다 decay
pup'aehan 부패한 rotten; corrupt
pup'aessŏng-ŭi 부패성의 septic
pup'e 부페 buffet
pup'iga k'ŭn 부피가 큰 bulky
pup'ullida 부풀리다 inflate; expand
pup'um 부품 part, piece; unit; spare part
pup'yo 부표 buoy
pural 불알 balls; testicles
puran 불안 alarm, unrest; ***puranhae hada*** 불안해 하다 feel uneasy about
purangja 부랑자 bum; street people
puranhada 불안하다 be uneasy
puranhaejida 불안해지다 get worked up, get nervous
puranhage hada 불안하게 하다 alarm, worry
puranhan 불안한 insecure, uneasy; unstable
puranjŏng 불안정 insecurity, instability
puranjŏnghage 불안정하게 precariously
puranjŏnghan 불안정한 precarious, unstable

purhaeng 불행 unhappiness; misfortune
purhaenghada 불행하다 be unhapp be unlucky
puraenghan 불행한 poor, unfortunate; unhappy
purhaenghi 불행히 unfortunately
purhamnihan 불합리한 irrational
purhandang 불한당 ruffian
purhwa 불화 split; feud; discord
purhwaksshilssŏng 불확실성 uncertainty
purhwaksshirhada 불확실하다 be doubt; be doubtful
purhwaksshirhan 불확실한 uncertain
purhwang-ida 불황이다 be in the doldrums
purhyŏp'waŭm 불협화음 discord, dissonance
puri 부리 beak
purilch'i 불일치 discrepancy; clash (*of personalities*)
purilch'ihada 불일치하다 clash; be inconsistent
purim 불임 infertility
purimk'ehada 불임케 하다 sterilize
purimŭi 불임의 infertile, sterile
purŏjida 부러지다 break; get broker
purŏjin 부러진 broken
purŏ nallida 불어 날리다 blow off
purŏttŭrida 부러뜨리다 break, snap
purŏumŭl sada 부러움을 사다 be envious of
purŏun 부러운 enviable
purŏwŏhada 부러워하다 be envious of
purŏwŏhanŭn 부러워하는 envious
purok 부록 appendix (*in book*)
purŭda 부르다 call; summon; ***...rago purŭda*** ...라고 부르다 address, call; describe as
purŭl puch'ida 불을 붙이다 ignite; light; set on fire
purŏ ponaeda 부르러 보내다 send for
puruhan 불우한 deprived, underprivileged
purun 불운 bad luck; disaster
purunhan 불운한 ill-fated
puruťunghaejida 부루퉁해지다 sulk

rut'unghan 부루퉁한 sulky

rwanjŏnhan 불완전한 imperfect; ncomplete

ryŏmŏktta 부려먹다 boss around

ryŏnsŏng-ŭi 불연성의 on(in)flammable

ryu 부류 class, category

sa 부사 adverb

sajang 부사장 vice president

san 부산 Pusan

sang 부상 injury; wound

sangja 부상자 injured; wounded

sanmul 부산물 by-product, spin-off

shik 부식 corrosion

shik'ada 부식하다 corrode

sŏ 부서 department, division, unit; post

sŏhada 부서하다 countersign

sŏjida 부서지다 break, come apart; shatter, smash

sŏjigi shwiun 부서지기 쉬운 brittle; fragile

sŏjin 부서진 broken

sŏng 부성 paternity ◊ paternal

sŭrŏgi 부스러기 crumb; *chandon pusŭrŏgi* 잔돈 부스러기 loose change

sŭrŏttŭrida 부스러뜨리다 crumble

sŭrŏjida 부스러지다 crumble

suda 부수다 break, shatter; force

sugo yŏlda 부수고 열다 break down *door*

uttchaptta 붙잡다 hold *prisoner etc*

ut-tta 붙다 adhere, stick; *shihŏme put-tta* 시험에 붙다 pass (*in exam*)

ut-tta 붓다 swell

ut-ttŭlgo iyagihada 붙들고 이야기하다 buttonhole

ut-ttŭrŏ tuda 붙들어 두다 keep; detain; keep in

ut'ak'ada 부탁하다 ask; ask for; arrange for; *mwŏ chom put'ak'aedo toemnikka?* 뭐 좀 부탁해도 됩니까? can I ask you something?

ut'an 부탄 Bhutan ◊ Bhutanese

ut'bagiŭi 불박이의 built-in

ut'ik'ŭ 부티크 boutique

ut'ingdoeda 부팅되다 boot (up)

ut'inghada 부팅하다 boot (up)

...put'ŏ ... kkaji ...부터 ... 까지 from ... to ...; ...(*esŏ*)*but'ŏ* ... (에서)부터 from (*in time*); *wŏryoilbut'ŏ suyoilkkaji* 월요일부터 수요일까지 from Monday to Wednesday

pu-ŭn 부은 swollen

puyang 부양 support; boost

puyangbi 부양비 maintenance (*money*)

puyanghada 부양하다 support, maintain

puyang kajok 부양 가족 dependents

puyŏhada 부여하다 attach

puyŏjaptta 부여잡다 grab

puyŏnhada 부연하다 elaborate

puyuhada 부유하다 be rich

puyuhan 부유한 rich, wealthy

pyŏk 벽 wall

pyŏkppo 벽보 placard

pyŏktchi 벽지 wallpaper

pyŏkttol 벽돌 brick

pyŏkttolgong 벽돌공 bricklayer

pyŏk'wa 벽화 mural

pyŏl 별 star ◊ different; unusual; *pyŏl il animnida* 별 일 아닙니다 it's no problem

pyŏlgaero 별개로 independently of

pyŏlgaeŭi 별개의 different; separate

pyŏlgŏ 별거 separation

pyŏlgŏhada 별거하다 separate; live apart; be (legally) separated

pyŏlgŏhan 별거한 separated

pyŏlgŏ sudang 별거 수당 alimony

pyŏlgwan 별관 annex

pyŏllada 별나다 be eccentric; be strange

pyŏllan 별난 eccentric, quirky

pyŏllo 별로 nothing much

pyŏllon 변론 defense; justification

pyŏlloyeyo 별로에요 not really, not much

pyŏlmashi ŏmnŭn 별맛이 없는 bland

pyŏlmyŏng 별명 nickname

pyŏlp'yo 별표 asterisk

pyŏlsŭrŏn 별스런 whimsical

pyŏltchong 별종 freak

pyŏnanhada 편안하다 feel at ease

pyŏnapkki 변압기 transformer

pyŏnbi 변비 constipation

pyŏnbie kŏllin 변비에 걸린

constipated

pyŏnbiyak 변비약 laxative

pyŏndŏk 변덕 freak (*event*); whim

pyŏndŏkssŭröptta 변덕스럽다 be fickle

pyŏndŏkssŭröun 변덕스러운 temperamental; fickle; variable

pyŏndong 변동 variation, fluctuation

pyŏndonghada 변동하다 fluctuate

pyŏndong shisega toeda 변동 시세가 되다 float FIN

pyŏnduri 변두리 outskirts

pyŏng 병 bottle; flask; illness

pyŏng-ari 병아리 chick

pyŏngch'am ŏmmu 병참 업무 logistics

pyŏngch'unghae kwalli 병충해 관리 pest control

pyŏngdong 병동 ward, room (*in hospital*)

pyŏngdŭlda 병들다 fall ill, be taken ill

pyŏng-e köllida 병에 걸리다 catch an illness

pyŏngga 병가 sick leave

pyŏng-i chaebarhada 병이 재발하다 have a relapse

pyŏn-gie naeryŏbonaeda 변기에 내려보내다 flush down the toilet

pyŏng-i nat-tta 병이 낫다 get better (*in health*)

pyŏngja 병자 invalid (*person*)

pyŏngkkahada 평가하다 estimate

pyŏng magae 병 마개 stopper

pyŏngmok 병목 bottleneck

pyŏngnallo 벽난로 fireplace

pyŏngnihak 병리학 pathology

pyŏngnihaktcha 병리학자 pathologist

pyŏngnyŏk 병력 case history

pyŏngnyŏng 병영 quarters

pyŏngsang-e innŭn 병상에 있는 bedridden

pyŏngse 병세 case MED

pyŏngtchŏgin 병적인 morbid, pathological

pyŏngtchŏk hŭngbun 병적 흥분 hysterics; hysteria; *pyŏngtchŏk hŭngbunsangt'aega toeda* 병적 흥분상태가 되다 become hysterical

pyŏngtchok hŭngbun sangt'aeŭi 병적 흥분 상태의 hysterical

pyŏngttagae 병따개 bottle-opener

pyŏng-wŏn 병원 hospital

pyŏngyak'an 병약한 sickly

pyŏn-gyŏng 변경 alteration; shift

pyŏn-gyŏnghada 변경하다 be deflected from

pyŏnhada 변하다 change, shift

pyŏnhagi shwiun 변하기 쉬운 unsettled, changeable

pyŏnhohada 변호하다 defend

pyŏnhosa 변호사 attorney, counsel, counselor

pyŏnhosabi 변호사비 fee (*of lawyer*)

pyŏnhwa 변화 change, shift; variety

pyŏnhwahada 변화하다 change; convert

pyŏnhwan 변환 conversion

pyŏnhwashik'ida 변화시키다 change

pyŏnhyŏng 변형 transformation

pyŏnhyŏngshik'ida 변형시키다 transform; deform

pyŏnjang 변장 disguise

pyŏnjanghada 변장하다 dress up, wear a disguise; dress up as; disguise oneself as

pyŏnje 변제 repayment

pyŏnjehada 변제하다 pay back

pyŏnjildoeda 변질되다 degenerate into

pyŏnmyŏng 변명 excuse

pyŏnmyŏnghal su ŏmnŭn 변명할 수 없는 inexcusable

pyŏnsaekssshik'ida 변색시키다 discolor; tarnish

pyŏnsŏnghada 변성하다 break (*of boy's voice*)

pyŏnsokki 변속기 transmission

pyŏnssu 변수 variable

pyŏnt'ae 변태 perversion

pyŏnt'aejŏgin 변태적인 kinky, bizarre; perverted

pyŏrak ch'ulssehan nom 벼락 출세한 놈 upstart

pyŏril ŏmnŭn 별일 없는 uneventful

pyŏruk 벼룩 flea

pyŏt 벗 crest

P'

a 파 scallion; faction; par (*in golf*)

aak'agi himdŭn 파악하기 힘든 *elusive meaning*

ach'ungnyu 파충류 reptile

ada 파다 dig; mine

ado 파도 wave

aebae 패배 defeat

aebaejuŭijŏgin 패배주의적인 defeatist

aebaeshik'ida 패배시키다 defeat

aeda 패다 chop; beat

aegŏri 패거리 crowd, crew

aein kumŏng 패인 구멍 pothole

aeja 패자 loser SP

aejiŏ konggyŏk'ada 패지어 몰격하다 gang up on

aek 팩 carton

aek'iji kwangwang 패키지 관광 package tour

aek'iji sangp'um 패키지 상품 package deal

aekssŭ 팩스 fax

aekssŭ munsŏ 팩스 문서 fax

aekssŭroponaeda 팩스로 보내다 fax; *Xŭl / rŭl p'aekssŭro ponaeda* X을 / 를 팩스로 Y에게 보내다 fax X to Y

aen 팬 fan, supporter

aendŏ kom 팬더 곰 panda

aengch'ang 팽창 expansion

aengch'anghada 팽창하다 expand

aengi 팽이 spinning top

aengp'aenghan 팽팽한 taut

aengp'aenghan chul 팽팽한 줄 tightrope

aenji 팬지 pansy

aenk'eik'ŭ 팬케이크 pancake

aenŏl 패널 panel

aenŏlt'i 패널티 penalty

aenŏlt'i kuyŏk 패널티 구역 penalty area

aen pelt'ŭ 팬 벨트 fan belt

aent'i 팬티 panties, underpants

p'aent'i sŭt'ak'ing 팬티 스타킹 pantyhose

p'aesshyŏn 패션 fashion

p'aesshyŏn tijainŏ 패션 디자이너 fashion designer

p'aesŭ 패스 pass

p'aesŭhada 패스하다 pass

p'aesŭt'ŭ'ŭp'udŭjŏm 패스트푸드점 fastfood restaurant

p'aet'ŏn 패턴 pattern

p'agidoenŭn 파기되는 doomed

p'agoe 파괴 destruction, demolition; ruin

p'agoehada 파괴하다 destroy, demolish; ruin

p'agoejŏgin 파괴적인 destructive

p'agŭp hyokkwa 파급 효과 repercussion

p'agyŏktchŏgin harin kagyŏk 파격적인 할인 가격 knockdown price

p'ahech'ida 파헤치다 dig up

p'ai 파이 pie

p'ail 파일 file COMPUT

p'aip'ŭ 파이프 pipe

p'ainaep'ŭl 파인애플 pineapple

p'aip'ŭrain 파이프라인 pipeline

p'ajang 파장 wavelength

p'ak'a 파카 parka

P'ak'isŭt'an 파키스탄 Pakistan ◊ Pakistani

p'al 팔 arm; eight

p'alda 팔다 sell

p'alkkumch'i 팔꿈치 elbow

p'al kup'yŏ p'yŏgi 팔 굽혀 펴기 push-up

p'allida 팔리다 fetch *price*, be sold for

P'almandaejanggyŏng 팔만대장경 Tripitaka Koreana

p'alsship 팔십 eighty

p'altchang-ŭl kkida 팔짱을 끼다 fold one's arms

p'altchi 팔찌 bracelet

p'ama 파마 perm

p'ama hada 파마 하다 perm

p'amp'ŭllet 팜플렛 pamphlet

p'amut-tta 파묻다 bury

p'amyŏl 파멸 destruction, doom

p'amyŏlshik'ida 파멸시키다 destroy; ruin

p'amyŏrhan 파멸한 ruined, in ruins

p'an 판 sheet (*of glass, metal*); tray; board; edition

p'anaeda 파내다 extract

p'andan 판단 opinion, judgment

p'andanhada 판단하다 judge;
kŏnmosŭburo p'andanhada 겉모습으로 판단하다 judge by appearances, take at face value

p'andannyŏk 판단력 judgment, discernment

p'andok chŏnyong kiŏk changch'i 판독 전용 기억 장치 ROM, read-only memory

p'andok chŏnyong p'ail 판독 전용 파일 read-only file

p'andok'ada 판독하다 decipher

p'an-gyŏl 판결 ruling, sentence

p'an-gyŏrhada 판결하다 judge;
nugurŭl mujoero / yujoero p'an-gyŏrhada 누구를 무죄로 / 유죄로 판결하다 find a person innocent / guilty; *p'ansanŭn ...rago p'an-gyŏrhaet-tta* 판사는 ...라고 판결했다 the judge ruled that ...

p'an-gyŏrŭl naerida 판결을 내리다 pass sentence; sentence

p'anhwa 판화 engraving

p'anja 판자 board

p'anjaro maktta 판자로 막다 board up

p'anji 판지 cardboard

p'anmae 판매 sale; selling; *p'anmae chung-ida* 판매 중이다 be on sale

p'anmaebusŏ 판매부서 sales (department)

p'anmae chŏmwŏn 판매 점원 sales clerk

p'anmae ch'oktchin 판매 촉진 promotion

p'anmaehada 판매하다 sell, market

p'anmaeja 판매자 seller

p'anmae kagyŏk 판매 가격 asking price

p'anmae kŭmaek 판매 금액 sales figures

p'anmae pujang 판매 부장 sales manager

p'anorama 파노라마 panorama

p'ansa 판사 judge

p'ansori 판소리 epic songs

p'antton 판돈 stake

p'aŏp 파업 strike

p'aŏptcha 파업자 striker

p'apk'on 팝콘 popcorn

p'apssong 팝송 pop song

p'ap'yŏn 파편 debris

p'aran 파란 blue

p'arangsaek 파랑색 blue

p'aranmanjanghan 파란만장한 checkered

p'arasol 파라솔 parasol, sunshade

p'arat'a 파랗다 be blue

p'ari 파리 fly (*insect*)

p'arwŏl 팔월 August

p'aryŏmch'ihan 파렴치한 shameless

p'asakp'asak'an 파삭파삭한 crisp

p'asan 파산 bankruptcy

p'asanhada 파산하다 go bankrupt; go bust; be ruined

p'asanshik'ida 파산시키다 bankrupt; ruin

p'ason 파손 breakage

p'asshijŭm 파시즘 fascism

p'asshisŭt'ŭ 파시스트 fascist

p'asŭlli 파슬리 parsley

p'asŭt'el 파스텔 pastel

p'at'anhada 파탄하다 fail; go bankrupt

p'at'i 파티 party

p'at'ibok 파티 복 evening wear; evening dress; party dress

p'at'ŭ 파트 part MUS

p'awŏ sŭt'iŏring 파워 스티어링 power steering

p'awŏ yunit 파워 유닛 power unit

p'ayŏl 파열 rupture

p'ayŏldoeda 파열되다 rupture

p'edal 페달 pedal

p'edarŭl paltta 페달을 밟다 pedal

p'eiji 페이지 page

p'eint'ŭ 페인트 paint

p'eint'ŭ sol 페인트 솔 paintbrush

p'elt'ŭp'en 펠트펜 felt-tip (pen)

p'eminijŭm 페미니즘 feminism

eminisŭt'ŭ 페미니스트 feminist
endŏ 펜더 fender
enishillin 페니실린 penicillin
enp'al ch'in-gu 펜팔 친구 pen pal
enshing 펜싱 fencing SP
i 피 blood
ianisŭt'ŭ 피아니스트 pianist
iano 피아노 piano
ibu 피부 skin
ida 피다 open; unroll; blossom
igo 피고 the accused
igoch'ŭk 피고측 defense
igoch'ŭk chŭngin 피고측 증인 defense witness
igoch'ŭk pyŏnhosa 피고측 변호사 defense lawyer
igoin 피고인 defendant
igonhada 피곤하다 be tired
igonhaejida 피곤해지다 get tired
igonhan 피곤한 tired
igosŏk 피고석 dock LAW
igyŏ sŭk'eit'ing 피겨 스케이팅 figure skating
ihada 피하다 avoid; ward off; shelter
ihae 피해 damage
ihaega maksshimhan 피해가 막심한 disastrous
ihae mangsang 피해 망상 paranoia
ihaerŭl ip'ida 피해를 입히다 damage
ihal su innŭn 피할 수 있는 sheltered
ihal su ŏmnŭn 피할 수 없는 inevitable
ihal su ŏpsshi 피할 수 없이 inevitably
ihugyŏnin 피후견인 ward (*child*)
iim 피임 contraception
iimhada 피임하다 use contraception
iim kigu 피임 기구 contraceptive device
iimyak 피임약 (contraceptive) pill
iimyong p'esari 피임용 페사리 diaphragm
ija 피자 pizza
ijangp'ajang-i toeda 피장파장이 되다 be quits with
iksel 픽셀 pixel

p'ik'et 피켓 picket
p'ik'et lain 피켓 라인 picket line
p'ik'ŭl 피클 pickles
p'ildŭ kyŏnggi 필드 경기 field events
P'illandŭ 핀란드 Finland ◊ Finnish
P'illandŭŏ 핀란드어 Finnish (*language*)
P'illandŭ saram 핀란드 사람 Finn
p'ille sŭt'eik'ŭ 필레 스테이크 fillet steak
P'illip'in 필리핀 Philippines ◊ Filipino
p'illŭm 필름 film
p'ilmyŏng 필명 pen name
p'ilssabon 필사본 manuscript
p'ilssajŏgin 필사적인 desperate
p'ilssu chokkŏn 필수 조건 precondition
p'ilssujŏgin 필수적인 vital, essential
p'ilssup'um 필수품 necessity
p'ilssuŭi 필수의 indispensable
p'iltchŏk'ada 필적하다 match; parallel; equal
p'ilt'ŏ 필터 filter; filter tip
p'ilt'ŏ innŭn tambae 필터 있는 담배 filter-tipped (cigarettes)
p'imang 피망 pepper, pimiento
p'in 핀 pin ◊ open *flower*
p'inanch'ŏ 피난처 refuge, shelter; retreat
p'inanhada 피난하다 take refuge
p'inggye 핑계 excuse, pretext
p'ing tolda 핑 돌다 whirl
p'i pŭi sshi 피 브이 씨 PVC
p'iri 피리 Korean oboe
p'iro 피로 fatigue
p'iroech'im 피로침 lightning rod
p'iryo 필요 need; **...***l p'iryoga it-tta* ...ㄹ 필요가 있다 it is necessary to ...
p'iryohada 필요하다 want; need, require, call for
p'iryohadamyŏn 필요하다면 if need be, as necessary
p'iryohan 필요한 necessary
p'iryoro hada 필요로 하다 need, require, take; entail, mean
p'iryossŏng 필요성 necessity
p'isaldanghada 피살당하다 be killed
p'isangjŏgin 피상적인 cursory
p'ishint'agin 피신탁인 trustee
p'isshi 피씨 PC, personal computer
p'isŭt'on 피스톤 piston

p'itchaguk 핏자국 bloodstain
p'it-ttŏng-ŏri 핏덩어리 (blood) clot
p'it'usŏng-iŭi 피투성이의 bloody
p'iuda 피우다 burn; smoke; give off *smell*; play *trick*
p'ŏbut-tta 퍼붓다 pour; pour on; *chilmun kongserŭl p'ŏbut-tta* 질문 공세를 퍼붓다 bombard with questions
p'ŏdakkŏrida 퍼덕거리다 flutter
p'ŏjida 퍼지다 spread
p'ŏjŭl 퍼즐 puzzle (*game*)
p'ŏllŏgida 펄럭이다 flap; flutter; wave
p'ŏlp'ŭ 펄프 pulp
p'ŏltchŏk ttwida 펄쩍 뛰다 jump
p'ŏmp'ŭ 펌프 pump
p'ŏng 펑 pop
p'ŏngk'ŭ 펑크 blow-out
p'ŏngp'ŏng sosanaoda 펑펑 솟아나오다 gush
p'ŏ ollida 퍼 올리다 scoop up
p'ŏreidŭ 퍼레이드 parade, procession
p'ŏsent'ŭ 퍼센트 percent
p'ŏtchi 버찌 cherry
p'ŏttŭrida 퍼뜨리다 spread; circulate *memo*
p'oak'ada 포악하다 be ruthless; be oppressive
p'oak'an 포악한 oppressive; ruthless
p'och'ak'ada 포착하다 capture, portray; seize
p'odae 포대 bag; sack
p'odaegi 포대기 baby quilt (*for carrying baby on mother's back*)
p'odo 포도 grape; *p'odo han song-i* 포도 한 송이 a bunch of grapes
p'odoju 포도주 wine
p'odoju menyu 포도주 메뉴 wine list
p'odoju pyŏng ttagae 포도주 병 따개 corkscrew
p'odonamu 포도나무 grapevine
p'odongp'odonghan 포동포동한 plump
p'odowŏn 포도원 vineyard
p'ogihada 포기하다 give up, renounce
p'ogŭmhada 폭음하다 drink too much
p'ogu 폭우 downpour
p'ogwaltchŏgin 포괄적인 comprehensive

p'ogyŏk 포격 gunfire
p'ogyŏk'ada 포격하다 shell
p'ohamhada 포함하다 include; add on
p'ohamhan 포함한 inclusive
p'ohamhayŏ 포함하여 including
p'ohwa 포화 shellfire
p'ojang 포장 packaging
p'ojang chaeryo 포장 재료 wrapping
p'ojanghada 포장하다 pack, package; giftwrap; *haembŏgo p'ojanghaejuseyo* 포장해주세요 hamburger to go
p'ojangji 포장지 wrapper; wrapping paper; tissue paper
p'ojangnyong laep 포장용 랩 clingfilm
p'ojin 포진 herpes
p'ojŭ ch'wihada 포즈 취하다 pose
p'oju 포주 pimp
p'ok 폭 width, breadth; *p'ok shim mit'ŏ* 폭 10미터 10m across
p'ok-kkun 폭군 tyrant
p'ok-kkyŏk 폭격 bomb attack
p'ok-kkyŏk-kki 폭격기 bomber
p'okkunjŏgin 폭군적인 tyrannical, domineering
p'okŏ 포커 poker
p'okppal 폭발 explosion
p'okppalmul 폭발물 explosive
p'okppal sshik'ida 폭발시키다 detonate
p'okpparhada 폭발하다 explode, go off; blow up; erupt
p'okp'ahada 폭파하다 blow up, bomb
p'okp'ashik'ida 폭파시키다 blast
p'okp'o 폭포 waterfall
p'okp'ung 폭풍 storm
p'okp'ungju-ŭibo 폭풍주의보 storm warning
p'okp'ung-u 폭풍우 rainstorm
p'okp'ung-u-ga ch'inŭn 폭풍우가 치는 stormy
p'oksshik 폭식 gluttony
p'oksshik'ada 폭식하다 eat too much
p'okssorŭl t'ŏttŭrida 폭소를 터뜨리다 burst out laughing

okttong 폭동 riot, uprising
okttongja 폭동자 rioter
okttongŭl irŭk'ida 폭동을 일으키다 riot
okt'an 폭탄 bomb
ok'aeng 폭행 assault
ok'aenghada 폭행하다 assault
ok'etyong kyesan-gi 포켓용 계산기 pocket calculator
ok'ŭ 포크 fork
ok'ŭttaensŭ 포크댄스 folkdance
oldŏ 폴더 folder
ollandŭ 폴란드 Poland ◊ Polish
ollandŭŏ 폴란드어 Polish
olliesŭt'erŭ 폴리에스테르 polyester
olliet'illen 폴리에틸렌 polyethylene
ollisŭt'iren 폴리스티렌 polystyrene
omaet'ada 포맷하다 format
ongnak'ada 폭락하다 drop sharply (of stock market)
ongnirŭl ch'wihada 폭리를 취하다 rip off; profiteer
ong-nŏlbŭn 폭넓은 wide experience
ongno 폭로 revelation, disclosure
ongnohada 폭로하다 expose; **uyŏnhi p'ongnohada** 우연히 폭로하다 give oneself away
ongnyŏk 폭력 force, violence; outrage
ongnyŏktchŏgin 폭력적인 violent; outrageous
ongnyŏkttanwŏn 폭력단원 mobster
o-ong 포옹 cuddle; hug
o-onghada 포옹하다 cuddle; hug
oro 포로 captive; **nugurŭl p'ororo chaptta** 누구를 포로로 잡다 take s.o. prisoner
orŭno 포르노 pornography ◊ pornographic
orŭt 버릇 habit
orŭt'ugal 포르투갈 Portugal ◊ Portuguese
orŭt'ugarin 포르투갈인 Portuguese
orŭt'ugarŏ 포르투갈어 Portuguese (language)
oshik'ada 포식하다 overeat **muŏsŭl p'oshik'ada** 무엇을 포식하다 gorge oneself on sth
osŭt'ŏ 포스터 poster

p'ot'eit'o ch'ipssŭ 포테이토 칩스 potato chips
p'ot'ŏbŭl 포터블 portable COMPUT
p'ot'ŭ 포트 port COMPUT
p'owihada 포위하다 surround; close in
p'owi konggyŏk 포위 공격 siege
p'owi konggyŏk'ada 포위 공격하다 lay siege to
p'owŏdŭ 포워드 forward SP
p'oyu tongmul 포유 동물 mammal
p'ŭllaent'eishyŏn 플랜테이션 plantation
p'ŭllaeshwi 플래쉬 flash PHOT
p'ŭllaetp'om 플랫폼 platform
p'ŭllaja 플라자 plaza, shopping mall
p'ŭllasŭt'ik 플라스틱 plastic
p'ŭllŏgŭ 플러그 plug
p'ŭllŏgŭrŭl kkot-tta 플러그를 꽂다 plug in
p'ŭllŏgŭrŭl ppoptta 플러그를 뽑다 unplug
p'ŭllop'i tisŭk'ŭ 플로피 디스크 floppy (disk)
p'ŭllot'ŏ 플로터 plotter COMPUT
p'ŭllut'ŭ 플루트 flute
P'ŭrangssŭ 프랑스 France ◊ French
P'ŭrangssŭin 프랑스인 Frenchman; Frenchwoman
P'ŭrangssŭŏ 프랑스어 French (language)
p'ŭrik'ik 프리킥 free kick
p'ŭrima 프리마 creamer (for coffee)
p'ŭrimiŏm 프리미엄 premium
p'ŭrint'ŏ 프린터 printer (machine)
p'ŭro 프로 professional
p'ŭromp'ŭt'ŭ 프롬프트 prompt COMPUT
p'ŭront'ŭ 프론트 reception, check-in
p'ŭrop'ellŏ 프로펠러 propeller
p'ŭro sŏnsuro 프로 선수로 professionally SP
p'uda 푸다 scoop
p'uk chamdŭlda 푹 잠들다 be (fast) asleep
p'ukssinhan 푹신한 soft
p'ul 풀 glue; grass; **p'urŭl ttŭdŏmŏktta** 풀을 뜯어먹다 graze
p'ulda 풀다 undo; unpack; disentangle; solve; release brake; **k'orŭl p'ulda** 코를 풀다 blow one's nose

p'ullida 풀리다 unwind
p'ullin 풀린 frayed
p'ullo puch'ida 풀로 붙이다 glue
p'umhaeng-i tanjŏnghan 품행이
단정한 well-behaved
p'umjil 품질 quality
p'umjil kwalli 품질 관리 quality
control
p'umjiri nappŭn 품질이 나쁜 poor
quality, shoddy
p'umjong 품종 brand; breed
p'umkkyŏk 유행 style, fashion
p'umsa 품사 part of speech
p'umwi innŭn 품위 있는 gracious;
dignified; classy
p'ungbu 풍부 abundance
p'ungbuhada 풍부하다 be abundant
p'ungbuhage hada 풍부하게 하다
enrich
p'ungbuhan 풍부한 abundant; lavish
◊ a wealth of
p'ungch'a 풍차 windmill
p'unggi sabŏm tansokppan 풍기
사범 단속반 vice squad
p'unggyŏng 풍경 scenery
p'unggyŏnghwa 풍경화 landscape
(painting)
p'ungja 풍자 irony; sarcasm; satire
p'ungjagŭi 풍작의 bumper crop, year
p'ungjajŏgin 풍자적인 satirical
p'ungja manhwa 풍자 만화
caricature
p'ungmanhan 풍만한 buxom
p'ungmunŭro 풍문으로 by hearsay
p'ungnyoropkke hada 풍요롭게
하다 enrich
p'ungsŏn 풍선 balloon
p'ungsŏnghan 풍성한 hearty
p'ungsŏnkkŏm 풍선껌 bubble gum
p'ung-yo 풍요 plenty
p'ung-yoroun sahoe 풍요로운 사회
affluent society
p'unnaegi 풋내기 squirt; greenhorn
p'uri chugŭn 풀이 죽은
downhearted, downcast
p'uri ugŏjin 풀이 우거진 grassy
p'urŏjuda 풀어주다 untie
p'ŭromp'ŭt'ŭ 프롬프트 prompt
COMPUT
p'urŏ naerida 풀어 내리다 let down
p'urŏ poda 풀어 보다 unwrap

p'ushwi maen 푸쉬맨 person who
pushes Seoul commuters into subw
trains at rush hour
p'ye 폐 lung
p'yeam 폐암 lung cancer
p'yegihada 폐기하다 discard, dump
p'yegimul 폐기물 waste, waste
product
p'yegishik'ida 폐기시키다 scrap,
drop, abandon
p'yegyŏnggi 폐경기 menopause
p'yehoeshik 폐회식 closing
ceremony
p'yejihada 폐지하다 abolish
p'yejŏm 폐점 closure
p'yejŏmhada 폐점하다 close down
p'yejŏm shigan 폐점 시간 closing
time
p'yemuri toen 폐물이 된 obsolete
p'yeŏp'ada 폐업하다 close down
p'yeryŏm 폐렴 pneumonia
p'yeswae 폐쇄 closure
p'yeswaehada 폐쇄하다 close; clos
up
p'yeswae hoero t'ellebijyŏn 폐쇄
회로 텔레비전 closed-circuit
television
p'yŏda 펴다 unfold; smooth out
p'yŏlch'ida 펼치다 spread, lay
p'yŏlch'ŏjida 펼쳐지다 unfold
p'yŏlli 편리 convenience
p'yŏllihada 편리하다 be convenient
p'yŏllihan 편리한 convenient, handy
p'yŏn 편 side; faction; means;
tendency; editing; volume; part,
section; k'ŭn/chagŭn p'yŏn
큰/작은 편 on the big/small side;
nuguŭi p'yŏni toeŏ chuda 누구의
편이 되어 주다 come to s.o.'s
defense
p'yŏnanhada 편안하다 be
comfortable
p'yŏnanhan 편안한 comfortable,
easy, relaxed
p'yŏnanhi hada 편안히 하다 make
oneself at home
p'yŏnch'in kajŏng 편친 가정 one-
parent family
p'yŏndosŏn 편도선 tonsil
p'yŏndosŏnnyŏm 편도선염
tonsilitis

yŏndo sŭngch'akkwŏn 편도
승차권 one-way ticket
yŏndŭt'ong 편두통 migraine
yŏngbang mit'ŏ 평방 미터 square
meter
yŏngbŏmhan 평범한 plain,
regular; commonplace
yŏngdŭng 평등 equality
yŏngdŭngjuŭiŭi 평등주의의
egalitarian
yŏnggyŏl 평결 verdict
yŏnggyun 평균 average;
o'yŏnggyun ...(ŭ)ro kyesandoeda
평균 ...(으)로 계산되다 average out
at
yŏnggyunnaeda 평균내다 average
out
yŏnggyunŭi 평균의 average
yŏnggyunŭro ... hada 평균으로 ...
하다 average
yŏnghaeng 평행 parallel (line)
yŏnghaenghanŭn 평행하는
parallel
yŏnghwa 평화 peace
yŏnghwajuŭi 평화주의 pacifism
yŏnghwajuŭija 평화주의자 pacifist;
dove
yŏnghwa Pongsadan 평화 봉사단
Peace Corps
yŏnghwaropkke 평화롭게
peacefully
yŏnghwaroptta 평화롭다 be
peaceful
yŏnghwaroun 평화로운 peaceful
yŏnghyŏng 평형 breaststroke
yŏng-il 평일 weekday; workday
yŏngkka 평가 evaluation;
appreciation
yŏngkka chŏrha 평가 절하
devaluation
yŏngkkahada 평가하다 assess;
appreciate; rate, rank, consider;
rank among
yŏngkkajŏlssang 평가절상
revaluation
yŏngmyŏndo 평면도 ground plan
yŏngnon 평론 write-up, review
yŏngnon-ga 평론가 reviewer
yŏngnyang 평양 P'yongyang

p'yŏn-gok 편곡 arrangement MUS
p'yŏn-gok'ada 편곡하다 arrange
MUS
p'yŏng-on 평온 calm
p'yŏng-onhada 평온하다 be tranquil
p'yŏng-onhan 평온한 serene,
tranquil
p'yŏngp'an 평판 reputation
p'yŏngp'ani chŏun 평판이 좋은
reputable
p'yŏngp'ani nappŭn 평판이 나쁜
disreputable
p'yŏngp'yŏnghada 평평하다 be
even, be flat
p'yŏngp'yŏnghage hada 평평하게
하다 flatten
p'yŏngp'yŏnghan 평평한 flat, level
p'yŏngsaeng 평생 lifetime; kŭnyŏ
p'yŏngsaeng-e 그녀 평생에 all her
life; nae p'yŏngsaeng-e 내 평생에
in my lifetime
p'yŏngsaeng-ŭi 평생의 lifelong
p'yŏngsangbok 평상복 casual wear
p'yŏngsangbok ch'arimŭi 평상복
차림의 informal
p'yŏngsangshich'ŏrŏm 평상시처럼
as usual
p'yŏngsang-ŭi 평상의 casual shirt etc
p'yŏng-ya 평야 plain; prairie
p'yŏn-gyŏn 편견 bias, prejudice; ...e
taehan p'yŏn-gyŏn ...에 대한 편견
bias against
p'yŏn-gyŏnŏmnŭn 편견없는
unbiased
p'yŏn-gyŏnŭl kajin 편견을 가진
biased, prejudiced
p'yŏnhan 편한 be comfortable;
tangshini p'yŏnhan shigane
당신이 편한 시간에 at your
convenience
p'yŏnhi shwida 편히 쉬다 relax
p'yŏnhyangshik'ida 편향시키다
deflect
p'yŏnida 편이다: ...nŭn p'yŏnida
...는 편이다 tend to
p'yŏnji 편지 letter; letters,
correspondence
p'yŏnjibin 편집인 editor
p'yŏnjihada 편지하다 mail
p'yŏnjiji 편지지 notepaper
p'yŏnjip 편집 editing ◊ editorial

p'yŏnjipkkwang 편집광 paranoia
p'yŏnjiptcha 편집자 editor
p'yŏnjiptchang 편집장 editor
p'yŏnjiptchŏgin 편집적인 paranoid
p'yŏnjip'ada 편집하다 edit, make corrections to; compile
p'yŏnjirŭl ponaeda 편지를 보내다 mail
p'yŏnjirŭl ssŭda 편지를 쓰다 write a letter
p'yŏnmo 편모 single mother
p'yŏnmul 편물 knitting
p'yŏnppŏp 편법 expedient
p'yŏnsŭnghada 편승하다 hitchhike
p'yŏnŭl tŭlda 편을 들다 take sides
p'yŏ parŭda 펴 바르다 apply ointment etc
p'yo 표 table (of figures); ticket
p'yobaek 표백 bleach
p'yobaek'ada 표백하다 bleach; whiten
p'yobŏm 표범 leopard
p'yobon 표본 sample, specimen
p'yo chadong p'anmaegi 표 자동 판매기 ticket machine
p'yogyŏrhada 표결하다 vote on
p'yohyŏn 표현 expression; display; wording
p'yohyŏnhada 표현하다 express
p'yohyŏnŭi p'ungbuhan 표현이 풍부한 expressive
p'yoje 표제 heading
p'yoji 표지 cover (of book, magazine)
p'yojip'an 표지판 (road) sign
p'yojŏk 표적 target
p'yojŏng 표정 appearance, expression, look
p'yojŏng-i p'ungbuhan 표정이 풍부한 expressive
p'yojŏrhada 표절하다 pirate software etc
p'yojun 표준 standard; p'yojune

midarhada 표준에 미달하다 not be up to standard; *p'yojune tarhada* 표준에 달하다 be up to standard
p'yojune mat-tchi annŭn 표준에 맞지 않는 nonstandard
p'yojun midarŭi 표준 미달의 substandard
p'yojun shiganttae 표준 시간대 tir zone
p'yo kŏmsawŏn 표 검사원 ticket inspector
p'yok'an 표칸 cell COMPUT
p'yomyŏn 표면 surface
p'yomyŏnghada 표명하다 voice *opinion*
p'yomyŏnjŏgin 표면적인 superficia cosmetic
p'yop'i 표피 cuticle
p'yoryuhada 표류하다 drift
p'yoshi 표시 indication, sign; *kam-saŭi p'yoshiro* 감사의 표시로 as a token of my / our appreciation
p'yoshidŭng 표시등 indicator
p'yoshihada 표시하다 display, indicate; stand for; mark up
p'yujŭ 퓨즈 fuse
p'yujŭrŭl kkŭnt'a 퓨즈를 끊다 (blo a) fuse

...rago ...라고 that; *chŏnŭn ...rago saenggak'amnida* 저는 ...라고 생각합니다 I think that ...
...ranŭn ...라는 that; *...ranŭn saeng gagŭl kosuhada* ...라는 생각을 고수하다 hold that, believe
...ro ...로 by; from, because of; of; into; in; with; to; toward
...robut'ŏ ...로부터 from
...rosŏ ...로서 as
...rŭl ...를 *object particle*
...ryŏgo hada ...려고 하다 try to do intend to; be going to

S

사 four
사악한 wicked; sinister
sam 사암 sandstone
sabang 사방 all directions
sabip kwanggo 삽입 광고 insert (*in magazine etc*)
sabip'ada 삽입하다 insert
sabŏm 사범 (martial arts) instructor
sabŏp 사법 judicature ◊ judicial
sabŏpkkwŏn 사법권 jurisdiction
sabok 사복 plain clothes ◊ plain-clothes
sabon 사본 duplicate, copy; transcript
sabunŭi il 사분의 일 quarter
sabunŭi sam 사분의 삼 three quarters
sabun ŭmp'yo 사분 음표 quarter note
sabyŏng 사병 private MIL
sabyŏrhan 사별한 bereaved
sach'i 사치 luxury, extravagance
sach'inhoe 사친회 parent-teacher association
sach'isŭrŏpta 사치스럽다 be extravagant; be luxurious
sach'isŭrŏun 사치스러운 extravagant; luxurious
sach'on 사촌 cousin
sach'un-gi 사춘기 adolescence; puberty
sach'un-giŭi 사춘기의 adolescent
sada 사다 buy; pay for
sadari 사다리 ladder
sae 새 bird ◊ new
saebarŭi p'i 새발의 피 chickenfeed, peanuts
saebyŏk 새벽 dawn, daybreak
saech'igihada 새치기하다 shove in, cut in *line*
saeda 새다 leak, seep
saedanjanghada 새단장하다 freshen up
saegan-gyŏng 색안경 sunglasses

saegida 새기다 carve; engrave
saegin 색인 index
saegin k'adŭ 색인 카드 index card
Saehae 새해 New Year; *Saehae Pok Mani Padŭseyo!* 새해 복 많이 받으세요! Happy New Year!
Saehae Ch'ŏnnal 새해 첫날 New Year's Day
sae irŭmŭro (chŏjang hagi) 새 이름으로 (저장하기) save as
saejang 새장 bird cage
saekch'aega p'ungbuhan 색채가 풍부한 colorful
saekch'aeŭi paehap 색채의 배합 color scheme
saekkaman 새까만 jet-black
saekki 새끼 cub, young animal; kid; brat
saekki koyang-i 새끼 고양이 kitten
saekkiyang 새끼양 lamb
saek-kkal 색깔 color
saek-kkal innŭn 색깔 있는 tinted
saekssŏp'on 색소폰 saxophone
saektchi 색지 tinted paper
saektchŏntchŭng 색전증 embolism
saektcho 색조 shade, tone
saek'omdalk'omhan 새콤달콤한 sweet and sour
saellŏdŭ 샐러드 salad
saem 샘 spring (*water*); envy; jealousy
saendŭl 샌들 sandal
saendŭwich'i 샌드위치 sandwich
saeng-ae 생애 career
saengbangsong 생방송 live broadcast
saengch'e konghak 생체 공학 biotechnology
saengdo 생도 cadet
saenggage chamgida 생각에 잠기다 muse, reflect
saenggage chamgin 생각에 잠긴 pensive

saenggagi kip'ŭn 생각이 깊은 thoughtful

saenggagŏmnŭn 생각없는 mindless, senseless

saenggak 생각 thought, idea; *chŏun saenggagiya!* 좋은 생각이야! good idea!

saenggak'ada 생각하다 think, consider; *...rago saenggakttoenda* ...라고 생각된다 it is considered to be ...

saenggak'aenaeda 생각해내다 come up with, hit on, think up

saenggak'al su choch'a ŏmnŭn 생각할 수 조차 없는 unthinkable; inconceivable

saenggak'al su innŭn 생각할 수 있는 conceivable

saenggang 생강 ginger

saenggangch'a 생강차 ginger tea

saenggi 생기 animation, liveliness

saenggida 생기다 occur; come into existence; *musŭn iri saeng-gyŏssŏyo* 무슨 일이 생겼어요 something has come up

saenggiga nada 생기가 나다 perk up, cheer up

saenggiinnŭn 생기있는 lively, fresh

saenggi tolge hada 생기 돌게 하다 cheer up

saenggye 생계 living, livelihood; *kyŏu saenggyerŭl iŏnagada* 겨우 생계를 이어나가다 eke out a living

saenghwal 생활 life, existence; living

saenghwalbi 생활비 cost of living; maintenance; budget; *saenghwal-birŭl pŏlda* 생활비를 벌다 earn one's living

saenghwal pangsshik 생활 방식 way of life, lifestyle

saenghwal pojo 생활 보조 welfare

saenghwal pojogŭm 생활 보조금 welfare check

saenghwalsa 생활사 life history

saenghwal sujun 생활 수준 standard of living

saeng-il 생일 birthday; *saeng-il ch'uk'ahamnida!* 생일 축하합니다! happy birthday!

saengjonhada 생존하다 exist; survive

saengjonhal ssu innŭn 생존할 수 있는 viable

saengjonja 생존자 survivor

saengjon kyŏngjaeng 생존 경쟁 struggle for survival

saeng k'ŭrim 생 크림 whipped cream

saengmaektchu 생맥주 draft (bee

saengmaeng 색맹 color-blindness color-blind

saengmul 생물 organism, being ◊ bio-

saengmurhak 생물학 biology

saengmurhaktchŏgin 생물학적인 biological

saengmyŏng 생명 life

saengmyŏng ŏmnŭn 생명 없는 lifeless

saengmyŏng pohŏm 생명 보험 li assurance

saengmyŏng-ŭl wihyŏp'anŭn 생명을 위협하는 life-threatening

saengni 생리 menstruation; period

saengnidae 생리대 sanitary napkir

saengnihada 생리하다 menstruate

saengnyak'ada 생략하다 leave ou omit

saengnyŏnwŏril 생년월일 date of birth

saengp'ohada 생포하다 capture (alive)

saengsaenghada 생생하다 be vivi

saengsaenghan 생생한 vivid, graphic

saengsan 생산 production, output

saengsanbi 생산비 production cost

saengsanbirŭl kyŏnjŏk'ada 생산비를 견적하다 cost, calculate the cost of

saengsanhada 생산하다 produce, output

saengsanja 생산자 maker, produce

saengsanmul 생산물 product

saengsannyŏk 생산력 production capacity

saengsanssŏng 생산성 productivi

saengsanŭl kadonghada 생산을 가동하다 come into production; come on stream

saengshikki 생식기 genitals

saengshik nŭngnyŏk 생식 능력

…irility

…engsŏn 생선 fish

…engsŏnppyŏ 생선뼈 fishbone

…engsu 생수 mineral water

…engt'aegye 생태계 ecosystem

…engt'aehak 생태학 ecology

…engt'aehaktcha 생태학자 naturalist, ecologist

…engt'aehaktchŏgin 생태학적인 ecological

…engt'aehaktchŏk kyunhyŏng 생태학적 균형 ecological balance

…aenŭn 새는 leaky

…aeŏ naoda 새어 나오다 leak out, seep out; filter through

…aeppalgak'e tan 새빨갛게 단 red-hot

…aeppalgan kŏjinmal 새빨간 거짓말 downright lie

…aero koch'im 새로 고침 reload COMPUT

…aeropkke nŭkkida 새롭게 느끼다 feel renewed

…aeroptta 새롭다 be new

…aeroun 새로운 fresh, new

…ae tanjanghada 새 단장하다 redecorate

…aeu 새우 shrimp

…agak'yŏng 사각형 square; quadrangle

…agi 사기 swindle, fraud, rip-off; con; morale, spirits ◊ fraudulent

…agi ch'ida 사기 치다 con, cheat

…agikkun 사기꾼 crook, con man

…agijik'ada 사직하다 resign

…ago 사고 accident, mishap; thought; *sagoro chuktta* 사고로 죽다 be killed in an accident; *sagorŭl tanghada* 사고를 당하다 have an accident

…agwa 사과 apology; apple

…agwa chusŭ 사과 주스 apple juice

…agwahada 사과하다 apologize

…agwan saengdo 사관 생도 cadet

…agwasosŭ 사과소스 apple sauce

…agwida 사귀다 get acquainted, make friends; *ch'in-gurŭl sagwida* 친구를 사귀다 make friends; *saramgwa sagwida* 사람과 사귀다 socialize

…agyogye saramdŭl 사교계 사람들 glitterati

sagyojŏgin 사교적인 sociable; *kŭnyŏnŭn sagyossŏng-i chot'a* 그녀는 사교성이 좋다 she's a good mixer

sahaktcha 사학자 historian

sahoe 사회 society, community ◊ social

sahoehak 사회학 sociology

sahoeja 사회자 chairperson; chairwoman; host; master of ceremonies

sahoejuŭi 사회주의 socialism

sahoejuŭija 사회주의자 socialist

sahoejuŭijŏgin 사회주의적인 socialist

sahoe kyegŭp 사회 계급 (social) class

sahoe poda 사회 보다 preside

sahoe saŏp 사회 사업 social work

sahoe saŏpkka 사회 사업가 social worker

sahoe ssŭregi 사회 쓰레기 lowlife

sahyŏng chip'aeng 사형 집행 execution

sahyŏng chip'aenghada 사형 집행하다 execute

sahyŏng chip'aeng-in 사형 집행인 executioner

sahyŏng sŏn-gorŭl pat-tta 사형 선고를 받다 be sentenced to death

sai 사이 interval, space; relationship; *kip'ŭn sai* 깊은 사이 intimacy (*sexual*); *kip'ŭn saiin* 깊은 사이인 intimate (*sexually*)

saie 사이에 between

saiga chot'a 사이가 좋다 get on; be friendly with

saiga t'ŭrŏjida 사이가 틀어지다 fall out, argue

saijok'e chinaeda 사이좋게 지내다 get along

saim 사임 resignation

saimhada 사임하다 resign

sain 사인 killer; autograph

sairen 사이렌 siren

saja 사자 lion

sajang 사장 boss; president

sajik 사직 resignation; *sajik'al kŏsŭl allida* 사직할 것을 알리다 hand in one's notice sajik'ada 사직하다 resign

sajin 사진 photo(graph); **sajini chal pannŭn** 사진이 잘 받는 photogenic

sajinaelbŏm 사진앨범 photo album

sajin ch'waryŏng 사진 촬영 photography

sajinsa 사진사 photographer

sajin tchiktta 사진 찍다 photograph

sajŏl 사절 delegation; envoy

sajŏn 사전 dictionary

sajŏng kŏri 사정 거리 range

sajŏng-ŏmnŭn 사정없는 relentless; ruthless

sajŏn kyŏnghŏm 사전 경험 foretaste

sajungju 사중주 quartet

sak-kkam 삭감 cut, cutback, reduction

sak-kkamhada 삭감하다 reduce, cut; slash

sakkŏn 사건 affair, matter, case; incident; **sakkŏnŭi sunsŏ** 사건의 순서 the sequence of events

sakpparhan 삭발한 shaven

saktche 삭제 deletion

saktchehada 삭제하다 delete

sak'arin 사카린 saccharin

sal 살 flesh, meat; years of age; arrow; spoke (of wheel)

salch'ungje 살충제 pesticide; insecticide

salda 살다 live

salgach'i kŏch'in 살갗이 거친 chapped

salgŭmŏni 살그머니 stealthily, furtively

salgŭmsalgŭm kŏt-tta 살금살금 걷다 creep

salgu 살구 apricot

salgyundoen 살균된 sterile MED

salgyunŭi 살균의 antiseptic

salk'ogi 살코기 lean meat

sallim kyŏngbiwŏn 산림 경비원 forest ranger

sallŏdŭ tŭreshing 샐러드 드레싱 salad dressing

sal ppaeda 살 빼다 slim

salp'yŏboda 살펴보다 see about, look into; check on; examine, look at; observe

salsal 살살 softly, lightly, gently

salssugi 살수기 sprinkler

sal su innŭn 살 수 있는 inhabitable

sal su ŏmnŭn 살 수 없는 uninhabitable

saltchak 살짝 furtively; easily; light

saltchak kkaemulda 살짝 깨물다 nibble

saltchak milch'ida 살짝 밀치다 jo elbow etc

saltchak sŭch'ida 살짝 스치다 brush, touch lightly

saltchida 살찌다 fill out, get fatter

sam 삼 three

samagwi 사마귀 wart

samak 사막 desert

samang 사망 death

samangjasu 사망자수 death toll

samangnyul 사망률 mortality, dea rate

sambunŭi il 삼분의 일 one third

samch'on 삼촌 uncle (father's brother, single)

samgahada 삼가하다 refrain, desis

samgak 삼각 triangle ◊ triangular

samgak-kki 삼각기 pennant

samgak-kkŏn 삼각건 sling (bandage)

samgakttae 삼각대 tripod

samgak'yŏng 삼각형 triangle

Samguk 삼국 The Three Kingdoms

samgyet'ang 삼계탕 chicken boile with ginseng

samgyŏpssal kui 삼겹살 구이 barbecued belly of pork

Samiltchŏl 삼일절 1 March Memorial Day

samja 삼자 third party

samjungju 삼중주 trio

samk'ida 삼키다 engulf, swallow

samnyu 삼류 third class ◊ third-rate

samohada 사모하다 adore

samonim 사모님 Madam, Mrs (respectful)

Samp'alssŏn 삼팔선 38th Parallel

samship 삼십 thirty

samtta 삶다 boil

samuguk 사무국 bureau, office

samugwan 사무관 clerk

samujang 사무장 steward

samujik sawŏn 사무직 사원 office worker, white-collar worker

samul 사물 thing

samushil 사무실 office (*room*)

samushillyong kŏnmul 사무실용 건물 office (*building*)

samushillyong koch'ŭng piltting 사무실용 고층 빌딩 office block

samwŏl 삼월 March

samyŏn 사면 amnesty, pardon; hill

samyŏng 사명 mission, vocation

samyŏnhada 사면하다 absolve, pardon

san 산 mountain; acid

sana chehan 산아 제한 birth control

sanae(sŏ) 사내에(서) in-house

sanaeŭi 사내의 in-house

sanagin 산악인 mountaineer

sanapke morach'ida 사납게 몰아치다 rage

sanaptta 사납다 be wild; be fierce; be unlucky

sanaun 사나운 rough, fierce

sanawajida 사나와지다 become abusive

sanbaltch'ŏgin 산발적인 sporadic; scattered; intermittent

sanbuinkkwa 산부인과 maternity hospital

sanbuinkkwa pyŏngdong 산부인과 병동 maternity ward

sanbuinkkwa ŭisa 산부인과 의사 gynecologist; obstetrician

sanch'aek 산책 ramble; rambling; stroll

sanch'aekshik'ida 산책시키다 walk *the dog*

sanch'aek'ada 산책하다 go for a walk; take a stroll; ramble

sanch'ul 산출 yield

sanch'urhada 산출하다 yield

sanch'urhae naeda 산출해 내다 calculate

sandaejŏguro 상대적으로 relatively

sandŏmi 산더미 mound, pile

sandŭlpparam 산들바람 breeze

sang 상 prize; icon (*cultural*); statue; table; mourning; *sang chung-ida* 상 중이다 be in mourning

sang-a 상아 ivory

sang-ajil 상아질 enamel (*on tooth*)

sangbandoen 상반된 opposite

sangbogŭl iptta 상복을 입다 wear mourning

sangbuŭi 상부의 top

sangbyŏng 상병 corporal

sangch'ŏ 상처 wound; sore; bruise

sangch'ŏ ibŭn 상처 입은 wounded, injured

sangch'ŏ ip'ida 상처 입히다 injure, wound

sangch'ŏnan 상처난 bruising, emotionally painful

sangch'ŏ ŏmnŭn 상처없는 uninjured

sangch'ŏ patkki shwiun 상처 받기 쉬운 vulnerable

sangch'ŏrŭl chuda 상처를 주다 bruise; hurt

sangch'ŏrŭl pat-tta 상처를 받다 get hurt

sangch'u 상추 lettuce

sangdae 상대 opponent; companion

sangdaejŏgin 상대적인 relative

sangdam 상담 consultancy; counseling; advice

sangdambi 상담비 (consultancy) fee

sangdamhada 상담하다 counsel

sangdamnyŏk 상담역 counselor, adviser

sangdanghada 상당하다 be appropriate; be considerable; be reasonable; be equivalent

sangdanghage 상당하게 substantially, considerably

sangdanghan 상당한 substantial, considerable, significant; equivalent

sangdanghi 상당히 reasonably, considerably, quite

sangdanghi chohŭn 상당히 좋은 decent, reasonable

... sang-e ... 상에 on

sangga 상가 (shopping) mall

sanggam 상감 inlay

sanggapp'an 상갑판 upper deck

sanggihada 상기하다 recall, remember; relive

sanggishikida 상기시키다 remind

sanggo mŏri 상고 머리 crew cut

Sanggong Hoeŭiso 상공 회의소 Chamber of Commerce

sanggŭm 상금 winnings

sanggŭp 상급 senior rank; advanced level ◊ senior, superior

sanggwanŏmnŭn 상관없는 immaterial, irrelevant; **chŏn, sanggwanŏpssŏyo** 전, 상관없어요 it's all the same to me

sanggwanŏpta 상관없다 be irrelevant; not mind; **chŏnŭn sanggwanŏpssŭmnida** 저는 상관없습니다 I don't mind; **kŭgŏsŭn sanggwanŏpta** 그것은 상관없다 it doesn't matter

sanghada 상하다 go bad; be injured; be emaciated; **muŏse kibun sanghada** 무엇에 기분 상하다 get upset about sth

sanghage hada 상하게 하다 wound

sanghan 상한 sour

sangho chagyong 상호 작용 interaction

sangho chagyonghanŭn 상호 작용하는 interactive

sanghoganŭi 상호간의 mutual; reciprocal

sangho ŭijonhanŭn 상호 의존하는 interdependent

sanghwang 상황 situation, circumstances; **ŏttŏn sanghwang-esŏdo** 어떤 상황에서도 under no circumstances

sanghwanhada 상환하다 redeem, pay off

sang-in 상인 merchant, dealer, trader

san-gisŭlk 산기슭 foot of a mountain

sangja 상자 case, box

sangjing 상징 symbol, emblem

sangjinghada 상징하다 symbolize

sangjingjŏgin 상징적인 symbolic

sangjingjuŭi 상징주의 symbolism

sangjŏm 상점 store, shop

sangk'waehada 상쾌하다 feel fresh

sangk'waehan 상쾌한 refreshing, invigorating; crisp

sangmak'ada 삭막하다 be bleak

sangmak'an 삭막한 stark, severe

sangnil 삯일 piecework

sangnokssu 상록수 evergreen

sangnyŏnghada 상영하다 show *movie*

sangnyu 상류 upper reaches; upper classes ◊ upper-class

sangnyuch'ŭng 상류층 upper classes

sangnyuch'ŭng-ŭi 상류층의 upper class

sangnyuro 상류로 upstream

sangnyu sahoe 상류 사회 high society

sangnyu sahoeŭi saenghwal 상류 사회의 생활 high life

sangŏ 상어 shark

sang-ŏp 상업 commerce, trade ◊ commercial

sang-ŏpssang-ŭi 상업상의 commercial

sangp'um 상품 goods, merchandise, stock

sangp'umhwahada 상품화하다 commercialize

sangp'umkkwŏn 상품권 token

sangp'umŭi imiji 상품의 이미지 brand image

sangp'yo 상표 brand, make

sangp'yomyŏng 상표명 brand name

sangsa 상사 boss

sangsang 상상 imagination

sangsanghada 상상하다 imagine, conceive of, envisage

sangsanghal su innŭn 상상할 수 있는 imaginable

sangsanghal su ŏmnŭn 상상할 수 없는 unimaginable

sangsangnyŏgi ŏmnŭn 상상력이 없는 unimaginative

sangsangnyŏgi p'ungbuhan 상상력이 풍부한 imaginative

sangsang-ŭl ch'owŏrhanŭn 상상을 초월하는 exorbitant

sangsehada 상세하다 be detailed

sangsehage 상세하게 minutely, in detail

sangsehan 상세한 detailed, full

sangsehi 상세히 fully, in minute detail

sangshik 상식 sense, common sense

sangshil 상실 loss

sangshirhada 상실하다 forfeit, give up, lose

sangsogin 상속인 heir

sangsok 상속 inheritance

sangsok-kkwŏnŭl pakt'arhada 상속권을 박탈하다 disinherit

sangsok'ada 상속하다 inherit

sangsŭng 상승 rise ◊ rising

angsŭnghada 상승하다 rise, ascend

angsŭngse-ŭi 상승세의 buoyant

angsŭptchŏgin 상승적인 habitual

angsŭrŏptta 상스럽다 be crude, be vulgar

angsŭrŏun 상스러운 crude, coarse, vulgar

angsudo 상수도 waterworks

angt'ae 상태 state, condition; circumstances

ang-ŭi 상의 top (*piece of clothing*); coat; consultation

ang-wŏn 상원 senate

ang-wŏnŭiwŏn 상원의원 senator

anho 산호 coral

anhwamul 산화물 oxide

anjaehanŭn 산재하는 sparse

anjŏk 산적 bandit; shish kebab

ankkil 산길 pass

anmaek 산맥 (mountain) range

anmanhada 산만하다 be loose; be vague

anmanhage 산만하게 loosely

anmanhan 산만한 loose, imprecise; vague; *mŏriga sanmanhan* 머리가 산만한 scatterbrained

anmun 산문 prose

annamul 산나물 wild greens

anŏp 산업 industry ◊ industrial

anŏp'yegimul 산업폐기물 industrial waste

anŏp'wahada 산업화하다 industrialize

ansanjogak naeda 산산조각 내다 smash to pieces

ansaram 산사람 hillbilly

ansat'ae 산사태 landslide

anshin 산신 mountain spirit

ansŏngbi 산성비 acid rain

anso 산소 oxygen; ancestral grave

ansul 산술 arithmetic

anttŏmi 산더미 heap, pile; *santtŏmigach'i manŭn il* 산더미같이 많은 일 a pile of work

anttŭngsŏng-i 산둥성이 ridge

Sant'ak'ŭllosŭ 산타클로스 Santa Claus

ant'okki 산토끼 hare

sanyang 사냥 hunt; hunting

sanyanghada 사냥하다 hunt

sanyangkkun 사냥꾼 hunter

saŏp 사업 business; enterprise; undertaking; project; *saŏpch'a* 사업차 on business

saŏpkka 사업가 businessman

saŏp kwan-gye 사업 관계 business relations

sap 삽 shovel; scoop; spade

sapsshigane 삽시간에 in an instant; *sapsshigane p'ŏjida* 삽시간에 퍼지다 spread like wildfire

sap'aiŏ 사파이어 sapphire

sap'alnun 사팔눈 squint

sap'o 사포 sandpaper

sap'oro taktta 사포로 닦다 sandpaper

sap'oro tangnŭn changch'i 사포로 닦는 장치 sander

sap'wa 삽화 illustration

sap'waga 삽화가 illustrator

sap'warŭl kŭrida 삽화를 그리다 illustrate

saragada 살아가다 live; keep on living

sara innŭn 살아 있는 live, living

sara innŭn tŭt'an 살아 있는 듯한 lifelike

sarait-tta 살아있다 be alive

sarajida 사라지다 disappear; decline; die out

saram 사람 person; man; people; human ◊ *countword for people*

saramdaun 사람다운 humane

sarami salji annŭn 사람이 살지 않는 uninhabited

saramŭi shilssu 사람의 실수 human error

saranada 살아나다 revive; survive

sara nagada 살아 나가다 survive; carry on living

saranamtta 살아남다 survive

sarang 사랑 love

sarang-e ppajida 사랑에 빠지다 fall in love; fall in love with

saranghada 사랑하다 love

saranghanŭn 사랑하는 beloved

sarang-ni 사랑니 wisdom tooth

sarangsŭrŏun 사랑스러운 lovely; lovable, endearing

sarhae 살해 killing, slaying, murder

sarhaehada 살해하다 kill, slay, murder

sari 사리 coil; self-interest; Buddhist saint's relic; reason

sarin 살인 murder, homicide

sarinböm 살인범 homicide; murderer

sarinhada 살인하다 murder

sarinja 살인자 killer, murderer

sarisayok 사리사욕 self-interest

sarojaptta 사로잡다 capture

sarojap'ida 사로잡히다 be obsessed by

sarül enündüshi 살을 에는듯이 bitterly cold

sarül enün tüt'an 살을 에는 듯한 sharp, bitter cold

saryŏ kip'ün 사려 깊은 thoughtful, considerate

saryŏnggwan 사령관 commander

saryŏŏmnün 사려없는 inconsiderate

saryo 사료 fodder

saryun-gudong 사륜구동 four-wheel drive

sasaeng-a 사생아 illegitimate child, bastard

sasaenghwal 사생활 privacy

sasandoeda 사산되다 be stillborn

sasang 사상 thought, ideology; in history; death and injury

sasangja 사상자 casualty

sashil 사실 fact; truth

sashilssang 사실상 in fact, actually; virtually, more or less

sashilssang-üi 사실상의 actual; virtual

sashiltchuüi 사실주의 realism

sashiltchuüija 사실주의자 realist

saship 사십 forty

sashirül türönaenün 사실을 드러내는 telltale signs

sashirün 사실은 in fact, as a matter of fact, actually

sashiüi 사시의 cross-eyed

sasŏ 사서 librarian

sasŏham 사서함 PO Box

sasŏl 사설 editorial

sasŏng changgun 사성 장군 four-star general

sasohada 사소하다 be trivial

sasohan 사소한 trivial, minor

sasohan il 사소한 일 detail, trifle

sasohan kŏt 사소한 것 triviality

sasohan sahang 사소한 사항 technicality

sasül 사슬 chain

sasüm 사슴 deer

sasüm kogi 사슴 고기 venison

Sasunjŏl 사순절 Lent

satchŏgin 사적인 private

satssach'i twijida 샅샅이 뒤지다 comb; ransack

sat'aguni 사타구니 groin

Sat'an 사탄 Satan

sat'ang 사탕 candy

sat'angsusu 사탕 수수 sugar cane

sat'uri 사투리 dialect

Saudi Arabia 사우디 아라비아 Saudi Arabia ◊ Saudi

sauna 사우나 sauna

saundü k'adü 사운드 카드 sound card

sawi 사위 son-in-law

sawŏl 사월 April

sawŏn 사원 temple REL

sayanghada 사양하다 decline with thanks; *sayangch'i mashigo kajiseyo* 사양치 마시고 가지세요 please keep it, I insist

sayanghal su ŏmnün 사양할 수 없 irresistible

sayŏrhada 사열하다 review *troops*

sayong 사용 use

sayonghada 사용하다 use, employ; exercise *control, restraint*; work

sayonghagi shwiun 사용하기 쉬운 user-friendly

sayongja 사용자 user

sayongppŏp 사용법 directions, instructions for use

sayong sŏlmyŏngsŏ 사용 설명서 instruction manual

sayuktcha 사육자 breeder

sebaero chünggahada 세배로 증가하다 treble

sebal chajŏn-gŏ 세발 자전거 tricycle

sebu chohang 세부 조항 small print

sebunhada 세분하다 subdivide

sebu sahang 세부 사항 detail

sech'ashik'ida 세차시키다 get the car washed

sech'a sŏbissü 세차 서비스 valet service

●ch'igi 세치기 cutting in line
●ch'ŏktche 세척제 detergent
●da 세다 count (up)
●dae 세대 generation
●dae ch'ai 세대 차이 generation gap
●dan 세단 sedan
●ge ch'ida 세게 치다 punch; push, jolt
●gehada 세게 하다 intensify
●ge tchirŭda 세게 찌르다 thrust
●gi 세기 century
●gŭm 세금 tax
●gŭm kiho 세금 기호 tax code
●gŭm kongjega kanŭnghan 세금 공제가 가능한 tax deductible
●gŭmŭl pugwahada 세금을 부과하다 tax
●gŭmŭl p'ohamhan 세금을 포함한 pre-tax
●gwan kŏmsa 세관 검사 customs inspection
●gwan t'onggwa 세관 통과 customs clearance
●gwanwŏn 세관원 customs officer
●gye 세계 world
●gyehwa 세계화 globalization
●gyejŏgin 세계적인 worldwide
●gyejŏgŭro 세계적으로 worldwide
●gyejŏk kangdaeguk 세계적 강대국 world power
●gye kyŏngje 세계 경제 global economy
●gye onnanhwa 세계 온난화 global warming
●gye P'yojunshi 세계 표준시 GMT, Greenwich Mean Time
●gye shijang 세계 시장 global market
●gye taejŏn 세계 대전 world war
●gyun 세균 germ
●gyunjŏn 세균전 germ warfare
●il chung-ida 세일 중이다 be on sale (at reduced prices)
●iljŭmaen 세일즈맨 salesman; representative
●ip 세입 revenue
●llŏri 셀러리 celery
●llop'an 셀로판 cellophane
●lp'ŭ set'aksso 셀프세탁소 laundromat

selp'ŭssŏbisŭ shikttang 셀프서비스 식당 self-service restaurant
selp'ŭssŏbisŭŭi 셀프서비스의 self-service
sel su omnŭn 셀 수 없는 countless
sem 셈 count; intention, design; ...ŭi semŭl ijŏbŏrida ...의 셈을 잊어버리다 lose count of; ...ŭl/rŭl hal semŭro ...을/를 할 셈으로 with the intention of
semina 세미나 seminar
semirhi chosadoeda 세밀히 조사되다 come under scrutiny
semŭro ch'ida 셈으로 치다 count, qualify
semu chosagwan 세무 조사관 tax-inspector
semyŏndae 세면대 basin
semyŏndogu kabang 세면도구 가방 sponge bag
semyŏn-gi 세면기 washbasin, washbowl
semyŏnjang 세면장 bathroom
semyŏn t'awŏl 세면 타월 washcloth
semyŏn yongp'um 세면 용품 toiletries
senoe 세뇌 brainwashing
senoehada 세뇌하다 brainwash
sensseisyŏn 센세이션 sensation
sent'i(mit'ŏ) 센티(미터) centimeter
sent'ŏ 센터 center
sent'ŭ 센트 cent
se pŏntchae 세 번째 third
se pŏntchaeŭi 세 번째의 third
sep'o 세포 cell
seriju 세리주 sherry
seroro 세로로 portrait print
serye 세례 baptism
seryehada 세례하다 baptize, christen
seryemyŏng 세례명 Christian name
seryŏk 세력 power, leverage; influence
seryŏndoen 세련된 cultured, sophisticated
seryok-kkwŏn 세력권 sphere of influence
sesang 세상 world; sesang-e! 세상에! oh God!; sesang-e nae-not'a 세상에 내놓다 bring out; sesang multchŏng-e palgŭn 세상 물정에 밝은 worldly; streetwise;

sesang-ŭl ttŏdŭlssŏk'age hanŭn
세상을 떠들썩하게 하는 sensational;
sesang-ŭl ttŭda 세상을 뜨다
depart this world, pass away
seshim 세심 carefulness; *...ŭl/rŭl
seshimhage poda* ...을 / 를
세심하게 보다 keep a wary eye on ...
seshimhan 세심한 meticulous
sesogŭi 세속의 secular
sesoktchŏgin 세속적인 material,
worldly
se ssangdung-i 세 쌍둥이 triplets
set sŏ 세 three
set'agŭl matkkida 세탁을 맡기다
have laundered
set'ak-kki 세탁기 washing machine
set'ak sŏbissŭ 세탁 서비스 valet
service
set'aksso 세탁소 laundry; dry
cleaner
set'ak'ada 세탁하다 launder
set'ak'age hada 세탁하게 하다 get
one's laundry done
set'angmul 세탁물 laundry (*clothes*)
set'inghada 세팅하다 set up
setŏp 셋업 set-up COMPUT
set'ŭ 세트 set
seuda 세우다 build; erect; establish,
set up; turn up *collar*; stop *person in
street*; *ttokpparo seuda* 똑바로
세우다 stand on end
shi 시 poetry, verse; poem; city;
o'clock; *tasŏt shie* 다섯 시에 at five
o'clock
shiabŏji 시아버지 father-in-law
(*husband's father*)
shibi 십이 twelve
shibil 십일 eleven
shibiwŏl 십이월 December
shibirwŏl 십일월 November
shibo 십오 fifteen
shibobun 십오분 fifteen minutes, a
quarter of an hour
shich'a 시차 time-lag
shich'al 시찰 inspection
shich'arhada 시찰하다 inspect
shich'e 시체 body, corpse, cadaver
shich'ŏng 시청 city hall; town hall
shich'ŏnggagŭi 시청각의
audiovisual
shich'ŏnghada 시청하다 view, tune

in to
shich'ŏngja 시청자 audience; view
follower
shich'o 시초 beginning, dawn
shida 시다 be sour
shidae 시대 era, epoch; *yojŭm
shidaega kŭrŏssŭmnida* 요즘
시대가 그렇습니다 it's a sign of th
times
shidaee twittŏrŏjin 시대에 뒤떨어
dated, old-fashioned
shidallida 시달리다 be harassed
shidallin 시달린 harassed;
kŏktchŏng-e shidallin 걱정에
시달린 careworn
shido 시도 attempt, endeavor; *sae
oun shido* 새로운 시도 new
departure
shidohada 시도하다 try, attempt,
endeavor
shidongdoeda 시동되다 start
shidonggi 시동기 starter MOT
shidongshik'ida 시동시키다 start
shidŭlda 시들다 droop, wilt, withe
shigaji 시가지 built-up area
shigak kyojae 시각 교재 visual ai
shigaktchŏgin 시각적인 visual
shigaktchŏgŭro 시각적으로 visua
shigaktchŏgŭro sonsangdoen
시각적으로 손상된 visually
impaired
shigan 시간 time; hour
shigan chŏryak 시간 절약
timesaving
shiganjero 시간제로 part-time
shigan kan-gyŏk 시간 간격 inter
shiganmada 시간 마다 every hou
shigan ŏmsu 시간 엄수 punctuali
shiganp'yo 시간표 schedule,
timetable
shiganŭl chik'inŭn 시간을 지키는
prompt, on time
shiganŭl hŏbihada 시간을 허비하
dawdle
shiganŭl match'uda 시간을 맞추
synchronize
shiganŭl match'uŏ 시간을 맞추어
time
shiganŭl ŏmsuhanŭn 시간을
엄수하는 punctual
shigi 시기 phase, period, stage;

higirŭl match'ugi 시기를 맞추기 timing

higisangjoŭi 시기상조의 premature

higi yoppŏp 식이 요법 diet (*as cure*)

higol 시골 countryside; hick town; **shigore(sŏ)** 시골에(서) in the country

higolkkil 시골길 country lane

higoltchip 시골집 cottage

higolttŭgi 시골뜨기 lout; hick

higorŭi 시골의 rural

higŭmch'i 시금치 spinach

higurhada 시굴하다 prospect for

higye 시계 clock; watch

higye chejoin 시계 제조인 watchmaker

higye panghyang-ŭro tora 시계 방향으로 돌아 clockwise

higye panŭl 시계 바늘 hand (*of clock*)

higyeradio 시계라디오 clock radio

higye t'aeyŏp changch'i 시계 태엽 장치 clockwork (mechanism)

higyogŭl todunŭn 식욕을 돋우는 appetizing

higyok 식욕 appetite

hihan p'okt'an 시한 폭탄 time bomb

hihap 시합 tournament; event; match; bout (*in boxing*)

hihŏm 시험 exam; test, trial

hihŏmgwan 시험관 examiner; test tube

hihŏmgwan agi 시험관 아기 test-tube baby

hihŏmhada 시험하다 examine, test

hihŏmhae poda 시험해 보다 try out; have on trial

hihŏmji 시험지 examination paper

hihŏm kigan 시험 기간 trial period

hihŏm kongjang 시험 공장 pilot plant

hiin 시인 confession; poet

hiinhada 시인하다 admit, confess

hijak 시작 beginning, start; onset; **choŭn/nappŭn shijagŭl hada** 좋은/나쁜 시작을 하다 get off to a good/bad start

hijakdoeda 시작되다 begin, start;

break out, start up; break (*of storm*)

shijak pŏt'ŭn 시작 버튼 start button; trigger; on switch

shijakttoeda 시작되다 begin, commence

shijak'ada 시작하다 begin, originate; institute; take up; get down to; log on; *...ki shijak'ada ...*기 시작하다 start ...ing; **irŭl shijak'ada** 일을 시작하다 set to work

shijang 시장 market; marketplace; mayor; **shijang-e** 시장에 on the market; **shijang-ŭl toktchŏmhada** 시장을 독점하다 corner the market

shijangboda 시장보다 store, shop

shijang chŏmnyuyul 시장 점유율 market share

shijang chosa 시장 조사 market research

shijang kyŏngje 시장 경제 market economy

shijangnyŏk 시장력 market forces

shije 시제 tense GRAM

shijŏl 시절 season; time; *kŭ shijŏrenŭn* 그 시절에는 in those days

shijungdŭlda 시중들다 serve

shijung tŭnŭn saram 시중 드는 사람 valet

shijung-ŭl tŭlda 시중을 들다 wait on

shik 식 event; ceremony; eclipse

shikch'o 식초 vinegar

shikkŭrŏptta 시끄럽다 be loud; be noisy

shikkŭrŏun 시끄러운 loud, noisy

shikkŭrŏun sori 시끄러운 소리 din, noise

shikppyŏllyŏgi innŭn 식별력이 있는 discriminating, discerning

shikppyŏrhada 식별하다 spot, identify; discern; distinguish

shikp'umjŏm 식품점 grocery (store)

shikssa 식사 meal

shikssahada 식사하다 dine

shikssa shigan 식사 시간 mealtime; sitting

shikssŏng 식성 taste, preference (*in food*); **shikssŏng-i kkadaroptta** 식성이 까다롭다 be a fussy eater

shiktchahada 식자하다 typeset, set

shiktchungdok 식중독 food

poisoning

shiktta 식다 cool, cool down

shikttan 식단 menu

shikttang 식당 restaurant; dining room

shikttangch'a 식당차 restaurant car

shikttanp'yo 식단표 menu

shiktto 식도 gullet

shik'ak 식탁 dining table

shik'akppo 식탁보 tablecloth

shik'ida 식히다 cool down

shik'ida 시키다 (*causative*): **shil-mangshik'ida** 실망시키다 disappoint; **t'ŭrimŭl shik'ida** 트림을 시키다 burp *baby*

shil 실 yarn, thread

shilch'ehwahada 실체화하다 materialize

shilk'ŏt mŏk-kki 실컷 먹기 blowout

shillae 실내 interior

shillae changshik-kka 실내 장식가 interior decorator

shillaee(sŏ) 실내에(서) indoors

shillae kyŏng-ŭmak 실내 경음악 piped music

shillalgat'ŭn hŭimang 실낱같은 희망 glimmer of hope

shillang 신랑 groom, bridegroom

shillang tŭllŏri 신랑 들러리 best man

shillarhan 신랄한 cutting, stinging; bitter

shillijŏgin 실리적인 practical, pragmatic

shillijŏguro 실리적으로 practically, pragmatically

shillik'on 실리콘 silicon

shillik'on ch'ip 실리콘 칩 silicon chip

shilloe 신뢰 trust, confidence; faith

shilloegam kanŭn 신뢰감 가는 credible

shilloehada 신뢰하다 trust, believe in

shilloehal su innŭn 신뢰할 수 있는 trustworthy; trusted; reliable

shilloehanŭn 신뢰하는 trustful, trusting

shilloessŏng 신뢰성 reliability; credibility

shilluet 실루엣 silhouette

shillye 실례 illustration

shillyehamnida 실례합니다 excuse me

shilmang 실망 disappointment

shilmanghada 실망하다 disappoin

shilmanghan 실망한 disappointed

shilmangshik'ida 실망시키다 disappoint

shilmangsŭröun 실망스러운 disappointing

shilmari 실마리 clue

shilmul k'ügiŭi 실물 크기의 life-siz

shilp'ae 실패 failure; breakdown; reel, spool

shilp'aehada 실패하다 fail; break down; lose out; be out

shilp'aehan 실패한 unsuccessful

shilp'aeja 실패자 loser, failure

shilp'aejagida 실패자이다 flop, fail

shilp'aejak 실패작 flop, failure

shilp'aero kkŭnnada 실패로 끝나다 end in failure; fall through

shilsshidoeda 실시되다 come into effect

shilsshigan 실시간 real time

shilsshiganŭi 실시간의 real-time

shilsshihada 실시하다 carry out

shilssu 실수 mistake

shilssuhada 실수하다 make a mistake, go wrong

shilssuip 실수입 take-home pay

shilssuro 실수로 by mistake

shiltchaehaji annŭn 실재하지 않는 unreal

shiltche 실제 truth; fact; practice ◊ practical

shiltchejŏgin 실제적인 practical; down-to-earth

shiltcheŭi 실제의 actual, real

shiltchik'ada 실직하다 lose one's job; be unemployed

shiltchik'an 실직한 unemployed, ou of work

shiltchiltchŏgin 실질적인 substantive

shiltchiltchŏguro 실질적으로 substantially

shiltchŏm 실점 lost points SP

shiltchong 실종 disappearance

shiltchŭng nada 실증 나다 be tired of

shiltta 싣다 load; **chimŭl shiltta** 짐을 싣다 load

shilt'an 실탄 live ammunition

hilt'ohada 실토하다 confess

him 심 pith

himburŭm 심부름 errand

himburŭmgada 심부름가다 run errands

himent'ŭ 시멘트 cement; **himent'ŭro parŭda** 시멘트로 바르다 cement

himgak'ada 심각하다 be serious

himgak'an 심각한 serious *illness*; deep *trouble*; heavy *loss*

himgiga twit'ŭllin 심기가 뒤틀린 cranky, bad-tempered

himgyehangjin 심계항진 palpitations

himhada 심하다 be awful

himhage 심하게 seriously; badly; severely

himhage nappŭn 심하게 나쁜 atrocious

himham 심함 severity

himhan 심한 bad, awful; heavy; severe

himin 시민 citizen

himin-gun 시민군 militia

himinkkwŏn 시민권 citizenship

himiŭi 시민의 civil; civic

himjang 심장 heart ◊ cardiac, coronary

himjang chŏngji 심장 정지 cardiac arrest

himjang ishik 심장 이식 heart transplant

himjang mabi 심장 마비 heart attack, coronary

himjang pakttong 심장 박동 heartbeat

himji 심지 wick

himjiga kujŭn 심지가 굳은 strong-minded, independent

himmijŏgin 심미적인 esthetic

himmun 심문 interrogation

himmunhada 심문하다 interrogate

himmunja 심문자 interrogator

himnanhage hada 심란하게 하다 distract

himnanhan 심란한 distracted, worried

himni 심리 hearing LAW

himnihak 심리학 psychology

himnihaktcha 심리학자 psychologist

shimnijŏgin 심리적인 psychological

shimnijŏgŭro 심리적으로 psychologically

shimnya 심야 small hours

shimnyŏngjuŭi 심령주의 spiritualism

shimnyŏngjuŭija 심령주의자 spiritualist

shimnyŏng-ŭi 심령의 psychic

shimoham 심오함 depth (*of thought*)

shimohan 심오한 deep, profound

shimp'an 심판 referee; umpire

shimp'an wiwŏnhoe 심판 위원회 tribunal

shimsahada 심사하다 judge

shimsasuk-kko 심사숙고 reflection

shimsasuk-kkohan 심사숙고한 thoughtful

shimsa wiwŏn 심사 위원 judge

shimsa wiwŏndan 심사 위원단 jury; panel

shimsulgujŭn 심술궂은 sour; bitchy; bad-tempered

shimsulgut-tta 심술궂다 be bad-tempered

shimtta 심다 plant

shimŭi 심의 debate

shimuruk'an 시무룩한 glum

shimwŏnhan 심원한 deep

shimyuk 십육 sixteen

shin 신 deity; god ◊ sour

shinae t'onghwa 시내 통화 local call

shinbal 신발 footwear; shoe

shinbalkkage 신발가게 shoestore

shinbalkkŭn 신발끈 shoelace

shinbi 신비 mystery

shinbihada 신비하다 be mysterious

shinbihage 신비하게 mysteriously

shinbihan 신비한 mysterious

shinbingssŏng 신빙성 credibility; authenticity

shinbingssŏng-ŭl ttŏrŏttŭrida 신빙성을 떨어뜨리다 discredit

shinbiroun 신비로운 magical; delightful

shinbongja 신봉자 believer

shinbu 신부 bride; (Catholic) priest

shinbun 신분 rank

shinbun chŭngmyŏngsŏ 신분 증명서 identity card

shinbuntchŭng 신분증 (identity) papers

shinbunŭi sangjing 신분의 상징 status symbol

shinbu tŭllŏri 신부 들러리 bridesmaid

shinbyŏng 신병 recruit

shinchunghan 신중한 discreet

shinch'am 신참 newcomer

shinch'e chang-ae 신체 장애 physical handicap, physical disability

shinch'e chang-aeja 신체 장애자 the disabled; cripple

shinch'e chang-aeja innŭn 신체 장애가 있는 physically handicapped

shinch'e kŏmsa 신체 검사 medical

shinch'ŏng 신청 application

shinch'ŏnghada 신청하다 apply for; *teit'ŭ shinch'ŏnghada* 데이트 신청하다 ask out, ask for a date

shinch'ŏngsŏ 신청서 application form

shinch'ukssŏng 신축성 elasticity

shinch'ukssŏng innŭn 신축성 있는 stretchy, elastic

shinch'ukssŏng-ŭl kajin 신축성을 가진 elasticized

shindong 신동 child prodigy

shingandang 시간당 hourly rate

Shinggap'orŭ 싱가포르 Singapore ◊ Singaporean

shinggŭt usŭm 싱긋 웃음 grin

shinggŭt ut-tta 싱긋 웃다 grin

shin-giru 신기루 mirage

shingk'ŭ 싱크 sink

shingminji 식민지 colony

shingminjiŭi 식민지의 colonial

Shingmogil 식목일 Arbor Day

shingmul 식물 plant ◊ botanical

shingmurhak 식물학 botany

shingnyo chap'wajŏm 식료 잡화점 grocery store

shin-gohada 신고하다 register; declare; inform; turn in (*to police*)

shin-gwan 신관 fuse (*of bomb*)

shin-gwanŭl chegŏhada 신관을 제거하다 defuse

shin-gyŏng 신경 creed; beliefs; nerve; *nuguŭi shin-gyŏng-ŭl kŏndŭrida* 누구의 신경을 건드리다 get on s.o.'s nerves

shin-gyŏng enŏji 신경 에너지 nervous energy

shin-gyŏng-i kŏsŭllinŭn 신경이 거슬리는 annoyed

shin-gyŏng-i kwaminhan 신경이 과민한 nervous

shin-gyŏng-i ssŭida 신경이 쓰이다 bother; *shin-gyŏng ssŭji maseyo!* 신경 쓰지 마세요! don't bother!; *shin-gyŏng ssŭl kŏt ŏpssŭmnida* 신경 쓸 것 없습니다! never mind!

shin-gyŏngjjiltchŏgin 신경질적인 fussy

shin-gyŏngkkwa ŭisa 신경과 의사 neurologist

shin-gyŏng kwaminŭi 신경 과민의 jumpy, nervous; neurotic

shin-gyŏng soeyage kŏllida 신경 쇠약에 걸리다 crack up, have a nervous breakdown

shin-gyŏng soeyagida 신경 쇠약이다 be a nervous wreck

shin-gyŏng soeyak 신경 쇠약 nervous breakdown

shin-gyŏng soeyaktcha 신경 쇠약 nervous wreck

shin-gyŏngssŭji annŭn 신경쓰지 않는 unconcerned

shin-gyŏngtchil 신경질 nervousness

shin-gyŏngtchilnage hada 신경질나게 하다 nettle, irritate

shin-gyŏngtchŭng 신경증 neurosis

Shin-gyodo 신교도 Protestant

Shin-gyodoŭi 신교도의 Protestant

shin-gyu mojip 신규 모집 recruitment

shin-gyu mojip k'aemp'ein 신규 모집 캠페인 recruitment drive

shinhak 신학 theology

shinho 신호 signal

shinhodŭng 신호등 traffic light

shinhohada 신호하다 signal

shinhon pubu 신혼 부부 newlyweds

shinhon yŏhaeng 신혼 여행 honeymoon

shinhwa 신화 myth

shinhwahak 신화학 mythology

shinhwaŭi 신화의 mythical

hinip 신입 newcomer

hinip sawŏn 신입 사원 recruit

hinip sawŏnŭl ppoptta 신입 사원을 뽑다 recruit

hinipssaeng 신입생 freshman

hinja 신자 believer

hinjakp'um 신작품 collection

hinjang 신장 kidney ANAT

hinjindaesa 신진대사 metabolism

hinjŏng 신정 New Year

hinjo 신조 doctrine

hinju 신주 spirit tablet

hinjung 신중 prudence, caution; good sense

hinjunghada 신중하다 be careful; be wary

hinjunghage 신중하게 carefully

hinmang innŭn 신망 있는 serious

hinmun 신문 newspaper

hinmun kap'andae 신문 가판대 newsstand

hinmun p'anmaeso 신문 판매소 newsdealer

hinmun p'anmaewŏn 신문 판매원 newsvendor

hinnyŏm 신념 conviction, belief

hinsa 신사 gentleman

hinsabok 신사복 lounge suit

hinse 신세 debt of gratitude; *nuguege shinserŭl chida* 누구에게 신세를 지다 be indebted to s.o.

hinsŏndo 신선도 freshness

hinsŏng 신성 sanctity

hinsŏnghan 신성한 divine, sacred

hinsŏnhada 신선하다 be fresh

hinsŏnhan 신선한 fresh

hinssok 신속 rapidity

hinssok'ada 신속하다 be rapid

hinssok'an 신속한 rapid

hintta 신다 put on *shoes*

hinŭmhada 신음하다 groan, moan

hinŭm sori 신음 소리 groan, moan

hinui 시누이 sister-in-law (*husband's sister*)

hinwŏn 신원 identity

hinwŏn pojŭng-in 신원 보증인 referee (*for job*)

Shinyak Sŏngsŏ 구약 성서 New Testament

hinyong 신용 credit

hinyong-i ttŏrŏjigehada 신용이 떨어지게 하다 discredit

shinyonginnŭn 신용있는 creditworthy

shinyong k'adŭ 신용 카드 credit card

shinyong taebu 신용 대부 credit, loan

shinyong taebuŭi hando 신용 대부의 한도 credit limit

shinyongtchang 신용장 letter of credit

shinyung 시늉 act, pretense

shiŏmŏni 시어머니 mother-in-law (*wife's*)

shiŏmŏnim 시어머님 mother-in-law (*wife's*) (*polite*)

shioe pŏsŭ 시외 버스 bus (*long-distance*)

ship 십 ten

shipch'il 십칠 seventeen

shipkku 십구 nineteen

ship nyŏn 십 년 decade

ship ŏk 십억 billion

shipp'al 십팔 eighteen

shipssa 십사 fourteen

shipssam 십삼 thirteen

ship ssent'ŭ 십 센트 dime

ship tae 십 대 teens ◊ teenage; *ship taega toeda* 십 대가 되다 reach one's teens; *ship tae sonyŏn / sonyŏ* 십 대 소년 / 소녀 teenage boy / girl, teenager

ship taeida 십 대이다 be in one's teens

shiptchaga 십자가 cross; *kasŭme shiptcharŭl kŭt-tta* 가슴에 십자를 긋다 cross (oneself)

shiptchungp'algu 십중팔구 in all likelihood; nine times out of ten

shiptta 싶다 want; seem; *...go ship'ŭn kibunida* ...고 싶은 기분이다 be in the mood for; *...ŭl / rŭl hago shipssŭmnikka?* ...을 / 를 하고 싶습니까? would you like to ...?

ship'ŭt'ŭ k'i 시프트 키 shift key

shirhaeng 실행 fulfillment; execution (*of plan*); return COMPUT

shirhaenghada 실행하다 carry out; execute, put into effect; fulfill; run *software*

shirhaeng kanŭnghan 실행 가능한 feasible, workable

shirhŏm 실험 experiment

shirhŏm chaeryo 실험 재료 guinea pig *fig*

shirhŏmhada 실험하다 experiment, test

shirhŏmhaeboda 실험해보다 experiment with, try out

shirhŏmshil 실험실 lab, laboratory

shirhŏmshil kisultcha 실험실 기술자 laboratory technician

shirhŏmŭi 실험의 experimental

shirhwang-ŭi 실황의 actual

shirhyŏn 실현 realization (*of goal*)

shirhyŏndoeda 실현되다 come true

shiriŏl 시리얼 cereal

shirŏhada 싫어하다 dislike

shirŏjida 싫어지다 go off, stop liking

shirŏmnŭn 실없는 frivolous

shirŏn 실언 slip of the tongue

shirŏp 시럽 syrup

shirŏp 실업 unemployment

shirŏpkka 실업가 industrialist

shirŏptcha 실업자 the unemployed

shirŭl kkweda 실을 꿰다 thread

shirŭl ppoptta 실을 뽑다 take the stitches out

shirŭm 싫음 distaste

shirŭn 싫은 distasteful

shiryŏk 시력 eyesight, vision

shiryŏn 실연 demonstration

shiryŏn 시련 ordeal

shiryŏnhada 실연하다 demonstrate

shiryongjŏgin 실용적인 practical, functional

shiryongjuŭi 실용주의 pragmatism

shisa 시사 current affairs; preview

shisa p'ŭroguraem 시사 프로그램 current affairs program

shisap'ungjaguk 시사풍자극 revue

shishihada 시시하다 be trivial; be wishy-washy; be tame (*of joke etc*); be stupid

shisŏl 시설 establishment; facilities

shisŏn 시선 line of vision; *nuguŭi shisŏnŭl kkŭlda* 누구의 시선을 끌다 catch s.o.'s eye

shiso 시소 seesaw

shisok 시속: *shisok 150mairŭi sokttoro* 시속 150마일의 속도로 at a speed of 150 mph

shisŭt'em 시스템 system

shisŭt'em punsŏk-kka 시스템 분석가 systems analyst

shitta 싣다 embark, go on board *sh*

shittchŏgin 시적인 poetic

shit'ŭk'om 시트콤 sitcom

shiŭi 시의 municipal, civic

shi ŭihoe 시 의회 town council

shiŭihoe ŭiwŏn 시의회 의원 councilman

shi ŭiwŏn 시 의원 councilman

shiwi 시위 demonstration, protest

shiwi ch'amgaja 시위 참가자 demonstrator, protester

shiwihada 시위하다 demonstrate

shiwŏl 시월 October

shiwŏnhada 시원하다 be cool

shiya 시야 visibility

shiyŏn 시연 preview

shiyŏnhada 시연하다 rehearse, run through

shŏlttŭk'ae poda 설득해 보다 reason with

shwida 쉬다 rest; be off; not be at work; *harurŭl / iltchuirŭl shwida* 하루를 / 일주일을 쉬다 take a day / week off

shwim ŏpsshi 쉼 없이 without respite

shwimp'yo 쉼표 comma

shwin 쉰 fifty

shwin mokssori 쉰 목소리 croak

shwin mokssoriŭi 쉰 목소리의 husky

shwin pŏntchaeŭi 쉰 번째의 fiftiet

shwinŭn nal 쉬는 날 day off

shwinŭn shigan 쉬는 시간 recess EDU

shwipkke 쉽게 easily

shwipkke hŭngbunhanŭn 쉽게 흥분하는 excitable

shwiptta 쉽다 be easy; *...gi shwiptt* ...기 쉽다 be prone to ...

shwishwihaebŏrida 쉬쉬해버리다 hush up, conceal

shwit sorirŭl naeda 쉿 소리를 내다 hiss

shwiun 쉬운 easy, simple; *...gi shwiun* ...기 쉬운 be easy to ...

shyaemi kajuk 섀미 가죽 chamois

leather)

hyaeshi 섀시 chassis

hyamp'ein 샴페인 champagne

hyamp'u 샴푸 shampoo

hyam ssangdung-i 샴 쌍둥이 Siamese twins

hyangdŭllie 샹들리에 chandelier

hyawŏ 샤워 shower

hyawŏhada 샤워하다 shower, take a shower

hyawŏ k'aep 샤워 캡 shower cap

hyawŏ k'ŏt'ŭn 샤워 커튼 shower curtain

hyeŏweŏ 셰어웨어 shareware

hyŏch'ŭ 셔츠 shirt

hyŏt'ŏ 셔터 shutter PHOT

hyŏt'ŭlppŏsŭ 셔틀버스 shuttlebus

hyŏt'ŭl sŏbissŭ 셔틀 서비스 shuttle service

hyo 쇼 show; vaudeville

hyok'ŭ 쇼크 shock ELEC

hyol 숄 shawl

hyo pijŭnisŭ 쇼 비즈니스 show business

hyop'ing 쇼핑 shopping

hyop'inghanŭn saram 쇼핑하는 사람 shopper

hyop'ingssent'ŏ 쇼핑센터 shopping center, shopping mall

hyo rum 쇼 룸 showroom

hyowindo 쇼윈도 store window

idŭ 시드 seed (in tennis)

ik'ye 식혜 malted rice drink

illa 신라 Silla (Ancient Kingdom)

iltchŭngnage hada 싫증나게 하다 bore

inggŭlp'an 싱글판 single MUS

ingnyop'um chŏjangso 식료품 저장소 larder

ŏ 서 west

ŏbissŭ 서비스 service

ŏbissŭ chegonghoesa 서비스 제공회사 service provider

ŏbissŭhada 서비스하다 service machine, car

ŏbissŭryo 서비스료 service charge

ŏbissŭ sanŏp 서비스 산업 service industry

ŏbissŭ sanŏp pubun 서비스 산업 부분 service sector

ŏbŏ 서버 server COMPUT

sŏbŭ 서브 serve (in tennis)

sŏbŭhada 서브하다 serve

sŏbu 서부 west

sŏbugŭk 서부극 western (movie)

sŏch'i 서치 search COMPUT

sŏch'ihada 서치하다 search, search for COMPUT

sŏda 서다 stand; stop

sŏdullŏ! 서둘러! come on! hurry up!

sŏdullŏ ttŏnada 서둘러 떠나다 dash off

sŏdurŭda 서두르다 hurry up, rush

sŏdurŭn 서두른 hurried

sŏgok 서곡 overture

sŏgŭlp'ŭn 서글픈 sad; lamentable

sŏgyŏnch'i anŭn 석연치 않은 dubious, suspect

sŏgyŏng 석영 quartz

sŏgyu 석유 oil; petroleum

sŏgyu hoesa 석유 회사 oil company

sŏgyu hwahak chep'um 석유 화학 제품 petrochemical

sŏgyu kulch'ak changch'i 석유 굴착 장치 oil rig

Sŏgyu Such'ulguk Kigu 석유 수출국 기구 OPEC, Organization of Petroleum Exporting Countries

Sŏhae 서해 West Sea, Yellow Sea

sŏjae 서재 study (room)

sŏjŏm 서점 bookstore

sŏkkarae 서까래 rafter

sŏkkida 섞이다 blend in

Sŏk-kkamoni 석가모니 Sakyamuni (Buddha)

sŏk-kkin 섞인 mixed

sŏk-kkosang 석고상 plaster cast

sŏkkŏ not'a 섞어 놓다 mix up, muddle up

sŏkkŭn kŏt 섞은 것 mix, mixture

sŏkppang 석방 release

sŏkppanghada 석방하다 free, release

sŏkp'an 석판 slab

sŏkssa(hagwi) 석사(학위) master's (degree)

sŏkssoe 석쇠 grill

sŏkssoero kuptta 석쇠로 굽다 grill

sŏkssu 석수 mason

sŏktcho 석조 stone (material)

sŏktta 섞다 mix, blend in; mingle

sŏkt'an 석탄 coal

sŏk'ŏsŭ 서커스 circus

sŏk'o 석호 lagoon

sŏk'oe 석회 lime (*substance*)

sŏk'oeam 석회암 chalk (*in soil*)

sŏlbi 설비 fixture

sŏlch'i 설치 installation

sŏlch'ihada 설치하다 install; *chiroerŭl sŏlch'ihada* 지뢰를 설치하다 mine, lay mines in

sŏlch'in 설친 fitful

sŏlch'iryu 설치류 rodent

sŏldŭngnyŏk innŭn 설득력 있는 forceful

sŏlgŏji hada 설거지하다 wash the dishes

sŏlgŏji kigye 설거지 기계 dishwasher

sŏlgŏji mul 설겆이 물 dishwater

sŏlguwŏjin 설구워진 soggy

sŏlgyedo 설계도 design; plan

sŏlgyehada 설계하다 design; shape

sŏlgyeja 설계자 designer

sŏlgyesa 설계사 architect

sŏlgyesang-ŭi munjetchŏm 설계상의 문제점 design fault

sŏlgyo 설교 sermon

sŏlgyodan 설교단 pulpit

sŏlgyohada 설교하다 preach

sŏlgyoja 설교자 preacher

Sŏllal 설날 Lunar New Year

sŏlliptcha 설립자 founder

sŏllip'ada 설립하다 establish

sŏllo 선로 track; platform

sŏllye 선례 precedent; *nuguŭi sŏllyerŭl ttarŭda* 누구의 선례를 따르다 follow in s.o.'s footsteps

sŏlma! 설마! surely; come on! (*in disbelief*)

sŏlmyŏng 설명 explanation

sŏlmyŏnghada 설명하다 explain; account for; set out; *Xege Ye taehan kaeyorŭl sŏlmyŏnghada* x에게 Y에 대한 개요를 설명하다 brief X on Y

sŏlmyŏnghal su ŏmnŭn 설명할 수 없는 inexplicable; unaccountable

sŏlmyŏng p'ail 설명파일 readme file

sŏlmyŏngsŏ 설명서 manual

sŏlssa 설사 diarrhea

sŏltchŏng 설정 institution, setting up

sŏlttŭk 설득 persuasion

sŏltttŭk'ada 설득하다 persuade

sŏlttŭngnyŏk innŭn 설득력 있는 convincing, persuasive

sŏlt'ang 설탕 sugar

sŏlt'ang-t'ong 설탕통 sugar bowl

sŏlt'ang-ŭl nŏt'a 설탕을 넣다 sugar, add sugar

sŏm 섬 island

sŏmgwang 섬광 flash

sŏmgwang chŏn-gu 섬광 전구 flashbulb

sŏmnyu 섬유 fiber

sŏmnyujil 섬유질 roughage

sŏmseham 섬세한 delicacy (*of fabric*)

sŏmsehan 섬세한 delicate, dainty; *chinach'ige sŏmsehan* 지나치게 섬세한 finicky

sŏmssaram 섬사람 islander

sŏmttŭk nollam 섬뜩 놀람 consternation

sŏmttŭk'an 섬뜩한 scary

sŏmun 서문 foreword, preface

sŏmyŏng 서명 signature

sŏmyŏnghada 서명하다 sign

sŏmyŏng-in 서명인 signatory

sŏmyŏnŭro 서면으로 in writing

sŏn 선 line; gland; (space) module; Zen; goodness

-sŏn -선 ship, vessel

sŏnbak 선박 boat, craft

sŏnbak soyuja 선박 소유자 shipowner

sŏnbal kwajŏng 선발 과정 selection process

sŏnban 선반 shelf; rack; lathe

sŏnbarhada 선발하다 choose, single out

sŏnbul 선불 advance (*money*) ◊ prepaid; *sŏnbullo* 선불로 cash in advance, cash up front

Sŏnbulgyo 선불교 Zen Buddhism

sŏnbul yogŭm 선불 요금 advance payment

sŏnburhada 선불하다 put down *deposit*

sŏnburŭi 선불의 prepaid

sŏnbyŏrhada 선별하다 screen (*for security reasons*)

sŏnch'e 선체 hull

sŏnch'ŏnjŏgin 선천적인 congenital,

söngkkwaga manŭn 성과가 많은 fruitful

söngkkyögŭl myosahada 성격을 묘사하다 characterize, describe

söngkkyök 성격 nature, character; personality; **urinŭn söngkkyögi an mat-tta** 우리는 성격이 안 맞다 we're not compatible; **söngkkyögi nanp'ok'ada** 성격이 난폭하다 have a violent temper

söng kwan-gyerŭl kajida 성 관계를 가지다 make love

söngk'ŭmsöngk'ŭm köt-tta 성큼성큼 걷다 stride

söngmarŭn 성마른 petulant; prickly, irritable

söngmiga koyak'an 성미가 고약한 ill-natured

söngmi kŭp'an 성미 급한 bad-tempered, irritable

söngmyŏng 성명 declaration, statement; name (on document)

söngnada 성나다 be angry, be cross

söngnan 성난 angry, cross

söngnip'ada 성립하다 materialize; be formed; be concluded

söngnŭng 성능 capacity, performance

söngnŭng-i usuhan ch'a 성능이 우수한 차 performance car

söngnyang 성냥 match

söngnyangkkap 성냥갑 box of matches

söngnyŏn 성년 manhood, maturity

Söngnyŏng 성령 Holy Spirit

sŏn-gŏ 선거 election; the polls

sŏn-gŏil 선거일 election day

sŏn-gŏin 선거인 elector

sŏn-gŏ pangshik 선거 방식 electoral system

sŏn-gŏ undong 선거 운동 election campaign

söngppyŏng 성병 sexually transmitted disease

söng pullŭng 성 불능 impotence (sexual)

söngsaenghwal 성생활 sex life

söngshil 성실 sincerity

söngshirhada 성실하다 be sincere

söngshirhan 성실한 sincere

söngsö-ŭi 성서의 biblical

söngsŭröptta 성스럽다 be holy

söngsŭröun 성스러운 holy

söngsuk-kki 성숙기 maturity, adulthood

söngsuk'ada 성숙하다 be mature; ripen; reach maturity

söngsuk'am 성숙함 maturity

söngsuk'an 성숙한 mature, adult

söngtchögin 성적인 sexual

söngtchögŭro hüironghada 성적으로 희롱하다 molest

söngtchögŭro hüngbunhan 성적으로 흥분한 horny

söngtchögŭro hüngbunshik'ida 성적으로 흥분시키다 turn on (sexually)

söngtchök hüngmirŭl ilk'e hada 성적 흥미를 잃게 하다 turn off (sexually)

söngtchök maeryögi innŭn 성적 매력이 있는 sexually attractive

söngtchök yok-kku pulman 성적 욕구 불만 sexual frustration

Söngt'anjöl 성탄절 Christmas; Christmas Day

sön-gŭm 선금 cash in advance

sön-guja 선구자 pioneer

sön-gujögin 선구적인 pioneering

söng-wön 성원 applause

söng-wönŭl ponaeda 성원을 보내다 applaud

sön-gyönjimyŏng 선견지명 foresig

sön-gyo 선교 bridge (of ship)

sön-gyosa 선교사 missionary

sönho 선호 preference

sönhohada 선호하다 prefer

söninjang 선인장 cactus

sönipkkyön 선입견 prejudice; preconception

sönjam 선잠 doze

sönjang 선장 captain, master, skipper

sönjin-guk 선진국 advanced countr

sönjök 선적 shipping

sönjök hwamul 선적 화물 cargo

sönjök'ada 선적하다 ship

sönjön 선전 publicity; promotion; advertisement

sönjönhada 선전하다 publicize;

promote; advertise

ŏnjŏn hwalttong 선전 활동 propaganda

ŏnjŏn munkku 선전 문구 blurb

ŏnjŏnnyong 선전용 demo

ŏnjŏnnyong tisŭk'ŭ 선전용 디스크 demo disk

ŏnjŏn p'ogo 선전 포고 declaration of war

ŏnjŏn p'ogohada 선포 하다 declare war

ŏnmul 선물 gift, present

ŏnmul kyeyak 선물 계약 futures

ŏnmul shijang 선물 시장 futures market

ŏnmyŏngdo 선명도 resolution, sharpness

ŏnmyŏnghada 선명하다 be vivid

ŏnmyŏngham 선명함 brilliance; vividness

ŏnmyŏnghan 선명한 vivid

ŏnnyul 선율 melody

ŏnŏn 선언 declaration

ŏnŏnhada 선언하다 declare, proclaim

ŏnoe mot'ŏ 선외 모터 outboard motor

ŏnp'ung 선풍 whirlwind

ŏnp'unggi 선풍기 fan

ŏnp'ungŭl irŭk'ida 선풍을 이르키다 create a sensation

ŏnsaeng 선생 teacher

ŏnsaengnim 선생님 teacher; sir; Mr

ŏnsashidaeŭi 선사시대의 prehistoric

ŏnshil 선실 cabin

ŏnshim 선심 linesman

ŏnshimŭl ssŭnŭn tŭt'ada 선심을 쓰는 듯하다 patronize, be condescending toward

ŏnsŏ 선서 oath

ŏnsŏ chŭng-ŏn 선서 증언 deposition

ŏnsŏhada 선서하다 swear

ŏnsu 선수 athlete; player

ŏnsuch'ida 선수치다 outwit

ŏnsugwŏn 선수권 championship (*title*)

ŏnsugwŏn taehoe 선수권 대회 championship (*event*)

ŏnttŭt 선뜻 readily

sŏnt'aegŭi 선택의 optional, elective

sŏnt'aegŭi pŏmwi 선택의 범위 choice, selection

sŏnt'aek 선택 choice, selection

sŏnt'aek-kkwŏn 선택권 option

sŏnt'aekttoen 선택된 elected

sŏnt'aek'ada 선택하다 choose, select

sŏnŭiŭi 선의의 well-meaning; well-meant

sŏnŭl kŭt-tta 선을 긋다 mark out

sŏnŭrhaejida 설늘해지다 cool down

sŏnwŏn 선원 seaman

sŏnyŏl 선열 glandular fever

sŏpsshi 섭씨 Celsius; centigrade

sŏp'ing 서핑 surfing

sŏp'ing podŭ 서핑 보드 surfboard

sŏp'ung 서풍 west wind

sŏrap 서랍 drawer

sŏraptchang 서랍장 bureau, chest of drawers

sŏri 서리 frost

sŏriga naerinŭn 서리가 내리는 frosty

sŏrirŭl ŏpssaeda 서리를 없애다 defrost *freezer, windshield*

sŏro 서로 one another, each other

sŏro kwan-gyega innŭn 서로 관계가 있는 interrelated

sŏro mannŭn 서로 맞는 compatible

sŏro mannŭn chŏngdo 서로 맞는 정도 compatibility

sŏron 서론 introduction

sŏrŭn 서른 thirty

sŏrŭn pŏntchaeŭi 서른 번째의 thirtieth

sŏryu 서류 documentation, papers; document

sŏryu chŏlttan-gi 서류 절단기 shredder

sŏryuch'ŏl 서류철 file

sŏryuham 서류함 file cabinet

sŏryu kabang 서류 가방 briefcase

sŏshiktchi 서식지 habitat

sŏshin wangnae 서신 왕래 correspondence

sŏshin wangnaehada 서신 왕래하다 correspond

sŏsŏhi kkŭlta 서서히 끓다 simmer

sŏsŏhi kkŭnnada 서서히 끝나다 wind down, quieten down

sŏsŏhi sarajida 서서히 사라지다

melt away, vanish

sŏsŏngdaeda 서성대다 prowl

sŏsŭp'enshyŏn 서스펜션 suspension

sŏsŭp'ensŭ 서스펜스 suspense

sŏtchogesŏ punŭn 서쪽에서 부는 westerly *wind*

sŏtchogŭi 서쪽의 western; westerly

sŏtchoguro 서쪽으로 west, westward

sŏtchok 서쪽 west; *...e sŏtchoge ...*의 서쪽에 west of

Sŏttal Kŭmnal 섣달 그믐날 New Year's Eve

sŏt'un 서툰 rusty

sŏt'urŭda 서투르다 be bad at; be out of practice

sŏt'urŭge hada 서투르게 하다 fumble; make a mess of

sŏt'urŭge mandŭlda 서투르게 만들다 bungle

sŏt'urŭn 서투른 bad, poor; clumsy

Sŏul 서울 Seoul

sŏyak 서약 vow

Sŏyang 서양 the West ◊ Western

sŏyang changgi 서양 장기 checkers

sŏyang changgip'an 서양 장기판 checkerboard

sŏyanghwadoen 서양화된 westernized

Sŏyang saram 서양 사람 Westerner

sŏye 서예 calligraphy

so 소 cattle

soakkwa 소아과 pediatrics

soakkwa ŭisa 소아과 의사 pediatrician

soamabi 소아마비 polio

sobangch'a 소방차 fire truck

sobangsŏ 소방서 fire department

sobangsu 소방수 firefighter, fireman

sobi 소비 consumption

sobihada 소비하다 consume, expend, use

sobija 소비자 consumer, purchaser

sobija sahoe 소비자 사회 consumer society

sobip'um 소비품 consumer goods

sobyŏn 소변 urine

sobyŏnŭl poda 소변을 보다 urinate

soch'aektcha 소책자 booklet

soch'ong 소총 rifle

sodae 소대 platoon

sodok'ada 소독하다 sterilize, disinfect

sodong 소동 disturbance, uproar

sodongnyak 소독약 disinfectant, antiseptic

sodŭk 소득 income, earnings

sodŭkkse 소득세 income tax

soe 쇠 iron

soech'angssal 쇠창살 grill, grille

soegogi 쇠고기 beef

soesalttae 쇠살때 grate

soesasŭl 쇠사슬 chain

soet'oe 쇠퇴 decay

soet'oehada 쇠퇴하다 decay; go downhill; slump

soet'oehanŭn 쇠퇴하는 decaying, dying

sogae 소개 introduction

sogaehada 소개하다 introduce, present

sogak'ae pŏrida 태워버리다 burn down

sogam 소감 opinion; sentiment

sogagno 소각로 incinerator

***...soge** ...속에 in

sogida 속이다 deceive, cheat; fiddle; rip off; *namŭl soginŭn* 남을 속이는 deceitful

sogim 속임 deception

sogimsu 속임수 deceit, cheat; hoax trick; *...ŭi sogimsue kŏllida* ...의 속임수에 걸리다 fall for, be deceived by

sogimsuro yuhok'ada 속임수로 유혹하다 lure

sogimsurŭl ssŭda 속임수를 쓰다 cheat

sogi pich'inŭn 속이 비치는 transparent

sogi pin 속이 빈 hollow

sogi shiwŏnhajiyo! 속이 시원하지요 I hope you're satisfied!

sogŏ 속어 slang

sogogi kukppap 소고기 국밥 beef soup with rice

sogot 속옷 underwear; briefs

sogŭl ch'ae-uda 속을 채우다 stuff

sogŭl ch'aeunŭn chaeryo 속을 채우는 재료 stuffing

sogŭl ppaenaeda 속을 빼내다 core

sogŭm 소금 salt

sogŭm kŭrŭt 소금 그릇 saltcellar

ogŭp'anŭn 소급하는 retroactive
ogŭp'ayŏ chŏgyongshik'ida 소급하여 적용시키다 backdate
ogŭro ssaida 속으로 쌓이다 smolder *fig*
ohorhan 소홀한 negligent
ohwa 소화 digestion
ohwagi 소화기 fire extinguisher
ohwahada 소화하다 digest, assimilate; extinguish; put out
ohwahagi ŏryŏun 소화하기 어려운 indigestible
ohwajŏn 소화전 fire hydrant
ohwa kyet'ong 소화 계통 digestive system
ohwanhada 소환하다 call; summons, subpoena; recall
ohwantchang 소환장 subpoena, summons
ohwa pullyang 소화 불량 indigestion
ohyŏng 소형 small size
ohyŏng chadongch'a 소형 자동차 subcompact (car)
ohyŏngch'a 소형차 compact (car)
ohyŏnghwahada 소형화하다 downsize
ohyŏng pŏsŭ 소형 버스 minibus
oin 소인 postmark
ojangp'um 소장품 collection
ojil 소질 talent; temperament
ojip'ada 소집하다 call, convene; summon
ojip'um 소지품 belongings
ojŏngŭi 소정의 prescribed; *sojŏngŭi ch'aek* 소정의 책 set book
oju 소주 distilled liquor
ojunghan saram 소중한 사람 treasure (*person*)
ojunghi hada 소중히 하다 take care of; cherish
ojunghi kanjik'ada 소중히 간직하다 cherish
ojunghi yŏgida 소중히 여기다 value
ok 속 core; filling; stuffing
okch'ima 속치마 underskirt
ok-kkan shinmun 석간 신문 evening paper
ok-kki 속기 shorthand
ok-kki shwiun 속기 쉬운 gullible

sokkŏsŏ mandŭlda 섞어서 만들다 concoct
sokppo 속보 news flash
sokp'yŏn 속편 sequel
sokssagida 속삭이다 murmur; whisper
sokssagim 속삭임 murmur; whisper
sokssanghada 속상하다 be upsetting
sokssanghan 속상한 upsetting
sokssŏng 속성 attribute
sokssŏng taiŏt'ŭ 속성 다이어트 crash diet
sokttam 속담 proverb, saying
sokttanhada 속단하다 come to a hasty conclusion
soktto 속도 speed; pace, tempo; velocity
soktto chehan 속도 제한 speed limit
soktto chojŏl changch'i 속도 조절 장치 throttle
sokttogye 속도계 speedometer
soktto naeda 속도 내다 speed up
sok'et 소켓 socket
sol 솔 brush, scrubbing brush
solgi 솔기 seam
soljirhada 솔질하다 brush
solmyŏnghal su ŏmnŭn 설명할 수 없는 mystifying
solppang-ŭl 솔방울 cone
solssŏnhada 솔선하다 lead the way; *muŏsŭl solssŏnhaesŏ hada* 무엇을 솔선해서 하다 do sth on one's own initiative
soltchik'ada 솔직하다 be frank, be candid; be blunt; be straight; be outspoken; *soltchik'i malhamyŏn* 솔직히 말하면 to be frank
soltchik'age 솔직하게 bluntly, plainly; honestly
soltchik'i 솔직히 frankly
som 솜 absorbent cotton
somae 소매 sleeve
somaech'igi 소매치기 shoplifter; pickpocket
somaega ŏmnŭn 소매가 없는 sleeveless
somae kagyŏk 소매 가격 retail price
somaero 소매로 retail; *...e somaero p'alda* ...에 소매로 팔다 retail at
somaesang-in 소매상인 shopkeeper; retailer

somaetppuri 소맷부리 cuff

somo chingmul 소모 직물 worsted

somsat'ang 솜사탕 cotton candy

somsshi 솜씨 workmanship

somsshi choŭn 솜씨 좋은 deft

somsshi innŭn 솜씨 있는 workmanlike

somt'ŏlgat'ŭn 솜털같은 fluffy

somun 소문 rumor

somyŏl 소멸 disappearance; demise

somyŏrhada 소멸하다 die out

son 손 hand; **soni tach'i annŭn kose** 손이 닿지 않는 곳에 out of reach; **soni tannŭn kose** 손이 닿는 곳에 within reach; **son tteseyo!** 손 떼세요! hands off!; **son tŭrŏ!** 손 들어! hands up!

sonagi 소나기 shower (of rain)

sonamu 소나무 pine (tree)

sonaraet saram 손아랫 사람 junior, subordinate

sonaraeŭi 손아래의 junior, subordinate

sonbal 손발 limb

sondokki 손도끼 hatchet

sone chwida 손에 쥐다 purchase, grip

song-aji 송아지 calf

songaji kogi 송아지 고기 veal

songbyŏrhoe 송별회 leaving party

songgŭmhada 송금하다 transfer

songgŭmhwan 송금환 transfer

song-i 송이 cluster ◊ countword for flowers, bunches of grapes etc

songmaŭmŭl t'ŏnot'a 속마음을 터놓다 open up (of person)

songmul 속물 snob

songmurŭi 속물의 snobbish

songnunssŏp 속눈썹 eyelash

songnyŏgŭl naeda 속력을 내다 lengthen one's stride

songnyŏgŭl nŭllyŏgada 속력을 늘려가다 gather speed

song-ŏ 송어 trout

son-gŏhada 선거하다 elect

songp'yŏn 송편 rice cake steamed with pine needles

songshin-gi 송신기 transmitter

songshinhada 송신하다 transmit,

beam

songwanhada 송환하다 repatriate

sonhae 손해 harm; loss

sonhae paesanggŭm 손해 배상금 damages LAW

sonik pun-gijŏm 손익 분기점 break even point

sonil 손일 manual labor

sonja 손자 grandson

sonjabi 손잡이 handle; knob; stem (of glass)

sonjirhada 손질하다 trim; groom; touch up

sonkkabang 손가방 pocketbook, purse

sonkkaragŭro karik'ida 손가락으로 가리키다 point; point to

sonkkarak 손가락 finger; **kŭnyŏnŭn sonkkaraktto kkadak'aji annŭnda** 그녀는 손가락도 까닥하지 않는다 she never lifts a finger

sonkkarak kkŭt 손가락 끝 fingertip

sonkkarak madi 손가락 마디 knuckle

sonmok 손목 wrist

sonmok shigye 손목 시계 wrist watch

sonnim 손님 guest; visitor; company

sonnimnyong ch'imshil 손님용 침 guestroom

sonnyŏ 손녀 granddaughter

sonppadaguro ch'alssak ttaerida 손바닥으로 찰싹 때리다 smack, spank

sonppadak 손바닥 palm (of hand)

sonppadangmanhan 손바닥만한 scanty

sonsang 손상 damage

sonsangdoeji anŭn 손상되지 않은 undamaged, intact

sonsangshik'ida 손상시키다 damage, prejudice

sonsangshik'inŭn 손상시키는 damaging

sonshil 손실 loss

sonshiri k'ŭn 손실이 큰 costly

sonsugŏn 손수건 handkerchief

sonsu mandŭlgi 손수 만들기 DIY do-it-yourself

sontchisŭro marhada 손짓으로 말하다 gesticulate

sot'anghada

ontchit 손짓 gesture

ontchit'ayŏ purŭda 손짓하여 부르다 beckon

ont'op 손톱 fingernail

ont'opkkak-kki 손톱깎이 nail clippers

ont'op kkangnŭn kawi 손톱 깎는 가위 nail scissors

ont'optchul 손톱줄 nail file

onŭl hŭndŭlda 손을 흔들다 wave; wave to

onŭl ppŏtch'ida 손을 뻗치다 reach out

onŭl taeda 손을 대다 touch; feel up (*sexually*); *chamkkan sonŭl taeda* 잠깐 손을 대다 dabble in

onŭl tteda 손을 떼다 back out

onŭro 손으로 by hand

onŭro hanŭn 손으로 하는 manual

onŭro manjida 손으로 만지다 paw

onŭro ssŭn 손으로 쓴 handwritten

onŭro tŏdŭmtta 손으로 더듬다 grope

onwiŭi 손위의 senior, older

onyŏ 소녀 girl

onyŏn 소년 juvenile; boy

onyŏn-kat'ŭn 소년같은 boyish

onyŏn pŏmjoe 소년 범죄 juvenile delinquency

onyŏn pŏmjoeja 소년 범죄자 juvenile delinquent

onyŏnŭi 소년의 juvenile

onyŏ tanwŏn 소녀단원 girl guide

o-oegam 소외감 sense of alienation

o-oeja 소외자 outcast

op'a 소파 couch, sofa

op'a sett'ŭ 소파 셋트 (three-piece) suite

op'ashik ch'imdae 소파식 침대 sofa bed

op'o 소포 parcel, package

op'ŭrano 소프라노 soprano

op'ŭt'ŭweŏ 소프트웨어 software

op'um 소품 (stage) prop

op'ung 소풍 outing, trip; picnic

oran 소란 uproar, tumult, commotion; scene; *soranŭl p'iuda* 소란을 피우다 make a scene

oranhada 소란하다 be noisy

oranhan 소란한 loud, noisy

oransŭrŏun 소란스러운 tumultuous

sori 소리 sound, noise; *k'ŭn soriro iltta* 큰 소리로 읽다 read out loud; *k'ŭn soriro marhada* 큰 소리로 말하다 speak up, speak louder

sorich'ida 소리치다 shout; scream

sorich'yŏ purŭda 소리쳐 부르다 call, call out, shout

sorijirŭm 소리지름 shouting

sorinop'yŏ ut-tta 소리높여 웃다 howl (with laughter)

sori ŏmnŭn 소리 없는 silent

soriŏpsshi kŏt-tta 소리없이 걷다 pad, move quietly

soriptcha 소립자 (elementary) particle

sorirŭl naeŏ 소리를 내어 aloud

sorŭm 소름 gooseflesh; *narŭl sorŭmkkich'ige handa* 나를 소름끼치게 한다 it gives me gooseflesh

soryang 소량 dab, splash; *soryang-ŭi...* 소량의 ... a little ...

Soryŏn 소련 Soviet Union

soryŏng 소령 major MIL

sosaeng 소생 revival

sosaengshik'ida 소생시키다 revive, resuscitate

sosa orŭda 솟아 오르다 soar; lift off; rise

soshiji 소시지 sausage

soshik 소식 news; *...(ŭ)ro put'ŏ soshigŭl tŭt-tta* ...(으)로 부터 소식을 듣다 have news from, hear from

sosŏl 소설 novel; fiction

sosŏlga 소설가 novelist

sosong 소송 lawsuit

sosong sakkŏn 소송 사건 court case

sossŭ 소스 sauce; dressing (*for salad*)

sosŭrach'ige hada 소스라치게 하다 petrify, terrify

sosŭrach'in 소스라친 petrified

sosu 소수 decimal

sosu minjok 소수 민족 ethnic minority

sosup'a 소수파 minority

sosup'aida 소수파이다 be in the minority

sosutchŏm 소수점 decimal point

sot'anghada 소탕하다 mop up

sot'ongdoeda 소통되다 flow
sot'ŭ 소트 sort COMPUT
soŭm 소음 sound, noise
souju 소우주 microcosm
sowi 소위 so-called *pej* ◊ second lieutenant
sowŏn 소원 wish
sowŏnhada 소원하다 be estranged; petition
sowŏnhaejin 소원해진 estranged
sowŏnhan 소원한 distant, aloof
soyo 소요 disturbances, civil unrest
soyongdori 소용돌이 whirlpool
soyongŏmnŭn 소용없는 pointless, futile, useless; *noryŏk'aedo soyong-ŏpssŏyo* 노력해도 소용없어요 it's pointless trying
soyu 소유 possession, ownership
soyuhada 소유하다 have, own; possess
soyuja 소유자 owner; holder
soyukkwŏn 소유권 ownership
soyukkyŏk 소유격 possessive GRAM
soyumul 소유물 belongings, things; property; possession
soyuŭi 소유의 own
soyuyogi kanghan 소유욕이 강한 possessive
ssaaollida 쌓아올리다 stack, heap up; build up
ssaa ollin tŏmi 쌓아 올린 더미 heap
ssada 싸다 wrap; pack; envelop; be cheap; be fast; excrete
ssaguryŏmulgŏn 싸구려물건 cheap goods
ssain nundŏmi 쌓인 눈더미 snowdrift
ssak 싹 germ; bud
ssal 쌀 rice (*uncooked*)
ssallongch'a 쌀롱차 sedan MOT
ssalssarhada 쌀쌀하다 be chilly
ssalssarhan 쌀쌀한 chilly; fresh; icy; standoffish
ssamjit-tton 쌈짓돈 loose change
ssan 싼 inexpensive, cheap; low
ssang 쌍 pair; couple; *namnyŏ han ssang* 남녀 한 쌍 couple
ssang-an-gyŏng 쌍안경 binoculars
ssangdung-i 쌍둥이 twins
ssang-ŭro toen 쌍으로 된 double
ssan mulgŏn 싼 물건 cheap goods

ssaragi nun 싸라기 눈 sleet
ssat'a 쌓다 stack; run up *debts*
ssauda 싸우다 fight, battle; comba ...*ŭl* / *rŭl wihae ssauda* ...을 / 를 위해 싸우다 fight for
ssaum 싸움 fight, scrap, brawl; struggle; row
ssaumjirhada 싸움질하다 brawl
ssayŏjida 쌓여지다 accumulate, build up
sseda 세다 be strong; turn gray; count
ssekssihan 섹시한 sexy
ssekssŭ 섹스 sex
ssen 센 strong
sshi 씨 Mr; Ms; seed, pip, stone; *Hong Kildongsshi* 홍길동씨 Mr Kildong Hong; *I Sunmisshi* 이 순미씨 Ms Sunmi Lee
sshibal! ∨ 씨발! fuck!
sshidaek 씨댁 care of
sshidirom 씨디롬 CD-ROM
sshidirom tŭraibŭ 씨디롬 드라이브 CD-ROM drive
sshiep'ŭsshi 씨에프씨 CFC, chlorofluorocarbon
sshigŭn-gŏrida 씨근거리다 wheeze
sshijok 씨족 clan
sshing chinagada 씽 지나가다 whizz by
sshing pulda 씽 불다 whistle (*of wind*)
sshiptta 씹다 chew
sshiriŏl p'ot'ŭ 씨리얼 포트 serial port
sshirŭm 씨름 (Korean-style) wrestling
sshirŭmhada 씨름하다 tackle *problem*; grapple with; wrestle
sshirŭm kyŏnggi 씨름 경기 (Korean-style) wrestling match
sshirŭm sŏnsu 씨름 선수 (Korean-style) wrestler
sshit-tta 씻다 clean; wash
sshit'ŭ 시트 sheet
ssŏbŏrida 써버리다 use, consume
ssŏgŭn 썩은 rotten, bad, rancid
ssŏk-kki shwiun 썩기 쉬운 perishable
ssŏktta 썩다 rot; go bad
ssŏlda 썰다 chop

sŏlmae 썰매 sled(ge), toboggan; sleigh

sŏlmul 썰물 ebb tide; low tide

sŏlmurida 썰물이다 the tide is out

sŏn k'urim 썬 크림 sun cream

sŏnt'en 썬텐 suntan

soa ttŏröttürida 쏘아 떨어뜨리다 shoot down, bring down

soda 쏘다 fire; shoot; sting; **ch'ongŭl ssoda** 총을 쏘다 fire a gun

soda put-tta 쏟아 붓다 pour

sonsalgach'i chinagada 쏜살같이 지나가다 fly past, pass quickly (of time)

sonsalgach'i naragada 쏜살같이 날아가다 dart

ssŭda 쓰다 use; spend; write; put on glasses; be bitter

ssŭdadŭmtta 쓰다듬다 stroke, caress; smooth hair

ssŭgi 쓰기 writing; use

ssŭiuda 씌우다 coat, cover; get on; crown tooth

ssŭium 씌움 coating, layer

ssŭlda 쓸다 sweep

ssŭlgae 쓸개 gall bladder

ssŭlmo 쓸모 usefulness

ssŭlmoinnŭn 쓸모있는 useful

ssŭlmoŏmnŭn 쓸모없는 useless, worthless; trashy; waste land, material

ssŭl su innŭn 쓸 수 있는 usable

ssŭltteŏmnŭn 쓸데없는 futile; idle threat

ssŭn 쓴 bitter

ssŭrarige hada 쓰라리게 하다 embitter

ssŭrebatkki 쓰레받기 dustpan

ssŭregi 쓰레기 garbage, litter; scum (people); crap

ssŭregi p'yegijang 쓰레기 폐기장 garbage dump

ssŭregi sujip 쓰레기 수집 garbage collection

ssŭregi tŏmi 쓰레기 더미 scrap heap

ssŭregi t'ong 쓰레기 통 garbage can, trashcan

ssŭregi t'ongno 쓰레기 통로 garbage chute

ssŭröjida 쓰러지다 fall, fall over; fall down; slump

ssŭröttürida 쓰러뜨리다 topple, bring down

ssukssuk charada 쑥쑥 자라다 shoot up (of children)

ssuktttŭm 쑥뜸 moxibustion

ssurŏ moŭda 쓸어 모으다 sweep up

ssushida 쑤시다 prod, poke; have a stitch; hurt, smart

ssushyŏ nŏt'a 쑤셔 넣다 jam, ram

sswabŏrida 쏴버리다 blaze away (with gun)

sswaegi 쌔기 wedge

sŭch'idŭt chinagada 스치듯 지나가다 skim

sŭk'ach'i 스카치 Scotch

sŭk'aen 스캔 scan

sŭk'aendŭl 스캔들 scandal

sŭk'aenhada 스캔하다 scan; scan in

sŭk'aenŏ 스캐너 scanner

sŭk'airain 스카이라인 skyline

sŭk'ap'ŭ 스카프 scarf

sŭk'aut'ŭ 스카우트 (boy) scout

sŭk'ech'i 스케치 sketch

sŭk'ech'ibuk 스케치북 sketchbook

sŭk'ech'ihada 스케치하다 sketch

sŭk'eit'ŭ 스케이트 skate

sŭk'eit'ŭbodŭ 스케이트보드 skateboard

sŭk'eit'ŭjang 스케이트장 ice rink

sŭk'eit'ŭ t'ada 스케이트 타다 skate

sŭk'eit'ŭ t'agi 스케이트 타기 skating

sŭk'i 스키 ski

sŭk'i chip'ang-i 스키 지팡이 ski pole

sŭk'i hwaltchuro 스키 활주로 ski run

sŭk'i k'ŭrosŭk'ŏnt'ŭri 스키 크로스컨트리 cross-country skiing

sŭk'i lip'ŭt'ŭ 스키 리프트 ski lift

sŭk'in taibing 스킨 다이빙 skin diving

sŭk'i t'ada 스키 타다 ski

sŭk'i t'agi 스키 타기 skiing

sŭk'it'o 스키토 ski tow

Sŭk'ot'ŭllaendŭ 스코틀랜드 Scotland ◊ Scottish

sŭk'ŭraep puk 스크랩 북 scrapbook

sŭk'ŭrin 스크린 screen

sŭk'ŭrin t'esŭt'ŭ 스크린 테스트 screen test

sŭk'ubŏ taibing 스쿠버 다이빙 scuba diving

sŭk'ut'ŏ 스쿠터 motorscooter

sŭk'wŏshi 스쿼시 squash SP

sŭlgaegol 슬개골 kneecap

sŭlgŭmŏni 슬그머니 stealthily

sŭllaeshwi 슬래쉬 slash, oblique

sŭllaidŭ 슬라이드 slide, transparency

sŭlleit'ŭ 슬레이트 slate

sŭllip'ing paek 슬리핑 백 sleeping bag

sŭllip'ŏ 슬리퍼 slipper

sŭllogŏn 슬로건 slogan

sŭllot mŏshin 슬롯 머신 slot machine

sŭlloumoshŏn 슬로우모션 slow motion; action replay

sŭlp'ŏhada 슬퍼하다 lament, mourn; **sŭlp'ŏhajima** 슬퍼하지마 don't be sad

sŭlp'ŭda 슬프다 be sad

sŭlp'ŭge 슬프게 sadly

sŭlp'ŭm 슬픔 sadness

sŭlp'ŭme chamgin 슬픔에 잠긴 mournful

sŭlp'ŭn 슬픈 sad

sŭltchŏk kajida 슬쩍 가지다 pocket, take

sŭltchŏk kajyŏgada 슬쩍 가져가다 sneak, steal

sŭltchŏk nagada 슬쩍 나가다 make oneself scarce

sŭmaeshi 스매시 smash (in tennis)

sŭmiŏ shihŏm 스미어 시험 smear MED

sŭmogŭ 스모그 smog

sŭmul 스물 twenty

sŭmu pŏntchaeŭi 스무 번째의 twentieth

sŭmyŏnaoda 스며나오다 ooze

sŭnaep sajin 스냅 사진 snap, snapshot

sŭnggaek 승객 passenger; occupant

sŭnggaeksŏk 승객석 passenger seat

sŭngganggi 승강기 elevator

sŭng-in 승인 approval

sŭng-inhada 승인하다 approve; recognize; grant

sŭng-in patta 승인 받다 pass; gain approval

sŭngjin 승진 promotion

sŭngjinhada 승진하다 promote

sŭngma 승마 riding; horse, mount

sŭngmahada 승마하다 ride horse

sŭngmuwŏn 승무원 cabin crew, flight crew

sŭngmuwŏn chŏnwŏn 승무원 전원 crew

sŭngmuwŏnshil 승무원실 cabin

sŭngnak 승낙 approval, blessing

sŭngni 승리 win, victory; triumph; **...e taehae sŭngnihada** ...에 대해 승리하다 win a victory over

sŭngnihan 승리한 victorious

sŭngnija 승리자 victor

sŭnok'ŭl 스노클 snorkel

sŭnou ch'ein 스노우 체인 snow chains

sŭpkki 습기 humidity; moisture

sŭpkkich'an 습기찬 damp

sŭpkki innŭn 습기 있는 moist

sŭpkkwan 습관 practice, custom, habit; **kŭŭi sŭpkkwanŭro** 그의 습관으로 as was his custom; **sŭpkkwani toeda** 습관이 되다 become a habit; **...nŭn sŭpkkwan tŭlda** ...는 습관이 들다 take to ...ing, get into the habit of ...ing

sŭpkkwanjŏgin 습관적인 customary, habitual

sŭpkkyŏk 습격 assault, attack

sŭpp'o 습포 compress MED

sŭptchi 습지 marsh

sŭptchin 습진 eczema

sŭptchiŭi 습지의 marshy

sŭptttŭk'ada 습득하다 acquire

sŭp'ai 스파이 spy

sŭp'ai haeng-wi 스파이 행위 espionage

sŭp'aijisŭl hada 스파이짓을 하다 s

sŭp'an 습한 humid

sŭp'eidŭ 스페이드 spades

Sŭp'ein 스페인 Spain ◊ Spanish

Sŭp'einŏ 스페인어 Spanish (language)

sŭp'eisŭ pa 스페이스 바 space bar

sŭp'iamint'ŭ 스피아민트 spearmint

sŭp'ik'ŏ 스피커 speaker

sŭp'och'ŭ 스포츠 sport

sŭp'och'ŭin 스포츠인 athlete

sŭp'och'ŭ kija 스포츠 기자 sports journalist

ŭp'och'ŭ k'a 스포츠 카 sportscar

ŭp'och'ŭ nyusŭ 스포츠 뉴스 sports news

ŭp'och'ŭran 스포츠란 sports page

ŭp'onji 스폰지 sponge

ŭp'onji komu 스폰지 고무 foam rubber

ŭp'onji k'eik'ŭ 스폰지 케이크 sponge cake

ŭp'otŭrait'ŭ 스포트라이트 spotlight

ŭp'ot'ihan 스포티한 sporty

ŭp'ŭredŭshit'ŭ 스프레드시트 spreadsheet

ŭp'ŭrei 스프레이 aerosol, spray

ŭrasoni 스라소니 lynx

ŭrillŏmul 스릴러물 thriller

ŭroin 스로인 throw-in

ŭsŭng-ŭi nal 스승의 날 Teachers' Day

ŭsŭro 스스로 by oneself

ŭt'a 스타 star

ŭt'aillisŭt'ŭ 스타일리스트 (hair)stylist

ŭt'ak'ing 스타킹 stocking

ŭt'eik'ŭ 스테이크 steak

ŭt'eindŭ kŭllasŭ 스테인드 글라스 stained glass

ŭt'einlesŭ 스테인레스 stainless steel

ŭt'eip'ŭl kŏn 스테이플 건 staple gun

ŭt'ereo 스테레오 stereo

ŭt'eroidŭ 스테로이드 steroids

ŭt'ik'ŏ 스티커 sticker

ŭt'im tarimi 스팀 다리미 steam iron

ŭt'ŏnt'ŭmaen 스턴트맨 stuntman

ŭt'obŭ 스토브 stove

ŭt'ok'ŏ 스토커 stalker

ŭt'op lait'ŭ 스톱 라이트 stoplight

ŭt'op wŏch'i 스톱 워치 stopwatch

ŭt'ŭraik'ŏ 스트라이커 striker

ŭt'ŭraik'ŭ 스트라이크 strike

ŭt'ŭreit'ŭ 스트레이트 straight (up) *whiskey etc*

ŭt'ŭresŭ 스트레스 stress; **sŭt'ŭresŭrŭl pat-tta** 스트레스를 받다 be under stress; **sŭt'ŭresŭga it-tta** 스트레스가 있다 be under pressure

ŭt'ŭresŭ chojŏlppŏp 스트레스 조절법 stress management

ŭt'ŭresŭga shimhan 스트레스가

심한 stressful

sŭt'ŭresŭrŭl shimhage pannŭn 스트레스를 심하게 받는 stressed out

sŭt'ŭripssho 스트립쇼 strip show, striptease

sŭt'ŭrip'ŏ 스트리퍼 stripper

sŭt'ŭro 스트로 straw

sŭt'yu 스튜 stew

sŭt'yudio pakkŭi pangsong 스튜디오 밖의 방송 outside broadcast

sŭt'yuŏdissŭ 스튜어디스 air hostess, stewardess

Sŭweden 스웨덴 Sweden ◊ Swedish

Sŭweden mal 스웨덴 말 Swedish

Sŭweden saram 스웨덴 사람 Swede

Sŭwedenŭi 스웨덴의 Swedish

sŭweidŭ 스웨이드 suede

sŭwet'ŏ 스웨터 sweater

sŭwet'ŭ shyŏch'ŭ 스웨트 셔츠 sweatshirt

sŭwich'i 스위치 switch

Sŭwisŭ 스위스 Switzerland ◊ Swiss

sŭwit'ŭ 스위트 suite

su 수 number; figure; quantity; move (*in chess*) ◊ hydro...

su 수: *...l su it-tta* ...ㄹ 수 있다 can; *...l su ŏptta* ...ㄹ 수 없다 cannot

suabŭi 수압의 hydraulic

suaek 수액 sap

subak 수박 water melon

subanhada 수반하다 involve, mean

subi 수비 defense SP

subisu 수비수 defense player

subunkonggŭpp'aek 수분공급팩 moisturizing face mask

subyŏng 수병 sailor

such'aehwa 수채화 watercolor

such'aehwa mulkkam 수채화 물감 watercolor

such'iga toeda 수치가 되다 disgrace

such'ishim 수치심 shame; *...e such'ishimŭl an-gyŏjuda* ...에 수치심을 안겨주다 bring shame on

such'isŭrŏptta 수치스럽다 be disgraceful

such'isŭrŏun 수치스러운 disgraceful, scandalous

such'ŏk'an 수척한 emaciated; gaunt; haggard

su ch'ŏnŭi 수 천의 thousands of

such'uk p'ojang 수축 포장 shrink-wrapping

such'uk'ada 수축하다 contract, shrink

such'uk p'ojanghada 수축 포장하다 shrink-wrap

such'ul 수출 export, exporting

such'ulguk 수출국 exporter (*country*)

such'ul k'aemp'ein 수출 캠페인 export campaign

such'urhada 수출하다 export

such'urŏptcha 수출업자 exporter (*person*)

such'wiin 수취인 recipient, receiver; payee

suda 수다 chatter

sudajaeng-i 수다쟁이 chatterbox

sudal 수달 otter

sudan 수단 means, way

sudasŭrŏun 수다스러운 chatty

suda ttŏlda 수다 떨다 chatter, talk

sudo 수도 capital (*of country*); metropolis; waterworks

sudongjŏgin 수동적인 passive

sudong pŭreik'ŭ 수동 브레이크 parking brake

sudongt'ae 수동태 passive GRAM

sudosa 수도사 monk

sudosŭng kat'ŭn 수도승 같은 monastic

sudowŏn 수도원 monastery; convent; abbey

sudu 수두 chicken pox

sugaeng 수갱 shaft

sugamja 수감자 inmate

suganghada 수강하다 take a course

sugap 수갑 handcuffs

sugida 숙이다 bow, lower

sugŏjip 숙어집 phrasebook

sugŏn 수건 towel; washcloth

sugŏn kŏri 수건 걸이 towel rail

sugo 수고 effort, struggle; *sugo-haseyo* 수고하세요 keep up the good work (*when taking one's leave of s.o. who is working*)

sugong 수공 handiwork

sugong-ŏptcha 수공업자 artisan

sugongp'um 수공품 handiwork; handmade goods

sugong-ŭi 수공의 handmade

sugong-ye 수공예 handicraft

sugorŭl akkiji annŭn 수고를 아끼지 않는 painstaking

sugŭrŏdŭlda 수그러들다 die down

sugu 수구 water polo

suhaenghada 수행하다 conduct, carry out

suhage nŭnghan 수학에 능한 mathematical

suhagŭi 수학의 mathematical

suhak 수학 mathematics, math

suhaktcha 수학자 mathematician

suhamul pogwanso 수하물 보관소 (baggage) checkroom

suhoja 수호자 protector

suhwa 수화 sign language

suhwagi 수화기 receiver TELEC

suhwak 수확 crop

suhwak'ada 수확하다 reap

suhwamul 수화물 baggage; luggage; hand baggage

suhwamul k'ŭlleim 수화물 클레임 baggage reclaim

suhwamul pogwantchŭng 수화물 보관증 baggage check

suhwamul unbanch'a 수화물 운반 baggage cart

suhwamul yŏlch'a 수화물 열차 baggage car

suhwa pŏt'ŭn 수화 버튼 hook TELE

suhyŏl 수혈 blood transfusion

suigi choŭn 수익이 좋은 profitable

suibi ch'ungbunhan 수입이 충분한 financially comfortable

suik 수익 proceeds

suikssŏng 수익성 profitability

suimnyo 수임료 retainer

suip 수입 import; receipts FIN

suiptcha 수입자 importer

suip'ada 수입하다 import

sujang 수장 burial at sea

suji 수지 resin

sujiga mat-tta 수지가 맞다 be profitable, pay

sujigŭi 수직의 vertical; perpendicul

sujigŭro ttŏrŏjida 수직으로 떨어지다 plummet

sujip 수집 collection

sujiptcha 수집가 collector

sujip'ada 수집하다 collect

sujŏ 수저 spoon and chopsticks

sujŏng 수정 amendment, modification, revision; crystal

sujŏng-aek 수정액 whiteout, correcting fluid

sujŏnghada 수정하다 amend, revise

sujŏngjuŭi 수정주의 revisionism

sujŏngshik'ida 수정시키다 fertilize

sujubŏhada 수줍어하다 be shy

sujubŏhanŭn 수줍어하는 shy; coy

sujubŭm 수줍음 shyness

sujun 수준 level

sujung hohŭpkki 수중 호흡기 air cylinder

sujung-iksŏn 수중익선 hydrofoil

sujung-ŭi 수중의 aquatic

sukch'ŏng 숙청 purge

sukch'ŏnghada 숙청하다 purge

sukch'wi 숙취 hangover

suk-kko 숙고 consideration, thought

suk-kkohada 숙고하다 contemplate, think about, deliberate; debate

sukppak shisŏl 숙박 시설 accommodations

sukssŏng 숙성 ripeness

sukssŏnghan 숙성한 ripe; mellow

suktche 숙제 assignment; homework

suk'ŏsŭi 수컷의 male

suk'ŏt 수컷 male (of animal, bird, fish); cock

suk'oyang-i 수코양이 tomcat

sul 술 liquor; fringe; tassel; tuft

sul chanch'i 술 잔치 drinking party

sul ch'wihan 술 취한 drunk; intoxicated

sulgorae 술고래 heavy drinker

sulkkun 술꾼 drunk

sullye 순례 pilgrimage

sullyeja 순례자 pilgrim

sulp'ŭm 슬픔 sorrow, sadness

sultchan 술잔 stemware

sultchip 술집 bar

sultchip yŏjong-ŏbwŏn 술집 여종업원 bartender

sum 숨 breath; sumŭl kip'i tŭrŏ mashida 숨을 깊이 들어 마시다 take a deep breath; sumi ch'ada 숨이 차다 be out of breath, pant; sumŭl chugida 숨을 죽이다 hold one's breath; gulp; sumŭl hŏltŏgida 숨을 헐떡이다 gasp for

breath; sumŭl naeshwida 숨을 내쉬다 breathe out; sumŭl tŭryŏ mashida 숨을 들여 마시다 breathe in

sumanŭn 수많은 a great many, a large number of

sumbakkoktchil 숨바꼭질 hide-and-seek

sumch'an 숨찬 breathless

sumgida 숨기다 hide, conceal; hold back

sumgimŏmnŭn 숨김없는 open, honest, frank

sumgimŏpsshi 숨김없이 openly, honestly, frankly

sumgyŏjin 숨겨진 hidden

summak'il chŏngdoŭi 숨막힐 정도의 breathtaking

sumnŭn kot 숨는 곳 hiding place

sumshwida 숨쉬다 breathe

sumtta 숨다 hide; go into hiding

sumt'ong 숨통 windpipe

sumyŏn 수면 surface; sumyŏni orŏbut-tta 수면이 얼어붙다 freeze over

sumyŏng 수명 life (of machine)

sumyŏnje 수면제 sleeping pill

sun 순 pure silver, gold; complete, total ◊ ten years

-sun -순 order; yŏllyŏngsunŭro 연령순으로 in order of age

sunch'al 순찰 patrol

sunch'alch'a 순찰차 patrol car

sunch'algwan 순찰관 patrolman

sunch'arhada 순찰하다 patrol; be on patrol

sun-gan 순간 moment, instant

sun-gan chŏngjishik'ida 순간 정지시키다 freeze video

sun-ganŭi 순간의 momentary

sungbae 숭배 worship

sungbaehada 숭배하다 worship; idolize

sungmyŏn 숙면 sound sleep

sungnyŏ 숙녀 lady

sungnyŏndoen 숙련된 skilled, expert

sungnyŏn-gong 숙련공 skilled worker

sun-gyŏrŭl ilt'a 순결을 잃다 lose one's virginity

sun-gyoja 순교자 martyr

sunhada 순하다 be gentle; be mild

sunhan 순한 mild; docile

sunhang 순항 cruise

sunhanghada 순항하다 cruise

sunhangsŏn 순항선 cruise liner

sunhan soktto 순항 속도 cruising speed

sunhwan 순환 cycle; circulation

suniik 순이익 net profit

sunjinhada 순진하다 be innocent, be pure

sunjinham 순진함 innocence

sunjinhan 순진한 innocent; naïve

sunjŏnhan 순전한 unadulterated, absolute

sunjong 순종 obedience

sunjonghada 순종하다 obey

sunjonghanŭn 순종하는 obedient

sunjongjŏgin 순종적인 submissive

sunjoroun 순조로운 smooth

sunmu 순무 turnip

sunnyang 숫양 ram

sunoe hoedam 수뇌 회담 summit POL

sunot'a 수놓다 embroider

sunp'ung 순풍 tail wind

sunshik-kkane 순식간에 in an instant, quickly

sunshik-kkanŭi 순식간의 instantaneous

sunsŏ 순서 sequence; system; *ajik tangshin sunsŏga animnida* 아직 당신 순서가 아닙니다 it's not your turn yet; *sunsŏga pakkwin* 순서가 바뀐 out of order, not in sequence

sunsŏdaero 순서대로 in sequence; *sunsŏdaero chŏngnihada* 순서대로 정리하다 order, put in sequence

sunsuhan 순수한 pure; natural; neat; net

sunsuibŭl ollida 순수입을 올리다 earn; clear, net

sunsuik 순수익 profit margin

sunŭnghada 순응하다 conform; *...e sunŭnghayŏ* ...에 순응하여 in line with

sunyŏ 수녀 nun

suŏbil 수업일 school days

suŏp 수업 tuition; lesson, class

sup 숲 forest; wood

suppŏp 수법 gimmick (*promotiona...*)

sup'ŏmak'et 수퍼마켓 supermarket

sup'ŭ 수프 soup

sup'ul 수풀 tuft

sup'yŏng kŏnnŏlmok 수평 건널목 grade crossing

sup'yŏngsŏn 수평선 horizon (*at sea...*)

sup'yo 수표 check FIN

sup'yoch'aek 수표책 checkbook

surak 수락 *fml* acceptance

surak'ada 수락하다 *fml* take up, accept *offer*; undertake, take on *tas...*

suran 수란 poached egg

sure ch'wihada 술에 취하다 get drunk

surigong 수리공 repairman

surihada 수리하다 repair, recondition

suri kkaeda 술이 깨다 sober up

surishik'ida 수리시키다 get fixed

suro 수로 waterway, channel; watercourse

surŭl mashida 술을 마시다 drink *alcohol*

surŭl seda 술를 세다 count

suryŏk chŏn-gi 수력 전기 hydroelectricity ◊ hydroelectric

suryŏn 수련 water lily

suryŏng-in 수령인 recipient

suryŏngtchŭng 수령증 delivery note

suryut'an 수류탄 grenade

susa 수사 rhetoric

susaek 수색 search, hunt

susaekttae 수색대 search party

susaek yŏngtchang 수색 영장 search warrant

susaek'ada 수색하다 search for; trace

susaek'anŭn 수색하는 searching

susang 수상 premier

susang ch'angnyuk'ada 수상 착륙하다 splash down

susanghada 수상하다 win a prize; be suspicious

susanghan 수상한 suspicious, fishy

susangja 수상자 prizewinner; medalist

susangsŭk'i 수상스키 waterskiing

seshik pyŏn-gi 수세식 변기 water closet, flush toilet

shin 수신 reception (*for phone etc*); for the attention of

shin-gi 수신기 receiver RAD

shinin 수신인 addressee

shinin pudamŭi chŏnhwa 수신인 부담의 전화 collect call

shinin pudamŭro chŏnhwahada 수신인 부담으로 전화하다 call collect

shinyŏburŭl allida 수신여부를 알리다 acknowledge

sŏk paiollinisŭt'ŭ 석 바이올리니스트 concert master

sŏk weit'ŏ 석 웨이터 head waiter

sŏn 수선 repair; alteration

sŏnhada 수선하다 mend, repair

so 수소 hydrogen

song 수송 transport; transportation; *susong chung-in* 수송 중인 in transit

songhada 수송하다 transport

so p'okt'an 수소 폭탄 hydrogen bomb

suham 수수함 modesty

suhan 수수한 modest; conservative

sukkekki 수수께끼 puzzle, mystery; riddle; enigma

sukkekkigat'ŭn 수수께끼같은 enigmatic

sul 수술 surgery; operation

sulshil 수술실 operating room

surŭl hada 수술을 하다 operate

surŭl pat-tta 수술을 받다 have an operation, undergo surgery

surhada 수술하다 operate on

susuryo 수수료 commission

sut 숟 thickness; *such'i manŭn mŏri* 숱이 많은 머리 thick hair

sut 숯 charcoal

sutcha 숫자 numeral, digit, figure

sutchap'an 숫자판 numeric keys

sutch'onggak 숫총각 virgin (*male*)

sutkkarak 숟가락 spoon

sutppure kuwŏjin 숯불에 구워진 charbroiled

sut'ak 수탉 cock (*chicken*)

suŭisa 수의사 veterinarian

suŭn 수은 mercury, quicksilver

suwi 수위 janitor; water level

suwŏnji 수원지 source

suwŏrhada 수월하다 be easy

suwŏrhan 수월한 easy, simple

suyang pŏdŭl 수양 버들 weeping willow

suyŏhada 수여하다 award, confer

suyŏk 수역 body of water

suyŏm 수염 whiskers; bristles

suyŏng 수영 swimming; swim

suyŏngbok 수영복 swimsuit

suyŏnghada 수영하다 swim

suyŏngjang 수영장 swimming pool

suyŏngppŏp 수영법 stroke (*swimming*)

suyo 수요 demand COM; *suyoga it-tta* 수요가 있다 be in demand

suyoil 수요일 Wednesday

suyong inwŏn 수용 인원 intake (*of people*)

suyongnyŏk 수용력 capacity

suyongso 수용소 camp

swaebingsŏn 쇄빙선 icebreaker

swaedo 쇄도 deluge; stampede

swaedohada 쇄도하다 deluge

swaegol 쇄골 collarbone

T

ta 다 completely, fully; **ta ssŏbŏrida** 다 써버리다 run out of; use up

tabal 다발 wad (*of paper*); wisp (*of hair*)

tabang 다방 café

tabunhi 다분히 no doubt, probably

ta charan 다 자란 full-grown

tach'aeropkke hada 다채롭게 하다 jazz up

tach'aeroun 다채로운 colorful

tach'ida 닫히다 close

tach'ige hada 다치게 하다 hurt

tach'iji anŭn 다치지 않은 unhurt

tach'in 닫힌 shut, closed

tach'in te ŏmnŭn 다친 데 없는 unhurt, unscathed

tach'ŭl naerida 닻을 내리다 anchor

tach'ŭl ollida 닻을 올리다 weigh anchor

tadarŭda 다다르다 span

tado 다도 tea ceremony

tadŭmtta 다듬다 polish, perfect; trim *hair*; smooth out; **k'allo tadŭmtta** 칼로 다듬다 scrape

tae 대 great; huge ◊ versus ◊ stem ◊ countword for vehicles, airplanes, machines, pipe tobacco, cigarettes

taean 대안 alternative

taebon 대본 script

taebu 대부 loan; godfather

taebubun 대부분 most

taebubunŭi 대부분의 most

taebubunŭn 대부분은 mostly, mainly

taebumo 대부모 godparent

taebyŏnin 대변인 spokesperson; mouthpiece

taebyŏnja 대변자 representative

taech'adaejop'yo 대차대조표 balance sheet

taech'ebup'um 대체부품 replacement part

taech'ehal su ŏmnŭn 대체할 수 없는 irreplaceable

taech'e ŏdie 대체 어디에 wherever

taech'ep'um 대체품 replacement

taech'ero 대체로 on the whole, as a rule

taech'ing 대칭 symmetry

taech'ingjŏgin 대칭적인 symmetric

taech'owŏn 대초원 prairie

taech'u 대추 date (*fruit*)

taech'ung hult'ŏboda 대충 흩어보 look over

taeda 대다 pad (*with material*)

taedamhada 대담한 bold

taedanhage 대단하게 enormously

taedanhan 대단한 enormous, tremendous; serious ◊ a great deal of; **kŭn taedanhan inmuriye** 그는 대단한 인물이예요 he's a real character; **tangshinŭn taedanha-gunyo** 당신은 대단하군요 you're incredible

taedanhi 대단히 very, extremely, remarkably; **taedanhi manŭn** 대단히 많은 a great many

taedap 대답 answer, reply

taedap'ada 대답하다 answer, reply

taedasu 대다수 majority

taedoshi 대도시 metropolis

taedoshiŭi 대도시의 metropolitan

taedŭlbo 대들보 girder

taedŭnghada 대등하다 equalize

taegae 대개 principally, mainly, chiefly

taegakssŏnŭi 대각선의 diagonal

taegang 대강 general features ◊ roughly; cursorily

taegang hult'ŏboda 대강 흩어보다 flip through

taegang miruŏ poda 대강 미루어 보다 judge, estimate

taegang-ŭi 대강의 approximate, rough; sweeping *generalization*

taegi 대기 atmosphere

taegihada 대기하다 stand by, be ready

taegihago innŭn 대기하고 있는 on

standby

egija myŏngdan 대기자 명단 waiting list

egi oyŏm 대기 오염 atmospheric pollution

egishil 대기실 waiting room

egŏlle 대걸레 mop

egŭm 대금 (large) flute

egŭmŏptcha 대금업자 money-lender

egŭm sanghwan 대금 상환 COD, collect on delivery

egyŏl 대결 confrontation; clash; dispute

egyumoŭi 대규모의 large scale

ehae(sŏ) 대해(서): **...e taehae(sŏ)** ...에 대해(서) about; regarding

ehagwŏn 대학원 graduate school

ehagwŏnsaeng 대학원생 graduate

ehak 대학 university, school

ehak-kkyo 대학교 university

ehak kyojŏng 대학 교정 university campus

ehakssaeng 대학생 university student

ehakssal 대학살 carnage, slaughter

ehak k'aemp'ŏsŭ 대학 캠퍼스 university campus

ehamul 대하물 epic

ehan 대한: **...e taehan** ...에 대한 about

ehanjeguk 대한제국 Great Han Empire

ehanmin-guk 대한민국 Republic of Korea, ROK

ehap chogae 대합 조개 clam

ehapsshil 대합실 departure lounge

ehayŏ 대하여: **...e taehayŏ** ...에 대하여 with respect to, with regard to

ehit'ŭ 대히트 smash hit

ehit'ŭjak 대히트작 blockbuster

ehoe 대회 convention, rally; contest

ehoe ch'amgaja 대회 참가자 conventioneer

ehollan 대혼란 chaos

ehongsu 대홍수 deluge

ehwa 대화 talk; conversation; dialog; **taehwarŭl chungdanhada** 대화를 중단하다 break off, stop

talking

taehwasangja 대화상자 dialog box COMPUT

taehyŏng 대형 large size

taeja 대자 godchild; godson

taejesajang 대제사장 high priest

taejŏnhada 대전하다 meet (*in competition*)

taejŏp 대접 dish; bowl; beaker

taejŏp'ada 대접하다 entertain; treat

taejo 대조 contrast

taejohada 대조하다 contrast

taejojŏgin 대조적인 contrasting

taejop'yo 대조표 checklist

taejo p'yoshirŭl hada 대조 표시를 하다 check off

taejung 대중 the public, the masses ◊ popular, mass

taejunggayo 대중가요 pop MUS

taejung kyot'ong 대중 교통 public transportation

taejung maech'e 대중 매체 mass media

taejungtchŏgin 대중적인 popular, general, widespread; mass, downmarket

taema 대마 hemp

taemach'o 대마초 cannabis, hashish

Taeman 대만 Taiwan ◊ Taiwanese

Taemanin 대만인 Taiwanese (*person*)

Taemanŏ 대만어 Taiwanese (*dialect*)

taemŏriŭi 대머리의 bald

taemo 대모 godmother

taemosŭro paktta 대못으로 박다 rivet

taemot 대못 rivet; spike

taemŭro maktta 댐으로 막다 dam

taemun 대문 gate

taemuntcha 대문자 capital (letter)

taemyŏngsa 대명사 pronoun; **...ŭi taemyŏngsaga toeda** ...의 대명사가 되다 be a byword for, be synonymous with

taemyŏnhago 대면하고 face to face

taenaje 대낮에 in broad daylight

taenamu 대나무 bamboo

taenggŭranghanŭn sori 댕그랑하는 소리 chink (*sound*)

taensŭ p'ati 댄스 파티 dance

taenyŏ 대녀 god-daughter

taep'ae 대패 plane (*tool*)

taep'ihada 대피하다 evacuate, leave

taep'iho 대피호 shelter

taep'ishik'ida 대피시키다 evacuate

taep'iro 대피로 pull-in

taep'iso 대피소 shelter

taep'o 대포 artillery

taep'ok ollida 대폭 올리다 bump up

taep'yodan 대표단 delegation

taep'yohada 대표하다 represent, stand for

taep'yoja 대표자 representative, delegate

taep'yojŏgin myŏn 대표적인 면 cross-section

taep'yoro immyŏnghada 대표로 임명하다 delegate

taeri 대리 deputy

taerihada 대리하다 represent, act as

taeriin 대리인 agent, representative, proxy; substitute

taerikkwŏn 대리권 proxy, authority

taerimo 대리모 surrogate mother

taerip 대립 conflict, disagreement

taerisŏk 대리석 marble

taeryagŭi 대략의 approximate

taeryak 대략 approximately

taeryang 대량 large quantity

taeryang hakssal 대량 학살 massacre, slaughter

taeryang saengsan 대량 생산 mass production

taeryang saengsanhada 대량 생산하다 mass-produce

taeryang-ŭi 대량의 wholesale, indiscriminate

taeryang-ŭro 대량으로 in bulk

taeryŏng 대령 colonel

taeryugŭi 대륙의 continental

taeryuk 대륙 continent

taesa 대사 speech; ambassador

taesagwan 대사관 embassy

taesang 대상 object

taesangja myŏngdan 대상자 명단 hit list

taesangp'ojin 대상포진 shingles

taesarŭl illŏjuda 대사를 일러주다 prompt *actor*

taeshi 대시 dash

taeshikka 대식가 glutton

taeshilp'ae 대실패 fiasco

taeshin 대신 substitute; compensation ◊ instead of; ***taeshin kiyonghada*** 대신 기용하다 make substitution SP

taeshine 대신에 instead; instead of

taeshinhada 대신하다 replace, stand in for; take over; substitute

taeshinhaesŏ hada 대신해서 하다 stand in for; ***narŭl / kŭrŭl taeshin haesŏ*** 나를 / 그를 대신해서 on my / his behalf

taeshinhal 대신할 alternative

taesŏnggong 대성공 coup

taesŏnggong-ida 대성공이다 be a success

taesŏnggong-ŭl kŏduda 대성공을 거두다 hit the bull's-eye

Taesŏyang 대서양 Atlantic

Taesŏyang hoengdanŭi 대서양 횡단의 transatlantic

taesuroptchi anŭn 대수롭지 않은 peripheral

taet'ongnyŏng 대통령 president

taet'ongnyŏng imgi 대통령 임기 presidency (*term*)

taet'ongnyŏngjik 대통령직 presidency (*office*)

taeŭnghanŭn 대응하는 corresponding, equivalent

taeu 대우 treatment

taeuhada 대우하다 treat, behave toward

taeyŏk 대역 double (*person*)

taeyŏl 대열 file; ranks MIL

taeyong 대용 substitution

taeyongp'um 대용품 substitute

taeyuhaeng 대유행 all the rage, fashionable ◊ craze, fad; ***ch'oegŭnŭi taeyuhaeng*** 최근의 대유행 the latest craze

tagagada 다가가다 walk up to

tagak'wa 다각화 diversification

tagak'washik'ida 다각화시키다 diversify

tagaoda 다가오다 close in, move closer

tagaonŭn 다가오는 forthcoming

tagugŏŭi 다국어의 multilingual

taguktchŏk 다국적 multinational

taguktchŏk kiŏp 다국적 기업 multinational company

gwa 다과 refreshments; tea and cookies

hada 다 하다 run out (*of time*); carry out, perform

haenghido 다행히도 thankfully, luckily

haengsŭröpkkedo 다행스럽게도 mercifully, thankfully

iamondŭ 다이아몬드 diamond

ibing 다이빙 (high) diving

ibing tae 다이빙 대 diving board

ibŏ 다이버 diver

inŏmait'ŭ 다이너마이트 dynamite

iŏl 다이알 dial; *taiŏrül tollida* 다이얼을 돌리다 dial

iŏri 다이어리 (appointments) diary

iŏt'ŭ 다이어트 diet

iŏt'ŭhada 다이어트하다 diet; be on a diet

jaedanŭnghan 다재다능한 versatile

jagŭ 다작의 prolific

jŏngdagamhan 다정다감한 warm-hearted

jŏnghada 다정하다 be affectionate; be friendly

jŏnghan 다정한 affectionate, loving; genial; pleasant, friendly

jung maech'e 다중 매체 multimedia

k 닭 chicken

kkanaeda 닦아내다 wipe off

k-kkogi 닭고기 chicken (*as food*)

ktta 닦다 wipe; clean; wash; mop up

kttari 닭다리 drumstick (*of poultry*)

k'yument'ŏri 다큐멘터리 documentary (program)

k'yument'ŏri tŭrama 다큐멘터리 드라마 docudrama

l 달 month; moon ◊ lunar

lch'angnyuksŏn 달착륙선 lunar module

lda 달다 fit, install; attach; be sweet

lge hada 달게 하다 sweeten

lgyal 달걀 egg

lgyal kkŏptchil 달걀 껍질 eggshell

lgyal wansuk 달걀 완숙 hard-boiled egg

lgyarhyŏng 달걀형 oval

talk'e hada 닳게 하다 wear; wear away; damage

talk'omhada 달콤하다 be sweet

tallabut-tta 달라붙다 stick, jam; stick to, adhere to; cling

tallak 단락 passage; short circuit

tallanggŏrida 달랑거리다 dangle

tallida 달리다 hang; depend; be attached; run short; not be enough; run, rush; drive

talligi 달리기 run; running SP

tallŏ 달러 dollar

tallyŏdŭlda 달려들다 tackle

tallyŏk 달력 calendar

tallyŏnhada 단련하다 build up

tallyŏnshik'ida 단련시키다 exercise

talppich'i örin 달빛이 어린 moonlit

talppit 달빛 moonlight

talp'aeng-i 달팽이 snail

taltta 닳다 run down

tam 담 wall

tambae 담배 tobacco; cigarette; *tambaerül samgahae chushigi paramnida* 담배를 삼가해 주시기 바랍니다 please refrain from smoking; *tambae p'iuda* 담배 피우다 smoke a cigarette

tambae kkongch'o 담배 꽁초 cigarette butt

tamdamhan 담담한 matter-of-fact, calm; unemotional

tamdang 담당 charge ◊ in charge

tamdanghada 담당하다 take charge of

tamdang-ida 담당이다 be in charge

tamgŭda 담그다 immerse, soak

tamhwangsaek 담황색 cream (*color*)

tamjaeng-i 담쟁이 ivy

tamkko it-tta 담고 있다 contain

tamnyo 담요 blanket

tamsŏk 담석 gallstone

tamtta 담다 hold, contain; resemble, take after; *nuguwa tamtta* 누구와 닮다 be like s.o.

tamyo 담요 rug

tan 단 column (*in newspaper*); rung; hit squad; tuck (*in dress*) ◊ sweet ◊ *countword for firewood, spinach etc*

tanbaektchil 단백질 protein

tanbal 단발 bob (*haircut*)

tanch'e 단체 society, organization

tanch'e chŏngshin 단체 정신 team spirit

tanch'e hyŏp'oe 단체 협회 association, organization

tanch'e kyosŏp 단체 교섭 collective bargaining

tanch'ŏl 단철 wrought iron

tan ch'ŏri 단처리 braid, trimming

tanch'ŭng 단층 rift (in earth)

tanch'u 단추 button

tanch'ukk'i 단축키 shortcut key COMPUT

tanch'u kumŏng 단추구멍 buttonhole

tanch'urŭl ch'aeuda 단추를 채우다 button (up)

tandanhada 단단하다 be solid; be firm; be tight

tandanhi 단단히 tight

tandanhi choida 단단히 조이다 tighten

tandanhi ch'unggyŏgŭl padŭn 단단히 충격을 받은 shattered, upset

tandanhi muktta 단단히 묶다 lash down (with rope)

tandanhi pak'in 단단히 박힌 stuck fast

tando 단도 dagger

tandogŭi 단독의 single-handed

tang 당 party; faction

tang- 당- this; that; the present; tangshi 당시 that time

-tang -당 per; irindang 일인당 per head, per person

tangbŏn 당번 rota

tangbun-gan 당분간 for the moment, for the time being

tangch'an 당찬 brisk

tangch'ŏmdoen 당첨된 winning

tangch'ŏmja 당첨자 winner

tangdanghan 당당한 regal

tanggida 당기다 pull

tanggŭn 당근 carrot

tanggu 당구 pool; snooker; billiards

tanggudae 당구대 pool table

tanggujang 당구장 pool hall

tangguk 당국 the authorities

tanghok 당혹 perplexity

tanghok'age hada 당혹하게 하다 perplex, puzzle

tanghok'an 당혹한 perplexed, puzzled

tanghwang 당황 alarm, panic

tanghwanghada 당황하다 be embarrassed; panic, get flustered

tanghwanghae hada 당황해 하다 baffled

tanghwanghage hada 당황하게 하 baffle; embarrass; disconcert

tanghwanghage hanŭn 당황하게 하는 embarrassing

tanghwanghan 당황한 embarrasse disconcerted

tan-gigan 단기간 short-term

tan-gijŏgŭro 단기적으로 in the sho term

tang-ilch'igi yŏhaeng 당일치기 여 daytrip

tangjang 당장 right now, immediately

tangjigida 당직이다 be on duty

tangjwa yegŭm kujwa 당좌 예금 구좌 checking account

tangmil 당밀 molasses

tangnagwi 당나귀 donkey

tangnyŏnhada 당연하다 be natural be right

tangnyŏnhan 당연한 natural, obvious; muŏsŭl tang-yŏnhan il yŏgida 무엇을 당연한 일로 여기다 take sth for granted

tangnyŏnhi 당연히 naturally, of course; automatically

tangnyoppyŏng 당뇨병 diabetes ◇ diabetic

tan-gŏri yukssang kyŏnggi 단거리 육상 경기 sprint

tan-gŏri yukssang sŏnsu 단거리 육상 선수 sprinter

tan-gol 단골 custom; regular (person)

tan-gollo tanida 단골로 다니다 patronize, be a customer of

tangshin 당신 (polite) you

tangshin chashin 당신 자신 (polit yourself

tangshindŭl chashin 당신들 자신 (polite) yourselves

tangshinŭi 당신의 (polite) your

tangsŏndoeda 당선되다 be electe sŏn-gŏro tangsŏndoen 선거로

당선된 elected

tangsŏnja 당선자 winner

tan-gye 단계 stage, period, phase

tan-gyejŏguro chegŏhada 단계적으로 제거하다 phase out

tan-gyejŏguro t'uip'ada 단계적으로 투입하다 phase in

tan-gyŏl 단결 solidarity

tang-yŏnhae! 당연해! no wonder!

tang-yŏnhi 당연히 of course, naturally

tan hanaŭi 단 하나의 sole, only; single, solitary, lone

anhohan 단호한 decisive, resolute, emphatic; purposeful, determined, relentless; stalwart

anilssŏng 단일성 unity

anja 단자 terminal ELEC

anji 단지 only, just ◊ mere ◊ jar; container; urn; housing development

anjŏl 단절 rupture

anjŏnghada 단정하다 determine, establish; be neat; be decent

anjŏnghan 단정한 tidy, neat; decent, upright

anjŏnghi hada 단정히 하다 tidy oneself up

anjŏngtchŏgin 단정적인 assertive

anjoroptta 단조롭다 be monotonous; be boring

anjoroum 단조로움 monotony

ankkwa taehak 단과 대학 college

anmal changch'i 단말 장치 terminal COMPUT

anmyŏnghan 단명한 short-lived

anmyŏm 단념 resignation

annyŏmhada 단념하다 relinquish, abandon

annyŏmshik'ida 단념시키다 deter; *Xi / ga Yŭl / rŭl tannyŏmhage hada* X이/가 Y을/를 단념하게 하다 put X off Y

anŏ 단어 word

anp'a 단파 short wave

anp'ungnamu 단풍나무 maple

anp'yŏn 단편 fragment, shred

anp'yŏnsosŏl 단편소설 short story

anp'yŏntchŏgin 단편적인 sketchy; piecemeal; fragmentary

ansang 단상 platform, stage

anshigan 단시간 a short time

tanshik 단식 singles (*in tennis*)

tansŏ 단서 proviso, stipulation

tanso 단소 bamboo flute

tansok 단속 crackdown

tansok'ada 단속하다 crack down, clamp down

tansu 단수 singular GRAM

tansume 단숨에 at a stretch, non-stop; *tansume ssŭda* 단숨에 쓰다 dash off, write quickly; *tansume tallyŏgada* 단숨에 달려가다 dash; make a dash for

tansunhada 단순하다 be simple; be unsophisticated

tansunhwahada 단순화하다 simplify

tansuro 단수로 in the singular

tansuŭi 단수의 singular GRAM

tantchŏm 단점 disadvantage, drawback

tantcho 단조 minor MUS

tanŭl naerida 단을 내리다 let down *dress etc*

tanwi 단위 unit (of measurement)

tanwi wŏnkka 단위 원가 unit cost

tanyŏnhi 단연히 easily, by far

tap 답 answer

tapp'ahada 답파하다 cover, travel

tapssahada 답사하다 travel; explore

taptchang 답장 reply (*letter*)

taptchanghada 답장하다 reply (*to letter*)

tapttap'ada 답답하다 be gloomy; be stifling; be hidebound; be anxious

tapttap'an 답답한 stifling

tap'ada 답하다 answer

tarajida 닳아지다 wear; wear away, wear out

tarakppang 다락방 attic, loft

taramjwi 다람쥐 squirrel

taranada 달아나다 run away, rush off

taraoruda 달아오르다 glow

tarappajin 닳아빠진 well-worn, worn-out

tara ttŏrojida 닳아 떨어지다 wear out

tari 다리 bridge; leg

tarimi 다리미 iron

tarimjil 다림질 ironing

tarimjilttae 다림질대 ironing board

tarimjirhada 다림질하다 iron; press; do the ironing

tarimjiri p'iryoŏmnŭn 다림질이
필요없는 non-iron
tarŭda 다르다 differ, be different
tarŭge 다르게 differently;
...wa/kwanŭn tarŭge ...와/과는
다르게 as distinct from
tarŭn 닳은 threadbare; dead *battery*
tarŭn 다른 different; distinct;
another; other
tarŭn kŏt 다른 것 another
tarŭn nugun-ga 다른 누군가
someone else
tarŭn ŏttŏn kŏt 다른 어떤 것
something else
taruda 다루다 handle; manage; treat
tarugi himdŭn 다루기 힘든 unruly;
tricky
tarugi ŏryŏun 다루기 어려운
awkward *customer*; not user-friendly
tarugi shwiun 다루기 쉬운
manageable; docile
taryang 다량 mass
tasahan 다사한 eventful
tasan 다산 fertility
tasanŭi 다산의 fertile
tashi 다시 again; *tashi han pŏn* 다시
한 번 once more
tashi chada 다시 자다 go back to
sleep
tashi ch'aeuda 다시 채우다 refill
tashi ch'irhada 다시 칠하다 repaint
tashi ch'usŭrida 다시 추스리다
reconstruct
tashi hwaginhada 다시 확인하다
doublecheck
tashi kamtta 다시 감다 rewind
tashi nat'anada 다시 나타나다
reappear
tashi padadŭrida 다시 받아들이다
take back, accept back
tashi pangmunhada 다시 방문하다
call back
tashi ssŭda 다시 쓰다 rewrite
tasŏt 다섯 five
tasŏt pŏntchaeŭi 다섯 번째의 fifth
taso 다소 rather, sort of, somewhat
tasŭrida 다스리다 govern, rule
tasuŭi 다수의 many
tat 닻 anchor
tatch'ida 닫히다 shut
tatki 닫기 close COMPUT

tatkki shwiun 닫기 쉬운 easy to
reach, accessible
tat-tta 닫다 close; fasten; be closed
tat'a 닿다 reach
tat'ŭ 다트 dart
tat'uda 다투다 fight; quarrel; ...ŭl/r
wihae tat'uda ...을/를 위해 다투다
contend for
tat'um 다툼 quarrel
taŭm 다음 next; *taŭmŭi kŏt* 다음의
것 the following
taŭme 다음에 after, next; *taŭme
kyesok* 다음에 계속 to be
continued; *taŭmgwa kat'ŭn* 다음과
같은 as follows; *taŭm pun?* 다음
분? who's next?
taŭmnal 다음날 the day after
Tau Chonsŭ P'yŏnggyun Chuga
다우 존스 평균 주가 Dow Jones
Average
taunnodŭ 다운로드 download
taunnodinghada 다운로딩하다
download
tayanghada 다양하다 be diverse
tayanghage twisŏkkin 다양하게
뒤섞인 miscellaneous
tayanghan 다양한 diverse, varied;
multiple
tayangssŏng 다양성 diversity,
variety
tayongdoŭi 다용도의 all-purpose;
adaptable
-tcha -자 *(suffix for persons)* → *-ja*
-자
tchada 짜다 structure, plan; press,
squeeze; weave; spin; wring; be salt
tchaenggŭrŏnghanŭn sori
쨍그렁하는 소리 clink
tchajangmyŏn 짜장면 noodles and
black bean sauce
tchajŭngnadorok 짜증나도록
frustratingly
tchajŭngnage hada 짜증나게 하다
irritate
tchajŭngnage hanŭn 짜증나게 하는
irritating
tchajŭngnanŭn 짜증나는 irritating;
frustrating; trying, annoying
tchajŭng-ŭl chal naenŭn 짜증을 잘
내는 irritable
tchak 짝 partner; mate *(of animal)*

:hakssuŭi 짝수의 even *number*

:haktchit-tta 짝짓다 mate

halbŭn 짧은 short

:halkke charŭda 짧게 자르다 cut shorter; crop

:halkke hada 짧게 하다 shorten

:halkke pomyŏn 짧게 보면 in the short run

:hallida 짤리다 ax *employee*

:halptta 짧다 be short

:ham 짬 slot (*in schedule*)

:ha match'uda 짜 맞추다 piece together

:han 짠 salty

:haptcharhan 짭짤한 savory

:hatchŭng 짜증 tantrum

:hiburŏttŭrida 찌부러뜨리다 mangle, crush

:hida 찌다 steam

:higŏ mŏktta 찍어 먹다 dip, dunk

:higŏ naegi 찍어 내기 chop

:higŭrŏttŭrida 찌그러뜨리다 crush; *nullŏ tchigŭrŏttŭrida* 눌러 찌그러뜨리다 squash, crush

:hijŏjida 찢어지다 split

:hijŏjige kananhan 찢어지게 가난한 poverty-stricken

:hijŏjigi shwiun 찢어지기 쉬운 flimsy

:hijŏjin 찢어진 ragged, tattered

:hijŏjin kot 찢어진 곳 slit; tear

:hijŏ yŏlda 찢어 열다 slit; rip open

:hikkŏgi 찌꺼기 dregs

:hiktchigi 찍찍이 Velcro®

:hiktchk-kkŏrida 찍찍거리다 squeak

:himt'ong 찜통 steamer (*for cooking*)

:hinggŭrida 찡그리다 scowl; contort; screw up *eyes*

:hinggŭrin ŏlgul 찡그린 얼굴 scowl

:hinŭn tŭshi tŏun 찌는 듯이 더운 scorching hot

:hinŭn tŭt'an 찌는 듯한 sweltering

:hip'urida 찌푸리다 frown

:hip'urin 찌푸린 threatening

:hip'urin ŏlgul 찌푸린 얼굴 frown

:hirŭda 찌르다 plunge; thrust; prick; jab; stab; lunge at; *k'allo tchirŭda* 칼로 찌르다 knife, stab

:hirŭregi 찌르레기 blackbird; starling

tchit-tta 찢다 rip, tear; split

tchit'ŭn 짙은 thick, dense

tchoch'abŏrida 쫓아버리다 chase away; turn away, send away

tchoch'anaeda 쫓아내다 eject; expel; evict

tchoch'a ponaeda 쫓아 보내다 see off, chase away

tchoda 쪼다 peck

tchogaeda 쪼개다 split

tchogaejida 쪼개지다 split

tchok 쪽 page; slice

tchok pŏnho 쪽 번호 page number

tchotkkyŏnada 쫓겨나다 be expelled, be kicked out

-tchŭm -쯤 around, approximately; *tushitchŭm* 두시쯤 around two o'clock

tchugŭlgŏrige hada 쭈글거리게 하다 shrivel

tchuk ppŏt-tta 쭉 뻗다 stretch

tebyu 데뷰 début

teda 데다 get burnt; get scalded

teit'ŏ 데이터 data

teit'ŏ chŏjang 데이터 저장 data storage

teit'ŏ ch'ŏri 데이터 처리 data processing

teit'ŏ peisŭ 데이터 베이스 database

teit'ŏ poho 데이터 보호 data protection

teit'ŏ sujip 데이터 수집 data capture

teit'ŭ 데이트 date, meeting

teit'ŭ hada 데이트하다 date, go out with

teit'ŭ sangdae 데이트 상대 date (*person*)

tek'ŭnosedae 테크노세대 techno music fans

temo 데모 demo, demonstration, protest

temohada 데모하다 demonstrate, protest

temo haengjin 데모 행진 demo, demonstration, march

temo haengjinhada 데모 행진하다 march

temoja 데모자 demonstrator, protester

tenim 데님 denim

Tenishwi p'aesŭch'yuri 데니쉬 패스츄리 Danish pastry

Tenmak'ŭ 덴마크 Denmark ◇ Danish

Tenmak'ŭŏ 덴마크어 Danish

terigo kada 데리고 가다 take, accompany

terigo nagada 데리고 나가다 take out (*to dinner etc*)

terigo oda 데리고 오다 fetch *person, animal*

terirŏ kada 데리러 가다 call for, collect

terirŏ oda 데리러 오다 come for, collect

teryŏdajuda 데려다주다 take back

teryŏgada 데려가다 draw, lead

teryŏoda 데려오다 bring; pick up

teshibel 데시벨 decibel

tesŭk'ŭ 데스크 (reception) desk

teuda 데우다 heat up

teun 데운 heated

tewŏjida 데워지다 warm up

tidimp'an 디딤판 tread

tidimttol 디딤돌 stepping stone

tijain 디자인 design

tijainhada 디자인하다 design, plan

tijain hak-kkyo 디자인 학교 design school

tijainŏ 디자이너 designer

tijel 디젤 diesel

tijit'ŏl 디지털 digital

tillŏ 딜러 dealer (*in card game*)

tinŏ p'at'i 디너 파티 dinner party

tioksshiribo haeksssan 디옥시리보 핵산 DNA, deoxyribonucleic acid

tip'olt'ŭkkap 디폴트값 default COMPUT

tisŭk'et 디스켓 disk

tisŭk'et t'ŭraibŭ 디스켓 드라이브 disk drive

tisŭk'o 디스코 disco

tisŭk'o t'ek 디스코 텍 discotheque

tisŭk'ŭ 디스크 disc

tisŭk'ŭ chak'i 디스크 자키 disc jockey

tisŭp'ŭllei 디스플레이 display COMPUT

tŏ 더 far, much; further; *tŏ chagŭn* 더 작은 fewer; *tŏ chal* 더 잘 better; *chogŭmman tŏ* 조금만 더 a little

more

tŏbinghada 더빙하다 dub

tŏbŭl 더블 double

tŏbŭlbedŭ 더블베드 double bed

tŏbŭlbeisŭ 더블베이스 double-bass

tŏbŭl k'ŭllik 더블클릭 double click COMPUT

tŏch'e kŏllida 덫에 걸리다 be trapped

toch'ŏng 도청 provincial office

tŏch'ŭro chaptta 덫으로 잡다 trap

tŏdŏl ttŏlda 덜덜 떨다 quake, tremble

tŏdŭmgŏrim 더듬거림 impediment (*in speech*)

tŏdŭmgŏrimyŏ ch'at-tta 더듬거리며 찾다 fumble around

tŏdŭmi 더듬이 feeler, antenna

tŏdŭmtta 더듬다 stumble over *words*; *marŭl tŏdŭmtta* 말을 더듬 stammer, stutter

tŏhada 더하다 add

tŏhagi 더하기 plus (sign)

tŏhayŏ 더하여 plus, in addition to

tŏ isang 더 이상 any more

tŏk 덕 goodness, virtue; *...tŏkt'aeg* ...덕택에 thanks to ...; *kŭ tŏkppune* 그 덕분에 because of that

tŏl 덜 less; incompletely

tŏlda 덜다 ease, alleviate, relieve

tŏldŏl ttŏllida 덜덜 떨리다 chatter (*of teeth*)

tŏlgŏdŏk'anŭn sori 덜거덕하는 소리 clatter

tŏl ik'in 덜 익힌 rare, underdone

tŏlk'ŏk-kkŏrida 덜컥거리다 rattle; jolt

tŏm 덤 bonus; freebie

tŏ manŭn 더 많은 more

tŏmbida 덤비다 pounce

tŏmbul 덤불 clump, group; undergrowth

tŏmbyŏdŭlda 덤벼들다 go for, attac

tŏmi 더미 pile, heap

tŏ mŏlli 더 멀리 farther

tŏ mŏn 더 먼 further

tŏmp'ŭlling 덤플링 dumpling

tŏ naajida 더 나아지다 be better; b on the mend

tŏ nappajida 더 나빠지다 worsen

tŏ nappŭge 더 나쁘게 worse

nappŭn 더 나쁜 worse
natkke 더 낫게 better
nggul shingmul 덩굴 식물 creeper
nggulwŏlgyul 덩굴월귤 cranberry
ng-ŏri 덩어리 lump, block; loaf
ng-ŏrijida 덩어리지다 cake, solidify
ng-ŏri t'usŏng-iŭi 덩어리 투성이의 lumpy
njida 던지다 throw; **Xege Yŭl/rŭl**
ŏnjida X에게 Y을/를 던지다 pelt X with Y
njigi 던지기 throw
nmun 덧문 shutter
ŏmnŭn haengbok 더 없는 행복 bliss, no greater happiness
pch'ida 덮치다 pounce; swoop on
pch'iryŏ tŭlda 덮치려 들다 attack, go for
pkkae 덮개 cover, hood;
ŏpkkaerŭl pŏtkkida 덮개를 벗기다 uncover
pssuruk'an 덥수룩한 shaggy
ptta 덥다 be hot (*of weather*); be warm (*of water*)
ptta 덮다 cover
p'ida 덮히다 be buried under, be covered by
p'in 덮인: **k'ŭrimŭro tŏp'in** 크림으로 덮힌 topped with cream
p'ŏ kkŭda 덮어 끄다 smother
rhada 덜하다 ease
rŏptta 더럽다 be dirty; be sordid
rŏp'ida 더럽히다 soil, stain, dirty; mudge; blemish; smear *character*
rŏwŏjida 더러워지다 stain
t 덫 trap
t-ch'angmun 덧창문 storm window
tch'il 덧칠 coat (*of paint etc*)
tppuch'ida 덧붙이다 add
tppuch'yŏ marhada 덧붙여 말하다 add
tssem 덧셈 addition
uk 더욱 more; **tŏuk chung-yohan** 더욱 중요한 more important; **tŏuk tŏ** 더욱 더 more and more, even more
ugi 더욱이 moreover; in addition; plus
un 더운 hot; warm
to ...도 too, also

to 도 province, *do*; degree
toan 도안 engraving
toan-ga 도안가 draftsman
tobaehada 도배하다 paper *room*, *walls*
tobak 도박 gambling
tobak-kkun 도박꾼 gambler
tobak'ada 도박하다 gamble
tobaldoeji anŭn 도발되지 않은 unprovoked; spontaneous
tobalshik'ida 도발시키다 whip up, arouse
tobo yŏhaeng 도보 여행 walk; walking; hike; hiking; walking tour
tobo yŏhaenghada 도보 여행하다 walk, hike
toboyŏhaengja 도보여행자 hiker
toch'ak 도착 arrival
toch'ak yejŏng shigan 도착 예정 시간 ETA, estimated time of arrival
toch'ak'ada 도착하다 arrive, reach
toch'ak'anŭn 도착하는 incoming
toch'ŏe 도처에 throughout
toch'ŏnggi 도청기 bug (*electronic*)
toch'ŏnggirŭl sŏlch'ihada 도청기를 설치하다 bug, wire up
toch'ŏnghada 도청하다 bug, tap
todaech'e 도대체 on earth, the hell; **todaech'e muŏsŭl hanŭn/wŏnhanŭn kŏmnikka?** 도대체 무엇을 하는/원하는 겁니까? what the hell are you doing/do you want?
todarhada 도달하다 arrive at
todŏk kwannyŏm 도덕 관념 morals; scruples
todŏkssŏng 도덕성 morality
todŏktchŏgin 도덕적인 moral; scrupulous
toduda 돋우다 boost
toduktchil 도둑질 theft
toduktchirhada 도둑질하다 steal
toebadach'ida 되받아치다 hit back, retaliate
toech'ajŭm 되찾음 recovery
toech'at-tta 되찾다 recover, regain
toeda 되다 amount to; become, get; **...ke/ge toeda** ...게 되다 turn out so that ...; be arranged so that; **ak'wadoeda** 악화되다 get worse, become worse

toedollyŏjuda 되돌려주다 return, give back; take back

toedollyŏnot'a 되돌려놓다 replace, put back

toedoragada 되돌아가다 go back, return; retrace

toedoraoda 되돌아오다 come back, return

toedorok imyŏn 되도록 이면 preferably, if possible

toejŏra! 뒈져라! go to hell!

toel ssu innŭn han 될 수 있는 한 as possible; if possible

toen 된 stiff

toenjang 된장 fermented soya paste

toeŏ it-tta 되어 있다 be scheduled; taŭmttare kkŭnmach'igiro toeŏ issŏyo 다음달에 끝마치기로 되어 있어요 it's scheduled for completion next month; ...giro toeŏ it-tta ...기로 되어 있다 be supposed to ...

toep'uridoenŭn 되풀이되는 repetitive

toep'urihada 되풀이하다 repeat; go over

toesallida 되살리다 revive; resuscitate; jog memory

toetch'atta 되찾다 retrieve

toetollida 되돌리다 reintroduce, bring back

toet'wida 되튀다 rebound

togani 도가니 melting pot

togi 도기 pottery

Togil 도일 Germany ◊ German

Togirin 독일인 German

Togirŏ 독일어 German (language)

togong 도공 potter

togŭl t'ada 독을 타다 poison

togu 도구 tool, device

Togyo 도교 Taoism

tohwasŏn 도화선 fuse wire

toip 도입 introduction; injection; input

toip'ada 도입하다 introduce; inject, contribute; input

tojagi 도자기 ceramics; porcelain

tojagiro toen 도자기로 된 ceramic

tojagiryu 도자기류 crockery

tojang 도장 paintwork; stamp, seal

tojang chaguk 도장 자국 stamp

tojang tchiktta 도장 찍다 stamp

tojŏhi 도저히 at all, by no means; tojŏhi ...l su ŏptta 도저히 ...ㄹ 수 없다 be completely unable to ...

tojŏn 도전 challenge

tojŏnhada 도전하다 challenge; dare

tojŏnja 도전자 challenger

toju ch'aryang 도주 차량 getaway car

tojung-e 도중에 on the way; kirŭl kŏnnŏnŭn tojung-e 길을 건너는 도중에 in crossing the road, while crossing the road

tojung-e tŭllŭda 도중에 들리다 stop off, break a journey

tok 독 poison; pot; dock

tokch'ang 독창 solo

tokch'angja 독창자 soloist

tokch'angjŏgin 독창적인 clever, ingenious

tokch'angnyŏk 독창력 ingenuity

tokch'angssŏng 독창성 originality

tokch'oktchang 독촉장 reminder COM

tokki 도끼 ax

tok-kkam 독감 flu, influenza

tokppaek 독백 monolog

tokppŏsŏt 독버섯 toadstool, poisonous mushroom

...tokppune ...덕분에 through, thank to

tokssarhada 독살하다 poison

toksshinin 독신인 unattached, single

toksshinja 독신자 single (person)

toksshirhan 독실한 devout

tokssŏ 독서 reading

tokssŏ chang-ae 독서 장애 dyslexia

tokssŏ chang-aeja 독서 장애자 dyslexic (person)

tokssŏga 독서가 reader (person)

tokssŏl 독설 sharp tongue

tokssŏnjŏgin 독선적인 dogmatic; self-righteous

tokssuri 독수리 eagle; vulture

toktchae chŏngkkwŏn 독재 정권 dictatorship

toktchaeja 독재자 dictator

toktchaejŏgin 독재적인 dictatorial

toktchajŏgin chosa podo 독자적인 조사 보도 investigative journalism

toktchŏm 독점 monopoly

toktchŏmhada 독점하다 monopolize

ktchŏmjŏgin 독점적인 exclusive, sole

ktchu 독주 solo

ktchuja 독주자 soloist

kttanjŏgin 독단적인 arbitrary

kt'ŭk'ada 독특하다 be unique

kt'ŭk'an 독특한 unique

k'ada 독하다 be poisonous; be strong (of coffee etc); be spiteful; be firm

k'ingshik'ida 도킹시키다 dock

ol 돌 rock, stone; **tori manŭn** 돌이 많은 stony

ol 돐 first birthday

olbal 돌발 outbreak

olbarhada 돌발하다 flare up

olboda 돌보다 look after

olbom 돌봄 care

olbwajuda 돌봐주다 watch, look after; **agirŭl tolbwajuda** 아기를 돌봐주다 baby-sit

olch'ul 돌출 bulge

olch'urhada 돌출하다 jut out

olda 돌다 turn, turn around; circulate

oldol mungch'ida 돌돌 뭉치다 screw up paper etc

olgi 돌기 turn

olgyŏk'ada 돌격하다 charge, attack

olkkorae 돌고래 dolphin

ollida 돌리다 turn, turn around; pass around; deal; direct

ollyŏbat-tta 돌려받다 have back, get back

ollyŏjuda 돌려주다 return, give back; pass on costs, savings

ollyŏnot'a 돌려놓다 return, put back

ollyŏ ponaeda 돌려 보내다 send back

ollyŏsŏ ŏn-gŭp'ada 돌려서 언급하다 allude to

olp'ari 돌팔이 itinerant tradesman ◊ unqualified, quack

olp'ung 돌풍 blast; gust, freak wind

ol segong 돌 세공 masonry

omabaem 도마뱀 lizard

omae 도매 wholesale

omaekkapssŭro 도매값으로 wholesale

omae-ŏptcha 도매업자 wholesaler

omal p'yobon kŏmsa 도말 표본 검사 smear (test)

tomang 도망 escape

tomangch'ida 도망치다 escape; break away; flee

tomanggada 도망가다 escape; run away; scram

tomangja 도망자 fugitive

ton 돈 money; cash; currency

tonan kyŏngbogi 도난 경보기 burglar alarm

tong 동 sub-district, dong

...tong-an ... 동안 during ◊ while; **...nŭn tong-ane** ...는 동안에 while ...ing; **...tong-an naenae** ...동안 내내 throughout, during

tongbanhada 동반하다 accompany

tongbanja 동반자 escort

tongbong 동봉 inclosure ◊ inclosed

tongbonghada 동봉하다 attach, inclose

tongbongmul 동봉물 inclosure (in letter etc)

tongbuk 동북 north-east

tongch'e 동체 fuselage

tongdŭnghada 동등하다 be equal

tongdŭnghage 동등하게 equally

tongdŭnghan 동등한 equal, equivalent; **tongdŭnghan kach'iga it-tta** 동등한 가치가 있다 be equivalent to

tonggamhada 동감하다 empathize with

tonggi 동기 incentive, motive

tonggi puyŏ 동기 부여 motivation

tonggirŭl puyŏhada 동기를 부여하다 motivate

tonggisaeng 동기생 contemporary

tonggŏhada 동거하다 live with; cohabit

tonggŭpssaeng 동급생 classmate

tonggŭrami 동그라미 circle; **tonggŭramirŭl ch'ida** 동그라미를 치다 circle, draw a circle around

tonggul 동굴 cave

tonggyŏldoeda 동결되다 ice up

Tonggyŏng 동경 Tokyo

tonggyŏng-ŭi taesang 동경의 대상 heart-throb

tonggyŏrhada 동결하다 freeze

Tonghae 동해 East Sea, Sea of Japan

tonghwa 동화 fairy tale

tonghyŏng-iŭiŏ 동형이의어 homograph

tong-irhan 동일한 identical

tongjaguro p'yohyŏnhada 동작으로 표현하다 mime

tongjak 동작 motion

tongji 동지 comrade

tongjŏn 동전 coin

tongjŏng 동정 pity; virginity; collar

tongjŏnghada 동정하다 pity; commiserate

tongjŏnghanŭn 동정하는 sympathetic, compassionate

tongjŏngshim 동정심 sympathy, pity, compassion

tongjŏngshimi manŭn 동정심이 많은 considerate

tongjoja 동조자 sympathizer

tongjongnyoppŏp 동종요법 homeopathy

tongjong pŏnshik 동종 번식 inbreeding

tongmaek 동맥 artery

tongmaeng 동맹 alliance

tongmaengguk 동맹국 ally (country)

tongmaeng p'aŏp 동맹 파업 strike; tongmaeng p'aŏp'ada 동맹 파업하다 go on strike; tongmaeng p'aŏp chung-ida 동맹 파업 중이다 be on strike

tongmedal 동메달 bronze medal

tongmu 동무 friend; comrade; companion

tongmul 동물 animal, creature

tongmurhak 동물학 zoology

tongmurhakssang-ŭi 동물학상의 zoological

tongmuro sagwigi 동무로 사귀기 companionship

tongmurwŏn 동물원 zoo

tongmyŏng-iin 동명이인 namesake

tongmyŏnhada 동면하다 hibernate

Tongnam Ashia 동남 아시아 Southeast Asia ◊ Southeast Asian

Tongnam Ashia Kuk-kka Yŏnhap 동남 아시아 국가 연합 ASEAN, Association of South East Asian Nations

tongnip 독립 independence ◊ independent

Tongnip Kinyŏmil 독립 기념일 Independence Day

tongnipkkuk 독립국 independent country

tongniptchŏgin 독립적인 independent, self-reliant

tongniptchŏgŭro 독립적으로 independently

tongnip'ada 독립하다 break away

tongnŏk 동력 movement; play

Tongnyang 동양 East Asia ◊ East Asian

Tongnyang saram 동양 사람 East Asian

tongnyŏguro chojonghanŭn 동력으로 조종하는 power-assisted

tongnyŏk 동력 power

tongnyo 동료 companion; colleague

tongnyo 동요 nursery rhyme; turbulence; chŏllyuŭi tongnyo 전류의 동요 surge ELEC

tongnyohanŭn 동요하는 turbulent

tongnyo kwan-gye 동료 관계 comradeship, friendship

tong-ŏp 동업 partnership

tong-ŏptcha 동업자 partner

tongp'o 동포 fellow citizen, fellow countryman

tongp'ung 동풍 easterly wind

tongsa 동사 verb

tongsamuso 동사무소 sub-district office

tongsang 동상 frostbite; chilblain

tongsang-e kŏllin 동상에 걸린 frostbitten

tongshi 동시 the same time ◊ simultaneous ◊ nursery rhyme

tongshie irŏnanŭn 동시에 at the same time, simultaneously

tongshie irŏnanŭn 동시에 일어나는 parallel, simultaneous

tongsŏ 동서 sister-in-law (husband's younger / elder brother's wife)

tongsŏng-ae hyŏmotchŭng 동성애 혐오증 homophobia

tongsŏng-aeja 동성애자 homosexual, gay

tongsŏng-aeŭi 동성애의 homosexual, gay

tongtchŏm 동점 draw, tie; tongtchŏmŭl mandŭlda 동점을 만들다 even the score; i tae iro

tongtchŏmin 이 대 이로 동점인 two all
ongtchŏmi toeda 동점이 되다 draw, tie
ongtchoguro 동쪽으로 east, eastward
ongtchok 동쪽 east
ongtŭnghan chonjae 동등한 존재 equal
ongt'ae chigae 동태 찌개 pollack chowder
ong-ŭi 동의 agreement, consent; arrangement; understanding
ong-ŭihada 동의하다 agree, consent; agree with, support
ong-ŭiŏ 동의어 synonym
ong-yo 동요 agitation
ong-yohan 동요한 agitated
ŏnŏt 도넛 donut
ŏnŭl kŏlda 돈을 걸다 back, put money on
ŏnŭl moktchŏguro hanŭn 돈을 목적으로 하는 mercenary
ŏnŭl naeda 돈을 내다 pay
ŏnŭl pŏlda 돈을 벌다 earn money
ŏŏ maen 도어 맨 doorman
ŏptta 돕다 help
ŏp'yo 도표 diagram, graph
ŏragada 돌아가다 go back, return
ŏrang 도랑 ditch; gutter
ŏraoda 돌아오다 come back, get back
ŏratanida 돌아다니다 move around; wander, roam
ŏrie mannŭn 도리에 맞는 honorable
ŏrie mat-tta 도리에 맞다 be in the right
ŏrik'il su ŏmnŭn 돌이킬 수 없는 irretrievable
ŏrip'ada 돌입하다 fall, plunge
ŏrirŭl anŭn 도리를 아는 honorable
ŏro 도로 roadway
ŏro chido 도로 지도 road map
ŏro kongsa 도로 공사 road works
ŏro p'yojip'an 도로 표지판 roadsign
ŏroŭi chung-ang pullidae 도로의 중앙 분리대 median strip
ŏroŭi taep'isŏn 도로의 대피선 hard shoulder

torŭrae 도르래 pulley
toryŏnhan 돌연한 freak
tosal 도살 slaughter
tosarhada 도살하다 slaughter
toshi 도시 city; town ◊ urban
toshihwa 도시화 urbanization
toshim-ŭi 도심의 down-town
toshirak 도시락 lunch box
toshiŭi 도시의 city, urban
toshiŭi chungshim 도시의 중심 city center
toshiŭi chungshimbue(sŏ) 도시의 중심부에(서) down-town
tosŏgwan 도서관 library
tot 돛 sail
totkkuda 돋구다 work up, develop
totppogi 돋보기 magnifying glass
tot-ttae 돛대 mast
totuk 도둑 thief
toŭi 도의 (moral) principle; **toŭisang** 도의상 on principle, as a matter of principle
touŏ moida 도우러 모이다 rally around
toum 도움 help, aid; **toumŭi p'iryohan** 도움이 필요한 in need
toumdatkki 도움닫기 run-up SP
toumi toenŭn 도움이 되는 helpful; conducive to
toummal hwamyŏn 도움말 화면 help screen
touŏ tallyŏoda 도우러 달려오다 rally around
toyak 도약 leap; vault
toyak sŏnsu 도약 선수 jumper
toye 도예 pottery; ceramics
toyeji 도예지 pottery (place)
ttabunhan 따분한 boring
ttada 따다 win; pick; unstop, pop cork
ttadollida 따돌리다 leave out; ostracize
ttadollimŭl pat-tta 따돌림을 받다 be alienated; be excluded
ttae 때 occasion; time; **-l ttae** -ㄹ 때 when; **naega ŏryŏssŭl ttae** 내가 어렸을 때 when I was a child; **...se ttaee** ...세 때에 at the age of ...; **-l ttaemada** -ㄹ 때마다 whenever; **ttaerŭl chal match'un** 때를 잘 맞춘 well-timed

ttae anin 때 아닌 untimely

ttaega toemyŏn 때가 되면 in due course, eventually

ttaekkaji 때까지 until; **-l ttaekkaji** -ㄹ 때까지 until

ttaelnamu 땔나무 firewood

ttaem 댐 dam

ttaemudŭn 때묻은 grimy

...ttaemune ...때문에 because ◊ because of; out of; **...gi ttaemune** ...기 때문에 since, because of; **...ttaemune irŏnada** ...때문에 일어나다 be due to, be caused by

...ttaemunŭro ...때문으로 because of

ttaerida 때리다 hit, beat (up)

ttaerigi 때리기 thrashing, beating

ttaettaero 때때로 sometimes, occasionally

ttagae 따개 tab

ttak 딱 punctually; exactly; just

ttakttak'ada 딱딱하다 be hard; be stiff

ttakkŭmgŏrida 따끔거리다 sting; tingle

ttakkŭmgŏrinŭn 따끔거리는 prickly

ttak tallabut-tta 딱 달라붙다 adhere

ttaktchi 딱지 scab

ttaktchŏngbŏlle 딱정벌레 beetle

ttakttaguri 딱따구리 woodpecker

ttakttak-kkŏrida 딱딱거리다 snap

ttakttak sorirŭl naeda 딱딱 소리를 내다 crackle

ttakttak'an 딱딱한 hard; stiff, stilted

ttakttak'an kkŏptchil 딱딱한 껍질 crust

ttak'anŭn sori 딱하는 소리 snap

ttal 딸 daughter

ttalgi 딸기 strawberry

ttalkkuktchil 딸꾹질 hiccup

ttalkkuktchirhada 딸꾹질하다 have the hiccups

ttallanggŏrida 딸랑거리다 jingle

ttallangttallang 딸랑딸랑 tinkling, jingling

ttam 땀 sweat, perspiration

ttami paen 땀이 밴 sweaty

ttamnae nanŭn 땀내 나는 sweaty

ttamt'usŏng-iin 땀투성이인 covered in sweat

ttamŭl hŭllida 땀을 흘리다 sweat, perspire

ttang 땅 property, land; estate

ttangbŏlle 땅벌레 grub (of insect)

ttangk'ong 땅콩 groundnut, peanut

ttangk'ong pŏt'ŏ 땅콩 버터 peanut butter

ttangttalmak'an 땅딸막한 squat, stocky

ttanim 따님 daughter

ttan 딴 another; different; separate; irrelevant; **ttan tero tollida** 딴 데로 돌리다 divert; **kŭgŏn ttan yaegi-yeyo** 그건 딴 얘기예요 that's beside the point

ttara 따라 down, along

ttaragada 따라가다 follow, come to

ttarajaptta 따라잡다 catch; catch up; overtake

ttarasŏ 따라서 therefore; thus ◊ in accordance with; along

ttarasŏ irŏnan 따라서 일어난 subsequent, later

ttaro 따로 separately, apart ◊ extra; additional; **kakki ttaro salda** 각기 따로 살다 live apart

ttarŭda 따르다 abide by, follow, conform; go along with; pour out liquid; **sanghwang-e ttara tarŭda** 상황에 따라 다르다 that depends (on the circumstances)

ttarŭmyŏn 따르면 according to

ttattŭt'ada 따뜻하다 be warm

ttattŭt'aejida 따뜻해지다 warm up

ttattŭt'age 따뜻하게 warmly

ttattŭt'age iptta 따뜻하게 입다 wrap up

ttattŭt'age kamssada 따뜻하게 감싸다 muffle up

ttattŭt'an 따뜻한 warm

ttat'a 땋다 braid

ttaŭn mŏri 땋은 머리 braid, pigtail

tte 떼 crowd; mob; herd; flock; swarm; **tte tonŭl pŏlda** 떼 돈을 벌다 make a killing; **tterŭl chiŏ moida** 떼를 지어 모이다 huddle together; **tterŭl chiŏ tallyŏdŭlda** 떼를 지어 달려들다 mob; **tterŭl chit-tta** 떼를 짓다 swarm

ttemilgi 떼밀기 shove

ttemilgo tŭrŏgada 떼밀고 들어가다 squeeze into room

ttenmok 뗏목 raft

...naeda 떼어내다 detach; pull off; separate; **t'ellebijŏnesŏ tteŏ not'a** 텔레비전에서 떼어 놓다 drag oneself away from the TV

...] sash

...doradanida 떠돌아다니다 wander, roam

...dori 떠돌이 hobo

...dŭlssŏk'an 떠들썩한 boisterous

...innŭn 떠 있는 afloat

...k 떡 rice cake

...kch'iri toeda 떡칠이 되다 be plastered with

...k-kkuk 떡국 rice cake soup

...k pŏrojin 떡 벌어진 broad

...kppok-kki 떡볶이 rice cake in hot sauce

...ch'yŏbŏrida 떨쳐버리다 dismiss

...da 떨다 shake, tremble; shiver

...lida 떨리다 quaver, tremble; judder; throb

...lim 떨림 shudder

...limŭm 떨림음 throb

...linŭn 떨리는 is wobbly

...mat-tta 떠맡다 take charge

...nada 떠나다 leave, go away

...naganŭn 떠나가는 outgoing

...nage hada 떠나게 하다 excuse; allow to leave

...ngmanduguk 떡만두국 rice cake and dumpling soup

...orŭda 떠오르다 occur to; haunt (of memory); surface, come up, rise

...rŏjida 떨어지다 fall, drop, decline; run out; run out of; come off (of candle etc); strike (of disaster); set (of sun); deteriorate; be apart; separate; be left behind; fail exam; miscarry; be evenly divisible; get finished; die; get over illness; **imail törŏjyŏit-tta** 2마일 떨어져있다 it's 2 miles away

...rŏjyŏsŏ 떨어져서 apart; **chudoroesŏ ttŏrŏjyŏ** 주도로에서 떨어져 off the main road; **...put'ŏ** 떨어져 있다 stay away from; **...esŏ ttŏrŏjyŏsŏ sŏda** ...에서 떨어져서 서다 stand clear of

...öröttŭrida 떨어뜨리다 drop, lower; shed *leaves*; strip *leaves*; throw off

ttŏröttŭryŏ 떨어뜨려 aside

tto 또 again; also; **tto poja!** 또 보자! see you!

ttohan 또한 also, too; either; **...to ttohan ...** ...도 또한 ... (+ *negative verb*) nor

tto hana 또 하나 another, additional

ttokkatchi anŭn 똑같지 않은 unequal

ttokkatkkehada 똑같게하다 equalize

ttok-kkat-tta 똑같다 be exactly like; **soriga ttok-kkat'ayo** 소리가 똑같아요 sound the same

ttokpparo 똑바로 straight; straight ahead; upright; **ttokpparo kada** 똑바로 가다 carry straight on; **ttokpparo antta** 똑바로 앉다 sit up (straight)

ttokpparŭge hada 똑바르게 하다 straighten

ttokpparŭn 똑바른 straight

ttokttak-kkŏrida 똑딱거리다 tick

ttokttok ttŏrojida 똑똑 떨어지다 drip, trickle

ttokttok'ada 똑똑하다 be intelligent

ttokttok'an 똑똑한 intelligent, smart, clever

ttolttol kamtta 똘똘 감다 coil

ttong 똥 dung; shit; poop; excrement

ttongkkumŏng 똥구멍 anus, rectum; bottom; butt

ttongppae 똥배 paunch, belly

ttonŭn 또는 or

tto tarŭn 또 다른 further, additional; **tto tarŭn kŏt** 또 다른 것 another (one)

ttŭda 뜨다 float; scoop

ttŭgaejil 뜨개질 knitting

ttŭgaejirhada 뜨개질하다 knit

ttŭgŏpta 뜨겁다 be hot; be burning

ttŭgŏun 뜨거운 hot

ttŭiŏmttŭiŏm 띄엄띄엄 sparsely; intermittently; slowly; **ttŭiŏmttŭiŏm iltta** 띄엄띄엄 읽다 browse through a book

ttŭiuda 띄우다 sail

ttŭkppakkŭi il 뜻밖의 일 contingency

ttŭl 뜰 garden

ttŭnaegi 뜨내기 hobo

ttŭnaegi ilkkun 뜨내기 일꾼 hobo (*itinerant worker*)

ttŭn-gurum chapkki뜬구름 잡기 wild-goose chase

ttŭsŭl palk'ida뜻을 밝히다 define, specify

ttŭsŭl palk'im뜻을 밝힘 definition

ttŭt뜻 sense, meaning; intention; aim, purpose

ttŭtppakk뜻밖 surprise

ttŭtppakke뜻밖에 unexpectedly

ttŭtppakkŭi뜻밖의 unexpected

ttŭtppakkŭi haeng-un뜻밖의 행운 stroke of luck

ttŭt'aji anŭn chang-ae뜻하지 않은 장애 snag, problem; twist (in story)

ttukkŏng뚜껑 lid; top, cap; flap

ttukttuk ttŏrŏjida뚝뚝 떨어지다 dribble

ttulkko nagada뚫고 나가다 negotiate obstacles; weather crisis

ttult'a뚫다 drill; pierce ears; unblock

ttungbo뚱보 fatty

ttungttungbo뚱뚱보 fatso

ttungttunghada뚱뚱하다 be fat

ttungttunghan뚱뚱한 fat

tturŏjige poda뚫어지게 보다 peer at

tturyŏt'ada뚜렷하다 be clear, distinct

tturyŏt'age뚜렷하게 clearly, distinctly

tturyŏt'aji anŭn뚜렷하지 않은 indistinct

tturyŏt'an뚜렷한 clear; distinct; definite

ttwida뛰다 pound, throb

ttwigi뛰기 spring, jump

ttwiŏdanida뛰어다니다 jump, bounce

ttwiŏdŭlda뛰어들다 dive; *pang anŭro ttwiŏdŭlda* 방 안으로 뛰어들다 burst into the room

ttwiŏdŭlgi뛰어들기 dive

ttwiŏdŭm뛰어듦 plunge, fall

ttwiŏnada뛰어나다 excel; excel at; be excellent; *poda ttwiŏnada* 보다 뛰어나다 outperform

ttwiŏ nagada뛰어 나가다 fly out, rush out

ttwiŏnage뛰어나게 extremely

ttwiŏnam뛰어남 excellence

ttwiŏnan뛰어난 excellent

ttwiŏnan somsshi뛰어난 솜씨 prowess

ttwiŏ nŏmtta뛰어 넘다 jump, va

ttwiŏ orŭda뛰어 오르다 jump

ttwiŏorŭgi뛰어오르기 jump

ttwiŏ orŭm뛰어 오름 jump

tŭkdŭk득득 profit, benefit; *...nŭn kŏsh tŭgi toeji anayo* ...는 것이 득이 되지 않아요 it doesn't pay to ...

tŭkp'yohada득표하다 poll, obtai

tŭksshiri ŏpkke toeda득실이 없 되다 break even

tŭktchŏm득점 score; goal; *tŭktchŏm maganaegi* 득점 막아내기 save SP

tŭktchŏmhada득점하다 score; to down

tŭktchŏmja득점자 scorer

tŭlch'angmun들창문 trapdoor

tŭlch'uŏnaeda들추어내다 dredge up, unearth

tŭlda들다 enter; join club; catch cold; contain; accommodate; get; begin; dye; be pleased, be satisfie cost; put up hand; take out insura policy; cut; grow older; hold pen; cite example; eat; drink

tŭlgo kada들고 가다 carry

tŭlkkae p'ohoegin들깨 포획인 do catcher

tŭlkkŏt들것 stretcher

tŭlkkŭlt'a들끓다 be overrun with; smolder

tŭllida들리다 hear; be audible; be rumored by; be obsessed by; be lifted up

tŭllinŭn pŏmwi ane(sŏ)들리는 범 안에(서) within hearing

tŭllinŭn pŏmwi pakke(sŏ)들리는 범위 밖에(서) out of hearing

tŭllŏbunnŭn들러붙는 clingy

tŭllida들르다 drop in, stop by

tŭlppo들보 beam

tŭlp'an들판 field

tŭlsso들소 buffalo

tŭltchungnaltchuk'an들쭉날쭉한 ragged, jagged

tŭmppuk듬뿍 plenty, lots

tŭmulda드물다 be rare

tŭmulge드물게 rarely, seldom, unusually

tŭmun드문 rare; infrequent; unusu

dŭnhan 든든한 stalwart, steadfast

ng등 back, spine (of book); light, ntern; *nuguege tŭng-ŭl tollida* 구에게 등을 돌리다 turn one's ack on s.o.

ngban 등반 climb

gbanhada 등반하다 climb

ngch'yŏmŏktta 등쳐먹다 prey on

ngdae 등대 lighthouse

nggamul 등가물 equivalent

nggŭbŭl maegida 등급을 매기다 ~ade, rank

nggŭp 등급 grade, quality

ng-i kuptta 등이 굽다 stoop

ngjang 등장 entrance THEAT

ngjanghada 등장하다 enter THEAT

ngjang inmul 등장 인물 haracters, cast THEAT

ngjida 등지다 desert

ngkkiro puch'ida 등기로 부치다 register; *pyŏnjirŭl tŭngkkiro onaeda* 편지를 등기로 보내다 end a letter registered

ngkki up'yŏn 등기 우편 registered etter

ngnogŭl hada 등록을 하다 register

ngnok 등록 entry; enrollment, egistration

ngnok pŏnho 등록 번호 license umber

ngnok sangp'yo 등록 상표 rademark

ngnok'ada 등록하다 register, nroll

ngppul 등불 lamp

ngsan 등산 mountaineering

ngsan-ga 등산가 mountaineer, limber

ngsanhwa 등산화 climbing boots

ngssu 등수 place, position

ngtcha 등자 stirrup

ngttaktchi 등딱지 shell (of ortoise)

ng-yu 등유 kerosene

nŏlbŭn 넓은 spacious

raibŏ 드라이버 screwdriver; driver COMPUT

raibŭ 드라이브 drive; outing

raik'ŭllining 드라이클리닝 dry-cleaning

raik'ŭllininghada 드라이클리닝하다

dry-clean

tŭraik'ŭllining set'aksso 드라이클리닝 세탁소 dry-cleaner

tŭraiŏro mŏrirŭl mallida 드라이어로 머리를 말리다 blow-dry

tŭrama 드라마 drama

tŭresŭ 드레스 dress

tŭribat-tta 들이받다 knock down; run into

tŭribŭrhada 드리블하다 dribble SP

tŭrida 드리다 give

tŭrimashida 들이마시다 suck in, gulp down; inhale

tŭrishwida 들이쉬다 breathe in; *k'oro tŭrishwida* 코로 들이쉬다 sniff

tŭrŏgada 들어가다 enter, go into; let in

tŭrŏ it-tta 들어 있다 be inside; *nae k'ameraga tŭrŏ issŏt-tta* 내 카메라가 들어 있었다 my camera was in it

tŭrŏjuda 들어주다 accommodate *requirement*; grant *wish*

tŭrŏm 드럼 drum

tŭrŏ mat-tta 들어 맞다 fit

tŭrŏmŏ 드러머 drummer

tŭrŏmt'ong 드럼통 drum (container)

tŭrŏnaeda 드러내다 reveal; take out; throw out; *kamjŏng-ŭl tŭrŏnaeda* 감정을 드러내다 be demonstrative

tŭrŏnuptta 드러눕다 lie down

tŭrŏoda 들어오다 come in, enter

tŭrŏ ollida 들어 올리다 lift; heave; hand

tŭrŏsŏda 들어서다 enter; *tarŭn killo tŭrŏsŏda* 다른 길로 들어서다 turn off

tŭryŏda ponŭn kumŏng 틀여다 보는 구멍 peephole

tŭryŏnot'a 들여놓다 stock up on

tŭryŏ ponaeda 들여 보내다 send in

tŭt-tta 듣다 hear; listen; listen to; *tŭrŭl su innŭn* 들을 수 있는 audible

tu 두 two

tubu 두부 tofu

tu chari su 두 자리 수 in double figures

tudŭrida 두드리다 beat; knock; pound

tudŭrŏjin 두드러진 conspicuous

tudŭrŏjinŭn 두드러지는 striking, marked

tudunhada 두둔하다 cover up for

tugaegol 두개골 skull

tugoboda 두고보다 watch, keep watch; *nŏ tugo poja!* 너 두고 보자! just you wait!

tugo kada 두고 가다 leave behind

tugo marhada 두고 말하다 be meant for, be aimed at

tugŭndugŭn ttwida 두근두근 뛰다 thump

tugŭn-gŏrida 두근거리다 flutter

tujŏl 두절 disruption

tujŏlshik'ida 두절시키다 disrupt

tuk 둑 dike; embankment; weir

tuk-kkil 둑길 embankment

tukkŏbi 두꺼비 toad

tukkŏbijip 두꺼비집 fusebox

tukkŏun 두꺼운 thick

tukkŏuptta 두껍다 be thick

tu kyŏbŭi 두 겹의 double *layer*

tul 둘 two; *kŭdŭl tul* 그들 둘 the two of them; *...wa / gwa ..., tul ta* ...와 / 과 ..., 둘 다 both... and ...

tulle 둘레 around

tullŏboda 둘러보다 look around; survey; view

tullŏdaeda 둘러대다 beat about the bush; dodge

tullŏdaenŭn kŏjinmal 둘러대는 거짓말 whitewash

tullŏ ssada 둘러 싸다 enclose; surround; *tullŏssaida* 둘러싸이다 be surrounded by

tullŏ ssŭiuda 둘러 씌우다 drape

tul ta 둘 다 both; *kŭdŭl tul ta* 그들 둘 다 both of them

tultchaero 둘째로 secondly

tumal hal kŏt ŏpsshi 두말 할 것 없이 it goes without saying; *tumal hal kŏt ŏpsshi ch'oegoimnida* 두말 할 것 없이 최고입니다 it is simply the best

tumesankkol 두메산골 the sticks, the boonies

tumok haengsehanŭn 두목 행세하는 bossy

tunbu 둔부 haunch

tun-gamhan 둔감한 stolid

tunggŭlda 둥글다 be round

tunggŭlge hada 둥글게 하다 round off *edges*

tunggŭlge ogŭradŭlda 둥글게 오그라들다 curl

tunggŭn 둥근 round, circular

tunggŭn ch'ŏnjang 둥근 천장 dome; vault

tungji 둥지 nest

tunhan 둔한 dull; thick; stupid

tunoe 두뇌 brain

tunt'ak'an 둔탁한 dull

tu pae 두 배 double *amount*

tu paega toeda 두 배가 되다 double

tu paero 두 배로 double

tu paero hada 두 배로 하다 double

tu paeŭi 두 배의 double, twice as much

tu pŏn 두 번 twice

tu pŏntchae 두 번째 second

tu pŏntchaero 두 번째로 second; *pŏntchaero chal hanŭn* 두 번째 잘 하는 second best

tu pŏntchaeŭi 두 번째의 second

tup'yoham 투표함 ballot box

turŏnada 들어나다 emerge

turŏ ollida 들어 올리다 take up *carpet etc*

turŭda 두르다 enclose

turumagi 두루마기 (traditional) long coat

turumari 두루마리 scroll, manuscript

turyŏptta 두렵다 be fearful

turyŏum 두려움 fear

turyŏum ŏmnŭn 두려움 없는 fearless

turyŏwŏhada 두려워하다 be afraid, be afraid of

tusŏnŏ kae 두서너 개 a couple of

tusŏnŏsŭi 두서넛의 a couple of (*people*)

tusŏŏmnŭn 두서없는 incoherent, rambling

tusŏŏpsshi iyagihada 두서없이 이야기하다 ramble

tut'ong 두통 headache

tu t'ong-ŭro 두 통으로 in duplicate

tuyu 두유 soy(a) milk

twaeji 돼지 hog, pig

twaeji chŏgŭmt'ong 돼지 저금통 piggybank

aeji chokppal 돼지 족발 pig's trotters
aejigogi 돼지고기 pork
aeji kajuk 돼지 가죽 pigskin
aejiuri 돼지우리 pigpen
aessŏyo 됐어요 that's plenty; that's it
aessŭmnida 됐습니다 there you are (completing sth)
engbŏl 뒝벌 bumblebee
esalligi 되살리기 undelete COMPUT
뒤 back, rear; (ch'aŭi) twit chwasŏge(sŏ) (차의) 뒷 좌석에(서) in back (of the car); ...bŏsŭ twit chwasŏge(sŏ) 버스 뒷 좌석에(서) at the back of the bus
...bŏmbŏk 뒤범벅 jumble
...ch'ŏgida 뒤척이다 stir, move
...ch'ŏk-kkŏrida 뒤척거리다 toss and turn; turn over
...ch'uk 뒤축 heel (of shoe)
...ch'yŏjige hada 뒤쳐지게 하다 set back
...idoraboda 뒤돌아보다 look back
...ie(sŏ) 뒤에(서) behind; at the back
...ie namgida 뒤에 남기다 leave behind
...ie namtta 뒤에 남다 stay behind
...iesŏ chidohada 뒤에서 지도하다 mastermind
...iŭn 뒤이은 succeeding, following
...ijibŏjida 뒤집어지다 turn over (of vehicle)
...ijibŏsŏ 뒤집어서 inside out
...ijibŭm 뒤집음 demolition (of argument)
...ijida 뒤지다 poke around; search
...ijiji ank'o ttaragada 뒤지지 않고 따라가다 keep up (when walking etc)
...ijipta 뒤집다 upset, overturn drink, glass; capsize; fold; back; demolish argument; turn inside out
...ijip'ida 뒤집히다 overturn, capsize
...ijukppaktchugin 뒤죽박죽인 topsy-turvy
...ijyŏ ch'ajanaeda 뒤져 찾아내다 rummage around

twijyŏsŏ 뒤져서 behind (in progress, order)
twikkumch'i 뒤꿈치 heel (of foot)
twinggulda 뒹굴다 roll over
twinmadang 뒷마당 backyard
twinmun 뒷문 backdoor
twinmyŏn 뒷면 back, reverse; *ammyŏn animyŏn twinmyŏn?* 앞면 아니면 뒷면? heads or tails?
twinŭjŭn kkaedarŭm 뒤늦은 깨달음 hindsight
twiŏlk'in 뒤얽힌 intricate
twiŏptta 뒤엎다 overturn, tip over
twiro chŏp'ae it-tta 뒤로 접혀 있다 back onto
twiro mungnŭn mŏri 뒤로 묶는 머리 ponytail
twiro tanggida 뒤로 당기다 draw back, pull back
twirŭl paltta 뒤를 밟다 stalk
twisŏk-kkida 뒤섞이다 be mixed up (of figures, papers)
twisŏktta 뒤섞다 shuffle; *ilburŏ twisŏktta* 일부러 뒤섞다 scramble *message*
twitchoch'a ch'ajanaeda 뒤쫓아 찾아내다 track down
twitchot-tta 뒤쫓다 chase
twitch'ŭnggye 뒷층계 backstairs
twitjwasŏk 뒷좌석 pillion
twitkkil 뒷길 back road
twitkŭlswe 뒷글쇠 backspace COMPUT
twitppatch'imhae chuda 뒷받침해 주다 back up *claim, argument*
twittchang 뒷장 back, reverse
twittchoge(sŏ) 뒷쪽에(서) behind (in position)
twittchoge innŭn 뒷쪽에 있는 back, at the back
twittchogŭi 뒷쪽의 backward; rear
twittchogŭro 뒷쪽으로 backward
twittchok 뒷쪽 back
twittchumŏni 뒷주머니 hip pocket
twittŏrŏjida 뒤떨어지다 lag behind
twit-ttŭl 뒤뜰 backyard
twittunggŏrimyŏ kŏt-tta 뒤뚱거리며 걷다 waddle
twiŭi 뒤의 rear
tyusŭ 듀스 deuce (in tennis)

T'

t'aak-kki 타악기 percussion; percussion instrument

t'abŏrida 타버리다 burn down

t'abŭlloidŭp'an shinmun 타블로이드판 신문 tabloid (newspaper)

t'ada 타다 get in (to car); board; catch bus etc; mount horse, bicycle; ride horse, bicycle; fly; burn; glow

t'adanghada 타당하다 be just; be valid

t'adanghan 타당한 just; valid

t'adangsŏng 타당성 validity

t'adangsŏng chosa 타당성 조사 feasibility study

t'aea 태아 embryo; fetus

t'aedo 태도 attitude, manner

T'aegugin 태국인 Thai

T'aegugŏ 태국어 Thai (language)

t'aegŭk-kki 태극기 (South Korean) national flag

T'aeguk 태국 Thailand ◊ Thai

T'aekkwŏndo 태권도 Taekwondo

t'aeksshi 택시 taxi, cab

t'aeksshi sŭngch'ajang 택시 승차장 taxi rank, cab stand

t'aeksshi unjŏnsa 택시 운전사 taxi driver, cab driver

t'aek'ŭl 태클 tackle SP

t'aek'ŭrhada 태클하다 tackle SP

t'aemanhada 태만하다 neglect, omit

t'aenggo 탱고 tango

t'aengk'ŭ 탱크 tank

t'aeŏnada 태어나다 be born

t'aeŏp 태업 slowdown, go-slow

t'aep 탭 tab

t'aepttaensŭ 탭댄스 tap dance

t'aep'ung 태풍 hurricane, typhoon

T'aep'yŏng-yang 태평양 Pacific (Ocean)

T'aep'yŏng-yang yŏnan 태평양 연안 Pacific Rim

t'aetchul 탯줄 umbilical cord

t'aeuda 태우다 burn; give a ride;

ch'a-e t'aeuda 차에 태우다 pick (in car)

t'aeugi 태우기 ride (in car)

t'aewŏbŏrida 태워버리다 burn out gut

t'aewŏ chuda 태워 주다 take, driv

t'aeyang 태양 sun

t'aeyang chŏnjip'an 태양 전지판 solar panel

t'aeyang enŏji 태양 에너지 solar energy

t'aeyŏnhan 태연한 nonchalant

t'agae 타개 breakthrough

t'agi shwiun 타기 쉬운 combustibl

t'agonan 타고난 innate; natural

t'agonan chaenŭng 타고난 재능 gift, natural ability

t'agonan kŭmbal 타고난 금발 natural blonde

t'agwŏrhan 탁월한 prominent, significant

t'agyŏk 타격 knock, blow

t'ahyŏp 타협 compromise

t'ahyŏpsshik'ida 타협시키다 compromise

t'ahyŏp'ada 타협하다 compromise

t'ahyŏp'aji annŭn 타협하지 않는 uncompromising

t'ail 타일 tile

t'aim aut 타임 아웃 time out

t'aiming 타이밍 timing

t'aimŏ 타이머 timer

t'aim süwich'i 타임 스위치 time switch

t'aiŏ 타이어 tire

t'aip'isŭt'ŭ 타이피스트 typist

t'airŭda 타이르다 preach, moralize

t'aja 타자 batter SP

t'aja ch'ida 타자 치다 type

t'ajagi 타자기 typewriter

t'ajagiro ch'ida 타자기로 치다 type

t'ak-kku 탁구 ping-pong

t'alch'um 탈춤 mask dance

t'alch'urhada 탈출하다 escape; get

...way; bail out
lch'urhan 탈출한 at large
lch'wi 탈취 hijack
lch'wibŏm 탈취범 hijacker
lch'wihada 탈취하다 hijack
lch'wije 탈취제 deodorant
lgok'ada 탈곡하다 thresh *corn*
lgushik'ida 탈구시키다 dislocate
llak 탈락 elimination
llak'ada 탈락하다 be eliminated
llo 탄로 exposure
llonada 탄로나다 be out (*of secret*)
llyŏginnŭn 탄력있는 elastic
lsse 탈세 tax evasion
lssŏndoeda 탈선되다 be derailed
lssudoen 탈수된 dehydrated
lssugi 탈수기 spin-dryer
lssuhada 탈수하다 spin-dry
ltchang 탈장 hernia
ltchimyŏn 탈지면 absorbent
otton
ltchi uyu 탈지 우유 skimmed milk
lt'oehada 탈퇴하다 break away
from organization)
m 탐 ride
mdok'ada 탐독하다 devour
mgujŏgin 탐구적인 inquisitive
mhŏm 탐험 expedition,
xploration
mhŏmdae 탐험대 expedition
mhŏmga 탐험가 explorer
mji 탐지 detection
mjigi 탐지기 detector
mjihada 탐지하다 detect
mjŏng sosŏl 탐정 소설 detective
ovel
mjodŭng 탐조등 searchlight
mnanŭn 탐나는 desirable, coveted
mnik 탐닉 indulgence
mnik'ada 탐닉하다 indulge
mp'on 탐폰 tampon
msa 탐사 probe
msaek 탐색 search
msaek'ada 탐색하다 explore, look
nto, examine; seek, search for
myokssŭrŏun 탐욕스러운
nsatiable
ando misail 탄도 미사일 ballistic
nissile
andu 탄두 warhead
an-gwang 탄광 coal mine

t'annyak 탄약 ammunition
t'ansaeng 탄생 birth
t'ansansu 탄산수 soda (water)
t'ansanŭi 탄산의 carbonated
t'ansŏng-i innŭn 탄성이 있는
springy
t'ansuhwamul 탄수화물
carbohydrate
t'anyakt'ong 탄약통 cartridge
t'aorŭda 타오르다 blaze; flare up
t'ap 탑 pagoda; tower
t'apssŭnggu 탑승구 gate (*at airport*)
t'apssŭngkkwŏn 탑승권 boarding
card
t'apssŭng susogŭl hada 탑승
수속을 하다 check in
t'apssŭng susok k'aunt'ŏ 탑승 수속
카운터 check-in (counter)
t'apssŭng susok shigan 탑승 수속
시간 check-in time
t'apssŭng taegija 탑승 대기자
standby passenger
t'arae 타래 lock (*of hair*)
t'arak 타락 corruption
t'araksshik'ida 타락시키다 corrupt
t'arak'ada 타락하다 degenerate; be
corrupt
t'arak'an 타락한 corrupt, sleazy
t'arhwan 탈환 recapture
t'arok'ada 탈옥하다 break out,
escape
t'arŭ 타르 tar
t'arŭishil 탈의실 cubicle; changing
room
t'aryŏng 탈영 desertion
t'aryŏngbyŏng 탈영병 deserter
t'aryŏnghada 탈영하다 desert MIL
t'at 탓 fault, blame; result; effect;
Xŭl / rŭl Yŭi t'asŭro tollida X을 / 를
Y의 탓으로 돌리다 put X down to Y
t'at'ada 탓하다 blame
t'awŏnhyŏng 타원형 ellipse
t'e 테 frame, rim; hoop
t'eduri 테두리 brim, rim
t'eibŭl 테이블 table
t'eibŭl po 테이블 보 table cloth
t'eip'ŭ 테이프 tape
t'eip'ŭ nogŭm 테이프 녹음 tape
recording
t'eip'ŭro puch'ida 테이프로 붙이다
tape (*with sticky tape*)

t'eksŭt'ŭ p'ail 텍스트 파일 text file

t'ellebi 텔레비 TV

t'ellebijŏn 텔레비전 television

t'ellebijŏn p'ŭrogŭraem 텔레비전 프로그램 television program

t'ellebijŏn set'ŭ 텔레비전 세트 television (set)

t'ellebijŏn susanggi 텔레비전 수상기 television (set)

t'ema 테마 theme

t'ema kong-wŏn 테마 공원 theme park

t'ema ŭmak 테마 음악 theme tune; signature tune

t'enissŭ 테니스 tennis

t'enissŭ chang 테니스 장 tennis court

t'enissŭ kong 테니스 공 tennis ball

t'enissŭ lak'et 테니스 라켓 tennis racket

t'enissŭ sŏnsu 테니스 선수 tennis player

t'enŏ 테너 tenor

t'erŏbŏm 테러범 terrorist

t'erŏ chojik 테러 조직 terrorist organization

t'erŏrijŭm 테러리즘 terrorism

t'erŭl talda 테를 달다 edge

t'i 티 tee

T'ibet'ŭ 티베트 Tibet ◊ Tibetan

T'ibet'ŭin 티베트인 Tibetan (person)

T'ibet'ŏ 티베트어 Tibetan (language)

t'ibi 티비 TV

t'ik'ŭ namu 티크 나무 teak

t'im 팀 team; crew

t'imjang 팀장 team captain

t'ineijŏ 틴에이저 teenager

t'i ŏmnŭn 티 없는 immaculate

t'ip 팁 tip, gratuity

t'ishyŏch'ŭ 티셔츠 T-shirt

t'ŏbin 터빈 turbine

t'ŏch'i 터치 touch SP

t'ŏch'idaun 터치다운 touchdown

t'ŏch'irain 터치라인 touchline

t'ŏjida 터지다 burst

t'ŏjin 터진 burst

t'ŏk 턱 chin; jaw; ledge

t'ŏkppaji 턱받이 bib

t'ŏksshido 턱시도 tuxedo

t'ŏkssuyŏm 턱수염 beard

T'ŏk'i 터키 Turkey ◊ Turkish

T'ŏk'iin 터키인 Turk

T'ŏk'iŏ 터키어 Turkish (language)

t'ŏl 털 hair; fur; bristles

t'ŏlshillo ttŭda 털실로 뜨다 knit

t'ŏlssŏk naeryŏnot'a 털썩 내려놓다 slam down

t'ŏminŏl 터미널 terminal

t'ŏmuniŏmnŭn 터무니없는 outrageous, ridiculous

t'ŏng pin 텅 빈 bare, empty

t'ŏnŏl 터널 tunnel

t'ŏ noch'i annŭn 터 놓지 않는 secretive

t'ŏnot'a 터놓다 pour out, tell troubles; songmaŭmŭl t'ŏnot'a 속마음을 터놓다 speak one's mind

t'ŏnt'eibŭl 턴테이블 turntable

t'ŏpssuruk'an 텁수룩한 bushy

t'ŏri manŭn 털이 많은 woolly

t'ŏri ŏmnŭn 털이 없는 hairless

t'ŏri p'ungsŏnghan 털이 풍성한 furry

t'ŏrŏnaeda 털어내다 brush off dust etc

t'ŏrŏnot'a 털어놓다 confide

t'ŏttŭrida 터뜨리다 burst; give vent to

t'obŭro charŭda 톱으로 자르다 saw

t'obŭro k'yŏda 톱으로 켜다 saw off

t'odae 토대 support

t'oebohada 퇴보하다 go backward; degenerate

t'oebohanŭn 퇴보하는 backward society

t'oegŏ myŏngnyŏng 퇴거 명령 deportation order

t'oehak 퇴학 expulsion

t'oejanghada 퇴장하다 leave; exit (of actor); walk out

t'oejangshik'ida 퇴장시키다 expel from the game

t'oejikkŭm 퇴직금 golden handshake

t'oejik sudang 퇴직 수당 unemployment compensation

t'oejŏkshik'ida 퇴적시키다 deposit

t'oep'yejŏgin 퇴폐적인 decadent

t'oerak'ada 퇴락하다 go to seed, become shabby

t'oetcha 퇴짜 brush-off

t'oewihada 퇴위하다 abdicate

ewŏn 퇴원 discharge

ewŏnshik'ida 퇴원시키다
scharge

ji 토기 earthenware

hada 토하다 vomit

i kaebarŏptcha 토지 개발업자
operty developer

kki 토끼 rabbit

kt'ok tudŭrida 톡톡 두드리다 rap

k'ŭn 토큰 token

mak 토막 fragment, chip

makch'ida 토막치다 cut up

mat'o 토마토 tomato

mat'o k'ech'ap 토마토 케찹
mato ketchup

mnibak'wi 톱니바퀴 cog

mni moyang-ŭi 톱니 모양의
egged

mok kisa 토목 기사 civil engineer

n 톤 ton

tong 통 pack; tub; barrel; *t'ong*,
ubdivision of a city ◊ countword for
tters or documents

ngch'al 통찰 insight

ngch'allyŏk innŭn 통찰력 있는
erceptive, shrewd

ngch'ihada 통치하다 rule (of
onarch)

ngch'ija 통치자 ruler (of state)

ngdok'ada 통독하다 go through,
ead through

nggi 통기 ventilation

nggi kumŏng 통기 구멍 vent

nggŭnhada 통근하다 commute

nggŭnja 통근자 commuter

nggŭn kyot'ong 통근 교통
ommuter traffic

nggŭn yŏlch'a 통근 열차
ommuter train

nggwashik'ida 통과시키다 carry
roposal, approve

nggwa yŏgaek 통과 여객 transit
assenger

nggwa yŏgaek taehapsshil 통과
객 대합실 transit lounge

nggye 통계 statistics, figures ◊
atistical

nggyehak 통계학 statistics

nggyejŏguro 통계적으로
atistically

nghada 통하다 flow; be

understood; be versed in; go
through; open onto

t'onghae chinagada 통해 지나가다
pass through

t'onghaengin 통행인 passer-by

t'onghaengkkwŏn 통행권 right of
way

t'onghaengnyo 통행료 toll

t'onghaeng usŏnkkwŏn 통행 우선권
priority, right of way

t'onghap'ada 통합하다 integrate

t'onghwa 통화 currency; telephone
call

t'onghwa chaep'aengch'ang 통화
재팽창 reflation

t'onghwa chung shinho 통화중 신호
busy signal TELEC

t'onghwahada 통화하다 get through
TELEC

t'onghwajung-in 통화중인 busy
TELEC

t'onghwajung shinhoŭm 통화중
신호음 busy tone TELEC

t'onghwa p'aengch'angshik'ida
통화 팽창 시키다 inflate

t'onghwaryo 통화료 toll TELEC

t'ong-il 통일 unification;
reunification

t'ong-irhada 통일하다 unify

t'ongjang 통장 bank book, pass
book; head of a *t'ong*, subdivision of
a city

t'ongjehada 통제하다 control,
regulate; master; *uriga t'ongjehal
su ŏmnŭn sanghwang-ida* 우리가
통제할 수 없는 상황이다 these are
circumstances beyond our control

t'ongjeshil 통제실 control center

t'ongji 통지 notice (to leave job,
house); *nuguege chibŭl nagarago
t'ongjihada* 누구에게 집을 나가라고
통지하다 give s.o. his/her notice

t'ongjorim 통조림 can

t'ongjorimdoen 통조림된 canned

t'ongjorimhada 통조림 하다 can

t'ongmilppang 통밀빵 wholemeal
bread

t'ongnamu 통나무 log

t'ongnamu odumaktchip 통나무
오두막집 log cabin

t'ongno 통로 aisle; passageway;

gangway

t'ongnye통례 custom

t'ongnyeŭi통례의 customary

t'ongnyŏrhan통렬한 scathing

t'ongp'ung통풍 draft

t'ongp'ung-i chal toenŭn통풍이 잘 되는 drafty

t'ongshin통신 communications; telecommunications

t'ongshin p'anmae ch'aektcha통신 판매 책자 mail-order catalog

t'ongshin p'anmae hoesa통신 판매 회사 mail-order firm

t'ongshinsa통신사 news agency

t'ongshin wisŏng통신 위성 communications satellite

t'ongsollyŏk통솔력 leadership

t'ongsorhada통솔하다 lead

t'ongtchaero kuptta통째로 굽다 barbecue

t'ongt'onghada통통하다 be chubby

t'ongt'onghan통통한 chubby

t'ongyŏk통역 interpretation

t'ongyŏk-kka통역가 interpreter

t'ongyŏk'ada통역하다 interpret

t'onik wŏt'ŏ토닉 워터 tonic water

t'onŏ토너 toner

t'op톱 saw

t'opkkiŏ톱기어 top (gear)

t'op-ppap톱밥 sawdust

t'op'i토피 toffee

t'op'ing토핑 topping

t'op'ŭllisŭ토플리스 topless

t'oron토론 discussion, debate

t'osŭt'ŭ토스트 toast

t'oyoil토요일 Saturday

t'ŭda트다 open bank account; sprout (of seed)

t'ŭgi ch'ejil특이 체질 peculiarity

t'ŭgihan특이한 peculiar to

t'ŭgiŏptcha투기업자 speculator

t'ŭgyuŭi특유의 distinctive

t'ŭkch'urhan특출한 outstanding; high-powered

t'ŭk-kkwŏnŭl kajin특권을 가진 privileged

t'ŭkppyŏl chosadan특별 조사단 task force

t'ŭkppyŏl kwallamsŏk특별 관람석 grandstand

t'ŭkppyŏl poryuji특별 보류지

reservation (special area)

t'ŭkppyŏrhada특별하다 be specia

t'ŭkppyŏrhage특별하게 particula especially

t'ŭkppyŏrhan특별한 particular, special

t'ŭkppyŏrhan yeoeŭi특별한 예오 exceptional, special

t'ŭkppyŏrhi특별히 especially, in particular, particularly

t'ŭkp'awŏn특파원 (special) correspondent

t'ŭkssang-ŭi특상의 choice, top quality

t'ŭkssŏng특성 characteristic, tra special quality

t'ŭkssŏng-ŭl nat'anaeda특성을 나타내다 characterize, be typical

t'ŭkssŏng-ŭl nat'anaenŭn특성을 나타내는 characteristic, typical

t'ŭkssu kidongdae특수 기동대 taskforce

t'ŭktchil특질 idiosyncrasy

t'ŭktching특징 character, feature

...ŭl / rŭl t'ŭktching-ŭro hada ...을 / 를 특징으로 하다 make a feature of; emphasize

t'ŭktching-ŏmnŭn특징없는 nondescript

t'ŭktchŏn특전 privilege; preroga

t'ŭktchŏnghada특정하다 specify

t'ŭktchŏnghan특정한 particular, specific

t'ŭktchong특종 scoop (in journalism)

t'ŭkttaehyŏng-ŭi특대형의 outsiz

t'ŭk'i특히 especially; specifically

t'ŭk'i choahanŭn특히 좋아하는 favorite

t'ŭk'ŏ특허 patent

t'ŭk'ŏrŭl ŏt-tta특허를 얻다 pater

t'ŭl틀 frame; casing; mold

t'ŭlda틀다 put on, turn on

t'ŭlli틀니 false teeth

t'ŭllida틀리다 be wrong; go wron make a mistake

t'ŭllige틀리게 incorrectly

t'ŭllimŏmnŭn틀림없는 unmistakable

t'ŭllimŏptta틀림없다 must be; 6shiime t'ŭllimŏptta 6시임에

림없다 it must be about 6 o'clock;
ŭllimŏpsshi ...l kŏshida 틀림없이
ㄹ 것이다 be bound to, be sure to
llin 틀린 incorrect, wrong,
mistaken
llin koshi manŭn 틀린 곳이 많은
corrupt COMPUT
llin parŭm 틀린 발음
mispronunciation
llin parŭmŭl hada 틀린 발음을
다 mispronounce
m 틈 space; gap; opening; **kip'ŭn
ŭm** 깊은 틈 gulf
nt'ŭnhada 튼튼하다 be robust, be
healthy
nt'ŭnhan 튼튼한 healthy, robust,
solid
raek 트랙 track
raekt'ŏ 트랙터 tractor
raemp'ollin 트램폴린 trampoline
raenjisŭt'ŏ 트랜지스터 transistor
raenjisŭt'ŏ ladio 트랜지스터
디오 transistor radio
raiaenggŭl 트라이앵글 triangle
MUS
redŭ 트레드 tread (of tire)
reillŏ 트레일러 trailer
re kkiuda 틀에 끼우다 frame
re nŏŏ mandŭlda 틀에 넣어
들다 mold
rim 트림 belch
rimhada 트림하다 belch
rŏk 트럭 truck
rŏk unjŏnsa 트럭 운전사 truck
river, teamster
rŏ maktta 틀어 막다 plug hole
rŏmbon 트롬본 trombone
rŏmp'et 트럼펫 trumpet
rŏngk'ŭ 트렁크 trunk
rŏollin mŏri 틀어올린 머리 bun (in
air)
rol ŏsŏn 트롤 어선 trawler
win pedŭ 트윈 베드 twin beds
dŏlgŏrida 투덜거리다 grumble
gi 투기 speculation FIN; jealousy

t'ugihada 투기하다 speculate FIN
t'ugijŏk saŏp 투기적 사업 venture
t'uguhada 투구하다 pitch SP
t'ugwang chomyŏng 투광 조명
floodlight
t'uhahada 투하하다 jettison, throw
overboard; drop bomb
t'uip chŏnyŏlgi 투입 전열기
immersion heater
t'uja 투자 stake, investment
t'ujaeng 투쟁 fight, conflict
t'ujaengtchŏgin 투쟁적인 militant
t'ujahada 투자하다 invest
t'ujaja 투자자 investor
t'uk t'wiŏ naon 툭 튀어 나온
prominent
t'umyŏnghan 투명한 transparent
t'ungmyŏngsŭrŏptta 퉁명스럽다 be
curt, be blunt
t'ungmyŏngssŭrŏun 퉁명스러운
abrupt, curt
t'uok 투옥 imprisonment
t'uok'ada 투옥하다 imprison
t'up'isŭ 투피스 two-piece
t'up'yo 투표 vote; voting;
t'up'yokwŏnŭl kajida 투표권을
가지다 have the vote
t'up'yohada 투표하다 vote
t'up'yoro chŏnghada 투표로 정하다
ballot
t'usa 투사 militant
t'usu 투수 pitcher SP
t'usuk shigan 투숙 시간 check-in
time (at hotel)
t'wida 튀다 bounce; splash
t'wige hada 튀게 하다 bounce
t'wigida 튀기다 splatter; deep-fry
t'wigim 튀김 (deep) fried food
t'winggida 튕기다 twang
t'wiŏ naoda 튀어나오다 bulge,
project
t'yubŭ 튜브 tube
t'yubŭga ŏmnŭn 튜브가 없는
tubeless tire
t'yullip 튤립 tulip
t'yunŏ 튜너 tuner

Ŭ

ŭddŭm direkt'ori 으뜸 디렉터리 root directory

...ŭi ...의 of; kŭ ch'aŭi saek 그 차의 색 the color of the car

ŭi-ahage yŏgida 의아하게 여기다 wonder, think

ŭibok 의복 garment

ŭibudadŭl 의붓아들 stepson

ŭibut-tchamae 의붓자매 stepsister

ŭibut-ttal 의붓딸 stepdaughter

ŭibut'yŏngje 의붓형제 stepbrother

ŭibyŏng 의병 righteous army

ŭichimhaji annŭn 의심하지 않는 unsuspecting

ŭich'i 의치 dentures

ŭido 의도 intention

ŭidohada 의도하다 mean, intend; muŏsŭl ŭidohada 무엇을 의도하다 intend to do sth, do sth on purpose

ŭidojŏgin 의도적인 intentional

ŭigiyangyang 의기양양 elation

ŭigiyangyanghan 의기양양한 elated

ŭigushim 의구심 doubt, uncertainty; reservation

ŭigyŏn 의견 opinion; naŭi ŭigyŏnŭronŭn 나의 의견으로는 in my opinion

ŭigyŏn ch'ai 의견 차이 disagreement, misunderstanding

ŭigyŏni mat-tchi ant'a 의견이 맞지 않다 disagree with

ŭigyŏnŭl murŏboda 의견을 물어보다 canvass, seek opinion of

ŭigyŏnŭl mut-tta 의견을 묻다 consult, seek the advice of

ŭigyŏnŭl tallihada 의견을 달리하다 differ, differ from, disagree

ŭihae 의해 by

ŭihak 의학 medicine (science) ◊ medical

ŭihak paksa 의학 박사 MD, Doctor of Medicine

ŭihoe 의회 assembly; council; parliament

ŭihoeŭi 의회의 parliamentary

ŭija 의자 chair

ŭijang 의장 chairman, the chair

ŭijangjigŭl mat-tta 의장직을 맡다 chair; take the chair

ŭiji 의지 will, willpower

ŭijiga kanghan 의지가 강한 strong-willed

ŭijiga kudŭn 의지가 굳은 resolute

ŭijihada 의지하다 rely on, look to

ŭijiryŏk 의지력 willpower

ŭijŏrhada 의절하다 disown

ŭijonhada 의존하다 depend; muŏ ŭijonhada 무엇에 의존하다 depe on sth; nanŭn nŏhant'e ŭijonha it-tta 난 너한테 의존하고 있다 depend on you

ŭijonhanŭn 의존하는 dependant

ŭimi 의미 sense, meaning

ŭimihada 의미하다 signify, mean

ŭimiinnŭn 의미있는 meaningful, constructive

ŭimu 의무 duty; obligation; responsibility

ŭimujŏgin 의무적인 compulsory, mandatory

ŭimu kyoyuk 의무 교육 compulso education

ŭimun 의문 query

ŭimunsa 의문사 interrogative

ŭimunŭl chegihada 의문을 제기ha query

ŭimurŭl chiuda 의무를 지우다 bin oblige

ŭimuŭi 의무의 obligatory

ŭinonhada 의논하다 discuss, talk over, talk

ŭiroe 의뢰 commission (job)

ŭiroehada 의뢰하다 commission (j a job)

ŭiroein 의뢰인 client

ŭirye 의례 protocol, etiquette

ŭiryo pohŏm 의료 보험 medical insurance

ŭiryu 의류 clothing
ŭisa 의사 doctor
ŭisa chŏndal 의사 전달 communication
ŭisa kyŏltchŏngja 의사 결정자 decision-maker
ŭisang 의상 outfit, costume
ŭisa p'yoshi 의사 표시 gesture
ŭisarok 의사록 minutes (of meeting)
ŭisarŭl sot'onghada 의사를 통하다 communicate
ŭishigi innŭn 의식이 있는 conscious
ŭishigŭi 의식의 ritual
ŭishigŭl hoebok'ada 의식을 회복하다 come to, regain consciousness
ŭishigŭl ilt'a 의식을 잃다 lose consciousness, black out
ŭishik 의식 ritual, ceremony; consciousness
ŭishik sangshil 의식 상실 blackout
ŭishiktchŏgin 의식적인 conscious, deliberate
ŭishim 의심 suspicion, doubt
ŭishimhada 의심하다 doubt, question, suspect; *ŭishimhal yŏji ŏpsshi* 의심할 여지 없이 undoubtedly, indisputably
ŭishimŏmnŭn 의심없는 unquestioning
ŭishimsŭrŏpkke 의심스럽게 doubtfully
ŭishimsŭrŏptta 의심스럽다 be doubtful (of person)
ŭishimsŭrŏun 의심스러운 dubious; suspicious; questionable
ŭishimtchŏgŭn 의심쩍은 doubtful; in question; shady
ŭishimtchŏk-kke saenggak'ada 의심쩍게 생각하다 doubt
ŭisŏk 의석 seat POL
ŭiwŏn 의원 councilor
ŭiyok 의욕 will, motivation; *nanŭn pyŏllo ŭiyogi annanda* 나는 별로 의욕이 안난다 I don't feel very motivated
ŭkkaeda 으깨다 mash
ŭkkaen kamja 으깬 감자 mashed potatoes
...ŭl ...을 object particle; future particle
(ŭ)lsurok -(으)ㄹ수록 the more... the

---

more ...; *manŭlsurok chohayo* 많을수록 좋아요 the more the better
ŭmak 음악 music
ŭmak hak-kkyo 음악 학교 music school, conservatory
ŭmakkat'ŭn 음악같은 musical, melodious
ŭmak-kka 음악가 musician
ŭmaktchŏgin 음악적인 musical person
ŭmaktchŏk sojiri ŏmnŭn 음악적 소질이 없는 unmusical
ŭmban 음반 album
ŭmch'imhan 음침한 bleak, dingy
ŭmgŭgŭi 음극의 negative ELEC
ŭmgye 음계 scale MUS
ŭmgyŏng 음경 penis
ŭmhŏmhan 음험한 underhand, devious; insidious
ŭmhyanghak 음향학 acoustics
ŭmjŏl 음절 syllable
ŭmjŏng-i mannŭn 음정이 맞는 in tune
ŭmjŏng-i t'ŭllin 음정이 틀린 out of tune
ŭmju 음주 drinking
ŭmju ch'ŭktchŏnggi 음주 측정기 Breathalyzer®, breath analyzer
ŭmjuja 음주자 drinker
ŭmju unjŏn 음주 운전 drink driving
ŭmmi 음미 taste, savor
ŭmmihada 음미하다 taste, savor
ŭmmo 음모 conspiracy, intrigue; pubic hair
ŭmmohada 음모하다 plot
ŭmmoja 음모자 conspirator
ŭmmorŭl kkumida 음모를 꾸미다 conspire
ŭmnanhada 음란하다 be obscene
ŭmnanhan 음란한 dirty; obscene; pornographic
ŭmnyang 음량 volume
ŭmnyang 음양 yin and yang
ŭmnyang chojŏlgi 음량 조절기 volume control
ŭmnyŏk 음역 range
ŭmnyŏk 음력 lunar calendar
ŭmnyŏk'ada 음역하다 transliterate
ŭmnyo 음료 beverage, drink
ŭmp'yo 음표 note MUS
ŭmsaek 음색 tone

ŭmsanhan 음산한 dismal

ŭmshik 음식 food

ŭmsŏng up'yŏn 음성 우편 voice mail

ŭn 은 silver

...ŭn... 은 → nŭn 는

ŭnbang-ul kkot 은방울 꽃 lily of the valley

ŭnch'ong 은총 blessing

ŭndunja 은둔자 recluse, hermit

ŭndunsaenghwal 은둔생활 secluded life

ŭngch'uk 응축 condensation

ŭngch'uk'ada 응축하다 condense

ŭngdal 응달 shade; ŭngdare(sŏ) 응달에(서) in the shade

ŭngdap 응답 answer

ŭngdap'ada 응답하다 answer

ŭnggohada 응고하다 set, congeal; curdle

ŭnggoshik'ida 응고시키다 coagulate

ŭnggŭp ch'iryo 응급 치료 first aid

ŭnghada 응하다 comply; comply with; k'waehi ŭnghada 쾌히 응하다 jump at, take eagerly

ŭngmoja 응모자 applicant

ŭngmojak 응모작 entry (for competition)

ŭngmo sŏryu 응모 서류 entry form

ŭngnak 응낙 compliance

ŭn-goe 은괴 silver ingot

ŭngshi 응시 gaze

ŭngshihada 응시하다 gaze; gaze at; contemplate

ŭngshija 응시자 entrant, candidate

ŭn-gŭnhi 은근히 politely; secretly; ...ranŭn ŭishimŭl ŭn-gŭnhi kajida ...라는 의심을 은근히 가지다 have a sneaking suspicion that

ŭng-wŏnhada 응원하다 cheer on

ŭngyong p'ŭrogŭraem 응용 프로그램 application (program)

ŭnhaeng 은행 bank

ŭnhaeng chan-go 은행 잔고 bank balance

ŭnhaengga 은행가 banker

ŭnhaeng t'ongjang 은행 통장 bank book

ŭnhaeng yungja 은행 융자 bank loan

ŭnhye 은혜 obligation, moral indebtedness; nuguege ŭnhyerŭl ipkko it-tta 누구에게 은혜를 입고 있다 be under an obligation to s.o.

ŭnhyerŭl pep'unŭn saram 은혜를 베푸는 사람 benefactor

...(ŭ)nji ...(으)ㄴ지 → ...inji ...인지

ŭnjong-i 은종이 tinfoil

ŭnmirhi 은밀히 secretly

ŭnnik 은닉 secretion, concealment

ŭnnik'ada 은닉하다 conceal, hide; chiharo ŭnnik'ada 지하로 은닉하다 go underground

ŭnŏ 은어 slang

ŭnppich'ŭi 은빛의 silver

ŭnp'ye 은폐 cover-up

ŭnshinch'ŏ 은신처 hideaway

ŭnshinhada 은신하다 be in hiding

ŭn togŭmhan 은 도금한 silver-plated

ŭnt'oe 은퇴 retirement

ŭnt'oehada 은퇴하다 retire

ŭnt'oehan 은퇴한 retired

ŭp 읍 large township

...ŭro ...으로 by; from, because of; c into; in; with; to; toward

...ŭrobut'ŏ ...으로부터 from

...ŭrosŏ ...으로서 as

ŭrŭrŏnggŏrida 으르렁거리다 growl snarl

~hada 우아하다 be graceful; be elegant
~han 우아한 graceful; elegant
~ak 우박 hail
~oi 우비 raincoat
~chahyŏng k'ŏbŭ U자형 커브 hairpin curve
~ch'ebu 우체부 mailman
~ch'eguk 우체국 post office
~ch'et'ong 우체통 mailbox
~ch'ŭgŭi 우측의 starboard; right
~ch'ŭk haendŭl unjŏn 우측 핸들 운전 right-hand drive
~ch'ŭk konggyŏkssu 우측 공격수 right wing
~daehanŭn 우대하는 preferential
~dumŏri 우두머리 head; boss; leader
~dunhan 우둔한 dense, dim, stupid
~gŏjin 우거진 dense foliage
~gŭlgŏrida 우글거리다 swarm, crowd
~hoe 우회 detour, diversion
~hoehada 우회하다 bypass, circumvent
~hoero 우회로 bypass
~hoeshik'ida 우회시키다 divert
~hoeŭi 우회의 roundabout
~hojŏgin 우호적인 amicable
~igŭi 우익의 right-wing
~ik 우익 right, right wing; **uige(sŏ)** 우익에(서) on the right
~ik chijija 우익 지지자 right winger
~jŏkujŏk sshiptta 우적우적 씹다 munch
~jŏng 우정 friendship
~ju 우주 space, outer space; universe
~jubok 우주복 spacesuit
~ju chŏnggŏjang 우주 정거장 space station
~juin 우주인 astronaut
~ju pihaengsa 우주 비행사 cosmonaut
~jusŏn 우주선 spaceship, spacecraft
~ju wangbokssŏn 우주 왕복선 space shuttle

ujuyŏhaeng 우주여행 voyage (*in space*)
ulbujit-tta 울부짖다 howl, wail
ulch'anghage charada 울창하게 자라다 thrive
ulda 울다 weep, cry; bawl, bellow
ullida 울리다 go off (*of alarm*); blow; ring; honk
ullim 울림 ring (*of bell*); roll (*of thunder*); echo
Ullŭngdo 울릉도 Ullung Island
ullyŏ p'ŏjida 울려 퍼지다 echo, reverberate; blare out
ultchŏk'ada 울적하다 be melancholy
ult'ari 울타리 fence; railings; hedge; barrier
ult'ariro tullŏ ssada 울타리로 둘러 싸다 fence in
ult'ungbult'unghada 울퉁불퉁하다 be bumpy
ult'ungbult'unghan 울퉁불퉁한 rough; bumpy; lumpy
umch'ŭrida 움츠리다 cower
umch'urida 움추리다 curl up
umjigida 움직이다 move, budge; dislodge; operate, run
umjigim 움직임 motion; move; movement; maneuver
umjiginŭn 움직이는 moving (*which can move*)
umk'yŏjaptta 움켜잡다 grasp
ummorŭl kkumida 움모를 꾸미다 frame, set up
ump'uk kkŏjida 움푹 꺼지다 cave in
ump'uk tŭrŏgage hada 움푹 들어가게 하다 dent
ump'uk tŭrŏgan 움푹 들어간 hollow
umtchirhada 움찔하다 flinch
umul 우물 well
un 운 luck, fortune; rhyme; **une matkkigo haeboda** 운에 맡기고 해보다 take a chance; **uni chot'a** 운이 좋다 be lucky, luck out; **uni mat-tta** 운이 맞다 rhyme with

unban 운반 haulage
unbanhada 운반하다 convey, carry
unbanin 운반인 porter
unban sudan 운반 수단 vehicle
un chok'e 운 좋게 luckily
un choŭn 운 좋은 lucky
undong 운동 campaign, drive; movement; exercise ◊ sporting, athletic
undongga 운동가 athlete; campaigner
undonggyŏnggi 운동경기 athletics
undonghada 운동하다 exercise, take exercise; work out; play SP
undonghwa 운동화 sneakers
undongjang 운동장 arena
undong pujogin 운동 부족인 unfit
undongshik'ida 운동시키다 exercise
undong-ŭl hada 운동을 하다 campaign
ungbyŏn-ga 웅변가 speaker, orator
ungdaehan 웅대한 epic; tremendous; impressive; majestic
ungdŏng-i 웅덩이 pool; puddle
ungjanghada 웅장하다 be grand
ungjanghan 웅장함 grandeur
ungjanghan 웅장한 grand
ungk'ŭrida 웅크리다 stoop, bend down
unha 운하 canal
unhaengdoeda 운행되다 run (of trains etc)
unim mit pohŏm p'oham kagyŏk 운임 및 보험 포함 가격 CIF, cost insurance freight
unjŏn 운전 drive; driving
unjŏnhada 운전하다 drive
unjŏn hagwŏn 운전 학원 driving school
unjŏnja 운전자 driver; motorist
unjŏn kyoyuk 운전 교육 driving lesson
unjŏn kyoyuk kangsa 운전 교육 강사 driving instructor
unjŏn myŏnhŏ shihŏm 운전 면허 시험 driving test
unjŏn myŏnhŏtchŭng 운전 면허증 driver's license
unjŏntae 운전대 steering column
unmyŏng 운명 fate, destiny
unmyŏng chiuda 운명 지우다 condemn

unmyŏng yejŏngsŏl 운명 예정설 predestination
unŏmnŭn 운없는 unlucky, unfortunate
unŏpkke 운없게 unluckily
unsŏk 운석 meteorite
unsong hoesa 운송 회사 carrier, haulage company
unsuŏptcha 운수업자 forwarding agent
unttaega mannŭn 운때가 맞는 luc
unyŏng 운영 operations
unyŏngdoeda 운영되다 operate
unyŏnghada 운영하다 run, manage
up'yŏn 우편 mail ◊ postal; *muŏsŭl up'yŏnŭro ponaeda* 무엇을 우편으로 보내다 put sth in the mai
up'yŏnham 우편함 mailbox
up'yŏnhwan 우편환 money order
up'yŏn pŏnho 우편 번호 zip code
up'yŏn yogŭm 우편 요금 postage
up'yo 우표 stamp
uranyum 우라늄 uranium
uri 우리 we; us ◊ cage; pen; pound
uri chashin 우리 자신 ourselves; *uri chashinŭro* 우리 자신으로 by ourselves; *urikkiriŭi yaegiijiman* 우리끼리의 얘기이지만 between yc and me
urida 우리다 infuse
uriŭi 우리의 our; my
uriŭi kŏt 우리의 것 ours; mine
urŏnada 우러나다 well up; soak out *chinshimesŏ urŏnan* 진심에서 우러난 heartfelt
urŭmŭl t'ŏttŭrida 울음을 터뜨리다 burst into tears
urŭrunggŏrida 우르릉거리다 roar
ururu taranada 우루루 달아나다 stampede
ururu taranam 우루루 달아남 stampede
uryang chushik 우량 주식 blue chip
uryangju 우량주 gilts
uryŏhada 우려하다 worry
usan 우산 umbrella
usang 우상 idol
use 우세 domination, superiority
usehan 우세한 prevailing
usŏn 우선 firstly

ŏng-ŭi 우성의 dominant

ŏn-gwŏnŭl chuda 우선권을 주다
 ve preference to

ŏnhada 우선하다 take precedence;
 ake precedence over

ŏnkkwŏni it-tta 우선권이 있다
 ave priority

ŏnkkwŏnŭl chuda 우선권을 주다
 rioritize, give priority to

ŏn sunwirŭl maegida 우선 순위를
 기다 prioritize, put in order of
 riority

ŏnŭn 우선은 first of all

ŏsŭl pŏtkko 웃옷을 벗고 in his
 hirt sleeves

ŭgae sori 우스개 소리 joke

ŭkkwangsŭrŏun 우스꽝스러운
 omical

ŭl iri anida 웃을 일이 아니다 it's
 o joke

ŭm 웃음 laugh; laughter

ŭmkkŏriga toeda 웃음거리가 되다
 ake a fool of oneself, become a
 ughing stock

ŭmŭl chaanaenŭn 웃음을
 아내는 hilarious

ŭngja 우승자 winner

ŭngk'ŏp 우승컵 trophy, cup

ŭngp'ae 우승패 shield, trophy

ŭpkkedo 우습게도 funnily enough

ŭpkke yŏgida 우습게 여기다 jeer

ŭptta 우습다 be funny

ŭun 우스운 funny, humorous

ŭchuldaenŭn 우쭐대는 big-headed

ŭkkida 웃기다 amuse

ŭkige 웃기게 comically

ŭkinŭn chit 웃기는 짓 farce

ŭkinŭn nom 웃기는 놈 joker,
 omedian, clown pej

ŭchuldaeda 우쭐대다 show off pej

ut-tta 웃다 laugh

uul 우울 gloom

uultchŭng 우울증 depression

uultchŭng hwanja 우울증 환자
 hypochondriac

uurhada 우울하다 be gloomy

uurhaehada 우울해하다 depress, get
 down; mope

uurhagehada 우울하게하다 depress,
 get down

uurhagehanŭn 우울하게하는
 depressing; oppressive

uurhan 우울한 depressed; gloomy;
 morose

uusorirŭl naeda 우우소리를 내다
 hoot

uyŏn 우연 chance, luck

uyŏnhada 우연하다 be accidental

uyŏnhan 우연한 casual; accidental;
 chance

uyŏnhan mannam 우연한 만남
 chance encounter

uyŏnhan sakkŏn 우연한 사건
 accident

uyŏnhi 우연히 by accident, by chance

uyŏnhi irŏnanŭn 우연히 일어나는
 incidental

uyŏnhi majuch'ida 우연히 마주치다
 meet by chance

uyŏnhi mannada 우연히 만나다
 bump into, meet by chance, run
 across

uyŏnhi palgyŏnhada 우연히
 발견하다 happen across, find by
 chance

uyŏnhi tŭt-tta 우연히 듣다 overhear

uyŏnŭi ilch'i 우연의 일치
 coincidence

uyu 우유 milk

uyubudan 우유부단 indecisiveness

uyubyŏng 우유병 bottle (for baby)

W

...wa ...와 and
wa! 와! wow!
wae 왜 why, what for; what is it?;
  wae andwae? 왜 안돼? why not?
waegari 왜가리 heron
waegŏn 왜건 station wagon
waegokttoen shigandae 왜곡된
  시간대 timewarp
waegok'ada 왜곡하다 distort
Waegu 왜구 Japanese marauders
waenyahamyŏn ...ki ttaemunida
  왜냐하면 ...기 때문이다 as, because
waip'ŏ 와이퍼 windshield wiper
waip'ŭ 와이프 wife
wajak-wajak soriga nada 와작와작
  소리가 나다 crunch
wakssŭ 왁스 wax
walch'ŭ 왈츠 waltz
wallyohyŏng 완료형 perfect GRAM
wanbyŏk 완벽 perfection
wanbyŏkjuŭija 완벽주의자
  perfectionist
wanbyŏk'ada 완벽하다 be perfect
wanbyŏk'age 완벽하게 perfectly;
  impeccably; soundly *beaten*; *muŏsŭl
  wanbyŏk'age alda* 무엇을 완벽하게
  알다 know sth inside out
wanbyŏk'an 완벽한 perfect;
  impeccable
wanbyŏk'i 완벽히 perfectly
wanch'ung changch'i 완충 장치
  buffer
wanch'unggi 완충기 shock absorber
wanch'ung kiŏk changch'i 완충
  기억 장치 memory buffer
wanch'ungnyŏk 완충역 buffer
wanduk'ong 완두콩 pea
wang 왕 king
wan-ganghada 완강하다 be
  stubborn, be dogged
wan-ganghan 완강한 determined,
  tenacious; stubborn
wangbok pihaenggi 왕복 비행기
  return flight

wangbok yŏhaeng 왕복 여행 rou
  trip
wangbok yŏhaengp'yo 왕복 여행
  round trip ticket
wangbok'ada 왕복하다 shuttle
wangguk 왕국 kingdom
wanggwan 왕관 crown
wangja 왕자 prince
wangjo 왕조 dynasty
wangjok 왕족 royalty
wangjwa 왕좌 throne
wan-gogŏ 완곡어 euphemism
wan-gohan 완고한 inflexible, rigi
  headstrong; pigheaded
wangsŏnghada 왕성하다 be heart
wangsŏnghan 왕성한 hearty;
  voracious
wang-wie ollida 왕위에 올리다
  crown
wanhwahada 완화하다 soften,
  cushion
wanhwashik'ida 완화시키다 relax
wanje 완제 wipe out
wanjep'um 완제품 end product
wanjŏnhada 완전하다 be perfect, b
  complete
wanjŏnhage 완전하게 perfectly,
  totally
wanjŏnhan 완전한 complete,
  thorough; pure; outright
wanjŏnhi 완전히 purely, nothing b
  absolutely, completely; entirely
  fully; outright *win*
wanjŏnhi chami kkaen 완전히 잠
  깬 wide awake
wanjŏnhi kkŭnnaeda 완전히 끝내
  terminate
wanjŏnhi mach'ida 완전히 마치다
  complete
wanjŏnhi mich'in 완전히 미친
  raving mad
wanjŏnhi pusuda 완전히 부수다
  completely destroy, wipe out
wanjŏnhi p'agoehada 완전히

...괴하다 obliterate

ank'waehada완쾌하다 make a
omplete recovery

anmanhan완만한 sluggish

anp'aeshik'ida완패시키다 bomb

ansŏng완성 completion

ansŏngdoen완성된 complete,
inished

ansŏnghada완성하다 complete

ap'ŭl와플 waffle

ashyŏ와셔 washer

atta katta hada왔다 갔다 하다
ace up and down

aebburaujŏ웹브라우저 web browser

eding k'eik'ŭ웨딩 케이크 wedding
cake

eding tŭresŭ웨딩 드레스 wedding
dress

eilju웨일즈 Wales ◊ Welsh

eip'ŏ웨이퍼 wafer

eit'ŏ웨이터 waiter

eit'ŭrisŭ웨이트리스 waitress

ep웹 the Web

ep p'eiji웹 페이지 web page

ep sa-it'ŭ웹 사이트 web site

i위 upper side; top; superiority;
rank; position; stomach ◊ gastric ◊
over, above

ian위안 comfort, consolation

ianhada위안하다 comfort, console

iban위반 violation, breach

ibanhada위반하다 break, violate,
contravene

ibŏp위법 offense ◊ illicit

ivich'i위치 position, location, setting;
situation

vich'ihada위치하다 lie, be situated,
be located; stand

vich'irŭl aranaeda위치를 알아내다
locate

vich'irŭl chŏnghada위치를 정하다
locate, site

vich'i sŏnjŏng위치 선정 location,
siting

vich'ŭng-e위층에 upstairs, on the
floor above

vich'ŭng-ŭi위층의 upstairs

vidaehada위대하다 be great

vidaeham위대함 greatness

vidaehan위대한 grand

wido위도 latitude; parallel

widok'ada위독하다 be critically ill

widok'an위독한 critical; critically ill

wie위에 up; above; on top of;
hanŭl/chibung wie 하늘/지붕 위에
up in the sky/up on the roof

wigi위기 crisis; *...a(ŏ, yŏ)ya hal
wigie mollyŏ it-tta* ...아(어, 여)야
할 위기에 몰려있다 be under
pressure to ...

wigie ch'ŏhada위기에 처하다 be at
stake, be at risk

wigijŏgin위기적인 critical, serious

wihae위해 for; *...gi wihae* ...기 위해
to, in order to; *...gi wihayŏ* ...기
위하여 in order to; *...ŭl/rŭl wihaesŏ* ...을/를 위해서 for the sake
of ...

wihan위한 for; *igŏsŭn nŏrŭl wihan
kŏshida* 이것은 너를 위한 것이다
this is for you

wihayŏ위하여 on behalf of; for the
sake of; in favor of

wihŏm위험 risk, chance; danger,
peril; *wihŏmŭl murŭpssŭda* 위험을
무릅쓰다 take a risk; *wihŏme
ppajige hada* 위험에 빠지게 하다
endanger

wihŏmhada위험하다 be dangerous

wihŏmhan위험한 risky, dangerous;
hazardous; treacherous

wihŏm inmul위험 인물 menace;
security risk (*person*)

wihŏmjidae위험 지대 minefield

wihŏm yoso위험 요소 hazard

wihyŏp위협 threat, menace

wihyŏp'ada위협하다 threaten,
menace, terrorize

wihyŏp'anŭn위협하는 threatening,
menacing

wiim위임 delegation

wiimhada위임하다 delegate

wiimkkwŏn위임권 power of
attorney

wijak위작 forgery (*painting*)

wijang위장 disguise, camouflage;
insides

wijanghada위장하다 disguise,
camouflage; impersonate

wijaryo위자료 alimony

wijo위조 forgery

wijo chip'ye 위조 지폐 forged bill, dud

wijodoen sŏryu 위조된 서류 forgery

wijohada 위조하다 falsify; forge, counterfeit

wijoja 위조자 forger

wijop'um 위조품 forgery

wijoŭi 위조의 counterfeit

wijŭng 위증 perjury

wijŭnghada 위증하다 perjure oneself

windou 윈도우 window COMPUT

windŭsŏp'ing 윈드서핑 windsurfing, sailboarding

windŭsŏp'ing podŭ 윈드서핑 보드 windsurfer, sailboard

wingk'ŭ 윙크 wink

wingk'ŭhada 윙크하다 wink

wing-winggŏrida 윙윙거리다 hum

wing-winghanŭn sori 윙윙하는 소리 buzz, drone

wingwing sorirŭl naeda 윙윙 소리를 내다 buzz

wingwing tolda 윙윙 돌다 whirr

wiŏmminnŭn 위엄있는 dignified, majestic

wiŏp 위업 exploit, feat

wiro 위로 up, upward ◊ consolation

wirohada 위로하다 console

wirohal kil ŏmnŭn 위로할 길 없는 inconsolable

wiro ollida 위로 올리다 scroll up

wiro tŏnjida 위로 던지다 throw up ball

wiro unbanhada 위로 운반하다 take up, carry up

wisaeng 위생 hygiene ◊ sanitary

wisaengch'ŏri 위생처리 sanitation

wisaengjŏgin 위생적인 sanitary

wisaengsang-ŭi 위생상의 hygienic

wisaengsŏlbi 위생설비 sanitation, sanitary installation

wishŏme ppattŭrida 위험에 빠뜨리다 risk

wisŏn 위선 hypocrisy

wisŏng t'ibŭi 위성 티브이 satellite TV

wisŏnja 위선자 hypocrite

wisŏnjŏgin 위선적인 hypocritical

wisŭk'i 위스키 whiskey

wit'aeroptta 위태롭다 be in jeopardy

wit'aeroun 위태로운 dangerous

wit'ak 위탁 consignment; trust FIN

witchoge 위쪽에 at the top of

wi tchogŭi 위 쪽의 upper

witppubun 윗부분 top

witssaram 윗사람 superior

wittchari 윗자리 superior position: **Xboda wittcharie innŭn** X보다 윗자리에 있는 be senior to X

wiŭi 위의 upper

wiwŏndan 위원단 panel, committee

wiwŏnhoe 위원회 committee, commission

wŏdŭ p'ŭrosesŏ 워드 프로세서 word processor

wŏdŭ p'ŭrosesŭrŭl sayong 워드 프로세스를 사용 word processing

wŏk'ŭmaen 워크맨 Walkman®

wŏk'ŭshyop 워크숍 workshop

wŏl 월 month; moon

wŏlbu 월부 monthly installment

Wŏldŭwaidŭwep 월드와이드웹 World Wide Web

wŏlganji 월간지 monthly (magazin

wŏlgŭp 월급 wage; salary

wŏlgŭp pongt'u 월급 봉투 wage packet

wŏlgyesu 월계수 laurel

wŏlgyŏng 월경 menstruation

wŏlgyŏnghada 월경하다 menstrua

wŏllae 원래 originally

wŏllyo 원료 raw materials

Wŏlnam 월남 Vietnam ◊ Vietname

Wŏlnamin 월남인 Vietnamese

Wŏlnamŏ 월남어 Vietnamese (language)

wŏlsshik 월식 eclipse of the moon

Wŏl Sŭt'ŭrit'ŭ 월 스트리트 Wall Street

wŏn 원 circle; won FIN

wŏnban 원반 discus (object)

wŏnbanhyŏng 원반형 disk (shape)

wŏnban tŏnjigi 원반 던지기 discus (event)

wŏnbon 원본 original manuscript

Wŏnbulgyo 원불교 Won Buddhism

wŏnch'ik 원칙 principle, rule; **wŏnch'iktchŏgŭro** 원칙적으로 in principle, in theory

wŏnch'ŏn 원천 source

wŏndongnyŏk 원동력 dynamism

wŏn-giwangsŏnghan 원기왕성한

vely, sprightly; forceful

ŏn-göri 원거리 long-range

ŏn-go 원고 claimant, plaintiff; manuscript

ŏn-gwang 원광 halo

ŏnhada 원하다 want, desire; *...ŭl / rŭl wŏnhamnikka?* ...을 / 를 원합니까? would you like ...?

ŏnhan 원한 rancor; *nuguege sain wŏnhanŭl p'ulda* 누구에게 진 원한을 풀다 have a score to settle with s.o.

ŏnhyŏng 원형 circle, ring; prototype

ŏnin 원인 cause; *...ŭihan wŏnini öeda* ...의한 원인이 되다 contribute to

ŏnin kyumyŏng 원인 규명 inquest

ŏnja 원자 atom ◊ atomic

ŏnjak 원작 original *painting etc*

ŏnja p'okt'an 원자 폭탄 atom bomb

ŏnjaro 원자로 nuclear reactor

ŏnjaryŏk 원자력 nuclear power, atomic energy

ŏnjaryŏk paltchŏnso 원자력 발전소 nuclear power station

ŏnjŏng shihap 원정 시합 away game

ŏnjohada 원조하다 assist; *kyŏng-ejŏgŭro wŏnjohada* 경제적으로 원조하다 stake, help financially

ŏnju 원주 circumference

ŏnjumin 원주민 native

ŏnkka 원가 cost, cost price

ŏnkkŭbŭi 원급의 positive GRAM

wŏnkkyŏk chŏpkkŭn 원격 접근 remote access

wŏnkkyŏk chojong 원격 조종 remote control

wŏnmang 원망 resentment

wŏnmanghada 원망하다 resent; bear a grudge; *Xttaemune Yŭl / rŭl wŏnmanghada* X때문에 Y을 / 를 원망하다 hold X against Y

wŏnmanhage haegyŏrhada 원만하게 해결하다 smooth things over

wŏnŏmin 원어민 native speaker

wŏnppul 원뿔 cone

wŏnshijŏgin 원시적인 primitive

wŏnshiŭi 원시의 primitive; far-sighted

wŏnso 원소 element

wŏnsu 원수 enemy

wŏnsuk'ada 원숙하다 mellow

wŏnsuk'an 원숙한 mellow

wŏnsung-i 원숭이 monkey

wŏntchang 원장 ledger

wŏntchŏm 원점 original point, square one; *urinŭn wŏntchŏmŭro torawat-tta* 우리는 원점으로 돌아왔다 we're back to square one

wŏnyang 원양 deep-sea, ocean ◊ ocean-going

wŏnye 원예 gardening; horticulture

wŏnyu 원유 crude (oil)

wŏnt'ong 원통 cylinder

wŏnt'ong moyang-ŭi 원통 모양의 cylindrical

wŏryoil 월요일 Monday

Wŏshingt'ŏn 워싱턴 Washington

XY

Xsŏn 선 X-ray (*picture*)
Xsŏn ch'waryŏng-ŭl hada 선
촬영을 하다 X-ray *patient*

yabihan nom 야비한 놈 jerk
yach'ae 야채 vegetable
yadanbŏpsŏgŭl p'iuda 야단법석을
피우다 play up (*of child*)
yadang 야당 opposition
yadŭ 야드 yard
yagan hak-kkyo 야간 학교 night
school
yagan kŭnmu 야간 근무 night shift
yagan kŭnmuida 야간 근무이다
work nights
yagan oech'ul kŭmji 야간 외출 금지
curfew
yagan suŏp 야간 수업 evening
classes
yagihada 야기하다 create, bring
about, produce, generate
yagishik'ida 야기시키다 precipitate,
cause to happen
yagŭn poi 야근 보이 night porter
yagu 야구 ball game, baseball
yagugong 야구공 baseball (*ball*)
yagujang 야구장 ballpark
yagu kŭllŏbŭ 야구 글러브 baseball
glove
yagu moja 야구 모자 baseball cap
yagu pangmang-i 야구 방망이
baseball bat
yagu sŏnsu 야구 선수 baseball
player
yagyŏngkkun 야경군 watchman
yagyong-ŭi 약용의 medicated
yahan 야한 gaudy; vulgar
yahoebok 야회복 evening dress; suit
yajanamu 야자나무 palm (tree)
yak 약 medicine; medication; drug ◊
in the region of, around; **yak 5,000
tallŏ** 약 5,000 달러 in the region of
$5,000; **yak ...tchŭm** 약 ...쯤 around
(*with expressions of time*); **yagŭl**

mŏgida 약을 먹이다 give medici
yakkan 약간 drop, dash, touch ◊
slightly, vaguely
yakkanŭi 약간의 slight, small
yak-kkuk 약국 pharmacy
yak-kkwan 약관 (insurance) polic
yakssa 약사 druggist, pharmacist
yaksshigŭi 약식의 informal
yaksshik 약식 informality
yaksshik ch'ayong chŭngsŏ 약식
차용 증서 IOU
yaksshik yahoebok 약식 야회복
dinner jacket, tuxedo
yakssok 약속 promise, undertakir
engagement, appointment
yakssok changso 약속 장소
meeting place
yakssok'ada 약속하다 promise,
pledge; *naega*
yakssok'agessumnida 내가
약속하겠습니다 you have my wor
yaktcha 약자 weakling; underdog
monogram; abbreviation
yaktchaga saegyŏjin 약자가 새겨
monogrammed
yaktchang 약장 medicine cabinet
yaktchin 약진 tremor
yaktchŏm 약점 weakness, weak
point
yakt'alp'um 약탈품 loot
yakt'altcha 약탈자 looter
yakt'arhada 약탈하다 loot
yak'ada 약하다 be weak; have a
weakness for; abridge; omit
yak'aejida 약해지다 weaken
yak'aejinŭn 약해지는 ailing
yak'agehada 약하게 하다 weaker
yak'an 약한 weak, frail; flimsy;
muted
yak'on 약혼 engagement
yak'onhada 약혼하다 get engaged
yak'onhan 약혼한 engaged
yak'onja 약혼자 fiancé
yak'onnyŏ 약혼녀 fiancée

k'on panji 약혼 반지 engagement
ing
k'wadoeda 악화되다 go downhill
(of health); slacken off
k'washik'ida 악화시키다 sap
lbda 얇다 be thin
lbŭn 얇은 thin, flimsy
lbŭn p'anyuri 얇은 판유리
aminated glass
lkke charŭda 얇게 자르다 slice
mang 야망 ambition
mjŏnhada 얌전하다 be meek; be
entle; be nice
mjŏnhan 얌전한 meek; gentle;
ice
ng 양 Ms; quantity, amount, level;
heep; tripe; *Kim yang* 김 양 Miss
Kim
ngbaech'u 양배추 cabbage
ngban 양반 aristocrat
ngbanghyang t'onghaengno
양방향 통행로 two-way traffic
ngbo 양보 concession, giving in
ngbohada 양보하다 give way,
ield; back down, climb down;
oncede
ngbok 양복 suit (*man's*)
ngbok chokki 양복 조끼 vest
ngbumo 양부모 foster parents
ngbunhwahada 양분화하다
olarize
ngch'iaek 양치액 mouthwash
ngch'ijirhada 양치질하다 brush
eeth
ngch'iryu 양치류 fern
ngch'o 양초 candle
ngdohada 양도하다 transfer
ngdong-i 양동이 bucket, pail
nggaguro 양각으로 in relief
nggajuk 양가죽 sheepskin
nggogi 양고기 lamb
nggŭgŭi 양극의 positive
nggwibi 양귀비 poppy
nghoshil 양호실 infirmary
ngjaesa 양재사 dressmaker
ngjohada 양조하다 brew
ngjojang 양조장 brewery
ngjoŏptcha 양조업자 brewer
ngmal 양말 sock
ngmo 양모 wool
ngnip'ada 양립하다 coexist; be

compatible
yangnowŏn 양로원 nursing home
yangnyŏm 양념 spice, seasoning;
relish; sauce
yangnyŏmtchang 양념장 dip
yangnyŏp'e kŏnŭrida 양옆에
거느리다 be flanked by
yangnyŏp'e tuda 양옆에 두다 be
flanked by
yangnyuk-kkwŏn 양육권 custody
yangnyuk'ada 양육하다 bring up
child
yangp'a 양파 onion
yangshik 양식 form, document;
pattern (*in behavior*); style;
Western-style food; food ◊ Western-
style
yangshik'wahada 양식화하다
format, lay out
yangshim 양심 conscience; *...e
taehae yangshimŭi kach'aegŭl
pat-tchi ant'a* ...에 대해 양심의
가책을 받지 않다 have no qualms
about ...
yangshimjŏgin 양심적인
conscientious
yangshimjŏgŭro 양심적으로
religiously, conscientiously
yangshimtchŏk pyŏngnyŏk kŏbuja
양심적 병역 거부자 conscientious
objector
yangshimŭi kach'aek 양심의 가책
qualm; guilty conscience
yangsŏng-aeja 양성애자 bisexual
yangsŏng-ŭi 양성의 positive; benign;
bisexual
yangtchok 양쪽 both; both sides
yang-ŭl chaeda 양을 재다 quantify
yaoe 야외 the open air ◊ outdoor,
open-air; *yaoe ch'waryŏngjung*
야외 촬영중 on location
yaoeesŏ 야외에서 outdoors, in the
open air
yaong 야옹 miaow
yasaeng 야생 wild
yasaeng tongmul 야생 동물 wildlife
yashiminnŭn 야심있는 ambitious
yat-tta 얕다 be shallow; be
superficial; be low
yatchababonŭn 얕잡아보는
contemptuous

yat'ŭn 얕은 shallow, superficial

yawida 야위다 waste away

yayŏngji 야영지 campsite, camp ground

yayu 야유 jeer

yayuhada 야유하다 jeer; heckle; boo

yayurŭl ponaeda 야유를 보내다 hiss

ye 예 example, instance; old times; ceremony; courtesy; salute; bow ◊ yes; *choŭn / nappŭn yega toeda* 좋은 / 나쁜 예가 되다 set a good / bad example

yebaedang 예배당 chapel

yebang 예방 prevention; precaution

yebang chŏptchong 예방 접종 vaccination, inoculation; *... yebang chŏptchong chusarŭl mat-tta* ... 예방 접종 주사를 맞다 be vaccinated against

yebang chŏptchonghada 예방 접종하다 vaccinate, inoculate

yebanghada 예방하다 ward off

yebang-ŭi 예방의 preventive, precautionary

yebihada 예비하다 anticipate

yebi kyehoek 예비 계획 pilot scheme

yebi pak'wi 예비 바퀴 spare wheel

yebip'um 예비품 spare (part)

yebisŏn-gŏ 예비선거 primary POL

yebi t'aiŏ 예비 타이어 spare tire

yebiŭi 예비의 preliminary; spare

yebok 예복 robe (of priest)

yech'ŭk'al su ŏmnŭn 예측할 수 없는 unpredictable

yegam 예감 premonition; hunch; idea

yegihada 예기하다 expect, anticipate

yegop'yŏn 예고편 trailer (of movie)

yegŭm 예금 savings; deposit; *yegŭmi it-tta* 예금이 있다 be in credit

yegŭmaek 예금액 credit (payment received)

yegŭmhada 예금하다 bank, deposit; *kyejwae yegŭmhada* 계좌에 예금하다 credit an amount to an account

yegyŏn 예견 prediction

yegyŏnhada 예견하다 predict, foresee, visualize

yeinsŏn 예인선 tug NAUT

yeji 예지 prognosis

yejŏn 예전 former times

yejŏne 예전에 way back

yejŏng 예정 schedule; *yejŏngbodnŭt-tta* 예정보다 늦다 be behind schedule; *yejŏngdaero* 예정대로 scheduled, duly, as expected; *...l yejŏng-ida* ...ㄹ 예정이다 be due

yejŏnghada 예정하다 schedule

yennal 옛날 old days; *yennal saenggagi nage handa* 옛날 생각이 나게 한다 that takes me back; *yennal yettchŏge ...i issŏt-tta* 옛날 옛적에 ...이 있었다 once upon a time there was ...

yeŏn 예언 prophecy

yeŏnhada 예언하다 foretell, prophesy

yeoe 예외 exception

yeppŭda 예쁘다 be pretty

yeppüjanghada 예쁘장하다 be lovely

yeppüjanghan 예쁘장한 pretty

yeppŭn 예쁜 pretty

yerihada 예리하다 be sharp

yerihan 예리한 sharp; acute

yerŭl tŭlmyŏn 예를 들면 e.g.

yerŭl tŭrŏ 예를 들어 for instance

yerŭl tŭrŏsŏ 예를 들어서 for example

yesan 예산 budget; projection; forecast

yesane nŏt'a 예산에 넣다 budget

yesanghada 예상하다 expect; forecast; anticipate; bargain for

yesang pakke 예상 밖에 unexpectedly

yesang sumyŏng 예상 수명 life expectancy

yesanhada 예산하다 project, work out in advance

yesanŭl seuda 예산을 세우다 budget

yeshihada 예시하다 illustrate (with examples)

yeshiktchang 예식장 wedding hall

yesang 예상 anticipation; forecast; prospect

yesŏnŭl t'onggwahada 예선을 통과하다 qualify

Yesu(nim) 예수(님) Jesus

yesul 예술 art

yesulga 예술가 artist

sulp'um 예술품 art; work of art

sultchŏgin 예술적인 artistic

sun 예순 sixty

sun pŏntchaeŭi 예순 번째의 xtieth

üi 예의 politeness; manners
üiga ŏptta 예의가 없다 have no manners

üi parŭge haengdonghada 예의
ㅏ르게 행동하다 behave (oneself)
üi parün 예의 바른 polite, well-nannered

uhada 예우하다 honor

yagi kkwak ch'ada 예약이 꽉
ㅏ다 booked up

yak 예약 reservation

yak-kkŭm 예약금 deposit

yaktoen 예약된 reserved

yak'ada 예약하다 book, reserve; rrange

baek 여백 margin

bo 여보 honey (form of address to usband)

boge! 여보게! buddy! (form of address)

boseyo 여보세요 hello TELEC

buni nama innŭn hando naeesŏ
ㅕ분이 남아 있는 한도 내에서
ubject to availability

dŏl 여덟 eight

dŏl pŏntchaeŭi 여덟 번째의
ighth

dün 여든 eighty

dün pŏntchaeŭi 여든 번째의
ightieth

dürüm 여드름 spot; pimple

dürümi nan 여드름이 난 spotty

ga 여가 leisure

gajang 여가장 matriarch

ga shigan 여가 시간 leisure time

gi 여기 here; yŏgi issümnida 여기
있습니다 here you are, there you
re; yŏgi itkkuna 여기 있구나 here
ve are (finding sth)

gida 여기다 consider, regard;
harangsürŏpkke yŏgida
ㅏ랑스럽게 여기다 pride oneself on

gie(sŏ) 여기에(서) here; in here

gijŏri 여기저기 here and there

gijŏgi toradanida 여기저기
ㅏ어다니다 wander around

yŏgijŏgi yŏhaenghada 여기저기
여행하다 get about, travel around

yŏgwagi 여과기 filter

yŏgwan 여관 guesthouse; inn; hostel

yŏgyŏng 여경 policewoman

yŏgyojang 여교장 principal, headmistress

yŏhaeng 여행 trip, journey; ride; travel; travels

yŏhaenggaek 여행객 traveler

yŏhaenghada 여행하다 travel

yŏhaengja sup'yo 여행자 수표 traveler's check

yŏhaeng kabang 여행 가방 travel bag; suitcase

yŏhaeng piyong 여행 비용 travel expenses

yŏhaeng pohŏm 여행 보험 travel insurance

yŏhaengsa 여행사 travel agency

yŏhaeng shigan 여행 시간 journey time; flight time

yŏhakssaeng 여학생 schoolgirl

Yŏhowaŭi Chŭng-in 여호와의 증인 Jehovah's Witness

yŏja 여자 woman

yŏja ch'in-gu 여자 친구 girl friend

yŏjadaun 여자다운 womanly

yŏjagat'ün 여자같은 effeminate

yŏja hwajangshil 여자 화장실 ladies' room

yŏja hyŏngje 여자 형제 sister

yŏjangbu 여장부 heroine

yŏjang-ŭl hago 여장을 하고 disguised as a woman; in drag

yŏja paeu 여자 배우 actress

yŏja sone chwiyŏ sanŭn 여자 손에 쥐여 사는 henpecked

yŏja undongga 여자 운동가 sportswoman

yŏje 여제 empress

yŏji 여지 scope, latitude

...yŏjida ...여지다 become ..., get ..., go ...

yŏjŏng 여정 itinerary; stage (of journey)

yŏjŏnhi 여전히 yet; still; as ever

yŏjong-ŏbwŏn 여종업원 hostess

yŏjuin 여주인 landlady; mistress

yŏk 역 station; part, role; Haemlit yŏgŭro 햄릿 역으로 in the role of

Hamlet, as Hamlet

yŏk-kkyŏpkke hada역겹게 하다
nauseate, disgust

yŏk-kkyŏptta역겹다 be nauseating;
be nauseated; feel nauseous

yŏk-kkyŏun역겨운 nauseating

yŏk-kkyŏwŏ hada역겨워 하다
sicken, disgust

yŏkkŏnaeda엮어내다 concoct

yŏkkwŏn여권 passport

yŏkkwŏnjuŭi여권주의 feminism

yŏkkwŏnjuŭija여권주의자 feminist

yŏkkwŏnjuŭijaŭi여권주의자의
feminist

yŏkkwŏnjuŭiŭi여권주의의 feminist

yŏkkwŏn kwalli여권 관리 passport
control

yŏkkyŏun역겨운 foul

yŏkssa역사 history

yŏkssajŏgin역사적인 historical

yŏkssasang-ŭro chungnyohan
역사상으로 중요한 historic

yŏksshi역시 too, also; still; after all;
but, nevertheless; yŏksshi
isanghagedo 역시 이상하게도
strangely enough

yŏkssŏl역설 paradox

yŏkssŏltchŏgin역설적인
paradoxical

yŏkssŭp역습 counter-attack

yŏkssŭp'ada역습하다 counter-
attack

yŏktto역도 weightlifting

yŏktto sŏnsu역도 선수 weightlifter

yŏk'al역할 role

yŏk'yokkwaga nada역효과가 나다
backfire, rebound

yŏk'yokkwaŭi역효과의 counter-
productive

yŏl열 ten; row, line; tier; heat; fever;
temperature

yŏlbyŏngshik열병식 review

yŏlda열다 open; be off (of lid, top);
inaugurate; throw party

yŏldasŏt열 다섯 fifteen

yŏldasŏt pŏntchaeŭi열 다섯 번째의
fifteenth

yŏldu kae열두 개 dozen

yŏldul열 둘 twelve

yŏldu pŏntchaeŭi열두 번째의
twelfth

yŏlgi열기 open

yŏlgŏhada열거하다 recite

yŏlgwang열광 fascination;

yŏlgwanghada열광하다 be crazy
about; go wild

yŏlgwanghan열광한 delirious,
ecstatic

yŏlgwangtchŏgin열광적인 wild,
rapturous; feverish; avid

yŏllagi it-tta연락이 있다
communicate; nuguwa yŏllagi
kkŭnkkida 누구와 연락이 끊기다
lose touch with s.o.

yŏllak연락 contact, liaison,
communication; ...wa / gwa
yŏllagŭl chugo pat-tta ...와 / 가
연락을 주고 받다 keep in contact
with; yŏllagŭl ch'wihada 연락을
취하다 liaise with

yŏllakch'ŏ연락처 contact number

yŏllak'ada연락하다 apply to;
contact, get in touch with; nuguw
kyesok yŏllak'ada 누구와 계속
연락하다 keep in touch with s.o.

yŏllet열 넷 fourteen

yŏllida열리다 open; take place

yŏllin열린 open

yŏllip chut'aek연립 주택 row ho

yŏllu연루 involvement; nugurŭl
muŏse yŏllu shik'ida 누구를
무엇에 연루 시키다 involve s.o. i
sth

yŏlludoeda연루되다 be a party to
be involved in; muŏse yŏlludoe
무엇에 연루되다 get involved wit
sth

yŏllyŏ innŭn열려 있는 open

yŏllyŏrhan열렬한 enthusiastic;
ardent, fervent; glowing

yŏllyo연료 fuel

yŏllyorŭl konggŭp'ada연료를
공급하다 refuel

yŏllyorŭl pogŭp pat-tta연료를 노
받다 refuel

yŏlne pŏntchaeŭi열 네 번째의
fourteenth

yŏl pat-tta열 받다 be steamed up

yŏl pŏntchaeŭi열 번째의 tenth

yŏlp'a열파 heatwave

yŏlshi pan열시 반 half past ten, h
after ten

ŏlsoe열쇠 key
ŏlsoe kori열쇠 고리 keyring
ŏlsoe kumŏng열쇠 구멍 keyhole
ŏlsoe mungch'i열쇠 뭉치 bunch of keys
ŏlssabyŏng열사병 heatstroke
ŏlsse pŏntchaeŭi열 세 번째의 thirteenth
ŏlsset열 셋 thirteen
ŏlsshim열심 zeal, enthusiasm
ŏlsshimhi열심히 enthusiastically, eagerly
ŏlsshimhi irhanŭn열심히 일하는 hard-working
ŏlsshimin열심인 enthusiastic
ŏlssŏltchŏgŭro역설적으로 paradoxically
ŏltchŏng열정 enthusiasm; zest; passion
ŏltchŏngjŏgin열정적인 passionate; fervent; impassioned
ŏltchunghada열중하다 be enthusiastic about; be absorbed in; *muŏsŭl hanŭnde yŏltchunghada* 무엇을 하는데 열중하다 concentrate on doing sth
ŏlttae chibang열대 지방 tropics
ŏlttaeŭi열대의 tropical
ŏlttae urim열대 우림 tropical rain forest
ŏlttŭng ŭishik열등 의식 inferiority complex
ŏlyŏdŏl열 여덟 eighteen
ŏlyŏdŏl pŏntchaeŭi열 여덟 번째의 eighteenth
ŏlyŏsŏt열 여섯 sixteen
ŏlyŏsŏt pŏntchaeŭi열 여섯 번째의 sixteenth
ŏm mosŭp옆 모습 profile (*of face*)
ŏmmyŏn옆면 side
ŏmnyŏ염려 concern, anxiety; misgiving
ŏmnyŏhada염려하다 be anxious
ŏmnyŏhanŭn염려하는 concerned, anxious
ŏmnyo염료 dye
ŏmsaek염색 tint
ŏmsaek'ada염색하다 color; tint; dye
ŏmso염소 goat; chlorine
ŏmtchŭng염증 inflammation

yŏn연 kite
yŏnae연애 romance
yŏnae kyŏrhon연애 결혼 love marriage, love match
yŏnae p'yŏnji연애 편지 love letter
yŏnae sakkŏn연애 사건 love affair
yŏnan연안 coast; *yŏnane(sŏ)* 연안에(서) at the coast
yŏnan kyŏngbidae연안 경비대 coastguard (*organization*)
yŏnan kyŏngbiwŏn연안 경비원 coastguard (*person*)
yŏnanŭi연안의 coastal
yŏnbal연발 torrent (*of words, abuse*)
yŏnbang chŏngbu연방 정부 federal government
yŏnbang chŏngbuŭi연방 정부의 federal
Yŏnbang Susaguk연방 수사국 FBI, Federal Bureau of Investigation
yŏnbong연봉 annual salary
yŏnbun연분 bond
yŏnch'ach'onghoe연차총회 annual general meeting
yŏnch'ak'ada연착하다 be delayed
yŏnch'ul연출 direction
yŏnch'ultcha연출자 director
yŏnch'urhada연출하다 direct
yŏndae연대 regiment; chronology; era
yŏndaesunŭi연대순의 chronological; *yŏndaesunŭro* 연대순으로 in chronological order
yŏndan연단 podium, dais; rostrum
yŏng영 zero
yŏng-anshil영안실 morgue, mortuary
yŏng-anso영안소 funeral home
yŏnggam영감 inspiration; old man; husband (*used by elderly persons*); sir; *nuguege / muŏse yŏnggamŭl pat-tta* 누구에게 / 무엇에 영감을 받다 be inspired by s.o. / sth
yŏnggong영공 airspace
yŏngguch'a영구차 hearse
Yŏnggugin영국인 the British; the English
yŏngguhi영구히 permanently
yŏnggujŏgin영구적인 permanent
Yŏngguk영국 Britain; United Kingdom; England ◊ British;

English

Yŏngguk saram 영국 사람 Briton

yŏnggwang 영광 glory; privilege; honor

yŏnggwangsŭrŏpta 영광스럽다 be glorious

yŏnggwangsŭrŏun 영광스러운 glorious; privileged, honored

yŏngha 10to 영하 10도 10 below zero

yŏnghae 영해 waters; territorial waters

yŏngha-ŭi 영하의 subzero

yŏnghon 영혼 soul, spirit

yŏnghwa 영화 movie, film

yŏnghwa chejakŭtcha 영화 제작자 film-maker

yŏnghwa ch'waryŏngso 영화 촬영소 film studio

yŏnghwagwan 영화관 movie theater

yŏnghwa sanŏp 영화 산업 cinema, movie industry

yŏnghwa sŭt'a 영화 스타 movie star

yŏnghyang 영향 effect, impact; influence; *yŏnghyang-ŭl mich'ida* 영향을 미치다 affect; have an effect; influence; *yŏnghyang-ŭl namgida* 영향을 남기다 leave one's mark

yŏnghyang chuda 영향 주다 influence

yŏnghyang kkich'ida 영향 끼치다 influence

yŏnghyangnyŏk 영향력 impact; influence

yŏnghyangnyŏk innŭn 영향력 있는 influential

yŏn-gi 연기 action; acting (*profession*); portrayal; smoke; delay, postponement

yŏn-gich'ŏrŏm sarajida 연기처럼 사라지다 evaporate; vanish

yŏn-gidoen 연기된 belated

yŏn-giga chauk'an 연기가 자욱한 smoky

yŏn-giga nada 연기가 나다 smoke

yŏn-gihada 연기하다 act; portray; delay, postpone; put off

yŏn-gija 연기자 act; actor

yŏn-giman p'iuda 연기만 피우다 smolder

yŏngmae 영매 medium, spiritualist

yŏngmun morŭl 영문 모를 puzzli..

yŏngmunŭl morŭge hada 영문을 모르게 하다 puzzle

yŏngnihada 영리하다 be smart, be clever

yŏngnihan 영리한 smart, clever

yŏngnyang 영양 nutrition

yŏngnyangbujogŭi 영양부족의 underfed

yŏngnyangbun 영양분 nourishme.. goodness; nutrient

yŏngnyang-innŭn 영양있는 nourishing, nutritious

yŏngnyang shiltcho 영양 실조 malnutrition

yŏngnyŏk 영역 sector

yŏngnyŏk'ada 역력하다 be clear; *kŭnŭn kamdong padŭn kŏshi yŏngnyŏk'aet-tta* 그는 감동 받은 것이 역력했다 he was visibly mov..

Yŏng-ŏ 영어 English (*language*)

yŏn-go 연고 ointment

yŏn-goja 연고자 relative

yŏn-gol 연골 gristle

yŏngsa 영사 consul

yŏngsagi 영사기 projector

yŏngsagwan 영사관 consulate

yŏngsahada 영사하다 project

yŏngsang p'yoshi changch'i 영상 표시 장치 visual display unit

yŏngsujŭng 영수증 receipt; bill of sale

yŏngtchang 영장 warrant, writ

yŏngt'o 영토 territory ◊ territorial

yŏn-gŭk 연극 theater; play ◊ theatrical

yŏn-gŭm 연금 pension

yŏn-gŭm chedo 연금 제도 pension scheme

yŏn-gu 연구 research, study; *...e taehan yŏn-gu* ...에 대한 연구 research into

yŏn-guhada 연구하다 research

yŏn-gu kaebal 연구 개발 R & D, research and development

yŏn-gu kyehoek 연구 계획 research plan

yŏng-ung 영웅 hero

yŏng-ungjŏgin 영웅적인 heroic

yŏn-gu pojowŏn 연구 보조원 research assistant

n-guso연구소 research institute

n-guwŏn연구원 researcher

n-gwan연관 link, connection

n-gwanjit-tta연관짓다 link

ngwŏn영원 eternity

ngwŏnhada영원하다 be eternal

ng-wŏnhage hada영원하게 하다 erpetuate

ngwŏnhan영원한 eternal, verlasting

ng-wŏnhi영원히 forever, ternally

ng-ye영예 kudos

ngyŏk영역 preserve, domain

n-gyŏl연결 connection; **yŏn-yŏldwaessŭmnida**연결됐습니다 ou're through TELEC

n-gyŏlp'yŏn연결편 connecting ight, connection

n-gyŏrhada연결하다 connect, oin, link

nhabüi연합의 federal

nhada연하다 be tender; be soft

nhan연한 weak; tender *steak*

nhan hŏrisal연한 허리살 fillet

nhan saektcho연한 색조 tint

nhap연합 union, confederation; oalition; federation

nhapttoen연합된 united

nhoe연회 banquet

niŏsŏ 연이어서 consecutively, in a ow

niyul연이율 APR, annual ercentage rate

njaeüi il hoebun연재의 일 회분 nstallment, episode

njang연장 extension

njanghada연장하다 extend, rolong

njang k'eibŭl연장 케이블 xtension cable

njangshik'ida연장시키다 extend; *kiganül yŏnjangshik'ida* 기간을 장시키다 roll over, renew

nju연주 rendering

njuhada연주하다 play (*of musician*)

njuhoe연주회 concert

njuja연주자 player, musician

njung연중 throughout the year ◊ nnual

yŏnjung haengsa연중 행사 annual event

yŏnjung-üi연중의 annual

yŏnmaeng연맹 league

yŏnmahada연마하다 sharpen *skills*

yŏnminül cha-anaenün연민을 자아내는 pitiful

yŏnmot연못 pond

yŏnnalligi연날리기 kite flying

yŏnŏ연어 salmon

yŏnp'il연필 pencil

yŏnp'il kkak-kki연필 깍기 pencil sharpener

yŏnsang연상 elder

yŏnsanghada연상하다 associate

yŏnsangshik'ida연상시키다 be reminiscent of

yŏnsang-üi연상의 elder

yŏnse연세 age

yŏnsŏl연설 speech, address

yŏnsŏlga연설가 orator

yŏnsŏlmun chakssŏngja연설문 작성자 speech writer

yŏnsŏltcha연설자 speaker

yŏnsŏrhada연설하다 speak; address; make a speech

yŏnso연소 combustion

yŏnsohada연소하다 burn, consume *fuel*

yŏnsok연속 series; succession; sequence

yŏnsok kong-yŏn연속 공연 run (*of play*)

yŏnsok kong-yŏndoeda연속 공연되다 run (*of play*)

yŏnsok pangyŏnghada연속 방영하다 serialize

yŏnsok sarhaebŏm연속 살해범 serial killer

yŏnsokssŏng연속성 continuity

yŏnsoktchŏgin연속적인 consecutive

yŏnsok türama연속 드라마 soap (opera)

yŏnsongmul연속물 serial

yŏnssüp연습 exercise; drill; practice; workout

yŏnssüptchang연습장 exercise book

yŏnssüp'ada연습하다 practice; exercise; train

yŏnsuip연수입 annual income

yŏnswae ch'ungdol연쇄 충돌 pile-up, crash

yŏnswaejŏm 연쇄점 chain store

yŏnswae panŭng 연쇄 반응 chain reaction

yŏntchul 연출 connection, personal contact; *chŏun yŏntchuri innŭn* 좋은 연출리가 있는 be well-connected

yŏnyak'an 연약한 feeble

yŏnyein 연예인 entertainer

yŏnyu 연유 condensed milk

yŏpch'ong 엽총 shotgun

yŏpkkuri 옆구리 side, flank

yŏp saram 옆 사람 neighbor

yŏpssŏ 엽서 (post)card

yŏptchip 옆집 next door

yŏp'a 여파 hangover

yŏp'e 옆에 next to, beside

yŏp'ŭi 옆의 adjoining

yŏp'ŭro 옆으로 sideways

yŏrahop 열 아홉 nineteen

yŏrahop pŏntchaeŭi 열 아홉 번째의 nineteenth

yŏrhana 열 하나 eleven

yŏrhan pŏntchaeŭi 열 한 번째의 eleventh

yŏri innŭn 열이 있는 feverish

yŏri it-tta 열이 있다 have a temperature

yŏrilgop 열 일곱 seventeen

yŏrilgop pŏntchaeŭi 열 일곱 번째의 seventeenth

yŏrŏ 여러 various; several; *yŏrŏ hae tong-an* 여러 해 동안 for several years; *yŏrŏmoro kŏmt'ohada* 여러모로 검토하다 examine from various angles

yŏrŏbun 여러분 everyone; ladies and gentlemen

yŏrŏgaeŭi sŏnban 여러개의 선반 shelves

yŏrŏgaji 여러가지 all sorts of, various kinds of, various

yŏrŏ myŏnesŏ 여러 면에서 in many respects

yŏrŏ pŏn 여러 번 many times

yŏrŏ puryuŭi saram 여러 부류의 사람 assortment of people

yŏron chosa 여론 조사 poll, survey

yŏron chosawŏn 여론 조사원 pollster

yŏronŭl mut-tta 여론을 묻다 poll

yŏrŭi 열의 enthusiasm

yŏrŭm 여름 summer; *yŏrŭme* 여름 in the summer

yŏsa 여사 Mrs (*honoring term generally used for famous or accomplished women*)

yŏse 여세 impetus

yŏshin 여신 goddess

yŏsŏng 여성 female (*person*); women; feminine

yŏsŏng haebang undong 여성 해 운동 women's lib

yŏsŏng haebang undongga 여성 해방 운동가 women's libber

yŏsŏngjŏgin 여성적인 feminine

yŏsŏng kyŏngnyŏng-in 여성 경영 proprietress

yŏsŏng saŏpka 여성 사업가 businesswoman

yŏsŏng-ŭi 여성의 female, feminir GRAM

yŏsŏnsaengnim 여선생님 womar teacher

yŏsŏt 여섯 six

yŏsŏt pŏntchaeŭi 여섯 번째의 six

yŏsong-yŏn 여송연 cigar

yŏttŭt-tta 엿듣다 intercept *messag* listen in, eavesdrop

yŏt'ŭn 열은 pale; *yŏt'ŭn punhon saek* 열은 분홍색 pale pink

yŏt'ŭn saektcho 열은 색조 tinge

yŏŭisa 여의사 woman doctor

yŏu 여우 fox

yŏwang 여왕 queen

yŏwangbŏl 여왕벌 queen bee

...yŏya handa ...여야 한다 have tc must; be bound to

...yŏyaman hada ...여야만 하다 h (got) to; should, must

yŏyuga it-tta 여유가 있다 afford

yŏyuitkke hada 여유있게 하다 ta things easy

yŏyuroun 여유로운 free and easy

yo 요 Korean-style mattress (*for sleeping on the floor*)

yoch'ŏng 요청 request; *yoch'ŏng ttara* 요청에 따라 on request

yoch'ŏnghada 요청하다 request, in for

yoga 요가 yoga

gŭl hada 욕을 하다 swear; swear
t
gŭm 요금 fare; fee; charge; rate
gŭm chingsuso 요금 징수소 toll
ooth
gŭm kyesan-gi 요금 계산기 meter
gŭmp'yo 요금표 tariff, price
gu 요구 demand, requirement
guga shimhan 요구가 심한 demanding
guhada 요구하다 demand, call for, require; urge
guja 요구자 claimant
gurŭt'ŭ 요구르트 yoghurt
gyŏk'ada 요격하다 intercept
haengsu 요행수: *yohaengsurŭl baraji anssŭmnida* 요행수를 바라지 않습니다 I'm not taking any chances
in 요인 factor
jŏl 요절 premature death
jŏng 요정 fairy
jŭŭm 요즈음 nowadays
ok 욕 abuse; abusive language; swearword
okku 욕구 appetite
oksshil 욕실 bathroom
oksshim 욕심 greed
oksshimi ŏmnŭn 욕심이 없는 selfless
oksshim manŭn 욕심 많은 greedy
okssŏl 욕설 bad language; curse; oath; derogatory remark
oktchŏng 욕정 passion, sexual desire
oktcho 욕조 tub, bathtub
ok'ada 욕하다 abuse; curse; call names
omojomo saenggak'ae poda 요모조모 생각해 보다 think through
ong 용 dragon
ongbyŏnboda 용변보다 relieve oneself
ongbyŏng 용병 mercenary MIL
onggamhada 용감하다 be brave
onggamham 용감함 bravery
onggamhan 용감한 brave, valiant
onggi 용기 container; courage; spirit
onggi innŭn 용기 있는 courageous
onggirŭl chunŭn 용기를 주는 encouraging

yonggirŭl naeda 용기를 내다 pluck up courage
yonggol 용골 keel
yonggu 용구 equipment, gear; utensil
yonggwangno 용광로 furnace; blast furnace
yonghaedoeji annŭn 용해되지 않는 insoluble
yong-i 용이 ease, simplicity
yongjŏk 용적 proportions; dimensions; capacity
yongjŏpkkong 용접공 welder
yongjŏp'ada 용접하다 weld
yongk'e haenaeda 용케 해내다 contrive
yongk'e kuhada 용케 구하다 wangle
yongmang 욕망 desire, lust; ambition
yongmo 용모 looks, beauty
yongnap'ada 용납하다 approve; countenance
yongnyang 용량 capacity; memory
yong-ŏ 용어 term, word
yong-ŏ p'uri 용어 풀이 glossary
yongsŏ 용서 forgiveness
yongsŏhada 용서하다 forgive; excuse; let off; condone
yongsŏhal su ŏmnŭn 용서할 수 없는 unforgivable
yongsuch'ŏl 용수철 spring (*device*)
yongtton 용돈 allowance
yoodŭ 요오드 iodine
yoram 요람 cradle
yoranhada 요란하다 be loud
yoranhage ullida 요란하게 울리다 blare out
yori 요리 cooking; dish; food
yorich'aek 요리책 cookbook
yorihada 요리하다 cook
yorippŏp 요리법 cookery
yorisa 요리사 cook
yoriŭi 요리의 culinary
yoriyong ch'ŏlp'an 요리용 철판 burner
yoriyong konno 요리용 곤로 stove
yoryŏng 요령 knack
yosae 요새 fort, fortress
yoso 요소 ingredient
yosul 요술 magic; magic trick
yosulgach'i 요술같이 like magic
yosuljaeng-i 요술쟁이 magician

yosurŭl purida 요술을 부리다 juggle

yotchŏm 요점 point (*in argument*); gist; **yotchŏmŭl marhada** 요점을 말하다 get to the point; **yotchŏmŭl pŏsŏnan** 요점을 벗어난 beside the point, irrelevant

yot'ong 요통 lumbago

yot'ŭ 요트 sailboat, yacht

yot'ŭ chojongja 요트 조종자 yachtsman

yot'ŭ kyeryujang 요트 계류장 marina

yot'ŭ kyŏnggi 요트 경기 sailing

yot'ŭ kyŏnggija 요트 경기자 yachtsman

yot'ŭ t'agi 요트 타기 yachting

yoyak 요약 summary; précis; round-up

yoyak'ada 요약하다 summarize; sum up; abridge; compress

yoyak'amyŏn 요약하면 in short

yoyangso 요양소 rest home; hospice; sanatorium

yua 유아 infant

yuabŭi 유압의 hydraulic (*using oil*)

yuagi 유아기 infancy

yuayong pyŏn-gi 유아용 변기 potty

yubalshik'ida 유발시키다 cause; prompt

yubal yoin 유발 요인 trigger

yubang 유방 breast

yubarhada 유발하다 provoke, trigger

yuboktcha 유복자 posthumous child

yubok'an 유복한 fortunate

yubunam 유부남 married man

yubyŏlnan kŏt 유별난 것 the odd one out (*thing*)

yubyŏlnan saram 유별난 사람 the odd one out (*person*)

yuch'anghada 유창하다 be fluent

yuch'anghage 유창하게 eloquently, fluently

yuch'anghan 유창한 eloquent, fluent

yuch'anghan hwasul 유창한 화술 eloquence

yuch'ihada 유치하다 be childish

yuch'ihan 유치한 childish, infantile

yuch'iwŏn 유치원 kindergarten

yuch'ung 유충 larva; caterpillar

Yudaegyoŭi 유대교의 Jewish

Yudaein 유대인 Jew ◊ Jewish

yudae kwan-gye 유대 관계 link

yudo 유도 judo

yudok'an 유독한 virulent *disease*; poisonous

yudong-aek 유동액 fluid

yudong chasan 유동 자산 liquidi▮ FIN

yudot'an 유도탄 guided missile

yudu 유두 nipple

Yuen 유엔 UN, United Nations

Yuen-gigu 유엔기구 United Natio▮

yugam 유감 regret; grudge; **Sŏurŭ▮ ttŏnani yugamimnida** 서울을 떠나니 유감입니다 I will be sorry ▮ leave Seoul; **yugamŭl kajida** 유감 가지다 bear a grudge

yugamsŭrŏn 유감스런 criminal, shameful

yugamsŭrŏn il 유감스런 일 crime, shameful thing to do

yugamsŭrŏpkkedo 유감스럽게도 regrettably

yugamsŭrŏptta 유감스럽다 be regrettable

yugamsŭrŏun 유감스러운 regrettable

yuganŭronŭn 육안으로는 to the naked eye

yugashil 육아실 nursery

yugi nongppŏbŭi 유기 농법의 organic

Yugio Tongnan 육이오 동란 Korea▮ War

yugiŭi 유기의 organic

yugoe 유괴 kidnapping

yugoebŏm 유괴범 kidnapper

yugoehada 유괴하다 kidnap

yugŭp koyong 유급 고용 paid employment

Yugyo 유교 Confucianism

yuhae 유해 remains

yuhaehada 유해하다 be harmful

yuhaehan kŏt 유해한 것 hazard

yuhaeng 유행 fashion, vogue; **yuhaeng chung-ida** 유행 중이다 be in fashion; **yuhaeng-e twijida** 유행에 뒤지다 be out of fashion; **yuhaeng-e min-gamhan** 유행에 민감한 fashion-conscious; **yuhaeng-i chinada** 유행이 지나다 go out of fashion; **yuhaeng-i chinan** 유행이 지난 old-fashioned, out of fashion

haenghago innŭn유행하고 있는 n, fashionable, popular

haenghanŭn유행하는 in fashion

haeng-ida유행이다 be around (*of lness*)

haengppyŏng유행병 epidemic

haeng-ŭi kyŏnghyang유행의 경향 fashion, trend

haeng-ŭl ttarŭnŭn유행을 따르는 ashionable, trendy

hok유혹 temptation; seduction; **uhoge kulbok'ada** 유혹에 굴복하다 succumb to temptation

hoktchŏgin유혹적인 tempting; seductive; alluring

hok'ada유혹하다 tempt, entice; educe; make advances to

hwa유화 oil painting

hwang유황 sulfur

hyŏl유혈 bloodshed

hyŏng유형 type, sort

hyŏrŭi유혈의 bloody

hyohaejida유효해지다 come into orce

hyohage hada유효하게 하다 validate

hyohan유효한 valid

hyo mallyoil유효 만료일 expiry late

uik'ada유익하다 be beneficial

uik'an유익한 beneficial, salutary

uinyong유인용 decoy

uihada유일하다 be unique

uirhan유일한 only, sole; unique

ujep'um유제품 dairy products

uji유지 upkeep, maintenance; grease

ujihada유지하다 hold; stay; keep; keep up; uphold, maintain; **kŏn-gang-ŭl yujihada** 건강을 유지하다 keep fit

ujŏk유적 ruins, vestige

ujŏn유전 inheritance (*characteristics*); oil field

ujŏndoenŭn유전되는 hereditary

ujŏng유정 oil well

ujŏnhak유전학 genetics

ujŏnhaktcha유전학자 geneticist

ujŏnja유전자 gene

ujŏnja chimun유전자 지문 genetic fingerprint

yujŏnjŏgin유전적인 genetic

yujŏnjŏguro유전적으로 genetically

yujŏn konghak유전 공학 genetic engineering

yujoch'a유조차 tanker, truck

yujoerŭl sŏn-gohada유죄를 선고하다 convict

yujoeŭi유죄의 guilty

yujoeŭi p'an-gyŏl유죄의 판결 conviction

yujok유족 bereaved family

yujosŏn유조선 oil tanker

yuk육 six

yukch'e육체 flesh ◊ physical

yukch'ejŏguro육체적으로 physically

yukch'e nodongja육체 노동자 manual worker, blue-collar worker

yukch'in육친 blood relative

yukka chŭngkkwŏn유가 증권 securities

yukka chŭngkkwŏn shijang유가 증권 시장 securities market

yuk-kkamjŏgin육감적인 voluptuous

yuk-kkun육군 army

yuk-kkun hasagwan육군 하사관 noncommissioned officer

yuk-kkun sagwan hak-kkyo육군 사관 학교 military academy

yukkwŏnja유권자 voter; electorate

yukkyo육교 footbridge, overpass

yukp'il육필 handwriting

yukssang-e(sŏ)육상에(서) on shore

yukssang up'yŏnmul육상 우편물 surface mail

yuksshik tongmul육식 동물 predator

yuksship육십 sixty

yuktchi육지 land, shore; **yuk-tchie(sŏ)** 육지에(서) on land

yuktchi tchogŭi육지 쪽의 inland

yuktchŭp육즙 gravy; juice

yukt'anjŏn육탄전 unarmed combat

yuk'waehada유쾌하다 be pleasant

yuk'waehan유쾌한 pleasant, delightful

yulli윤리 ethics

yullijŏgin윤리적인 ethical, moral

yumanghan유망한 rosy *future*

yumŏ kamgak유머 감각 sense of humor

yumo 유모 nanny

yumoch'a 유모차 buggy, stroller; baby carriage

yulmuch'a 율무차 Job's tears tea

yumul 유물 remnant, relic

yumullon 유물론 materialism

yumullonja 유물론자 materialist

yumullonjŏgin 유물론적인 materialistic

yumyŏng 유명 fame

yumyŏnghada 유명하다 be famous; be famous for

yumyŏnghaejida 유명해지다 make a name for oneself

yumyŏnghan 유명한 famous, renowned

yumyŏng-in 유명인 personality, celebrity

yumyŏng insa 유명 인사 celebrity

yun 윤 gloss, shine

yunggi 융기 bump

yunghap 융합 fusion

yungja 융자 financing; loan

yungnoro 육로로 by land, overland

yungt'ongssŏng innŭn 융통성 있는 flexible

yun-gwagŭl chaptta 윤곽을 잡다 outline

yun-gwak 윤곽 outline, contour

yunhwaltche 윤활제 lubricant

yunhwalyu 윤활유 grease

yunip'om 유니폼 uniform, strip

yun naeda 윤 내다 rub, polish

yunnyŏn 윤년 leap year

yunyŏm 유념 regard, attention

yunyŏmhada 유념하다 pay heed to

yuraehada 유래하다 stem from

yuri 유리 glass

yuri chŏp'aptche 유리 접합제 putty

yurihada 유리하다 be profitable; be advantageous; *kŭgŏshi nŏege yurihada* 그것이 너에게 유리하다 it's to your advantage

yurihan 유리한 advantageous

yurihan chŏm 유리한 점 advantage

yuriŏptcha 유리업자 glazier

yuri sujokkwan 유리 수족관 aquarium

Yurŏbin 유럽인 European

Yurŏp 유럽 Europe ◊ European

yuryŏhage 유려하게 fluently

yuryŏhan 유려한 fluent

yuryŏk'an 유력한 strong, dominant

yuryŏng 유령 ghost; *igosŭn yuryŏng-i nat'ananŭn koshida* 이곳은 유령이 나타나는 곳이다 this place is haunted

yuryo kosokttoro 유료 고속도로 turnpike

yuryo toro 유료 도로 toll road

yusa 유사 similarity, resemblance; analogy; quicksand

yusahan 유사한 close, similar; comparable

yusan 유산 heritage; estate, legacy; miscarriage MED

yusanŭro namgida 유산으로 남기 bequeath

yusashie 유사시에 in an emergenc

yusassŏng 유사성 affinity

yusattchŏm 유사점 parallel

yusehada 유세하다 canvass POL

yusŏ 유서 will

yusŏng 유성 meteor, falling star

yusŏnggat'ŭn 유성같은 meteoric

yusŏng-ŭi 유성의 oily

yusŏnhyŏng 유선형 streamlined shape ◊ streamlined

yusu hosŭt'el 유스 호스텔 youth hostel

yusu 유수 running water

yut 윷 Four-Stick Game

yut'an 유탄 shell MIL

yut'illit'i 유틸리티 utility COMPUT

yut'ŏn U턴 U-turn

yut'ong 유통 distribution

yut'onghada 유통하다 distribute

yut'ong hyŏptchŏng 유통 협정 distribution arrangement

yuwŏl 유월 June

yuwŏnji 유원지 amusement park; recreation ground

yuyak 유약 enamel; glaze

yuyŏnhan 유연한 supple

yuyonghage hada 유용하게 하다 utilize

yuyongssŏng 유용성 utility, usefulness

a ◊ (*no equivalent in Korean*): *a book about Korea* Han-guge kwanhan ch'aek 한국에 관한 책; *he bought a car* kŭnŭn ch'arŭl sassŏyo 그는 차를 샀어요 ◊ (*with a countword*) hanaŭi 하나의, han 한; *a cup of coffee* k'ŏp'i han chan 커피 한 잔; *five men and a woman* tasŏt namjawa han yŏja 다섯 남자와 한 여자 ◊ (*per*) han 한; *$50 a ride* 50tallŏ 50달러; *$15 a head* han saram tang 15tallŏ 한 사람 당 15달러

abandon *object* pŏryŏduda 버려두다; *person* pŏrigo ttŏnada 버리고 떠나다; *plan* p'ogihada 포기하다

abbreviate churyŏssŭda 줄여쓰다

abbreviation yaktcha 약자

abdomen pokppu 복부

abdominal pokppuŭi 복부의

abduct napch'ihada 납치하다

abide by ttarŭda 따르다

ability nŭngnyŏk 능력

ablaze: *be ~* pult'aorŭ it-tta 불타오르고 있다

able (*skillful*) nŭngnyŏginnŭn 능력있는; *be ~ to ...* ...hal su it-tta ...할 수 있다; *I wasn't ~ to see / hear* nanŭn pol / tŭrŭl su ŏpssŏt-tta 나는 볼 / 들을 수 없었다

abnormal pijŏngsang-ŭi 비정상의

aboard 1 *prep* ...e t'ago ...에 타고 **2** *adv*: *be ~* t'ago it-tta 타고 있다; *go ~* t'ada 타다

abolish p'yejihada 폐지하다

abort *v/t mission, rocket launch,* COMPUT chungjihada 중지하다

abortion nakt'ae 낙태; *have an ~* nakt'aehada 낙태하다

about 1 *prep* (*concerning*) ...e kwanhan ...에 관한, ...e taehan ...에 대한; *what's it ~?* (*book, movie*) muŏse kwanhan kŏshimnikka? 무엇에 관한 것입니까? **2** *adv*

(*roughly*) yak 약; (*in the area*) chuwie 주위에; *~ 20 books* yak 20kwŏn 약 20권; *be ~ to ...* mak ...haryŏgo hada 막 ...하려고 하다; *I was just ~ to leave* nanŭn mak ...ttŏnaryŏgo haessŏyo 나는 막 ...떠나려고 했어요; *how ~ ...?* ...i/ga ŏttaeyo? ...이/가 어때요?; *how ~ going to the movies?* yŏnghwagwane kanŭn kŏshi ŏttaeyo? 영화관에 가는 것이 어때요?

above 1 *prep* (*higher than*) ... poda wi ... 보다 위; (*more than*) ... poda tŏ ... 보다 더; *~ all* muŏtppodado 무엇보다도 **2** *adv* wie 위에; *on the floor ~* wich'ŭng-e 위층에

above-mentioned sanggihan 상기한

abrasion pŏtkkyŏjin kot 벗겨진 곳

abrasive *personality* kŏsŭllinŭn 거슬리는

abridge yoyak'ada 요약하다

abroad *live* haeoeesŏ 해외에서; *go* haeoero 해외로

abrupt *departure* kaptchakssŭrŏn 갑작스런; *manner* t'ungmyŏngsŭrŏun 퉁명스러운

abscess nong-yang 농양

absence (*of person*) pujae 부재; (*from school*) kyŏlssŏk 결석; (*from work*) kyŏlgŭn 결근; (*lack*) kyŏlp'ip 결핍

absent *adj* (*from school*) kyŏlssŏk'an 결석한; (*from work*) kyŏlgŭnhan 결근한

absent-minded mŏnghan 멍한

absolute *power* chŏlttaejŏgin 절대적인; *idiot* wanjŏnhan 완전한

absolutely (*completely*) wanjŏnhi 완전히; *~ not!* chŏlttae andoemnida! 절대 안됩니다!; *do you agree? ~ ~* tong-ŭihaseyo? – kŭya mullonimnida 동의하세요? – 그야 물론입니다

absolve samyŏnhada 사면하다

absorb *liquid, shock, group* hŭppsuhada 흡수하다; *changes, information* padadŭrida 받아들이다; **~ed in** ...e molttuhan ...에 몰두한

absorbent hŭpssussŏng-ŭi 흡수성의

absorbent cotton t'alchimyŏn 탈지면, som 솜

abstain *(from voting)* kikkwŏnhada 기권하다

abstention *(in voting)* kikkwŏn 기권

abstract *adj* ch'usangjŏgin 추상적인

absurd ŏrisŏgŭn 어리석은

absurdity ŏrisŏgŭm 어리석음

abundance p'ungbu 풍부

abundant p'ungbuhan 풍부한

abuse[1] *n (insults)* yok 욕; *(of child)* hakttae 학대; *(of machine etc)* namyong 남용

abuse[2] *v/t (physically, sexually)* hakttaehada 학대하다; *(verbally)* yok'ada 욕하다

abusive: ~ language yok 욕; **become ~** sanawajida 사나와지다

abysmal *(very bad)* hyŏngp'yŏnŏmnŭn 형편없는

abyss kurŏngt'ŏng-i 구렁텅이

academic[1] *n* kyosa 교사 [2] *adj* kodŭnggyoyugŭi 고등교육의; *person* hak-kkujŏgin 학구적인; **~ year** hangnyŏn 학년

academy hagwŏn 학원

accelerate[1] *v/i* ppallajida 빨라지다 [2] *v/t production* kasokshik'ida 가속시키다

acceleration *(of car)* kasokto 가속도

accelerator aksellŏreit'ŏ 액셀러레이터

accent *(when speaking)* aksent'ŭ 악센트; *(emphasis)* kangjo 강조

accentuate kangjohada 강조하다

accept[1] *v/t offer, present* padadŭrida 받아들이다; *behavior, conditions* kyŏndida 견디다 [2] *v/i* padadŭrida 받아들이다

acceptable padadŭril su innŭn 받아들일 수 있는

acceptance padadŭrim 받아들임

access[1] *n (to secrets, one's children)* chŏpkkŭn 접근; *(to a building)* ch'urip 출입; **have ~ to** *computer*

...e chŏpkkŭnhal su it-tta ...에 접근할 수 있다; *child* ...ŭl/rŭl mannal kwŏllirŭl kat-tta ...을/를 만날 권리를 갖다 [2] *v/t* chŏpkkŭnhada 접근하다; COMPUT ipch'ullyŏk'ada 입력력하다

access code COMPUT ipch'ullyŏk k'odŭ 입출력 코드

accessible *(easy to reach)* tatkki shwiun 닿기 쉬운; *house* kagi shwiun 가기 쉬운; *information* ipssuhagi shwiun 입수하기 쉬운

accessory *(for wearing)* changshin gu 장신구; LAW chongbŏm 종범

access road chinimno 진입로

access time COMPUT hoch'ul shiga 호출 시간

accident uyŏnhan sakkŏn 우연한 사건; *(crash etc)* sago 사고; **by ~** uyŏnhi 우연히

accidental uyŏnhan 우연한

acclimate, acclimatize *v/t* chŏgŭnghada 적응하다

accommodate chinael kosŭl chegonghada 지낼 곳을 제공하다; *special requirements* tŭrŏjuda 들어주다

accommodations sukppak shisŏl 숙박 시설; **have you found ~?** chinael kosŭn ch'ajŭsyŏssŏyo? 지낼 곳은 찾으셨어요?

accompaniment MUS panju 반주

accompany tongbanhada 동반하다; MUS panjurŭl hada 반주를 하다

accomplice kongbŏm 공범

accomplish *task* sŏngch'wihada 성취하다

accomplished *(person)* ttwiŏnan 뛰어난

accord: of one's own ~ chabalchŏgŭro 자발적으로

accordance: in ~ with ...e ttarasŏ ...에 따라서

according: ~ to ...e ttarŭmyŏn ...에 따르면

accordingly *(consequently)* kŭrŏmŭro 그러므로; *(appropriately)* kŭe match'uŏ 그에 맞추어

account *n (financial)* kujwa 구좌; *(report, description)* pogo 보고; **give an ~ of** ...ŭi iyagirŭl hada ...의

이야기를 하다; *on no ~ must you tell anybody* chŏlttaero amuegedo yagihaesŏnŭn andoemnida 절대로 누구에게도 이야기해서는 안됩니다; *on ~ of* …ttaemune …때문에; *take ... into ~, take ~ of* …ŭl/rŭl koryŏhada …을/를 고려하다

account for (*explain*) sŏlmyŏnghada 설명하다; (*make up, constitute*) pijung-ŭl ch'ajihada 비중을 차지하다

accountability ch'aegim 책임

accountable: be held ~ ch'aegimŭl chida 책임을 지다

accountant hoegyesa 회계사

account number kujwa pŏnho 구좌 번호

accounts hoegye 회계

accumulate 1 *v/t* moŭda 모으다 **2** *v/i* moida 모이다

accuracy chŏnghwak 정확

accurate chŏnghwak'an 정확한

accusation pinan 비난

accuse pinanhada 비난하다; *he ~d me of lying* kŭnŭn naega kŏjinmarŭl haet-ttago pinanhaet-tta 그는 내가 거짓말을 했다고 비난했다; *be ~d of* LAW …(ŭ)ro kobaldoeda …(으)로 고발되다

accused: the ~ LAW p'igo 피고

accustom: get ~ed to …e …에 ikssuk'aejida …에 익숙해지다; *be ~ed to* …nŭn supkkwani it-tta …는 습관이 있다

ace (*in cards, tennis: shot*) eisŭ 에이스

ache 1 *n* ap'ŭm 아픔 **2** *v/i* ap'ŭda 아프다

achieve sŏngch'wihada 성취하다

achievement (*of ambition*) sŏngch'wi 성취; (*thing achieved*) ŏptchŏk 업적

acid *n* san 산

acid rain sansŏngbi 산성비

acid test *fig* kyŏltchŏngjŏgin kŏmt'o 결정적인 검토

acknowledge injŏnghada 인정하다; *receipt* sushinyŏburŭl allida 수신여부를 알리다

acknowledg(e)ment injŏng 인정; (*of a letter*) sushinyŏburŭl allinŭn kŏt 수신여부를 알리는 것

acoustics ŭmhyanghak 음향학

acquaint: be ~ed with (*with person*) …wa/kwa mannan chŏgi it-tta …와/과 만난 적이 있다; (*with things, poem*) …ŭl/rŭl algo it-tta …을/를 알고 있다

acquaintance (*person*) anŭn saram 아는 사람

acquire *skill, knowledge* sŭpttŭk'ada 습득하다; *property* hoekttŭk'ada 획득하다

acquisitive ŏtkkoja hanŭn 얻고자 하는

acquit LAW mujoeimŭl sŏnŏnhada 무죄임을 선언하다

acre eik'ŏ 에이커

acrobat kogyesa 곡예사

acrobatics kogye 곡예

across 1 *prep* ◊ (*on the other side of*) …ŭi majŭn p'yŏne(sŏ) …의 맞은 편에(서); *the person sitting ~ the table from me* shikt'agŭi majŭn p'yŏne anjŭn saram 식탁의 맞은 편에 앉은 사람; *~ the street* kŏriŭi majŭn p'yŏne(sŏ) 거리의 맞은 편에(서) ◊ (*to the other side of*) …ŭi majŭn p'yŏnŭro …의 맞은 편으로; *walk ~ the street* kirŭl kŏnnŏda 길을 건너다; *sail ~ the Pacific* T'aep'yŏng-yang-ŭi majŭn p'yŏnŭro hanghaehada 태평양의 맞은 편으로 항해하다 **2** *adv* (*to the other side*) kŏnnosŏ 건너서; *10 meters ~* p'ok 10mit'ŏ 폭 10미터

act 1 *v/i* THEA yŏn-gihada 연기하다; (*pretend*) kajanghada 가장하다; (*take action*) haengdonghada 행동하다; *~ as* …ŭl/rŭl taerihada …을/를 대리하다 **2** *n* (*deed*) haengdong 행동; (*of play*) mak 막; (*in vaudeville*) yŏn-gija 연기자; (*pretense*) shinyung 시늉; (*law*) pŏmnyŏng 법령

acting 1 *n* yŏn-gi 연기 **2** *adj* (*temporary*) imshiŭi 임시의

action haengwi 행위; *out of ~* (*not functioning*) chakttong-i andoenŭn 작동이 안되는; *take ~* choch'wirŭl ch'wihada 조처를 취하다; *bring an ~ against* LAW kobarhada 고발하다

action replay TV kyŏnggi chaeyŏn

경기 재연; (*in slow motion*)
sŭlloumoshŏn 슬로우모션
active hwalttongjŏgin 활동적인;
GRAM nŭngdongt'aeŭi 능동태의
activist POL hwalttongga 활동가
activity (*being busy*) hwalbarhan
umjigim 활발한 움직임; (*pastime*)
hwalttong 활동
actor namja paeu 남자 배우
actress yŏja paeu 여자 배우
actual (*real*) shiltcheŭi 실제의
actually (*in fact, to tell the truth*)
sashirŭn 사실은; (*surprised*)
chŏngmallo 정말로; ~ **I do know
him** (*stressing converse*) nanŭn
chŏngmallo kŭrŭl arayo 나는 정말로
그를 알아요
acupressure massage chiap 지압
acupuncture ch'imsul 침술
acute *pain* kŭksshimhan 극심한; *sense
of smell* min-gamhan 민감한;
analysis, mind yerihan 예리한
ad kwanggo 광고, (*on TV*) sŏnjŏn
선전
adapt 1 *v/t* chŏk'ap'age hada 적합하게
하다 **2** *v/i* chŏgŭnghada 적응하다
adaptable *person, plant*
chŏgŭngnyŏgi innŭn 적응력이 있는;
vehicle etc tayongdoŭi 다용도의
adaptation (*of play etc*) kakssaek
각색
adapter ELEC ŏdaept'ŏ 어댑터
add 1 *v/t* MATH tŏhada 더하다; (*say*)
tŏtppuch'yŏ marhada 덧붙여 말하다;
comment tŏtppuch'ida 덧붙이다;
sugar, salt etc puŏ nŏt'a 부어 넣다
2 *v/i* (*of person*) tŏhada 더하다
♦ **add on** *15% etc* p'ohamhada
포함하다
♦ **add up 1** *v/t* hapkkyehada 합계하다
2 *v/i fig* ihaedoeda 이해되다
addict chungdoktcha 중독자
addicted *be* ~ ...e chungdogida
...에 중독이다
addiction (*to drugs, TV etc*)
chungdok 중독
addictive *be* ~ chungdokssŏng-ida
중독성이다
addition MATH tŏtssem 덧셈; (*to list,
company etc*) ch'uga 추가; *in* ~
ch'ugaro 추가로; *in* ~ *to* ...e tŏhayŏ

...에 더하여
additional ch'ugaŭi 추가의
additive (*in food*) ch'ŏmgaje 첨가제
add-on ch'uga hangmok 추가 항목
address 1 *n* chuso 주소; *form of* ~
ch'ingho 칭호 **2** *v/t letter* chusorŭl
ssŭda 주소를 쓰다; *audience*
yŏnsŏrhada 연설하다; *person* ...ra
purŭda ...라고 부르다
address book chusorok 주소록
addressee sushinin 수신인
adequate chŏkttanghan 적당한;
(*satisfactory*) manjokssŭrŏun
만족스러운
adhere ttak tallabut-tta 딱 달라붙다
♦ **adhere to** *surface* ...e tallabut-tta
...에 달라붙다; *rules* ...ŭl / rŭl
chik'ida ...을 / 를 지키다; *opinion*
...ŭl / rŭl kosuhada ...을 / 를 고수하
adhesive *n* chŏpch'aktche 접착제
adhesive plaster panch'anggo
반창고
adhesive tape panch'anggo 반창고
adjacent injŏp'an 인접한
adjective hyŏng-yongsa 형용사
adjoining yŏp'ŭi 옆의
adjourn *v/i* (*of court*) hyujŏnghadoe
휴정되다; (*of meeting*)
chungdandoeda 중단되다
adjust *v/t* match'uda 맞추다
adjustable chojŏnghal su innŭn
조정할 수 있는
administer *medicine* pogyongshik'
복용시키다; *company* kwallihada
관리하다; *country* tasŭrida 다스리다
administration (*of company etc*)
kwalli 관리; (*of country*) haengjŏn
행정; (*government*) chŏngbu 정부
administrative haengjŏng-ŭi 행정의
administrator kwalliin 관리인; (*of
company*) kwallija 관리자; (*in
government*) haengjŏnggwan 행정
admirable hullyunghan 훌륭한
admiral haegun changsŏng 해군 장
admiration kamt'an 감탄
admire kamt'anhada 감탄하다
admirer ch'anmija 찬미자
admissible padadŭril su innŭn
받아들일 수 있는
admission (*confession*) shiin 시인; (*
building*) iptchang hŏga 입장 허가

(to country) ipkkuk hŏga 입국 허가; *(to organization)* ip'oe hŏga 입회 허가; *(fee)* iptchangnyo 입장료; **~ free** muryo iptchang 무료 입장

dmitinjŏnghada 인정하다; *(allow in)* tŭrŏonŭn kŏsŭl hŏgahada 들어오는 것을 허가하다; *(confess)* shiinhada 시인하다; *(accept)* padadŭrida 받아들이다; *he was ~ted to the hospital* kŭnŭn pyŏng-wŏne ibwŏnhaet-tta 그는 병원에 입원했다

dmittance no ~ iptchang kŭmji 입장 금지

dolescencesach'un-gi 사춘기

dolescent 1 *n* sach'un-giŭi namnyŏ 사춘기의 남녀 2 *adj* sach'un-giŭi 사춘기의

doptchild ibyanghada 입양하다; plan ch'aet'aek'hada 채택하다

doption(of child) ibyang 입양; (of plan) ch'aet'aek 채택

dorablepanhal manhan 반할 만한

doresamohada 사모하다

dult 1 *n* ŏrŭn 어른; (over 20) sŏng-in 성인; (animal) sŏngjanghan tongmul 성장한 동물 2 *adj* sŏngsuk'an 성숙한; person ŏrŭnŭi 어른의; (over 20) sŏng-inŭi 성인의; ~ movie sŏng-inyŏnghwa 성인영화

dulterykant'ŏng kwan-gye 간통 관계

advance 1 *n* (money) sŏnbul 선불; (in science etc) chinbo 진보; MIL chŏnjin 전진; **in ~** miri 미리; get money sŏnbullo 선불로; 48 hours in ~ saship'al'shigan chŏne 48시간 전에; make ~s (progress) chinbohada 진보하다; (sexually) yuhok'ada 유혹하다 2 *v/i* MIL chŏnjinhada 전진하다; (make progress) chinbohada 진보하다 3 *v/t* theory cheanhada 제안하다; sum of money miri naeda 미리 내다; human knowledge, a cause paltchŏnhada 발전하다

advance bookingyeyak 예약

advancedap sŏn 앞 선; ~ country sŏnjin-guk 선진국; ~ learner sanggŭptcha 상급자; ~ level sanggŭp 상급

advance paymentsŏnbul yogŭm 선불 요금

advantageyurihan chŏm 유리한 점; it's to your ~ kŭgŏshi nŏege yurihada 그것이 너에게 유리하다; take ~ of sth of opportunity muŏsŭl iyonghada 무엇을 이용하다

advantageousyurihan 유리한

adventuremohŏm 모험

adventurousmohŏmjŏk 모험적; person mohŏmŭl chŭlginŭn 모험을 즐기는

adverbpusa 부사

adversarychŏk 적

advertise *v/t & v/i* kwanggohada 광고하다

advertisementkwanggo 광고

advertiserkwanggoju 광고주

advertisingkwanggo 광고; (industry) kwanggo-ŏp 광고업

advertising agencykwanggo taehaengsa 광고 대행사

advicechoŏn 조언; take s.o.'s ~ nuguŭi choŏnŭl padadŭrida 누구의 조언을 받아들이다

advisablehyŏnmyŏnghan 현명한

adviseperson choŏnhada 조언하다; caution etc ch'unggohada 충고하다; ~ s.o. to … nuguege …rago choŏnhada 누구에게 …라고 조언하다

adviserkomun 고문

aerial 1 *n* ant'ena 안테나 2 *adj* kongjung-ŭi 공중의

aerial photographhanggongsajin 항공사진

aerobicssŏrobik 에어로빅

aerodynamickonggi yŏk'agŭi 공기 역학의

aeronauticalhanggonghagŭi 항공학의

aerosolsŭp'ŭrei 스프레이

aerospace industryhanggong-ujugonghak 항공우주공학

affair(matter) il 일; (business) ŏmmu 업무; (love) pullyun 불륜; foreign ~s oemuŏmmu 외무업무; have an ~ with …wa / kwa param p'iuda …와 / 과 바람피우다; that's my ~ kŭgŏsŭn che ŏmmuimnida 그것은 제 업무입니다

affectMED palbyŏnghada 발병하다; (influence) yŏnghyang-ŭl mich'ida

affection

영향을 미치다; (*concern*) kŏktchŏng-ŭl kkich'ida 걱정을 끼치다
affection aejŏng 애정
affectionate tajŏnghan 다정한
affinity yusassŏng 유사성
affirmative: *answer in the ~* yerago tap'ada 예라고 답하다
affluent puyuhan 부유한; *~ society* p'ung-yoroun sahoe 풍요로운 사회
afford (*financially*) yŏyuga it-tta 여유가 있다
Afghan 1 *adj* Ap'ŭganisŭt'anŭi 아프가니스탄의 **2** *n* (*person*) Ap'ŭganisŭt'anin 아프가니스탄인
Afghanistan Ap'ŭganisŭt'an 아프가니스탄
afloat *boat* ttŏ innŭn 떠 있는
afraid: *be ~* turyŏwŏhada 두려워하다; *be ~ of* ...ŭl/rŭl musŏwŏhada ...을/를 무서워하다; *of upsetting s.o.* ...ŭl/rŭl turyŏwŏhada ...을/를 두려워하다; *I'm ~ ...* (*expressing regret*) choesonghajiman ... 죄송하지만 ...; *I'm ~ he will lose his job* kŭga iltchariŭl irŭlkkabwa kŏktchŏng imnida 그가 일자리를 잃을까봐 걱정입니다; *I'm ~ so* choesonghajiman, kŭrŏn kŏt kat'ayo 죄송하지만, 그런 것 같아요; *I'm ~ not* choesonghajiman, andoelgŏt kat'ayo 죄송하지만, 안될 것 같아요
Africa Ap'ŭrik'a 아프리카
African 1 *adj* Ap'ŭrik'aŭi 아프리카의 **2** *n* Ap'ŭrik'a saram 아프리카 사람
after 1 *prep* (*in order, time*) hue 후에; (*in position*) taŭme 다음에; *~ all* kyŏlguk 결국; *~ that* kŭ ihue 그 이후에; *it's ten ~ two* tushi shippunimnida 두시 십분입니다 **2** *adv* (*afterward*) taŭme 다음에, hue 후에; *the day ~* taŭmnal 다음날
afternoon ohu 오후; *in the ~* ohue 오후에; *this ~* onŭl ohue 오늘 오후에; *good ~* annyŏnghaseyo 안녕하세요
after sales service aep'ŭt'ŏ sŏbisŭ 애프터 서비스; **aftershave** aep'ŭt'ŏ shyeibŭ loshyŏn 애프터 셰이브 로션; **aftertaste** kkŭnmat 끝맛
afterward najung-e 나중에
again tashi 다시

against (*opposed to*) ...e pandaeha ...에 반대하여; (*leaning on*) ...e kidaeŏ ...에 기대어; *America v Brazil* SP Miguk tae Pŭrajil 미국 [브라질; *I'm ~ the idea* nanŭn kŭ ŭigyŏne pandaehamnida 나는 그 의견에 반대합니다; *what do you have ~ him?* wae kŭrŭl pandaehanŭn kŏyeyo? 왜 그를 반대하는 거예요?; *be ~ the law* pŏbe ŏgŭnnada 법에 어긋나다
age 1 *n* (*of person, object*) nai 나이; (*respectful: of older person*) yŏnse 연세; (*era*) ki 기; *at the ~ of* ...se ttae ...세 때에; *under ~* misŏngnyŏnŭi 미성년의; *she's five years of ~* kŭnyŏnŭn tasŏt sarimnida 그녀는 다섯 살입니다 **2** nai tŭlda 나이 들다
agency chunggaeŏp 중개업
agenda iltchŏng 일정; *on the ~* iltchŏngsang 일정상
agent taeriin 대리인
aggravate ak'washik'ida 악화시키디
aggression konggyŏk 공격
aggressive konggyŏktchŏgin 공격적인; (*dynamic*) chinch'wijŏgin 진취적인
agile chaepparŭn 재빠른
agitated tong-yohan 동요한
agitation tong-yo 동요
agitator sŏndongja 선동자
ago: *3 days ~* samil chŏne 3일 전어 *long ~* orae chŏne 오래 전에; *how long ~?* ŏlmana chŏne? 얼마나 전에?
agonizing kot'ongsŭrŏun 고통스러윈
agony kot'ong 고통
agree 1 *v/i* tong-ŭihada 동의하다; (*o figures, accounts*) ilch'ihada 일치하다; (*reach agreement*) habŭihada 합의하다; *I ~* nanŭn ton ŭihanda 나는 동의한다; *I don't ~* nanŭn tong-ŭihaji annŭnda 나는 동의하지 않는다; *it doesn't ~ with me* (*of food*) nanŭn i ŭmshigi pate annŭnda 나는 이 음식이 받지 않는다 **2** *v/t price* ilch'ishik'ida 일치시키다; *~ that something should be done* muŏsŭl haeyahamŭl tong-ŭihada 무엇을

...여함을 동의하다
...reeable (*pleasant*) kibunjoŭn
...분좋은; (*in agreement*) tong-ŭihal
...anhan 동의할 만한
...reement (*consent*) tong-ŭi 동의;
(*contract*) kyeyak 계약; **reach ~ on**
...he habŭihada ...에 합의하다
...ricultural nong-ŏpŭi 농업의
...riculture nong-ŏp 농업
...ead **be ~ of** ...ŭi ap'e ...의 앞에;
...lan / think ~ miraeeŭi
...yehoek / saenggak 미래에의
...획 / 생각
...d1 n toum 도움 2 v/t toptta 돕다
...dseijŭ 에이즈, huch'ŏnssŏng
...nyŏnnyŏk kyŏlp'iptchŭng 후천성
...역 결핍증
...ling economy yak'aejinŭn 약해지는
...m1 n (*in shooting*) kyŏnyang 겨냥;
(*objective*) moktchŏk 목적 2 v/i (*in*
shooting) kyŏnyanghada 겨냥하다; ~
...t **doing sth, ~ to do sth** muŏsŭl
...anŭn kŏsŭl mokp'yoro samtta
...릇을 하는 것을 목표로 삼다 3 v/t
...e **~ed at** (*of remark etc*) ...ŭl / rŭl
...yŏnun kŏshida ...을 / 를 겨눈
...이다; (*of guns*) ...ŭl / rŭl
...yŏnyanghada ...을 / 를 겨냥하다
...r1 n kongjung 공중; (*what we*
reathe) konggi 공기; **by ~ travel**
...pihaenggiro 비행기로; **send mail**
...anggongp'yŏnŭro 항공편으로; **in**
...he **open ~** yaoeesŏ 야외에서; **on**
...he **~** RAD, TV pangsong chung-e
...방송 중에 2 v/t room hwan-
...gishik'ida 환기시키다; *fig*: views
...balk'ida 밝히다
...rbase konggun kiji 공군 기지; **air-**
conditioned naengbangjung 냉방중;
air-conditioning naengbang 냉방,
...ŏk'ŏn 에어컨; **aircraft** hanggonggi
...항공기; **aircraft carrier**
...hanggongmoham 항공모함; **air cyl-**
inder sujung hohŭpkki 수중 호흡기;
airfield pihaengjang 비행장; **air**
force konggun 공군; **air hostess**
...sŭt'yuŏdissŭ 스튜어디스; **air letter**
...hanggongbonghamnyŏpssŏ
...항공봉함엽서; **airline** hanggongsa
...항공사; **airmail by ~** hanggong-
...up'yŏnŭro 항공우편으로; **airplane**

pihaenggi 비행기; **air pollution**
taegioyŏm 대기오염; **airport**
konghang 공항; **airsick get ~**
pihaenggi mŏlmirŭl hada 비행기
멀미를 하다; **airspace** yŏnggong
영공; **air terminal** konghang
t'ŏminŏl 공항 터미널; **airtight**
container konggiga ant'onghanŭn
공기가 안통하는; **air traffic**
hanggong kyot'ong 항공 교통; **air-**
traffic control hanggong kyot'ong
kwanje 항공 교통 관제; **air-traffic**
controller hanggong kyot'ong
kwanjewŏn 항공 교통 관제원
airy *room* konggiga shinsŏnhan
공기가 신선한; *attitude* kabyŏun
가벼운
aisle t'ongno 통로
aisle seat t'ongno tchok chari 통로
쪽 자리
alarm1 n (*feeling*) puran 불안;
(*warning*) kyŏnggo 경고; (*device*)
kyŏngbogi 경보기; **raise the ~**
kyŏnggohada 경고하다 2 v/t
puranhage hada 불안하게 하다
alarm clock chamyŏngjong shigye
자명종 시계
album (*for photographs*) aelbŏm
앨범; (*record*) ŭmban 음반
alcohol alk'o-ol 알코올
alcoholic 1 n alk'o-ool chungdoktcha
알코올 중독자 2 adj alk'o-olssŏng-ŭi
알코올성의
alert1 n (*signal*) kyŏngboŭm 경보음;
be on the ~ kyŏnggyehada 경계하다
2 v/t kyŏnggohada 경고하다 3 adj
kyŏnggyehanŭn 경계하는
alibi allibai 알리바이
alien1 n (*foreigner*) oegugin 외국인;
(*from space*) oegyein 외계인 2 adj
ijiltchŏgin 이질적인; **be ~ to**
...wa / kwa mat-tchi ant'a ..와 / 과
맞지 않다
alienate sowŏnhage hada 소원하게
하다; **be ~d** ttadollimŭl pat-tta
따돌림을 받다
alight adj: **be ~** pult'aorŭda
불타오르다
alike1 adj: **be ~** pisŭt'ada 비슷하다
2 adv: **old and young ~** nŭlgŭnina
chŏlmŭnina ttokkach'i 늙은이나

젊은이나 똑같이

alimony wijaryo 위자료

alive: *be ~* sarait-tta 살아있다

all 1 *adj* modŭn 모든; *~ the cars* modŭn ch'a 모든 차; *~ the time* hangsang 항상 **2** *pron* modu 모두; *~ of us/them* uridŭl/kŭdŭl modu 우리들/그들 모두; *he ate ~ of it* kŭga modu ta mŏgŏssŏyo 그가 모두 다 먹었어요; *that's ~, thanks* twaessŭmnida, kamsahamnida 됐습니다. 감사합니다; *for ~ I care* naega al pa aniyeyo 내가 알 바 아니에요; *for ~ I know* naega anŭn paronŭn 내가 아는 바로는; *~ but ...* (*except*) ...man ppaego ...만 빼고; *~ but agreed* modu tong-ŭihaessŏyo 존만 빼고 모두 동의했어요 **3** *adv*: *~ at once* (*suddenly*) kaptchagi 갑자기; *~ but* (*nearly*) kŏŭi ta 거의 다; *~ right* choayo 좋아요; *be ~ the better* ohiryŏ tŏ nat-tta 오히려 더 낫다; *it is ~ the better for having been cleaned* ch'ongsoga ta toeŏsŏ ohiryŏ tŏ natkkunnyo 청소가 다 되어서 오히려 더 낫군요; *they're not at ~ alike* kŭdŭrŭn chŏnhyŏ tamtchi anassŏyo 그들은 전혀 닮지 않았어요; *not at ~!* (*please do*) chŏnmaneyo! 천만에요!; *two ~* (*in score*) i tae iro tongtchŏm 이 대 이로 동점

allegation chujang 주장

alleged chujangdoen 주장된

allergic: *be ~ to* ...e allerŭgi panŭng-i it-tta ...에 알레르기 반응이 있다

allergy allerŭgi 알레르기

alley (*between buildings*) kolmok 골목; (*in a garden*) osolkkil 오솔길

alliance tongmaeng 동맹

alligator agŏ 악어

allocate punbaehada 분배하다

allot paebunhada 배분하다

allow (*permit*) hŏrak'ada 허락하다; *money, time* chuda 주다; *it's not ~ed* kŭgŏsŭn kŭmjisahang-imnida 그것은 금지사항입니다; *~ s.o. to ...* nuguegen ...ŭl/rŭl hŏrak'ada 누구에게 ...을/를 허락하다

♦ **allow for** ...ŭl/rŭl koryŏhada ...을/를 고려하다

allowance (*money*) kŭbyŏ 급여; (*pocket money*) yongtton 용돈; *make ~s* (*for thing, weather etc*) koryŏhada 고려하다; (*for person*) kamanhaejuda 감안해주다

alloy hapkkŭm 합금

all-purpose tayongdoŭi 다용도의;

all-round mannŭng-ŭi 만능의; **all time**: *be at an ~ low* chŏgŭn chŏllyeŏpss ... 적은

♦ **allude to** tollyŏsŏ ŏn-gŭp'ada 돌려서 언급하다

alluring yuhoktchŏgin 유혹적인

all-wheel drive saryun-gudong 사륜구동

ally *n* (*country*) tongmaengguk 동맹국; (*person*) hyŏmnyŏktcha 협력자

almond amondŭ 아몬드

almost kŏŭi 거의

alone honja 혼자

along 1 *prep* ...ŭl/rŭl ttarasŏ ...을 따라 **2** *adv* hamkke 함께; *~ with* ...wa/kwa hamkke ...와/과 함께; *~* (*all the time*) naenae 내내

aloud sorirŭl naeŏ sori-rŭl naeŏ: *thi* chung-ŏl kŏrimyŏ 중얼 거리며

alphabet alp'abet 알파벳

alphabetical alp'abesŭi 알파벳의

already pŏlssŏ 벌써, imi 이미

alright: *that's ~* (*doesn't matter*) kwaench'anayo 괜찮아요; (*when s says thank you*) ch'ŏnmaneyo 천만에요; (*is quite good*) choŭnde 좋은데요; *I'm ~* (*not hurt*) chŏn, kwaench'anayo 전, 괜찮아요; (*hav got enough*) chŏn, kŭman twaessŭmnida 전, 그만 됐습니다; *that's enough!* kŭgŏllo twaessŏy 그걸로 됐어요

also ttohan 또한

altar chedan 제단

alter ... bi pakkuda 바꾸다

alteration pyŏn-gyŏng 변경; (*to clothes*) susŏn 수선

alternate 1 *v/i* kyoch'ehada 교체하 **2** *adj* pŏn-gara hanŭn 번갈아 하는 on *~ days* kyŏgillo 격일로

alternating current kyoryu 교류

ternative 1 *n* taean 대안 2 *adj*
aeshinhal 대신할
ternatively taeshin 대신
though pirok ... haljirado 비록
...할지라도; ~ *I don't like it* pirok
naega choahaji anŭltchirado 비록
내가 좋아하지 않을지라도
titude haebalgodo 해발고도; (*of
plane*) kodo 고도
together (*completely*) wanjŏnhi
완전히; (*in all*) chŏnbu 전부
truistic aet'ajŏgin 애타적인
luminum alluminyum 알루미늄
lways hangsang 항상, ŏnjena 언제나,
nŭl 늘
m. ojŏn 오전
malgamate *v/i* (*of companies*) happyŏnghada 합병하다
mateur *n* amach'uŏ 아마추어
maze kkamtchak nollage hada 깜짝
놀라게 하다
mazement kkamtchak nollam 깜짝
놀람
mazing (*surprising*) aju nollaun 아주
놀라운; (*very good*) aju chohŭn 아주
좋은
mbassador taesa 대사
mber. *at* ~ hwangsaek shinho-e 황색
신호에
mbiguous aemaemohohan
애매모호한
mbition yamang 야망; (*something
desired*) kkum 꿈; *pej* yongmang
욕망
mbitious *person, plan* yashiminnŭn
야심있는
mbulance kugŭpch'a 구급차
mbush 1 *n* maebok 매복 2 *v/t*
maepok'ayŏ sŭpkkyŏk'ada 매복하여
습격하다
mend sujŏnghada 수정하다
mendment sujŏng 수정
mends: *make* ~ posangŭl hada
보상을 하다
menities (*leisure facilities*)
orakssishisŏl 오락시설
merica Miguk 미국
merican 1 *adj* Migugŭi 미국의 2 *n*
Miguk saram 미국 사람
miable hogamŭl chunŭn 호감을
주는

amicable uhojŏgin 우호적인
Amitabha Buddha Amit'abul
아미타불
ammunition t'annyak 탄약; *fig* mugi
무기
amnesty *n* samyŏn 사면
among(st) kaunde 가운데
amount yang 양; (*sum of money*)
kŭmaek 금액
♦ amount to ...i/ka toeda ...이/가
되다
ample ch'ungbunhan 충분한
amplifier aemp'ŭ 앰프
amplify *sound* chŭngp'ok'ada
증폭하다
amputate chŏlttanhada 절단하다
amuse (*make laugh etc*) utkkida
웃기다; (*entertain*) chŭlgŏpkkehada
즐겁게하다
amusement (*merriment*) chaemi
재미; (*entertainment*) chŭlgŏum
즐거움; ~**s** (*games*) orangmul 오락물;
to our great ~ usŭpkkedo 우습게도
amusement park yuwŏnji 유원지
amusing chaemiinnŭn 재미있는
anabolic steroid kŭnyuk
chŭnggangje 근육 증강제
analog COMPUT anallogŭ 아날로그
analogy yusa 유사
analysis punsŏk 분석; PSYCH
chŏngshinbunsŏk 정신분석
analyze punsŏk'ada 분석하다
anarchy mujŏngbu sangt'ae 무정부
상태
anatomy haebuhak 해부학
ancestor chosang 조상; ~ *worship*
chosang sungbae 조상 숭배
ancestral grave sanso 산소
ancestral rite chesa 제사
anchor NAUT 1 *n* tat 닻 2 *v/i* tach'ŭl
naerida 닻을 내리다
anchor man TV aengk'ŏ 앵커
anchovies myŏlch'i 멸치
ancient *adj* kodaeŭi 고대의
and ◊ (*joining nouns*) wa/kwa 와/과;
you ~ *me* tangshin-gwa na 당신과
나 ◊ (*joining adjectives*) ...go ...고 ;
tall ~ *thin* k'iga k'ŭgo marŭn 키가
크고 마른 ◊ (*joining verbs*) ...hago
...하고; *I did some exercises* ~ *had
a shower* nanŭn undong-ŭl hago

shyawŏrŭl haet-tta 나는 운동을 하고 샤워를 했다; *they were eating ~ drinking* kŭdŭrŭn mŏk-kko mashigo issŏssŏyo 그들은 먹고 마시고 있었어요 ◊ (*starting a new sentence*) kŭrigo 그리고; *And it was expensive* kŭrigo pissassŏyo 그리고 비쌌어요 ◊ (*expressing a result*) ...haesŏ ...해서; *he fell ~ broke his leg* kŭnŭn nŏmŏjyŏsŏ tariga purŏjyŏt-tta 그는 넘어져서 다리가 부러졌다 ◊: *it's getting hotter ~ hotter* chŏmjŏm tŏ tŏwŏjinda 점점 더 더워진다

anemia pinhyŏltchŭng 빈혈증
anemic *be ~* MED pinhyŏltchŭng-ida 빈혈증이다
anesthetic mach'wije 마취제
anesthetist mach'wisa 마취사
anger 1 *n* noyŏum 노여움 2 *v/t* hwanaege hada 화나게 하다
angina hyopsshimtchŭng 협심증
angle *n* kak 각
angry hwaga nan 화가 난; *be ~ with s.o.* nuguege hwaga nada 누구에게 화가 나다
anguish k'ŭn kot'ong 큰 고통
animal tongmul 동물
animated hwalbarhan 활발한
animated cartoon manhwa yŏnghwa 만화 영화
animation (*liveliness*) saenggi 생기; (*cinematic*) aenimeishyŏn 애니메이션
animosity chŭng-o 증오
ankle palmok 발목
annex 1 *n* (*building*) pyŏlgwan 별관 2 *v/t state* hap-ppyŏnghada 합병하다
anniversary (*wedding ~*) kinyŏmil 기념일
announce kongshiktchŏgŭro allida 공식적으로 알리다
announcement allim 알림; (*official*) konggo 공고
announcer TV, RAD anaunsŏ 아나운서
annoy sŏnggashigehada 성가시게 하다; *be ~ed* hwanada 화나다
annoyance (*anger*) hwa 화; (*nuisance*) sŏnggashim 성가심
annoying sŏnggashin 성가신

annual *adj* (*once a year*) illyŏne ha ponŭi 일년에 한 번의; (*of a year*) yŏnjung-ŭi 연중의; *~ salary* yŏnbong 연봉; *an ~ income* yŏns 연수입; *an ~ event* yŏnjung haeng 연중 행사
annul *marriage* muhyorohada 무효 하다
anonymous ingmyŏng-ŭi 익명의
anorexia kŏshiktchŭng 거식증
anorexic *be ~* kŏshiktchŭng-ŭl alt 거식증을 앓다
another 1 *adj* (*different*) tarŭn 다른 (*additional*) tto hana 또 하나 2 *pr* (*different one*) tarŭn kŏt 다른 것; (*additional one*) tto tarŭn kŏt 또 다른 것; *one* ~ sŏro 서로
answer 1 *n* tap 답; (*to problem*) haedap 해답 2 *v/t* tap'ada 답하다; *~ the door* munŭl yŏllŏ kada 문을 열러 가다; *~ the telephone* chŏnhwarŭl pat-tta 전화를 받다
♦ answer back 1 *v/t person* ...ege maldaekkuhada ...에게 말대꾸하ㄷ 2 *v/i* maldaekkuhada 말대꾸하다
♦ answer for ch'aegimŭl chida 책임 지다
answerphone chadong-ŭngdapkki 자동응답기
ant kaemi 개미
antagonism chŏktaeshim 적대심
Antarctic *n* Namgŭk-kkwŏn 남극권
antenatal ch'ulssan chŏnŭi 출산 전
antenna (*of insect*) tŏdŭmi 더듬이; (*for TV*) ant'ena 안테나
antibiotic *n* hangsaeng multchil 항 물질
antibody hangch'e 항체
anticipate (*expect*) yesanghada 예상하다
anticipation yesang 예상
anti-Communism pan-gongjuŭi 반공주의
antidote haedoktche 해독제
antifreeze pudong-aek 부동액
antipathy pan-gam 반감
antiquated kushigŭi 구식의
antique n kolttongp'um 골동품
antique dealer kolttongp'um sang- 골동품 상인
antiseptic 1 *adj* salgyunŭi 살균의 2

odongnyak 소독약

atisocial pisagyojŏgin 비사교적인; *I'm feeling very ~* nanŭn pyŏllo ugurŭl mannal kibuni anida 나는 별로 누구를 만날 기분이 아니다

ntivirus program COMPUT pairŏsŭ baeksshin p'ŭrogŭraem 바이러스 백신 프로그램

nxiety kŏktchŏng

nxious kŏktchŏnghanŭn 걱정하는; *(eager)* maeu paranŭn 매우 바라는; *be ~ for (for news etc)* ...ŭl/rŭl kodaehada ...을/를 고대하다

ny **1** *adj* ◊ *(no translation): are there ~ diskettes / glasses?* tisŭk'eshi / chani issŏyo? 디스켓이/잔이 있어요?; *is there ~ bread / improvement?* ppang-i / hyangsang-i issŭmnikka? 빵이/향상이 있습니까? ◊ *(in negatives)* amu ~ 아무; *there aren't ~ diskettes / glasses* amu tisŭk'et-tto / chando ŏpssŏyo 아무 디스켓도/잔도 없어요; *there isn't ~ bread / improvement* amu ppangdo / hyangsangdo ŏpssŭmnida 아무 빵도/향상도 없습니다; *take ~ one you like* choahanŭn kŏsŭn muŏidŭn kajiseyo 좋아하는 것은 무엇이든 가지세요 ◊ *(emphatic)* ŏttŏn ~ 어떤; *have you ~ idea at all?* ŏttŏn saenggagi issŭmnikka? 어떤 생각이 있습니까? **2** *pron (thing)* amu kŏt 아무 것; *(person)* nuguegedo 누구에게도; *don't you have ~?* amu kŏtto ŏpssŭseyo? 아무 것도 없으세요?; *there isn't / aren't ~ left* namŭn kŏshi ŏptta 남은 것이 없다; *~ of them could be guilty* kŭdŭl chung nuguegedo choega issŭl su issŏyo 그들 중 누구에게도 죄가 있을 수 있어요 **3** *adv* chogŭm 조금; *is that ~ better / easier?* chogŭmirado tŏ nassŭmnikka / shwissŭmnikka? 조금이라도 더 낫습니까/쉽습니까?; *I don't like it ~ more* nanŭn tŏ isang kŭgŏsŭl choahaji annŭnda 나는 더이상 그것을 좋아하지 않는다

anybody nugun-ga 누군가; *was ~ at home?* nugun-ga chibe issŏssŏyo? 누군가 집에 있었어요? ◊ *(with negatives)* amudo ... (+ negative verb) 아무도 ...; *there wasn't ~ there* amudo kŏgi ŏpssŏssŏyo 아무도 거기 없었어요; *wasn't ~ at home?* amudo chibe ŏpssŏssŏyo 아무도 집에 없었어요 ◊ *(emphatic)* nugurado 누구라도; *~ can do that* kŭgŏsŭn nugurado hal su issŏyo 그것은 누구라도 할 수 있어요

anyhow ŏtchaet-ttŭn 어쨌든

anyone → **anybody**

anything muŏt 무엇; *(with negatives)* amu kŏt-tto 아무 것도; *I didn't hear ~* nanŭn amu kŏt-tto tŭt-tchi anat-tta 나는 아무 것도 듣지 않았다; *~ but ...* chŏnhyŏ ...haji ant'a 전혀 ...하지 않다; *she was ~ but helpful* kŭnyŏnŭn chŏnhyŏ toumi toeji anassŏyo 그녀는 전혀 도움이 되지 않았어요; *~ else?* tarŭn kŏsŭnyo? 다른 것은요?

anyway → **anyhow**

anywhere ŏdidŭnji 어디든지; *if you see one ~, buy it* ŏdidŭnji kŭgŏsŭl pomyŏn saseyo 어디든지 그것을 보면 사세요 ◊ *(with negatives)* amudedo 아무데도; *he won't go ~ without me* kŭnŭn naŏpsshinŭn amudedo kaji anŭl kŏyeyo 그는 나 ŏpsinŭn 아무데도 가지 않을 거예요

apart *(in distance)* ttŏrŏjyŏsŏ 떨어져서; *live ~ (of people)* kakki ttaro salda 각기 따로 살다; *~ from (excepting)* cheoehago 제외하고; *(in addition to)* ...edaga tŏ ...에다가 더

apartment ap'at'ŭ 아파트

apartment block ap'at'ŭ tanji 아파트 단지

apathetic mukwanshimhan 무관심한

ape *n* k'ŭn wŏnsung-iryu 큰 원숭이류

aperture PHOT kugyŏng 구경

apologize sagwahada 사과하다

apology sagwa 사과

apostrophe GRAM ŏp'asŭt'ŭrop'i 어퍼스트로피

appall chilgŏp'age hada 질겁하게 하다

appalling musŭun 무서운; *language* chijŏbunhan 지저분한

apparatus changch'i 장치

apparent myŏngbaek'an 명백한;
become ~ that ... ranŭn kŏshi
punmyŏnghaejida ...라는 것이
분명해지다

apparently pogie 보기에; *~ they are
married* pogie kŭdŭrŭn kyŏrhonhan
kŏt kat'ayo 보기에 그들은 결혼한 것
같아요

appeal 1 *n* (*charm*) maeryŏk 매력;
(*for funds etc*) kanch'ŏng 간청; LAW
hangso 항소 2 *v/i* LAW hangsohada
항소하다

♦ **appeal to** (*be attractive to*) ...ŭl/rŭl
kkŭlda ...을/를 끌다

♦ **appeal for** ...ŭl/rŭl hosohada
...을/를 호소하다

appear nat'anada 나타나다; (*in
movie*) ch'uryŏnhada 출연하다; (*of
new product*) ch'ulsshihada
출시하다; (*in court*) ch'ulttuhada
출두하다; *he ~s calm* kŭnŭn
choyonghae poinda 그는 조용해
보인다; *it ~s that* ...in kŏt kat-tta ...
인 것 같다

appearance (*arrival*) ch'urhyŏn 출현;
(*in movie etc*) ch'uryŏn 출연; (*in
court*) ch'ulttu 출두; (*look*) p'yojŏng
표정; *put in an ~* chamkkan
ch'amsŏk'ada 잠깐 참석하다

appendicitis maengjangnyŏm 맹장염,
ch'ungsuyŏm 충수염

appendix MED maengjang 맹장,
ch'ungsu 충수; (*of book etc*) purok
부록

appetite shigyok 식욕; *fig* yokku 욕구

appetizer (*food*) chŏnch'ae 전채;
(*drink*) shiktchŏnŭi ŭmnyo 식전의
음료

appetizing shigyogŭl todunŭn 식욕을
돋우는

applaud 1 *v/i* sŏng-wŏnŭl ponaeda
성원을 보내다 2 *v/t* ...ege paksurŭl
ponaeda ...에게 박수를 보내다; *fig*
ch'ingsonghada 칭송하다

applause sŏng-wŏn 성원; (*praise*)
ch'ingsong 칭송

apple sagwa 사과

apple pie sagwa p'ai 사과 파이

apple sauce sagwasosŭ 사과소스

appliance kigye 기계; (*household*)
kajŏnjep'um 가전제품; *electrical ~*
chŏnja chep'um 전자 제품

applicable chŏgyonghal su innŭn
적용할 수 있는

applicant ŭngmoja 응모자

application (*for job, university etc*)
chiwŏn 지원; (*for passport, visa*)
shinch'ŏng 신청

application form chiwŏnsŏ 지원서;
(*for passport, visa*) shinch'ŏngsŏ
신청서; (*for university*) ip'ak wŏnsŏ
입학 원서

apply 1 *v/t* chŏgyonghada 적용하다;
ointment p'yŏ parŭda 펴 바르다 2
(*of rule, law*) chŏgyongdoeda
적용되다

♦ **apply for** *job, university*
chiwŏnhada 지원하다; *passport*
shinch'ŏnghada 신청하다

♦ **apply to** *address, department etc*
...(ŭ)ro yŏllak'ada ...(으)로
연락하다; *person* ...ege yŏllak'ada
...에게 연락하다; (*affect*) ...e
chŏgyongdoeda ...에 적용되다

appoint (*to position*) immyŏnghada
임명하다

appointment (*to position*) immyŏng
임명; (*meeting*) yakssok 약속

appointments diary taiŏri 다이어리

appreciate 1 *v/t* (*value*)
p'yŏngkkahada 평가하다; (*be
grateful for*) kamsahada 감사하다;
(*acknowledge*) alda 알다; *thanks, I
~ it* ch'injŏre kamsadŭrimnida
친절에 감사드립니다 2 *v/i* FIN
kagyŏgi orŭda 가격이 오르다

appreciation (*of kindness etc*) kamsa
감사; (*of music etc*) p'yŏngkka 평가;
as a token of our ~ kamsaŭi
p'yoshiro 감사의 표시로

apprehensive puranhan 불안한

apprentice kyŏnsŭpsaeng 견습생

approach 1 *n* chean 제안; (*offer etc*)
kyosŏp 교섭; (*to problem*) chŏpkkŭn
pangbŏp 접근 방법 2 *v/t* (*get near
to*) kakkai tagagada 가까이
다가가다; (*contact*) chŏpch'ok'ada
접촉하다; *problem* taruda 다루다

approachable *person* kakkai hagi
shwiun 가까이 하기 쉬운

appropriate *adj* chŏktchŏrhan 적절한

approval sŭng-in 승인

approve¹ *v/i* ch'ansŏnghada 찬성하다 **2** *v/t* sŭng-inhada 승인하다

approve of injŏnghada 인정하다

approximate *adj* taeryagŭi 대략의

approximately taeryak 대략

APR (= *annual percentage rate*) yŏniyul 연이율

apricot salgu 살구

April sawŏl 사월

apt *pupil* chaenŭng-innŭn 재능있는; *remark* chŏkttanghan 적당한; *be ~ to* (*likely*) …hanŭn kyŏnghyang-i it-tta …하는 경향이 있다

aptitude chŏkssŏng 적성

aquarium yuri sujokkwan 유리 수족관

aquatic sujung-ŭi 수중의

Arab1 *adj* Arabŭi 아랍의 **2** *n* Arabin 아랍인

Arabic1 *adj* Arabŭi 아랍의; *~ numerals* Arabia suttcha 아라비아 숫자 **2** *n* Arabŏ 아랍어

arable nonggyŏng-e almajŭn 농경에 알맞은

arbitrary *decision*, *remark* tokttanjŏgin 독단적인; *attack* mujagwihan 무작위한

arbitrate *v/i* chungjaehada 중재하다

arbitration chungjae 중재

arch *n* ach'i 아치

archeologist kogohaktcha 고고학자

archeology kogohak 고고학

archer kungsu 궁수

architect sŏlgyesa 설계사

architecture (*subject*) kŏnch'uk'ak 건축학; (*style*) kŏnch'ungnyangshik 건축양식

archives kirok 기록

archway ach'i mich'ŭi t'ongno 아치 밑의 통로

Arctic *n* Pukkŭkkwŏn 북극권

ardent yŏllyŏrhan 열렬한

area (*region*) chiyŏk 지역; (*of activity*, *study etc*) punya 분야; (*square meters etc*) myŏnjŏk 면적

area code TELEC chiyŏk pŏnho 지역 번호

arena SP undongjang 운동장

Argentina Arŭhent'ina 아르헨티나

Argentinian1 *adj* Arŭhent'inaŭi 아르헨티나의 **2** *n* Arŭhent'inain

아르헨티나인

arguably ama t'ŭllimŏpsshi 아마 틀림없이

argue1 *v/i* (*quarrel*) maldat'umhada 말다툼하다; (*reason*) nonhada 논하다 **2** *v/t*: *~ that* …rago chujanghada …라고 주장하다

argument (*quarrel*) nonjaeng 논쟁; (*reasoning*) nolli 논리

argumentative nonjaeng-ŭl choahanŭn 논쟁을 좋아하는

arid *land* kŏnjohan 건조한

arise (*of situation*, *problem*) irŏnada 일어나다

aristocrat kwijok 귀족

arithmetic sansul 산술

arm¹ *n* (*of person*) p'al 팔; (*of chair*) p'algŏri 팔걸이

arm² *v/t* mujangshik'ida 무장시키다

armaments kunbi 군비

armchair allak ŭija 안락 의자

armed mujanghan 무장한

armed forces kukkun 국군

armed robbery mujang kangdo 무장 강도

armor pangt'an chokki 방탄 조끼

armored vehicle changgapch'a 장갑차

armpit kyŏdŭrang-i 겨드랑이

arms (*weapons*) kunbi 군비

army yuk-kkun 육군

aroma hyanggi 향기

around1 *prep* (*in circle*) …ŭi chuwi …의 주위, …ŭi tulle …의 둘레; (*roughly*) taeryak … 대략 …; (*with expressions of time*) yak … tchŭm 약 … 쯤; *it's ~ the corner* igŏsŭn chŏ kusŏktchŭme it-tta 이것은 저 구석 쯤에 있다 **2** *adv* (*in the area*) kŭnch'ŏe 근처에; (*encircling*) tullee 둘레에; *be ~* (*somewhere near*) kŭnch'ŏe it-tta 근처에 있다; *he's ~ somewhere* kŭnŭn ŏdi kŭnch'ŏe issŏyo 그는 어디 근처에 있어요; *there are a lot of people ~* sabang-e manŭn saramdŭri issŏyo 사방에 많은 사람들이 있어요; *there's a nasty flu ~* tok-kkami yuhaeng-ida 독감이 유행이다; *he lives ~ here* kŭnŭn i kŭnch'ŏe sanda 그는 이 근처에 산다; *walk ~* kŏrŏdanida

걸어다니다; **she has been ~** (*has traveled, is experienced*) kŭnyŏnŭn insaenggyŏnghŏmi mant'a 그녀는 인생경험이 많다

arouse *interest, feelings* pullŏ irŭk'ida 불러 일으키다; (*sexually*) chaguk'ada 자극하다

arrange (*put in order*) paeyŏrhada 배열하다; *furniture* paech'ihada 배치하다; *flowers, books* kajirŏnhi kkot-tta 가지런히 꽃다; *music* p'yŏn-gok'ada 편곡하다; *meeting, party etc* chunbihada 준비하다; *time and place* yeyak'ada 예약하다; **I've ~d to meet him** nanŭn kŭwa mannagiro haet-tta 나는 그와 만나기로 했다
♦ **arrange for** ...ege put'ak'ada ...에게 부탁하다

arranged marriage chungmae kyŏrhon 중매 결혼

arrangement (*plan*) kyehoek 계획; (*agreement*) tong-ŭi 동의; (*of furniture etc*) paech'i 배치; (*of flowers*) kkotkkoji 꽃꽂이; (*of music*) p'yŏn-gok 편곡

arrears minapkkŭm 미납금; **be in ~** (*of person*) minap'ada 미납하다; **I'm paid in ~** nanŭn hubullo chigŭppannŭnda 나는 후불로 지급받는다

arrest 1 *n* ch'ep'o 체포; **be under ~** kugŭm sangt'aee it-tta 구금 상태에 있다 2 *v/t criminal* ch'ep'ohada 체포하다

arrival toch'ak 도착; **~s** (*at airport*) ipkkuk 입국

arrive toch'ak'ada 도착하다
♦ **arrive at** *place* ...e toch'ak'ada ...에 도착하다; *decision etc* ...e todarhada ...에 도달하다

arrogance kŏman 거만

arrogant kŏmanhan 거만한

arrow hwasal 화살

arrow key COMPUT hwasalp'yo külsoe 화살표 글쇠

arson panghwa 방화

art yesul 예술; (*things produced*) yesul'p'um 예술품; (*skill*) kisul 기술; **the ~s** munhwayesul 문화예술; **~s degree** munhaksa 문학사

arterial road kansŏndoro 간선도로

artery MED tongmaek 동맥

art gallery misulgwan 미술관

arthritis kwanjŏllyŏm 관절염

article (*item*) han p'ummok 한 품목; (*in newspaper*) kisa 기사; (*section*) chohang 조항; GRAM kwansa 관사

articulate *adj* myŏnghwak'an 명확한

artificial in-gongjŏgin 인공적인; *pearls, leather, flowers* injoŭi 인조의 (*not sincere*) inwijŏgin 인위적인

artificial intelligence in-gongjinŭng 인공지능

artillery taep'o 대포

artisan sugong-ŏptcha 수공업자

artist (*painter*) misulga 미술가; (*artistic person*) yesulga 예술가

artistic yesultchŏgin 예술적인

as 1 *conj* ◊ (*while, when*) ...hal ttae ...할 때; **he came in ~ I was going out** naega nagaryŏgo hal ttae kŭga tŭrŏwassŏyo 내가 나가려고 할 때 그가 들어왔어요 ◊ (*because*) waenyahamyŏn ...(i)ki ttaemunida 왜냐하면 ...(이)기 때문이다; **it's so rainy today** waenyahamyŏn onŭl piga nŏmu ogi ttaemuniyeyo 왜냐하면 오늘 비가 너무 오기 때문이에요 ◊ (*like*) ...ch'ŏrŏm ...처럼 **she married a miner, ~ her sister had done** kŭnyŏnŭn ŏnnich'ŏrŏm kwangbuwa kyŏrhonhaet-tta 그녀는 언니처럼 광부와 결혼했다; **~ if ...** in-gŏt ch'ŏrŏm ...인것 처럼; **don't treat me ~ if I was a child** narŭl aiin-gotch'ŏrŏm ch'igŭp'aji maseyo 나를 아이인것 처럼 취급하지 마세요; **~ usual** p'yŏngsoch'ŏrŏm 평소처럼; **~ necessary** p'iryohadamyŏn 필요하다면 2 *adv* mank'ŭm 만큼; **~ high/pretty ...** ...mank'ŭm nop'ŭn/yeppŭn ...만큼 높은/예쁜; **~ much/that?** kŭrŏke mani? 그렇게 많습니까? 3 *prep* ...(ŭ)rosŏ ...(으)로서; **~ a child** ŏryŏssŭl ttae ŏryŏng ul ttae 어렸을 때; **work ~ a teacher/translator** sŏnsaengnimŭro/pŏnyŏkkaro irhada 선생님으로/번역가로 일하다; **~ for you** nŏnŭn nŏ nŭn 너는; **~ Hamlet** haemlit yŏgŭro 햄릿 역으로

asap (= *as soon as possible*)

anŭnghanhan ppalli 가능한한 빨리

ṢEAN (= *Association of South East Asian Nations*) Tongnam Ashia Kuk-kka Yŏnhap 동남 아시아 국가 연합

hchae 재; **~es** chae 재

hamed *be ~* pukkŭrŏwŏhada ᄅ끄러워하다; *be ~ of* …ege ukkŭrŏpke yŏgida …에게 ᄅ끄럽게 여기다; *you should be ~ of yourself* tangshinŭn chashinege ᄅ끄럽게 여기다; *you should be ~ of yourself* tangshinŭn chashinege ᄅ끄러운 churŭl arayadoeyo 당신은 자신에게 부끄러운 줄을 알아야되요

sh can ssŭregi t'ong 쓰레기 통

shore mut'e 뭍에; *go ~* mut'e orŭda 뭍에 오르다

shtray chaettŏri 재떨이

sia Ashia 아시아

sian 1 *adj* Ashiaŭi 아시아의 2 *n* Ashiain 아시아인

side ttŏrŏttŭryŏ 떨어뜨려; *~ from* …ŭl / rŭl cheoehago …을 / 를 제외하고; *(in addition to)* …edaga tŏ …에다가 더

sk 1 *v/t (put a question to)* …ege mut-tta …에게 묻다; *(invite)* ch'odaehada 초대하다; *question* chilmunhada 질문하다; *favor* put'ak'ada 부탁하다; *can I ~ you something?* mwŏ chom 부탁해도 됩니까? *~ s.o. about sth* nuguege muŏse kwanhayŏ mut-tta 누구에게 무엇에 관하여 묻다; *~ s.o. for* nuguege …ŭl / rŭl put'ak'ada 누구에게 …을 / 를 부탁하다; *~ s.o. to* nuguege … haedallago hada 누구에게 … 해달라고 하다 2 *v/i* mut-tta 묻다

♦ **ask after** *person* …ŭi kŭnhwang-ŭl mut-tta …의 근황을 묻다

♦ **ask for** …ŭl / rŭl put'ak'ada …을 / 를 부탁하다; *person* …ŭl / rŭl ch'at-tta …을 / 를 찾다

♦ **ask out** teit'ŭ shinch'ŏnghada 데이트 신청하다

asking price p'anmae kagyŏk 판매 가격

asleep *be (fast) ~* p'uk chamdŭlda 푹 잠들다; *fall ~* chamdŭlda 잠들다

asparagus asŭp'aragŏsŭ 아스파라거스

aspect myŏn 면

aspirin asŭp'irin 아스피린

ass[1] *(idiot)* pabo 바보

ass[2] V *(backside)* ŏngdŏng-i 엉덩이; *(sex)* seksŭ 섹스

assassin amsalbŏm 암살범

assassinate amsarhada 암살하다

assassination amsal 암살

assault 1 *n* p'ok'aeng 폭행 2 *v/t* p'ok'aenghada 폭행하다

assemble 1 *v/t parts* chorip'ada 조립하다 2 *v/i (of people)* moida 모이다

assembly *(of parts)* chorip 조립; POL ŭihoe 의회

assembly line ilgwanjagŏp yŏl 일관작업 열

assembly plant chorip kongjang 조립 공장

assent *v/i* tong-ŭihada 동의하다

assert *~ oneself* chagirŭl chujanghada 자기를 주장하다

assertive *person* tanjŏngtchŏgin 단정적인

assess *situation, value* p'yŏngkkahada 평가하다

asset FIN, *fig* chasan 자산

asshole V ttongkkumŏng 똥구멍; *(idiot)* kaesaekki 개새끼

assign *task* chuda 주다; *room* halttanghada 할당하다

assignment *(task)* immu 임무; EDU suktche 숙제

assimilate *v/t facts* sohwahada 소화하다; *person into group* padadŭrida 받아들이다

assist toptta 돕다

assistance toum 도움

assistant chosu 조수

assistant director pujang 부장; *(for movie)* chogamdok 조감독

assistant manager pugyŏng-yŏng-in 부경영인; *(of hotel, restaurant, store)* pujibaein 부지배인

associate 1 *v/t* kwallyŏnshik'ida 관련시키다; *(in one's mind)* yŏnsanghada 연상하다 2 *v/i: ~ with* kyojehada 교제하다 3 *n* tongnyo 동료

associate professor pugyosu 부교수

association tanch'e hyŏp'oe 단체 협회; *in ~ with* ...wa/kwa hyŏmnyŏk'ayŏ ...와/과 협력하여

assortment kajigakssaek 가지각색

assume (*suppose*) kajŏnghada 가정하다

assumption kajŏng 가정

assurance pojŭng 보증; (*confidence*) chashin 자신

assure (*reassure*) pojanghada 보장하다

assured (*confident*) hwakssine ch'an 확신에 찬

asterisk pyŏlp'yo 별표

asthma ch'ŏnshik 천식

astonish kkamtchak nollagehada 깜짝 놀라게하다; *be ~ed* kkamtchak nollada 깜짝 놀라다

astonishing maeu nollaun 매우 놀라운

astonishment kkamtchak nollam 깜짝 놀람

astrologer chŏmsŏngga 점성가

astrology chŏmsŏngsul 점성술

astronaut ujuin 우주인

astronomer ch'ŏnmunhaktcha 천문학자

astronomical ch'ŏnmunhaktchŏgin 천문학적인; *price* ŏmch'ŏngnage nop'ŭn 엄청나게 높은

astronomy ch'ŏnmunhak 천문학

asylum (*mental*) chŏngshinppyŏng-wŏn 정신병원; (*political*) mangmyŏng 망명; *seek political ~* chŏngch'ijŏk mangmyŏng-ŭl shinch'ŏnghada 정치적 망명을 신청하다

at (*with places*) ...e(sŏ) ...에(서); *~ the cleaner's* set'akssoe(sŏ) 세탁소에(서); *~ Joe's* cho nechibesŏ(sŏ) 조 네집에(서); *~ the door* mune 문에; *~ 10 dollars* 10tallŏro 10달러로; *~ the age of 18* yoryŏdŏl sal ttaee 열여덟 살 때에; *~ 5 o'clock* 5shie 5시에; *~ 150 km/h* shisok 150k'illomit'ŏro 시속 150 킬로미터로; *be good/bad ~ sth* muŏse nŭngsuk'ada/nŭngsuk'aji mot'ada 무엇에 능숙하다/능숙하지 못하다

atheist mushillonja 무신론자

athlete undonga 운동가, sŭp'och'i 스포츠인

athletic undong-ŭi 운동의; *person* ch'eryŏginnŭn 체력있는

athletics undonggyŏnggi 운동경기

Atlantic *n* Taesŏyang 대서양

atlas chidoch'aek 지도책

ATM (= *automated teller machine*) hyŏn-gŭm inch'ulgi 현금 인출기

atmosphere (*of earth*) taegi 대기; (*ambiance*) punwigi 분위기

atmospheric pollution taegi oyŏm 대기 오염

atom wŏnja 원자

atom bomb wŏnja p'okt'an 원자 폭탄

atomic wŏnjaŭi 원자의

atomic energy wŏnjaryŏk 원자력

atomic waste haekssŭregi 핵쓰레기

atomizer punmugi 분무기

atrocious shimhage nappŭn 심하게 나쁜

atrocity hyung-ak 흉악

attach puch'ida 붙이다; *importance* puyŏhada 부여하다; (*to letter*) tongbonghada 동봉하다; *be ~ed to* (*fond of*) ...e(ge) maŭmi kkŭllida ...에(게) 마음이 끌리다

attachment (*with e-mail*) ch'ŏmga 첨가

attack 1 *n* konggyŏk 공격 2 *v/t* konggyŏk'ada 공격하다

attempt 1 *n* shido 시도 2 *v/t* shidohada 시도하다

attend ch'amsŏk'ada 참석하다

♦ **attend to** ch'ŏrihada 처리하다; *customer* moshida 모시다; (*pay attention to*) chuŭihada 주의하다

attendance ch'amsŏk 참석; (*at school*) ch'ulssŏk 출석

attendant (*in museum*) chigwŏn 직원

attention chuŭi 주의; *bring X to the ~ of Y* Xe taehan chuŭirŭl Yege hwan-gishik'ida X에 대한 주의를 Y에게 환기시키다; *your ~ please* chumok'ae chushipssimio 주목해 주십시오; *pay ~* chuŭihada 주의하다

attentive *listener* chuŭigip'ŭn 주의깊은

attic tarakppang 다락방

attitude t'aedo 태도

attn (= *for the attention of*) sushin 수신

attorney pyŏnhosa 변호사; *power of ~* wiimkkwŏn 위임권

attract *person, attention* kkŭlda 끌다; *be ~ed to s.o.* nuguege maŭmi kkŭllida 누구에게 마음이 끌리다

attraction (*also romantic*) maeryŏk 매력

attractive maeryŏginnŭn 매력있는

attribute[1] *v/t: ~ sth to* muŏshi … ttaemunŭro ch'ujŏngdoeda 무엇이 … 때문으로 추정되다; *painting, poem* muŏsŭl …ŭi chakp'umŭro ch'ujŏnghada 무엇을 …의 작품으로 추정하다

attribute[2] *n* sokssŏng 속성

auction 1 *n* kyŏngmae 경매 **2** *v/t* kyŏngmaehada 경매하다

auction off kyŏngmaehada 경매하다

audacious *plan* taedamhan 대담한

audacity taedamhan haengdong 대담한 행동

audible tŭrŭl su innŭn 들을 수 있는

audience ch'ŏngjung 청중; (*in theater, at show*) kwanjung 관중; TV shich'ŏngja 시청자; (*of radio program*) ch'ŏngch'wija 청취자

audio *adj* odioŭi 오디오의

audiovisual shich'ŏnggagŭi 시청각의

audit 1 *n* kamsa 감사 **2** *v/t* kamsahada 감사하다; *course* ch'ŏngganghada 청강하다

audition 1 *n* odishyŏn 오디션 **2** *v/i* odishyŏnŭl pat-tta 오디션을 받다

auditor FIN kamsagwan 감사관; (*of course*) ch'ŏnggangsaeng 청강생

auditorium (*of theater etc*) kwanjungsŏk 관중석

August p'arwŏl 팔월

aunt (*own, sister of father*) komo 고모; (*own, sister of mother*) imo 이모; (*own, wife of uncle on father's side*) sungmo 숙모; (*own, wife of uncle on mother's side*) oesungmo 외숙모; (*somebody else's*) ajumma 아줌마

austere *interior, style* kkumijianŭn 꾸미지 않은; *person, face* chunŏmhan 준엄한; *life* kŭmyoktchŏgin 금욕적인

austerity (*economic*) naep'ip 내핍

Australasia Oseania 오세아니아

Australia Hoju 호주

Australian 1 *adj* Hojuŭi 호주의 **2** *n* Hojuin 호주인

Austria Osŭt'ŭria 오스트리아

Austrian 1 *adj* Osŭt'ŭriaŭi 오스트리아의 **2** *n* Osŭt'ŭriain 오스트리아인

authentic chintchaŭi 진짜의

authenticity shinbingssŏng 신빙성

author chakka 작가; (*of report etc*) chipp'iltcha 집필자

authoritative kwŏniinnŭn 권위있는

authority kwŏnwi 권위; (*permission*) hŏga 허가; *be an ~ on* …ŭi kwŏnwijaida …의 권위자이다; *the authorities* tangguk 당국

authorize kwŏnhanŭl chuda 권한을 주다; *be ~d to* …ㄹ/을 hŏga pat-tta …ㄹ/을 허가 받다

autistic chap'yetchŭng-ŭi 자폐증의

auto *n* chadongch'a 자동차

autobiography chasŏjŏn 자서전

autograph *n* sain 사인

automate chadonghwahada 자동화하다

automatic 1 *adj* chadong-ŭi 자동의 **2** *n* (*car, gun etc*) chadongkigye 자동기계

automatically chadong-ŭro 자동으로

automation chadonghwa 자동화

automobile chadongch'a 자동차

automobile industry chadongch'a sanŏp 자동차 산업

autonomy chach'i 자치

autopilot chadong chojong changch'i 자동 조종 장치

autopsy pugŏm 부검

auxiliary *adj* pojoŭi 보조의

available *facility, service* ŏdŭl su innŭn 얻을 수 있는; *book, information* ch'ajŭl su innŭn 찾을 수 있는; *person* shiganinnŭn 시간있는

avalanche nunsat'ae 눈사태

avenue *also fig* kil 길

average 1 *adj* p'yŏnggyunŭi 평균의; (*ordinary*) pot'ong-ŭi 보통의; (*mediocre*) pot'ong chŏngdoŭi 보통

정도의 **2** *n* p'yŏnggyun 평균; *above / below* ~ p'yŏnggyun wiŭi / araeŭi 평균 위의 / 아래의; *on* ~ pot'ong 보통 **3** *v/t* p'yŏnggyunŭro … hada 평균으로 … 하다; *I ~ six hours sleep a night* nanŭn harue p'yŏnggyun yŏsŏt shiganŭl chanda 나는 하루에 평균 여섯 시간을 잔다

♦ **average out** *v/t* p'yŏnggyunnaeda 평균내다

♦ **average out at** p'yŏnggyun …(ŭ)ro kyesandoeda 평균 …(으)로 계산되다

aversion: *have an* ~ *to* …ŭl / rŭl aju shirŏhada …을 / 를 아주 싫어하다

avert *one's eyes* p'ihada 피하다; *crisis* maktta 막다

aviary k'ŭn saejang 큰 새장

aviation hanggong 항공

avid yŏlgwangtchŏgin 열광적인

avoid p'ihada 피하다

awake *adj* kkaeŏinnŭn 깨어있는; *it's keeping me* ~ kŭgŏshi chamŭl sŏlch'ige haet-tta 그것이 잠을 설치게 했다

award 1 *n* (*prize*) sang 상 **2** *v/t* suyŏhada 수여하다; *he was ~ed $10,000 in damages* kŭnŭn mandallŏŭi sonhae paesang-ŭl padat-tta 그는 10,000달러의 손해 배상을 받았다

aware: *be* ~ *of sth* muŏsŭl alda 무엇을 알다; *become* ~ *of sth*

muŏsŭl arach'arida 무엇을 알아차리다

awareness inshik 인식

away: *be* ~ (*traveling, sick etc*) ŏptt 없다; *I'll be* ~ *until next Friday* nanŭn taŭm chu kŭmnyoilkkaji ŏpssŭl kŏyeyo 나는 다음 주 금요일까지 없을 거예요; *walk / run* ~ kŏrŏgada / tomanggada 걸어가다 / 도망가다; *look* ~ nunkkirŭl tollida 눈길을 돌리다; *it's 2 miles* ~ 2mail ttŏrŏjyŏit-tta 2마일 떨어져있다; *Christmas is still six weeks* ~ Sŏngt'anjŏlkkajinŭn yŏjŏnhi yuk chuna nama issŏyo 성탄절까지는 여전히 육 주나 남아 있어요; *take sth* ~ *from s.o.* nugurobut'ŏ muŏsŭl ppaeat-tta 누구로부터 무엇을 빼앗다; *put sth* ~ muŏsŭl ch'iuda 무엇을 치우다

away game SP wŏnjŏng shihap 원정 시합

awesome F (*terrific*) koengjanghan 굉장한

awful shimhan 심한

awkward (*clumsy*) sŏt'urŭn 서투른; (*difficult*) himdŭn 힘든; (*embarrassing*) kŏbuk'an 거북한; *feel* ~ kŏbuk'aehada 거북해하다

awning ch'ayang 차양

ax 1 *n* tokki 도끼 **2** *v/t job etc* tchallida 짤리다; *budget* sak-kkamhada 삭감하다

axle ch'ach'uk 차축

B

A (= *Bachelor of Arts*) haksa
agwi 학사 학위
aboon kaek'owŏnsung-i 개코원숭이
aby n agi 아기
aby carriage yumoch'a 유모차;
baby quilt (*for carrying baby*)
'odaegi 포대기; **baby-sit** agirŭl
olbwajuda 아기를 돌봐주다; **baby-
sitter** agirŭl tolbwajununŭn saram
아기를 돌봐주는 사람
achelor ch'onggak 총각
ack 1 n (*of person, book, knife,
chair*) tŭng 등; (*of car, bus, paper*)
winmyŏn 뒷면; (*of house*) twittchok
뒷쪽; SP huwi 후위; **in ~** anthoge(sŏ)
안쪽에(서); **in ~** (*of the car*)
(ch'aŭi) twit chwasŏge(sŏ) (차의) 뒷
좌석에(서); **at the ~ of the bus**
bŏsŭ twit chwasŏge(sŏ) 버스 뒷
좌석에(서); **~ to front** kŏkkuro
거꾸로; **at the ~ of beyond** mopsshi
oejin kose(sŏ) 몹시 외진 곳에(서)
2 adj twittchoge innŭn 뒷쪽에 있는;
~ road twitkkil 뒷길 **3** adv: **please
move / stand ~** twiro mullŏna
chushipsshiyo / twie sŏ chushipsshiyo
뒤로 물러나 주십시요 / 뒤에 서
주십시요; **2 meters ~ from the
edge** kajangjariesŏ 2mit'ŏ tŭrŏgasŏ
가장자리에서 2미터 들어가서; **~ in
1935** 1935nyŏnŭro kŏsŭllŏ ollagasŏ
1935년으로 거슬러 올라가서; **give X
~ to Y** Xŭl / rŭl Yege toedollyŏjuda
X을/를 Y에게 되돌려주다; **~
tomorrow** kŭnyŏnŭn naeil toraol
kŏshimnida 그녀는 내일 돌아올
것입니다; **when are you coming ~?**
ŏnje tora-ol kŏmnikka? 언제 돌아올
겁니까?; **take X ~ to the store**
(*because unsatisfactory*) Xŭl / rŭl
kagee murŭda X을 / 를 가게에
무르다; **they wrote / phoned ~**
kŭdŭrŭn hoeshin haet-tta / hoedap
haet-tta 그들은 회신 했다 / 회답

했다; **he hit me ~** kŭnŭn narŭl
toettaeryŏt-tta 그는 나를 되때렸다
4 v/t (*support*) huwŏnhada 후원하다;
car hujinshik'ida 후진시키다; *horse*
tonŭl kŏlda 돈을 걸다 **5** v/i (*of car*)
hujinhada 후진하다; ida 이다
♦ **back away** mullŏsŏda 물러서다
♦ **back down** yangbohada 양보하다
♦ **back off** twiro mullŏnada 뒤로
물러나다; (*from danger*) …esŏ
mullŏnada …에서 물러나다
♦ **back onto** …wa / kwa twiro
chŏp'ae it-tta …와 / 과 뒤로 접해
있다
♦ **back out** (*of commitment*) sonŭl
tteda 손을 떼다
♦ **back up 1** v/t (*support*) huwŏnhada
후원하다; *claim, argument*
twittppatch'imhae chuda 뒷받침해
주다; *file* paegŏp'ada 백업하다; **be
backed up** (*of traffic*) millyŏ it-tta
밀려 있다 **2** v/i (*in car*) hujinhada
후진하다
back burner: **put sth on the ~**
muŏsŭl yŏn-gihada 무엇을 연기하다;
backdate sogŭp'ayŏ
chŏgyongshik'ida 소급하여
적용시키다; **backdoor** twinmun
뒷문
backer huwŏnja 후원자
backfire v/i fig yŏk'yokkwaga nada
역효과가 나다; **background**
paegyŏng 배경; (*of person*)
ch'ulsshin sŏngbun 출신 성분; (*of
situation*) paehu 배후; **she prefers
to stay in the ~** kŭnyŏnŭn ohiryŏ
nasŏji ankirŭl choahanda 그녀는
오히려 나서지 않기를 좋아한다;
backhand n (*in tennis*) paek
haendŭ 백 핸드
backing (*support*) chiji 지지; MUS
panju 반주
backing group MUS panjudan 반주단
backlash panbal 반발; **backlog**

mich'ŏribun 미처리분; **backpack**
1 *n* paenang 배낭 **2** *v/i* paenang
maego yŏhaenghada 배낭 매고
여행하다; **backpacker** paenang
yŏhaengja 배낭 여행자; **backpedal**
fig ch'ŏlhoehada 철회하다;
backslash COMPUT paeksŭllaeshi
억슬래시; **backspace (key)** COMPUT
paeksssŭp'eisŭ k'i 백스페이스 키;
backstairs twitch'ŭnggye 뒷층계;
backstroke SP paeyŏng 배영;
backup (*support*) chiwŏn 지원;
COMPUT paegŏp 백업; *take a ~*
COMPUT paegŏbŭl hada 백업을 하다;
backup disk COMPUT paegŏp
tisŭk'ŭ 백업 디스크

backward 1 *adj child* twittŏrojin
뒤떨어진; *society* t'oebohanŭn
퇴보하는; *glance* twittchogŭi 뒷쪽의
2 *adv* twittchogŭro 뒷쪽으로

backyard twit-ttŭl 뒷뜰; *fig* kŭnch'ŏ
근처

bacon peik'ŏn 베이컨

bacteria pakt'eria 박테리아

bad nappŭn 나쁜; *spelling* sŏt'urŭn
서투른; *cold, headache etc* shimhan
심한; (*rotten*) ssŏgŭn 썩은; *it's not ~
kwaench'anayo 괜찮아요; *that's
really too ~* (*shame*) nŏmu
andwaessŏyo 너무 안됐어요; *feel ~
about* ...e taehae choech'aek-
kkamŭl nŭkkida ...에 대해 죄책감을
느끼다; *be ~ at* ...e sŏt'urŭda ...에
서투르다; *Friday's ~, how about
Thursday?* kŭmnyoirŭn
andoenŭnde, mogyoirŭn ŏttaeyo?
금요일은 안되는데, 목요일은
어때요?

bad debt pullyang puch'ae 불량 부채

badge paeji 배지

badger *v/t* chorŭda 조르다

bad language yoksssŏl 욕설

badly nappŭge 나쁘게; (*making
mistakes, errors*) chalmot 잘못;
injured, damaged shimhage 심하게;
he ~ needs a haircut / rest kŭnŭn
chŏngmal mŏrirŭl challayagessŏyo /
shwiŏyagessŏyo 그는 정말 머리를
잘라야겠어 요 / 쉬어야겠어요; *he is ~
off* (*poor*) kŭnŭn kananhada 그는
가난하다

badminton paedŭmint'ŏn 배드민턴

baffle tanghwanghage hada 당황하게
하다; *be ~d* tanghwanghae hada
당황해 하다

baffling ihaehal su ŏmnŭn 이해할 수
없는

bag (*travel ~*) yŏhaeng kabang 여행
가방; (*plastic, paper*) kabang 가방;
(*for school*) ch'aek-kkabang 책가방;
(*pocketbook*) haendŭbaek 핸드백

baggage suhwamul 수화물

baggage car RAIL suhwamul yŏlch'a
수화물 열차; **baggage cart**
suhwamul unbanch'a 수화물 운반차;
baggage check suhwamul
pogwantchŭng 수화물 보관증;
baggage reclaim suhwamul
k'ŭlleim 수화물 클레임

baggy hŏllŏnghan 헐렁한

bail *n* LAW posŏk 보석; (*money*)
posŏk-kkŭm 보석금; *on ~* posŏk-
kkŭmŭl naego 보석금을 내고

♦ **bail out 1** *v/t* LAW posŏgŭl patkke
hada 보석을 받게 하다; *fig* kon-
gyŏng-esŏ ...ŭl / rŭl kuhaenaeda
곤경에서 ...을 / 를 구해내다 **2** *v/i*
(*from airplane*) nak'asanŭro
t'alch'urhada 낙하산으로 탈출하다

bait *n* mikki 미끼

bake *v/t* kuptta 굽다

baked potato kuun kamja yori 구운
감자 요리

baker cheppang-ŏptcha 제빵업자

bakery ppangjip 빵집

balance 1 *n* kyunhyŏng 균형;
(*remainder*) chanyŏgŭm 잔여금; (*of
bank account*) chan-go 잔고 **2** *v/t*
...ŭi kyunhyŏng-ŭl chaptta ..의
균형을 잡다; *~ the books* hoegye
kyŏlssanhada 회계 결산하다 **3** *v/i*
kyunhyŏng chaptta 균형 잡다; (*of
accounts*) kyŏlssandoeda 결산되다

balanced (*fair*) kongjŏnghan 공정한
diet kyunhyŏng chap'in 균형 잡힌;
personality anjŏngdoen 안정된

balance of payments kuktche suji
국제 수지; **balance of trade** muyŏk
suji 무역 수지; **balance sheet**
taech'adaejp'yo 대차대조표

balcony (*of house*) peranda 베란다;
(*in theater*) ich'ŭng chwasŏk 이층

좌석

aldman taemŏriŭi 대머리의; *he's going ~* kŭnŭn taemŏriga toeŏ kanda 그는 대머리가 되어 간다

allkong 공; *on the ~* fig pint'ŭm ŏmnŭn 빈틈 없는; *play ~* fig hyŏmnyŏk'ada 협력하다; *the ~'s in this court* fig taŭmŭn kŭŭi ch'aryeida 다음은 그의 차례이다

all bearingpol pŏring 볼 베어링

allerinapallerina 발레리나

alletpalle 발레

allet dancerpalle muyongga 발레 무용가

all game(baseball game) yagu 야구; *that's a different ~* kŭgŏn tarŭn chongnyuŭi munjeimnida 그건 다른 종류의 문제입니다

allistic missilet'ando misail 탄도 미사일

alloon(child's) p'ungsŏn 풍선; (for flight) kigu 기구

allot1 n t'up'yo 투표 2 v/t members t'up'yoro chŏnghada 투표로 정하다

allot boxtup'yoham 투표함

allpark(baseball) yagujang 야구장; *be in the right ~* fig kŏŭi mat-tta 거의 맞다; *~ figure* taegang-ŭi ŏrim 대강의 어림

ballpoint (pen)polp'en 볼펜

alls√ pural 불알; (courage) paetchang 배짱

bambootaenamu 대나무

oan1 n kŭmji 금지 2 v/t kŭmjihada 금지하다

bananapanana 바나나

bandakdan 악단; (pop) paendŭ 밴드; (of material) kkŭn 끈

bandage1 n pundae 붕대 2 v/t pungdaerŭl kamtta 붕대를 감다

Band-Aid®panch'anggo 반창고

banditsanjŏk 산적

bandwagon *jump on the ~* shiryurŭl t'ada 시류를 타다

bandylegs hwin 휜

bang1 n (noise) k'wang hanŭn sori 쾅 하는 소리; (blow) k'wang pudich'im 쾅 부딪힘 2 v/t door k'wang tat-tta 쾅 닫다; (hit) k'wang pudich'ida 쾅 부딪히다 3 v/i (of door) k'wang tach'ida 쾅 닫히다

BangladeshPanggŭlladeshi 방글라데시

Bangladeshi1 adj Panggŭlladeshiŭi 방글라데시의 2 n Panggŭlladeshiin 방글라데시인

banjopaenjo 밴조

bank1(of river) chebang 제방

bank2 1 n FIN ŭnhaeng 은행 2 v/i: *~ with* ...wa/kwa kŏraehada ...와/과 거래하다 3 v/t money yegŭmhada 예금하다

♦**bank on**...ŭl/rŭl kidaehada ...을/를 기대하다; *don't ~ it* nŏmu hwakssinhaji mara 너무 확신하지 마라

bank accountŭnhaeng kujwa 은행 구좌; **bank balance**ŭnhaeng chango 은행 잔고; **bank bill**chip'ye 지폐

bankerŭnhaengga 은행가

banker's cardŭnhaeng shinyong k'adŭ 은행 신용 카드

banker's orderchadong taech'e 자동 대체

bank loanŭnhaeng yungja 은행 융자; **bank manager**ŭnhaeng chijŏmjang 은행 지점장; **bank rate**(chung-ang ŭnhaeng-ŭi) ijayul (중앙 은행의) 이자율; **bankroll**v/t chagŭmŭl taeda 자금을 대다

bankrupt1 adj (person, company) p'asanhan 파산한; *go ~* p'asanhada 파산하다 2 v/t p'asanshik'ida 파산시키다

bankruptcyp'asan 파산

bank statementchan-go chohoe 잔고 조회

bannerki 기

bannskyŏrhon yego 결혼 예고

banquetyŏnhoe 연회

bantern kabyŏun nongdam 가벼운 농담

baptismserye 세례

baptizeseryehada 세례하다

bar1(iron) pitchang 빗장; (of chocolate) makttaegi 막대기; (for drinks) sultchip 술집; (counter) kyesandae 계산대; *a ~ of soap* pinu hanjang 비누 한 장; *be behind ~s* kamoge it-tta 감옥에 있다

bar2v/t kŭmhada 금하다

bar3prep (except) ...ŭl/rŭl cheoehago

…을/를 제외하고
barbecue 1 *n* pabek'yu 바베큐;
(*equipment*) pabegabŏsŭn
바베큥용 철판 **2** *v*/*t* t'ongtchaero
kuptta 통째로 굽다
barbecued beef pulgogi 불고기
barbed wire kashi ch'ŏlssa 가시 철사
barber ibalssa 이발사
bar code pak'odŭ 바코드
bare *adj* (*naked*) palgabŏsŭn
발가벗은; *room* t'ŏng pin 텅 빈; **~
floor** maenmaru 맨마루
barefoot: be ~ maenbarida 맨발이다
bare-headed mojarŭl ssŭji anŭn
모자를 쓰지 않은
barely kanshinhi 간신히
bargain 1 *n* (*deal*) yakssok 약속;
(*good buy*) ssan mulgŏn 싼 물건; **it's
a ~!** (*deal*) kyŏltchŏngnassŏyo!
결정났어요! **2** *v*/*i* hŭngjŏnghada
흥정하다
♦ **bargain for** (*expect*) yesanghada
예상하다
barge *n* NAUT kŏrutppae 거룻배
bark[1] **1** *n* (*of dog*) kae chinnŭn sori 개
짖는 소리 **2** *v*/*i* chit-tta 짖다
bark[2] (*of tree*) kkŏptchil 껍질
barley *n* pori 보리
barn hŏtkkan 헛간
barometer kiapkkye 기압계; *fig*
chip'yo 지표
barracks MIL makssa 막사
barrel (*container*) t'ong 통
barren *land* pulmoŭi 불모의
barrette mŏrip'in 머리핀
barricade *n* parik'eidŭ 바리케이드
barrier ult'ari 울타리; (*cultural*)
chang-ae 장애; **language ~** ŏnŏ
chang-ae 언어 장애
bar tender pat'endŏ 바텐더
barter 1 *n* mulmul kyohwan 물물
교환 **2** *v*/*t* mulmul kyohwanhada
물물 교환하다
base 1 *n* (*bottom*) mit 밑; (*center*)
ponbu 본부; MIL chaktchŏn kiji 작전
기지 **2** *v*/*t*: **~ on** …e pat'angŭl tuda
…에 바탕을 두다; **~ X on Y** Xŭi
pat'angŭl Y(으)ro hada X의 바탕을
Y(으)로 하다; **be ~d in** (*in city,
country*) …e kŭn-gŏjirŭl tugo it-tta
…에 근거지를 두고 있다

baseball (*ball*) yagugong 야구공;
(*game*) yagu 야구
baseball bat yagu pangmang-i 야구
방망이; **baseball cap** yagu moja
야구 모자; **baseball player** yagu
sŏnsu 야구 선수
base camp peisŭ k'emp'ŭ 베이스
캠프
basement (*of house*) chihashil
지하실; (*of store*) chihach'ŭng 지하
base rate FIN chung-ang ŭnhaeng-ŭ
kibon kŭmni 중앙 은행의 기본 금라
basic (*rudimentary*) kibonjŏgin
기본적인; (*fundamental*)
kŭnbonjŏgin 근본적인; *level*
kich'ojŏgin 기초적인; **a ~ hotel**
susuhan hot'el 수수한 호텔
basically kibonjŏgŭro 기본적으로
basics: the ~ kich'o 기초; **get dow**
to ~ kich'obut'ŏ hada 기초부터 하ㄷ
basin (*for washing*) semyŏndae
세면대
basis kich'o 기초; (*of argument*) kŭ
gŏ 근거
bask haetppyŏch'ŭl tchoeda 햇볕을
쬐다
basket paguni 바구니; (*in basketbal*
pasŭk'et 바스켓
basketball nonggu 농구
bass 1 *n* (*part, singer*) peisŭ 베이스;
(*instrument*) pasŭ 바스 **2** *adj*
chŏŭmŭi 저음의; **~ clef** najŭn
ŭmjarip'yo 낮은 음자리표
bastard sasaeng-a 사생아; F
kaesaekki 개새끼; *poor / stupid ~*
pulssanghan / pabokat'ŭn nyŏsŏk
불쌍한 /바보같은 녀석
bat[1] **1** *n* (*for baseball*) pangmang-i
방망이; (*for table tennis*) ch'ae 채
2 *v*/*i* (*in baseball*) pangmang-iro
ch'ida 방망이로 치다
bat[2]: **he didn't ~ an eyelid** kŭnŭn
nun hana kkamtchak'aji anat-tta
그는 눈 하나 깜짝하지 않았다
bat[3] (*animal*) paktchwi 박쥐
batch *n* (*of students*) ilttan 일단; (*of
data*) paech'i 배치; (*of goods
produced*) han mukkŭm 한 묶음; (*
bread*) han kama 한 가마
bath mogyok 목욕; **have a ~, take a**
~ mogyok'ada 목욕하다

...the v/i (have a bath) mogyok'ada 목욕하다
...th mat mogyokt'ang kkalgae 목욕탕 깔개; **bathrobe** mogyok kaun 목욕 가운; **bathroom** (for ...ath) yokshil 욕실; (for washing ...ands) semyŏnjang 세면장; (toilet) wajangshil 화장실; **bath towel** ...nogyok sugŏn 목욕 수건; **bathtub** ...oktcho 욕조

...tter¹ n (in cooking) milkkaru ...anjuk 밀가루 반죽

...tter² (in baseball) t'aja 타자

...ttery chŏnji 전지; MOT paet'ŏri ...터리

...ttle n chŏnt'u 전투; fig t'ujaeng ...투쟁

battle against illness etc ....wa/kwa ssauda ...와/과 싸우다

...ttlefield, battleground ...hŏnjaengt'ŏ 전쟁터

...wdy oesŭlsŭrŏun 외설스러운

...wl (shout) kohamch'ida 고함치다; (weep) ulda 울다

...bawl out v/t hot'ong-ŭl ch'ida ...호통을 치다

...y (inlet) man 만

...y window naeminch'ang 내민창

...BS (= **Buddhist Broadcasting ...System**) Pulgyo Pangsong 불교 ...방송

...e◊ ida 이다; (exist) itta 있다; **I am ...e student** nanŭn hakssaeng-iyeyo ...는 학생이에요; **was she there?** ...ŏgi kŭ yŏjaga itssŏssŏyo? 거기 그 ...녀자가 있었어요?; **it's me** chŏyeyo ...여요; **how much is/are ...?** ...ŏ..ŭn/nŭn ŏlmaimnikka? ...은/는 ...얼마입니까?; **there is, there are** ...i/ga it-tta ...이/가 있다; **there are ...ome books in my bag** nae kabang ...oge ch'aegi it-tta 내 가방 속에 책이 ...있다 ◊ (with adjectives) ...ta ...다; **she ...s pretty** kŭnyŏnŭn yeppŭda 그녀는 ...예쁘다; **I am tired** nanŭn p'igonhada 나는 피곤하다; **~ careful** ...hoshimhaseyo 조심하세요; **don't ~ ...ad** sŭlp'ŏhajima 슬퍼하지마 ◊: **has ...he mailman been?** uch'ebuga ...üllŏt-tta kassŏyo? 우체부가 들렀다 ...어요?; **I've never been to Korea**

nanŭn Han-guge kabon chŏgi ŏptta 나는 한국에 가본 적이 없다; **I've been here for hours** nanŭn yŏgi myŏt shiganina kyesŏk issŏt-tta 나는 여기 몇 시간이나 계속 있었다 ◊ (tag questions) ...jiyo? ...지요?; **that's right, isn't it?** mat-chiyo? 맞지요?; **she's Korean, isn't she?** kŭ yŏjanŭn Han-guk saram ijiyo? 그 여자는 한국 사람 이지요? ◊ (auxiliary) ... hago it-tta ... 하고 있다; **I am thinking** nanŭn saenggak'ago issŏyo 나는 생각하고 있어요; **he was running** kŭnŭn ttwigo issŏt-tta 그는 뛰고 있었다; **you're ~ing silly** nŏnŭn pabosŭrŏun chisŭl hago issŏ 너는 바보스러운 짓을 하고 있어 ◊ (obligation) ... haeya handa ... 해야 한다; **you are to do what I tell you** nŏnŭn naega marhanŭn taero haeya handa 너는 내가 말하는 대로 해야 한다; **I was to tell you this** nanŭn nŏege igŏsŭl marhaessŏya haessŏ 나는 너에게 이것을 말했어야 했어; **you are not to tell anyone** amuegedo marhaesŏn andwae 아무에게도 말해선 안돼 ◊ (passive): **he was killed** kŭnŭn p'isaldanghaet-tta 그는 피살당했다; **they have been sold** kŭgŏt-ttŭrŭn p'allyŏt-tta 그것들은 팔렸다; **it was discovered** kŭgŏsŭn palgyŏndoeŏt-tta 그것은 발견되었다 ♦ **be in for** ...ŭl/rŭl yesanghago it-tta ...을/를 예상하고 있다

beach haebyŏn 해변

beachwear pich'iwcŏ 비치웨어

beads kusŭl 구슬

beak puri 부리

beaker taejŏp 대접

be-all the ~ and end-all kajang chungnyohan kŏt 가장 중요한 것

beam 1 n (in ceiling etc) tŭlppo 들보 **2** v/i (smile) hwaltchak ut-tta 활짝 웃다 **3** v/t (transmit) songshinhada 송신하다

beans k'ong 콩; **be full of ~** kiuni nŏmch'yŏ nanŭn 기운이 넘쳐 나는

bear¹ (animal) kom 곰

bear² 1 v/t weight chit'aenghada 지탱하다; costs pudamhada 부담하다;

(tolerate) kyŏndida 견디다; *child* ch'ulssanhada 출산하다 2 *v/i:* **bring pressure to ~ on** ...e amnyŏgŭl kahada ...에 압력을 가하다
♦ **bear out** *(confirm)* chijihada 지지하다

bearable kyŏndil su innŭn 견딜 수 있는

beard t'ŏkssuyŏm 턱수염

bearing *(in machine)* pŏring 베어링; *that has no ~ on the case* kŭ ilgwanŭn amurŏn kwallyŏni ŏptta 그 일과는 아무런 관련이 없다

bear market FIN hahyang shiseŭi shijang 하향 시세의 시장

beast *(animal)* chimsŭng 짐승

beat 1 *n (of heart)* kodong 고동; *(of music)* paktcha 박자 **2** *v/i (of heart)* kodongch'ida 고동치다; *(of rain)* t'ungt'ung tudŭrida 퉁퉁 두드리다; **~ around the bush** tullŏdaeda 둘러대다 **3** *v/t (in competition)* igida 이기다; *(hit)* ttaerida 때리다; *(pound)* tudŭrida 두드리다; **~ it!** F kkŏjyŏ pŏryŏ! 꺼져 버려!; *it ~s me* F nanŭn todaech'e ihae hal su ŏptta 나는 도대체 이해할 수 없다
♦ **beat up** kut'ahada 구타하다

beaten: off the ~ track sandorŭl pŏsŏnan 상도를 벗어난

beating *(physical)* kut'a 구타

beat-up F nalgŭn 낡은

beautician miyongsa 미용사

beautiful arŭmdaun 아름다운; *day* mŏtchin 멋진; *weather* hwach'anghan 화창한; *thanks, that's just ~!* komawŏyo, nŏmu mashissŭmnida 고마워요, 너무 맛있습니다

beautifully *cooked, done* hullunghage 훌륭하게; *simple* koengjanghi 굉장히

beauty arŭmdaum 아름다움

beauty parlor miyongshil 미용실
♦ **beaver away** pujirŏnhi irhada 부지런히 일하다

because ... ttaemune ... 때문에; *it was too expensive* kŭgŏshi nŏmu pissatkki ttaemunida 그것이 너무 비쌌기 때문이다; *~ of* ... ttaemune ... 때문에; *~ of the weather* nalsshi ttaemune 날씨 때문에

beckon *v/i* sontchit'ayŏ purŭda 손짓하여 부르다

become ◊ *(+ adj)* ... haejida ... 해지다; *the weather became colder* nalsshiga ch'uwŏjyŏt-tta 날씨가 추워졌다 ◊ *(+ noun)* ...i/ga toeda ...이/가 되다; *he became priest* kŭnŭn shibuga toeŏt-tta 그 신부가 되었다; *what's ~ of her?* yŏjanŭn ŏttŏk'e toeottchiyo? 그 여자는 어떻게 되었지요?

bed ch'imdae 침대; *(of flowers)* hwadan 화단; *(of sea, river)* mitppadak 밑바닥; *go to ~* chamjarie tŭlda 잠자리에 들다; *he still in ~* kŭnŭn ajiktto chago it-tta 그는 아직도 자고 있다; *go to ~ with* ...wa/kwa kach'i chada ...와/과 같이 자다

bedclothes ch'imgu 침구

bedding ch'imgu 침구

bedridden pyŏngsang-e innŭn 병상에 있는; **bedroom** ch'imshil 침실; **bedspread** ch'imdaebo 침대보; **bedtime** ch'wich'im shigan 취침 시간

bee pŏl 벌

beech nŏdobamnamu 너도밤나무

beef 1 *n* soegogi 쇠고기; F *(complain)* pulp'yŏng 불평 **2** *v/i* F *(complain)* pulp'yŏnghada 불평하다
♦ **beef up** poganghada 보강하다

beefburger pip'ŭbŏgŏ 비프버거

beehive pŏltchip 벌집

beeline: make a ~ for ...(ŭ)ro kot tchang tallyŏgada ...(으)로 곧장 달려가다

beep 1 *n* shinhoŭm 신호음 **2** *v/i* shimhoŭmi ullida 신호음이 울리다 **3** *v/t (call on pager)* hoch'urhada 호출하다

beeper hoch'ulgi 호출기

beer maektchu 맥주

beetle ttaktchŏngbŏlle 딱정벌레

before 1 *prep (in time, order)* ... chŏne ... 전에; **~ 8 o'clock** 8shi chŏne 8시 전에 **2** *adv* ijŏne 이전에; *you should have let me know ~* ijŏne na-ege allyŏjuŏssŏya haessŏ 이전에 내게 알려주었어야 했어; *~ week/day ~* kŭ chŏnjue/chŏnna

그 전주에 / 전날에 3 *conj* ...hagi
chŏne ...하기 전에; **~ he leaves**
xŭga ttŏnagi chŏne 그가 떠나기 전에
eforehand miri 미리
eg 1 *v/i* kugŏrhada 구걸하다 2 *v/t*: **~**
s.o. to ... nuguege ...hae tallago
canch'ŏnghada 누구에게 ... 해
달라고 간청하다
eggar kŏji 거지
egin 1 *v/i* shijakttoeda 시작되다; **to**
~ with (*at first*) ch'ŏumenŭn
처음에는; (*in the first place*) ch'ŏt-
chaero 첫째로 2 *v/t* shijak'ada
시작하다
eginner ch'oboja 초보자
eginner driver unjŏnŭl paeunŭn
saram 운전을 배우는 사람
eginning shijak 시작; (*origin*)
hich'o 시초
ehalf: **on** or **in ~ of** ...ŭl / rŭl wihayŏ
...을 / 를 위하여; **on my / his ~**
harŭl / kŭrŭl taeshinhaesŏ 나를 / 그를
대신해서
ehave *v/i* haengdonghada 행동하다;
~ (oneself) yeŭi parŭge
haengdonghada 예의 바르게
행동하다; **~ (yourself)!** yeŭi parŭge
haengdonghaera 예의바르게
행동해라
ehavior haengdong 행동
ehind 1 *prep* (*in position*) ...
wittchoge(sŏ) ... 뒷쪽에(서); (*in*
progress, order) ...e twijyŏsŏ ...에
뒤져서; **be ~ ...** (*responsible for*) ...e
ch'aegimi it-tta ...에 책임이 있음; (*support*) chijihada 지지하다 2 *adv*
(*at the back*) twie(sŏ) 뒤에(서); **be ~**
with ... ...i / ga millyŏ it-tta ...이 / 가
밀려있다
eijing Puk-kkyŏng 북경
eing (*existence*) chonjae 존재;
(*creature*) saengmul 생물
elated yŏn-gidoen 연기된
elch 1 *n* t'ŭrim 트림 2 *v/i* t'ŭrimhada
트림하다
elgian 1 *adj* Pelgieŭi 벨기에의 2 *n*
Pelgiein 벨기에인
elgium Pelgie 벨기에
elief midŭm 믿음; (*religious*) shinang
신앙
elieve mit-tta 믿다

♦ **believe in ...** ...ŭl / rŭl mit-tta ...을 / 를
믿다; *ghosts* ...ŭi chonjaerŭl mit-tta
...의 존재를 믿다; *a person*
shilloehada 신뢰하다
believer shinja 신자; *fig* shinbongja
신봉자
bell chong 종
bellhop pelboi 벨보이
belligerent *adj* hojŏnjŏgin 호전적인
bellow 1 *n* koham 고함; (*of bull*) soga
unŭn sori 소가 우는 소리 2 *v/i*
kohamch'ida 고함치다; (*of bull*) ulda
울다
belly (*of person*) pae 배; (*fat stomach*)
ttongppae 똥배; (*of animal*) wi 위
bellyache *v/i* F pulp'yŏng-ŭl nŭrŏnot-
tta 불평을 늘어놓다
belong *v/i*: **where does this ~?** ŏdie
noŭlkkayo? 어디에 놓을까요?; **I**
don't ~ here nanŭn yŏgie mat-tchi
anayo 나는 여기에 맞지 않아요
♦ **belong to ...** ...ŭi kŏshida ...의
것이다; *club, organization* ...ŭi
irwŏnida ...의 일원이다
belongings sojip'um 소지품
beloved *adj* saranghanŭn 사랑하는
below 1 *prep* ... araee(sŏ) ...
아래에(서); (*in amount, rate, level*) ...
iharo ... 이하로 2 *adv* araet-
tchoge(sŏ) 아랫쪽에(서); (*in text*)
araee(sŏ) 아래에(서); **see ~** araet-
tchogŭl poseyo 아랫쪽을 보세요; **10**
degrees ~ yŏngha shiptto 영하 십도
belt hŏritti 허리띠; **tighten one's ~**
fig hŏrittirŭl chollamaeda 허리띠를
졸라매다
bench (*seat*) pench'i 벤치; (*work~*)
chagŏpttae 작업대
benchmark kijun 기준
bend 1 *n* man-gok 만곡 2 *v/t* kuburida
구부리다 3 *v/i* hwida 휘다; (*of*
person) kuburida 구부리다
♦ **bend down** kuburida 구부리다
bender F sul mashigo
hŭngch'ŏnggŏrim 흥청거림; **go on a**
~ chint'ang surŭl mashida 진탕 술을
마시다
beneath 1 *prep* ...ŭi araee(sŏ) ...의
아래에(서); (*in status, value*) ... poda
natkke ... 보다 낮게 2 *adv* araee(sŏ)
아래에(서)

benefactor ŭnhyerŭl pep'unŭn saram 은혜를 베푸는 사람

beneficial yuik'an 유익한

benefit 1 n iik 이익 **2** v/t ...ŭi iigi toeda ...의 이익이 되다 **3** v/i iigŭl ŏt-tta 이익을 얻다

benevolent injong manŭn 인정 많은

benign onhwahan 온화한; MED yangsŏng-ŭi 양성의

bequeath yusanŭro namgida 유산으로 남기다; fig chŏnhada 전하다

bereaved 1 adj sabyŏrhan 사별한; **the ~ family** yujok yujok 유족 **2** n: **the ~** sabyŏrhan saramdŭl 사별한 사람들

berry ttalgiryuŭi yŏlmae 딸기류의 열매

berserk: **go ~** kwangp'ok'aejida 광폭해지다

berth (for sleeping) ch'imdaek'an 침대칸; (for ship) chŏngbaktchang 정박장; **give a wide ~ to** ...ŭl/rŭl p'ihada ...을/를 피하다

beside ...ŭi kyŏt'e(sŏ) ...의 곁에(서); **be ~ oneself** chejŏngshinŭl ilt'a 제정신을 잃다; **that's ~ the point** kŭgŏn ttan yaegiyeyo 그건 딴 얘기예요

besides 1 adv kedaga 게다가 **2** prep (apart from) ...ioe-e ... 이외에

best 1 adj kajang chŏun 가장 좋은, ch'oegoŭi 최고의 **2** adv kajang chal 가장 잘, cheil cheil 제일; **it would be ~ if** ... hanŭn kŏshi kajang chŏul tŭt'ada ... 하는 것이 가장 좋을 듯하다; **I like her ~** nanŭn kŭnyŏrŭl cheil choahanda 나는 그녀를 제일 좋아한다 **3** n: **do one's ~** ch'oesŏnŭl tahada 최선을 다하다; **the ~** (thing) ch'oego 최고; (person) ch'oegoro chal hanŭn saram 최고로 잘 하는 사람; **make the ~ of** ...ŭl/rŭl ch'oedaehanŭro iyonghada ...을/를 최대한으로 이용하다; **all the ~!** haeng-uni itkkirŭl! 행운이 있기를!

best before date ch'oego p'umjil pojŭng kigan 최고 품질 보증 기간; **best man** (at wedding) shillang tŭllŏri 신랑 들러리; **best-seller** pesŭt'ŭsellŏ 베스트셀러

bet 1 n naegi 내기 **2** v/i naegirŭl kŏlda 내기를 걸다; **you ~!** mullonijyo! 물론이죠! **3** v/t (reckon) t'ŭllimŏpss ...hal kŏshirago saenggak'ada 틀림없이 ...할 것이라고 생각하다

betray paebanhada 배반하다

betrayal paeban 배반

better 1 adj poda naŭn 보다 나은; **g ~** (skills) hyangsangdoeda 향상되다 (in health) pyŏng-i nat-tta 병이 낫다 **he's ~** (in health) kŭŭi kŏn-gang-i choajyŏt-tta 그의 건강이 좋아졌다 **2** adv tŏ chal 더 잘, tŏ natkke 더 낫게; **she sings ~ than I do** kŭnyŏnŭn naboda noraerŭl tŏ chal handa 그녀는 나보다 노래를 더 잘 한다; **you look ~ today** onŭl tŏ naa poinda 오늘 더 나아 보인다; **you'd ~ ask permission** tangshin-ŭn hŏragŭl pannŭn kŏshi natkkessŏyo 당신은 허락을 받는 것이 낫겠어요; **I'd really ~ not** nanŭn haji annŭn p'yŏni natkkessŏyo 나는 하지 않는 편이 낫겠어요; **all the ~ for us** urihant'enŭn tŏ chaldoen irimnida 우리한테는 더 잘된 일입니다; **I like her ~** nanŭn kŭnyŏrŭl tŏ choahamnida 나는 그녀를 더 좋아합니다

better-off yubok'an 유복한

between prep saie 사이에; **~ you ar me** urikkirriŭi yaegijiman 우리끼리의 얘기지만

beverage fml ŭmnyo 음료

beware: **~ of** ...ŭl/rŭl choshimhada ...을/를 조심하다

bewilder tanghwanghage hada 당황하게 하다

beyond 1 prep (in time) ...ŭl/rŭl chinasŏ ...을/를 지나서; (in space) ...ŭl/rŭl nŏmŏsŏ ...을/를 넘어서; (in degree) ...ŭi pŏmwirŭl nŏmŏsŏ ...의 범위를 넘어서; **it's ~ me** (don't understand) narosŏn al su ŏmnŭn irida 나로선 알 수 없는 일이다; (can't do it) nae nŭngnyŏk pakkŭi irida 내 능력 밖의 일이다 **2** adv chŏp'yŏnŭro 저편으로

Bhutan Put'an 부탄

Bhutanese 1 adj Put'anŭi 부탄의 **2** (person) Put'anin 부탄인

bias n p'yŏn-gyŏn 편견

as(s)ed p'yŏn-gyŏnŭl kajin 편견을
가진

b (for baby) t'ŏkppaji 턱받이

ble Sŏnggyŏng 성경

bliography munhŏn mongnok 문헌
목록

ceps p'arŭi alt'ong 팔의 알통

cker v/i maldat'umhada 말다툼하다

cycle n chajŏn-gŏ 자전거

d 1 n (at auction) ipch'al 입찰;
attempt) shido 시도 2 v/i (at
uction) ipch'arhada 입찰하다

ennial adj kyŏng-nyŏnŭi 격년의

g 1 adj k'ŭn 큰; **my ~**
rother / sister (man's) naŭi k'ŭn
yŏng / nuna 나의 큰 형 / 누나;
woman's) naŭi k'ŭn oppa / ŏnni
.의 큰 오빠 / 언니; **~ name**
umyŏnghan irŭm 유명한 이름
adv: **talk ~** hŏp'ung ttŏlda 허풍
떨다

gamy chunghon 중혼

g-headed utchuldaenŭn 우쭐대는

ke 1 n chajŏn-gŏ 자전거 2 v/i
hajŏn-gŏrŭl t'ada 자전거를 타다

kini pik'ini 비키니

lingual tu nara marŭl hanŭn 두
나라 말을 하는

l 1 n (money) chip'ye 지폐; (for gas,
lectricity) ch'ŏngguso 청구서; (in
otel, restaurant etc) kyesansŏ
계산서; POL pŏban 법안; (poster)
wanggo p'osŭt'ŏ 광고 포스터 2 v/t
invoice) kyesansŏro ch'ŏngguhada
계산서로 청구하다

lboard kwanggop'an 광고판

lfold chigap 지갑

liards tanggu 당구

lion ship ŏk 십억

l of exchange hwanŏŭm 환어음

l of sale yŏngsujŭng 영수증

n (for storage) chŏjangt'ong 저장통

nary ijinppŏbŭi 이진법의

nd v/t (connect) yŏn-gyŏrhada
연결하다; (tie) muktta 묶다; (LAW:
oblige) ...ŭi ŭimurŭl chiuda ...의
의무를 지우다

nder (for papers) paindŏ 바인더

nding 1 adj agreement, promise
.usongnyŏgi innŭn 구속력이 있는
n (of book) changjŏng 장정

binoculars ssang-an-gyŏng 쌍안경

biodegradable misaengmure ŭihae
punhaega toenŭn 미생물에 의해
분해가 되는

biography chŏn-gi 전기

biological saengmurhagŭi 생물학의; ~
parents ch'inbumo 친부모; ~ **de-**
tergent ch'inhwan-gyŏng
sech'ŏktche 친환경 세척제

biology saengmurhak 생물학

biotechnology saengch'e konghak
생체 공학

bird sae 새

bird of prey sanaun naljimsŭng
사나운 날짐승

bird sanctuary choryu poho kuyŏk
조류 보호 구역

birth (of child) t'ansaeng 탄생; (labor)
ch'ulssan 출산; (of country) kiwŏn
기원; **give ~ to** child airŭl nat'a
아이를 낳다; **date of ~**
saengnyŏnwŏri 생년월일; **place of**
~ ch'ulssaengji 출생지

birth certificate ch'ulssaeng
chŭngmyŏngsŏ 출생 증명서; birth
control sana chehan 산아 제한;
birthday saeng-il 생일; **happy ~!**
saeng-il ch'uk'ahamnida! 생일
축하합니다!; birthplace ch'ulssaengji
출생지; birthrate ch'ulssaengnyul
출생률

biscuit pisŭk'et 비스켓

bisexual 1 adj yangsŏng-ŭi 양성의 2 n
yangsŏng-aeja 양성애자

bishop chugyo 주교

bit n (piece) chogak 조각; (part of a
whole) pubun 부분; COMPUT pit'ŭ
비트; **a ~** (a little) chogŭm 조금; (a
while) chamkkan 잠깐; **a ~ of** (a
little) chogŭm 조금; **a ~ of**
news / advice yakkanŭi
soshik / ch'unggo 약간의 소식 / 충고;
~ by ~ chogŭmsshik 조금씩; **I'll be**
there in a ~ nanŭn chamshi hue
kŏgi toch'ak'al kŏmnida 나는 잠시
후에 거기 도착할 겁니다

bitch 1 n (dog) amk'ae 암캐; F
(woman) nappŭn nyŏn 나쁜 년 2 v/i
F (complain) pulp'yŏnghada
불평하다

bitchy F person, remark shimsulgujŭn

심술궂은

bite 1 n mum 물음; (*of food*) han ip 한 입; **get a ~** (*of angler*) mikkirŭl mulda 미끼를 물다; **let's have a ~ (to eat)** shikssahapsshida 식사합시다 **2** v/t mulda 물다 **3** v/i mulda 물다; (*of fish*) mikkirŭl mulda 미끼를 물다

bitmap COMPUT pit'ŭmaep 비트맵
bitmap font COMPUT chŏm kŭlkkol 점 글꼴

bitter *taste* ssŭn 쓴; *person* pit'onghan 비통한; *weather* hokttok'an 혹독한; *argument* shillahan 신랄한

bitterly *cold* sarŭl enŭndŭshi 살을 에는듯이

black 1 *adj* kŏmŭn 검은; *music, history* hŭginŭi 흑인의; *coffee* pŭllaek 블랙; *fig* amdamhan 암담한 **2** n (*color*) kŏmjŏngsaek 검정색; (*person*) hŭgin 흑인; **in the ~** FIN hŭktcharo 흑자로
♦**black out** v/i ŭishigŭl ilt'a 의식을 잃다

blackberry pŭllaekppperi 블랙베리; **blackbird** tchirŭregi 찌르래기; **blackboard** ch'ilp'an 칠판; **black box** pŭllaek paksŭ 블랙 박스; **black economy** pulppŏp koyong 불법 고용

blacken *person's name* omyŏng-ŭl ssŭiuda 오명을 씌우다

black eye mŏngdŭn nun 멍든 눈; **black ice** pŭllaek aisŭ 블랙 아이스, *toro wiŭi kŏmkke poinŭn pingp'an* 도로 위의 검게 보이는 빙판; **blacklist 1** n pŭllaekrisŭt'ŭ 블랙리스트 **2** v/t pŭllaekrisŭt'ŭe ollida 블랙리스트 에 올리다; **blackmail 1** n konggal 공갈; *emotional* ~ shimtchŏk konggal 심적 공갈 **2** v/t konggal ch'ida 공갈 치다; **blackmailer** konggal ch'inŭn saram 공갈 치는 사람; **black market** amshijang 암시장

blackness amhŭk 암흑
blackout ELEC chŏngjŏn 정전; MED ŭishik sangshil 의식 상실; **blacksmith** taejangjang-i 대장장이; **black tea** hongch'a 홍차
bladder panggwang 방광

blade (*of knife*) k'allal 칼날; (*of helicopter*) nalgae 날개; (*of grass*) 잎

blame 1 n pinan 비난; (*responsibili...*) ch'aegim 책임 **2** v/t pinanhada 비난하다; **~ X for Y** Xŭi ch'aegimi Yege it-ttago pinanhada Y의 책임 X에게 있다고 비난하다

bland *smile, answer* kimppajin 김빠...; *food* pyŏlmashi ŏmnŭn 별맛이 없는

blank 1 *adj* (*not written on*) kongbaegŭi 공백의; *look* mŏnghan 멍한; **~ tape** kongt'eip'ŭ 공테이프 **2** n (*empty space*) kongbaek 공백; **my mind's a ~** chŏngshini mŏnghada 정신이 멍하다

blank check paektchi sup'yo 백지 수표

blanket n tamnyo 담요; **a ~ of** *fig* ...(ŭ)ro ont'ong tŏp'in ...(으)로 온 덮인; **a ~ of snow** onnurirŭl tŏp'ŭn nun 온누리를 덮은 눈

blare v/i yoranhage ullida 요란하게 울리다
♦**blare out 1** v/i ullyŏp'ŏjida 울려퍼지다 **2** v/t yoranhage ullida 요란하게 울리다

blaspheme v/i modok'ada 모독하다

blast 1 n (*explosion*) p'okppal 폭발; (*gust*) tolp'ung 돌풍 **2** v/t p'okp'ashik'ida 폭파시키다; **~!** pirŏmŏgŭl 빌어먹을!
♦**blast off** (*of rocket*) palssashik'id... 발사시키다

blast furnace yonggwangno 용광로
blast-off palssa 발사
blatant ppŏnppŏnsŭrŏun 뻔뻔스러운
blaze 1 n (*fire*) hwajae 화재; **a ~ of color** manbarhan saek ch'ae 만발한 색채 **2** v/i (*of fire*) t'aorŭda 타오르...
♦**blaze away** (*with gun*) sswabŏric... 쏴버리다

blazer pŭlleijyŏ chak'et 블레이져 자켓

bleach 1 n p'yobaek 표백; (*for hair*) kŭmballo yŏmsaek 금발로 염색 **2** v/t p'yobaek'ada 표백하다; *hair* kŭmballo yŏmsaek'ada 금발로 염색하다

bleak *countryside* hwangnyanghan 황량한; *weather* ŭmch'imhan 음침...

future ŏduun 어두운

bleary-eyed nuni ch'imch'imhan 눈이 침침한

bleat v/i (of sheep) maeaehago ulda 매애하고 울다

bleed v/i ch'urhyŏhada 출혈하다; *my nose is ~ing* nanŭn k'op'iga nanda 나는 코피가 난다 2 v/t fig tonŭl ch'akch'wihada 돈을 착취하다

bleeding n ch'urhyŏl 출혈

bleep 1 n ppii hanŭn sori 삐이 하는 소리 2 v/i ppii hanŭn soriga nada 삐이 하는 소리가 나다

bleeper hoch'ulgi 호출기

blemish 1 n hŭm 흠 2 v/t hŭmnaeda 흠내다; *reputation* tŏrŏp'ida 더럽히다

blend 1 n honhap 혼합 2 v/t honhap'ada 혼합하다

  blend in 1 v/i sŏkkida 섞이다 2 v/t (in cooking) sŏkta 섞다

blender mikssŏgi 믹서기

bless ch'ukppok'ada 축복하다; *~ you!* (when s.o. sneezes) chŏrŏn! 저런!; *be ~ed with* ...(ŭ)ro ch'ukppok pat-tta ...(으)로 축복 받다

blessing REL ŭnch'ong 은총; fig (approval) sŭngnak 승낙

blind adj nun mŏn 눈 먼; corner ap'i poiji annŭn 앞이 보이지 않는; *~ to* ...ŭl / rŭl poji mot'anŭn ...을 / 를 보지 못하는 2 n: the ~ maeng-in 맹인; 3 v/t nun mŏlge hada 눈 멀게 하다; fig poji mot'age hada 보지 못하게 하다

blind alley makttarŭn kolmok 막다른 골목; **blind date** p'ullaindŭ teit'ŭ 블라인드 데이트, mit'ing 미팅

blindfold 1 n nun karigae 눈 가리개 2 v/t nunŭl karida 눈을 가리다 3 adv nunŭl karigo 눈을 가리고

blinding light nun pushige hanŭn 눈 부시게 하는; headache nuni mŏl chŏngdoŭi 눈이 멀 정도의

blind spot (in road) chadongch'a unjŏnjaŭi sagak 자동차 운전자의 사각; fig maengchŏm 맹점

blink v/i (of person, light) kkamppakkŏrida 깜박거리다

blip (on radar screen) leida yŏngsang 레이더 영상; fig ilsshijŏk pyŏndong 일시적 변동

bliss tŏ ŏmnŭn haengbok 더 없는 행복

blister 1 n multchip 물집 2 v/i multchibi saenggida 물집이 생기다; (of paint) kip'oga saenggida 기포가 생기다

blizzard shimhan nunbora 심한 눈보라

bloated puŏn 부은

blob (of liquid) han pang-ul 한 방울

bloc POL kwŏn 권

block 1 n tŏng-ŏri 덩어리; (in town) kuhoek 구획; (of shares) han cho 한 조; (blockage) chang-aemul 장애물 2 v/t maktta 막다

  ◆ **block in** (with vehicle) pongswaehada 봉쇄하다

  ◆ **block out** light ch'adanhada 차단하다

  ◆ **block up** sink etc maktta 막다

blockade 1 n pongswae 봉쇄 2 v/t pongswaehada 봉쇄하다

blockage mak'yŏ innŭn kŏt 막혀있는 것

blockbuster taehit'ŭjak 대히트작

block letters taemuntcha 대문자

blog 블로그 pŭllogŭ

blond adj kŭmbarŭi 금발의

blonde (woman) kŭmbal mŏri yŏja 금발 머리 여자

blood p'i 피; *in cold ~* naenghok'age 냉혹하게

blood bank hyŏraek ŭnhaeng 혈액 은행; **blood donor** hŏnhyŏltcha 헌혈자; **blood group** hyŏraek'yŏng 혈액형

bloodless coup muhyŏrŭi 무혈의

blood poisoning p'yehyŏltchŭng 폐혈증; **blood pressure** hyŏrap 혈압; **blood relation blood relative** yukch'in 육친; **blood sample** hyŏraek saemp'ŭl 혈액 샘플; **bloodshed** yuhyŏl 유혈; **bloodshot** ch'unghyŏldoen 충혈된; **bloodstain** p'itchaguk 핏자국; **bloodstream** hyŏllyu 혈류; **blood test** hyŏraek kŏmsa 혈액 검사; **blood transfusion** suhyŏl 수혈; **blood vessel** hyŏlgwan 혈관

bloody hands etc p'it'usŏng-iŭi 피투성이의; battle yuhyŏrŭi 유혈의

bloody mary p'ŭllŏdi maeri 블러디

매리

bloom 1 *n* kkot 꽃; *in full ~* hwaltchak p'in hwaltchak 활짝 핀 **2** *v/i* kkoch'i p'ida 꽃이 피다; *fig* pŏnyŏnghada 번영하다

blossom 1 *n* kkot 꽃 **2** *v/i* p'ida 피다; *fig* k'waehwarhaejida 쾌해해지다

blot 1 *n* ŏlluk 얼룩; *fig* hŭm 흠 **2** *v/t* (*dry*) mulkkirŭl tudŭryŏ chiuda 물기를 두드려 지우다
♦ **blot out** *memory* chiuda 지우다; *view* kamch'uda 감추다; *sun* karida 가리다

blotch panjŏm 반점

blotchy ŏllukt'usŏng-iŭi 얼룩투성이의

blouse p'ŭllausŭ 블라우스

blow[1] kangt'a 강타; (*shock*) ch'unggyŏk 충격

blow[2] *v/t* (*of wind, whistle*) pulda 불다; *smoke* naeppumtta 내뿜다; F (*spend*) nallida 날리다; F *opportunity* nallyŏ pŏrida 날려 버리다; *~ one's nose* k'orŭl p'ulda 코를 풀다 **2** *v/i* (*of wind*) pulda 불다; (*of whistle*) ullida 울리다; (*breathe out*) ipkkimŭl pulda 입김을 불다; (*of fuse*) kkŭnŏjida 끊어지다; (*of tire*) t'ŏjida 터지다
♦ **blow off 1** *v/t* purŏ nallida 불어 날리다 **2** *v/i* parame nallida 바람에 날리다
♦ **blow out 1** *v/t* candle kkŭda 끄다 **2** *v/i* (*of candle*) kkŏjida 꺼지다
♦ **blow over 1** *v/t* purŏ nŏmŏttŭrida 불어 넘어뜨리다 **2** *v/i* karaantta 가라앉다; (*of argument*) musahi chinagada 무사히 지나가다
♦ **blow up 1** *v/t* (*with explosives*) p'okp'ahada 폭파하다; *balloon* pulda 불다; *photograph* hwakttaehada 확대하다 **2** *v/i* p'okpparhada 폭발하다; F (*get angry*) hwanaeda 화내다

blow-dry *v/t* tŭraiŏro mŏrirŭl mallida 드라이어로 머리를 말리다; **blow job** ∨ p'ellach'io 펠라치오; **blow-out** (*of tire*) p'ŏngk'ŭ 펑크; F (*big meal*) shilk'ŏt mŏk-kki 실컷 먹기; **blow-up** (*of photo*) hwakttae 확대

blue 1 *adj* p'aran 파란; *movie* p'orŭno 포르노 **2** *n* p'arangsaek 파랑색

blueberry p'ŭlluberi 블루베리; **blue chip** uryang chushik 우량 주식; **blue-collar worker** yukch'e nodongja 육체 노동자; **Blue House** Ch'ŏng-wadae 청와대; **blueprint** ch'ŏngsajin 청사진; *fig* (*plan*) sangsehan kyehoek 상세한 계획

blues MUS p'ŭllusŭ 블루스; *have the ~* ultchŏk'ada 울적하다

blues singer p'ŭllusŭ kasu 블루스 가수

bluff 1 *n* (*deception*) ŏmp'o 엄포 **2** *v/i* ŏmp'orŭl not'a 엄포를 놓다

blunder 1 *n* k'ŭn shilssu 큰 실수 **2** *v/i* k'ŭn shilssurŭl hada 큰 실수를 하다

blunt *adj* mudin 무딘; *person* soltchik'an solchik'an 솔직한

bluntly *speak* soltchik'age 솔직하게

blur 1 *n* hŭrim 흐림 **2** *v/t* hŭrige hada 흐리게 하다

blurb (*on book*) sŏnjŏn munkku 선전 문구
♦ **blurt out** pulssuk marhada 불쑥 말하다

blush 1 *n* hongjo 홍조 **2** *v/i* ŏlgurŭl pulk'ida 얼굴을 붉히다

blusher (*cosmetic*) poryŏnji 볼연지

BO (= *body odor*) amnae 암내

board 1 *n* p'anja 판자; (*for game*) p'an 판; (*for notices*) keship'an 게시판; *~* (*of directors*) isahoe 이사회; *on ~* (*on plane*) pihaenggi ane 비행기 안에; (*on train*) kich'a ane 기차 안에; (*on boat*) pae ane 배 안에; *take on ~ comments etc* koryŏhada 고려하다; (*fully realize truth of*) hwaksshirhi ihaehada 확실히 이해하다; *across the ~* chŏnmyŏnjŏgŭro 전면적으로 **2** *v/t* airplane etc t'ada 타다 **3** *v/i* t'ada 타다
♦ **board up** p'anjaro maktta 판자로 막다
♦ **board with** …e hasuk'ada …에 하숙하다

board and lodging hasuk 하숙

boarder hasugin 하숙인; EDU hasukssaeng 하숙생

board game podŭ keim 보드 게임

boarding card t'apssŭngkkwŏn 탑승권; **boarding house** hasuktchi

하숙집; **boarding pass** t'apssŭngk'wŏn 탑승권; **boarding school** kisuk hak-kyo 기숙 학교; **board meeting** isa hoeŭi 이사 회의; **board room** isa hoeŭishil 이사 회의실; **boardwalk** p'anjarŭl kkan podo 판자를 깐 보도

boast 1 *n* charang kŏri 자랑 거리 **2** *v/i* charanghada 자랑하다

oat pae 배; (*small, for leisure*) pot'ŭ 보트; **go by** ~ paero kada 배로 가다

ob¹ (*haircut*) tanbal 단발

ob² *v/i* (*of boat etc*) wi araero kabyŏpkke umjigida 위 아래로 가볍게 움직이다

bob up pulssuk nat'anada 불쑥 나타나다

obsleigh, bobsled popssŭllei 봅슬레이

odhisattva posal 보살

odily 1 *adj* momŭi 몸의 **2** *adv* eject momŭro 몸으로

ody mom 몸; (*dead*) shich'e 시체; ~ **of water** suyŏk 수역; ~ (*suit*) (*undergarment*) podisut'ŭ 보디수트

odyguard kyŏnghowŏn 경호원; **body language** momtchit ŏnŏ 몸짓 언어; **body odor** amnae 암내; **body shop** MOT ch'ach'e kongjang 차체 공장; **bodywork** MOT ch'ach'e 차체

oggle: *it* ~**s the mind!** sangsangdo hal su ŏmnŭn irida! 상상도 할 수 없는 일이다!

ogus katchaŭi 가짜의

oil¹ *n* (*swelling*) chonggi 종기

oil¹ **1** *v/i liquid* kkŭrida 끓이다; *egg, vegetables* samtta 삶다 **2** *v/i* kkŭlt'a 끓다

boil down to kyŏlguk …(ŭ)ro toeda 결국 …(으)로 되다

boil over (*of milk etc*) kkŭrŏ nŏmch'ida 끓어 넘치다

oiler poillŏ 보일러

oisterous ttŏdŭlssŏk'an 떠들썩한

old 1 *adj* taedamhan 대담한 **2** *n* (*print*) kulgŭn kŭlsshich'e 굵은 글씨체; *in ~* kulgŭn kŭlsshich'ero 굵은 글씨체로

olster *v/t confidence* pukttoduda 북돋우다

olt 1 *n* polt'ŭ 볼트; (*on door*)

chamulssoe 자물쇠; (*of lightning*) pŏn-gae 번개; **like a ~ from the blue** ch'ŏngch'ŏnbyŏngnyŏk-kwa kach'i 청천벽력과 같이 **2** *adv*: ~ **upright** ttokpparo 똑바로 **3** *v/t* (*fix with bolts*) polt'ŭro choeda 볼트로 죄다; (*close*) chamulssoero chamgŭda 자물쇠로 잠그다 **4** *v/i* (*run off*) tomangch'ida 도망치다

bomb 1 *n* p'okt'an 폭탄 **2** *v/t* p'okp'ahada 폭파하다

bombard: ~ **with questions** chilmun kongserŭl p'ŏbut-tta 질문 공세를 퍼붓다

bomb attack p'ok-kkyŏk 폭격

bomber (*airplane*) p'ok-kkyŏk-kki 폭격기; (*terrorist*) p'okp'abŏm 폭파범

bomber jacket kunnyong chamba 군용 잠바

bomb scare p'okt'anŭi uryŏ 폭탄의 우려

bond 1 *n* (*tie*) kkŭn kkŭn 끈 끈; (*of matrimony*) yŏnbun 연분; FIN ch'aekkwŏn 채권 **2** *v/i* (*of glue*) chŏpch'ak'ada 접착하다

bone 1 *n* ppyŏ 뼈 **2** *v/t meat, fish* ppyŏrŭl pallanaeda 뼈를 발라내다

bonfire modakppul 모닥불

bonsai punjae 분재

bonus (*money*) ponŏsŭ 보너스; (*something extra*) tŏm 덤

boo 1 *n* yayuhanŭn sori 야유하는 소리 **2** *v/t & v/i* yayuhada 야유하다

book 1 *n* ch'aek 책; ~ **of matches** sŏngnyangkkap 성냥갑 **2** *v/t* (*reserve*) yeyak'ada 예약하다; (*for crime*) pŏlgŭm changbue ollida 벌금 장부에 올리다 **3** *v/i* (*reserve*) yeyak'ada 예약하다

bookcase ch'aektchang 책장

booked up *hotel, flight* yeyagi kkwak ch'ada 예약이 꽉 차다; *person* iltchŏng-i kkwak ch'ada 일정이 꽉 차다

bookie F makkwŏnŏptcha 마권업자

booking (*reservation*) yeyak 예약

booking clerk maep'yogyewŏn 매표계원

bookkeeper hoegyejangburŭl chŏngnihanŭn saram 회계장부를

정리하는 사람

bookkeeping pugi 부기

booklet soch'aektcha 소책자

bookmaker magwŏnŏptcha 마권업자

books (*accounts*) hoegyejangbu
회계장부; *do the ~* hoegyejangburŭl
chŏngnihada 회계장부를 정리하다

bookseller ch'aek changsa 책 장사;
bookstall maejŏm 매점; **bookstore**
sŏjŏm 서점

boom¹ 1 *n* (*economic*) kyŏnggi
p'okttŭng 경기 폭등, pum 붐 2 *v/i* (*of
business*) kyŏnggiga p'okttŭnghada
경기가 폭등하다

boom² *n* (*noise*) koeng-ŭm 굉음

boonies: *out in the ~* F ojie(sŏ)
오지에(서)

boost 1 *n* (*to sales*) ch'oktchin 촉진;
(*to confidence*) kyŏngnyŏ 격려; (*to
economy*) puyang 부양 2 *v/t*
production, sales ch'oktchinshik'ida
촉진시키다; prices kkŭrŏ ollida 끌어
올리다; confidence, morale toduda
돋우다

boot *n* changhwa 장화; *climbing ~s*
tŭngsanhwa 등산화

♦ **boot out** F naetchot-tta 내쫓다

♦ **boot up** 1 *v/t* COMPUT put'inghada
부팅하다 2 *v/i* COMPUT put'ingdoeda
부팅된다

booth (*at market, fair*) chŏmp'o 점포;
(*in restaurant*) k'anmagihan
chwasŏk 칸막이한 좌석; (*at
exhibition*) kwallamsŏk 관람석

booze *n* F sul 술

booze-up *Br* F sul chanch'i 술 잔치

border 1 *n* (*between countries*) kuk-
kkyŏng 국경; (*edge*) kajangjari
가장자리 2 *v/t country, river* ...e
chŏp'ae it-tta ...에 접해 있다

♦ **border on** *country* ...e iut'ada ...에
이웃하다; (*be almost*) kŏŭi ...ida
거의 ...이다

borderline: *a ~ case* idojŏdo anin
kyŏng-u 이도저도 아닌 경우

bore¹ *v/t hole* ttult'a 뚫다

bore² 1 *n* (*person*) ttabunhan saram
따분한 사람 2 *v/t* siltchŭngnage hada
싫증나게 하다; *be ~d* chiruhaejida
지루해지다

boredom kwŏnt'ae 권태

boring ttabunhan 따분한

born: *be ~* t'aeŏnada 태어나다;
where were you ~? kohyang-i
ŏdiimnikka? 고향이 어디입니까?; *be
a ~ ...* t'agonan ... ida 타고난 ...
이다

borrow pilda 빌다

bosom (*of woman*) chŏtkkasŭm
젖가슴

boss (*one's own*) sangsa 상사; (*of
company*) sajang 사장

♦ **boss around** puryŏmŏktta
부려먹다

bossy tumok haengsehanŭn 두목
행세하는

botanical shingmulŭi 식물의

botany shingmurhak 식물학

botch *v/t* sŏt'urŭge haesŏ
mangch'yŏbŏrida 서투르게 해서
망쳐버리다

both 1 *adj* yangtchogŭi 양쪽의 2 *pron*
tul ta 둘 다; *I know ~ of the brothers* nanŭn kŭ hyŏngjerŭl tul ta alge
issŏyo 나는 그 형제를 둘 다 알고
있어요; *~ of the brothers were
there* tu hyŏngjega ta kŏgie
issŏssŏyo 두 형제가 다 거기에
있었어요; *~ of them* (*things*) kŭgŏt
tul ta 그것 둘 다; (*people*) kŭdŭl tu
ta 그들 둘 다 3 *adv*: *~ ... and ...*
(*with nouns*) ...wa/kwa ..., tul ta ...
와/과 ..., 둘 다; (*with adjs*) ... go
...ta ...고 ...다; *~ my sister and*
ŏnni wa na, tul ta 언니와 나, 둘 다
it's ~ easy and interesting
kŭgŏsŭn shwipkko chaemiit-tta
그것은 쉽고 재미있다; *is it business
or pleasure? ~* illo hanŭn
kŏmnikka, animyŏn chaemiro
hanŭn kŏmnikka? ~ tul tayeyo 일로
하는 겁니까, 아니면 재미로 하는
겁니까? ~ 둘 다예요

bother 1 *n* kolch'itkkŏri 골칫거리; *it's
no ~* pyŏl il animnida 별 일
아닙니다 2 *v/t* (*disturb*) kwich'ank'e
hada 귀찮게 하다; *person working*
sŏnggashige hada 성가시게 하다;
(*worry*) kŏktchŏngdoege hada
걱정되게 하다 3 *v/i* shin-gyŏng-i
ssŭida 신경이 쓰이다; *don't ~!* shin-
gyŏng ssŭji maseyo! 신경 쓰지

...세요!; *you needn't have ~ed*
...in-gyŏng ssŭl p'iryo ŏpssŏssŏyo
...경 쓸 필요 없었어요

...ttle 1 *n* pyŏng 병; (*for baby*)
...yubyŏng 우유병 2 *v/t* pyŏng-e
...mtta 병에 담다

...ottle up *feelings* ŏngnurŭda
...누르다

...ttle bank chaehwaryongppyŏng
...njppsso 재활용병 수집소

...ttled water p'anŭn mul 파는 물

...ttleneck *n* (*in road*) pyŏngmok
...목; (*in production*) aero sahang
...로 사항

...ttle-opener pyŏngttagae 병따개

...ttom 1 *adj* maen mitppadagŭi 맨
...바닥의 2 *n* (*on the inside*) antchok
...padak 안쪽 바닥; (*underside*)
...nitppadak 밑바닥; (*of hill*) ŭi kajang
...raetppubun 가장 아랫부분; (*of pile*)
...naen araetchok 맨 아래쪽; (*of*
...*treet*) kkŭt 끝; (*of garden*) maen
...atchok 맨 가쪽; (*buttocks*)
...ngdŏng-i 엉덩이; *at the ~ of the*
...*creen* hwamyŏnŭi hadane 화면의
...단에

...ottom out padagŭl pŏsŏnada
...닥을 벗어나다

...ttom line *fig* (*financial outcome*)
...h'ongkyŏlssan 총결산; (*the real*
...*ssue*) kajang chungnyohan sahang
...장 중요한 사항

...ulder k'ŭn chagal 큰 자갈

...unce 1 *v/t ball* t'wige hada 튀게
...다 2 *v/i* (*of ball, rain etc*) t'wida
...다; (*on sofa etc*) ttwiŏdanida
...어다니다; (*of check*) pudoga toeŏ
...oedoraoda 부도가 되어 되돌아오다

...uncer kyŏngbiwŏn 경비원

...und¹: *be ~ to ...* (*sure to*)
...üllimŏpsshi ...hal kŏshida 틀림없이
...할 것이다; (*obliged to*) ... haeya
...anda ... 해야 한다

...und²: *be ~ for* (*of ship*) ... haeng
... 행; *a plane ~ for Seoul*
...ŏurhaeng pihaenggi 서울행 비행기

...und³ 1 *n* (*jump*) ttwiŏorŭgi
...어오르기 2 *v/i* ttwiŏdanida
...어다니다

...undary kyŏnggye 경계

...undless muhanŭi 무한의

bouquet (*flowers*) kkot-ttabal 꽃다발;
(*of wine*) hyanggi 향기
bourbon pŏbŏn wisŭk'i 버번 위스키
bout MED palppyŏng 발병; (*in boxing*)
shihap 시합
boutique put'ik'ŭ 부티크
bow¹ 1 *n* (*as greeting*) chŏl 절 2 *v/i*
insahada 인사하다 3 *v/t head* sugida
숙이다
bow² (*knot*) maedŭp 매듭; MUS,
(*weapon*) hwal 활
bow³ (*of ship*) paenmŏri 뱃머리
bowels ch'angja 창자
bowl¹ (*container*) kŭrŭt 그릇; (*for
rice*) konggi 공기; (*for soup*) taejŏp
대접; (*for cooking, salad*) k'ŭn kŭrŭt
큰 그릇
bowl² *v/i* (*in bowling*) pollinghada
볼링하다
♦ bowl over *fig* ...ŭl / rŭl kkamtchak
nollage hada ...을 / 를 깜짝 놀라게
하다
bowling polling 볼링
bowling alley pollingjang 볼링장
bow tie nabi nekt'ai 나비 넥타이
box¹ *n* (*container*) sangja 상자; (*on
form*) pin k'an 빈 칸
box² *v/i* kwŏnt'uhada 권투하다
boxer kwŏnt'u sŏnsu 권투 선수
boxing kwŏnt'u 권투
boxing match kwŏnt'u shihap 권투
시합
box office maep'yoso 매표소
boy sonyŏn 소년; (*son*) adŭl 아들
boycott 1 *n* poik'ot 보이콧 2 *v/t*
poik'ot'ada 보이콧하다
boyfriend namja ch'in-gu 남자 친구;
(*lover*) aein 애인
boyish sonyŏn-kat'ŭn 소년같은
boyscout poisŭk'aut 보이스카웃
bra pŭrejiŏ 브레지어
brace (*on teeth*) ch'iyŏl kyojŏnggi
치열 교정기
bracelet p'altchi 팔찌
bracket (*for shelf*) kkach'ibal 까치발;
(*in text*) kwarho 괄호
brag *v/i* charanghada 자랑하다
braid *n* (*in hair*) ttaün mŏri 땋은 머리;
(*trimming*) tan ch'ŏri 단처리
braille chŏmtcha 점자
brain tunoe 두뇌

brainless F mŏriga nappŭn 머리가 나쁜

brains (*intelligence*) chinŭng 지능

brainstorm → **brainwave**; **brainstorming** p'ŭreinsŭt'oming 브레인스토밍; **brain surgeon** noe chŏnmun oekkwa ŭisa 뇌 전문 외과 의사; **brainwash** senoehada 세뇌하다; **brainwashing** senoe 세뇌; **brainwave** (*brilliant idea*) myoan 묘안

brainy F ch'ongmyŏnghan 총명한

brake 1 n p'ŭreik'ŭ 브레이크; *fig* kyŏnje 견제 **2** v/i p'ŭreik'ŭrŭl kŏlda 브레이크를 걸다

brake light p'ŭreik'ŭ lait'ŭ 브레이크 라이트

brake pedal p'ŭreik'ŭ p'edal 브레이크 페달

branch n (*of tree*) kaji 가지; (*of bank, company*) chijŏm 지점

♦ **branch off** (*of road*) kallajida 갈라지다

♦ **branch out** saŏbŭl hwaktchanghada 사업을 확장하다

brand 1 n (*of product*) sangp'yo 상표 **2** v/t: ~ **s.o. a liar** nuguege kŏjitmaltchang-iŭi numyŏng-ŭl ssŭiuda 누구에게 거짓말장이의 누명을 씌우다

brand image sangp'umŭi imiji 상품의 이미지

brandish hwidurŭda 휘두르다

brand leader kajang chal naganŭn sangp'yo 가장 잘 나가는 상표; **brand loyalty** p'ŭraendŭ loyŏlt'i 브랜드 로열티; **brand name** sangp'yomyŏng 상표명; **brand-new** shinp'umŭi 신품의

brandy p'ŭraendi 브랜디

brass (*alloy*) notssoe 놋쇠

brass band ch'wiji akttan 취주 악단

brassière p'ŭrejiŏ 브레지어

brat pej saekki 새끼

bravado hŏse 허세

brave adj yonggamhan 용감한

bravery yonggamham 용감함

brawl 1 n ssaum 싸움 **2** v/i ssaumjirhada 싸움질하다

brawny kŏnjanghan 건장한

Brazil P'ŭrajil 브라질

Brazilian 1 adj P'ŭrajirŭi 브라질의 P'ŭrajil saram 브라질 사람

breach (*violation*) wiban 위반; (*in party*) purhwa 불화

breach of contract LAW kyeyak wiban 계약 위반

bread n ppang 빵

breadcrumbs (*for cooking*) ppan karu 빵 가루; (*for birds*) ppang pusŭrŏgi 빵 부스러기

breadth p'ok 폭

breadwinner chibanŭi pŏrihanŭn saram 집안의 벌이하는

break 1 n (*in bone etc*) kŭm 금; (*re* hyushik 휴식; (*in relationship*) hyushik-kki 휴식기; *give ... a ~* (*opportunity*) ...ege kihoerŭl chu …에게 기회를 주다; *take a ~* chamshi chungdanhada 잠시 중단하다; *without a ~ work, trav* shwiji ank'o 쉬지 않고 **2** v/t *mach device, toy* pusuda 부수다; *stick, o leg* purŏttŭrida 부러뜨리다; *china, glass, egg* kkaettŭrida 깨뜨리다; *rules, law, promise* wibanhada 위반하다; *news* chŏnhada 전하다; *record* kkaeda 깨다 **3** v/i (*of machine, device, toy*) pusŏjida 부서지다; (*of china, glass, egg*) kkaejida 깨지다; (*of stick*) purŏjic 부러지다; (*of news*) allyŏjida 알려지다; (*of storm*) shijakdoeda 시작되다; (*of boy's voice*) pyŏnsŏnghada 변성하다

♦ **break away** v/i (*escape*) tomangch'ida 도망치다; (*from family*) tongnip'ada 독립하다; (*fr organization*) t'alt'oehada 탈퇴하(*from tradition*) pŏsŏnada 벗어나

♦ **break down 1** v/i (*of vehicle, machine*) kojangnada 고장나다; (*talks*) shilp'aehada 실패하다; (*in tears*) urŭmŭl t'ŏttŭrida 울음을 터뜨리다; (*mentally*) shin-gyŏng-i soeyak'aejida 신경이 쇠약해지다 **2** v/t *door* pusugo yŏlda 부수고 열 *figures* pullyuhada 분류하다

♦ **break even** COM tŭksshiri ŏpkke toeda 득실이 없게 되다

♦ **break in** (*interrupt*) pyŏran-gan malch'amgyŏnhada 발언간

갈참견하다; (of burglar) ch'imip'ada 침입하다

break off 1 v/t kkŏkkŏnaeda 꺾어내다; branch kkŏkitta 꺾다; relationship kkaettŭrida 깨뜨리다; *they've broken it off* kŭdŭl saiga kkaeŏjyŏt-tta 그들 사이가 깨어졌다 **2** v/i (stop talking) taehwarŭl chungdanhada 대화를 중단하다

break out (start up) shijakdoeda 시작되다; (of disease) palppyŏnghada 발병하다; (of prisoners) t'arok'ada 탈옥하다; *he broke out in a rash* kŭnŭn kaptchagi paltchini nat-tta 그는 갑자기 발진이 났다

break up 1 v/t (into component parts) haech'ehada 해체하다; fight mallida 말리다 **2** v/i (of ice) kkaeŏjida 깨어지다; (of couple) heŏjida 헤어지다; (of band, meeting) haech'ehada 해체하다

breakable kkaeŏjigi shiun 깨어지기 쉬운

breakage p'ason 파손

breakdown (of vehicle, machine) kojang 고장; (of talks) shilp'ae 실패; (nervous ~) shin-gyŏng soeyak 신경 쇠약; (of figures) punsŏk 분석

break-even point sonik pun-gitchŏm 손익 분기점

breakfast n ach'im 아침; *have ~* ach'imŭl mŏkta 아침을 먹다

break-in ch'imip 침입

breakthrough (in talks) t'agae 타개; (in science, technology) k'ŭn paltchŏn 큰 발전

breakup (of partnership etc) purhwa 불화

breast (of woman) yubang 유방

breastfeed v/t moyurŭl mŏgida 모유를 먹이다

breaststroke p'yŏnghyŏng 평형

breath sum 숨; *be out of ~* sumi ch'ada 숨이 차다; *take a deep ~* sumŭl kip'i tŭrŏ mashida 숨을 깊이 들어 마시다

breathalyzer®, **breath analyzer** ŭmju ch'ŭktchŏnggi 음주 측정기

breathe 1 v/i sumshwida 숨쉬다 **2** v/t (inhale) tŭri mashida 들이 마시다;

(exhale) naeshwida 내쉬다
♦ **breathe in 1** v/i p'umjong tŭryŏ mashida ~ 들여 마시다 **2** v/t tŭrishwida 들이쉬다
♦ **breathe out** v/i sumŭl naeshwida 숨을 내쉬다

breathing hohŭp 호흡

breathless sumch'an 숨찬

breathlessness hohŭp kollan 호흡 곤란

breathtaking summak'il chŏngdoŭi 숨막힐 정도의

breed 1 n p'umjong 품종 **2** v/t kirŭda 기르다; fig irŭk'ida 일으키다 **3** v/i (of animals) pŏnshik'ada 번식하다

breeding (of animals) pŏnshik 번식

breeding ground fig onsang 온상

breeze sandŭlpparam 산들바람

brew 1 v/t beer yangjohada 양조하다; tea kkŭrida 끓이다 **2** v/i (of storm) ilda 일다; (of trouble) irŏnaryŏgo hada 일어나려고 하다

brewer yangjoŏptcha 양조업자

brewery yangjojang 양조장

bribe 1 n noemul 뇌물 **2** v/t maesuhada 매수하다

bribery noemul susu 뇌물 수수

brick pyŏkttol 벽돌

bricklayer pyŏkttolgong 벽돌공

bride shinbu 신부

bridegroom shillang 신랑

bridesmaid shinbu tŭllŏri 신부 들러리

bridge¹ 1 n tari 다리; (of nose) k'onmaru 콧마루; (of ship) sŏn-gyo 선교 **2** v/t gap chunggae yŏk'arŭl hada 중개 역할을 하다

bridge² (card game) pŭritchi 브릿지

brief¹ adj kan-gyŏrhan 간결한; time tanshiganŭi 단시간의

brief² 1 n (mission) immu 임무 **2** v/t: *~ X on Y* Xege Ye taehan kaeyorŭl sŏlmyŏnghada X에게 Y에 대한 개요를 설명하다

briefcase sŏryu kabang 서류 가방

briefing pŭrip'ing 브리핑

briefly (for a short period of time) chamshidong-an 잠시동안; (in a few words) kan-gyŏrhage 간결하게; (to sum up) yoyak'ajamyŏn 요약하자면

briefs p'aench'ŭ 팬츠

bright *color, future, room* palgŭn
밝은; *smile* hwanhan 환한; (*sunny*)
hwach'anghan 화창한; (*intelligent*)
ttokttok'an 똑똑한
♦ **brighten up 1** *v/t* hwanhage hada
환하게 하다 **2** *v/i* (*of weather*)
malgajida 맑아지다

brighten (*of face, person*) palgajida
밝아지다

brightly hwanhage 환하게

brightness (*of weather*) malgŭm
맑음; (*of smile*) hwanham 환함;
(*intelligence*) ch'ongmyŏngham
총명함

brilliance (*of person*) chitchŏgin
t'agwŏrham 지적인 탁월함; (*of
color*) sŏnmyŏngham 선명함

brilliant *sunshine etc* palgŭn 밝은;
(*very good*) hullyunghan 훌륭한;
(*very intelligent*) much'ŏk
ttokttok'an 무척 똑똑한; *idea* aju
hullyunghan 아주 훌륭한

brim (*of container*) kajangjari
가장자리; (*of hat*) t'eduri 테두리

brimful nŏmch'ildŭt'an 넘칠듯한

bring *object* kajyŏoda 가져오다;
person teryŏoda 데려오다; *peace,
happiness* ch'oraehada 초래하다; ~ *it
here, will you?* iriro kŭgŏsŭl
kajyŏo chullaeyo? 이리로 그것을
가져다 줄래요? *can I ~ a friend?*
ch'in-gurŭl terigo kado twaeyo?
친구를 데리고 가도 돼요?
♦ **bring about** yagihada 야기하다
♦ **bring around** *from a faint* chŏnsin
ch'arigehada 정신 차리게 하다;
(*persuade*) sŏlttŭk'ada 설득하다
♦ **bring back** (*return*) tollyŏjuda
돌려주다; (*re-introduce*) toetollida
되돌리다; *memories* saenggangnage
hada 생각나게 하다
♦ **bring down** *fence, tree* ssŭrŏjige
hada 쓰러지게 하다; *government*
chŏnbokshik'ida 전복시키다; *bird,
airplane* ssoa ttŏrŏttŭrida 쏘아
떨어뜨리다; *rates, inflation, price*
naerige hada 내리게 하다
♦ **bring in** *interest, income* kajyŏoda
가져오다; *legislation* chech'urhada
제출하다; *verdict* naerida 내리다;
(*involve*) kwallyŏnshik'ida

kwallyŏnshik'ida
관련시키다
♦ **bring out** *sesang-e naenot'a* 세상
내놓다; *book* ch'ulp'anhada
출판하다; *video, CD* ch'ulsshihada
출시하다; *new product* palmaehada
발매하다
♦ **bring to** (*from a faint*) chŏnsin
ch'arigehada 정신 차리게 하다
♦ **bring up** *child* yangnyuk'ada
양육하다; *subject* marŭl kkŏnaeda
말을 꺼내다; (*vomit*) t'ohada 토하다

brink kajangjari 가장자리; *fig*
kyŏltchŏngjŏk shigi 결정적 시기

brisk *person, voice, walk* taegt'an
당찬; *trade* hwalbarhan 활발한

bristles (*on chin*) suyŏm 수염; (*of
brush*) t'ŏl 털

bristling: be ~ with ...(ŭ)ro kadŭk
ch'ait-tta ...(으)로 가득 차있다

Britain Yŏngguk 영국

British 1 *adj* Yonggugŭi 영국의 **2** *n*
the ~ Yŏnggugin 영국인,
Yŏngguginŭi 영국인의

Briton Yŏngguk saram 영국 사람

brittle *adj* pusŏjigi shwiun 부서지기
쉬운

broach *subject* marŭl kkŏnaeda 말을
꺼내다

broad 1 *adj* *street, hips* p'ok nŏlbŭn
폭 넓은; *shoulders* ttŏk pŏrŏjin 떡
벌어진; *smile* hwanhan 환한;
(*general*) ilbanjŏgin 일반적인; *in ~
daylight* taenaje 대낮에 **2** *n* F
(*woman*) yŏja 여자

broadcast 1 *n* pangsong 방송 **2** *v/t*
pangsonghada 방송하다

broadcaster pangsong-in 방송인

broadcasting pangsong 방송

broaden *v/i* nŏlbŏjida 넓어지다 **2**
nŏlp'ida 넓히다

broadjump nŏlbi ttwigi 넓이 뛰기;

broadly: ~ speaking ilbanjŏgŭro
marhajamyŏn 일반적으로 말하자면

broadminded kwandaehan 관대한

broccoli pŭrok'olli 브로콜리

brochure pŭrosyŏ 브로셔

broil *v/t* kuptta 굽다

broiler *n* (*on stove*) kumnŭn kigu 굽
기구; (*chicken*) kuiyong yŏnggye
구이용 영계

broke F muilp'unŭi 무일푼의;

bankrupt) p'asanhan 파산한; **go ~** p'asanhada 파산하다

...ken *adj* pusŏjin 부서진; *window,* ...romise kkaejin 깨진; *neck, arm* ...urŏjin 부러진; *home* kyŏlssonŭi ...손의; *English etc* ŏngt'ŏriŭi ...터리의

...ken-hearted maŭmŭi sangch'ŏrŭl ...ŭn 마음의 상처를 입은

...ker chunggaeŏptcha 중개업자

...onchitis kigwanjiyŏm 기관지염

...onze *n* (*metal*) ch'ŏngdong 청동; ...*color*) ch'ŏngdongsaek 청동색; ~ ...**medal** tongmedal 동메달

...ooch purŏch'i 브로치

...ood *v/i* (*of person*) komgomhi ...aenggak'ada 곰곰히 생각하다

...oom pitcharu 빗자루

...oth (*soup*) mulgŭn sup'ŭ 묽은 수프; ...*stock*) kungmul 국물

...othel maech'un-gul 매춘굴

...other (*man's elder*) hyŏng 형; ...*woman's elder*) oppa 오빠; ...*younger*) namdongsaeng 남동생; ...**hey're ~s** kŭdŭrŭn hyŏngjeyeyo ...그들은 형제예요; **~s and sisters** ...yŏngje chamae 형제 자매

...other-in-law (*woman's elder* ...*ister's husband*) hyŏngbu 형부; ...*wife's younger brother*) ch'ŏ-nam ...너남; (*man's elder sister's husband*) ...naehyŏng 매형

...otherly hyŏngjeŭi 형제의

...owbeat mallo wihyŏp'ada 말로 ...위협하다

...ow (*forehead*) ima 이마; (*of hill*) ...maru 마루

...own 1 *n* kalsaek 갈색 2 *adj* ...kalsaegŭi 갈색의; (*tanned*) ...naeppyŏch'e t'an 햇볕에 탄 3 *v/t* (*in* ...*cooking*) norŭnnorŭt'age kuptta ...노릇노릇하게 굽다 4 *v/i* (*in cooking*) ...norŭnnorŭt'age toeda 노릇노릇하 ...게되다

...ownbag: **~ it** toshiragŭl ssaoda ...도시락을 싸오다

...ownie kŏlsŭk'aut'ŭŭi yunyŏn ...tanwŏn 걸스카우트의 유년 단원; ...(*cake*) ch'ok'ollit k'eik 초콜릿 케익

...ownie points: **earn ~** ach'ŏmŭro ...ŏdŭn shinyong 아첨으로 얻은 신용

brown-nose *v/t* F ...ege ach'ŏmhada ...에게 아첨하다

browse (*in store*) kugyŏngman hago tanida 구경만 하고 다니다; **~ through a book** ttŭiŏmttŭiŏm iltta 띄엄띄엄 읽다

browser COMPUT pŭraujŏ 브라우저

bruise 1 *n* mŏng 멍; (*emotional*) sangch'ŏ 상처 2 *v/t person, fruit* mŏngdŭlge hada 멍들게 하다 3 *v/i* (*of person*) mŏngdŭlda 멍들다; (*of fruit*) hŭmi saenggida 흠이 생기다

bruising *adj fig* sangch'ŏnan 상처난

brunch ach'im kyŏm chŏmshim 아침 겸 점심

brunette kalssaek mŏriŭi yŏja 갈색 머리의 여자

brunt: **bear the ~ of** ...(ŭ)ro cheil shimhage kot'ongbat-tta ...(으)로 제일 심하게 고통받다

brush 1 *n* sol 솔; (*conflict*) yakkanŭi ch'ungdol 약간의 충돌 2 *v/t hair, floor* pitchirhada 빗질하다; *teeth* yangch'ijirhada 양치질하다; *jacket* soljirhada 솔질하다; (*touch lightly*) saltchak sŭch'ida 살짝 스치다; (*remove*) ch'iuda 치우다

♦ **brush against** saltchak sŭch'imyŏnsŏ chinagada 살짝 스치면서 지나가다

♦ **brush aside** mushihada 무시하다

♦ **brush off** t'ŏrŏnaeda 털어내다; *criticism* mushihada 무시하다

♦ **brush up** pokssŭp'ada 복습하다

brushoff F t'oetcha 퇴짜; **get the ~** t'oetacharŭl mat-tta 퇴짜를 맞다

brusque muttukttuk'an 무뚝뚝한

Brussels sprouts yangbaech'uŭi iltchong 양배추의 일종

brutal *person* chaninhan 잔인한; *treatment* hokttok'an 혹독한; *honesty* naeng-ŏmhan 냉엄한

brutality chaninham 잔인함

brutally chaninhage 잔인하게; **be ~ frank** chinach'ige soltchik'ada 지나치게 솔직하다

brute chimsŭng kat'ŭn saram 짐승 같은 사람

brute force p'ongnyŏk 폭력

bubble *n* kŏp'um 거품

bubble gum p'ungsŏnkkŏm 풍선껌

buck¹ n F (dollar) tallŏ 달러

buck² v/i (of horse) p'ŏltchŏk ttwida 펄쩍 뛰다

buck³: pass the ~ ch'aegimŭl chŏngahada 책임을 전가하다

bucket n yangdong-i 양동이

buckle¹ 1 n pŏk'ŭl 버클 2 v/t belt pelt'ŭrŭl maeda 벨트를 매다

buckle² v/i (of wood, metal) kuburŏjida 구부러지다

bud n BOT ssak 싹

Buddha Puch'ŏ 부처

Buddha's Birthday Puch'ŏnim Oshin Nal 부처님 오신 날

Buddhism Pulgyo 불교

Buddhist 1 n pulgyo shinja 불교 신자 **2** adj pulgyoŭi 불교의

Buddhist Broadcasting System Pulgyo Pangsong 불교 방송

buddy F ch'in-gu 친구; (form of address) yŏboge 여보게

budge 1 v/t umjigida 움직이다; (make reconsider) maŭmŭl pakkuge hada 마음을 바꾸게 하다 **2** v/i umjigida 움직이다; (change one's mind) maŭmŭl pakkuda 마음을 바꾸다

budgerigar ingkko 잉꼬

budget 1 n yesan 예산; (of a family) saenghwalbi 생활비; **be on a ~** kyŏlp'ip saenghwarŭl hada 결핍 생활을 하다 **2** v/i yesanŭl seuda 예산을 세우다

♦ **budget for** yesane nŏt'a 예산에 넣다

buff¹ adj color hwanggalsaek 황갈색

buff²: a movie/jazz ~ yŏnghwagwang / chaejŭgwang 영화광 / 재즈광

buffalo tŭlsso 들소

buffer RAIL wanch'ung changch'i 완충 장치; fig wanch'ungnyŏk 완충력; **memory ~** COMPUT wanch'ung kiŏk changch'i 완충 기억 장치

buffet¹ n (meal) pup'e 부페

buffet² v/t (of wind) ch'ida 치다

bug 1 n (insect) pŏlle 벌레; (virus) pairŏsŭ 바이러스; (spying device) toch'ŏnggi 도청기; COMPUT pŏgŭ 버그 **2** v/t room toch'ŏnggirŭl sŏlch'ihada 도청기를 설치하다; telephones toch'ŏnghada 도청하다; F

(annoy) koerop'ida 괴롭히다

buggy (for baby) yumoch'a 유모차

build 1 n (of person) ch'egyŏk 체격 **2** v/t seuda 세우다

♦ **build up 1** v/t strength tallyŏnhada 단련하다; relationship ssaa ollida 쌓아 올리다; collection moŭda 모으다 **2** v/i ssayŏjida 쌓여지다

builder (company) kŏnch'ugŏp 건축업; (person) kŏnch'ugŏptcha 건축업자

building kŏnmul 건물; (activity) kŏnch'uk 건축

building site kongsajang 공사장

building trade kŏnch'ugŏp 건축업

build-up (accumulation) ssayŏjim 쌓여짐; (publicity) sŏnjŏn 선전

built-in put'bagiŭi 붙박이의; flash naejangdoeŏ innŭn 내장되어 있는

built-up area shigaji 시가지

bulb BOT kŭbun 구근; (light ~) chŏn-gu 전구

bulge 1 n tolch'ul 돌출; (in number quantity) ilsshijŏk chŭngga 일시적 증가 **2** v/i (of pocket) pulluk'ada 불룩하다; (of wall, eyes) t'wiŏ naoda 튀어 나오다

bulk taebubun 대부분; **in ~** taeryanŭro 대량으로

bulky pup'iga k'ŭn 부피가 큰

bull hwangso 황소

bulldoze (demolish) puldoujŏro chegŏhada 불도우저로 제거하다; **~ into Y** fig Xŭl / rŭl kangjero Yhadorok mandŭlda X을 / 를 강제 Y하도록 만들다

bulldozer puldouŏ 불도우저

bullet ch'ong-al 총알

bulletin keshi 게시

bulletin board (on wall) keship'an 게시판; COMPUT chŏnja keship'an 전자 게시판

bullet-proof pangt'anŭi 방탄의

bull market FIN kangse chusik shijang 강세 주식 시장

bull's-eye kwanyŏgŭi hanbokp'an 과녁의 한복판; **hit the ~** kwanyŏgŭl match'uda 과녁을 맞추다; fig taesŏnggong-ŭl kŏduda 대성공을 거두다

bullshit V **1** n hŏp'ung 허풍 **2** v/i

hŏp'ung-ŭl ttŏlda 허풍을 떨다
ully 1 *n* **kkangp'ae** 깡패 **2** *v/t* **mot salge kulda** 못 살게 굴다
um 1 *n* F (*tramp*) **purangja** 부랑자; (*worthless person*) **mangnani** 망나니 **2** *adj* (*useless*) **ssŭlmoŏmnŭn** 쓸모없는 **3** *v/t* **cigarette etc kŏjŏ ŏt-tta** 거저 얻다
◆ **bum around** F (*travel*)
pangnanghada 방랑하다; (*be lazy*)
pindungbindung chinaeda 빈둥빈둥 지내다
umblebee twengbŏl 뒝벌
ump 1 *n* (*swelling*) **hok** 혹; (*in road*) **yunggi** 융기; *get a ~ on the head* **mŏrirŭl handae mat-tta** 머리를 한대 맞다 **2** *v/t* **puditch'ida** 부딪히다
◆ **bump into** ...**e puditch'ida** ...에 부딪히다; (*meet*) ...**wa/kwa uyŏnhi mannada** ...와/과 우연히 만나다
◆ **bump off** F (*murder*) **chugida** 죽이다
◆ **bump up** F **prices taep'ok ollida** 대폭 올리다
umper *n* MOT **pŏmp'ŏ** 범퍼
umpy flight tŏlk'ŏk-kkŏrinŭn 덜커거리는; *road* **ult'ungbult'unghan** 울퉁불퉁한
un (*hairstyle*) **t'ŭrŏollin mŏri** 틀어올린 머리; (*for eating*) **chagŭn lolppang** 작은 롤빵
unch (*of people*) **muri** 무리; *a ~ of keys* **yŏlsoe mungch'i** 열쇠 뭉치; *a ~ of flowers* **kkot hantabal kwa** 꽃 한 다발; *a ~ of grapes* **p'odo han song-i** 포도 한 송이; *thanks a ~* (*ironic*) **nunmulnage komapkkunyo** 눈물나게 고맙군요
undle (*of clothes*) **kkurŏmi** 꾸러미; (*of wood*) **mungch'i** 뭉치
◆ **bundle up kkurida** 꾸리다; (*dress warmly*) **ttattŭt'a-ge ip'ida** 따뜻하게 입히다
ungle *v/t* **sŏt'urŭge mandŭlda** 서투르게 만들다
unk sŏnban moyang-ŭi ch'imdae 선반 모양의 침대
unk beds ich'ŭng ch'imdae 이층 침대
uoy *n* **pup'yo** 부표
buoyant hwallyŏgi innŭn 활력이

있는; *fig* **sangsŭngse-ŭi** 상승세의
burden 1 *n* **chim** 짐; *fig* **pudam** 부담 **2** *v/t*: *~ X with Y* **Xŭl / rŭl Y(ŭ)ro pudam chiuda** X을 / 를 Y(으)로 부담 지우다
bureau (*chest of drawers*)
sŏraptchang 서랍장; (*office*)
samuguk 사무국
bureaucracy (*red tape*) **pŏn-gŏroun haengjŏng chŏlch'a** 번거로운 행정 절차; (*system*) **kwallyoje** 관료제
bureaucrat kwallyo 관료
bureaucratic kwallyojŏgin 관료적인
burger haembŏgŏ 햄버거
burglar kangdo 강도
burglar alarm tonan kyŏngbogi 도난 경보기
burglarize kangdojirhada 강도질하다
burglary kangdo 강도
burial maejang 매장; *~ at sea* **sujang** 수장
burly kŏnjanghan 건장한
Burma Pŏma 버마
Burmese 1 *adj* **Pŏmaŭi** 버마의 **2** *n* (*person*) **Pŏmain** 버마인; (*language*) **Pŏmaŏ** 버마어
burn 1 *n* **hwasang** 화상 **2** *v/t* **t'aeuda** 태우다; *fuel* **yŏnsohada** 연소하다 **3** *v/i* **t'ada** 타다
◆ **burn down 1** *v/t* **t'aewŏbŏrida** 태워버리다 **2** *v/i* **t'abŏrida** 타버리다
◆ **burn out** *v/t*: *burn oneself out* **chŏngnyŏgŭl tahada** 정력을 다하다; *a burned-out car* **pult'abŏrin ch'a** 불타버린 차
burner (*on cooker*) **naembirŭl ollyŏdunŭn tae** 냄비를 올려두는 대
burp 1 *n* **t'ŭrim** 트림 **2** *v/i* **t'ŭrimhada** 트림하다 **3** *v/t* *baby* **t'ŭrimŭl shik'ida** 트림을 시키다
burst 1 *n* (*in water pipe*) **p'ayŏl** 파열; (*of gunfire*) **chiptchung sagyŏk** 집중 사격; *in a ~ of energy* **kiuni p'ŏlp'ŏl nŏmch'yŏnasŏ** 기운이 펄펄 넘쳐나서 **2** *adj* *tire* **t'ŏjin** 터진 **3** *v/t* *balloon* **t'ŏttŭrida** 터뜨리다 **4** *v/i* (*of balloon, tire*) **t'ŏjida** 터지다; *~ into a room* **pang anŭro ttwiŏdŭlda** 방 안으로 뛰어들다; *~ into tears* **urŭmŭl t'ŏttŭrida** 울음을 터뜨리다; *~ out laughing* **p'oksorŭl t'ŏttŭrida**

폭소를 터뜨리다

bury *person, animal* p'amut-tta
파묻다; (*conceal*) sumgida 숨기다; *be
buried under* (*covered by*) ...(ŭ)ro
tŏp'ida ...(으)로 덮히다; *~ oneself
in one's work* ire molttuhada 일에
몰두하다

bus[1] 1 *n* (*local*) pŏsŭ 버스; (*long
distance*) shioe pŏsŭ 시외 버스 2 *v/t*
pŏsŭro idonghada 버스로
이동하다

bus[2] COMPUT pŏsŭ 버스

busboy weit'ŏŭi chongnyu 웨이터의 조수

bush (*plant*) kwanmok 관목; (*terrain*)
oji 오지

bushed F (*tired*) p'igonhan 피곤한

bushy *beard* t'ŏpssuruk'an 텁수룩한

business (*trade*) muyŏk 무역;
(*company*) hoesa 회사; (*work*) il 일;
(*sector*) saŏbŭi chongnyu 사업의
종류; (*affair, matter*) sakkŏn 사건; (*as
subject of study*) kyŏngnyŏnghak
경영학; *on ~* saŏpch'a 사업차; *that's
none of your ~!* nega sanggwan hal
paga anida! 네가 상관 할 바가
아니다!; *mind your own ~!* ne irina
haera! 네 일이나 해라!

business card myŏngham 명함;
business class pijŭnisŭ k'ŭllaesŭ
비즈니스 클래스; **business hours**
ŏmmu shigan 업무 시간;
businesslike nŭngnyultchŏgin
능률적인; **business lunch** saŏpch'a
hanŭn shikssa 사업차 하는 식사;
businessman saŏpkka 사업가;
business meeting pijŭnisŭ mit'ing
비즈니스 미팅; **business school**
kyŏngnyŏng taehagwŏn 경영 대학원;
business studies kyŏngnyŏnghak
경영학; **business trip** ch'ultchang
출장; **businesswoman** yŏsŏng
saŏpkka 여성 사업가

bus station pŏsŭ t'ŏminŏl 버스
터미널

bus stop pŏsŭ chŏngnyujang 버스
정류장

bust[1] *n* (*of woman*) kasŭm 가슴

bust[2] 1 *adj* F (*broken*) pusŏjin 부서진;
go ~ (*bankrupt*) p'asanhada
파산하다 2 *v/t* pusuda 부수다

♦ **bustle around** punjuhi irhada

분주히 일하다

bust-up F kyŏlbyŏl 결별

busty kasŭmi p'ungmanhan 가슴이
풍만한

busy 1 *adj* pappŭn 바쁜; *street*
pŏnhwahan 번화한; (*making money*)
pumbinŭn 붐비는; (*full of people*)
saramdŭri puktchŏkttaenŭn
사람들이 북적대는; TELEC
t'onghwajung-in 통화중인; *be ~
doing ...* ...ŭl/rŭl hanŭra pappŭda
...을/를 하느라 바쁘다 2 *v/t*: *~ one
self with ...*(ŭ)ro pappŭda ...(으)로
바쁘다

busybody ch'am-gyŏn chal hanŭn
saram 참견 잘 하는 사람

busy signal TELEC t'onghwa chung
shinho 통화중 신호

but 1 *conj* ...hajiman ...하지만; *I tried
to tell him ~ he wouldn't listen*
kŭege marharyŏgo haet-tchiman tŭt
tchi anassŏyo 그에게 말하려고
했지만 듣지 않았어요; *it's not me
my father you want* tangshini
wŏnhan saramŭn naega anira nae
abŏjigunyo 당신이 원한 사람은 내가
아니라 내 아버지군요; *~ then
(again)* kŭrŏt'adorado 그렇다
하더라도; *~ that's not fair* hajiman
kŭgŏn kongp'yŏnghaji anayo 하지만
그건 공평하지 않아요 2 *prep*: *all ~
him* kŭ saramŭl cheoehago modŭ ta
그 사람을 제외하고 모두 다; *the
last ~ one* hana ppaego maen
majimak 하나 빼고 맨 마지막; *the
next ~ one* hana kŏnnŏ ap'e 하나
건너 앞에; *~ for you* nega
ŏpssŏymyŏn 네가 없으면; *nothing ~
the best* ojik ch'oegoman 오직
최고만

butcher chŏngnyuktchŏm chuin
정육점 주인; (*murderer*) hakssaltcha
학살자

butt 1 *n* (*of cigarette*) tambae
kkongch'o 담배 꽁초; (*of joke*)
nongdamŭi p'yojŏk 농담의 표적; F
(*buttocks*) ŏngdŏng-i 엉덩이 2 *v/t*
mŏriro pat-tta 머리로 받다; (*of goat,
bull*) pat-tta 받다

♦ **butt in** panghaehada 방해하다

butter 1 *n* pŏt'ŏ 버터 2 *v/t* pŏt'ŏrŭl

arŭda 버터를 바르다

utter up F ach'ŏmhada 아첨하다

tterfly (*insect*) nabi 나비

ttocks ŏngdŏng-i 엉덩이

ŏt'ŭn 버튼; (*badge*) paeji 배지 2 *v/t* anch'urŭl ch'aeuda 단추를 채우다

utton up → **button**

ttonhole 1 *n* (*in suit*) tanch'u **umŏng** 단추구멍 2 *v/t* put-ttŭlgo agihada 붙들고 이야기하다

xom p'ungmanhan 풍만한

y 1 *n* san mulgŏn 산 물건 2 *v/t* sada 나다; *can I ~ you a drink?* chega an chan sado toelkkayo? 제가 한 ‍ 사도 될까요?; *$50 doesn't ~ nuch* 50tallŏronŭn pyŏllo sal kŏshi ptta 50달러로는 별로 살 것이 없다 **uy off** (*bribe*) maesuhada 배수하다

uy out COM hoesa chibunŭl adŭrida 회사 지분을 사들이다 **uy up** maejŏmhada 매점하다 **yer** kumaeja 구매자; (*for a ompany*) paiŏ 바이어

zz 1 *n* wing-winghanŭn sori 윙윙하는 소리; F (*thrill*) sŭril 스릴 ‍ *v/i* (*of insect*) wingwing sorirŭl aeda 윙윙 소리를 내다; (*with uzzer*) pujŏrŭl ullida 부저를 울리다 ‍ *v/t* (*with buzzer*) pujŏro purŭda ‍부저로 부르다

uzz off F kkŏjyŏ pŏrida 꺼져 ‍리다; *~!* kkŏjyŏ pŏryŏ! 꺼져 버려! **zzer** pujŏ 부저

1 *prep* ◊ (*agency*) ...e ŭihae ...에 ‍의해; *she was murdered ~ her usband* kŭnyŏnŭn namp'yŏne iihae sarhaedanghaet-tta 그녀는

남편에 의해 살해당했다; *a play ~ ...*
...i/ga ssŭn yŏn-gŭk ...이/가 쓴 연극
◊ (*near, next to*) ...yŏp'e ...옆에; *a seat ~ the window* ch'angmun yŏp'e innŭn chari 창문 옆에 있는 자리; *side ~ side* naranhi 나란히 ◊ (*no later than*) ...kkaji ...까지; *~ midnight* chajŏngkkaji 자정까지; *~ this time tomorrow* naeil i shigankkaji 내일 이 시간까지 ◊ (*past*) ...ŭl/rŭl chinasŏ ...을/를 지나서; *as we walked ~ the church* uriga kyohoerŭl china kŏrŏgassŭl ttae 우리가 교회를 지나 걸어갔을 때 ◊ (*mode of transport*)
...(ŭ)ro ...(으)로; *~ bus/train* pŏsŭro/kich'aro 버스로/기차로; *~ day/night* naje/pame 낮에/밤에 ◊ (*measuring*): *~ the hour/ton* shigandang/t'ondang 시간당/톤당; *~ a couple of minutes* myŏt pun ch'airo 몇 분 차이로; *2 ~ 4* p'ogi 2, kiriga 4in nŏlbi p'ogi 2, 길이가 4인 넓이; *~ my watch* nae shigyero 내 시계로 ◊: *~ oneself* honjasŏ 혼자서 2 *adv*: *~ and ~* (*soon*) kot 곧

bye(-bye) annyŏng 안녕
bygone: *let ~s be ~s* chinan irŭn kŭnyang chŏbŏduja 지난 일은 그냥 접어두자
bypass 1 *n* (*road*) uhoero 우회로;
MED hyŏlgwan ishik 혈관 이식 2 *v/t* uhoehada 우회하다
by-product pusanmul 부산물
bystander panggwanja 방관자
byte COMPUT pait'ŭ 바이트
byword: *be a ~ for* ...ŭi taemyŏngsaga toeda ...의 대명사가 되다

C

cab (*taxi*) t'aeksshi 택시; (*of truck*) unjŏnsŏk 운전석
cabaret k'yabare 카바레
cabbage yangbaech'u 양배추
cab driver t'aeksshi unjŏnsa 택시 운전사
cabin (*of plane, for crew*) sŭngmuwŏnshil 승무원실; (*of plane, for passengers*) kaekshshil 객실; (*on ship*) sŏnshil 선실
cabin crew sŭngmuwŏn 승무원
cabinet changshiktchang 장식장; POL naegak 내각; **medicine** ~ yaktchang 약장
cable (*of electrical appliance, telephone etc*) k'eibŭl 케이블; ~ (*TV*) yusŏn pangsong 유선 (방송)
cable car k'eibŭlk'a 케이블카
cable television yusŏn pangsong 유선 방송
cab stand t'aeksshi t'anŭn kot 택시 타는 곳
cactus sŏninjang 선인장
cadaver shich'e 시체
CAD-CAM k'aedŭ/k'aem 캐드/캠
caddie 1 *n* (*in golf*) k'aedi 캐디 2 *v/i*: ~ **for** …ŭl/rŭl wihan k'aediro irhada …을/를 위한 캐디로 일하다
cadet (*in police etc*) saengdo 생도; MIL sagwan saengdo 사관 생도
cadet corps hakssaeng kunsa kyoryŏndan 학생 군사 련단
cadge: ~ **X from Y** Y(ŭ)robut'ŏ Xŭl/rŭl kugŏrhada Y(으)로부터 X을/를 구걸하다
café tabang 다방
cafeteria k'ap'et'eria 카페테리아
caffeine k'ap'ein 카페인
cage (*for bird*) saejang 새장; (*for lion*) uri 우리
cagey t'ŏnourŏ haji annŭn 터놓으려 하지 않는
cahoots: **be in ~ with** …wa/kwa kongmohada …와/과 공모하다

cake 1 *n* k'eik'ŭ 케이크; **be a piece of ~** *fig* maeu shwiun irida 매우 쉬 일이다 2 *v/i* tŏng-ŏrijida 덩어리지다
calcium k'alshyum 칼슘
calculate (*work out*) sanch'urhae naeda 산출해 내다; (*in arithmetic*) kyesanhada 계산하다
calculating *adj* kyesanjŏgin 계산적
calculation kyesan 계산
calculator kyesan-gi 계산기
calendar tallyŏk 달력
calf[1] (*young cow*) song-aji 송아지
calf[2] ANAT chong-ari 종아리
caliber (*of gun*) kugyŏng 구경; **a m of his ~** suwan choŭn saram 수완 좋은 사람
call 1 *n* TELEC chŏnhwa 전화; (*shou* oech'im 외침; (*demand*) yogu 요구 **there's a ~ for you** tangshinhant' chŏnhwaga wassŏyo 당신한테 전화가 왔어요 2 *v/t* TELEC chŏnhwarŭl kŏlda 전화를 걸다; (*summon*) purŭda 부르다; (*meeting* sojip'ada 소집하다; (*summons*) sohwanhada 소환하다; (*describe as* …rago purŭda …라고 부르다; (*shout*) sorich'yŏ purŭda 소리쳐 부르다; **what have they ~ed the baby?** kŭdŭrŭn agi irŭmŭl mwŏra chiŏt-tchiyo? 그들은 아기 이름을 뭐라고 지었지요?; **but we ~ him Tom** kŭrŏch'iman urinŭn kŭrŭl T'omirago pullŏyo 그렇지만 우리는 그를 톰이라고 불러요; ~ **s.o. nam** nugurŭl yok'ada 누구를 욕하다 3 TELEC chŏnhwahada 전화하다; (*shout*) sorich'yŏ purŭda 소리쳐 부르다; (*visit*) pangmunhada 방문하다
♦ **call at** (*stop at*) …e tŭllida …에 들리다; (*of train*) …e chŏngch'ahac …에 정차하다
♦ **call back 1** *v/t* TELEC najung-e tas chŏnhwahada 나중에 다시 전화하다

summon) pullŏsŏ toedoraoge hada
불러서 되돌아오게 하다 **2** *v/i* TELEC
najung-e tashi chŏnhwahada 나중에
다시 전화하다; (*visit*) tashi
pangmunhada 다시 방문하다
call for (*collect*) ...ŭl/rŭl kajirŏ
kada ...을/를 가지러 가다; *person*
...ŭl/rŭl terirŏ kada ...을/를 데리러
가다; (*demand*) yoguhada 요구하다;
(*require*) ...i/ga p'iryohada ...이/가
필요하다
call in 1 *v/t* (*summon*) pullŏ tŭrida
불러 들이다 **2** *v/i* TELEC chŏnhwaro
allida 전화로 알리다
call off (*cancel*) ch'wisohada
취소하다
call on (*urge*) yoguhada 요구하다;
(*visit*) pangmunhada 방문하다
call out sorich'yŏ purŭda 소리쳐
부르다; (*summon*) ch'ulttongshik'ida
출동시키다
call up *v/t* TELEC chŏnhwahada
전화하다; COMPUT yŏlda 열다
caller TELEC chŏnhwa kŏn saram
전화 건 사람; (*visitor*) sonnim 손님
call girl maech'unbu 매춘부
calligraphy sŏye 서예
callous mugamgak'an 무감각한
calm 1 *adj sea*, *weather* koyohan
고요한; *person* ch'imch'ak'an 침착한
2 *n* (*of the countryside etc*) p'yŏng-
on 평온; (*of person*) ch'imch'ak 침착
calm down 1 *v/t* karaanch'ida
가라앉히다 **2** *v/i* (*of sea*, *weather*)
koyohaejida 고요해지다; (*of person*)
ch'imch'ak'aejida 침착해지다
calorie k'allori 칼로리
Cambodia K'ambodia 캄보디아
Cambodian 1 *adj* K'ambodiaŭi
캄보디아의 **2** *n* (*person*) K'ambodia
saram 캄보디아 사람
camcorder k'aemk'odŏ 캠코더
camera k'amera 카메라
cameraman ch'waryŏng kisa 촬영
기사
camouflage 1 *n* wijang 위장 **2** *v/t*
wijanghada 위장하다
camp 1 *n* k'aemp'ŭ 캠프; (*for
prisoners*, *refugees*) suyongso 수용소
2 *v/i* ch'ŏnmagŭl ch'ida 천막을 치다
campaign 1 *n* undong 운동 **2** *v/i*

undong-ŭl hada 운동을 하다
campaigner undongga 운동가
camper (*person*) k'aemp'inghanŭn
saram 캠핑하는 사람; (*vehicle*)
k'aemp'ŭyong t'ŭreillŏ 캠프용
트레일러
camp ground yayŏngji 야영지
camping k'aemp'ing 캠핑
campsite yayŏngji 야영지
campus: *university ~* taehak
kyojŏng 대학 교정, taehak
k'aemp'ŏsŭ 대학 캠퍼스
can[1] ◊ (*ability*) ...hal su it-tta ...할 수
있다; *~ you hear me?* nae marŭl
tŭrŭl su issŏyo? 내 말을 들을 수
있어요?; *~ you speak French?*
Puŏrŭl marhal su issŏyo? 불어를
말할 수 있어요?; *~ you help me?*
towajul su issŏyo? 도와줄 수
있어요?; *~ he call me back?* kŭnŭn
na-ege najung-e chŏnhwahae chul su
issŏyo? 그는 내게 나중에 전화해 줄
수 있어요?; *I ~ do it by tomorrow*
naeil kkaji hal su issŏyo 내일까지 할
수 있어요 ◊ (*in negative*) ...hal su
ŏptta ...할 수 없다; *I ~'t see* pol su
ŏpssŏyo 볼 수 없어요; *you ~'t give
up now* tangshinŭn chigŭm p'ogihal
su ŏpssŏyo 당신은 지금 포기할 수
없어요; *that ~'t be right* majŭl li
ŏpssŏ 맞을 리 없어 ◊ (*permission*)
...hayŏdo chot'a ...하여도 좋다; *I
use the phone?* chŏnhwarŭl ssŏdo
toemnikka? 전화를 써도 됩니까?; *~ I
help you?* towadŭrilkkayo?
도와드릴까요?; *~ I have a
beer / coffee?* maektchuga /
k'ŏp'iga issŏyo? 맥주가 / 커피가
있어요?
can[2] 1 *n* (*for drinks etc*) kkangt'ong
깡통; (*of preserved food*) t'ongjorim
통조림 **2** *v/t* t'ongjorimhada 통조림
하다
Canada K'aenada 캐나다
Canadian 1 *adj* K'aenadaŭi 캐나다의
2 *n* K'aenada saram 캐나다 사람
canal (*waterway*) unha 운하
canary k'anaria 카나리아
cancel ch'wisohada 취소하다
cancellation ch'wiso 취소
cancer am 암

c & f (= *cost and freight*) unim p'oham kagyŏk 운임 포함 가격
candid soltchik'an 솔직한
candidacy ip'ubo 입후보
candidate (*for position*) huboja 후보자; (*in exam*) ŭngsija 응시자
candle yangch'o 양초
candlestick ch'ot-ttae 촛대
candor hŏshim t'anhoe 허심 탄회
candy sat'ang 사탕
cannabis taemach'o 대마초
canned *fruit etc* t'ongjorimdoen 통조림된; (*recorded*) nogŭmdoen 녹음된
cannot → *can¹*
canoe k'anu 카누
can opener kkangt'ong ttagae 깡통 따개
can't → *can¹*
canteen (*in factory*) kunae shikttang 구내 식당
canvas (*for painting*) kaenbŏsŭ 캔버스; (*material*) chŭk'ŭ 즈크
canvass 1 *v/t* (*seek opinion of*) …ŭi ŭigyŏnŭl murŏboda …의 의견을 물어보다 **2** *v/i* POL yusehada 유세하다
canyon kip'ŭn hyŏkkkok 깊은 협곡
cap (*hat*) k'aep 캡; (*of bottle, pen, lens etc*) ttukkŏng 뚜껑
capability (*of person*) nŭngnyŏk 능력; (*of military*) kunsaryŏk 군사력
capable (*efficient*) nŭngnyŏk innŭn 능력 있는; **be ~ of** …hal nŭngnyŏgi it-tta …할 능력이 있다
capacity (*of container, engine*) yongnyang 용량; (*of building*) yongjŏk 용적; (*of elevator*) suyongnyŏk 수용력; (*of factory*) ch'oedae saengsannyŏk 최대 생산력; (*ability*) nŭngnyŏng 능력; **in my ~ as** nanŭn …(ŭ)rosŏ 나는 …(으)로서
capital *n* (*of country*) sudo 수도; (*letter*) taemuntcha 대문자; (*money*) chabon 자본
capital expenditure ch'ongbiyong 총비용; **capital gains tax** chasan sodŭksse 자산 소득세; **capital growth** chabon chŭngga 자본 증가
capitalism chabonjuŭi 자본주의
capitalist 1 *adj* chabonjuŭijŏk

자본주의적 **2** *n* chabonjuŭija 자본주의자; (*businessman*) chabon ga 자본가
capital letter taemuntcha 대문자
capital punishment kŭk'yŏng 극형
capitulate hangbok'ada 항복하다
capsize 1 *v/i* twijip'ida 뒤집히다 **2** *v* twijiptta 뒤집다
capsule MED, (*in space*) k'aepsshyu 캡슐
captain *n* (*of ship*) sŏnjang 선장; (*of aircraft*) kijang 기장; (*of team*) t'imjang 팀장
caption *n* k'aepsshyŏn 캡션
captivate maŭmŭl sarojaptta 마음을 사로잡다
captive (*of war*) p'oro 포로
captivity kamgŭm 감금
capture 1 *n* (*of city*) chŏmnyŏng 점; (*of criminal*) saengp'o 생포; (*of animal*) p'ohoek 포획 **2** *v/t person, animal* sarojaptta 사로잡다; *city, building* chŏmnyŏnghada 점령하다; *market share etc* hoekttŭk'ada 획득하다; (*portray*) p'och'ak'ada 포착하다
car chadongch'a 자동차; (*of train*) ch'aryang 차량; **by ~** chadongch'a 자동차로
carafe pyŏng 병
carat k'aerŏt 캐럿
carbohydrate t'ansuhwamul 탄수화물
carbonated *drink* t'ansanŭi 탄산의
carbon monoxide ilssanhwat'anso 일산화탄소
carburetter, carburetor k'aburet'ŏ 카뷰레터
carcinogen param multchil 발암 물질
carcinogenic paramsŏng-ŭi 발암성의
card k'adŭ 카드; (*post~*) yŏpssŏ 엽서; (*business ~*) myŏngham 명함
cardboard p'anji 판지
cardiac shimjang-ŭi 심장의
cardiac arrest shimjang chŏngji 심장 정지
cardigan k'adigŏn 카디건
card index k'adŭshik saegin 카드식 색인

...rd key k'adŭro toen yŏlssoe 카드로 열쇠

...re 1 n (of baby, pet) tolbom 돌봄; (of the elderly) posalp'im 보살핌; (of sick person) kanho 간호; (medical ~) n'iryo ch'iryo; (worry) kŏkchŏng 걱정; ~ of → c/o; take ~ (be cautious) choshimhada 조심하다; take ~ (of yourself)! (goodbye) choshimhaesŏ kaseyo! 조심해서 가세요!; take ~ of baby, dog tolboda 돌보다; tool, house, garden sojunghi hada 소중히 하다; (deal with) ch'ŏrihada 처리하다; (handle) with ~! (on label) ch'wigŭp chuŭi 취급 주의; ~ of 2 v/i kwanshimŭl kajida 관심을 가지다; I don't ~! sanggwan ŏpssŏ! 상관 없어!; I couldn't ~ less chŏnhyŏ kwanshimi ŏpssŏ 전혀 관심이 없어

♦care about ...e kwanshimŭl kajida ...에 관심을 가지다

♦care for (look after) tolboda 돌보다; (like, be fond of) choahada 좋아하다; would you ~ ...? ...ŭl/rŭl chom tŭshigessŏyo? ...을/를 좀 드시겠어요?

...reer (profession) kyŏngnyŏk 경력; (path through life) saeng-ae 생애

...refree amu kŏktchŏng ŏmnŭn 아무 걱정 없는

...reful (cautious) choshimsŏng innŭn 조심성 있는; (thorough) shinjunghan 신중한; (be) ~! choshimhae! 조심해!

...refully (with caution) choshimsŭrŏpkke 조심스럽게; worded etc shinjunghage 신중하게

...reless choshimsŏng ŏmnŭn 조심성 없는; you are so ~! nŏnŭn nŏmu choshimsŏng-i ŏpkkuna! 너는 너무 조심성이 없구나!

...aress 1 n aemu 애무 2 v/t aemuhada 애무하다

...aretaker kwalliin 관리인

...areworn kŏktchŏng-e shidallin 걱정에 시달린

...argo sŏnjŏk hwamul 선적 화물

...aricature n p'ungja manhwa 풍자 만화

...aring adj chal tolbonŭn 잘 돌보는

...arnage taehaksal 대학살

carnation k'aneishyŏn 카네이션

carnival (at carnival) hoejŏnshik k'onbeiŏ 회전식 콘베이어; (amusement park) yuwŏnji 유원지

carol n ch'uk-kka 축가

carousel (at airport) hoejŏnshik k'onbeiŏ 회전식 콘베이어; (for slide projector) hwandŭnggi p'illŭm k'arusel 환등기 필름 카루셀; (merry-go-round) hoejŏn mongma 회전 목마

carpenter mokssu 목수

carpet k'ap'et 카펫

carpool 1 n chagayong-ŭi hapssŭng iyong 자가용의 합승 이용 2 v/i chagayong-ŭl hapssŭng-ŭro iyonghada 자가용을 합승을 이용하다

car port kani ch'ago 간이 차고

carrier (company) unsong hoesa 운송 회사; (of disease) pogyunja 보균자

carrot tanggŭn 당근

carry 1 v/t (in hand) tŭlgo kada 들고 가다; (from one place to another) narŭda 나르다; (have on one's person) chinigo tanida 지니고 다니다; (of pregnant woman) paego it-tta 배고 있다; disease omgida 옮기다; (of ship, plane, bus etc) narŭda 나르다; proposal t'onggwashik'ida 통과시키다; get carried away nŏkssŭl ilt'a 넋을 잃다 2 v/i (of sound) irŭda 이르다

♦carry on 1 v/i (continue) kyesok'ada 계속하다; (make a fuss) soranŭl p'iuda 소란을 피우다; (have an affair) paramŭl p'iuda 바람을 피우다 2 v/t (conduct) haenagada 해나가다

♦carry out survey etc shilsshihada 실시하다; orders etc shirhaenghada 실행하다

car seat (for child) ŏriniyong chwasŏk 어린이용 좌석

cart chimmach'a 짐마차

cartel k'arŭt'el 카르텔

carton (for storage, transport) pakssŭ 박스; (for eggs) kwak 곽; (for milk etc) p'aek 팩; (of cigarettes) kap 갑

cartoon (in newspaper, magazine) manhwa 만화; (on TV, movie) manhwa yŏnghwa 만화 영화

cartridge (*for gun*) t'anyakt'ong 탄약통

carve *meat* charǔda 자르다; *wood* saegida 새기다

carving (*figure*) chogak 조각

car wash ch'a sech'ŏk 차 세척

case¹ (*container*) k'eisǔ 케이스; (*of Scotch, wine*) sangja 상자; *Br* (*suitcase*) otkkabang 옷가방

case² *n* (*instance*) kyŏng-u 경우; (*argument*) chujang 주장; (*for investigation*) sakkŏn 사건; MED pyŏngse 병세; LAW sosong sakkŏn 소송 사건; **in ~ ...** manil ... hal kyŏng-urǔl saenggak'ayŏ 만일 ... 할 경우를 생각하여; **in ~ it rains** manil piga ol kyŏng-urǔl saenggak'ayŏ 만일 비가 올 경우를 생각하여; **in any ~** ŏtchaettǔn 어쨌든; **in that ~** kǔrŏn kyŏng-ue 그런 경우에

case history MED pyŏngnyŏk 병력

cash 1 *n* hyŏn-gǔm 현금; **~ down** kǔ chariesŏ hyŏn-gǔmǔro 그 자리에서 현금으로; **pay** (**in**) ~ hyŏn-gǔmǔro naeda 현금으로 내다; **~ in advance** sŏn-gǔm 선금 **2** *v/t check* hyŏn-gǔmǔro pakkuda 현금으로 바꾸다

♦ **cash in on** ...(ǔ)ro tonǔl pŏlda ...(으)로 돈을 벌다

cash cow kiŏbǔi hǔktcha hoesa 기업의 흑자 회사; **cash desk** kyesandae 계산대; **cash discount** hyŏn-gǔm harin 현금 할인; **cash flow** hyŏn-gǔm yuch'urip 현금 유출입

cashier *n* (*in store etc*) ch'ullabwŏn 출납원

cash machine hyŏn-gǔm inch'ulgi 현금 인출기

cashmere *adj* k'aeshimiŏ 캐시미어

cash register kǔmjŏn tǔngnok-kki 금전 등록기

casino k'ajino 카지노

casket (*coffin*) kwan 관

cassette nogǔm t'eip'ǔ 녹음 테이프

cassette player nogǔmgi 녹음기

cassette recorder nogǔmgi 녹음기

cast 1 *n* (*of play*) ch'uryŏnjin 출연진; (*mold*) chuhyŏng 주형 **2** *v/t doubt, suspicion* irǔk'ida 일으키다; *play* paeurǔl

chŏnghada 배우를 정하다; *actor* paeyŏgǔl chŏnghada 배역을 정하

♦ **cast off** *v/i* (*of ship*) pattchurǔl p'ulda 밧줄을 풀다

caste k'asǔt'ǔ chedo 카스트 제도

caster (*on chair etc*) tari pak'wi 다 바퀴

cast iron *n* musoe 무쇠

cast-iron *adj* musoero mandǔn 무쇠로 만든

castle sŏng 성

castrate kŏsehada 거세하다

casual (*chance*) uyŏnhan 우연한; (*offhand*) mugwanshimhan 무관심한; (*not formal*) p'yŏngsang 평상의; (*not permanent*) ilsshijŏgin 일시적인

casualty sasangja 사상자

casual wear p'yŏngsangbok 평상복

cat koyang-i 고양이

catalog *n* mongnok 목록

catalyst *fig* ch'oktchinje 촉진제

catalytic converter ch'ongmae k'ŏnbŏt'ŏ 촉매 컨버터

catastrophe ch'ŏnjaejibyŏn 천재지

catch 1 *n* chapkki 잡기; (*of fish*) nakkǔn kŏt 낚은 것; (*locking device* kori 고리; (*problem*) munje 문제 **2** *v/t ball, escaped prisoner, fish* chaptta 잡다; (*bus, train*) chaba t'a 잡아 타다; (*in order to speak to*) ttarajaptta 따라잡다; (*hear*) ara tǔt tta 알아 듣다; *illness ...e* kŏllida ... 걸리다; **~ (a) cold** kamgie kŏllida 감기에 걸리다; **~ s.o.'s eye** (*of person, object*) nuguǔi shisŏnǔl kkǔlda 누구의 시선을 끌다; **~ sigh of ...**ǔl/rǔl hŭllkkŭt poda ...을/를 흘끗 보다; **~ X doing Y** Xi/ga Yhago innŭn changmyŏnǔl puttchaptta X이/가 Y하고 있는 장면을 붙잡다

♦ **catch on** (*become popular*) in-gir ŏt-tta 인기를 얻다; (*understand*) ihaehada 이해하다

♦ **catch up** *v/i* ttarajaptta 따라잡다

♦ **catch up on** ...ǔl/rǔl poch'unghada ...을/를 보충하다

catch-22: *it's a ~ situation* pujorihan sanghwang-ida 부조리한 상황이다

tcher (*in baseball*) k'aech'ŏ 캐처
tching *disease* chŏnyŏmsŏng-ŭi
전염성의; *fear, panic* ŏmssŭp'anŭn
겁심하는
tchy *tune* kŭmbang shwipkke
cewŏjinŭn 금방 쉽게 외워지는
tegory pŏmju 범주
cater for (*meet the needs of*) …ŭi
umie mat-tta …의 구미에 맞다;
(*provide food for*) …ŭl / rŭl wihan
corirŭl chegonghada …을 / 를 위한
요리를 제공하다
terer yori chodaltcha 요리 조달자
terpillar yuch'ung 유충
thedral sŏngdang 성당
atholic 1 *adj* Ch'ŏnjugyoŭi 천주교의
n Ch'ŏnjugyo shinja 천주교 신자
tsup k'ech'ŏp 케첩
ttle so 소
tty pianyanggŏrinŭn 비아냥거리는
auliflower k'ollip'ŭllawŏ 콜리플라워
use 1 *n* wŏnin 원인; (*grounds*) iyu
기유; (*aim of movement*) moktchŏk
목적 **2** *v/t* irŭk'ida 일으키다
aution 1 *n* (*care*) choshim 조심; *~ is*
advised choshimhaeya hamnida
조심해야 합니다 **2** *v/t* (*warn*)
chuŭihashik'ida 주의시키다
autious choshimsŭrŏun 조심스러운
ave tonggul 동굴
cave in (*of roof*) ump'uk kkŏjida
옴폭 꺼지다
aviar ch'ŏlgap sang-ŏ aljŏt 철갑 상어
알젓
avity ch'ungch'i 충치
BS (= *Christian Broadcasting
System*) Kidok-kkyo Pangsong
기독교 방송
1 *n* saboni ponaejim 사본이 보내짐
2 *v/t* sabonŭl ponaeda 사본을 보내다
(= *compact disc*) k'omp'aekt'ŭ
tisŭk'ŭ 콤팩트 디스크
player CD p'ŭlleiŏ CD 플레이어
-ROM sshidirom 씨디롬
-ROM drive sshidirom tŭraibŭ
씨디롬 드라이브
ase 1 *v/i* chungdanhada 중단하다
2 *v/t* chungdanshik'ida 중단시키다
asefire hyujŏn 휴전
eiling (*of room*) ch'ŏnjang 천장;
(*limit*) ch'oego hando 최고 한도

celadon ware ch'ŏngja 청자
celebrate 1 *v/i* ch'uk'ahada 축하하다
2 *v/t* ch'uk'ahada 축하하다; (*observe*)
chinaeda 지내다
celebrated yumyŏnghan 유명한; *be ~
for* …(ŭ)ro yumyŏnghada ..(으)로
유명하다
celebration ch'uk'ayŏn 축하연
celebrity yumyŏng insa 유명 인사
celery sellŏri 샐러리
cell (*for prisoner*) kambang 감방; BIO
sep'o 세포; COMPUT p'yok'an 표칸
cellar chihashil 지하실
cello ch'ello 첼로
cellophane sellop'an 셀로판
cell(ular) phone haendŭp'on 핸드폰,
idong chŏnhwa 이동 전화
Celsius sŏpsshi 섭씨
cement 1 *n* shiment'ŭ 시멘트 **2** *v/t*
shiment'ŭro parŭda 시멘트로
바르다; *friendship* kuch'ida 굳히다
cemetery myoji 묘지
censor *v/t* kŏmyŏrhada 검열하다
censorship kŏmyŏl chedo 검열 제도
cent sent'ŭ 센트
centennial paek chunyŏn 백 주년
center 1 *n* (*middle*) han-gaunde
한가운데; (*building*) sent'ŏ 센터;
(*region*) chungshimji 중심지; POL
chungdop'a 중도파; *in the ~ of* …ŭi
han-gaundee(sŏ) …의
한가운데에(서) **2** *v/t* han-gaundero
tuda 한가운데로 두다
♦ **center on** …e chungshimŭl tuda
…에 중심을 두다
centigrade sŏpsshi 섭씨; *10 degrees
~* sŏpsshi 10to sgsshi 섭씨 10도
centimeter sent'i(mit'ŏ) 센티(미터)
central chungshimŭi 중심의; *location,
apartment* chungshimbue innŭn
중심부에 있는; (*main*) chuyohan
주요한; *~ France* P'ŭrangsŭ
chungbu 프랑스 중부; *be ~ to sth*
muŏse chungshimjŏgida 무엇에
중심적이다
central heating chung-ang chamgŭm
changch'i 중앙 잠금 장치
centralize chiptchung kyŏruihada
집중 결의하다
central locking MOT chung-ang
anjŏn changch'i 중앙 안전 장치

central processing unit → **CPU**

century segi 세기

CEO (= **Chief Executive Officer**) ch'oego kyŏngnyŏngja 최고 경영자

ceramic tojagiro toen 도자기로 된

ceramics (*objects*) tojagi 도자기; (*art*) toye 도예

cereal (*grain*) kongmul 곡물; **breakfast** ~ shiriŏl 시리얼

ceremonial 1 *adj* ŭishigŭl wihan 의식을 위한 **2** *n* ŭishik 의식

ceremony (*event*) shik 식; (*ritual*) ŭishik 의식; **the Oscars** ~ Osŭk'a shisangshik 오스카 시상식; **opening ~ / closing ~** kaehoeshik / p'yehoeshik 개회식 / 폐회식

certain (*sure*) hwaksshinhanŭn 확신하는; (*particular*) ottŏn 어떤; (*specific*) iltchŏnghan 일정한; **it's ~ that** …라는 것은 확실하다; **a ~ Mr Park** Pak mosshi 박 모씨; **make ~** hwaginhada 확인하다; **know / say for ~** hwaksshirhi alda / marhada 확실히 알다 / 말하다

certainly (*definitely*) hwaksshirhi 확실히; (*of course*) mullon 물론; **~ not!** mullon andwaeji! 물론 안돼지!

certainty (*confidence*) hwaksshin 확신; (*inevitability*) hwaksshilssŏng 확실성; **it's / he's a ~** kŭgŏsŭn / kŭnŭn hwaksshirhada 그것은 / 그는 확실하다

certificate (*qualification*) chagyŏktchŭng 자격증; (*official paper*) chŭngmyŏngsŏ 증명서

certified public accountant kong-in hoegyesa 공인 회계사

certify pojŭnghada 보증하다

Cesarean *n* chewang chŏlgae 제왕 절개

cessation chungji 중지; **~ of hostilities** hyujŏn 휴전

CFC (= **chlorofluorocarbon**) sshiep'ŭsshi 씨에프씨

chain 1 *n* (*for animal, anchor*) soesasŭl 쇠사슬; (*jewelry*) mokkkŏrijul 목걸이줄; (*for bicycle, tire*) ch'ein 체인; (*of stores, hotels*) ch'einjŏm 체인점 **2** *v/t*: **~ X to Y** Xŭl / rŭl Ye sasŭlo muktta X을 / 를

Y에 사슬로 묶다

chain reaction yŏnswae panŭng 연쇄 반응; **chain smoke** chuldambaerŭl p'iuda 줄담배를 피우다; **chain smoker** chuldambaerŭl p'iunŭn saram yŏnswaejŏm 연쇄점; **chain store** yŏnswaejŏm 연쇄점

chair 1 *n* ŭija 의자; (*arm~*) allak ŭija 안락 의자; (*at university*) chŏnggyosujik 정교수직; **the ~** (*electric*) chŏn-gi ŭija 전기 의자; (*meeting*) ŭijang 의장; **take the ~** ŭijangjigŭl mat-tta 의장직을 맡다 **2** *v/t meeting* ŭijangjigŭl mat-tta 의장직을 맡다

chair lift ch'eŏ lip'ŭt'ŭ 체어 리프트; **chairman** ŭijang 의장; **chairperson** sahoeja 사회자; **chairwoman** sahoeja 사회자

chalk (*for writing*) punp'il 분필; (*in soil*) sŏk'oeam 석회암

challenge 1 *n* (*difficult task*) haebol manhan il 해볼 만한 일; (*in race, competition*) tojŏn 도전 **2** *v/t* (*to race, debate*) tojŏnhada 도전하다; (*call into question*) hwan-gishik'ida 환기시키다

challenger tojŏnja 도전자

challenging nŭngnyŏgŭl shihŏmhaebonŭn nŭngnyŏgŭl 능력을 시험해보는

chambermaid kaekshil tamdang yŏjong-ŏbwŏn 객실 담당 여종업원

Chamber of Commerce Sanggong-hoeŭiso 상공 회의소

chamois (*leather*) shyaemi kajuk 섀미 가죽

champagne shyamp'ein 샴페인

champion 1 *n* SP ch'aemp'iŏn 챔피언; (*of cause*) onghoja 옹호자 **2** *v/t* (*cause*) onghohada 옹호하다

championship (*event*) sŏnsugwŏn taehoe 선수권 대회; (*title*) sŏnsugwŏn 선수권

chance (*possibility*) kamang 가망; (*opportunity*) kihoe 기회; (*risk*) wihŏm 위험; (*luck*) uyŏn 우연; **by chance** uyŏnhi 우연히; **take a ~** une matkkigo haeboda 운에 맡기고 해보다; **I'm not taking any ~s** yohaengsurŭl paraji ansssŭmnida 요행수를 바라지 않습니다

andelier shyangdŭllie 샹들리에

ange 1 *n* (*to plan, idea etc*.)
yŏnhwa 변화; (*small coins, from
urchase*) chandon 잔돈; (*different
tuation etc*) kibun chŏnhwan 기분
변환; *for a* ~ kibun chŏnhwanŭro
분 전환으로; *a ~ of clothes*
araibŭl ot 가라입을 옷 2 *v/t* (*alter*)
akkuda 바꾸다; (*world, society*)
yŏnhwashik'ida 변화시키다;
ankbill pakkuŏ chuda 바꾸어 주다;
replace) kalda 갈다; *trains, planes*
arat'ada 갈아타다; *one's clothes*
akkuŏ iptta 바꾸어 입다 3 *v/i*
akkuŏjida 바뀌어지다; (*of world,
ociety*) pyŏnhwahada 변화하다; (*put
n different clothes*) pakkuŏ iptta
꾸어 입다; (*take different train etc*)
arat'ada 갈아타다

annel (*on TV, radio*) ch'aenŏl
널; (*waterway*) suro 수로

ant 1 *n* norae 노래 2 *v/i* noraehada
래하다

aos taehollan 대혼란

aotic hollansŭrŏun 혼란스러운

apel yebaedang 예배당

apped salgach'i t'ŭn salgaʼi t'ŭn 틈

apter (*of book*) chang 장; (*of
rganization*) chibu 지부

aracter (*nature*) sŏngkkyŏk 성격;
person) inmul 인물; (*in book, play*)
ingjang inmul 등장 인물; (*special
ura*) t'ŭktching 특징; (*letter*)
uantcha 문자; *he's a real ~* kŭnŭn
edanhan inmuriyeyo 그는 대단한
물이에요

aracteristic 1 *n* t'ŭkssŏng 특성
adj t'ŭkssŏng-ŭl nat'anaenŭn
특성을 나타내는

aracterize (*be typical of*) …ŭi
ŭkssŏng-ŭl nat'anaeda …의 특성을
타내다; (*describe*) sŏngkkyŏgŭl
yosahada 성격을 묘사하다

aracter set COMPUT munjap'yo
글자표

arbroiled sutppure kuwŏjin 숯불에
구워진

arcoal (*for barbecue*) sut 숯; (*for
rawing*) mokt'an 목탄

arge 1 *n* (*fee*) yogŭm 요금; LAW
yŏmŭi 혐의; *free of ~* muryoro
무료로; *will that be cash or ~?*
hyŏn-gŭmimnikka, oesang-imnikka?
현금입니까, 외상입니까?; *be in ~*
tamdang-ida 담당이다; *take ~*
ttŏmat-tta 떠맡다 2 *v/t sum of money*
ch'ŏngguhada 청구하다; (*put on
account*) ap'ŭro taranot'a 앞으로
달아놓다; LAW kobarhada 고발하다;
battery ch'ungjŏnshik'ida 충전시키다
3 *v/i* (*attack*) tolgyŏk'ada 돌격하다

charge account oesang kŏrae 외상
거래

charge card shinyong k'adŭ 신용
카드

charisma k'arisŭma 카리스마

charitable *institution, donation*
chasŏnŭi 자선의; *person* chasŏnshimi
manŭn 자선심이 많은

charity (*assistance*) chasŏn 자선;
(*organization*) chasŏn tanch'e 자선
단체

charm 1 *n* (*appealing quality*)
maeryŏk 매력 2 *v/t* (*delight*)
maehok'ada 매혹하다

charming maehoktchŏgin 매혹적인

charred kŭsŭllin 그슬린

chart (*diagram*) top'yo 도표; NAUT
haedo 해도; (*for airplane*) ch'yat'ŭ
차트; *the ~s* MUS hit'ŭgok sunwi
히트곡 순위

charter *v/t* chŏnse naeda 전세 내다

charter flight chŏnsegi 전세기

chase 1 *n* ch'ugyŏk 추격 2 *v/t*
twitchot-tta 뒤쫓다

♦ **chase away** tchoch'abŏrida
쫓아버리다

chaser (*drink*) ch'eisŏ 체이서

chassis (*of car*) shyaeshi 섀시

chat 1 *n* chapttam 잡담 2 *v/i*
chapttamhada 잡담하다

chatter 1 *n* suda 수다 2 *v/i* (*talk*) suda
ttŏlda 수다 떨다; (*of teeth*) tŏldŏl
ttŏllida 덜덜 떨리다

chatterbox sudajaeng-i 수다쟁이

chatty *person* sudasŭrŏun 수다스러운;
letter hŏmurŏmnŭn 허물없는

chauffeur *n* chagayong unjŏnsa
자가용 운전사

chauvinist (*male ~*) namsŏng
uwŏltchuŭija 남성 우월주의자

cheap *adj* (*inexpensive*) ssan 싼;

(*nasty*) p'iyŏrhan 비열한; (*mean*) insaek'an 인색한

cheat 1 *n* (*person*) sogimsu 속임수 **2** *v/t* sogida 속이다; **~ X out of Y** Yŭl/rŭl sogyŏsŏ Xŭl/rŭl ppaeat-tta Y을/를 속여서 X을/를 빼앗다 **3** *v/i* (*in exam, cards etc*) sogimsurŭl ssŭda 속임수를 쓰다; **~ on one's wife** anae mollae param p'iuda 아내 몰래 바람 피우다

check¹ *adj shirt* ch'ek'ŭ munŭiŭi 체크 무늬의 **2** *n* ch'ek'ŭ munŭi ch'ek'ŭ munŭi 체크 무늬

check² FIN sup'yo 수표; (*in restaurant etc*) kyesansŏ 계산서; **~ please** kyesanhae chuseyo 계산해 주세요

check³ 1 *n* (*to verify sth*) hwagin 확인; **keep in ~, hold in ~** ŏktchehada 억제하다; **keep a ~ on** hwaginhae tuda 확인해 두다 **2** *v/t* (*verify*) hwaginhada 확인하다; (*inspect*) chŏmgŏmhada 점검하다; (*restrain*) ŏktchehada 억제하다; (*stop*) maktta 막다; (*with a ~mark*) ch'ek'ŭ p'yoshirŭl hada 첵크 표시를 하다; *coat, package etc* pogwansoe matkkida 보관소에 맡기다 **3** *v/i* hwaginhae chuda 확인해 주다; **~ for** hwaginhada 확인하다

♦ **check in** (*at airport*) t'apsŭng susogŭl hada 탑승 수속을 하다; (*at hotel*) ch'ek'ŭinhada 체크인하다

♦ **check off** taejo p'yoshirŭl hada 대조 표시를 하다

♦ **check on** salp'yŏboda 살펴보다

♦ **check out 1** *v/i* (*of hotel*) ch'ek'ŭaut'ada 체크아웃하다 **2** *v/t* (*look into*) chosahada 조사하다; *club, restaurant etc* tŭllyŏboda 들러보다

♦ **check up on** ... ŭl/rŭl naeryŏgŭl chosahada ...을/를 내력을 조사하다

♦ **check with** (*of person*) ...wa/kwa mŏnjŏ araboda ... 와/과 먼저 알아보다; (*of information*) ...wa/kwa ilch'ihada ...와/과 일치하다

checkbook sup'yoch'aek 수표책

checked *material* ch'ek'ŭ munŭiŭi 체크 무늬의

checkerboard sŏyang changgip'an

서양 장기판

checkered *pattern* ch'ek'ŭ munŭiŭi 체크 무늬의; *career* p'aranmanjanghan 파란만장한

checkers sŏyang changgi 서양 장기

check-in (*counter*) t'apsŭng suso k'aunt'ŏ 탑승 수속 카운터

checking account tangjwa yegŭm kujwa 당좌 예금 구좌

check-in time (*in hotel*) t'usuk shigan 투숙 시간; (*at airport*) t'apsŭng susok shigan 탑승 수속 시간; **checklist** taejop'yo 대조표; **checkmark** ch'ek'ŭ p'yoshi 체크 표시; **checkmate** *n* changgun 장 **checkout** kyesandae 계산대; **checkout time** pang-ŭl naeŏjul shigan 방을 내어줄 시간; **check-point** MIL kŏmmunso 검문소; (*in race etc*) ch'ek'ŭp'oint'ŭ 체크포인 **checkroom** (*for coats*) hyudaep pogwanso 휴대품 보관소; (*for baggage*) suhamul pogwanso 수하 보관소; **checkup** MED kŏn-gang chindan 건강 진단; (*dental*) ch'ia kŏmsa 치아 검사

cheek (*of face*) ppyam 뺨

cheekbone kwangdaeppyŏ 광대뼈

cheer 1 *n* hwanho 환호; **~s!** (*toast*) kŏnbae! 건배! **2** *v/t* & *v/i* hwanhohada 환호하다

♦ **cheer on** ŭng-wŏnhada 응원하다

♦ **cheer up 1** *v/i* kiuni nada 기운이 나다; **~!** kiun nae! 기운 내! **2** *v/t* kiunŭl na-ege hada 기운을 내게 하

cheerful myŏngnanghan 명랑한

cheering hwanho 환호

cheerleader ch'iŏridŏ 치어리더

cheese ch'ijŭ 치즈

cheeseburger ch'ijŭbŏgŏ 치즈버

cheesecake ch'ijŭk'eik 치즈케익

chef chubangjang 주방장

Cheju Island Chejudo 제주도

chemical 1 *adj* hwahagŭi 화학의 **2** hwahak chep'um 화학 제품

chemical warfare hwahaktchŏn 화학전

chemist hwahaktcha 화학자

chemistry hwahak 화학; *fig* sŏnggyŏgi mannŭn yŏbu 성격이 되 여부

emotherapy hwahak yoppŏp 화학
요법
erish sojunghi hada 소중히 하다;
memory, hope sojunghi kanjik'ada
소중히 간직하다
erry (*fruit*) p'ŏtchi 버찌; (*tree*)
pŏnnamu 벚나무
ess ch'esŭ 체스
essboard ch'esŭp'an 체스판
est (*of person*) kasŭm 가슴; (*box*)
changnong 장롱
estnut pam 밤; (*tree*) pamnanu
밤나무
est of drawers sŏraptchang
서랍장
ew v/t shiptta 씹다
ew out F hodoege kkujit-tta
호되게 꾸짖다
ewing gum kkŏm 껌
ick pyŏng-ari 병아리; F (*girl*)
kyejibae 계집애
icken 1 n (*food*) tak-kkogi
닭고기; F kŏptchaeng-i 겁쟁이 2 *adj* F
(*cowardly*) kŏbŭl mŏgŭn 겁을 먹은
chicken out kŏbŭl mŏk-kko
mullŏsŏda 겁을 먹고 물러서다
ickenfeed F saebarŭi p'i 새발의 피
icken pox sudu 수두
ief 1 n (*head*) chang 장; (*of tribe*)
choktchang 촉장 2 *adj* chuyohan
주요한
iefly churo 주로
ilblain tongsang 동상
ild ai 아이; *pej* yuch'ihan saram
유치한 사람
ildbirth haesan 해산
ildhood ŏrinshijŏl 어린시절
ildish *pej* yuch'ihan 유치한
ildless ai ŏmnŭn 아이 없는
ildlike ch'ŏnjinhan 천진한
ildren's Day Ŏrininal 어린이날
ill 1 n (*in air*) han-gi 한기; (*illness*)
kamgi 감기 2 v/t (*wine*) ch'age hada
차게 하다
illi (*pepper*) koch'u 고추
illi (*pepper*) **powder** koch'ugaru
고추가루
illy *weather* ssalssarhan 쌀쌀한;
welcome naengdamhan 냉담한; *I'm*
~ ssalssarhaneyo 쌀쌀하네요
ime v/i chong-i ullida 종이 울리다

chimney kulttuk 굴뚝
chimpanzee ch'imp'anji 침판지
chin t'ŏk 턱
China Chungguk 중국
china chagi 자기; (*material*) chagi
kŭrŭt 자기 그릇
Chinese 1 *adj* Chunggugŭi 중국의 **2** n
(*language*) Chunggugŏ 중국어;
(*person*) Chungguk saram 중국 사람
Chinese cabbage paech'u 배추;
Chinese character hantcha 한자;
Chinese character dictionary
okp'yŏn 옥편; **Chinese herbal**
medicine hanyak 한약; **Chinese**
medicine clinic hanŭiwŏn 한의원
Chin Island Chindo 진도
chink (*gap*) t'ŭm 틈; (*sound*)
taenggŭranghanŭn sori 댕그랑하는
소리
chip 1 n (*fragment*) t'omak 토막;
(*damage*) i ppajin chaguk 이 빠진
자국; (*in gambling*), COMPUT ch'ip
칩; ~**s** p'ot'eit'o ch'ipssŭ 포테이토
칩스 **2** v/t (*damage*) iga ppajida 이가
빠지다
♦ **chip in** n (*interrupt*)
malch'amgyŏnhada 말참견하다;
(*with money*) chogŭmsshik tonŭl
naeda 조금씩 돈을 내다
chipset COMPUT ch'ipset 칩셋
chiropractor ch'ŏkch'u chiapssa 척추
지압사
chirp v/i chijŏgwida 지저귀다
chisel n kkŭl 끌
chivalrous kisadojŏgin 기사도적인
chives kolp'aŭi ip 골파의 잎
chlorine yŏmso 염소
chockfull kkwak tŭrŏch'an 꽉 들어찬
chocolate ch'okollit 초콜릿; *hot ~*
hat ch'okollit 핫 초콜릿
chocolate cake ch'okollit k'eik
초콜릿 케이
choice 1 n sŏnt'aek 선택; (*selection*)
sŏnt'aegŭi pŏmwi 선택의 범위; *I had*
no ~ sŏnt'aegŭi yŏjiga ŏpssŏt-tta
선택의 여지가 없었다 **2** *adj* (*top*
quality) t'ŭkssang-ŭi 특상의
choir hapch'angdan 합창단
choke 1 n MOT ch'ok'ŭ 초크 **2** v/i
mogi maeida 목이 매이다; *he ~d on*
a bone kŭnŭn kashiga kŏllyŏ mogi

maeyŏt-tta 그는 가시가 걸려 목이 매였다 **3** *v/t* mogŭl chorŭda 목을 조르다

cholesterol k'ollesŭt'erol 콜레스테롤

choose *v/t* & *v/i* sŏnt'aek'ada 선택하다

choosey F kkadaroun 까다로운

chop 1 *n* chigŏ naegi 찍어 내기; (*meat*) tukkŏpkke charŭn kogittchŏm 두껍게 자른 고깃점 **2** *v/t wood* p'aeda 패다; *meat, vegetables* ssŏlda 썰다

♦ **chop down** *tree* p'aenŏmgida 패넘기다

chopper (*tool*) tokki 도끼; F (*helicopter*) hellik'opt'ŏ 헬리콥터

chopsticks chŏtkkarak 젓가락

chord MUS hyŏn 현

chore chiban il 집안 일

choreographer anmuga 안무가

choreography anmu 안무

chorus (*singers*) hapch'angdan 합창단; (*of song*) hapch'ang 합창

Choson Chosŏn 조선

Christ Kŭrisŭdo 그리스도; **~!** chegirŏl! 제기럴!

christen seryehada 세례하다

Christian 1 *n* Kidok-kkyo shinja 기독교 신자 **2** *adj* Kidok-kkyoŭi 기독교의; *attitude* in-ganjŏgin 인간적인

Christian Broadcasting System Kidok-kkyo Pangsong 기독교 방송

Christianity Kidok-kkyo 기독교

Christian name seryemyŏng 세례명

Christmas Sŏngt'anjŏl 성탄절; **at ~** Sŏngt'anjŏre 성탄절에; **Merry ~!** meri K'ŭrisŭmasŭ! 메리 크리스마스!

Christmas card K'ŭrisŭmasŭ k'adŭ 크리스마스 카드; **Christmas Day** Sŏngt'anjŏl 성탄절; **Christmas Eve** K'ŭrisŭmasŭ ibŭ 크리스마스 이브; **Christmas present** K'ŭrisŭmasŭ sŏnmul 크리스마스 선물; **Christmas tree** K'ŭrisŭmasŭ t'ŭri 크리스마스 트리

chrome, chromium k'ŭrom 크롬

chronic mansŏng-ŭi 만성의

chronological yŏndaesunŭi 연대순의; *in ~ order* yŏndaesunŭro 연대순으로

chrysanthemum kuk'wa 국화

chubby t'ongt'onghan 통통한

chuck *v/t* F naedŏnjida 내던지다

♦ **chuck out** *object* naebŏrida 내버리다; *person* naetchot-tta 내쫓다

chuckle 1 *n* k'ilk'il usŭm 킬킬 웃음 **2** *v/i* k'ilk'il ut-tta 킬킬 웃다

chunk k'ŭn tŏng-ŏri 큰 덩어리

church kyohoe 교회

chute hwalgangno 활강로; (*for garbage*) ssŭregi t'ongno 쓰레기 통로

CIA (= *Central Intelligence Agency*) Miguk chung-ang chŏngbobu 미국 중앙 정보부

cider sagwa chusŭ 사과 주스

CIF (= *cost insurance freight*) un mit pohŏm p'oham kagyŏk 운임 및 보험 포함 가격

cigar yŏsong-yŏn 여송연

cigarette tambae 담배

cinema (*industry*) yŏnghwa sanŏp 영화 산업; Br (*building*) yŏnghwagwan 영화관

cinnamon kyep'i 계피

circle 1 *n* wŏn 원; (*group*) chipttan 집단 **2** *v/t* (*draw circle around*) tonggŭramirŭl ch'ida 동그라미를 치다 **3** *v/i* (*of plane, bird*) pingbing tolda 빙빙 돌다

circuit hoero 회로

circuit board hoero kyegip'an 회로 계기판

circuit breaker hoero ch'adan-gi 회로 차단기

circular 1 *n* (*giving information*) hoeram 회람 **2** *adj* tunggŭn 둥근

circulate 1 *v/i* tolda 돌다 **2** *v/t* (*memo*) p'ŏttŭrida 퍼뜨리다

circulation BIO sunhwan 순환; (*of newspaper, magazine*) parhaeng pusu 발행 부수

circumference wŏnju 원주

circumstances sanghwang 상황; (*financial*) sangt'ae sangt'ae 상태; **under no ~** ŏttŏn sanghwang-esŏdo (+ *negative verb*) 어떤 상황에서도; **under the ~** kŭrŏn sanghwang-esŏnŭn 그런 상황에서는

circus sŏk'ŏsŭ 서커스

cistern mul t'aengk'ŭ 물 탱크

citizen shimin 시민

enship shiminkkwŏn 시민권
toshi 도시; ~ *center* toshiŭi
ungshim 도시의 중심; ~ *hall*
ch'ŏng 시청
c *adj* shiŭi 시의; *pride*,
sponsibilities shiminŭi 시민의;
(*not military*) min-ganŭi 민간의;
sobedience *etc* shiminŭi 시민의;
olite) yeŭi parŭn 예의 바른
defense minbang-wi 민방위
engineer t'omok kisa 토목 기사
lian 1 *n* min-ganin 민간인 2 *adj*
thes ilbaninŭi 일반인의
ization munmyŏng 문명
lize *person* kaehwahada 개화하다
rights kongmin
yŏngdŭngkkwŏn 공민 평등권; civil
rvant kongmuwŏn 공무원; civil
rvice haengjŏng samu 행정 사무;
vil war naejŏn 내전
m 1 *n* (*for damages*) ch'ŏnggu
구; (*right*) kwŏlli 권리; (*assertion*)
ujang 주장 2 *v/t* (*ask for as a right*)
ŏngguhada 청구하다; (*assert*),
operty chujanghada 주장하다;
ey have ~ed responsibility for
e attack kŭdŭrŭn konggyŏge
chan ch'aegimŭl yoguhaet-tta
들은 공격에 대한 책임을 요구했다
mant yoguja 요구자; LAW wŏn-go
고
n taehap chogae 대합 조개
am up F ibŭl tamulda 입을 다물다
nmy ch'ago kŭnjŏk-kŭnjŏk'an
고 끈적끈적한
nor (*noise*) ttŏdŭlssŏk'am
썩함; (*outcry*) ausŏng 아우성
amor for shikkŭrŏpkke yoguhada
끄럽게 요구하다
np 1 *n* (*fastener*) choemsoe 죔쇠
v/t (*fasten*) choemsoero choeda
쇠로 죄다
amp down tansok'ada 단속하다
amp down on kangnyŏk'i
nsok'ada 강력히 단속하다
sshijok 씨족
ndestine pimirŭi 비밀의
ag 1 *n* ch'ŏlk'ŏdŏnghanŭn sori
커덩하는 소리 2 *v/i*
ŏlk'ŏdŏnghanhan soriga nada
커덩하는 소리가 나다

clap 1 *v/i* (*applaud*) paksurŭl ch'ida
박수를 치다 2 *v/t* paksu ch'ida 박수
치다
clarify myŏnghwak'age hada 명확하게
하다
clarinet k'ŭllarinet 클라리넷
clarity myŏnghwak'am 명확함
clash 1 *n* ch'ungdol 충돌; (*of*
personalities) purilch'i 불일치 2 *v/i*
ch'ungdorhada 충돌하다; (*of*
opinions) purilch'ihada 불일치하다;
(*of colors*) ŏulliji ant'a 어울리지
않다; (*of events*) kyŏpch'ida 겹치다
clasp 1 *n* kŏlssoe 걸쇠 2 *v/t* (*in hand*)
kkwak chwida 꽉 쥐다; (*to self*)
kkyŏantta 껴안다
class 1 *n* (*lesson*) suŏp 수업; (*students*
in a ~) hak-kkŭp 학급; (*social*)
kyegŭp 계급; (*category*) puryu 부류
2 *v/t* pullyuhada 분류하다
classic 1 *adj* (*typical*)
chŏnhyŏngjŏgin 전형적인; (*definitive*) kwŏnwi innŭn 권위 있는
2 *n* kojŏn 고전
classical *music* k'ŭllaeshik 클래식
classification (*activity*) tŭnggŭbŭl
maegim 등급을 매김; (*category*)
pullyu 분류
classified *information* kimirŭi 기밀의
classified ad(vertisement)
hangmokppyŏl kwanggo 항목별
광고
classify (*categorize*) pullyuhada
분류하다
classmate tonggŭpssaeng 동급생;
classroom kyoshil 교실; class
warfare kyegŭp t'ujaeng 계급 투쟁
classy F kogŭbin 고급인; *person*
p'umwi innŭn 품위 있는
clatter 1 *n* tŏlgŏdŏk'anŭn sori
덜거덕하는 소리 2 *v/i* soransŭrŏn
sorirŭl naemyŏ ppalli umjigida
소란스런 소리를 내며 빨리 움직이다
clause (*in agreement*) chohang 조항;
GRAM chŏl 절
claustrophobia milshil
kongp'otchŭng 밀실 공포증
claw 1 *n* palt'op 발톱; *fig* ansanghage
marŭn son-garak 앙상하게 마른
손가락 2 *v/t* (*scratch*) halk'wida
할퀴다

clay chinhŭk 진흙
clean 1 *adj* kkaekkŭt'an 깨끗한 **2** *adv* F (*completely*) kkaekkŭshi 깨끗이 **3** *v/t* kkaekkŭt'age hada 깨끗하게 하다; *teeth, shoes* taktta 닦다; *house, room* ch'ŏngsohada 청소하다; *car, hands, face* sshit-tta 씻다; *clothes* ppalda 빨다; **have sth ~ed** muŏsŭl set'age matkkida 무엇을 세탁에 맡기다
♦ **clean out** *room, cupboard* kkaekkŭt'age ch'ŏngsohada 깨끗하게 청소하다; *fig* pint'ŏlt'ŏriro mandŭlda 빈털털이로 만들다
♦ **clean up 1** *v/t* ch'ŏngsohada 청소하다; *fig* ilssohada 일소하다 **2** *v/i* ch'ŏngsohada 청소하다; (*wash*) malssuk'aejida 말쑥해지다; (*on stock market etc*) k'ŭn tonŭl pŏlda 큰 돈을 벌다
cleaner ch'ŏngsobu 청소부; **dry ~** tŭraik'ŭllining set'akso 드라이클리닝 세탁소
cleaning woman ch'ŏngsohanŭn ajumma 청소하는 아줌마
cleanse (*skin*) kkaekkŭt'age sshit-tta 깨끗하게 씻다
cleanser (*for skin*) k'ŭllenjŏ 클렌저
clear 1 *adj voice, weather, water, skin* malgŭn 맑은; (*bright*) palgŭn 밝은; *photograph, vision* tturyŏt'an 뚜렷한; (*easy to understand*) punmyŏnghan 분명한; (*obvious*) myŏngbaek'an 명백한; *thinker* myŏngsŏk'an 명석한; **I'm not ~ about it** musŭn irinji punmyŏnghaji anayo 무슨 일인지 분명하지 않아요; **I didn't make myself ~** nae shimjung-ŭl tturyŏt'age marhaji anassŏ 내 심중을 뚜렷하게 말하지 않았어 **2** *adv*: **stand ~ of** …esŏ ttŏrŏjyŏsŏ sŏda …에서 떨어져서 서다; **steer ~ of** …e chŏpkkŭnhaji ant'a …에 접근하지 않다 **3** *v/t roads etc* ch'iuda 치우다; (*acquit*) mujoero hada 무죄로 하다; (*authorize*) hŏgahada 허가하다; (*earn*) …ŭi sunsuibŭl ollida …의 순수입을 올리다; **~ one's throat** hŏtkki'imhada 헛기침하다 **4** *v/i* (*of sky, mist*) kaeda 개다; (*of face*) palgajida 밝아지다

♦ **clear away** *v/t* ch'iuda 치우다
♦ **clear off** *v/i* sarajida 사라지다
♦ **clear out 1** *v/t closet* piuda 비우다 **2** *v/i* kabŏrida 가버리다
♦ **clear up 1** *v/i* chŏngdonhada 정돈하다; (*of weather*) kaeda 개다; (*of illness, rash*) nat-tta 낫다 **2** *v/t* (*tidy*) chŏngdonhada 정돈하다; *mystery, problem* p'ulda 풀다
clearance (*space*) t'ŭm 틈; (*authorization*) hŏga 허가
clearance sale chaego chŏngni se… 재고 정리 세일
clearly (*with clarity*) tturyŏt'age 뚜렷하게; (*evidently*) punmyŏngh… 분명히
clemency kwannyŏng 관용
clench *teeth* angmulda 악물다; *fist* kkwak chwida 꽉 쥐다
clergy sŏngjiktchadŭl 성직자들
clergyman sŏngjiktcha 성직자
clerk (*administrative*) samugwan 사무관; (*in store*) chŏmwŏn 점원
clever *person, animal* ttokttok'an 똑똑한; *idea* hyŏnmyŏnghan 현명…; *gadget* tokch'angjŏgin 독창적인
click 1 *n* COMPUT k'ŭllik 클릭 **2** *v/i* (*make noise*) ch'alk'ak'anŭn sori nada 찰칵하는 소리가 나다
♦ **click on** COMPUT k'ŭllik'ada 클릭하다
client (*of lawyer etc*) ŭiroein 의뢰… (*customer*) kogaek 고객
cliff chŏlbyŏk 절벽
climate kihu 기후
climax *n* chŏltchŏng 절정
climb 1 *n* (*up mountain*) tŭngban 등반 **2** *v/t* orŭda 오르다 **3** *v/i* orŭda 오르다; *mountain* tŭngbanhada 등반하다; *fig* (*of inflation etc*) chŭnggahada 증가하다
♦ **climb down** naerida 내리다; *fig* yangbohada 양보하다
climber (*person*) tŭngsan-ga 등산…
clinch: **~ a deal** kŏraerŭl maedŭp chit-tta 거래를 매듭 짓다
cling (*of clothes*) tallabut-tta 달라…
♦ **cling to** (*of child*) …e maedallid… …에 매달리다; *ideas, tradition* … chipch'ak'ada …에 집착하다
clingfilm p'ojangnyong laep 포장용…

...앵

ngy *child, boyfriend* 뚤뚤분눈
들러붙는

nic chillyoso 진료소

nical imsang-ŭi 임상의

ori 쨍그렁하는 소리 *v/i*
chaenggŭrŏnghanŭn
쨍그렁하는 소리가 나다

p' 1 *n* (*fastener*) k'ŭllip 클립 2 *v/t*
k'ŭllibŭro kojŏngshik'ida 클립으로
고정시키다; ~ *X to Y* Xŭl/rŭl Ye
에 클립으로 고정시키다

p² 1 *n* (*extract*) palch'we 발췌 2 *v/t*
hair, hedge, grass kawiro charŭda
가위로 자르다

pboard k'ŭllip-ppodŭ 클립보드

ppers (*for hair*) parik'ang 바리캉;
(*for nails*) son't'op kkak-kki 손톱
깎기; (*for gardening*) chŏng-
wŏnnyong kawi 정원용 가위

pping (*from newspaper etc*)
oryŏnaen kŏt 오려낸 것

ock shigye 시계

ock radio shigyega innŭn ladio
시계가 있는 라디오

ockwise shigye panghyang-ŭro
ora 시계 방향으로 돌아

ockwork shigye t'aeyŏp changch'i
시계 태엽 장치; *it went like ~*
nansaga chal chinhaengdoeŏt-tta
각사가 잘 진행되었다

clog up 1 *v/i* mak'ida 막히다 2 *v/t*
mak'ige hada 막히게 하다

ose¹ 1 *adj family* kakkaun 가까운;
friend ch'inhan 친한; *resemblance*
yusahan 유사한 2 *adv* kakkapke
가깝게; ~ *at hand* paro kakkaie 바로
가까이에; ~ *by* paro kyŏt'e 바로
곁에; *be ~ to* (*emotionally*)
…wa/kwa ch'inhada …와/과
친하다

ose² *v/t* tat-tta 닫다; *eyes* kamtta
감다; *factory* p'yeswaehada 폐쇄하다;
(*permanently*) p'yeŏp'ada 폐업하다
2 *v/i* (*of door, store*) tach'ida 닫히다;
(*of eyes*) kamgida 감기다; (*of store:
permanently*) p'yeŏp'ada 폐업하다

close down 1 *v/t* p'yeŏpsshik'ida
폐업시키다 2 *v/i* (*permanently*)

p'yeŏp'ada 폐업하다

◆ **close in** *v/i* (*of fog*) tagaoda
다가오다; (*of troops*) p'owihada
포위하다

◆ **close up** 1 *v/t building*
p'yeswaehada 폐쇄하다 2 *v/i* (*move
closer*) tagaoda 다가오다

closed *store* tach'in 닫힌; *eyes* kamgin
감긴

closed-circuit television p'yeswae
hoero t'ellebijŏn 폐쇄 회로
텔레비전

closely *listen, watch* yŏlsshimhi
열심히; *cooperate* ŏmmirhi 엄밀히

closet ot-tchang 옷장

close-up k'ŭllojŏŏp 클로즈업

closing time (*of store*) p'yejŏm
shigan 폐점 시간; (*of museum,
library*) p'yegwan shigan 폐관 시간

closure *permanent* p'yeswae 폐쇄; (*of
shop*) p'yejŏm 폐점

clot 1 *n* (*of blood*) p'it-ttŏng-ŏri
핏덩어리 2 *v/i* (*of blood*) ŏnggida
엉기다

cloth (*fabric*) ch'ŏn 천; (*for kitchen*)
haengju 행주; (*for cleaning*) kŏlle
걸레

clothes ot 옷

clothes brush ott'ŏri 옷털이

clothes hanger otkkŏri 옷걸이

clothing ŭiryu 의류

cloud *n* kurŭm 구름; *a ~ of
smoke/dust* sabang-e kkin yŏn-
gi/mŏnji 사방에 낀 연기/먼지

◆ **cloud over** ont'ong hŭryŏjida 온통
흐려지다

cloudburst p'ogu 폭우

cloudy hŭrin 흐린

clout *fig* (*influence*) yŏnghyangnyŏk
영향력

clown *n* (*in circus*) ŏritkkwangdae
어릿광대; (*joker*) chaemiinnŭn
saram 재미있는 사람; *pej* utkkinŭn
nom 웃기는 놈

club *n* (*weapon*) konbong 곤봉; (*golf
iron, organization*) k'ŭllŏp 클럽; ~*s*
(*in cards*) k'ŭllŏp 클럽

clue shilmari 실마리; *I haven't a ~*
orimujung-iya 오리무중이야

clued-up F …e taehae chal algo it-tta
…에 대해 잘 알고 있다

clump n (*of earth*) hŭktttŏng-ŏri 흙덩어리; (*group*) tŏmbul 덤불

clumsiness kkolsanaum 꼴사나움; (*lack of tact*) sŏt'urŭm 서투름

clumsy *person* haengdong-i ŏsusŏnhan 행동이 어수선한; (*tactless*) nunch'i ŏmnŭn 눈치 없는

cluster 1 n (*of people*) muri 무리; (*of houses*) miltchip chiyŏk 밀집 지역 **2** v/i (*of people*) muri chit-tta 무리 짓다; (*of houses*) moyŏ it-tta 모여 있다

clutch 1 n MOT k'ŭllŏch'i 클러치 **2** v/t kkwak chaptta 꽉 잡다

♦ **clutch at** chabŭryŏ tŭlda 잡으려 들다

Co. (= *Company*) hoesa 회사

c/o (= *care of*) ...sshidaek ...씨댁

coach 1 n (*trainer*) k'och'i 코치 **2** v/t karŭch'ida 가르치다

coagulate (*of blood*) ŭnggoshik'ida 응고시키다

coal sŏkt'an 석탄

coalition yŏnhap 연합

coalmine t'an-gwang 탄광

coarse kŏch'in 거친

coast n yŏnan 연안; *at the ~* yŏnane(sŏ) 연안에(서)

coastal yŏnanŭi 연안의

coastguard yŏnan kyŏngbidae 연안 경비대; (*person*) yŏnan kyŏngbiwŏn 연안 경비원

coastline haeansŏn 해안선

coat 1 n sang-ŭi 상의; (*over-*) oet'u 외투; (*of animal*) oep'i 외피; (*of paint etc*) tŏtch'il tŏlgal 덧칠 2 v/t (*cover*) ssŭiuda 씌우다; (*of paint*) ch'irhada 칠하다

coathanger otkkŏri 옷걸이

coating ssŭium 씌움

coax kusŭllida 구슬리다

cobweb kŏmijul 거미줄

cocaine k'ok'ain 코카인

cock n (*chicken*) sut'ak 수탉; (*any male bird*) suk'ŏt 수컷

cockeyed *idea etc* ŏch'ŏguniŏmnŭn 어처구니없는

cockpit (*of plane*) chojongshil 조종실

cockroach pak'wi pŏlle 바퀴 벌레

cocktail k'akt'eil 칵테일

cocoa (*plant, drink*) k'ok'oa 코코아

coconut k'ok'oyaja yŏlmae 코코야자

yŏlmae 열매

coconut palm k'ok'oyaja namu 코코야자 나무

COD (= *collect on delivery*) taegŭm sanghwan 대금 상환

coddle *sick person* momjorishik'ida 몸조리시키다; *child* kwaing pohohada 과잉 보호하다

code n k'odŭ 코드

coeducational namnyŏ konghagŭi 남녀 공학의

coerce kangyohada 강요하다

coexist kongjonhada 공존하다

coexistence kongjon 공존

coffee k'ŏp'i 커피; *two ~s please* k'ŏp'i tu jan chuseyo 커피 두 잔 주세요

coffee break kabyŏun hyushik shigan 가벼운 휴식 시간; **coffee maker** k'ŏp'i kkŭrinŭn kigu 커피 끓이는 기구; **coffee pot** k'ŏp'i p'ot'ŭ 커피 포트; **coffee shop** k'ŏp'i shyop 커피 숍; **coffee table** k'ŏp'iyong chagŭn t'aktcha 커피용 작은 탁자

coffin kwan 관

cog t'omnibak'wi 톱니바퀴

cognac k'onyak 코냑

cogwheel manmullinŭn t'omnibak'wi 맞물리는 톱니바퀴

cohabit tonggŏhada 동거하다

coherent chŏnghaptchŏgin 정합적인; (*in speech*) choriga sŏnŭn 조리가 서는

coil 1 n (*of rope*) sari 사리 **2** v/t kamtta 감다

coin n tongjŏn 동전

coincide tongshie irŏnada 동시에 일어나다

coincidence uyŏnŭi ilch'i 우연의 일치

coke F (*cocaine*) k'ok'ain 코카인

Coke® k'ok'a k'olla 코카 콜라

cold 1 *adj weather, day, room* ch'uun 추운; *air, water, character* ch'agaun 차가운; *I'm (feeling)* ~ ch'uwŏyo 추워요; *it's* ~ ch'uptta 춥다; *in* ~ *blood* naenghyŏrhage naenghyŏrhage냉혈하게; *get* ~ *feet* fig kŏmmŏktta 겁먹다 2 n ch'uwi 추위; *I have a* ~ kamgi kŏllyŏt-tta 감기 걸렸다

d-blooded naenghyŏrŭi 냉혈의;
ㅈ naenghyŏrhan 냉혈한; **cold cuts**
ㅐng-yuk 냉육; **cold sore** ipkkaŭi
altchin 입가의 발진
eslaw k'osŭllo 코슬로
laborate kongdong-ŭro irhada
ㅓ동으로 일하다; (with enemy)
yŏmnyŏk'ada 협력하다; (in
esearch) kongdong yŏn-guhada
ㅕ동 연구하다; (on book etc)
ongdong-ŭro chŏjak'ada 공동으로
ㅓ작하다
llaboration hyŏpttong 협동; (on
ook etc) kongjŏ 공저
llaborator hyŏmnyŏktcha 협력자;
with enemy) ijŏk haeng-wija 이적
ㅐ위자; (in writing book etc)
ongdong chŏja 공동 저자
llapse munŏjida 무너지다; (of
erson) chwajŏrhada 좌절하다
llapsible chŏbŭl su innŭn 접을 수
ㅣ는
llar kit 깃; (for dog) kae mok-kkŏri
ㅐ 목걸이
llarbone swaegol 쇄골
lleague tongnyo 동료
llect 1 v/t person terirŏ kada 데리러
ㅏ다; tickets, cleaning etc kajirŏ kada
ㅏ지러 가다; (as hobby) sujip'ada
ㅜ집하다; (gather) moŭda 모으다
2 v/i (gather together) moida 모이다
ㅣ adv: **call** ~ sushinin pudamŭro
hŏnhwahada 수신인 부담으로
ㅓ화하다
llect call sushinin pudamŭi
hŏnhwa 수신인 부담의 전화
llected moŭn 모은; person
ch'imch'ak'an 침착한; ~ **works**
chŏnjip 전집
llection sujip 수집; (in church)
kibugŭm mojip 기부금 모집; (in art)
sojangp'um 소장품; (in fashion)
shinjakp'um 신작품
llective chipttanjŏgin 집단적인
llective bargaining tanch'e
kyosŏp 단체 교섭
llector sujipkka 수집가
llege tankkwa taehak tan-gwa 대학
llide ch'ungdorhada 충돌하다
llision ch'ungdol 충돌
lloquial ilssang hoehwaŭi 일상

회화의
colon (punctuation) k'ollon 콜론;
ANAT kyŏltchang 결장
colonel taeryŏng 대령
colonial adj shingminjiŭi 식민지의
colonize shingminjiro mandŭlda
식민지로 만들다
colony shingminji 식민지
color 1 n saek-kkal 색깔; (in cheeks)
ansaek 안색; **in** ~ **movie** k'allaro
toen 칼라로 된; ~**s** MIL kun-gi 군기
2 v/t hair yŏmsaek'ada 염색하다
color-blind saengmaeng-ŭi 색맹의
colored adj person hŭginŭi 흑인의
color fast paraeji annŭn 바래지 않는
colorful saekch'aega p'ungbuhan
색채가 풍부한; fig tach'aeroun
다채로운
coloring ansaek 안색
color photograph k'alla sajin 칼라
사진; **color scheme** saekch'aeŭi
paehap 색채의 배합; **color TV** k'alla
t'ellebijŏn 칼라 텔레비전
colt mang-aji 망아지
column (of figures, people) chul 줄;
(architectural) kidung 기둥; (of text)
tan 단; (newspaper feature) nan 난
columnist kigoga 기고가
coma honsu sangt'ae 혼수 상태
comb 1 n pit 빗 2 v/t pit-tta 빗다; area
satssach'i twijida 샅샅이 뒤지다
combat 1 n chŏnt'u 전투 2 v/t ssauda
싸우다
combination kyŏrhap 결합; (of safe)
chamulssoeŭi pŏnho 자물쇠의 번호
combine 1 v/t kyŏrhap'ada 결합하다;
ingredients hapch'ida 합치다 2 v/i (of
chemical elements) kyŏrhap'ada
결합하다
combine harvester k'ombain 콤바인
combustible t'agi shwiun 타기 쉬운
combustion yŏnso 연소
come (toward speaker) oda 오다;
(toward listener) kada 가다; **you'll** ~
to like it choahage toel kŏyeyo
좋아하게 될 거에요; **how** ~? ㄷ
ŏtchidoen iriya? 어찌된 일이야?
♦ **come about** (happen) irŏnada
일어나다
♦ **come across 1** v/t (find)
palgyŏnhada 발견하다 2 v/i (of idea,

humor) ihaedoeda 이해되다; **she comes across as ...** kŭnyŏnŭn ... chŏrŏm poinda 그녀는 ... 처럼 보인다

♦ **come along** (*come too*) kach'i oda 같이 오다; (*turn up*) nat'anada 나타나다; (*progress*) chinhaengdoeda 진행되다

♦ **come apart** punhaedoeda 분해되다; (*break*) pusŏjida 부서지다

♦ **come around** (*to s.o.'s home*) tŭllida 들리다; (*regain consciousness*) ŭishigŭl hoebok'ada 의식을 회복하다

♦ **come away** (*leave*) ttŏnada 떠나다; (*of button etc*) ttŏrŏjida 떨어지다

♦ **come back** toraoda 돌아오다; *it came back to me* tashi saenggangnassŏ 다시 생각났어

♦ **come by** 1 *v/i* tŭllida 들리다 2 *v/t* (*acquire*) ŏt-tta 얻다; (*find*) kuhada 구하다

♦ **come down** *v/i* naeryŏoda 내려오다; (*in price, amount etc*) ttŏrŏjida 떨어지다; (*of rain, snow*) naerida 내리다; *he came down the stairs* kyedanŭl naeryŏwat-tta 그는 계단을 내려왔다

♦ **come for** (*collect*) kaijrŏ oda 가지러 오다; *person* terirŏ oda 데리러 오다; (*attack*) tŏpch'iryŏ tŭlda 덮치려 들다

♦ **come forward** (*present oneself*) ap'ŭro nasŏda 앞으로 나서다

♦ **come from** ...esŏ oda ...에서 오다

♦ **come in** tŭrŏoda 들어오다; *~!* tŭrŏoseyo! 들어오세요!

♦ **come in for**: *~ criticism* pip'anŭl pat-tta 비판을 받다

♦ **come in on**: *~ a deal* kŏraee ch'amgahada 거래에 참가하다

♦ **come off** (*of handle etc*) ttŏrŏjida 떨어지다

♦ **come on** (*progress*) chinhaengdoeda 진행되다; *~!* sŏdullŏ! 서둘러!; (*in disbelief*) sŏlma! 설마!

♦ **come out** (*of person, sun, results, new product*) naoda 나오다; (*of stain*) ppajida 빠지다

♦ **come to** 1 *v/t place* ...e irŭda ...에 이르다; (*of hair, dress, water*) ...kkaji

irŭda ...까지이르다; *that comes $70* chŏgŏsŭn 70tallŏe irŭda 저 70달러에 이른다 2 *v/i* (*regain consciousness*) ŭishigŭl hoebok'a 의식을 회복하다

♦ **come up** ollaoda 올라오다; (*of s ...* ttŏorŭda 떠오르다; *something h come up* musŭn iri saenggyŏssŏ 무슨 일이 생겼어요

♦ **come up with** *new idea etc* saenggak'aenaeda 생각해내다

comeback: *make a ~* pok-kkwiha 복귀하다

comedian k'omidiŏn 코미디언; *pe* utkkinŭn nyŏsŏk 웃기는 녀석

comedown mollak 몰락

comedy hŭigŭk 희극

comet hyesŏng 혜성

comeuppance: *he'll get his ~* kŭnŭn ŭngborŭl padŭl kŏshida 그 응보를 받을 것이다

comfort 1 *n* allak 안락; (*consolatio* wian 위안 2 *v/t* wianhada 위안하디

comfortable *chair* p'yŏnanhan 편안한; *house, room* allak'an 안락 *be ~* (*of person*) p'yŏnhan 편함; (*financially*) suibi ch'ungbunhan 수입이 충분한

comic 1 *n* (*magazine*) manhwa chaptchi 만화 잡지 2 *adj* hŭigŭgŭi 희극의

comical usŭkkwangsŭrŏun 우스꽝스러운

comic book manhwa ch'aek 만화

comics manhwaran 만화란

comma shwimp'yo 쉼표

command 1 *n* myŏngnyŏng 명령 2 myŏngnyŏnghada 명령하다

commander saryŏnggwan 사령관

commander-in-chief ch'oego saryŏnggwan 최고 사령관

commemorate kinyŏmhada 기념힌

commemoration: *in ~ of* ...ŭi kinyŏmŭro ...의 기념으로

commence 1 *v/i* shijakdoeda 시작되다 2 *v/t* shijak'ada 시작하다

comment 1 *n* ŏn-gŭp 언급; *no ~* mal ŏpssŭmnida 할 말 없습니다 2 *v/i* ŏn-gŭp'ada 언급하다

commentary haesŏl 해설

commentator haesŏltcha 해설자

>mmerce sang-ŏp 상업

>mmercial 1 *adj* sang-ŏbŭi 상업의; *success, failure* sang-ŏpssang-ŭi 상업상의 **2** *n* (*advert*) kwanggo 광고

>mmercial break kwanggo >angsong 광고 방송

>mmercialize *v/t* >angp'umhwahada 상품화하다

>mmercial traveler oep'anwŏn 외판원

>mmiserate tongjŏnghada 동정하다

>mmission 1 *n* (*payment*) susuryo 수수료; (*job*) ŭiroe 의뢰; (*committee*) >iwŏnhoe 위원회 **2** *v/t* (*for a job*) ŭiroehada 의뢰하다

>mmit *crime* pŏmhada 범하다; *money* halttanghada 할당하다; ~ **>neself** ŏnjirŭl chuda 언질을 주다

>mmitment (*in professional relationship*) chŏllyŏm 전념; (*in personal relationship*) hŏnshin 헌신; (*responsibility*) ch'aegim 책임

>mmittee wiwŏnhoe 위원회

>mmodity iryongp'um 일용품

>mmon (*not rare*) pot'ong-ŭi 보통의; (*shared*) kongt'ong-ŭi 공통의; **in ~** kongt'ong-ŭro 공통으로; **>ave sth in ~ with s.o.** muŏsŭl >uguwa kongt'ong-ŭro kajigo it-tta 무엇을 누구와 공통으로 가지고 있다

>mmon law wife naeyŏnŭi ch'ŏ 내연의 처; **commonplace** *adj* 'yŏngbŏmhan 평범한; **common sense** sangshik 상식

>mmotion soran 소란

>mmunal kongdong-ŭi 공동의

>mmunicate 1 *v/i* (*be in contact*) >ŏllagi it-tta 연락이 있다; (*make self understood*) ŭisarŭl sot'onghada 의사를 소통하다 **2** *v/t* chŏndarhada 전달하다

>mmunication ŭisa chŏndal 의사 전달

>mmunications t'ongshin 통신

>mmunications satellite t'ongshin wisŏng 통신 위성

>mmunicative *person* marhagi 'hoahanŭn 말하기 좋아하는

>mmunism Kongsanjuŭi 공산주의

>mmunist 1 *adj* Kongsanjuŭiŭi 공산주의의; (*of Communist party*)

Kongsandang-ŭi 공산당의 **2** *n* Kongsanjuŭija 공산주의자

Communist Party Kongsandang 공산당

community kongdongch'e 공동체; (*social group*) sahoe 사회

commute 1 *v/i* t'onggŭnhada 통근하다 **2** *v/t* LAW kamhyŏnghada 감형하다

commuter t'onggŭnja 통근자

commuter traffic t'onggŭn kyot'ong 통근 교통

commuter train t'onggŭn yŏlch'a 통근 열차

compact 1 *adj* apch'ukttoen 압축된; *house* adamhan 아담한; MOT sohyŏng-ŭi 소형의 **2** *n* MOT sohyŏngch'a 소형차

compact disc k'omp'aekt'ŭ tisŭk'ŭ 콤팩트 디스크

companion tongnyo 동료

companionship tongmuro sagwigi 동무로 사귀기

company COM hoesa 회사; (*companionship*) tongmuro sagwigi 동무로 사귀기; (*guests*) sonnim 손님; **keep ... ~** ...wa/kwa kyojehada ...와/과 교제하다

company car hoesa ch'a 회사 차

company law hoesapŏp 회사법

comparable (*can be compared*) pigyodoel su innŭn 비교될 수 있는; (*similar*) yusahan 유사한

comparative 1 *adj* (*relative*) pigyojŏgin 비교적인; *study* pigyoŭi 비교의; GRAM pigyogŭbŭi 비교급의 **2** *n* GRAM pigyogŭp 비교급

comparatively pigyojŏgŭro 비교적으로

compare 1 *v/t* pigyohada 비교하다; **~ X with Y** Xŭl/rŭl Ywa/gwa pigyohada X을/를 Y와/과 비교하다; **~d with** ...wa/kwa pigyohaesŏ ...와/과 비교해서 **2** *v/i* pigyodoeda 비교되다

comparison pigyo 비교; **there's no ~** pigyohal su ŏpssŏyo 비교할 수 없어요

compartment k'an 칸

compass nach'imban 나침반; (*for geometry*) k'ŏmp'ŏsŭ 컴퍼스

compassion tongjŏngshim 동정심

compassionate tongjŏnghanŭn 동정하는

compatibility sŏro mannŭn chŏngdo 서로 맞는 정도; (*of systems*) chŏk'apssŏng 적합성; (*of software*) hohwansŏng 호환성; (*of blood types*) ilch'i yŏbu 일치 여부

compatible *people* sŏro mannŭn 서로 맞는; *blood types, lifestyles* ilch'ihanŭn 일치하는; COMPUT hohwanhal su innŭn 호환할 수 있는; *we're not ~* urinŭn sŏngkkyŏgi an mat-tta 우리는 성격이 안 맞다

compel ŏkchiro …shik'ida 억지로 …시키다; *be ~led to* hal su ŏpsshi …hada 할 수 없이 …하다

compelling *argument* sŏlttŭngnyŏk innŭn 설득력 있는; *movie, book* hŭngmirŭl todunŭn 흥미를 돋우는

compensate 1 *v/t* (*with money*) paesanghada 배상하다 **2** *v/i: ~ for* …ŭl/rŭl posanghada …을/를 보상하다

compensation (*money*) paesang 배상; (*reward*) posang poch'ung 보상 보충; (*comfort*) wianmul 위안물

compete kyŏngjaenghada 경쟁하다; (*take part*) ch'ultchŏnhada 출전하다; *~ for* …ŭl/rŭl wihae kyŏngjaenghada …을/를 위해 경쟁하다

competence, competency nŭngnyŏk 능력

competent *person* nŭngnyŏk innŭn 능력 있는; *work* chungbunhan 충분한; *I'm not ~ to judge* nanŭn p'andanhal chagyŏgi ŏptta 나는 판단할 자격이 없다

competition kyŏngjaeng 경쟁; (*competitors*) kyŏngjaengja 경쟁자; *the government wants to encourage ~* chŏngbunŭn kyŏngjaeng-ŭl puch'uk'igo ship'ŏhanda 정부는 경쟁을 부추키고 싶어한다

competitive kyŏngjaengjŏgin 경쟁적인; *price, offer* kyŏngjaengnyŏk innŭn 경쟁력 있는

competitor (*in contest*) kyŏngjaengja 경쟁자; COM kyŏngjaeng sangdae 경쟁 상대

compile p'yŏnjip'ada 편집하다

complacency chagi manjok 자기 만족

complacent chagi manjoktchŏgin 자기 만족적인

complain *v/i* pulp'yŏnghada 불평하다; *~ of* MED …ŭl/rŭl hosohada …을/를 호소하다

complaint pulp'yŏng 불평; MED pyŏng 병

complement *v/t* powanhada 보완하다; *they ~ each other* kŭdŭrŭn sŏro powanhanda 그들은 서로 보완한다

complementary powanhanŭn 보완하는

complete 1 *adj* (*utter*) wanjŏnhan 완전한; (*whole, entire*) chŏnbuŭi 전부의; (*finished*) wansŏngdoen 완성된 **2** *v/t task, building etc* wansŏnghada 완성하다; *course* wanjŏnhi mach'ida 완전히 마치다; *form* ch'aeuda 채우다

completely wanjŏnhi 완전히

completion wansŏng 완성

complex 1 *adj* poktchap'an 복잡한 **2** *n* PSYCH k'omp'ŭllĕkssŭ 콤플렉스; (*of buildings*) chip'apch'e 집합체

complexion (*facial*) ansaek 안색

compliance ŭngnak 응낙

complicate poktchap'age hada 복잡하게 하다

complicated poktchap'an 복잡한

complication poktchap'age hanŭn kŏt 복잡하게 하는 것; *~s* MED happyŏngtchŭng 합병증

compliment 1 *n* ch'ansa 찬사 **2** *v/t* ch'ansahada 찬사하다

complimentary ch'ansahanŭn 찬사하는; (*free*) muryoŭi 무료의

compliments slip kŭnjŏng tchokchi 근정 쪽지

comply ŭnghada 응하다; *~ with* …ŭnghada …에 응하다

component (*constituent part*) kusŏ yoso 구성 요소; (*of machine etc*) pup'um 부품

compose *v/t* kusŏnghada 구성하다; MUS chak-kkok'ada 작곡하다; *be of* …(ŭ)ro kusŏngdoeŏ it-tta

(으)로 구성되어 있다; ~ *oneself* aŭmŭl karaanch'ida 마음을 라앉히다

nposed (*calm*) ch'imch'ak'an 착한

nposer MUS chak-kkok-kka 곡가

nposition (*make-up*) kusŏng 구성; JS chak-kkok 작곡; (*essay*) angmun 작문

nposure ch'imch'ak 침착

npound *n* CHEM hapssŏngmul 성물

npound interest pongni 복리

nprehend (*understand*) ihaehada 해하다

nprehension ihae 이해

nprehensive p'ogwaltchŏgin 괄적인

nprehensive insurance onghap pohŏm 종합 보험

npress 1 *n* MED sŭpp'o 습포 2 *v/t* *, gas, file* apch'uk'ada 압축하다; *formation* yoyak'ada 요약하다

nprise kusŏngdoeda 구성되다; *be d of* ...(ŭ)ro kusŏngdoeŏ it-tta (으)로 구성되어 있다

npromise 1 *n* t'ahyŏp 타협 2 *v/i* hyŏp'ada 타협하다 3 *v/t principles* hyŏpssik'ida 타협시키다; *amage: reputation etc* nsangshik'ida 손상시키다; ~ *one- lf* chagiŭi ch'emyŏnŭl nsangshik'ida 자기의 체면을 상시키다

npulsion PSYCH kangbak vannyŏm 강박 관념

npulsive *behavior* kangbak vannyŏme sarojap'in 강박 관념에 로잡힌; *reading* murihanŭn 리하는

npulsory ŭimujŏgin 의무적인; ~ *lucation* ŭimu kyoyuk 의무 교육

nputer k'ŏmp'yut'ŏ 컴퓨터; *put h on* ~ muŏsŭl k'ŏmp'yut'ŏe nyŏk'shik'yŏ not'a 무엇을 퓨터에 입력시켜 놓다

nputer-controlled k'ŏmp'yut'ŏro ngjedoenŭn 컴퓨터로 통제되는

nputer game k'ŏmp'yut'ŏ keim 퓨터 게임

computerize chŏnsanhwahada 전산화하다

computer literate k'ŏmp'yut'ŏrŭl tarul chul anŭn 컴퓨터를 다룰 줄 아는; **computer science** k'ŏmp'yut'ŏ kwahak 컴퓨터 과학; **computer scientist** k'ŏmp'yut'ŏ kwahaktcha 컴퓨터 과학자

computing k'ŏmp'yut'ŏ sayong 컴퓨터 사용

comrade (*friend*) tongnyo 동료; POL tongji 동지

comradeship tongnyo kwan-gye 동료 관계

con F 1 *n* (*trick*) sagi 사기 2 *v/t* sagi ch'ida 사기 치다

conceal kamch'uda 감추다

concede *v/t* (*admit*) injŏnghada 인정하다

conceit chaman 자만

conceited chamanhanŭn 자만하는

conceivable saenggak'al su innŭn 생각할 수 있는

conceive *v/i* (*of woman*) imshinhada 임신하다; ~ *of* (*imagine*) ...ŭl/rŭl sangsanghada ...을/를 상상하다

concentrate 1 *v/i* chiptchunghada 집중하다; (*on task*) chŏnnyŏmhada 전념하다 2 *v/t one's attention, energies* chiptchungshik'ida 집중시키다

concentrated *juice etc* nongch'ukttoen 농축된

concentration chiptchung 집중

concept kaenyŏm 개념

conception (*of child*) imshin 임신

concern 1 *n* (*anxiety*) kŏktchŏng 걱정; (*care*) yŏmnyŏ 염려; (*business*) kwanshimsa 관심사; (*company*) hoesa 회사 2 *v/t* (*involve*) ...e kwan-gyehada ...에 관계하다; (*worry*) kŏktchŏnghada 걱정하다; ~ *oneself with* ...e kwanyŏhada ...에 관여하다

concerned (*anxious*) kŏktchŏnghanŭn 걱정하는; (*caring*) yŏmnyŏhanŭn 염려하는; (*involved*) kwan-gyedoenŭn 관계되는; *as far as I'm* ~ naega pogienŭn 내가 보기에는

concerning *prep* ...e kwanhayŏ ...에 관하여

concert yŏnjuhoe 연주회
concerted (*joint*) habŭidoen 합의된
concertmaster susŏk paiollinisŭt'ŭ 수석 바이올리니스트
concerto hyŏptchugok 협주곡
concession (*giving in*) yangbo 양보
conciliatory hoeyujŏgin 회유적인
concise kan-gyŏrhan 간결한
conclude 1 *v/t* (*deduce*) kyŏllonŭl naerida 결론을 내리다; (*end*) kkŭnnaeda 끝내다; **~ X from Y** Y(ŭ)robut'ŏ Xranŭn kyŏllonŭl naerida Y(으)로부터 X라는 결론을 내리다 2 *v/i* kkŭnnaeda 끝나다
conclusion (*deduction*) kyŏllon 결론; (*end*) kyŏlmal 결말; **in ~** kkŭt'ŭro 끝으로
conclusive kyŏltchŏngjŏgin 결정적인
concoct *meal, drink* sokkŏsŏ mandŭlda 섞어서 만들다; *excuse, story* yŏkkŏnaeda 엮어내다
concoction (*food, drink*) honhammul 혼합물
concrete[1] *adj* (*not abstract*) kuch'ejŏgin 구체적인
concrete[2] *n* k'onk'ŭrit'ŭ 콘크리트
concur *v/i* tong-ŭihada 동의하다
concussion noejint'ang 뇌진탕
condemn *action* pinanhada 비난하다; *building* p'yegi ch'ŏbunŭl sŏn-gohada 폐기 처분을 선고하다; (*fate*) unmyŏng chiuda 운명 지우다
condemnation (*of action*) pinan 비난
condensation ŭngch'uk 응축
condense 1 *v/t* (*shorten*) apch'uk'ada 압축하다 2 *v/i* (*of steam*) ŭngch'uk'ada 응축하다
condensed milk yŏnyu 연유
condescend: *he ~ed to speak to me* kŭnŭn hwangsonghagedo na-ege marŭl kŏrŏssŏ 그가 황송하게도 내게 말을 걸었어
condescending kyŏmsonhan ch'ŏk'anŭn 겸손한 척하는
condition 1 *n* (*state*) sangt'ae 상태; (*of health*) kŏn-gang sangt'ae 건강 상태; MED chirhwan 질환; (*requirement, term*) chokkŏn 조건; **~s** (*circumstances*) hwan-gyŏng 환경; **on ~ that** ...ranŭn chokkŏnŭro ...라는 조건으로 2 *v/t*

PSYCH chokkŏn pansarŭl irŭk'ige hada 조건 반사를 일으키게 하다
conditional 1 *adj acceptance* chokkŏnbuŭi 조건부의 2 *n* GRAM chokkŏnppŏp 조건법
conditioner (*for hair, fabric*) k'ondishyŏnŏ 콘디셔너
conditioning PSYCH chŏgŭngshik 적응시키기
condo k'ondo 콘도
condolences aedo 애도
condom k'ondom 콘돔
condominium k'ondominium 콘도미니움
condone *actions* yongsŏhada 용서하다
conducive: **~ to** ...e toumi toenŭ ...에 도움이 되는
conduct 1 *n* (*behavior*) haeng-wi 행위 2 *v/t* (*carry out*) suhaengha 수행하다; ELEC chŏndohada 전도하다; MUS chihwihada 지휘하 **~ oneself** ch'ŏshinhada 처신하ㄷ
conducted tour kwan-gwang an 관광 안내
conductor MUS chihwija 지휘자; (*train*) ch'ajang 차장
cone (*in geometry*) wŏnppul 원뿔 (*for ice cream*) k'on 콘; (*of pine* solppang-ul 솔방울; (*on highway* wŏnppul 원뿔
confectioner (*shop*) chegwajŏm 제과점
confectioners' sugar chŏngje sŏlt'ang 정제 설탕
confectionery (*candy*) kwajaryu 과자류
confederation yŏnhap 연합
confer 1 *v/t* (*bestow*) suyŏhada 수여하다 2 *v/i* (*discuss*) hyŏbŭih 협의하다
conference hoeŭi 회의
conference room hoeŭishil 회으
confess 1 *v/t sin, guilt* kobaek'ad 고백하다; (*to police*) chabaek'ad 자백하다; REL kohaehada 고해하 **~ I don't know** morŭndanŭn kŏ kobaek'amnida 모른다는 것을 고백합니다 2 *v/i* kobaek'ada 고백하다; (*to police*) chabaek'ad 자백하다; REL kohaehada 고해하

~ to a weakness for sth muŏse yak'adanŭn kŏsŭl shilt'ohada 무엇에 약하다는 것을 실토하다

confession kobaek 고백; *(to police)* chabaek 자백; REL kohae 고해

confessional REL kohaeshil 고해실

confessor REL kohae shinbu 고해 신부

confide 1 v/t t'ŏronot'a 털어놓다 **2** v/i: **~ in s.o.** nuguege pimirŭl t'ŏronot'a 누구에게 비밀을 털어놓다

confidence *(assurance)* hwaksshin 확신; *(trust)* shilloe 신뢰; *(secret)* pimil 비밀; **in ~** pimillo 비밀로

confident *(self-assured)* chashinhanŭn 자신하는; *(convinced)* hwaksshinhanŭn 확신하는

confidential kŭkppiŭi 극비의

confine *(imprison)* kamgŭmhada 감금하다; *(restrict)* chehanhada 제한하다; **be ~d to one's bed** ara nuwŏ it-tta 앓아 누워 있다

confined *space* chehandoen 제한된

confinement *(imprisonment)* kamgŭm 감금; MED haesan 해산

confirm v/t hwaginhada 확인하다; *theory, statement, fears* hwakchŭnghada 확증하다

confirmation hwagin 확인; *(of theory, statement, fears)* hwakchŭng 확증

confirmed *(inveterate)* kudŏbŏrin 굳어버린

confiscate apssuhada 압수하다

conflict 1 n *(disagreement)* taerip 대립; *(clash)* ch'ungdol 충돌; *(war)* t'ujaeng 투쟁 **2** v/i *(clash)* ch'ungdorhada 충돌하다

conform sunŭnghada 순응하다; *(of product)* ttarŭda 따르다; **~ to government standards** chŏngbu kyugyŏge ttarŭda 정부 규격에 따르다

conformist n chunsuja 준수자

confront *(face)* majuhada 마주하다; *(tackle)* matssŏda 맞서다

confrontation taegyŏl 대결

Confucianism Yugyo 유교

Confucius Kongja 공자

confuse *(muddle)* hollanshik'ida 혼란시키다; *(one thing with another)* hondonghada 혼동하다; **~ X with Y**

Xŭl/rŭl Ywa/gwa hondonghada X을/를 Y와/과 혼동하다

confused hollansŭrŏun 혼란스러운

confusing hollanshik'inŭn 혼란시키는

confusion hollan 혼란

congeal ŭnggohada 응고하다

congenial maŭme mannŭn 마음에 맞는

congenital MED sŏnch'ŏnjŏgin 선천적인

congested *roads* honjap'an 혼잡한

congestion *(on roads)* honjap 혼잡; *(in chest)* mak'im 막힘; **traffic ~** kyot'ong honjap 교통 혼잡

conglomerate chaebŏl 재벌

congratulate ch'uk'ahada 축하하다

congratulations ch'uk'a 축하; **~ on** ...ŭl/rŭl ch'uk'ahamnida ...을/를 축하합니다

congregate *(gather)* moida 모이다

congregation REL chip'oe 집회

congress *(conference)* hoeŭi 회의; **Congress** *(of US)* Kuk'oe 국회

congressional kuk'oeŭi 국회의

congressman kuk'oe ŭiwŏn 국회 위원

congresswoman yŏja kuk'oe ŭiwŏn 여자 국회 의원

conifer ch'imnyŏpssu 침엽수

conjecture n *(speculation)* ch'uch'ŭk 추측

conjugate v/t GRAM hwaryongshik'ida 활용시키다

conjunction GRAM chŏpssoksssa 접속사; **in ~ with** ...wa/kwa hamkke ...와 / 과 함께

conjunctivitis kyŏlmangnyŏm 결막염

♦ conjure up *(produce)* nun kkamtchak'al saie mandŭlda 눈 깜짝할 사이에 만들다; *(evoke)* pullŏ irŭk'ida 불러 일으키다

conjurer, conjuror masulsa 마술사

conjuring tricks masul 마술

con man sagikkun 사기꾼

connect *(join)* TELEC yŏn-gyŏrhada 연결하다; *(link)* kwallyŏnshik'ida 관련시키다; *(to power supply)* chŏpssoksshik'ida 접속시키다

connected: be well-~ chŏun yŏntchuri innŭn 좋은 연줄이 있는; **be ~ with** ...wa/kwa kwallyŏndoeda …와/과 관련되다

connecting flight yŏn-gyŏlp'yŏn 연결편

connection (*in wiring*) yŏn-gyŏl 연결; (*link*) kwallyŏn 관련; (*when traveling*) yŏn-gyŏlp'yŏn 연결편; (*personal contact*) yŏnchul 연줄; *in ~ with* …wa/kwa kwallyŏnhayŏ …와/과 관련하여

connoisseur kamjŏngga 감정가

conquer chŏngbok'ada 정복하다; *fear etc* kŭppok'ada 극복하다

conqueror chŏngboktcha 정복자

conquest (*of territory*) chŏngbok 정복

conscience yangshim 양심; *a guilty ~* yangshimŭi kach'aek 양심의 가책; *it has been on my ~* kŭgŏshi maŭme kŏllyŏssŏyo 그것이 마음에 걸렸어요

conscientious yangshimjŏgin 양심적인

conscientious objector yangshimtchŏk pyŏngnyŏk kŏbuja 양심적 병역 거부자

conscious *adj* (*aware*) chigagi innŭn 지각이 있는; (*deliberate*) ŭishiktchŏgin 의식적인; MED ŭishigi innŭn 의식이 있는; *be ~ of* …ŭl/rŭl algo it-tta …을/를 알고 있다

consciousness (*awareness*) chigak 지각; MED ŭishik 의식; *lose/regain ~* ŭishigŭl ilt'a/hoebok'ada 의식을 잃다/회복하다

consecutive yŏnsoktchŏgin 연속적인

consensus ilch'i 일치

consent 1 *n* tong-ŭi 동의 **2** *v/i* tong-ŭihada 동의하다

consequence (*result*) kyŏlkwa 결과

consequently (*therefore*) ttarasŏ 따라서

conservation (*preservation*) pojon 보존

conservationist *n* chawŏn pohoronja 자원 보호론자

conservative *adj* (*conventional*) posujŏgin 보수적인; *clothes* susuhan 수수한; *estimate* chuljabŭn 줄잡은

conservatory (*for plants*) onshil 온실; MUS ŭmak hak-kkyo 음악 학교

conserve 1 *n* (*jam*) chaem 잼 **2** *v/t*

energy, strength pojonhada 보존하▮

consider (*regard*) yŏgida 여기다; (*show regard for*) koryŏhada 고려하다; (*think about*) saenggak'ada 생각하다; *it is ~ed t▮ be* …rago saenggakttoenda …라고 생각된다

considerable sangdanghan 상당한

considerably sangdanghi 상당히

considerate tongjŏngshimi manŭn 동정심이 많은

consideration (*thought*) suk-kko 숙고; (*thoughtfulness, concern*) koryŏ 고려; (*factor*) koryŏhal saha▮ 고려할 사항; *take X into ~* Xŭl/r▮ koryŏhada X을/를 고려하다

consignment COM wit'ak 위탁

♦ **consist of** …(ŭ)ro iruŏjyŏ it-tta …(으)로 이루어져 있다

consistency (*texture*) nongdo 농도; (*of attitude, behavior*) ilgwansŏng 일관성

consistent *attitude, behavior* ilgwansŏng innŭn 일관성 있는

consolation wiro 위로

console *v/t* wirohada 위로하다

consonant *n* GRAM chaŭm 자음

consortium ch'agwandan 차관단

conspicuous tudŭrŏjin 두드러진

conspiracy ŭmmo 음모

conspire ŭmmorŭl kkumida 음모를 꾸미다

constant (*continuous*) kyesokttoenŭn 계속되는

consternation sŏmttŭk nollam 섬뜩 놀람

constipated pyŏnbie kŏllin 변비에 걸린

constipation pyŏnbi 변비

constituent *n* (*component*) kusŏng yoso 구성 요소

constitute (*account for*) kusŏnghac 구성하다; (*represent*) nat'anaeda 나타내다

constitution POL hŏnppŏp 헌법; (*o▮ person*) ch'ejil 체질

constitutional *adj* POL hŏnppŏpssang-ŭi 헌법상의

Constitution Day Chaehŏnjŏl 재헌▮

constraint (*restriction*) ŏktche 억제

construct *v/t* building etc seuda

...우다
nstruction (of building etc) kŏnsŏl
설; (building etc) kŏnch'ungmul
축물; (trade) kŏnsŏrŏp 건설업;
nder ~ kongsa chung 공사 중
nstruction industry kŏnsŏrŏp
설업; construction site
ongsajang 공사장; construction
orker kongsajang inbu 공사장
부

nstructive kŏnsŏltchŏgin 건설적인
nsul yŏngsa 영사
nsulate yŏngsagwan 영사관
nsult (seek the advice of) ...ŭi
igyŏnŭl mut-tta ...의 의견을 묻다;
ictionary ch'amgohada 참고하다
nsultancy (company)
'ŏnssŏlt'ŏnt'ŭŏp 컨설턴트업;
advice) sangdam 상담
nsultant (adviser) k'ŏnssŏlt'ŏnt'ŭ
설턴트
nsultation sang-ŭi 상의
nsume (eat) mŏgŏbŏrida
어버리다; (drink) mashyŏbŏrida
셔버리다; (use) ssŏbŏrida 써버리다
nsumer (purchaser) sobija 소비자
nsumer confidence kumae ŭiji
매 의지; consumer goods
obip'um 소비품; consumer soci-
ty sobija sahoe 소비자 사회
nsumption sobi 소비
ntact 1 n (person) chunggyein
계인; (communication) yŏllak
락; (social) kyoje 교제; (by radio)
yoshin 교신; (physical) chŏpch'ok
촉; *keep in* ~ *with X* Xwa/gwa
ŏllagŭl chugo pat-tta X와/과 연락을
고 받다 2 v/t yŏllak'ada 연락하다;
by radio) kyoshinhada 교신하다
ntact lens k'ont'aekt'ŭrenjŭ
택트렌즈
ntact number yŏllakch'ŏ 연락처
ntagious illness, laughter
hŏnyŏmdoenŭn 전염되는
ntain tamkko it-tta 담고 있다;
it ~ed my camera nae
'ameraga tŭrŏ issŏt-tta 내 카메라가
들어 있었다; ~ *oneself* ch'amtta
다
ntainer (recipient) yonggi 용기;

COM k'ŏnt'einŏ 컨테이너
container ship k'ŏnt'einŏsŏn
컨테이너선
contaminate oyŏmshik'ida
오염시키다
contamination oyŏm 오염
contemplate v/t (look at) ŭngshihada
응시하다; (think about) suk-kkohada
숙고하다
contemporary 1 adj hyŏndaeŭi
현대의 2 n tongnyŏnbaeŭi saram
동년배의 사람; (at school)
tonggisaeng 동기생
contempt kyŏngmyŏl 경멸; *be beneath* ~ kyŏngmyŏrhal kach'ijoch'a
ŏmnŭn 경멸할 가치조차 없는
contemptible kyŏngmyŏrhal manhan
경멸할 만한
contemptuous yatchababonŭn
얕잡아보는
contend: ~ *for* ...ŭl/rŭl wihae
tat'uda ...을/를 위해 다투다; ~ *with*
ch'ŏrihada 처리하다
contender (in sport, competition)
kyŏngjaengja 경쟁자; (against
champion) tojŏnja 도전자
content[1] n naeyong 내용
content[1] 1 adj manjok'anŭn 만족하는
2 v/t: ~ *oneself with* ...(ŭ)ro
manjok'ada ...(으)로 만족하다
contented majok'ago innŭn 만족하고
있는
contention (assertion) chujang 주장;
be in ~ *for* ...ŭl/rŭl wihae
kyŏngjaenghada ...을/를 위해
경쟁하다
contentment manjok 만족
contents naeyong 내용
contest[1] (competition) taehoe 대회;
(struggle, for power) kyŏngjaeng
경쟁
contest[2] leadership etc kyŏruda
겨루다; (oppose) pandaehada
반대하다
contestant kyŏngjaengja 경쟁자
context munmaek 문맥; *look at X in*
~ /*out of* ~ Xŭl/rŭl munmaege
match'wŏ/munmaegŭl pŏsŏna poda
X을/를 문맥에 맞춰/문맥을 벗어나
보다
continent n taeryuk 대륙

continental taeryugйi 대륙의
contingency ttйkppakkйi il 뜻밖의 일
continual kyesoktchŏgin 계속적인
continuation kyesok 계속
continue 1 v/t kyesok'ada 계속하다; **to be ~d** taйme kyesok toeda 다음에 계속 **2** v/i kyesokttoeda 계속되다
continuity yŏnsoksŏng 연속성
continuous kkйnimŏmnйn 끊임없는
contort face tchinggйrida 찡그리다; body pit'йlda 비틀다
contour yun-gwak 윤곽
contraception p'iim 피임
contraceptive n (device) p'iim kigu 피임 기구; (pill) p'iimyak 피임약
contract¹ n kyeyak 계약
contract² 1 v/i (shrink) such'uk'ada 수축하다 2 v/t illness ...e kŏllida ...에 걸리다
contractor kyeyaktcha 계약자
contractual kyeyakssang-йi 계약상의
contradict statement puinhada 부인하다; person panbak'ada 반박하다
contradiction mosun 모순
contradictory account mosundoen 모순된
contraption F sae koanmul 새 고안물
contrary¹ 1 adj pandaeйi 반대의; **~ to** ...e panhayŏ ...에 반하여 2 n: **on the ~** pandaero 반대로
contrary² (perverse) pandaeroman hanйn 반대로만 하는
contrast 1 n taejo 대조 2 v/t taejohada 대조하다 3 v/i taejodoeda 대조되다
contrasting taejojŏgin 대조적인
contravene wibanhada 위반하다
contribute 1 v/i (with money, material) kibuhada 기부하다; (with time) konghŏnhada 공헌하다; (to magazine, paper) kigohada 기고하다; (to discussion) kiyŏhada 기여하다; **~ to** (help to cause) ...йihan wŏnini toeda ...의한 원인이 되다 2 v/t money kibuhada 기부하다
contribution (money) kibu 기부; (of time, effort) konghŏn 공헌; (to discussion) kiyŏ 기여; (to magazine) kigo 기고

contributor (of money) kibuja 기부자; (to magazine) kigoga 기고
contrive yongk'e haenaeda 용케 해내다
control 1 n (of country, organizati chibae 지배; (of emotions) chŏ 저 (of ball) cheguryŏk 제구력; **be in of** ...йl/rйl chibaehada ...을/를 지배하다; **bring X under ~** Xйl/r cheŏhada X을/를 제어하다; **get o of ~** cheŏhal su ŏpkke toeda 제어 수 없게 되다; **lose ~ of** ...йl/rйl cheŏhal su ŏpkke toeda ...을/를 제어할 수 없게 되다; **lose ~ of self** chashinйl ŏktchehal su ŏpkk toeda 자신을 억제할 수 없게 되다 **the situation is under ~** sanghwang-йn t'ongjedoeŏt-tta 상황은 통제되었다; **circumstance beyond our ~** uriga t'ongjehal su ŏmnйn sanghwang-ida 우리가 통제할 수 없는 상황이다; **~s** (of aircraft, vehicle) chojong changch 조종 장치; (restrictions) chehan 저 2 v/t (govern) chibaehada 지배하 (restrict) chehanhada 제한하다; (regulate) t'ongjehada 통제하다; **~ oneself** chajehada 자제하다
control center t'ongjeshil 통제실
control freak F kwŏllyŏk chungdoktcha 권력 중독자
controlled substance kyuje yangmul 규제 약물
controlling interest FIN chibaejŏk ikkwŏn 지배적 이권
control panel cheŏban 제어판
control tower kwanjet'ap 관제탑
controversial nonjaeng-йl irйk'inʼ 논쟁을 일으키는
controversy nonjaeng 논쟁
convalesce kŏn-gang-йl hoebok'a 건강을 회복하다
convalescence hoebok-kki 회복기
convene v/t sojip'ada 소집하다
convenience (of location, time) p'yŏlli 편리; **at your/my ~** tangshini/naega p'yŏllihan ttaee 당신이/내가 편리한 때에; **all** (mod ern) **~s** modйn hyŏndaejŏgin p'yŏnйi shisŏl 모든 현대적인 편의 시설

nvenience food insŭt'ŏnt'ŭ
hikp'um 인스턴트 식품
nvenience store iryong chap'wa
hikp'umjŏm 일용 잡화 식품점
nvenient p'yŏllihan 편리한
nvent sudowŏn 수도원
nvention (tradition) kwansŭp 관습;
conference) taehoe 대회
nventional chŏnt'ongjŏgin
전통적인
nvention center k'ŏnbenshyŏn
ent'ŏ 컨벤션 센터
nventioneer taehoe ch'amgaja
대회 참가자
nversant: be ~ with …ŭl/rŭl chal
anŭn …을/를 잘 아는
nversation taehwa 대화
nversational hoehwaŭi 회화의
nverse n (opposite) pandae 반대
nversely pandaero 반대로
nversion chŏnhwan 전환; (of unit
of measurement) hwansan 환산; (of
building) kaejo 개조
nversion table hwansanp'yo
환산표
nvert 1 n chŏnhyang 전향 2 v/t
pyŏnhage hada 변하게 하다; unit of
measurement hwansanhada
환산하다; building kaejohada
개조하다; person chŏnhyangshik'ida
전향시키다
nvertible n (car) kŏnbŏt'ŏbŭl
컨버터블
nvey (transmit) chŏndarhada
전달하다; (carry) unbanhada
운반하다
nveyor belt k'ŏnbeiŏ pelt'ŭ
컨베이어 벨트
nvict 1 n kigyŏlssu 기결수 2 v/t
AW yujoerŭl sŏn-gohada 유죄를
선고하다; ~ X of Y Xege Yŭi p'an-
gyŏrŭl naerida X에게 Y의 판결을
내리다
nviction LAW yujoeŭi p'an-gyŏl
유죄의 판결; (belief) shinnyŏm 신념
nvince hwaksshinshik'ida
확신시키다
nvincing sŏlttŭngnyŏk innŭn
설득력 있는
nvivial (friendly) k'waehwarhan
쾌활한

convoy (of ships) hosonghada
호송하다; (of vehicles) howihada
호위하다
convulsion MED kyŏngnyŏn 경련
cook 1 n yorisa 요리사 2 v/t yorihada
요리하다; a ~ed meal yoridoen
shikssa 요리된 식사 3 v/i yorihada
요리하다
cookbook yorich'aek 요리책
cookery yorippŏp 요리법
cookie k'uk'i 쿠키
cooking (food) yori 요리
cool 1 n F keep one's ~
ch'imch'ak'ada 침착하다; lose one's
~ hŭngbunhada 흥분하다 2 adj
weather, breeze shiwŏnhan 시원한;
drink ch'agaun 차가운; (calm)
naengjŏnghan 냉정한; (unfriendly)
naengdamhan 냉담한; F (great)
kimak'ige kŭnsahan 기막히게 근사한
3 v/i (of food) shiktta 식다; (of
tempers, interest) karaantta 가라앉다
4 v/t F: ~ it ch'imch'ak'aseyo
침착하세요
♦ cool down 1 v/i (of food, person)
shiktta 식다; (of weather)
sŏnŭrhaejida 서늘해지다; (of
tempers) karaantta 가라앉다 2 v/t
food shik'ida 식히다; fig
karaanch'ida 가라앉히다
cooperate hyŏmnyŏk'ada 협력하다
cooperation hyŏmnyŏk 협력
cooperative 1 n COM hyŏpttong
chohap 협동 조합 2 adj COM
hyŏpttong-ŭi 협동의; (helpful)
hyŏmnyŏktchŏgin 협력적인
coordinate activities chojŏng
chohwashik'ida 조정 조화시키다
coordination (of activities) chojŏng
chohwa 조정 조화; (of body) undong
shin-gyŏng 운동 신경
cop F kyŏngch'al 경찰
cope ch'ŏrihada 처리하다; ~ with
…ŭl/rŭl ch'ŏrihada …을/를
처리하다
copier (machine) pokssagi 복사기
copilot pujojongsa 부조종사
copious amount p'ungbuhan 풍부한;
notes chasehan 자세한
copper n (metal) kuri 구리
copy 1 n (duplicate, photocopy)

pokssa 복사; (*imitation*) mobang 모방; (*of book*) pu bu; (*of record, CD*) chang 장; (*of newspaper material*) kisa kŏri 기사 거리; (*in advertisement*) kwanggo munan 광고 문안; ***make a ~ of a file*** COMPUT p'airŭl pokssahada 파일을 복사하다 **2** *v/t* (*imitate*) mobanghada 모방하다; (*duplicate, photocopy*) pokssahada 복사하다; (*in writing*) pekkyŏ ssŭda 베껴 쓰다; (*in order to cheat*) mollae pekkida 몰래 베끼다

copy cat F mobanghanŭn saram 모방하는 사람; **copycat crime** mobang pŏmjoe 모방 범죄; **copyright** *n* chŏjak-kkwŏn 저작권; **copywriter** k'ap'irait'ŏ 카피라이터

coral (*on seabed*) sanho 산호

cord (*string*) nokkŭn 노끈; (*cable*) chŏnsŏn 전선

cordial *adj* ch'ungshimŭrobut'ŏŭi 충심으로부터의

cordless phone musŏn chŏnhwagi 무선 전화기

cordon pisang kyŏnggyesŏn 비상 경계선

♦ **cordon off** pisang kyŏnggyesŏnŭl ch'ida 비상 경계선을 치다

cords (*pants*) kolden paji 골덴 바지

corduroy kolden 골덴

core 1 *n* (*of fruit*) sok 속; (*of problem*) koltcha 골자; (*of organization, party*) haeksshim 핵심 **2** *adj* issue haeksshimjŏgin 핵심적인

cork (*in bottle*) k'orŭk'ŭ magae 코르크 마개; (*material*) k'orŭk'ŭ 코르크

corkscrew p'odoju pyŏng ttagae 포도주 병 따개

corn okssusu 옥수수

corner 1 *n* (*of page, room*) kusŏk 구석; (*of table, street*) mot'ung-i 모퉁이; (*bend: on road*) kilmot'ung-i 길모퉁이; (*in soccer*) k'onŏk'ik 코너킥; ***in the ~*** kusŏge(sŏ) 구석에(서); ***on the ~*** (*of street*) mot'ung-ie(sŏ) 모퉁이에(서) **2** *v/t* person kusŏgŭro molda 구석으로 몰다; ***~ the market*** shijang-ŭl toktchŏmhada 시장을 독점하다 **3** *v/i* (*of driver, car*) mot'ung-irŭl tolda

모퉁이를 돌다

corner kick k'onŏk'ik 코너킥

cornstarch nongmal 녹말

corny F (*trite*) chinbuhan 진부한; (*sentimental*) kamsangjŏgin 감상적

coronary 1 *adj* shimjang-ŭi 심장의; shimjang mabi 심장 마비

coroner kŏmshigwan 검시관

corporal *n* sangbyŏng 상병

corporal punishment ch'ehyŏng 체형

corporate COM pŏbinŭi 법인의; ***~ image*** kiŏp imiji 기업 이미지; ***sense of ~ loyalty*** kiŏbe taehan ch'ungsŏngshim 기업에 대한 충성

corporation (*business*) chushik hoe 주식 회사

corps kundan 군단

corpse shich'e 시체

corpulent pimanhan 비만한

corpuscle hyŏlgu 혈구

corral *n* kach'uk uri 가축 우리

correct 1 *adj* orŭn 옳은; *time* chŏnghwak'an 정확한 **2** *v/t* koch'ida 고치다; *proofs* kyojŏnghada 교정하

correction koch'in kŏt 고친 것

correspond (*match*) ilch'ihada 일치하다; (*write letters*) sŏshin wangnaehada 서신 왕래하다; ***~ to*** ...e haedanghada ...에 해당하다; ***~ with*** ...wa/kwa puhap'ada ...와/과 부합하다

correspondence (*match*) ilch'i 일치; (*letters*) p'yŏnji 편지; (*exchange of letters*) sŏshin wangnae 서신 왕래

correspondent (*letter writer*) p'yŏnjirŭl ssŭnŭn saram 편지를 쓰는 사람; (*reporter*) t'ŭkp'awŏn 특파원

corresponding *adj* taeŭnghanŭn 대응하는

corridor (*in building*) poktto 복도

corroborate hwaksshirhage hada 확실하게 하다

corrode *v/t & v/i* pushik'ada 부식하

corrosion pushik 부식

corrugated cardboard kolp'anji 골판지

corrugated iron korhamsŏk 골함석

corrupt 1 *adj* t'arak'an 타락한; COMPUT t'ŭllin koshi manŭn 틀린 곳이 많은 **2** *v/t* t'arakshik'ida

락시키다; (*bribe*) maesuhada
수하다

rruption t'arak 타락

smetic *adj* hwajangnyŏng-ŭi
장용의; *fig* p'yomyŏnjŏgin
면적인

smetics hwajangp'um 화장품

smetic surgeon sŏnghyŏng-
ekkwa ŭisa 성형외과 의사

smetic surgery sŏnghyŏng-
ekkwa 성형외과

smonaut uju pihaengsa 우주
행사

smopolitan *city* taguktchogŭi
국적의

st 1 *n* kagyŏk 가격; (~ *price, in
manufacturing*) wŏnkka 원가; *fig
ŭisaeng* 희생; ~**s** piyong 비용 2 *v/t
money, time* tŭlda 들다; FIN *project*
aengsanbirŭl kyŏnjŏk'ada 생산비를
견적하다; *how much does it* ~?
iyong-i ŏlmana tŭmnikka? 비용이
마나 듭니까?; *it* ~ *me my health
ŭgŏt-ttaemune kŏn-gang-ŭl irŏt-tta
그것때문에 건강을 잃었다

st and freight COM unim p'oham
agyŏk 운임 포함 가격; **cost-
onscious** kyŏngbirŭl
hŏlgamhanŭn 경비를 절감하는;
cost-effective piyong
yokkwajŏgin 비용 효과적인; **cost,
nsurance and freight** COM pohŏm
nit unim p'oham kagyŏk 보험 및
운임 포함 가격

stly *error* sonshiri k'ŭn 손실이 큰

st of living saenghwalbi 생활비

st price wŏnkka 원가

stume (*for actor*) ŭisang 의상

stume jewelry mojo posŏngnyu
교조 보석류

t (*camp-bed*) kani ch'imdae 간이
침대

ttage shigoltchip 시골집

tton 1 *n* myŏn 면 2 *adj* myŏnŭro
nandŭn 면으로 만든

cotton on F ihaehada 이해하다

cotton on to F ...ŭl/rŭl
kkaedatkke toeda ...을/를 깨닫게
다

cotton to F ...ege hogamŭl kajida
...에게 호감을 가지다

cotton candy somsat'ang 솜사탕

couch *n* sop'a 소파

couch potato F t'edori 테돌이

couchette chimdaech'atkkan
침대찻간

cough 1 *n* kich'im 기침; (*to get
attention*) kich'im sori 기침 소리
2 *v/i* kich'imhada 기침하다; (*to get
attention*) kich'im sorirŭl naeda 기침
소리를 내다

♦ **cough up** 1 *v/t blood etc*
kich'imhayŏ naebaet-tta 기침하여
내뱉다; F *money* maji mot'ae
naejuda 마지 못해 내주다 2 *v/i* F
(*pay*) maji mot'ae naeda 마지 못해
내다

cough medicine, cough syrup
kich'im yak/shirŏp 기침 약/시럽

could: *I have my key?* che
yŏlsoerŭl chushigessŏyo? 제 열쇠를
주시겠어요?; ~ *you help me?* chŏl
towajushil su issŏyo? 절 도와주실 수
있어요?; *this* ~ *be our bus* uri
pŏsŭinjido morŭnda 우리
버스인지도 모른다; *you* ~ *be right*
nega majŭl sudo issŏ 네가 맞을 수도
있어; *I* ~*n't say for sure*
hwaksshirhadago marhal sunŭn
ŏpssŏyo 확실하다고말할 수는
없어요; *he* ~ *have got lost* kŭnŭn
kirŭl irŏbŏryŏssŭltchido morŭnda
그는 길을 잃어버렸을지도 모른다;
you ~ *have warned me!* nahant'e
miri yaegirŭl haessŏyaji! 나한테 미리
얘기를 했어야지!

council (*assembly*) hoeŭi 회의; POL
ŭihoe 의회

councilman shiŭihoe ŭiwŏn 시의회
의원

councilor ŭiwŏn 의원

counsel 1 *n* (*advice*) choŏn 조언;
(*lawyer*) pyŏnhosa 변호사 2 *v/t*
(*advise*) choŏnhada 조언하다;
(*because of problems*) ...wa/kwa
sangdamhada ...와/과 상담하다

counseling sangdam 상담

counselor (*adviser*) sangdamnyŏk
상담녁; LAW pyŏnhosa 변호사

count 1 *n* (*number arrived at*)
ch'onggye 총계; (*counting*) sem 셈;
(*in baseball, boxing*) k'aunt'ŭ

카운트; **keep ~ of** ...ŭl/rŭl kyesok
seda ...을/를 계속 세다; **lose ~ of**
...ŭi semŭl ijŏbŏrida ...의 셈을
잊어버리다; **at the last ~**
ch'oejongsuro 최종수로 2 v/i (to ten
etc) surŭl seda 수를 세다; (calculate)
kyesanhada 계산하다; (be important)
kach'iga it-tta 가치가 있다; (qualify)
semŭro ch'ida 셈으로 치다 3 v/t (~
up) seda 세다; (calculate)
kyesanhada 계산하다; (include)
ch'ida 치다
♦ **count on** ...ege kidaeda ...에게
기대다
countdown ch'o ilkki 초 읽기
countenance v/t yongnap'ada
용납하다
counter¹ (in shop, café) k'aunt'ŏ
카운터; (in game) san-gaji 산가지
counter² 1 v/t ...ŭi hyŏkkwarŭl
churida ..의 효과를 줄이다 2 v/i
(retaliate) matssŏda 맞서다
counter³: **run ~ to** ...e pandaedoeda
...에 반대되다
counteract chunghwahada 중화하다;
counter-attack 1 n yŏkssŭp 역습
2 v/i yŏkssŭp'ada 역습하다; **coun-
terclockwise** panshigye panghyang
반시계 방향; **counterespionage**
pangch'ŏp pangbŏp
방첩 방법
counterfeit 1 v/t wijohada 위조하다
2 adj wijoŭi 위조의
counterpart (person) kat'ŭn chiwiŭi
saram 같은 지위의 사람; **counter-
productive** yŏk'yokkwaŭi yŏk'gwaŭi;
countersign v/t pusŏhada 부서하다
countless sel su ŏmnŭn 셀 수 없는
country nara 나라; (not town) shigol
시골; **in the ~** shigore(sŏ) 시골에(서)
country and western MUS k'ŏnt'ŭri
myujik 컨트리 뮤직
countryman (fellow ~) kat'ŭn nara
saram 같은 나라 사람
countryside shigol 시골
county kun 군
coup POL k'udet'a 쿠데타; fig
taesŏnggong 대성공
couple (married) pubu 부부; (man &
woman) namnyŏ han ssang 남녀 한
쌍; (two people) han ssang 한 쌍;
just a ~ chogŭm 조금; **a ~ of**

(people) tusŏnŏsŭi 두서너의; (thir
tusŏnŏ kae 두서너 개; **a ~ of day**
isahŭl 이사흘
coupon (form) shinch'ŏngkkwŏn
신청권; (voucher) k'up'on 쿠폰
courage yonggi 용기
courageous yonggi innŭn 용기 있
courier (messenger) paedal 배달;
(with tourist party) annaewŏn 안내
course n (series of lessons) kyokk
kwajŏng 교과 과정; (part of meal
for race) k'osŭ 코스; (of ship, plar
haengno 행로; **of ~** (certainly)
mullon 물론; (naturally) tang-yŏn
당연히; **of ~ not** mullon aniyo 물
아니죠; **~ of action** haengdong
pangch'im 행동 방침; **~ of treatment** chillyo kwajŏng 진료 과정;
the ~ of ... tong-ane ... 동안에
court n LAW pŏptchŏng 법정;
(courthouse) pŏbwŏn 법원; SP k'o
코트; **take X to ~** Xŭl/rŭl chaep'
kŏlda X을/를 재판에 걸다
court case sosong sakkŏn 소송 사
courteous chŏngjunghan 정중한
courtesy chŏngjungham 정중함
courthouse pŏbwŏn 법원; **court
martial** 1 n kunppŏp hoeŭi 군법
회의 2 v/t kunppŏp hoeŭie
hoebuhada 군법 회의에 회부하다
court music aak 아악; **court ord**
pŏbwŏn myŏngnyŏng 법원 명령;
courtroom pŏptchŏng 법정; **cour**
yard anmadang 안마당
cousin sach'on 사촌
cove (bay) humijin kot 후미진 곳
cover 1 n (protective) tŏpkkae 덮개
(of book, magazine) p'yoji 표지; (
bed) ch'imdaeppo 침대보; (shelter
ŏmhomul 엄호물; (shelter from ra
etc) p'inanch'ŏ 피난처; (insurance
pohŏm 보험 2 v/t tŏpta 덮다; (in
blood, mud etc) ssŭiuda 씌우다;
(hide) sumgida 숨기다; (of insura
policy) pohŏme kŏlda 보험에 걸
distance tapp'ahada 답파하다; (of
journalist) podohada 보도하다
♦ **cover up** 1 v/t tŏpta 덮다; fig
kamch'uda 감추다 2 v/i fig
kamch'uda 감추다; **~ for X** Xŭl/r
tudunhada X을/를 두둔하다

verage (by media) podo 보도
vering letter ch'ŏmbusŏ 첨부서
vert pimirŭi 비밀의
verup (of crime) ŭnp'ye 은폐
w n amso 암소
ward kŏptchaeng-i 겁쟁이
wardice pigŏp 비겁
wardly pigŏp'an 비겁한
wboy k'auboi 카우보이
wer umch'ŭrida 움츠리다
y (evasive) hoep'ihanŭn 회피하는;
flirtatious) sujubŏhanŭn 수줍어하는;
zy anŭk'an 아늑한
⊃U (= *central processing unit*)
hung-ang ch'ŏri changch'i 중앙
러리 장치
ab n ke 게
ack 1 n kallajin kŭm 갈라진 금;
joke) pikkonŭn nongdam 비꼬는
농담 2 v/t cup, glass kŭmgage hada
금가게 하다; nut kkaeda 깨다; code
⊃'ulda 풀다; F (solve) haegyŏrhada
해결하다; ~ *a joke* nongdamhada
농담하다 3 v/i kŭmi kada 금이 가다;
get ~ing F irŭl shijak'ada 일을
시작하다
crack down on …ŭl/rŭl ŏmhage
tasŭrida …을/를 엄하게 다스리다
crack up v/i (have breakdown)
shin-gyŏng soeyage kŏllida 신경
쇠약에 걸리다; F (laugh) kaptchagi
utkki shijak'ada 갑자기 웃기
시작하다
ackdown tansok 단속
acked cup, glass kŭmi kan 금이 간
acker (to eat) k'ŭraek'ŏ 크래커
ackle v/i (of fire) ttakttak sorirŭl
naeda 딱딱 소리를 내다
adle n (for baby) yoram 요람
aft¹ NAUT sŏnbak 선박
aft² (art) kong-ye 공예; (skill)
kinŭng 기능
aftsman chang-in 장인
afty kyohwarhan 교활한
ag (rock) hŏmhan pawi 험한 바위
am v/t mirŏ nŏt'a 밀어 넣다
ramped room pijobŭn 비좁은
ramps kŭpkkyŏk'an pokt'ong
급격한 복통
ranberry tŏnggulwŏlgyul 덩굴월귤
rane 1 n (machine) kijunggi 기중기;

(bird) hak 학 2 v/t: ~ **one's neck**
mogŭl kilge ppaeda 목을 길게 빼다
crank n (strange person) koetcha 괴짜
crankshaft kŭraengk'ŭch'uk
크랭크축
cranky (bad-tempered) shimgiga
twit'ŭllin 심기가 뒤틀린
crap F (garbage) ssŭregi 쓰레기
crash 1 n (noise) k'wang hanŭn sori
쾅 하는 소리; (accident) ch'ungdol
충돌; (plane ~) ch'urak 추락; COM
munŏjim 무너짐; COMPUT kojang
고장 2 v/i (make noise) k'wang
hanŭn sorirŭl naeda 쾅 하는 소리를
내다; (of thunder) ch'ida 치다; (of
car) ch'ungdorhada 충돌하다; (of
airplane) ch'urak'ada 추락하다;
(COM: of market) punggoehada
붕괴하다; COMPUT kojangnada
고장나다 3 v/t car ch'ungdolshik'ida 충돌시키다
♦ crash out F (fall asleep) kora
ttŏrŏjida 곯아 떨어지다
crash course chiptchung kangjwa
집중 강좌; crash diet soksssŏng
taiŏt'ŭ 속성 다이어트; crash helmet
anjŏn helmet 안전 헬멧; crash
landing pulshich'ak 불시착
crate namu sangja 나무 상자
crater (of volcano) punhwagu 분화구
crave kalmanghada 갈망하다
craving kalmang 갈망
crawl 1 n (stroke) k'ŭrol suyŏng 크롤
수영; *at a ~* (slowly) nŭrinnŭrit'age
느릿느릿하게 2 v/i (on floor) kida
기다; (move slowly) nŭrinnŭrit kada
느릿느릿 가다
♦ crawl with …(ŭ)ro ugŭlgŏrida
…(으)로 우글거리다
crayon k'ŭreyong 크레용
craze ilsshijŏk taeyuhaeng 일시적
대유행; *the latest ~* ch'oegŭnŭi
taeyuhaeng 최근의 대유행
crazy adj mich'in 미친; *be ~ about*
…e yŏlgwanghada …에 열광하다
creak 1 n ppigŭk-kkŏrinŭn sori
삐걱거리는 소리 2 v/i ppigŭk-
kkŏrida 삐걱거리다
cream 1 n (for skin, coffee, cake)
k'ŭrim 크림; (color) tamhwangsaek
담황색 2 adj tamhwangsaegŭi
담황색의

담황색의
cream cheese k'ŭrim ch'iju 크림
치즈
creamer (*pitcher*) k'ŭrim kŭrŭt 크림
그릇; (*for coffee*) p'ŭrima 프리마
creamy (*with lots of cream*) k'ŭrimi
mani tŭrŏgan k'ŭrimi 많이 들어간
crease 1 *n* (*accidental*) kugimsal
구김살; (*deliberate*) churŭm 주름
2 *v/t* (*accidentally*) kugida 구기다
create 1 *v/t* ch'angjohada 창조하다;
uncertainty, problem yagihada
야기하다 **2** *v/i* ch'angjohada 창조하다
creation ch'angjo 창조; (*sth created*)
ch'angjomul 창조물; *the Creation*
REL Ch'ŏnji ch'angjo 천지 창조
creative ch'angjojŏgin 창조적인
creator ch'angjoja 창조자; (*author*)
ch'angjaktcha 창작자; (*founder*)
ch'angsŏltcha 창설자; *the Creator*
REL Chomultchu 조물주
creature (*animal*) tongmul 동물;
(*person*) saram 사람
credibility (*of person*) shilloesŏng
신뢰성; (*of story*) shinbingsŏng
신빙성
credible (*believable*) midŭl manhan
믿을 만한; *candidate etc* shilloegam
kanŭn 신뢰감 가는
credit 1 *n* FIN oesang 외상; (*loan*)
shinyong taebu 신용 대부; (*honor*)
kongno 공로; (*payment received*)
yegŭmaek 예금액; *be in ~* yegŭmi it-
tta 예금이 있다; *get the ~ for X* Xe
taehan kongnorŭl injŏngpat-tta X에
대한 공로를 인정받다 **2** *v/t* (*believe*)
mit-tta 믿다; *~ an amount to an
account* kyejwae yegŭmhada
계좌에 예금하다
creditable ch'ingch'anhal manhan
칭찬할 만한
credit card shinyong k'adŭ 신용 카드
credit limit (*of credit card*) shinyong
taebuŭi hando 신용 대부의 한도
creditor ch'aegwŏnja 채권자
creditworthy shinyonginnŭn
신용있는
credulous chal minnŭn 잘 믿는
creed (*beliefs*) shin-gyŏng 신경
creek (*stream*) chagŭn nae 작은 내
creep 1 *n pej* anikkoun saram

아니꼬운 사람 **2** *v/i* salgŭmsalgŭm
kŏt-tta 살금살금 걷다
creeper BOT tŏnggul shingmul 덩굴
식물
creeps: *the house* / *he gives me
the ~* kŭ chibi / kŭga narŭl
sŏmttŭk'age handa 그 집이 / 그가
나를 섬뜩하게 한다
creepy sŏmttŭk'an 섬뜩한
cremate hwajanghada 화장하다
cremation hwajang 화장
crematorium hwajangjang 화장장
crescent ch'osŭngttal moyang 초승
모양
crest (*of hill*) kkokttaegi 꼭대기; (*of
bird*) pyŏt 벗
crestfallen p'uri chugŭn 풀이 죽은
crevice kallajin t'ŭm 갈라진 틈
crew *n* (*of ship, airplane*)
sŭngmuwŏn chŏnwŏn 승무원 전원;
(*of repairmen etc*) t'im 팀; (*group*)
p'aegŏri 패거리
crew cut sanggo mŏri 상고 머리
crew neck swet'aŭi tunggŭn mok
쉐타의 둥근 목
crib *n* (*for baby*) yuayong ch'imdae
유아용 침대
crick: *~ in the neck* mogŭl ppida
목을 삐다
cricket (*insect*) kwitturami 귀뚜라미
crime pŏmjoe 범죄; (*shameful act*)
yugamsŭrŏn il 유감스런 일
criminal 1 *n* pŏmjoeja 범죄자 **2** *adj*
pŏmjoeŭi 범죄의; (*LAW: not civil*)
hyŏngsasang-ŭi 형사상의; (*shamef*)
yugamsŭrŏn 유감스런
crimson *adj* chinhongsaegŭi 진홍색
cringe momŭl umsshirhada 몸을
움씰하다
cripple 1 *n* (*disabled person*) shinch
chang-aeja 신체 장애자 **2** *v/t pers*
pulguga toege hada 불구가 되게
하다; *fig* munŭnghage hada 무능하
하다
crisis wigi 위기
crisp *adj weather, air* sangk'waehar
상쾌한; *apple, bacon* p'asakp'asak'
파삭파삭한; *new shirt, bills*
ppatpat'an 빳빳한
criterion (*standard*) kijun 기준
critic pip'yŏngga 비평가

ical (*making criticisms*)
p'anjŏgin 비판적인; (*serious*)
igijŏgin 위기적인; *moment etc*
yŏltchŏngjŏgin 결정적인; MED
idok'an 위독한
ically *speak etc* pip'anjŏguro
판적으로; ~ *ill* widok'an 위독한
icism pip'yŏng 비평
icize *v/t* pip'yŏnghada 비평하다
ak *v/i* (*of frog*) kaegulgaegul ulda
굴개굴 울다; (*of person*) shwin
oksorirŭl naeda 쉰 목소리를 내다
ckery tojagiryu 도자기류
codile agŏ 악어
ny F ch'in-gu 친구
ok *n* (*dishonest*) sagikkun 사기꾼
oked (*twisting*) kuburŏjin
부러진; *necktie, picture* pitturŏjin
뒬어진; (*dishonest*) pujŏnghan
정한
p 1 *n* nongjangmul 농작물; *fig*
ahwak 수확 2 *v/t hair, photo*
halkke charŭda 짧게 자르다
rop up kaptchagi saenggida 갑자기
기다
ss 1 *adj* (*angry*) sŏngnan 성난 2 *n*
X) kopp'yo 곱표; (*Christian
mbol*) shiptchaga 십자가 3 *v/t* (*go
cross*) kŏnnŏgada 건너가다; ~ *one-
elf* REL kasŭme shiptcharŭl kŭt-tta
슴에 십자를 긋다; ~ *one's legs*
arirŭl kkoda 다리를 꼬다; *keep
ne's fingers ~ed* haeng-unŭl pilda
운을 빌다; *it never ~ed my mind*
ŭ saenggagŭn na-ege ttŏorŭji anat-
a 그 생각은 내게 떠오르지 않았다
v/i (*go across*) kŏnnŏgada
너가다; (*of lines*) kyoch'ahada
차하다
ross off, cross out chiuda 지우다
ssbar (*of goal*) kolttae 골대; (*of
icycle*) chungshimdae 중심대; (*in
igh jump*) pa 바
oss-country (skiing) sŭk'i
'ŭrosŭk'ŏnt'ŭri 스키 크로스컨트리
ssed check hoengsŏn sup'yo
선 수표
oss-examine LAW pandae
himmunhada 반대 심문하다
oss-eyed sashiŭi 사시의
ossing NAUT hoengdan 횡단

crossroads kyoch'aro 교차로; **cross-section** (*of people*) taep'yojŏgin myŏn 대표적인 면; **crosswalk** hoengdan podo 횡단 보도; **crossword** (**puzzle**) kŭltcha match'ugi nori 글자 맞추기 놀이
crouch *v/i* momŭl kuburida 몸을 구부리다
crow *n* (*bird*) kkamagwi 까마귀; *as the ~ flies* iljikssŏnŭro 일직선으로
crowd *n* kunjung 군중; (*at sports event*) kwanjung 관중
crowded pumbinŭn 붐비는
crown 1 *n* wanggwan 왕관; (*on tooth*) ch'igwan 치관 2 *v/t* wang-wie ollida 왕위에 올리다; *tooth* ssŭiuda 씌우다
crucial kyŏltchŏngjŏgin 결정적인
crude 1 *adj* (*vulgar*) sangsŭrŏun 상스러운; (*unsophisticated*) chojap'an 조잡한 2 *n*: ~ (**oil**) wŏnyu 원유
cruel chaninhan 잔인한
cruelty chaninham 잔인함
cruise 1 *n* sunhang 순항 2 *v/i* (*in ship*) sunhanghada 순항하다; (*of car*) kyŏngje sokttoro kada 경제 속도로 가다; (*of plane*) sunhang sokttoro nalda 순항 속도로 날다
cruise liner sunhangsŏn 순항선
cruising speed sunhan sokttto 순항 속도; (*of project*) sunjoroun sokttto 순조로운 속도
crumb pusŭrŏgi 부스러기
crumble 1 *v/t* pusŭrŏttŭrida 부스러뜨리다 2 *v/i* (*of bread, stone*) pusŭrojida 부스러지다; *fig* (*of opposition etc*) munŏjida 무너지다
crumple 1 *v/t* (*crease*) kugida 구기다 2 *v/i* (*collapse*) munŏjida 무너지다
crunch 1 *n*: *when it comes to the ~* F kyŏltchŏngjŏgin shigiga omyŏn 결정적인 시기가 오면 2 *v/i* (*of snow, gravel*) wajak-wajak soriga nada 와작와작 소리가 나다
crusade *n fig* kaehyŏk undong 개혁 운동
crush 1 *n* (*crowd*) kunjung 군중; *have a ~ on* …ege holttak panhada …에게 홀딱 반하다 2 *v/t* pakssarŭl naeda 박살을 내다; (*crease*) kugida 구기다; *they were ~ed to death*

kŭdŭrŭn pakssalla chugŏt-tta 그들은
박살나 죽었다 **3** *v/i* (*crease*)
kugyŏjida 구겨지다

crust (*on bread*) ttakttak'an
kkŏptchil 딱딱한 껍질

crutch (*for walking*) mokttari 목다리

cry 1 *n* (*call*) oech'im 외침; **have a ~**
ulda 울다 **2** *v/t* (*call*) oech'ida 외치다
3 *v/i* (*weep*) ulda 울다

♦ **cry out 1** *v/t* oech'yŏ purŭda 외쳐
부르다 **2** *v/i* koham chirŭda 고함
지르다

♦ **cry out for** (*need*) …ŭl/rŭl p'iryoro
hada …을/를 필요로 하다

crystal (*mineral*) sujŏng 수정; (*glass*)
k'urisŭt'ŏl 크리스털

crystallize *v/t & v/i* kuch'ehwahada
구체화하다

cub saekki 새끼

cube (*shape*) ip-ppangch'e 입방체

cubic ip-ppang-ŭi 입방의

cubic capacity TECH ip-ppang
yongnyang 입방 용량

cubicle (*changing room*) t'arŭishil
탈의실

cucumber oi 오이

cuddle 1 *n* p'oong 포옹 **2** *v/t* kkok
kkyŏantta 꼭 껴안다

cuddly *kitten etc* kkyŏanko ship'ŭn
껴안고 싶은; (*liking cuddles*)
kkyŏanko ship'ŏhanŭn 껴안고
싶어하는

cue *n* (*for actor, pool etc*) k'yu 큐

cuff 1 *n* (*of shirt*) somaetppuri
소맷부리; (*of pants*) pajittan 바지단;
(*blow*) ch'alssak ttaerim 찰싹 때림;
off the ~ chŭkssŏgŭi 즉석의 **2** *v/t*
(*hit*) ch'alssak ttaerida 찰싹 때리다

cuff link k'ŏp'ŭsŭ tanch'u 커프스 단추

culinary yoriŭi 요리의

culminate: **~ in** …(ŭ)ro chŏltchŏng-e
tarhada …(으)로 절정에 달하다

culmination chŏltchŏng 절정

culprit pŏmin 범인

cult (*sect*) sagyo chipttan 사교 집단

cultivate *land* kyŏngjak'ada 경작하다;
person chal sagwida 잘 사귀다

♦ **cultivated** *person* seryŏndoen 세련된

cultivation (*of land*) kyŏngjak 경작

cultural munhwajŏgin 문화적인

culture *n* munhwa 문화

cultured (*cultivated*) seryŏndoen
세련된

culture shock munhwajŏk
ch'unggyŏk 문화적 충격

cumbersome sŏnggashin 성가신

cunning 1 *n* kyohwarham 교활함
2 *adj* kyohwarhan 교활한

cup *n* chan 잔; (*trophy*) usŭngk'ŏp
우승컵; **a ~ of tea** ch'a han chan 차
한 잔

cupboard ch'antchang 찬장

curable ch'iryohal su innŭn 치료할 수
있는

curator k'yureit'ŏ 큐레이터

curb 1 *n* (*of street*) yŏnsŏk 연석; (*on
powers etc*) ŏktche 억제 **2** *v/t*
ŏktchehada 억제하다

curdle *v/i* (*of milk*) ŭnggohada
응고하다

cure 1 *n* MED ch'iryo 치료 **2** *v/t* MED
ch'iryohada 치료하다; *meat, fish*
pojon ch'ŏrihada 보존 처리하다

curfew yagan oech'ul kŭmji 야간
외출 금지

curiosity (*inquisitiveness*) hogishim
호기심

curious (*inquisitive*) hogishim man
호기심 많은; (*strange*) isanghan
이상한

curiously (*inquisitively*) hogishime
호기심에서; (*strangely*) isanghage
이상하게; **~ enough** isanghagedo
이상하게도

curl 1 *n* (*in hair*) kopssŭlgŏrim
곱슬거림; (*of smoke*) maemdom mun
2 *v/t hair* kopssŭlgŏrige hada
곱슬거리게 하다; (*wind*) kamtta 감
3 *v/i* (*of hair*) kopssŭlgŏrida
곱슬거리다; (*of paper etc*) tunggŭl
ogŭradŭlda 둥글게 오그라들다

♦ **curl up** umch'urida 움추리다

curly *hair* kopssŭlgŏrinŭn 곱슬거리;
tail kkobulgŏrinŭn 꼬불거리는

currant (*dried fruit*) kŏnp'odo 건포

currency (*money*) t'onghwa 통화;
foreign ~ oehwa 외화

current 1 *n* hŭrŭm 흐름; (*tidal*)
choryu 조류; ELEC chŏllyu 전류 **2** *a*
(*present*) chigŭmŭi 지금의

current affairs shisa 시사

current affairs program shisa

'ürograem 시사 프로그램

'rently chigŭm 지금

'riculum kyokkwa kwajŏng 교과
 과정

rse 1 n (spell) chŏju 저주; (swear-
 ord) yokssŏl 욕설 2 v/t chŏjuhada
 저주하다; (swear at) yok'ada 욕하다
 v/i (swear) yok'ada 욕하다

rsor COMPUT k'ŏsŏ 커서

rsory p'isangjŏgin 피상적인

rt t'ungmyŏngsŭrŏun 퉁명스러운

rtail churida 줄이다

rtain k'ŏt'ŭn 커튼; THEA mak 막

rtain k'ŏt'ŭn 커튼; THEA mak 막

rve 1 n kokssŏn 곡선 2 v/i (bend)
 uburŏjida 구부러지다

shion 1 n (for couch etc) k'ushyŏn
 쿠션 2 v/t fall wanhwahada 완화하다

stard k'ŏsŭt'ŏdŭ 커스터드

stody (of children) yangnyuk-
 kwŏn 양육권; in ~ LAW kuryu
 hung 구류 중

stom (tradition) kwansŭp 관습;
 'OM tan-gol 단골; as was his ~ kŭŭi
 ŭpkkwanŭro 그의 습관으로

stomary sŭpkkwanjŏgin 습관적인;
 socially) t'ongnyeŭi 통례의; it is ~
 o ... hanŭn kŏshi t'ongnyeida ...
 하는 것이 통례이다

stomer kogaek 고객

stomer relations kogaek kwalli
 고객 관리

stoms kwanse 관세

stoms clearance segwan
 'onggwa 세관 통과; customs inspection segwan kŏmsa 세관 검사;
 customs officer segwanwŏn 세관원

t 1 n (with knife) pegi 베기; (with
 cissors) charŭgi 자르기; (injury) pen
 angch'ŏ 벤 상처; (of garment, hair)
 narŭmjil 마름질; (reduction) sak-
 kam 삭감; my hair needs a ~
 ianŭn mŏrirŭl challayagessŏyo 나는
 l리를 잘라야겠어요 2 v/t (with
 knife) peda 베다; (with scissors)
 charŭda 자르다; (reduce) sak-
 kamhada 삭감하다; get one's hair
 ~ mŏrirŭl charŭda 머리를 자르다

ut back 1 v/i (in costs)
 ch'uksssohada 축소하다 2 v/t
 mployees sak-kkamhada 삭감하다

cut down 1 v/t peŏ nŏmŏttŭrida

베어 넘어뜨리다 2 v/i (in smoking
 etc) churida 줄이다
 ♦ cut down on smoking etc ...ŭl / rŭl
 churida ...을 / 를 줄이다
 ♦ cut off (with knife etc) peŏnaeda
 베어내다; (with scissors) challanaeda
 잘라내다; (isolate) koripsshik'ida
 고립시키다; TELEC kkŭnt'a 끊다; we
 were ~ chŏnhwaga kkŭnk'yŏssŏyo
 전화가 끊겼어요
 ♦ cut out (with scissors) oryŏnaeda
 오려내다; (eliminate) chungdanhada
 중단하다; (exclude) ch'adanhada
 차단하다; cut that out! F kŭman
 twŏ! 그만 둬!; be ~ for X Xe ttak
 chŏk'ap'ada X에 딱 적합하다
 ♦ cut up v/t meat etc t'omakch'ida
 토막치다

cutback sak-kkam 삭감

cute (pretty) kwiyŏun 귀여운;
 (sexually) maeryŏktchŏgin 매력적인;
 (clever) yŏngnihan 영리한

cuticle p'yop'i 표피

cut-price harinkkaŭi 할인가의

cut-throat competition ch'iyŏrhan
 치열한

cutting 1 n (from newspaper)
 oryŏnaen kŏt 오려낸 것 2 adj
 remark shillarhan 신랄한

cyberspace kasang konggan 가상
 공간

cycle 1 n (bicycle) chajŏn-gŏ 자전거;
 (series of events) sunhwan 순환 2 v/i
 chajŏn-gŏro kada 자전거로 가다

cycling chajŏn-gŏ t'agi 자전거
 타기

cyclist chajŏn-gŏ t'anŭn saram 자전거
 타는 사람

cylinder (container) wŏnt'ong 원통;
 (in engine) kit'ong 기통

cylindrical wŏnt'ong moyang-ŭi 원통
 모양의

cynic pikkonŭn saram 비꼬는 사람

cynical naengsojŏgin 냉소적인

cynicism naengso 냉소

cyst p'onang 포낭

Czech 1 adj Ch'ek'oŭi 체코의; the ~
 Republic Ch'ek'o konghwaguk 체코
 공화국 2 n (person) Ch'ek'o saram
 체코 사람; (language) Ch'ek'oŏ
 체코어

D

DA (= *district attorney*) chibang kŏmsa 지방 검사

dab 1 *n* (*small amount*) soryang 소량 **2** *v/t* (*remove*) saltchak takkkanaeda 살짝 닦아내다; (*apply*) kabyŏpkke parŭda 가볍게 바르다
◆ **dabble in** chamkkan sonŭl taeda 잠깐 손을 대다

dad appa 아빠

dagger tando 단도

daily 1 *n* (*paper*) shinmun 신문 **2** *adj* maeirŭi 매일의; **~ newspaper** ilgan shinmun 일간 신문

dainty sŏmsehan 섬세한

dairy products yujep'um 유제품

dais yŏndan 연단

dam 1 *n* (*for water*) ttaem 댐 **2** *v/t river* taemŭro maktta 댐으로 막다

damage 1 *n p'ihae* 피해; *fig* (*to reputation etc*) sonsang 손상 **2** *v/t p'ihaerŭl ip'ida* 피해를 입히다; *fig: reputation etc* sonsangshik'ida 손상시키다

damages LAW sonhae paesanggŭm 손해 배상금

damaging sonsangshik'inŭn 손상시키는

dame F (*woman*) yŏja 여자

damn 1 *interj* F chegirŏl 제기랄 **2** *n* F: **I don't give a ~!** naega alkke mwŏya! 내가 알게 뭐야! **3** *adj* F pirŏmŏgŭl 빌어먹을 **4** *adv* F pirŏmŏk-kke 빌어먹게 **5** *v/t* (*condemn*) hŏlttŭt-tta 헐뜯다; **~ it!** F chenjanghal! 젠장할!; **I'm ~ed if** F nanŭn chŏlttaero … haji ank'et-tta 나는 절대로 … 하지 않겠다

damned → **damn** *adj & adv*

damp *cloth* ch'ukch'uk'an 축축한; *building, room* sŭpkkich'an 습기찬

dampen ch'ukch'uk'age hada 축축하게 하다

dance 1 *n* ch'um 춤; (*social event*) taensŭ p'ati 댄스 파티 **2** *v/i*

ch'umch'uda 춤추다; **would you I to ~?** ch'um ch'ushigessŏyo? 춤 추시겠어요?

dancer ch'umch'unŭn saram 춤추는 사람; (*performer*) muyongga 무용.

dancing muyong 무용

dandruff pidŭm 비듬

Dane Tenmak'ŭ saram 덴마크 사람

danger wihŏm 위험; **out of ~** (*of patient*) chungt'ae-esŏ pŏsŏnan 중태에서 벗어난

dangerous wihŏmhan 위험한; *assumption* wit'aeroun 위태로운

dangle *v/t & v/i* tallanggŏrida 달랑거리다

Danish 1 *adj* Tenmak'ŭŭi 덴마크의 **2** *n* (*language*) Tenmak'ŭŏ 덴마크 (

Danish (*pastry*) tenishwi p'aesŭch'yuri 데니쉬 패스츄리

dare 1 *v/i: he didn't ~* kŭnŭn kamh hal su ŏpssŏssŏyo 그는 감히 할 수 없었어요; **how ~ you!** nega kamhi ŏttŏk'e! 네가 감히 어떻게! **2** *v/t: ~ to do Y* Xege Yŭl/rŭl tojŏhae porago hada X에게 Y을/를 도전히 보라고 하다

daring *adj* taedamhan 대담한

dark 1 *n* ŏdum 어둠; **after ~** haejin hue 해진 후에; **keep s.o. in the ~** *fig* nuguege morŭge hada 누구에가 모르게 하다 **2** *adj room, night* ŏduun 어두운; *hair, eyes* kŏmusŭrŭmhan 거무스름한; *color* chinhan 진한; *clothes* ŏduun pitkkarŭi 어두운 빛깔의; **~ green / blue** chinhan ch'orokssaek / p'aransaek 진한 초록색 / 파란색

darken (*of sky*) ŏduwŏjida 어두워지다

dark glasses saegan-gyŏng 색안경

darkness amhŭk 암흑

darling 1 *n* kajang sarangsŭrŏn sar 가장 사랑스런 사람; **~!** chagiya!

...기야! 2 *adj* kajang saranghanün
...장 사랑하는

m¹ *n* 1 (*mend*) kkwemaen chari
...맨 자리 2 *v/t* (*mend*) kkwemaeda
...매다

m², darned → **damn**

t 1 *n* (*for throwing*) tat'ü 다트 2 *v/i*
...sonsalgach'i naragada 쏜살같이
...아가다

sh 1 *n* (*punctuation*) taeshi 대시; (*small amount*) yakkan 약간; (MOT-*ashboard*) kyegip'an 계기판; *a ~ of brandy* yakkanüi püraendi 약간의
...랜디; *make a ~ for* ...(ü)ro nsume tallyŏgada ...(으)로 단숨에
...려가다 2 *v/i* tansume tallyŏgada
...에 달려가다 3 *v/t* hopes kkŏkta

lash off 1 *v/i* sŏdullŏ ttŏnada
...들러 떠나다 2 *v/t* (*write quickly*) ansume ssüda 단숨에 쓰다

shboard kyegip'an 계기판

ta charyo 자료, teit'ŏ 데이터; (*information*) chŏngbo 정보

tabase teit'ŏ peisü 데이터 베이스; **data capture** teit'ŏ sujip 데이터 수집; **data processing** teit'ŏ ch'ŏri 데이터 처리; **data protection** teit'ŏ poho 데이터 보호; **data storage** teit'ŏ chŏjang 데이터 저장

te¹ (*fruit*) taech'u 대추

te² 1 *n* naltcha 날짜; (*meeting*) teit'ŭ 데이트; (*person*) teit'ü sangdae 데이트 상대; *what's the ~ today?* onŭl myŏch'irijyo? 오늘 몇일이죠?; *out of ~ clothes* yuhaeng-i chinan 유행이 지난; *passport* naltchaga chinan 날짜가 지난; *up to ~* ... 2 *v/t letter, check* naltcharül chŏkta 날짜를 적다; (*go out with*) ...wa/kwa teit'ü hada ...와/과 데이트하다; *that ~s you* kŭgŏsŭro nŏüi nairül kanŭmhal su t-tta 그것으로 너의 나이를 가늠할 수 있다

ated shidaee twittŏrŏjin 시대에 뒤떨어진

aub *v/t* sŏt'urüge ch'irhada 서투르게 칠하다; *~ paint on a wall* pyŏge sŏt'urüge p'eint'ü ch'irül hada 벽에 서투르게 페인트 칠을 하다

daughter ttal 딸; (*somebody else's*) ttanim 따님
daughter-in-law myŏnüri 며느리; (*somebody else's*) myŏnnim 며느님
daunt *v/t* kirül kkŏkta 기를 꺾다
dawdle (*waste time*) shiganül hŏbihada 시간을 허비하다; (*move slowly*) kkumulgŏrida 꾸물거리다; *~ over* nŭgŭt'age ... hada 느긋하게 ... 하다
dawn 1 *n* saebyŏk 새벽; *fig* (*of new age*) shich'o 시초 2 *v/i: it ~ed on me that* ...ranŭn kŏsül nanün kkaedatkki shijak'aet-tta ...라는 것을 나는 깨닫기 시작했다
day nal 날; *all ~* haru chong-il 하루 종일; *what ~ is it today?* onŭrün musün yoiriyeyo? 오늘은 무슨 요일이에요?; *~ off* shwinün nal 쉬는 날; *~ by ~* naje 낮에; *~ off* nanari 나날이; *the ~ after* kŭ taŭmnal 그 다음날; *the ~ after tomorrow* more 모레; *the ~ before* kŭ chŏnnal 그 전날; *the ~ before yesterday* küjökke 그저께; *~ in ~ out* maeilmaeil kyesok'aesŏ 매일 매일 계속해서; *in those ~s* kŭ shijŏrenün 그 시절에는; *one ~* ŏnjen-ganün 언젠가는; *the other ~* (*recently*) iltchŏne 일전에; *let's call it a ~!* küman kkŭnnaepsshida! 그만 끝냅시다!
daybreak saebyŏk 새벽; **daydream** 1 *n* paegilmong 백일몽 2 *v/i* kongsang-e chamgida 공상에 잠기다; **daylight** nat 낮; **daytime: *in the ~*** naje 낮에; **daytrip** tang-ilch'igi yŏhaeng 당일치기 여행
dazed (*by news*) ŏridungjŏrhaejin 어리둥절해진; (*by a blow*) chŏngshini mŏnghan 정신이 멍한
dazzle *v/t* nunbushige hada 눈부시게 하다; *fig* apttodanghada 압도당하다
dead 1 *adj person, plant* chugŭn 죽은; *battery* tarün 닮은; *phone* kkŭnŏjin 끊어진; *flashlight, engine* kkŏjin 꺼진; *bulb* nagan 나간; F (*boring: place*) hwalgi ŏmnün 활기 없는 2 *adv* F *~ beat, ~ tired* nokch'oga toeŏ 녹초가 되어; *that's ~ right* chŏntchŏgŭro

matsŭmnida 전적으로 맞습니다 **3** n: **the ~** koin 고인; **in the ~ of night** han pamtchung-e 한 밤중에

deaden pain, sound chugida 죽이다

dead end (street) makttarŭn 막다른; **dead-end job** changnaesŏng ŏmnŭn chigŏp 장래성 없는 직업; **dead heat** musŭngbu 무승부; **deadline** (day) magamil 마감일; (hour) magamshigan 마감시간; **deadlock** n (in talks) kyoch'ak sangt'ae 교착 상태

deadly adj (fatal) ch'imyŏngjŏgin 치명적인; F (boring) chiruhaesŏ mich'ilkkŏt kat'ŭn 지루해서 미칠것 같은

deaf kwimŏgŭn 귀먹은

deaf-and-dumb (of child) nong-aŭi 농아의

deafen kwimŏk-kke hada 귀먹게 하다

deafening kwich'ŏng-i ttŏrŏjil ttŭt'an 귀청이 떨어질 듯한

deafness ch'ŏnggak chang-ae 청각 장애

deal **1** n (contract) kyeyak 계약; (in business) kŏrae 거래; **it's a ~!** (agreed) habŭidoen kŏmnida! 합의된 겁니다!; (it's a promise) yakssok'an kŏmnida! 약속한 겁니다!; **a good ~** (bargain) charhan hŭngjŏng 잘한 흥정; (a lot) mani 많이; **a great ~ of** (lots) manŭn 많은 **2** v/t cards tollida 돌리다; **~ a blow to** …ege t'agyŏgŭl chuda …에게 타격을 주다

♦ **deal in** (trade in) kŏraehada 거래하다

♦ **deal out** cards nanuŏ chuda 나누어 주다

♦ **deal with** (handle) ch'ŏrihada 처리하다; (do business with) kŏraehada 거래하다

dealer (merchant) sang-in 상인; (drug ~) mayak tillŏ 마약 딜러; (in cards) tillŏ 딜러

dealing (drug ~) mayak kŏrae 마약 거래

dealings (business) kŏrae 거래

dean (of college) haktchang 학장

dear adj ch'inaehanŭn 친애하는; (expensive) kagyŏgi pissan 가격이 비싼; **Dear Sir** chon-gyŏnghanŭn

sŏnsaengnimkke chonjŏnghanŭn 선생님 존경하는 선생님 **Dear Richard / Margaret** saranghanŭn Rich'adŭ / Magaret 사랑하는 리차드 / 마가렛; **be sentenced ~ sahyŏng sŏn-gorŭl pat-tta** **dearly** love kkŭmtchigi 끔찍이

death chugŭm 죽음; **~s** (fatalities) samangja 사망자; **be sentenced ~** sahyŏng sŏn-gorŭl pat-tta 사형 선고를 받다

death penalty sahyŏng 사형

death toll samangjasu 사망자수

debatable nonjaeng-ŭi yŏjiga innŭn 논쟁의 여지가 있는

debate 1 n nonjaeng 논쟁; POL shimsim-ŭi 2 v/i suk-kkohada 숙고하다 3 nonjaenghada 논쟁하다

debauchery pangt'ang 방탕

debit 1 n chan-goran 잔고란 2 v/t account, amount chan-gorane kiip'ada 잔고란에 기입하다

debris p'ap'yŏn 파편

debt pit 빚; **be in ~** piji it-tta 빚이 있다

debtor ch'aemuja 채무자

debug room toch'ŏng changch'irŭl chegŏhada 도청 장치를 제거하다; COMPUT kyŏrhamŭl koch'ida 결함 고치다

début n tebyu 데뷔

decade ship nyŏn 십 년

decadent t'oep'yejŏgin 퇴폐적인

decaffeinated k'ap'eini chegŏdoen 카페인이 제거된

decapitate mogŭl charŭda 목을 자르다

decay 1 n (process) pup'ae 부패; (civilization) soet'oe 쇠퇴; (decayed matter) ssŏgŭm 썩음 2 v/i pup'aehada 부패하다; (of civilization) soet'oehada 쇠퇴하다; (of teeth) ch'ungch'iga saenggida 충치가 생기다

deceased: **the ~** chugŭn saram 죽은 사람

deceit sogimsu 속임수

deceitful namŭl soginŭn 남을 속이는

deceive sogida 속이다

December shibiwŏl 십이월

decency yeŭi parŭm 예의 바름; **he had the ~ to …** kŭnŭn … hal

nŏngdŏui yeŭinŭn issŏt-tta 그는 …
정도의 예의는 있었다
cent person nŏgŭrŏun 너그러운;
cceptable) kwaench'anŭn
nŏngdŏui kwaench'ŭn 정도의;
easonable) sangdanghi choŭn
당히 좋은; (meal, sleep)
nŏkttanghan 적당한
centralize administration chibang
unkkwŏnhwa hada 지방 분권화
다
ception sogim 속임
ceptive (in appearance)
ogiwanŭn tarŭn 보기와는 다른
ceptively: it looks ~ simple
ogiwanŭn taruge kandanhaji ant'a
기와는 다르게 간단하지 않다
cibel teshibel 데시벨
cide 1 v/t (make up one's mind)
yŏlsshimhada 결심하다; (conclude)
yŏltchŏnghada 결정하다; (settle)
yŏltchŏng-ŭl naerida 결정을 내리다
v/i kyŏltchŏnghada 결정하다; you
nega kyŏltchŏnghae 네가 결정해
cided (definite) tturyŏt'an 뚜렷한
cider (match etc) kyŏlssŭngjŏn
승전
cimal n sosu 소수
cimal point sosutchŏm 소수점
cimate manŭn surŭl chugida 많은
를 죽이다
cipher p'andok'ada 판독하다
cision kyŏltchŏng 결정;
conclusion) kyŏllon 결론: come to
~ kyŏllone irŭda 결론에 이르다
cision-maker ŭisa kyŏltchŏngja
사 결정자
cisive (resolute) tanhohan 단호한;
crucial) kyŏltchŏngjŏgin 결정적인
ck (of ship) kapp'an 갑판; (of bus)
h'ŭng 층; (of cards) han pŏl 한 벌
ckchair hyudaeyong ŭija 휴대용
자
claration (statement) sŏngmyŏng
명; (of independence) sŏnŏn 선언;
~ of war sŏnjŏn p'ogo 선전 포고
clare (state) kongp'yohada
표하다; independence sŏnŏnhada
언하다; (at customs) sin-gohada
고하다; ~ war sŏnjŏn p'ogohada
전 포고하다

decline 1 n (fall) kamso 감소; (in standards) harak 하락; (in health) ak'wa 악화 2 v/t invitation kŏjŏrhada 거절하다; ~ to comment ŏn-gŭbŭl kŏbuhada 언급을 거부하다; ~ to accept padadŭriji ant'a 받아들이지 않다 3 v/i (refuse) kŏjŏrhada 거절하다; (decrease) kamsohada 감소하다; (of health) ak'wadoeda 악화되다

declutch k'ŭllŏch'irŭl p'ulda 클러치를 풀다

decode haedok'ada 해독하다

decompose pup'aehada 부패하다

décor changsshik 장식

decorate (with paint, paper) changsshik'ada 장식하다; (adorn) kkumida 꾸미다; soldier hunjang-ŭl suyŏhada 훈장을 수여하다

decoration (paint, paper, ornament) changshik 장식

decorative changshingnyong-ŭi 장식용의

decorator (interior ~) shillae changshik-kka 실내 장식가

decoy n yuinyong 유인용

decrease 1 n kamso 감소 2 v/t churida 줄이다 3 v/i chulda 줄다

dedicate book etc pach'ida 바치다; ~ oneself to …e chŏnnyŏmhada …에 전념하다

dedication (in book) hŏnjŏngsa 헌정사; (to cause, work) chŏnnyŏm 전념

deduce ch'uronhada 추론하다

deduct: ~ X from Y Yesŏ Xŭl / rŭl ppaeda Y에서 X를 / 를 빼다

deduction (from salary) kongje 공제; (conclusion) ch'uron 추론

deed n (act) haeng-wi 행위; LAW kimyŏng narinhan chŭngsŏ 기명 날인한 증서

deep hole, water, sleep kip'ŭn 깊은; trouble shimgak'an 심각한; voice chŏŭmŭi 저음의; color chinhan 진한; thinker shimwŏnhan 심원한

deepen 1 v/t kipkke hada 깊게 하다 2 v/i kip'ŏjida 깊어지다; (of crisis, mystery) shimgak'aejida 심각해지다

deep freeze n kŭpssok naengdong naengjanggo 급속 냉동 냉장고;

deep-frozen food naengdong shikp'um 냉동 식품; **deep-fry** tümppuk t'wigida 듬뿍 튀기다

deer sasům 사슴

deface woegwanŭl sonsangshik'ida 외관을 손상시키다

defamation pibang 비방

defamatory pibanghanŭn 비방하는

default *adj* COMPUT miri sŏltchŏnghaen 미리 설정된; **~ value** tip'olt'ŭkkap 디폴트값

defeat **1** *n* p'aebae 패배 **2** *v/t* p'aebaeshik'ida 패배시키다; (*of task*) chwajŏlsshik'ida 좌절시키다

defeatist *adj attitude* p'aebaejuŭijŏgin 패배주의적인

defect *n* kyŏltchŏm 결점

defective kyŏltchŏmi innŭn 결점이 있는

defend chik'ida 지키다; (*back up*) onghohada 옹호하다; (*justify*) chŏngdanghwahada 정당화하다; LAW pyŏnhohada 변호하다

defendant (*in criminal case*) p'igoin 피고인

defense *n* (*protection*) pang-ŏ 방어; MIL, POL pang-wi 방위; SP subi 수비; LAW p'igoch'ŭk 피고측; (*justification*) pyŏllon 변론; (*of cause, support*) ongho 옹호; **come to s.o.'s ~** nuguŭi p'yŏni toeŏ chuda 누구의 편이 되어 주다

defense budget POL kukppangbi yesan 국방비 예산

defense lawyer p'igoch'ŭk pyŏnhosa 피고측 변호사

defenseless mubangbiŭi 무방비의

defense player SP subisu 수비수; **Defense Secretary** POL Kukppangbuhanggwan 국방부 장관; **defense witness** LAW p'igoch'ŭk chŭng-in 피고측 증인

defensive **1** *n:* **on the ~** pang-ŏhanŭn chasero 방어하는 자세로; **go on the ~** pangŏjŏgin chaserŭl ch'wihada 방어적인 자세를 취하다 **2** *adj weaponry* pang-ŏyong-ŭi 방어용의; *person* pang-ŏjŏgin 방어적인

defer *v/t* yŏn-gihada 연기하다

deference chon-gyŏng 존경

deferential chŏngjunghan 정중한

defiance panhang 반항; **in ~ of** ...ŭl/rŭl mushihago ...을/를 무시하고

defiant panhangjŏgin 반항적인

deficiency (*lack*) kyŏlp'ip 결핍

deficient: **be ~ in** ...i/ga kyŏlp'ipttoeda ...이/가 결핍되다

deficit chŏktcha 적자

define *word* chŏng-ŭirŭl naerida 정의를 내리다; *objective* ttŭsŭl palk'ida 뜻을 밝히다

definite *date, time* chŏnghwak'an 정확한; *answer, improvement* myŏnghwak'an 명확한; (*certain*) hwaksshinhanŭn 확신하는; **are you ~ about that?** hwaksshin-hamnikka? 확신합니까?; **nothing has been arranged** hwaktchŏng-doen kŏn, amu kŏtto ŏpssŭmnida 확정된 건, 아무 것도 없습니다

definite article chŏnggwansa 정관사

definitely hwaksshirhi 확실히

definition (*of word*) chŏng-ŭi chŏngŭi 정의; (*of objective*) ttŭsŭl palk'im 뜻을 밝힘

definitive kyŏltchŏngjŏgin 결정적인

deflect *ball, blow* pinnagage hada 빗나가게 하다; *criticism* p'yŏnhyang-shik'ida 편향시키다; (*from course of action*) pŏsŏnage hada 벗어나게 하다; **be ~ed from** ...ŭl/rŭl pyŏn-gyŏnghada ...을/를 변경하다

deform pyŏnhyŏngshik'ida 변형시키다

deformity kihyŏng 기형

defraud sach'wihada 사취하다

defrost *v/t food* nogida 녹이다; *fridge* sŏrirŭl ŏpssaeda 서리를 없애다

deft *person* somsshi choŭn 솜씨 좋은; *fingers* nŭngsuk'an 능숙한

defuse *bomb* shin-gwanŭl chegŏhada 신관을 제거하다; *situation* chinjŏngshik'ida 진정시키다

defy panhanghada 반항하다

degenerate *v/i t'arak'ada 타락하다; **into** ...(ŭ)ro pyŏnjildoeda ...(으)로 변질되다

degrade ch'emyŏnŭl sonsangshik'ida 체면을 손상시키다

degrading *position, work* ch'emyŏn sonsangshik'inŭn 체면을 손상시키는

...ree (*from university*) hagwi 학위;
...f temperature, angle, latitude) to
...; (*amount*) chŏngdo 정도; **by ~s**
...'ach'a 차차; **get one's ~** hagwirŭl
...ada 학위를 따다
...ydrated t'alssudoen 탈수된
...ice windshield chebinghada
... 빙하다; *airplane wings*
...angbinghada 방빙하다
...icer (*spray*) chebingje 제빙제
...gn: ~ **to** komapkkedo … hae
...ushida 고맙게도 … 해 주시다
...ty shin 신
...ected nakttamhan 낙담한
...ay 1 *n* yŏn-gi 연기 2 *v/t* yŏn-gihada
...기하다; **be ~ed** (*of person*)
...igak'ada 지각하다; (*of train,*
...ane) yŏnch'ak'ada 연착하다 3 *v/i*
...ich'ehada 지체하다
...egate 1 *n* taep'yoja 대표자 2 *v/t*
...sk wiimhada 위임하다; *person*
...ep'yoro immyŏnghada 대표로
...명하다
...egation (*of task*) wiim 위임; (*of*
...*people*) taep'yodan 대표단
...ete saktchehada 삭제하다; (*cross*
...*ut*) chiuda 지우다
...etion (*act*) malsso 말소; (*that*
...*eleted*) saktche 삭제
...ti shikp'umjŏm 식품점
...iberate 1 *adj* koŭijŏgin 고의적인
...*v/i* suk-kkohada 숙고하다
...iberately ilburŏ 일부러
...icacy (*of fabric*) sŏmseham
... 세함; (*of problem*) mimyoham
...묘함; (*of health*) hŏyak'am 허약함;
...*act*) paeryŏ 배려; (*food*) chinmi
...미
...icate fabric sŏmsehan 섬세한; *health*
...*roblem* mimyohan 미묘한; *health*
...ŏyak'an 허약한
...icatessen shikp'umjŏm 식품점
...icious mashinnŭn 맛있는; *that*
...*as ~* mashissŏssŏyo 맛있었어요
...ight *n* kippŭm 기쁨
...ighted kippŏhanŭn 기뻐하는
...ightful *evening* chŭlgŏun 즐거운;
...*erson* yuk'waehan 유쾌한; *house*
...'waejŏk'an 쾌적한
...imit han-gyerŭl chŏnghada 한계를
...하다

delirious MED ilsshijŏk chŏngshin
ch'angnanŭi 일시적 정신 착란의;
(*ecstatic*) yŏlgwanghan 열광한
deliver paedarhada 배달하다; *message*
chŏndarhada 전달하다; *baby*
punmanshik'ida 분만시키다; **~ a
speech** yŏnsŏrŭl hada 연설을 하다
delivery (*of goods, mail*) paedal 배달;
(*of baby*) punman 분만
delivery date paedal naltcha 배달
날짜; **delivery note** suryŏngtchŭng
수령증; **delivery van** paedalch'a
배달차
delude sogida 속이다; **you're deluding
yourself** tangshin sŭsŭro ch'ak-
kkak'ago innŭn kŏyeyo 당신 스스로
착각하고 있는 거예요
deluge 1 *n* taehongsu 대홍수; *fig*
swaedo 쇄도 **2** *v/t fig* swaedohada
쇄도하다
delusion ch'ak-kkak 착각
de luxe hohwaroun 호화로운
demand 1 *n* yogu 요구; COM suyo
수요; **be in ~** suyoga it-tta 수요가
있다 **2** *v/t* yoguhada 요구하다;
(*require*) yoguhada 요구하다
demanding *job* sangdanghan noryŏgi
yogudoenŭn 상당한 노력이
요구되는; *person* yoguga shimhan
요구가 심한
demented chŏngshin ch'angnane
kŏllin 정신 착란에 걸린
Demilitarized Zone Pimujang
Chidae 비무장 지대
demise samang 사망; *fig* somyŏl 소멸
demitasse chagŭn k'ŏp'itchan 작은
커피잔
demo (*protest*) temo 데모; (*of video
etc*) sŏnjŏnnyong 선전용
democracy minjujuŭi 민주주의
democrat minjujuŭija 민주주의자;
Democrat POL Minjudang-wŏn
민주당원; (*supporter*) Minjudang
chijija 민주당 지지자
democratic minjujuŭiŭi 민주주의의
**Democratic People's Republic of
Korea** Chosŏn Minjujuŭi Inmin
Konghwaguk 조선 민주주의 인민
공화국
demo disk sŏnjŏnnyong tisŭk'ŭ
선전용 디스크

demolish *building* p'agoehada
파괴하다; *argument* twijiptta 뒤집다

demolition (*of building*) p'agoe 파괴;
(*of argument*) twijibŭm 뒤집음

demon angma 악마

demonstrate 1 *v/t* (*prove*)
iptchŭnghada 입증하다; *machine*
shiryŏnhada 실연하다 **2** *v/i*
(*politically*) shiwihada 시위하다

demonstration (*display*) kwashi
과시; (*protest*) shiwi 시위; (*of
machine*) shiryŏn 실연

demonstrative: *be ~* kamjŏng-ŭl
tŭrŏnaeda 감정을 드러내다

demonstrator (*protester*) shiwi
ch'amgaja 시위 참가자

demoralized kiga kkŏkkin 기가 꺾인

demoralizing kirŭl kkŏngnŭn 기를
꺾는

den (*study*) sŏjae 서재

denial (*of rumor, accusation*) pujŏng
부정; (*of request*) kŏjŏl 거절

denim tenim 데님

denims (*jeans*) ch'ŏngbaji 청바지

Denmark Tenmak'ŭ 덴마크

denomination (*of money*) aengmyŏn
kŭmaek 액면 금액; (*religious*)
chongp'a 종파

dense tchit'ŭn 짙은; *foliage* ugŏjin
우거진; *crowd* miltchip'an 밀집한;
(*stupid*) udunhan 우둔한

densely: *~ populated* in-guga
chomirhan 인구가 조밀한

density (*of population*) in-gu miltto
인구 밀도

dent 1 *n* ump'uk p'aein kot 움푹 패인
곳 **2** *v/t* ump'uk tŭrŏgage hada 움푹
들어가게 하다

dental *treatment* ch'iaŭi 치아의;
school etc ch'ikkwa 치과; *~ clinic*
ch'ikkwa 치과

dentist ch'ikkwa ŭisa 치과 의사

dentures ŭich'i 의치

deny *charge, rumor* puinhada
부인하다; *right, request* kŏjŏrhada
거절하다

deodorant t'alch'wije 탈취제

depart ch'ulbarhada 출발하다: *~
from* (*deviate*) …esŏ pŏsŏnada
…에서 벗어나다

department (*of company*) pusŏ 부서;

(*of university*) hak-kkwa 학과; (*of
government*) puch'ŏ 부처; (*of store*
maejang 매장; *Department of Defense* Kukppangbu 국방부; *Department of the Interior* Hwan-
gyŏngch'ŏ 환경처; *Department of
State* (Mi)Kungmusŏng (미)국무ᄉ

department store paek'wajŏm
백화점

departure (*of train, bus etc*) ch'ulba
출발; (*of person from job*)
kŭmandum 그만둠; (*deviation*) it'a
이탈; *a new ~* (*for government,
organization*) sae ch'ulbŏm 새 출ᄇ
(*for company*) sae ch'ulbal 새 출ᄇ
(*for actor, artist, writer*) saeroun
shido 새로운 시도

departure lounge taehapsshil
대합실

departure time ch'ulbal shigak 출ᄇ
시각

depend ŭijonhada 의존하다; *that ~*
sanghwang-e ttara tarŭda 상황에
따라 다르다; *it ~s on the weathe*
nalsshie tallyŏit-tta 날씨에 달려있ᄃ
~ on sth (*need*) muŏse ŭijonhada
무엇에 의존하다; *I ~ on you* nanŭr
nŏhant'e ŭijonhago it-tta 나는
너한테 의존하고 있다

dependable ŭijonhal su innŭn 의존
수 있는

dependence, dependency ŭijon
의존

dependent 1 *n* puyang kajok 부양
가족 **2** *adj* ŭijonhanŭn 의존하는

depict myosahada 묘사하다

deplorable hant'anhal 한탄할

deplore hant'anhada 한탄하다

deport kugoero ch'ubanghada 국외ᄇ
추방하다

deportation kugoe ch'ubang 국외
추방

deportation order t'oegŏ
myŏngnyŏng 퇴거 명령

deposit 1 *n* (*in bank*) yegŭm 예금; (
mineral) maejangmul 매장물; (*on
purchase*) yeyak-kkŭm 예약금; (*for
the lease on an apartment*)
chŏnsegŭm 전세금 **2** *v/t money*
yegŭmhada 예금하다; (*put down*)
not'a 놓다; *silt, mud* t'oejŏkshik'ida

적시키다
-osition LAW sŏnsŏ chŭng-ŏn 선서
-ot (train station) chŏnggŏjang
거장; (bus station) chŏngnyujang
류장; (for storage) ch'anggo 창고
-reciate v/i FIN kach'iga ttŏrŏjida
-치가 떨어지다
-reciation FIN kach'i harak 가치
-락
-ress person uurhagehada
-울하게하다
-ressed person uurhan 우울한
-ressing uurhagehanŭn
-울하게하는
-ression MED uultchŭng 우울증;
-conomic) pulgyŏnggi 불경기;
-neteorological) chŏgiap
-기압
-rive: ~ X of Y Xegesŏ Yŭl/rŭl
-paeat-tta X에게서 Y을/를 빼앗다
-rived child puruhan 불우한; area
-ananhan 가난한
-oth kip'i 깊이; (of shelf) kip'ŭm
-음; (of color) chit'ŭm 짙음; (of
-ought) shimoham 심오함; in ~
-h'ŏltchŏhage 철저하게; in the ~s of
-'inter han kyŏure 찬 겨울에; he
-vas out of his ~ (in water) kŭui
-'irŭl nŏmnŭn kip'iyŏt-tta 그의 키를
-는 깊이였다; (in discussion) kŭui
-haega mich'iji anat-tta 그의 이해가
-치치 않았다
-outation taep'yodan 대표단
-eputize for ...ŭl/rŭl taerihada
-을/를 대리하다
-outy taeri 대리
-outy leader pudaep'yo 부대표
-rail: be ~ed (of train)
-alssŏndoeda 탈선되다
-ranged hollandoen 혼란된
-relict adj building pŏryŏjin 버려진
-ride piut-tta 비웃다
-rision piusŭm 비웃음
-risive remarks, laughter piunnŭn
-웃는
-isory amount chwikkorimanhan
-꼬리만한
-rivative (not original)
-okch'angjŏgi anin 독창적이 아닌
-rive v/t ŏt-tta 얻다; **be ~d from** (of

derogatory kyŏngmyŏrhanŭn
경멸하는; ~ remark yokssŏl 욕설
descend 1 v/t naeryŏgada 내려가다;
she ~ed the staircase kŭnyŏnŭn
kyedanŭl naeryŏgat-tta 그녀는
계단을 내려갔다; be ~ed from ...ŭi
chasonida ...의 자손이다 2 v/i (of
airplane) haganghada 하강하다; (of
climber) naeryŏgada 내려가다; (of
road) kyŏngsajida 경사지다; (of
darkness) naeryŏantta 내려앉다
descendant chason 자손
descent (from mountain) hasan 하산;
(of airplane) hagang 하강; (ancestry)
kagye 가계; of Korean ~ Han-guk-
kkyeŭi 한국계의
describe myosahada 묘사하다; ~ X
as Y Xŭl/rŭl Y(ŭ)ro myosahada
X을/를 Y(으)로 묘사하다
description myosa 묘사
desegregate injong ch'abyŏl p'yeji
인종 차별 폐지
desert[1] n samak 사막; fig hwangmuji
황무지
desert[2] 1 v/t (abandon) pŏrida 버리다;
friends tŭngjida 등지다 2 v/i (of
soldier) t'aryŏnghada 탈영하다
deserted injŏgi kkŭnk'in 인적이 끊긴
deserter MIL t'aryŏngbyŏng 탈영병
desertion (abandoning) pŏrim 버림;
MIL t'aryŏng 탈영
deserve padŭl manhada 받을 만하다;
~ to ... ... hal manhada ... 할 만하다
design 1 n tijain 디자인; (drawing)
mitkkŭrim 밑그림; (for building, car
etc) sŏlgyedo 설계도; (pattern)
munŭi 무늬 2 v/t tijainhada
디자인하다; building, car, machine
sŏlgyehada 설계하다; not ~ed for
use in the home kajŏngnyong-i
anin 가정용이 아닌
designate v/t person immyŏnghada
임명하다; area etc chijŏnghada
지정하다
designer tijainŏ 디자이너; (of car,
building) sŏlgyeja 설계자
designer clothes yumyŏng tijainŏŭi
ot 유명 디자이너의 옷
design fault sŏlgyesang-ŭi

munjetchŏm 설계상의 문제점
design school tijain hak-kkyo 디자인
학교
desirable (*advisable*) paramjik'an
바람직한; (*coveted*) t'amnanŭn
탐나는
desire *n* param 바람; (*sexual*)
yongmang 욕망
desk ch'aekssang 책상; (*in hotel*)
tesŭk'ŭ 데스크
desk clerk chŏpssu kyewŏn 접수
계원
desktop publishing kŏmp'yut'ŏ
ch'ulp'an 컴퓨터 출판
desolate *adj place* hwangnyanghan
황량한
despair 1 *n* chŏlmang 절망; **in ~**
chŏlmanghayŏ 절망하여 **2** *v/i*
chŏlmanghada 절망하다; **~ of** …e
taehae chŏlmanghada …에 대해
절망하다
desperate *person, action* p'ilssajŏgin
필사적인; *situation* chŏlmangjŏgin
절망적인; **be ~ for a drink/**
cigarette surŭl mashigo/tambaerŭl
p'iugo ship'ŏ chugŭl chigyŏng-ida
술을 마시고/담배를 피우고 싶어
죽을 지경이다
desperation p'ilssajŏgim 필사적임;
an act of ~ chap'ojagishig-ŭi
haengdong 자포자기식의 행동
despise kyŏngmyŏrhada 경멸하다
despite …edo pulguhago …에도
불구하고
despondent nakttamhan 낙담한
despot p'ok-kkun 폭군
dessert hushik 후식
destination moktchŏktchi 목적지
destiny unmyŏng 운명
destitute pin-gonhan 빈곤한
destroy p'agoehada 파괴하다; *fig*
p'amyŏlshik'ida 파멸시키다; *trust,*
friendship, marriage mangch'ida
망치다
destroyer NAUT kuch'uk'am 구축함
destruction p'agoe 파괴; *fig* p'amyŏl
파멸
destructive *power* p'agoejŏgin
파괴적인; *criticism* pujŏngjŏgin
부정적인
detach tteŏnaeda 떼어내다

detachable pullihal su innŭn 분리할
수 있는
detached (*objective*) kongp'yŏngh
공평한
detachment (*objectivity*)
kongp'yŏngham 공평함
detail *n* (*small point*) sebu sahang
세부 사항; (*piece of information*)
chasehan naeyong 자세한 내용;
(*trifle*) sasohan il 사소한 일; **in ~**
chasehage 자세하게
detailed sangsehan 상세한
detain chich'eshik'ida 지체시키다;
prisoner kamgŭmhada 감금하다
detainee ŏngnyuja 억류자
detect arach'aeda 알아채다; (*of*
device) t'amjihada 탐지하다
detection (*of criminal*) palgyŏn 발
(*of crime*) palgak 발각; (*of smoke*)
t'amji 탐지
detective (*policeman*) hyŏngsa 형
detective novel t'amjŏng sosŏl 탐
소설
detector t'amjigi 탐지기
détente POL kinjang wanhwa 긴장
완화
detention (*imprisonment*) kamgŭm
감금
deter tannyŏmshik'ida 단념시키다;
X from doing Y Xi/ga Yhanŭn
kŏsŭl mot'age hada X이/가 Y하는
것을 못하게 하다
detergent sech'ŏktche 세척제
deteriorate ak'wadoeda 악화되다
determination (*resolution*) kyŏlssh
결심
determine (*decide*) kyŏltchŏnghad
결정하다; (*establish*) tanjŏnghada
단정하다
determined kyŏlsshimhan 결심한;
effort hwakkohan 확고한
deterrent *n* panghaemul 방해물
detest hyŏmohada 혐오하다
detonate 1 *v/t* p'okppal sshik'ida
폭발시키다 **2** *v/i* p'okpparhada
폭발하다
detour *n* uhoe 우회; (*diversion*) tar
kil 다른 길
detract: ~ from …ŭi kach'irŭl
ttŏrŏttŭrida …의 가치를 떨어뜨리
detriment: to the ~ of …e haerŭl

igo …에 해를 입히고

rimental haeroun 해로운

ice (in tennis) tyusŭ 듀스

aluation FIN p'yŏngkka chŏrha
가 절하

alue currency p'yŏngkka
ŏrhashik'ida 평가 절하시키다

astate p'agoehada 파괴하다; fig:
rson nŏkssil ilk'e hada 넋을 잃게
다

astating apttohanŭn 압도하는

elop 1 v/t land, (invent)
ebarhada 개발하다; activity,
siness paltchŏnshik'ida
전시키다; film hyŏnsanghada
상하다; (progress) palttalshik'ida
달시키다; illness, cold …e kŏllida
.에 걸리다 2 v/i (grow)
altchŏnhada 발전하다; (of country,
siness) kaebarhada 개발하다
eveloper (of property) kaebaltcha
발자

eloping country
ebaldosangguk 개발도상국

elopment (of land) kaebal 개발;
f business, country) sŏngjang 성장;
vent) nyussŭ 뉴스; (of film)
ŏnsang 현상; (progression)
altchŏn 발전

ice changch'i 장치; (tool) togu
구

il angma 악마

ious (sly) kyohwarhan 교활한

ise koanhada 고안하다

void: ~ of …i/ga chŏnhyŏ ŏmnŭn
.이/가 전혀 없는

ote time, money, life pach'ida
…; effort kiurida 기울이다

voted son etc hŏnshinjŏgin
신적인; be ~ to s.o.
ŏnshinjŏgida 누구에게 헌신적이다

otion (to a person) hŏnshin 헌신;
o one's job) chŏnnyŏm 전념

vour food kegŏlssŭrŏpkke mŏkta
걸스럽게 먹다; book t'amdok'ada
독하다

out tokssirhan 독실한

w isŭl 이슬

xterity somsshi choŭm 솜씨 좋음

betes tangnyoppyŏng 당뇨병

betic 1 n tangnyoppŏng hwanja

당뇨병 환자 2 adj tangnyoppyŏng-ŭi
당뇨병의

diagonal adj taegakssŏnŭi 대각선의

diagram top'yo 도표

dial 1 n (of clock) chap'an 자판; (of
meter) nun-gŭmp'an 눈금판 2 v/i
TELEC chŏnhwarŭl kŏlda 전화를
걸다 3 v/t TELEC: number taiŏrŭl
tollida 다이얼을 돌리다

dialect sat'uri 사투리

dialog taehwa 대화

dial tone palsshinŭm 발신음

diameter chik-kkyŏng 직경

diametrically: ~ opposed
chŏngbandaeŭi 정반대의

diamond (jewel, in cards) taiamondŭ
다이아몬드; (shape) taiamondŭ
moyang 다이아몬드 모양

Diamond Sutra Kŭmgganggyŏng
금강경

diaper kijŏgwi 기저귀

diaphragm ANAT hoenggyŏngmak
횡격막; (contraceptive) p'iimyong
p'esari 피임용 페사리

diarrhea sŏlssa 설사

diary (for thoughts) ilgi 일기; (for
appointments) iltchi 일지

dice 1 n chusawi 주사위 2 v/t (cut)
kkakttugi moyang-ŭro ssŏlda 깍두기
모양으로 썰다

dichotomy ibunppŏp 이분법

dictate v/t letter, novel kusurhada
구술하다

dictation padassŭgi 받아쓰기

dictator POL toktchaeja 독재자

dictatorial tone of voice
myŏngnyŏngjŏgin 명령적인; person
toktchaejŏgin 독재적인; powers
hoengp'orŭl purinŭn 횡포를 부리는

dictatorship toktchae chŏngkkwŏn
독재 정권

dictionary sajŏn 사전

die chuktta 죽다; ~ of cancer / aids
amŭro / eijŭro chuktta
암으로 / 에이즈로 죽다; I'm dying to
know / leave algo / ttŏnago ship'ŏ
chuk-kket-tta 알고 / 떠나고 싶어
죽겠다

♦ die away (of noise) chŏmjŏm
sarajida 점점 사라지다

♦ die down (of noise) churŏdŭlda

줄어들다; (*of storm, fire*)
sugŭrŏdŭlda 수그러들다; (*of excitement*) chŏmjŏm sarajida 점점 사라지다

♦ **die out** (*of custom*) sarajida 사라지다; (*of species*) somyŏrhada 소멸하다

diesel (*fuel*) tijel 디젤

diet 1 *n* (*regular food*) shikttan 식단; (*for losing weight*) taiŏt'ŭ 다이어트; (*for health reasons*) shigi yoppŏp 식이 요법 2 *v/i* (*to lose weight*) taiŏt'ŭhada 다이어트하다

differ (*be different*) tarŭda 다르다; (*disagree*) ŭigyŏnŭl tallihada 의견을 달리하다

difference ch'ai 차이; (*disagreement*) igyŏn 이견; **it doesn't make any ~** (*doesn't change anything*) amurŏn ch'aiga ŏptta 아무런 차이가 없다; (*doesn't matter*) sanggwan ŏpssŏyo 상관 없어요

different tarŭn 다른, pyŏlgaeŭi 별개의

differentiate ~ **between** between people ch'abyŏrhada 차별하다; ~ **between X and Y** Xwa/kwa Yŭl/rŭl kubyŏrhada X와/과 Y을/를 구별하다

differently tarŭge 다르게

difficult himdŭn 힘든

difficulty ŏryŏum 어려움; **with ~** ŏryŏpkke 어렵게

dig 1 *v/t* p'ada 파다 2 *v/i*: **it was ~ging into me** narŭl k'ukk'uk tchillŏt-tta 나를 쿡쿡 찔렀다

♦ **dig out** (*find*) ch'ajanaeda 찾아내다

♦ **dig up** p'ahech'ida 파헤치다; *information* ch'ajanaeda 찾아내다

digest *v/t* sohwahada 소화하다

digestible *food* sohwaga chal toenŭn 소화가 잘 되는

digestion sohwa 소화

digit (*number*) arabia suttcha 아라비아 숫자; **a four ~ number** arabia suttcha negae 아라비아 숫자 네개

digital tijit'ŏl 디지털; **~ camera** tijit'ŏl k'amera 디지털 카메라

dignified wiŏm innŭn 위엄 있는

dignitary kowi insa 고위 인사

dignity chonŏm 존엄

digress pinnagada 빗나가다

digression pinnagam 빗나감

dike (*wall*) tuk 둑

dilapidated *house* hŏmurŏjin 허물어진; *car, sofa* hŏrŏppajin 헐어빠진

dilate (*of pupils*) nŏlp'ida 넓히다

dilemma chint'oeyangnan 진퇴양난; **be in a ~** chint'oeyangnane ch'ŏhada 진퇴양난에 처하다

diligent pujirŏnhan 부지런한

dilute *v/t* muk-kke hada 묽게 하다

dim 1 *adj room, light* ŏdumch'imch'imhan 어둠침침한; *outline* hŭrit'an 흐릿한; (*stupid*) udunhan 우둔한; *prospects* irŏnal kattchi anŭn 일어날 것 같지 않은 2 *v/t*: **~ the headlights** hedŭrait'ŭrŭl kŭn-gŏriyong-ŭro pakkuda 헤드라이트를 근거리용으로 바꾸다 3 *v/i* (*of lights*) hŭrige hada 흐리게 하다

dime ship ssent'ŭ 십 센트

dimension (*measurement*) ch'isu 치수

diminish 1 *v/t* churida 줄이다 2 *v/i* chulda 줄다

diminutive 1 *n* churin irŭm 줄인 이름 2 *adj* chagŭmahan 자그마한

dimple pojogae 보조개

din *n* shikkŭrŏun sori 시끄러운 소리

dine shikssahada 식사하다

diner (*person*) shikssahanŭn saram 식사하는 사람

dinghy chagŭn pae 작은 배

dingy (*gloomy*) ŭmch'imhan 음침한; (*dirty*) tŏrŏun 더러운; **a rather ~ white** taso ch'ikch'ik'an hayanssaek 다소 칙칙한 하얀색

dining car shikttangch'a 식당차; **dining room** shikttang 식당; **dining table** shikt'ak 식탁

dinner (*in the evening*) manch'an 만찬; (*at midday*) och'an 오찬; (*gathering*) hyang-yŏn 향연

dinner guest manch'an sonnim 만찬 손님; **dinner jacket** yaksshik yahoebok 약식 야회복; **dinner party** tinŏ p'at'i 디너 파티

dinosaur kongnyong 공룡

dip 1 *n* (*swim*) mure ttwiŏdŭm 물에 뛰어듦; (*for food*) yangnyŏmtchang

…념장; (in road) kyŏngsajin kot 사진 곳 2 v/t (in liquid etc) …ltchak tamgŭda 살짝 담그다; ~ the **headlights** hedŭrait'ŭrŭl kŭn-…riyong-ŭro pakkuda 헤드라이트를 …거리용으로 바꾸다 3 v/i (of road) yŏngsaga chida 경사가 지다

…loma chŭngsŏ 증서

…lomacy oegyo 외교; (tact) …gyosul 외교술

…lomat oegyogwan 외교관

…lomatic oegyoŭi 외교의; (tactful) …uwani choŭn 수완이 좋은

…e (appalling) hyŏngp'yŏnŏmnŭn …편없는; (extreme) kŭkttanjŏgin …단적인

…ect 1 adj chiktchŏptchŏgin 직접적인; flight, train chik'aeng-ŭi …행의; person nogoltchŏgin …골적인; a ~ descendant of … …골-kkye chason …의 직계 …손 2 v/t (to a place) annaehada …내하다; play yŏnch'urhada 연출하다; movie kamdok'ada 감독하다; attention tollida 돌리다

…ect current ELEC chingnyu 직류

…ection panghyang 방향; (of movie) …amdok 감독; (of play) yŏnch'ul …출; ~s (instructions) annae 안내; (to a place) panghyang 방향; (for use) sayongppŏp 사용법; (for medicine) pogyongppŏp 복용법

…ection indicator MOT panghyang …yoshidŭng 방향 표시등

…ectly 1 adv (straight) paro 바로; (soon) kot 곧; (immediately) …ŭmbang 금방 2 conj …hajamaja ….하자마자; ~ I've finished naega …kŭnnaejamaja 내가 끝내자마자

…ector (of company) isa 이사; (of …lay) yŏnch'ultcha 연출자; (of …ovie) kamdok 감독

…ectory chuso sŏngmyŏngnok 주소 …명록; TELEC chŏnhwa pŏnhobu …화 번호부; COMPUT tirekt'ori …렉토리

…t mŏnji 먼지

…t cheap aju hŏlkkapssŭi 아주 …값의

…ty 1 adj tŏrŏun 더러운; (pornographic) ŭmnanhan 음난한

2 v/t …ŭl/rŭl tŏrŏp'ida …을/를 더럽히다

dirty trick piyŏrhan ch'aengnyak 비열한 책략

disability shinch'e chang-ae 신체 장애

disabled 1 n: **the ~** shinch'e chang-aeja 신체 장애자 **2** adj pulguŭi 불구의

disadvantage (drawback) tantchŏm 단점; **be at a ~** pullihan iptchang-e it-tta 불리한 입장에 있다

disadvantaged hyet'aekppat-tchi mot'an 혜택받지 못한

disadvantageous pullihan 불리한

disagree ŭigyŏni tarŭda 의견이 다르다

♦ **disagree with** …wa/gwa ŭigyŏni mat-tchi ant'a …와/과 의견이 맞지 않다; (of food) …ŭi soge mat-tchi ant'a …�\ 구의 속에 맞지 않다

disagreeable pulk'waehan 불쾌한

disagreement ŭigyŏn ch'ai 의견 차이; (argument) maldat'um 말다툼

disappear sarajida 사라지다; (run away) chach'wi-rŭl kamch'uda 자취를 감추다

disappearance (of thing) somyŏl 소멸; (of person) shiltchong 실종

disappoint shilmangshik'ida 실망시키다

disappointed shilmanghan 실망한

disappointing shilmangsŭrŏun 실망스러운

disappointment shilmang 실망

disapproval pulch'ansŏng 불찬성

disapprove pulch'ansŏnghada 불찬성하다; **~ of** …e pulch'ansŏnghada …에 불찬성하다

disarm 1 v/t robber mugirŭl ppaeat-tta 무기를 빼앗다; militia mujang haejeshik'ida 무장 해제시키다 **2** v/i mujang-ŭl haejehada 무장을 해제하다

disarmament mujang haeje 무장 해제

disarming ch'ŏninjinhan 천진한

disaster (natural) ch'ŏnjaejibyŏn 천재지변; (fiasco) shilp'ae 실패

disaster area chaehae chiyŏk 재해 지역; fig (person) kujebullŭng-in saram 구제불능인 사람

disastrous p'ihaega makssshimhan 피해가 막심한

disbelief: *in* ~ mitkkiji annŭn mosŭbŭro 믿기지 않는 모습으로

disc tisŭk'ŭ 디스크

discard *old clothes* pŏrida 버리다; *boyfriend* ch'abŏrida 차버리다; *theory, habits* p'yegihada 폐기하다

discern (*see*) shikppyŏrhada 식별하다

discernible arabol su innŭn 알아볼 수 있는

discerning anmogi nop'ŭn 안목이 높은

discharge 1 *n* (*from hospital*) t'oewŏn 퇴원; (*from army*) chedae 제대 **2** *v/t* (*from hospital*) t'oewŏnshik'ida 퇴원시키다; (*from army*) chedaeshik'ida 제대시키다; (*from job*) haegoshik'ida 해고시키다

disciple (*religious*) cheja 제자

disciplinary chinggyeŭi 징계의

discipline 1 *n* kyuyul 규율 **2** *v/t pŏrŭsŭl karŭch'ida 버릇을 가르치다; *employee* chinggyehada 징계하다

disc jockey tisŭk'ŭ chak'i 디스크 자키

disclaim puinhada 부인하다

disclose tŭrŏnaeda 드러내다

disclosure (*of information*) nusŏl 누설; (*about scandal*) p'ongno 폭로

disco tisŭk'o 디스코

discolor pyŏnsaeksshik'ida 변색시키다

discomfort (*pain*) ap'ŭm 아픔; (*embarrassment*) ŏsaek'am 어색함

disconcert tanghwanghage hada 당황하게 하다

disconcerted tanghwanghan 당황한

disconnect pullishik'ida 분리시키다; (*supply*) chungdanshik'ida 중단시키다; *telephone* kkŭnt'a 끊다

disconsolate sŏgŭlp'ŭn 서글픈

discontent pulman 불만

discontented pulmansŭrŏun 불만스러운

discontinue chungjihada 중지하다

discord MUS purhyŏp'waŭm 불협화음; (*in relations*) purhwa 불화

discotheque tisŭk'o t'ek 디스코 텍

discount 1 *n* harin 할인 **2** *v/t goods*

harinhada 할인하다; *theory* mushihada 무시하다

discourage (*dissuade*) mot'age ha~ 못하게 하다; (*dishearten*) nakttamshik'ida 낙담시키다

discover palgyŏnhada 발견하다; *talent* palgurhada 발굴하다

discoverer palgyŏnhan saram 발견 사람

discovery palgyŏn 발견

discredit *v/t person* ...ŭi shinyong-i ttŏrŏjigehada ...의 신용이 떨어지 하다; *theory* ...ŭi shinbingssŏng-ŭl ttŏrŏttŭrida ...의 신빙성을 떨어뜨리다

discreet *person* shinjunghan 신중한

discrepancy (*in story*) mosun 모순; (*in accounts etc*) purilch'i 불일치

discretion shinjungham 신중함; *at your* ~ tangshinŭi chaeryang-ŭro 당신의 재량으로

discriminate: ~ *against* ...ŭl/rŭl ch'abyŏrhada ...을/를 차별하다; ~ *between X and Y* (*distinguish*) Xwa/gwa Yŭl/rŭl kubyŏrhada X와/과 Y을/를 구별하다

discriminating shikppyŏllyŏgi innŭ 식별력이 있는

discrimination (*sexual, racial etc*) ch'abyŏl 차별

discus (*object*) wŏnban 원반; (*even* wŏnban tŏnjigi 원반 던지기

discuss (*talk about*) hwaje sama yaegihada 화제 삼아 얘기하다; (*of article*) nonŭihada 논의하다; (*in negotiations*) ŭinonhada 의논하다

discussion (*debate*) t'oron 토론; *have a* ~ *with s.o.* nuguwa ŭinonhada 누구와 의논하다; *it's st under* ~ ajik nonŭijung-ida 아직 논의중이다

disease chilbyŏng 질병

disembark *v/i* naerida 내리다

disenchanted: ~ *with* ...e tŏ isang maeryŏgŭl nŭkkiji mot'anŭn ...에 이상 매력을 느끼지 못하는

disengage noajuda 놓아주다

disentangle p'ulda 풀다

disfigure *person* oemorŭl ch'uhage mandŭlda 외모를 추하게 만들다; *thing* oegwanŭl sonsangshik'ida

관을 손상시키다

grace 1 n pulmyŏng-ye 불명예; *a
(person)* ch'iyok 치욕; *it's a ~*
'iyoktchŏgin iriyeyo 치욕적인
이예요; *in ~* pulmyŏng-yesŭrŏpkke
yŏnmogŭl irŭn 불명예스럽게
목을 잃은, ch'emyŏnŭl irŭn 체면을
은 2 *v/t* ...ŭi such'iga toeda ...의
치가 되다
graceful such'isŭrŏun 수치스러운
gruntled pulmansŭrŏun
만스러운
guise 1 n wijang 위장; *(costume,
ake-up)* pyŏn-jang 변장 2 *v/t*
ijanghada 위장하다;
iaesaek'aji ant'a 내색하지 않다; *~
neself as ...*(ŭ)ro pyŏnjanghada
.(으)로 변장하다; *he was ~d as
inŭn ...*(ŭ)ro wijanghaet-tta 그는
.(으)로 위장했다
gust 1 n hyŏmo 혐오 2 *v/t*
yŏmogamŭl irŭk'ida 혐오감을
으키다
gusting *habit* hyŏmosŭrŏun
오스러운; *smell, food* kuyŏktchil
anŭn 구역질 나는; *it is ~ that ...
.ranŭn kŏsŭn hyŏmosŭrŏptta
.라는 것은 혐오스럽다
h *(part of meal)* yori 요리;
container) kŭrŭt 그릇; *(for rice)*
ongi 공기; *(for soup)* taejŏp 대접
hcloth haengju 행주
heartened nakttamhan 낙담한
heartening nakttam shik'inŭn
담시키는
heveled *hair* hŏngk'ŭrŏjin
켜러진; *clothes* tanjŏngch'i mot'an
정치 못한; *person* hŭt'ŭrŏjin
트러진
honest pujŏngjik'an 부정직한
honesty pujŏngjik 부정직
honor n pulmyŏng-ye 불명예;
*ring ~ on ...*ŭl / rŭl
nangshinshik'ida ...을 / 를
앙신시키다
honorable pulmyŏng-yesŭrŏun
명예스러운
hwasher *(person)* sŏlgŏjihanŭn
aram 설거지하는 사람; *(machine)*
ŏlgŏji kigye 설거지 기계
hwashing liquid chubangyong

seje 주방용 세제
dishwater sŏlgŏji mul 설겆이 물
disillusion *v/t* hwansang-ŭl pŏrige
hada 환상을 버리게 하다
disillusionment hwanmyŏl 환멸
disinclined maŭmi naek'iji annŭn
마음이 내키지 않는
disinfect sodok'ada 소독하다
disinfectant sodongnyak 소독약
disinherit sangsok-kkwŏnŭl
pakt'arhada 상속권을 박탈하다
disintegrate hŏmurŏjida 허물어지다;
(of marriage, building)
punggoedoeda 붕괴되다
disinterested *(unbiased)*
kongp'yŏnghan 공평한
disjointed chal yŏn-gyŏri toeji annŭn
잘 연결이 되지 않은
disk *(shape)* wŏnbanhyŏng 원반형;
COMPUT tisŭk'et 디스켓; *on ~*
tisŭk'ese chŏjangdoen 디스켓에
저장된
disk drive COMPUT tisŭk'et tŭraibŭ
디스켓 드라이브
diskette tisŭk'et 디스켓
dislike 1 n shirŏham 싫어함 2 *v/t*
shirŏhada 싫어하다
dislocate t'algushik'ida 탈구시키다
dislodge umjigida 움직이다
disloyal pulch'ungsshirhan 불충실한
disloyalty pulch'ungsshil 불충실
dismal *weather* ŭmsanhan 음산한;
news, prospect ch'imurhan 침울한;
(depressed) uurhan 우울한;
(pessimistic) pujŏngjŏgin 부정적인;
failure hyŏngp'yŏnŏmnŭn 형편없는
dismantle haech'ehada 해체하다
dismay 1 n *(alarm)* tanghwang 당황;
(disappointment) nakttam 낙담 2 *v/t*
tanghwanghage hada 당황하게 하다
dismiss *employee* haegoshik'ida
해고시키다; *suggestion* kŏjŏrhada
거절하다; *idea, thought*
ttŏlch'yŏbŏrida 떨쳐버리다;
possibility mushihada 무시하다
dismissal *(of employee)* haego 해고
disobedience pulboktchong 불복종
disobedient marŭl tŭt-tchi annŭn
말을 듣지 않는
disobey kŏyŏk'ada 거역하다
disorder *(untidiness)* chijŏbunham

지저분함; (*unrest*) hollan 혼란; MED chang-ae 장애

disorderly *room, desk* ŏjillŏ noŭn 어질러 놓은; (*unruly*) mubŏbŭi 무법의

disorganized mujilssŏhan 무질서한

disoriented panghyang kamgagŭl irŏbŏrin 방향 감각을 잃어버린

disown ŭijŏrhada 의절하다

disparaging hŏlttŭnnŭn 헐뜯는

disparity pulgyunhyŏng 불균형

dispassionate naengjŏnghan 냉정한

dispatch *v/t* (*send*) palssonghada 발송하다

dispensary (*in pharmacy*) chojeshil 조제실

dispense: ~ *with* ... ŏpsshi hada ... 없이 하다

disperse 1 *v/t* hŭt'ŏjige hada 흩어지게 하다 **2** *v/i* (*of crowd*) hŭt'ŏjida 흩어지다; (*of mist*) hŭt'ŏ ŏpssŏjida 흩어 없어지다

displace (*supplant*) pakkwŏ not'a 바꾸어 놓다

display 1 *n* chŏnshi 전시; (*in store window*) chinyŏl 진열; COMPUT tisŭp'ŭllei 디스플레이; **be on ~** (*at exhibition*) chŏnshi chung-ida 전시 중이다; (*in store*) chinyŏl chung-ida 진열 중이다 **2** *v/t emotion* p'yoshihada 표시하다; (*at exhibition*) chŏnshihada 전시하다; (*in store*) chinyŏrhada 진열하다; COMPUT hwamyŏne p'yoshihada 화면에 표시하다

display cabinet chinyŏltchang 진열장

displease pulk'waehage hada 불쾌하게 하다

displeasure pulk'wae 불쾌

disposable ssŭgo pŏril su innŭn 쓰고 버릴 수 있는; ~ *income* kach'ŏbun sodŭk 가처분 소득

disposal ch'ŏbun 처분; (*of pollutants, nuclear waste*) p'yegi 폐기; **I am at your** ~ ŏnjedŭn malman haseyo 언제든 말만 하세요; **put X at Y's** ~ Xŭl/rŭl Yŭi maŭmdaero ssŭge hada X을/를 Y의 마음대로 쓰게 하다

dispose: ~ *of* ...ŭl/rŭl ch'ŏbunhada ...을/를 처분하다

disposed: **be** ~ **to do** ... (*willing*) ...

hagop'ŭ maŭmi nada ... 하고픈 마음이 나다; **be well** ~ **toward** ...ege hogamŭl kajida ...에게 호감 가지다

disposition (*nature*) kijil 기질

disproportionate pulgyunhyŏnghan 불균형한

disprove panjŭnghada 반증하다

dispute 1 *n* nonjaeng 논쟁; (*between countries*) punjaeng 분쟁; (*industrial*) chaeng-ŭi 쟁의 **2** *v/t* (*disagree with*) pallonhada 반론하다; (*fight over*) ...ŭl/rŭl ŏdŭryŏgo ssauda ...을/를 얻으려고 싸우다

disqualify chagyŏgŭl pakt'arhada 자격을 박탈하다

disregard 1 *n* mushi 무시 **2** *v/t* mushihada 무시하다

disrepair: **in a state of** ~ hwangp'yehan sangt'aee 황폐한 상태에

disreputable *person* hyŏngp'yŏnŏmnŭn 형편없는; *area* p'yongp'ani nappŭn 평판이 나쁜

disrespect murye 무례

disrespectful muryehan 무례한

disrupt *train service* tujŏlshik'ida 두절시키다; *meeting, class* chungdanshik'ida 중단시키다

disruption (*of train service*) tujŏl 두절; (*of meeting, class*) chungdan 중단

disruptive punyŏlsshik'inŭn 분열시키는

dissatisfaction pulman 불만

dissatisfied pulmansŭrŏun 불만스러운

dissension ŭigyŏnŭi ch'ai 의견의 차이

dissent 1 *n* pandae ŭigyŏn 반대 의견 **2** *v/i*: ~ **from** ...e pandaehada ...에 반대하다

dissident *n* pandaeja 반대자

dissimilar tarŭn 다른

dissociate: ~ **oneself from** ...wa/kwa kwan-gyerŭl kkŭnt'a ...와/과 관계를 끊다

dissolute pangt'anghan 방탕한

dissolve 1 *v/t substance* nogida 녹이다 **2** *v/i* (*of substance*) noktta 녹다

dissuade mallida 말리다; ~ **X from**

i / ga Yhanŭn kŏsŭl mallida 지이 / 가
하는 것을 말리다
tance 1 n kŏri 거리; **in the ~** mŏn
ose(sŏ) 먼 곳에(서) 2 v/t: **~ one-
elf from** …(ŭ)robut'ŏ kŏrirŭl tuda
.(으)로부터 거리를 두다
tant place, time mŏn 먼; fig (aloof)
wŏnhan 소원한
taste shirŭm 싫음
tasteful shirŭn 싫은
tilled liquor soju 소주
tilled rice wine chŏngjong 정종
tinct (clear) tturyŏt'an 뚜렷한;
different) tarŭn 다른; **as ~ from**
.wa / kwanŭn tarŭge …와 / 과는
나르게
tinction (differentiation) kubyŏl
별; **hotel / product of ~**
agwŏrhan hot'el / sangp'um 탁월한
텔 / 상품
tinctive t'ŭgyuŭi 특유의
tinctly tturyŏt'age 뚜렷하게;
decidedly) hwaksshirhi 확실히
tinguish (see) pun-ganhada
분간하다; **~ between X and Y**
Kwa / gwa Yŭl / rŭl shikppyŏrhada
와 / 과 Y을 / 를 식별하다
tinguished (famous)
hŏmyŏnghan 저명한; (dignified)
ip'um innŭn 기품 있는
tort waegok'ada 왜곡하다
tract person shimnanhage hada
란하게 하다; attention ttan tero
ollige hada 딴 데로 돌리게 하다
tracted (worried) shimnanhan
란한
traction (of attention) ttan tero
ollim 딴 데로 돌림; (amusement)
ibun chŏnhŭ 기분 전환; **drive**
.o. to ~ nugurŭl mich'ige
nandŭlda 누구를 미치게 만들다
straught mich'il tŭt'an 미칠 듯한
stress 1 n (mental) komin 고민,
(physical pain) kot'ong 고통; **in ~**
hip, aircraft chonan sangt'aeŭi 조난
상태의 2 v/t (upset) koerop'ida
괴롭히다
stress signal chonan shinho 조난
신호
stribute nanuda 나누다; wealth
punbaehada 분배하다; COM

yut'onghada 유통하다
distribution (handing out) nanuŏ
chum 나누어 줌; (of wealth) punbae
분배; COM yut'ong 유통
distribution arrangement COM
yut'ong hyŏptchŏng 유통 협정
distributor COM paegŭbŏptcha
배급업자
district chiyŏk 지역; (of city) ku 구
district attorney chibang kŏmsa 지방
검사
district office kuch'ŏng 구청
distrust 1 n pulshinhom 불신 2 v/t
pulshinhada 불신하다
disturb (interrupt) panghaehada
방해하다; (upset) …ŭi maŭmŭl
ŏjirŏp'ida …의 마음을 어지럽히다;
do not ~ panghaehaji mashio
방해하지 마시오
disturbance (interruption) panghae
방해; **~s** soyo 소요
disturbed (concerned, worried)
maŭmi ŏjirŏun 마음이 어지러운;
(mentally) chŏngshin isang-ŭi 정신
이상의
disturbing maŭmŭl ŏjirŏp'inŭn
마음을 어지럽히는
disused sayongdoeji annŭn 사용되지
않는
ditch 1 n torang 도랑 2 v/t F (get rid
of) pŏrida 버리다; (drop)
kŭmanduda 그만두다
dive 1 n ttwiŏdŭlgi 뛰어들기;
(underwater) chamsu 잠수; (of
plane) kŭpkkangha 급강하; F (bar)
ssaguryŏ sultchip 싸구려 술집; **take
a ~** (of dollar etc) p'ongnak'ada
폭락하다 2 v/i ttwiŏdŭlda 뛰어들다;
(underwater) chamsuhada 잠수하다;
(of plane) kŭpkkanghahada
급강하다
diver (off board) taibŏ 다이버;
(underwater) chamsubu 잠수부
diverge kallajida 갈라지다
diverse tayanghan 다양한
diversification COM saŏbŭi tagak'wa
사업의 다각화
diversify v/i COM saŏbŭl
tagak'washik'ida 사업을 다각화시키
다
diversion (for traffic) uhoe 우회; (to

distract attention) chuŭirŭl ttan tero tollim 주의를 딴 데로 돌림

diversity tayangssŏng 다양성

divert *traffic* uhoeshik'ida 우회시키다; *attention* ttan tero tollida 딴 데로 돌리다

divest: ~ *X of Y* Xegesŏ Yŭl/rŭl ppaeat-tta X에게서 Y을/를 빼앗다

divide nanuda 나누다

dividend FIN paedanggŭm 배당금; *pay* ~*s* fig idŭgi toeda 이득이 되다

divine REL shinsŏnghan 신성한; F aju mŏtchin 아주 멋진

diving (*from board*) taibing 다이빙; (*scuba* ~) sŭk'ubŏ taibing 스쿠버 다이빙

diving board taibing tae 다이빙 대

divisible nanul su innŭn 나눌 수 있는

division MATH nanutssem 나눗셈; (*in party etc*) punyŏl 분열; (*splitting into parts*) pulli 분리; (*of company*) pusŏ 부서

divorce 1 *n* ihon 이혼; *get a* ~ ihonhada 이혼하다 2 *v/t* ...wa/kwa ihonhada ...와/과 이혼하다 3 *v/i* ihonhada 이혼하다

divorced ihonhan 이혼한; *get* ~*d* ihonhada 이혼하다

divorcee (*man*) ihonnam 이혼남; (*woman*) ihonnyŏ 이혼녀

divulge nusŏrhada 누설하다; *secret* palk'ida 밝히다

DIY (= *do-it-yourself*) sonsu mandŭlgi 손수 만들기

DIY store tiaiwai kage 디아이와이 가게

dizzy: *feel* ~ hyŏn-gitchŭng-i nada 현기증이 나다

DMZ (= *Demilitarized Zone*) Pimujang Chidae 비무장 지대

DNA (= *deoxyribonucleic acid*) tioksshiribo haekssan 디옥시리보 핵산

do 1 *v/t* hada 하다; *one's hair* sonjirhada 손질하다; *French, chemistry* kongbuhada 공부하다; *100mph etc* ...ŭi sokttorŭl naeda ...의 속도를 내다; *what are you* ~*ing tonight?* onŭl chŏnyŏk mwŏ halkkŏyeyo? 오늘 저녁에 뭐 할꺼예요?; *I don't know what to* ~

ŏttŏk-kke haeya haltchi morŭgessŏyo 어떻게 해야 할지 모르겠어요; *no, I'll* ~ *it* aniyo, chegahagessŭmnida 아니요, 제가 하겠습니다; ~ *it right now!* chigŭm tangjang hae! 지금 당장 해!; *have you done this before?* chŏne haebon chŏgi issŏyo? 전에 해 본 적이 있어요?; *have one's hair done* mŏrirŭl sonjirhada 머리를 손질하다 2 *v/i* (*be suitable, enough*) kwaench'an'ta 괜찮다; *that will* ~! kŭ chŏngdomyŏn twaessŏ! 그 정도면 됐어!; ~ *well* (*of person*) chal haenaeda 잘 해내다; (*of business*) saŏbi chal toeda 사업이 잘 되다; *well done!* (*congratulations!*) chal haessŏyo! 잘 했어요; *how* ~ *you* ~ chŏŭm poepkkessŭmnida 처음 뵙겠습니다 3 (*auxiliary*): ~ *you know him?* kŭ saramŭl algo issŭmnikka? 그 사람을 알고 있습니까?; *I don't know* morŭgessŏyo 모르겠어요; ~ *you like Seoul?* - *yes I* ~ Sŏurŭl choahaeyo - ne, choahaeyo 서울을 좋아해요? - 네, 좋아해요; *he works hard, doesn't he?* kŭnŭn chŏngmal yŏlsshimhiirhajyo? 그는 정말 열심히 일하죠?; *don't you believe me?* narŭl mittchi annayo? 나를 믿지 않아요?; *you* ~ *believe me, don't you?* narŭl mittchyo? 나를 믿죠?

♦ **do away with** p'yejihada 폐지하다

♦ **do in**: *I'm done in* F nanŭn nokch'oga toeŏt-tta 나는 녹초가 되었다

♦ **do out of**: *do X out of Y* Xŭl/rŭl sogyŏ Yŭl/rŭl ppaeat-tta X을/를 속여 Y을/를 빼앗다

♦ **do over** (*do again*) toep'urihada 되풀이하다

♦ **do up** (*renovate*) posuhada 보수하다; (*fasten*) chamgŭda 잠그다; *buttons* ch'aeuda 채우다; *laces* muktta 묶다

♦ **do with**: *I could* ~ ... nanŭn ...i/ga p'iryohada 나는 ...이/가 필요하다; *he won't have anything to* ~ *it* kŭnŭn kŭ ilgwa mugwanhada 그는 그 일과 무관하다

o without 1 v/i kyŏndida 견디다 v/t … ŏpsshi chinaeda … 없이 내다

cile person sunhan 순한; animal ...rugi shwiun 다루기 쉬운

ck¹ 1 n NAUT pudu 부두 pudue taeda 부두에 대다; (of ...ip) pudue taeda 부두에 대다; (of ...aceship) tok'ingshik'ida 도킹시키다

ck² LAW p'igosŏk 피고석

kyard chosŏnso 조선소

ctor n MED ŭisa 의사; (form of ...dress) ŭisa sŏnsaengnim 의사 선생님

ctorate paksa hagwi 박사 학위

ctrine shinjo 신조

cudrama tak'yument'ŏri tŭrama 다큐멘터리 드라마

cument n sŏryu 서류

cumentary (program) ...k'yument'ŏri 다큐멘터리

cumentation (documents) sŏryu 서류

dge v/t blow p'ihada 피하다; ...erson, issue kyomyohi hoep'ihada 교묘히 회피하다; question tullŏdaeda 둘러대다

e (deer) amssasŭm 암사슴

g 1 n kae 개 **2** v/t (follow) ...ihaenghada 미행하다; (of bad ...uck) kyesok'aesŏ irŏnada 계속해서 일어나다

g catcher tŭlkkae p'ohoegin 들개 포획인

gged kkŭnjilgin 끈질긴

ggie mŏngmŏng-i 멍멍이

ggy bag namŭn ŭmshigŭl ssajunŭn kŏt 남은 음식을 싸주는 것

ghouse: be in the ~ ch'emyŏnŭl ...t'a 체면을 잃다

gma kyori 교리

gmatic toksssŏnjŏgin 독선적인

-gooder kongsangjŏk sahoe ...aeryangga 공상적 사회 개량가

g tag MIL kuninŭi insshikp'yo 군인의 인식표

g-tired kijinmaektchinhan 기진맥진한

-it-yourself sonsu mandŭlgi 손수 ...ak'dŭlgi 만들기

oldrums: be in the ~ (of economy) purhwang-ida 불황이다; (of person) ch'imurhae it-tta 침울해 있다

♦ **dole out** paebunhada 배분하다

doll (toy) inhyŏng 인형; F (woman) maeryŏktchŏgin yŏja 매력적인 여자

♦ **doll up: get dolled up** mŏttchige ch'aryŏ iptta 멋지게 차려 입다

dollar tallŏ 달러

dollop n tŏng-ŏri 덩어리

dolmen koindol 고인돌

dolphin tolkkorae 돌고래

dome (of building) tunggŭn ch'ŏnjang 둥근 천장

domestic adj chores kasaŭi 가사의; news, policy kungnaeŭi 국내의

domestic animal (for agriculture) kach'uk 가축

domesticate animal kiltŭrida 길들이다; **be ~d** (of person) kasa irŭl hada 가사 일을 하다

domestic flight kungnaesŏn pihaenggi 국내선 비행기

dominant chuyohan 주요한; (influential) yuryŏk'an 유력한; BIO usŏng-ŭi 우성의

dominate chibaehada 지배하다; landscape apttohada 압도하다

domination (control) chibae 지배; (superiority) use 우세

domineering chibaejŏgin 지배적인; husband p'okkunjŏgin 폭군적인

donate money kibuhada 기부하다; time pach'ida 바치다; toys, books hŭisahada 희사하다; MED kijŭnghada 기증하다

donation (of money) kibuhada 기부; (of time) hŏnshin 헌신; (of toys, books) hŭisa 희사; MED kijŭng 기증

donkey tangnagwi 당나귀

donor (of money) kibuja 기부자; MED kijŭngja 기증자

donut tonŏt 도넛

doom n (fate) agun 악운; (ruin) p'amyŏl 파멸

doomed project p'agidoenŭn 파기되는; **we are ~** (bound to fail) urinŭn shilp'aehage toeŏit-tta 우리는 실패하게 되어있다; (going to die) urinŭn chukke toeŏit-tta 우리는 죽게 되어있다; **the ~ ship** nanp'ahal

unmyŏng-ŭi pae 난파할 운명의 배
door mun 문; (*entrance, exit*) ch'urimmun 출입문; **there's some-one at the ~** nugun-ga mune it-tta 누군가 문에 있다
doorbell ch'oinjong 초인종; **door-knob** munjabi 문잡이; **doorman** toŏ maen 도어 맨; **doormat** hyŏn-gwane innŭn kudu tak-kkae 현관에 있는 구두 닦개; **doorstep** muntchibang 문지방; **doorway** ch'uripkku 출입구
dope 1 *n* (*drugs*) mayak 마약; F (*idiot*) mŏngch'ŏng-i 멍청이; F (*information*) pimil chŏngbo 비밀 정보 2 *v/t* yagŭl mŏgida yak을 먹이다
dormant *plant* paryuk chŏngji chung-in 발육 정지 중인; **~ volcano** hyuhwasan 휴화산
dormitory kisukssa 기숙사
dosage pogyongnyang 복용량
dose *n* irhoe pogyongnyang 일회 복용량
dot *n* (*also in e-mail address*) chŏm 점; **on the ~** chŏnghwak'i 정확히
♦ **dote on** …e holttak ppajida …에 홀딱 빠지다
dotted line chŏmsŏn 점선
double 1 *n* (*amount*) tu pae 두 배; (*person*) kkok talmŭn saram 꼭 닮은 사람; (*of movie star*) tu taeyŏk 대역; (*room*) iinyong pang 이인용 방 2 *adj* (*twice as much*) tu paeŭi 두 배의; *whiskey* tŏbŭl 더블; *sink, oven* ssang-ŭro toen 쌍으로 된; *door* yangtchoguro yŏnŭn mun 양쪽으로 여는 문; *layer* tu kyŏbŭi 두 겹의; **in ~ figures** tu chari su 두 자리 수 3 *adv* tu paero 두 배로 4 *v/t* tu paero hada 두 배로 하다; (*fold*) panŭro chŏptta 반으로 접다 5 *v/i* tu paega toeda 두 배가 되다
♦ **double back** *v/i* (*go back*) toedoragada 되돌아가다
♦ **double up** (*in pain*) ap'asŏ momŭl kuburida 아파서 몸을 구부리다; (*share a room*) pang-ŭl nanŭŏ ssŭda 방을 나누어 쓰다
double-bass tŏbŭlbeisŭ 더블베이스; **double bed** tŏbŭlbedŭ 더블베드; **double-breasted** tanch'uga 단추가

yangtchoguro tallin 양쪽으로 달린; **doublecheck** *v/t & v/i* tashi hwaginhada 다시 확인한다; **double chin** ijungt'ŏk 이중턱; **double clic** *n* tŏbŭl k'ŭllik 더블클릭; **double-cross** *v/t* paebanhada 배반하다; **double glazing** ijung yuri 이중 유리; **doublepark** *v/i* ijung chuch'ashik'ida 이중 주차시키다; **double-quick**: **in ~ time** hwanggŭp'i 황급히; **double room** iinyong pang 이인용 방
doubles (*in tennis*) pokssik 복식
doubt 1 *n* (*suspicion*) ŭishim 의심; (*mistrust*) pulsshin 불신; (*uncertainty*) ŭigushim 의구심; **be ~ purhwaksshirhada** 불확실하다; **n ~** (*probably*) tabunhi 다분히 2 *v/t* ŭishimhada 의심하다
doubtful *remark, look* ŭishimtchŏg 의심쩍은; **be ~** (*of person*) ŭishimsŭrŏptta 의심스럽다; **it is ~ whether** … halji purhwaksshirhac … 할지 불확실하다
doubtfully ŭishimsŭrŏpkke 의심스럽게
doubtless hwaksshirhi 확실히
dough milkkaru panjuk 밀가루 반죽 F (*money*) ton 돈
dove pidulgi 비둘기; *fig* p'yŏnghwajuŭija 평화주의자
dowdy ch'onsŭrŏun 촌스러운
Dow Jones Average Tau Chonsŭ p'yŏnggyun chuga 다우 존스 평균 주가
down¹ *n* (*feathers*) kitt'ŏl 깃털
down² 1 *adv* (*downward*) najŭn tchoguro 낮은 쪽으로; (*onto the ground*) araetchoguro 아래쪽으로; **there** chŏgi araetchoge 저기 아래쪽에; **fall ~** ttŏrŏjida 떨어지다; **look ~** naeryŏda poda 내려다 보다 **$200 ~** (*as deposit*) kyeyak-kkŭm 200tallŏ 계약금 200달러; **go ~ sout** namtchoguro naeryŏgada 남쪽으로 내려가다; **be ~** (*of price, rate*) naerida 내리다; (*of numbers, amount*) churŏdŭro it-tta 줄어들어 있다; (*not working*) kojangna it-tta 고장나 있다; (*depressed*) ŭltchŏk'ae hada 울적해 하다 2 *prep* …ŭi

aetchogŭro ...의 아래쪽으로;
long) ...ŭl/rŭl ttara ...을/를 따라;
~ the stairs kyedanŭi
aetchogŭro tallyŏ naeryŏgada
단의 아래쪽으로 달려 내려가다;
alk ~ the road kirŭl ttara kŏt-tta
을 따라 걷다 3 *v/t* (swallow)
ashida 마시다; (destroy) ssoa
ŏmŏttŭrida 쏘아 넘어뜨리다
wn-and-out *n* pint'ŏlt'ŏri
털터리;**downcast** (dejected) p'uri
ugŭn 풀이 죽은;**downfall** *n*
ollak 몰락; (cause of ruin)
ilp'aeŭi wŏnin 실패의 원인;
wngrade *v/t person*
angdŭngshik'ida 강등시키다;
 document, forecast chŏngdorŭl
ŏröttŭrida 정도를 떨어뜨리다,
wnhearted p'uri chugŭn 풀이
은;**downhill** *adv*: **go ~** (of road)
aerimak-kkiri toeda 내리막길이
다; (of quality of work) ttŏrŏjida
어지다; (of health) yak'wadoeda
화되다; (of country) soet'oehada
퇴하다;**downhill skiing** hwalgang
ik'i 활강 스키;**download** COMPUT
unrodinghada 다운로딩하다;
ownmarket *adj* taejungtchŏgin
중적인;**down payment** kyeyak-
kŭm 계약금;**downplay** *v/t*
yŏngshihada 경시하다;**downpour**
ogu 폭우;**downright** 1 *adj idiot*
anjŏnhan 완전한; **~ lie** saeppalgan
ŏjinmal 새빨간 거짓말 2 *adv*
angerous, stupid etc aju 아주;
ownside (disadvantage) tantchŏm
점;**downsize** 1 *v/t car*
hyŏnghwahada 소형화하다;
ompany kyumorŭl churida 규모를
이다 2 *v/i* (of company) kyumoga
nulda 규모가 줄다;**downstairs**
adj araech'ŭng-ŭi 아래층의 2 *adv*
raech'ung-e(sŏ) 아래층에(서);
own-to-earth approach
niltchejŏgin 실제적인; person
yŏnshiljŏgin 현실적인;**down-town**
adj toshim-ŭi 도심의 2 *adv* toshiŭi
hungshimbue(sŏ) 도시의
 심부에(서);**downturn** (economic)
yŏnggi ch'imch'e 경기 침체
nward 1 *adj* araetchogŭroŭi

아래쪽으로의 2 *adv* araetchogŭro
아래쪽으로
doze 1 *n* sŏnjam 선잠 2 *v/i* cholda
졸다
♦**doze off** kkubŏk-kkubŏk cholda
꾸벅꾸벅 졸다
dozen yŏldu kae 열두 개; **~s of** aju
manŭn 아주 많은
DPRK (= **Democratic People's**
Republic of Korea) Chosŏn
Minjujuŭi Inmin Konghwaguk 조선
민주주의 인민 공화국
drab tanjoroun 단조로운
draft 1 *n* (of air) t'ongp'ung 통풍; (of
document) ch'ogo 초고; MIL
chingbyŏng 징병; **~ (beer)**
saengmaektchu 생맥주 2 *v/t*
document ch'ogorŭl chakssŏnghada
초고를 작성하다; MIL
chingbyŏnghada 징병하다
draft dodger chingbyŏng kip'ija 징병
기피자
draftee chingjip-ppyŏng 징집병
draftsman (of technical drawing)
toan-ga 도안가; (of plan) ibanja
입안자
drafty t'ongp'ung-i chal toenŭn
통풍이 잘 되는
drag 1 *n*: **it's a ~ having to ...** ...
haeya hanŭn kŏshi sŏnggashida ...
해야 하는 것이 성가시다; **he's a ~**
kŭnŭn ttabunhan saramida 그는
따분한 사람이다; **the main ~** han-gil
한길; **in ~** yŏjang-ŭl hago yŏjang을
하고 2 *v/t* (pull) tanggida 당기다
끌어
당기다; (search) hultta 훑다; **~**
X into Y (involve) Xŭl/rŭl Y(ŭ)ro
kkŭrŏ tŭrida X을/를 Y(으)로 끌어
들이다; **~ X out of Y** (get
information from) Y(ŭ)robut'ŏ
Xŭl/rŭl kanshinhi ppaenaeda
Y(으)로부터 X을/를 간신히 빼내다
3 *v/i* (of time) kkŭlda 끌다; (of show,
movie) chiruhada 지루하다
♦**drag away**: **drag oneself away**
from the TV t'ellebijŏnesŏ ttŏ
not'a 텔레비전에서 떼어 놓다
♦**drag in** (into conversation) ...e
taehan marŭl kkŏnaeda ...에 대한
말을 꺼내다

- **drag on** chijil kkŭlda 질질 끌다
- **drag out** (*prolong*) kkŭlda 끌다
- **drag up** (*mention*) kkŭjibŏ naeda 끄집어 내다

dragon yong 용; *fig* ŏmkkyŏk'an saram 엄격한 사람

drain 1 *n* (*pipe*) paesuro 배수로; (*under street*) hasugu 하수구; **a ~ on resources** chawŏn kogal 자원 고갈 **2** *v/t water* ppaenaeda 빼내다; *engine oil* paech'ulshik'ida 배출시키다; *vegetables* mulkkirŭl ppaeda 물기를 빼다; *land* paesu shisŏrŭl hada 배수 시설을 하다; *glass, tank* piuda 비우다; (*exhaust: person*) chich'ige hada 지치게 하다 **3** *v/i* (*of dishes*) mulkkiga marŭda 물기가 마르다

- **drain away** (*of liquid*) ppajida 빠지다
- **drain off** *water* ppaeda 빼다

drainage (*drains*) paesu 배수; (*of water from soil*) ppajim 빠짐

drainpipe paesugwan 배수관

drama (*art form*) hŭigok 희곡; (*excitement*) kŭktchŏgin sanghwang 극적인 상황; (*play: on TV*) tŭrama 드라마

dramatic yŏn-gŭgŭi 연극의; (*exciting*) kŭktchŏgin 극적인; *gesture* kwajangdoen 과장된

dramatist kŭktchak-kka 극작가

dramatization (*play*) kŭk'wa 극화

dramatize *story* kŭk'wahada 극화하다; *fig* kwajanghayŏ p'yohyŏnhada 과장하여 표현하다

drape *v/t cloth, coat* tullŏ ssŭiuda 둘러 씌우다; **~d in** (*covered with*) …(ŭ)ro tullŏ ssayŏjin …(으)로 둘러 싸여진

drapery hwijang 휘장

drapes k'ŏt'ŭn 커튼

drastic (*extreme*) chinach'in 지나친; *measures* kwagamhan 과감한; *change* kyŏngnyŏrhan 격렬한

draw 1 *n* (*in match, competition*) tongtchŏm 동점; (*in lottery*) chebi ppopkki 제비 뽑기; (*attraction*) inkkiinnŭn kŏt 인기있는 것 **2** *v/t picture, map* kŭrida 그리다; *cart* kkŭrŏ tanggida 끌어 당기다; *curtain* ch'ida 치다; *gun, knife* ppaeda 빼다; (*attract*) …ŭi chuŭirŭl kkŭlda …의

주의를 끌다; (*lead*) teryŏgada 데려가다; (*from bank account*) inch'urhada 인출하다 **3** *v/i kŭrimŭl kŭrida 그림을 그리다; (*in match, competition*) pigida 비기다; **~ near** kakkai tagagada 가까이 다가가다; (*of time*) kakkai tagaoda 가까이 다가오다

- **draw back 1** *v/i* (*recoil*) twiro mullŏnada 뒤로 물러나다 **2** *v/t* (*pull back*) twiro tanggida 뒤로 당기다
- **draw on 1** *v/i* (*advance*) kip'ŏgada 깊어가다 **2** *v/t* (*make use of*) iyonghada 이용하다
- **draw out** *v/t pocketbook* kkŏnaeda 꺼내다; *money from bank* inch'urhada 인출하다
- **draw up 1** *v/t document* chakssŏnghada 작성하다; *chair* nŭrŏnot'a 늘어놓다 **2** *v/i* (*of vehicle*) mŏmch'uda 멈추다

drawback kyŏltchŏm 결점

drawer[1] (*of desk etc*) sŏrap 서랍

drawer[2] (*person*) hwaga 화가

drawing kŭrim 그림

drawing board chedop'an 제도판; **go back to the ~** ch'ŏŭmbut'ŏ tashi shijak'ada 처음부터 다시 시작하다

drawl *n* nŭrin malt'u 느린 말투

dread *v/t* turyŏwŏhada 두려워하다

dreadful *movie, book* mushimushihan 무시무시한; *weather* pity chidok'an 지독한

dreadfully (*extremely*) mopsshi 몹시; *behave* hyŏngp'yŏnŏpsshi 형편없이

dream 1 *n* kkum 꿈 **2** *adj house etc* kkumgat'ŭn 꿈같은 **3** *v/t* kkumkkuda 꿈꾸다; (*day~*) mongsanghada 몽상하다 **4** *v/i* kkumŭl kkuda 꿈을 꾸다; (*day~*) mongsanghada 몽상하다

- **dream up** ŏngttunghan saenggagŭl haenaeda 엉뚱한 생각을 해내다

dreamer (*day~*) mongsangga 몽상가

dreamy *voice, look* kkumkkyŏlgat'ŭn 꿈결같은

dreary chiruhan 지루한

dredge *harbor, canal* chunsŏrhada 준설하다

- **dredge up** *fig* tŭlch'uŏnaeda 들추어내다

gs (*of coffee*) tchikkŏgi 찌꺼기;
~e ~ *of society* sahoe ssŭregi 사회
쓰레기

nch v/t hŭmppŏk chŏksshida 흠뻑
시다; *get ~ed* hŭmppŏk chŏt-tta
뻑 젖다

ss 1 *n* (*for woman*) tŭresŭ 드레스;
lothing) ot 옷 2 v/t *person* osŭl
'ida 옷을 입히다; *wound*
ngdaerŭl kamtta 붕대를 감다; *get
ed* osŭl iptta 옷을 입다 3 v/i (*get
ed*) ot iptta 옷 입다; ~ *in*
ack / *conservatively* kkaman
egŭro / posujŏgŭro osŭl iptta 까만
으로 / 보수적으로 옷을 입다; ~
ell osŭl chal iptta 옷을 잘 입다
ress up v/i sŏngjanghada
장하다; (*wear a disguise*)
*yŏnjanghada 변장하다; ~ *as*
…(ŭ)ro pyŏnjanghada …(으)로
장하다

ss **circle** kŭktchang-ŭi
ŭkppyŏlssŏk 극장의 특별석
sser (*dressing table*) hwajangdae
장대; (*in kitchen*) ch'antchang 찬장
ssing (*for salad*) sosŭ 소스; (*for
ound*) pungdae 붕대
ssing **room** THEA punjangshil
장실
ssing **table** hwajangdae 화장대
ssmaker yangjaesa 양재사
ss **rehearsal** ŭisang lihŏsŏl 의상
허설
ssy uahan 우아한
oble v/i (*of person*, *baby*) ch'imŭl
ŭllida 침을 흘리다; (*of liquid*)
ŭkttuk ttŏrŏjida 뚝뚝 떨어지다; sp
riburhada 드리블하다
ed *fruit etc* mallin 말린
er kŏnjogi 건조기
ft 1 *n* (*of snow*) nundŏmi 눈더미
v/i (*of snow*) parame nallyŏ ssaida
람에 날려 쌓이다; (*of ship*)
*yoryuhada 표류하다; (*go off
ourse*) hangnoesŏ pŏsŏnada
로에서 벗어나다; (*of person*)
ŏngch'ŏŏpsshi pangnanghada
처없이 방랑하다
rift apart (*of couple*) maŭmi
ŏrŏjida 마음이 멀어지다
iter pangnangja 방랑자

---

drill 1 *n* (*tool*) ch'ŏn-gonggi 천공기;
(*exercise*) yŏnssŭp 연습; MIL hullyŏn
훈련 2 v/t *hole* ttult'a 뚫다 3 v/i (*for
oil*) kumŏng naeda 구멍 내다; MIL
hullyŏnhada 훈련하다
drilling rig (*platform*) chŏn-gongdae
천공대
drily *remark* pikkoasŏ 비꼬아서
drink 1 *n* mashil kŏt 마실 것; *a ~ of
… han chan …* 한 잔; *a ~ of water*
mul han chan 물 한 잔; *go for a ~*
han chan harŏ kada 한 잔 하러 가다
2 v/t mashida 마시다 3 v/i mashida
마시다; (*consume alcohol*) surŭl
mashida 술을 마시다; *I don't ~*
nanŭn surŭl ibe taeji ansssŭmnida
나는 술을 입에 대지 않습니다
♦ **drink up** v/t & v/i ta mashida 다
마시다
drinkable mashil su innŭn 마실 수
있는
drinker ŭmjuja 음주자
drinking (*of alcohol*) ŭmju 음주
drinking water mashinŭn mul 마시는
물
drip 1 *n* pang-ul 방울; MED chŏmjŏk
점적 2 v/i ttokttok ttŏrŏjida 똑똑
떨어지다
dripdry nŏrŏsŏ mallida 널어서 말리다
dripping: ~ (**wet**) hŭmppŏk chŏjŭn
흠뻑 젖은
drive 1 *n* unjŏn 운전; (*outing*) tŭraibŭ
드라이브; (*energy*) hwallyŏk 활력;
COMPUT tŭraibŭ 드라이브;
(*campaign*) undong 운동; *it's a
long ~ to the station from here*
yŏgisŏ yŏk-kkajinŭn ch'aro orae
kayo 여기서 역까지는 차로 오래
가요; *left-* / *right-hand ~* MOT
oenson / orŭnson chabi unjŏn
왼손 / 오른손 잡이 운전 2 v/t *vehicle*
molda 몰다; (*take in car*) ch'aro
teryŏda chuda 차로 데려다 주다;
TECH chakttongshik'ida 작동시키다;
that noise / *he is driving me mad*
chŏ soŭmi / kŭga narŭl mich'ige
mandŭrŏyo 저 소음이 / 그가 나를
미치게 만들어요 3 v/i unjŏnhada
운전하다
♦ **drive at**: *what are you driving at?*
musŭn marŭl haryŏnŭn kŏyeyo?

무슨 말을 하려는 거예요?

♦ **drive away 1** *v/t* ch'ae t'aeugo kaböridda 차에 태우고 가버리다; (*chase off*) tchoch'aböridda 쫓아버리다 **2** *v/i* ch'arŭl t'ago kaböridda 차를 타고 가버리다

♦ **drive in** *v/t* nail paktta 박다

♦ **drive off** → **drive away**

drive-in *n* (*movie theater*) tŭraibŭin kŭktchang 드라이브인 극장

driver unjŏnja 운전자; COMPUT tŭraibŏ 드라이버

driver's license unjŏn myŏnhŏtchŭng 운전 면허증

driveway ch'ado 차도

driving 1 *n* unjŏn 운전 **2** *adj* rain ŏkssugat'ŭn 억수같은

driving force ch'ujinnyŏk 추진력; **driving instructor** unjŏn kyoyuk kangsa 운전 교육 강사; **driving lesson** unjŏn kyoyuk 운전 교육; **driving school** unjŏn hagwŏn 운전 학원; **driving test** unjŏn myŏnhŏ shihŏm 운전 면허 시험

drizzle 1 *n* isŭlbi 이슬비 **2** *v/i* isŭlbiga naerida 이슬비가 내리다

drone (*noise*) wingwinghanŭn sori 윙윙하는 소리

droop *v/i* ch'uk nŭrŏjida 축 늘어지다; (*of plant*) shidŭlda 시들다

drop 1 *n* (*of rain*) pang-ul bangul 방울; (*small amount*) yakkan 약간; (*in price, temperature*) harak 하락; (*in number*) kamso 감소 **2** *v/t object* ttŏrŏttŭrida 떨어뜨리다; *person from car* naeryŏjuda 내려주다; *person from team* chemyŏngshik'ida 제명시키다; (*stop seeing*) ...wa/kwa chŏlgyohada ...와/과 절교하다; (*give up*) kŭmanduda 그만두다; *charges, demand etc* ch'wisohada 취소하다; **~ a line to** ...ege kallyak'i p'yŏnjirŭl ssŭda ...에게 간략히 편지를 쓰다 **3** *v/i* ttŏrŏjida 떨어지다; (*of prices, temperature*) harak'ada 하락하다; (*of wind*) chada 자다

♦ **drop in** (*visit*) tŭllŭda 들리다

♦ **drop off 1** *v/t person* ch'a-esŏ naeryŏjuda 차에서 내려주다; (*deliver*) chŏndarhada 전달하다 **2** *v/i* (*fall asleep*) chami tŭlda 잠이 들다;

(*decline*) sarajida 사라지다

♦ **drop out** (*withdraw*) kŭmanduda 그만두다; (*of school*) chungt'oeha 중퇴하다

dropout (*from school*) chungt'oeja 중퇴자; (*from society*) nagoja 낙오

drops (*for eyes*) chŏmanje 점안제

drought kamum 가뭄

drown 1 *v/i* ikssahada 익사하다 **2** *v/ person* ikssashik'ida 익사시키다; *sound* tŭlliji ank'e hada 들리지 않 하다; **be ~ed** ikssahada 익사하다

drowsy narŭnhan 나른한

drudgery tanjoroun il 단조로운 일

drug 1 *n* MED yak'ut 약; (*illegal*) maya 마약; **be on ~s** mayagŭl hada 마약 하다 **2** *v/t* mach'wihada 마취하다

drug addict mayak sang-yongja 마 상용자

drug dealer mayak p'anmaeja 마약 판매자

druggist yakssa 약사

drugstore *yak-kkugi ttallin chap'wajŏm* 약국이 딸린 잡화점

drug trafficking mayak kŏrae 마약 거래

drum 1 *n* MUS puk 북; (*in western music*) tŭrŏm 드럼; (*container*) tŭrŏmt'ong 드럼통

♦ **drum into**: **drum X into Y** Xŭl/r Yege panbok'ayŏ karŭch'ida X을 / Y에게 반복하여 가르치다

♦ **drum up**: **~ support** chijirŭl kwŏnyuhada 지지를 권유하다

drummer pugŭl ch'inŭn saram 북을 치는 사람; (*western or ethnic music* tŭrŏmŏ 드러머; (*Korean music*) ko 고수

drumstick MUS pukch'ae 북채; (*of poultry*) takttari 닭다리

drunk 1 *n* (*habitually*) sulkkun 술꾼 (*on one occasion*) sul ch'wihan saram 술 취한 사람 **2** *adj* sul ch'wihan 술 취한; **get ~** sure ch'wihada 술에 취하다

drunk driving ŭmju unjŏn 음주 운전

drunken *voices, laughter* ch'wijung 취중의; *party* manch'wihan 만취한

dry 1 *adj clothes* marŭn 마른; *skin, mouth, ground* kŏnjohan 건조한; *wine* talji anŭn 달지 않은; (*ironic)* kkonŭn 비꼬는; (*where alcohol is* ...nned) kŭmjuŭi 금주의 **2** *v/t* *clothes* ...allida 말리다; *dishes* mallida ...리다; **~ one's eyes** nunmurŭl ...ktta 눈물을 닦다 **3** *v/i* marŭda ...르다

...**ry out** (*of alcoholic*) alk'ool ...nungdok ch'iryorŭl pat-tta 알코올 ...독 치료를 받다

...**ry up** (*of river*) passak marŭda ...싹 마르다; (*be quiet*) choyonghi ...ada 조용히 하다

...**v-clean** *v/t* tŭraik'ŭllininghada ...라이클리닝하다

...**v-cleaner** set'aksso 세탁소

...**v-cleaning** (*clothes*) tŭraik'ŭllining ...라이클리닝

...**er** (*machine*) kŏnjogi 건조기

...**y field** pat 밭

...**P** (= *desktop publishing*) ...ŏmp'yut'ŏ ch'ulp'an 컴퓨터 출판

...**al** ijung-ŭi 이중의; **have ~ nation-** ...**lity** ijung kuktchŏgŭl kajida 이중 ...적을 가지다

...**b** *movie* tŏbinghada 더빙하다

...**bious** (*suspect*) sŏgyŏnch'i anŭn ...연치 않은; (*having doubts*) ...uishimsŭrŏun 의심스러운

...**ck 1** *n* ori 오리 **2** *v/i* mŏrirŭl hwaek ...ugida 머리를 홱 숙이다 **3** *v/t head* ...hwaek sugŭrida 홱 수그리다; ...*uestion* p'ihada 피하다

...**d** *n* (*false bill*) wijo chip'ye 위조 ...지폐

...**e** (*owed*) chiburhagiro toeŏ innŭn ...지불하기로 되어 있는; (*proper*) ...nattanghan 마땅한; **be ~** (*of train,* ...*baby etc*) ... hal yejŏng-ida ... 할 ...예정이다; **when is your husband** ...**~?** namp'yŏnŭn ŏnje ol yejŏng-...yeyo? 남편은 언제 올 예정이에요?; ...**when is the baby ~?** ainŭn ŏnje ...t'aeŏnal yejŏng-in-gayo? 아이는 ...언제 태어날 예정인가요?; **~ to** ...(*because of*) ... ttaemune ... 때문에; ...**be ~ to** (*be caused by*) ... ttaemune ...irŏnada ... 때문에 일어나다; **in ~** ...**course** ttaega toemyŏn 때가 되면

...**ull** *weather* hŭrin 흐린; *sound* ...tunt'ak'an 둔탁한; *pain* tunhan 둔한; ...(*boring*) chiruhan 지루한

duly (*as expected*) yejŏngdaero 예정대로; (*properly*) ch'ungbunhi 충분히

dumb (*mute*) pŏng-ŏriŭi 벙어리의; (*stupid*) ŏrisŏgŭn 어리석은

dummy (*for clothes*) manek'ing 마네킹

dump 1 *n* (*for garbage*) ssŭregi pŏrinŭn kot 쓰레기 버리는 곳; (*unpleasant place*) chijŏbunhan changso 지저분한 장소 **2** *v/t* (*throw away*) naebŏrida 내버리다; (*dispose of*) pŏrida 버리다; *toxic waste, nuclear waste* p'yegihada 폐기하다

dumpling tŏmp'ŭlling 덤플링

dune morae ŏndŏk 모래 언덕

dung ttong 똥

dungarees melppang paji 멜빵 바지

dunk *biscuit* tchigŏ mŏktta 찍어 먹다

duo (*singers*) ijungch'ang 이중창; (*instrumentalists*) ijungju 이중주

duplex (**apartment**) chungch'ŭnghyŏng-ŭi ap'at'ŭ 중층형의 아파트

duplicate 1 *n* sabon 사본; **in ~** tu t'ong-ŭro 두 통으로 **2** *v/t* (*copy*) pokssahada 복사하다; (*repeat*) toep'urihada 되풀이하다

duplicate key pokssadoen yŏlssoe 복사된 열쇠

durable *material* naegusŏng-i innŭn 내구성이 있는; *relationship* orae kanŭn 오래 가는

duration chisok kigan 지속 기간

duress: under ~ hyŏp-ppagŭl pada 협박을 받아

during ... tong-an ... 동안; **~ the week** chu tong-an 주 동안

dusk haejil muryŏp 해질 무렵

dust 1 *n* mŏnji 먼지 **2** *v/t* mŏnjirŭl t'ŏlda 먼지를 털다; **~ X with Y** (*sprinkle*) Yŭl/rŭl Xe ppurida Y을/를 X에 뿌리다

dust cover (*for furniture*) mŏnji magi tŏpkkae 먼지 막이 덮개

duster (*cloth*) mŏnji tangnŭn hŏnggŏp 먼지 닦는 헝겊

dust jacket (*of book*) ch'aek k'ŏbŏ 책 커버

dustpan ssŭrebatkki 쓰레받기

dusty mŏnjit'usŏng-iŭi 먼지투성이의

Dutch 1 *adj* Nedŏllandŭŭi 네덜란드의; *go* ~ kaktcha tonŭl naeda 각자 돈을 내다 **2** *n* (*language*) Nedŏllandŭŏ 네덜란드어; *the* ~ Nedŏllandŭin 네덜란드인

duty ŭimu 의무; (*task*) immu 임무; (*on goods*) kwanse 관세; *be on* ~ tangjigida 당직이다; *be off* ~ pibŏnida 비번이다

duty-free 1 *adj* myŏnseŭi 면세의 **2** *n* myŏnsep'um 면세품

duty-free shop myŏnsejŏm 면세점

dwarf 1 *n* nanjaeng-i 난쟁이 **2** *v/t* chaga poige hada 작아 보이게 하다

♦ **dwell on** …e taehae komgomhi saenggak'ada …에 대해 곰곰히 생각하다

dwindle chŏmjŏm chagajida 점점 작아지다

dye 1 *n* yŏmnyo 염료 **2** *v/t* yŏmsaek'ada 염색하다

dying *person* chugŏganŭn 죽어가는; *industry, tradition* soet'oehanŭn 쇠퇴하는

dynamic *person* hwalttongjŏgin 활동적인

dynamism wŏndongnyŏk 원동력

dynamite *n* tainŏmait'ŭ 다이너마이트

dynamo TECH paltchŏn-gi 발전기

dynasty wangjo 왕조

dyslexia tokssŏ chang-ae 독서 장애

dyslexic 1 *adj* tokssŏ chang-aeŭi 독서 장애의 **2** *n* tokssŏ chang-aeja 독서 장애자

E

h 1 adj kak-kkagŭi 각각의 2 adv
k-kkak 각각; **they're \$1.50 ~**
ıgŏttŭrŭn kak-kkak hana-e 1.50
llŏida 그것들은 각각 하나에 1.50
러이다 3 pron kak-kkak 각각; **~**
ther sŏro 서로; **we don't like ~**
ther urinŭn sŏro joahaji annŭnda
리는 서로 좋아하지 않는다
er kanjŏrhan 간절한; **be ~ to do**
에 열심이다
er beaver ilbŏlle 일벌레
erly kanjŏrhi 간절히
erness kalmang 갈망
le tokssuri 독수리
¹ (of person, animal) kwi 귀
² (of corn) isak 이삭
ache kwiari 귀앓이
drum komak 고막
ly 1 adj (not late) iltchigin 일찍인;
ahead of time) irŭn 이른; (farther
ack in time) ch'ogiŭi 초기의; (in the
ear future) pparŭn 빠른; **in the ~**
ours of the morning ojŏn irŭn
nigane 오전 이른 시간에; **in ~**
March / June samwŏl / yuwŏl ch'oe
ᅦ월/유월 초에 2 adv (not late)
tchik iljjik; (ahead of time) irŭge
ᅵ르게
rly bird (in the morning) iltchik
rŏnanŭn saram 일찍 일어나는 사람;
who arrives early) iltchik onŭn
saram 일찍 오는 사람
mark: **~ X for Y** Xŭl/rŭl Yro
aedanghada X을/를 Y로 배당하다
rn pŏlda 벌다; holiday, drink etc ŏt-
ta 얻다; respect pat-tta 받다
nest chinjihan 진지한; **in ~**
hinjihage 진지하게
mings sodŭk 소득
rphones hedŭp'on 헤드폰; (inside
ear) ip'on 이어폰; **ear-piercing** adj
kwich'ŏng-i ttŏrojil tŭt'an 귀청이
ᅥ러질 듯한; **earring** kwigori 귀고리;

earshot: **within ~** kach'ŏng
chiyŏgesŏ 가청 지역에서; **out of ~**
nanch'ŏng chiyŏgesŏ 난청 지역에서
earth (soil) hŭk 흙; (world, planet)
chigu 지구; **where on ~ have you**
been? todaech'e ŏdie issŏssŏyo?
도대체 어디에 있었어요?
earthenware n t'ogi 토기
earthly chisang-ŭi 지상의; **it's no ~**
use … …ŭn/nŭn chŏnhyŏ
ssŭlmoŏmnŭn irida …은/는 전혀
쓸모없는 일이다
earthquake chijin 지진
earth-shattering ch'unggyŏktchŏgin
충격적인
ease 1 n (comfort) p'yŏnanham
편안함; (simplicity) yong-i 용이; **feel**
at ~ p'yŏnanhada 편안하다; **feel ill at**
~ maŭmŭl p'yŏnhi noch'i mot'ada
마음을 편히 놓지 못하다 2 v/t
(relieve) tŏlda 덜다 3 v/i (of pain)
tŏrhada 덜하다
♦ ease off 1 v/t (remove) salsal
pŏtkkida 살살 벗기다 2 v/i (of pain,
rain) nugŭrŏjida 누그러지다
easel ijel 이젤
easily (with ease) shwipkke 쉽게; (by
far) tanyŏnhi 단연히
east 1 n tongtchok 동쪽 2 adj
tongtchogŭi 동쪽의 3 adv travel
tongtchogŭro 동쪽으로
East Asia Tongnyang 동양
East Asian 1 adj Tongnyang 동양 2 n
Tongnyang saram 동양 사람
Easter Puhwalchŏl 부활절
easterly tongtchogŭrobut'ŏŭi
동쪽으로부터의; **an ~ wind**
tongp'ung 동풍
eastern tongbuŭi 동부의; (Oriental)
tongnyang-ŭi 동양의
easterner tongbu saram 동부 사람
East Sea Tonghae 동해
eastward(s) tongtchogŭro 동쪽으로
easy (not difficult) shwiun 쉬운;

(*relaxed*) p'yŏnanhan 편안한; **take things ~** (*slow down*) yŏyuitkke hada 여유있게 하다; **take it ~!** (*calm down*) nŏmu hŭngbunhaji maseyo! 너무 흥분하지 마세요!

easy chair allak ŭija 안락 의자

easy-going nŭgŭt'an 느긋한

eat v/t & v/i mŏktta 먹다

♦ **eat out** oeshik'ada 외식하다

♦ **eat up** *food* ta mŏgŏ pŏrida 다 먹어 버리다; *fig* ta ssŭge hada 다 쓰게 하다

eatable mŏgŭl su innŭn 먹을 수 있는

eaves ch'ŏma 처마

eavesdrop yŏt-ttŭt-tta 엿듣다

ebb v/i (*of tide*) ppajida 빠지다

♦ **ebb away** *fig* ppajyŏ yŏttŭt-tta 빠져 나가다

ebb tide ssŏlmul 썰물

eccentric 1 *adj* pyŏllan 별난 **2** *n* koetcha 괴짜

echo 1 *n* ullim 울림; (*in mountains*) meari 메아리 **2** v/i ullyŏ p'ŏjida 울려 퍼지다 **3** v/t *words* toep'uri hada 되풀이 하다; *views* tong-ŭihada 동의하다

eclipse 1 *n* shik 식; **~ of the sun** ilsshik 일식; **~ of the moon** wŏlsshik 월식 **2** v/t *fig* kŭnŭljige hada 그늘지게 하다

ecological saengt'aehaktchŏgin 생태학적인

ecological balance saengt'aehaktchŏk kyunhyŏng 생태학적 균형

ecologically friendly ch'inhwan-gyŏngjŏgin 친환경적인

ecologist saengt'aehaktcha 생태학자

ecology saengt'aehak 생태학

economic kyŏngjeŭi 경제의

economical (*cheap*) kyŏngjejŏgin 경제적인; (*thrifty*) chŏryak'anŭn 절약하는

economically (*in terms of economics*) kyŏngjejŏgŭro 경제적으로; (*thriftily*) chŏryagajŏ 절약하여

economics (*science*) kyŏngjehak 경제학; (*financial aspects*) kyŏngjejŏk ch'ŭngmyŏn 경제적 측면

economist kyŏngjehaktcha 경제학자

economize chŏryak'ada 절약하다

♦ **economize on** ...ŭl / rŭl chŏryak'ada ...을 / 를 절약하다

economy (*of a country*) kyŏngje 경제; (*saving*) chŏryak 절약

economy class pot'ongsŏk 보통석

economy drive chŏryak undong 절약 운동; **economy size** chŏryak'yŏng 절약형

ecosystem saengt'aegye 생태계

ecstasy hwanghol 황홀

ecstatic hwanghorhan 황홀한

eczema sŭptchin 습진

edge 1 *n* (*of knife*) nal 날; (*of table seat*) mosŏri 모서리; (*of lawn, road*) kajang chari 가장 자리; (*of cliff*) kkŭt 끝; (*in voice*) nalk'aroum 날카로움; **on ~** ch'ojohan 초조한 **2** v/t ...e t'erŭl talda ...에 테를 달 **3** v/i (*move slowly*) ch'ŏnch'ŏnhi umjigida 천천히 움직이다

edgewise: **I couldn't get a word** ~ nanŭn mal han madi hal su ŏpssŏssŏyo 나는 말 한 마디 할 수 없었어요

edgy ch'ojohan 초조한

edible mŏgŭl su innŭn 먹을 수 있는

edit p'yŏnjip'ada 편집하다

edition p'an 판

editor p'yŏnjiptcha 편집자; (*of newspaper*) p'yŏnjiptchang 편집장; **sports / political ~** sŭp'och'ŭran / chŏngch'iran p'yŏnjibwiwŏn 스포츠란 / 정치란 편집위원

editorial 1 *adj* p'yŏnjibŭi 편집의 **2** *n* sasŏl 사설

EDP (= *electronic data processing*) chŏnja chŏngbo ch'ŏ 전자 정보 처리

educate *children, consumers* kyoyuk'ada 교육하다

educated *person* kyoyukppadŭn 교육받은

education kyoyuk 교육

educational kyoyuge kwanhan 교육에 관한; (*informative*) kyoyuktchŏgin 교육적인

eel chang-ŏ 장어

eerie ossak'an 오싹한

effect *n* yŏnghyang 영향; **take ~** (*o medicine, drug*) hyoryŏgŭl nat'anaeda 효력을 나타내다; **com**

to ~ *(of law)* shilssishidoeda 시되다

ctive *(efficient)* hyokkwajŏgin 과적인; *(striking)* insangjŏgin 상적인; *~ May 1* owŏl irilbut'ŏ hyohan 오월 일일부터 유효한

minate yŏjagat'ŭn 여자같은

rvescent kŏp'umnanŭn 거품나는

rsonality hwalgich'an 활기찬

ciency *(of person)* nŭngnyul nŭngryul 능률; *f machine, method)* hyoyul 효율 적인; *machine, method* oyultchŏgin 효율적인

ciently nŭngnyultchŏgŭro 률적으로

rt *(struggle)* sugo 수고; *(attempt)* oryŏk 노력; *make an ~ to …* ...ŭl / rŭl hagi wihae noryŏk'ada 을 / 를 하기 위해 노력하다

rtless suwŏrhan 수월한

ontery ppŏnppŏnham 뻔뻔함

usive kamjŏng-i nŏmch'inŭn 정이 넘치는

yerŭl tŭlmyŏn 예를 들면

litarian *adj* p'yŏngdŭngjuŭiŭi 등주의의

al al *(of chicken)* talgyal 달걀, eran 계란

g on puch'ugida 부추기다

cup *salmŭn talgyarŭl nonnŭn kŏp* 삶은 달걀을 놓는 컵; **egghead** **int'elli** 인텔리; **eggplant** kaji 가지; **gshell** talgyal kkŏptchil 달걀 껍질; ► PSYCH chaa 자아; *(self-esteem)* abushim 자부심

centric chagi chungshimŭi 자기 심의

pt Ijipt'ŭ 이집트

ptian 1 *adj* Ijipt'ŭŭi 이집트의 **2** *n* ipt'ŭ saram 이집트 사람

erdown *(quilt)* orit'ŏl ibul 오리털 불

nt yŏdŏl 여덟, p'al 팔

nteen yŏlyŏdŏl 열 여덟, shipp'al 팔

nteenth yŏlyŏdŏl pŏntchaeŭi 열 덟 번째의

nth yŏdŏl pŏntchaeŭi 여덟 번째의

ntieth yŏdŭn pŏntchaeŭi 여든 번째의 째의

eighty yŏdŭn 여든, p'alship 팔십

either 1 *adj* ŏnŭ han tchogŭi 어느 한 쪽의; *(both)* yangtchogŭi 양쪽의; *which one do you want? - ~ one* ŏnŭ kŏsŭl hashigessŏyo? - ŏnŭ tchoidŭn kwaench'anayo 어느 것을 하시겠어요? - 어느 쪽이든 괜찮아요 **2** *pron* ŏnŭ tchogina 어느 쪽이나; *~ can do it* ŏnŭ tchogina kŭirŭl hal su it-tta 어느 쪽이나 그 일을 할 수 있다 **3** *adv* ttohan 또한; *I won't go ~* na ttohan kaji ank'essŏyo 나 또한 가지 않겠어요 **4** *conj: ~ X or Y* Xna Y xLㅏ Y; *~ my mother or my sister will come* uri ŏmŏnina nae tongsaeng-i olgŏyeyo 우리 어머니나 내 동생이 올 거에요

eject 1 *v/t demonstrators* tchoch'anaeda 쫓아내다; *cartridge, diskette* ppaenaeda 빼내다 **2** *v/i (from plane)* t'alch'urhada 탈출하다

♦ **eke out** …ŭi pujogŭl meuda …의 부족을 메우다; *~ a living* kyŏu saenggyerŭl iŏnagada 겨우 생계를 이어나가다

el → *elevated railroad*

elaborate 1 *adj* kongdŭrin 공들인 **2** *v/i* puyŏnhada 부연하다

elapse kyŏnggwahada 경과하다

elastic 1 *adj* t'allyŏginnŭn 탄력있는 **2** *n* komujul 고무줄

elastic band komu paendŭ 고무 밴드

elasticity shinch'uksŏng 신축성

elasticized shinch'uksŏng-ŭl kajin 신축성을 가진

elated ŭigiyangyanghan 의기양양한

elation ŭigiyangnyang 의기양양

elbow 1 *n* p'alkkumch'i 팔꿈치 **2** *v/t: ~ s.o. out of the way* nugurŭl p'alkkumch'iro mirŏjech'ida 누구를 팔꿈치로 밀어제치다

elder 1 *adj* yŏnsang-ŭi 연상의 **2** *n* yŏnsang 연상

elderly nai chigŭt'an 나이 지긋한

eldest 1 *adj* naiga kajang manŭn 나이가 가장 많은 **2** *n: the ~ (in family)* maji maïl 맏이 맏이

elect *v/t* son-gŏhada 선거하다; *~ to … * …ŭl / rŭl sŏnt'aek'ada …을 / 를 선택하다

elected sŏn-gŏro tangsŏndoen 선거로

당선된
election sŏn-gŏ 선거
election campaign sŏn-gŏ undong 선거 운동
election day sŏn-gŏil 선거일
elective sŏnt'aegŭi 선택의
elector sŏn-gŏin 선거인
electoral system sŏn-gŏ pangshik 선거 방식
electorate yukkwŏnja 유권자
electric chŏn-giŭi 전기의; *fig* chagŭktchŏgin 자극적인
electrical chŏn-giŭi 전기의
electric blanket chŏn-gi tamnyo 전기 담요
electric chair chŏn-gi ŭija 전기 의자
electrician chŏn-gi kisa 전기 기사
electricity chŏn-gi 전기
electrify chŏn-girŭl t'onghage hada 전기를 통하게 하다; *fig* hŭngbunshik'ida 흥분시키다
electrocute kamjŏnsashik'ida 감전시키다
electrode chŏn-gŭk 전극
electron chŏnja 전자
electronic chŏnjaŭi 전자의
electronic data processing chŏnja chŏngbo ch'ŏri 전자 정보 처리
electronic mail chŏnja up'yŏn 전자 우편
electronics chŏnja konghak 전자 공학
electronics industry chŏnja sanŏp 전자 산업
elegance kosang 고상
elegant kosanghan 고상한
element CHEM wŏnso 원소
elementary (*rudimentary*) kibonŭi 기본의
elementary school ch'odŭnghak-kkyo 초등학교
elementary teacher ch'odŭnghak-kkyo kyosa 초등학교 교사
elephant k'okkiri 코끼리
elevate nop'ida 높이다
elevated railroad koga ch'ŏltto 고가 철도
elevation (*altitude*) nop'i 높이
elevator sŭngganggi 승강기, ellibeit'ŏ 엘리베이터
eleven yŏrhana 열 하나, shibil 십일
eleventh yŏrhan pŏntchaeŭi 열 한

번째의; *at the ~ hour* majimak su gane 마지막 순간에
eligible chagyŏgi innŭn 자격이 있는
eligible bachelor mattanghan shillangkkam 마땅한 신랑감
eliminate (*get rid of*) chegŏhada 제거하다; (*rule out*) cheoehada 제외하다; (*kill*) chugyŏ ŏpssaeda 죽여 없애다; *be ~d* (*from competition etc*) t'allak'ada 탈락하다
elimination (*from competition*) t'allak 탈락; (*of poverty*) chegŏ 제거; (*murder*) sarin ch'ŏngbu 살인 청부
elite 1 *n* chŏng-ye 정예 **2** *adj* chŏng-yeŭi 정예의
elk k'ŭn sasŭm 큰 사슴
ellipse t'awŏnhyŏng 타원형
elm nŭrŭmnamu 느릅나무
elope nun maja taranada 눈 맞아 달아나다
eloquence yuch'anghan hwasul 유창한 화술
eloquent yuch'anghan 유창한
eloquently yuch'anghage 유창하게
else: *anything ~?* kŭbakkŭi tarŭn kŏsŭn? 그밖의 다른 것은?; *if you have nothing ~ to do* manyak tarŭn hal iri ŏpttamyŏn 만약 다른 일이 없다면; *no one ~ spoke/came* tarŭn nugudo marhaji/oji anat-tta 다른 누구도 말하지/오지 않았다; *everyone ~ is going* kŭbakke moduga kanda 그밖에 모두가 간다; *who ~ was there?* kŭgose ttonuga issŏssŏyo? 그곳에 또누가 있었어요?; *someone ~* tarŭ nugun-ga 다른 누군가; *something ~* tarŭn ŏttŏn kŏt 다른 어떤 것; *let's go somewhere ~* ŏdi tarŭn kosŭro kapsshida 어디 다른 곳으로 갑시다; *or ~* kŭrŏch'i anŭmyŏn 그렇지 않으면
elsewhere (*position*) ŏttŏn tarŭn kosesŏ 어떤 다른 곳에서; (*motion toward*) ŏttŏn tarŭn kosŭro 어떤 다른 곳으로
elude (*escape from*) pŏsŏnada 벗어나다; (*avoid*) p'ihada 피하다; *her name ~s me* kŭnyŏŭi irŭmi saenggangnaji anat-tta 그녀의

름이 생각나지 않았다

...sive (*hard to define*) p'aak'agi ...mdŭn 파악하기 힘든; *person* ...'atkki himdŭn 찾기 힘든

...aciated such'ŏk'an 수척한

...ail 1 *n* imeil 이메일 2 *v/t person* ...ege imeirŭl ponaeda ...에게 ...메일을 보내다; *text* imeillo ...naeda 이메일로 보내다

...ail address imeil chuso 이메일 ...소

...ancipated haebangdoen 해방된; ...*oman* chayurowajin 자유로와진 ...ancipation haebang 해방

...balm pangbu ch'ŏrihada 방부 ...리하다

...bankment *of river* tuk 둑; RAIL ...k-kkil 둑길

...bargo *n* ch'urip'ang kŭmji 출입항 ...지

...bark shitta 싣다

...mbark on shijak'ada 시작하다

...barrass tanghwanghage hada ...황하게 하다

...barrassed tanghwanghan 당황한

...barrassing tanghwanghage hanŭn ...황하게 하는

...barrassment tanghwangham ...황함

...bassy taesagwan 대사관

...bellish changshik'ada 장식하다; ...*ory* kkumida 꾸미다

...bers kkambugibul 깜부기불

...bezzle hoengnyŏnghada 횡령하다

...bezzlement hoengnyŏng 횡령

...bitter ssŭrarige hada 쓰라리게 하다

...blem sangjing 상징

...bodiment hwashin 화신

...body kuch'ewahada 구체화하다

...bolism MED saektchŏntchŭng ...전증

...boss *metal, paper, fabric* ...dŭrajinŭn saegimŭl hada ...드라지는 새김을 하다

...brace 1 *n* po-ong 포옹 2 *v/t* (*hug*) ...'o-onghada 포옹하다; (*take in*) ...ohamhada 포함하다 3 *v/i* (*of two* ...*eople*) p'o-onghada 포옹하다

...broider sunot'a 수놓다; *fig* ...kumida 꾸미다

...broidery chasu 자수

embryo pae 배; (*of human*) t'aea 태아

emerald (*precious stone*) emeraldŭ 에메랄드; (*color*) palgŭn ch'orokssaek 밝은 초록색

emerge (*appear*) nat'anada 나타나다; *it has ~d that* ...ranŭn kŏshi turŏnat-tta ...라는 것이 들어났다

emergency pisang 비상; *in an ~* pisangshie 비상시에

emergency exit pisanggu 비상구

emergency landing pisang ch'angnyuk 비상 착륙

emigrant *n* imin 이민

emigrate iminhada 이민하다

emigration iju 이주

eminent chŏmyŏnghan 저명한

eminently (*extremely*) ttwiŏnage 뛰어나게

emission (*of gases*) palssan 발산

emotion kamjŏng 감정

emotional *problems, development* kamjŏngjŏgin 감정적인; (*full of emotion*) kamdongjŏgin 감동적인

empathize: *~ with* ...ŭl/rŭl tonggamhada ...을/를 동감하다

emperor hwangje 황제

emphasis kangjo 강조

emphasize kangjohada 강조하다

emphatic tanhohan 단호한

empire *also fig* cheguk 제국

employ koyonghada 고용하다; (*use*) sayonghada 사용하다; *he's ~ed as a ...* kŭnŭn ...(ŭ)ro koyongdoeŏ it-tta 그는 ...(으)로 고용되어 있다

employee koyong-in 고용인

employer koyongju 고용주

employment chigŏp 직업; (*work*) il 일; *be seeking ~* kujik'ada 구직하다

employment agency chigŏp annaeso 직업 안내소

empress yŏje 여제

emptiness konghŏham 공허함

empty 1 *adj* pin 빈; *promises* muŭimihan 무의미한 2 *v/t drawer, pockets, glass* piuda 비우다; 3 *v/i* (*of room, street*) pida 비다

emulate ponttŭda 본뜨다

enable kanŭnghage hada 가능하게 하다

enact *law* chejŏnghada 제정하다; THEA kongnyŏnhada 공연하다

enamel *n* enamel 에나멜; (*on tooth*) sang-ajil 상아질; (*paint*) yuyak 유약

enchanting maehoktchŏgin 매혹적인

encircle ewŏssada 에워싸다

encl (= **enclosure(s)**) tongbong 동봉

enclose (*in letter*) tongbonghada 동봉하다; *area* turŭda 두르다; **please find ~d ...** tongbonghan ...ŭl/rŭl poseyo 동봉한 ...을/를 보세요

enclosure (*with letter*) tongbongmul 동봉물

encore *n* angk'orŭ 앙코르, chaech'ŏng 재청

encounter 1 *n* uyŏnhan mannam 우연한 만남 **2** *v/t person* uyŏnhi mannada 우연히 만나다; *problem* mat-ttakttŭrida 맞닥뜨리다

encourage kyŏngnyŏhada 격려하다

encouragement kyŏngnyŏ 격려

encouraging yonggirŭl chunŭn 용기를 주는

♦ **encroach on** *land* ch'imip'ada 침입하다; *rights* ch'imhaehada 침해하다; *time* ppaeat-tta 빼앗다

encyclopedia paek-kkwa sajŏn 백과사전

end 1 *n* (*extremity, conclusion*) kkŭt 끝; (*of month, year*) mal 말; (*purpose*) moktchŏk 목적; **at the ~ of this month** idal mare 이달 말에; **in the ~** mach'imnae 마침내; **for ~ hours on ~** kyesok myŏt shigan tong-an 계속 몇 시간 동안; **stand X on ~** Xŭl/rŭl ttokpparo seuda X을/를 똑바로 세우다; **at the ~ of July** ch'irwŏl mal 칠월 말; **put an ~ to** ...ŭl/rŭl kkŭttchangnaeda ...을/를 끝장내다 **2** *v/t* kkŭnnaeda 끝내다 **3** *v/i* kkŭnnada 끝나다

♦ **end up**: **you'll ~ in the hospital** tangshinŭn pyŏng-wŏnesŏ insaengŭl mach'ige toelkkŏyeyo 당신은 병원에서 인생을 마치게 될거에요; **we ended up going to his place** urinŭn kyŏlguk kŭŭi chibe kage toego marat-tta 우리는 결국 그의 집에 가게 되고 말았다

endanger wihŏme ppajigehada 위험에 빠지게 하다

endangered species myŏltchong wigiŭi p'umjong 멸종 위기의 품종

endearing sarangsŭrŏun 사랑스러

endeavor 1 *n* shido 시도 **2** *v/t* shidohada 시도하다; **~ to be ear** ppalli odorok hada 빨리 오도록

ending kyŏlmal 결말; GRAM ŏmi 어

endless kkŭdŏmnŭn 끝없는

endorse *check* isŏhada 이서하다; *candidacy* chijihada 지지하다; *product* ch'uch'ŏnhada 추천하다

endorsement (*of check*) isŏ 이서; *candidacy* chiji 지지; (*of product* ch'uch'ŏn 추천

end product wanjep'um 완제품

end result ch'oejong kyŏlgwa 최종 결과

endurance chiguryŏk 지구력

endure 1 *v/t* kyŏndida 견디다 **2** *v/i* (*last*) chisok'ada 지속하다

enduring chisoktchŏgin 지속적인

end-user ch'oejong sayongja 최종 사용자

enemy chŏk 적

energetic hwalttongjŏgin 활동적인 *fig*: *measures* kangnyŏk'an 강력한

energy (*gas, electricity etc*) enŏji 에너지; (*of person*) him 힘

energy-saving *device* enŏjirŭl chŏryak'anŭn 에너지를 절약하는

enforce kangnyŏk shilsshihada 강실시하다

engage 1 *v/t* (*hire*) koyonghada 고용하다 **2** *v/i* TECH chakttonghac 작동하다

♦ **engage in** ...e kwallyŏndoeda ..관련되다

engaged (*to be married*) yak'onha 약혼한; **get ~** yak'onhada 약혼하다

engagement (*appointment*) yaksse 약속; (*to be married*) yak'on 약혼, MIL kyojŏn 교전

engagement ring yak'on panji 약혼 반지

engaging maeryŏktchŏgin 매력적

engine enjin 엔진

engineer 1 *n* kisa 기사; NAUT, RAIL kigwansa 기관사 **2** *v/t coup, meeti* kkoehada 꾀하다

engineering konghak 공학

England Yŏngguk 영국

English 1 *adj* Yŏnggugŭi 영국의 **2** (*language*) Yŏng-ŏ 영어; **the ~**

önggugin 영국인
glishman Yŏngguk namja 영국
자
glishwoman Yŏngguk yŏja 영국
자
rave saegida 새기다
raving (*drawing*) p'anhwa 판화;
design) toan 도안
rossed: **~ in** ...e molttudoen ...에
두된
ulf samk'ida 삼키다
ance nop'ida 높이다
gma susukkekki 수수께끼
gmatic susukkekkigat'ün
수께끼같은
oy chülgida 즐기다; **~ oneself**
hülgŏpke chinaeda 즐겁게 지내다;
(*said to s.o. eating*) mashikke
seyo! 맛있게 드세요!
oyable chülgŏun 즐거운
oyment chülgŏum 즐거움
arge k'üge hada 크게 하다
argement hwakttae 확대
ghten kyemonghada 계몽하다
ghtened (*liberal*) kyemongdoen
몽된
ist 1 *v/i* MIL chawŏn iptaehada
원 입대하다 2 *v/t*: **~ the help of**
üi toumül ŏt-tta ...의 도움을 얻다
iven hwalgirül purŏnŏt'a 활기를
어넣다
ormity (*of crime*) hyung-akssŏng
악성; (*of task*) kŏdaeham 거대함
ormous kŏdaehan 거대한; *satis-*
ction, patience taedanhan 대단한
ormously taedanhage 대단하게
ough 1 *adj* ch'ungbunhan 충분한
pron ch'ungbunhan yang 충분한
; **will $50 be ~?** 50tallŏmyŏn
분합니까?; **I've had ~!** ije
분해!; **that's ~,**
ümanhae! 이제 그만해!; **calm down!** ije twaessünikka
ümanhae! 이제 됐으니까 그만해!
adv ch'ungbunhi 충분히; **big / old**
h'ungbunhi k'ün/naidün 충분히
/나이든; **strangely ~** yŏkssi
sanghagedo 역시 이상하게도
quire, enquiry → **inquire, inquiry**
raged hwaga nan 화가 난
rich *vocabulary* p'ungbuhage hada

풍부하게 하다; *s.o.'s life*
p'ungnyoropkke hada 풍요롭게 하다
enroll *v/i* tüngnok'ada 등록하다
enrollment tüngnok 등록
ensure hwakssirhage hada 확실하게 하다
entail p'iryoro hada 필요로 하다
entangle: **become ~d in** (*in rope*)
...wa/kwa ŏlk'ida ...와/과 얽히다;
(*in love affair*) ...e kkomtchagŏpsshi yŏlludoeda ...에 꼼짝없이 연루되다
enter 1 *v/t* (*go into*) ...e tŭrŏgada
...에 들어가다; (*come into*) ...(ŭ)ro tŭrŏoda ...(으)로 들어오다;
competition ...e ch'amgahada ...에 참가하다; *person, horse in race* ch'amgashik'ida 참가시키다; (*write down*) kiip'ada 기입하다; COMPUT imnyŏkshik'ida 입력시키다 **2** *v/i* (*go in*) tŭrŏgada 들어가다; (*come in*) tŭrŏoda 들어오다; THEA tüngjanghada 등장하다; (*in competition*) ch'amgahada 참가하다
3 *n* COMPUT imnyŏk 입력
enterprise (*initiative*) chinch'wijŏk kisang 진취적 기상; (*venture*) saŏp 사업
enterprising chinch'wijŏgin 진취적인
entertain 1 *v/t* (*amuse*) chülgŏpke hada 즐겁게 하다; *idea* saenggak'ada 생각하다 **2** *v/i* (*have guests*) taejŏp'ada 대접하다
entertainer yŏnyein 연예인
entertaining *adj* chaemiinnün 재미있는
entertainment orak 오락
enthrall ...üi maümül sarojaptta ...의 마음을 사로잡다
enthusiasm yŏltchŏng 열정
enthusiast: ... ~ ...kwang ...광; *jazz ~* chaejügwang 재즈광
enthusiastic yŏllyŏrhan 열렬한
entice yuhok'ada 유혹하다; (*persuade*) kkoeda 꾀다
entire chŏnch'eüi 전체의
entirely wanjŏnhi 완전히
entitle chagyŏgül chuda 자격을 주다
entitled *book* ...(i)ranün chemogüi ...(이)라는 제목의
entrance *n* ipkku 입구; (*entering, admission*) iptchang 입장; THEA

tŭngjang 등장

entranced maeryodoen 매료된

entrance fee iptchangnyo 입장료

entrant (*in competition*) ch'amgaja 참가자; (*for exam*) ŭngshija 응시자

entrenched *attitudes* ppuribak'in 뿌리박힌

entrepreneur kiŏpka 기업가

entrepreneurial kiŏpkaŭi 기업의

entrust: ~ *X with Y*, ~ *Y to X* Xege Yŭl/rŭl matkkida X에게 Y을/를 맡기다

entry (*way in*) ipku 입구; (*act of entering*) iptchang 입장; (*to country*) ipkkuk 입국; (*for competition: person*) ch'amgaja 참가자; (*for competition: item submitted*) ŭngmojak 응모작; (*in diary, accounts*) tŭngnok 등록

entry form ŭngmo sŏryu 응모 서류

entry visa ipkkukpija 입국비자

envelop ssada 싸다

envelope pongt'u 봉투

enviable purŏun 부러운

envious purŏwŏhanŭn 부러워하는; *be ~ of s.o.* nugurŭl purŏwŏhada 누구를 부러워하다

environment hwan-gyŏng 환경

environmental hwan-gyŏng-ŭi 환경의

environmentalist hwan-gyŏngbohoronja 환경보호론자

environmentally friendly ch'inhwan-gyŏngjŏgin 친환경적인

environmental pollution hwan-gyŏng-oyŏm 환경오염

environmental protection hwan-gyŏngboho 환경보호

environs kŭn-gyo 근교

envoy sajŏl 사절

envy 1 *n* saem 샘; *be the ~ of* …ŭi purŏumŭl sada …의 부러움을 사다 2 *v/t*: ~ *s.o. sth* nuguŭi muŏsŭl purŏwŏhada 누구의 무엇을 부러워하다

epic 1 *n* taehamul 대하물 2 *adj voyage, deed* ungdaehan 웅대한; ~ *journey* changjŏng 장정; ~ *songs* p'ansori 판소리; *a task of ~ proportions* ŏmch'ongnan halttangnyang-ŭi il 엄청난

활당량의 일

epicenter chinwŏnji 진원지

epidemic *n* (*of flu, measles*) yuhaengppyŏng 유행병; *fig* sŏnghaeng 성행

epilepsy kanjilppyŏng 간질병

epileptic *n* kanjilppyŏng hwanja 간질병 환자

epileptic fit kanjirŭi paltchak 간질 발작

epilog hugi 후기

episode (*of story, soap opera*) sap'il 삽회; (*happening*) ep'isodŭ 에피소

epitaph pimun 비문

epoch shidae 시대

epoch-making hoek-kkijŏgin 획기적인

equal 1 *adj* kat'ŭn 같은; *standing, rank* tongdŭnghan 동등한; *be ~ to* task …ŭl/rŭl ch'ungbunhi hal su itta …을/를 충분히 할 수 있다 2 *n* tongtŭnghan chonjae 동등한 존재 3 *v/t* MATH …wa/kwa kat-tta …와/과 같다; (*be as good as*) p'iltchŏk'ada 필적하다; *four plus five ~s nine* sa toehagi onŭn kud 더하기 5는 9이다

equality p'yŏngdŭng 평등

equalize 1 *v/t* ttokkatkkehada 똑같게하다 2 *v/i* SP taedŭnghada 대등하다

equally kyundŭnghage 균등하게; ~ … tongdŭnghage, … 동등하게, …

equate: ~ *X with Y* Xŭl/rŭl Ywa/kwa kat-ttago saenggak'ada X을/를 Y와/과 같다고 생각하다

equation MATH pangjŏngshik 방정식

equator chŏktto 적도

equilibrium kyunhyŏng 균형

equinox chuya p'yŏngbunshi 주야 평분시; *the autumnal* ~ ch'ubun 추분; *the spring* ~ ch'unbun 춘분

equip *v/t* katch'uŏ chuda 갖추어 주; *he's not ~ped to handle it fig* kŭnŭn kŭirŭl halmanhan yŏngnyang-i katch'uŏjyŏ it-tchi an tta 그는 그일을 할만한 역량이 갖추어져 있지 않다

equipment changbi 장비

equity capital FIN chagi chabon 자 자본

ivalent 1 *adj* tongdŭnghan 동등한;
~ to ...wa/kwa tongdŭnghan
ch'iga it-tta ...와/과 동등한
치가 있다 2 *n* tŭnggamul 등가물
shidae 시대

dicate pangmyŏrhada 박멸하다

se chiuda 지우다

ser chiugae 지우개

ct 1 *adj* kotpparo sŏn 곧바로 선
v/t paro seuda 바로 세우다
ction (*of building etc*) paro seugi
로 세우기; (*of penis*) palgi 발기
de ch'imshik'ada 침식하다; *rights*,
ower chommŏktta 좀먹다
sion ch'imshik 침식; *fig*
ommŏgŭm 좀먹음
tic kwannŭngjŏgin 관능적인
ticism kwannŭngjuŭi 관능주의
and shimburŭm 심부름; **run ~s**
imburŭmgada 심부름가다
atic *driving* chigŭjaegŭshigŭi
그재그식의; *performance, behavior*
chŏnghaji anŭn 일정하지 않은
or chalmot 잘못
or message COMPUT erŏ meseji
러 메세지
pt (*of volcano*) punch'urhada
출하다; (*of violence*) palbarhada
발하다; (*of person*) pokpparhada
발하다
ption (*of volcano*) punhwa 분화;
f violence) palbal 발발
alate hwakttaehada 확대하다
alation hwakttae 확대
alator esŭk'ŏlleitŏ 에스컬레이터
ape 1 *n* (*of prisoner, animal*)
omang 도망; (*of gas*) nuch'ul 누출;
OMPUT isŭk'eip'ŭ 이스케이프; **have
narrow ~** (*from death*) kakkasŭro
ranamtta 가까스로 살아남다;
from arrest) kakkasŭro
pajyŏnagada 가까스로 빠져나가다
v/i (*of prisoner, animal*)
omanggada 도망가다; (*of gas*)
uch'uldoeda 누출되다 3 v/t: **the
ord ~s me** kŭ mari saenggangnaji
ssŭmnida 그 말이 생각나지
습니다
ape chute pisangnyong
walgangno 비상용 활강로
cort 1 *n* tongbanja 동반자; (*guard*)

kyŏnghowŏn 경호원 2 v/t (*socially*)
paraedajuda 바래다주다; (*act as
guard to*) kyŏnghohada 경호하다
especial → **special**
especially t'ŭkppyŏrhi 특별히
espionage sŭp'ai haeng-wi 스파이
행위
essay *n* changmun 작문; (*at
university*) lep'ot'ŭ 레포트
essential *adj* (*necessary*)
p'ilssŭujŏgin 필수적인; (*very
important*) haeksshimjŏgin 핵심적인
essentially ponjiltchŏgŭro 본질적으로
establish *company* sŏllip'ada
설립하다; (*create*) mandŭlda 만들다;
(*determine*) iptchŭnghada 입증하다;
~ oneself as ...(ŭ)ro
yumyŏnghaejida ...(으)로
유명해지다
establishment (*firm, store etc*) shisŏl
시설; **the Establishment** kwŏllyŏk
chipttan 권력 집단
estate (*land*) ttang 땅; (*of dead
person*) yusan 유산
esthetic shimmijŏgin 심미적인
estimate 1 *n* kyŏnjŏk 견적 2 v/t
pyŏngkkahada 평가하다
estimation: **he has gone up** / **down
in my ~** kŭedaehan naŭi
p'yŏnggganŭn tŏ nop'ajyŏt-tta /
najajyŏt-tta 그에대한 나의 평가는 더
높아졌다 / 낮아졌다; **in my ~** naega
pogienŭn 내가 보기에는
estranged *wife, husband*
sowŏnhaejin 소원해진
estuary nŏlbŭn kang-ŏgwi 넓은
강어귀
ETA (= *estimated time of arrival*)
toch'ak yejŏng shigan 도착 예정 시간
etching ech'ing 에칭
eternal yŏngwŏnhan 영원한
eternity yŏngwŏn 영원
ethical yullijŏgin 윤리적인
ethics yulli 윤리
ethnic minjogŭi 민족의
ethnic group minjokchipttan
민족집단
ethnic minority sosu minjok 소수
민족
euphemism wan-gogŏ 완곡어
euphoria k'ŭn haengbok-kkam 큰

행복감

Europe Yurŏp 유럽

European 1 *adj* Yurŏbŭi 유럽의 **2** *n* Yurŏbin 유럽인

euthanasia allakssa 안락사

evacuate (*clear people from*) taep'ishik'ida 대피시키다; (*leave*) taep'ihada 대피하다

evade kyomyohi hoep'ihada 교묘히 회피하다

evaluate p'yŏngkkahada 평가하다

evaluation p'yŏngkka 평가

evangelist pogŭm chŏndosa 복음 전도사

evaporate (*of water*) chŭngbarhada 증발하다; (*of confidence*) yŏngich'ŏrŏm sarajida 연기처럼 사라지다

evasion (*of responsibilities etc*) hoep'i 회피

evasive aemaehan 애매한

eve chŏnya 전야

even 1 *adj* (*regular*) korŭn 고른; (*level*) p'yŏngp'yŏnghan 평평한; *number* tchakssuŭi 짝수의; *get ~ with* …ege anggap'ŭmŭl hada …에게 앙갚음을 하다 **2** *adv* choch'ado 조차도; ~ *my father* naŭi abŏji choch'ado 나의 아버지 조차도; ~ *bigger/better* tŏuk tŏ k'ŭn/naŭn 더욱 더 큰/나은; *not* ~ choch'a ant'a 조차 않다; *so* kŭrŏt'a hadŏrado 그렇다 하더라도; ~ *if …* pirok …l/ŭltchirado 비록 …ㄹ/을지라도 **3** *v/t:* ~ *the score* tongtchŏmŭl mandŭlda 동점을 만들다

evening chŏnyŏk 저녁; *in the* ~ chŏnyŏge 저녁에; *this* ~ onŭl chŏnyŏk 오늘 저녁; *good* ~ annyŏnghaseyo 안녕하세요

evening classes yagan suŏp 야간 수업; **evening dress** (*for woman, man*) yahoebok 야회복; **evening paper** sok-kkan shinmun 석간 신문

evenly (*regularly*) korŭge 고르게

event haengsa 행사; SP shihap 시합; *at all ~s* amut'ŭn 아무튼

eventful tasahan 다사한

eventual kunggŭktchŏgin 궁극적인

eventually kunggŭktchŏgŭro 궁극적으로

ever *adv* ◊ (*with if, in future*) ŏnjen 언젠가; *if you ~ visit here, pleas call me* ŏnjen-ga yŏgi oshimyŏn chege chŏnhwarŭl chuseyo 언제가 여기 오시면 제게 전화를 주세요 ◊ (*with past tense*) chigŭmkkaji 지금까지; *have you ~ been to K rea?* chigŭmkkaji Han-guge kab chŏgi issŏyo? 지금까지 한국에 가 적이 있어요? ◊: *for* ~ ŏnjena 언제나; ~ *since* kŭ hu chulgot 그 줄곧

evergreen *n* sangnokssu 상록수

everlasting yŏng-wŏnhan 영원한

every modŭn 모든; onŭ …(i)na ta 어느 …(이)나 다; ~ *day/week/ month/year* maeil/maeju/ maewŏl/maenyŏn 매일/매주/매월 매년; ~ *other day* it'ŭlmada 이틀마다; ~ *now and then* ttaettaero 때때로

everybody → *everyone*

everyday ilsangjŏgin 일상적인

everyone nuguna 누구나, modu ㄷ

everything modŭn kŏt 모든 것

everywhere modŭn kot 모든 곳; (*wherever*) ŏdidŭnji 어디든지

evict tchoch'anaeda 쫓아내다

evidence chŭnggŏ 증거; LAW chŭn ŏn 증언; *give* ~ chŭng-ŏnhada 증언하다

evident myŏngbaek'an 명백한

evidently punmyŏnghi 분명히

evil 1 *adj* ak'an 악한 **2** *n* ak sŏ 악

evoke *image* hwan-gishik'ida 환기시키다

evolution chinhwa 진화

evolve *v/i* (*of animals*) chinhwaha 진화하다; (*develop*) paltchŏnhada 발전하다

ewe amnyang 암양

ex- ijŏnŭi 이전의

ex *n* F (*former wife*) chŏnbuin 전부 (*former husband*) chŏnnamp'yŏn 전남편

exact *adj* chŏnghwak'an 정확한

exactly chŏnghwak'i 정확히; ~! pa kŭrŏssŭmnida! 바로 그렇습니다!; *not* ~ pandŭshi kŭroch'inŭn anssŭmnida 반드시 그렇지는

...습니다
...ggerate v/t & v/i kwajanghada
...장하다
...ggeration kwajang 과장
...m shihŏm 시험; **take an ~**
...ihŏmŭl poda 시험을 보다;
...**ass** / **fail an ~** shihŏme put-tta /
...ŏrŏjida 시험에 붙다 / 떨어지다
...mination (of facts, patient) kŏmsa
...사; EDU shihŏm 시험
...mine (study) chosahada 조사하다;
...patient chinch'arhada 진찰하다; EDU
...ihŏmhada 시험하다
...miner EDU shihŏmgwan 시험관
...mple ye 예; **for ~** yerŭl tŭrŏsŏ
...를 들어서; **set a good** / **bad ~**
...houn / nappŭn yega toeda
...은 / 나쁜 예가 되다
...asperated hwanan 화난
...cavate v/t (dig) p'ada 파다; (of
...rcheologist) palgurhada 발굴하다
...cavation palgul 발굴
...cavator kulch'ak-kki 굴착기
...ceed (be more than) ch'ogwahada
...초과하다; (go beyond) nŏmŏsŏda
...넘어서다
...ceedingly taedanhi 대단히
...cel 1 v/i ttwiŏnada 뛰어나다; **~ at**
...e ttwiŏnada …에 뛰어나다 2 v/t: **~**
...oneself chagi nŭngnyŏk isang-ŭl
...arhwihada 자기 능력 이상을
...발휘하다
...cellence ttwiŏnam 뛰어남
...cellent ttwiŏnan 뛰어난
...cept …ŭl / rŭl cheoehago …을 / 를
...제외하고; **~ for** …i / ga ŏpssŭmyŏn
...이 / 가 없으면; **~ that …** …ranŭn
...kŏsŭl cheoehamyŏn …라는 것을
...제외하면
...ception yeoe 예외; **with the ~ of**
...ŭl / rŭl cheoehagonŭn …을 / 를
...제외하고는; **take ~ to** …e taehan
...ŭiŭl shinch'ŏnghada …에 대한
...이의를 신청하다
...ceptional (very good) iryejŏgŭro
...ttwiŏnan 이례적으로 뛰어난;
...(special) t'ŭkppyŏrhan yeoeŭi
...특별한 예외의
...ceptionally (extremely) maeu
...yeoejogŭro 매우 예외적으로
...cerpt palch'we 발췌

excess 1 n: **eat to ~** p'oksshik'ada
폭식하다; **drink to ~** p'ogŭmhada
폭음하다; **in ~ of** …ŭl / rŭl
ch'ogwahanŭn …을 / 를 초과하는
2 adj kwadahan 과다한
excess baggage ch'ogwa suhamul
초과 수하물
excess fare ch'ogwa yogŭm 초과
요금
excessive chinach'in 지나친
exchange 1 n (of views, between
schools) kyohwan 교환; **in ~ for**
kyohwanŭro 교환으로; **in ~ for**
…wa / kwa kyohwanŭro …와 / 과
교환으로 2 v/t (in store) pakkuda
바꾸다, kyohwanhada 교환하다;
addresses matpakkuda 맞바꾸다,
kyohwanhada 교환하다; currency
hwanjŏnhada 환전하다; **~ X for Y**
Xŭl / rŭl Y(ŭ)ro kyohwanhada
X을 / 를 Y(으)로 교환하다
exchange rate FIN hwannyul 환율
excitable shwipkke hŭngbunhanŭn
쉽게 흥분하는
excite (make enthusiastic)
hŭngbunshik'ida 흥분시키다
excited hŭngbundoen 흥분된; **get ~**
hŭngbunhada 흥분하다; **get ~ about**
…e hŭngbunhada …에 흥분하다
excitement hŭngbun 흥분
exciting hŭngbunshik'inŭn
흥분시키는
exclaim oech'ida 외치다
exclamation kamt'an 감탄
exclamation point nŭkkimp'yo
느낌표
exclude (not include) cheoehada
제외하다; possibility paejehada
배제하다; (from club etc) tŭrŏoji
mot'age hada 들어오지 못하게 하다
excluding …ŭn / nŭn cheoehago
…은 / 는 제외하고
exclusive restaurant etc paet'ajŏgin
배타적인; rights, interview
toktchŏmjŏgin 독점적인
excruciating pain komun pannŭn
tŭt'an 고문 받는 듯한
excursion tchalbŭn yŏhaeng 짧은
여행
excuse 1 n pyŏnmyŏng 변명 2 v/t
(forgive) yongsŏhada 용서하다;

(*allow to leave*) ttŏnage hada 떠나게 하다; **~ X from Y** Xŭl/rŭl Yesŏ myŏnjehae chuda X을/를 Y에서 면제해 주다; **~ me** (*to get attention, to get past, interrupting s.o.*) shillyehamnida 실례합니다; (*apologizing*) choesonghamnida 죄송합니다; **~ me?** (*what did you say?*) mwŏragoyo? 뭐라고요?

execute *criminal* sahyŏng chip'aenghada 사형 집행하다; *plan* shirhaenghada 실행하다

execution (*of criminal*) sahyŏng chip'aeng 사형 집행; (*of plan*) shirhaeng 실행

executioner sahyŏng chip'aeng-in 사형 집행인

executive *n* kanbu 간부

executive briefcase kanbuyong sŏryu kabang 간부용 서류 가방

executive washroom kanbuyong hwajangshil 간부용 화장실

exemplary mobŏmjŏgin 모범적인

exempt: **be ~ from** …(ŭ)ro put'ŏ myŏnjedoeda …(으)로 부터 면제되다

exercise 1 *n* (*physical*) undong 운동; EDU yŏnsŭp 연습; MIL hullyŏn 훈련; **take some ~** undonghada 운동하다 **2** *v/t dog* undongshik'ida 운동시키다; *muscle* tallyŏnshik'ida 단련시키다; *caution, restraint* sayonghada 사용하다 **3** *v/i* undonghada 운동하다

exercise book EDU yŏnsŭptchang 연습장

exert *authority* parwihihada 발휘하다; **~ oneself** noryŏk'ada 노력하다

exertion noryŏk 노력

exhale naeshwida 내쉬다

exhaust 1 *n* (*fumes*) paech'ul 배출; (*pipe*) paegigwan 배기관 **2** *v/t* (*pipe*) nokch'oro mandŭlda 녹초로 만들다; (*use up*) ta ssŏ pŏrida 다 써 버리다

exhausted (*tired*) nokch'oga toen 녹초가 된

exhaust fumes paegi kasŭ 배기 가스

exhausting nokch'oga toege hanŭn 녹초가 되게 하는

exhaustion kŭkttoŭi p'iro 극도의 피로

exhaustive ch'ŏltchŏhan 철저한

exhaust pipe paegigwan 배기관

exhibit 1 *n* (*in exhibition*) chŏnship'um 전시품 **2** *v/t* (*of gallery, artist*) chŏnshihada 전시하다; (*give evidence of*) poida 보이다

exhibition chŏnshi 전시; (*of bad behavior*) ch'ut'ae 추태; (*of skill*) parhwi 발휘

exhibitionist chagi sŏnjŏn-ga 자기 선전가

exhilarating kibunŭl todunŭn 기분 돋우는

exile 1 *n* (*forced*) ch'ubang 추방; (*political, voluntary*) mangmyŏng 망명; (*person*) ch'ubangja 추방자; (*person: voluntary*) mangmyŏngja 망명자 **2** *v/t* ch'ubanghada 추방하다

exist chonjaehada 존재하다; **~ on** …(ŭ)ro saragada …(으)로 살아가

existence chonjae 존재; (*life*) saenghwal 생활; **in ~** hyŏnjonhanŭn 현존하는; **come into ~** saenggida 생기다

existing hyŏnjonhanŭn 현존하는

exit *n* ch'ulgu 출구

exonerate mujoerŭl chŭngmyŏnghada 무죄를 증명하다

exorbitant sangsang-ŭl ch'owŏrhanŭn 상상을 초월하는

exotic igukttchŏgin 이국적인

expand 1 *v/t* nŏlp'ida 넓히다 **2** *v/i* nŭlda 늘다; (*of metal*) p'aengch'anghada 팽창하다

♦ **expand on** tŏ chasehi sŏlmyŏnghada 더 자세히 설명하다

expanse: **a vast ~ of** nŏlkke p'yŏlch'yŏjin 넓게 펼쳐진

expansion hwaktchang 확장; (*of metal*) p'aengch'ang 팽창

expansion card COMPUT hwakchang k'adŭ 확장카드

expect 1 *v/t* kidaehada 기대하다; *baby* imshinhada 임신하다; (*suppose*) ch'uch'ŭk'ada 추측하다; (*demand*) yoguhada 요구하다 **2** *v/i*: **be ~ing** imshinjung-ida 임신 중이 **I ~ so** kŭrŏl kŏyeyo 그럴 거예요

expectant yegihago innŭn 예기하고 있는

expectant mother imshinbu 임신부

ectation kidae 기대; **~s**
(*demands*) changnaeŭi hŭimang
래의 희망

edient *n* p'yŏnppŏp 편법

edition t'amhŏm 탐험; (*group*)
amhŏmdae 탐험대; (*to do*
opping, sightseeing) tchalbun
haeng 짧은 여행

el *person* tchoch'anaeda 쫓아내다

end *energy* sobihada 소비하다

endable *person* hŭisaengdoel su
inŭn 희생될 수 있는

enditure chich'ul 지출

ense piyong 비용; **at the com-**
any's ~ hoesa piyong-ŭro 회사
용으로; **a joke at my ~** narŭl tugo
an nongdam 나를 두고 한 농담; **at**
he ~ of his health kŭŭi kŏn-gang-
 haech'imyŏnsŏ 그의 건강을
쳐치면서

ense account piyong myŏngse
용 명세

enses kyŏngbi 경비

ensive pissan 비싼

perience 1 *n* (*event*) ch'ehŏm 체험;
(*in life*) kyŏnghŏm 경험; (*in*
particular field) kyŏngnyŏk 경력
 v/t pain, pleasure nŭkkida 느끼다;
difficulty kyŏktta 겪다

perienced kyŏnghŏmminnŭn
경험있는

periment 1 *n* shirhŏm 실험 **2** *v/i*
hirhŏmhada 실험하다; **~ on ani-**
mals tongmul shirhŏmŭl hada 동물
실험을 하다; **~ with** (*try out*)
..ŭl / rŭl shirhŏmhaeboda ...을 / 를
실험해보다

perimental shirhŏmŭi 실험의

pert 1 *adj* sungnyŏndoen; **~ advice**
hŏnmun-gaŭi ch'unggo 전문가의
충고 **2** *n* chŏnmun-ga 전문가

pertise chŏnmun chishik / kisul
전문 지식 / 기술

pire man-gidoeda 만기되다

piry kihan mallyo 기한 만료

piry date yuhyo mallyoil 유효
관료일

xplain *v/t & v/i* sŏlmyŏnghada
설명하다

xplanation sŏlmyŏng 설명

xplicit *instructions* myŏngbaek'an
명백한

explicitly *state* myŏngbaek'i 명백히;
forbid punmyŏnghi 분명히

explode 1 *v/i* (*of bomb*)
p'okpparhada 폭발하다 **2** *v/t bomb*
p'okp'ashik'ida 폭파시키다

exploit¹ *n* wiŏp 위업

exploit² *v/t person* ch'akch'wihada
착취하다; *resources* kaebarhayŏ
iyonghada 개발하여 이용하다

exploitation (*of person*) ch'akch'wi
착취

exploration t'amhŏm 탐험

exploratory *surgery* kŏmsa 검사

explore *country etc* tapssahada
답사하다; *possibility* t'amsaek'ada
탐색하다

explorer t'amhŏmga 탐험가

explosion p'okppal 폭발; (*in*
population) kŭptchŭng 급증

explosive *n* p'okppalmul 폭발물

export 1 *n* (*action*) such'ul 수출;
(*item*) such'ulp'um 수출품 **2** *v/t*
goods such'urhada 수출하다;
COMPUT chŏnsonghada 전송하다

export campaign such'ul k'aemp'ein
수출 캠페인

exporter (*person*) such'urŏptcha
수출업자; (*country*) such'ulguk
수출국

expose (*uncover*) tŭrŏnaeda
드러내다; *scandal* p'ongnohada
폭로하다; *person* poyojuda 보여주다;
he's been ~d as ... kŭga ... imi
tŭrŏnat-tta 그가 ... 임이 드러났다; **~**
X to Y Xŭl / rŭl Ye noch'ulshik'ida
x을 / 를 Y에 노출시키다

exposure noch'ul 노출; (*of dishonest*
behavior) t'allo 탄로; (*part of film*)
chang 장

express 1 *adj* (*fast*) kŭp'aeng-ŭi
급행의; (*explicit*) myŏngbaek'an
명백한; **~ train / bus** kŭp'aeng
yŏlch'a / pŏssŭ 급행 열차 / 버스 **2** *n*
kŭp'aeng 급행 **3** *v/t* (*speak of, voice*)
mallo p'yohyŏnhada 말로 표현하다;
feelings p'yohyŏnhada 표현하다; **~**
oneself well / clearly chagi
chashinŭl chal / punmyŏnghi
p'yohyŏnhada 자기 자신을
잘 / 분명히 표현하다

express elevator kosok ellibeit'ŏ
고속 엘리베이터

expression (*voicing, phrase*)
p'yohyŏn 표현; (*on face*) p'yojŏng
표정; **with ~** p'yohyŏni p'ungbuhage
표현이 풍부하게

expressive p'yohyŏni p'ungbuhan
표현이 풍부한; *face* p'yojŏng-i
p'ungbuhan 표정이 풍부한

expressly (*explicitly*) myŏnghwak'i
명확히; (*deliberately*) ilburŏ 일부러

expressway kosokttoro 고속도로

expulsion (*from school*) t'oehak
퇴학; (*of diplomat*) ch'ubang 추방

exquisite (*beautiful*) chŏlmyohan
절묘한

extend 1 *v/t* nŏlp'ida 넓히다; *runway,
path* nŭrida 늘이다; *contract, visa*
yŏnjanghada 연장하다; *thanks,
congratulations* p'yohyŏnhada
표현하다 **2** *v/i* (*of garden etc*)
ppŏdŏit-tta 뻗어있다

extension (*to house*) hwaktchang
확장; (*of contract, visa*) yŏnjang 연장;
TELEC naesŏn 내선

extension cable yŏnjang k'eibŭl 연장
케이블

extensive kwangbŏmwihan 광범위한

extent pŏmwi 범위; **to such a ~
that ...** ...ranŭn hankkajinŭn ...라는
한까지는; **to a certain ~** ŏnŭ
chŏngdokkaji 어느 정도까지

exterior 1 *adj* oegwansang-ŭi
외관상의 **2** *n* (*of building*) oegwan
외관; (*of person*) kŏnmosŭp 겉모습

exterminate *vermin*
chŏnmyŏlshik'ida 전멸시키다; *race*
myŏltchongshik'ida 멸종시키다

external (*outside*) oebuŭi 외부의

extinct *species* myŏltchongdoen
멸종된

extinction (*of species*) myŏltchong
멸종

extinguish *fire, light* kkŭda 끄다

extinguisher sohwagi 소화기

extort: **~ money from** ...(ŭ)robut'ŏ
tonŭl kangyohada ...(으)로부터 돈을
강요하다

extortion kangt'al 강탈

extortionate t'ŏmuniŏpsshi manŭn
터무니없이 많은

extra 1 *n* ch'ugaŭi kŏt 추가의 것 **2**
ch'ugaŭi 추가의; **be ~** (*cost more*)
ch'ugaida 추가이다 **3** *adv*
t'ŭkppyŏrhi 특별히

extra charge ch'uga yogŭm 추가 요금

extract 1 *n* inyong 인용 **2** *v/t*
kkŏnaeda 꺼내다; *coal, oil* p'anaeda
파내다; *tooth* ppoptta 뽑다;
information ŏryŏpkke ŏdŏnaeda
어렵게 얻어내다

extraction (*of oil, coal*) ch'uch'ul
추출; (*of tooth*) ppopkki 뽑기

extradite indohada 인도하다

extradition pŏmjoein indo 범죄인
인도

extradition treaty pŏmjoein indo
hyŏptchŏng 범죄인 인도 협정

extramarital kant'ong-ŭi 간통의

extraordinarily ŏmch'ŏngnage
엄청나게

extraordinary ŏmch'ŏngnan 엄청난

extravagance sach'i 사치

extravagant (*with money*)
sach'isŭrŏun 사치스러운

extreme 1 *n* kŭkttan 극단 **2** *adj*
kŭksshimhan 극심한; *views*
kŭkttanjŏgin 극단적인

extremely taedanhi 대단히

extremist *n* kwagyŏngnonja 과격론자

extricate kuch'urhada 구출하다

extrovert *n* oehyangtchŏgin saram
외향적인 사람

exuberant hwalgiga ch'ungmanhan
활기가 충만한

exult kippŏnalttwida 기뻐날뛰다

eye 1 *n* nun 눈; (*of needle*) panŭlgwi
바늘귀; **keep an ~ on** (*look after*)
...ŭl/rŭl chik'yŏboda ...을/를
지켜보다; (*monitor*) ...ŭl/rŭl
kamshihada ...을/를 감시하다 **2** *v/t*
poda 보다

eyeball nunal 눈알; **eyebrow** nunss
눈썹; **eyeglasses** an-gyŏng 안경;
eyelash songnunssŏp 속눈썹; **eye**
nunkkŏp'ul 눈꺼풀; **eyeliner** airai
아이라이너; **eyeshadow** aishyaed
아이섀도우; **eyesight** shiryŏk 시력
eyesore pogi hyunghan kŏt 보기
흉한 것; **eye strain** nunŭi p'iro 눈
피로; **eyewitness** mok-kkyŏktcha
목격자

F

= **Fahrenheit**) Hwasshi 화씨; **45° ~** wasshi 45to 화씨 45도
...**ric** chingmul 직물
...**ulous** koengjanghan 굉장한
...**ade** (*of building*) chŏngmyŏn 면; (*of person*) kŏnmosŭp 겉모습
...**e 1** *n* ŏlgul 얼굴; (*look, expression*) yojŏng 표정; **~ to ~** taemyŏnhago 면하고; **lose ~** ch'emyŏnŭl ilt'a 면을 잃다 **2** *v/t person, the sea* majuboda 마주보다; *fact* ...ingmyŏnhada 직면하다
...**elift** churŭm chegŏsul 주름 제거술
...**e value** aengmyŏnkka 액면가;
...**ke at ~** kŏnmosŭburo andanhada 겉모습으로 판단하다
...**ilitate** shwipkke hada 쉽게 하다
...**ilities** shisŏl 시설
...**t** sashil 사실; **in ~, as a matter of** sashirŭn 사실은
...**tor** yoin 요인; MATH insu 인수
...**tory** kongjang 공장
...**ulty** (*hearing etc*) nŭngnyŏk 능력; *...t university*) hakppu 학부; (*teaching staff*) kyojigwŏn 교직원
...**e** *v/i* (*of colors*) paraeda 바래다; (*of sounds, memories*) hŭimihaejida 미해지다
...**ed** *color, jeans* paraen 바랜
...**F** (*homosexual*) homo 호모
...**arenheit** Hwasshi 화씨
...*v/i* shilp'aehada 실패하다; (*in ...am*) ttŏrŏjida 떨어지다
...**ure** shilp'ae 실패
...**t 1** *adj* hŭimihan 희미한; **feel ~** ...irŏpta 어지럽다 **2** *v/i* kijŏrhada ...절하다
...**¹** *n* (*trade show*) muyŏk ...angnamhoe 무역 박람회; *...gricultural*) p'ump'yŏnghoe 품평회
...**²** *adj hair* kŭmbarŭi 금발의; *...omplexion* palgŭn 밝은; (*just*) ...ongjŏnghan 공정한; **it's not ~** ...ŭgŏsŭn kongjŏnghaji anssŭmnida

그것은 공정하지 않습니다
fairly *treat* kongjŏnghage 공정하게; (*quite*) kkwae 꽤
fairness (*of treatment*) kongjŏngham 공정함
fairy yojŏng 요정
fairy tale tonghwa 동화
faith shilloe 신뢰; REL shinang 신앙
faithful ch'ungshirhan 충실한; **be ~ to one's partner** sangdaeege ch'ungshirhada 상대에게 충실하다
fake 1 *n* katcha 가짜 **2** *adj* katchaŭi 가짜의
fall¹ 1 *v/i* (*of person, price, temperature etc*) ttŏrŏjida 떨어지다; (*stumble*) nŏmŏjida 넘어지다; (*of building, government*) munŏjida 무너지다; (*of tree*) ssŭrŏjida 쓰러지다; (*of night*) oda 오다; **my birthday ~s on a Tuesday this year** nae saeng-irŭn orhae hwayoirida 내 생일은 올해 화요일이다; **~ ill** pyŏng-e kŏllida 병에 걸리다 **2** *n* (*from high place*) ch'urak 추락; (*stumble*) nŏmŏjim 넘어짐; (*of government*) punggoe 붕괴; (*in temperature*) hagang 하강; (*of minister*) saim 사임; (*in price*) harak 하락
♦**fall back on** pisangshie sayonghada 비상시에 사용하다
♦**fall down** (*trip*) nŏmŏjida 넘어지다; (*because ill*) ssŭrŏjida 쓰러지다; (*of wall, building*) munŏjida 무너지다
♦**fall for** *person* ...wa/kwa sarang-e ppajida ...와/과 사랑에 빠지다; (*be deceived by*) ...ŭi sogimsue kŏllida ...의 속임수에 걸리다
♦**fall out** (*of hair*) ppajida 빠지다; (*argue*) saiga t'ŭrŏjida 사이가 틀어지다
♦**fall over** (*of person*) nŏmŏjida 넘어지다; (*of tree*) ssŭrŏjida 쓰러지다
♦**fall through** (*of plans*) shilp'aero

kkŭnnada 실패로 끝나다

fall² n (autumn) kaŭl 가을

fallout pangsasŏng naktchin 방사성 낙진

false kŭrŭttoen 그릇된

false teeth t'ŭlli 틀니

falsify wijohada 위조하다

fame myŏngsŏng 명성

familiar adj (intimate) ch'in-gŭnhan 친근한; (well-known) chal anŭn 잘 아는; form of address hŏmul ŏmnŭn 허물 없는; be ~ with X Xŭl/rŭl chal alda X을/를 잘 알다

familiarity (with subject etc) chŏngt'ong 정통; (of behavior) hŏmul ŏpssŭm 허물 없음

familiarize ik'ida 익히다; ~ oneself with …wa/kwa ikssuk'aejida …와/과 익숙해지다

family kajok 가족

family doctor chuch'iŭi 주치의; family name sŏng 성; family planning kajok kyehoek 가족 계획

famine kigŭn 기근

famous yumyŏnghan 유명한; be ~ for …(ŭ)ro yumyŏnghada …(으)로 유명하다

fan¹ n (supporter) p'aen 팬

fan² n (for cooling: electric) sŏnp'unggi 선풍기; (handheld) puch'ae 부채; (on ceiling) hwanp'unggi 환풍기 2 v/t: ~ oneself puch'aejirhada 부채질하다

fanatic n kwangsinja 광신자

fanatical kwangsinjŏgin 광신적인

fan belt MOT p'aen pelt'ŭ 팬 벨트

fancy adj design mŏtchin 멋진

fancy dress kajang mudobok 가장 무도복

fancy-dress party kajang mudohoe 가장 무도회

fan dance puch'aech'um 부채춤

fang ŏmni 엄니

fanny pack hŏri chigap 허리 지갑

fantastic (very good) hwansangjŏgin 환상적인; (very big) ŏmch'ŏngnan 엄청난

fantasy hwansang 환상

far adv mŏlli 멀리; (much) tŏ 더; ~ away mŏlli ttŏrŏjin 멀리 떨어진; how ~ is it to …? … kkaji ŏlmana

mŏn-gayo? … 까지 얼마나 먼가요

as ~ as the corner / hotel kusŏkkaji / hot'elkkaji 구석까지 / 호텔까지; as ~ as I can see naega pol su innŭn han 내가 볼 수 있는 한; ~ as I know naega anŭn han 내가 아는 한; you've gone too ~ (in behavior) nega nŏmu chinach'yŏtta 네가 너무 지나쳤다; so ~ so good chigŭmkkajinŭn choayo 지금까지는 좋아요

farce (ridiculous goings-on) utkkinŭn chit 웃기는 짓

fare n (for travel) yogŭm 요금

Far East Kŭkttong 극동

farewell n ibyŏl 이별

farewell party songbyŏrhoe 송별회

farfetched murihan 무리한; a ~ story hŏhwangdoen iyagi 허황된 이야기

farm n nongjang 농장

farmer nongbu 농부

farmhouse nongga 농가

farmworker nongjang-ŭi ilkkun 농장의 일꾼

farsighted sŏn-gyŏnjimyŏng-i innŭn 선견지명이 있는; (optically) wŏnshiŭi 원시의

fart F n panggwi 방귀 2 v/i panggwi kkwida 방귀 뀌다

farther adv tŏ mŏlli 더 멀리

farthest travel etc kajang mŏlli 가장 멀리

fascinate v/t maehoksshik'ida 매혹시키다; be ~d by …e maehokttoeda …에 매혹되다

fascinating maehoktchŏgin 매혹적

fascination (with subject) yŏlgwan 열광

fascism p'asshijŭm 파시즘

fascist 1 n p'asshisŭt'ŭ 파시스트 2 p'asshijŭmŭi 파시즘의

fashion n yuhaeng 유행; (in clothes) p'aesshyŏn 패션; (manner) pangsik 방식; in ~ yuhaenghanŭn 유행하는; out of ~ yuhaeng-i chinan 유행이 지난

fashionable clothes yuhaeng-ŭl ttarŭnŭn 유행을 따르는; idea, restaurant inkkiinnŭn 인끼있는; person mŏsŭl chal naenŭn 멋을 잘 내는

...ion-conscious yuhaeng-e min-/...mhan 유행에 민감한
...ion designer p'aesshyŏn tijainŏ/...션 디자이너
...¹ **1** *adj* pparŭn 빠른; **be ~** (*of ...ock*) pparŭda 빠르다 **2** *adv* ...barŭge 빠르게; **stuck ~** tandanhi ...k'in 단단히 박힌; **~ asleep** kip'i ...amdŭn 깊이 잠든
...² *n* (*not eating*) kŭmshik 금식
...ten **1** *v/t* (*fix*) kojŏnghada ...정하다; *belt, zipper* chaeuda ...우다; *dress, bag* chamgŭda 잠그다; ...*l, window* tat-tta 닫다; **~ your ...eatbelt** anjŏnbelt'ŭrŭl ...'agyonghashio 안전벨트를 ...jŏnghada X을/를 Y에 고정하다 ...*v/i* (*of dress etc*) chamgida 잠기다 ...tener (*for dress, lid*) chamgŭnŭn ...ŏt 잠그는 것
...t food chŭkssŏk shikp'um 즉석 ...품; (*hamburger, fried chicken*) ...aesŭt'ŭp'udŭ 패스트푸드; **fast-...d restaurant** p'aesŭt'ŭp'udŭjŏm ...스트푸드점; **fast forward 1** *n* (*on ...deo etc*) kosok kamkki 고속 감기 ...*v/i* kosoguro kamtta 고속으로 ...다; **fast lane** (*on road*) kosok ...'asŏn 고속 차선; **fast train** kosok ...ŏlch'a 고속 열차
...**1** *adj* ttungttunghan 뚱뚱한 **2** *n* (*on ...eat*) chibang 지방
...al *illness, error* ch'imyŏngjŏgin ...명적인
...lity samangja 사망자
...ally: **~ injured** ch'imyŏngsang-ŭi ...명상의
...e unmyŏng 운명
...her *n* aboji 아버지
...herhood aboji toegi 아버지 되기
...her-in-law (*husband's father*) ...iabŏji 시아버지; (*wife's father*) ...nang-in 장인
...erly aboji kat'ŭn 아버지 같은
...nom *n* NAUT kil 길
...gue *n* p'iro 피로
...so *n* F ttungttungbo 뚱뚱보
...ty **1** *adj* chibang-i manŭn 지방이 ...은 **2** *n* F (*person*) ttungbo 뚱보
...cet mulkkoktchi 물꼭지

fault *n* (*defect*) kyŏltchŏm 결점; **it's your/my ~** nŏŭi/naŭi chalmoshida 너의/나의 잘못이다; **find ~ with** ...ŭl/rŭl hŭmjaptta ...을/를 흠잡다
faultless *person, performance* hŭmjabŭlde ŏmnŭn 흠잡을데 없는
faulty *goods* kyŏltchŏm innŭn 결점 있는
favor hoŭi 호의; **in ~ of** (*resign, withdraw*) ...ŭl/rŭl wihayŏ ...을/를 위하여; **be in ~ of** ...e ch'ansŏnghada ...에 찬성하다; **do s.o. a ~** nuguege hoŭirŭl pep'ulda 누구에게 호의를 베풀다; **do me a ~!** (*don't be stupid*) utkkinŭn sori hajima! 웃기는 소리 하지마!
favorable *reply etc* hoŭijŏgin 호의적인
favorite 1 *n* (*thing*) cheil choahanŭn kŏt 제일 좋아하는 것; (*person*) cheil choahanŭn saram 제일 좋아하는 사람; (*food*) cheil choahanŭn ŭmshik 제일 좋아하는 음식 **2** *adj* cheil choahanŭn 제일 좋아하는
fax 1 *n* (*machine*) p'aekssŭ 팩스; (*document*) p'aekssŭ munsŏ 팩스 문서; **send X a ~** Xŭl/rŭl ponaeda 팩스로 X을/를 보내다 **2** *v/t* p'aekssŭroponaeda 팩스로 보내다; **~ X to Y** Xŭl/rŭl p'aekssŭroY ponaeda 팩스로 Y에게 보내다
FBI (= *Federal Bureau of Investigation*) Yŏnbang Susaguk 연방 수사국
fear 1 *n* turyŏum 두려움 **2** *v/t* turyŏwŏhada 두려워하다
fearless turyŏum ŏmnŭn 두려움 없는
feasibility study t'adangsŏng chosa 타당성 조사
feasible shirhaeng kanŭnghan 실행 가능한
feast *n* (*meal*) manch'an 만찬; (*event*) ch'uktche 축제
feat wiŏp 위업
feather kit'ŏl 깃털
feature 1 *n* (*on face, of city, style etc*) t'ŭktching 특징; (*article in paper*) kisa 기사; (*movie*) changp'yŏn yŏnghwa 장편 영화; **make a ~ of** ...ŭl/rŭl t'ŭktching-ŭro hada

…을/를 특징으로 하다 **2** *v/t (of movie)* chuyŏnŭro hada 주연으로 하다

February iwŏl 이월

federal *(allied)* yŏnhabŭi 연합의; *court, police* yŏnbang chŏngbuŭi 연방 정부의; **~ government** yŏnbang chŏngbu 연방 정부

federation *(alliance)* yŏnhap 연합

fed up *adj* F chillin 질린; **be ~ with** …e(ge) chillida …에(게) 질리다

fee *(of doctor)* chillyobi 진료비; *(of consultant)* sangdambi 상담비; *(for entrance)* iptchangnyo 입장료; *(for school)* ip'akkŭm 입학금; *(for membership)* hoewŏnnyo 회원료

feeble *person* yŏnyak'an 연약한; *attempt* miyak'an 미약한; *laugh* himŏmnŭn 힘없는

feed *v/t* mŏgida 먹이다; *animal* mŏgirŭl chuda 먹이를 주다

feedback p'idŭbaek 피드백

feel 1 *v/t (touch)* manjida 만지다; *pain, pleasure, sensation* nŭkkida 느끼다; *(think)* saenggak'ada 생각하다 **2** *v/i (of cloth etc)* nŭkkimi it-tta 느낌이 있다; **it ~s like silk/cotton** shilk'ŭwa/myŏn-gwa kat'ŭn kamch'ogida 실크와/면과 같은 감촉이다; **your hand ~s hot/cold** tangshin soni ttŭgŏpkkunyo/ch'agapkkunyo 당신 손이 뜨겁군요/차갑군요; **I ~ hungry/tired** nanŭn paegop'ŭda/p'igonhada 나는 배고프다/피곤하다; **how are you ~ing today?** onŭl kibuni ŏttŏseyo? 오늘 기분이 어떠세요?; **how does it ~ to be rich?** pujaga toenikka ŏttŏn kibuni tŭseyo? 부자가 되니까 어떤 기분이 드세요?; **do you ~ like a drink/meal?** mwŏ mashirŏ/mŏgŭrŏ kallaeyo? 뭐 마시러/먹으러 갈래요?; **I ~ like going/staying** nanŭn kago/mŏmulgo ship'ŏyo 나는 가고/머물고 싶어요; **I don't ~ like it** pyŏllo naek'iji anneyo 별로 내키지 않네요

◆ **feel up to** …hal su issŭl kŏt kat-tta …할 수 있을 것 같다

feeler *(of insect)* tŏdŭmi 더듬이

feelgood factor hoŭng 호응

feeling *(of happiness etc)* nŭkkim 느낌; *(emotion)* kamjŏng 감정; *(sensation)* kamgak 감각; **what are your ~s about it?** igŏse taehayŏ ŏttŏk'e saenggak'ashimnikka? 이것에 대하여 어떻게 생각하십니까?; **I have mixed ~s about him** nanŭn kŭege ch'aktchap'an shimjŏng-ŭl kajigo tta 나는 그에게 착잡한 심정을 가지고 있다

fellow *n (man)* saram 사람

fellow citizen kat'ŭn shimin 같은 시민; **fellow countryman** tongp'o 동포; **fellow man** kat'ŭn in-gan 같은 인간

felony chungjoe 중죄

felt *n* p'elt'ŭ 펠트

felt tip, felt-tip(ped) pen p'elt'ŭp 펠트펜

female 1 *adj animal, plant* amk'ŏsŭi 암컷의; *(relating to people)* yŏsŏngŭi 여성의 **2** *n (of animals, plants)* amk'ŏt 암컷; *(person)* yŏsŏng 여성 *(pej: woman)* kyejip 계집

feminine 1 *adj qualities* yŏsŏngjŏgin 여성적인; GRAM yŏsŏng-ŭi 여성의; **she's very ~** kŭnyŏnŭn aju yŏsŏngjŏgida 그녀는 아주 여성적이다 **2** *n* GRAM yŏsŏng 여성

feminism yŏkkwŏnjuŭi 여권주의, p'eminijŭm 페미니즘

feminist 1 *n* yŏkkwŏnjuŭija 여권주의자, p'eminisŭt'ŭ 페미니스트 **2** *adj group* yŏkkwŏnjuŭijaŭi 여권주의자의; *ideas* yŏkkwŏnjuŭiŭi 여권주의의

fence *n* ult'ari 울타리

◆ **fence in** *land* ult'ariro tullŏ ssada 울타리로 둘러 싸다

fencing SP p'enshing 펜싱

fend: ~ for oneself che himŭro kkuryŏnagada 제 힘으로 꾸려나가

fender MOT p'endŏ 펜더

ferment[1] *v/i (of liquid)* parhyohada 발효하다

ferment[2] *n (unrest)* puran 불안

fermentation parhyo 발효

fermented soya paste toenjang 된

fern yangch'iryu 양치류

ocious *animal* hyungp'ohan
포함; *attack* chaninhan 잔인한

y *n* narutppae 나룻배

ile *soil* piok'an 비옥한; *woman,
imal* tasanŭi 다산의

ility (*of soil*) piok piyok (*of
oman, animal*) tasan 다산

ility drug paeran ch'oktchinje
란 촉진제

ilize *v/t ovum* sujŏngshik'ida
. 정시키다

ilizer (*for soil*) piryo 비료

vent *admirer* yŏllyŏrhan 열렬한

er *v/i* (*of wound*) komtta 곪다

ival ch'uktche 축제

tive ch'uktcheŭi 축제의; *the ~
eason* sŏngt'anjŏl kigan 성탄절

tivities ch'uk'a haengsa 축하
사

person terigo oda 데리고 오다;
ing kajyŏ oda 가져 오다; *price ...e*
allida …에 팔리다

us t'aea 태아

d *n* purhwa 불화

er yŏl 열

erish yŏri innŭn 열이 있는; *fig:
xcitement* yŏlgwangtchŏgin
광적인

1 *adj* (*not many*) manch'i anŭn
지 않은; *a ~* (*things*) chogŭmŭi
금의; *quite a ~, a good ~* (*a lot*)
kwae manŭn 꽤 많은; *we have ~
iends* urinŭn ch'in-guga manch'i
nt'a 우리는 친구가 많지 않다; *we
e a ~ friends* urinŭn ch'in-guga
hom it-tta 우리는 친구가 좀 있다
pron (*not many people*) chŏgŭn
iŭi saram 적은 수의 사람; (*not
any: things*) chogŭn suŭi kŏt 적은
의 것; *a ~* (*people*) myŏnmyŏt
aram 몇몇 사람; (*things*)
iyŏnmyŏsŭi kŏt 몇몇의 것; *quite a
, a good ~* (*people*) kkwae manŭn
aram 꽤 많은 사람; (*things*) kkwae
anŭn kŏt 꽤 많은 것

ver *adj* tŏ chagŭn 더 작은; *~ than
.* poda chagŭn … 보다 작은

ncé yak'onja 약혼자

ncée yak'onnyŏ 약혼녀

sco taeshilp'ae 대실패

fib *n* sasohan kŏjinmal 사소한 거짓말

fiber *n* sŏmnyu 섬유

fiberglass *n* sŏmnyu yuri 섬유 유리;
fiber optic kwangsŏmnyuŭi
광섬유의; **fiber optics**
kwangsŏmnyu 광섬유

fickle pyŏndŏksŭrŏun 변덕스러운

fiction (*novels*) sosŏl 소설; (*made-up
story*) kkumin iyagi 꾸민 이야기

fictitious hŏguŭi 허구의

fiddle 1 *n* F (*violin*) kkaengkkaeng-i
깽깽이 **2** *v/i*: **~ around with** …ŭl/rŭl
majijak-kkŏrida …을/를
만지작거리다 **3** *v/t accounts* sogida
속이다

fidelity ch'ungshil 충실

fidget *v/i* anjŏlbujŏl mot'ada 안절부절
못하다

field *n* tŭlp'an 들판; (*for crops*) pat 밭;
(*for animals*) mokch'oji 목초지; (*of
rice*) non 논; (*for sport*) kyŏnggijang
경기장; (*competitors in race*) kyŏnggi
ch'amgaja 경기 참가자; (*of research,
knowledge etc*) punya 분야; **that's
not my ~** che punyaga animnida 제
분야가 아닙니다

field events p'ildŭ kyŏnggi 필드 경기

fierce sanaun 사나운

fiery *personality, temper* pul kat'ŭn 불
같은

fifteen yŏldasŏt 열 다섯, shibo 십오

fifteenth yŏldasŏt pŏntchaeŭi 열 다섯
번째의

fifth tasŏt pŏntchaeŭi 다섯 번째의

fiftieth shwin pŏntchaeŭi 쉰 번째의

fifty shwin 쉰, oship 오십

fifty-fifty *adv* oship tae oshibŭro 오십
대 오십으로

fig muhwagwa 무화과

fight 1 *n* ssaum 싸움; *in war* chŏnt'u
전투; *fig* (*for survival, championship
etc*) t'ujaeng 투쟁; (*in boxing*)
kyŏnggi 경기 **2** *v/t enemy, person,
disease, injustice* …wa/kwa ssauda
…와/과 싸우다; (*in boxing*)
…wa/kwa ssŏuda …와/과 겨루다
3 *v/i* ssauda 싸우다

♦ **fight for** *one's rights, a cause*
…ŭl/rŭl wihae ssauda …을/를 위해
싸우다

fighter chŏnsa 전사; (*airplane*)

chŏnt'ugi 전투기; (*boxer*) sŏnsu 선수; **she's a ~** kŭnyŏnŭn pulgurŭl ŭijirŭl kajigo it-tta 그녀는 불굴의 의지를 가지고 있다

figurative *use of word* piyujŏgin 비유적인; *art* chohyŏngjŏgin 조형적인

figure 1 *n* (*digit*) sutcha 숫자; (*of person*) mommae 몸매; (*form, shape*) hyŏngsang 형상 2 *v/t* F (*think*) saenggak'ada 생각하다

♦ **figure on** F (*plan*) kyehoek'ada 계획하다

♦ **figure out** (*understand*) ihaehada 이해하다; *calculation* kyesanhada 계산하다

figure skating p'igyŏ sŭk'eit'ing 피겨 스케이팅

file[1] 1 *n* (*of documents*) sŏryuch'ŏl 서류철; COMPUT hwail 화일 2 *v/t documents* ch'ŏrhada 철하다

♦ **file away** *documents* ch'ŏrhayŏ pogwanhada 철하여 보관하다

file[2] *n* (*for wood, fingernails*) chul 줄

file cabinet sŏryuham 서류함

file manager COMPUT hwail maenijŏ 화일 매니저

filial piety hyo 효

Filipino 1 *adj* P'illip'inŭi 필리핀의 2 *n* (*person*) P'illip'in saram 필리핀 사람

fill 1 *v/t* ch'aeuda 채우다 2 *n*: **eat one's ~** chanttŭk mŏkta 잔뜩 먹다

♦ **fill in** *form* kiip'ada 기입하다; *hole* meuda 메우다

♦ **fill in for** …ŭl/rŭl taesinhada …을/를 대신하다

♦ **fill out** 1 *v/t* *form* kiip'ada 기입하다 2 *v/i* (*get fatter*) saltchida 살찌다

♦ **fill up** 1 *v/t* kadŭk ch'aeuda 가득 채우다 2 *v/i* (*of stadium, theater*) kadŭk ch'ada 가득 차다

fillet *n* ppyŏ parŭn saltchŏm 뼈 바른 살점

fillet steak p'ille sŭt'eik'ŭ 필레 스테이크

filling 1 *n* (*in sandwich*) sok 속; (*in tooth*) p'illing 필링 2 *adj food* paeburŭge hanŭn 배부르게 하는

filling station chuyuso 주유소

film 1 *n* (*for camera*) p'illŭm 필름;

(*movie*) yŏnghwa 영화 2 *v/t perso event* ch'waryŏnghada 촬영하다

film-maker yŏnghwa chejaktcha ᄋ 제작자

film star yŏnghwa sŭt'a 영화 스타

filter 1 *n* p'ilt'ŏ 필터, yŏgwagi 여과 2 *v/t coffee, liquid* kŏrŭda 거르다

♦ **filter through** (*of news reports*) saeŏ naoda 새어 나오다

filter tip (*cigarette*) p'ilt'ŏ 필터

filth pulgyŏrhan kŏt 불결한 것

filthy pulgyŏrhan 불결한; *language* sangsŭrŏun 상스러운

fin (*of fish*) chinŭrŏmi 지느러미

final 1 *adj* (*last*) majimagŭi 마지막의 *decision* ch'oejŏng-ŭi 최종의 2 *n* S kyŏlssŭng 결승

finalist kyŏlssŭngjŏn ch'ultchŏn sŏnsu 결승전 출전 선수

finalize mamurihada 마무리하다

finally majimagŭro 마지막으로; (*at last*) mach'imnae 마침내

finance 1 *n* chaejŏng 재정; (*provisi of funds*) kŭmnyung 금융 2 *v/t* …(chagŭm chiwŏnŭl hada …에 자금 지원을 하다

financial chaejŏng-ŭi 재정의; *a ~ magazine* kyŏngje chaptchi 경제 잡지

financial year hoegye yŏndo 회계 연도

financier chaejŏngga 재정가

find *v/t* ch'at-tta 찾다; *if you ~ it to hot weather* nŏmu tŏpttago saenggakttoemyŏn 너무 덥다고 생각되면; *food* nŏmu ttŭgŏpttago saenggakttoemyŏn 너무 뜨겁다고 생각되면; *~ s.o. innocent / guilty* LAW nugurŭl mujoero / yujoero p'a gyŏrhada 누구를 무죄로 / 유죄로 판결하다

♦ **find out** 1 *v/t* aranaeda 알아내다 2 *v/i* (*inquire*) palk'yŏnaeda 밝혀내다; (*discover*) aranaeda 알아내다

fine[1] *adj day, weather* malgŭn 맑은; *wine, performance, city* hullyunghe 훌륭한; *distinction* misehan 미세한; *line* kanŭn 가는; *powder* kou 고운 *print* chŏnggyohan 정교한; *how's that? – that's ~* ŏttŏssŭmnikka?

ossŭmnida 어떻습니까? -
습니다; *that's ~ by me* nanŭn
ㅇoŭndeyo 나는 좋은데요; *how are
ou? ~ ~* ŏttŏk'e chinaeseyo? – chal
sŭmnida 어떻게 지내세요? - 잘
습니다
▸ *n* pŏlgŭm 벌금
▸er *n* sonkkarak 손가락
▸ernail sont'op 손톱; **fingerprint** *n*
imun 지문; **fingertip** sonkkarak
▸kkŭt 손가락 끝; *have X at one's ~s*
ŭl / rŭl hwŏnhi alda X을 / 를 훤히
다
▸cky *person* kkadaroun 까다로운;
▸esign chinach'ige sŏmsehan
나치게 섬세한
▸sh 1 *v/t* kkŭnnaeda 끝내다; ~
▸ing sth muŏt'agirŭl kkŭnnaeda
▸엇하기를 끝내다 2 *v/i* kkŭnnada
▸나다 3 *n* (*of product*) kkŭnmaejŭm
▸맺음; (*of race*) kyŏlssŭngjŏm
▸승점
▸nish off *v/t* kkŭnmach'ida
▸마치다
▸nish up *v/t* ta kkŭnnaebŏrida 다
▸내버리다; *he finished up liking
/ living there* kŭnŭn kŭgŏsŭl
▸noahage toego / kŭgose salge toego
▸arat-tta 그는 그것을 좋아하게
▸고 / 그곳에 살게 되고 말았다
▸nish with *boyfriend etc*
▸.wa / kwaŭi kwan-gyerŭl
▸kkŭnnaeda …와 / 과의 관계를 끝내다
▸shing line kyŏlssŭngsŏn 결승선
▸land P'illandŭ 핀란드
▸n P'illandŭ saram 핀란드 사람
▸nish 1 *adj* P'illandŭŭi 핀란드의 2 *n*
▸anguage) P'illandŭŏ 핀란드어
▸chŏnnamu 전나무
▸ *1 n* pul 불; (*electric, gas*) nanbang
▸방; (*blaze*) hwajae 화재; *be on ~*
▸ul t'ago it-tta 불 타고 있다; *catch
▸* pur put-tta 불 붙다; *set X on ~,
▸et ~ to X* Xe purŭl puch'ida X에
▸을 붙이다 2 *v/i* (*shoot*) ssoda 쏘다
▸ *v/t* F (*dismiss*) haegohada 해고하다;
▸ ~d haegodoeda 해고되다
▸ alarm hwajae kyŏngbogi 화재
▸보기; **firearm** ch'ong 총; **fire de-
▸artment** sobangsŏ 소방서; **fire
▸scape** hwajae p'inan changch'i

화재 피난 장치; **fire extinguisher**
sohwagi 소화기; **firefighter, fireman**
sobangsu 소방수; **fireplace**
pyŏngnallo 벽난로; **fire truck**
sobangch'a 소방차; **firewood**
ttaelnamu 땔나무; **fireworks**
pulkkonnori 불꽃놀이
firm[1] *adj grip, handshake* himinnŭn
힘있는; *flesh, muscles* tandanhan
단단한; *voice, decision* hwakkohan
확고한; *a ~ deal* hwaksshirhage toen
kŏrae 확실하게 된 거래
firm[2] *n* COM hoesa 회사
first 1 *adj* ch'ŏŭmŭi 처음의; *who's ~
please?* ŏnŭ pun mŏnjŏimnikka?
어느 분 먼저입니까? 2 *n* (*person*)
ch'ŏŭmŭi saram 처음의 사람; (*thing*)
ch'ŏŭmŭi kŏt 처음의 것; *~, please*
ch'ŏŭm pun oshipssshio 처음 분
오십시오 3 *adv* arrive, finish
ch'ŏŭmŭro 처음으로; (*beforehand*)
mŏnjŏ mŏnjŏ 먼저; *~ of all* (*for one reason*)
usŏnŭn 우선은; *at ~* ch'ŏŭme 처음에
first aid ŭnggŭp ch'iryo 응급 치료;
first-aid box, first-aid kit
kugŭmnyak sangja 구급약 상자; **first
birthday** tol tŭt; **first-born** *adj*
majiro t'aeŏnan mal-iro t'aeŏnan 맏이로 태어난; **first
class 1** *adj ticket* ilttŭngshirŭi
일등실의; (*very good*) ch'oegogŭbŭi
최고급의 2 *adv travel* ilttŭngshillo
일등실로; **first floor** ilch'ŭng 일층;
firsthand *adj* chiktchŏptchŏgin
직접적인
firstly usŏn 우선
first name irŭm 이름
first-rate illyuŭi 일류의
fiscal *policy, measures* choseŭi
조세의
fiscal year hoegye yŏndo 회계 연도
fish 1 *n* mulkkogi 물고기; (*to eat*)
saengsŏn 생선 2 *v/i* nakssihada
낚시하다
fishbone saengsŏnppyŏ 생선뼈
fisherman ŏbu 어부
fishing nakssi 낚시
fishing boat ŏsŏn 어선; **fishing line**
naksshitchul nakssŭl 낚싯줄; **fishing rod**
naksshit-ttae 낚싯대
fishmonger saengsŏn changsu 생선
장수

fish stick saengsŏn t'wigim 생선 튀김

fishy F (*suspicious*) susanghan 수상한

fist chumŏk 주먹

fit[1] *n* MED paltchak 발작; ***a ~ of rage / jealousy*** sun-ganjŏgin pokssushim / chilt'ushim 순간적인 복수심 / 질투심

fit[2] *adj* (*physically*) kŏn-ganghan 건강한; (*morally*) chŏk'ap'an 적합한; ***keep ~*** kŏn-gang-ŭl yujihada 건강을 유지하다

fit[1] **1** *v/t* (*of clothes*) ...ege mat-tta ...에게 맞다; (*attach*) talda 달다 **2** *v/i* (*of clothes*) mat-tta 맞다; (*of piece of furniture etc*) tŭrŏ mat-tta 들어 맞다 **3** *n*: ***it's a good ~*** chal mat-tta 잘 맞다; ***it's a tight ~*** kkok mat-tta 꼭 맞다

♦ **fit in** (*of person in group*) murie ŏullida 무리에 어울리다; ***it fits in with our plans*** kŭgŏsŭn uriŭi kyehoege tŭrŏ mannŭnda 그것은 우리의 계획에 들어 맞는다

fitful *sleep* sŏlch'in 설친

fitness (*physical*) kŏn-gangham 건강함

fitness center helssŭ k'ŭllŏp 헬스 클럽

fitted kitchen match'um puŏk 맞춤 부엌

fitter *n* chŏngbigong 정비공

fitting *adj* chŏktchŏrhan 적절한

fittings kŏnmul naebu changch'i 건물 내부 장치

five tasŏt 다섯, ㅇ 오

fix 1 *n* (*solution*) haegyŏl 해결; ***be in a ~*** F kon-gyŏng-e ch'ŏhae it-tta 곤경에 처해 있다 **2** *v/t* (*attach*) kojŏnghada 고정하다; (*repair*) koch'ida 고치다; (*arrange: meeting etc*) ilssirŭl chŏnghada 일시를 정하다; *lunch* chunbihada 준비하다; (*dishonestly: match etc*) chojak'ada 조작하다; ***~ X onto Y*** Xŭl / rŭl Ye kojŏngshik'ida X을 / 를 Y에 고정시키다; ***I'll ~ you a drink*** chega mashil kŏsŭl mandŭrŏ tŭrigessŭmnida 제가 마실 것을 만들어 드리겠습니다

♦ **fix up** *meeting* ilssirŭl chŏnghada 일시를 정하다; ***it's all fixed up*** ta

chŏnghaejyŏt-tta 다 정해졌다

fixed *part, exchange rate* kojŏngdoe 고정된

fixture (*in room*) sŏlbi 설비; SP chŏnggijŏn 정기전

flab (*on body*) kunsal 군살

flabbergast: ***be ~ed*** F ch'unggyŏ pat-tta 충격을 받다

flabby *muscles, stomach* nŭrŏjin 늘어진

flag[1] *n* kitppal 깃발; (*national ~*) kukki 국기

flag[2] *v/i* (*tire*) chich'ida 지치다

flair (*talent*) chaenŭng 재능; ***have natural ~ for*** ...e t'agonan chaenŭng-i it-tta ...에 타고난 재능 있다

flake *n* yalbŭn chogak 얇은 조각

♦ **flake off** *v/i* pŏtkkyŏjyŏ ttŏrŏjida 벗겨져 떨어지다

flaky *adj* pŏtkkyŏjigi shwiun 벗겨 쉬운; F (*odd*) pyŏllan 별난

flaky pastry p'asak'an p'aiyong panjuk 파삭한 파이용 반죽

flamboyant *personality* chashini nŏmch'yŏboinŭn 자신이 넘쳐보이

flame *n* pulkkot 불꽃; ***~s*** pulkkil 불

flammable kayŏnssŏng-ŭi 가연성의

flan op'ŭn p'ai 오픈 파이

flank 1 *n* (*of horse etc*) yŏpkkuri 옆구리; MIL taeyŏrŭi ch'ŭngmyŏn 대열의 측면 **2** *v/t*: ***be ~ed by*** (*by person*) ...ŭl / rŭl yangnyŏp'e kŏnŭrida ...을 / 를 양옆에 거느리 (*by building, person etc*) ...ŭl / rŭl yangnyŏp'e tuda ...을 / 를 양옆에 두다

flap 1 *n* (*of envelope, pocket*) ttukkŏng 뚜껑; ***be in a ~*** F anjŏlbujŏl mot'ada 안절부절 못하 **2** *v/t wings* p'ŏllŏgida 펄럭이다 **3** (*of flag etc*) p'ŏllŏgida 펄럭이다; F (*panic*) ch'ojohaehada 초조해하다

flare 1 *n* (*distress signal*) chomyŏngt'an 조명탄; (*in dress*) p'ŭllleŏ 플레어 **2** *v/t nostrils* pŏrida 벌이다

♦ **flare up** (*of violence, illness*) tolbarhada 돌발하다; (*of fire*) t'aorŭda 타오르다; (*get very angry*) hwaga ch'isot-tta 화가 치솟다

flight time

sh 1 n (of light) sŏmgwang 섬광;
HOT p'ŭllaeshwi 플래쉬; **in a ~** F
un kkamtchak'al saie 눈 깜짝할
이에; **have a ~ of inspiration**
ŏnggami pŏntchŏk ttorŭda 영감이
쩍 떠오르다; **~ of lightning** pŏn-
aetppurŭi pŏntchŏgim 번갯불의
쩍임 2 v/i (of light) pich'ida 비치다
v/t headlights pich'uda 비추다

shback n (in movie) kwagŏ
hoesang changmyŏn 과거 회상 장면
shbulb sŏmgwang chŏn-gu 섬광
전구
sher MOT chadong chŏmmyŏl
changch'i 자동 점멸 장치
shlight hoejung chŏndŭng 회중
등; PHOT p'ŭllaeshwi 플래쉬
shy pej yoranhan 요란한

sk pyŏng 병
t 1 adj surface, land
p'yŏngp'yŏnghan 평평한; beer kim
pajin 김 빠진; battery, tire ta tarŭn
닳은; shoes najŭn kubŭi 낮은
굽의; MUS panŭm naerimŭi 반음
내림의; **and that's ~** F tŏ isang-ŭn
marhaji ank'essŏ 더 이상은 말하지
않겠어 2 adv MUS panŭm naerimŭro
반음 내림으로; **~ out**
hŏnsŏngnyŏguro hada 전속력으로
하다

t-chested kasŭmi pinyak'an
가슴이 빈약한
t rate iltchŏng-aek 일정액
tten v/t land, road
p'yŏngp'yŏnghage hada 평평하게
하다; (by bombing, demolition)
nunŏttŭrida 무너뜨리다
tter v/t ach'ŏmhada 아첨하다
ttering comments ach'ŏmhanŭn
아첨하는; color, clothes shilmulboda
otpoige hanŭn 실물보다 돋보이게
하는
ttery ach'ŏm 아첨
vor 1 n mat 맛 2 v/t food mannaeda
맛내다
voring chomiryo 조미료
aw n hŭm 흠
awless hŭmŏmnŭn 흠없는
ea pyŏruk 벼룩
ee v/i tomangch'ida 도망치다
et n NAUT hamdae 함대

fleeting visit etc chamkkan tong-anŭi
잠깐 동안의; **catch a ~ glimpse of**
ŏlp'it poda 얼핏 보다
flesh (of people, fruit etc) sal 살; **the ~**
yukch'e 육체; **meet/see a person
in the ~** nugurŭl shilchero
mannada/poda 누구를 실제로
만나다/보다
flex v/t muscles such'uksshik'ida
수축시키다
flexible material kuburigi shwiun
구부리기 쉬운; arrangement, hours
yungt'ongsŏng innŭn 융통성 있는;
I'm quite ~ about the timing
chŏnŭn amu ttaerado chossŭmnida
저는 아무 때라도 좋습니다
flick v/t hwidurŭda 휘두르다; **he
~ed a fly off his hand** kŭnŭn sonŭl
hwidullŏsŏ p'arirŭl naetchoch'at-tta
그는 손을 휘둘러서 파리를
내쫓었다; **she ~ed her hair out of
her eyes** kŭnŭn shiyarŭl karinŭn
mŏrik'aragŭl ssŭrŏnŏmgyŏt-tta 그는
시야를 가리는 머리카락을
쓸어넘겼다
♦ **flick through** book, magazine
taegang hult'ŏboda 대강 훑어보다
flicker v/i (of light, screen)
kkamppagida 깜박이다
flies (on pants) paji ammun 바지 앞문
flight (in airplane) pihaeng 비행;
(flying) nalgi 날기; (fleeing) tomang
도망; **~ (of stairs)** han ch'ŭrŭi
kyedan 한 줄의 계단; **three ~s a
day** iril samhoŭi hanggongp'yŏn
1일 3회의 항공편; **a direct ~**
chik'ang 직항; **it's a long ~** igŏsŭn
kin yohaeng-iyeyo 이것은 긴
여행이에요; **when is your ~?**
tangshinŭi pihaenggi shiganŭn
ŏnjeimnikka? 당신의 비행기 시간은
언제입니까?
flight crew sŭngmuwŏn 승무원; **flight
deck** (in airplane) chojongshil
조종실; **flight number**
hanggongp'yŏn pŏnho 항공편 번호;
flight path pihaeng kyŏngno 비행
경로; **flight recorder** pŭllaek pakssŭ
블랙 박스; **flight time** (departure)
ch'ulbal shigan 출발 시간; (duration)
yŏhaeng shigan 여행 시간

flighty pyŏndŏkssŭrŏun 변덕스러운

flimsy *structure, furniture* yak'an 약한; *dress* yalbŭn 얇은; *material* tchijŏjigi shwiun 찢어지기 쉬운; *excuse* pinyak'an 빈약한

flinch umtchirhada 움찔하다

fling *v/t* naedŏnjida 내던지다; ~ **open** kŏch'ilge yŏlda 거칠게 열다; ~ **oneself into a chair** ŭijae t'ŏlssŏk ant'a 의자에 털썩 앉다

♦ **flip through** *book, magazine* taegang hult'ŏboda 대강 훑어보다

flipper (*for swimming*) mulgalk'wi 물갈퀴

flirt 1 *v/i* saeronggŏrida 새롱거리다 **2** *n* saeronggŏrinŭn saram 새롱거리는 사람

flirtatious saeronggŏrinŭn 새롱거리는

float *v/i* ttŭda 뜨다; FIN pyŏndong shisega toeda 변동 시세가 되다

flock *n* (*of sheep*) tte 떼

flog *v/t* (*whip*) ch'aetchiktchirhada 채찍질하다

flood 1 *n* hongsu 홍수; (*of river*) pŏmnam 범람 **2** *v/t* (*of river*) pŏmnamhada 범람하다; ~ **its banks** kangttugi nŏmch'ida 강둑이 넘치다

flooding pŏmnam 범람

floodlight *n* t'ugwang chomyŏng 투광 조명

floor *n* (*of a room*) marutppadak 마룻바닥; (*story*) ch'ŭng 층

floorboard padangnŏl 바닥널; **floor cloth** maru kŏlle 마루 걸레; **floor lamp** sŭt'aendŭ 스탠드

flop 1 *v/i* t'ŏlssŏk momŭl tŏnjida 털썩 몸을 던지다; F (*fail*) shilp'aejagida 실패작이다 **2** *n* F (*failure*) shilp'aejak 실패작

floppy *adj* (*not stiff*) hŏllŏnghan 헐렁한; (*weak*) narŭnhan 나른한

floppy (**disk**) p'ŭllop'i tisŭk'ŭ 플로피 디스크

florist kkotchangsu 꽃장수

flour milkkaru 밀가루

flourish *v/i* (*of plants*) chal charada 잘 자라다; (*of business*) pŏnch'anghada 번창하다; (*of civilization*) pŏnyŏnghada 번영하다

flourishing *business, trade*

pŏnch'anghanŭn 번창하는

flow 1 *v/i* (*of river*) hŭrŭda 흐르다; *electric current*) t'onghada 통하다; (*of traffic*) sot'ongdoeda 소통되다; (*of work*) chinhaengdoeda 진행되다; **the traffic ~s better** kyot'ong sot'ong-i wŏnhwarhaejida 교통 소통이 원활해지다 **2** *n* (*of river, information*) hŭrŭm 흐름; (*of ideas*) kyohwan 교환

flowchart chagŏp kongjŏngdo 작업 공정도

flower 1 *n* kkot 꽃 **2** *v/i* kkoch'i p'ida 꽃이 피다

flowerbed hwadan 화단; **Flower Garland Sutra** Hwaŏmgyŏng 화엄경; **flowerpot** hwabyŏng 화병

flowery *pattern* kkŏnmunŭiŭi 꽃무늬의; *style of writing* misayŏgŭi 미사여구의

flu tok-kkam 독감

fluctuate *v/i* pyŏndonghada 변동하다

fluctuation pyŏndong 변동

fluency yuch'angham 유창함

fluent *adj speaker* yuch'anghan 유창한; *he speaks ~ Korean* kŭ Han-gungmarŭl yuch'anghage handa 그는 한국말을 유창하게 한다

fluently *speak* yuch'anghage 유창하게; *write* yuryŏhage 유려하게

fluff: *a bit of ~* (*material*) yakkanŭi pop'ul 약간의 보풀

fluffy *adj material, hair* somt'ŏlgat'ŭn 솜털같은; ~ *clouds* somt'ŏl kurŭm 솜털 구름

fluid *n* (*in body*) aek 액; (*for brake*) yudong-aek 유동액

flunk *v/t* F (*subject*) …e naktcherŭl pat-tta …에 낙제를 받다

fluorescent hyŏnggwang-ŭi 형광의

flush 1 *v/t toilet* …ŭi murŭl naeridai …의 물을 내리다; ~ *X down the toilet* Xŭl / rŭl pyŏn-gie naeryŏ ponaeda X을/를 변기에 내려 보니 **2** *v/i* (*of toilet*) muri naeryŏgada 물이 내려가다; (*go red in the face*) ppalgaejida 빨개지다 **3** *adj* (*level*) kat'ŭn nop'iŭi 같은 높이의; *be ~ with* …wa / kwa kat'ŭn nop'iida …와/과 같은 높이이다

♦ **flush away** (*down toilet*) pyŏn-g

eryŏ ponaeda 변기에 내려 보내다
sh out *rebels etc* naogehada
오게 하다
ter *v/t* tanghwanghage hada
황하게 하다; *get ~ed*
nghwanghada 당황하다
e p'ŭllut'ŭ 플루트; (*large*) taegŭm
금; (*bamboo*) tanso 단소
er *v/i* (*of bird, wings*)
ŏdókkŏrida 퍼덕거리다; (*of flag*)
ŏllŏgida 펄럭이다; (*of heart*)
gŭn-gŏrida 두근거리다
n (*insect*) p'ari 파리
n (*on pants*) paji ammun 바지
문
1 *v/i* (*of bird, airplane*) nalda 날다;
airplane) pihaenghada
haenghada 비행기로 여행하다; (*of
g*) keyangdoeda 계양되다; (*rush*)
wiŏ nagada 뛰어 나가다; *~ into a
ge* pŏlk'ŏk sŏngnaeda 벌컥
내다 2 *v/t airplane* chojonghada
종하다; *airline* t'ada 타다;
ransport by air*) hanggong
nsonghada 항공 운송하다
away naragada 날아가다
back v/i (*travel back*)
haenggiro toragada 비행기로
아가다
in 1 *v/i* (*of airplane, passengers*)
ch'ak'ada 도착하다 2 *v/t supplies*
pihaenggiro unbanhada 비행기로
반하다
off (*of hat etc*) naragada
아가다
out v/i naragada 날아가다
past (*in formation*) kongjung
haenghada 공중 비행하다; (*of
ne*) ssonsalgach'i chinagada
살같이 지나가다
ng *n* pihaeng 비행
m *n* (*on liquid*) kŏp'um 거품
m rubber sŭp'onji komu 스폰지
무
B (= *free on board*) ponsŏn indo
선 인도
us *n* (*of attention*), PHOT
h'otchŏm 초점; *be in / out of ~*
HOT ch'otchŏmi mat-tta / mat-tchi
nt'a 초점이 맞다 / 맞지 않다
ocus on *also fig* …e ch'otchŏmŭl

match'uda …에 초점을 맞추다
fodder saryo 사료
fog an-gae 안개
foggy an-gae kkin 안개 낀
foil¹ *n* (*silver ~ etc*) hoil 호일
foil² *v/t* (*thwart*) chwajŏlsshik'ida
좌절시키다
fold 1 *v/t paper* chŏptta 접다; *cloth*
kaeda 개다; *~ one's arms*
p'altchang-ŭl kkida 팔짱을 끼다
2 *v/i* (*of business*) manghada 망하다
3 *n* (*in cloth etc*) chŏbŭn chari 접은
자리
◆**fold up 1** *v/t* chŏptta 접다 **2** *v/i* (*of
chair, table*) chŏp'ida 접히다
folder *also* COMPUT p'oldŏ 폴더
folding *adj* chŏmnŭn 접는
foliage ip 잎
folk (*people*) saram 사람; *my ~s*
(*family*) nae kajok 내 가족; *come
in, ~s* F tŭrŏoseyo, yŏrŏbun
들어오세요, 여러분
folk dance (*traditional*) minsok
ch'um 민속 춤; (*western*)
p'ok'ŭttaensŭ 포크댄스; **folk medicine** min-gan yoppŏp 민간 요법;
folk music minsok ŭmak 민속 음악;
folk painting minhwa 민화; **folk
singer** minyo kasu 민요 가수; **folk
song** minyo 민요
follow 1 *v/t person, road* ttaragada
따라가다; *guidelines, instructions*
ttarŭda 따르다; *TV series, news*
kyesok shich'ŏnghada 계속
시청하다; (*understand*) ihaehada
이해하다; *~ me* (*come*) chŏrŭl
ttaraoseyo 저를 따라오세요 **2** *v/i*
ttaragada 따라가다; (*logically*)
sŏngnip'ada 성립하다; *it ~s from
this that ...* kŭraesŏ ...ranŭn mari
mat-tta 그래서 ...라는 말이 맞다; *as
~s* taŭmgwa kat'ŭn 다음과 같은
◆**follow up** *v/t inquiry* poganghada
보강하다
follower (*of politician etc*) chijija
지지자; (*of football team*) p'aen 팬;
(*of TV program*) shich'ŏngja 시청자
following 1 *adj day, night* kŭ taŭmŭi
그 다음의; *pages* taŭmŭi 다음의 **2** *n*
(*people*) chijija 지지자; *the ~* taŭmŭi
kŏt 다음의 것

follow-up meeting pogang hoeŭi 보강 회의

follow-up visit chaebangmun 재방문; (*to doctor*) chaejin 재진

folly (*madness*) ŏrisŏgŭn chit 어리석은 짓

fond (*loving*) tajŏnghan 다정한; *memory* arŭmdaun 아름다운; *be ~ of* …ŭl/rŭl choahada …을/를 좋아하다

fondle v/t ssŭdadŭmtta 쓰다듬다

fondness aejŏng 애정; (*for wine, food*) aeho 애호

font (*in printing*) kŭltchach'e 글자체

food ŭmshik 음식

food freak F misshik-kka 미식가; **food mixer** mikssŏ 믹서; **food poisoning** shiktchungdok 식중독

fool n pabo 바보; *make a ~ of one-self* usŭmkkŏriga toeda 웃음거리가 되다

♦ **fool around** changnanch'ida 장난치다; (*sexually*) param p'iuda 바람피우다

♦ **fool around with** *knife, drill etc* …ŭl/rŭl kajigo changnanch'ida …을/를 가지고 장난치다

foolish ŏrisŏgŭn 어리석은

foolproof chalmot toel suga ŏmnŭn 잘못 될 수가 없는

foot pal 발; (*measurement*) p'it'ŭ 피트; *on ~* kŏrŏsŏ 걸어서; *at the ~ of the page/hill* chang-ŭi/ŏndŏgŭi mit'e 장의/언덕의 밑에; *put one's ~ in it* F k'ŭn shilssurŭl hada 큰 실수를 하다

football (*soccer*) ch'uk-kku 축구; (*American-style*) mishik ch'uk-kku 미식 축구; (*ball*) ch'uk-kkugong 축구공; **football player** (*soccer*) ch'uk-kku sŏnsu 축구 선수; (*American-style*) mishik ch'uk-kku sŏnsu 미식 축구 선수; **footbridge** yukkyo 육교; **foothills** san-gisŭlgŭi chagŭn ŏndŏk 산기슭의 작은 언덕

footing (*basis*) kiban 기반; *lose one's ~* hŏt-ttidida 헛디디다; *be on the same/a different ~* tongdŭnghan/tarŭn chagyŏgida 동등한/다른 자격이다; *be on a friendly ~ with* …wa/kwa uhojŏk …와/과 우호

kwan-gyerŭl kajida …와/과 우호 관계를 가지다

footlights kak-kkwang 각광; **foot-note** kaktchu 각주; **footpath** ind.. 인도; **footprint** paltchaguk 발자국.. **footstep** paltchaguk sori 발자국 소리; *follow in s.o.'s ~s* nuguŭi sŏllyerŭl ttarŭda 누구의 선례를 따르다; **footwear** shinbal 신발

for ◊ (*purpose, destination*) …ŭl/r.. wihan …을/를 위한; *clothes ~ c..dren* aidŭrŭl wihan ot 아이들을.. 옷; *I did it ~ John* Jonŭl wihaesŏ hassŏyo 존을 위해서 했어요; *a tr..* ~ *Seoul* Sŏullo kanŭn kich'a 서울.. 가는 기차; *it's too big/small ~ y.* kŭgŏsŭn nŏege nŏmu k'ŭda/cha.. 그것은 너에게 너무 크다/작다; *here's a letter ~ you* yŏgi nŏeg.. p'yŏnjiga it-tta 여기 너에게 온 편지가 있다; *this is ~ you* ikŏsŭn nŏrŭl wihan kŏshida 이것은 너.. 위한 것이다; *what is there ~ lunch?* chŏmshimŭro muŏshi issŭmnikka? 점심으로 무엇이 있습니까?; *the steak is ~ me* kŭ sŭt'eik'ŭnŭn che kŏshimnida 그 스테이크는 제 것입니다; *what is this ~?* ikŏsŭn muŏse sayongdoennŭn kŏshimnikka? 이것은 무엇에 사용되는 것입니까.. *what ~?* wae kŭron-gayo? 왜 그런가요? ◊ (*time*) … tong-an … 동안; *~ three days/two hours ..* il/tu shikan tong-an sam 일/두 시.. 동안; *please get it done ~ Mon..* wŏryoire kkŭnnaejuseyo 월요일(.. 끝내주세요 ◊ (*distance*): *I walke.. a mile* nanŭn il mairŭl kŏrŏtssŏ.. 나는 일 마일을 걸었어요; *it stretches ~ 100 miles* kŭgŏsŭn 100mairina ppŏdŏ issŏyo 그것은 100마일이나 뻗어 있어요 ◊ (*in fa.. of*): *I am ~ the idea* nanŭn kŭ saenggagi choayo 나는 그 생각.. 좋아요 ◊ (*instead of, in behalf of*) *let me do that ~ you* chega taes.. haedŭrigessŭmnida 제가 대신 해드리겠습니다; *we are agents ~* urinŭn …ŭl/rŭl taehaenghamnid.. 우리는 …을/를 대행합니다 ◊ (*in*

exchange for): **I bought it ~ $25**
25tallŏrŭl chugo sat-tta 25달러를
주고 샀다; **how much did you sell
t ~?** kŭgŏsŭl ŏlmae
p'aratssŭmnikka? 그것을 얼마에
팔았습니까?

rbid kŭmjihada 금지하다; **~ X to do
Y** Xege Yhanŭn kŏsŭl kŭmjihada
X에게 Y하는 것을 금지하다
rbidden adj kŭmjidoen 금지된; **~
city** chagŭmsŏng 자금성; **it's ~**
kŭgŏsŭn kŭmjidoeŏ issŭmnida
그것은 금지되어 있습니다; **smok-
ing / parking** ~ kŭmnyŏn / chuch'a
kŭmji 금연 / 주차 금지

rbidding hŏmak'an 험악한
rce **1** *n* (*violence*) p'ongnyŏk 폭력;
(*of explosion, wind, punch*) him 힘;
come into ~ (*of law etc*)
yuhyohaejida 유효해지다; **the ~s**
MIL chŏn-gun 전군 **2** *v/t door, lock*
pusuda 부수다; **~ X to do Y** Xege
Yhal kŏsŭl kangyohada X에게 Y할
것을 강요하다; **~ X open** Xŭl / rŭl
ŏktchiro yŏlda X을 / 를 억지로 열다
rced laugh, smile ŏktchiŭi 억지의;
confession kangjejŏgin 강제적인
rced landing pisang ch'angnyuk
비상 착륙
rceful argument himch'an 힘찬;
speaker sŏldŭngnyŏk innŭn 설득력
있는; *character* wŏn-giwangsŏnghan
원기왕성한
rceps kyŏmja 겸자
rcible entry kangjejŏgin 강제적인;
argument kangnyŏk'an 강력한
ord n yat'ŭn yŏul 얕은 여울
ore: **come to the ~** yumyŏnghaejida
유명해지다
reboding pulgirhan yegam 불길한
예감; **forecast 1** *n* yesang 예상; (*of
weather*) kisang yebo 기상 예보 **2** *v/t*
yesanghada 예상하다; **forecourt** (*of
service station*) kŭbyuhanŭn kot
급유하는 곳; **forefathers** chosang
조상; **forefinger** chipkke sonkkarak
집게 손가락; **foregone: that's a ~
conclusion** kŭgŏsŭn ch'ŏŭmbut'ŏ
ppŏnhan kyŏllonida 그것은 처음부터
뻔한 결론이다; **foreground** chŏn-
gyŏng 전경; **forehand** (*in tennis*)

p'ohaendŭ 포핸드; **forehead** ima
이마
foreign oegugŭi 외국의
foreign affairs oemu 외무
foreign currency oehwa 외화
foreigner oegugin 외국인
foreign exchange oeguk'wan 외국환;
foreign language oegugŏ 외국어;
Foreign Office *Br* Oemubu 외무부;
foreign policy oemu chŏngch'aek
외무 정책; **Foreign Minister** *Br*
oemu changgwan 외무 장관
foreman kongjangjang 공장장; LAW
paeshimwŏnjang 배심원장; **fore-
most** kajang chungnyohan 가장
중요한; **forerunner** sŏndu chuja 선두
주자; **foresee** yegyŏnhada 예견하다;
foreseeable yegyŏnhal su innŭn
예견할 수 있는; **in the ~ future**
kakkaun changnaee 가까운 장래에;
foresight sŏn-gyŏnjimyŏng 선견지명
forest sup 숲
forestry imhak 임학
foretaste sajŏn kyŏnghŏm 사전 경험
foretell yeŏnhada 예언하다
forever yŏng-wŏnhi 영원히
foreword sŏmun 서문
forfeit *v/t* sangshirhada 상실하다
forge *v/t* (*counterfeit*) mojohada
모조하다; *signature* wijohada
위조하다
forger wijoja 위조자
forgery (*bank bill, document*) wijo
위조
forget it-tta 잊다
forgetful chal ijŏbŏrinŭn 잘
잊어버리는
forget-me-not (*flower*)
mulmangch'o 물망초
forgive *v/t & v/i* yongsŏhada 용서하다
forgiveness yongsŏ 용서
fork *n* p'ok'ŭ 포크; (*in road*) pun-
gitchŏm 분기점
♦ **fork out** *v/i* F (*pay*) tonŭl naeda
돈을 내다
forklift (*truck*) chigech'a 지게차
form 1 *n* (*shape*) hyŏngt'ae 형태;
(*document*) yangshik 양식 **2** *v/t* (*in
clay etc*) mandŭlda 만들다;
friendship maet-tta 맺다; *opinion*
seuda 세우다; *past tense etc*

hwaryonghada 활용하다 **3** *v/i* (*take shape, develop*) kuch'ehwadoeda 구체화되다

formal hyŏngshiktchŏgin 형식적인; *recognition etc* kongtchŏgin 공적인

formality hyŏngshik 형식; *it's just a ~* kŭnyang hyŏngshigil ppunimnida 그냥 형식일 뿐입니다

formally *adv speak, behave* hyŏngshiktchŏgŭro 형식적으로; *recognized* kongtchŏgŭro 공적으로

format 1 *v/t diskette* p'omaet'ada 포맷하다; *document* yangshik'wahada 양식화하다 **2** *n* (*size: of magazine, paper etc*) k'ŭgi 크기; (*make-up: of program*) hyŏngshik 형식

formation (*act of forming*) hyŏngsŏng 형성; *~ flying* p'yŏndae pihaeng 편대 비행

formative hyŏngsŏnghanŭn 형성하는; *in his ~ years* kŭŭi in-gyŏk hyŏngsŏnggie 그의 인격 형성기에

former chŏnŭi 전의; *the ~* chŏnja 전자

formerly ijŏne 이전에

formidable musŏun 무서운

formula MATH, CHEM kongshik 공식; (*for success etc*) pangbŏp 방법

formulate (*express*) myŏnghwak'i p'yohyŏnhada 명확히 표현하다

fort MIL yosae 요새

forth: *back and ~* apttwiro 앞뒤로; *and so ~* kit'a tŭngdŭng 기타 등등

forthcoming (*future*) tagaonŭn 다가오는; *personality* saenggagŭl t'ŏnonnŭn 생각을 터놓는

fortieth mahŭn pŏntchaeŭi 마흔 번째의

fortnight *Br* tu chu 두 주

fortress MIL yosae 요새

fortunate un choŭn 운 좋은

fortunately un chok'edo 운 좋게도

fortune un 운; (*lot of money*) k'ŭn ton 큰 돈; *good ~* haeng-un haeng 행운

fortune-teller chŏmjaeng-i 점쟁이

forty mahŭn 마흔, saship 사십

forward 1 *adv* ap'ŭro 앞으로 **2** *adj pej*: *person* kŏnbangjin 건방진 **3** *n* SP p'owŏdŭ 포워드 **4** *v/t letter* hoesonghada 회송하다

forwarding agent COM unsuŏptch 운수업자

fossil hwasŏk 화석

foster child ibyang-a 입양아

foster parents yangbumo 양부모

foul 1 *n* SP panch'ik 반칙 **2** *adj smel taste* yŏkkyŏun 역겨운; *weather* chidok'an 지독한 **3** *v/t* SP panch'igŭro panghaehada 반칙으로 방해하다

found *v/t school etc* sŏllip'ada 설립하다

foundation (*of theory etc*) kŭn-gŏ 근거; (*organization*) chaedan 재단

foundations (*of building*) kich'o 기

founder *n* sŏlliptcha 설립자

foundry chujo kongjang 주조 공장

fountain punsu 분수

four net 넷, sa 사

four-star *hotel* mugunghwa nesŭi 무궁화 넷의

four-stick game yut 윷

fourteen yŏllet 열 넷, shipssa 십사

fourteenth yŏlne pŏntchaeŭi 열 네 번째의

fourth ne pŏntchaeŭi 네 번째의

fowl kagŭmnyu 가금류

fox n yŏu 여우

fraction ilbubun 일부분; (*decimal*) punsu 분수

fracture 1 *n* kŭm 금 **2** *v/t ...e* kŭmgage hada …에 금가게 하다

fragile kkaejigi shwiun 깨지기 쉬운

fragment *n* (*of vase etc*) chogak 조각 (*of story, conversation*) tanp'yŏn 단편

fragmentary tanp'yŏntchŏgin 단편적인

fragrance hyanggi 향기

fragrant hyangginanŭn 향기나는

frail yak'an 약한

frame 1 *n* (*of picture, window*) t'ŭl 틀 (*of eyeglasses*) t'e 테; (*of bicycle*) ppyŏdae 뼈대; *~ of mind* kibun 기분 **2** *v/t picture* t'ŭre kkiuda 틀에 끼우다; F *person* numyŏng ssŭiuda 누명 씌우다

framework kusang 구상

France P'ŭrangssŭ 프랑스

frank soltchik'an 솔직한

frankly soltchik'i 솔직히

ntic mich'in tŭt'an 미친 듯한
ternal hyŏngjeŭi 형제의
ud sagi 사기; (*person*) sagikkun
사기꾼
udulent sagiŭi 사기의
yed *cuffs* p'ullin 풀린
ak 1 *n* (*unusual event*) pyŏndŏk
변덕; (*two-headed person, animal
tc*) kihyŏng 기형; F (*strange person*)
yŏltchong 별종; *movie* | *jazz* ~ F
(*fanatic*) yŏnghwagwang /
haejŭgwang 영화광 / 재즈광 **2** *adj*
orm etc toryŏnhan 돌연한; ~ *wind*
olp'ung 돌풍
ckle chugŭnkkae 주근깨
e 1 *adj* (*at liberty*) chayuŭi 자유의;
(*no cost*) muryoŭi 무료의; *room,
able* pin 빈; *are you ~ this after-
oon?* onŭl ohue shigan issŭseyo?
늘 오후에 시간 있으세요?; ~ *and
asy* yŏyuroun 여유로운; *for* ~
nuryoro 무료로 **2** *v/t prisoners*
ŏkppanghada 석방하다
eebie F tŏm 덤
eedom chayu 자유
eedom of the press ŏllonŭi chayu
언론의 자유
ee kick (*in soccer*) p'ŭrik'ik 프리킥;
reelance 1 *adj* chayu kyeyagŭi 자유
계약의 **2** *adv work* chayu kyeyagŭro
자유 계약으로; **freelancer**
'ŭriraensŏ 프리랜서; **free market
economy** chayu shijang kyŏngje
자유 시장 경제; **free sample** muryo
yŏnbon 무료 견본; **free speech**
ŏllonŭi chayu 언론의 자유; **freeway**
kosokttoro 고속도로; **freewheel** *v/i*
on bicycle) p'edarŭl tteda 페달을
떼다
eeze 1 *v/t food, river* ŏllida 얼리다;
ages, bank account tonggyŏrhada
동결하다; *video* sun-gan
chŏngjishik'ida 순간 정지시키다 **2** *v/i*
of water) ŏlda 얼다
reeze over (*of river*) sumyŏni
ŏrŏbut-tta 수면이 얼어붙다
eezer naengdongshil 냉동실
eezing 1 *adj* mopsshi ch'uun 몹시
추운; *water* mopsshi ch'agaun 몹시
가운; *it's* ~ (*cold*) (*of weather*)
nopsshi ch'upssŭmnida 몹시

춥습니다; (*of water*) mopsshi
ch'agapssŭmnida 몹시 차갑습니다;
I'm ~ (*cold*) chŏnŭn mopsshi
ch'uwŏyo 저는 몹시 추워요 **2** *n*
naengdong 냉동; *10 below* ~ yŏngha
10to 영하 10도
freezing compartment
naengdongshil 냉동실
freezing point pingtchŏm 빙점
freight *n* hwamul hwaul; (*costs*)
hwamul unsongnyo 화물 운송료
freight car hwamulch'a 화물차
freighter (*ship*) hwamulsŏn 화물선;
(*airplane*) hwamul pihaenggi 화물
비행기
freight train hwamul yŏlch'a 화물
열차
French 1 *adj* P'ŭrangssŭŭi 프랑스의
2 *n* (*language*) P'ŭrangssŏ 프랑스어;
the ~ P'ŭrangssŭin 프랑스인
French doors ssang-yŏdaji yurimun
쌍여닫이 유리문; **French fries**
kamja t'wigim 감자 튀김; (*fast food*)
hurench'ihurai 후렌치후라이;
Frenchman P'ŭrangssŭ namja
프랑스 남자; **Frenchwoman**
P'ŭrangssŭ yŏja 프랑스 여자
frequency pinbŏnham 빈번함; RAD
chup'asu 주파수; *the increasing ~
of X* Xi / ga palsaenghanŭn hoessuŭi
chŭngga X이/가 발생하는 횟수의
증가
frequent[1] *adj* chajŭn 잦은; *visitor*
chaju onŭn 자주 오는
frequent[2] *v/t bar* chaju ch'at-tta 자주
찾다
frequently chaju 자주
fresh *air, water, food* shinsŏnhan
신선한; *complexion* saenggiinnŭn
생기있는; (*cold*) ssalssarhan 쌀쌀한;
start saeroun 새로운; (*impertinent*)
kŏnbangjin 건방진; *feel* ~
sangk'wehada 상쾌하다
♦ **freshen up 1** *v/i* sshit-tta 씻다 **2** *v/t
room, paintwork* saedanjanghada
새단장하다
freshman shinipssaeng 신입생
freshness (*of fruit, meat*) shinsŏndo
신선도; (*of style, approach*)
shinsŏnham 신선함; (*of weather*)
ssalssarham 쌀쌀함

freshwater *adj* minmurŭi 민물의
fret *v/i* kominhada 고민하다
friction mach'al 마찰
friction tape chŏn-gisŏnyong komut'eip'ŭ 전기선용 고무테이프
Friday kŭmyoil 금요일
fridge naengjanggo 냉장고
friend ch'in-gu 친구; **make ~s** (*of one person*) ch'in-gurŭl sagwida 친구를 사귀다; (*of two people*) ch'in-guga toeda 친구가 되다; **make ~s with X** Xwa/kwa ch'in-guga toeda X와/과 친구가 되다
friendly *adj atmosphere* tajŏnghan 다정한; *person* ch'inhan 친한; (*easy to use*) shwiun 쉬운; **be ~ with X** (*be friends*) Xwa/kwa ch'inhage toeda X와/과 친하게 되다
friendship ujŏng 우정
fries hurench'ihurai 후렌치후라이
fright kkamtchak nollam 깜짝 놀람; **give X a** Xŭl/rŭl kkamtchak nollage hada X을/를 깜짝 놀라게 하다
frighten *v/t* kŏptchuda 겁주다; **be ~ed** kŏmnada 겁난다; **don't be ~ed** kŏmnaeji maseyo 겁내지 마세요; **be ~ed of** ...i/ga kŏmnada ...이/가 겁난다
frightening kŏmnanŭn 겁나는
frigid (*sexually*) pulgamtchŭng-ŭi 불감증의
frill (*on dress etc*) p'ŭril 프릴; (*fancy extra*) pugamul 부가물
fringe (*on dress, curtains etc*) sul 술; (*in hair*) ammŏri 앞머리; (*edge*) kajangjari 가장자리
frisk *v/t* momsusaek'ada 몸수색하다
frisky *puppy etc* kiun chok'e ttwiŏdaninŭn 기운 좋게 뛰어다니는
♦ **fritter away** *time, fortune* hŏbihada 허비하다
frivolous shirŏmnŭn 실없는
frizzy *hair* kopssŭlgŏrinŭn 곱슬거리는
frog kaeguri 개구리
frogman chamsubu 잠수부
from ◊ (*in time*) ...(esŏ)but'ŏ ...(에서)부터; **~ 9 to 5** (*o'clock*) ahopshibut'ŏ tasŏsshikkaji 9시부터 5시까지; **~ the 18th century** 18segibut'ŏ 18세기부터; **~ today on**

onŭlbut'ŏ 오늘부터; **~ next Tues•** taŭm chu hwayoilbut'ŏ 다음 주 화요일부터 ◊ (*in space*) ...esŏ(but ...에서(부터); **~ here to there** yŏgiesŏ chŏgiro 여기에서 저기로; **drove here ~ Seoul** urinŭn Sŏur yŏgikkaji unjŏnhae wassŭmnida 우리는 서울에서 여기까지 운전해 왔습니다 ◊ (*origin: of people*) ...(ŭ)robut'ŏ ...(으)로부터; **a letter Jo** Chorobut'ŏ on p'yŏnji 조로부터 온 편지; **a gift ~ the manageme** kyŏng-yŏngjinŭrobut'ŏŭi sŏnmul 경영진으로부터의 선물; **it doesn'** **say who it's ~** igŏsŭn nuguegesŏ kŏshinji palk'yŏit-tchi ant'a 이것은 누구에게서 온 것인지 밝혀있지 않다; **I am ~ New Jersey** chŏnŭn Nyujŏji ch'ulsshinimnida 저는 뉴저지 출신입니다; **made ~ ba-nanas** pananaro mandŭn 바나나로 만든 ◊ (*because of*) ...(ŭ)ro ...(으). **tired ~ the journey** yŏhaeng-ŭro chich'in 여행으로 지친; **it's ~ ove** **eating** nŏmu mani mŏgŏsŏ kŭrŏt' 너무 많이 먹어서 그렇다
front 1 *n* (*of building, book*) ap 앞; (*cover organization*) kanp'an 간판 MIL, (*of weather*) chŏnsŏn 전선; **a cold/warm ~** hannaeng/onnan chŏnsŏn 한랭/온난 전선; **in ~** ap'e(sŏ) 앞에(서); **in ~ of ...** aptchoge(sŏ) ...의 앞쪽에(서); **at the ~** ap'e(sŏ) 앞에(서); (*in a race*) sŏndue(sŏ) 선두에(서); **in ~ of ...** aptchoge(sŏ) ...의 앞쪽에(서 **2** *adj wheel, seat* aptchogŭi 앞쪽의 **3** *v/t TV program* chinhaenghada 진행하다
front cover p'yoji 표지; **front door** ammun 앞문; **front entrance** chŏngmun 정문
frontier kuk-kkyŏng 국경; *fig* (*of knowledge, science*) ch'oech'ŏmda 최첨단
front page (*of newspaper*) ilmyŏn 일면; **front page news** ilmyŏn ki 일면 기사; **front row** aptchul 앞줄 **front seat passenger** (*in car*) aptchwasŏk sŭnggaek 앞좌석 승가 **front-wheel drive** ap-ppak'wi

ullim 앞바퀴 굴림

ost sŏri 서리

ostbite tongsang 동상

ostbitten tongsang-e kŏllin 동상에
걸린

osted glass pult'umyŏnghan yuri
불투명한 유리

osting (on cake) sŏlt'ang-ŭl ip'im
설탕을 입힘

osty weather sŏriga naerinŭn 서리가
내리는; welcome naengdamhan
냉담한

oth n kŏp'um 거품

othy cream etc kŏp'umi manŭn
거품이 많은

own 1 n tchip'urin ŏlgul 찌푸린 얼굴
2 v/t tchip'urida 찌푸리다

ozen ŏrŭn 얼은; wastes of Siberia
kŭk'anŭi 극한의; I'm ~ F ch'uwŏsŏ ŏl
higyŏng-ieyo 추워서 얼
지경이에요; a ~ chicken / pizza
naengdong tak / p'ija 냉동 닭 / 피자

ozen food naengdong shikp'um
냉동 식품

uit kwail 과일

uitful discussions etc sŏngkkwaga
nanŭn 성과가 많은

uit juice kwail chussŭ 과일 쥬스

uit salad kwail saellŏdŭ 과일 샐러드

ustrate v/t person, plans
chwajŏlshik'ida 좌절시키다

ustrated look, sigh chwajŏldoen
좌절된

ustrating tchajŭngnanŭn 짜증나는

ustratingly slow, hard
tchajŭngnadorok 짜증나도록

ustration chwajŏlgam 좌절감;
sexual ~ sŏngtchŏk yok-kku
pulman 성적 욕구 불만; the ~s of
modern life hyŏndaejŏk salme
taehan chwajŏl 현대적 삶에 대한
좌절

y v/t chijida 지지다; (stir-~) poktta
볶다; (deep-~) t'wigida 튀기다

ied egg kyeran hurai 계란 후라이

ied potatoes kamja t'wigim 감자
튀김

ying pan huraip'aen 후라이팬

ck v/t V ...wa / kwa sŏnggyohada
...와 / 과 성교하다; ~! sshibal 씨발!; ~
him / that! sshibal nom / nomŭi kŏt!

씨발 놈 / 놈의 것!

◆fuck off V kkŏjida 꺼지다; ~!
kkojyŏbŏryŏ! 꺼져버려!

fucking V 1 adj chidok'an 지독한
2 adv chidok'age 지독하게

fuel n yŏllyo 연료

fugitive n tomangja 도망자

fulfill shirhaenghada 실행하다; feel
~ed (in job, life) manjok'ada
만족하다

fulfilling job manjokssŭrŏun
만족스러운

fulfillment (of contract etc) shirhaeng
실행; (spiritual) manjok-kkam
만족감

full bottle kadŭk ch'an 가득 찬; hotel,
bus, diskette kkwak ch'an 꽉 찬;
account, report sangsehan 상세한;
life pappŭn 바쁜; schedule, day
ppadŭt'an 빠듯한; ~ of ...(ŭ)ro
kadŭk'an ...(으)로 가득한; ~ up
hotel etc kadŭk ch'ada 가득 차다;
(with food) paeburŭda 배부르다;
pay in ~ chŏnaegŭl naeda 전액을
내다; sorry, we're ~ (at hotel)
choesonghajiman, ta ch'assŭmnida
죄송하지만, 다 찼습니다

full cover (insurance) chonghap
pohŏm 종합 보험; full-grown ta
charan 다 자란; full-length dress
chŏnshindaeŭi 전신대의; movie
changp'yŏnŭi 장편의; full moon
porŭmttal 보름달; full stop
mach'imp'yo 마침표; full-time 1 adj
worker, job chŏnshiganjeŭi
전시간제의 2 adv work
chŏnshiganjero 전시간제로

fully ta 다, wanjŏnhi 완전히; describe
sangsehi 상세히

fumble v/t catch sŏt'urŭge chaptta
서투르게 잡다

◆fumble around tŏdŭmgŏrimyŏ
ch'at-tta 더듬거리며 찾다

fume: be fuming F kyŏngnohada
격노하다

fumes maeyŏn 매연

fun chaemi 재미; it was great ~
kŭgŏsŭn chŏngmal chaemiissŏssŏyo
그것은 정말 재미있었어요; bye,
have ~! annyŏnghi kyeseyo,
chaemiitkke chinaeseyo! 안녕히

function 계세요. 재미있게 지내세요!; **for ~** chaemiro 재미로; **make ~ of** ...ŭl/rŭl nollida ...을/를 놀리다

function 1 n (of employee) chingnŭng 직능; (of machine part) kinŭng 기능; (reception etc) haengsa 행사 **2** v/i chakttonghada 작동하다; **~ as** ...ŭi kinŭng-ŭl hada ...의 기능을 하다

function key COMPUT kinŭngk'i 기능키

fund 1 n chagŭm 자금 **2** v/t project etc ...e chagŭmŭl chegonghada ...에 자금을 제공하다

fundamental (basic) kibonjŏgin 기본적인; (substantial) ponjiltchŏgin 본질적인; (crucial) chung-yohan 중요한

fundamentally different, altered ponjiltchŏgŭro 본질적으로

funeral changnyeshik 장례식

funeral home yŏng-anso 영안소

funfair yuwŏnji 유원지

funicular (railway) k'eibŭl ch'ŏltto 케이블 철도

funnel n (of ship) kulttuk 굴뚝

funnily (oddly) isanghage 이상하게; (comically) utkkige 웃기게; **~ enough** isanghagedo 이상하게도

funny (comical) usŭun 우스운; (odd) isanghan 이상한

fur (of coat, animal) t'ŏl 털

furious (angry) kyŏngnohanŭn 격노하는; **at a ~ pace** maengnyŏrhan sokttoro 맹렬한 속도로

furnace hwadŏk 화덕; (for metal) yonggwangno 용광로

furnish room ...e kagurŭl tŭryŏ not'a ...에 가구를 들여 놓다; (supply) konggŭp'ada 공급하다

furniture kagu 가구; **a piece of ~** kagu han chŏm 가구 한 점

furry animal, coat t'ŏri p'ungsŏnghan 털이 풍성한

further 1 adj (additional) tto tarŭn 또 다른; (more distant) tŏ mŏn 더 먼;

until ~ notice ch'uhu t'ongjiga iss ttaekkaji 추후 통지가 있을 때까지

have you anything ~ to say? tŏ marhal kŏshi issŭshimnikka? 더 말할 것이 있으십니까? **2** adv walk drive tŏ 더; **~, I want to say ...** chega tŏtppuch'yŏ marhago ship'ŭ kŏsŭn ... imnida 제가 덧붙여 말하ᄀ 싶은 것은 ... 입니다; **2 miles ~ (o** 2mailboda tŏ mŏn 2마일보다 더 먼 **3** v/t cause etc chojanghada 조장하ᄃ

furthest 1 adj kajang mŏn 가장 먼 **2** adv kajang mŏlli 가장 멀리

furtive glance ŭnmirhan 은밀한

fury (anger) kyŏngno 격노

fuse ELEC **1** n p'yujŭ 퓨즈 **2** v/i p'yujŭga kkŭnk'ida 퓨즈가 끊기다 **3** v/t p'yujŭrŭl kkŭnt'a 퓨즈를 끊디

fusebox tukkŏbijip 두꺼비집

fuselage tongch'e 동체

fuse wire tohwasŏn 도화선

fusion yunghap 융합

fuss n nallibŏpssŏk 난리법석; **make ~** (complain) nallich'ida 난리치다; (behave in exaggerated way) nallibŏpssŏk ttŏlda 난리법석 떨다; **make a ~ of** (be very attentive to) ...ege modŭn kwanshimŭl ssot-tta ...에게 모든 관심을 쏟다

fussy person kkadaroun 까다로운; design etc chinach'ige kkumin 지나치게 꾸민; **be a ~ eater** shikssŏng-i kkadaroptta 식성이 까다롭다

futile ssŭlte ŏmnŭn 쓸데 없는

future n mirae 미래; GRAM miraehyŏng 미래형; **in ~** miraenŭ 미래에는

futures FIN sŏnmul kyeyak 선물 계 **futures market** FIN sŏnmul shijang 선물 시장

futuristic design ch'ohyŏndaejŏgin 초현대적인

fuzzy hair kopssŭlgopssŭrhan 곱슬곱슬한; (out of focus) hŭrit'an 흐릿한

G

dget kanttanhan togu 간단한 도구

g 1 n chaegal 재갈; (*joke*) kaegŭ 그 **2** v/t person ...ege chaegarŭl mullida ...에게 재갈을 물리다; *the ress* ogap'ada 억압하다

in v/t (*acquire*) ŏt-tta 얻다; **~ speed** okttorŭl naeda 속도를 내다; **~ 5 ounds** op'aundŭga nŭlda 파운드가 늘다

le kangp'ung 강풍

ll bladder ssŭlgae 쓸개

llery (*for art*) hwarang 화랑; (*in eater*) maen wich'ŭng kwallamsŏk 위층 관람석

lley (*on ship*) chubang 주방

llon kaellŏn 갤런

llop v/i chiltchuhada 질주하다

llows kyosudae 교수대

llstone tamsŏk 담석

mble tobak'ada 도박하다

mbler tobak-kkun 도박꾼

mbling tobak 도박

me n shihap 시합; (*of baseball, ootball*) kyŏnggi 경기; (*children's*) ori 놀이; (*in tennis*) keim 게임

ng p'aegŏri 패거리; (*of criminals*) aeng 갱

gang up on p'aejiŏ konggyŏk'ada 지어 공격하다

ngster nappŭn muri 나쁜 무리

ngway t'ongno 통로

p (*in wall, teeth*) t'ŭm 틈; (*for arking, in figures*) pin-got 빈 곳; (*in me, conversation*) kongbaek 공백; (*between opinions, characters*) ch'ai 이

pe v/i (*of person*) ibŭl ttak pŏlligo araboda 입을 딱 벌리고 바라보다

pe at ibŭl ttak pŏllin ch'ae ŏkssŭl ilk'o ch'yŏdaboda 입을 딱 린 채 넋을 잃고 쳐다보다

ping **~ hole** k'ŭge pŏrŏjin kumŏng 게 벌어진 구멍

rage (*for parking*) ch'ago 차고;

(*for gas*) chuyuso 주유소; (*for repairs*) chadongch'a suriso 자동차 수리소

garbage ssŭregi 쓰레기; fig (*useless stuff*) ssŭlmoŏmnŭn kŏt 쓸모없는 것; (*poor quality item*) pullyangp'um 불량품; (*nonsense*) maldo an toenŭn sori 말도 안 되는 소리; *don't talk ~!* mal katchi anŭn sori hajido mara! 말 같지 않은 소리 하지도 마라!

garbage can ssŭregi t'ong 쓰레기 통; **garbage collection** ssŭregi sujip 쓰레기 수집; **garbage dump** ssŭregi p'yegijang 쓰레기 폐기장

garden chŏng-wŏn 정원, ttŭl 뜰

gardener (*professional*) chŏng-wŏnsa 정원사; *he's an enthusiastic ~* kŭnŭn chŏng-wŏnesŏ irhanŭn kŏsŭl choahaeyo 그는 정원에서 일하는 것을 좋아해요

gardening wŏnye 원예

gargle v/i ibanŭl kashida 입안을 가시다

garish chinach'ige hwaryŏhan 지나치게 화려한

garland n hwahwan 화환

garlic manŭl 마늘

garment ŭibok 의복

garnish v/t komyŏng-ŭro changshik'ada 고명으로 장식하다

garrison n (*place*) kun chudunji 군 주둔지; (*troops*) chudun-gun 주둔군

garter kat'ŏ 가터

gas n kich'e 기체; (*for cooking*) kasŭ 가스; (*gasoline*) hwibaryu 휘발유

gash n kilgo kipkke pein sangch'ŏ 길고 깊게 베인 상처

gasket kasŭk'et 가스켓

gasoline hwibaryu 휘발유

gasp 1 n hŏltttŏk-kkŏrim 헐떡거림; *with a ~* hŏltttŏk-kkŏrimyŏ 헐떡거리며 **2** v/i hŏltttŏk-kkŏrida 헐떡거리다; **~ for breath** sumŭl hŏlttŏgida 숨을 헐떡이다

gas pedal aekssellŏreit'ŏ p'edal 액셀러레이터 페달; **gas pump** chuyu p'ŏmp'ŭ 주유 펌프; **gas station** chuyuso 주유소

gate taemun 대문 (at airport) t'apssŭnggu 탑승구

gatecrash ch'odaebat-tchi ank'o kada 초대받지 않고 가다

gateway (entrance) ipkku 입구; (passage) t'ongno 통로; fig kwanmun 관문

gather 1 v/t facts, information moŭda 모으다; **~ speed** songnyŏgŭl nŭllyŏgada 속력을 늘려가다; **am I to ~ that …?** …rago ihaehamyŏn matssŭmnikka? …라고 이해하면 맞습니까? **2** v/i (understand) ch'uch'ŭk'ada 추측하다
♦ **gather up** possessions …ŭl/rŭl chuwŏ moŭda …을/를 주워 모으다

gathering n (group of people) moim 모임

gaudy ch'onsŭrŏpkke hwaryŏhan 촌스럽게 화려한

gauge 1 n kyegi 계기 **2** v/t pressure ch'ŭktchŏnghada 측정하다; opinion p'andanhada 판단하다

gaunt such'ŏk'an 수척한

gauze kŏjŭ 거즈

gay 1 n (homosexual) tongsŏngaeja 동성애자 **2** adj tongsŏngaeŭi 동성애의

gaze 1 n ŭngshi 응시 **2** v/i ŭngshihada 응시하다
♦ **gaze at** …ŭl/rŭl ŭngshihada …을/를 응시하다

GB (= **Great Britain**) Yŏngguk 영국

GDP (= **gross domestic product**) kungnae ch'ongsaengsan 국내 총생산

gear n (equipment) yonggu 용구; (in vehicles) kiŏ 기어

gear shift kiŏ chŏnhwan changch'i 기어 전환 장치

gel (for hair) chel 젤; (for shower) mulbinu 물비누

gem posŏk 보석; fig (book etc) myŏngjak 명작; (person) pobaegat'ŭn saram 보배같은 사람

gender sŏng 성

gene yujŏnja 유전자; **it's in his ~**s saramŭi ch'ŏnsŏng-ida 그 사람의 천성이다

genealogy book chokppo 족보

general 1 n (in army) changgun 장 **in ~** ilbanjŏgŭro 일반적으로 **2** adj ilbanjŏgin 일반적인; (overall) chŏnch'ejŏgin 전체적인

general anesthetic chŏnshin mach'wi 전신 마취

general election ch'ongsŏn-gŏ 총선거

generalization ilbanhwa 일반화

generalize ilbanhwahada 일반화하

generally ilbanjŏgŭro 일반적으로

generate (create) nat-tta 낳다; electricity palssaengshik'ida 발생시키다; (in linguistics) saengsŏnghada 생성하다; feeling irŭk'ida 일으키다; accident, new situation etc yagihada 야기하다

generation (of family) sedae 세대

generation gap sedae ch'ai 세대 차이

generator paltchŏn-gi 발전기

generosity nŏgŭrŏum 너그러움

generous (with money) inshim ch 인심 좋은; (not too critical) kwandaehan 관대한; portion etc p'ungbuhan 풍부한

genetic yujŏnjŏgin 유전적인

genetically yujŏnjŏgŭro 유전적으로

genetic engineering yujŏn kongh 유전 공학

genetic fingerprint yujŏnja chimu 유전자 지문

geneticist yujŏnhaktcha 유전학자

genetics yujŏnhak 유전학

genial person, company tajŏnghan 다정한

genitals saengshikki 생식기

genius ch'ŏnjae 천재

gentle pudŭrŏun 부드러운; person onhwahan 온화한

gentleman shinsa 신사

gents (toilet) namja hwajangshil 남 화장실

genuine chintchaŭi 진짜의; person chinshinhan 진실한

geographical features chirijŏk 지ㄹ

geography (of area, subject) chiri

...리

...ological *features* chijirŭi 지질의;
...*urvey* chijirhaktchŏk 지질학적
...ologist chijirhaktcha 지질학자
...ology (*of area*) chijil 지질; (*subject*)
...hijirhak 지질학
...ometric(al) kihahaktchŏk
...|하학적
...ometry kihahak 기하학
...riatric 1 *adj* noinppyŏng-ŭi
...인병의 2 *n* noin 노인
...rm segyun 세균; (*of idea etc*) ssak
...싹
...erman 1 *adj* Togirŭi 독일의 2 *n*
...*person*) Togirin 독일인; (*language*)
...Togirŏ 독일어
...ermany Togil 독일
...rm warfare segyunjŏn 세균전
...sticulate sontchisŭro marhada
...손짓으로 말하다
...sture *n* (*with hand*) sontchit 손짓;
...*g* (*of friendship*) ŭisa p'yoshi 의사
...표시
...t 1 *v/t* ◊ (*obtain*) ŏt-tta 얻다; (*fetch*)
...kajyŏoda 가져오다; (*receive*) pat-tta
...받다; (*catch: bus, train etc*) t'ada
...타다; (*understand*) alda 알다; *I don't*
...*~ it* (*don't understand*) ihaehal su
...ŏpssŏyo 이해할 수 없어요 ◊
...*become*) ...haejida ...해지다; *~*
...*ired / careless* p'igonhaejida /
...pujuŭihaejida 피곤해지다 /
...부주의해지다; *be ~ting older /*
...*warmer* chŏmjŏm nŭlgŏgada /
...tŏwŏjida 점점 늙어가다 / 더워지다 ◊
...*causative*): *~ sth done* muŏsŭl
...hage hada 무엇을 하게 하다; *~ s.o.*
...*to do sth* nuguege muŏsŭl harago
...hada 누구에게 무엇을 하라고 하다; *~*
...*you must ~ him to agree* kŭrŭl
...pandŭshi sŏlttŭkshik'yŏya hamnida
...그를 반드시 설득시켜야 합니다; *~*
...*one's hair cut* mŏrirŭl charŭda
...머리를 자르다; *~ the car washed*
...sech'ashik'ida 세차시키다; *~ the car*
...*fixed* ch'arŭl surishik'ida 차를
...수리시키다; *~ sth ready* muŏsŭl hal
...chunbirŭl kach'uda 무엇을 할
...준비를 갖추다; *~ going* (*leave*)
...ttŏnada 떠나다 ◊ (*have*
...*opportunity*): *~ to do sth* muŏsŭl

haepoda 무엇을 해보다; *~ to know*
alge toeda 알게 되다 ◊ *have got*
kajida 가지다; *I've got some*
money tonŭl chom kajigo issŏyo
돈을 좀 가지고 있어요; *I've got*
something for you tangshinhant'e
chul kŏshi issŏyo 당신한테 줄 것이
있어요; *I've got a headache*
mŏriga ap'ayo 머리가 아파요
◊ (*have ~ to*) ...haeya hada ...해야
하다; *I have got to study / see him*
nanŭn kongbuhaeya hamnida / kŭrŭl
mannaboaya hamnida 나는 공부해야
합니다 / 그를 만나보아야 합니다; *I*
don't want to, but I've got to
wŏnhajinŭn anch'iman
haeyahamnida 원하지는 않지만
해야합니다 2 *v/i* (*arrive*) toch'ak'ada
도착하다

◆ **get about** (*travel*) yŏgijŏgi
yŏhaenghada 여기저기 여행하다; (*be*
mobile) toratanida 돌아다니다
◆ **get along** (*progress*) chinaeda
지내다; (*to party etc*) kada 가다;
(*with s.o.*) saiga chot'a 사이가 좋다
◆ **get at** (*criticize*) pinjŏngdaeda
빈정대다; (*imply, mean*)
marharyŏhada 말하려하다
◆ **get away 1** *v/i* (*leave*) ttŏnada
떠나다 2 *v/t*: *get sth away from*
s.o. nuguegesŏ muŏsŭl ppaeat-tta
누구에게서 무엇을 빼앗다
◆ **get away with** *crime etc* pŏl pat-
tchi ank'o haenaeda 벌 받지 않고
해내다
◆ **get back 1** *v/i* toraoda 돌아오다; *I'll*
~ to you on that kŭgŏse taehan
ŭngdabŭl tŭrigessŭmnida 그것에
대한 응답을 드리겠습니다 2 *v/t*
(*obtain again*) toech'at-tta 되찾다
◆ **get by** (*pass*) chinagada 지나가다;
(*financially*) kkuryŏnagada
꾸려나가다
◆ **get down 1** *v/i* (*from ladder etc*)
naeryŏgada 내려가다; (*duck etc*)
ŏpttŭrida 엎드리다 2 *v/t* (*depress*)
uurhaehada 우울해하다
◆ **get down to** *work* shijak'ada
시작하다; *real facts* tat'a 닿다
◆ **get in 1** *v/i* (*of train, plane*)
toch'ak'ada 도착하다; (*come home*)

chibe tŭrŏoda 집에 들어오다; (*to car*) t'ada 타다; **how did they ~?** (*of thieves, snakes etc*) ŏttŏk'e tŭrŏgassŭlkkayo? 어떻게 들어갔을까요? **2** *v/t* (*to suitcase etc*) chibŏ nŏt'a 집어 넣다

♦ **get off 1** *v/i* (*from bus etc*) naerida 내리다; (*finish work*) iri kkŭnnada 일이 끝나다; (*not be punished*) pŏrŭl myŏnhada 벌을 면하다 **2** *v/t clothes, hat, footwear* pŏt-tta 벗다; *lid, top* pŏtkkida 벗기다; **~ the grass!** chandie tŭrŏgaji mashio! 잔디에 들어가지 마시오!

♦ **get off with** *Br* (*sexually*) …wa/kwa chŭlgida …와/과 즐기다; **~ a small fine** kabyŏun pŏlgŭmŭro momyŏnhada 가벼운 벌금으로 모면하다

♦ **get on 1** *v/i* (*to bike, bus, train*) t'ada 타다; (*be friendly*) saiga chot'a 사이가 좋다; (*become old*) naidŭrŏ kada 나이들어 가다; (*make progress*) chinch'ŏkttoeda 진척되다; *it's getting on* (*late*) shigani nŭjŏjinda 시간이 늦어진다; *he's getting on* kŭnŭn kkwae naidŭrŏganda 그는 꽤 나이들어간다; *he's getting on for 50* kŭnŭn nai oshibi ta toeŏt-tta 그는 나이 50이 다 되었다; *he's getting on well at school* kŭnŭn hak-kkyoesŏ chal haenaagago it-tta 그는 학교에서 잘 해나가고 있다 **2** *v/t lid, top of box* ssŭiuda 씌우다; *boots* shintta 신다; **~ the bus / one's bike** pŏssŭe / chajŏn-gŏe t'ada 버스에 / 자전거에 타다; *I can't get these pants on* i pajirŭl ibŭl suga ŏpssŭmnida 이 바지를 입을 수가 없습니다

♦ **get out 1** *v/i* (*from car etc*) naerida 내리다; (*of prison*) naoda 나오다; **~!** nagayo! 나가요; *let's ~ of here* yŏgiesŏ nagapsshida 여기에서 나갑시다; *I don't ~ much these days* yojŭm pyŏllo pakke nagaji anssŭmnida 요즘 별로 밖에 나가지 않습니다 **2** *v/t nail, sth jammed, gun, pen* ppaenaeda 빼내다; *stain* ŏpssaeda 없애다

♦ **get over** *fence, disappointment etc* igyŏnaeda 이겨내다, kŭkppok'ada 극복하다; *lover* it-tta 잊다

♦ **get over with:** *let's get it over with* kŭnyang huttak haebŏripsshi 그냥 후딱 해버립시다

♦ **get through** (*on telephone*) t'onghwahada 통화하다; (*make self understood*) ihaeshik'ida 이해시키

♦ **get up 1** *v/i* (*in morning, from ch etc*) irŏnada 일어나다; (*of wind*) ild 일다 **2** *v/t hill* orŭda 오르다

getaway (*from robbery*) tomang 도망; **~ car** toju ch'aryang 도주 차

get-together ch'in-gyo moim 친교 모임

ghastly (*horrible*) chidok'an 지독한

gherkin chagŭn oi 작은 오이

ghetto pinmin-ga 빈민가

ghost kwishin 귀신

ghostly kwishin-gat'ŭn 귀신같은

giant 1 *n* kŏin 거인; *fig* kŏjang 거장 **2** *adj* kŏdaehan 거대한

gibberish hoengsŏlsusŏl 횡설수설

giblets choryuŭi naejang 조류의 내

giddiness hyŏn-gitchŭng 현기증

giddy ŏjirŏun 어지러운

gift sŏnmul 선물; (*natural ability*) t'agonan chaenŭng 타고난 재능

gifted t'agonan chaenŭng-i innŭn 타고난 재능이 있는

giftwrap *v/t* p'ojanghada 포장하다

gigabyte COMPUT kigabait'ŭ 기가바이트

gigantic pangdaehan 방대한

giggle 1 *v/i* kkilkkil ut-tta 낄낄 웃다 **2** *n* kkilkkil usŭm 낄낄 웃음

gill (*of fish*) agami 아가미

gilt *n* kŭmbak 금박; **~s** FIN uryangju 우량주

gimmick (*promotional*) suppŏp 수법 (*new invention*) koanmul 고안물

gin chin 진; **~ and tonic** chint'onik 진토닉

ginger *n* (*spice*) saenggang 생강

gingerbeer chinjŏ piŏ 진저 비어; **gingerbread** saenggangppang 생강빵; **ginger tea** saenggangch'a 생강차

ginseng insam 인삼

gipsy chipsshi 집시

giraffe kirin 기린

...der n taedŭlbo 대들보
...i yŏja 여자; (young) sonyŏ 소녀
...friend yŏja ch'in-gu 여자 친구;
...(lover) aein 애인
...guide sonyŏ tanwŏn 소녀단원
...lie magazine p'orŭno chaptchi
르노 잡지
...scout kŏlsŭk'aut'ŭ 걸스카우트
...t yotchŏm 요점
...e chuda 주다; fml tŭrida 드리다;
...supply: electricity etc) konggŭp'ada
급하다; ~ a talk iyagirŭl haejuda
이야기를 해주다; ~ a cry ulda 울다;
~ a groan shinŭmhada 신음하다; ◆
...er my regards kŭnyŏege anburŭl
...hŏnhaejuseyo 그녀에게 안부를
...해주세요
give away (as present) chuda 주다;
...betray) paebanhada 배반하다; give
...neself away uyŏnhi p'ongnohada
...우연히 폭로하다
give back tollyŏjuda 돌려주다
give in 1 v/i (surrender) kulbok'ada
...굴복하다 2 v/t (hand in)
...hech'urhada 제출하다
give off smell, fumes naeda 내다
give onto (open onto) ...(ŭ)ro
...'onghada ...(으)로 통하다
give out 1 v/t leaflets etc paebuhada
...배부하다 2 v/i (of supplies, strength)
...ahada 다하다
give up 1 v/t smoking etc kkŭnt'a
...끊다; give oneself up to the police
...kyŏngch'are chasuhada 경찰에
...자수하다 2 v/i (cease habit) kkŭnt'a
...끊다; (stop making effort) p'ogihada
...포기하다
give way (of bridge etc) munŏjida
...무너지다
...ven name sŏng-ŭl cheoehan irŭm
...성을 제외한 이름
...acier pingha 빙하
...lad kippŭn 기쁜; ~ to see you
...mannasŏ pan-gapssŭmnida 만나서
...반갑습니다; yes, I will be ~ to ye,
...kikkŏi hagessŏyo 예, 기꺼이
...하겠어요
...ladly kikkŏi 기꺼이
...lamor maeryŏk 매력
...lamorous maeryŏgi nŏmch'inŭn
...매력이 넘치는

glance 1 n hŭlgŭt pom 흘긋 봄 2 v/i:
~ at ...ŭl/rŭl hŭlgŭt poda ...을/를
흘긋 보다
gland sŏn 선
glandular fever sŏnyŏl 선열
glare 1 n (of sun, headlights)
nunbushinŭn pit 눈부시는 빛 2 v/i
(of sun, headlights) nunbushige
pinnada 눈부시게 빛나다
◆ glare at noryŏboda 노려보다
glaring adj mistake nune hwak
ttŭinŭn 눈에 확 띄는
glass (material) yuri 유리; (for drink)
k'ŏp 컵
glasses an-gyŏng 안경
glaze n yuyak 유약
◆ glaze over (of eyes) nune
saenggirŭl ilt'a 눈에 생기를 잃다
glazed expression hŭrit'an 흐릿한
glazier yuriŏptcha 유리업자
glazing (glass) yuri 유리
gleam 1 n ŏsŭrehan pit 어스레한 빛
2 v/i ŏsŭrehage pich'ida 어스레하게
비치다
glee kippŭm 기쁨
gleeful kippŏhanŭn 기뻐하는
glib ipsshim choŭn 입심 좋은
glide (of bird, plane) hwalgonghada
활공하다; (of person, furniture)
mikkŭrojida 미끄러지다
glider SP kŭllaidŏ 글라이더
gliding n SP kŭllaidŏ kyŏnggi
글라이더 경기
glimmer 1 n (of light) hŭimihan pit
희미한 빛; - of hope shillalgat'ŭn
hŭimang 실낱같은 희망 2 v/i
kkamppagida 깜빡이다
glimpse 1 n hŭlkkŭt pom 흘끗 봄;
catch a ~ of ...ŭl/rŭl hŭlkkŭt poda
...을/를 흘끗 보다 2 v/t hŭlkkŭt
poda 흘끗 보다
glint 1 n pantchak 반짝 2 v/i (of light)
pantchak pinnada 반짝 빛나다; (of
eyes) pŏnttŭgida 번득이다
glisten v/i pantchak-kkŏrida
반짝거리다
glitter v/i pantchakpantchak pinnada
반짝반짝 빛나다
glitterati sagyogye saramdŭl 사교계
사람들
gloat v/i kosohaehada 고소해하다; ~

over kosohaehada 고소해하다

global (*worldwide*) chŏnsegyeŭi 전세계의; (*without exception*) t'onggwaljŏgin 통괄적인

global economy segye kyŏngje 세계 경제

globalization segyehwa 세계화

global market segye shijang 세계 시장

global warming segye onnanhwa 세계 온난화

globe (*the earth*) chigu 지구; (*model of earth*) chigubon 지구본

gloom (*darkness*) ŏduk'ŏmk'ŏmham 어두컴컴함; (*mood*) uul 우울

gloomy *room* ŏduk'ŏmk'ŏmhan 어두컴컴한; *mood, person* uurhan 우울한

glorious *weather* malgŭn 맑은; *victory* yŏnggwangsŭrŏun 영광스러운

glory *n* yŏnggwang 영광

gloss *n* (*shine*) yun 윤; (*general explanation*) chusŏk 주석

glossary yong-ŏ p'uri 용어 풀이

gloss paint kwangt'aek p'eint'ŭ 광택 페인트

glossy **1** *adj paper* kwangt'aek nanŭn 광택 나는 **2** *n* (*magazine*) kogŭp chaptchi 고급 잡지

glove changgap 장갑; (*in baseball*) yagu kŭllŏbŭ 야구 글러브

glow **1** *n* (*of light*) paengnyŏl 백열; (*of fire*) t'aorŭm 타오름; (*in cheeks*) taraorŭm 다라오름 **2** *v/i* (*light*) pich'ŭl naeda 빛을 내다; (*fire*) t'ada 타다 **2** *v/i* (*cheeks*) taraorŭda 다라오르다

glowing *description* yŏllyŏrhan 열렬한

glue **1** *n* p'ul 풀 **2** *v/t* p'ullo puch'ida 풀로 붙이다; ~ *X to Y* Xŭl/rŭl Ye p'ullo puch'ida X을/를 Y에 풀로 붙이다

glum shimuruk'an 시무룩한

glutinous rice ch'apssal 찹쌀

glutton taeshikka 대식가

gluttony p'oksshik 폭식

GMT (= *Greenwich Mean Time*) segye p'yojunshi 세계 표준시

gnarled *branch* madit'usŏng-iin 마디투성이인; *hands* kŏch'in 거친

gnat kakttagwi 각다귀

gnaw *v/t bone* kaltta 갉다

GNP (= *gross national product*) kungmin ch'ongsaengsan 국민 총생산

Go (*game*) Paduk 바둑

go 1 *n*: **on the** ~ chulgot irhayŏ 줄곧 일하여 **2** *v/i* kada 가다; (*leave: of train, plane*) ch'ulbarhada 출발하다; (*leave: of people*) ttŏnada 떠나다; (*work, function*) chakttonghada 작동하다; (*become*) ...haejida ...해지다; (*come out: of stain etc*) ŏpssŏjida 없어지다; (*cease: of pain etc*) sarajida 사라지다; (*match: of colors etc*) ŏullida 어울리다; ~ *quiet* choyonghaejida 조용해지다; ~ *shopping* / *jogging* shyop'ingharŏ / chogingharŏ kada 쇼핑하러 / 조깅하러 가다; *I must be* ~*ing* ije kayaman hamnida 이제 가야만 합니다; *let's* ~! kappsshida! 갑시다! *for a walk* sanch'aek'ada 산책하다; ~ *to bed* charŏ kada 자러 가다; ~ *to school* hak-kkyoe kada 학교에 가다; *how's the work* ~*ing*? iri ŏttŏk'e toeŏgamnikka? 일이 어떻게 되어갑니까? *they're* ~ *for $50* kŭgŏsŭn 50tallŏe p'amnida 그것은 50달러에 팝니다; *hamburger to* ~ haembŏgŏ p'ojanghaejuseyo 햄버거 포장해주세요; *it's all gone* ta ŏpssŏjyŏt-tta 다 없어졌다; *be* ~*ing to do sth* muŏsŭl hal kŏshida 무엇을 할 것이다

♦ **go ahead** kŭrŏk'e haseyo 그렇게 하세요

♦ **go ahead with** *plans etc* ch'ujinhada 추진하다

♦ **go along with** *suggestion* ...e ttarŭda ...에 따르다

♦ **go at** (*attack*) tŏmbyŏdŭlda 덤벼들다

♦ **go away** (*of person*) ttŏnada 떠나다; (*of rain*) kŭch'ida 그치다; (*pain, clouds*) sarajida 사라지다

♦ **go back** (*return*) toragada 돌아가다; (*date back*) kŏsŭllŏ ollagada 거슬러 올라가다; ~ *to sleep* tashi chada 다시 자다; *we* ~ *a long way* urinŭn orae algo chinaen saiyeyo 우리는 오래 알고 지내온 사이예요

2래 알고 지낸 사이예요

go by (*go past*) chinagada 지나가다
go down 1 v/t *stairs etc* naeryŏgada
내려가다 **2** v/i (*of sun*) chida 지다; (*of hip, swelling*) karaantta 가라앉다; ~ **well / badly** (*of suggestion etc*) chok'e / nappŭge padadŭryŏjida 좋게 / 나쁘게 받아들여지다
go for (*attack*) tŏmbyŏdŭlda 덤벼들다; (*like*) choahada 좋아하다
go in (*to room, of sun*) turŏgada 들어가다; (*fit: of part etc*) mat-tta 맞다
go in for *competition, race* ch'ultchŏnhada 출전하다; (*like*) hŭlgida 즐기다
go off 1 v/i (*leave*) kabŏrida 가버리다; (*of bomb*) p'okpparhada 폭발하다; (*of gun*) palssadoeda 발사되다; (*of alarm*) ullida 울리다; (*of milk etc*) sanghada 상하다 **2** v/t *stop liking* …i / ga shirŏjida …이 / 가 싫어지다
go on (*continue*) kyesok'ada 계속하다; (*happen*) irŏnada 일어나다; ~, **do it!** (*encouraging*) kwaench'anayo, haeboseyo! 괜찮아요. 해보세요!; **what's going on?** musŭn il issŏyo? 무슨 일 있어요?; ~ **about** …e taehae kyesok tŏdŭrŏdaeda …에 대해 계속 떠들어대다
go on at (*nag*) …ege chansorihada …에게 잔소리하다; *husband* …ŭl / rŭl pagaji kŭltta …을 / 를 바가지 긁다
go out (*of person*) nagada 나가다; (*of light, fire*) kkŏjida 꺼지다
go over v/t (*check*) kŏmt'ohada 검토하다
go through v/t *illness, hard times* kyŏktta 겪다; (*check*) myŏnmirhi chosahada 면밀히 조사하다; (*read through*) t'ongdok'ada 통독하다
go under (*sink*) karaantta 가라앉다; (*of company*) manghada 망하다
go up (*climb, in price*) ollagada 올라가다
go without 1 v/t *food etc* … ŏpsshi saragada … 없이 살아가다 **2** v/i

ŏpsshi chinaeda 없이 지내다
goad v/t koerop'ida 괴롭히다
go-ahead 1 n hŏga 허가; **get the ~** hŏgabat-tta 허가받다 **2** adj (*enterprising, dynamic*) chinch'wijŏgin 진취적인
goal SP (*target*) kol 골; (*points*) tŭktchŏm 득점; (*objective*) mokp'yo 목표
goalkeeper kolk'ip'ŏ 골키퍼
goalpost kolttae 골대
goat yŏmso 염소
♦ **gobble up** kegŏlsŭrŏpkke mŏktta 게걸스럽게 먹다
go-between chunggaeja 중개자
God Hanŭnim 하느님; **thank ~!** a, sarat-tta 아, 살았다; **oh ~!** sesang-e! 세상에!
god shin 신
goddess yŏshin 여신
godfather taebu 대부
godforsaken *place, town* hwangnyanghan 황량한
goggles poan-gyŏng 보안경; (*for skiing*) kogŭl 고글; (*for swimming*) muran-gyŏng 물안경
going adj *price etc* hyŏnjaeŭi 현재의; ~ **concern** sujiga mannŭn saŏp 수지가 맞는 사업
goings-on pinan padŭl manhan haeng-wi 비난 받을 만한 행위
gold 1 n kŭm 금 **2** adj kŭmŭi 금의
golden *hair* kŭmsaegŭi 금색의
golden handshake t'oejikkŭm 퇴직금
golden wedding anniversary kŭmhonshik 금혼식
goldfish kŭmbung-ŏ 금붕어; **gold medal** kŭmmedal 금메달; **goldsmith** kŭmsegongsa 금세공사
golf kolp'ŭ 골프
golf club (*organization, stick*) kolp'ŭ k'ŭllŏp 골프 클럽
golf course kolp'ŭjang 골프장
golfer kolp'ŭ ch'inŭn saram 골프 치는 사람
gong (*iron*) ching 징; (*brass*) kkwaenggwari 꽹과리
good choŭn 좋은; **a ~ many** aju manŭn 아주 많은; **be ~ at** …ŭl / rŭl charhada …을 / 를 잘하다; **be ~ for**

s.o. nuguege chot'a 누구에게 좋다
goodbye annyŏng 안녕; (*polite: to the person who is leaving*) annyŏnghi kaseyo 안녕히 가세요; (*polite: to the person who is staying*) annyŏnghi kyeseyo 안녕히 계세요; **say ~ to s.o.** nuguege chakppyŏl insarŭl hada 누구에게 작별 인사를 하다
good-for-nothing *n* amu ssŭlmo ŏmnŭn saram 아무 쓸모없는 사람; **Good Friday** Sŏnggŭmnyoil 성금요일; **good-humored** myŏngnanghan 명랑한; **good-looking** chal saenggin 잘 생긴; **good-natured** sŏnggyŏgi chŏun 성격이 좋은
goodness (*moral*) tŏk 덕; (*nutritional*) yŏngnyangbun 영양분; **thank ~!** komawŏra! 고마워라!
goods COM sangp'um 상품
goodwill hoŭi 호의
goody-goody *n* F ch'ak'an ch'ŏk'anŭn saram 착한 척하는 사람
gooey kkŭnjŏk-kkŭnjok'an 끈적끈적한
goof *v/i* F pabojisŭl hada 바보짓을 하다
goose kŏwi 거위
gooseberry kujŭberi 구즈베리
gooseflesh: it gives me ~ narŭl sorŭmkkich'ige handa 나를 소름끼치게 한다
gorge 1 *n* hyŏpkkok 협곡 **2** *v/t*: **~ oneself on sth** muŏsŭl p'oshik'ada 무엇을 포식하다
gorgeous *weather* hwach'anghan 화창한; *dress, woman, hair, smell* kŭnsahan 근사한
gorilla korilla 고릴라
go-slow t'aeŏp 태업
Gospel (*in Bible*) Pogŭmsŏ 복음서
gossip 1 *n* chapttam 잡담; (*person*) hŏmdam 험담 **2** *v/i* chapttamhada 잡담하다
govern *country* tasŭrida 다스리다
government chŏngbu 정부
governor (*of province*) chisa 지사
gown (*long dress*) kin kŏt'ot 긴 겉옷; (*wedding dress*) weding tŭresŭ 웨딩 드레스; (*of judge*) pŏp-ppok 법복; (*of surgeon*) kaun 가운

grab *v/t* puyŏjaptta 부여잡다; **~ something to eat** kanshigŭl mŏk 간식을 먹다; **~ a nap** hansum cha 한숨 자다
grace (*quality*) ua 우아
graceful uahan 우아한
gracious *person, style, living* p'um innŭn 품위 있는; **good ~!** chŏrŏn 저런!
grade 1 *n* (*quality*) tŭnggŭp 등급; (*year in school*) hangnyŏn 학년; (*exam*) sŏngjŏk 성적 **2** *v/t* tŭnggŭb maegida 등급을 매기다; EDU *pape* sŏngjŏgŭl ŏt-tta 성적을 얻다;
grade crossing RAIL sup'yŏng kŏnnŏlmok 수평 건널목
gradient kyŏngsado 경사도
gradual chŏmch'ajŏgin 점차적인
gradually chŏmch'ajŏgŭro 점차적으
graduate 1 *n* chorŏpssaeng 졸업생; (*at graduate school*) taehagwŏn hakssaeng 대학원 학생 **2** *v/i* chorŏp'ada 졸업하다
graduate school taehagwŏn 대학원
graduation chorŏp 졸업
graffiti naksssŏ 낙서
graft *n* BOT chŏppuch'igi 접붙이기; MED ishik chojik 이식 조직; F (*corruption*) pujong pup'ye 부정 부폐
grain nadal 낟알; (*in wood*) namutkkyŏl 나뭇결; **go against th ~** sŏngjire mat-tchi ant'a 성질에 맞 않다
gram kŭraem 그램
grammar munppŏp 문법
grammatical munppŏpssang-ŭi 문법상의
grand 1 *adj* ungjanghan 웅장한; F (*very good*) widaehan 위대한 **2** *n* F ($1000) ch'ŏn tallŏ 천 달러
grandad harabŏji 할아버지; **grandchild** (*male*) sonja 손자; (*female*) sonnyŏ 손녀; **granddaughter** sonnyŏ 손녀
grandeur ungjangham 웅장함
grandfather harabŏji 할아버지
grandma halmŏni 할머니; **grandmother** halmŏni 할머니; **grandpa** harabŏji 할아버지; **grandparents** chobumo 조부모; **grand piano**

ŭraendŭ p'iano 그랜드 피아노;
randson sonja 손자; **grandstand**
ŭkppyŏl kwallamsŏk 특별 관람석
anite hwagang-am 화강암
anny halmŏni 할머니
ant 1 n (*money*) pojogŭm 보조금;
(*or university, school*) changhak-
kŭm 장학금 **2** v/t wish, peace
arŏjuda 들어주다; visa hŏgahada
)가하다; request sŭng-inhada
)인하다; **take sth for ~ed** muŏsŭl
ng-yŏnhan illo yŏgida 무엇을
연한 일로 여기다; **take s.o. for
ed** nugurŭl tang-yŏnhage yŏgida
구를 당연하게 여기다
anule chagŭn algaeng-i 작은 알갱이
ape p'odo 포도
apefruit kŭreip'ŭp'ŭrut'ŭ
레이프프루트; **grapefruit juice**
kŭreip'ŭp'ŭrut'ŭ chusŭ
레이프프루트 주스; **grapevine:
ear sth through the ~** muŏsŭl
)munŭro tŭt-tta 무엇을 소문으로
)다
aph top'yo 도표
aphic 1 adj (*vivid*) saengsaenghan
생생한 **2** n COMPUT kŭraep'ik 그래픽
aphics COMPUT kŭraep'iksŭ
그래픽스
rapple with attacker ...wa/kwa
)atpput'ŏ ssauda ...와/과 맞붙어
)우다; problem etc ...wa/kwa
)shirŭmhada ...와/과 씨름하다
asp 1 n (*physical*) umk'yŏjapki
)켜잡기; (*mental*) ihaeryŏk 이해력
v/t (*physically*) umk'yŏjaptta
)켜잡다; (*understand*) ihaehada
)해하다
ass p'ul 풀
asshopper mettugi 메뚜기; **grass
idow** kwabugat'ŭn shinse 과부같은
)세; **grass widower** horabigat'ŭn
hinse 홀아비같은 신세
assy p'uri ugŏjin 풀이 우거진
ate n (*metal*) soesalttae 쇠살대
ate² 1 v/t carrots etc pibyŏ
usŭrŏttŭrida 비벼 부스러뜨리다
v/i (*of sound*) kŏsŭllida 거슬리다
ateful komapke yŏginŭn 고맙게
1기는; **be ~ to** ...ŭl/rŭl komapke
)ŏgida ...을/를 고맙게 여기다

grater kangp'an 강판
gratification manjoksshik'igi
만족시키기
gratify manjoksshik'ida 만족시키다
grating 1 n soe kyŏktcha ttukkŏng 쇠
격자 뚜껑 **2** adj sound, voice kwie
kŏsŭllinŭn 귀에 거슬리는
gratitude kamsa 감사
gratuity t'ip 팁
grave¹ n mudŏm 무덤
grave² adj error chungdaehan 중대한;
face, voice kŭnŏmhan 근엄한
gravel n chagal 자갈
gravestone chagal 자갈
graveyard myoji 묘지
gravity PHYS chungnyŏk 중력
gravy yuktchŭp 육즙
gray adj hoesaegŭi 회색의; **be going
~** paekppari toeda 백발이 되다
gray-haired paekpparŭi 백발의
grayhound kŭreihaundŭ
그레이하운드
graze¹ v/i (*of cow, horse*) p'urŭl
ttŭdŏmŏktta 풀을 뜯어먹다
graze² 1 v/t arm etc kabyŏpkke
sŭch'ida 가볍게 스치다 **2** n (*on arm
etc*) ch'algwasang 찰과상
grease (*for cooking*) yuji 유지; (*for
car*) yunhwalyu 윤활유
greasy kirŭmkki manŭn 기름기 많은
great (*in size*) koengjanghi k'ŭn
굉장히 큰; (*in amount*) koengjanghi
manŭn 굉장히 많은; (*outstanding*)
hyŏnjŏhan 현저한; (*very important*)
chungdaehan 중대한; composer,
writer tae... 대...; F (*very good*)
koengjanghi chŏŭn 굉장히 좋은; **~
composer** taejak-kkok-kka
대작곡가; **how was it? - ~**
ŏttaessŏyo? - koengjanghi
choassŏyo 어땠어요? - 굉장히
좋았어요; **~ to see you!** mannasŏ
nŏmu pan-gapssŭmnida! 만나서
너무 반갑습니다!
Great Britain Yŏngguk 영국
Great Han Empire Taehanjeguk
대한제국
greatly koengjanghi 굉장히
greatness widaeham 위대함
greed yoksshim 욕심
greedy yoksshim manŭn 욕심 많은

green nokssaegŭi 녹색의;
(*environmentally*) hwan-gyŏng
pohoŭi 환경 보호의
greenhorn F p'unnaegi 풋내기;
greenhouse onshil 온실; greenhouse effect onshil hyokkwa 온실
효과; greenhouse gas
isanhwat'anso 이산화탄소; green
tea nokch'a 녹차
greet insahada 인사하다
greeting insa 인사
grenade suryut'an 수류탄
grid kyŏktcha 격자
gridiron SP mishik ch'uk-kku
kyŏnggijang 미식 축구 경기장
gridlock (*in traffic*) kyot'ongmang
chŏngch'e 교통망 정체
grief pit'ong 비통
grievance pulp'yŏngkkŏri 불평거리
grieve pit'onghaehada 비통해하다; ~
for s.o. nugurŭl irŏ pit'onghaehada
누구를 잃어 비통해하다
grill 1 n (*on window*) soech'angssal
쇠창살 2 v/t (*interrogate*)
shimmunhada 심문하다
grille soech'angssal 쇠창살
grim *look, person* ŏmhan 엄한;
prospect, future naenghok'an 냉혹한
grimace n ŏlgurŭl tchip'urim 얼굴을
찌푸림
grime ttae 때
grimy ttaemudŭn 때묻은
grin 1 n shinggŭt usŭm 싱긋 웃음
2 v/i shinggŭt ut-tta 싱긋 웃다
grind v/t *coffee, meat* kalda 갈다
grip 1 n (*on rope etc*) kkwak chabŭm
꽉 잡음; *be losing one's ~* (*losing
one's skills*) nŭngnyŏgi ŏpssŏjida
능력이 없어지다 2 v/t kkwak chaptta
꽉 잡다
gristle yŏn-gol 연골
grit n (*dirt*) mŏnji 먼지; (*for roads*)
chan morae 잔 모래
groan 1 n shinŭm sori 신음 소리 2 v/i
shinŭmhada 신음하다
grocer shingnyo chap'wasang 식료
잡화상
groceries shingnyo chap'waryu 식료
잡화류
grocery store shingnyo chap'wajŏm
식료 잡화점

groin sat'aguni 사타구니
groom 1 n (*for bride*) shillang 신랑;
(*for horse*) mabu 마부 2 v/t *horse*
sonjirhada 손질하다; (*train, prepa*
hullyŏnshik'ida 훈련시키다; *well
~ed* (*in appearance*) chal sonjildo
잘 손질된
groove n hŭm 홈
grope 1 v/i (*in the dark*) sonŭro
tŏdŭmtta 손으로 더듬다 2 v/t
(*sexually*) sonŭro tŏdŭmtta 손으로
더듬다
♦ grope for *door, word* ch'at-tta 찾
gross adj (*coarse, vulgar*) sangsŭrŏ
상스러운; *exaggeration* ŏmch'ŏngr
엄청난; FIN ch'onggye 총계
gross domestic product kungnae
ch'ongsaengsan 국내 총생산
gross national product kungmin
ch'ongsaengsan 국민 총생산
ground 1 n ttang ttang 땅; (*reason*) kŭn-g
kŭn-gŏ 근거; ELEC chŏptchi 접지; *on the ~*
hyŏnjang-e(sŏ) 현장에(서) 2 v/t EL
chŏptchihada 접지하다
ground control chisang kwanje 지
관제
ground crew chisang kŭnmuwŏn
지상 근무원
groundless kŭn-gŏ ŏmnŭn 근거 없
ground meat kan kogi 간 고기;
groundnut ttangk'ong 땅콩; grour
plan p'yŏngmyŏndo 평면도; grour
staff SP chŏngbiwŏn 정비원; (*at
airport*) chisang kŭnmuwŏn 지상
근무원; groundwork kich'o chagŏ
기초 작업
group 1 n muri 무리; (*of companies*)
kŭrup 그룹 2 v/t murijit-tta 무리짓다
grow 1 v/i charada 자라다; (*of
number, amount*) k'ŏjida 커지다; (*
business*) sŏngjanghada 성장하다; ~
old / ~ *tired* nŭlgŏjida / p'igonhaeji
늙어지다 / 피곤해지다 2 v/t *flowers*
kirŭda 기르다
♦ grow up (*of person*) charanada
자라나다; (*of city*) paltchŏnhada
발전하다; ~! nai kapssŭl hae! 나이
값을 해!
growl 1 n ŭrŭrŏnggŏrinŭn sori
으르렁거리는 소리 2 v/i
ŭrŭrŏnggŏrida 으르렁거리다

own-up 1 n 어른 öŭrŭn 어른 **2** adj
ŏrŭnsŭrŏun 어른스러운
owth (of person, company)
sŏngjang 성장; (increase) chŭngga
증가; MED chongyang 종양
ub (of insect) ttangbŏlle 땅벌레
ubby tŏrŏun 더러운
udge 1 n yugam 유감; **bear a ~**
yugamŭl kajida 유감을 가지다 **2** v/t:
don't ~ him his success kŭga
sŏnggonghaedo pae anap'ayo 그가
성공해도 배 안아파요
udging insaek'an 인색한
ueling climb, task nokch'oro
mandŭnŭn 녹초로 만드는
uff kulkko t'ak'an mokssori 굵고
탁한 목소리
umble v/i t'udŏlgŏrida 투덜거리다
umbler t'udŏlgŏrinŭn saram
투덜거리는 사람
unt 1 n (of pig) kkulkkulgŏrim
꿀꿀거림; (of person) kŏch'in shinŭm
거친 신음 **2** v/i (of pig)
kkulkkulgŏrida 꿀꿀거리다; (of
person) kŏch'ilge shinŭmhada
거칠게 신음하다
uarantee 1 n (of sth) pojŭng 보증; **~ period**
pojŭng kigan 보증 기간 **2** v/t
pojŭnghada 보증하다
uarantor pojŭng-in 보증인
uard 1 n (security ~) kyŏngbiwŏn
경비원; MIL poch'o 보초; (in prison)
kyodogwan 교도관; **be on one's ~**
against ...ŭl/rŭl kyŏnggyehada
...을/를 경계하다 **2** v/t chik'ida
지키다
guard against ...ŭl/rŭl
choshimhada ...을/를 조심하다
uarded reply choshimsŏng innŭn
조심성 있는
uardian LAW hugyŏnin 후견인
uerrilla kerilla 게릴라
uess 1 n ch'uch'ŭk 추측 **2** v/t answer
ch'uch'ŭk'ada 추측하다; **I ~ so**
kŭrŏn kŏt kat'ayo 그런 것 같아요; **I
~ not** kŭrŏch'i anŭn kŏt kat'ayo
그렇지 않은 것 같아요 **3** v/i
ch'uch'ŭk'ada 추측하다
uesswork ŏrimjimjak 어림짐작
uest sonnim 손님
uesthouse yŏgwan 여관

gunshot

guestroom sonnimnyong ch'imshil
손님용 침실
guffaw 1 n kaptchakssŭrŏn k'ŭn
usŭm 갑작스런 큰 웃음 **2** v/i
kaptchagi k'ŭge ut-tta 갑자기 크게
웃다
guidance annae 안내
guide 1 n (person) annaeja 안내자;
(book) annaesŏ 안내서 **2** v/t
annaehada 안내하다
guidebook annaesŏ 안내서
guided missile yudot'an 유도탄
guided tour kaidŭ t'uŏ 가이드 투어
guidelines chich'im 지침
guilt LAW pŏmjoe 범죄; (moral) choe
죄; (guilty feeling) choech'aek-kkam
죄책감
guilty LAW yujoeŭi 유죄의;
(responsible) choe chiŭn 죄 지은;
look, smile choe chiŭndŭt'an 죄
지은듯한; **have a ~ conscience**
choech'aek-kkamŭl nŭkkida
죄책감을 느끼다
guinea pig morŭmot'ŭ 모르모트; fig
shirhŏm chaeryo 실험 재료
guitar kit'a 기타
guitarist kit'a yŏnjuga 기타 연주가
gulf man 만; fig kip'ŭn t'ŭm 깊은 틈
gull kalmaegi 갈매기
gullet shiktto 식도
gullible sok-kki shwiun 속기 쉬운
gulp 1 n (of water etc) kkulkkŏk-
kkulkkŏk mashim 꿀꺽꿀꺽 마심
2 v/i (in surprise) sumŭl chugida
숨을 죽이다
♦**gulp down** drink, kkulkkŏk-
kkulkkŏk mashida 꿀꺽꿀꺽 마시다;
breakfast, food kŭp'i mŏktta 급히
먹다
gum¹ (in mouth) inmom 잇몸
gum² (glue) chŏmsŏng komu 점성
고무; (chewing ~) kkŏm 껌
gun ch'ong 총
♦**gun down** ssoa nŏmŏttŭrida 쏘아
넘어뜨리다
gunfire p'ogyŏk 포격; **gunman**
ch'onggi hyudaeja 총기 휴대자;
(robber) mujang kangdo 무장 강도;
gunpowder hwayak 화약; **gunshot**
palp'o 발포; **~ wound** ch'ongsang
총상

gurgle *v/i (of baby)* mogŭl kkolttak-
kkŏrida 목을 꼴딱거리다; *(of drain)*
k'walk'wal hŭllŏnaoda 콸콸
흘러나오다

gush *v/i (of liquid)* p'ŏngp'ŏng
sosanaoda 펑펑 솟아나오다

gushy F *(very enthusiastic)*
chinach'ige kamsangjŏgin 지나치게
감상적인

gust *n* tolp'ung 돌풍

gusty *weather* parami shimhan 바람이
심한; **~ wind** tolp'ung 돌풍

gut 1 *n* ch'angja 창자; F *(stomach)* pae
배; **~s** F *(courage)* yonggi 용기 **2** *v/t*
(of fire) t'aewŏbŏrida 태워버리다;
(roof) homt'ong 홈통

gutter *(on sidewalk)* torang 도랑; (~
roof) homt'ong 홈통

guy F namja 남자; ***hey, you ~s*** ŏi,
yŏrŏbun 어이, 여러분

gym ch'eyuk-kkwan 체육관

gymnasium ch'eyuk-kkwan 체육관

gymnast ch'eyuk kyosa 체육 교사

gymnastics ch'ejo 체조

gynecologist sanbuinkkwa ŭisa
산부인과 의사

gypsy chipsshi 집시

H

it p'orŭt 버릇, sŭpkkwan 습관
itable kŏjuhal su innŭn 거주할 수
는
itat sŏshiktchi 서식지
itual sŭpkkwanjŏgin 습관적인;
noker, drinker sangsŭptchŏgin
습적인
ck n (poor writer) samnyu chakka 삼류 작가
cker COMPUT haek'ŏ 해커
kneyed chinbuhan 진부한
ddock taeguŭi iltchong 대구의
종
gard such'ŏk'an 수척한
ggle (over price) kkaktta 깎다
l n ubak 우박
r t'ŏl 털; (on person's head) mŏri
리; (single human ~) mŏrik'arak
리카락; short ~ / long ~
halbŭn / kin mŏri 짧은 / 긴 머리
rbrush mŏri sol 머리 솔; haircut:
ave a ~ mŏrirŭl charŭda 머리를
르다; hairdo mŏrihyŏng 머리형;
airdresser miyongsa 미용사; at
we ~'s miyongshiresŏ 미용실에서;
airdrier, hairdryer heŏdŭraiŏ
어드라이어
rless t'ŏri ŏmnŭn 털이 없는
rpin mŏrip'in 머리핀; hairpin
rve Uchahyŏng k'ŏbŭ U자형 커브
air-raising mŏrikkŭch'i
huppyŏt'aejinŭn 머리끝이
빳해지는; hair remover
hemoyongp'um 제모용품; hair-
splitting n: that's just ~ sasohan
in-gyŏngssŭnŭn kŏshieyo 사소한
에 신경쓰는 것이에요; hairstyle
ŏrihyŏng 머리형
ry arm, animal t'ori manŭn 털이
은; F frightening musŏun 무서운
f 1 n pan 반; ~ (past) ten yŏlshi
an yŏlshi ban 열시 반; ~ an hour pan shigan
시간; ~ a pound pan p'aundŭ 반
운드 2 adj panŭi 반의 3 adv: ~

eaten / finished panŭn mŏgŭn /
kkŭnnan 반은 먹은 / 끝난; only ~
understood panman ihaedoen 반만
이해된
half-hearted maŭmi naek'iji annŭn
마음이 내키지 않는; half time n SP
chunggan hyushik 중간 휴식; halfway 1 adj stage, point chunggan
chijŏmŭi 중간 지점의 2 adv
chunggane 중간에
hall (large room) hol 홀; (hallway in
house) poktto 복도
halo wŏn-gwang 원광
halt 1 v/i mŏmch'uda 멈추다 2 v/t
mŏmch'ugehada 멈추게하다 3 n
chŏngji 정지; come to a ~
mŏmch'uda 멈추다
halve v/t panŭro hada 반으로 하다
ham haem 햄
hamburger haembŏgŏ 햄버거
hammer 1 n mangch'i 망치 2 v/i
mangch'ijirhada 망치질하다; ~ at
the door munŭl k'wangk'wang
tudŭrida 문을 쾅쾅 두드리다
hammock haemŏk 해먹
hamper¹ n (for food) paguni 바구니
hamper² v/t (obstruct) panghaehada
방해하다
hamster haemsŭt'ŏ 햄스터
hand 1 n son 손; (of clock) shigye
panŭl 시계 바늘; (worker) ilsson
일손; at ~, to ~ kakkaie 가까이에; at
first ~ chiktchŏptchogŭro
직접적으로; by ~ sonŭro 손으로;
deliver inp'yŏnŭro 인편으로; on the
one ~ ..., on the other ~
hanp'yŏnŭronŭn ..., tarŭn
hanp'yŏnŭronŭn hanp'yŏn-ŭronŭn ..., 다른
한편으로는; in ~ (being done)
kkŭnnanŭn chung-in 끝나는 중인;
on your right ~ orŭntchok
panghyang-ŭro 오른쪽 방향으로; ~s
off! son tteseyo! 손 떼세요!; ~s up!
son tŭrŏ! 손 들어!; change ~s

imjaga pakkwida 임자가 바뀌다
♦ **hand down** *heirloom etc*
mullyŏjuda 물려주다
♦ **hand in** chech'urhada 제출하다
♦ **hand on** chŏnhada 전하다
♦ **hand out** nanuŏ chuda 나누어 주다
♦ **hand over** kŏnnejuda 건네주다; (*to authorities*) nŏmgyŏjuda 넘겨주다
handbag *Br* son-gabang 손가방, haendŭbaeg 핸드백; **handbook** annaech'aektcha 안내책자; **handcuffs** sugap 수갑
handicap *n* (*physical*) shinch'e chang-ae 신체 장애; *fig* pullihan chokkŏn 불리한 조건
handicapped (*physically*) shinch'e chang-aeja innŭn 신체 장애가 있는; (*mentally*) chŏngshin chang-aeja innŭn 정신 장애가 있는; **~ *by a lack of funds*** chagŭm pujogŭro pullihan 자금 부족으로 불리한
handicraft sugong-ye 수공예
handiwork sugong 수공; (*handmade goods*) sugongp'um 수공품
handkerchief sonsugŏn 손수건
handle 1 *n* sonjabi 손잡이 **2** *v/t* taruda 다루다; *let me ~ this* chega tarugessŭmnida 제가 다루겠습니다
handlebars chajŏn-gŏ haendŭl 자전거 핸들
hand luggage suhwamul 수화물; **handmade** sugong-ŭi 수공의; **handrail** nan-gan 난간; **handshake** akssu 악수
hands-off kansŏp'aji annŭn 간섭하지 않는
handsome chal saenggin 잘 생긴
hands-on shilmurŭl chiktchŏp'anŭn 실무를 직접하는; *get some ~ experience* chiktchŏp kyŏnghŏmŭl ŏt-tta 직접 경험을 얻다
handwriting yukp'il 육필
handwritten sonŭro ssŭn 손으로 쓴
handy *tool, device* p'yŏllihan 편리한; *it might come in ~* ama ssŭlmo issŭl kŏshida 아마 쓸모 있을 것이다
hang 1 *v/t picture* kŏlda 걸다; *person* mok maedalda 목 매달다 **2** *v/i* (*of dress, hair*) nŭrŏjida 늘어지다 **3** *n*: *get the ~ of* ...ŭl/rŭl ihaehage toeda ...을/를 이해하게 되다

♦ **hang around** ŏsŭllŏnggŏrida 어슬렁거리다
♦ **hang on** *v/i* (*wait*) kidarida 기다리다
♦ **hang on to** (*keep*) kyesok ...ŭl/▸ kajigo it-tta 계속 ...을/를 가지고 있다
♦ **hang up** *v/i* TELEC chŏnhwarŭl kkŭnt'a 전화를 끊다
hangar kyŏngnapkko 격납고
hanger (*for clothes*) otkkŏri 옷걸이
hang glider (*person*) haenggŭllaidŏrŭl t'anŭn saram 행글라이더를 타는 사람; (*device*) haenggŭllaidŏ 행글라이더; **hang gliding** haenggŭllaidŏ pihaeng 행글라이더 비행; **hangover** sukch'wi 숙취; (*idea, attitude*) yŏp'a 여파
♦ **hanker after** ... ŭl/rŭl mopsshi katkko ship'ŏhada ...을/를 몹시 갖싶어하다
hankie, hanky F sonsugŏn 손수건
Han River Han-gang 한강
haphazard magujabiŭi 마구잡이의
happen irŏnada 일어나다; *if you ~ see him* manyak nega kŭrŭl uyŏn▸ mannandamyŏn 만약 네가 그를 우연히 만난다면; *what has ~ed t▸ you?* musŭn iri issŏssŭmnikka? 무▸ 일이 있었습니까?
♦ **happen across** uyŏnhi palgyŏnhada 우연히 발견하다
happening palsaeng 발생
happily haengbok'age 행복하게; (*gladly*) kippŭge 기쁘게; (*luckily*) chok'e un 좋게
happiness haengbok 행복
happy haengbok'an 행복한
happy-go-lucky nakch'ŏnjŏgin 낙천적인
happy hour t'ŭkpyŏl yŏmkka pong▸ kigan t'ŭkpyŏl 염가 봉사 기간
harass koerop'ida 괴롭히다
harassed shidallin 시달린
harassment koerop'im 괴롭힘; *sexual ~* sŏnghŭirong 성희롱
harbor 1 *n* hanggu 항구 **2** *v/t crimin▸* sumgida 숨기다; *grudge* maŭme p'umtta 마음에 품다
hard tandanhan 단단한; (*difficult*) ŏryŏun 어려운; *facts, evidence* hwa▸

kohan 확고한; **~ of hearing** kwiga
mŏn 귀가 먼
'**dback** changjŏngbon 장정본;
ard-boiled egg talgyal wansuk
갈 완숙; **hard copy** hadŭ k'ap'i
드 카피; **hard core** n
aeksshimch'ŭng 핵심층;
pornography) nogoltchŏgin
'orŭno 노골적인 포르노; **hard**
urrency kyohwan kanŭng
onghwa 교환 가능 통화; **hard disk**
adŭ tisŭk'ŭ 하드 디스크
rden 1 v/t kuch'ida 굳히다 **2** v/i (of
ue) kut-tta 굳다; (of attitude)
anghaejida 강해지다
rdheaded naengjŏnghan 냉정한
rdliner kanggyŏngnonja 강경론자
rdly kŏŭi ...haji ant'a 거의 ...하지
다; **he ~ ever studies** kŭnŭn kŏŭi
ongbuhaji anayo 그는 거의
부하지 않아요; **I can ~ hear** kŏŭi
illiji anayo 거의 들리지 않아요; **did**
ou agree? - ~! tong-ŭihaessŏyo? –
n'ŏnmaneyo! 동의했어요? **~**
네요!
rdness kutkki 굳기; (difficulty)
ryŏum 어려움
rd sell chŏkkŭk p'anmae 적극 판매
rdship kollan 곤란
rd shoulder toroŭi taep'isŏn
로의 대피선; **hard up** toni
unghan 돈이 궁한; **hardware**
n'ŏlmul 철물; COMPUT hadŭwŏ
드웨어; **hardware store**
n'ŏlmultchŏm 철물점; **hard-**
orking yŏlssimhi irhanŭn 열심히
하는
rdy kanghan 강한
re sant'okki 산토끼
rm 1 n hae 해; **it wouldn't do any**
~ to ... ... haedo kwaench'anŭl
ŏshida ... 해도 괜찮을 것이다 **2** v/t
aech'ida 해치다
rmful haeroun 해로운
rmless muhaehan 무해한
rmonious chohwadoen 조화된
rmonize chohwashik'ida
조화시키다
rmony MUS hwasŏng 화성; (in
elationship etc) chohwa 조화
rp hap'ŭ 하프

♦ **harp on about** F kyesok ...ŭl/rŭl
toep'uri marhada 계속 ...을/를
되풀이 말하다
harpoon n chakssal 작살
harsh criticism, words kahok'an
가혹한; color, light kŏsŭllinŭn
거슬리는
harvest n ch'usu 추수
Harvest Festival Ch'usŏk 추석
hash: make a ~ of F ...ŭl/rŭl
ŏngmang-ŭro mandŭlda ...을/를
엉망으로 만들다
hash browns kamja t'wigim 감자
튀김
hashish taemach'o 대마초
haste sŏdurŭm 서두름
hasty kŭp'an 급한
hat moja 모자
hatch n (for serving food) ch'anggu
창구; (on ship) haech'i 해치
♦ **hatch out** (of eggs) puhwahada
부화하다
hatchback haech'ibaek 해치백
hatchet sondokki 손도끼
hate 1 n mium 미움 **2** v/t miwŏhada
미워하다
hatred chŭng-o 증오
haughty kŏmanhan 거만한
haul 1 n (of fish) ŏhoengnyang 어획량
2 v/t (pull) chabattanggida
잡아당기다
haulage unban 운반
haulage company unsong hoesa
운송 회사
haulier unsong hoesa 운송 회사
haunch tunbu 둔부
haunt 1 v/t nat'anada 나타나다; (of
memory) ttŏorŭda 떠오르다; **this**
place is ~ed igosŭn yuryŏng-i
nat'ananŭn koshida 이곳은 유령이
나타나는 곳이다 **2** n (place) chŭlgyŏ
ch'annŭn kot 즐겨 찾는 곳
haunting tune noerirŭl ttŏnaji annŭn
뇌리를 떠나지 않는
have ◊ kajida 가지다; **I ~ some**
money tonŭl chom kajigo issŏyo
돈을 좀 가지고 있어요; **I ~ some-**
thing for you tangshinhant'e chul
kŏshi issŏyo 당신한테 줄 것이
있어요; **I ~ a headache** mŏriga
ap'ayo 머리가 아파요; **~ a cold**

kamgie kŏllida 감기에 걸리다; **can I ~ ...?** *(please give me)* ...ŭl/rŭl chushigetssŭmnikka? ...을/를 주시겠습니까?; **do you ~ ...?** ...i/ka issŭmnikka? ...이/가 있습니까?; **I ~ no family** nanŭn kajogi amudo ŏptta 나는 가족이 아무도 없다; **I had no choice** sŏnt'aegŭi yŏjiga ŏpssŏt-tta 선택의 여지가 없었다 ◊ *(own)* kajida 가지다, soyuhada 소유하다 ◊ *breakfast, lunch* mŏktta 먹다 ◊: **~ to** *(must)* ...haeya hada ...해야 하다; **I ~ to study / see him** nanŭn kongbuhaeya hamnida / kŭrŭl mannaboaya hamnida 나는 공부해야 합니다 / 그를 만나보아야 합니다; **you ~ to try** nŏnŭn noryŏk'aeya hahanda 너는 노력해야 한다 ◊ *(causative)*: **~ sth done** muŏsŭl haet-tta 무엇을 했다; **I had my hair cut** nanŭn mŏrirŭl challat-tta 나는 머리를 잘랐다; **~ sth cleaned** muŏsŭl set'agŭl matkkida 무엇을 세탁을 맡기다 ◊ *(auxiliary)*: **I ~ decided** nanŭn kyŏltchŏnghaet-tta 나는 결정했다; **~ you seen her?** kŭnyŏrŭl pon chŏgi issŭmnikka? 그녀를 본 적이 있습니까?

◆ **have back** tollyŏbat-tta 돌려받다; **when can I have it back?** ŏnje kŭgŏsŭl tollyŏbadŭl su issŭmnikka? 언제 그것을 돌려받을 수 있습니까?

◆ **have on** *(wear)* iptta 입다; *(have planned)* kyehoek'aet-tta 계획했다; **do you have anything on for tonight?** onŭl pame mwŏ hal il issŭmnikka? 오늘 밤에 뭐 할 일 있습니까?

haven *fig* anshikch'ŏ 안식처

havoc ŏngmangjinch'ang 엉망진창; **play ~ with** ...ŭl/rŭl ŏngmang-ŭro mandŭlda ...을/를 엉망으로 만들다

hawk mae 매; *fig* kanggyŏngnonja 강경론자

hay kŏnch'o 건초

hay fever kŏnch'oyŏl 건초열

hazard *n* wihŏm yoso 위험 요소

hazard lights MOT pisangdŭng 비상등

hazardous wihŏmhan 위험한

haze ajirang-i 아지랑이

hazel *(tree)* kaeamnamu 개암나무

hazelnut kaeam 개암

hazy *view, memories* hŭrin 흐린; **I'm a bit ~ about it** nanŭn kugŏse taehayŏ punmyŏnghaji ant'a 나는 그것에 대하여 분명하지 않다

he kŭ 그; **~ is American** kŭnŭn Miguk saramieyo 그는 미국 사람이에요 ◊ *(omission of pronoun)*: **who is ~? - - is my teacher** nuguyeyo? - che sŏsaengnimieyo 누구예요? - 제 선생님이에요

head 1 *n* mŏri 머리; *(boss, leader)* udumŏri 우두머리; *(on beer)* kŏp'um 거품; *(of nail)* monmŏri 못머리; *(of queue, line)* sŏndu 선두; **$15 a ~** han saram tang 15tallŏ 한 사람 당 15달러; **~s** ammyŏn 앞면; **heads or tails?** ammyŏn animyŏn twinmyŏn? 앞면 아니면 뒷면?; **at the ~ of the list** myŏngdanŭi ch'ŏnmŏrie 명단의 첫머리에; **~ over heels** *fall* kokkurajida 고꾸라지다; *fall in love* holttak 홀딱; **lose one's ~** *(go crazy)* che chŏngshinŭl ilt'a 제 정신을 잃다 **2** *v/t* *(lead)* ikkŭlda 이끌다; *ball* mŏriro pat-tta 머리로 받다

headache tut'ong 두통

header *(in soccer)* heding 헤딩; *(in document)* mŏrinmal 머릿말

headhunter COM injae sŭk'aut'ŭ tamdangja 인재 스카우트 담당자

heading *(in list)* p'yoje 표제

headlamp, headlight hedŭrait'ŭ 헤드라이트; **headline** mŏritkkisa 머릿기사; **make the ~s** mŏritkkisa k'ŭge ch'wigŭpttoeda 머릿기사로 크게 취급되다; **headlong** *adv fall* kŏndubaktchillo 곤두박질로; **head master** kyojang 교장; **headmistress** yŏgyojang 여교장; **head of** *(of company)* ponsa 본사; **head-on 1** *adv crash* chŏngmyŏnch'ungdoruro 정면충돌로 **2** *adj crash* chŏngmyŏnch'ungdorŭi 정면충돌의; **headphones** hedŭp'on 헤드폰; **headquarters** ponbu 본부; **headrest** mŏri patch'im 머리 받침; **headroom** *(under bridge)* wit konggan-ŭi nop'i 윗 공간의 높이; *(car)* ch'ŏnjang-ŭi nop'i 천장의 높이

eadscarf mŏri sŭk'ap'ŭ 머리
카프; **headstrong** wan-gohan
고한; **head waiter** susŏk weit'ŏ
석 웨이터; **headwind** matpparam
바람

ady *wine etc* ppalli ch'wihage
anŭn 빨리 취하게 하는

al **1** *v/t* natkke hada 낫게 하다 **2** *v/i*
at-tta 낫다

alth kŏn-gang 건강; *your ~!*
ngshinŭi kŏn-gang-ŭl wihae!
신의 건강을 위해!

alth club helssŭ k'ŭllŏp 헬스 클럽;
ealth food kŏn-gang shikp'um
강 식품; **health food store** kŏn-
ang shikp'umjŏm 건강 식품점;
alth insurance kŏn-gang pohŏm
강 보험; **health resort** poyangji
양지

althy *person* kŏn-ganghan 건강한;
ood, lifestyle kŏn-gang-e choŭn
강에 좋은; *economy* t'ŭnt'ŭnhan
튼튼한

ap n ssaa ollin tŏmi 쌓아 올린 더미
eap up ssaa ollida 쌓아 올리다

ar tŭt-tta 듣다

.ear about …e kwanhae tŭt-tta
..에 관해 듣다

.ear from …(ŭ)ro put'ŏ soshigŭl
tŭt-tta …(으)로 부터 소식을 듣다
지리; *within ~* tŭllinŭn pŏmwi
ane(sŏ) 들리는 범위 안에(서); *out of*
~ tŭllinŭn pŏmwi pakke(sŏ) 들리는
범위 밖에(서)

earing aid poch'ŏnggi 보청기
earsay: *by ~* p'ungmunŭro 풍문으로
earse yŏngguch'a 영구차

eart shimjang 심장; (*emotional
senses*) maŭm 마음; (*of problem*)
haeksshim 핵심; (*of city,
organization*) haeksshimbu 핵심부;
know sth by ~ muŏsŭl oeugo it-tta
구엇을 외우고 있다

eart attack shimjang mabi 심장
마비; **heartbeat** shimjang pakttong
심장 박동; **heartbreaking** aekkŭlk'e
hanŭn 애끓게 하는; **heartburn**
kasŭmari 가슴앓이; **heart failure**
shimjang mabi 심장 마비; **heartfelt**
sympathy chinshimesŏ urŏnan

진심에서 우러난
hearth pyŏngnallo padak 벽난로 바닥
heartless maejŏnghan 매정한
heartrending *plea, sight* pit'onghan
비통한
hearts (*in cards*) hat'ŭ 하트
heart throb F tonggyŏng-ŭi taesang
동경의 대상
heart transplant shimjang ishik 심장
이식
hearty *appetite* wangsŏnghan 왕성한;
meal p'ungsŏnghan 풍성한; *person*
tajŏngdagamhan 다정다감한
heat *n* yŏl 열
♦**heat up** teuda 데우다
heated *discussion* kyŏk'an 격한; ~
floor ondol 온돌; ~ **swimming pool**
onsu suyŏngjang 온수 수영장
heater nanbang changch'i 난방 장치
heathen *n* igyodo 이교도
heating nanbang changch'i 난방 장치
heatproof, heat-resistant
naeyŏlssŏng-ŭi 내열성의; **heatstroke** yŏlssabyŏng 열사병; **heatwave** yŏlp'a 열파
heave *v/t* (*lift*) tŭrŏollida 들어올리다
heaven ch'ŏnguk 천국; *good ~s!*
chŏrŏn! 저런!
heavy mugŏun 무거운; *rain* manŭn
많은; *traffic, cold, bleeding* shimhan
심한; *accent* kanghan 강한; *food*
sohwaga chal andoenŭn 소화가 잘
안되는; *financial loss* shimgak'an
심각한; *loss of life* maksshimhan
막심한; ~ **smoker** kolch'o 골초; ~
drinker sulgorae 술고래
heavy-duty aju t'ŭnt'ŭnhan 아주
튼튼한
heavyweight SP hebikkŭp 헤비급
heckle *v/t* yayuhada 야유하다
hectic mopsshi pappŭn 몹시 바쁜
hedge *n* ult'ari 울타리
hedgehog kosŭmdoch'i 고슴도치
heed: *pay ~ to* yunyŏmhada 유념하다
heel (*of foot*) twikkumch'i 뒤꿈치; (*of
shoe*) twich'uk 뒤축
heel bar kudu susŏntchip 구두 수선집
hefty mugŏun 무거운
height nop'i 높이; (*of person*) k'i 키;
(*of airplane*) kodo 고도; (*of season*)
chŏltchŏng 절정

heighten *effect, tension* nop'ida 높이다

heir sangsogin 상속인

heiress yŏja sangsogin 여자 상속인

helicopter hellik'opt'ŏ 헬리콥터

hell chiok 지옥; *what the ~ are you doing / do you want?* F todaech'e muŏsŭl hanŭn / wŏnhanŭn kŏmnikka? 도대체 무엇을 하는 / 원하는 겁니까?; *go to ~!* F kkŏjyŏ pŏryŏ! 꺼져 버려!; *a ~ of a lot* F ŏmch'ŏng manŭn 엄청 많은; *one ~ of a nice guy* F koengjanghi choŭn saram 굉장히 좋은 사람

hello (*polite, to older people*) annyŏnghashimnikka 안녕하십니까; (*to friend, younger people*) annyŏng 안녕; TELEC yŏboseyo 여보세요; (*on entry phone*) nuguseyo 누구세요

helm NAUT k'i chojong changch'i 키 조종 장치

helmet helmet 헬멧

help 1 *n* toum 도움 **2** *v/t* toptta 돕다; *~ oneself* (*to food*) maŭmkkŏt tŭlda 마음껏 들다; *I can't ~ it* ŏtchŏl su ŏpssŏyo 어쩔 수 없어요; *I couldn't ~ laughing* utchi anŭl su ŏpssŏssŏyo 웃지 않을 수 없었어요

helper towajunŭn saram 도와주는 사람

help file COMPUT toummal p'ail 도움말 파일

helpful toumi toenŭn 도움이 되는

helping (*of food*) han kŭrŭt 한 그릇

helpless (*unable to cope*) ŏtchŏl su ŏmnŭn 혼자서 어쩔 수 없는; (*powerless*) muryŏk'an 무력한

help screen COMPUT toummal hwamyŏn 도움말 화면

hem *n* (*of dress etc*) ot-ttan 옷단

hemisphere pan-gu 반구

hemorrhage 1 *n* ch'urhyŏl 출혈 **2** *v/i* ch'urhyŏrhada 출혈하다

hemp taema 대마

hen amt'ak 암탉; (*of any bird*) amsae 암새

henchman *pej* shimbok 심복

henpecked yŏja sone chwiyŏ sanŭn 여자 손에 쥐여 사는; *~ husband* kongch'ŏga 공처가

hepatitis kannyŏm 간염

her 1 *adj* kŭnyŏŭi 그녀의; *~ ticket* kŭnyŏŭi p'yo 그녀의 표 **2** *pron* kŭnyŏrŭl 그녀; *I know ~* nanŭn kŭnyŏrŭl anda 나는 그녀를 안다; *this is for ~* igŏsŭn kŭnyŏŭi kŏsh 이것은 그녀의 것이다

herb shigyong p'ullip 식용 풀잎, hŏ 허브

herb(al) tea hŏbŭ ch'a 허브 차

herd *n* tte 떼

here yŏgie(sŏ) 여기에(서); *~'s to you!* (*as toast*) kŏnbae! 건배!; *~ yc are* (*giving sth*) yŏgi issŭmnida 여 있습니다; *~ we are!* (*finding sth*) yŏgi itkkuna! 여기 있구나!

hereditary *disease* yujŏndoenŭn 유전되는

heritage yusan 유산

hermit ŭndunja 은둔자

hernia MED t'altchang 탈장

hero yŏng-ung 영웅

heroic yŏng-ungjŏgin 영웅적인

heroin heroin 헤로인

heroine yŏjangbu 여장부

heron waegari 왜가리

herpes MED p'ojin 포진

herring ch'ŏng-ŏ 청어

hers kŭnyŏŭi kot 그녀의 것; *it's ~* igosŭn kunyŏŭi kŏshida 이것은 그녀의 것이다; *a cousin of ~* kŭnyŏŭi sach'on 그녀의 사촌

herself kŭnyŏ chashin 그녀 자신; *s hurt ~* kŭnyŏga tach'yŏt-tta 그녀 다쳤다; *by ~* kŭnyŏ sŭsŭro 그녀 스스로

hesitate mangsŏrida 망설이다

hesitation mangsŏrim 망설임

heterosexual *adj* isŏng-aeŭi 이성애

heyday chŏnsŏnggi 전성기

hi annyŏng 안녕

hibernate tongmyŏnhada 동면하다

hiccup *n* ttalkkuktchil 딸꾹질; (*min problem*) yak-kkanŭi munje 약간의 문제; *have the ~s* ttalkkuktchirha 딸꾹질하다

hick *pej* F shigolttŭgi 시골뜨기

hick town *pej* F shigol 시골

hidden *meaning, treasure* sumgyŏji 숨겨진, kamch'wŏjin 감춰진

hide[1] *v/t* sumgida 숨기다, kamch' 감추다 **2** *v/i* sumtta 숨다

…e² n (of animal) kajuk 가죽
…e-and-seek sumbakkoktchil
바꼭질
…eaway ǔnshinch'ǒ 은신처
…eous weather, taste kkǔmtchik'an
찍한; crime hyung-ak'an 흉악한;
…ce hyunghan 흉한
…ing¹ (beating) maejil 매질
…ing²: be in ~ ǔnshinhada 은신하다;
…o into ~ sumtta 숨다
…ing place sumnǔn kot 숨는 곳
…rarchy kyegǔp chojik 계급 조직
…fi haip'ai 하이파이
…h 1 adj nop'ǔn 높은; wind kanghan
강한; (on drugs) ch'wihan 취한; have
… ~ opinion of s.o. nugurǔl nop'i
…'yǒngkkahada 누구를 높이
…가하다; it is ~ time … ijen kǔman
…. hal ttaeda 이젠 그만 … 할 때다
…n MOT koso kiǒ 고속 기어; (in
…atistics) nop'ǔn sujun 높은 수준;
…DU kodǔnghak-kkyo 고등학교
…adv nopke 높게; ~ in the sky
…anǔl nopke 하늘 높게; that's as ~
…s we can go uriga hal su innǔn
…h'oedaehanimnida 우리가 할 수
…있는 최대입니다
…ghbrow adj chishiginǔi 지식인의;
…ighchair yuayong nop'ǔn ǔija
…우아용 높은 의자; highclass
…ogǔbǔi 고급의; high diving taibing
…다이빙; high-frequency kojup'a
…고주파; high-grade kogǔbǔi 고급의;
…igh-handed koaptchǒgin 고압적인;
…igh-heeled nop'ǔn kubǔi 높은
…굽의; high jump nop'i ttwigi 높이
…뛰기; high-level kowi kogwanǔi
…고위 고관의; high life sangnyu
…sahoeǔi saenghwal 상류 사회의
…생활; highlight 1 n (main event, in
…air) hailait'ǔ 하이라이트 2 v/t (with
…pen) kangjohada 강조하다; COMPUT
…pullogǔl ssǔiuda 블록을 씌우다;
…highlighter (pen) hyǒnggwangp'en
…형광펜
…ghly desirable, likely k'ǔge 크게; be
… ~ paid nop'ǔn ponggǔbǔl pat-tta
…높은 봉급을 받다; think ~ of s.o.
…nugurǔl nop'i p'yǒngkkahada 누구를
…높이 평가하다
…gh-performance drill, battery

kosǒngnǔng 고성능; high-pitched
koǔmǔi 고음의; high point (of life,
career, program) chǒltchǒng 절정;
high-powered engine kosǒngnǔng-
ǔi 고성능의; intellectual t'ǔkch'urhan
특출한; salesman kkǔnjilgin 끈질긴;
high pressure 1 n (weather) kogiap
고기압 2 adj TECH koabǔi 고압의;
salesman kangnyohanǔn 강요하는;
job, lifestyle kodoǔi kinjang-ǔl
yohanǔn 고도의 긴장을 요하는; high
priest taejesajang 대제사장; fig (of
fashion etc) chidoja 지도자; high
school kodǔnghak-kkyo 고등학교;
high society sangnyu sahoe 상류
사회; high-speed train kosok
yǒlch'a 고속 열차; high strung min-
gamhan 민감한; high tech 1 n
ch'ǒmdan kisul 첨단 기술 2 adj
ch'ǒmdan kisurǔi 첨단 기술의; high
technology ch'ǒmdan kisul 첨단
기술; high-tension cable koabǔi
고압의; high tide manjo 만조; high
water ch'oego suwi 최고 수위; highway kosokttoro 고속도로; high
wire (in circus) chult'agi chul 줄타기
줄
hijack 1 v/t plane kongjung
napch'ihada 공중 납치하다; bus
t'alch'wihada 탈취하다 2 n (of
plane) kongjung napch'i 공중 납치;
(of bus) t'alch'wi 탈취
hijacker (of plane) kongjung
napch'ibǒm 공중 납치범; (of bus)
t'alch'wibǒm 탈취범
hike¹ 1 n toboyǒhaeng 도보여행 2 v/i
toboyǒhaenghada 도보여행하다
hike² n (in prices) insang 인상
hiker toboyǒhaengja 도보여행자
hilarious usǔmǔl chaanaenǔn 웃음을
자아내는
hill ǒndǒk 언덕; (slope) samyǒn 사면
hillbilly pej F sansaram 산사람
hillside ǒndǒgǔi samyǒn 언덕의 사면
hilltop ǒndǒk kkokttaegi 언덕 꼭대기
hilly kurǔngjidaeǔi 구릉지대의
hilt charu 자루
him kǔrǔl 그를; I know ~ nanǔn
kǔrǔl anda 나는 그를 안다; this is
for ~ igǒsǔn kǔǔi kǒshida 이것은
그의 것이다

himself kŭ chashin 그 자신; **he hurt ~** kŭnŭn tach'yŏt-tta 그는 다쳤다; **by ~** kŭ sŭsŭro 그 스스로

hinder panghaehada 방해하다

hindrance chang-ae 장애

hindsight twinŭjŭn kkaedarŭm 뒤늦은 깨달음; **with ~** twinŭjŭn kkaedarŭmŭro 뒤늦은 깨달음으로

hinge kyŏngch'ŏp 경첩

hint (clue) hint'ŭ 힌트; (piece of advice) choŏn 조언; (implied suggestion) amshi 암시; (of red, sadness etc) miyak'an chinghu 미약한 징후

hip kungdungi 궁둥이, ŏngdŏng-i 엉덩이

hip pocket twittchumŏni 뒷주머니

hippopotamus hama 하마

hire v/t room, car tonŭl chugo pillida 돈을 주고 빌리다; person koyonghada 고용하다

his 1 adj kuŭi 그의; **~ ticket** kuŭi p'yo 그의 표 2 pron kuŭi kŏt 그의 것; **it's ~** igosŭn kuŭi kŏshida 이것은 그의 것이다; **a cousin of ~** kuŭi sach'on 그의 사촌

hiss v/i (of snake) shwit sorirŭl naeda 쉿 소리를 내다; (of audience) yayurŭl ponaeda 야유를 보내다

historian sahaktcha 사학자

historic yŏkssasang-ŭro chungnyohan 역사상으로 중요한

historical yŏkssajŏgin 역사적인

history yŏkssa 역사

hit 1 v/t ch'ida 치다; (collide with) ch'ungdorhada 충돌하다; **he was ~ by a bullet** kŭnŭn t'anarŭl majat-tta 그는 탄알을 맞았다; **it suddenly ~ me** (I realized) nanŭn kaptchagi kkaedarat-tta 나는 갑자기 깨달았다; **~ town** (arrive) tongnee todarhada 동네에 도달하다 2 n (blow) t'agyŏk 타격; MUS hit'ŭ 히트; (success) sŏnggong 성공

♦ hit back toebadach'ida 되받아치다

♦ hit on idea saenggak'aenaeda 생각해내다

♦ hit out at (criticize) maengnyŏrhi pinanhada 맹렬히 비난하다

hit-and-run adj: **~ accident** ppaengsoni sago 뺑소니 사고; **~ driver** ppaengsoni unjŏnsu 뺑소니 운전수

hitch 1 n (problem) chang-ae 장애; **without a ~** chang-aeŏpsshi 장애없이 2 v/t kŏrŏmaeda 걸어매다; **~ X to Y** Xŭl/rŭl Ye kŏrŏmaeda X을/를 Y에 걸어매다; **~ a ride** p'yŏnsŭnghada 편승하다 3 v/i (hitchhike) p'yŏnsŭnghada 편승하다

♦ hitch up trailer kkŭrŏollida 끌어올리다

hitchhike p'yŏnsŭnghada 편승하다

hitchhiker p'yŏnsŭng yŏhaengja 편승 여행자

hitchhiking p'yŏnsŭnghagi 편승하기

hi-tech 1 n ch'ŏmdan kisul 첨단 기술 2 adj ch'ŏmdan kisurŭi 첨단 기술의

hitlist taesangja myŏngdan 대상자 명단; hitman ch'ŏngbu sarinja 청부 살인자; hit-or-miss toenŭndaeroŭi 되는대로의; hit squad amsalttan 암살단

HIV Inch'e Myŏnyŏk Kyŏlp'ip Pairŏsŭ 인체 면역 결핍 바이러스

hive (for bees) pŏlt'ong 벌통

♦ hive off v/t (COM: separate off) pullihada 분리하다

HIV-positive Eijŭ yangsŏng panŭng 에이즈 양성 반응

hoard 1 n pich'uk 비축 2 v/t pich'uk'ada 비축하다

hoarse moksshwin 목쉰

hoax n sogimsu 속임수

hobble v/i chŏllŭmgŏrida 절름거리다

hobby ch'wimi 취미

hobo ttŭnaegi 뜨내기; (itinerant worker) ttŭnaegi ilkkun 뜨내기 일꾼

hockey (ice ~) aisŭ hak'i 아이스 하키

hog n (pig) twaeji 돼지

hoist 1 n kijunggi 기중기 2 v/t kkŭrŏ ollida 끌어 올리다

hokum (nonsense) hŏt'ŭn sori 허튼 소리; (sentimental stuff) ssaguryŏm 싸구려물

hold 1 v/t (in hands) chaptta 잡다, chibŏdŭlda 집어들다; (support, keep in place) chit'aenghada 지탱하다; passport, job kajida 가지다; prisoner, suspect puttchaptta 붙잡다; (contain) tamtta 담다; course yujihada 유지하다; **~ one's breath** sumŭl

ugida 숨을 죽이다; *he can ~ his
rink kŭnŭn surŭl kyesok mashil su
tta 그는 술을 계속 마실 수 있다; ~
o. responsible nuguege
aegimit-ttago saenggak'ada
구에게 책임있다고 생각하다; ~
at ... (*believe, maintain*) ...ranŭn
enggagŭl kosuhada ...라는 생각을
수하다; ~ *the line* TELEC
kŭntchimalgo kidariseyo 끊지말고
다리세요 **2** *n* (*in ship, plane*)
wamulsshil 화물실; *catch ~ of sth*
uŏsŭl chaptta 무엇을 잡다; *lose
ne's ~ on sth* (*on rope*) muŏsŭl
och'ida 무엇을 놓치다
old against: hold X against Y
taemune Yŭl/rŭl wŏnmanghada
때문에 Y을/를 원망하다
old back 1 *v/t crowds* maktta 막다;
cts, information sumgida 숨기다
v/i (*not tell all*) ta marhaji ant'a 다
하지 않다
old on *v/i* (*wait*) kidarida 기다리다;
ELEC kŭŭntchiank'o it-tta 끊지않고
다; *now ~ a minute!*
amkkanman kidaryŏ poseyo!
깐만 기다려 보세요!
old on to (*keep*) kyesok kajigo it-
a 계속 가지고 있다; *belief*
osuhada 고수하다
old out 1 *v/t hand* naemilda
밀다; *prospect* cheanhada 제안하다
v/i (*of supplies*) kyesok namait-tta
속 남아있다; (*survive*) pŏt'ida
티다
old up *v/t hand* tŭrŏ ollida 들어
리다; *bank etc* kangt'arhada
탈하다; (*make late*) chich'ehage
da 지체하게 하다; *hold sth up as
example* muŏsŭl yero
eshihada 무엇을 예로 제시하다
old with (*approve of*) injŏnghada
정하다
der (*container*) kwak 곽; (*of
assport, ticket etc*) soyuja 소유자;
of record) poyuja 보유자
ding company mohoesa 모회사
dup (*robbery*) kangdo 강도;
elay) chich'e 지체
e kumŏng 구멍
iday (*single day*) hyuil 휴일;

(*period*) hyuga 휴가
Holland Nedŏllandŭ 네덜란드
hollow *object* sogi pin sogi 속이 빈; *cheeks*
ump'uk tŭrŏgan 움푹 들어간; *words*
konghŏhan 공허한
holly horanggashinamu 호랑가시나무
holocaust Yut'aein taehakssal 유태인
대학살
hologram hollograem 홀로그램
holster kwŏnch'ongjip 권총집
holy sŏngsŭrŏun 성스러운
Holy Spirit Sŏngnyŏng 성령
Holy Week Sŏng Chugan 성 주간
home 1 *n* kajŏng 가정, chip 집; (*native
country*) koguk 고국; (*town, part of
country*) kohyang 고향; (*for old
people*) yangnowŏn 양로원; *at ~* (*in
my house*) nae chibe 내 집에; (*in my
country*) nae koguge 내 고국에; SP
hom kyŏnggijang-esŏ 홈 경기장에서;
make oneself at ~ p'yŏnanhi hada
편안히 하다; *at ~ and abroad*
kungnaeoeesŏ 국내외에서; *work
from ~* chat'aek kŭnmu 자택 근무
2 *adv* chibe 집에; (*in own country*)
koguge 고국에; (*in own town, part of
country*) kohyang-e 고향에; *go ~*
chibe kada 집에 가다; (*to own
country*) koguge kada 고국에 가다;
(*to town, part of country*) kohyang-e
kada 고향에 가다
home address chiptchuso 집주소;
homecoming kwiga 귀가; **home
computer** kajŏngnyong
k'ŏmp'yut'ŏ 가정용 컴퓨터; **home
education** kajŏng kyoyuk 가정
교육; **home game** hom kyŏnggi 홈
경기
homeless 1 *adj* chibŏmnŭn 집없는
2 *n: the ~* mujut'aektcha 무주택자
homeloving kajŏngjŏgin 가정적인
homely (*homeloving*) kajŏngjŏgin
가정적인; (*not good-looking*)
motssaenggin 못생긴
homemade chibesŏ mandŭn 집에서
만든; **home movie** chaga chejak
yŏnghwa 자가 제작 영화; **home
page** COMPUT homp'eiji 홈페이지
homeopathy tongjongnyoppŏp
동종요법
homesick: *be ~* hyangsuppyŏng-ŭl

alt'a 향수병을 앓다; **home town** kohyang 고향; **home tutor** kajŏng kyosa 가정 교사; **homeward** *adv* (*to own house*) kwiga kire 귀가 길에; (*to own country*) kwiguk kire 귀국 길에; **homework** EDU suktche 숙제; **homeworking** COM chat'aek kŭnmu 자택 근무

homicide (*crime*) sarin 살인; (*police department*) kyŏngch'al sarin chŏndam pusŏ 경찰 살인 전담 부서

homograph tonghyŏng-iŭiŏ 동형이의어

homophobia tongsŏng-ae hyŏmotchŭng 동성애 혐오증

homosexual 1 *adj* tongsŏng-aeŭi 동성애의 **2** *n* tongsŏng-aeja 동성애자

honest chŏngjik'an 정직한

honestly soltchik'age 솔직하게; **~!** chŏngmalloyo! 정말로요!

honesty chŏngjik 정직

honey kkul 꿀; F (*darling*) chagi 자기; (*to husband*) yŏbo 여보

honeycomb pŏltchip 벌집

honeymoon *n* shinhon yŏhaeng 신혼 여행

Hong Kong Hongk'ong 홍콩

honk *v/t horn* ullida 울리다

honor 1 *n* myŏng-ye 명예 **2** *v/t* yeuhada 예우하다

honorable *person* torirŭl anŭn 도리를 아는; *thing to do* torie mannŭn 도리에 맞는

honorific kyŏng-ŏppŏbŭi 경어법의

hood (*over head*) ose tallin moja 옷에 달린 모자; (*over cooker*) tŏpkkae 덮개; MOT enjin ttukkŏng 엔진 뚜껑; F (*gangster*) kkangp'ae 깡패

hoodlum kkangp'ae 깡패

hoof palkkup 발굽

hook kalgori 갈고리; (*to hang clothes on*) kori 고리; (*for fishing*) nakssippanŭl 낚시바늘; **off the ~** TELEC suhwagirŭl pŏsŏna 수화기를 벗어나

hooked: be ~ on (*on drugs, fig*) ...e ppajida ...에 빠지다

hooker F ch'angnyŏ 창녀

hooky: play ~ mudan kyŏlssŏk'ada 무단 결석하다

hooligan pullyangbae 불량배

hooliganism pullyangbae kijil 불량배 기질

hoop t'e 테

hoot 1 *v/t horn* uusorirŭl naeda 우우소리를 내다 **2** *v/i* (*of car*) kyŏngjŏgŭl ullida 경적을 울리다; (*owl*) puŏngbuŏng ulda 부엉부엉 울다

hop[1] *n* (*plant*) hop 홉

hop[2] *v/i* kabyŏpkke twiŏ orŭda 가볍게 뛰어 오르다

hope 1 *n* hŭimang 희망; **there's no of that** chŏnhyŏ kŭrŏl kamang-i ŏptta 전혀 그럴 가망이 없다 **2** *v/i* parada 바라다, hŭimanghada 희망하다; **~ for sth** muŏsŭl parad 무엇을 바라다; **I ~ so** kŭrŏgil paramnida 그러길 바랍니다; **I ~ n** kŭrŏch'i ank'irŭl paramnida 그렇 않기를 바랍니다 **3** *v/t*: **I ~ you like** maŭme tŭlmyŏn chok'essŏyo 마음 들면 좋겠어요

hopeful hŭimang-e ch'an 희망에 ㅊ (*promising*) kamang-innŭn 가망있

hopefully *say, wait* kidaehamyŏ 기대하며; (*I/we hope*) paragŏnde 바라건데

hopeless *position, prospect* hŭimar ŭl irŭn 희망을 잃은; (*useless: pers* kamang ŏmnŭn 가망 없는

horizon (*on land*) chip'yŏngsŏn 지평선; (*at sea*) sup'yŏngsŏn 수평(

horizontal sup'yŏng-ŭi 수평의

hormone horŭmon 호르몬

horn (*of animal*) ppul 뿔; MOT kyŏngjŏk 경적

hornet malbŏl 말벌

horn-rimmed spectacles ppult'e an-gyŏng 뿔테 안경

horny (*sexually*) sŏngtchŏgŭro hŭngbunhan 성적으로 흥분한

horoscope chŏmsŏngsul 점성술

horrible chidok'an 지독한

horrify: I was horrified ch'unggyŏktchŏgiŏssŏyo 충격적이었어요

horrifying *experience* kkŭmtchik'a'a 끔찍한; *idea, prices* ch'unggyŏktchŏgin 충격적인

horror kongp'o 공포; **the ~s of wa** chŏnjaeng-ŭi ch'amsa 전쟁의 참사

ror movie kongp'o yŏnghwa 공포
화
s d'oeuvre chŏnch'ae 전채
se mal 말
seback: *on* ~ marŭl t'ago 말을
고; horse chestnut maronie
lmae 마로니에 열매; horsehair
at kat 갓; horsepower maryŏk
력; horse race kyŏngma 경마;
orseshoe malgup 말굽
se hosŭ 호스
spice yoyangso 요양소
spitable hwandaehanŭn 환대하는
spital pyŏng-wŏn 병원; *go into*
e ~ ibwŏnhada 입원하다
spitality hwandae 환대
st *n (at party, reception)* chuin
인; *(of TV program)* sahoeja
회자
stage injil 인질; *be taken* ~ injillo
ap'ida 인질로 잡히다
stage taker injilbŏm 인질범
stel *(inexpensive accommodations)*
ŏgwan 여관; *(youth* ~) yusuhŏsŭt'el
스호스텔
stess *(at party, reception)* antchuin
주인; *(on airplane)* sŭt'yuŏdisŭ
튜어디스; *(in bar)* yŏjong-ŏbwŏn
종업원; *(prostitute)* hosŭt'essŭ
스테스
stile chŏkttaejŏgin 적대적인
stility *(of attitude)* chŏkttaesim
대심; *hostilities* chŏnt'u 전투
t *water, food* ttŭgŏun 뜨거운
eather tŏun 더운; *(spicy)* maeun
운; F *(good)* maeu chal hanŭn 매우
하는; *I'm* ~ tŏwŏyo 더워요; *it's so
today* onŭl nalsshiga maeu
ŏpkkunnyo 오늘 날씨가 매우
군요
t dog hattogŭ 핫도그
tel hot'el 호텔
tplate yoriyong ch'ŏlp'an 요리용
판
t spot *(military, political)* punjaeng
niyŏk 분쟁 지역
ur shigan 시간
urglass drum changgo 장고
urly *adj* shiganmadaŭi 시간마다의
use *n* chip 집; *at your* ~ nŏŭi

chibesŏ 너의 집에서
houseboat chugŏyong pae 주거용
배; housebreaking kat'aek ch'imip
가택 침입; household kajok 가족;
household name chal allyŏjin irŭm
잘 알려진 이름; house husband
kasarŭl tolbonŭn namp'yŏn 가사를
돌보는 남편; housekeeper
kajŏngbu 가정부; housekeeping
(activity) kasa 가사; *(money)* kagye
가계; House of Representatives
Hawŏn 하원; housewarming
(party) chipttŭri 집들이; housewife
chubu 주부; housework chiban il
집안 일
housing chut'aek 주택; TECH t'ŭl 틀
housing conditions chut'aek sajŏng
주택 사정
hovel nuch'uhan chip 누추한 집
hover pingbing maemdolda 빙빙
맴돌다
hovercraft hobŏk'ŭrap'ŭt'ŭ
호버크라프트
how ŏttŏk'e 어떻게; ~ *are you?*
annyŏnhaseyo? 안녕하세요?; ~
about ...? ...hanŭn kŏshi
ŏttŏgessŭmnikka? ...하는 것이
어떻겠습니까?; ~ *much?*
ŏlmank'ŭm? 얼마큼?; ~ *much do
you want?* ŏlmank'ŭm wŏnhaseyo?
얼마큼 원하세요?; ~ *much is it?*
ŏlmaimnikka? 얼마입니까?; ~
many? ŏlmana mani? 얼마나 많이?;
~ *often?* ŏlmana chaju? 얼마나
자주?; ~ *funny!* ŏlmana
chaemiinnŭnji! 얼마나 재미있는지!
however kŭrŏna 그러나; ~ *big* / *rich
they are* amuri k'ŭda / puyuhada
hadŏrado 아무리 크다 / 부유하다
하더라도
howl *v/i (of dog, person in pain)*
ulbujit-tta 울부짖다; *(with laughter)*
sorinop'yŏ ut-tta 소리높여 웃다
hub *(of wheel)* pak'wiŭi chungshimbu
바퀴의 중심부
hubcap chadongch'aŭi hwilk'aep
자동차의 휠캡
♦ huddle together tterŭl chiŏ moida
떼를 지어 모이다
huff: *be in a* ~ palkkŭn hwarŭl naeda
발끈 화를 내다

hug v/t p'o-onghada 포옹하다, antta 안다

huge kŏdaehan 거대한; (*in amount*) makttaehan 막대한

hull n sŏnch'e 선체

hullabaloo soran 소란

hum 1 v/t *song, tune* k'onnoraero puruda 콧노래로 부르다 **2** v/i (*of person*) k'onnoraerŭl puruda 콧노래를 부르다; (*of machine*) wing-winggŏrida 윙윙거리다

human 1 n in-gan 인간, saram 사람 **2** adj *species, characteristics* in-ganŭi 인간의; *weakness* in-ganjŏgin 인간적인; **~ error** saramŭi shilssu 사람의 실수

human being in-gan 인간

humane injŏng-innŭn 인정있는

humanitarian indojuŭiŭi 인도주의의

humanity (*human beings*) illyu 인류; (*of attitude etc*) saramdaum 사람다움, in-ganssŏng 인간성

human race illyu 인류

human resources insakkwa 인사과

humble *attitude, person* kyŏmsonhan 겸손한; *origins* ch'ŏnhan 천한; *meal, house* ch'orahan 초라한

humdrum maeu p'yŏngbŏmhan 매우 평범한

humid sŭp'an 습한

humidifier kasŭpkki 가습기

humidity sŭpkki 습기; **90% ~** kuship p'ŏsent'ŭŭi sŭpdo 구십 퍼센트의 습도

humiliate kuryogŭl chuda 굴욕을 주다

humiliating kuryoktchŏgin 굴욕적인

humiliation kuryok 굴욕

humility kyŏmson 겸손

humor haehak 해학, usŭgae sori 우스개 소리; (*mood*) kibun 기분; **sense of ~** yumŏ kamgak 유머 감각

humorous usŭun 우스운

hump 1 n (*of camel, person*) hok 혹; (*on road*) hŏmp'ŭ 험프, *sokttorŭl churige hagi wihan toro sang-ŭi changch'i* 속도를 줄이게 하기 위한 도로 상의 장치 **2** v/t (*carry*) chilmŏjida 짊어지다

hunch (*idea*) yegam 예감

hundred paek 백

hundred day ceremony (*after birth*) paegil 백일

hundredth adj paek pŏntchaeŭi 백 번째의

hundredweight 100p'aundŭ 100파운드; *Br* 112p'aundŭ 112파운드

Hungarian 1 adj Hŏnggariŭi 헝가리의 **2** n (*person*) Hŏnggari saram 헝가리 사람 (*language*) Hŏnggariŏ 헝가리어

Hungary Hŏnggari 헝가리

hunger paegop'ŭm 배고픔

hung-over sukch'wiŭi 숙취의

hungry paegop'ŭn 배고픈; **I'm ~** paega kop'ayo 배가 고파요

hunk: great ~ F (*man*) mŏtchin namja 멋진 남자

hunky-dory F mansa p'yŏnanhan 만사 편안한

hunt 1 n (*for animals*) sanyang 사냥 (*for new leader, actor*) ch'ajŭm 찾음 (*for criminal, missing child*) susaek 수색 **2** v/t *animal* sanyanghada 사냥하다

♦ **hunt for** ch'at-tta 찾다

hunter sanyangkkun 사냥꾼

hunting sanyang 사냥

hurdle SP chang-aemul 장애물; *fig* (*obstacle*) chang-ae 장애

hurdler SP chang-aemul kyŏngjuja 장애물 경주자

hurdles SP chang-aemul kyŏngju 장애물 경주

hurl himkkŏt naedŏnjida 힘껏 내던지다

hurray hwanoŭi sori 환호의 소리; **manse!** 만세!

hurricane t'aep'ung 태풍

hurried sŏdurŭn 서두른

hurry 1 n sŏdurŭm 서두름; **be in a ~** sodullŏ hada 서둘러 하다 **2** v/i sodurŭda 서두르다

♦ **hurry up 1** v/i sŏdurŭda 서두르다 sŏdurŭseyo! 서두르세요! **2** v/t chaech'ok'ada 재촉하다

hurt 1 v/i ap'ŭda 아프다; **my leg ~s** tariga ap'ayo 다리가 아파요; **does it ~?** ap'ŭmnikka? 아픕니까? **2** v/t tach'ige hada 다치게 하다; (*emotionally*) ...ŭi maŭmŭl sanghage hada ...의 마음을 상하게

hysterics

...다
...sband namp'yŏn 남편
...sh n choyongham 조용함; ~!
...oyonghi! 조용히!
...ush up scandal etc
...wishwihaebŏrida 쉬쉬해버리다
...sk (of grain) kkŏptchil 껍질
...sky adj shwin mokssoriŭi 쉰 소리의, hŏsŭk'iŭi 허스키의
...stle 1 n: ~ and bustle hwalgich'an onjap 활기찬 혼잡 2 v/t person ŏdurŭge hada 서두르게 하다
...t odumak 오두막
...acinth hiashinsŭ 히아신스
...orid n (plant, animal) chaptchong ...종
...drant kŭpssugwan 급수관; fire ~ ...ohwajŏn 소화전
...draulic (using water) suabŭi ...압의; (using oil) yuabŭi 유압의
...droelectric suryŏk chŏn-giŭi 수력 ...기의
...drofoil (boat) sujung-iksŏn ...중익선
...drogen suso 수소
...drogen bomb suso p'okt'an 수소 ...탄
...giene wisaeng 위생
...gienic wisaengsang-ŭi 위생상의
...mn ch'ansongga 찬송가, sŏngga ...가
...pe n kwadae sŏnjŏn 과대 선전
...peractive chinach'ige sŏlch'inŭn ...나치게 설치는; hypermarket ...aehyŏng shyup'ŏmak'et 대형

슈퍼마켓; hypersensitive kwaminhan 과민한; hypertension kohyŏrap 고혈압; hypertext COMPUT haip'ŏt'ekssŭt'ŭ 하이퍼텍스트
hyphen iŭmp'yo 이음표
hypnosis ch'oemyŏnsul 최면술
hypnotherapy ch'oemyŏn yoppŏp 최면 요법
hypnotize ch'oemyŏnsurŭl kŏlda 최면술을 걸다
hypochondriac n uultchŭng hwanja 우울증 환자
hypocrisy wisŏn 위선
hypocrite wisŏnja 위선자
hypocritical wisŏnŭi 위선의
hypothermia chŏch'eontchŭng 저체온증
hypothesis kasŏl 가설
hypothetical kasŏrŭi 가설의
hysterectomy chagung chŏkch'ulssul 자궁 적출술
hysteria hisŭt'eri 히스테리
hysterical person pyŏngtchok hŭngbun sangt'aeŭi 병적 흥분 상태의, hisŭt'erisŏng-ŭi 히스테리성의; laughter paltchaktchŏgin 발작적인; (very funny) ŏmch'ŏngnage usŭun 엄청나게 우스운; become ~ pyŏngtchŏk hŭngbunsangt'aega toeda 병적 흥분상태가 되다
hysterics hisŭt'eri 히스테리; (laughter) paltchaktchŏgin usŭm 발작적인 웃음

I

I ◊ na 나; H chŏ 저; **~ am American /
a student** nanŭn Migugin /
hakssaengiyeyo 나는 미국인 /
학생이예요; **can ~ buy you a
drink?** chega han chan sado
toelkkayo? 제가 한 잔 사도 될까요?
◊ (omission of pronoun): **~ can't
see** pol su ŏpssŏyo 볼 수 없어요; **~
don't know** mollayo 몰라요
ice ŏrŭm 얼음; **break the ~** fig
ŏsaek'an punwigirŭl kkaeda 어색한
분위기를 깨다
♦ **ice up** (of engine etc)
tonggyŏldoeda 동결되다
iceberg pingsan 빙산; **icebox** aisŭ
pakssŭ 아이스 박스; **icebreaker**
(ship) swaebingsŏn 쇄빙선; **ice
cream** aisŭ k'ŭrim 아이스 크림; **ice-
cream parlor** aisŭ k'ŭrim kage
아이스 크림 가게; **ice cube** kak
ŏrŭm 각 얼음
iced drink ŏrŭmŭl nŏhŭn 얼음을 넣은
iced coffee aisŭ k'ŏp'i 아이스 커피
ice hockey aisŭ hak'i 아이스 하키
ice rink sŭk'eit'ŭjang 스케이트장
icicle kodŭrŭm 고드름
icon (cultural) sang sang 상 상; COMPUT
aik'on 아이콘
icy road, surface ŏrŭmi ŏrŭn 얼음이
ŏrŭn; welcome ssalssarhan 쌀쌀한
idea saenggak 생각; **good ~!** chŏun
saenggagiya! 좋은 생각이야!; **I have
no ~** nan chal morŭgennŭndeyo 난
잘 모르겠는데요; **it's not a good ~
to ...** ...hanŭn kŏsŭn chŏun
saenggagi animnida ...하는 것은
좋은 생각이 아닙니다
ideal (perfect) isangjŏgin 이상적인
idealistic isangjujŭijŏgin 이상주의적인
identical tong-irhan 동일한; **~ twins**
illanssŏng ssangdung-i 일란성 쌍둥이
identification hwagin 확인; (papers
etc) chŭngmyŏngsŏ 증명서
identify hwaginhada 확인하다

identity shinwŏn 신원; **their sense
national ~** kŭdŭrŭi kungmin
chuch'eŭishik 그들의 국민 주체의
identity card shinbun chŭngmyŏng,
신분 증명서
ideological inyŏmjŏgin 이념적인
ideology ideollogi 이데올로기
idiom (saying) kwanyong-ŏ 관용어
idiomatic kwanyongjŏgin 관용적인
idiosyncrasy t'ŭktchil 특질
idiot pabo 바보
idiotic ŏrisŏgŭn 어리석은
idle 1 adj person nat'aehan 나태한;
threat ssŭltteŏmnŭn 쓸데없는;
machinery nolgo innŭn 놀고 있는;
an ~ moment hangahan ttaee
한가한 때에 2 v/i (of engine)
kongjŏnhada 공전하다
♦ **idle away** time etc pindunggŏrida
빈둥거리다
idol usang 우상
idolize sungbaehada 숭배하다
idyllic nagwŏn-gat'ŭn 낙원같은
if manyak ...myŏn 만약 ...면; (wheth
or not) ...inji aninji ...인지 아닌지;
you catch a cold manyak kamgi
kŏllimyŏn 만약 감기에 걸리면; **as
him ~ he will be there** kŭege kŏ
issŭl kŏshinji aninji murŏposeyo
그에게 거기 있을 것인지 아닌지
물어보세요
igloo igŭllu 이글루
ignite v/t purŭl puch'ida 불을 붙이
ignition (in car) chŏmhwa changch
점화 장치; **~ key** igŭnishyŏn k'i
이그니션 키
ignorance muji 무지
ignorant morŭnŭn 모르는; (rude)
muryehan 무례한
ignore mushihada 무시하다
ill ap'ŭn 아픈; **fall ~, be taken ~**
pyŏngdŭlda 병들다
illegal pulppŏbŭi 불법의
illegible ilkki ŏryŏun 읽기 어려운

gitimate pulppŏpǔi 불법의; **an ~
hild** sasaeng-a 사생아
ated purunhan 불운한
eit wibŏbǔi 위법의
erate munmaeng-ǔi 문맹의
mannered muryehan 무례한
natured sŏngmiga koyak'an 성미가
약한
ess pyŏng 병
gical pinollijŏgin 비논리적인
tempered sŏngkkal innǔn 성깔
는
eat hakttaehada 확대하다
minate *building etc*
homyŏnghada 조명하다
minating *remarks etc*
unmyŏnghage hanǔn 분명하게 하는
sion hwanyŏng 환영
strate *book* sap'warǔl kǔrida
화를 그리다; (*with examples*)
eshihada 예시하다
stration kǔrim 그림; (*example*)
hillye 실례
strator sap'waga 삽화가
will agǔi 악의
age (*picture*) imiji 이미지; (*exact
keness*) ppaedalmǔn mosǔp 빼닮은
습; (*of politician, company*) insang
인상
age-conscious ch'emyŏnǔl
h'arinǔn 체면을 차리는
aginable sangsanghal su innǔn
상상할 수 있는; **the biggest/
smallest size ~** sangsanghal su
innǔn ch'oedaeǔi/ch'oesoǔi k'ǔgi
상상할 수 있는 최대의/최소의 크기
aginary kasang-ǔi 가상의
agination sangsang 상상; **it's all in
your ~** kǔgŏsǔn chŏnbu tangshinǔi
sangsang-imnida 그것은 전부 당신의
상상입니다
aginative sangsangnyŏgi
ǔ'ungbuhan 상상력이 풍부한
agine sangsanghada 상상하다; **I
can just ~ it** sangsang-i kamnida
상상이 갑니다; **you're imagining
things** tangshini sangsanghanǔn
kŏyeyo 당신이 상상하는 거예요
nbecile chŏngshin pagyaktcha 정신
박약자
MF (= **International Monetary**

Fund) Kuktche T'onghwa Kigǔm
국제 통화 기금, Aiemep'ǔ
아이엠에프
imitate mobanghada 모방하다
imitation (*copying*) mobang 모방;
(*something copied*) mojop'um
모조품
Imjin River Imjin-gang 임진강
immaculate t'i ŏmnǔn 티 없는
immaterial sanggwanŏmnǔn 상관없는
immature misŏngsugǔi 미성숙의
immediate chǔksshiǔi 즉시의; **the ~
family** paeuja ttonǔn pumo hyŏngje,
chashik 배우자 또는 부모 형제,
자식; **in the ~ neighborhood**
injŏp'an kose 인접한 곳에
immediately chǔksshiro 즉시로; **~
after the bank/church**
ǔnhaeng/kyohoe paro yŏp'e
은행/교회 바로 옆에
immense ŏmch'ŏngnan 엄청난
immerse tamgǔda 담그다; **~ oneself
in** molttuhada 몰두하다
immersion heater t'uip chŏnyŏlgi
투입 전열기
immigrant *n* ijuja 이주자
immigrate ijuhada 이주하다
immigration (*act*) iju 이주
Immigration Bureau Ch'urip
Kwalliguk 출입 관리국
imminent chŏlbak'an 절박한
immobilize *factory* kadonghaji
mot'age hada 가동하지 못하게 하다;
person umjigiji mot'age hada
움직이지 못하게 하다; *car*
kadongshik'iji mot'age hada
가동시키지 못하게 하다
immoderate mujŏltchehan 무절제한
immoral pudodŏk'an 부도덕한
immorality pudodŏk 부도덕
immortal pulmyŏrǔi 불멸의
immortality pulmyŏl 불멸
immune (*to illness, infection*)
myŏnyŏgǔi 면역의; (*from ruling,
requirement*) myŏnjedoen 면제된
immune system MED myŏnyŏk
ch'egye 면역 체계
immunity (*to infection*) myŏnyŏk
면역; (*from ruling*) myŏnje 면제;
diplomatic ~ oegyomyŏnch'aek
외교면책

impact n (*of meteorite, vehicle*) ch'ungdol 충돌; (*of new manager etc*) yŏnghyangnyŏk 영향력; (*effect*) yŏnghyang 영향

impair haech'ida 해치다

impaired sonsangdoen 손상된

impartial kongjŏnghan 공정한

impassable *road* t'onghaenghal su ŏmnŭn 통행할 수 없는

impasse (*in negotiations etc*) kongyong 곤경

impassioned *speech, plea* yŏltchŏngjŏgin 열정적인

impassive naengjŏnghan 냉정한

impatience sŏnggŭp'am 성급함

impatient sŏnggŭp'an 성급한

impatiently sŏnggŭp'age 성급하게

impeccable *turnout* namural te ŏmnŭn 나무랄 데 없는; *English* wanbyŏk'an 완벽한

impeccably *dressed* namural te ŏpsshi 나무랄 데 없이; *speak Korean* wanbyŏk'age 완벽하게

impede panghaehada 방해하다

impediment (*in speech*) tŏdŭmgŏrim 더듬거림

impending imbak'an 임박한

impenetrable hearil su ŏmnŭn 헤아릴 수 없는

imperative 1 *adj* kkok haeya hal 꼭 해야 할; *it is ~ that we go now* urinŭn chigŭm kkok kaya handa 우리는 지금 꼭 가야 한다 **2** n GRAM myŏngnyŏngppŏp 명령법

imperceptible nŏmu chaga kamjihal su ŏmnŭn 너무 작아 감지할 수 없는

imperfect 1 *adj* purwanjŏnhan 불완전한 **2** n GRAM miwallyo 미완료

imperial chegugŭi 제국의

impersonal piin-ganjŏgin 비인간적인

impersonate (*as a joke*) hyungnaenaeda 흉내내다; (*illegally*) wijanghada 위장하다

impertinence kŏnbangjim 건방짐

impertinent kŏnbangjin 건방진

imperturbable ch'abunhan 차분한

impervious: ~ *to* ...e mudŏmdŏmhan ...에 무덤덤한

impetuous ch'ungdongjŏgin 충동적인

impetus (*of campaign etc*) yŏse 여세

implement 1 n togu 도구 **2** v/t

measures etc shirhaenghada 실행하

implicate: ~ *s.o. in sth* nugurŭl muŏse yŏllu shik'ida 누구를 무엇에 연루 시키다

implication hamch'uk 함축

implicit hamch'uktchŏgin 함축적인; *trust* chŏlttaejŏgin 절대적인

implore kanch'ŏnghada 간청하다

imply amshihada 암시하다

impolite pŏrŭt ŏmnŭn 버릇 없는

import 1 n suip 수입 **2** v/t suip'ada 수입하다

importance chungnyosŏng 중요성

important chungnyohan 중요한

importer suiptcha 수입자

impose *tax* pugwahada 부과하다; ~ *oneself on s.o.* nuguege pudamŭl chuda 누구에게 부담을 주다

imposing insangjŏgin 인상적인

impossibility pulganŭng 불가능

impossible pulganŭnghan 불가능한

impostor sagikkun 사기꾼

impotence sŏng pullŭng 성 불능

impotent muryŏk'an 무력한; MED sŏng pullŭng-ŭi 성 불능의

impoverished pin-gone tchidŭn 빈곤에 찌든

impractical *person, suggestion* pihyŏnshiltchŏgin 비현실적인

impress kammyŏng chuda 감명 주다; *be ~ed by s.o. / sth* nuguege / muŏse kammyŏng pat-tta 누구에게 / 무엇에 감명 받다; *I'm not ~ed* chŏrŭl shilmangshik'inŭn-gunyo 저를 실망시키는군요

impression nŭkkim 느낌; (*impersonation*) hyungnaenaegi 흉내내기; *make a good / bad ~ on s.o.* nuguege choŭn / nappŭn insangŭl chuda 누구에게 좋은 / 나쁜 인상을 주다; *get the ~ that ...* ...ranŭn insang-ŭl pat-tta ...라는 인상을 받다

impressionable kamsusŏng-i yeminhan 감수성이 예민한

impressive insangjŏgin 인상적인

imprint n (*of credit card*) nullŏ tchigŭn chaguk 눌러 찍은 자국

imprison t'uok'ada 투옥하다

imprisonment t'uok 투옥

improbable irŏnal kŏt kattchi anŭn

...어날 것 같지 않은

proper *behavior* pujŏktchŏrhan 적절한

prove 1 *v/t* hyangsangshik'ida 향상시키다 **2** *v/i* hyangsanghada 향상하다

provement hyangsang 향상

provise *v/i* (*in music*) chŭk'ŭng-ro hada 즉흥으로 하다; (*in plans*) nŭkssŏgesŏ mandŭlda 즉석에서 ...들다

pudent ppŏnppŏnsŭrŏun ...뻔스러운

pulse ch'ungdong 충동; **do sthon ~** ch'ungdongjŏguro muŏsŭl ...ada 충동적으로 무엇을 하다; **~ buy** ch'ungdong kumae 충동 구매

pulsive ch'ungdongjŏgin 충동적인

punity: with ~ pŏrŭl pat-tchi ank'o ...을 받지 않고

pure pulssunhan 불순한

1 *prep* ...e(sŏ) ...에(서); **~ Wash-ngton / Seoul** Wŏshingt'ŏne(sŏ) / ...ŏure(sŏ) 워싱턴에(서) / 서울에(서); **the street** kŏrie(sŏ) 거리에(서); **ounded ~ the leg / arm** ...arie / pare pusang-ŭl ibŭn ...다리에 / 팔에 부상을 입은 ◊ (*inside*) ...ane / soge ...안에 / 속에; **~ the box** ...angja ane 상자 안에; **put it ~ your pocket** chumŏni soge nŏŏ twŏra ...머니 속에 넣어 둬라 ◊ **~ his ovel** kŭŭi sosŏl soge(sŏ) 그의 소설 속에(서); **~ Faulkner** P'ok'ŭnŏŭi ...hakp'um soge(sŏ) 포크너의 작품 속에(서) ◊ (*time*) ...e ...에; **~ 1999** ...999nyŏne 1999년에; **~ two hours from now** tu shigan ane 두 시간 ...에, tu shigan inaee 두 시간 이내에; **~ the morning** ach'ime 아침에; **~ he summer** yŏrŭme 여름에; **~ August** p'arwŏre 팔월에 ◊ (*manner*) ...(ŭ)ro ...(으)로; **~ Eng-ish / Korean** Yŏng-ŏro / Han-gugŏro 영어로 / 한국어로; **~ a loud voice** k'ŭn mokssoriro 큰 목소리로; **~ yellow** noransaeguro 노란색으로 ◊ (*while*): **~ crossing the road** kirŭl kŏnnŏnŭn tojung-e 길을 건너는 도중에; **~ agreeing to this** (*by virtue of*) igŏse tong-ŭihamŭrossŏ

이것에 동의함으로써 ◊: **three ~ all** t'ongt'ŭrŏ se se 통틀어 세 개; **one ~ ten** yŏl kae chung han kae 열 개 중 한 개 **2** *adv*: **be ~** (*at home, in the building etc*) ane it-tta 안에 있다; (*arrived: of train*) toch'ak'an 도착한; **when the diskette is ~** tisŭk'eshi ane issŭl ttae 디스켓이 안에 있을 때; **~ here** yŏgie 여기에 **3** *adj* (*fashionable, popular*) yuhaenghanŭn 유행하는; **pink is ~** punhongsaegi yuhaeng-iyeyo 분홍색이 유행이예요

inability munŭng 무능

inaccessible chŏpkkŭnhagi ŏryŏun 접근하기 어려운

inaccurate pujŏnghwak'an 부정확한

inactive hwalttonghaji annŭn 활동하지 않는

inadequate pujŏkttanghan 부적당한

inadvisable kwŏnhal su ŏmnŭn 권할 수 없는

inanimate musaengmurŭi 무생물의

inapplicable chŏgyonghal su ŏmnŭn 적용할 수 없는

inappropriate pujŏkttanghan 부적당한

inarticulate marŭl ttokttok'i mot'anŭn 말을 똑똑히 못하는

inattentive pujuŭihan 부주의한

inaudible tŭlliji annŭn 들리지 않는

inaugural *speech* ch'wiimŭi 취임의

inaugurate *new building* kaegwanhada 개관하다; *new era* yŏlda 열다; *president* ...ŭi ch'wiimshigŭl kŏhaenghada ...의 취임식을 거행하다

inborn t'agonan 타고난

inbreeding tongjong pŏnshik 동종 번식

inc. (= *incorporated*) pŏbin hoesa 법인 회사

incalculable *damage* makttaehan 막대한

incapable nŭngnyŏgi ŏmnŭn 능력이 없는; **be ~ of doing sth** muŏsŭl hanŭn kŏse munŭnghada 무엇을 하는 것에 무능하다

incendiary device panghwajangch'i 방화장치

incense¹ *n* hyang 향

incense² v/t maeu hwanage hada 매우 화나게 하다

incentive tonggi 동기

incessant kkŭnimŏmnŭn 끊임없는

incessantly kkŭnimŏpsshi 끊임없이

incest kŭnch'insanggan 근친상간

inch n inch'i 인치

incident sakkŏn 사건

incidental uyŏnhi irŏnanŭn 우연히 일어나는; ~ **remark** uyŏnhi naon mal 우연히 나온 말; ~ **expenses** chap-ppi 잡비

incidentally mari nan-gime 말이 난김에

incinerator sogangno 소각로

incision chŏlgae 절개

incisive mind, analysis nalk'aroun 날카로운

incite kyŏngnyŏhada 격려하다; ~ s.o. to do sth nuguege muŏsŭl hadorok kyŏngnyŏhada 누구에게 무엇을 하도록 격려하다

inclement weather hŏmak'an 험악한

inclination (tendency, liking) sŏnghyang 성향

incline: be ~d to do sth muŏsŭl hanŭn kyŏnghyang-i it-tta 무엇을 하는 경향이 있다

inclose → **enclose**

include p'ohamhada 포함하다

including prep ...ŭl/rŭl p'ohamhayŏ ...을/를 포함하여

inclusive 1 adj price p'ohamhan 포함한 **2** prep p'ohamhayŏ 포함하여; ~ of ...ŭl/rŭl p'ohamhayŏ ...을/를 포함하여 **3** adv ilch'erŭl p'ohamhayŏ 일체를 포함하여; from Monday to Thursday ~ wŏryoilbut'ŏ mogyoilkkaji 월요일부터 목요일까지

incoherent tusŏŏmnŭn 두서없는

income sodŭk 소득

income tax sodŭkkse 소득세

incoming flight toch'ak'anŭn 도착하는; phone call kŏllyŏonŭn 걸려오는; president huimŭi 후임의; ~ tide milmul 밀물

incomparable pihal te ŏmnŭn 비할 데 없는

incompatibility (of personalities) yangnip'al su ŏpssŭm 양립할 수 없음; (of systems) hohwan

incompatible personalities yangnip su ŏmnŭn 양립할 수 없는; formats, systems hohwandoeji annŭn 호환되지 않는

incompetence munŭngnyŏk 무능력

incompetent munŭngnyŏk'an 무능력한

incomplete purwanjŏnhan 불완전한

incomprehensible ihaehal su ŏmn 이해할 수 없는

inconceivable saenggakhal su choch'a ŏmnŭn 생각할 수 조차 없

inconclusive kyŏltchŏngjŏgiji anŭr 결정적이지 않은

incongruous chohwadoeji annŭn 조화되지 않는

inconsiderate saryoŏmnŭn 사려없

inconsistent mosundoenŭn 모순되

inconsolable wirohal kil ŏmnŭn 위로할 길 없는

inconspicuous nune ttŭiji annŭn 눈에 띄지 않는

inconvenience n pulp'yŏn 불편

inconvenient pulp'yŏnhan 불편한

incorporate p'ohamhada 포함하다

incorporated COM pŏbin hoesa 법인 회사

incorrect t'ŭllin 틀린

incorrectly t'ŭllige 틀리게

incorrigible ŏtchŏl su ŏmnŭn 어쩔 없는

increase 1 v/t chŭnggashik'ida 증가시키다 **2** v/i chŭnggahada 증가하다 **3** n chŭngga 증가

increasing chŭnggahanŭn 증가하는

increasingly kalssurok tŏ 갈수록 더

incredible (amazing, very good) midŏjiji annŭn 믿어지지 않는

incriminate choerŭl ssŭiuda 죄를 씌우다; ~ oneself choerŭl chainha 죄를 자인하다

in-crowd naebu haeksshim chipttan 내부 핵심 집단

incubator ink'yubeit'ŏ 인큐베이터

incur ch'oraehada 초래하다

incurable pulch'iŭi 불치의

indebted: be ~ to s.o. nuguege shinserŭl chida 누구에게 신세를 지다

indecent chŏmjanch'i mot'an 점잖지

453

한

ecisive kyŏlttanssŏng-i ŏmnŭn 단성이 없는

ecisiveness uyubudan 우유부단

eed (*in fact*) chinshillo 진실로; *es, agreeing*) kŭraeyo 그래요; *very **uch** ~ chŏngmal kŭraeyo 정말 그래요

efinable magyŏnhan 막연한

efinite muhanjŏnghan 무한정한; *rticle* GRAM pujŏng kwansa 부정 사

efinitely mugihanŭro 무기한으로

elicate mushin-gyŏnghan 무신경한

ent 1 *n* (*in text*) anŭro tŭryŏssŭgi 으로 들여쓰기 **2** *v/t line* anŭro iryŏsŏ ssŭda 안으로 들여서 쓰다

ependence tongnip 독립

ependence Day Tongnip inyŏmil 독립 기념일

ependent tongniptchŏgin 립적인

ependently *deal with* ongniptchŏgŭro 독립적으로; *~ of* yŏlgaero 별개로

escribable hyŏng-ŏnhal su mnŭn 형언할 수 없는

escribably *bad, beautiful* hyŏng-ŏnhal su ŏpttorok 형언할 수 없도록

estructible p'agoehal su ŏmnŭn 파괴할 수 없는

eterminate pujŏnghwak'an 정확한

ex (*for book*) saegin 색인

ex card saegin k'adŭ 색인 카드

ex finger chipkke sonkkarak 집게 손가락

dia Indo 인도

dian 1 *adj* Indoŭi 인도의 **2** *n* Indoin 도인; (*American*) Indian 인디안

dian summer hwach'anghan nalssi 화창한 날씨

dicate 1 *v/t* karik'ida 가리키다 **2** *v/i* (*when driving*) (tonŭn panghyang-ŭl) p'yoshihada (도는 방향을) 표시하다

dication p'yoshi 표시

dicator (*on car*) p'yoshidŭng 표시등

dict kisohada 기소하다

difference mugwanshim 무관심

different mugwanshimhan

무관심한; (*mediocre*) pot'ong-ŭi 보통의

indigestible sohwahagi ŏryŏun 소화하기 어려운

indigestion sohwa pullyang 소화 불량

indignant pun-gaehan 분개한

indignation pun-gae 분개

indirect kanjŏptchŏgin 간접적인

indirectly kanjŏptchŏgŭro 간접적으로

indiscreet mubunbyŏrhan 무분별한

indiscretion (*act*) mubunbyŏl 무분별

indiscriminate much'abyŏrŭi 무차별의

indispensable p'ilssuŭi 필수의

indisposed (*not well*) momi pulp'yŏnhan 몸이 불편한

indisputable nonŭiŭi yŏjiga ŏmnŭn 논의의 여지가 없는

indisputably ŭishimhal yŏji ŏpsshi 의심할 여지 없이

indistinct tturyŏt'aji anŭn 뚜렷하지 않은

indistinguishable pun-gan hal su ŏmnŭn 분간 할 수 없는

individual 1 *n* kaein 개인 **2** *adj* (*separate*) kaegaeŭi 개개의; (*personal*) kaeinŭi 개인의

individualist kaeinjuŭija 개인주의자

individually kaebyŏltchŏgŭro 개별적으로

indivisible pulgabunŭi 불가분의

indoctrinate chuip'ada 주입하다

indolence keŭrŭm 게으름

indolent nat'aehan 나태한

Indochina Indoch'aina 인도차이나

Indochinese *adj* Indoch'ainaŭi 인도차이나의

Indonesia Indoneshia 인도네시아

Indonesian 1 *adj* Indoneshiaŭi 인도네시아의 **2** *n* (*person*) Indoneshiain 인도네시아인

indoor shillaeŭi 실내의

indoors shillae(sŏ) 실내에(서)

induction ceremony orient'eishyŏn 오리엔테이션

indulge 1 *v/t* (*oneself, one's tastes*) t'amnik'ada 탐닉하다 **2** *v/i*: ~ *in sth* muŏse ppajida 무엇에 빠지다

indulgence (*of tastes, appetite etc*) t'amnik 탐닉; (*laxity*) ŭngsŏk padŭm

응석 받음
indulgent (*not strict enough*) kwandaehan 관대한
industrial sanŏbŭi 산업의
industrial action nodong chaeng-ŭi haeng-wi 노동 쟁의 행위
industrial dispute nosaganŭi purhwa 노사간의 불화
industrialist shirŏpkka 실업가
industrialize 1 *v/t* sanŏp'wahada 산업화하다 2 *v/i* sanŏp'wadoeda 산업화되다
industrial park kong-ŏpttanji 공업 단지
industrial waste sanŏpp'yegimul 산업폐기물
industrious kŭnmyŏnhan 근면한
industry sanŏp 산업
ineffective *person* munŭnghan 무능한; *measures, device* hyokkwaga ŏmnŭn 효과가 없는
ineffectual *person* munŭnghan 무능한
inefficient pinŭngnyultchŏgin 비능률적인
ineligible chagyŏgi ŏmnŭn 자격이 없는
inept nŭngnyŏgi ŏmnŭn 능력이 없는
inequality pulp'yŏngdŭng 불평등
inescapable p'ihal su ŏmnŭn 피할 수 없는
inestimable hearil su ŏmnŭn 헤아릴 수 없는
inevitable p'ihal su ŏmnŭn 피할 수 없는
inevitably p'ihal su ŏpsshi 피할 수 없이
inexcusable pyŏnmyŏnghal su ŏmnŭn 변명할 수 없는
inexhaustible *person* chich'il tchul morŭnŭn 지칠 줄 모르는; *supply* mujinjanghan 무진장한
inexpensive kapsshi ssan 값이 싼
inexperienced kyŏnghŏmi ŏmnŭn 경험이 없는
inexplicable sŏlmyŏnghal su ŏmnŭn 설명할 수 없는
inexpressible *joy* hyŏngŏnhal su ŏmnŭn 형언할 수 없는
infallible chŏltttae t'ŭllilli ŏmnŭn 절대 틀릴리 없는

infamous angmyŏng nop'ŭn 악명 높은
infancy yuagi 유아기; *fig* ch'ogi 초기
infant yua 유아
infantile *pej* yuch'ihan 유치한
infantry pobyŏngdae 보병대
infantry soldier pobyŏng 보병
infatuated: be ~ with s.o. nuguege holttak panhada 누구에게 홀딱 반하다
infect kamyŏmshik'ida 감염시키다; (*of person*) muldŭrida 물들이다; *food, water* oyŏmshik'ida 오염시키다; **become ~ed** (*of person*) muri tŭlda 물이 들다; (*of wound*) kamyŏmdoeda 감염되다
infected *wound* kamyŏmdoen 감염
infection kamyŏm 감염
infectious *disease* chŏnyŏmssŏng-ŭ 전염성의; *laughter* omgyŏjigi shwiu 옮겨지기 쉬운
infer: ~ X from Y Yesŏ Xŭl / rŭl ch'uronhada Y에서 X을 / 를 추론하
inferior *quality* iryuŭi 이류의; (*in rank*) hagŭbŭi 하급의; (*in company* hawiŭi 하위의
inferiority (*in quality*) iryu 이류
inferiority complex yŏltttŭng ŭishik 열등 의식
infertile *soil* pulmoŭi 불모의; *woman* purimŭi 불임의
infertility (*of soil*) pulmo 불모; (*of woman*) purim 불임
infidelity pujŏng 부정
infiltrate *v/t* ch'imip'ada 침입하다
infinite muhanhan 무한한
infinitive GRAM pujŏngsa 부정사
infinity muhan 무한
infirm hŏyak'an 허약한
infirmary (*in boarding school*) yanghoshil 양호실; MIL chillyoso 진료소
infirmity hŏyak 허약
inflame pul t'aorŭge hada 불 타오르게 하다
inflammable inhwassŏng-ŭi 인화성으
inflammation MED yŏmtchŭng 염증
inflatable *dinghy* komu pot'ŭ 고무 보트
inflate *v/t tire, dinghy* pup'ullida 부풀리다; *economy* t'onghwa

aengch'angshik'ida 통화
창시키다
ation inp'ŭlle(ishyŏn)
플레(이션)
ationary (of inflation)
p'ŭlleishyŏnŭi 인플레이션의;
ausing inflation) inp'ŭlleishyŏnŭl
barhanŭn 인플레이션을 유발하는
ection (of voice) ŏgyang 억양
exible attitude, person kup'il su
mnŭn 굽힐 수 없는
ict: ~ X on Y Xŭl/rŭl Yege
ahada X을/를 Y에게 가하다
flight paehaeng chung-ŭi 비행 중의;
entertainment kinaeorak
내오락
uence 1 n yŏnghyang 영향;
power to influence) yŏnghyangnyŏk
향력; *be a good/bad ~ on s.o.*
uguege choŭn/nappŭn yŏnghyang
chuda 누구에게 좋은/나쁜 영향을
다 2 v/t s.o.'s thinking yŏnghyang
kich'ida 영향 끼치다; decision
ŏnghyang chuda 영향 주다
uential yŏnghyangnyŏk innŭn
향력 있는
luenza tok-kkam 독감
orm 1 v/t allida 알리다; ~ X of Y
ege Yrŭl allyŏjuda X에게 Y를
려주다; *please keep me ~ed*
yesok'aesŏ allyŏjuseyo 계속해서
려주세요 2 v/i shin-gohada
고하다; ~ on s.o. nugurŭl shin-
ohada 누구를 신고하다
ormal meeting, conversation
igongshigŭi 비공식의; form of
ddress, agreement yaksshigŭi
식의; dress p'yŏngsangbok
h'arimŭi 평상복 차림의
ormality (of meeting, conversation)
igongshik 비공식; (of form of
ddress, agreement) yaksshik 약식
ormant chŏngbo chegongja 정보
공자
ormation chŏngbo 정보
ormation science chŏngbo
wahak 정보 과학; information
cientist chŏngbo kwahaktcha 정보
학자; information technology
hŏngbo kisul 정보 기술
ormative chŏngboga manŭn

정보가 많은
informer milgoja 밀고자
infra-red adj chŏgoesŏnŭi 적외선의
infrastructure (of economy, society)
kigan shisŏl 기간 시설; (of
organization) habu chojik 하부 조직
infrequent tŭmun 드문
infuriate kyŏngno shik'ida 격노
시키다; *be ~ed at* …e
nobaldaebarhada …에 노발대발하다
infuriating kyŏngnok'e hanŭn 격노케
하는
infuse v/i (of tea) urida 우리다
infusion (herb tea) uryŏnaem 우려냄
ingenious tokch'angjŏgin 독창적인
ingenuity tokch'angnyŏk 독창력
ingot (gold) kŭmgoe 금괴; (silver)
ŭn-goe 은괴
ingratiate: *~ oneself with s.o.*
nuguŭi piwirŭl match'uda 누구의
비위를 맞추다
ingratitude paeŭnmangdŏk 배은망덕
ingredient chaeryo 재료; fig yoso 요소
inhabit kŏjuhada 거주하다
inhabitable sal su innŭn 살 수 있는
inhabitant kŏjuja 거주자
inhale 1 v/t pparadŭrida 빨아들이다
2 v/i (when smoking) hŭbip'ada
흡입하다
inhaler hŭbipkki 흡입기
inherit sangsok'ada 상속하다
inheritance sangsok 상속;
(characteristics) yujŏn 유전
inhibit growth, conversation etc
ŏktchehada 억제하다
inhibited ŏktchedoen 억제된
inhibition ŏktche 억제
inhospitable city, people
pulch'injŏrhan 불친절한; climate
hwangp'yehan 황폐한
in-house 1 adj sanaeŭi 사내의 2 adv
work sanaee(sŏ) 사내에(서)
inhuman injŏng ŏmnŭn 인정 없는
initial 1 adj ch'oech'oŭi 최초의 2 n
inishyŏl 이니셜 3 v/t (write initials
on) inishyŏllo ssŭda 이니셜로 쓰다
initially ch'ŏŭmbut'ŏ 처음부터
initiate kaeshihada 개시하다
initiation kaeshi 개시
initiative chudo 주도; *do sth on
one's own ~* muŏsŭl solssŏnhaesŏ

hada 무엇을 솔선해서 하다
inject *medicine, drug* chusahada
주사하다; *fuel* nŏt'a 넣다; *capital*
t'uip'ada 투입하다
injection MED chusa 주사; (*of fuel*)
chuip 주입; (*of capital*) t'uip 도입
injure sangch'ŏ ip'ida 상처 입히다
injured 1 *adj leg, feelings* sangch'ŏ
ibŭn 상처 입은 **2** *n:* **the ~** pusangja
부상자
injury pusang 부상
injustice pujŏng 부정
ink ingk'ŭ 잉크
inkjet (printer) ingk'ŭ chet p'ŭrint'ŏ
잉크 젯 프린터
inland *sea* yuktchi tchogŭi 육지 쪽의;
mail, areas, trade naeryugŭi 내륙의
in-laws inch'ŏk 인척
inlay *n* sanggam 상감
inlet (*of sea*) humi 후미; (*in machine*)
chuipku 주입구
inmate (*of prison*) sugamja 수감자;
(*of mental hospital*) ibwŏn hwanja
입원 환자
inn yŏgwan 여관
innate t'agonan 타고난
inner naebuŭi 내부의; *thoughts*
naetchŏgin 내적인
inner city toshi chungshimŭi 도시 중심의
(pinmin) chiyŏk 도시 중심의 (빈민)
지역
innermost kajang kipssuk'an 가장
깊숙한
inner tube (chajŏn-gŏ) t'yubŭ
(자전거) 튜브
innocence LAW kyŏlbaek 결백; (*of
child*) sunjinham 순진함
innocent LAW kyŏlbaek'an 결백한;
child sunjinhan 순진한
innovation hyŏksshin 혁신
innovative hyŏksshinjŏgin 혁신적인
innovator (*person*) hyŏksshin-ga
혁신가; (*company*) hyŏksshinhanŭn
hoesa 혁신하는 회사
innumerable musuhan 무수한
inoculate yebang chŏptchonghada
예방 접종하다
inoculation yebang chŏptchong 예방
접종
inoffensive *animal* muhaehan 무해한;
person, attitude agŭiga ŏmnŭn

악의가 없는
inorganic mugiŭi 무기의
in-patient ibwŏnhwanja 입원환자
input 1 *n* (*into project etc*) t'uip 투입;
COMPUT imnyŏk 입력 **2** *v/t* (*into
project*) t'uip'ada 투입하다; COMP┃
imnyŏk'ada 입력하다
input port COMPUT imnyŏk tanja 입┃
단자
inquest wŏnin kyumyŏng 원인 규┃
inquire munŭihada 문의하다; *~ int*
sth muŏse taehae chosahada 무엇┃
대해 조사하다
inquiry munŭi 문의
inquisitive t'amgujŏgin 탐구적인
insane mich'in 미친
insanitary piwisaengjŏgin 비위생적┃
insanity chŏngshin isang 정신 이상
insatiable t'amyoksssŭrŏun
탐욕스러운
inscription (*in book*) chemyŏng 제┃
inscrutable pulgasaŭihan 불가사의┃
insect konch'ung 곤충
insecticide salch'ungje 살충제
insect repellent pangch'ungje 방충┃
insecure puranhan 불안한
insecurity puranjŏng 불안정
insensitive mugamgak'an 무감각한
insensitivity mugamgak 무감각
inseparable *two issues* pullihal su
ŏmnŭn 분리할 수 없는; *two peopl*
heŏjil su ŏmnŭn 헤어질 수 없는
insert 1 *n* (*in magazine etc*) sabip
kwanggo 삽입 광고 **2** *v/t* kkiwŏ
nŏt'a 끼워 넣다; *~ X into Y* Xŭl / ┃
Ye kkiwŏ nŏt'a X를 / 를 Y에 끼워
넣다
insertion (*act*) sabip 삽입
inside 1 *n* (*of house, box*) naebu 내┃
(*of road*) antchok 안쪽; *someboc*
on the ~ naebuin 내부인; *~ out*
twijibŏsŏ 뒤집어서; *turn sth ~ ou*
muŏsŭl twijiptta 무엇을 뒤집다;
know sth ~ out muŏsŭl
wanbyŏk'age alda 무엇을 완벽하┃
알다 **2** *prep* ane(sŏ) 안에(서); *~ th*
house chibane(sŏ) 집안에(서); *~ ┃*
2 hours tushigan inae 두시간 이나┃
3 adv stay, remain naebue(sŏ)
내부에(서); *go, carry* anŭro 안으로;
we went ~ urinŭn anŭro tŭrŏgat-

리는 안으로 들어갔다 **4** *adj*
aebue innŭn 내부에 있는; **~ infor-**
nation naebu chŏngbo 내부 정보; (*on*
bad) antchok kil 안쪽 길; **~ pocket**
ntchumŏni 안주머니
ider naebuin 내부인
ider trading FIN insaidŏ kŏrae
사이더 거래
ides wijang 위장
idious *disease* chamhaengssŏng-ŭi
행성의
ight t'ongch'al 통찰
ignificant *amount* chagŭmahan
그마한; *person, problem*
ach'anŭn 하찮은
incere musŏng-ŭihan 무성의한
incerity musŏng-ŭi 무성의
inuate (*imply*) nŏnjishi pich'ida
진시 비치다
ist chujanghada 주장하다; *please*
eep it, I ~ sayangch'i mashigo
ajiseyo 사양치 마시고 가지세요
nsist on kangyohada 강요하다
istent chibyohan 집요한
istent chibyohan 집요한
olent kŏnbangjin 건방진
oluble *problem* haegyŏrhal su
mnŭn 해결할 수 없는; *substance*
onghaedoeji annŭn 용해되지 않는
olvent chibul pullŭng-ŭi 지불
능의
omnia pulmyŏntchŭng 불면증
pect *work, tickets, baggage*
hŏmgŏmhada 점검하다; *building,*
actory, school shich'arhada
찰하다
pection (*of work, tickets, baggage*)
hŏmgŏm 점검; (*of building, factory,*
chool) shich'al 시찰
pector (*in factory etc*)
amch'altcha 감찰자
piration (*business etc*) yŏngam 영감; (*very good*
dea) kibarhan saenggak 기발한 생각
pire *respect etc* pullŏ irŭk'ida 불러
을으키다; *be ~d by s.o. / sth*
uguege / muŏse yŏnggamŭl pat-tta
구에게 / 무엇에 영감을 받다
tability puranjŏng 불안정
tal(l) *equipment, software*
ŏlch'ihada 설치하다
tallation (*of equipment, software*)

installment (*of story, TV drama etc*)
(yŏnjaeŭi) il hoebun (연재의) 일
회분; (*payment*) punhal purip 분할
불입; **monthly ~s** wŏlbu 월부
installment plan punhal purip
pangshik 분할 불입 방식
instance (*example*) ye 예; **for ~** yerŭl
tŭrŏ 예를 들어
instant **1** *adj* chŭk-kkaktchŏgin
즉각적인 **2** *n* sun-gan 순간; *in an ~*
sunshik-kkane 순식간에
instantaneous sunshik-kkanŭi
순식간의
instant coffee insŭt'ŏnt'ŭ k'ŏp'i
인스턴트 커피
instantly chŭksshi 즉시
instead taeshine 대신에; **~ of** ...
taeshine ... 대신에
instep palttŭng 발등
instinct ponnŭng 본능
instinctive ponnŭngjŏgin 본능적인
institute **1** *n* yŏn-guso 연구소;
(*academic*) hak'oe 학회; (*special*
home) konggong kigwan 공공 기관
2 *v/t inquiry* shijak'ada 시작하다
institution (*governmental*) kigwan
기관; (*something traditional*)
kwansŭp 관습; (*setting up*) sŏltchŏng
설정
instruct (*order*) chishihada 지시하다;
(*teach*) karŭch'ida 가르치다; **~ X to**
do Y (*order*) Xege Y hal kŏsŭl
chishihada X에게 Y할 것을 지시하다
instruction chishi sahang 지시 사항;
~s for use sayongppŏp 사용법
instruction manual sayong
sŏlmyŏngsŏ 사용 설명서
instructive kyoyuktchŏgin 교육적인
instructor kangsa 강사; (*in martial*
arts) sabŏm 사범
instrument MUS ak-kki 악기; (*gadget,*
tool) togu 도구
insubordinate pulboktchonghanŭn
불복종하는
insufficient pulch'ungbunhan
불충분한
insulate ELEC chŏryŏnhada 절연하다;
(*against cold*) panghanhada 방한하다
insulation ELEC chŏryŏn 절연;

(*against cold*) panghan 방한

insulin inshyullin 인슐린

insult 1 *n* moyok 모욕 **2** *v/t* moyok'ada 모욕하다

insurance pohŏm 보험

insurance company pohŏm hoesa 보험 회사

insurance policy pohŏm chŭngsŏ 보험 증서

insure pohŏme tŭlda 보험에 들다; *be ~ed* pohŏme tŭrŏit-tta 보험에 들어있다

insurmountable kŭkppok'al su ŏmnŭn 극복할 수 없는

intact (*not damaged*) sonsangdoeji anŭn 손상되지 않은

intake (*of college etc*) suyong inwŏn 수용 인원

integrate *v/t* t'onghap'ada 통합하다

integrated circuit chiptchŏk hoero 집적 회로

integrity (*honesty*) chŏngjik 정직

intellect chisŏng 지성

intellectual 1 *adj* chitchŏgin 지적인 **2** *n* chisŏng-in 지성인

intelligence chinŭng 지능; (*news*) chŏngbo 정보

intelligence service chŏngbo kigwan 정보 기관

intelligent ttokttok'an 똑똑한

intelligible chal ihaehal su innŭn 잘 이해할 수 있는

intend ... hal chaktchŏng-ida ... 할 작정이다; *~ to do sth* (*do on purpose*) muŏsŭl ŭidohada 무엇을 의도하다; (*plan to do*) muŏsŭl hal chaktchŏng-ida 무엇을 할 작정이다; *that's not what I ~ed* kŭgŏn naega ŭidohan ke animnida 그건 내가 의도한 게 아닙니다

intense *sensation, pleasure* kangnyŏrhan 강렬한; *heat, pressure* kangnyŏk'an 강력한; *personality, concentration* kanghan 강한

intensify 1 *v/t effect, pressure* sege hada 세게 하다 **2** *v/i* (*of pain*) kanghaejida 강해지다; (*of fighting*) kyŏngnyŏrhaejida 격렬해지다

intensive *study, training, treatment* chiptchungjŏgin 집중적인

intensity (*of sensation, heat, pain*) kangdo 강도; (*of fighting*) kyŏngnyŏl 격렬

intensive care (**unit**) chunghwanjashil 중환자실

intensive course (*of language stud*) chiptchung k'osŭ 집중 코스

intent: *be ~ on doing sth* (*determined to do*) muŏsŭl haryŏgo chaktchŏnghada 무엇을 하려고 작정하다; (*concentrating on*) muŏs hanŭnde yŏltchunghada 무엇을 하는데 열중하다

intention ŭido 의도; *I have no ~ o* (*refuse to*) nanŭn ... hal ŭidoga ŏpssŏyo 나는 ... 할 의도가 없어요

intentional ŭidojŏgin 의도적인

intentionally koŭijŏgŭro 고의적으로

interaction sangho chagyong 상호 작용

interactive sangho chagyonghanŭn 상호 작용하는

intercede chungjaehada 중재하다

intercept *ball* karoch'aeda 가로채다 *message* yŏt-tŭt-tta 엿듣다; *missile* yogyŏk'ada 요격하다

interchange *n* (*of highways*) int'ŏch'einji 인터체인지

interchangeable pakku kul su innŭn 바꿀 수 있는

intercom int'ŏk'ŏm 인터컴

intercourse (*sexual*) sŏnggyo 성교

interdependent sangho ŭijonhanŭn 상호 의존하는

interest 1 *n* kwanshim 관심; (*financial*) ija 이자; *take an ~ in s* muŏse hŭngmirŭl kajida 무엇에 흥미를 가지다 **2** *v/t* hŭngmirŭl irŭk'ige hada 흥미를 일으키게 하다; *does that offer ~ you?* kŭ chewŏ maŭme tŭmnikka? 그 제의가 마음 드니까

interested kwanshimi innŭn 관심이 있는; *be ~ in sth* muŏse kwanshir kajida 무엇에 관심을 가지다; *thanks, but I'm not ~* komaptchiman, chŏn kwanshimi ŏmnŭndeyo 고맙지만, 전 관심이 없는데요

interesting chaemiinnŭn 재미있는

interest rate ijayul 이자율

interface 1 *n* chŏpch'ok yŏng-yŏk

촉 영역, int'ŏpeisŭ 인터페이스 **2** *v/i* ...ŏpssok'ada 접속하다

...erfere kansŏp'ada 간섭하다
...terfere with *controls, plans* anghaehada 방해하다

...erference kansŏp 간섭; RAD ...nsŏn 혼선

...erior 1 *adj* shillaeŭi 실내의 **2** *n* (*of ...ouse*) shillae 실내; (*of country*) ...aeryuk 내륙; **Department of the ...iterior** Naemubu 내무부

...erior decorator shillae changshik-ka 실내 장식가; **interior design** ...-t'eriŏ tijain 인테리어 디자인; **inte-...or designer** int'eriŏ tijainŏ ...테리어 디자이너

...erlude (*at theater, concert*) mak-...kan 막간; (*period*) kigan 기간

...ermediary *n* chungjaeja 중재자
...ermediate *adj* chungganŭi 중간의
...ermission (*in theater, movie ...eater*) hyuge shigan 휴게 시간
...ern *v/t* kusok'ada 구속하다

...ernal *measurements* anŭi 안의; ...ade kung-naeŭi 국내의; (*within ...rganization*) naebuŭi 내부의

...ernal combustion engine naeyŏn ...gwan 내연 기관

...ernally (*in body*) ch'enaee(sŏ) ...내에(서); (*within organization*) ...aebujŏgŭro 내부적으로

...ernal Revenue (Service) ...ŭksssech'ŏng 국세청

...ernational *adj* kuktchejŏgin ...제적인

...ernational Court of Justice ...uktche Sabŏp Chaep'anso 국제 ...법 재판소

...ernationally kuktchejŏgŭro ...제적으로

...ernational Monetary Fund ...uktche T'onghwa Kigŭm 국제 통화 ...금

...ernet Int'ŏnet 인터넷; **on the ~** ...nt'ŏnet sangesŏ 인터넷 상에서
...ernist naekkwa chŏnmun ŭisa 내과 ...문 의사

...erpret 1 *v/t* (*linguistically*) ...ongyŏk'ada 통역하다; *music,* ...omment etc* haesŏk'ada 해석하다 ...*v/i* t'ongyŏk'ada 통역하다

interpretation (*linguistic*) t'ongyŏk 통역; (*of music, of meaning*) haesŏk 해석

interpreter t'ongyŏk-kka 통역가
interrelated *facts* sŏro kwan-gyega innŭn 서로 관계가 있는
interrogate shimmunhada 심문하다
interrogation shimmun 심문
interrogative *n* GRAM ŭimunsa 의문사
interrogator shimmunja 심문자
interrupt 1 *v/t speaker* chungdanshik'ida 중단시키다 **2** *v/i* chungdanhada 중단하다
interruption chungdan 중단
intersect kyoch'ahada 교차하다
intersection (*crossroads*) kyoch'a 교차
interstate *n* chugan kosok toro 주간 고속 도로
interval shigan kan-gyŏk 시간 간격; (*in theater, at concert*) hyuge shigan 휴게 시간
intervene (*of person, police etc*) chungjaehada 중재하다
intervention chungjae 중재
interview 1 *n* (*on TV, in paper*) int'ŏbyu 인터뷰; (*for job*) myŏnjŏp 면접 **2** *v/t* (*on TV, for paper*) int'ŏbyuhada 인터뷰하다; (*for job*) myŏnjŏp'ada 면접하다
interviewee (*on TV*) int'ŏbyu pannŭn saram 인터뷰 받는 사람; (*for job*) myŏnjŏp pannŭn saram 면접 받는 사람
interviewer (*on TV, for paper*) int'ŏbyuhanŭn saram 인터뷰하는 사람; (*for job*) myŏnjŏpkkwan 면접관
intestine ch'angja 창자
intimacy (*of friendship*) ch'insuk'am 친숙함; (*sexual*) kip'ŭn sai 깊은 사이
intimate *friend* ch'insuk'an 친숙한; (*sexually*) kip'ŭn saiin 깊은 사이인; *thoughts* kaeintchŏgin 개인적인
intimidate hyŏp-ppak'ada 협박하다
intimidation hyŏp-ppak 협박
into anŭro 안으로; (*change, transition*) ...(ŭ)ro ...(으)로; **he put it ~ his suitcase** kŭnŭn kŭgŏsŭl otkkabang anŭro nŏŏt-tta 그는 그것을 옷가방

안으로 넣었다; *translate ~ English* Yŏng-ŏro pŏnyŏk'ada 영어로 번역하다; *be ~ sth* F (*like*) muŏsŭl choahada 무엇을 좋아하다; (*be interested in*) muŏse kwanshimi it-tta 무엇에 관심이 있다; *when you're ~ the job* nega chomdŏ kŭ ire iksuk'aejil ttae 네가 좀더 그 일에 익숙해질 때

intolerable ch'amŭl su ŏmnŭn 참을 수 없는

intolerant ch'amŭlssŏng ŏmnŭn 참을성 없는

intoxicated sul ch'wihan 술 취한

intransitive chadongsaŭi 자동사의

intravenous chŏngmaeng-naeŭi 정맥내의

intrepid taedamhan 대담한

intricate twiŏlk'in 뒤얽힌

intrigue 1 n ŭmmo 음모 **2** v/t hŭngmi kkŭlda 흥미 끌다; *I would be ~d to know ...* chŏnŭn ...ŭl/rŭl algo shipssŭmnida 저는 ...을/를 알고 싶습니다

intriguing hogishimŭl chaguk'anŭn 호기심을 자극하는

introduce sogaehada 소개하다; *new technique etc* toip'ada 도입하다; *may I ~ ...?* ...ŭl/rŭl sogaehaedo toelkkayo? ...을/를 소개해도 될까요?

introduction (*to person, new food, sport etc*) sogae 소개; (*in book*) sŏron 서론; (*of new techniques etc*) toip 도입

introvert n naehyangjŏgin saram 내향적인 사람

intrude ch'imbŏmhada 침범하다

intruder ch'imiptcha 침입자

intrusion ch'imbŏm 침범

intuition chik-kkwan 직관

invade ch'imnyak'ada 침략하다

invalid¹ *adj* muhyoŭi 무효의

invalid² n MED pyŏngja 병자

invalidate *claim, theory* muhyohwahada 무효화하다

invaluable *help* kapssŭl hearil su ŏmnŭn 값을 헤아릴 수 없는

invariably (*always*) hangsang 항상

invasion ch'imnyak 침략

invent palmyŏnghada 발명하다

invention palmyŏng 발명

inventive ch'ang-ŭijŏgin 창의적인

inventor palmyŏngga 발명가

inventory mongnok 목록

inverse *adj order* kŏkkuro toen 거꾸로 된

invert kŏkkuro hada 거꾸로 하다

invertebrate n much'ŏkch'u tongmul 무척추 동물

inverted commas inyong puho 인용 부호

invest 1 v/t t'ujadoeda 투자되다 **2** v/i t'ujahada 투자하다

investigate chosahada 조사하다

investigation chosa 조사

investigative journalism toktchajŏgin chosa podo 독자적인 조사 보도

investment t'uja 투자

investor t'ujaja 투자자

invigorating *climate* kiuni nage hanŭn 기운이 나게 하는

invincible mujŏgŭi 무적의

invisible nune poiji annŭn 눈에 보이지 않는

invitation ch'odae 초대

invite ch'odaehada 초대하다

invoice 1 n inboisŭ 인보이스 **2** v/t *customer* kumaesŏrŭl ponaeda 구매서를 보내다

involuntary muŭishiktchŏgin 무의식적인; (*forced*) kangjejŏgin 강제적인

involve *hard work, expense* subanhada 수반하다; (*concern*) kwan-gyehada 관계하다; *what does it ~?* kŭgŏsŭn muŏsŭl subanhamnikka? 그것은 무엇을 수반합니까?; *get ~d with sth* muŏe kwan-gyedoeda 무엇에 관계되다; (*negative*) muŏse yŏlludoeda 무엇에 연루되다; *get ~d with s.o.* nuguwa kwan-gyedoeda 누구와 관계되다

involved (*complex*) poktchap'an 복잡한

involvement (*in a project etc*) kwallyŏn 관련; (*in a crime, accident*) yŏllu 연루

invulnerable haech'il su ŏmnŭn 해칠 수 없는

inward 1 *adj* antchoguŭi 안쪽의 **2** *adv*

ntchŏgŭro 안쪽으로
...vardly maŭmsogŭro 마음속으로
...ine yoodŭ 요오드
...U (= *I owe you*) yaksshik ch'ayong
chŭngsŏ 약식 차용 증서
... (= *intelligence quotient*) aik'yu
아이큐
...n Iran 이란
...nian 1 *adj* Iranŭi 이란의 **2** *n*
(*person*) Iranin이란인; (*language*)
Iranŏ 이란어
...q Irak'ŭ 이라크
...qi 1 *adj* Irak'ŭŭi 이라크의 **2** *n*
(*person*) Irak'ŭin 이라크인
...land Aillaendŭ 아일랜드
...s (*of eye*) hongch'ae 홍채; (*flower*)
airisŭ 아이리스
...ish *adj* Aillaendŭŭi 아일랜드의
...shman Aillaendŭ namja 아일랜드
남자
...shwoman Aillaendŭ yŏja 아일랜드
여자
...n 1 *n* (*substance*) soe 쇠; (*for
clothes*) tarimi 다리미 **2** *v/t shirts etc*
tarimjirhada 다림질하다
...nic(al) panŏjŏgin 반어적인
...ning tarimjil 다림질; **do the ~**
tarimjirhada 다림질하다
...ning board tarimjilttae 다림질대
...nworks ch'ŏlgongso 철공소
...ny airŏni 아이러니; (*in prose style*)
p'ungja 풍자
...ational purhamnihan 불합리한
...econcilable hwahaehal su ŏmnŭn
화해할 수 없는
...ecoverable hoebok'al su ŏmnŭn
회복할 수 없는
...egular *intervals, sizes*
pulgyuch'iktchŏgin 불규칙적인;
behavior panch'igŭi 반칙의
...elevant kwallyŏni ŏmnŭn 관련이
없는
...eparable koch'il su ŏmnŭn 고칠 수
없는
...eplaceable *object, person*
taech'ehal su ŏmnŭn 대체할 수 없는
...epressible *sense of humor*
ŏngnurŭl su ŏmnŭn 억누를 수 없는;
person mallil su ŏmnŭn 말릴 수 없는
...eproachable namural te ŏmnŭn
나무랄 데 없는

irresistible *offer* sayanghal su ŏmnŭn
사양할 수 없는; *pleasure* ŏktchehal
su ŏmnŭn 억제할 수 없는
irrespective: **~ of** ...e kwan-
gyeŏpsshi ...에 관계없이
irresponsible much'aegimhan
무책임한
irretrievable torik'il su ŏmnŭn 돌이킬
수 없는
irreverent pulssonhan 불손한
irrevocable ch'wisohal su ŏmnŭn
취소할 수 없는
irrigate kwan-gaehada 관개하다
irrigation kwan-gae 관개
irrigation canal kwan-gaeyong suro
관개용 수로
irritable tchajŭng-ŭl chal naenŭn
짜증을 잘 내는
irritate tchajŭngnage hada 짜증나게
하다
irritating tchajŭngnage hanŭn
짜증나게 하는
irritation ch'ajŭngnanŭn kŏt 짜증나는
것
Islam (*religion*) Isŭllamgyo 이슬람교;
(*race*) Isŭllam minjok 이슬람 민족;
(*Islamic state*) Isŭllam kuk-kka
이슬람 국가
Islamic Isŭllamŭi 이슬람의
island sŏm 섬
islander sŏmssaram 섬사람
isolate (*from society*) koripshik'ida
고립시키다; (*separate*) pullihada
분리시키다; (*in prison, hospital*)
kyŏngnishik'ida 격리시키다;
(*identify*) ppobanaeda 뽑아내다
isolated *house* oettan 외딴;
occurrence ttaro 따로
isolation (*of a region*) korip 고립; **in
~** kyŏngnihayŏ 따로 분리해서
isolation ward kyŏngni pyŏngdong
격리 병동
Israel Isŭrael 이스라엘
Israeli 1 *adj* Isŭraerŭi 이스라엘의 **2** *n*
Isŭraerin 이스라엘인
issue 1 *n* (*matter*) chaengtchŏm 쟁점;
(*topic*) nontchŏm 논점; (*of
magazine*) ho 호 **2** *v/t passport, visa*
palgŭp'ada 발급하다; *coins*
parhaenghada 발행하다; *supplies*
chigŭp'ada 지급하다; *warning*

kongp'yohada 공표하다; **the point at ~** nonŭi sahang 논의 사항; **take ~ with s.o. / sth** nugue / muŏse iŭirŭl chegihada 누구에 / 무엇에 이의를 제기하다

IT (= *information technology*) chŏngbo kisul 정보 기술

it ◊ (*as subject*) kŭgŏsun 그것은; (*as object*) kŭgŏsŭl 그것을 ◊ (*not translated*): **what is ~?** - **~'s a novel** muŏshiyeyo? - sosŏriyeyo 무엇이에요? – 소설이에요; **~'s on the table** ch'aekssang-wie issŏyo 책상위에 있어요; **~'s me / him** chŏyeyo / kŭyeyo 저예요 / 그예요; **~'s Charlie here** TELEC chŏ, Ch'alliyeyo 저, 찰리예요; **~'s your turn** tangshin ch'aryeyeyo 당신 차례예요; **that's ~!** (*that's right*) majayo! 맞아요!; (*I've finished*) twaessŏyo! 됐어요!

Italian 1 *adj* It'alliaŭi 이탈리아의 **2** (*person*) It'alliain 이탈리아인; (*language*) It'alliaŏ 이탈리아어

italic it'aellikch'eŭi 이탈릭체의

italics: in ~ it'aellikch'aero 이탈릭체로

Italy It'allia 이탈리아

itch 1 *n* karyŏum 가려움 **2** *v/i* karyŏptta 가렵다

item hangmok 항목

itemize *invoice* myŏngserŭl palk'ida 명세를 밝히다

its kŭgŏsŭi 그것의

itself kŭgŏt chach'e 그것 자체; **by ~** (*alone*) hollo 홀로; (*automatically*) chŏjŏllo 저절로

ivory (*substance*) sang-a 상아

ivy tamjaeng-i 담쟁이

v/t k'uk tchirŭda 쿡 찌르다
k MOT chaek 책; (in cards) chaek

ck up MOT chaegŭro mirŏ ollida
으로 밀어 올리다
ket chaek'it 재킷; (of book) k'ŏbŏ
버
ket potato kuun kamja yori 구운
자 요리
k-knife v/i chaengnaip'ŭch'ŏrŏm
aburŏjida 잭나이프처럼 구부러지다
kpot kŏaegŭi sanggŭm 거액의
금; **hit the** ~ kŏaegŭi sanggŭmŭl
ada 거액의 상금을 타다
e n pich'wi 비취
ged t'omni moyang-ŭi 톱니 모양의
kyodoso 교도소
¹ chaem 잼
² 1 n MOT kyot'ong honjap 교통
잡; F (difficulty) kon-gyŏng 곤경;
e in a ~ kon-gyŏng-e ch'ohada
경에 처하다 2 v/t (ram) ssushyŏ
t'a 쑤셔 넣다; broadcast
anghaehada 방해하다; **be ~med** (of
ads) kkwak ch'ait-tta 꽉 차있다; (
f door, window) umjigiji ank'e
eda 움직이지 않게 되다 3 v/i (
tick) umjigiji ant'a 움직이지 않다; (
queeze) ttemilgo tŭrŏgada 떼밀고
어가다
a-packed ppaekppaek'age kkwak
'an 빽빽하게 꽉 찬
tor suwi 수위
uary irwŏl 일월
an Ilbon 일본
anese 1 adj Ilbonŭi 일본의 2 n (
erson) Ilbon saram 일본 사람; (
language) Ilbonŏ 일본어
n (container) tanji 단지
v/i (of noise) ppigŏk-kkŏrida
격거리다; ~ **on** ...e kŏsŭllida ...에
슬리다
jon chŏnmun yong-ŏ 전문 용어
ndice hwangdal 황달

jaw n t'ŏk 턱
jaywalker mudan hwoengdanhanŭn
saram 무단 횡단하는 사람
jazz chaejŭ 재즈
♦jazz up F tach'aeropkke hada
다채롭게 하다
jealous chilt'uhanŭn 질투하는; **be ~
of** ...ŭl/rŭl chilt'uhada ...을/를
질투하다
jealousy chilt'u 질투
jeans ch'ŏngbaji 청바지
jeep chip'ŭch'a 지프차
jeer 1 n yayu 야유 2 v/i yayuhada
야유하다; ~ **at** ...ŭl/rŭl usŭpkke
yŏgida ...을/를 우습게 여기다
Jehovah's Witness Yŏhowaŭi
Chŭng-in 여호와의 증인
jelly chaem 잼
jelly bean chelli kwaja 젤리 과자
jellyfish haep'ari 해파리
jeopardize wit'aeropkke hada
위태롭게 하다
jeopardy: **be in** ~ wit'aeroptta
위태롭다
jerk¹ 1 n kaptchagi umjigim 갑자기
움직임 2 v/t kaptchagi umjigida
갑자기 움직이다
jerk² n F (fool) mŏngch'ŏng-i 멍청이
jerky movement kaptchagi umjiginŭn
갑자기 움직이는
jest 1 n nongdam 농담; **in** ~
nongdamŭro 농담으로 2 v/i
nongdamhada 농담하다
Jesus Yesu(nim) 예수(님)
jet 1 n (of water) punch'ul 분출;
(nozzle) punch'ulgu 분출구;
(airplane) chet'ŭgi 제트기 2 v/i
(travel) chet'ŭgiro yŏhaenghada
제트기로 여행하다
jet-black saekkaman 새까만; jet
engine chet'ŭ enjin 제트 엔진; jet-
lag shich'aro inhan p'iro 시차로
인한 피로
jettison t'uhahada 투하하다; fig

pŏrida 버리다
jetty pudu 부두
Jew Yut'aein 유태인
jewel posŏk 보석; *fig (person)* pobae 보배
jeweler posŏkssang 보석상
jewelry posŏngnyu 보석류
Jewish *religion* Yut'aegyoŭi 유태교의; *people* Yut'aeinŭi 유태인의
jiffy: *in a ~* F kot 곧
jigsaw (puzzle) chogak kŭrim match'ugi 조각 그림 맞추기
jilt ch'abŏrida 차버리다
jingle 1 *n (song)* kwanggoyong ŭmak 광고용 음악 **2** *v/i (of keys, coins)* ttallanggŏrida 딸랑거리다
jinx *(person)* chaesuŏmnŭn saram 재수없는 사람; *(bad luck)* ma 마; *there's a ~ on this project* i kihoegenŭn maga kkiŏt-tta 이 기획에는 마가 끼었다
jitters: *get the ~* F anjŏlbujŏl mot'ada 안절부절 못하다
jittery F anjŏlbujŏl mot'anŭn 안절부절 못하는
job *(employment)* chigŏp 직업; *(task)* il 일; *out of a ~* shiltchik'ayŏ 실직하여; *it's a good ~ you ...* nega ... hagil charhaet-tta 네가 ... 하길 잘됐다; *you'll have a ~ (it'll be difficult)* himdŭl kŏyeyo 힘들 거예요
job description chingmu naeyong sŏlmyŏngsŏ 직무 내용 설명서
job hunt: *be job hunting* chigŏbŭl kuhago it-tta 직업을 구하고 있다
jobless shiltchik'an 실직한
job satisfaction chigŏp manjoktto 직업 만족도
Job's tears tea yulmuch'a 율무차
jockey *n* kisu 기수
jog 1 *n* choging 조깅; *go for a ~* chogingharŏ kada 조깅하러 가다 **2** *v/i (as exercise)* choginghada 조깅하다 **3** *v/t elbow etc* saltchak milch'ida 살짝 밀치다; *~ one's memory* kiŏgŭl toesallida 기억을 되살리다
jogger *(person)* choginghanŭn saram 조깅하는 사람; *(shoe)* choging shyujŭ 조깅 슈즈
jogging choging 조깅; *go ~*

chogingharŏ kada 조깅하러 가다
jogging suit chogingbok 조깅복
john F *(toilet)* hwajangshil 화장실
join 1 *n* iŭn chari 이은 자리 **2** *v/i (of roads, rivers)* hapch'yŏjida 합쳐지다; *(become a member)* kaip'ada 가입하다 **3** *v/t (connect)* yŏn-gyŏrhada 연결하다; *person* hamnyuhada 합류하다; *club* ip'oehada 입회하다; *(go to work for)* ipssahada 입사하다; *(of road)* mannada 만나다
♦ **join in** kach'i hada 같이 하다
joiner mokssu 목수
joint 1 *n* ANAT kwanjŏl 관절; *(in woodwork)* chŏp'ap pubun 접합 부분; *(of meat)* k'ŭn kogit-ttŏng-ŏri 큰 고깃덩어리; F *(place)* kot 곳; *(of cannabis)* marihwana 마리화나 **2** *adj (shared)* kongdong-ŭi 공동의
joint account kongdong kujwa 공동 구좌; **joint-stock company** hapthoesa 합자 회사; **joint venture** haptchak t'uja 합작 투자
joke 1 *n (story)* nongdam 농담; *(practical ~)* chittkkujŭn changnan 짓궂은 장난; *play a ~ on* ...ŭl / rŭl nollida ...을 / 를 놀리다; *it's no ~* usŭl iri anida 웃을 일이 아니다 **2** *v/i (pretend)* ikssalburida 익살부리다; *(have a ~)* nongdamhada 농담하다
joker *pej* utkkinŭn nom 웃기는 놈; *(cards)* chok'ŏ 조커
joking: *~ apart* nongdam kŭmanhago 농담 그만하고
jokingly nongdamŭro 농담으로
jolly *adj* yuk'waehan 유쾌한
jolt 1 *n (jerk)* tŏlk'ŏk-kkŏrim 덜커덕거림 **2** *v/t (push)* sege ch'ida 세게 치다
jostle *v/t* nanp'ok'age milda 난폭하게 밀다
♦ **jot down** chŏgŏduda 적어두다
journal *(magazine)* chaptchi 잡지; *(diary)* ilgi 일기
journalism *(writing)* ŏllon 언론; *(profession)* ŏllon-gye 언론계
journalist kija 기자
journey *n* yŏhaeng 여행
joy kippŭm 기쁨
jubilant hwanhohanŭn 환호하는

ilation hwanho 환호
ige 1 n LAW p'ansa 판사; (in
ompetition) shimsa wiwŏn 심사
위원 **2** v/t p'andanhada 판단하다;
ompetition) shimsahada 심사하다;
estimate) taegang miruŏ poda 대강
미루어 보다
gment LAW chaep'an 재판;
opinion) p'andan 판단; (good sense)
'andannyŏk 판단력
icial sabŏbŭi 사법의
icious punbyŏl innŭn 분별 있는
lo yudo 유도
igle yosurŭl purida 요술을 부리다;
g chaejurŭl purida 재주를 부리다
ce chusŭ 쥬스
cy chŭbi manŭn 즙이 많은; news,
ossip hŭngmijinjinhan 흥미진진한
ly ch'irwŏl 칠월
nble n twibŏmbŏk 뒤범벅
umble up twibŏmbŏgŭl mandŭlda
뒤범벅을 만들다
np 1 n twiŏ orŭm 뛰어 오름;
increase) kŭpsangsŭng 급상승;
ive a ~ (of surprise) (nollasŏ)
'ŏltchŏk ttwida (놀라서) 펄쩍 뛰다
v/i ttwiŏ orŭda 뛰어 오르다; (in
urprise) p'ŏltchŏk ttwida 펄쩍 뛰다;
increase) kŭpsangsŭnghada
상승하다; **~ to one's feet** pŏlttŏk
ŏnada 벌떡 일어나다; **~ to conclu-**
ions kŭp'age kyŏllon chit-tta
하게 결론 짓다 **3** v/t fence etc ttwiŏ
ŏmtta 뛰어 넘다; F (attack)
ombyŏdŭlda 덤벼들다
ump at opportunity k'waehi
nghada 쾌히 응하다
mper sp toyak sŏnsu 도약 선수;
horse) chang-aemul kyŏngjuma
애물 경주마; COMPUT chŏmp'ŏ
퍼
mpy shin-gyŏng kwaminŭn 신경
민의
nction (of roads) kyoch'ajŏm 교차점
ne yuwŏl 유월
igle millim 밀림
ior 1 adj (subordinate) sonaraeŭi
오래의; (younger) ŏrin 어린 **2** n
subordinate) sonaraet saram 손아랫

사람; **she is ten years my ~**
kŭnyŏnŭn naboda yŏl sal ŏrida
그녀는 나보다 열 살 어리다
junk (garbage) komul 고물
junk food chŏngk'ŭ p'udŭ 정크 푸드
junkie chungdoktcha 중독자
junk mail ssŭregi up'yŏnmul 쓰레기
우편물
junkyard komul sujipsso 고물 수집소
jurisdiction LAW sabŏpkkwŏn 사법권
juror paeshimwŏn 배심원
jury paeshimwŏndan 배심원단;
(panel) shimsawiwŏndan
심사위원단
just 1 adj law kongjŏnghan 공정한;
war, cause t'adanghan 타당한 **2** adv
(barely) kyŏu 겨우; (exactly)
mach'im 마침; (only) tanji 단지; **I've**
~ seen her mak kŭnyŏrŭl poassŏyo
막 그녀를 보았어요; **~ about**
(almost) kŏŭi 거의; **I was ~ about**
to leave nanŭn mak ttŏnaryŏdŏn
ch'amiŏssŏyo 나는 막 떠나려던
참이었어요; **~ like that** (abruptly)
kŭnyang kŭrŏk'e 그냥 그렇게;
(exactly like that) paro kŭrŏk'e 바로
그렇게; **~ now** (a few moments ago)
panggŭm pang-gŭm 방금; (at the moment)
chigŭm paro chigŭm 바로 지금; **~ you wait!** nŏ
tugo poja! 너 두고 보자!; **~ be**
quiet! chom choyonghi hae! 좀
조용히 해!
justice chŏng-ŭi 정의; (of cause)
t'adang 타당
justifiable chŏngdanghwa hal su
innŭn 정당화할 수 있는
justifiably chŏngdanghage 정당하게
justification chŏngdanghwa 정당화
justify chŏngdanghwahada
정당화하다; text match'uda 맞추다
justly (fairly) chŏngdanghage
정당하게; (deservedly) mattanghage
마땅하게
♦ **jut out** v/i tolch'urhada 돌출하다
juvenile 1 adj sonyŏnŭi 소년의; pej
misuk'an 미숙한 **2** n fml sonyŏn 소년
juvenile delinquency sonyŏn pŏmjoe
소년 범죄
juvenile delinquent sonyŏn
pŏmjoeja 소년 범죄자

K

k (= **kilobyte**) k'ilobait'ǔ 킬로바이트;
(= **thousand**) ch'ǒn 천
Kanghwa Island Kanghwado 강화도
karaoke karaok'e 가라오케
karaoke room noraebang 노래방
karate k'arat'e 카라테
karate chop k'arat'e ilgyǒk 카라테
일격
KBS (= **Korean Broadcasting
System**) Han-guk Pangsong
Kongsa 한국 방송 공사
keel n NAUT yonggol 용골
keen (*intense*) kanghan 강한
keep 1 n: for ~s F ǒnjekkajina
언제까지나 2 v/t pogwanhada
보관하다; (*not give back*) chagi
kǒsǔro hada 자기 것으로 하다; (*not
lose*) yujihada 유지하다; (*detain*) put-
ttǔrǒ tuda 붙들어 두다; (*store*)
kansuhada 간수하다; *family*
puyanghada 부양하다; *animals*
kirǔda 기르다; ~ **a promise**
yakssogǔl chik'ida 약속을 지키다; ~
... *waiting* ...ǔl/rǔl kyesok kidarige
hada ...을/를 계속 기다리게 하다; ~
... *to oneself* (*not tell*) ...ǔl/rǔl
alliji ant'a ...을/를 알리지 않다; ~ **X
from Y** Xǔl/rǔl Yege alliji ant'a
X을/를 Y에게 알리지 않다; ~ (**on**)
trying kyesok noryŏk'ada 계속
노력하다; ~ (**on**) *interrupting*
kyesok panghaehada 계속 방해하다
3 v/i (*remain*) ... it-tta ... 있다; (*of
food, milk*) ssŏktchi ank'o kyŏndida
썩지 않고 견디다; ~ **calm**
ch'imch'ak'age it-tta 침착하게 있다
◆ keep away 1 v/i mullŏna it-tta
물러나 있다; ~ **from** ...(ŭ)robut'ŏ
mullŏna it-tta ...(으)로부터 물러나
있다 2 v/t kakkai kaji mot'age hada
가까이 가지 못하게 하다
◆ keep back v/t (*hold in check*)
maktta 막다; *information* kamch'uda
감추다

◆ keep down v/t voice, noise
natch'uda 낮추다; costs, inflation e
chinjŏngshik'ida 진정시키다; food
padadǔrida 받아들이다
◆ keep in (*in hospital*) kyesok
ibwŏnhae itkke hada 계속 입원해
있게 하다; (*in school*) put-ttǔro tu
붙들어 두다
◆ keep off 1 v/t (*avoid*) p'ihada
피하다; ~ **the grass!** chandirŭl
paltchi mashiyo! 잔디를 밟지
마시요! 2 v/i (*of rain*) oji ant'a 오지
않다
◆ keep out v/i tŭrogaji ant'a 들어가
않다; ~! (*as sign*) tŭrogaji mashiyo
들어가지 마시요!
◆ keep out of argument, trouble ...
kkiŏ tŭrogaji ant'a ...에 끼어
들어가지 않다
◆ keep to path, rules chik'ida 지키디
◆ keep up 1 v/i (*when running etc*)
twijiji ank'o ttaragada 뒤지지 않고
따라가다 2 v/t pace, payments
yujihada 유지하다; bridge, pants
chit'aenghada 지탱하다
◆ keep up with ...e twittŏrŏjiji ant
...에 뒤떨어지지 않다; (*stay in tou*
with) ...wa/kwa kyesok yŏllak'ad
...와/과 계속 연락하다
keeping: in ~ with ...wa/kwa
chohwahayŏ ...와/과 조화하여;
(*with promises*) ...wa/kwa
ilch'ihayŏ ...와/과 일치하여
kennel kaejip 개집
kennels kae sayuktchang 개 사육징
kernel haek 핵
kerosene tŭng-yu 등유
ketchup k'ech'ŏp 케첩
kettle chujŏnja 주전자
key 1 n (*to door, drawer*) yŏlsoe 열
COMPUT, (*on piano*) k'i 키; MUS c
조 調 2 adj (*vital*) maeu chungnyoha
매우 중요한 3 v/t COMPUT k'irǔl
ch'ida 키를 치다

ey in *data* imnyŏk'ada 입력하다
yboard COMPUT, MUS k'ibodŭ
보드; (*of piano*) kŏnban 건반;
eyboarder COMPUT charyorŭl
mnyŏk'anŭn saram 자료를 입력하는
람; **keycard** k'adŭro toen yŏlsoe
드로 된 열쇠
yed-up kinjangdoen 긴장된
yhole yŏlsoe kumŏng 열쇠 구멍;
eynote speech kijo yŏnsŏl 기조
설; **keyring** yŏlsoe kori 열쇠 고리
k 1 *n* ch'agi 차기; F (*thrill*)
ungbun 흥분; **get a ~ out of …**
.i /ga ssŏk chaemiit-tta …이 /가 썩
미있다; (*just*) **for ~s** chaemiro
미로 **2** *v/t* ch'ada 차다; F *habit*
kŭnt'a 끊다 **3** *v/i* ch'ada 차다
ick around *ball* molgo tanida 몰고
니다; (*treat harshly*) hamburo
aruda 함부로 다루다; F (*discuss*)
ŏromoro ŭnon'ohada 여러모로
토하다
ick in 1 *v/t* F (*money*) naeda 내다
v/i (*of boiler etc*) chakttonghada
동하다
ick off *v/i* k'ik'op'ŭhada
오프하다; F (*start*) shijak'ada
작하다
ick out *v/t* tchoch'anaeda
아내다; **~ of the company** /**army**
oesaesŏ /kundaeesŏ
chotkkyŏnada 회사에서 /군대에서
겨나다
ckback F (*bribe*) chŏngch'i hŏn-
ŭm 정치 헌금
koff k'ik'op'ŭ 킥오프
d 1 *n* (*child*) ai 아이; **~**
rother /**sister** namdongsaeng /
ŏdongsaeng 남동생 /여동생 **2** *v/t*
ollida 놀리다 **3** *v/i* nongdamhada
담하다; *I was only ~ding* kŭnyang
ongdamiyeyo 그냥 농담이에요
dder F nongdam chal hanŭn saram
담 잘 하는 사람
dnap napch'ihada 납치하다; *child*
ugoehada 유괴하다
dnap(p)er napch'ibŏm 납치범; (*of*
hild) yugoebŏm 유괴범
dnap(p)ing napch'i 납치; (*of child*)
ugoe 유괴
dney ANAT shinjang 신장; (*to eat*)

k'ongp'at 콩팥
kill *v/t also time* chugida 죽이다; *be*
~ed in an accident sagoro chuktta
사고로 죽다; *~ oneself* chasarhada
자살하다
killer sarinja 살인자; (*cause of death*)
sain 사인
killing sarhae 살해; *make a ~* (*lots of*
money) tte tonŭl pŏlda 떼 돈을 벌다
kiln kama 가마
kilo k'illo 킬로
kilobyte k'illobait'ŭ 킬로바이트
kilogram k'illogŭraem 킬로그램
kilometer k'illomit'ŏ 킬로미터
kimchee kimch'i 김치
kimono k'imono 키모노
kind¹ *adj* ch'injŏrhan 친절한
kind² *n* chongnyu 종류; *what ~ of …?*
ŏttŏn chongnyuŭi …? 어떤 종류의
…?; *what ~ of dog is that?*
chŏgŏsŭn ŏttŏn chongnyuŭi
kaeimnikka? 저것은 어떤 종류의
개입니까?; *all ~s of people* oman
chongnyuŭi saram 오만 종류의 사람;
nothing of the ~ kyŏlk'o kŭrŏn
kŏshi anida 결코 그런 것이 아니다;
~ of sad /*strange* F ŏnŭ chŏngdo
sŭlp'ŭda /isanghada 어느 정도
슬프다 /이상하다
kindergarten yuch'iwŏn 유치원
kind-hearted maŭmsshi koun 마음씨
고운
kindly 1 *adj* ch'injŏrhan 친절한 **2** *adv*
ch'injŏrhage 친절하게; (*please*)
chebal 제발
kindness ch'injŏl 친절
king wang 왕
kingdom wangguk 왕국
king-size(d) F k'ing saijŭ 킹 사이즈
kink (*in hose etc*) kkoim 꼬임
kinky F pyŏnt'aejŏgin 변태적인
kiosk kani maejŏm 간이 매점
kiss 1 *n* k'isŭ 키스 **2** *v/t* k'isŭhada
키스하다 **3** *v/i* k'isŭhada 키스하다
kit (*equipment*) changbi 장비; (*for*
assembly) chorimnyongp'um
조립용품
kitchen puŏk 부엌
kite yŏn 연
kite flying yŏnnalligi 연날리기
kitten saekki koyang-i 새끼 고양이

kitty (*money*) kongdong chŏngnipkkŭm 공동 적립금

klutz F (*clumsy*) tŏlch'ŏngi tŏll ryŏngi 덜렁이

knack yoryŏng 요령

knead *dough* panjuk'ada 반죽하다

knee *n* murŭp 무릎

kneecap *n* sŭlgaegol 슬개골

kneel murŭp kkult'a 무릎 꿇다

knick-knacks chajilgurehan changshin-gu 자질구레한 장신구

knife 1 *n* k'al 칼 2 *v/t* k'allo tchirŭda 칼로 찌르다

knit 1 *v/t* t'ŏlshillo ttŭda 털실로 뜨다 2 *v/i* ttŭgaejirhada 뜨개질하다

♦ **knit together** (*of bone*) itta 잇다

knitting (*sth being knitted*) p'yŏnmul 편물; (*activity*) ttŭgaejil 뜨개질

knitwear nit'ŭ weŏ 니트 웨어

knob (*on door*) sonjabi 손잡이

knock 1 *n* (*on door*) mun tudŭrinŭn sori 문 두드리는 소리; (*blow*) t'agyŏk 타격 2 *v/t* (*hit*) ch'ida 치다; F (*criticize*) kkalboda 깔보다 3 *v/i* (*on the door*) nok'ŭhada 노크하다; ~ **at the door** munŭl nok'ŭhada 문을 노크하다

♦ **knock around** 1 *v/t* (*beat*) magu tudŭlgyŏ p'aeda 마구 두들겨 패다 2 *v/i* F (*travel*) magu toradanida 마구 돌아다니다

♦ **knock down** (*of car*) ch'iŏ nŏmŏttŭrida 치어 넘어뜨리다; *object, building etc* hŏrŏ nŏmŏttŭrida 헐어 넘어뜨리다; F (*reduce the price of*) …ŭi kapssŭl naerida …의 값을 내리다

♦ **knock out** (*make unconscious*) naga ttŏrŏjige hada 나가 떨어지게 하다; (*of medicine*) chamdŭlge hada 잠들게 하다; *power lines etc* munŏttŭrida 무너뜨리다

♦ **knock over** nŏmŏttŭrida 넘어뜨리다; (*of car*) ch'iŏ nŏmŏttŭrida 치어 넘어뜨리다

knockout *n* SP nogaut'ŭ 녹아우트

knot 1 *n* maedŭp 매듭 2 *v/t* maeda 매다

knotty *problem* haegyŏri kollanhan 해결이 곤란한

know 1 *v/t* alda 알다; *language* …e chŏngt'onghada …에 정통하다;

(*recognize*) araboda 알아보다 2 *v/i* algo it-tta 알고 있다; *I don't ~* mollayo 몰라요; *yes, I ~* ye, algo issŏyo 예, 알고 있어요 3 *n*: *be in the* ~ naebu sajŏng-ŭl chal algo it-tta 내부 사정을 잘 알고 있다

knowhow nohau 노하우

knowing alget-ttanŭn shigŭi 알겠다는 식의

knowingly (*wittingly*) algosŏdo 알고서도; *smile etc* anŭn tŭt'an ara ~dŭt'an 아는 듯한

know-it-all F anŭn ch'e hanŭn sara ~sara 아는 체 하는 사람

knowledge chishik 지식; *to the be* ~ *of my* ~ naega algo itkkironŭn 내 ~ 알고 있기로는; *have a good* ~ *of* …e chŏngt'onghada …에 정통한

knowledgeable chishigi innŭn 지식 ~ 있는

knuckle sonkkarak madi 손가락 마 ~

♦ **knuckle down** chinjihage ch'akssuhada 진지하게 착수하다

♦ **knuckle under** kulbok'ada 굴복하다

KO k'ei ou 케이 오우

Koje Island Kŏjedo 거제도

Korea (*South*) Han-guk 한국; (*Nor* Puk'an 북한

Korean 1 *adj* (*South*) Han-gugŭi 한국의; (*North*) Puk'anŭi 북한의 2 (*South*) Han-guk saram 한국 사람 (*North*) Puk'an saram 북한 사람; (*language*) Han-gugŏ 한국어

Korean Broadcasting System H. ~guk Pangsong Kongsa 한국 방송 공사; **Korean chess** changgi 장기 ~ **Korean costume** hanbok 한복; **Korean oboe** p'iri 피리; **Korean script** Han-gŭl 한글; **Korean Stra** Taehanhaehyŏp 대한해협, Namha 남해; **Korean-style hotel** yŏgwa ~ 여관; **Korean-style mattress** yo ~ **Korean War** Han-guk Chŏnjaeng ~ 한국 전쟁; **Korean wrestling** sshirŭm 씨름

kosher REL Yut'aein yulppŏbe ~ mannŭn 유태인 율법에 맞는; F ~ chŏngdanghan 정당한

kudos yŏng-ye 영예

Kum River Kŭmgang 금강

shirhŏmshil 실험실
el 1 *n* kkorip'yo 꼬리표 **2** *v/t* aggage kkorip'yorŭl puch'ida
리표를 붙이다
or *n* nodong 노동; (*giving birth*)
unman 분만; **be in ~** punman
hung-ida 분만 중이다
oratory shirhŏmshil 실험실
oratory technician shirhŏmshil
isultcha 실험실 기술자
ored *style, speech* ŏsaek'an 어색한
orer nodongja 노동자
orious himdŭnŭn 힘드는
or union nodong chohap 노동
합
or ward punmanshil 분만실
e *n* leisŭ 레이스; (*for shoe*) kkŭn 끈
ace up *shoes* kkŭnŭl maeda 끈을
다
k 1 *n* pujok 부족 **2** *v/t* ...i/ga ŏptta
..i/가 없다; **he ~s confidence**
ŭnŭn chashin-gami ŏptta 그는
신감이 없다 **3** *v/i*: **be ~ing**
ujok'ada 부족하다
quer *n* (*for hair*) heŏsŭp'ŭrei
어스프레이
cquerware ch'ilgi 칠기
chŏlmŭn namja 젊은 남자
dder sadari 사다리
den chŏktchaehan 적재한
dies' room yŏja hwajangshil 여자
장실
dle *n* kuktcha 국자
ly sungnyŏ 숙녀
ybug mudangbŏlle 무당벌레
v/t pipes p'iboktchaero ssada
복재로 싸다
ag behind twittŏrŏjida 뒤떨어지다
ger lagŏ 라거 비어
goon sŏk'o 석호
dback nŭgŭt'an 느긋한
ke hosu 호수
mb saekkiyang 새끼양; (*meat*)
anggogi 양고기

lame *person* chŏllŭmbariŭi
절름발이의; *excuse* ŏsŏlp'ŭn 어설픈
lament 1 *n* kit'an 비탄 **2** *v/t*
sŭlp'ŏhada 슬퍼하다
lamentable sŏgŭlp'ŭn 서글픈
laminated k'ot'inghan 코팅한; ~
glass yalbŭn p'anyuri 얇은 판유리
lamp tŭngppul 등불
lamppost karodŭng kidung 가로등
기둥
lampshade chŏndŭnggat 전등갓
land 1 *n* ttang 땅; (*shore*) yuktchi
육지; (*country*) nara 나라; **by ~**
yungnoro 육로로; **on ~** yuktchie(sŏ)
육지에(서); **work on the ~** (*as
farmer*) nongsa chitkko salda 농사
짓고 살다 **2** *v/t airplane*
ch'angnyukshik'ida 착륙시키다; *job*
ŏt-tta 얻다 **3** *v/i* (*of airplane*)
ch'angnyuk'ada 착륙하다; (*of ball,
sth thrown*) ttorŏjida 떨어지다
landing (*of airplane*) ch'angnyuk
착륙; (*top of staircase*)
ch'ŭnggyech'am 층계참
landing field pihaengjang 비행장;
landing gear ch'angnyuk changch'i
착륙 장치; **landing strip** kasŏl
hwaltchuro 가설 활주로
landlady (*of hostel etc*) yŏjuin 여주인;
landlord (*of hostel etc*) chuin 주인;
landmark yumyŏnghan
kŏnch'ungmul 유명한 건축물; *fig*
hoek-kkijŏgin sakkŏn 획기적인 사건;
land owner chiju 지주; **landscape
1** *n* kyŏngch'i 경치; (*painting*)
p'unggyŏnghwa 풍경화 **2** *adv print*
karo panghyang-ŭro 가로 방향으로;
landslide sansat'ae 산사태; ~ **victory** apssŭng 압승
lane (*in country*) shigolkkil 시골길;
(*alley*) chobŭn kil 좁은 길; (*on
highway*) ch'asŏn 차선
language ŏnŏ 언어
lank *hair* kirŭmgi kkin 기름기 낀

lanky *person* horihorihan 호리호리한

lantern tŭng 등

Lao (*language*) Laosŏ 라오스어

Laos Laosŭ 라오스

Laotian 1 *adj* Laosŭŭi 라오스의 **2** *n* (*person*) Laosŭin 라오스인

lap[1] *n* (*of racetrack*) han pak'wi 한 바퀴

lap[2] *n* (*of water*) chanmulkkyŏrŭi sori 잔물결의 소리

♦ **lap up** *milk* halt'amŏktta 핥아먹다; *flattery* koji kot-ttaero padadŭrida 곧이 곧대로 받아들이다

lap[3] *n* (*of person*) murŭp 무릎

lapel chŏbŭn otkkit 접은 옷깃

laptop COMPUT laept'ap 랩탑

larceny chŏlttotchoe 절도죄

large k'ŭn 큰; *at ~* (*criminal, wild animal*) t'alch'urhan 탈출한

largely (*mainly*) churo 주로

lark (*bird*) chongdalssae 종달새

larva yuch'ung 유충

laryngitis huduyŏm 후두염

larynx hudu 후두

laser leijyŏ 레이저

laser beam leijyŏ kwangsŏn 레이저 광선

laser printer leijyŏ p'urint'ŏ 레이저 프린터

lash[1] *v/t* (*with whip*) ch'aetchiktchirhada 채찍질하다

lash[2] *n* (*eyelash*) songnunssŏp 속눈썹

♦ **lash down** (*with rope*) tandanhi mukta 단단히 묶다

last[1] *adj* (*in series*) majimak 마지막; (*preceding*) chŏnbŏnŭi 전번의; *~ but one* majimagesŏ tu pŏntchae 마지막에서 두 번째; *~ night* ŏjetppam 어젯밤; *~ but not least* kkŭch'ijiman chungnyohage tŏtppuch'inŭn kŏsŭn kkŭt'ijiman chungnyohage tŏtppuch'inŭn kŏsŭn 끝이지만 중요하게 덧붙이는 것은; *at ~* mach'imnae 마침내

last[2] *v/i* chisokttoeda 지속되다

lastly majimaguro 마지막으로

latch *n* kŏlssoe 걸쇠

late (*behind time*) nŭjŭn 늦은; (*at night*) pam nŭjŭn 밤 늦은; *it's getting ~* nŭjŏjinda 늦어진다; *of ~* ch'oegŭne 최근에; *the ~ 19th/20th century* shipkku/iship segi mal

십구/이십 세기 말; *sleep ~* nŭttcham chada 늦잠자다

lately ch'oegŭne 최근에

later *adv* najung-e 나중에; *see you ~* najung-e poja! 나중에 보자!; *~ on* najung-e 나중에

latest *news, developments* ch'oesh 최신의; *girlfriend* ch'oegŭnŭi 최근

lathe *n* sŏnban 선반

lather (*from soap*) kŏp'um 거품

Latin America Nammi 남미

Latin American 1 *adj* Lat'in Amerik'aŭi 라틴 아메리카의 **2** *n* Lat'in Amerik'ain 라틴 아메리카ᄂ

latitude (*geographical*) wido 위도; (*freedom to maneuver*) hŏyong pŏmwi 허용 범위

latter hujaŭi 후자의

laugh 1 *n* usŭm 웃음; *it was a ~* chaemiissŏt-tta 재미있었다 **2** *v/i* u tta 웃다

♦ **laugh at** (*mock*) …ŭl/rŭl piut-tt …을/를 비웃다

laughing stock: make oneself a sŭsŭrorŭl usŭmkkŏriro mandŭlda 스스로를 웃음거리로 만들다; *become a ~* usŭmkkŏriga toeda 웃음거리가 되다

laughter usŭm 웃음

launch 1 *n* (*boat*) chinsusŏn 진수선 (*of rocket*) palssa 발사; (*of ship*) chinsu 진수; (*of new product*) palmae 발매 **2** *v/t rocket* palssahae 발사하다; *ship* chinsuhada 진수하ᄂ *product* palmaehada 발매하다

launch(ing) ceremony (*for ship*) chinsushik 진수식; (*for product*) palmae ch'uk'ayŏn 발매 축하연

launch(ing) pad palssadae 발사대ᄂ

launder set'ak'ada 세탁하다

laundromat selp'ŭ set'aksso 셀프세탁소

laundry (*place*) set'aksso 세탁소; (*clothes*) set'angmul 세탁물; *get one's ~ done* set'ak'age hada 세탁하게 하다

laurel wŏlgyesu 월계수

lavatory hwajangshil 화장실

lavender labendŏ 라벤더

laver (*seaweed*) kim 김

lavish *adj* p'ungbuhan 풍부한

pŏp 법; (*as subject*) pŏp'ak 법학;
ainst the ~ pulppŏbin 불법인;
rbidden by ~ pŏbŭro kŭmjidoen
으로 금지된
' **court** pŏptchŏng 법정
ful hap-ppŏptchŏgin 합법적인
less mubŏbŭi 무법의
'n chandi 잔디
'n **mower** chandi kkangnŭn kigye
디 깎는 기계
'suit sosong 소송
yer pyŏnhosa 변호사
nŭsŭnhan 느슨한
ative *n* pyŏnbiyak 변비약
v/t (*put down*) not'a 놓다; *eggs*
it'a 낳다; ∨ (*sexually*) sŏnggyohada
교하다
y **into** (*attack*) konggyŏk'ada
격하다
y **off** *workers* haegohada 해고하다
y **on** (*provide*) maryŏnhada
련하다
y **out** *objects* chinyŏrhada
열하다; *page* leiausŭl hada
이아웃을 하다
er *n* ch'ŭng 층
man amach'uŏ 아마추어
but paech'i 배치
ze **around** pindŭnggŏrida
둥거리다
y *person* keŭrŭn 게으른; *day*
arirŏmnŭn 하릴없는
= *pound(s)*) p'aundŭ 파운드
D (= *liquid crystal display*)
ktchŏng p'yoshi changch'i 액정
시 장치
d[1] 1 *v/t procession, race* sŏndue
da 선두에 서다; *company, team*
kŭlda 이끌다; (*guide, take*)
dohada 인도하다 2 *v/i* (*in race,
mpetition*) sŏndue sŏda 선두에
다; (*provide leadership*)
ngsorhada 통솔하다; *a street*
ng off the square kwangjangesŏ
ŏŏdŏnaonŭn kil 광장에서
어나오는 길; *where is this ~ing?*
liro hŭllŏgago innŭn kŏmnikka?
디로 흘러가고 있는 겁니까? 3 *n*
n race) sŏndu 선두; *be in the ~*
ndue it-tta 선두에 있다; *take the*
sŏndue tŭrŏsŏda 선두에 들어서다;

lose the ~ sŏnduesŏ millyŏnada
선두에서 밀려나다
♦**lead on** (*go in front*) aptchang sŏda
앞장 서다
♦**lead up to** ...(ŭ)ro ikkŭlgo kada
...(으)로 이끌고 가다
lead[2] *n* (*for dog*) kae chul 개 줄
lead[3] *n* (*metal*) nap 납
leader chidoja 지도자
leadership (*of party etc*) t'ongsollyŏk
통솔력; *under his* ~ kŭŭi chido ha-e
그의 지도 하에; ~ *skills* chidoryŏk
지도력
leadership contest chidoja sŏn-gŏ
hoeŭi 지도자 선거 회의
lead-free *gas* muyŏnŭi 무연의
leading *runner* sŏnduŭi 선두의;
company, product chudojŏgin
주도적인
leading-edge *adj company,
technology* ch'ŏmdanŭi 첨단의
leaf ip 잎
♦**leaf through** taech'ung pomyŏ
nŏmgida 대충 보며 넘기다
leaflet chŏndan 전단
league yŏnmaeng 연맹
leak 1 *n* saeŏ naom 새어 나옴; (*of
information*) nuch'ul 누출 2 *v/i* saeda
새다
♦**leak out** (*of air, gas*) saeŏ naoda
새어 나오다; (*of news*) nusŏldoeda
누설되다
leaky *pipe, boat* saenŭn 새는
lean[1] *v/i* (*be at an angle*) kidaeda
기대다; ~ *against sth* muŏse
kidaeda 무엇에 기대다 2 *v/t* ~
sth against sth muŏsŭl muŏse
kidaeŏ not'a 무엇을 무엇에 기대어
놓다
lean[2] *adj meat* salk'ogiŭi 살코기의;
style, prose kundŏdŏgi ŏmnŭn
군더더기 없는
leap 1 *n* toyak 도약; *a great ~ forward* tae chinbo 대 진보 2 *v/i*
hultchŏk ttwida 훌쩍 뛰다
leap year yunnyŏn 윤년
learn paeuda 배우다; ~ *how to do
sth* muŏsŭl hanŭn pangbŏbŭl
paeuda 무엇을 하는 방법을
배우다

learner paenŭn saram 배우는 사람

learning n (*knowledge*) chishik 지식; (*act*) haksŭp 학습

learning curve haksŭp koksŏn 학습 곡선; **be on the ~** shin-gisurŭl sŭptŭkt'aeya handa 신기술을 습득해야 한다

lease 1 n imdae 임대 **2** v/t *apartment, equipment* imdaehada 임대하다
♦ **lease out** imdaehada 임대하다

leash n (*for dog*) kae chul 개 줄

least 1 adj (*slightest*) kajang chagŭn 가장 작은 **2** adv kajang an 가장 안; **~ difficult** kajang anŏryŏun 가장 안어려운 **3** n ch'oesoryang 최소량; **not in the ~ surprised/disappointed** chogŭmdo nollaji/shilmanghaji annŭn 조금도 놀라지/실망하지 않은; **at ~** chŏgŏdo 적어도

leather 1 n kajuk 가죽 **2** adj kajugŭi 가죽의

leave 1 n (*vacation*) hyuga 휴가; **on ~** hyugarŭl ŏdŏ 휴가를 얻어 **2** v/t *city, place, person* ttŏnada 떠나다; *husband, wife* pŏrida 버리다; *food on plate* namgyŏ tuda 남겨 두다; *scar, memory, message* namgida 남기다; (*forget, leave behind*) ijŏbŏrigo tugo kada 잊어버리고 두고 가다; **let's ~ things as they are** kŭnyang kŭdaero tugiro hapshida 그냥 그대로 두기로 합시다; **how did you ~ things with him?** kŭ saramgwaŭi irŭn ŏttŏk'e hagiro haessŭmnikka? 그 사람과의 일은 어떻게 하기로 했습니까?; **~ alone** (*not touch*) kŭnyang kŭdaero tuda 그냥 그대로 두다; (*not interfere with*) kansŏp'aji ant'a 간섭하지 않다; (*not damage*) haerŭl ip'iji ant'a 해를 입히지 않다; **be left** namtta 남다; **there is nothing left** namŭn kŏshi ŏpssŭmnida 남은 것이 없습니다 **2** v/i (*of person*) ttŏnada 떠나다; (*of plane, train, bus*) ch'ulbarhada 출발하다
♦ **leave behind** *person* twie namgida 뒤에 남기다; *object* tugo kada 두고 가다; (*forget*) ijŏ pŏrigo tugo kada 잊어 버리고 두고 가다
♦ **leave on** *hat* ssŭn ch'aero tuda 쓴

채로 두다; *coat* ibŭn ch'aero tuda 입은 채로 두다; *TV, computer* k'yŏ ch'aero tuda 켠 채로 두다
♦ **leave out** *word* saengnyak'ada 생략하다; (*not put away*) naenoŭn ch'ae pŏryŏduda 내놓은 채 버려두다; **leave me out of this** chŏnŭn i iresŏ cheoeshik'yŏ chushipssshio 저는 이 일에서 제외시켜 주십시오

leaving party songbyŏrhoe 송별회

lecture 1 n kang-ŭi 강의 **2** v/i (*at university*) kang-ŭihada 강의하다

lecture hall kang-ŭishil 강의실

lecturer kangsa 강사

LED (= *light-emitting diode*) palgwang taiodŭ 발광 다이오드

ledge t'ŏk 턱

ledger COM wŏntchang 원장

leek puch'u 부추

leer n (*sexual*) ch'up'a 추파

left 1 adj oentchogŭi 왼쪽의; POL chwaigŭi 좌익의 **2** n oentchok 왼쪽; POL chwaik 좌익; **on the ~** oentchoge(sŏ) 왼쪽에(서); **on the ~ of sth** muŏsŭi oentchoge(sŏ) 무엇의 왼쪽에(서); **to the ~** turn, look oentchoguro 왼쪽으로 **3** adv turn, look oentchoguro 왼쪽으로

left-hand bend oenp'yŏnŭro hanŭn 왼편으로 하는; **left-hand drive** chwach'ŭk haendŭl unjŏn 좌측 핸들 운전; **left-handed** oensonjabi 왼손잡이; **left-overs** (*food*) namkŏt nam은 것; **left-wing** POL chwai 좌익

leg tari 다리; **pull s.o.'s ~** nugurŭl nollida 누구를 놀리다

legacy yusan 유산

legal (*allowed*) hap-ppŏptchŏgin 합법적인; (*relating to the law*) pŏptchŏgin 법적인

legal adviser pŏptchŏk chojŏnja 법적 조언자

legality hap-ppŏp 합법

legalize hap-ppŏp'wahada 합법화하다

legend chŏnsŏl 전설

legendary chŏnsŏljŏgin 전설적인

legible ilkki shwiun 읽기 쉬운

legislate chejŏnghada 제정하다

legislation (*laws*) pŏmnyul 법률;

...assing of laws) ip-ppŏp 입법
islative powers, assembly ip-pŏbŭi 입법의
islature POL ip-ppŏp-ppu 입법부
itimate claim chŏkppŏbŭi 적법의; ...mplaint, cause chŏngdanghan 당한; child chŏkch'urŭi 적출의
room: there's no ~ tarirŭl 'yŏnhage noŭl su ŏpssŏyo 다리를 ...하게 놓을 수 없어요
sure yŏga 여가; at your ~ tangshini 'yŏnhan shigane 당신이 편한 ...간에
sure center lejŏ sent'ŏ 레저 센터
surely pace nŭgŭt'an 느긋한
sure time yŏga shigan 여가 시간
...on lemon 레몬
...onade lemoneidŭ 레모네이드
...on juice lemon chusŭ 레몬 주스
...on tea lemonch'a 레몬차
...d: ~ s.o. sth nuguege muŏsŭl 누구에게 무엇을 빌려주다
...gth kiri 길이; at ~ describe, explain ...lge 길게; (eventually) mach'imnae ...침내
...gthen nŭllida 늘리다
...gthy speech, stay kin 긴
...ient kwandaehan 관대한
...s lenjŭ 렌즈
...s cover lenjŭ ttukkŏng 렌즈 ...껑
...nt sasunjŏl 사순절
...til lenjŭ k'ong 렌즈 콩
...til soup lenjŭ k'ong sŭp'ŭ 렌즈 콩 ...프
...pard p'yobŏm 표범
...tard ch'ejobok 체조복
...bian 1 n lejŭbiŏn 레즈비언 2 adj ...jŭbiŏnŭi 레즈비언의
...s: eat/talk ~ tŏl mŏkta/marhada ... 먹다/말하다; ~ interest-...g/serious tŏl hŭngmiroun/simgak'an 덜 흥미로운/심각한; it ...ost ~ toni tŏl tŭnda 돈이 덜 든다; ...than $200 200tallŏ miman ...0달러 미만
...son suŏp 수업
...v/t (allow): ~ s.o. do sth nuga ...uŏt'age haejuda 누가 무엇하게 ...주다; ~ me go! noajwŏ! 놓아줘!; ...im come in kŭrŭl tŭrŏoge haseyo

그를 들어오게 하세요; ~'s go/stay kaja/mŏmŭlja 가자/머물자; ~'s not argue ssauji malja 싸우지 말자; ~ alone … kinŭn k'ŏnyŏng …기는 커녕; he can't read, ~ alone write kŭnŭn ssŭginŭn k'ŏnyŏng iltchido mot'anda 그는 쓰기는 커녕 읽지도 못한다; ~ go of sth (of rope, handle) muŏsŭl noa pŏrida 무엇을 놓아 버리다

◆let down hair p'urŏ naerida 풀어 내리다; shades naerida 내리다; (disappoint) shilmangshik'ida 실망시키다; (make longer) tanŭl naerida 단을 내리다
◆let in (to house) tŭrŏgada 들어가다
◆let off (not punish) yongsŏhada 용서하다; (from car) naeryŏ chuda 내려 주다; let a student off homework hakssaeng-ege suktcherŭl myŏnjehae chuda 학생에게 숙제를 면제해 주다
◆let out (of room, building) nagage hada 나가게 하다; jacket etc nŭllida 늘리다; groan, yell ip ppakkŭro naeda 입 밖으로 내다
◆let up v/i (stop) mŏt-tta 멎다
lethal ch'imyŏngjŏgin 치명적인
lethargic nogonhan 노곤한
letter (of alphabet) kŭltcha 글자; (in mail) p'yŏnji 편지
letterhead (heading) p'yŏnjiji wiŭi inswae munkku 편지지 위의 인쇄 문구; (headed paper) wit pubune inswae munkkuga innŭn p'yŏnjiji 윗 부분에 인쇄 문구가 있는 편지지
letter of credit COM shinyongtchang 신용장
letter of guarantee pojŭngsŏ 보증서
lettuce sangch'u 상추
letup: without a ~ shwiji ank'o 쉬지 않고
leukemia paek'yŏlppyŏng 백혈병
level 1 adj field, surface p'yŏngp'yŏnghan 평평한; (in competition, scores) kat'ŭn sujunŭi 같은 수준의; draw ~ with s.o. nuguwa makssangmak'a-e irŭda 누구와 막상막하에 이르다 2 n (on scale, in hierarchy) sujun 수준; (amount, quantity) yang 양; on the

~ (on ~ ground) p'yŏngp'yŏnghan kose(sŏ) 평평한 곳에(서); be on the ~ F (honest) chŏngjik'ada 정직하다

level-headed punbyŏl innŭn 분별 있는

lever 1 n chire 지레 2 v/t chirero umjigida 지레로 움직이다; ~ sth open muŏsŭl pijibŏ yŏlda 무엇을 비집어 열다

leverage chirŭl chagyong 지레의 작용; (influence) seryŏk 세력

levy v/t taxes chingsuhada 징수하다

lewd ch'ujap'an 추잡한

liability (responsibility) ch'aegim 책임

liability insurance ch'aegim pohŏm 책임 보험

liable (answerable) ch'aegimjyŏya hanŭn 책임져야 하는; be ~ to (likely) …hanŭn kyŏnghyang-i it-tta …하는 경향이 있다

♦ **liaise with** yŏllagŭl ch'wihada 연락을 취하다

liaison (contacts) yŏllak 연락

liar kŏjitmaljaeng-i 거짓말쟁이

libel 1 n munsŏe ŭihan myŏng-ye hweson 문서에 의한 명예 훼손 2 v/t myŏng-ye hwesonhada 명예 훼손하다

liberal adj (broad-minded) maŭmi nŏlbŭn 마음이 넓은; portion etc insaek'aji anŭn 인색하지 않은; POL chayujuŭiŭi 자유주의의

♦ **liberate** haebangshik'ida 해방시키다

liberated woman haebangdoen 해방된

Liberation Day Kwangboktchŏl 광복절

liberty chayu 자유; at ~ (prisoner etc) chayuro 자유로; be at ~ to do sth muŏsŭl maŭmdaero hada 무엇을 마음대로 하다

librarian sasŏ 사서

library tosŏgwan 도서관

Libya Libia 리비아

Libyan 1 adj Libiaŭi 리비아의 2 n Libiain 리비아인

license 1 n (for car) myŏnhŏtchŭng 면허증; (for imports, exports, TV, gun) hŏgatchŭng 허가증 2 v/t: be ~d (of car) myŏnhŏ pat-tta 면허 받다; (of gun, equipment) hŏga pat-tta

허가 받다

license number tŭngnok pŏnho 등 번호

license plate pŏnhop'an 번호판

lick 1 n halkki 핥기 2 v/t haltta 핥다; one's lips immasŭl tashida 입맛을 다시다

licking: get a ~ F (defeat) chida 지

lid ttukkŏng 뚜껑

lie[1] 1 n (untruth) kŏjinmal 거짓말; kŏjinmarhada 거짓말하다

lie[2] v/i (of person) nuptta 눕다; (of object) it-tta 있다; (be situated) wich'ihada 위치하다

♦ **lie down** nuptta 눕다

lieutenant: first ~ chung-wi 중위; second ~ sowi 소위

life saengmyŏng 생명; (living) saenghwal 생활; (~ span) sumyŏn 수명; all her ~ kŭnyŏ p'yŏngsaeng 그녀 평생에; that's ~! insaeng-ira kŭrŏn kŏshimnida! 인생이란 그런 것입니다!

life belt kumyŏng tti 구명 띠; **life** kumyŏngjŏng 구명정; **life expectancy** yesang sumyŏng 예상 수명; **lifeguard** kujowŏn 구조원; **life history** saenghwalsa 생활사; **life insurance** saengmyŏng pohŏm 생명 보; **life jacket** kumyŏng chokki 구명 조끼

lifeless saengmyŏng ŏmnŭn 생명 없는

lifelike sara innŭn tŭt'an 살아 있는 듯한; **lifelong** p'yŏngsaeng-ŭi 평생; **life preserver** (for swimmer) kumyŏnggu 구명구; **life-saving** a equipment kumyŏng-ŭi 구명의; medicine, drug saengmyŏng-ŭl kuhanŭn 생명을 구하는; **lifesized** shilmul k'ŭgiŭi 실물 크기의; **lifethreatening** saengmyŏng-ŭl wihyŏp'anŭn 생명을 위협하는; **life time** p'yŏngsaeng 평생; in my ~ p'yŏngsaeng-e 내 평생에

lift 1 v/t tŭrŏ ollida 들어 올리다 2 v/ (of fog) kŏch'ida 걷히다 3 n (in ca t'aeugi 태우기; Br (elevator) ellibeit'ŏ 엘리베이터; give s.o. a nugurŭl t'aewŏ chuda 누구를 태워 주다

ft off v/i (of rocket) sosa orŭda 솟아 오르다

off (of rocket) iryuk 이륙

ament indae 인대

ht¹ **1** n pit 빛; (lamp) tŭng 등; **in the of** ...e pich'uŏsŏ ...에 비추어서; **ave you got a ~?** pul issŭmnikka? 불 있읍니까? **2** v/t fire, cigarette pul uch'ida 불 붙이다; (illuminate) nomyŏnghada 조명하다 **3** adj (not ark) palgŭn 밝은

ht¹ **1** adj (not heavy) kabyŏun 벼운 **2** adv: **travel ~** chimŭl mani ajiji ank'o yŏhaenghada 짐을 많이 지지 않고 여행하다

ght up 1 v/t (illuminate) palkke 하다 **2** v/i (start to smoke) uri nada 불이 나다

ht bulb paegyŏl chŏn-gu 백열 전구

hten¹ v/t color palkke hada 밝게 다

hten² v/t load kabyŏpkke hada 볍게 하다

ighten up (of person) kibun p'ulda 분 풀다

hter (for cigarettes) lait'ŏ 라이터

ht-headed (dizzy) ŏjirŏun 지러운

ht-hearted maŭm kabyŏun 마음 벼운

hthouse tŭngdae 등대

hting chomyŏng 조명

htly touch kabyŏpkke 가볍게; **get ff ~** kabyŏpkke momyŏnhada 볍게 모면하다

htness¹ (of room) palgŭm 밝음

htness² (in weight) kabyŏum 벼움

htning pŏn-gae 번개

htning conductor p'iroech'im 리회침

ht pen lait'ŭ p'en 라이트 펜

htweight (in boxing) lait'ŭkkŭp ŏnsu 라이트급 선수

ht year kwangnyŏn 광년

kable hogami kanŭn 호감이 가는

ke¹ **1** prep kat'ŭn 같은; **be ~ s.o.** nuguwa tamtta 누구와 닮다; **be ~ sth** muŏtkkwa kat-tta 무엇과 같다; **what is she ~?** kŭ yŏjanŭn ŏttŏn saramimnikka? 그 여자는 어떤

사람입니까?; **it's not ~ him** (not his character) kŭ saramdaptchi anssŭmnida 그 사람답지 않습니다; **do it ~ this** irŏk'e haseyo 이렇게 하세요 **2** conj F: **I said** naega marhaettŭshi 내가 말했듯이

like² v/t choahada 좋아하다; **I ~ her** nanŭn kŭnyŏrŭl choahamnida 나는 그녀를 좋아합니다; **I would ~ ...** nanŭn ...ŭl/rŭl wŏnhamnida 나는 ...을/를 원합니다; **I would ~ a bigger room** nanŭn tŏ k'ŭn pang-ŭl wŏnhaeyo 나는 더 큰 방을 원해요; **I would ~ to ...** nanŭn ...hago shipssŭmida 나는 ...하고 싶습니다; **I would ~ to leave** nanŭn ttŏnago ship'ŏyo 나는 떠나고 싶어요; **would you ~ ...?** ...ŭl wŏnhamnikka? ...을/를 원합니까?; **would you ~ to ...?** ...hago shipssŭmnikka? ...하고 싶습니까?; **~ to do sth** muŏsŭl hago shiptta 무엇을 하고 싶다; **if you ~** tangshini chot'amyŏn 당신이 좋다면

likeable hogami kanŭn 호감이 가는

likelihood kanŭngssŏng 가능성; **in all ~** shiptchungp'algu 십중팔구

likely (probable) amado 아마도; **not ~!** maldo andoemnida! 말도 안됩니다!

likeness (resemblance) yusa 유사

liking: to your ~ tangshin maŭme tŭnŭn 당신 마음에 드는; **take a ~ to s.o.** nuguga choajida 누구가 좋아지다

lilac (flower, color) laillak 라일락

lily paek'ap 백합

lily of the valley ŭnbang-ul kkot 은방울 꽃

limb sonbal 손발

lime¹ (fruit, tree) laim 라임

lime² (substance) sŏk'oe 석회

limegreen laim nokssaek 라임 녹색

limelight: be in the ~ mut saramŭi chumogŭl pat-tta 뭇 사람의 주목을 받다

limit 1 n han-gye 한계; (of s.o.'s land) kyŏnggye 경계; **within ~s** chŏkttanghage 적당하게; **off ~s** ch'urip kŭmji 출입 금지; **that's the ~!** ijen tŏ isang ch'amŭl suga ŏpssŏyo! 이젠 더 이상 참을 수가

없어요! **2** *v/t* hanjŏnghada 한정하다

limitation han-gye 한계

limited company *Br* yuhan ch'aegim hoesa 유한 책임 회사

limo, limousine limujin 리무진

limp¹ *adj* hŭnŭjŏk-kkŏrinŭn 흐느적거리는

limp² *n* chŏlttuk-kkŏrim 절뚝거림; *he has a ~* kŭnŭn parŭl chŏlttuk-kkŏrinda 그는 발을 절뚝거린다

line¹ *n* (*on paper, road, for telephone*) sŏn 선; (*of people, text, trees*) chul 줄; (*of business*) saŏp 사업; *the ~ is busy* t'onghwa chung imnida 통화 중 입니다; *hold the ~* chamshiman kidariseyo 잠시만 기다리세요; *draw the ~ at sth* muŏsŭl handoro chŏnghada 무엇을 한도로 정하다; *~ of inquiry* chosaŭi panghyang 조사의 방향; *~ of reasoning* ch'uron 추론; *stand in ~* churŭl sŏda 줄을 서다; *in ~ with* (*conforming with*) …e sunŭnghayŏ …에 순응하여

line² *v/t* (*with material*) …(ŭ)ro anŭl taeda …(으)로 안을 대다

♦ **line up** *v/i* chul sŏda 줄 서다

linen (*material, sheets etc*) linen 리넨

liner (*ship*) chŏnggisŏn 정기선

linesman *SP* sŏnshim 선심

linger nama it-tta 남아 있다

lingerie lanjeri 란제리

linguist ŏnŏhakcha 언어학자; (*good at languages*) ŏhage nŭnghan saram 어학에 능한 사람

linguistic ŏhagŭi 어학의

lining (*of clothes*) ankkam 안감; (*of pipe, brakes*) laining 라이닝

link **1** *n* (*connection*) yŏn-gwan 연관; (*in chain*) kori 고리; (*of friendship*) yudae kwan-gye 유대 관계 **2** *v/t* yŏn-gyŏrhada 연결하다

♦ **link up** *v/i* mannada 만나다; *TV* yŏn-gyŏrhada 연결하다

lion saja 사자

lip ipssul 입술

lipread *v/t & v/i* immoyang-ŭro iltta 입모양으로 읽다

lipstick lipssŭt'ik 립스틱

liqueur lik'yurŭ 리큐르

liquid **1** *n* aekch'e 액체 **2** *adj* aekch'eŭi 액체의

liquidation ch'ŏngsan 청산; *go int* ch'ŏngsanhada 청산하다

liquidity *FIN* yudong chasan 유동 ᅎ

liquor sul ㅅ개

liquorice kamch'o 감초

liquor store churyu p'anmaejŏm ᅎ 판매점

lisp **1** *n* hyŏ tchalbŭn sori 혀 짧은 소리 **2** *v/i* hyŏ tchalbŭn soriro marhada 혀 짧은 소리로 말하다

list **1** *n* mongnok 목록 **2** *v/t* mongnŏ ollida 목록에 올리다

listen tŭt-tta 듣다

♦ **listen in** yŏt-ttŭt-tta 엿듣다

♦ **listen to** *radio, person* …ŭl / rŭl tta …을 / 를 듣다

listener (*to radio*) ch'ŏngch'wija 청취자; *he's a good ~* kŭnŭn sar marŭl chal tŭrŏjumnida 그는 사ᄅ 말을 잘 들어줍니다

listings magazine pangsong p'ŭrogŭraem chaptchi 방송 프로ᄀ 잡지

listless maŭm naek'iji annŭn 마음 내키지 않는

liter lit'ŏ 리터

literal *adj* kŭltcha kŭdaeroŭi 글자 그대로의

literary munhagŭi 문학의

literate: *be ~* kŭrŭl ilkko ssŭl chul anda 글을 읽고 쓸 줄 안다

literature munhak 문학

litter ssŭregi 쓰레기; (*of young animals*) han pae saekki 한 배 새끼

little **1** *adj* chagŭn 작은; *the ~ one* aidŭl 아이들 **2** *n* chogŭm 조금; *the I know* naega kŏŭi morŭnŭn kŏt 내가 거의 모르는 것; *a ~* chogŭm 조금; *a ~ bread / wine* ppang / p'odoju chogŭm 빵 / 포도주 조금; *a ~ is better than nothing* chogŭmirado ŏmnŭn kŏshi ŏmnŭn kotppoda nat-tta 조금이라도 있는 것이 없는 것보다 낫다 **3** *adv* chogŭmŭn 조금은; *~ by ~* chogŭmshik 조금씩; *a ~ bet-ter / bigger* chogŭm tŏ choŭn / k'ŭ 조금 더 좋은 / 큰; *a ~ before 6* yŏsŏtshi chogŭm chŏne 6시 조금 전에

live¹ *v/i* salda 살다

ve on 1 v/t *rice, bread* ...ŭl/rŭl
ŏk-kko salda ...을/를 먹고 살다
v/i (*continue living*) kyesok salda
|속 살다

ve up: **live it up** sach'issŭrŏpkke
alda 사치스럽게 살다

ve up to ...e mannŭn saenghwarŭl
ada ...에 맞는 생활을 하다

ve with *person* ...wa/kwa
ŏnggŏhada ...와/과 동거하다

a² *adj* (*living*) sara innŭn salla innŭn;
ELEC chŏn-giga t'onghago innŭn
기가 통하고 있는; ~ **ammunition**
hilt'an silt'an; ~ **broadcast**
aengbangsong 생방송

elihood saenggye 생계

ely hwalgi ch'an hwalgi ch'an
r ANAT kanjang 간장; (*food*) kan
|

estock kach'uk 가축

d (*angry*) nobaldaebarhan
·발대발한

ng 1 *adj* sara innŭn 살아 있는 2 *n*
aenghwal 생활; (*means of support*)
aenggye 생계; **earn one's** ~
aenghwalbirŭl pŏlda 생활비를 벌다

ing room kŏshil 거실

ard tomabaem 도마뱀

d 1 *n* chim 짐; ELEC puha 부하; ~**s**
f manŭn 많은 2 v/t *car, truck* chimŭl
hilt'a 짐을 싣다; *camera* p'illŭmŭl
ŏt'a 필름을 넣다; *gun*
hangjŏnhada 장전하다; *software*
ŏdŭhada 로드하다; ~ **sth onto sth**
uŏsŭl muŏse shilt'a 무엇을 무엇에
|넣다

aded F (*very rich*) toni manŭn 돈이
|은; (*drunk*) ch'wihan 취한
f tŏng-ŏri 덩어리; **a ~ of bread**
pang han tŏng-ŏri 빵 한 덩어리

oaf around nolgo chinaeda 놀고
|내다

afer (*shoe*) kanp'yŏnhwa 간편화

an 1 *n* taebu 대부; **on ~** pillin 빌린
v/t: ~ **s.o. sth** nuguege muŏsŭl
illyŏjuda 누구에게 무엇을 빌려주다

athe mopsshi shirŏhada 몹시
|어하다

oby (*in hotel*) lobi 로비; (*in theater*)
yugeshil 휴게실; POL amnyŏk
anch'e 압력 단체

lobster padatkkajae 바닷가재

local 1 *adj* chibang-ŭi 지방의; **I'm not
~** nanŭn igot sarami aniyeyo 나는
이곳 사람이 아니예요 **2** *n* (*person*)
chibang saram 지방 사람

local anesthetic kukppu mach'wi
국부 마취; **local call** TELEC shinae
t'onghwa 시내 통화; **local government** chibang chach'i 지방 자치

locality changso 장소

locally *live, work* kakkaie(sŏ)
가까이에(서)

local produce chibang t'ŭkssanmul
지방 특산물

local time hyŏnji shigan 현지 시간

locate *new factory etc* wich'irŭl
chŏnghada 위치를 정하다; (*identify
position of*) wich'irŭl aranaeda
위치를 알아내다; **be ~d** wich'ihada
위치하다

location (*siting*) wich'i sŏnjŏng 위치
선정; (*identifying position of*)
wich'irŭl aranaem 위치를 알아냄; **on
~** *movie* yaoe ch'waryŏngjung 야외
촬영중

lock¹ (*of hair*) t'arae 타래

lock² 1 *n* (*on door*) chamulsswe
자물쇠 2 v/t *door* chamgŭda 잠그다;
~ **sth in position** muŏsŭl chejarie
kojŏngshik'ida 무엇을 제자리에
고정시키다

♦**lock away** chamulssoerŭl ch'aewŏ
nŏt'a 자물쇠를 채워 넣다

♦**lock in** *person* kaduda 가두다

♦**lock out** (*of house*) mot tŭrŏoge
chamgŭda 못 들어오게 잠그다; **I
was locked out of my office**
yŏlssoega ŏpssŏsŏ samushire mot
tŭrŏgassŏyo 열쇠가 없어서 사무실에
못 들어갔어요

♦**lock up** (*in prison*) kamgŭmhada
감금하다

locker lok'ŏ 로커

locksmith chamulsswe chejogong
자물쇠 제조공

locust mettugi 메뚜기

lodge 1 v/t *complaint* chech'urhada
제출하다 **2** v/i (*of bullet, ball*)
pak'ida 박히다

lodger hasugin 하숙인

loft tarakppang 다락방; (*apartment*)

kŏnmul maen wich'ŭng-ŭi chugŏ konggan 건물 맨 윗층의 주거 공간

lofty *heights* maeu nop'ŭn 매우 높은; *ideals* chigohan 지고한

log (*wood*) t'ongnamu 통나무; (*written record*) ilchi 일지

♦ **log off** chongnyohada 종료하다

♦ **log on** shijak'ada 시작하다

♦ **log on to** …ŭl/rŭl shijak'ada …을/를 시작하다

logbook ilchi 일지

log cabin t'ongnamu odumaktchip 통나무 오두막집

logic nolli 논리

logical nollijŏgin 논리적인

logistics MIL pyŏngch'am ŏmmu 병참 업무; COM sangsehan kyehoek 상세한 계획

logo logo 로고

loiter pindunggŏrida 빈둥거리다

London Lŏndŏn 런던

loneliness oeroum 외로움; (*of place*) korip 고립

lonely *person* oeroun 외로운; *place* koripttoen 고립된

loner honja itkki choahanŭn saram 혼자 있기 좋아하는 사람

long[1] *adj* kin 긴; *it's a ~ way* mŏrŏyo 멀어요; *for a ~ time* oraettong-an 오랫동안 2 *adv* orae 오래; *don't be ~* kkumulgŏriji mara 꾸물거리지 마라; *5 weeks is too ~* tasŏt chunŭn nŏmu kilda 다섯 주는 너무 길다; *will it take ~?* orae kŏllyŏyo? 오래 걸려요?; *that was ~ ago* aju orae chŏniyeyo 아주 오래 전이예요; *~ before then* hwŏlsshin kŭ chŏne 훨씬 그 전에; *before ~* kot 곧; *we can't wait any ~er* urinŭn tŏ isang kidaril su ŏpssŏyo 우리는 더 이상 기다릴 수 없어요; *he no ~er works here* kŭnŭn tŏ isang yŏgi irhaji anayo 그는 더 이상 여기 일하지 않아요; *so ~ as* (*provided*) …hanŭn han …하는 한; *so ~!* annyŏng! 안녕!

long[2] *v/i*: *~ for sth* muŏsŭl aet'age parada 무엇을 애타게 바라다; *be ~ing to do sth* muŏt hanŭn kŏsŭl aet'age parada 무엇 하는 것을 애타게 바라다

long-distance *adj phonecall, race, flight* changgŏriŭi 장거리의

longing *n* kalmang 갈망

longitude kyŏngdo 경도

long jump nŏlbi ttwigi 넓이 뛰기; **long-range** *missile* wŏn-gŏriŭi 원거리의; *forecast* changgijŏgin 장기적인; **long-sighted** sŏn-gyŏnjimyŏng-i innŭn 선견지명이 있는; **long-sleeved** kin somaeŭi 소매의; **long-standing** orae kyesokttoenŭn 오래 계속되는; **long term** *adj* changgiŭi 장기의; **long wave** changp'a 장파

loo *Br* hwajangshil 화장실

look 1 *n* (*appearance*) moyang 모양; (*glance*) pom 봄; *give s.o. / sth a ~ at sth* (*examine*) muŏsŭl / nugurŭl hult'ŏboda 무엇을 / 누구를 훑어보다; *have a ~ at sth* (*examine*) muŏsŭl salp'yŏboda 무엇을 살펴보다; *can I have a ~?* pwado toelkkayo? 봐도 될까요?; *can I have a ~ around?* (*in store etc*) tullŏbwado toelkkayo? 둘러봐도 될까요?; *~s* (*beauty*) yongmo 용모 2 *v/i* poda 보다; (*search*) ch'ajaboda 찾아보다; (*seem*) poida 보이다; *you ~ tired / different* nŏnŭn p'igonhae / talla poinda 너는 피곤해 / 달라보인다

♦ **look after** …ŭl / rŭl posalp'ida …을 / 를 보살피다

♦ **look around** *museum, city* …ŭl / tullŏboda …을 / 를 둘러보다

♦ **look at** …ŭl / rŭl poda …을 / 를 보다; (*examine*) …ŭl / rŭl salp'yŏboda …을 / 를 살펴보다; (*consider*) …ŭl / rŭl koch'arhada …을 / 를 고찰하다

♦ **look back** twidoraboda 뒤돌아보다

♦ **look down on** (*despise*) …ŭl / rŭl natch'uŏ poda …을 / 를 낮추어 보다

♦ **look for** …ŭl / rŭl ch'at-tta …을 / 를 찾다

♦ **look forward to** …ŭl / rŭl kidaehada …을 / 를 기대하다

♦ **look in on** (*visit*) …ŭl / rŭl pangmunhada …을 / 를 방문하다

♦ **look into** (*investigate*) …ŭl / rŭl chosahada …을 / 를 조사하다

♦ **look on** 1 *v/i* (*watch*)

nggwanhada 방관하다 **2** v/t: ~
sth as (consider)
gurŭl/muŏsŭl …(ŭ)ro kanjuhada
구를／무엇을 …(으)로 간주하다
ok onto garden, street …(ŭ)ro
yŏnhada …(으)로 면하다
ok out (of window etc)
kkach'ŭl naedaboda 바깥을
다보다; (pay attention) chuŭihada
의하다; **~!** choshimhae! 조심해!
ok out for …ŭl/rŭl ch'ajaboda
을/를 찾아보다; (be on guard
ainst) …ŭl/rŭl kyŏnggyehada
을/를 경계하다
ok out of window pakkach'ŭl
edaboda 바깥을 내다보다
ok over house, translation
ŭl/rŭl taech'ung hult'ŏboda
을/를 대충 훑어보다
ok through magazine, notes
ŭl/rŭl ch'ŏltchŏhi chosahada
을/를 철저히 조사하다
ok to (rely on) …e ŭijihada …에
지하다
ok up 1 v/i (from paper etc)
'ajaboda 찾아보다; (improve)
altchŏnhada 발전하다; **things are
oking up** iri choajigo it-tta 일이
아지고 있다 **2** v/t word, phone
mber ch'ajaboda 찾아보다; (visit)
angmunhada 방문하다
ok up to (respect) chon-
ŏnghada 존경하다
kout (person) mangbogi 망보기;
e on the ~ for …ŭl/rŭl
ŏnggyehada …을/를 경계하다
om up ŏryŏmp'ushi nat'anada
렴풋이 나타나다
ny F **1** n mich'igwang-i 미치광이
adj mich'in 미친
p n kori 고리
phole (in law etc) hŏtchŏm 허점
se connection, button nŭsŭnhan
슨한; clothes hŏlgŏun 헐거운;
orals pangjonghan 방종한; wording
anmanhan 산만한; **~ change**
andon pusŭrŏgi 잔돈 부스러기; **tie
e ~ ends** kyŏlmarŭl chit-tta
알을 짓다
sely tied hŏlgŏpke 헐겁게;
orded sanmanhage 산만하게

loosen collar, knot nŭsŭnhage hada
느슨하게 하다
loot 1 n yakt'alp'um 약탈품 **2** v/i
yakt'arhada 약탈하다
looter yakt'altcha 약탈자
♦ **lop off** sak-kkamhada 삭감하다
lop-sided hantchogŭro kiurŏjin
한쪽으로 기울어진
Lord (God) Chu 주; **~'s Prayer** Chu
Kidomun 주 기도문
lorry Br t'ŭrŏk 트럭
lose 1 v/t object ilt'a 잃다; match chida
지다 **2** v/i sp chida 지다; (of clock)
nŭjŏjida 늦어지다; **I'm lost** nanŭn
kirŭl irŏbŏryŏssŏyo 나는 길을
잃어버렸어요; **get lost!**
kkŏjyŏbŏryŏ! 꺼져버려!
♦ **lose out** shilp'aehada 실패하다
loser sp p'aeja 패자; (in life) shilp'aeja
실패자
loss (of object) sonshil 손실; (of loved
one) sangshil 상실; (in business)
sonhae 손해; **make a ~** sonhaerŭl
iptta 손해를 입다; **be at a ~** ŏtchihal
parŭl mŏrŭda 어찌할 바를 모르다
lost irŭn 잃은
lost-and-found (office) punshilmul
sent'ŏ 분실물 센터
lot: **a ~ of**, **~s of** manŭn 많은; **a ~**, **~s**
eat, talk etc mani 많이; **a ~ bet-
ter/easier** hwŏlsshin toe
choŭn/shiun 훨씬 더 좋은／쉬운
lotion loshyŏn 로션
loud shikkŭrŏun 시끄러운; color
yoranhan 요란한
loudspeaker hwakssŏnggi 확성기
lounge launji 라운지
♦ **lounge around** pindunggŏrida
빈둥거리다
louse i 이
lousy F (bad) hyŏngp'yŏnŏmnŭn
형편없는
lout shigolttŭgi 시골뜨기
lovable sarangsŭrŏun 사랑스러운
love 1 n sarang 사랑; (in tennis)
mudŭktchŏm 무득점; **be in ~**
saranghago it-tta 사랑하고 있다; **fall
in ~** sarang-e ppajida 사랑에 빠지다;
make ~ sŏng kwan-gyerŭl kajida 성
관계를 가지다; **yes my ~** kŭraeyo
yŏbo 그래요 여보 **2** v/t person,

country saranghada 사랑하다; **~ to do sth** muôt hanŭn kŏsŭl koengjanghi choahada 무엇 하는 것을 굉장히 좋아하다

love affair yŏnae sakkŏn 연애 사건; **love life** sŏngsaenghwal 성생활; **love letter** yŏnae p'yŏnji 연애 편지

lovely *face, hair, color, tune* arŭmdaun 아름다운; *person, character* sarangsŭrŏun 사랑스러운; *holiday, weather, meal* mŏtchin 멋진; **we had a ~ time** urinŭn chŏngmal chŭlgŏpkke ponaessŏyo 우리는 정말 즐겁게 보냈어요

love marriage yŏnae kyŏrhon 연애 결혼

lover aein 애인

loving *adj* aejŏng-i innŭn 애정이 있는

low 1 *adj bridge, wall, voice, quality* najŭn 낮은; *price* ssan 싼; *salary* chagŭn 작은; **be feeling ~** ch'imurhage nŭkkida 침울하게 느끼다; **be ~ on gas/tea** kasŭga/ch'aga kŏŭi ta ttŏrŏjida 가스가/차가 거의 다 떨어지다 **2** *n* (*in weather*) chŏgiap 저기압; (*in sales, statistics*) chŏjo 저조

lowbrow *adj movie, writing* sujuni najŭn 수준이 낮은; *person* kyoyang-i ŏmnŭn 교양이 없는; **low-calorie** chŏk'alloriŭi 저칼로리의; **low-cut** *dress* kasŭmi mani p'ain 가슴이 많이 파인

lower *v/t boat, sth to the ground* naerida 내리다; *flag, hemline* natch'uda 낮추다; *pressure, price* ttŏrŏttŭrida 떨어뜨리다

low-fat chŏjibang-ŭi 저지방의; **lowkey** chajehanŭn 자제하는; **lowlands** chŏji 저지; **low-pressure area** chŏgiap chidae 저기압 지대; **low season** pisugi 비수기; **low tide** ssŏlmul 썰물

loyal ch'ungsŏngsŭrŏun 충성스러운

lozenge (*shape*) marŭmmokkol 마름모꼴; (*tablet*) marŭmmokkol chŏngje 마름모꼴 정제

Ltd (= *limited*) yuhanhoesa 유한회사

lubricant *n* yunhwalche 윤활제

lubricate mikkŭrŏpkke hada

mikkŭrŏpkke hada 미끄럽게 하다

lubrication mikkŭrŏpkke ham 미끄럽게 함

lucid (*clear*) algi shwiun 알기 쉬운 (*sane*) chejŏngshinŭi 제정신의

luck un 운; **bad ~** purun 불운; **hard ~** chaesuŏpkkun! 재수없군!; **good ~** haeng-un 행운; **good ~!** haeng-u pimnida! 행운을 빕니다!

♦**luck out** Γ uni chot'a 운이 좋다

luckily un chok'e 운 좋게

lucky *person* un choŭn 운 좋은; *d number* haeng-unŭl kajyŏonŭn 행운을 가져오는; *coincidence* unttaega mannŭn 운때가 맞는; **yc were ~** nŏn uni choassŏ 넌 운이 좋았어; **he's ~ to be alive** kŭnŭr chok'edo sara namat-tta 그는 운 좋게도 살아 남았다; **that's ~!** kŭ un chŏassŏyo! 그거 운 좋았어요!

ludicrous pabosŭrŏun 바보스러운

luggage suhwamul 수화물

lukewarm *water* mijigŭnhan 미지근한; *reception* naengdamha 냉담한

lull 1 *n* (*in storm, fighting*) chinjŏn 진정; (*in conversation*) chamshi chungdandoem 잠시 중단됨 **2** *v/ s.o. into a false sense of secu* nugurŭl kŏjisŭro anshimshik'ida 누구를 거짓으로 안심시키다

lullaby chajangga 자장가

lumbago yot'ong 요통

lumber *n* (*timber*) chaemok 재목

luminous pich'ŭl naenŭn 빛을 내

lump (*of sugar*) chogak 조각; (*swelling*) hok 혹

♦**lump together** ilgwaljŏgŭro ch'wigŭp'ada 일괄적으로 취급하

lump sum ilsshibul 일시불

lumpy *liquid, sauce* tŏng-ŏri t'usŏ iŭi tŏng-ŏri 투성이의; *mattress* ult'ungbult'unghan 울퉁불퉁한

lunacy mich'in chit 미친 짓

lunar tarŭi 달의

lunar calendar ŭmnyŏk 음력

Lunar New Year Sŏllal 설날

lunatic *n* mich'igwang-i 미치광이

lunch chŏmshim 점심; **have ~** chŏmshimŭl mŏktta 점심을 먹다

lunch box toshirak 도시락; **lunch**

break, lunchtime chŏmshimshigan
점심시간
...ng p'ye 폐
...ng cancer p'yeam 폐암
...lunge at tchirŭda 찌르다
...rch *v/i* pit'ŭlgŏrida 비틀거리다
...re 1 *n* maeryŏk 매력 2 *v/t* sogimsuro
yuhok'ada 속임수로 유혹하다
...rid *color* yoranhan 요란한; *details*
mushimushihan 무시무시한
...rk (*of person*) chambok'ada
잠복하다; (*of doubt*) chamjaehada
잠재하다

luscious *fruit, dessert* talk'omhan
달콤한; *woman, man* kwannŭngjŏgin
관능적인
lust *n* yongmang 욕망
luxurious sach'isŭrŏun 사치스러운
luxury 1 *n* sach'i 사치 2 *adj*
sach'isŭrŏun 사치스러운
lymph gland limp'ŭsaem 림프샘
lynch chipttan p'ok'aeng-ŭl kahada
집단 폭행을 가하다
lynx sŭrasoni 스라소니
lyricist chakssaga 작사가
lyrics kasa 가사

M

MA (= *Master of Arts*) munhak sŏksa 문학 석사
ma'am (*to married woman*) samonim 사모님; (*to unmarried woman*) agassi 아가씨
machine 1 *n* kigye 기계 2 *v/t* (*on sewing machine*) chaebongt'ŭllo pakta 재봉틀로 박다; TECH kigyero saengsanhada 기계로 생산하다
machine gun *n* kigwanch'ong 기관총
machine-readable k'ŏmp'yut'ŏ ch'ŏriga kanŭnghan 컴퓨터 처리가 가능한
machinery (*machines*) kigyeryu 기계류; (*of government, organization*) kigwan 기관
machismo namjadaumŭl kangjoham 남자다움을 강조함
macho namjadaumŭl kangjohan 남자다움을 강조한
mackintosh pangsu oet'u 방수 외투
macro COMPUT maek'ŭro 매크로
mad (*insane*) mich'in 미친; F (*angry*) mich'il tŭshi hwanan 미칠 듯이 화난; **be ~ about** F (*enthusiastic*) …ŭl/rŭl mich'idŭshi choahada …을/를 미치듯이 좋아하다; **drive s.o. ~** nugurŭl mich'igehada 누구를 미치게 하다; **go ~** (*become insane*) mich'yŏgada 미쳐가다; (*with enthusiasm*) kippŏsŏ mich'in tŭshi nalttwida 기뻐서 미친 듯이 날뛰다; **like ~** F run, work mich'in tŭshi 미친 듯이
madden (*infuriate*) mich'il tŭshi hwanage hada 미칠 듯이 화나게 하다
maddening hwaga nasŏ mich'ige hanŭn 화가 나서 미치게 하는
made-to-measure match'umŭi 맞춤의
madhouse *fig* nanjangp'an 난장판
madly mich'in tŭshi 미친 듯이; **~ in love** sarang-e mich'yŏsŏ 사랑에

mich'yŏsŏ
madman mich'igwang-i 미치광이
madness kwangki 광기
Mafia: the ~ Map'ia chojik 마피아 조직
magazine (*printed*) chaptchi 잡지
maggot kudŏgi 구더기
magic 1 *n* masul 마술; (*tricks*) yosul 요술; **like ~** yosulgach'i 요술같이 2 *adj* masurŭi 마술의
magical masuljŏgin 마술적인; *moment* shinbiroun 신비로운
magician (*performer*) masulssa 마술사
magic spell chumun 주문
magic trick yosul 요술
magnanimous kwandaehan 관대한
magnet chasŏk 자석
magnetic chagiŭi 자기의; *personalit* maehoktchŏgin 매혹적인
magnetism chagi 자기; (*of person*) maehok 매혹
magnificence changnyŏham 장려함
magnificent changnyŏhan 장려한; **what a ~ day!** ŏlmana mŏtchin nariyeyo! 얼마나 멋진 날이에요!
magnify hwaktttaehada 확대하다; *difficulties* kwajanghada 과장하다
magnifying glass totppogi 돋보기
magnitude kyumo 규모
mah-jong majak 마작
maid (*servant*) hanyŏ 하녀; (*in hotel*) hot'el chong-ŏbwŏn 호텔 종업원
maiden name kyŏrhon chŏnŭi sŏng 결혼 전의 성
maiden voyage ch'ŏnyŏ hanghae 처녀 항해
mail 1 *n* up'yŏn 우편; **put sth in the ~** muŏsŭl up'yŏnŭro ponaeda 무엇을 우편으로 보내다 2 *v/t letter* p'yŏnjihada 편지하다
mailbox (*in street*) uch'et'ong 우체통; (*of house*) up'yŏnham 우편함; COMPUT meilbakssŭ 메일박스

ailing list chusorok 주소록
ailman uch'ebu 우체부; **mail-order**
catalog t'ongshin p'anmae
ch'aektcha 통신 판매 책자; **mail-
order firm** t'ongshin p'anmae hoesa
통신 판매 회사
aim pulguro mandŭlda 불구로
만들다
ain adj chudoen 주된
ainboard COMPUT meinbodŭ
메인보드; **mainframe** n k'ŏmp'yut'ŏ
ponch'e 컴퓨터 본체; **mainland**
pont'o 본토; **on the ~** pont'oesŏ
본토에서; **mainland China**
Chungguk pont'o 중국 본토
ainly churo 주로
ain road chudoro 주도로
ain street chungshimga 중심가
aintain law and order, speed,
machine, house yujihada 유지하다;
relationship chisok'ada 지속하다; old
building pojonhada 보존하다; family
puyanghada 부양하다; innocence,
guilt chujanghada 주장하다; **~ that**
... ...ranŭn kosŭl chujanghada
...라는 것을 주장하다
aintenance (of machine, house, law
and order) yuji 유지; (of old
building) pojon 보존; (money)
puyangbi 부양비
aitreya Buddha Mirŭkppul 미륵불
ajestic ungdaehan 웅대한
ajor 1 adj (significant) chuyohan
주요한; **in E ~** MUS ta changjo 다
장조 **2** n MIL soryŏng 소령
ajor in ... ŭl/rŭl chŏn-gonghada
...을/를 전공하다
ajority taedasu 대다수; POL
kwabansu 과반수; **be in the ~**
kwabansuida 과반수이다
ake 1 n (brand) sangp'yo 상표 **2** v/t
mandŭlda 만들다; (earn) pŏlda 벌다;
MATH ida 이다; **two and two ~ four**
i tŏhagi inŭn saida 이 더하기 이는
사이다; **~ a decision** kyŏltchŏng-ŭl
hada 결정을 하다; **~ a telephone
call** chŏnhwarŭl hada 전화를 하다;
made in Korea Han-gukssan
한국산; **~ it** (catch bus, train) che
shigane t'ada 제 시간에 타다;
(come) oda 오다; (succeed)

sŏnggonghada 성공하다; (survive)
saranada 살아나다; **I just made it to
the station** kyŏu che shigane yŏge
toch'akaessŏyo 겨우 제 시간에 역에
도착했어요; **what time do you ~ it?**
tangshin shigyenŭn myŏt
shiimnikka? 당신 시계는 몇
시입니까? **~ believe** ...inch'ehada
...인체 하다; **~ do with** ...(ŭ)ro
manjok'ada ...(으)로 만족하다; **what
do you ~ of it?** tangshinŭi
saenggagŭn ŏttŏssŭmnikka? 당신의
생각은 어떻습니까? ◊: **~ s.o. do sth**
(force to) nuguege muŏsŭl shik'ida
누구에게 무엇을 시키다; (cause to)
nugurŭl muŏt'age hada 누구를
무엇하게 하다; **you can't ~ me do
it!** tangshini nahant'e kŭgŏsŭl shik'il
su ŏpssŏyo! 당신이 나한테 그것을
시킬 수 없어요! ◊: **~ s.o.
happy / angry** nugurŭl
haengbok'age / hwanage hada 누구를
행복하게 / 화나게 하다
◆ **make for** (go toward) ...ro kada
...로 가다
◆ **make off** taranada 달아나다
◆ **make off with** (steal) humch'ida
훔치다
◆ **make out** v/t list chakssŏnghada
작성하다; check ssŭda 쓰다; (see)
poda 보다; (imply) nŏnjishi pich'uda
넌지시 비추다
◆ **make over: make X over to Y**
Xrŭl Yege mullyŏjuda X를 Y에게
물려주다
◆ **make up 1** v/i (of woman, actor)
hwajanghada 화장하다; (after
quarrel) hwahaehada 화해하다 **2** v/t
story, excuse kkumida 꾸미다; face
hwajanghada 화장하다; (constitute)
kusŏnghada 구성하다; **be made up
of** ...(ŭ)ro kusŏngdoeŏ itta ...(으)로
구성되어 있다; **~ one's mind**
maŭmŭl chŏnghada 마음을 정하다;
make it up (after quarrel)
hwahaehada 화해하다
◆ **make up for** (compensate for)
pŏlch'unghada 벌충하다
make-believe n kkumin kŏt 꾸민 것
maker saengsanja 생산자
makeshift imshi sudan 임시 수단

make-up (*cosmetics*) hwajangp'um 화장품

maladjusted chŏgŭng-ŭl mot'anŭn 적응을 못하는

Malay (*language*) Malleiŏ 말레이어; (*person*) Malleishia saram 말레이시아 사람

Malaysia Malleishia 말레이시아

Malaysian Malleishiain 말레이시아인

male 1 *adj* (*masculine*) namsŏng-ŭi 남성의; *animal, bird, fish* suk'ŏsŭi 수컷의 **2** *n* (*man*) namja 남자; (*animal, bird, fish*) suk'ŏt 수컷

male chauvinist (*pig*) namsŏng uwŏltchuŭija 남성 우월주의자

male nurse namja kanhosa 남자 간호사

malevolent agŭi innŭn 악의 있는

malfunction 1 *n* chakttong pullyang 작동 불량 **2** *v/i* chakttong-i chal toeji ant'a 작동이 잘 되지 않다

malice agŭi 악의

malicious agŭi innŭn 악의 있는

malignant *tumor* akssŏng-ŭi 악성의

mall (*shopping ~*) sangga 상가

malnutrition yŏngnyang shiltcho 영양 실조

malpractice kwashil 과실

maltreat hakttaehada 학대하다

maltreatment hakttae 학대

mammal p'oyu tongmul 포유 동물

mammoth *adj* (*enormous*) kŏdaehan 거대한

man *n* namja 남자; (*human being*) saram 사람; (*humanity*) illyu 인류; (*in chess, checkers*) mal 말

manage 1 *v/t business* kwallihada 관리하다; *big company* kyŏngnyŏnghada 경영하다; *money* kkuryŏgada 꾸려가다; *bags* taruda 다루다; *~ to ...* irŏktchŏrŏk ... haenaeda 이럭저럭 ... 해내다 **2** *v/i* (*cope*) kyŏndida 견디다; (*financially*) kkuryŏnagada 꾸려나가다; *can you ~?* tangshini hal su issŭmnikka? 당신이 할 수 있습니까?

manageable tarugi shwiun 다루기 쉬운

management kwalli 관리; (*of big company*) kyŏngnyŏng 경영;

(*managers*) kyŏngnyŏngjin 경영진 *under his ~* kuŭi kwalliha-e 그의 관리하에; (*of big company*) kuŭi kyŏngnyŏngha-e 그의 경영하에

management buyout kyŏngnyŏngkkwŏn maemae 경영권 매매; **management consultant** kyŏngnyŏng sangdamja 경영 상담자; **management studies** kyŏngnyŏnghak 경영학; **management team** kyŏngnyŏngt'im 경영팀

manager (*of department*) kwalliin 관리인; (*of factory, of people*) kwallija 관리자; (*of company*) kyŏngnyŏngja 경영자; (*executive*) kyŏngnyŏng-in 경영인; (*of shop, restaurant, hotel*) chibaein 지배인

managerial kwalliŭi 관리의

managing director pujang 부장

Mandarin (*language*) Chungguk Pukkyŏng-ŏ 중국 북경어

mandarin (*in China*) kwalli 관리

mandarin orange kyul 귤

mandate (*authority*) kwŏnhan puyŏ 권한 부여; (*task*) immu 임무

mandatory ŭimujŏgin 의무적인

mane (*of horse*) kalgi 갈기

maneuver 1 *n* umjigim 움직임; *fig* ch'aengnyak 책략 **2** *v/t* kyomyohi umjigida 교묘히 움직이다

mangle *v/t* (*crush*) tchiburŏttŭrida 찌부러뜨리다

manhandle *person* kŏch'ilge taeha 거칠게 대하다; *object* illyŏgŭro umjigida 인력으로 움직이다

manhood (*maturity*) sŏngnyŏn 성년; (*virility*) namjadaum 남자다움

man-hour irindang han shiganŭi nodongnyang 일인당 한 시간의 노동량

manhunt pŏmin susaek 범인 수색

mania (*craze*) ...kwang ...광

maniac mich'in saram 미친 사람

manicure *n* maenik'yuŏ 매니큐어

manifest 1 *adj* myŏngbaek'an 명백한 **2** *v/t* myŏngbaek'age hada 명백하게 하다; *~ itself* nat'anada 나타나다

manipulate *person* chojonghada 조종하다; *bones* kyojŏnghada 교정하다

manipulation (*of person*) chojong

조종; (*of bones*) kyojŏng 교정
anipulative chojonghanŭn 조종하는
ankind illyu 인류
anly namjadaun 남자다운
an-made in-gong 인공
annequin (*for clothes*) manek'ing
마네킹
anner (*of doing sth*) pangshik 방식;
(*attitude*) t'aedo 태도
anners: **good/bad ~** yeŭi
parŭm/ŏpssŭm 예의 바름/없음;
have no ~ yeŭiga ŏptta 예의가 없다
anpower illyŏk 인력
ansion chŏt'aek 저택
antelpiece pyŏngnallo wiŭi sŏnban
벽난로 위의 선반
anual 1 *adj* sonŭro hanŭn 손으로
하는; **~ labor** sonil 손일; **a ~ worker**
yukch'e nodongja 육체 노동자 2 *n*
sŏlmyŏngsŏ 설명서
anufacture 1 *n* chejoŏp 제조업 2 *v/t*
equipment chejohada 제조하다
anufacturer chejoŏptcha 제조업자
anufacturing (*industry*) kong-ŏp
공업
anure piryo 비료
anuscript wŏn-go 원고; **original ~**
wŏnbon 원본
any 1 *adj* manŭn 많은; **~ times** yŏrŏ
pŏn 여러 번; **not ~ people/taxis**
kŭri manch'i anŭn saram/t'aeksshi
그리 많지 않은 사람/택시; **too ~**
problems/beers nŏmu manŭn
munjedŭl/maektchu 너무 많은
문제들/맥주 2 *pron* manŭn kŏt 많은
것; (*people*) manŭn saram 많은 사람;
a great ~, a good ~ taedanhi
manŭn 대단히 많은; **how ~ do you
need?** ŏlmana mani
p'iryohashimnikka? 얼마나 많이
필요하십니까?
ap *n* chido 지도
map out *career etc* sangsehi
kyehoek'ada 상세히 계획하다
aple tanp'ungnamu 단풍나무
ar mangch'yŏnot'a 망쳐놓다
arathon (*race*) marat'on 마라톤
arble (*material*) taerisŏk 대리석
arch samwŏl 삼월; **1st ~ Memorial
Day** Samiltchŏl 삼일절; **~ First
Movement** Samil Undong 삼일

운동
march 1 *n* haengjin 행진;
(*demonstration*) temo haengjin 데모
행진 2 *v/i* haengjinhada 행진하다; (*in
protest*) temo haengjinhada 데모
행진하다
Mardi Gras Osunjŏrŭi Hwayoil
오순절의 화요일
mare ammal 암말
margarine magarin 마가린
margin (*of page*) yŏbaek 여백; (*profit
~*) imun 이문; **by a narrow ~** kyŏu
겨우
marginal (*slight*) chŏgŭn 적은
marginally (*slightly*) chogŭm 조금
marihuana, marijuana taemach'o
대마초
marina yot'ŭ kyeryujang 요트 계류장
marinade *n* maerineidŭ 매리네이드
marinate chŏrida 절이다
marine 1 *adj* padaŭi 바다의 2 *n* MIL
haegun 해군
Marine Corps Haebyŏngdae 해병대
marital kyŏrhonŭi 결혼의
maritime haeyangŭi 해양의
mark 1 *n* (*stain*) ŏlluk 얼룩; (*sign,
token*) p'yoshi 표시; (*trace*) chach'wi
자취; EDU sŏngjŏk 성적; **leave one's
~** yŏnghyang-ŭl namgida 영향을
남기다 2 *v/t* (*stain*) chagugŭl naeda
자국을 내다; EDU sŏngjŏgŭl ŏt-tta
성적을 얻다; (*indicate*) p'yoshihada
표시하다; (*commemorate*)
kinyŏmhada 기념하다 3 *v/i* (*of
fabric*) chagungnada 자국나다
♦ **mark down** *price* kagyŏgŭl naerida
가격을 내리다
♦ **mark out** (*with a line etc*) sŏnŭl kŭt-
tta 선을 긋다; *fig* (*set apart*) karŭda
가르다
♦ **mark up** *price* kagyŏgŭl ollida
가격을 올리다; *goods* p'yoshihada
표시하다
marked (*definite*) hwaksshirhan
확실한
marker (*highlighter*)
hyŏnggwangp'en 형광펜
market 1 *n* shijang 시장; (*stock ~*)
chushik shijang 주식 시장; **on the ~**
shijang-e 시장에 2 *v/t* p'anmaehada
판매하다

market economy shijang kyŏngje 시장 경제

market forces shijangnyŏk 시장력

marketing maemae 매매

market leader shijang-ŭi sŏndujuja 시장의 선두주자; **marketplace** (*in town*) shijang 시장; (*for commodities*) maemae changso 매매 장소; **market research** shijang chosa 시장 조사; **market share** shijang chŏmmyuyul 시장 점유율

mark-up kagyŏk insang 가격 인상

marmalade mamalleidŭ 마말레이드

marquee taehyŏng ch'ŏnmak 대형 천막

marriage (*institution*) kyŏrhon 결혼; (*state of being married*) kyŏrhon saenghwal 결혼 생활; (*event*) kyŏrhonshik 결혼식

marriage certificate kyŏrhon chŭngmyŏngsŏ 결혼 증명서

marriage counselor kyŏrhon sangdamwŏn 결혼 상담원

married kihonŭi 기혼의, kyŏrhonhan 결혼한; **a ~ man** kihon namsŏng 기혼 남성, yubunam 유부남; **be ~ to …** …wa/kwa kyŏrhonhada …와/과 결혼하다

marry kyŏrhonhada 결혼하다; (*perform ceremony*) churyehada 주례하다; **get married** kyŏrhonhada 결혼하다

marsh sŭptchi 습지

marshal *n* (*police officer*) kyŏngch'algwan 경찰관; (*official*) haengsa wiwŏn 행사 위원

marshmallow mashimaello 마시맬로

marshy sŭptchiŭi 습지의

martial arts musul 무술

martial law kyeŏmnyŏng 계엄령

martyr *n* sun-gyoja 순교자; *fig* hŭisaengja 희생자

marvel *n* nollaŭn kŏt 놀라운 것; **you're a ~** tangshinŭn taedanhagunyo 당신은 대단하군요 ◆ **marvel at** …e nollada …에 놀라다

marvelous koengjanghi chŏun 굉장히 좋은

Marxism Marŭk'ŭsŭjuŭi 마르크스주의

Marxist 1 *adj* Marŭk'ŭsŭjuŭiŭi

마르크스주의의 **2** *n* Marŭk'ŭsŭjuŭi 마르크스주의자

mascara masŭk'ara 마스카라

mascot haeng-unŭl kajyŏonŭn kŏt 행운을 가져오는 것, masŭk'ot'ŭ 마스코트

masculine *also* GRAM namsŏngjŏg 남성적인

masculinity namsŏngmi 남성미

mash *v/t* ŭkkaeda 으깨다

mashed potatoes ŭkkaen kamja 으깬 감자, maeshit'ŭ p'ot'eit'o 매시트 포테이토

mask 1 *n* kamyŏn 가면 **2** *v/t feelings* kamch'uda 감추다

mask dance t'alch'um 탈춤

masochism maejŏk'ijŭm 매저키즘

masochist maejŏk'isŭt'ŭ 매저키스트

mason sŏkssu 석수

masonry tol segong 돌 세공

masquerade 1 *n fig* kajang 가장 **2 ~ as** … in ch'ŏk'ada … 인 척하다

mass[1] **1** *n* (*great amount*) taryang 다량; (*body*) k'ŭn tŏng-ŏri 큰 덩어리; **a solid ~** koch'e 고체; **the ~es** taejung 대중; **~es of** aju manŭn 아주 많은 **2** *v/i* moida 모이다

mass[2] REL misa 미사

massacre 1 *n* taeryang hakssal 대량 학살; F (*in sport*) ch'amp'ae 참패 **2** *v/t* hakssarhada 학살하다; F (*in sport*) ch'ampaeshik'ida 참패시키다

massage 1 *n* anma 안마, masaji 마사지 **2** *v/t* anmahada 안마하다; *figures* ŏlbŏmurida 얼버무리다

massage parlor *euph* maech'un-gul 매춘굴

masseur (*namja*) anmasa (남자) 안마사

masseuse (*yŏja*) anmasa (여자) 안마사

massive kŏdaehan 거대한

mass media taejung maech'e 대중 매체; **mass-produce** taeryang saengsanhada 대량 생산하다; **mass production** taeryang saengsan 대량 생산

mast (*of ship*) tot-ttae 돛대; (*for radio*) taehyŏng ant'ena 대형 안테나

master 1 *n* (*of dog*) chuin 주인; (*of ship*) sŏnjang 선장; **be a ~ of** …e

hŏngt'onghada ..에 정통하다 **2** *v/t*
kill, language chŏngt'onghada
통하다; *situation* t'ongjehada
통제하다
aster bedroom anppang 안방
aster key masŭt'ŏk'i 마스터키
asterly hullyunghan 훌륭한
astermind 1 *n* ch'idoja 지도자 **2** *v/t*
wiesŏ chidohada 뒤에서 지도하다;
Master of Arts munhak sŏksa 문학
석사; **master of ceremonies**
ahoeja 사회자; **masterpiece**
nyŏngjak 명작; **master's (degree)**
ŏksa(hagwi) 석사(학위)
astery chŏngbok 정복
asturbate chawihada 자위하다
at *n* (*for floor*) chari 자리, maet'ŭ
매트; (*for table*) t'eibŭl po 테이블 보
atch¹ (*for cigarette*) sŏngnyang 성냥
atch² **1** *n* (*competition*) shihap 시합;
e no - for s.o. nuguŭi sandaega
andoeda 누구의 상대가 안되다;
meet one's - hojŏkssurŭl mannada
호적수를 만나다 **2** *v/t* (*go with*)
ŏullida 어울리다; (*equal*) …e
piltchŏk'ada …에 필적하다 **3** *v/i* (*of
colors, patterns*) ŏullida 어울리다
atchbox sŏngnyangkkap 성냥갑
atching *adj* ŏullinŭn 어울리는
ate 1 *n* (*of animal*) tchak 짝; NAUT
anghaesa 항해사 **2** *v/i* tchaktchit-tta
작짓다
aterial 1 *n* (*fabric*) otkkam 옷감;
substance) chaeryo 재료 **2** *adj*
multchirŭi 물질의; (*not spiritual*)
esoktchŏgin 세속적인
aterialism yumullon 유물론
aterialist yumullonja 유물론자
aterialistic yumullonjŏgin
유물론적인
aterialize shilch'ehwahada
실체화하다
aterials charyo 자료
aternal ŏmŏniŭi 어머니의; *relative*
mogyeŭi 모계의; **- grandfather**
oeharabŏji 외할아버지
aternity mosŏng 모성
aternity dress imsanbok 임산복;
maternity hospital sanbuinkkwa
산부인과; **maternity leave** ch'ulsan
hyuga 출산 휴가; **maternity ward**

sanbuinkkwa pyŏngdong 산부인과
병동
math suhak 수학
mathematical *calculations, formula*
suhagŭi 수학의; *mind, person* suhage
nŭnghan 수학에 능한
mathematician suhaktcha 수학자
mathematics suhak 수학
matinée (*of play*) chugan kongnyŏn
주간 공연; (*of movie*) chugan
sangnyŏng 주간 상영
matriarch yŏgajang 여가장
matrimony kyŏrhon 결혼
matt kwangt'aegi ŏmnŭn 광택이 없는
matter (*affair*) sakkŏn 사건; PHYS
multchil 물질; **as a - of course**
tangnyŏnhi 당연히; **as a - of fact**
sashirŭn 사실은; **what's the -?**
musŭn iri issŭmnikka? 무슨 일이
있습니까?; **no - what she says**
kunyŏga muŏshirago marhadŭn
kane 그녀가 무엇이라고 말하든 간에
2 *v/i* chungnyohada 중요하다; **it
doesn't -** kŭgŏsŭn sanggwanŏptta
그것은 상관없다
matter-of-fact tamdamhan 담담한
mattress maet'ŭrisŭ 매트리스
mature 1 *adj* sŏngsuk'an 성숙한 **2** *v/i*
(*of person*) sŏngsuk'ada 성숙하다;
(*of insurance policy etc*) man-giga
toeda 만기가 되다
maturity (*adulthood*) sŏngsuk-kki
성숙기; (*in behavior, attitude*)
sŏngsuk'am 성숙함
maximize ch'oedaehwahada
최대화하다
maximum 1 *adj* ch'oedaeŭi 최대의
2 *n* ch'oedae 최대
May owŏl 오월
may ◊ (*possibility*) …iltchido
morŭnda …일지도 모른다; **it - rain**
piga oltchido morŭnda 비가 올지도
모른다; **you - be right** nega majŭl
chido morŭnda 네가 맞을 지도
모른다; **it - not happen** irŏnaji
annŭl jido mŏrŭnda 일어나지 않을
지도 모른다 ◊ (*permission*) …haedo
chot'a …해도 좋다; **you - go now**
inje kado chossŭmnida 인제 가도
좋습니다; **- I help?** towa
tŭrilkkayo? 도와 드릴까요?; **- I**

smoke? tambae p'iwodo toegessŭmnikka? 담배 피워도 되겠습니까?; *you ~ if you like* wŏnhashindamyŏn, hasyŏdo kwanch'ansŭmnida 원하신다면, 하셔도 괜찮습니다 ◊ *(wish, hope)* ...hagirŭl parada ...하기를 바라다; *~ you both be very happy* tubuni haengbok'ashigirŭl paramnida 두분이 함께 항상 행복하시기를 바랍니다

maybe amado 아마도

May Day Nodongjŏl 노동절

mayo, mayonnaise mayonejŭ 마요네즈

mayor shijang 시장

maze miro 미로

MB (= *megabyte*) megabait'ŭ 메가바이트

MBA (= *Master's in Business Administration*) kyŏngnyŏnghak sŏkssa 경영학 석사

MBO (= *management buyout*) kyŏngnyŏngkkwŏn maemae 경영권 매매

MD (= *Doctor of Medicine*) ŭihak paksa 의학 박사

me na 나; ㅂ chŏ 저; *it's ~* nada 나다; ㅂ chŏimnida 저입니다; *he knows ~* kŭnŭn narŭl anda 그는 나를 안다; *that's for ~* naŭi kŏshida 나의 것이다

meadow ch'owŏn 초원

meager pulch'ŭngbunhan 불충분한

meal shikssa 식사

mealtime shikssa shigan 식사 시간

mean¹ *(with money)* insaek'an 인색한; *(nasty)* mot-ttoen 못된

mean² 1 *v/t (intend)* ŭidohada 의도하다; *(signify)* ŭimihada 의미하다; *~ to do sth* muŏsŭl haryŏgo hada 무엇을 하려고 하다; *be ~t for* ...ŭl/rŭl wihan kŏshida ...을/를 위한 것이다; *(of remark)* ...ŭl/rŭl tugo marhada ...을/를 두고 말하다; *doesn't it ~ anything to you?* *(doesn't it matter?)* tangshinege amu sanggwan ŏpssŏyo? 당신에게 아무 상관 없어요? 2 *v/i: ~ well* chŏŭn ŭidorŭl

kajida 좋은 의도를 가지다

meaning *(of word)* ŭimi 의미

meaningful *(comprehensible)* ihaeganŭn 이해가는; *glance* ŭimiinnŭn 의미있는

meaningless muŭimihan 무의미한

means *(financial)* chaesan 재산; *(way)* sudan 수단; *~ of transport* kyot'ong sudan 교통 수단; *by all ~ (certainly)* mullon 물론; *by no ~ poor* kyŏlk'o kananhaji ant'a 결코 가난하지 않다; *by ~ of* ...ŭl/rŭl ssŏsŏ ...을/를 써서

meantime: *in the ~* kŭ saie 그 사이

measles hongnyŏk 홍역

measure 1 *n (step)* pangch'aek 방책 *(certain amount)* ŏnŭ chŏngdo 어느 정도 2 *v/t ch'issurŭl chaeda 치수를 재다 3 *v/i* chaeŏjida 재어지다

♦ measure out pullyang-ŭl chaeda 분량을 재다

♦ measure up to ... mank'ŭm chal hada ... 만큼 잘 하다

measurement *(action)* ch'ŭktchŏng 측정; *~s (dimensions)* ch'issu 치수; *system of ~* ch'ŭktchŏngppŏp 측정법

meat kogi 고기

meatball kogi wanja 고기 완자

meatloaf mitŭ lop'ŭ 미트 로프, chŏmin kogiwa ppanggaru, kyeran nŏk'o obŭne kuun tŏng-ŏri 저민 고기와 빵가루, 계란을 넣고 오븐에 구운 덩어리

mechanic kigyegong 기계공

mechanical *device* kigyeŭi 기계의; *gesture* kigyejŏgin 기계적인

mechanically *do sth* kigyejŏgŭro 기계적으로

mechanism kigye changch'i 기계 장치

mechanize kigyehwahada 기계화하다

medal medal 메달

medalist susangja 수상자

meddle kansŏp'ada 간섭하다; *~ with* ...ŭl/rŭl manjijak-kkŏrida ...을/를 만지작거리다

media: *the ~* maesŭk'ŏm 매스컴

media hype maesŭk'ŏmŭi kwajang 매스컴의 과장

median strip chung-ang pullidae 중잉

분리대
mediate chungjaehada 중재하다
mediation chungjae 중재
mediator chungjaein 중재인
medical 1 adj ŭihagŭi 의학의; ~
treatment ch'iryo 치료; ~ **insurance** ŭiryo pohŏm 의료 보험; ~
problem kŏn-gang munje 건강 문제
2 n shinch'e kŏmsa 신체 검사
medical certificate chindansŏ 진단서
Medicare noin ŭiryo pojang chedo
노인 의료 보장 제도
medicated yagyong-ŭi 약용의
medication yak 약
medicinal yagŭi 약의
medicine (science) ŭihak 의학;
(medication) yak 약
medieval chungseŭi 중세의; fig
kushigŭi 구식의
mediocre chillajŭn 질낮은
mediocrity (of work etc) chillajŭm
질낮음; (person) chŏjil 저질
meditate myŏngsanghada 명상하다;
(of Christian) mukssanghada
묵상하다; (of Buddhist monk)
ch'amsŏnhada 참선하다
meditation myŏngsang 명상; (in
Christianity) mukssang 묵상; (in
Buddhism) ch'amsŏn 참선
medium 1 adj (average) chungganŭi
중간의; (steak) pantch'ŭm ik'in 반쯤
익힌 **2** n (in size) chunggan k'ŭgi
중간 크기; (vehicle) maech'e 매체;
(spiritualist) yŏngmae 영매
medium-sized chunggan k'ŭgiŭi 중간
크기의
medium wave RAD chungp'a 중파
medley (mixture) kagyanggakssaek
각양각색; (of songs) medŭlli 메들리
meek yamjŏnhan 얌전한
meet 1 v/t mannada 만나다; (collect)
majunghagada 마중나가다; (in
competition) matssŏda 맞서다; (of
eyes) majuch'ida 마주치다; (satisfy)
ch'ungjokshik'ida 충족시키다 **2** v/i
mannada 만나다; (in competition)
taejŏnhada 대전하다; (of eyes)
majuch'ida 마주치다; (of committee
etc) moida 모이다 **3** n SP kyŏnggi
경기
♦ **meet with** person …wa/kwa

mannada …와/과 만나다; approval
pat-tta 받다; success, failure
majihada 맞이하다
meeting mannam 만남; (of
committee, in business) hoeŭi 회의;
he's in a ~ kŭnŭn hoeŭi chung-ida
그는 회의 중이다
meeting place yakssok changso 약속
장소
megabyte COMPUT megabait'ŭ
메가바이트
melancholy adj ultchŏk'an 울적한
mellow 1 adj kammiroun 감미로운;
fruit, wine sukssŏnghan 숙성한; color
pudŭroun 부드러운; person
wŏnsuk'an 원숙한 **2** v/i (of person)
wŏnsuk'ada 원숙하다
melodious koktchoga arŭmdaun
곡조가 아름다운
melodramatic melodŭramagat'ŭn
멜로드라마같은
melody melodi 멜로디, sŏnnyul 선율
melon melon 멜론
melt 1 v/i noktta 녹다 **2** v/t nogida
녹이다
♦ **melt away** fig sŏsŏhi sarajida
서서히 사라지다
♦ **melt down** metal nogida 녹이다
melting pot fig togani 도가니
member irwŏn 일원; ~ **of Congress**
kuk'oe ŭiwŏn 국회 의원
membership hoewŏn chagyŏk 회원
자격; (number of members) hoewŏn
su 회원 수
membership card hoewŏntchŭng
회원증
membrane mak 막
memento kinyŏmmul 기념물
memo memo 메모, kirok 기록
memoirs hoegorok 회고록
memorable kiŏk'al manhan 기억할
만한
memorial 1 adj kinyŏmŭi 기념의 **2** n
kinyŏmbi 기념비
Memorial Day Hyŏnch'ung-il 현충일
memorize amgihada 암기하다
memory (recollection) kiŏk 기억;
(emotionally tinged) ch'uŏk 추억;
(power of recollection) kiŏngnyŏk
기억력; COMPUT yongnyang 용량,
memori 메모리; **have a good/bad**

~ kiŏngnyŏgi chot'a / nappŭda 기억력이 좋다 / 나쁘다; **in ~ of** ...ŭl / rŭl kinyŏmhamyŏ ...을 / 를 기념하며

menace 1 n (threat) wihyŏp 위협; (person) wihŏm inmul 위험 인물 **2** v/t wihyŏp'ada 위협하다

menacing wihyŏp'anŭn 위협하는

mend v/t koch'ida 고치다; clothes, shoes susŏnhada 수선하다; **be on the ~** (after illness) tŏ naajida 더 나아지다

menial adj ch'ŏnhan 천한

meningitis noemangnyŏm 뇌막염

menopause p'yegyŏnggi 폐경기

men's room namja hwajangshil 남자 화장실

menstruate wŏlgyŏnghada 월경하다, saengnihada 생리하다

menstruation wŏlgyŏng 월경, saengni 생리

mental chŏngshinŭi 정신의; torture, suffering maŭmŭi ch'ŏthe 마음의; F (crazy) chŏngshinppyŏng-ŭi 정신병의

mental arithmetic amsan 암산; **mental cruelty** chŏngshintchŏk hakttae 정신적 학대; **mental hospital** chŏngshin pyŏng-wŏn 정신 병원; **mental illness** chŏngshinppyŏng 정신병

mentality chŏngshin sangt'ae 정신 상태

mentally (inwardly) maŭm sogŭro 마음 속으로; calculate chitchŏgŭro 지적으로; **~ handicapped** chŏngshintchŏk chang-aeja innŭn 정신적 장애가 있는; **~ ill** chŏngshinppyŏng-i innŭn 정신병이 있는

mention 1 n ŏn-gŭp 언급 **2** v/t ŏn-gŭp'ada 언급하다; **don't ~ it** (you're welcome) ch'ŏnmaneyo 천만에요

mentor choryŏktcha 조력자

menu (for food) shikttan 식단, menyu 메뉴; COMPUT menyu 메뉴

mercenary 1 adj tonŭl moktchŏgŭro hanŭn 돈을 목적으로 하는 **2** n MIL yongbyŏng 용병

merchandise sangp'um 상품

merchant sang-in 상인

merciful chabiroun 자비로운

mercifully (thankfully) tahaengsŭrŏpkkedo 다행스럽게도

merciless mujabihan 무자비한

mercury suŭn 수은

mercy chabi 자비; **be at s.o.'s ~** nuguŭi maŭmdaero toeda 누구의 마음대로 되다

mere tanji 단지

merely tanji 단지

merge v/i (of two lines etc) hapch'ida 합치다; (of companies) happyŏnghada 합병하다

merger COM hap-pyŏng 합병

merit 1 n (worth) kach'i 가치; (advantage) changtchŏm 장점 **2** v/t ...hal kach'iga it-tta ...할 가치가 있다

merry yuk'waehan 유쾌한; **Merry Christmas!** chŭlgŏun Sŏngt'ani toegirŭl paramnida! 즐거운 성탄이 되기를 바랍니다!

merry-go-round hoejŏn mongma 회전 목마

mesh n kŭmul 그물

mess n (untidiness) ŏngmang-in kŏt 엉망인 것; (trouble) kon-gyŏng 곤경 **be a ~** (of room, desk, hair) ŏngmang-ida 엉망이다; (of situation s.o.'s life) hollansŭrŏpt-tta 혼란스럽다

♦ **mess around 1** v/i pindanggŏrida 빈둥거리다 **2** v/t person hollanshik'ida 혼란시키다

♦ **mess around with** ...ŭl / rŭl katkko nolda ...을 / 를 갖고 놀다; s.o.'s wife ...wa / kwa param p'iuda ...와 / 과 바람 피우다

♦ **mess up** room, papers ŏjirŭda 어지르다; plans, marriage mangch'yŏ not'a 망쳐 놓다

message chŏnhanŭn mal 전하는 말, mesiji 메시지; (of movie, book) kyohun 교훈

messenger meshinjŏ 메신저; (courier) paedalbu 배달부

messy room ŏjiroun 어지러운; person hollanhage hanŭn 혼란하게 하는; job chijŏbunhan 지저분한; divorce, situation nanch'ŏhan 난처한

metabolism shinjindaesa 신진대사

metal 1 n kŭmsok 금속 **2** adj

ŭmsogŭi 금속의

etallic kŭmsoksŏng-ŭi 금속성의

eteor yusŏng 유성

eteoric *fig* yusŏnggat'ŭn 유성같은

eterorite unsŏk 운석

eteorological kisanghagŭi 기상학의

eteorologist kisanghaktcha 기상학자

eterology kisanghak 기상학

eter¹ *(for gas etc)* kyeryanggi 계량기; *(parking ~, in cab)* yogŭm yesan-gi 요금 계산기

eter² *(unit of length)* mit'ŏ 미터

ethod pangbŏp 방법

ethodical iltchŏnghan pangshige tarŭn 일정한 방식에 따른

ethodically iltchŏnghan pangshigŭro 일정한 방식으로

ethodist Church Kamni Kyohoe 감리 교회

eticulous seshimhan 세심한

etric mit'ŏppŏbŭi 미터법의

etropolis taedoshi 대도시; *(capital city)* sudo 수도

etropolitan *adj* taedoshiŭi 대도시의

ew → *miaow*

exican 1 *adj* Mekshik'oŭi 멕시코의 **2** *n* Mekshik'oin 멕시코인

exico Mekshik'o 멕시코

ezzanine *(floor)* chungch'ŭng 중층

iaow 1 *n* yaong 야옹 **2** *v/i* yaonghago ulda 야옹하고 울다

ickey mouse *adj* F *pej: course, qualification* kach'iŏmnŭn 가치없는

icrochip maik'ŭroch'ip 마이크로칩;

icrocosm souju 소우주; **microelectronics** kŭkso chŏnja konghak 극소 전자 공학; **microfilm** maik'ŭrop'illŭm 마이크로필름; **microphone** maik'ŭ마이크; **microprocessor** maik'ŭrop'ŭrosesŏ 마이크로프로세서; **microscope** hyŏnmigyŏng 현미경; **microscopic** kŭk'i chagŭn 극히 작은; **microwave** *(oven)* chŏnjarenji 전자렌지

idair: *in ~* kongjung-esŏ 공중에서

idday chŏng-o 정오

iddle 1 *adj* chunggan-ŭi 중간의 **2** *n* kaunde 가운데; *in the ~ of (floor, room)* ...ŭi chung-ang-esŏ ...의 중앙에서; *(period of time)* ... chung-

---

e ... 중에; *in the ~ of the night* hanbam chung-e 한밤 중에; *be in the ~ of doing sth* muŏsŭl hanŭn chung-ida 무엇을 하는 중이다

middle-aged chungnyŏnŭi 중년의; **Middle Ages** Chungse 중세; **middle-class** *adj* chungsanch'ŭng-ŭi 중산층의; **middle class(es)** chungsanch'ŭng 중산층; **Middle East** Chungdong 중동; **middleman** chunggan sang-in 중간 상인; **middle name** chunggan irŭm 중간 이름; **middleweight** *n (boxer)* chunggankkŭp 중간급

middling kŭjŏ kŭrŏn 그저 그런

midget *adj* ch'osohyŏng-ŭi 초소형의

midnight chajŏng 자정; *at ~* chajŏng-e 자정에; **midsummer** hannyŏrŭm 한여름; **midway** chungdo-e 중도에; **midweek** *adv* chujung-e 주중에; **Midwest** Chungsŏbu 중서부; **midwife** chosanwŏn 조산원; **midwinter** hangyŏul 한겨울

might¹ ...iltchido morŭnda ...일지도 모른다; *I ~ be late* chŏnŭn ama nŭjŭltchido morŭgessŭmnida 저는 아마 늦을지도 모르겠습니다; *it ~ rain* piga oltchido morŭgessŭmnida 비가 올지도 모르겠습니다; *it ~ never happen* kŭgŏsŭn ama tashinŭn irŏnaji anŭl kŏshimnida 그것은 아마 다시는 일어나지 않을 것입니다; *I ~ have lost it* chŏnŭn kŭgŏsŭl irŏpoaryŏnnŭnjido morŭgessŭmnida 저는 그것을 잃어버렸는지도 모르겠습니다; *he ~ have left* hokshi kŭga ttŏnassŭltchi morŭgessŭmnida 혹시 그가 떠났을지 모르겠습니다; *you ~ as well spend the night here* tanshindo yŏgisŏ pamŭl ponaeya haltchi morŭmnida 당신도 여기서 밤을 보내야 할지 모릅니다; *you ~ have told me!* chinjak naege marŭl haessŏyaji! 진짝 내게 말을 했어야지!

might² *n (power)* him 힘

mighty 1 *adj* himinnŭn 힘있는 **2** *adv* F *(extremely)* maeu 매우

migraine p'yŏndŭt'ong 편두통

migrant worker iju nodongja 이주 노동자

migrate ijuhada 이주하다

migration iju 이주

mike maik'ǔ 마이크

mild *weather, climate, person* onhwahan 온화한; *taste* sunhan 순한; *voice* pudǔrǒun 부드러운

mildly pudǔrǒpke 부드럽게

mildew komp'ang-i 곰팡이

mildness (*of weather, climate*) onhwaham 온화함; (*of voice*) pudǔrǒum 부드러움; (*of taste*) sunham 순함

mile mail 마일; **~s better** / **easier** F hwǒlsshin naǔn / shwiun 훨씬 나은 / 쉬운

mileage mail su 마일 수

milestone *fig* ijǒngp'yo 이정표

militant 1 *adj* t'ujaengtchǒgin 투쟁적인 **2** *n* t'usa 투사

military 1 *adj* kunǔi 군의 **2** *n*: **the ~** kun 군

military academy yuk-kkun sagwan hak-kkyo 육군 사관 학교

militia shimin-gun 시민군

milk 1 *n* uyu 우유 **2** *v/t* chǒjǔl tchada 젖을 짜다

milk chocolate milk'ǔ chyok'olit 밀크 쵸콜릿

milk shake milk'ǔ shweik'ǔ 밀크 쉐이크

mill *n* (*factory*) kongjang 공장; (*for grinding*) punswaegi 분쇄기

♦ **mill around** mujilssǒhage umjigida 무질서하게 움직이다

millennium ch'ǒnnyǒn 천년

milligram milligǔraem 밀리그램

millimeter millimit'ǒ 밀리미터

million paengman 백만

millionaire paengman changja 백만 장자

mime *v/t* tongjagǔro p'yohyǒnhada 동작으로 표현하다

mimic 1 *n* hyungnae 흉내 **2** *v/t* hyungnaenaeda 흉내내다

mince *v/t* chǒmida 저미다

mincemeat minsǔ p'ai sok 민스 파이 속

mince pie minsǔ p'ai 민스 파이

mind 1 *n* chǒngshin 정신; **it's all in your ~** kügǒsǔn ta nǒǔi sangsang-ida 그것은 다 너의 상상이다; **be out of one's ~** chǒngshini nagada 정신이 나가다; **bear sth in ~** muǒ kiǒk'ago it-tta 무엇을 기억하고 있[...]; **change one's ~** maǔmǔl pakkud[...] 마음을 바꾸다; **it didn't enter my** [...] kügǒsǔn na-ege sangsangdo kaji anat-tta 그것은 나에게 상상도 가[...] 않았다; **give s.o. a piece of one's** [...] nugurǔl namurada 누구를 나무라[...]; **make up one's ~** maǔmǔl chǒnghada 마음을 정하다; **have s[...] on one's ~** (*be worried*) muǒsǔl kǔnshimhada 무엇을 근심하다; **ke[...] one's ~ on** ...e chǒnnyǒmhada ...[...] 전념하다 **2** *v/t* (*look after*) tolboda 돌보다; (*object to*) ǒntchananhada 언짢아하다; (*heed*) maǔme tuda 마음에 두다; **I don't ~ what we d[...]** nanǔn uriga muǒsǔl hadǔn sanggwanǒptta 나는 우리가 무엇을 하든 상관없다; **do you ~ if I smoke?** tambaerǔl p'iwǒdo kwaench'ank'essǔmnikka? 담배를 피워도 괜찮겠습니까?; **would you mind opening the window?** ch'angmunǔl yǒrǒ chushigessǔmnikka? 창문을 열어 주시겠습니까?; **no, I don't ~** anio, kwaench'ansǔmnida 아니오, 괜찮습니다; **~ the step!** kyedanǔl choshimhaseyo! 계단을 조심하세요 **3** *v/i*: **~!** (*be careful*) choshimhaseyo[!] 조심하세요!; **never ~!** shin-gyǒng ssǔl kǒt ǒpssǔmnida! 신경 쓸 것 없습니다!; **I don't ~** chǒnǔn sanggwanǒpssǔmnida 저는 상관없습니다

mind-boggling nollaun 놀라운

mindless *violence* saenggagǒmnǔn 생각없는

mine *pron* naǔi kǒt 나의 것; H chǒǔi kǒt 저의 것; **a cousin of ~** naǔi sach'on 나의 사촌; H chǒǔi sach'on 저의 사촌

mine *n* (*for coal etc*) kwangsan 광산 **2** *v/i* (*for coal etc*) p'ada 파다; **for** ch'aegurhada 채굴하다

mine *n* (*explosive*) chiroe 지뢰 **2** *v* ...e chiroerǔl sǒlch'ihada ...에 지뢰를 설치하다

minefield MIL chiroepat 지뢰밭; *fig*

vihŏmjidae 위험 지대

iner kwangbu 광부

ineral *n* kwangmul 광물

ineral water kwangch'ŏnsu 광천수, aengsu 생수

inesweeper NAUT chiroe 'amsaeksŏn 지뢰 탐색선

ingle *v/i* (*of sounds, smells*) sŏktta 섞다; (*at party*) toradanimyŏ manŭn 'aramdŭrege marhada 돌아다니며 갆은 사람들에게 말하다

ini → **miniskirt**

iniature *adj* sohyŏng-ŭi 소형의

inibus sohyŏng pŏsŭ 소형 버스

inimal ch'oesoŭi 최소의

inimize ch'oesohwahada 최소화하다; (*downplay*) kwaso ɔ'yŏngkkahada 과소 평가하다

inimum 1 *adj* ch'oesohanŭi 최소한의 **2** *n* ch'oeso 최소

inimum wage ch'oejŏ ponggŭp 최저 봉급

ining kwang-ŏp 광업

iniskirt mini sŭk'ot'ŭ 미니 스커트

inister POL changgwan 장관; REL moksa 목사

inisterial changgwan-ŭi 장관의

inistry POL pu 부; (*in US, Japan*) sŏng 성

ink (*fur*) mingk'ŭ 밍크; (*coat*) mingk'ŭ k'ot'ŭ 밍크 코트

inor 1 *adj* poda chagŭn 보다 작은; *in G ~* MUS sa tantchoŭi 사 단조의 **2** *n* LAW misŏngnyŏnja 미성년자

inority sosup'a 소수파; *be in the ~* sosup'aida 소수파이다

int *n* (*herb*) pak'a 박하, mint'ŭ 민트; (*chocolate*) mint'ŭ chyok'ollit 민트 쵸콜릿; (*hard candy*) pak'a sat'ang 박하 사탕

inus 1 *n* (~ *sign*) ppaegi puho 빼기 부호 **2** *prep* ŭmŭi 음의; *42 ~ 18 is 24* sashibi ppaegi shipp'arŭn ishipssaida 42 빼기 18은 24이다; *temperatures of ~ 18 degrees* yŏngha shipp'alto 영하 18도

inuscule aju chagŭn 아주 작은

inute[1] *n* (*of time*) pun 분; *in a ~* (*soon*) kot 곧; *just a ~* chamshiman kidariseyo 잠시만 기다리세요

inute[2] *adj* (*tiny*) aju chogŭman 아주

조그만; (*detailed*) sangsehan 상세한; *in ~ detail* sangsehi 상세히

minutely (*in detail*) sangsehage 상세하게

minutes (*of meeting*) ŭisarok 의사록

miracle kijŏk 기적

miraculous kijŏktchŏgin 기적적인

miraculously kijŏkkach'i 기적같이

mirage shin-giru 신기루

mirror 1 *n* kŏul 거울; MOT paengmirŏ 백미러 **2** *v/t* pich'uda 비추다

misanthropist saramŭl shirŏhanŭn saram 사람을 싫어하는 사람

misapprehension: *be under a ~* chalmot saenggak'ada 잘못 생각하다

misbehave nappŭge haengdonghada 나쁘게 행동하다

misbehavior nappŭn haengdong 나쁜 행동

miscalculate *v/t & v/i* chalmot kyesanhada 잘못 계산하다

miscalculation osan 오산

miscarriage MED yusan 유산; *~ of justice* oshim 오심

miscarry (*of plan*) shilp'aehada 실패하다

miscellaneous kajigakssaegŭi 가지각색의

mischief (*naughtiness*) chitkkujŭn changnan 짓궂은 장난

mischievous *child* changnankkurŏgiŭi 장난꾸러기의; *behavior* chitkkujŭn 짓궂은

misconception ohae 오해

misconduct pujŏng haeng-wi 부정 행위

misconstrue chalmot haesŏk'ada 잘못 해석하다

misdemeanor kyŏngbŏmtchoe 경범죄; *youthful ~s* ch'ŏngsonyŏn pihaeng 청소년 비행

miser kudusoe 구두쇠

miserable (*unhappy*) purhaenghan 불행한; *weather* koyak'an 고약한; *performance* hyŏngp'yŏnŏmnŭn 형편없는

miserly insaek'an 인색한

misery (*unhappiness*) purhaeng 불행; (*wretchedness*) pich'amham 비참함

misfire (*of joke, scheme*) pinnagada 빗나가다

misfit (*in society*) pujŏgŭngja 부적응자

misfortune purhaeng 불행

misgiving yŏmnyŏ 염려

misguided chalmot chidodoen 잘못 지도된

mishandle chalmot taruda 잘못 다루다

mishap sago 사고

misinterpret chalmot haesŏk'ada 잘못 해석하다

misinterpretation chalmot-ttoen haesŏk 잘못된 해석

misjudge *person, situation* chalmot p'andanhada 잘못 판단하다

mislay tun kosŭl ijŏbŏrida 둔 곳을 잊어버리다

mislead odohada 오도하다

misleading odohanŭn 오도하는

mismanage chalmot unyŏnghada 잘못 운영하다

mismanagement chalmot-ttoen unyŏng 잘못된 운영

mismatch chalmot match'uda 잘못 맞추다

misplaced *loyalty* chalmot chun 잘못 준

misprint *n* chalmot-ttoen inswae 잘못된 인쇄

mispronounce t'ŭllin parŭmŭl hada 틀린 발음을 하다

mispronunciation t'ŭllin parŭm 틀린 발음

misread *word, figures* chalmot iltta 잘못 읽다; *situation* ohaehada 오해하다

misrepresent t'ŭllige chŏnhada 틀리게 전하다

miss[1]: **Miss Smith** Sŭmisŭ yang 스미스 양; **~!** agasshi! 아가씨!

miss[2] *n* SP shiltchŏm 실점; **give sth a ~** *meeting, party etc* muŏse ppajida 무엇에 빠지다 *2 v/t* (*not hit*) noch'ida 놓치다; (*not meet*) ŏtkkallida 엇갈리다; (*emotionally*) kŭriwŏhada 그리워하다; *bus, train, plane* noch'ida 놓치다; (*not notice*) arach'aeji mot'ada 알아채지 못하다; (*not be present at*) …e ppajida …에 빠지다 *3 v/i* noch'ida 놓치다

misshapen pijŏngsangchŏgin

moyang-ŭi 비정상적인 모양의

missile (*rocket*) misail 미사일

missing irŏbŏrin 잃어버린; **be ~** ŏpssŏjida 없어지다

mission (*task*) samyŏng 사명; (*people*) sajŏl 사절

missionary REL sŏn-gyosa 선교사

misspell chalmot ch'ŏltchahada 잘못 철자하다

mist an-gae 안개

♦ **mist over** (*of eyes*) hŭryŏjida 흐려지다

♦ **mist up** (*of mirror, window*) kimi sŏrida 김이 서리다

mistake *1 n* shilssu 실수; **make a ~** shilssuhada 실수하다; **by ~** shilssuro 실수로 *2 v/t* ch'ak-kkak'ada 착각하다; **~ X for Y** Xŭl/rŭl Y(ŭ)ro chak-kkak'ada X을/를 Y(으)로 착각하다

mistaken: **be ~** t'ŭllin 틀린

mister → **Mr**

mistress (*lover*) chŏngbu 정부; (*of servant*) yŏjuin 여주인; (*of dog*) chuin 주인

mistrust *1 n* pulshin 불신 *2 v/t* pulshinhada 불신하다

misty *weather* an-gae kkin 안개 낀; *eyes* hŭryŏjin 흐려진; *color* hŭrin 흐린

misunderstand ohaehada 오해하다

misunderstanding (*mistake*) ohae 오해; (*argument*) ŭigyŏn ch'ai 의견 차이

misuse *1 n* oyong 오용 *2 v/t* chalmot sayonghada 잘못 사용하다

mitigating circumstances kyŏnggam sayu 경감 사유

mitt (*in baseball*) mit'ŭ 미트

mitten pŏng-ŏri changgap 벙어리 장갑

mix *1 n* (*mixture*) sŏkkŭn kŏt 섞은 것; (*in cooking*) honhammul 혼합물; (*ready to use*) miri mandŭrŏjin yori chaeryo 미리 만들어진 요리 재료 *2 v/t* sŏktta 섞다 *3 v/i* (*socially*) ŏullida 어울리다

♦ **mix up** (*confuse*) hŏtkkallida 헛갈리다; (*muddle up*) sŏkkŏ noŭta 섞어 놓다; **mix X up with Y** Xŭl/rŭl Ywa/kwa hondonghada X을/를

와/과 혼동하다; *be mixed up
emotionally*) hollansŭrŏwŏ hada
...란스러워 하다; (*of figures, papers*)
wisŏk-kkida 뒤섞이다; *be mixed up
...*e kwallyŏndoeda ...에 관련되다;
et mixed up with ...wa/kwa
wan-gyehada ...와/과 관계하다
nix with (*associate with*) ...wa/kwa
ullida ...와/과 어울리다
xed *feelings* hollanhan 혼란한;
eactions, reviews sŏk-kkin 섞인
xed **marriage** kuktche kyŏrhon
국제 결혼
xer (*for food*) mikssŏ 믹서; (*drink*)
...'akt'eillyong mualk'ool ŭmnyo
...태일용 무알코올 음료; *she's a
...ood ~* kŭnyŏnŭn sagyossŏng-i
...hot'a 그녀는 사교성이 좋다
xture honhap 혼합; (*medicine*)
...nulyak 물약
x-up hollan 혼란
...an 1 *n* (*of pain*) shinŭm sori 신음
...리; (*complaint*) pulp'yŏng 불평
... *v/i* (*in pain*) shinŭmhada 신음하다;
...complain) pulp'yŏnghada 불평하다
...ob 1 *n* p'oktto 폭도 2 *v/t* tterŭul chiŏ
...allyŏdŭlda 떼를 지어 달려들다
...obile¹ *adj person* umjigil su innŭn
...직일 수 있는
...obile² *n* (*for decoration*) mobil 모빌
...obile home idongshik chut'aek
...동식 주택
...obile phone *Br* haendŭp'on
...앤드폰, idong chŏnhwa 이동 전화
...obility idong 이동
...obster p'ongnyŏk tanwŏn 폭력
...원
...ock 1 *adj* hyungnaenaen 흉내낸;
xams, elections moŭiŭi 모의의 2 *v/t*
...yungnaenaemyŏ choronghada
...흉내내며 조롱하다
...ockery chorong 조롱; (*travesty*)
...hojak 조작
...ock-up (*model*) mohyŏng 모형
...ode (*form*) pangshik 방식; COMPUT
...nodŭ 모드
...del 1 *adj employee, husband*
...nobŏmŭi 모범의; *boat, plane*
...nohyŏngŭi 모형의 2 *n* (*miniature*)
...nohyŏng 모형; (*pattern*) ponbogi
...본보기; (*fashion ~*) model 모델;

male ~ namja model 남자 모델 3 *v/t*
...ŭi moderŭl hada ...의 모델을 하다
4 *v/i* (*for designer*) moderida
모델이다; (*for artist, photographer*)
moderŭl hada 모델을 하다
modem modem 모뎀
moderate 1 *adj* chŏkttanghan 적당한,
almajŭn 알맞은; POL on-gŏnhan
온건한 2 *n* POL on-gŏnp'a 온건파
3 *v/t* chŏkttanghi hada 적당히 하다
moderately chŏkttanghage 적당하게
moderation (*restraint*) chungnyong
중용; *in ~* chŏkttanghage 적당하게
modern hyŏndaeŭi 현대의
modernization hyŏndaehwa 현대화
modernize 1 *v/t* hyŏndaejŏgŭro
pakkuda 현대적으로 바꾸다 2 *v/i* (*of
business, country*) hyŏndaehwahada
현대화하다
modest *house, apartment* susuhan
수수한; (*small*) chogŭmahan
조그마한; (*not conceited*)
kyŏmsonhan 겸손한
modesty (*of house, apartment*)
susuham 수수함; (*of wage,
improvement*) chogŭmaham
조그마함; (*lack of conceit*) kyŏmson
겸손
modification sujŏng 수정
modify sujŏnghada 수정하다
modular *furniture* choribŭi 조립의
module chorip tanwi 조립 단위;
(*space ~*) sŏn 선
moist sŭpkki innŭn 습기 있는,
ch'ukch'uk'an 축축한
moisten ch'ukch'uk'age hada
축축하게 하다
moisture sŭpkki 습기
moisturizer (*for skin*) moisch'yŏraijŏ
모이스처라이저
molar ŏgŭmni 어금니
molasses tangmil 당밀
mold¹ *n* (*on food*) komp'ang-i 곰팡이
mold² 1 *n* t'ŭl 틀 2 *v/t clay etc* t'ŭre
nŏŏ mandŭlda 틀에 넣어 만들다;
character, person hyŏngsŏnshik'ida
형성시키다
moldy *food* komp'ang-i p'in 곰팡이
핀
mole (*on skin*) chŏm 점
molecular punjaŭi 분자의

molecule punja 분자
molest *child, woman* sŏngtchŏguro hüironghada 성적으로 희롱하다
mollycoddle chinach'ige posalp'ida 지나치게 보살피다
molten nogŭn 녹은
mom F ŏmma 엄마
moment sun-gan 순간; **at the ~** chigŭmŭn 지금은; **at that ~** kŭ ttaeenŭn 그 때에는; **at the very ~** paro kŭ sun-gane 바로 그 순간에; **for the ~** tangbun-gan 당분간
momentarily *(for a moment)* chamshi tong-an 잠시 동안; *(in a moment)* kot 곧
momentary sun-ganŭi 순간의
momentous chungdaehan 중대한
momentum him 힘
monarch kunju 군주
monastery sudowŏn 수도원
monastic sudosŭng kat'ŭn 수도승 같은
Monday wŏryoil 월요일
monetary kŭmnyung-ŭi 금융의
money ton 돈
money-lender taegŭmŏptcha 대금업자; **money market** kŭmnyung shijang 금융 시장; **money order** up'yŏnhwan 우편환
Mongolia Monggo 몽고
Mongolian 1 *adj* Monggoŭi 몽고의 2 *n (person)* Monggoin 몽고인
mongrel chaptchonggyŏn 잡종견
monitor 1 *n* COMPUT monit'ŏ 모니터 2 *v/t* chik'yŏboda 지켜보다
monk sudosa 수도사
monkey wŏnsŭng-i 원숭이; F *(child)* ŏrin nom 어린 놈
♦ **monkey around with** F ...ŭl/rŭl kajigo changnanch'ida ...을/를 가지고 장난치다
monkey wrench mŏngk'i sŭp'aenŏ 멍키 스패너
monogram *n* yaktcha 약자
monogrammed yaktchaga saegyŏjin 약자가 새겨진
monolog tokp+paek 독백
monopolize toktchŏmhada 독점하다
monopoly toktchŏm 독점
monotonous tanjoroun 단조로운
monotony tanjoroum 단조로움

monsoon monsun 몬순
monsoon season monsun kyejŏl 몬순 계절
monster *n* koemul 괴물
monstrosity hyungmul 흉물
monstrous *(frightening)* koemulgat'ŭn 괴물같은; *(enormou* kŏdaehan 거대한; *(shocking)* ch'unggyŏktchŏgin 충격적인
month tal 달, wŏl 월
monthly 1 *adj* maedarŭi 매달의 2 *a* maedalmada 매달마다 3 *n (magazine)* wŏlganji 월간지
monument kinyŏmbi 기념비; *(sculpture)* kinyŏm tongsang 기념 동상
mood *(frame of mind)* kibun 기분; *(bad ~)* kibuni nappŭn sangt'ae 기분이 나쁜 상태; *(of meeting, country)* punwigi 분위기; **be in a good/bad ~** kibuni chot'a/ nappŭda 기분이 좋다/나쁘다; **be i the ~ for** ... hago ship'ŭn kibunid ...하고 싶은 기분이다
moody kibuni chaju pyŏnhanŭn 기분이 자주 변하는; *(bad-tempere* kibuni nappŭn 기분이 나쁜
moon *n* tal 달
moonlight 1 *n* talppit 달빛 2 *v/i* F pame puŏbŭl hada 밤에 부업을 하
moonlit talppich'i ŏrin 달빛이 어린
moor *v/t boat* chŏngbaksshik'ida 정박시키다
moorings chŏngbaktchang 정박장
moose k'ŭn sasŭm 큰 사슴
mop 1 *n* taegŏlle 대걸레 2 *v/t floor* taegŏllero takta 대걸레로 닦다; *eyes, face* takta 닦다
♦ **mop up** takta 닦다; MIL sot'anghada 소탕하다
mope uurhaehada 우울해하다
moral 1 *adj person, behavior etc* todŏktchŏgin 도덕적인 2 *n (of story* kyohun 교훈; **~s** todŏk kwannyŏm 도덕 관념
morale sagi 사기
morality todŏksssŏng 도덕성
morbid pyŏngtchŏgin 병적인
more 1 *adj* tŏ manŭn 더 많은; **some ~ tea?** ch'arŭl chom tŏ tŭshigessŭmnikka? 차를 좀 더

三시겠습니까?; ~ **and ~ stu-
dents/time** chŏmjŏm tŏ manŭn
haksaengdŭl/shigan 점점 더 많은
학생들/시간 **2** adv tŏuk tŏ욱; ~ **important** tŏ chung-yohan 더 중요한;
~ **often** tŏuk chaju 더욱 자주; **~ and
~** tŏuk tŏ tŏ욱 더; **~ or less** (about)
chŏngdo 정도; (virtually) sashilssang
사실상; **once ~** hanbŏn tŏ 한번 더; **~
than ...** poda tŏ mani ... 보다 더
같이; **~ than 80 people were injured** 80myŏngboda tŏ manŭn
sarami pusang-ŭl tanghaet-tta
80명보다 더 많은 사람이 부상을
당했다; **I don't live there any ~**
nanŭn tŏ isang kŏgi salji ansŭmnida
나는 더 이상 거기 살지 않습니다
3 pron tŏ 더; **do you want some ~?**
tŏ wŏnhashimnikka? 더
원하십니까?; **a little ~** chogŭm tŏ
조금 더
moreover kŏgidaga 거기다가
morgue yŏng-anshil 영안실
Mormonism Molmon-gyo 몰몬교
morning ach'im 아침; **in the ~** (early)
ach'ime 아침에; (before noon) ojŏne
오전에; (tomorrow) naeil ach'im 내일
아침; **four o'clock in the ~** ojŏn
neshi 오전 네시; **this ~** onŭl ach'im
오늘 아침; **tomorrow ~** naeil ach'im
내일 아침; **good ~** annyŏnghaseyo
안녕하세요; (on waking up)
annyŏnghi chumusyŏssŏyo 안녕히
주무셨어요
moron pabo 바보
morose uurhan 우울한
morphine morŭp'in 모르핀
morsel: a ~ of han chogagŭi 한
조각의
mortal 1 adj chugŏyahal unmyŏng-ŭi
죽어야할 운명의; **blow**
ch'imyŏngjŏgin 치명적인; ~ **enemy**
pulgu taech'ŏnŭi wŏnsu 불구 대천의
원수 **2** n pot'ong saram 보통 사람
mortality chugŭl unmyŏng chae 운명;
(death rate) samangnyul 사망률
mortar[1] MIL pakkyŏkp'o 박격포
mortar[2] (cement) hoebanjuk 회반죽
mortgage 1 n chŏdang 저당 **2** v/t
chŏdang chap'ida 저당 잡히다
mortician chang-ŭisa 장의사

mortuary yŏng-anshil 영안실
mosaic mojaik'ŭ 모자이크
mosquito mogi 모기
mosquito coil mogihyang 모기향
mosquito net mogijang 모기장
moss ikki 이끼
mossy ikki kkin 이끼 낀
most 1 adj taebubunŭi 대부분의; ~
people would agree with you
taebubunŭi saramdŭri tangshin
ŭigyŏne tong-ŭihal kŏshimnida
대부분의 사람들이 당신 의견에
동의할 것입니다 **2** adv kajang 가장;
(very) maeu 매우; **the ~ beauti-
ful/interesting** kajang
arŭmdaun/chaemiinnŭn 가장
아름다운/재미있는; **that's the one I
like ~** kŭgŏshi naega kajang
choahanŭn kŏshida 그것이 내가
가장 좋아하는 것이다; **~ of all**
muŏtppodado 무엇보다도 **3** pron
taebubun 대부분; (maximum)
ch'oedaehanŭi kŏt 최대한의 것; **at
(the) ~** manaya 많아야; **make the ~
of** ch'oedaehan hwaryonghada
최대한 활용하다
mostly taebubunŭn 대부분은, churo
주로
motel mot'el 모텔
moth nabang 나방
mother 1 n ŏmŏni 어머니 **2** v/t
ŏmŏnigach'i tolboda 어머니같이
돌보다
motherboard COMPUT madŏbodŭ
마더보드; **motherhood** ŏmŏniim
어머니임; **mother-in-law** shiŏmŏni
시어머니
motherly ŏmŏnigat'ŭn 어머니같은
mother-of-pearl chagae 자개; ~ **inlay**
chagae changshik 자개 장식;
Mother's Day ŏmŏninal 어머니날;
mother tongue mogugŏ 모국어
motif chuje 주제
motion 1 n umjigim 움직임; (of the
body) tongjak 동작; (proposal)
chean 제안; **set things in ~**
ch'ujinhada 추진하다 **2** v/t: **he ~ed
me forward** kŭga na-ege ap'ŭro
orago sonjit'aet-tta 그가 나에게
앞으로 오라고 손짓했다
motionless umjigiji annŭn 움직이지

않는

motivate *person* tonggirŭl puyŏhada 동기를 부여하다; *I don't feel very ~d* nanŭn pyŏllo ŭiyogi annanda 나는 별로 의욕이 안난다

motivation tonggi puyŏ 동기 부여

motive tonggi 동기

motor naeyŏn-gigwan 내연기관, mot'ŏ 모터

motorbike ot'obai 오토바이; **motorboat** mot'ŏbot'ŭ 모터보트; **motorcade** chadongch'a haengnyŏl 자동차 행렬; **motorcycle** ot'obai 오토바이; **motorcyclist** ot'obairŭl t'anŭn saram 오토바이를 타는 사람; **motor home** idong chut'aekch'a 이동 주택차

motorist unjŏnja 운전자

motorscooter sŭk'ut'ŏ 스쿠터

motor vehicle chadongch'a 자동차

motto chwaumyŏng 좌우명, mot'o 모토; *school* ~ kyohun 교훈

mound (*hillock*) chagŭn ŏndŏk 작은 언덕; (*in baseball*) maundŭ 마운드; (*pile*) sandŏmi 산더미

mount 1 *n* (*mountain*) san 산; (*horse*) sŭngma 승마 **2** *v/t steps* orŭda 오르다; *horse, bicycle* t'ada 타다; *campaign* ch'akssuhada 착수하다; *photo etc* tandanhan tee puch'ida 단단한 데에 붙이다 **3** *v/i* orŭda 오르다

♦ **mount up** nŭlda 늘다

mountain san 산

mountain bike sanak chajŏn-gŏ 산악 자전거

mountaineer tŭngsan-ga 등산가, sanagin 산악인

mountaineering tŭngsan 등산

mountainous sanjiŭi 산지의

mountain spirits sanshin 산신

mourn 1 *v/t* ch'udohada 추도하다 **2** *v/i: ~ for* …ŭi chugŭmŭl sŭlp'ŏhada …의 죽음을 슬퍼하다

mourner chogaek 조객

mournful sŭlp'ŭme chamgin 슬픔에 잠긴

mourning sang 상; *be in* ~ sang chung-ida 상 중이다; *wear* ~ sangbogŭl ipta 상복을 입다

mouse chwi 쥐; COMPUT mausŭ 마우스

mouse mat COMPUT mausŭ maet'ŭ 마우스 매트

mouth *n* ip 입; (*of river*) ŏgwi 어귀, hagu 하구

mouthful han ip kadŭk 한 입 가득

mouthorgan hamonik'a 하모니카; **mouthpiece** (*of instrument*) ibe taego punŭn pubun 입에 대고 부는 부분; (*spokesperson*) taebyŏnin 대변인; **mouthwash** yangch'iaek 양치액; **mouthwatering** kunch'im tolge hanŭn 군침 돌게 하는

move 1 *n* (*in chess, checkers*) su 수; (*step, action*) umjigim 움직임; (*change of house*) isa 이사; *get a ~ on!* sŏdŭrŭshipssio! 서두르십시오! *don't make a ~!* umjigiji ma! 움직이지 마!; *it's your ~* (*in chess etc*) tangshin ch'aryeimnida 당신 차례입니다 **2** *v/t object* umjigida 움직이다; (*transfer*) omgida 옮기다; (*emotionally*) kamdongshik'ida 감동시키다 **3** *v/i* umjigida 움직이다; (*transfer*) omgida 옮기다; ~ *house* isahada 이사하다

♦ **move around** (*in room*) toradanida 돌아다니다; (*from place to place*) idonghada 이동하다

♦ **move away** mullŏnada 물러나다; (*move house*) isahada 이사하다

♦ **move in** isaoda 이사오다

♦ **move on** (*to another town*) isahada 이사하다; (*to another job*) chŏnjinhada 전직하다; (*to another subject*) pakkuda 바꾸다

♦ **move out** (*of house*) isanagada 이사나가다; (*of area*) ttŏnada 떠나다

♦ **move up** (*be promoted*) sŭngjinhada 승진하다; (*make room*) charirŭl mandŭlda 자리를 만들다; *they have moved up to second position* kŭdŭrŭn che iwie ollat-tta 그들은 제 이위에 올랐다

movement umjigim 움직임; (*organization*) undong 운동; MUS aktchang 악장

movers isatchim unsong-ŏptcha 이삿짐 운송업자

movie yŏnghwa 영화; *go to a* / *the ~s* yŏnghwa porŏ kada 영화 보러 가다

⋅viegoer: be a big ~ yŏnghwa 關畫 보러 가는 것을 매우 좋아하다

⋅vie theater yŏnghwagwan 영화관

⋅ving (which can move) umjiginŭn 움직이는; (emotionally) 感動적인 amdongjŏgin 감동적인

⋅w grass peda 베다

⋅wer p'ulbenŭn kigye 풀베는 기계

⋅oxibustion ssukttŭm 쑥뜸

⋅P (= Military Policeman)

⋅h (= miles per hour) shisok 시속; **st 50 ~** shisok 50maillo 시속 50마일로

⋅: ~ Kevin Brown K'ebin 'ŭraunsshi 케빈 브라운씨

⋅rs: ~ Margo MacDonald Mago Maekttonaldŭ yŏsa 마고 맥도날드 여사

⋅s: ~ Sunmi Lee I Sunmisshi 이 ㅅ미씨

⋅uch 1 adj manŭn 많은; **I have as ~ ⋅ime as you need** shiganŭn ⋅lmadŭnji issŏyo 시간은 얼마든지 있어요; **there's not ~ difference** ⋅yŏllo tarŭji anayo 별로 다르지 않아요 **2** adv mani 많이; **very ~** aju ⋅nani 아주 많이; **too ~** nŏmu mani ⋅⋅무 많이; **do you like it? - not - ⋅** ⋅ŭgŏsŭl choahaeyo? - pyŏlloyo ⋅것을 좋아해요? - 별로요; **as ~ as ⋅⋅ ...**mank'ŭm mani ...만큼 많이; **I ⋅ thought as ~** nado kŭrŏk'e ⋅saenggak'aessŏyo 나도 그렇게 ⋅생각했어요 **3** pron manŭn kŏt 많은 ⋅것; **he earns as ~ as me** kŭnŭn ⋅namank'ŭm tonŭl pŏnda 그는 ⋅나만큼 돈을 번다; **nothing ~** pyŏllo ⋅별로

⋅uck (dirt) tŏrŏun kŏt 더러운 것

⋅ucus chŏmaek 점액; (in nose) ⋅k'onmul 콧물

⋅ud chinhŭk 진흙

⋅uddle 1 n (mess) ŏmmang-in ⋅sangt'ae ŏmmang-in 상태; (confusion) ⋅hollan 혼란 **2** v/t hŏllanshik'ida 혼란시키다

muddle up ŏngmang-ŭro mandŭlda 엉망으로 만들다; (confuse) hŏtkkallida 헛갈리다

muddy adj chinhŭkt'usŏng-iŭi 진흙투성이의

muffin mŏp'in 머핀

muffle chal andŭllige hada 잘 안들리게 하다

♦ muffle up v/i ttattŭt'age kamssada 따뜻하게 감싸다

muffler MOT pang-ŭm changch'i 방음 장치; (scarf) mŏkttori 목도리

mug¹ n (for tea, coffee) mŏgŭjan 머그잔; F (face) ŏlgul 얼굴

mug² v/t (attack) nosang kangdojirŭl hada 노상 강도질을 하다

mugger nosang kangdo 노상 강도

mugging nosang kangdo haeng-wi 노상 강도 행위

muggy hut'ŏptchigŭnhan 후텁지근한

mule nosae 노새; (slipper) myul 뮬, twiga t'ŭin kudu 뒤가 트인 구두

♦ mull over chuŭi kipkke saenggak'ada 주의 깊게 생각하다

multilingual tagugŏŭi 다국어의

multimedia n mŏlt'imidiŏ 멀티미디어, tajung maech'e 다중 매체

multinational 1 adj taguktchŏgŭi 다국적의 **2** n COM taguktchŏk kiŏp 다국적 기업

multiple adj tayanghan 다양한

multiplication MATH kopssem 곱셈

multiply 1 v/t kop'ada 곱하다 **2** v/i chŭnggahada 증가하다

mumble 1 n chung-ŏlgŏrim 중얼거림 **2** v/t & v/i chung-ŏlgŏrida 중얼거리다

mumps ihasŏnnyŏm 이하선염

munch v/t & v/i ujŏkujŏk sshiptta 우적우적 씹다

municipal shiŭi 시의

mural n pyŏk'wa 벽화

murder 1 n sarin 살인 **2** v/t person sarinhada 살인하다; song mangch'yŏ not'a 망쳐 놓다

murderer sarinja 살인자

murderous rage, look sarinhal kŏt kat'ŭn sŏnginŭl 살인할 것 같은

murmur 1 n sokssagim 속삭임 **2** v/t sokssagida 속삭이다

muscle kŭnyuk 근육

muscular pain, strain kŭnyugŭi 근육의; person kŭnyuktchirŭi 근육질의

muse v/i saenggage chamgida 생각에

잠기다

museum pangmulgwan 박물관

mushroom 1 *n* pŏsŏt 버섯 **2** *v/i* ppalli charada 빨리 자라다

music ŭmak 음악; (*written*) akppo 악보

musical 1 *adj* ŭmagŭi 음악의; *person* ŭmaktchŏgin 음악적인; *voice* ŭmakkat'ŭn 음악같은 **2** *n* myujik'ŏl 뮤지컬

musical instrument akki 악기

musician ŭmak-kka 음악가

mussel honghap 홍합

must ◇ (*necessity*) ...haeya hada ...해야 하다; *I ~ be on time* nanŭn pandŭshi cheshigane issŏya handa 나는 반드시 제시간에 있어야 한다; *I ~ kŭraeyaman handa 그래야만 한다; I ~ kŭraeyaman handa 그래야만 한다; *I ~n't be late* nanŭn nŭjŏsŏnŭn andoenda 나는 늦어서는 안된다 ◇ (*probability*): *it ~ be about 6 o'clock* 6shi tchŭm toessŭl kŏyeyo 6시 쯤 됐을 거예요; *they ~ have arrived by now* kŭdŭrŭn chigŭmimyŏn toch'ak'aekketchyo 그들은 지금이면 도착했겠죠

mustache k'otssuyŏm 콧수염

mustard kyŏja 겨자

musty komp'angnae nanŭn 곰팡내 나는

mute *adj* muŏnŭi 무언의

muted *color* pudŭrŏun 부드러운; *opposition, criticism* yak'an 약한

mutilate *person* sanghaerŭl ip'ida 상해를 입히다; *thing* hwesonhada

훼손하다

mutiny 1 *n* pallan 반란 **2** *v/i* pallanŭ irŭk'ida 반란을 일으키다

mutter *v/t & v/i* chung-ŏlgŏrida 중얼거리다

mutual sanghoganŭi 상호간의

muzzle 1 *n* (*of animal, dog*) chudu i 주둥이; (*device*) immagae 입마개 **2** *v/t*: *~ the press* ŏllon podorŭl maktta 언론 보도를 막다

my ◇ naŭi 나의; ㅐ chŏŭi 저의; *~ decision / money* naŭi kyŏltchŏng / ton 나의 결정 / 돈; *~ leg hurts* tariga ap'ayo 다리가 아파요 (*referring to family, groups etc, Korean usually uses the pronoun 'our'*) uriŭi 우리의; *~ house / mother* uri chip / ŏmŏni 우리 집 / 어머니; *~ family* uri kajok 우리 가족; *~ country / company* uri nara / hoesa 우리 나라 / 회사

myopic kŭnshianŭi 근시안의

myself na chashin 나 자신; *by ~* (*alone*) honja 혼자; (*without any help*) sŭsŭro 스스로

mysterious shinbihan 신비한

mysteriously shinbihage 신비하게

mystery shinbi 신비; (*fact which is mysterious*) pulgasaŭi 불가사의

mystify pulgahaehage mandŭlda 불가해하게 만들다; *I'm mystified* ihaehal su ŏpssŏyo 이해할 수 없어

myth shinhwa 신화; *fig* mangsang 망

mythical shinhwaŭi 신화의

mythology shinhwahak 신화학

N

b (*take for oneself*) nakka ch'aeda
낙아 채다

g *v/t & v/i* chansorihada
잔소리하다; ~ *s.o. to do sth*
uguege muŏsŭl harago
hansorihada 누구에게 무엇을
하라고 잔소리하다

agging *person* chansorihanŭn
잔소리하는; *doubt* sŏnggashin 성가신;
ain kkŭnjilgin 끈질긴

il (*for wood*) mot 못; (*on finger,
oe*) sont'op 손톱

il clippers sont'opkkak-kki
손톱깎이; **nail file** sont'optchul
손톱줄; **nail polish** maenik'yuŏ
매니큐어; **nail polish remover**
maenik'yuŏ chiunŭn yak 매니큐어
지우는 약; **nail scissors** sont'op
kkangnŭn kawi 손톱 깎는 가위; **nail
varnish** maenik'yuŏ 매니큐어

aive sunjinhan 순진한

aked pŏlgŏbŏsŭn 벌거벗은; *truth,
aggression* chŏngnarahan 적나라한;
to the ~ eye yuganŭronŭn
육안으로는

ame 1 *n* irŭm 이름; (*on document*)
sŏngmyŏng 성명; *what's your ~?*
irŭmi muŏsshimnikka? 이름이
무엇입니까?; (*polite*) sŏnghami
ŏttŏk'e toeshimnikka? 성함이
어떻게 되십니까?; *what's his ~?*
kŭŭi irŭmŭn muŏshimnikka? 그의
이름은 무엇입니까?; *call s.o. ~s*
nugurŭl yok'ada 누구를 욕하다;
make a ~ for oneself
yumyŏnghaejida 유명해지다 **2** *v/t*
irŭmŭl chit-tta 이름을 짓다

name for: name X for Y Yŭi
irŭmŭl ttasŏ Xŭi irŭmŭl chit-tta Y의
이름을 따서 X의 이름을 짓다

amely chŭk 즉

amesake tongmyŏng-iin 동명이인

ametag irŭmp'yo 이름표

lamhae Island Namhaedo 남해도

nanny *n* yumo 유모

nap *n* nattcham 낮잠; *have a ~*
nattchamŭl chada 낮잠을 자다

nape: ~ *of the neck* mokttŏlmi
목덜미

napkin (*table ~*) naepk'in 냅킨;
(*sanitary ~*) saengnidae 생리대

narcotic *n* mayak 마약

narcotics agent mayak tansokppan
마약 단속반

narrate iyagihada 이야기하다

narration (*telling*) iyagihagi
이야기하기

narrative 1 *n* (*story*) iyagi 이야기
2 *adj* poem, style iyagishigŭi
이야기식의

narrator iyagihanŭn saram
이야기하는 사람

narrow street, bed, views chobŭn 좁은;
victory kakkasŭro ŏdŭn 가까스로
얻은

narrowly win, escape kakkasŭro
가까스로

narrow-minded maŭmi chobŭn
마음이 좁은

nasal *voice* k'ŏssoriŭi 콧소리의

nasty person, thing to say mot-tten
못된; *smell, weather* pulk'waehan
불쾌한; *cut, wound, disease* shimhan
심한

nation kuk-kka 국가, nara 나라

national 1 *adj* kuk-kkaŭi 국가의,
naraŭi 나라의 **2** *n* kungmin 국민

national anthem kuk-kka 국가;
(*South Korean*) Aeguk-kka 애국가;
National Assembly Kuk'oe 국회;
national debt kukch'ae 국채; **national flag** (*South Korean*) t'aegŭk-
kki 태극기; **National Foundation
Day** Kaech'ŏnjŏl 개천절

nationalism minjoktchuŭi 민족주의

nationality kuktchŏk 국적

nationalize industry etc
kugyŏnghwahada 국영화하다

national park kungnip kong-wŏn 국립 공원

native 1 *adj* ch'ulssaeng-ŭi 출생의; **~ language** mogugŏ 모국어 **2** *n* ch'ulssŭninŭi saram 출신의 사람; (*tribesman*) wŏnjumin 원주민

native country ch'ulssaengguk 출생국

native speaker wŏnŏmin 원어민

NATO (= *North Atlantic Treaty Organization*) Pukttaesŏyang Choyak Kigu 북대서양 조약 기구

natural *resources* ch'ayŏnŭi 자연의; *flavor* sunsuhan 순수한; (*obvious*) tangnyŏnhan 당연한; **~ blonde** t'agonan kŭmbal 타고난 금발; **~ death** chayŏnsa 자연사

natural gas ch'ŏnyŏn kassŭ 천연 가스

naturalist saengt'aehaktcha 생태학자

naturalize: *become* **~d** kwihwahada 귀화하다

naturally (*of course*) tangnyŏnhi 당연히; *behave, speak* chayŏnsŭrŏpkke 자연스럽게; (*by nature*) pollae 본래

natural science chayŏn kwahak 자연 과학

natural scientist chayŏn kwahaktcha 자연 과학자

nature chayŏn 자연; (*of person*) ch'ŏnsŏng 천성; (*of problem*) sŏngkkyŏk 성격

nature reserve chayŏn pohogu 자연 보호구

naughty chitkkujŭn 짓궂은; *photograph, word etc* yahan 야한

nausea mesŭkkŏum 메스꺼움; *fig* yŏk-kkyŏum 역겨움

nauseate *fig* (*disgust*) yŏk-kkyŏpkke hada 역겹게 하다

nauseating *fig* yŏk-kkyŏun 역겨운

nauseous: *feel* **~** t'ohal kŏt kat-tta 토할 것 같다

nautical hanghaeŭi 항해의

nautical mile haeri 해리

naval haegunŭi 해군의

naval base haegun kiji 해군 기지

navel paekkop 배꼽

navigable *river* hanghaehal su innŭn 항해할 수 있는

navigate *v/i* (*in ship, airplane*) hanghaehada 항해하다; (*in car*) kil annaerŭl hada 길 안내를 하다; COMPUT kŏmsaek'ada 검색하다

navigation hanghaesul 항해술; (*in car*) kil annaehagi 길 안내하기

navigator (*in ship, airplane*) hanghaesa 항해사; (*in car*) kil annaerŭl hanŭn saram 길 안내를 하는 사람

navy haegun 해군

navy blue 1 *n* namsaek 남색 **2** *adj* namsaegŭi 남색의

near 1 *adv* kakkai 가까이 **2** *prep* kakkaie 가까이에; **~ the bank** ŭnhaeng kakkaie 은행 가까이에; **do you go ~ the bank?** ŭnhaeng kŭnch'ŏro kamnikka? 은행 근처로 갑니까? **3** *adj* kakkaun 가까운; **the ~est bus stop** kajang kakkaun pŏssŭ chŏngnyujang 가장 가까운 버스 정류장; **in the ~ future** kakkaun mirae-e 가까운 미래에

nearby *adv live* kakkapkke 가깝게

nearly kŏŭi 거의

near-sighted kŭnshiŭi 근시의

neat *room, desk* kkaekkŭt'an 깨끗한 *person* tanjŏnghan 단정한; *whiskey* sunsuhan 순수한; *solution* hyŏnmyŏnghan 현명한; F (*terrific*) kŭnsahan 근사한

necessarily pandŭshi 반드시

necessary p'iryohan 필요한; **it is ~ to …** …hal p'iryoga it-tta …할 필요가 있다

necessitate p'iryoro hada 필요로 하다

necessity p'iryosŏng 필요성; (*sth necessary*) p'ilssup'um 필수품

neck mok 목

necklace mok-kkŏri 목걸이; **neckline** (*of dress*) mokssŏn 목선; **necktie** net'ai 넥타이

née mihon ttaeŭi sŏng 미혼 때의 성

need 1 *n* p'iryo 필요; **if ~ be** p'iryohadamyŏn 필요하다면; **in ~** toumŭi p'iryohan 도움이 필요한; **be in ~ of sth** muŏshi p'iryohada 무엇이 필요하다; **there's no ~ to be upset** kibun nappahal p'iryonŭn

anado ŏpta 기분 나빠할 필요는
나도 없다 2 *v/t* p'iryohada
요하다; **you'll ~ to buy one**
ŏnŭn hanarŭl sayahal kŏshida 너는
나를 사야할 것이오; **you don't ~**
o wait kidaril p'iryoga ŏpta 기다릴
요가 없다; **I ~ to talk to you**
angshin-gwa iyagihaeyagessŏyo
신과 이야기해야겠어요; **~ I say**
nore? tŏ marhal p'iryoga
ssŭmnikka? 더 말할 필요가
습니까?

edle (*for sewing, on dial*) panŭl
늘; (*for injection*) chusa panŭl 주사
늘
edlework panŭjil 바느질
edy pin-gunghan 빈궁한
gative 1 *adj* GRAM pujŏng-ŭi
정의; *attitude, person* pujŏngjŏgin
정적인; ELEC ŭmgŭgŭi 음극의 2 *n*:
answer in the ~ anirago taedap'ada
니라고 대답하다
glect 1 *n* pangch'i 방치 2 *v/t*
garden, one's health tolboji ant'a
돌보지 않다; **to do X** Xŭl/rŭl haji
ant'a X을/를 하지 않다
glected *garden, author* pŏryŏjin
려진; *feel ~* pŏryŏjin tŭt'an
nŭkkimi tŭlda 버려진 듯한 느낌이
들다
gligence t'aeman 태만
gligent sohorhan 소홀한
gligible *amount* mushihaedo
choŭn 무시해도 좋은
gotiable *salary, terms*
hyŏpssanghal su innŭn 협상할 수
있는
gotiate 1 *v/i* hyŏpssanghada
협상하다 2 *v/t* *deal, settlement*
hyŏpssanghada 협상하다; *obstacles*
ttulkko nagada 뚫고 나가다; *curve*
chal tolda 잘 돌다
gotiation hyŏpssang 협상
gotiator hyŏpssangga 협상가
egro Hŭgin 흑인
eigh *v/i* hinghinggŏrida
힝힝거리다
eighbor iut saram 이웃 사람; (*at
table*) yŏp saram 옆 사람
eighborhood iut 이웃; **in the ~ of**
fig ... kakkai ... 가까이

neighboring *house, state* iushin
이웃인
neighborly iutkkach'i tajŏnghan
이웃같이 다정한
neither 1 *adj* ŏnŭ ...to anin 어느 ...도
아닌 (+ *negative verb*); **~ applicant**
was any good ŏnŭ hubojado
mattanghaji anat-tta 어느 후보자도
마땅하지 않았다 2 *pron* ŏnŭ
tchoktto ... 어느 쪽도 ... (+ *negative
verb*); **which do you want? ~,**
thanks ŏttŏn kŏsŭl wŏnhaseyo? –
komaptchina, ŏnŭ tchoktto
animnida 어떤 것을 원하세요? -
고맙지만, 어느 쪽도 아닙니다 3 *adv*:
~ X nor Y ... Xto Yto ... X도 Y도 ...
(+ *negative verb*); **Jane nor Sally**
knew where it was Cheindo
Saellido kŭgŏshi ŏdi innŭnji mollat-
tta 제인도 샐리도 그것이 어디
있는지 몰랐다 4 *conj*: **~ do I** nadoyo
나도요, chŏdoyo 저도요; **I don't like**
it - ~ do I nanŭn kŭgŏt choahaji
anayo – nado choahaji anayo 나는
그것 좋아하지 않아요 – 나도
좋아하지 않아요; **I can't see it - ~**
can I nanŭn anboinŭn teyo – chŏdo
anboyŏyo 나는 안보이는 데요 – 저도
안보여요
neon light neon ssain 네온 싸인
Nepal Nep'al 네팔
Nepalese 1 *adj* Nep'arŭi 네팔의 2 *n*
(*person*) Nep'arin 네팔인
nephew chok'a 조카
nerd F ŏlgani 얼간이
nerve shin-gyŏng 신경; (*courage*)
yonggi 용기; (*impudence*)
ppŏnppŏnham 뻔뻔함; **it's bad for**
my ~s shin-gyŏng ssŭige handa 신경
쓰이게 한다; **get on s.o.'s ~s**
nuguŭi shin-gyŏng-ŭl kŏndŭrida
누구의 신경을 건드리다
nerve-racking chomajomahage
hanŭn 조마조마하게 하는
nervous *person* shin-gyŏng-i
kwaminhan 신경이 과민한; **be ~**
about doing sth muŏt hanŭn kŏsŭl
puranhaehada 무엇 하는 것을
불안해하다
nervous breakdown shin-gyŏng
soeyak 신경 쇠약

nervous energy shin-gyŏng enŏji 신경 에너지

nervousness shin-gyŏngtchil 신경질

nervous wreck shin-gyŏng soeyaktcha 신경 쇠약자

nervy (*fresh*) ppŏnppŏnhan 뻔뻔한

nest *n* tungji 둥지

♦ **nestle up to** – *s.o.* nuguege momŭ p'yŏnhi kidaeda 누구에게 몸을 편히 기대다

net[1] (*for fishing*) kŭmul 그물; (*for tennis*) net'ŭ 네트

net[2] *adj amount* sunsuhan 순수한; *price* chŏngkka 정가; *weight* p'ojangŭl cheoehan 포장을 제외한

net curtain mangsa k'ŏt'ŭn 망사 커튼

net profit suniik 순이익

nettle *v/t* shin-gyŏngtchilnage hada 신경질나게 하다

network (*of contacts, cells*) kŭmulmang 그물망; COMPUT net'ŭwŏk'ŭ 네트워크

neurologist shin-gyŏngkkwa ŭisa 신경과 의사

neurosis shin-gyŏngtchŭng 신경증

neurotic *adj* shin-gyŏng kwaminŭi 신경 과민의

neuter *v/t animal* kŏsehada 거세하다

neutral 1 *adj country* chungnibŭi 중립의; *color* chunggansaegŭi 중간색의 2 *n* (*gear*) chungnip wich'i 중립 위치; **in** – chungnibe 중립에

neutrality chungnipssŏng 중립성

neutralize muryŏk'age hada 무력하게 하다

never chŏlttae (+ *negative verb*) 절대; *you're* – *going to believe this* tangshinŭn chŏlttaero kŭgŏsŭl midŭl su ŏpssŭl kŏshimnida 당신은 절대로 그것을 믿을 수 없을 것입니다; *you* – *promised, did you?* tangshinŭn chŏlttaero yakssok'aji anatchyo? 당신은 절대로 약속하지 않았죠? ◊ (*past*) han pŏndo (+ *negative verb*) 한 번도; *I have* – *eaten kimchee* han pŏndo kimch'irŭl mŏgŏbon chŏgi ŏpssŏyo 한 번도 김치를 먹어본 적이 없어요

never-ending kkŭdŏmnŭn 끝없는

nevertheless kŭrŏmedo pulguhago 그럼에도 불구하고

new saeroun 새로운; *this system is still* – *to me* i pangshigŭn na-ege yŏjŏnhi saerop-tta 이 방식은 나에게 여전히 새롭다; *I'm* – *to the job* nanŭn kŭ ire ikssuk'aji ant'a 나는 일에 익숙하지 않다; *that's nothir*[?] – saeroun kŏsŭn amu kŏt-tto ŏptt[?] 새로운 것은 아무 것도 없다

newborn *adj* kannan gŏt나

newcomer saero on saram 새로 온 사람; (*to organization*) shinip 신입

newly (*recently*) ch'oegŭn 최근

newly-weds shinhon pubu 신혼 부

new moon ch'ossŭngttal 초승달

news soshik 소식; (*on TV, radio*) nyusŭ 뉴스; *that's* – *to me* kŭmsh[?] ch'omunida 금시 초문이다

news agency t'ongshinsa 통신사;

newscast TV nyusŭ pangsong 뉴스 방송; **newscaster** TV nyusŭ pangsonghanŭn saram 뉴스 방송하는 사람; **news dealer** shinmun p'anmaeso 신문 판매소; **news flash** sokppo 속보; **newspaper** shinmun 신문; **newsreader** TV *etc* nyusŭ pangsonghanŭn saram 뉴스 방송하는 사람; **news report** nyusŭ podo 뉴스 보도; **newsstand** shinmun kap'andae 신문 가판대; **newsvendor** shinmun p'anmaewŏ[?] 신문 판매원

New Year Saehae 새해; (*public holiday*) Shinjŏng 신정; *Happy* –*!* Saehae pok mani padŭseyo! 새해 많이 받으세요!; **New Year's Day** Saehae Ch'ŏnnal 새해 첫날; (*lunar*) Sŏllal 설날; **New Year's Eve** Sŏtta[?] Kŭmŭmnal 섣달 그믐날; **New Yor**[?] Nyuyok 뉴욕; **New Zealand** Nyujillaendŭ 뉴질랜드; **New Zealander** Nyujillaendŭin 뉴질랜드인

next 1 *adj* taŭmŭi 다음의; *the* – *week / month he came back again* taŭm chu / tare kŭga tashi torawat-tta 다음 주 / 달에 그가 다시 돌아왔다; *who's* –*?* taŭm pun? 다음 분? 2 *adv* taŭme 다음에; – *to* (*beside*) …ŭi yŏp'ye …의 옆에; (*in comparison with*) …e ihŏŏ …에 이어서

next-door 1 *adj neighbor* yŏptchibŭ

옆집의 2 adv live 옆ptchibe 옆집에
xt of kin kǔnch'in 근친
oble v/t kalga mŏktta 갉아 먹다;
.o.'s ear saltchak kkaemulda 살짝
깨물다
ce mŏtchin 멋진; be ~ to your
ather ne abŏjihant'e charhae 네
아버지한테 잘해; that's very ~ of
you chŏngmal ch'injŏrhagunnyo
정말 친절하군요
cely written, presented chal 잘;
pleasantly) kippǔge 기쁘게
ceties: social ~ sagyoppŏp 사교법
che (in market) t'ǔmsae 틈새;
special position) chŏktchŏrhan
changso 적절한 장소
ck n (cut) hǔm 흠; in the ~ of time
paro che ttaee bȧro 제 때에
ckel nik'el 니켈; (coin)
ossent'ǔtchari tongjŏn 오센트짜리
동전
ckname n pyŏlmyŏng 별명
iece yŏja chok'a 여자 조카
ggardly adj insaek'an 인색한
ght pam 밤; (in hotel) pak 박; tomorrow ~ naeil pam 내일 밤;
(evening) naeil chŏnyŏk 내일 저녁;
11 o'clock at ~ pam yŏrhanshi 밤
11시; travel by ~ pam yŏhaeng 밤
여행; during the ~ pam saie 밤
사이에; stay the ~ pamǔl chinaeda
밤을 지내다; a room for 3 ~s samil
밤을 mugǔl pang 3일 밤을 묵을
방; work ~s yagan kǔnmuida 야간
근무이다; good ~ annyŏnghi
chumushipsshiyo 안녕히 주무십시요,
chal cha 잘 자
ghtcap (drink) chagi chŏne
mashinǔn sul 자기 전에 마시는 술;
nightclub nait'ǔ k'ŭllŏp 나이트클럽;
nightdress chamot 잠옷; nightfall:
at ~ ch'ojŏnyŏge 초저녁에; night
flight pambihaenggi 밤비행기;
nightgown chamot 잠옷
ghtingale nait'inggeil 나이팅게일
ightlife pam yuhǔng 밤 유흥
ightly 1 adj maeil pamǔi 매일 밤의
2 adv maeil pame 매일 밤에
ightmare angmong kkum 악몽; fig
angmonggat'ǔn kŏt 악몽같은 것
ight porter yagǔn poi 야간 보이;

night school yagan hak-kkyo 야간
학교; night shift yagan kǔnmu 야간
근무; nightshirt chamot 잠옷; nightspot nait'ǔ k'ŭllŏp 나이트 클럽;
nighttime: at ~, in the ~ pame 밤에
nimble chaepparǔn 재빠른
nine ahop 아홉, ku 구
nineteen yŏrahop 열 아홉, shipkku
십구
nineteenth yŏrahop pŏntchaeǔi 열
아홉 번째의
ninetieth ahǔn pŏntchaeǔi 아흔
번째의
ninety ahǔn 아흔, kuship 구십
ninth ahop pŏntchaeǔi 아홉 번째의
nip n (pinch) kkojipk-kki 꼬집기;
(bite) mulgi 물기
nipple chŏtkkoktchi 젖꼭지, yudu
유두
nitrogen chilso 질소
no 1 adv ◊ aniyo 아니오 ◊ (using 'yes',
ie yes, that is right): you don't know
the answer, do you? – ~, I don't
tabǔl morǔjyo? - ye, mollayo 답을
모르죠? - 예. 몰라요 2 adj: there's
~ coffee/tea left namǔn
k'ŏp'i/ch'aga ŏptta 남은 커피/차가
없드; I have ~ family nanǔn kajogi
amudo ŏptta 나는 가족이 아무도
없드; I'm ~ linguist nanǔn
ŏnŏhaktchaga anida 나는
언어학자가 아니다; ~ smoking/~
parking kǔmyŏn/chuch'agǔmji
금연/주차금지; ~ man is perfect
nugudo wanjŏnhaji ant'a 누구도
완전하지 않다
nobility kip'um 기품; the ~ kwijok
귀족
noble adj kogwihan 고귀한
nobody amudo (+ negative verb)
아무도; ~ knows amudo morǔnda
아무도 모른다; there was ~ at
home chibenǔn amudo ŏpssŏt-tta
집에는 아무도 없었다; who was
there? - ~ kŏgi nuga issŏssŏyo? -
amudo ŏpssŏssŏyo 거기 누가
있었어요? - 아무도 없었어요
nod 1 n kkǔdŏgim 끄덕임 2 v/i
kogaerǔl kkǔdŏgida 고개를 끄덕이다
♦ nod off (fall asleep) kkubŏk-
kkubŏk cholda 꾸벅꾸벅 졸다

no-hoper F munŭngnyŏktcha 무능력자

noise sori 소리; (*loud, unpleasant*) soŭm 소음

noisy shikkŭrŏun 시끄러운

nominal *amount* irŭmppunin 이름뿐인

nominate (*appoint*) immyŏnghada 임명하다; **~ s.o. for a post** (*propose*) nugurŭl kongch'ŏnhada 누구를 공천하다

nomination (*appointing*) immyŏng 임명; (*proposal*) kongch'ŏn 공천; (*person proposed*) kongch'ŏnja 공천자

nominee (*person proposed*) kongch'ŏnja 공천자; (*for prize*) hubo 후보; (*person appointed*) immyŏngja 임명자

nonalcoholic alk'oori ŏmnŭn 알코올이 없는

nonaligned chungniptchŏgin 중립적인

nonchalant t'aeyŏnhan 태연한

noncommissioned officer yuk-kkun hasagwan 육군 하사관

noncommittal *response* aemaemohohan 애매모호한; **he was very ~** kŭnŭn koengjanghi aemaemohohan t'aedorŭl chihaettta 그는 굉장히 애매모호한 태도를 취했다

nondescript t'ŭktching-ŏmnŭn 특징없는

none amu kŏtto (+ *negative verb*) 아무 것도; (*person*) amudo (+ *negative verb*) 아무도; **~ of the students is American** hakssaengdŭl chung amudo Miguk sarami anida 학생들 중 아무도 미국 사람이 아니다; **~ of the chocolate was sold** amu ch'yok'ollitto p'alliji anattta 아무 초콜릿도 팔리지 않았다; **there is / are ~ left** amu kŏtto namŭn kŏshi ŏptta 아무 것도 남은 것이 없다

nonentity pojal kŏt ŏmnŭn 보잘 것 없는

nonetheless kŭrŏmedo pulguhago 그럼에도 불구하고

nonexistent chonjaehaji annŭn 존재하지 않는

nonfiction nonp'iksshyŏn 논픽션;

non(in)flammable puryŏnsŏng-ŭi 불연성의; **noninterference, nonintervention** pulgansŏp 불간섭; **non-iron** *shirt* tarimjiri p'iryoŏmnŭn 다림질이 필요없는

no-no F: **that's a ~** kŭgŏsŭn haesŏnŭn andoenda 그것은 해서는 안된다

no-nonsense *approach* hyŏnshiltchŏgin 현실적인

nonpayment mibul 미불; **nonpolluting** mugonghaeŭi 무공해의; **nonresident** *n* pigŏjuja 비거주자; **nonreturnable** *deposit* hwanbul pulgaŭi 환불 불가의

nonsense maldo andoenŭn kŏt 말도 안되는 것; **don't talk ~** maldo andoenŭn sori haji mara 말도 안되는 소리 하지 마라; **~, it's easy!** musŭn sori, shwiun kŏshiya! 무슨 소리, 쉬운 것이야!

nonskid *tires* mikkŭrŏjiji annŭn 미끄러지지 않는; **nonslip** *surface* mikkŭrŏjiji annŭn 미끄러지지 않는; **nonsmoker** (*person*) pihŭbyŏnja 비흡연자; **nonstandard** p'yojune mat-tchi annŭn 표준에 맞지 않는; **nonstick** *pan* nurŏputtchi annŭn 눌어붙지 않는; **nonstop 1** *adj flight, train* chik'aengŭi 직행의; (*chatter*) chungdan ŏmnŭn 중단 없는 **2** *adv fly, travel* chik'aeng-ŭro 직행으로; *chatter, argue* chungdan ŏpsshi 중단 없이; **nonswimmer** suyŏng-ŭl mot'anŭn saram 수영을 못하는 사람; **nonunion** *adj* chohabe kaip'aji anŭn 조합에 가입하지 않은; **nonviolence** pip'ongnyŏk 비폭력; **nonviolent** pip'ongnyŏgŭi 비폭력의

noodles kukssu 국수; (*instant*) ramyŏn 라면; (*chilled*) naengmyŏn 냉면

nook kusŏk 구석

noon chŏng-o 정오; **at ~** chŏng-o-e 정오에

noose olgami 올가미

nor ...to ttohan (+ *negative verb*) ...또한; **~ do I** nado anida 나도 아니다

norm chŏngsang 정상

rmal chŏngsang-ŭi 정상의
rmality chŏngsang sangt'ae 정상
태
rmalize *relationships*
ŏngsanghwahada 정상화하다
rmally (*usually*) pot'ong-ŭro
통으로; (*in a normal way*)
ŏngsang-ŭro 정상으로
rth 1 *n* puk 북; **to the ~ of** ...ŭi
ŭktchoge ...의 북쪽에 2 *adj*
ŭktchogŭi 북쪽의 3 *adv travel*
ŭktchoguro 북쪽으로; **~ of** ...ŭi
ŭkppang-e ...의 북방에
rth America Pungmi 북미
rth American 1 *adj* Pungmiŭi
미의 2 *n* Pungmiin 북미인
rtheast *n* tongbuk 동북
rtherly *adj* puk'yang-ŭi 북향의
rthern pukppuŭi 북부의
rtherner pukppu chibaram saram
부 지방 사람
rth Korea Puk'an 북한
rth Korean 1 *adj* Puk'anŭi 북한의
n Puk'an saram 북한 사람
rth Pole Pukkŭk 북극
rthward *travel* puktchoguro
쪽으로
rthwest *n* puksssŏ 북서
rway Norŭwei 노르웨이
rwegian 1 *adj* Norŭweiŭi
르웨이의 2 *n* (*person*) Norŭweiin
르웨이인; (*language*) Norŭweiŏ
르웨이어
se k'o 코; **it was right under my**
! paro nae nun ap'esŏ irŏnat-tta!
로 내 눈 앞에서 일어났다!
ose around k'aeda 캐다
sebleed k'op'i 코피
stalgia hyangsu 향수
stalgic hyangsuŭi 향수의
stril k'otkkumŏng 콧구멍
sy ch'amgyŏnhagi choahanŭn
견하기 좋아하는
t: **~ this one, that one** igŏshi
nira chŏgŏt 이것이 아니라 저것,
gŏt malgo chŏgŏt 이것 말고 저것; **~**
ow chigŭm malgo 지금 말고; **~**
ere kŭgŏt malgo 그곳 말고; **~**
efore Tuesday / next week
wayoil / taŭm chu chŏnenŭn
ndoego 화요일 / 다음 주 전에는

안되고; **~ for me, thanks**
komaptchiman, chŏnŭn
kwanch'anssŭmnida 고맙지만, 저는
괜찮습니다; **~ a lot** pyŏllo 별로 ◊
(*with verbs*): **it's ~ ready / allowed**
igŏsŭn chunbitoeji / hŏgadoeji anat-
tta 그것은 준비되지 / 허가되지
않았다; **I don't know** nanŭn
morŭnda 나는 모른다; **I am ~**
American nanŭn Migugini
animnida 나는 미국인이 아닙니다;
he didn't help kŭnŭn toptchi anat-
tta 그는 돕지 않았다; **don't do it**
like that kŭrŏk'e haji maseyo
그렇게 하지 마세요
notable chumok'al manhan 주목할
만한
notary kongjŭng-in 공증인
notch *n* pen chaguk 벤 자국
note *n* (*short letter*) tchalbŭn p'yŏnji
짧은 편지; MUS ŭmp'yo 음표; (*to self*)
memo 메모; (*comment on text*) chu
주; **take ~s** chŏktta 적다; **take ~ of**
sth muŏsŭl arach'aeda 무엇을
알아채다
♦ **note down** chŏgŏduda 적어두다
notebook kongch'aek 공책; COMPUT
not'ŭbuk 노트북
notepad memojich'ŏp 메모지첩
notepaper p'yŏnjiji 편지지
nothing amu kŏt-tto (+ *negative verb*)
아무 것도; **there's ~ left** amu kŏt-
tto namtchi anat-tta 아무 것도 남지
않았다; **what did you do? - ~**
muŏsŭl mŏgŏssŏyo? - amu kŏt-tto
무엇을 먹었어요? - 아무 것도; **~ for**
me thanks chŏnŭn kwaench'anayo
저는 괜찮아요; **~ can change it**
ŏttŏn kŏt-tto kŭgŏsŭl pakkul su
ŏptta 어떤 것도 그것을 바꿀 수
없다; **but... ...il ppun** ...일 뿐; **he's**
~ but trouble kŭnŭn munjekkŏriil
ppunida 그는 문제거리일 뿐이다; **~**
much pyŏllo 별로; **for ~** (*for free*)
muryoro 무료로; (*for no reason*)
amu iyu ŏpsshi 아무 이유 없이; **I'd**
like ~ better naega cheil choahanŭn
kŏshida 내가 제일 좋아하는 것이다
notice 1 *n* (*on bulletin board, in*
street) keshi 게시; (*advance warning*)

chuŭi 주의; *(in newspaper)* konggo 공고; *(to leave job, to leave house)* t'ongji 통지; *at short ~* tchalbŭn shihanŭl namgin ch'ae 짧은 시한을 남긴 채; *until further ~* ch'uhu t'ongjiga issŭl ttaekkaji 추후 통지가 있을 때까지; *give s.o. his/her ~ (to quit job)* nuguege haeim t'ongjirŭl hada 누구에게 해임 통지를 하다; *hand in one's ~ (to employer)* sajik'al kŏsŭl allida 사직할 것을 알리다; *four weeks' ~* saju chŏnŭi t'ongjihanŭn kŏt 사주 전의 통지하는 것; *take ~ of* ...e chuŭihada ...에 주의하다; *take no ~ of* ...e amurŏn chuŭirŭl haji ant'a ...에 아무런 주의를 하지 않다 2 *v/t* arach'aeda 알아채다

noticeable chumok'al manhan 주목할 만한
notify konggohada 공고하다
notion saenggak 생각
notions panŭjil yongp'um 바느질 용품
notorious angmyŏng nop'ŭn 악명 높은
nougat nuga 누가
noun myŏngsa 명사
nourishing yŏngnyang-innŭn 영양있는
nourishment yŏngnyangbun 영양분
novel *n* sosŏl 소설
novelist sosŏlga 소설가
novelty *(being novel)* chamshinham 참신함; *(sth novel)* saeroum 새로움
November shibirwŏl 십일월
novice ch'oshimja 초심자
now chigŭm 지금; *~ and again, ~ and then* ttaettaero 때때로; *by ~* chigŭmtchŭm 지금쯤; *from ~ on* chigŭmbut'ŏ 지금부터; *right ~* paro chigŭm 바로 지금; *just ~ (at this moment)* chigŭm paro 지금 바로; *(a little while ago)* paro chŏne 바로 전에; *~, ~!* cha, cha! 자, 자!; *where did I put it?* ŏ, naega kŭgŏsŭl ŏdie tuŏssŭlkka? 어, 내가 그것을 어디에 두었을까?
nowadays yojŭm 요즈음
nowhere amu kosedo 아무 곳에도; *it's ~ near finished* hanado

kkŭnnaji anat-tta 하나도 끝나지 않았다
nozzle kkŭt 끝
nuclear haegŭi 핵의, haek 핵
nuclear energy haek enŏji 핵 에너
nuclear fission haek punnyŏl 핵 분열; **nuclear-free** pihaegŭi 비핵의 **nuclear physics** haek mullihak 핵 물리학; **nuclear power** wŏnjaryŏk 원자력; **nuclear power station** wŏnjaryŏk paltchŏnso 원자력 발전소; **nuclear reactor** wŏnjaro 원자로; **nuclear waste** haek p'yegimul 핵 폐기물; **nuclear weapons** haek mugi 핵 무기
nude 1 *adj* almomŭi 알몸의 2 *n (painting)* nach'ehwa 나체화; *in th ~* nach'ero 나체로
nudge *v/t* p'alkkumch'iro k'ukk'uk tchirŭda 팔꿈치로 쿡쿡 찌르다
nudist *n* nach'ejuŭija 나체주의자
nuisance kwich'anŭn kŏt 귀찮은 것 *make a ~ of oneself* namege p'yerŭl kkich'ida 남에게 폐를 끼치다; *what a ~!* irŏk'e kwich'ant suga! 이렇게 귀찮을 수가!
nuke *v/t* haek konggyŏk'ada 핵 공격하다
null and void muhyoŭi 무효의
numb kamgagŏmnŭn 감각없는; *(emotionally)* mugamgak'an 무감각한
number 1 *n (figure, quantity)* su 수; *(of hotel room, house, phone ~ etc)* pŏnho 번호; *quite a ~ of* manŭn 많은; *a small ~ of* chŏgŭn 적은 2 *v (put a number on)* pŏnhorŭl maegida 번호를 매기다
numeral sutcha 숫자
numerate kyesanŭl hal su innŭn 계산을 할 수 있는
numeric keys COMPUT sutchap'an 숫자판
numerous manŭn 많은
nun sunyŏ 수녀
nurse kanhosa 간호사
nursery yugashil 육아실; *(for plants)* onshil 온실
nursery rhyme tongnyo 동요; **nursery school** poyugwŏn 보육원; **nursery school teacher** poyugwŏn

yosa 보육원 교사

~sing kanho ŏmmu 간호 업무

~sing home (for old people) ~angnowŏn 양로원

~t kyŏn-gwa 견과; (for bolt) nŏt'ŭ 너트; **~s** F (testicles) pural 불알

~crackers hodu kkanŭn kigu 호두 까는 기구

~trient yŏngnyangbun 영양분

~trition yŏngnyang 영양

~tritious yŏngnyang-i innŭn 영양이 있는

nuts adj F (crazy) mich'in 미친; **be ~ about s.o.** nugue mich'ida 누구에 미치다

nutshell: in a ~ aju kanttanhage 아주 간단하게

nutty taste kyŏn-gwa mashi nanŭn 견과 맛이 나는; F (crazy) mich'in 미친

nylon 1 n naillon 나일론 **2** adj naillonŭi 나일론의

O

oak (*tree*) ok'ŭnamu 오크나무; (*wood*) ok'ŭ 오크
oar no 노
oasis oashissŭ 오아시스; *fig* hyushikch'ŏ 휴식처
oath LAW sŏnsŏ 선서; (*swearword*) yokssŏl 욕설; *you are on ~* tangshinŭn sŏnsŏrŭl haessŭmnida 당신은 선서를 했습니다
oatmeal ot'ŭmil 오트밀
oats kwiri 귀리
obedience sunjong 순종
obedient sunjonghanŭn 순종하는
obey …e sunjonghada …에 순종하다
obituary n pugo 부고
object¹ n (*thing*) mulch'e 물체; (*of love, pity*) taesang 대상; (*aim*) moktchŏk 목적; GRAM moktchŏgŏ 목적어
object² v/i pandaehada 반대하다
♦ object to …e pandaehada …에 반대하다
objection pandae 반대
objectionable (*unpleasant*) pulk'waehan 불쾌한
objective 1 adj kaekkwanjŏgin 객관적인 2 n mokp'yo 목표
obligation ŭimu 의무; *be under an ~ to s.o.* nuguege ŭnhyerŭl ipkko itta 누구에게 은혜를 입고 있다
obligatory ŭimuŭi 의무의
oblige: *much ~d!* chŏngmal komawŏyo! 정말 고마워요!
obliging chal tolbwajunŭn 잘 돌봐주는
oblique 1 adj reference kanjŏptchŏgin 간접적인 2 n (*in punctuation*) pitkkŭm 빗금
obliterate city wanjŏnhi p'agoehada 완전히 파괴하다; memory chiuda 지우다
oblivion ich'yŏjin sangt'ae 잊혀진 상태; *fall into ~* ich'yŏjida 잊혀지다
oblivious: *be ~ of* …ŭl/rŭl arach'ariji

mot'ada …을/를 알아차리지 못하다
oblong adj chikssagak'yŏng-ŭi 직사각형의
obnoxious aju pulk'waehan 아주 불쾌한
obscene ŭmnanhan 음란한; poverty kkŭmtchik'an 끔찍한
obscure (*hard to see*) chal poiji annŭn 잘 보이지 않는; (*hard to understand*) nanhaehan 난해한; (*little known*) mumyŏng-ŭi 무명의
observance (*of festival*) haengsa 행사
observant kwanch'allyŏgi yerihan 관찰력이 예리한
observation (*of nature*) kwanch'al 관찰; (*comment*) kwanch'al kyŏlgwa 관찰 결과
observatory kwanch'ŭ̆ksso 관측소
observe (*notice*) nunch'ich'aeda 눈치채다; natural phenomena kwanch'arhada 관찰하다; *he was leaving the …* kŭga …ŭl/rŭl ttŏnanŭn kŏshi mok-kkyŏkttoeŏt-… 그가 …을/를 떠나는 것이 목격되었다
observer kwanch'altcha 관찰자; (*at conference, elections*) ip'oein 입회인
obsess: *be ~d with* …e(ge) sarojap'ida …에(게) 사로잡히다
obsession kangbak kwannyŏm 강박 관념
obsessive kangbak kwanyŏme sarojap'in 강박 관념에 사로잡힌
obsolete p'yemuri toen 폐물이 된
obstacle chang-ae 장애; (*to progress etc*) panghae 방해
obstetrician sanbuinkkwa ŭisa 산부인과 의사
obstinacy kojip 고집
obstinate kojibi sen 고집이 센
obstruct road, passage maktta 막다; investigation, police panghaehada 방해하다
obstruction (*on road etc*)

anghaemul 방해물

structive *tactics* panghaehanŭn
방해하는

tain hoekttŭk'ada 획득하다; *advice*
-tta 얻다

tainable *products* kuibi kanŭnghan
제품이 가능한

vious myŏngbaek'an 명백한; (*not
btle*) nogoltchŏgin 노골적인
! mullonijiyo! 물론이지요!

casion ttae 때

casional kakkŭmŭi 가끔의

casionally ttaettaero 때때로

cult 1 *adj* mabŏbŭi 마법의 2 *n: the
~ mabŏp 마법

cupant (*of vehicle*) sŭnggaek 승객;
of house) chugŏja 주거자

cupation (*job*) chigŏp 직업; (*of
ountry*) chŏmnyŏng 점령

cupy ch'ajihada 차지하다; *country
hŏmnyŏnghada 점령하다

cur irŏnada 일어나다; *it ~red to
ne that ...* na-ege ...ranŭn
aenggagi ttollat-tta 나에게 ...라는
각이 떠올랐다

currence sakkŏn 사건

ean pada 바다

clock: at five / six ~ tasŏt / yŏsŏt
hie 다섯 / 여섯 시에

ctober shiwŏl 시월

topus munŏ 문어; (*very small*)
aktchi 낙지

ld (*strange*) isanghan 이상한; (*not
ven*) holssu 홀수; *the ~ one out*
person) yubyŏlnan saram 유별난
람; (*thing*) yubyŏlnan kŏt 유별난

lds: be at ~ with ...wa / kwa
h'ungdorhada ...와 / 과 충돌하다
lds and ends chapttongsani
동사니; (*to do*) chapttahan kŏttŭl
답다한 것들

lometer chuhaeng kŏrigye 주행
리계

lor naemsae 냄새
  (*possession*) ...ŭi ...의; *the color ~
he car* kŭ ch'aŭi saek 그 차의 색;
he works ~ Dickens Tik'insŭŭi
hakp'um 디킨스의 작품; *five / ten
minutes ~ twelve* yŏldushi obun /

shippun jŏn 열두시 오분 / 십분 전;
die ~ cancer / pneumonia
amŭro / p'yeryŏmŭro chuktta
암으로 / 폐렴으로 죽다; *love ~
money / adventure* tone / mohŏme
taehan sarang 돈에 / 모험에 대한
사랑; *~ the three this is ...* set
chung-e igŏshi ...ida 셋 중에 이것이
...이다

off 1 *prep* ...esŏ ttŏrŏjyŏsŏ ...에서
떨어져서; *~ the main road* (*away
from*) chudoroesŏ ttŏrŏjyŏ
주도로에서 떨어져; (*leading off*)
chudoroesŏ pŏsŏna 주도로에서
벗어나; *$20 ~ the price* 20tallŏ
harinhayŏ 20달러 할인하여; *he's ~
his food* kŭnŭn immasŭl irŏt-tta
그는 입맛을 잃었다 2 *adv: be ~* (*of
light, TV, machine*) kkŏjyŏ it-tta
꺼져 있다; (*of brake*) p'ullyŏ it-tta
풀려 있다; (*of lid*) yŏllyŏ it-tta
있다; (*not at work*) shwida 쉬다;
(*canceled*) ch'wisodoeda 취소되다;
we're ~ tomorrow (*leaving*) urinŭn
naeil ttŏnanda 우리는 내일 떠난다;
I'm ~ to New York nanŭn Nyuyoge
kal kŏshida 나는 뉴욕에 갈 것이다;
with his pants / hat ~ pajirŭl /
mojarŭl pŏsŭnch'ae 바지를 / 모자를
벗은채; *take a day ~* haru shwida
하루 쉬다; *it's 3 miles ~* 3mail
ttŏrŏjyŏ it-tta 3마일 떨어져 있다; *it's
a long way ~* (*in the distance*) mŏlli
ttŏrŏjyŏ it-tta 멀리 떨어져 있다; (*in
the future*) mŏn amnarŭi irida 먼
앞날의 일이다; *drive / walk ~* ch'arŭl
molgo / kŏrŏsŏ ka pŏrida 차를
몰고 / 걸어서 가 버린다 3 *adj: the ~
switch* chŏngji pŏt'ŭn 정지 버튼

offend *v/t* (*insult*) kibun sanghage
hada 기분 상하게 하다

offender LAW pŏmjoeja 범죄자

offense LAW wibŏp 위법

offensive 1 *adj* pulk'waehan 불쾌한
2 *n* MIL konggyŏk 공격; *go onto the
~* konggyŏk'ada 공격하다

offer 1 *n* chegong 제공 2 *v/t*
chegonghada 제공하다; *~ s.o. sth*
nuguege muŏsŭl kwŏnhada 누구에게
무엇을 권하다

offhand *adj attitude* amurŏk'ena

hanŭn 아무렇게나 하는
office (*building*) samushillyong kŏnmul 사무실용 건물; (*room*) samushil 사무실; (*position*) kwanch'ŏng 관청
office block samushillyong koch'ŭng piltting 사무실용 고층 빌딩
office hours ŏmmu shigan 업무 시간
officer MIL changgyo 장교; (*in police*) kyŏnggwan 경관
official 1 *adj organization, statement* kongshigŭi 공식의; *view, theory* kongtchŏgin 공적인; (*confirmed*) kongshik'wadoen 공식화된 **2** *n* kongmuwŏn 공무원
officially (*strictly speaking*) kongshiktchŏguro 공식적으로
off-line *adj* chŏpssogŭl anhan sangt'aeŭi 접속을 안한 상태의; **go ~** chŏpssogŭl kkŭnt'a 접속을 끊다
off-peak *rates* hansanhan ttaeŭi 한산한 때의; *season* pisugiŭi 비수기의
off-season 1 *adj* pisugiŭi 비수기의 **2** *n* pisugi 비수기
offset *v/t losses* sangswaehada 상쇄하다
offside 1 *adj wheel etc* ch'ado tchogŭi 차도 쪽의 **2** *adv* SP op'ŭsaidŭ 오프사이드
offspring chashik 자식
off-white *adj* misaegŭi 미색의
often chaju 자주
oil 1 *n* kirŭm 기름; (*for machine*) sŏgyu 석유; (*for skin*) oil 오일 **2** *v/t hinges, bearings* kirŭmch'irŭl hada 기름칠을 하다
oil company sŏgyu hoesa 석유 회사; **oil painting** yuhwa 유화; **oil rig** sŏgyu kulch'ak changch'i 석유 굴착 장치; **oil tanker** yujosŏn 유조선; **oil well** yujŏng 유정
oily kirŭmkki manŭn 기름기 많은
ointment yŏn-go 연고
ok: can I? - ~ haedo toelkkayo? - kŭraeyo 해도 될까요? - 그래요; **is it ~ with you if ...?** ... haedo kwaench'angessŭmnikka? ... 해도 괜찮겠습니까?; **that's ~ by me** nanŭn kwaench'anayo 나는 괜찮아요; **are you ~?** (*well, not hurt*)

kwaench'anŭseyo? 괜찮으세요?; *are you ~ for Friday?* kŭmnyoire kwaench'anŭseyo? 금요일에 괜찮으세요?; *he's ~* (*is a good guy*) kŭnŭn kwaench'anŭn saramida 그는 괜찮은 사람이다; *is this bus ~ for ...?* i pŏssŭ ...e kamnikka? 이 버스 ...에 갑니까?; *the car's going ~ now* ch'aga ijenŭn chal kanda 차가 이제는 잘 간다
old *person* nŭlgŭn 늙은; *building, car etc* oraedoen 오래된; *custom* oraen 오랜; (*previous*) yejŏnŭi 예전의; (*no longer fresh*) nalgŭn 낡은; *how ~ are you / is he?* tangshinŭn / kŭnŭn myŏtssarimnikka? 당신은 / 그는 몇살입니까?
old age nonyŏn 노년
Old Choson Kojosŏn 고조선
old-fashioned kushigŭi 구식의
olive ollibŭ 올리브
olive oil ollibŭ kirŭm 올리브 기름
Olympic Games Ollimp'ik Keim 올림픽 게임
omelet omŭllet 오믈렛
ominous pulgirhan 불길한
omission (*act*) t'aeman 태만; (*that omitted*) ppajin kŏt 빠진 것
omit ppaeda 빼다; **~ to do sth** muŏsŭl hagirŭl it-tta 무엇을 하기를 잊다
on 1 *prep* ... wie ... 위에; **~ the table** t'eibŭl wie 테이블 위에; **~ the wall** pyŏge 벽에; **~ the bus / train** pŏsŭ kich'a-e 버스에 / 기차에; **~ TV / the radio** t'ibŭiro / radioro TV로 / 라디오로; **~ Sunday** iryoire 일요일에; **~ the 1st of ...** ...ŭi ch'ŏtchaenare ...의 첫째날에; **this is ~ me** (*I'm paying*) chega naegessŭmnida 제가 내겠습니다; **his arrival / departure** kŭga toch'ak'aja / ch'ulbarhaja kot 그가 도착하자 / 출발하자 곧 **2** *adv* **be ~** (*of light, TV, computer etc*) k'yŏjyŏ it-tta 켜져 있다; (*of brake*) kŏllyŏ tta 걸려 있다; (*of lid, top*) tach'yŏ tta 닫혀 있다; (*of program*) pangsongdoeda 방송되다; (*of meeting etc: be scheduled to happen*) itkket-tta 있겠다; **what's ~ tonight**

on TV etc) onŭrŭn muŏsŭl
amnikka? 오늘은 무엇을 합니까?;
hat's planned?) onŭrŭn muŏsŭl
al kŏsimnikka? 오늘은 무엇을 할
입니까?; *with his jacket / hat ~*
et'urŭl ipkko / mojarŭl ssŭgo 외투를
고 / 모자를 쓰고; *you're ~ (I accept
our offer etc)* chossŭmnida
습니다; *~ you go (go ahead)*
yesok'ahipsshio 계속하십시오;
alk / talk ~ kyesok kŏt-tta / iyagi
ada 계속 걷다 / 이야기 하다; *and so
~* ... kit'adŭngdŭng 기타 등등; *~ and
alk etc* kkŭnimŏpsshi kyesok'aesŏ
임없이 계속해서 3 *adj: the ~
witch* shijak pŏt'ŭn 시작 버튼
ce 1 *adv (one time)* han pŏn 한 번;
formerly) hanttaee 한때에; *~ again,
more* tashi han pŏn 다시 한 번; *at
(immediately)* chŭksshi 즉시; *all at
(suddenly)* kaptchagi 갑자기; *(all)
t ~ (together)* hankkŏbŏne
한까번에; *~ upon a time there was
..* yennal yettchŏge ... i issŏt-tta
날 옛적에 ... 이 있었다 2 *conj:
..hal ttae ...*할 때; *~ you have fin-
shed* nega ta kkŭnnaessŭl ttae 네가
끝냈을 때

e 1 *(number)* hana 하나, il 2 *adj*
anaŭi 하나의; *~ day* ŏnŭ nal 어느
날 3 *pron* hana 하나; *which ~?
person)* ŏnŭ saram? 어느 사람?
thing) ŏnŭ kŏt? 어느 것?; *~ by
enter, deal with* hanasshik 하나씩;
another sŏro 서로; *what can ~
say / do?* nuga muŏsŭl marhal / hal
su itkketssŭmnikka? 누가 무엇을
할 / 할 수 있겠습니까?; *the little
~s* aidŭl 아이들
ne-off n *(unique event, person)*
yuirhan kŏt 유일한 것; *(exception)*
yeoeŏpsshi han pŏn ppunin kŏt
예외없이 한 번 뿐인 것
ne-parent family p'yŏnch'in kajŏng
편친 가정
neself chagi chashin 자기 자신; *do
sth by ~* muŏsŭl sŭsŭro hada 무엇을
스스로 하다
ne-sided *discussion, fight*
ilbangjŏgin 일방적인; **one-way**
street ilbang t'onghaengno 일방

통행로; **one-way ticket** p'yŏndo
sŭngch'akkwŏn 편도 승차권
onion yangp'a 양파
on-line *adj* ollainŭi 온라인의; *go ~ to*
...wa / kwa chŏpssok'ada ...와 / 과
접속하다
on-line service COMPUT ollain
sŏbissŭ 온라인 서비스
onlooker kugyŏngkkun 구경꾼
only 1 *adv* tanji 단지; *not ~ X but Y
also* Xppunman anira Ydo ttohan
X뿐만 아니라 Y도 또한; *~ just*
kanshinhi 간신히, kyŏu 겨우 2 *adj*
yuirhan 유일한; *~ son* oeadŭl 외아들;
~ daughter oedongttal 외동딸
onset shijak 시작
onside *adv* SP chŏnggyuŭi wich'ie
정규의 위치에
onto: *put X ~ Y (on top of)* Xŭl / rŭl
Ywie not'a X을 / 를 Y위에 놓다
onward ap'ŭro 앞으로; *from ... ~*
...esŏbut'ŏ ...에서부터
ooze 1 *v/i (of liquid, mud)*
sŭmyŏnaoda 스며나오다 2 *v/t: he ~s
charm* kŭegenŭn nŏmch'yŏnanŭn
maeryŏgi it-tta 그에게는 넘쳐나는
매력이 있다
opaque *glass* pult'umyŏnghan
불투명한
OPEC (= *Organization of Petroleum Exporting Countries*) Sŏgyu
Such'ulguk Kigu 석유 수출국 기구
open 1 *adj door, shop, window* yŏllyŏ
innŭn 열려 있는; *flower* p'in 핀;
COMPUT *file* yŏllin 열린; *(honest,
frank)* sumgimŏmnŭn 숨김없는;
market, society kaebangdoen 개방된;
relationship sŏro kusok'aji annŭn
서로 구속하지 않는; *countryside*
hwŏni t'ŭin 훤히 트인; *in the ~ air*
yaoeesŏ 야외에서 2 *v/t also* COMPUT
file yŏlda 열다; *book, paper* p'ida
피다; *bank account* t'ŭda 트다;
meeting shijak'ada 시작하다 3 *v/i (of
door, shop)* yŏllida 열리다; *(of
flower)* p'ida 피다
♦ **open up** *v/i (of person)*
songmaŭmŭl t'ŏnot'a 속마음을
터놓다
open-air *adj meeting, concert* yaoeŭi
야외의; *pool* ogoeŭi 옥외의

open-ended *contract etc* handaga ŏmnŭn 한도가 없는

opening (*in wall etc*) t'ŭm 틈; (*of movie, novel etc*) appubun 앞부분; (*job going*) kongsŏk 공석

openly (*honestly, frankly*) sumgimŏpssi 숨김없이

open-minded hŏshimt'anhoehan 허심탄회한; **open plan office** op'ŭn p'üllaen samushil 오픈 플랜 사무실, kubunŏpsshi yŏrŏshi hamkke ssŭnŭn samushil 구분없이 여럿이 함께 쓰는 사무실; **open ticket** op'ŭnt'ik'et 오픈티켓, sayong-irŭl chehanhaji annŭn p'yo 사용일을 제한하지 않은 표

opera op'era 오페라

opera glasses op'era mang-wŏn-gyŏng 오페라 망원경; **opera house** op'era haussŭ 오페라 하우스; **opera singer** op'era kasu 오페라 가수

operate 1 *v/i* (*of company*) unyŏngdoeda 운영되다; (*of airline etc*) chojongdoeda 조종되다; (*of machine*) chakttonghada 작동하다; MED susurŭl hada 수술을 하다 2 *v/t machine* chojonghada 조종하다

♦ **operate on** MED susurhada 수술하다

operating instructions sayongppŏp 사용법; **operating room** MED susulshil 수술실; **operating system** COMPUT op'ŏreit'ing shisŭt'em 오퍼레이팅 시스템

operation MED susul 수술; (*of machine*) chojong 조종; ~**s** (*of company*) unyŏng 운영; **have an ~** MED susurŭl pat-tta 수술을 받다

operator TELEC kyohwansu 교환수; (*of machine*) kisa 기사; (*tour ~*) kwan-gwang-ŏptcha 관광업자

ophthalmologist an-kkwa ŭisa 안과 의사

opinion ŭigyŏn 의견; **in my ~** naŭi ŭigyŏnŭronŭn 나의 의견으로는

opponent (*in game*) sangdae 상대; (*of tax reforms etc*) pandaeja 반대자

opportunity kihoe 기회

oppose pandaehada 반대하다; **be ~d to** …e pandaehada …에 반대하다; **as ~d to** …wa/kwa pandaero …와/과 반대로

opposite 1 *adj side, direction, meaning* pandaeŭi 반대의; *views, characters* sangbandoen 상반된; **the ~ sex** isŏng 이성 2 *n* pandae 반대

opposition (*to plan*) pandae 반대; POL yadang 야당

oppress *the people* appak'ada 압박하다

oppressive *rule* kahok'an 가혹한; *dictator* p'oak'an 포악한; *weather* uurhagehanŭn 우울하게하는

optical illusion ch'aksshi 착시

optician an-gyŏngsang 안경상

optimism nakch'ŏnjuŭi 낙천주의

optimist nakch'ŏnjuŭija 낙천주의자

optimistic *attitude, person* nakch'ŏnjŏgin 낙천적인; *view, speech* nakkwanjŏgin 낙관적인

optimum 1 *adj* ch'oejŏgŭi 최적의 2 *n* ch'oejŏk 최적

option sŏnt'aek-kkwŏn 선택권

optional sŏnt'aegŭi 선택의

optional extras opsshŏn sangp'um 옵션 상품

or hogŭn 혹은, ttonŭn 또는; **~ else!** kŭroch'i anŭmyŏn! 그렇지 않으면!

oral *exam* kusurŭi 구술의; *hygiene* kugang-ŭi 구강의; **~ sex** oral sekssŭ 오랄 섹스

orange 1 *adj* (*color*) chuhwangsaegŭi 주황색의 2 *n* (*fruit*) orenji 오렌지; (*color*) chuhwangsaek 주황색

orange juice orenji chusŭ 오렌지 주스

orator yŏnsŏlga 연설가

orbit 1 *n* (*of earth*) kwedo 궤도; **send sth into** ~ muŏsŭl kwedo-e ollida 무엇을 궤도에 올리다 2 *v/t* kongjŏnhada 공전하다

orchard kwasuwŏn 과수원

orchestra ok'esŭt'ŭra 오케스트라

orchid nanch'o 난초

ordeal shiryŏn 시련

order 1 *n* (*command*) myŏngnyŏng 명령; (*sequence*) sunsŏ 순서; (*being well arranged*) paeyŏl 배열; (*for goods, in restaurant*) chumun 주문; **in ~ to** … hagi wihayŏ … 하기 위하여; **out of ~** (*not functioning*) kojangnan 고장난; (*not in sequence*)

nsŏga pakkwin 순서가 바뀐 2 v/t
...ut in sequence, layout) sunsŏdaero
nŏnginhada 순서대로 정리하다;
oods, meal chumunhada 주문하다;
s.o. to do sth nuguege muŏsŭl
arago myŏngnyŏnghada 누구에게
...ŏt을 하고 명령하다 3 v/i (in
...staurant) chumunhada 주문하다
...erly 1 adj lifestyle parŭn 바른 2 n
(...n hospital) pyŏng-wŏnŭi
...nabyŏkppu 병원의 잡역부
...inary pot'ong-ŭi 보통의
...e kwangsŏk 광석
...gan ANAT chojik 조직; MUS orŭgan
...르간
...ganic food yugi nongppŏbŭi 유기
...법의; fertilizer yugiŭi 유기의
...ganism saengmul 생물
...ganization kigu 기구; (organizing)
...hojik 조직
...ganize chojik'ada 조직하다
...ganizer (person) chojiktcha 조직자
...gasm orŭgajŭm 오르가즘
...ent Tongnyang 동양
...ent v/t: **the teacher ~ed me**
ward ... sŏnsaengnimi naŭi
...wanshimŭl ... tchogŭro ikkŭro
...huŏt으로 이끌어 주었다; **~ oneself**
...get bearings) chagi wich'irŭl
...okpparo alda 자기 위치를 똑바로
...다
...ental 1 adj tongnyang-ŭi 동양의
...n Tongnyang saram 동양 사람
...gin kiwŏn 기원; **person of Chi**
ese ~ Chunggugesŏ on saram
...국에서 온 사람
...ginal 1 adj (not copied) chintchaŭi
...짜의; (first) ch'oech'oŭi 최초의 2 n
(...painting etc) wŏnjak 원작
...ginality tokch'angssŏng 독창성
...ginally wŏllaenŭn 원래는; (at first)
...h'ŏŭmenŭn 처음에는
...ginate 1 v/t scheme, idea shijak'ada
...작하다 2 v/i (of idea, belief)
...irot'ada 비롯하다; (of family)
...h'ulsshinida 출신이다
...ginator (of scheme etc) ch'angshija
...시자; **he's not an ~** kŭnŭn ch'ang...
...ijŏgin sarami anida 그는 창의적인
...람이 아니다

ornament n changsshikp'um 장식품
ornamental changshingnyong-ŭi
장식용의
ornate style, architecture hwaryŏhage
changshik'an 화려하게 장식한
orphan n koa 고아
orphanage koawŏn 고아원
orthopedic chŏnghyŏng oekkwaŭi
정형 외과의
ostentatious kwashihanŭn 과시하는
other 1 adj tarŭn 다른; **the ~ day**
(recently) chinan pŏne 지난 번에;
every ~ day haru kŏnnŏ 하루 건너;
every ~ person han myŏng kŏnnŏ
한 명 건너 2 n (thing) tarŭn hanaŭi
kŏt 다른 하나의 것; (person) tarŭn
han myŏng 다른 한 명; **the ~s**
(objects) namŏji kŏt 나머지 것;
(people) namŏji saram 나머지 사람
otherwise kŭrŏch'i anŭmyŏn 그렇지
않으면; (differently) tarŭge 다르게
otter sudal 수달
ought ...haeya hada ...해야 하다;
I/you ~ to know ... nanŭn/nŏnŭn
...ŭl/rŭl araya handa 나는/너는
...을/를 알아야 한다; **you ~ to have
done it** nŏnŭn kŭgŏsŭl haessŏya
haet-tta 너는 그것을 했어야 했다
ounce onsŭ 온스
our uriŭi 우리의
ours uriŭi kŏt 우리의 것; **an idea of
~** uri saenggak 우리 생각
ourselves uri chashin 우리 자신; **by ~**
uri chashinŭro 우리 자신으로
oust (from office) naetchot-tta 내쫓다
out: **be ~** (of light, fire) kkŏjyŏ it-tta
꺼져 있다; (of flower, sun) chyŏ it-
tta 져 있다; (not at home, not in
building) ŏptta 없다; (of
calculations) t'ŭllida 틀리다; (be
published) ch'ulp'andoeda 출판되다;
(of secret) t'allonada 탄로나다; (no
longer in competition) t'allak'ada
탈락하다; (no longer in fashion)
yuhaeng-e twijida 유행에 뒤지다; **~
here in Dallas** i kot Tallasŭesŏ 이
곳 달라스에서; **he's ~ in the garden** kŭnŭn chŏng-wŏne nagait-tta
그는 정원에 나가있다; (get) **~!**
nagaseyo! 나가세요!; (get) **~ of my
room!** naebang-esŏ nagaseyo! 내

outboard motor sŏnoe mot'ŏ 선외 모터

outbreak (*of violence, war*) tolbal 돌발

outburst kamjŏng-ŭi p'okppal 감정의 폭발

outcast so-oeja 소외자

outcome kyŏlkkwa 결과

outcry kangnyŏrhan hang-ŭi 강렬한 항의

outdated kushigŭi 구식의

outdo poda tŏ charhada 보다 더 잘하다

outdoor *toilet, activities, life* yaoeŭi 야외의

outdoors *adv* yaoeesŏ 야외에서

outer *wall etc* oebuŭi 외부의

outer space uju 우주

outfit (*clothes*) ŭisang 의상; (*company, organization*) chojik 조직

outgoing *flight* ttŏnaganŭn 떠나가는; *personality* oehyangtchŏgin 외향적인

outgrow *old ideas* pŏsŏnada 벗어나다

outing (*trip*) sop'ung 소풍

outlet (*of pipe*) paech'ulgu 배출구; (*for sales*) maejang 매장; ELEC sok'et 소켓

outline 1 *n* (*of person, building etc*) yun-gwak 윤곽; (*of plan, novel*) kaeyo 개요 **2** *v/t plans etc* …ŭi yun-gwagŭl chaptta …의 윤곽을 잡다

outlive poda tŏ orae salda 보다 더 오래 살다

outlook (*prospects*) chŏnmang 전망

outlying *areas* oejin 외진

outnumber poda suga mant'a 보다 수가 많다

out of ◇ (*motion*) …esŏ pakkŭro …에서 밖으로; *run ~ the house* chibesŏ pakkŭro tallyŏnaoda 집에서 밖으로 달려나오다 ◇ (*position*) …(ŭ)robut'ŏ ttŏrŏjin …(으)로부터 떨어진; *Tit'ŭroit'ŭro put'ŏ 20mail ttŏrŏjin* 디트로이트로 부터 20마일 떨어진 ◇ (*cause*) ttaemune 때문에; *~ jeal-*

ousy/curiosity chilt'ushim/ hogishim ttaemune 질투심/호기심 때문에 ◇ (*without*) ta ttŏrŏjin 다 떨어진; *we're ~ beer* urinŭn maektchuga ta ttŏrŏjyŏt-tta 우리는 맥주가 다 떨어졌다; *we're ~ gas* urinŭn hwiballyuga ta ttŏrŏjyŏt-tta 우리는 휘발유가 다 떨어졌다 ◇ (*from a group*): *5 – 10* yŏl chun tasŏt 10중 5

out-of-date kushigŭi 구식의

out-of-the-way oejin 외진

outperform poda ttwiŏnada 보다 뛰어나다

output 1 *n* (*of factory*) saengsan 생산 COMPUT ch'ullyŏk 출력 **2** *v/t* (*produce*) saengsanhada 생산하다; COMPUT *signal* ch'ullyŏk'ada 출력하다

outrage 1 *n* (*feeling*) pun-gae 분개; (*act*) p'ongnyŏk 폭력 **2** *v/t* maeu hwanage hada 매우 화나게 하다; *I was ~d to hear …* nanŭn …ŭl/rŭl tŭtkko mopshi hwaga nat-tta 나는 …을/를 듣고 몹시 화가 났다

outrageous *acts* p'ongnyŏktchŏgin 폭력적인; *prices* t'ŏmuniŏmnŭn 터무니없는

outright 1 *adj winner* wanjŏnhan 완전한 **2** *adv win* wanjŏnhi 완전히; *kill* chŭksshi 즉시

outrun poda ppalli tallida 보다 빨리 달리다

outset shijak 시작; *from the ~* shijak'al ttaebut'ŏ 시작할 때부터

outside 1 *adj surface, wall, lane* pakkach'ŭi 바깥의 **2** *adv sit* pakka바깥에; *go* pakkŭro 밖으로 **3** *prep* …ŭi pakke …의 밖에; (*apart from*) … oeŭi … 외의; *~ Seoul* oegwage sŏul 외곽에 **4** *n* (*of building, case etc*) pakat myŏn 면; *at the ~* ch'oedaehanŭro 최대한으로

outside broadcast sŭt'yudio pakk pangsong 스튜디오 밖의 방송

outsider oebusaram 외부사람

outsize *adj clothing* t'ŭkttaehyŏng특대형의

outskirts pyŏnduri 변두리

outspoken soltchik'an 솔직한

tstanding t'ŭkch'urhan 특출한; FIN
voice, suns miburŭi 미불의
tward adj appearance oegwanŭi
관의; ~ *journey* ttŏnanŭn yŏhaeng
나는 여행
twardly kŏt'ŭronŭn 겉으로는
tweigh poda chungnyohada 보다
요하다
twit sŏnsuch'ida 선수치다
t adj talgyarhyŏng-ŭi 달걀형의
ary (of animals, people) nanso 난소
en obŭn 오븐
er 1 prep (above) ...ŭi witchoge ...의
쪽에; (across) ...ŭi chŏtchok
'yŏne ...의 저쪽 편에; (more than)
oda tŏ poda 더; (during) tong-ane
안에; *travel all* ~ *Korea* Han-guk
hŏnyŏgŭl yŏhaenghada 한국 전역을
행하다; *you find them all* ~ *Ko-*
ea kŭgŏsŭn Han-guk ŏdiena it-tta
것은 한국 어디에나 있다; *let's*
alk ~ *a drink* / *meal* mashimyŏnsŏ /
nŏgŭmyŏnsŏ iyagihapsshida
시면서 / 먹으면서 이야기합시다;
ve're ~ *the worst* urinŭn ch'oeagŭi
anghwang-ŭl nŏmgyŏt-tta 우리는
최악의 상황을 넘겼다 2 *adv*: *be* ~
(finished) kkŭnnada 끝나다; (left)
amtta 남다; ~ *to you* (your turn)
ŏŭi ch'arye 너의 차례; ~ *in Europe*
ŭrŏbesŏnŭn 유럽에서는; ~
ere / there yŏgie / chŏgie
기에 / 저기에; *it hurts all* ~
nmomi ssushida 온몸이 쑤시다;
ainted white all ~ chŏnbu hayak'e
'eit'ŭ ch'irhaejin 전부 하얗게
페인트 칠해진; *it's all* ~ ta kkŭnnat-
ta 다 끝났다; ~ *and* ~ *again*
nyŏtppŏnigo toep'urihaesŏ 몇번이고
되풀이해서; *do sth* ~ (again)
nŭosŭl tashi toep'urihada 무엇을
시 되풀이하다
erall 1 *adj length* chŏnch'eŭi 전체의
adv modify chŏnbanjŏgin 전반적인
erawe: *be* ~*d by s.o.* / *sth*
uguege / muŏse kŏmmŏktta
구에게 / 무엇에 겁먹다
erboard: *man* ~! sarami ppajyŏt-
ta! 사람이 빠졌다!; *go* ~ *for*
.o. / *sth* nuguege / muŏsege ppajida
구에게 / 무엇에게 빠지다

overcast day, sky hŭrin 흐린
overcharge v/t customer pagaji
ssŭiuda 바가지 씌우다
overcoat oet'u 외투
overcome difficulties kŭkppok'ada
극복하다; *be* ~ *by emotion*
kamjŏng-ŭl ŏngnurŭji mot'ada
감정을 억누르지 못하다
overcrowded nŏmu honjap'an 너무
혼잡한
overdo (exaggerate) chinach'ige hada
지나치게 하다; (in cooking) nŏmu
ik'ida 너무 익히다; *you're ~ing*
things tangshinŭn irŭl chinach'ige
hanŭn-gunnyo 당신은 일을 지나치게
하는군요
overdone meat chinach'ige ik'in
지나치게 익힌
overdose n kwaing pogyong 과잉
복용
overdraft chanaegŭl ch'ogwahanŭn
inch'ul 잔액을 초과하는 인출; *have*
an ~ chanaekppoda tŏ inch'urhada
잔액보다 더 인출하다
overdraw account ...esŏ
chanaekppoda tŏ inch'ulshik'ida
...에서 잔액보다 더 인출시키다; *be*
$800 ~*n* chanaekppoda
p'albaektallŏrŭl tŏ inch'ulshik'ida
잔액보다 800달러를 더 인출시키다
overdrive MOT obŏdŭraibŭ
오버드라이브
overdue apology, change nŭjŭn 늦은
overestimate abilities, value kwadae
p'yŏngkkahada 과대 평가하다
overexpose photograph chinach'ige
noch'urhada 지나치게 노출하다
overflow 1 n (pipe) nŏmch'im 넘침
2 v/i (of water) nŏmch'ida 넘치다
overgrown garden musŏnghan
무성한; *he's an* ~ *baby* kŭnŭn
aich'ŏrŏm kunda 그는 아이처럼 군다
overhaul v/t engine chŏngmil
kŏmsahada 정밀 검사하다; plans
chŏngmilkŏmt'ohada 정밀 검토하다
overhead 1 adj lights mŏri wiesŏ 머리
위에서; railroad kokkaŭi 고가의 2 n
FIN kanjŏppi 간접비
overhear uyŏnhi tŭt-tta 우연히 듣다
overjoyed taedanhi kippŭn 대단히
기쁜

overland 1 *adj route* yungnoŭi 육로의 **2** *adv travel* yungnoro 육로로

overlap *v/i (of tiles etc)* pubunjŏgŭro kyŏpch'ida 부분적으로 겹치다; *(of periods, theories)* chungbokdoeda 중복되다

overload *v/t vehicle* nŏmu mani shiltta 너무 많이 싣다; ELEC kwabuhahada 과부하하다

overlook *(of building etc)* naeryŏdaboda 내려다보다; *(not see)* motppoda 못보다; *(pretend not to see)* nun-gama chuda 눈-감아 주다

overly chinach'ige 지나치게; **not ~ ...** chinach'iji ank'e ... 지나치지 않게 ...

overnight *adv travel* pamsae 밤새; **stay ~** haruppamŭl chinaeda 하룻밤을 지내다

overnight bag chagŭn yŏhaeng-yong kabang 작은 여행용 가방

overpaid kwadahage chibuldoen 과다하게 지불된

overpass *(for car)* kokka toro 고가 도로; *(for people)* yukkyo 육교

overpower *v/t (physically)* muryŏk'age hada 무력하게 하다

overpowering *smell* aju kanghan 아주 강한; *sense of guilt* aju k'ŭn 아주 큰

overpriced nŏmu pissan 너무 비싼

overrated kwadae p'yŏngkkadoen 과대 평가된

overrule *decision* muhyohwahada 무효화하다

overrun *country* wanjŏnhi ch'imnyak'ada 완전히 침략하다; *time* ch'ogwahada 초과하다; **be ~ with** ...(ŭ)ro tŭlkkŭlt'a ...(으)로 들끓다

overseas 1 *adv* haeoero 해외로 **2** *adj* haeoeŭi 해외의

overseas Koreans haeoe kyop'o 해외 교포

oversee kamdok'ada 감독하다

oversight kan-gwaro inhan shilssu 간과로 인한 실수

oversleep nŭttcham chada 늦잠자다

overtake *(in work, development)* ttarajaptta 따라잡다; *Br* MOT ch'uwŏrhada 추월하다

overthrow chŏnbok 전복

overtime 1 *n* ch'ogwa kŭnmu 초과 근무; SP yŏnjangjŏn 연장전 **2** *adv work* kŭnmu shigan oero 근무 시간 외로

overture MUS sŏgok 서곡; **make ~s to** ...ege cheŭihada ...에게 제의하다

overturn 1 *v/t object* twiŏptta 뒤엎다; *government* chŏnbok'ada 전복하다 **2** *v/i (of vehicle)* twijip'ida 뒤집히다

overweight *baggage* chungnyang ch'ogwaŭi 중량 초과의; *person* ch'ejung kwadaŭi 체중 과다의

overwhelm *(with work)* apttohada 압도하다; *(with emotion)* kaptchagi tanghwanghage hada 갑자기 당황하게 하다; **be ~ed by** *(by response)* ...(ŭ)ro ŏtchŏl chul morŭda ...(으)로 어쩔 줄 모르다

overwork 1 *n* kwaro 과로 **2** *v/i* kwarohada 과로하다 **3** *v/t* kwaroshik'ida 과로시키다

owe *v/t pitchida* 빚지다; **~ s.o. $500** nuguege 500tal:lŏrŭl pitchida 누구에게 500달러를 빚지다; **~ s.o. an apology** nuguege sagwahal kŏsit-tta 누구에게 사과할 것이 있다; **how much do I ~ you?** chega tangshinege ŏlmana tŏ tŭryŏya hamnikka? 제가 당신에게 얼마나 더 드려야 합니까?

owing to ...ttaemune ...때문에; **~ the weather** nalsshittaemune 날씨때문에

owl olppaemi 올빼미

own[1] *v/t* soyuhada 소유하다

own[2] **1** *adj* soyuŭi 소유의 **2** *pron: a car/an apartment of my ~** nae soyuŭi ch'a/ap'at'ŭ 내 소유의 차/아파트; **on my/his ~** honja 혼자

♦ **own up** mojori chabaek'ada 모조리 자백하다

owner chuin 주인; *(of hotel, company etc)* soyuja 소유자

ownership soyukkwŏn 소유권

ox hwangso 황소

oxide sanhwamul 산화물

oxygen sanso 산소

oyster kul 굴

ozone ojon 오존

ozone layer ojonch'ŭng 오존층

P

e 1 n (step) kŏrŭm 걸음; (speed)
kktto 속도 2 v/i: ~ up and down
atta katta hada 왔다 갔다 하다

emaker MED maekppak
ojŏngi 맥박 조정기; SP sŏndu
uja 선두 주자

cific: the ~ (Ocean) T'aep'yŏng-
ang 태평양

ific Rim: the ~ T'aep'yŏng-yang
ǒnan 태평양 연안; ~ countries
'aep'yŏng-yang yŏnan kuk-kka
평양 연안 국가

cifier komu chŏtkkoktchi 고무
꼭지

cifism p'yŏnghwajuŭi 평화주의
cifist n p'yŏnghwajuŭija
화주의자

cify chinjŏngshik'ida 진정시키다

k 1 n (back~) paenang 배낭; (of
real, food) t'ong 통; (of
garettes,cards) kap 갑 2 v/t bag,
em of clothing, groceries etc ssada
다; goods p'ojanghada 포장하다
v/i chim kkurida 짐 꾸리다

kage 1 n sop'o 소포; (of offers
c) ilgwal 일괄 2 v/t (in packs, for
omotion) p'ojanghada 포장하다

kage deal ilgwal kŏrae 일괄 거래

kage tour p'aek'iji kwangwang
키지 관광

kaging (of product) p'ojang p'ojang 포장,
of rock star etc) sangp'umhwa
품화

ked (crowded) honjap'an 혼잡한

cket pongji 봉지; (of envelopes)
ukkum 묶음

ct kyeyak 계약

d¹ 1 n (piece of cloth etc)
h'ŏntchogak 천조각; (for writing)
hong-i mukkŭm 종이 묶음 2 v/t
vith material) taeda 대다; speech,
eport kilge nŭllida 길게 늘리다

d² v/i (move quietly) soriŏpsshi
ŏt-tta 소리없이 걷다

padded: ~ jacket nubi chaek'it 누비
재킷; ~ shoulders ŏkkaeshimŭl taen
어깨심을 댄

padding (material) p'aeding 패딩; (in
speech etc) pulp'iryohan sabibŏgu
불필요한 삽입어구

paddle¹ 1 n (for canoe) no 노 2 v/i (in
canoe) chŏt-tta 젓다

paddle² v/i (in water) multchangnanŭl
ch'ida 물장난을 치다

paddock ul ch'in chandipat 울 친
잔디밭

padlock 1 n chamulsoe 자물쇠 2 v/t
chamulsoero chamgŭda 자물쇠로
잠그다; ~ X to Y Xŭl/rŭl Ykkaji
chamgŭda X을/를 Y까지 잠그다

page¹ n (of book etc) p'eiji 페이지; ~
number tchok pŏnho 쪽 번호

page² v/t (call) hoch'urhada 호출하다

pager hoch'ulgi 호출기

pagoda t'ap 탑

paid employment yugŭp koyong
유급 고용

pail yangdong-i 양동이

pain ap'ŭm 아픔; be in ~ ap'ahada
아파하다; take ~s to ... ... hagi
wihae mopsshi aessŭda ... 하기 위해
몹시 애쓰다; a ~ in the neck F
nunŭi kashi 눈의 가시

painful arm, leg etc ap'ŭn 아픈;
(distressing) kot'ongsŭrŏun
고통스러운; (laborious) himdŭn 힘든

painfully (extremely, acutely)
kot'ongsŭrŏpkke 고통스럽게

painkiller chint'ongje 진통제

painless mut'ong-ŭi 무통의

painstaking work himdŭnŭn 힘드는;
worker sugorŭl akkiji annŭn 수고를
아끼지 않는

paint 1 n (for wall, car) p'eint'ŭ
페인트; (for artist) mulkkam 물감
2 v/t wall etc ch'irhada 칠하다;
picture kŭrida 그리다 3 v/i (as art
form) kŭrida 그리다

paintbrush (for wall, ceiling etc) p'eint'ŭ sol 페인트 솔; (of artist) kŭrim put 그림 붓

painter (decorator) changshik-kka 장식가; (artist) hwaga 화가

painting (activity) kŭrim kŭrigi 그림 그리기; (picture) hoehwa chakp'um 회화 작품

paintwork tojang 도장

pair (of people, animals, objects) ssang 쌍; (of shoes) k'yŏlle 켤레; **a ~ of shoes/sandals** shinbal/saendŭl han k'yŏlle 신발/샌들 한 켤레; **a ~ of pants** paji han pŏl 바지 한 벌

pajama jacket chamot wit-ttori 잠옷 윗도리

pajama pants chamot paji 잠옷 바지

pajamas chamot 잠옷

Pakistan P'ak'isŭt'an 파키스탄

Pakistani 1 adj P'ak'isŭt'anŭi 파키스탄의 2 n P'ak'isŭt'anin 파키스탄인

pal F (friend) ch'in-gu 친구; **hey ~, got a light?** ŏi, igŏt pwa, pul chom issŏ? 어이, 이것 봐, 불 좀 있어?

palace kunggwŏl 궁궐

palate kugae 구개; fig migak 미각

palatial kunggwŏlgat'ŭn 궁궐같은

pale person ch'angbaek'an 창백한; **~ pink/blue** yŏt'ŭn punhongsaek/ p'aransaek 열은 분홍색/파란색

pallet hwamul unbanttae 화물 운반대

pallor ch'angbaek 창백

palm[1] (of hand) sonppadak 손바닥

palm[2] (tree) yajanamu 야자나무

palpitations MED shimgyehangjin 심계항진

paltry chwikkorimanhan 쥐꼬리만한

pamper aejijungjihada 애지중지하다

pamphlet p'amp'ŭllet 팜플렛

pan 1 n (for cooking) nambi 남비 2 v/t F (criticize) hokp'yŏnghada 혹평하다

♦ **pan out** (develop) chŏn-gaehada 전개하다

pancake p'aenk'eik'ŭ 팬케이크; (Korean-style) chŏn 전

panda p'aendŏ kom 팬더 곰

pandemonium asurajang 아수라장

pane (of glass) ch'ang-yuri 창유리

panel (section) k'an 칸; (in TV discussion) p'aenŏl 패널; (investigating) chosadan 조사단; (committee) wiwŏndan 위원단

paneling p'annerhagi 판넬하기

panhandle v/i F kugŏrhada 구걸하다

panic 1 n tanghwang 당황 2 v/i tanghwanghada 당황하다; **don't ~** tanghwanghaji mara 당황하지 마라

panic selling FIN pisangshiŭi kŭmmae 비상시의 급매

panic-stricken kŏbe chillin 겁에 질린

panorama p'anorama 파노라마

panoramic view hwak t'ŭin hwak t'ŭin 확 트인

pansy (flower) p'aenji 팬지

pant v/i sumi ch'ada 숨이 차다

panties p'aent'i 팬티

pantihose → **pantyhose**

pants paji 바지; **a pair of ~** paji han pŏl 바지 한 벌

pantyhose p'aent'i sŭt'ak'ing 팬티 스타킹

paper 1 n (material) chong-i 종이; (news~) shinmun 신문; (wall~) pyŏkchi 벽지; (academic) nonmun 논문; (examination) shihŏmji 시험지; **~s** (documents) sŏryu 서류 (identity ~s) shinbunchŭng 신분증 **piece of ~** chong-i han chang 종이 한 장 2 adj chong-iro mandŭn 종이로 만든 3 v/t room, walls tobaehada 도배하다

paperback chong-ip'yojiŭi yŏmkkap'an ch'aek 종이표지의 염가판 책; **paper bag** chong-i kabang 종이 가방; **paper clip** k'ŭllip 클립; **paper cup** chong-ik'ŏp 종이컵; **paperwork** munsŏ ŏmmu 문서 업무

par (in golf) p'a 파; **be on a ~ with** ...wa/kwa kat-tta ...와/과 같다; **feel below ~** k'ŏndishyŏni nappŭn k'ŏndishyŏni nappŭ 컨디션이 나쁘다

parachute 1 n nak'asan 낙하산 2 v/i nak'asanŭro naeryŏoda 낙하산으로 내려오다 3 v/t troops, supplies nak'asanŭro t'uhahada 낙하산으로 투하하다

parachutist nak'asankanghaja 낙하산강하자

parade 1 n (procession) p'ŏreidŭ 퍼레이드 2 v/i haengjinhada 행진하

v/t (show off) kwashihada 과시하다

radise nagwŏn 낙원

radox yŏksŏl 역설

radoxical yŏkssŏltchŏgin 역설적인

radoxically yŏkssŏltchŏguro 역설적으로

ragraph mundan 문단

rallel 1 *n* p'yŏnghaeng 평행; *(of atitude)* wido 위도; *fig* yusattchŏm 유사점; **do two things in ~** tugaji *rŭl tongshie hada 두가지 일을 동시에 하다 2 *adj lines* *'yŏnghaenghanŭn 평행하는; *fig* ongshie irŏnanŭn 동시에 일어나는 *v/t (match)* p'iltchŏk'ada 필적하다

ralysis mabi 마비

ralyze mabishik'ida 마비시키다; *fig* muryŏk'ehada 무력케하다

ramedic chun ŭiryo hwalltong chongsaja 준 의료 활동 종사자

rameter chehan pŏmwi 제한 범위

ramilitary 1 *adj* chun kunsajŏgin 준 군사적인 2 *n* chun kunsayowŏn 준 군사요원

ramount kajang chung-yohan 가장 중요한; *be ~* kajang chung-yohada 가장 중요하다

ranoia p'ihae mangsang 피해 망상

ranoid *adj* p'ihae mangsang-ŭi 피해 망상의

raphernalia chapttongsani 잡동사니

raphrase *n* pakkwŏ ssŭgi 바꾸어 쓰기

raplegic *n* habanshin mabihwanja 하반신 마비환자

rasite kisaeng tongshingmul 기생 동식물; *fig* kisaengch'unggat'ŭn saram 기생충같은 사람

rasol p'arasol 파라솔

ratrooper nak'asanbyŏng 낙하산병

rcel n sop'o 소포

parcel up kkurŏmiro ssada 꾸러미로 싸다

rch *v/t: be ~ed (of person)* mogi t'ada 목이 타다

ardon 1 *n* LAW samyŏn 사면; *I beg your ~? (what did you say?)* mwŏrago hashyŏttchyo? 뭐라고 하셨죠?; *I beg your ~ (I'm sorry)* choesonghamnida 죄송합니다 2 *v/t*

yongsŏhada 용서하다; LAW samyŏnhada 사면하다; *~ me?* mwŏraguyo? 뭐라구요?

pare *(peel)* kkŏptchirŭl pŏtkkida 껍질을 벗기다

parent pumo 부모

parental pumo-ŭi 부모의

parent company mohoesa 모회사;
Parents' Day Ŏbŏinal 어버이날;
parent-teacher association sach'inhoe 사친회

park[1] *(area)* kong-wŏn 공원

park[2] *v/i & v/t* MOT chuch'ahada 주차하다

parka p'ak'a 파카

parking MOT chuch'a 주차; *no ~* chuch'agŭmji 주차금지

parking brake sudong pŭreik'ŭ 수동 브레이크; **parking garage** ch'ago 차고; **parking lot** chuch'ajang 주차장; **parking meter** chuch'a yogŭmgi 주차 요금기; **parking place** chuch'a changso 주차 장소; **parking ticket** chuch'a wiban ttaktchi 주차 위반 딱지

parliament ŭihoe 의회; *(in Korea)* Kuk'oe 국회

parliamentary ŭihoeŭi 의회의; *~ buildings* kuk'oe ŭisadang 국회 의사당

parole 1 *n* kasŏkppang 가석방; *be on ~* kasŏkppangdoeda 가석방되다 2 *v/t* kasŏkppanghada 가석방하다

parrot aengmusae 앵무새

parsley p'asŭlli 파슬리

part 1 *n (portion)* pubun 부분; *(section)* p'yŏn 편; *(area)* chiyŏk 지역; *(of machine)* pup'um 부품; *(in play, movie)* yŏk 역; MUS p'at'ŭ 파트; *(in hair)* karŭma 가르마; *take ~ in* ch'amyŏhada 참여하다 2 *adv (partly)* pubuntchŏgŭro 부분적으로 3 *v/i* heŏjida 헤어지다 4 *v/t: ~ one's hair* karŭmarŭl t'ada 가르마를 타다
◆ **part with** ch'ŏbunhada 처분하다

part exchange ton taeshin mulgŏnŭro chugo patkki 돈 대신 물건으로 주고 받기; *take sth in ~* ton taeshin mulgŏnŭl kajida 돈 대신 물건을 가지다

partial *(incomplete)* purwanjŏnhan

불완전한; *be ~ to* choahada 좋아하다
partially pubuntchŏguro 부분적으로
participant ch'amgaja 참가자
participate ch'amgahada 참가하다; *~ in sth* muŏse ch'amgahada 무엇에 참가하다
participation ch'amga 참가
particle PHYS soriptcha 소립자; (*small amount*) kŭkssoryang 극소량
particular (*specific*) t'ŭktchŏnghan 특정한; (*special*) t'ŭkppyŏrhan 특별한; (*fussy*) kkadaroun 까다로운; *in ~* t'ŭkppyŏrhi 특별히
particularly t'ŭkppyŏrhage 특별하게
parting (*of people*) ibyŏl 이별
partition 1 *n* (*screen*) k'anmagi 칸막이; (*of country*) pulli 분리 **2** *v/t country* pullihada 분리하다
♦ **partition off** k'anmagirŭl hada 칸막이를 하다
partly pubuntchŏguro 부분적으로
partner COM tong-ŏptcha 동업자; (*personal*) paeuja 배우자; (*professional*) tong-ŏptcha 동업자; (*in particular activity*) tchak 짝
partnership COM tong-ŏp 동업; (*in particular activity*) hyŏmnyŏk kwan-gye 협력 관계
part of speech p'umsa 품사; **part owner** kongdong soyuja 공동 소유자; **part-time 1** *adj* shiganjeŭi 시간제의 **2** *adv work* shiganjero 시간제로
party 1 *n* (*celebration*) p'at'i 파티; POL chŏngdang 정당; (*group of people*) muri 무리; *be a ~ to* yŏlludoeda 연루되다 **2** *v/t* F p'at'irŭl hada 파티를 하다
pass 1 *n* (*permit*) SP p'aesŭ 패스; (*in mountains*) sankkil 산길; *make a ~ at* kuaehada 구애하다 **2** *v/t* (*hand*) chŏnhaejuda 전해주다; (*go past*) chinagada 지나가다; MOT ch'uwŏrhada 추월하다; (*go beyond*) nŏmŏsŏda 넘어서다; (*approve*) sŭng-in pat-tta 승인 받다; *~* SP p'aesŭhada 패스하다; *~ an exam* shihŏme hapkkyŏk'ada 시험에 합격하다; *~ sentence* LAW p'an-gyŏrŭl naerida 판결을 내리다; *~ the time* shiganŭl ponaeda 시간을 보내다 **3** *v/i* (*of

time) ponaeda 보내다; (*in exam*) shihŏme put-tta 시험에 붙다; SP p'aesŭhada 패스하다; (*go away*) ŏpssŏjida 없어지다
♦ **pass around** tollida 돌리다
♦ **pass away** (*die*) sesang-ŭl ttŭda 세상을 뜨다
♦ **pass by** *v/t & v/i* (*go past*) chinagada 지나가다
♦ **pass on 1** *v/t information, book* chŏnhada 전하다; *costs, savings* tollyŏjuda 돌려주다 **2** *v/i* (*die*) sesang-ŭl ttŭda 세상을 뜨다
♦ **pass out** (*faint*) kijŏrhada 기절하다
♦ **pass through** *town* t'onghae chinagada 통해 지나가다
♦ **pass up** *chance* noch'ida 놓치다
passable *road* chinagal su innŭn 지나갈 수 있는; (*acceptable*) kwaench'anŭn 괜찮은
passage (*corridor*) poktto 복도; (*from poem*) chŏl 절; (*from book*) tallak 단락; (*of time*) kyŏnggwa 경과
passageway t'ongno 통로
passenger sŭnggaek 승객
passenger seat sŭnggaeksŏk 승객석
passer-by t'onghaengin 통행인
passion (*emotion*) kyŏngnyŏrhan kamjŏng 격렬한 감정; (*sexual desire*) yoktchŏng 욕정; (*fervor*) yŏltchŏng 열정
passionate *lover* chŏngnyŏltchŏgin 정열적인; (*fervent*) yŏltchŏngjŏgin 열정적인
passive 1 *adj* sudongjŏgin 수동적인 **2** n GRAM sudongt'ae 수동태; *in the ~* sudongt'aero 수동태로
pass mark hapkkyŏktchŏm 합격점
passport yŏkkwŏn 여권; **passport control** yŏkkwŏn kwalli 여권 관리; **password** amho 암호
past 1 *adj* (*former*) mŏnjŏtppŏnŭi 먼젓번의; *the ~ few days* chinan myŏch'il ijin 며칠; *that's all ~ now* kŭgŏn ije ta chinagassŏyo 그건 이제 다 지나갔어요 **2** n kwagŏ 과거; *in the ~* kwagŏe 과거에 **3** *prep* (*in time*) nŏmŏ 넘어; (*in position*) chinasŏ 지나서; *it's ~ 7 o'clock* ilgop shiga nŏmŏssŏyo 일곱 시가 넘었어요; *it's half ~ two* tushi

...aniyeyo 두시 반이에요 4 adv: **run /
walk ~** ttwiŏsŏ/kŏrŏsŏ chinagada
...이어서/걸어서 지나가다

...ste 1 n (adhesive) p'ul 풀 2 v/t
(stick) puch'ida 붙이다

...stel 1 n (color) p'asŭt'el 파스텔
adj p'asŭt'erŭi 파스텔의

...stime ch'wimi 취미

...or 1 n kabyŏpke tudŭrigi 가볍게
두드리기; **give s.o. a ~ on the back**
...ig nugurŭl ch'uk'ahada 누구를
...개볍게 두드리다 2 v/t kabyŏpke tudŭrida
...가볍게 두드리다

...tch 1 n (on clothes) hŏnggŏp 헝겊;
(period) kigan 기간; (area) kot 곳;
(of fog) charak 자락; **not be a ~ on**
...wa/kwa pigyodo toeji ant'a
...와/과 비교도 되지 않다 2 v/t
...clothes hŏnggŏp'ŭl taeda 헝겊을
...대다

...patch up (repair) mibongjŏgŭro
...koch'ida 미봉적으로 고치다; quarrel
...haegyŏrhada 해결하다

...atchwork 1 n (needlework)
...p'aech'iwŏk'ŭ 패치워크 2 adj quilt
...p'aech'iwŏk'ŭŭi 패치워크의

...atchy quality, work korŭji mot'an
...고르지 못한

...tent 1 adj (obvious) punmyŏnghan
...분명한 2 n (for invention) t'ŭk'ŏ 특허
...3 v/t invention t'ŭk'ŏrŭl ŏt-tta 특허를
...얻다

...atent leather enamel kajuk 에나멜
...가죽

...atently (clearly) punmyŏnghi 분명히

...aternal relative pugyeŭi 부계의;
pride, love pusŏngŭi 부성의

...aternalism kajoktchuŭi 가족주의

...aternalistic kajoktchŏgin 가족적인

...aternity pusŏng 부성

...ath kil 길; fig chillo 진로

pathetic aech'ŏroun 애처로운; F
(very bad) hyŏngp'yŏnŏmnŭn
형편없는

pathological pyŏngtchŏgin 병적인

pathologist pyŏngnihaktcha 병리학자

pathology pyŏngnihak 병리학

patience ch'amŭlssŏng 참을성

patient 1 n hwanja 환자 2 adj
ch'amŭlssŏng innŭn 참을성 있는;
just be ~! ch'amara! 참아라!

patiently ch'amŭlssŏng itkke 참을성
있게

patio anttŭl 안뜰

patriot aeguktcha 애국자

patriotic aeguktchŏgin 애국적인

patriotism aeguksshim 애국심

patrol 1 n (of police) sunch'al 순찰;
be on ~ sunch'arhada 순찰하다 2 v/t streets,
border sunch'arhada 순찰하다

patrol car sunch'alch'a 순찰차; patrolman sunch'algwan 순찰관; patrol wagon choesu hosongch'a 죄수
호송차

patron (of store, movie house)
kogaek 고객; (of artist, charity etc)
huwŏnja 후원자

patronize store tan-gollo tanida
단골로 다니다; person sŏnshimŭl
ssŭnŭn tŭt'ada 선심을 쓰는 듯하다

patronizing sŏnshimŭl ssŭnŭn tŭt'an
선심을 쓰는 듯한

patter 1 n (of rain etc) hududuk'anŭn
sori 후두둑하는 소리; F (of salesman)
ppalli chikkŏrinŭn mal 빨리
지껄이는 말 2 v/i hududuk ttŏrŏjida
후두둑 떨어지다

pattern n (fabric) munŭi 무늬; (for
knitting, sewing) p'aet'ŏn 패턴;
(model) ponbogi 본보기; (in
behavior, events) yangshik 양식

patterned munŭi innŭn 무늬 있는

paunch ttongppae 똥배

pause 1 n chungdan 중단 2 v/i
chungdanhada 중단하다 3 v/t tape
chungdanshik'ida 중단시키다

pave kkalda 깔다; **~ the way for**
...eŭi kirŭl yŏlda ...의 길을 열다

pavement (asphalt) asŭp'alt'ŭ
아스팔트

paving stone p'osŏk 포석

paw 1 n (of animal) pal 발; F (hand)

son 손 2 v/t F sonŭro manjida 손으로
만지다
pawn¹ n (in chess) chol 졸; fig iyong
tanghanŭn saram 이용 당하는 사람
pawn² v/t chŏdang-ŭl chap'ida 저당을
잡히다
pawnbroker chŏndangp'o chuin
전당포 주인
pawnshop chŏndangp'o 전당포
pay 1 n posu 보수; **in the ~ of**
koyongdoen 고용된 2 v/t employee
posurŭl chuda 보수를 주다; sum
chiburhada 지불하다; bill nap-
ppuhada 납부하다; ~ attention
chuŭirŭl kiurida 주의를 기울이다; ~
s.o. a compliment nuguege
ch'ingch'anŭl hada 누구에게 칭찬을
하다 3 v/i chiburhada 지불하다; (be
profitable) sujiga matta 수지가 맞다;
it doesn't ~ to ... ... hanŭn kŏshi
tŭgi toeji anayo ... 하는 것이 득이
되지 않아요; ~ for purchase sada
사다; you'll ~ for this! fig i ire
taehan taetkkarŭl ch'irŭge
toelkkŏyeyo! 이 일에 대한 댓가를
치르게 될꺼예요!
♦ **pay back** person kaptta 갚다; loan
pyŏnjehada 변제하다; (get revenge
on) anggap'ŭmŭl hada 앙갚음을
하다
♦ **pay in** (bank) yegŭmhada 예금하다
♦ **pay off 1** v/t debt kaptta 갚다;
corrupt official noemurŭl chuda
뇌물을 주다 2 v/i (be profitable)
idŭgi toeda 이득이되다
♦ **pay up** chiburhada 지불하다
payable chiburhaeya hal 지불해야 할
pay check ponggŭp 봉급
payday ponggŭmnal 봉급날
payer such'wiin 수취인
pay envelope ponggŭp pongt'u 봉급
봉투
payer chiburin 지불인
payment (of bill) nabip 납입;
(money) chibul 지불
pay phone kongjung chŏnhwa 공중
전화
payroll (money) chibul ponggŭp
ch'ongaek 지불 봉급 총액;
(employees) chongŏbwŏn ch'ongsu
종업원 총수; be on the ~

koyongdoeda 고용되다
PC (= personal computer) p'isshi
피씨; (= politically correct) p'yŏn
gyŏni omnŭn 편견이 없는
pea wanduk'ong 완두콩
peace (not war) p'yŏnghwa 평화;
(quietness) koyo 고요
peaceable person onsunhan 온순한
Peace Corps P'yŏnghwa Pongsada
평화 봉사단
peaceful p'yŏnghwaroun 평화로운
peacefully p'yŏnghwaropkke
평화롭게
peach pokssung-a 복숭아
peacock kongjakssae 공작새
peak 1 n (of mountain) chŏngsang
정상; (mountain) san 산; fig
ch'oegoch'i 최고치 2 v/i ch'oegoch'i
tarhada 최고치에 달하다
peak consumption ch'oedae
sobiryang 최대 소비량
peak hours p'ik'ŭ shigan 피크 시간
peanut ttangk'ong 땅콩; get paid ~
F chwikkorimank'ŭm tonŭl
pannŭnda 쥐꼬리만큼 돈을 받는다;
that's ~s to him F kŭ saramegen
sae parŭi p'iyeyo 그 사람에겐 새
발의 피예요
peanut butter ttangk'ong pŏt'ŏ 땅콩
버터
pear pae 배
pearl chinju 진주
peasant nongmin 농민
pebble chagal 자갈
pecan p'ik'an 피칸
peck 1 n (bite) tchogi 쪼기; (kiss)
ppoppo 뽀뽀 2 v/t (bite) tchoda 쪼다;
(kiss) ppoppohada 뽀뽀하다
peculiar (strange) kimyohan 기묘한;
~ to (special) ...t'ŭgŭi ...특유의
peculiarity (strangeness) kimyoham
기묘함; (special feature) tokt'ŭk'am
독특함
pedal 1 n p'edal 페달 2 v/i (turn ~s)
p'edarŭl paltta 페달을 밟다; (cycle)
chajŏn-gŏrŭl t'ada 자전거를 타다
pedantic hyŏnhaktchŏgin 현학적인
pedestal (for statue) (chogagŭi)
patch'imttae (조각의) 받침대
pedestrian n pohaengja 보행자
pedestrian precinct pohaengja

hŏnyong kuyŏk 보행자 전용 구역

●diatrician soakkwa ŭisa 소아과
의사

●diatrics soakkwa 소아과

●dicab samnyun t'aeksi 삼륜 택시

●degree 1 *n* hyŏlt'ong 혈통 **2** *adj*
yŏlt'ong-i punmyŏnghan 혈통이
분명한

●e *v/i* F ojum nuda 오줌 누다

●ek 1 *n* saltchak yŏtppogi 살짝
엿보기 **2** *v/i* saltchak yŏtppoda 살짝
엿보다

●el 1 *n* kkŏptchil 껍질 **2** *v/t fruit,
vegetables* kkŏptchirŭl pŏtkkida
껍질을 벗기다 **3** *v/i* (*of nose,
shoulders*) kkŏptchiri pŏtkkyŏjida
껍질이 벗겨지다

●eep → peek

●eephole tŭryŏda ponŭn kumŏng
들여다 보는 구멍

●eer¹ *n* (*in status*) taedŭnghan saram
대등한 사람; (*in age*) tongbae 동배

●eer² *v/i* chasehi poda 자세히 보다; **~
through the mist** an-gae sogŭl
tturŏjige poda 안개 속을 뚫어지게
보다; **~ at** tturŏjige poda 뚫어지게
보다

●eeved F shin-gyŏng-i kŏsŭllinŭn
신경이 거슬리는

●eg *n* (*for coat*) mot 못; (*for tent*)
malttuk 말뚝; **off the ~** kisŏngbok
기성복

●ejorative kyŏngmyŏrŏ 경멸어

●ellet chagŭn kong 작은 공; (*air rifle
bullet*) chagŭn ch'ong-al 작은 총알

●elt 1 *v/t*: **~ X with Y** Xege Yŭl/rŭl
tŏnjida X에게 Y을/를 던지다 **2** *v/i*:
they ~ed along the road kŭdŭrŭn
kirŭl ttaraso kŭp'i kat-tta 그들은
길을 따라서 급히 갔다; **it's ~ing
down** piga sech'age naeryŏch'yŏyo
비가 세차게 내려쳐요

●elvis kolbanppyŏ 골반뼈

●en¹ *n* (*ballpoint ~*) polp'en 볼펜;
(*fountain ~*) mannyŏnp'il 만년필

●en² (*enclosure*) uri 우리

●en³ → penitentiary

●enalize ch'ŏbŏrhada 처벌하다

●enalty ch'ŏbŏl 처벌; SP p'aenŏlt'i
패널티

●enalty area SP p'aenŏlt'i kuyŏk

패널티 구역

penalty clause (kyeyagŭi) wiyak
pŏlch'ik chohang (계약의) 위약 벌칙
조항

pencil yŏnp'il 연필

pencil sharpener yŏnp'il kkak-kki
연필 깎기

pendant (*necklace*) mok-kkŏri 목걸이

pending 1 *prep* …ŭl/rŭl ttaekkaji
…을/를 때까지 **2** *adj*: **be ~**
(*awaiting decision*) kyŏltchŏngi
naogikkaji kidarinŭn 결정이
나오기까지 기다리는; (*about to
happen*) imbak'an 임박한

penetrate kwant'onghada 관통하다;
market chinch'urhada 진출하다

penetrating *stare, sound* nalk'aroun
날카로운; *analysis* kanp'ahanŭn
간파하는

penetration ch'imt'u 침투; (*of
market*) chinch'ul 진출

penicillin p'enishillin 페니실린

peninsula pando 반도

penis ŭmgyŏng 음경

penitence huhoe 후회

penitent *adj* nwiuch'inŭn 뉘우치는

penitentiary kyodoso 교도소

pen name p'ilmyŏng 필명

pennant samgak-kki 삼각기

penniless muilp'unŭi 무일푼의

penpal p'enp'al ch'in-gu 펜팔 친구

pension yŏn-gŭm 연금

♦ **pension off** myŏng-ye
t'oejiksshik'ida 명예 퇴직시키다

pension fund yŏn-gŭmchohap 연금
조합

pension scheme yŏn-gŭm chedo
연금 제도

pensive saenggage chamgin 생각에
잠긴

Pentagon: the ~ Miguk
kukppangssŏng 미국 국방성

penthouse p'aent'ŭhausŭ 팬트하우스

pent-up ŏngnullin 억눌린

penultimate ŏmiesŏ tubŏntchae
ŭmjŏrŭi 어미에서 두번째 음절의

people saram 사람; (*race, tribe*)
minjok 민족; **the ~** kungmin 국민;
the American ~ Miguk kungmin

미국 국민; **~ say ...** saramdŭrŭn ... rago marhanda 사람들은 ... 라고 말한다

pepper (*spice*) huch'u 후추; (*chilli*) koch'u 고추; (*pimiento*) p'imang 피망

peppermint (*candy*) pak'asat'ang 박하사탕; (*flavoring*) pak'ahyang 박하향

pep talk kyŏngnyŏ yŏnsŏl 격려 연설

per tang 당; **~ annum** illyŏne 일년에

perceive (*with senses*) kamjihada 감지하다; (*view, interpret*) arach'arida 알아차리다

percent p'ŏsent'ŭ 퍼센트; **10/20 ~** ship/iship p'ŏsent'ŭ 십/이십 퍼센트

percentage piyul 비율

perceptible chigak'al su innŭn 지각할 수 있는

perceptibly arach'aril su itkke 알아차릴 수 있게

perception (*through senses*) kamji 감지; (*of situation*) inji 인지; (*insight*) chigak 지각

perceptive t'ongch'allyŏk innŭn 통찰력 있는

perch 1 *n* (*for bird*) hwaet-ttae 횃대 **2** *v/i* (*of bird*) hwaet-ttaee antta 횃대에앉다; (*of person*) chamshi antta 잠시 앉다

percolate *v/i* (*of coffee*) k'ŏp'irŭl naerida 커피를 내리다

percolator k'ŏp'i meik'ŏ 커피 메이커

percussion t'aak-kki 타악기

percussion instrument t'aak-kki 타악기

perfect 1 *n* GRAM wallyohyŏng 완료형 **2** *adj* wanbyŏk'an 완벽한 **3** *v/t* wanbyŏk'age hada 완전하게 하다

perfection wanbyŏk 완벽; **to ~** wanbyŏk'i 완벽히

perfectionist *n* wanbyŏkjuŭija 완벽주의자

perfectly wanbyŏk'age 완벽하게; (*totally*) wanjŏnhage 완전하게

perforated *line* chŏlch'wisŏn 절취선

perforations chŏlch'wisŏn 절취선

perform 1 *v/t* (*carry out*) tahada 다하다; (*of actor, musician*) kong-yŏnhada 공연하다 **2** *v/i* (*of actor,*

musician, dancer) kong-yŏnhada 공연하다; (*of machine*) chakttonghada 작동하다

performance (*by actor, musician*) kong-yŏn 공연; (*of employee, company etc*) ŏmmu suhaeng 업무 수행; (*by machine*) sŏngnŭng 성능

performance car sŏngnŭng-i usuhan ch'a 성능이 우수한 차

performer kong-yŏnja 공연자

perfume hyangsu 향수; (*of flower*) hyanggi 향기

perfunctory hyŏngshiktchŏgin 형식적인

perhaps amado 아마도

peril wihŏm 위험

perilous wihŏmhan 위험한

perimeter chubyŏn 주변; (*of circle*) chuwi 주위

perimeter fence kyŏnggyesŏn ult'a 경계선 울타리

period (*time*) kigan 기간; (*menstruation*) saengni 생리; (*punctuation mark*) mach'imp'yo 마침표; **I don't want to, ~!** tŏ isang marhal p'iryodo ŏpssi nan hago shiptchi anayo! 더 이상 말할 필요도 없이 난 하고 싶지 않아요!

periodic chugijŏgin 주기적인

periodical *n* chŏnggi kanhaengmul 정기 간행물

periodically chŏnggijŏgŭro 정기적으로

peripheral 1 *adj* (*not crucial*) taesuroptchi anŭn 대수롭지 않은 **2** COMPUT chubyŏn changch'i 주변 장치

periphery chuwi 주위

perish (*of rubber*) ssŏktta 썩다; (*of person*) sesang-ŭl ttŭda 세상을 뜨다

perishable ssŏk-kki shwiun 썩기 쉬운

perjure: ~ oneself wijŭnghada 위증하다

perjury wijŭng 위증

perk *n* (*of job*) itchŏm 이점

♦ **perk up 1** *v/t* saenggi tolge hada 생기 돋게 하다 **2** *v/i* saenggiga nada 생기가 나다

perky (*cheerful*) kiun ch'an 기운 찬

perm 1 *n* p'ama 파마 **2** *v/t* p'ama hada 파마 하다

manent yŏnggujŏgin 영구적인

manently yŏngguhi 영구히

missible hŏyongdoel su innŭn 용될 수 있는

mission hŏrak 허락

missive kwandaehan 관대한

mit 1 n hŏgasŏ 허가서 **2** v/t ŏrak'ada 허락하다; **~ X to do Y** ...i/ga Yhanŭn kŏsŭl hŏrak'ada 이/가 Y하는 것을 허락하다

pendicular adj sujigŭi 수직의

petual kkŭnimŏmnŭn 끊임없는

petually kyesok'aesŏ 계속해서

petuate yŏng-wŏnhage hada 원하게 하다

plex tanghok'age hada 당혹하게 -다

plexed tanghok'an 당혹한

plexity tanghok 당혹

secute pak'aehada 박해하다

secution pak'ae 박해

severance kkŭn-gi 끈기

severe kyesok'aesŏ hada 계속해서 -다

sist chisok'ada 지속하다; **~ in** kŭndŏktchige toep'urihada 덕지게 되풀이하다

sistence (perseverance) kkŭn-gi 기; (continuation) chisok 지속

sistent person, questions kŭndŏktchige toep'urihanŭn 덕지게 되풀이하는; rain, nemployment etc chisoktchŏgin 속적인

sistently (continually) yesok'aesŏ 계속해서

rson saram 사람; **in ~** ponini hiktchŏp 본인이 직접

rsonal (private) kaeintchŏgin 인적인; (relating to a particular dividual) kaeinŭi 개인의; **don't make ~ remarks** satchŏgin marŭn aji maseyo 사적인 말은 하지 세요

rsonal assistant kaeinbisŏ 개인 서; **personal computer** aeinnyong k'ŏmp'yut'ŏ 개인용 퓨터; **personal hygiene** kaein wisaeng 개인 위생

rsonality sŏngkkyŏk 성격; celebrity) yumyŏng-in 유명인

personally (for my part) narossŏnŭn 나로서는; (in person) chiktchŏp 직접; **don't take it ~** tangsin mariragonŭn saenggak'aji maseyo 당신 말이라고는 생각하지 마세요

personal pronoun inch'ing taemyŏngsa 인칭 대명사; **personal seal** ,**personal stamp** tojang 도장; **personal stereo** kaeinyong sŭt'ereo 개인용 스테레오

personnel (employees) chigwŏn 직원; (department) insakwa 인사과

personnel manager insa tamdang pujang 인사 담당 부장

perspiration ttam 땀

perspire ttamŭl hŭllida 땀을 흘리다

persuade sŏlttŭk'ada 설득하다; **~ s.o. to do sth** nugurŭl muŏt'adorok sŏlttŭk'ada 누구를 무엇하도록 설득하다

persuasion sŏlttŭk 설득

persuasive sŏlttŭngnyŏk innŭn 설득력 있는

pertinent chŏktchŏrhan 적절한

perturb uryŏhada 우려하다

perturbing uryŏdoenŭn 우려되는

pervasive influence, ideas nŏlli p'ŏjyŏ innŭn 널리 퍼져 있는

perverse (awkward) isanghan 이상한

perversion (sexual) pyŏnt'ae 변태

pervert n (sexual) pyŏnt'ae sŏngnyŏktcha 변태 성욕자

pessimism pigwanjuŭi 비관주의

pessimist pigwanjuŭija 비관주의자

pessimistic pigwanjŏgin 비관적인

pest yuhaehan kŏt 유해한 것; F (person) koltchitkkŏri 골칫거리

pest control pyŏngch'unghae kwalli 병충해 관리

pester kwich'ank'e kulda 귀찮게 굴다; **~ s.o. to do sth** nuguege muŏsŭl hae tallago chorŭda 누구에게 무엇을 해 달라고 조르다

pesticide salch'ungje 살충제

pet 1 n (animal) aewandongmul 애완동물; (favorite person) t'ŭk'i choahanŭn saram 특히 좋아하는 사람 **2** adj (favorite) t'ŭk'i choahanŭn 특히 좋아하는 **3** v/t animal ssŭdadŭmtta 쓰다듬다 **4** v/i (of couple) aemuhada 애무하다

petal kkonnip 꽃잎

♦ peter out chŏmch'ajŏguro ŏpssŏjida 점차적으로 없어지다

petite momtchibi chagŭn 몸집이 작은

petition n ch'ŏng-wŏnsŏ 청원서

petrified sosŭrach'in 소스라친

petrify sosŭrach'ige hada 소스라치게 하다

petrochemical sŏgyu hwahak chep'um 석유 화학 제품

petroleum sŏgyu 석유

petty person, behavior piyŏrhan 비열한; details shishihan 시시한

petty cash ssamjit-tton 쌈짓돈

petulant sŏngmarŭn 성마른

pew kyohoeŭi shindosŏk 교회의 신도석

pewter paengnap 백랍

pharmaceutical cheyagŭi 제약의

pharmaceuticals cheyak 제약

pharmacist (in store) yakssa 약사

pharmacy (store) yak-kkuk 약국

phase shigi 시기

♦ phase in tan-gyejŏguro t'uip'ada 단계적으로 투입하다

♦ phase out tan-gyejŏguro chegŏhada 단계적으로 제거하다

PhD (= *Doctor of Philosophy*) paksa 박사

phenomenal koengjanghan 굉장한

phenomenally koengjanghi 굉장히

phenomenon hyŏnsang 현상

philanthropic injŏng-i manŭn 인정이 많은

philanthropist chasŏn-ga 자선가

philanthropy chasŏn 자선

Philippines: *the* ~ P'illip'in 필리핀

philistine n kyoyang ŏmnŭn saram 교양 없는 사람

philosopher ch'ŏrhaktcha 철학자

philosophical ch'ŏrhaktchŏgin 철학적인

philosophy ch'ŏrhak 철학

phobia kongp'otchŭng 공포증

phone 1 n chŏnhwa 전화 2 v/t chŏnhwa kŏlda 전화 걸다 3 v/i chŏnhwahada 전화하다

phone book chŏnhwabŏnhobu 전화번호부; **phone booth** kongjung chŏnhwa pakssŭ 공중 전화 박스; **phonecall** chŏnhwa 전화; **phone**

number chŏnhwa pŏnho 전화 번│

phon(e)y adj katchaŭi 가짜의; *a ~ ten dollar bill* ship tallŏ tchari wij│ chip'ye 십 달러 짜리 위조 지폐│

photo n sajin 사진

photo album sajinaelbŏm 사진앨범│

photocopier pokssagi 복사기; **photocopy** 1 n pokssa 복사 2 v/t pokssahada 복사하다

photogenic sajini chal pannŭn 사진 잘 받는

photograph 1 n sajin 사진 2 v/t saji│ tchiktta 사진 찍다

photographer sajinsa 사진사

photography sajin ch'waryŏng 사진│ ch'waryŏng 촬영

phrase 1 n munkku 문구 2 v/t mall│ p'yohyŏnhada 말로 표현하다

phrasebook sugŏjip 숙어집

physical 1 adj (*relating to the body*) yukch'eŭi 육체의 2 n MED shinch'e│ kŏmsa 신체 검사

physical handicap shinch'e chang│ 신체 장애

physically yukch'ejŏguro 육체적으│

physician naekkwa ŭisa 내과 의사

physicist mullihaktcha 물리학자

physics mullihak 물리학

physiotherapist mulli ch'iryosa│ ch'iryosa 치료사

physiotherapy mulli ch'iryo 물리│ ch'iryo 치료

physique mommae 몸매

pianist p'ianisŭt'ŭ 피아니스트

piano p'iano 피아노

pick 1 n: *take your* ~ korŭseyo│ 고르세요 2 v/t (*choose*) sŏnt'aek'a│ 선택하다; *flowers, fruit* ttada 따다; *one's nose* k'orŭl hubida 코를│ 후비다 3 v/i: ~ *and choose* korŭd│ 고르다

♦ pick at: ~ *one's food* saech'ŏrŏm│ chogŭmsshik mŏktta 새처럼 조금│ 먹다

♦ pick on (*treat unfairly*) ch'abyŏrhada 차별하다; (*select*)│ kollanaeda 골라내다

♦ pick out (*identify*) araboda│ 알아보다

♦ pick up 1 v/t chibŏ tŭlda 집어 들다│ (*from ground*) chuwŏ ollida 주워│

올리다; *person, the kids etc* 터져오다
데려오다; *dry cleaning etc* 가져오다
가ㅅ오다; *information* 입수하다
입수하다; *(from airport etc)* 마중
나오다 마중 나오다; *(in car)* 차에 태우다
차에 태우다; *(sexually)*
친해지다; *language, skill*
배우다 배우다; *habit* 습뜩들이다
습득하다; *illness* ...-에 걸리다 ...에
걸리다; *(buy)* 사다; *criminal*
체포하다 체포하다 2 *v/i*
(improve) 호전되다; *(of
weather)* 좋아지다

cket *1 n (of strikers)* 피켓
2 *v/t* 감시하다

cket fence 말뚝 울타리

cket line 피켓 라인

ckle *v/t* (소금/식초에) 절이다

ckles 피클

ckpocket 소매치기

ck-up **(truck)** 트럭

cky F 까다로운

cnic *1 n* 소풍 2 *v/i* 소풍 가다

cture *1 n (photo)* 사진;
(painting) 회화; *(illustration)* 그림; *keep s.o.
in the ~* 누구에게 알려주다 2 *v/t* 상상하다

cture book 그림책

cturesque 그림과 같은

ie 파이

iece *(fragment)* 조각;
(component) 부품; *(in board
game)* 말; *a ~ of pie/bread* 빵 한 조각; *a ~ of advice* 충고 한 마디; *go to ~s*
좌절하다; *take to ~s* 분해하다

♦ piece together *broken plate*
조각들을 모으다; *facts, evidence* 짜 맞추다

iecemeal *adv* 한 번에 한 가지씩

iecework *n* 상일 삯일

pierce *(penetrate)* 관통하다; *ears* 뚫다

piercing *noise* 귀를 찢는 듯한; *eyes* 날카로운; *wind* 매서운

pig 돼지; *(unpleasant person)* 돼지같은 놈

pigeon 비둘기

pigheaded 완고한; **pigpen** 돼지우리; *fig* 지저분하고 불결한 곳; **pigskin** 돼지 가죽; **pigtail** 땋은 머리

pile 더미; *a ~ of work* 산더미같이 많은 일

♦ pile up *1 v/i (of work, bills)* 모이다 2 *v/t* 쌓다

piles MED 치질

pile-up MOT 연쇄 충돌

pilfering 좀도둑질

pilgrim 순례자

pilgrimage 순례

pill 알약; *the ~* 먹는 피임약; *be on the ~* 피임하다

pillar 기둥

pillion *(of motorbike)* 뒷좌석

pillow *n* 베개

pillowcase 베갯잇

pilot *1 n (of airplane)* 조종사 2 *v/t airplane* 조종하다

pilot plant 시험 공장

pilot scheme 예비 계획

pimp *n* 포주

pimple 여드름

PIN (= *personal identification
number*) 개인 확인 번호

pin *1 n (for sewing)* 핀; *(in bowling)* 볼링핀; *(badge)* 배지; *a 2-~ electric plug* 핀이 두 개인 플러그 2 *v/t (hold down)* 꼼짝 못하게 누르다;

(*attach*) kkot-tta 꽂다

♦ **pin down**: *pin s.o. down to a date* nugurŭl t'ŭktchŏng naltcha-e tongŭihadorok mandŭlda 누구를 특정 날짜에 동의하도록 만들다

♦ **pin up** *notice* puch'ida 붙이다

pincers p'ench'i 펜치; (*of crab*) chipkkebal 집게발

pinch 1 *n* kkojipkki 꼬집기; (*of salt, sugar etc*) son-garagŭro chogŭm chipkki 손가락으로 조금 집기; *at a ~* yusashie 유사시에 2 *v/t* kkojiptta 꼬집다 3 *v/i* (*of shoes*) kkok kkida 꼭 끼다

pine[1] *n* (*tree, wood*) sonamu 소나무

pine[2] *v/i*: *~ for* kŭriwŏhada 그리워하다

pineapple p'ainaep'ŭl 파인애플

ping *n* p'inghanŭn sori 핑하는 소리

ping-pong t'ak-kku 탁구

pink (*color*) punhongsaegŭi 분홍색의

pinnacle *fig* chŏngsang 정상

pinpoint chŏngbhwak'i aranaeda 정확히 알아내다

pins and needles chŏrim 저림

pinstripe *adj* kanŭn serojul munŭiŭi 가는 세로줄 무늬의

pint p'aint'ŭ 파인트

pin-up (**girl**) p'in ŏp(yŏja) 핀 업(여자)

pioneer 1 *n fig* sŏn-guja 선구자 2 *v/t* kaech'ŏk'ada 개척하다

pioneering *adj* sŏn-gujŏgin 선구적인

pious kyŏnggŏnhan 경건한

pip *n* (*of fruit*) sshi 씨

pipe 1 *n* (*for smoking*) p'aip'ŭ 파이프; (*for water, gas, sewage*) kwan 관 2 *v/t* kwanŭro ponaeda 관으로 보내다

♦ **pipe down** choyonghi hada 조용히 하다

piped music shillae kyŏng-ŭmak 실내 경음악

pipeline p'aip'ŭrain 파이프라인; *in the ~* chinhaeng chung-in 진행 중인

piping hot kimi solsol nage ttŭgŏun 김이 솔솔 나게 뜨거운

pirate *v/t software* p'yojŏrhada 표절하다

piss *v/i* ∨ (*urinate*) ojum nuda 오줌 누다

pissed F (*annoyed*) hwaga nan 화가 난; *Br* (*drunk*) ch'ihan 취한

pistol kwŏnch'ong 권총

piston p'isŭt'on 피스톤

pit *n* (*hole*) kumŏng 구멍; (*coal mine*) kaeng 갱; (*in fruit*) sshi 씨

pitch[1] *n* MUS karak 가락

pitch[2] 1 *v/i* (*in baseball*) t'uguhada 투구하다 2 *v/t tent* ch'ida 치다; *ball* tŏnjida 던지다

pitch black ch'irhŭk 칠흑

pitcher[1] (*baseball player*) t'usu 투수

pitcher[2] (*container*) mulchuga 주전자

piteous pulssanghan 불쌍한

pitfall hamjŏng 함정

pith (*of citrus fruit*) sŏm shim 섬 심

pitiful *sight* yŏnminŭl cha-anaenŭn 연민을 자아내는; *excuse, attempt* hanshimhan 한심한

pitiless maejŏnghan 매정한

pittance aju chŏgŭn ton 아주 적은 돈

pity 1 *n* tongjŏng 동정; *it's a ~ that …* … hadani aesŏk'agunyo … 하다니 애석하군요; *what a ~!* andwaetkkunyo! 안됐군요!; *take ~ on* pulssanghi yŏgida 불쌍히 여기다 2 *v/t person* tongjŏnghada 동정하다

pivot *v/i* hoejŏnhada 회전하다

pixel COMPUT p'iksel 픽셀

pizza p'ija 피자

placard pyŏkkppo 벽보

place 1 *n* changso 장소; (*restaurant*) shikttang 식당; (*bar*) sultchip 술집; (*apartment, house*) chip 집; (*in book*) iktthŭn kot 읽던 곳; (*in race, competition*) tŭngssu 등수; (*seat*) chari 자리; *at my / his ~* naŭi / kŭŭi chibesŏ 나의 / 그의 집에서; *in ~ of* taeshine 대신에; *feel out of ~* pulp'yŏnhada 불편하다; *take ~* yŏllida 열리다; *in the first ~* (*firstly*) ch'ŏt-tchaero 첫째로; (*in beginning*) ch'ŏŭmenŭn 처음에는 2 *v/t* (*put*) not'a 놓다; (*identify*) ŏttŏk'e algo innŭn saraminji aranaeda 어떻게 알고 있는 사람인지 알아내다; *~ an order* chumunhada 주문하다

place mat shikt'agyong maet'ŭ 식탁용 매트

placid ch'abunhan 차분한

...ague 1 *n* chŏnyŏmppyŏng 전염병 *v/t* (*bother*) koeropida 괴롭히다
...in¹ *n* p'yŏng-ya 평야
...in² 1 *adj* (*clear, obvious*) nyŏngbaek'an 명백한; (*not fancy*) 'yŏngbŏmhan 평범한; (*not pretty*) ...otssaengin 못생긴; (*not patterned*) ...nujiŭn 무지의; (*blunt*) soltchik'an ...직한; **~ chocolate** p'ŭllein ...ch'ok'ollit 플레인 초콜릿 2 *adv crazy* ...tc wanjŏnhi 완전히
...in clothes: in ~ saboguŭi 사복의
...inly (*clearly*) punmyŏnghage ...명하게; (*bluntly*) soltchik'age ...직하게; (*simply*) kanttanhi 간단히
...in-spoken soltchik'i marhanŭn ...직히 말하는
...intiff wŏn-go 원고
...intive kusŭlp'ŭn 구슬픈
...it 1 *n* (*in hair*) ttaŭn mŏri 땋은 ...리 2 *v/t hair* ttat'a 땋다
...an 1 *n* (*project, intention*) kyehoek ...계; (*drawing*) sŏlgyedo 설계도 2 *v/t* (*prepare*) chunbihada 준비하다; (*design*) tijainhada 디자인하다; **~ to ...lo** ...hal kŏsŭl kyehoek'ada ...할 ...것을 계획하다 3 *v/i* kyehoek'ada ...계획하다
...ane¹ *n* (*airplane*) pihaenggi 비행기
...ane² *n* (*tool*) taep'ae 대패
...anet haengsŏng 행성
...ank nŏlppanji 널빤지; *fig* (*of policy*) ...hŏngdang kangnyŏng hangmok ...당 강령 항목
...anning chunbi 준비; **at the ~ stage** ...hunbihanŭn tan-gye-esŏ 준비하는 ...단계에서
...ant¹ 1 *n* shingmul 식물 2 *v/t* shimtta ...다
...ant² *n* (*factory*) kongjang 공장; (*equipment*) changbi 장비
...antation p'ŭllaent'eishyŏn 플랜테이션
...aque¹ (*on wall*) kinyŏm aektcha 기념 액자
...aque² (*on teeth*) ch'isŏk 치석
...aster 1 *n* (*on wall, ceiling*) ...hoebanjuk 회반죽 2 *v/t wall, ceiling* ...hoebanjugŭl parŭda 회반죽을 ...바르다; **be ~ed with ...** (ŭ)ro ...tŏkch'iri toeda ... (으)로 떡칠이

되다
plaster cast sŏk-kkosang 석고상, kibsŭ 깁스
plastic 1 *n* p'ŭllasŭt'ik 플라스틱 2 *adj* (*made of ~*) p'ŭllasŭt'igŭi 플라스틱의
plastic bag pinil pongji 비닐 봉지; **plastic money** shinyong k'adŭ 신용 카드; **plastic surgeon** sŏnghyŏng ŭisa 성형 의사; **plastic surgery** sŏnghyŏng susul 성형 수술
plate *n* (*for food*) chŏpssi 접시; (*sheet of metal*) p'an-gŭm 판금
plateau kowŏn 고원
platform (*stage*) tansang 단상; RAIL p'ŭllaetp'om 플랫폼; *fig* (*political*) chŏngdang kangnyŏng 정당 강령
platinum 1 *n* paek-kkŭm 백금 2 *adj* paek-kkŭmŭi 백금의
platitude chinbuhan mal 진부한 말
platonic *relationship* chŏngshintchŏgin 정신적인
platoon (*of soldiers*) sodae 소대
platter (*for food*) taehyŏng chŏpssi 대형 접시
plausible kŭrŏl ttŭt'an 그럴 듯한
play 1 *n* (*in theater, on TV*) yŏn-gŭk 연극; (*of children*) nori 놀이; TECH tongnŏk 동력; SP kyŏnggi 경기 2 *v/i* (*of children*) nolda 놀다; (*of musician*) yŏnjuhada 연주하다; (SP: *perform*) undonghada 운동하다; (SP: *take part*) ch'amgahada 참가하다 3 *v/t musical instrument, piece of music* yŏnjuhada 연주하다; *game* hada 하다; *opponent* kyŏruda 겨루다; *Macbeth etc* yŏn-gihada 연기하다; **~ a joke on** nollida 놀리다
◆ **play around** (*be unfaithful*) paramŭl p'iuda 바람을 피우다
◆ **play down** kyŏngshihada 경시하다
◆ **play up** (*of machine*) kojang-i nada 고장이 나다; (*of child*) yadanbŏpsŏgŭl p'iuda 야단법석을 피우다; (*of tooth etc*) sangt'aega nappajida 상태가 나빠지다
playact (*pretend*) ch'ŏk'ada 척하다; **playback** chaesaeng 재생; **playboy** paramdung-i 바람둥이
player SP kyŏnggija 경기자; MUS yŏnjuja 연주자; THEA yŏn-gija 연기자

playful *punch etc* changnanŭi 장난의

playground norit'ŏ 놀이터

playing card k'adŭ 카드

playing field kyŏnggijang 경기장

playmate norich'in-gu 놀이친구

playwright kŭktchak-kka 극작가

plaza (*for shopping*) p'ŭllaja 플라자

plea *n* kanch'ŏng 간청

plead *v/i*: ~ **for** kanch'ŏnghada
간청하다; ~ **guilty** / **not guilty**
yujoe / mujoerŭl hangbyŏnhada
유죄 / 무죄를 항변하다; ~ **with**
kanch'ŏnghada 간청하다

pleasant yuk'waehan 유쾌한

please 1 *adv* chebal 제발; *more tea?*
- *yes*, ~ ch'a tŏ hashigessŏyo? - ne,
tŏ chuseyo 차 더 하시겠어요? - 네,
더 주세요; ~ *do* mullonimnida
물론입니다 **2** *v/t* kippŭge hada 기쁘게
하다; ~ *yourself* cho-ŭshil taero
haseyo 좋으실 대로 하세요

pleased kippŭn 기쁜; (*satisfied*)
manjok'an 만족한; *be* ~ *with sth*
musŏse manjok'ada 무엇에서
만족하다; ~ *to meet you* mannasŏ
pan-gapssŭmnida 만나서 반갑습니다

pleasing chŭlgŏun 즐거운

pleasure (*happiness, satisfaction*)
manjok 만족; (*not business*) orak
오락; (*delight*) kippŭmŭl chunŭn kŏt
기쁨을 주는 것; *it's a* ~ (*you're
welcome*) ch'ŏnmaneyo 천만에요;
with ~ kikkŏi 기꺼이

pleat *n* (*in skirt*) churŭm 주름

pledge 1 *n* (*promise*) yakssok 약속;
Pledge of Allegiance kuk-kkie
taehan maengse 국기에 대한 맹세
2 *v/t* (*promise*) yakssok'ada 약속하다

plentiful nŏngnŏk'an 넉넉한

plenty (*abundance*) p'ung-yo 풍요; ~
of manŭn 많은; *that's* ~ - twaessŏyo
됐어요; *there's* ~ *for everyone*
moduege toragal mank'ŭm
ch'ungbunhamnida 모두에게 돌아갈
만큼 충분합니다

pliable hwigi shwiun 휘기 쉬운

pliers p'ench'i 펜치; *a pair of* ~
p'ench'i han pŏl 펜치 한 벌

plight kon-gyŏng 곤경

plod *v/i* (*walk*) mugŏun kŏrŭmŭro
ch'ŏnch'ŏnhi kŏt-tta 무거운

걸음으로 천천히 걷다
♦ **plod along, plod on** (*with a job*)
yŏrŭi ŏpssi kŭrŏktchŏrŏk hada
열의 없이 그럭저럭 하다

plodder (*at work, school*) kkujunh
irhanŭn saram 꾸준히 일하는 사람

plot[1] *n* (*land*) chagŭn kuhoegŭi tta
작은 구획의 땅

plot[2] **1** *n* (*conspiracy*) kyeryak 계략
(*of novel*) kusŏng 구성 **2** *v/t*
hoech'aek'ada 획책하다 **3** *v/i*
ŭmmohada 음모하다

plotter ŭmmoja 음모자; COMPUT
p'ŭllot'ŏ 플로터

plow 1 *n* chaenggi 쟁기 **2** *v/t* kalda
갈다 **3** *v/i* kyŏngjak'ada 경작하다
♦ **plow back** *profits* chaet'ujahada
재투자하다

pluck *v/t* *eyebrows* ppoptta 뽑다;
chicken t'ŏrŭl chaba ppoptta 털을
잡아 뽑다
♦ **pluck up**: ~ *courage* yonggirŭl
naeda 용기를 내다

plug 1 *n* (*for sink, bath*) magae 마개
(*electrical*) p'ŭllŏgŭ 플러그; (*spark
chŏmhwa p'ŭllŏgŭ 점화 플러그; (*f
new book etc*) sŏnjŏnyong
ch'uch'ŏnsa 선전용 추천사 **2** *v/t* ha
t'ŭrŏ maktta 틀어 막다; *new book
etc* sŏnjŏnhada 선전하다
♦ **plug away** F yŏlsshimhi
kkujunhage hada 열심히 꾸준하게
하다
♦ **plug in** *v/t* p'ŭllŏgŭrŭl kkot-tta
플러그를 꽂다

plum 1 *n* chadu 자두 **2** *adj* *job* taeng
t'ukppyŏrhan 대우가 특별한

plumage kitt'ŏl 깃털

plumb *adj* sujigŭi 수직의

plumber paegwangong 배관공

plumbing (*pipes*) paegwan 배관
plummet (*of airplane*) sujigŭro
ttŏrŏjida 수직으로 떨어지다; (*of
prices*) chik kangha 직 강하

plump *adj* p'odongp'odonghan
포동포동한
♦ **plump for** korŭda 고르다

plunge 1 *n* ttwiŏdŭm 뛰어듦; (*in
prices*) harak 하락; *take the* ~
mohŏmŭl hada 모험을 하다 **2** *v/i*
torip'ada 돌입하다; (*of prices*)

arak'ada 하락하다 **3** v/t tchirŭda
니르다; **the city was ~d into darkness** toshiga ŏdum sogŭro ppajyŏ
urŏt-tta 도시가 어둠 속으로 빠져
들었다; **the news ~d him into de-
pair** kŭ soshigŭro, kŭnŭn
hŏlmang-e ppajyŏt-tta 그 소식으로,
그는 절망에 빠졌다

ural 1 adj pokssuŭi 복수의 **2** n
okssuhyŏng 복수형
us 1 prep t'ohayŏ 더하여 **2** adj isang-
ŭi 이상의; **$500 ~** 500 tallŏ isang 오
백 달러 이상 **3** n (symbol) tŏhagi
더하기; (advantage) itchŏm 이점
~ conj (moreover) tŏugi 더욱이
ush hwaryŏhan 화려한
ywood happ'an 합판
m. ohu 오후
neumatic kich'eŭi 기체의
neumatic drill konggi tŭril 공기
드릴
neumonia p'yeryŏm 폐렴
ach¹ v/t (cook) ttŭgoun mure
amtta 뜨거운 물에 삶다
ach² v/t (hunt) salmon etc mollae
haptta 몰래 잡다
ached egg suran 수란
.O. Box sasŏham 사서함
ocket 1 n hojumŏni 호주머니; **line
ne's own ~s** chagi hojumŏnirŭl
h'aeuda 자기 호주머니를 채우다;
e out of ~ pint'ŏlt'ŏriga toeda
빈털터리가 되다 **2** adj (miniature)
ohyŏng-ŭi 소형의 **3** v/t sŭltchŏk
ajida 슬쩍 가지다
ocketbook (purse) chagŭn
onkkabang 작은 손가방; (billfold)
chigap 지갑; (book) p'ok'etyong
h'aek 포켓용 책; **pocket calcula-
or** p'ok'etyong kyesan-gi 포켓용
계산기; **pocketknife** chumŏnik'al
주머니칼
dium yŏndan 연단
em shi 시
et shiin 시인
etic shittchŏgin 시적인
etic justice sap'ilgwijŏng 사필귀정
etry shi 시

poignant kamdongjŏgin 감동적인
point 1 n (of pencil, knife) kkŭt 끝; (in
competition, exam) chŏmsu 점수;
(purpose) moktchŏk 목적; (moment)
sun-gan 순간; (in argument,
discussion) yotchŏm 요점; (in
decimals) sosutchŏm 소수점; **5~3**
otchŏm sam 오점 삼; **beside the ~**
yotchŏmŭl pŏsŏnan 요점을 벗어난;
be on the ~ of mak haryŏgo hada
막 하려고 하다; **get to the ~**
yotchŏmŭl marhada 요점을 말하다;
the ~ is ... yotchŏmŭn ... 요점은…;
there's no ~ in waiting / trying
kidaril / shidohal iyuga ŏpssŏyo
기다릴 / 시도할 이유가 없어요 **2** v/i
sonkkaragŭro karik'ida 손가락으로
가리키다 **3** v/t gun kyŏnuda 겨누다
♦ **point at** (with finger) karik'ida
가리키다
♦ **point out** sights, advantages
chijŏk'ada 지적하다
♦ **point to** (with finger) sonkkaragŭro
karik'ida 손가락으로 가리키다; fig
(indicate) amshihada 암시하다
point-blank 1 adj refusal
nogoltchŏgin 노골적인; **at ~ range**
chikssa kŏrieső 직사 거리에서 **2** adv
refuse nogoltchŏgŭro 노골적으로
pointed remark nalk'aroun 날카로운
pointer (for teacher) kyop'yŏn 교편;
(hint) choŏn 조언; (sign, indication)
amshi 암시
pointless soyongŏmnŭn 소용없는; **it's
~ trying** noryŏk'aedo soyong-
ŏpssŏyo 노력해도 소용없어요
point of sale (place) maejang 매장;
(promotional material) sŏnjŏnyong
mulp'um 선전용 물품
point of view kwantchŏm 관점
poise ch'imch'ak 침착
poised person ch'imch'ak'an 침착한
poison 1 n tok 독 **2** v/t tokssarhada
독살하다; water togŭl t'ada tokŭl
t'ada; fig: relationship mangch'ida
망치다
poisonous yudok'an 유독한
poke 1 n tchirŭgi 찌르기 **2** v/t (prod)
ssushida 쑤시다; (stick) k'uk tchirŭda
쿡 찌르다; **~ fun at** nollida 놀리다; **~
one's nose into** ch'amgyŏnhada

참견하다

♦ **poke around** (*in a place*) twijida 뒤지다; (*ask about a person*) kkoch'ikkoch'i k'aeda 꼬치꼬치 캐다

poker (*card game*) p'okŏ 포커

poky (*cramped*) pijobŭn 비좁은

Poland P'ollandŭ 폴란드

polar kükch'iŭi 극지의

polar bear puk-kük kom 북극 곰

polarize *v/t* yangbunhwahada 양분화하다

Pole P'ollandŭin 폴란드인

pole[1] (*of wood, metal*) kidung 기둥

pole[2] (*of earth*) kük 극

polevault changttae nop'i ttwigi 장대 높이 뛰기

police *n* kyŏngch'al 경찰

policeman kyŏngch'algwan 경찰관; **police state** kyŏngch'al kuk-kka 경찰 국가; **police station** kyŏngch'alsŏ 경찰 서; **policewoman** yŏgyŏng 여경

policy[1] chŏngch'aek 정책

policy[2] (*insurance ~*) yak-kkwan 약관

polio soamabi 소아마비

Polish 1 *adj* P'ollandŭŭi 폴란드의 2 *n* P'ollandŏ 폴란드어

polish 1 *n* kwangt'aekche 광택제; (*nail ~*) maenik'yuŏ 매니큐어 2 *v/t* kwangnaeda 광내다; *speech* tadŭmtta 다듬다

♦ **polish off** *food* ta mŏgŏ ch'iuda 다 먹어 치우다

♦ **polish up** *skill* kalgo tadŭmtta 갈고 다듬다

polished *performance* chal tadŭmjin 잘 다듬어진

polite kongsonhan 공손한

politely kongsonhage 공손하게

politeness kongsonham 공손함

political chŏngch'ijŏgin 정치적인

politically correct p'yŏn-gyŏni ŏmnŭn 편견이 없는

politician chŏngch'iga 정치가

politics chŏngch'i 정치; *what are his ~?* kŭ saramŭi chŏngch'ijŏk sogyŏni mwŏn-gayo? 그 사람의 정치적 소견이 뭔가요?

poll 1 *n* (*survey*) yŏron chosa 여론 조사; *the ~s* (*election*) sŏn-gŏ 선거; *go to the ~s* t'up'yohada 투표하다

2 *v/t people* yŏronŭl mut-tta 여론을 묻다; *votes* tŭkp'yohada 득표하다

pollen hwabun 화분

pollen count hwabunnyang 화분량

polling booth kip'yoso 기표소

pollster yŏron chosawŏn 여론 조사

pollutant oyŏmmultchil 오염물질

pollute oyŏmshik'ida 오염시키다

pollution oyŏm 오염

polo neck t'ŏt'ŭlnek 터틀넥

polo shirt p'olo shyŏch'ŭ 폴로 셔츠

polyethylene p'olliet'illen 폴리에틸렌

polyester p'olliesŭt'erŭ 폴리에스테르

polystyrene p'ollisŭt'iren 폴리스티렌

polyunsaturate kodo pulp'ohwa multchil 고도 불포화 물질

pompous kŏdŭrŭm p'iunŭn 거드름 피우는

pond yŏnmot 연못

ponder *v/i* komgomi saenggak'ada 곰곰이 생각하다

pony chorangmal 조랑말

ponytail ttwiro mungnŭn mŏri 뒤로 묶는 머리

poodle p'udŭl 푸들

pool[1] (*swimming ~*) suyŏngjang 수영장; (*of water, blood*) ungdŏng-ung'i 웅덩이

pool[2] (*game*) Migukshik tanggu 미국식 당구

pool[3] 1 *n* (*fund*) kongdonggigŭm 공동기금 2 *v/t resources* kongdong ikkwŏnŭro hada 공동 이권으로 하다

pool hall tanggujang 당구장

pool table tanggudae 당구대

pooped F nokch'oga toen 녹초가 된

poor 1 *adj* (*not wealthy*) kananhan 가난한; (*not good*) sŏt'urŭn 서투른; (*unfortunate*) purhaenghan 불행한; *be in ~ health* kŏn-gang-i choch'i antta 건강이 좋지 않다; *~ old Tony* pulssanghan Toni! 불쌍한 토니! 2 *the ~* pinja 빈자

poorly 1 *adv* hyŏngp'yŏnŏpssi 형편없이 2 *adj* (*unwell*) momi choch'i anŭn 몸이 좋지 않은

pop[1] 1 *n* (*noise*) p'ŏng hanŭn sori 펑 하는 소리 2 *v/i* (*of balloon etc*) p'ŏng hanŭn soriga nada 펑 하는 소리가 나다 3 *v/t cork* ttada 따다; *balloon* p'ŏng hago t'ŏjida 펑 하고 터지다

...[2] 1 *n* MUS taejunggayo 대중가요
adj taejung-ŭi 대중의

...[4] F (*father*) appa 아빠

...[5] F (*put*) noa tuda 놓아 두다

op up *v/i* (*appear suddenly*)
ŭlssuk nat'anada 불쑥 나타나다

...corn p'apk'on 팝콘

...pe kyohwang 교황

...ppy yanggwibi 양귀비

...psicle® aisŭ k'eik'ŭ 아이스 케이크

...p song p'apssong 팝송

...pular inkki innŭn 인기 있는; *belief*,

...pport taejungtchŏgin 대중적인

...pularity inkki 인기

...pulate kŏjuhada 거주하다

...pulation in-gu 인구

...rcelain 1 *n* tojagi 도자기 **2** *adj*
...jagiŭi 도자기의

...rch peranda 베란다

...rcupine hojŏ 호저

...e (*of skin*) mogong 모공

...ore over chasehi poda 자세히
...다

...k twaejigogi 돼지고기

...n *n* p'orŭno 포르노

...n(o) *adj* p'orŭnoŭi 포르노의

...nographic oesŏltchŏgin 외설적인

...nography p'orŭno 포르노

...ous t'ugwassŏngi choŭn 투과성이
...은

...t[1] *n* (*town*) hanggu 항구; (*area*)
...ŭdu 부두

...t[2] *adj* (*left-hand*) chwach'ugŭi
...측의

...t[3] COMPUT p'ot'ŭ 포트

...table 1 *adj* hyudaeyong-ŭi
대용의 **2** COMPUT, TV p'ot'ŏbŭl
터블

...ter unbanin 운반인; (*doorkeeper*)
...unjigi 문지기

...thole NAUT hyŏnch'ang 현창

...tion *n* pubun 부분; (*of food*) inbun
...분

...trait 1 *n* (*painting, photograph*)
...'osanghwa 초상화; (*depiction*)
...yosa 묘사 **2** *adv* print seroro 세로로

...tray (*of artist, photographer*)
...'osanghwarŭl kŭrida / tchikta
...상화를 그리다 / 찍다; (*of actor*)
...n-gihada 연기하다; (*of author*)
...yosahada 묘사하다

portrayal (*by actor*) yŏn-gi 연기; (*by author*) myosa 묘사

Portugal P'orŭt'ugal 포르투갈

Portuguese 1 *adj* P'orŭt'ugarŭi
포르투갈의 **2** *n* (*person*)
P'orŭt'ugarin 포르투갈인; (*language*)
P'orŭt'ugarŏ 포르투갈어

pose 1 *n* (*pretense*) kŏtch'ire 걸치레
2 *v/i* (*for artist, photographer*) p'ojŭ
ch'wihada 포즈 취하다; **~ as** (*of person*) ... in ch'ŏk'ada ... 인 척하다
3 *v/t*: **~ a problem / a threat**
munje / wihyŏbŭl yagihada
문제 / 위협을 야기하다

position 1 *n* (*location*) wich'i 위치;
(*stance*) chase 자세; (*in race,
competition*) sun wi 위; (*occupied by
soldiers*) chinji 진지; (*point of view*)
kwantchŏm 관점; (*situation*)
iptchang 입장; (*job*) chigŏp 직업;
(*status*) chiwi 지위 **2** *v/t* paech'ihada
배치하다

positive *attitude* chŏk-kkŭktchŏgin
적극적인; *response* kŭngjŏngjŏgin
긍정적인; *test results* yangsŏng-ŭi
양성의; GRAM wŏnkkŭbŭi 원급의;
ELEC yanggŭgŭi 양극의; **be ~** (*sure*)
hwaksshinhada 확신하다

positively (*decidedly*) punmyŏnghi
분명히; (*definitely*) hwakssirhi
확실히

possess soyuhada 소유하다

possession (*ownership*) soyu 소유;
(*thing owned*) soyumul 소유물; **~s**
chaesan 재산

possessive *person* soyuyogi kanghan
소유욕이 강한; GRAM soyukkyŏk
소유격

possibility kanŭngssŏng 가능성

possible kanŭnghan 가능한;
the quickest ~ ... kanŭnghan
kajang pparŭn ... 가능한 가장 빠른
...; *the best ~* ... kanŭnghan
ch'oesŏnŭi ... 가능한 최선의 ...

possibly (*perhaps*) amado 아마도;
how could I ~ have known that?
chega kwayŏn ŏttŏk'e kŭgŏsŭl al su
issŏtkkessŭmnikka? 제가 과연
어떻게 그것을 알 수 있었겠습니까?;
that can't ~ be right kŭgŏn
chŏlttaero orŭl li ŏpssŏyo 그건

post 절대로 옳을 리 없어요; *could you ~ tell me ...?* ...ül/rül malssümhae chushil su innünjiyo? ...을/를 말씀해 주실 수 있는지요?

post¹ **1** n (of wood, metal) kidung 기둥 **2** v/t notice keshihada 게시하다; profits kongshihada 공시하다; *keep s.o. ~ed* nuguege kyesok soshigül chŏnhada 누구에게 계속 소식을 전하다

post² **1** n (place of duty) pusŏ 부서 **2** v/t soldier, employee paesok'ada 배속하다; guards paech'ihada 배치하다

postage up'yŏn yogüm 우편 요금
postal up'yŏnüi 우편의
postcard yŏpssŏ 엽서
postdate shiltcheboda naltcharŭl nütch'uŏ chŏkta 실제보다 날짜를 늦추어 적다
poster p'osŭt'ŏ 포스터
posterior n F kungdung-i 궁둥이
posterity hudae hurae 후대
postgraduate 1 n taehagwŏn hakssaeng 대학원 학생 **2** adj taehagwŏn대학원의
posthumous sahuüi 사후의; *a ~ child* yuboktcha 유복자
posthumously sahue 사후에
posting (assignment) immyŏng 임명
postmark soin 소인
postmortem kŏmshi 검시
post office uch'eguk 우체국
postpone yŏn-gihada 연기하다
postponement yŏn-gi 연기
posture chase 자세
postwar chŏnhuüi 전후의
pot¹ (for cooking) naembi 냄비; (for coffee, tea) chujŏnja 주전자; (for plant) hwabun 화분
pot² F (marijuana) taemach'o 대마초
potato kamja 감자
potato chips kamja ch'ip 감자 칩
potent kangnyŏk'an 강력한
potential 1 adj chamjaejŏgin 잠재적인 **2** n chamjaeyŏk 잠재력
potentially chamjaejŏgŭro 잠재적으로
pothole (in road) p'aein kumŏng 패인 구멍
potter n togong 도공
pottery (activity) toye 도예; (items) togi 도기; (place) toyeji 도예지

potty n (for baby) yuayong pyŏn-gi 유아용 변기
pouch (bag) chagŭn chumŏni 작은 주머니
poultry (birds) kagŭm 가금; (meat) kagŭm kogi 가금 고기
pounce v/i (of animal) tŏmbida 덤비다; fig tŏpch'ida 덮치다
pound¹ n (weight) p'aundŭ 파운드
pound² (for strays) uri 우리; (for c ch'aryang kyŏninso 차량 견인소
pound³ v/i (of heart) ttwida 뛰다; ~ on (hammer on) magu tudŭrida ㄷ 두드리다
pound sterling p'aundŭ ton 파운드 돈
pour 1 v/t liquid ssoda put-tta 쏟아 붓다 **2** v/i: it's ~ing (with rain) (piga) ŏkssugach'i p'ŏbunnŭnda (비가) 억수같이 퍼붓는다
♦ **pour out** liquid ttarŭda 따르다; troubles t'ŏ not'a 터 놓다
pout v/i ppurut'unghada 뿌루퉁하ㄷ
poverty kanan 가난
poverty-stricken tchijŏjige kananhan 찢어지게 가난한
powder 1 n karu 가루; (for face) pu 분 **2** v/t face pun parŭda 분 바르다
powder room hwajangshil 화장실
power 1 n (strength) him 힘; (authority) kwŏllyŏk 권력; (energy enŏji 에너지; (electricity) chŏn-gi 전기; in ~ POL chipkkwŏnhanŭn 집권하는; fall from ~ POL kwŏnjw esŏ ttŏŏjida 권좌에서 떨어지다 **2** v/t: be ~ed by ...(ŭ)ro umjigida ...(으)로 움직이다
power cut chŏngjŏn 정전
powerful kangnyŏk'an 강력한
powerless muryŏk'an 무력한; be ~ to ... tojŏhi ...hal su ŏptta 도저히 ...할 수 없다
power line chŏn-gisŏn 전기선;
power outage chŏngjŏn 정전;
power station paltchŏnso 발전소;
power steering p'awŏ sŭt'iŏring 파워 스티어링; **power unit** (of computer) p'awŏ yunit 파워 유닛; (motor) enjin 엔진
PR (= *public relations*) hongbo 홍

actical *experience* shiltchejŏgin
실제적인; *person* shillijŏgin 실리적인;
functional) shiryongjŏgin 실용적인
actical joke haengdong-ŭro hanŭn
not-ttoen changnan 행동으로 하는
못된 장난
actical Learning Shirhak 실학
actically *behave, think* shillijŏgŭro
실리적으로; *(almost)* kŏŭi 거의
actice 1 *n* shiltche 실제; *(training)*
yŏnssŭp 연습; *(rehearsal)* lihŏsŏl
리허설; *(custom)* sŭpkkwan 습관; *in
~ (in reality)* hyŏnshiltchŏgŭro
현실적으로; **be out of ~** sŏt'urŭda
서투르다 2 *v/i* hullyŏnhada 훈련하다
3 *v/t* yŏnssŭp'ada 연습하다; *law,
medicine* chongsahada 종사하다
agmatic shillijŏgin 실리적인
agmatism shiryongjuŭi 실용주의
airie taech'owŏn 대초원
aise 1 *n* ch'ing'ch'an 칭찬 2 *v/t*
ch'ingch'anhada 칭찬하다
aiseworthy ch'ing'ch'an hal
nanhan 칭찬 할 만한
ank changnan 장난
attle *v/i* chaejalgŏrida 재잘거리다
ay kidohada 기도하다
ayer kido 기도
each 1 *v/i* REL sŏlgyohada
설교하다; *(moralize)* t'airŭda
타이르다 2 *v/t* sŏlgyohada 설교하다
eacher sŏlgyoja 설교자
ecarious puranjŏnghan 불안전한
ecariously puranjŏnghage
불안정하게
ecaution yebang 예방
ecautionary *measure* yebang-ŭi
계방의
ecede *v/t (in time)* miri
naenghaejida 미리 행해지다; *(walk
in front of)* apssŏ kada 앞서 가다
ecedence: **take ~** usŏnhada
우선하다; **take ~ over** …e usŏnhada
…에 우선하다
ecedent sŏllye 선례
eceding *week etc* chŏn(ŭi) 전(의);
chapter ap'ŭi 앞의
ecinct *(district)* haengjŏng kuyŏk
행정 구역
ecious kwijunghan 귀중한
ecipitate *v/t crisis* yagishik'ida

야기시키다
précis *n* yoyak 요약
precise chŏnghwak'an 정확한
precisely chŏnghwak'age 정확하게
precision chŏnghwak 정확
precocious *child* chosuk'an 조숙한
preconceived *idea* sŏnibŭi 선입의
precondition p'ilssu chokkŏn 필수
조건
predator *(animal)* yuksshik tongmul
육식 동물
predecessor *(in job)* chŏnimja
전임자; *(machine)* ijŏn model 이전
모델
predestination unmyŏng yejŏngsŏl
운명 예정설
predicament kungji 궁지
predict yegyŏnhada 예견하다
predictable yegyŏnhal su innŭn
예견할 수 있는
prediction yegyŏn 예견
predominant chuyohan 주요한
predominantly churo 주로
predominate chuga toeŏ it-tta 주가
되어 있다
prefabricated choripsshigŭi 조립식의
preface *n* sŏmun 서문
prefer sŏnhohada 선호하다; **~ X to Y**
Xŭl / rŭl Ypoda tŏ choahada X을 / 를
Y보다 더 좋아하다; **~ to do** ohiryŏ
…nŭn kŏshi natkket-tta 오히려 …는
것이 낫겠다
preferable ohiryŏ naŭn 오히려 나은;
be ~ to poda nat-tta 보다 낫다
preferably toedorok imyŏn 되도록
이면
preference sŏnho 선호
preferential udaehanŭn 우대하는
prefix *n* chŏpttusa 접두사
pregnancy imshin 임신
pregnant imshinhan 임신한
prehistoric sŏnsashidaeŭi 선사시대의;
fig shidaee aju twittŏrŏjin 시대에
아주 뒤떨어진
prejudice 1 *n* sŏnipkkyŏn 선입견 2 *v/t*
person p'yŏn-gyŏnŭl p'umkke hada
편견을 품게 하다; *chances*
sonsangshik'ida 손상시키다
prejudiced p'yŏn-gyŏnŭl kajin 편견을
가진
preliminary *adj* yebiŭi 예비의

premarital honjŏnŭi 혼전의; **~ sex** honjŏn sŏnggyo 혼전 성교

premature shigisangjoŭi 시기상조의; **~ baby** misuga 미숙아; **~ death** yojŏl 요절

premeditated kyehoektchŏgin 계획적인

premier *n* POL susang 수상

première *n* ch'oyŏn 초연

premises kunae 구내

premium *n* (*in insurance*) p'ŭrimiŏm 프리미엄

premonition yegam 예감

prenatal ch'ulssaeng chŏnŭi 출생 전의

preoccupied molttuhan 몰두한

preparation (*act*) chunbi 준비; **in ~ for** ...ŭl/rŭl chunbihaesŏ ...을/를 준비해서; **~s** chunbi 준비

prepare *v/t room, meal* chunbihada 준비하다; **be ~d to do sth** (*willing*) muŏsŭl hal chunbiga toeŏ it-tta 무엇을 할 준비가 되어 있다 2 *v/i* chunbihada 준비하다

preposition chŏnch'isa 전치사

preposterous t'ŏmuni ŏmnŭn 터무니 없는

prerequisite chŏnjejokŏn 전제조건

Presbyterian Church Changno Kyohoe 장로 교회

prescribe (*of doctor*) ch'ŏbanghada 처방하다

prescription MED ch'ŏbangjŏn 처방전

presence (*of doctor*) ch'ambihada 있음; **in the ~ of** myŏnjŏnesŏ 면전에서

presence of mind ch'imch'ak'am 침착함

present[1] 1 *adj* (*current*) hyŏnjaeŭi 현재의; **be ~** ch'amsŏk'ada 참석하다 2 *n*: **the ~** hyŏnjae 현재; GRAM hyŏnjaehyŏng 현재형; **at ~** chigŭm 지금

present[2] 1 *n* (*gift*) sŏnmul 선물 2 *v/t award, bouquet* suyŏhada 수여하다; *program* sogaehada 소개하다; **~ X with Y** Yŭl/rŭl Xege chŭngjŏnghada Y을/를 X에게 증정하다

presentation (*to audience*) palp'yo 발표

present-day onŭllarŭi 오늘날의

presently (*now*) hyŏnjaeronŭn 현재로는; (*soon*) kot 곧

preservation pojon 보존

preservative *n* pangbuje 방부제

preserve 1 *n* (*domain*) yŏngyŏk 영역 2 *v/t standards, peace etc* pojonhada 보존하다; *wood etc* pohohada 보호하다; *food* chŏjanghada 저장하다

preside *v/i* (*at meeting*) sahoe poda 사회 보다; **~ over** *meeting* ŭijang norŭt'ada 의장 노릇하다

presidency (*term*) taet'ongnyŏng imgi 대통령 임기; (*office*) taet'ongnyŏngjik 대통령직

president POL taet'ongnyŏng 대통령; (*of company*) sajang 사장

presidential taet'ongnyŏngŭi 대통령의

press 1 *n*: **the ~** ŏllon 언론 2 *v/t button* nurŭda 누르다; (*urge*) kangyohada 강요하다; *hand* kkwak chwida 꽉 쥐다; *grapes* tchada 짜다; *clothes* tarimjirhada 다림질하다 3 *v/i* **~ for** chŏruda 조르다

press conference kijahoegyŏn 기자회견

pressing *adj* chŏlssirhan 절실한

pressure 1 *n* amnyŏk 압력; (*air ~*) kiap 기압; (*of work, demands*) amnyŏk 압력; **be under ~** sŭt'ŭresŭga it-tta 스트레스가 있다; **be under ~ to** ... haeya hal wigie mollyŏit-tta ...해야 할 위기에 몰려있다 2 *v/t* amnyŏgŭl kahada 압력을 가하다

prestige myŏngsŏng 명성

prestigious myŏngsŏng-i nainnŭn 명성이 나있는

presumably amado 아마도

presume ch'ujŏnghada 추정하다; **~ ...** ... kamhi...hada 감히 ...하다

presumption (*of innocence, guilt*) ch'ujŏng 추정

presumptuous kŏnbangjin 건방진

pre-tax segŭmŭl p'ohamhan 세금을 포함한

pretend 1 *v/t* ... in ch'ŏk'ada ...인 척하다 2 *v/i* ch'ŏk'ada 척하다

pretense kŏjit 거짓

pretentious challan ch'ŏk'anŭn 잘난 척하는

etext p'inggye 핑계

etty 1 adj yeppŭn 예쁜 2 adv (quite) angdanghi 상당히

evail igida 이기다

evailing usehan 우세한

event maktta 막다; **~ X (from)** ...oing Y Xi/ga Yhanŭn kŏsŭl mot'age hada X이/가 Y하는 것을 ...하게 하다

evention yebang 예방

eventive yebangŭi 예방의

eview n (of movie) shisa 시사; (of exhibition) shiyŏn 시연

evious ijŏnŭi 이전의

eviously chŏne 전에

ewar chŏnjaeng chŏnŭi 전쟁 전의

ey n mŏgi 먹이

prey on chabamŏktta 잡아먹다; fig (of conman etc) tŭngch'yŏmŏktta 등쳐먹다

ice 1 n kagyŏk 가격 2 v/t COM kagyŏgŭl maegida 가격을 매기다

iceless kapssŭl maegil su ŏmnŭn 값을 매길 수 없는

ice war kagyŏk harin kyŏngjaeng 가격 할인 경쟁

ick¹ 1 n (pain) tchirŭm 찌름 2 v/t (jab) tchirŭda 찌르다

ick² n ∨ (penis) chot 좆; (person) yabihan nom 야비한 놈

prick up: **~ one's ears** (of dog) kwirŭl tchonggŭt seuda 귀를 쫑긋 세우다; (of person) kwi kiurida 귀 기울이다

ickle (on plant) kashi 가시

ickly beard, plant ttakkŭmgŏrinŭn 따끔거리는; (irritable) sŏngmarŭn 성마른

ide 1 n (in person, achievement) charang 자랑; (self-respect) chajonshim 자존심 2 v/t: **~ oneself on** charangsŭrŏpkke yŏgida 자랑스럽게 여기다

iest sŏngjiktcha 성직자; (Catholic) shinbu 신부

imarily ponjiltchŏgŭro 본질적으로

imary 1 adj chuyohan 주요한 2 n POL yebisŏn-gŏ 예비선거

ime 1 n: **be in one's ~** hanch'ang ttaeida 한창 때이다 2 adj example, reason kajang chungnyohan 가장 중요한; **of ~ importance** aju chungdaehan 아주 중대한

prime minister kungmuch'ongni 국무총리

prime time TV hwanggŭmshiganttae 황금시간대

primitive wŏnshiŭi 원시의; conditions wŏnshijŏgin 원시적인

prince wangja 왕자

princess kongju 공주

principal 1 adj chuyohan 주요한 2 n (of school) kyojang 교장

principally taegae 대개

principle (in moral sense) toŭi 도의; (rule) wŏnch'ik 원칙; **on ~** toŭisang 도의상; **in ~** wŏnch'iktchŏgŭro 원칙적으로

print 1 n (in book, newspaper etc) inswae 인쇄; (photograph) inhwa 인화; **out of ~** chŏlp'andoen 절판된 2 v/t book, newspaper parhaenghada 발행하다; COMPUT inswaehada 인쇄하다; (using block capitals) taemuntcharo ssŭda 대문자로 쓰다

♦ print out inswaehada 인쇄하다

printed matter inswaemul 인쇄물

printer (person) inswaeŏptcha 인쇄업자; (machine) p'ŭrint'ŏ 프린터

printing press inswaegi 인쇄기

printout p'ŭrint'ŭdoen kŏt 프린트된 것

prior 1 adj ijŏnŭi 이전의 2 prep: **~ to** chŏne 전에

prioritize (put in order of priority) usŏn sunwirŭl maegida 우선 순위를 매기다; (give priority to) usŏnkkwŏnŭl chuda 우선권을 주다

priority ch'oeusŏn sahang 최우선 사항; **have ~** usŏnkkwŏni it-tta 우선권이 있다

prison kamok 감옥

prisoner choesu 죄수; **take s.o. ~** nugurŭl p'ororo chaptta 누구를 포로로 잡다

prisoner of war chŏnjaeng p'oro 전쟁 포로

privacy sasaenghwal 사생활

private 1 adj satchŏgin 사적인 2 n MIL sabyŏng 사병; **in ~** naemirhage 내밀하게

privately (in private) naemirhage

내밀하게; *funded, owned* min-gane ŭihae 민간에 의해; (*inwardly*) maŭm sogŭro 마음 속으로

private sector min-gan pumun 민간 부문

privilege (*special treatment*) t'ŭktchŏn 특전; (*honor*) yŏnggwang 영광

privileged t'ŭk-kkwŏnŭl kajin 특권을 가진; (*honored*) yŏnggwangsŭrŏun 영광스러운

prize 1 *n* sang 상 **2** *v/t* kach'i itkke yŏgida 가치 있게 여기다

prizewinner susangja 수상자

prizewinning ipssanghan 입상한

pro¹ *n*: *the ~s and cons* ch'anban yangnon 찬반 양론

pro² → *professional*

pro³: *be ~ …* (*in favor of*) …e ch'ansŏnghada …에 찬성하다

probability kamangsŏng 가망성

probable kŭrŏlttŭt'an 그럴듯한

probably ama 아마

probation (*in job*) kyŏnsŭp 견습; LAW chip'aeng yuye 집행 유예

probation officer poho kamch'algwan 보호 감찰관

probation period (*in job*) kyŏnsŭpkkigan 견습기간

probe 1 *n* (*investigation*) ch'ŏltchŏhan chosa 철저한 조사; (*scientific*) t'amsa 탐사 **2** *v/t* (*investigate*) chasehi chosahada 자세히 조사하다

problem munje 문제; *no ~* muje ŏpssŏyo 문제 없어요

procedure chŏlch'a 절차

proceed *v/i* (*of people*) kada 가다; (*of work etc*) chinhaengdoeda 진행되다; *~ with the lesson* tashi suŏbŭl kyesok'ada 다시 수업을 계속하다 **2** *v/t*: *~ to do sth* kŭrigonasŏ muŏsŭl hada 그리고나서 무엇을 하다

proceedings (*events*) haengsa 행사

proceeds suik 수익

process 1 *n* kwajŏng 과정; *in the ~* (*while doing it*) kŭrŏnŭn kwajŏng-e 그러는 과정에 **2** *v/t* *food, raw materials* kagonghada 가공하다; *data, application etc* ch'ŏrihada 처리하다

procession haengjin 행진

processor COMPUT p'ŭrosesŏ 프로세서

proclaim sŏnŏnhada 선언하다

prod 1 *n* tchirŭgi 찌르기 **2** *v/t* ssushi 쑤시다

prodigy: (*child*) ~ shindong 신동

produce 1 *n* nongsanmul 농산물 **2** *commodity* saengsanhada 생산하다; (*bring about*) yagihada 야기하다; (*bring out*) kkŏnaeda 꺼내다; *play, movie, TV program* chejak'ada 제작하다

producer (*of commodity*) saengsanja 생산자; (*of play, movie, TV program*) chejaktcha 제작자

product saengsanmul 생산물; (*result*) kyŏlgwa 결과

production saengsan 생산; (*of play, movie, TV program*) chejak 제작

production capacity saengsannyŏk 생산력

production costs saengsanbi 생산비

productive saengsanjŏgin 생산적인

productivity saengsanssŏng 생산성

profane *language* pulgyŏnghan 불경한

profess *…in* ch'ŏk'ada …인 척하다

profession chigŏp 직업

professional 1 *adj* (*not amateur*) p'ŭroŭi 프로의; *advice, help* chigŏbtchŏgin 직업적인; *piece of work* chŏnmunjŏgin 전문적인; *turn ~* p'ŭroro chŏnhyanghada 프로로 전향하다 **2** *n* (*doctor, lawyer etc*) chŏnmunjik chongsaja 전문직 종사자; (*not an amateur*) p'ŭro 프로

professionally *play sport* p'ŭro sŏnsuro 프로 선수로; (*well, skillfully*) chŏnmunjŏgŭro 전문적으로

professor kyosu 교수

proficiency nŭngsuk 능숙

proficient nŭngsuk'an 능숙한

profile (*of face*) yŏm mosŭp 옆 모습; (*description*) p'ŭrop'il 프로필

profit 1 *n* iik 이익 **2** *v/t*: *~ from* …(ŭ)ro iigŭl ŏt-tta …(으)로 이익을 얻다

profitability suikssŏng 수익성

profitable suigi chohŭn 수익이 좋은

ofit margin sunsuik 순수익

ofound *shock* kip'ŭn 깊은; *hatred* ppuri kip'ŭn 뿌리 깊은; **a ~ thinker** himohan sasaek-kka 심오한 사색가

ognosis yeji 예지

ogram 1 *n* kyehoek 계획; RAD, TV, COMPUT, THEA p'ŭrogŭraem 프로그램 2 *v/t* COMPUT p'ŭrogŭraem chada 프로그램 짜다

ogrammer COMPUT p'ŭrogŭraemŏ 프로그래머

ogress 1 *n* chinhaeng 진행; *make ~* (*of patient*) ch'adorŭl poida 차도를 보이다; (*of building work*) chinch'ŏkdoeda 진척되다; *in ~* chinhaeng chung-in 진행 중인 2 *v/i* (*in time*) chinhaengdoeda 진행되다; (*move on*) chindoga nagada 진도가 나가다; (*improve*) hyangsanghada 향상하다; *how is the work ~ing?* irŭn ŏttŏk'e toeŏ kago issŏyo? 일은 어떻게 되어 가고 있어요?

ogressive *adj* (*enlightened*) chinbojŏgin 진보적인; *disease* chinhaenghanŭn 진행하는

ogressively chŏmch'ajŏgŭro 점차적으로

ohibit kŭmjihada 금지하다

ohibition kŭmji 금지; *Prohibition* Kŭmjuppŏp 금주법

ohibitive *prices* koengjanghi pissan 굉장히 비싼

oject 1 *n* (*plan*) kyehoek 계획; (*undertaking*) saŏp 사업; EDU kwaje 과제; (*housing area*) chut'aek tanji 주택 단지

oject 2 1 *v/t figures, sales* yesanhada 예산하다; *movie* yŏngsahada 영사하다 2 *v/i* (*stick out*) t'wiŏnaoda 튀어나오다

ojection (*forecast*) yesan 예산

ojector (*for slides*) yŏngsagi 영사기

olong yŏnjanghada 연장하다

om (*school dance*) hak-kkyo ch'uktche 학교 축제

ominent *nose, chin* t'uk t'wiŏ naon 툭 튀어 나온; (*significant*) t'agwŏrhan 탁월한

omiscuity hon-gyo 혼교

promiscuous nanjap'an 난잡한

promise 1 *n* yakssok 약속 2 *v/t* yakssok'ada 약속하다; **~ to …** hagiro yakssok'ada … 하기로 약속하다; **~ X to Y** Xege Yŭl/rŭl yakssok'ada X에게 Y을/를 약속하다 3 *v/i* yakssok'ada 약속하다

promising chŏndoga ch'angch'anghan 전도가 창창한

promote *employee* sŭngjinhada 승진하다; (*encourage, foster*) ch'oktchinhada 촉진하다; COM sŏnjŏnhada 선전하다

promoter (*of sports event*) p'ŭromot'ŏ 프로모터

promotion (*of employee*) sŭngjin 승진; (*of scheme, idea*) sŏnjŏn 선전; COM p'anmae ch'oktchin 판매 촉진

prompt 1 *adj* (*on time*) shiganŭl chik'inŭn 시간을 지키는; (*speedy*) chŭk-kkaktchŏgin 즉각적인 2 *adv*: *at two o'clock ~* chŏnggak tu shie 정각 두 시에 3 *v/t* (*cause*) yubalshik'ida 유발시키다; *actor* taesarŭl illŏjuda 대사를 일러주다 4 *n* COMPUT p'ŭromp'ŭt'ŭ 프롬프트

promptly (*on time*) cheshigane 제시간에; (*immediately*) chŭksshi 즉시

prone: *be ~ to do …* … hagi shwiptta … 하기 쉽다

pronoun taemyŏngsa 대명사

pronounce *word* parŭmhada 발음하다; (*declare*) kongp'yohada 공표하다

pronounced *accent* kanghan 강한; *views* hwak-kkohan 확고한

pronunciation parŭm 발음

proof *n* chŭnggŏ 증거; (*of book*) kyojŏngswae 교정쇄

prop 1 *v/t* kidaeŏ not'a 기대어 놓다 2 *n* (*in theater*) sop'um 소품

♦ **prop up** ollyŏ patch'ida 올려 받치다; *regime* chijihada 지지하다

propaganda sŏnjŏn hwalttong 선전 활동

propel ch'ujinhada 추진하다

propellant (*in aerosol*) koap kkassŭ 고압 가스

propeller (*of boat*) p'ŭrop'ellŏ 프로펠러

proper (*real*) chŏngshigŭi 정식의; (*correct*) parŭn 바른; (*fitting*) almajŭn 알맞은

properly (*correctly*) chedaero 제대로; (*fittingly*) chŏk'ap'age 적합하게

property soyumul 소유물; (*land*) ttang 땅

property developer t'oji kaebarŏptcha 토지 개발업자

prophecy yeŏn 예언

prophesy yeŏnhada 예언하다

proportion (*ratio*) piyul 비율; (*number, amount*) pubun 부분; **~s** (*dimensions*) yongjŏk 용적

proportional piryehanŭn 비례하는

proposal (*suggestion*) chean 제안; (*of marriage*) ch'ŏnghon 청혼

propose 1 *v/t* (*suggest*) cheanhada 제안하다; (*plan*) kyehoek'ada 계획하다 2 *v/i* (*make offer of marriage*) ch'ŏnghonhada 청혼하다

proposition 1 *n* cheŭi 제의 2 *v/t* woman yuhok'ada 유혹하다

proprietor kyŏngnyŏng-in 경영인

proprietress yŏsŏng kyŏngnyŏng-in 여성 경영인

prose sanmun 산문

prosecute *v/t* LAW kisohada 기소하다

prosecution LAW kiso 기소; (*lawyers*) kisojach'ŭk 기소자측

prosecutor kŏmsa 검사

prospect 1 *n* (*chance, likelihood*) kamang 가망; (*thought of something in the future*) yesang 예상 ; **~s** chŏnmang 전망 2 *v/i*: **~ for gold** shigurhada 시굴하다

prospective kidaedoenŭn 기대되는

prosper (*of person*) sŏnggonghada 성공하다; (*of business, city*) pŏnch'anghada 번창하다

prosperity pŏnch'ang 번창

prosperous *person* sŏnggonghan 성공한; *business, city* pŏnch'anghanŭn 번창하는

prostitute *n* maech'unbu 매춘부; **male ~** namch'ang 남창

prostitution maech'un 매춘

prostrate: **be ~ with grief** sŭlp'ŭme ppajyŏ it-tta 슬픔에 빠져 있다

protect pohohada 보호하다

protection poho 보호

protection money poho pannŭn taekkaro ttŭkkinŭn ton 보호 받는 대가로 뜯기는 돈

protective pohohanŭn 보호하는

protector suhoja 수호자

protein tanbaektchil 단백질

protest 1 *n* hang-ŭi 항의; (*demonstration*) temo 데모 2 *v/t* hang-ŭihada 항의하다; (*object to*) iŭirŭl chegihada 이의를 제기하다 3 *v/i* panbak'ada 반박하다; (*demonstrate*) temohada 데모하다

Protestant 1 *n* Shin-gyodo 신교도 2 *adj* Shin-gyodoŭi 신교도의

Protestantism Kaeshin-gyo 개신교

protester temoja 데모자

protocol ŭirye 의례

prototype wŏnhyŏng 원형

protracted orae kkŭnŭn 오래 끄는

protrude *v/i* pulssuk t'wiŏ naoda 불쑥 튀어 나오다

proud charangsŭrŏun 자랑스러운; (*independent*) chajonshimi kangh... 자존심이 강한; **be ~ of** charangsŭrŏpkke yŏgida 자랑스럽... 여기다

proudly charangsŭrŏpkke 자랑스럽...

prove chŭngmyŏnghada 증명하다

proverb sokttam 속담

provide chegonghada 제공하다; ~ **to X, ~ X with Y** Xege Yŭl / rŭl chegonghada X에게 Y을 / 를 제공하다; **~d** (*that*) ... ...ranŭn chokkŏnŭro ...라는 조건으로

♦ **provide for** *family* puyanghada 부양하다; (*of law etc*) kyujŏnghad... 규정하다

province chibang 지방

provincial *city* chibang-ŭi 지방의; ch'onssŭrŏun 촌스러운

provision (*supply*) konggŭp 공급; (*law, contract*) chohang 조항

provisional imshijŏgin 임시적인

proviso tansŏ 단서

provocation hwanage hanŭn kŏt 화나게 하는 것

provocative (*intended to annoy*) chagŭk'anŭn 자극하는; (*controversial*) nonjaengjŏgin 논쟁적인; (*sexually*) chagŭktchŏgin 자극적인

provoke (*cause*) yubarhada 유발하...

-nnoy) sŏnggashige hada 성가시게 하다
-w NAUT paenmŏri 뱃머리
-wess ttwiŏnan somsshi 뛰어난 솜씨 씨
-wl v/i (of tiger etc) ŏsŭllŏnggŏrida 슬렁거리다; (of burglar) -sŏngdaeda 서성대다
-wler sŏsŏngdaenŭn saram 서성대는 사람
-ximity kŭnjŏp 근접
-xy (authority) taerikkwŏn 대리권; -person) taeriin 대리인
-de ssungmaek 쑥맥
-dence shinjung 신중
-dent punbyŏl innŭn 분별 있는
-dish ssungmaegin 쑥맥인
-ne¹ *n* mallin chadu 말린 자두
-ne² *v/t plant* (kajirŭl) ch'ida 가지를) 치다; *expenditure, labor* -rce sak-kkamhada 삭감하다; *essay* -an-gyŏrhi hada 간결히 하다
-' k'aego tanida 캐고 다니다
-ry into kkoch'ikkoch'i -'aemutkko tanida 꼬치꼬치 캐묻고 -니다
-' (= *postscript*) ch'ushin 추신
-eudonym ka-myŏng 가명
-ychiatric chŏngshinkkwaŭi 정신과의
-ychiatrist chŏngshinkkwa ŭisa 정신과 의사
-ychiatry chŏngshinŭihak 정신의학
-ychic *adj* shimnyŏng-ŭi 심령의
-ychoanalysis chŏngshin punsŏk 정신 분석
-ychoanalyst chŏngshin punsŏk -aktcha 정신 분석 학자
-ychoanalyze chŏngshin -unsŏk'ada 정신 분석하다
-ychological shimnijŏgin 심리적인
-ychologically shimnijŏguro 심리적으로
-ychologist shimnihaktcha 심리학자
-ychology shimnihak 심리학
-ychopath chŏngshinppyŏngja 정신병자
-berty sach'un-gi 사춘기
-bic hair ŭmmo 음모
-blic 1 *adj* (in ~) konggaejŏgin 공개적인 공개적인; (of the masses) taejung-ŭi 대중의; (open to the ~) konggong-ŭi 공공의 **2** *n*: **the ~** taejung 대중; **in ~** kongtchŏgin changso-e(sŏ) 공적인 장소에(서)

publication (of book, report) ch'ulp'an 출판; (by newspaper) parhaeng 발행; (book) ch'ulp'an 출판; (newspaper) parhaeng 발행
publicity sŏnjŏn 선전
publicize (make known) sŏnjŏnhada 선전하다; COM kwanggohada 광고하다
publicly konggaejŏguro 공개적으로
public prosecutor kŏmch'algwan 검찰관; **public relations** hongbo 홍보; **public school** konggip hak-kkyo 공립 학교; **public sector** konggong pumun 공공 부문
publish ch'ulp'anhada 출판하다
publisher (person) ch'ulp'anŏptcha 출판업자; (company) ch'ulp'ansa 출판사
publishing ch'ulp'anŏp 출판업
publishing company ch'ulp'ansa 출판사
puddle *n* ungdŏng-i 웅덩이
puff 1 *n* (of wind, smoke) hanbŏn huk pulgi 한번 훅 불기 **2** *v/i* (pant) hŏlttŏk-kkŏrida 헐떡거리다
puffy eyes, face puŏorŭn 부어오른
pull 1 *n* (on rope) chaba tanggigi 잡아 당기기; F (appeal) hoŭng 호응; F (influence) yŏnghyangnyŏk 영향력 **2** *v/t* kkŭlda 끌다; rope, hair chaba tanggida 잡아 당기다; tooth ppoptta 뽑다; muscle murihage ssŭda 무리하게 쓰다 **3** *v/i* tanggida 당기다
♦ **pull apart** (separate) tteŏnaeda 떼어내다
♦ **pull away** *v/t* chabach'aeda 잡아채다
♦ **pull down** naerida 내리다; (demolish) hŏmulda 허물다
♦ **pull in** (of bus, train) toch'ak'ada 도착하다
♦ **pull off** leaves etc tteŏnaeda 떼어내다; coat etc pŏt-tta 벗다; F deal etc sŏnggongjŏguro haenaeda 성공적으로 해내다
♦ **pull out 1** *v/t* kkŏnaeda 꺼내다;

troops hut'oeshik'ida 후퇴시키다
2 *v/i* (*of an agreement*)
ch'ŏrhoehada 철회하다; (*of a competition*) ppajida
빠지다; (*of troops*) hut'oehada
후퇴하다; (*of ship*) ch'urhanghada
출항하다

♦ **pull through** (*from an illness*)
wank'waehada 완쾌하다

♦ **pull together 1** *v/i* (*cooperate*)
hyŏpttonghada 협동하다 **2** *v/t*: **pull
oneself together** maŭmŭl
karaanch'ida 마음을 가라앉히다

♦ **pull up 1** *v/t* kkŭroollida 끌어올리다;
plant, weeds chaba ppoptta 잡아
뽑다 **2** *v/i* (*of car etc*) sŏda 서다

pulley torŭrae 도르래
pulp kwayuk 과육; (*for paper-
making*) p'ŏlp'ŭ 펄프
pulpit sŏlgyodan 설교단
pulsate (*of heart, blood*)
kodongch'ida 고동치다; (*of rhythm*)
chindonghada 진동하다
pulse maekppak 맥박
pulverize karuro mandŭlda 가루로
만들다
pump 1 *n* p'ŏmp'ŭ 펌프 **2** *v/t water*
p'ŏmp'ŭro p'ŏ ollida 펌프로 퍼
올리다; *air* mirŏnaeda 밀어내다

♦ **pump up** konggirŭl chuip'ada
공기를 주입하다

pumpkin hobak 호박
pun tong-ŭmiŭiŭi maltchangnan
동음이의의 말장난
punch 1 *n* (*blow*) chumŏktchil
주먹질; (*implement*) kumŏng ttullŭn
kigu 구멍 뚫는 기구 **2** *v/t* (*with fist*)
huryŏch'ida 후려치다; *hole* kumŏng-
ŭl ttult'a 구멍을 뚫다; *ticket*
kaech'arhada 개찰하다
punch line nongdam chung utkkinŭn
taemok 농담 중 웃기는 대목
punctual shiganŭl ŏmsuhanŭn 시간을
엄수하는
punctuality shigan ŏmsu 시간 엄수
punctually chŏnghwak'i 정확히
punctuate kuduttchŏmŭl tchiktta
구두점을 찍다
punctuation kudutppŏp 구두법
punctuation mark kuduttchŏm
구두점
puncture 1 *n* kumŏng 구멍 **2** *v/t*

kumŏng ttult'a 구멍 뚫다
pungent chagŭk'anŭn 자극하는
punish *person* ch'ŏbŏrhada 처벌하
punishing *pace, schedule* chich'ige
hanŭn 지치게 하는
punishment ch'ŏbŏl 처벌
puny *person* hŏyak'an 허약한
pup (*young dog*) kang-aji 강아지
pupil[1] (*of eye*) nunttongja 눈동자
pupil[2] (*student*) hakssaeng 학생
puppet kkokttugaksshi 꼭두각시
puppet government koeroe
chŏngbu 괴뢰 정부
puppy kang-aji 강아지
purchase[1] *n* kumae 구매 **2** *v/t*
kumaehada 구매하다
purchase[2] (*grip*) sone chwida 손에
쥐다
purchaser maeiptcha 매입자
pure *silk* sunsuhan 순수한; *air, wat*
kkaekkŭt'an 깨끗한; *sound* malgŭn
맑은; (*morally*) kyŏlbaek'an 결백;
~ **wool** / **gold** / **white** sunmo / sun
gŭm / sunbaek 순모 / 순금 / 순백
purely wanjŏnhi 완전히
purge 1 *n* (*of political party*)
sukch'ŏng 숙청 **2** *v/t* sukch'ŏngha
숙청하다
purify *water* chŏnghwahada 정화하
puritan ch'ŏnggyodo 청교도
puritanical ŏmkkyŏk'an 엄격한
purity ch'ŏnggyŏl 청결; (*moral*)
kyŏlbaek 결백
purple *adj* chajuppich'ŭi 자주빛의
Purple Heart MIL myŏng-ye sang-
hunjang 명예 상이 훈장
purpose moktchŏk 목적; **on** ~
koŭijŏgŭro 고의적으로
purposeful tanhohan 단호한
purposely ilburŏ 일부러
purr *v/i* (*of cat*) kŭrŭrŏng-gŏrida
그르렁거리다
purse *n* (*pocketbook*) haendŭbaeg
핸드백
pursue *v/t person* ch'ujŏk'ada
추적하다; *career* ch'uguhada
추구하다; *course of action*
kyesok'ada 계속하다
pursuer ch'ujŏktcha 추적자
pursuit (*chase*) ch'ujŏk 추적; (*of
happiness etc*) ch'ugu 추구; (*activ*

il 일

us korům 고름

usan Pusan 부산

ush 1 n (shove) milgi 밀기; (of button) nurŭgi 누르기 2 v/t (shove) milda 밀다; button nurŭda 누르다; (pressure) kaap'ada 가압하다; drugs mayak milmaehada 마약 밀매하다; be ~ed for mojarada 모자라다; be ~ing 40 kǒŭi mahŭni ta toeda 거의 마흔이 다 되다 3 v/i milda 밀다

push along cart etc milgo kada 밀고 가다

push away mirŏ chech'ida 밀어 제치다

push off 1 v/t lid mirŏnaeda 밀어내다 2 v/i F (leave) ttŏnada 떠나다; ~! chŏri ka! 저리 가!

push on v/i (continue) kyesok'ada 계속하다

push up prices ollida 올리다

push-button nurŭm tanch'ushigüi 누름 단추식의

usher (of drugs) mayak milmaeja 마약 밀매자

push-up p'al kup'yŏ p'yŏgi 팔 굽혀 펴기

ushy ppŏnppŏnsŭrŏun 뻔뻔스러운

uss, pussy (cat) koyang-i 고양이

ut not'a 놓다; question mut-tta 묻다; ~ the cost at ... ...(ǔ)ro kagyǒgŭl ŏrimjaptta ...(으)로 가격을 어림잡다

put aside money chŏgŭmhada 저금하다; work chŏboduda 접어두다

put away (in closet etc) ch'iuda 치우다; (in institution) kamgŭmhada 감금하다; drink mashida 마시다; money chŏgŭmhada 저금하다; animal allakssashik'ida 안락사시키다

put back (replace) chejarie tollyǒnot'a 제자리에 돌려놓다

put by money chŏgŭmhada 저금하다

put down not'a 놓다; deposit sŏnburhada 선불하다; rebellion chinap'ada 진압하다; (belittle) nach'uda 낮추다; (in writing) ssŭda 쓰다; put one's foot down (in car) kasok'ada 가속하다; (be firm) kutkke kyŏlshimhada 굳게 결심하다; put X down to Y

(attribute) Xǔl/rŭl Yǔi t'asŭro tollida X을/를 Y의 탓으로 돌리다

♦ put forward idea etc cheanhada 제안하다

♦ put in nŏt'a 넣다; time ponaeda 보내다; request, claim cheshihada 제시하다

♦ put in for yoch'ŏnghada 요청하다

♦ put off light, radio, TV kkŭda 끄다; (postpone) yŏn-gihada 연기하다; (deter) tannyŏmshik'ida 단념시키다; (repel) pulk'waehada 불쾌하다; put X off Y Xi/ga Y을/를 tannyŏmhage hada X이/가 Y을/를 단념하게 하다

♦ put on light, radio, TV k'yŏda 켜다; tape, music t'ǔlda 틀다; jacket ipta 입다; shoes shintta 신다; eyeglasses ssŭda 쓰다; make-up hada 하다; brake chakttongshik'ida 작동시키다; (perform) kongyŏnhada 공연하다; (assume) kajanghada 가장하다; ~ weight ch'ejung-ŭl nŭrida 체중을 늘이다; she's just putting it on kŭ yŏjanŭn kŭ-nyang kŭrŏn ch'ŏk'ago innŭn kŏyeyo 그 여자는 그냥 그런 척하고 있는 거예요

♦ put out hand naemilda 내밀다; fire sohwahada 소화하다; light kkŭda 끄다

♦ put through (on phone) pakkwŏ chuda 바꿔 주다

♦ put together (assemble) chorip'ada 조립하다; (organize) chojik'ada 조직하다

♦ put up hand tǔlda 들다; person chaewŏjuda 재워주다; (erect) seuda 세우다; prices ollida 올리다; poster, notice puch'ida 붙이다; money naeda 내다; ~ for sale p'allyŏgo naenot'a 팔려고 내놓다

♦ put up with (tolerate) ch'amtta 참다

putty yuri chŏp'aptche 유리 접합제

puzzle 1 n (mystery) susukkekki 수수께끼; (game) p'ŏjŭl 퍼즐 2 v/t yŏngmunŭl morŭge hada 영문을 모르게 하다

puzzling yŏngmun morŭl 영문 모를

PVC p'i pǔi sshi 피 브이 씨

pylon koapssŏnnyong ch'ŏlt'ap 고압선용 철탑

P'yongyang P'yŏngnyang 평양

Q

quack¹ **1** *n* (*of duck*) kkwaek-kkwaek
unŭn sori 꽥꽥 우는 소리 **2** *v/i*
kkwaek-kkwaek ulda 꽥꽥 울다

quack² F (*bad doctor*) tolp'ari ŭisa
돌팔이 의사

quadrangle (*figure*) sagak'yŏng
사각형; (*courtyard*) anttŭl 안뜰

quadruped ne pal chimsŭng 네 발
짐승

quadruple *v/i* ne paero hada 네 배로
하다

quadruplets ne ssangdung-i 네
쌍둥이

quaint *cottage* yeppŭjanghan
예쁘장한; *ideas etc* kimyohan 기묘한

quake 1 *n* (*earth~*) chijin 지진 **2** *v/i*
(*of earth*) hŭndŭllida 흔들리다; (*with
fear*) tŏdŏl ttŏlda 덜덜 떨다

qualification (*from university etc*)
chagyŏk 자격; (*of remark etc*)
chehan 제한; **have the right ~s for
a job** ŏttŏn chigŏbe chŏk'ap'an
chagyŏgŭl kajida 어떤 직업에 적합한
자격을 가지다

qualified *doctor, engineer etc*
chagyŏktchŭng-i innŭn 자격증이
있는; (*restricted*) chehandoen 제한된;
I am not ~ to judge nanŭn
p'andanhal chagyŏgi ŏpssŭmnida
나는 판단할 자격이 없습니다

qualify 1 *v/t* (*of degree, course etc*)
chagyŏgŭl chuda 자격을 주다;
remark etc chehanhada 제한하다
2 *v/i* (*get degree etc*) chagyŏgŭl ŏt-tta
자격을 얻다; (*in competition*)
yesŏnŭl t'onggwahada 예선을
통과하다; *our team has qualified
for the semi-final* uri t'imŭn chun-
gyŏlssŭngjŏne chinch'urhaet-tta 우리
팀은 준결승전에 진출했다; *that
doesn't ~ as …* kŭgŏsŭn …(ŭ)rosŏ
chagyŏgi ŏptta 그것은 …(으)로서
자격이 없다

quality p'umjil 품질; (*characteristic*)
sŏngjil 성질

quality control p'umjil kwalli 품질
관리

qualm yangshimŭi kach'aek 양심의
가책; *have no ~s about …e taehae
yangshimŭi kach'aegŭl pat-tchi ant
…에 대해 양심의 가책을 받지 않[다]

quantify yang-ŭl chaeda 양을 재다

quantity yang 양

quarantine (*for animals*) kŏmnyŏk
검역; (*for people*) kyŏngni 격리

quarrel 1 *n* tat'um 다툼 **2** *v/i* tat'uda
다투다

quarrelsome tat'ugi choahanŭn
다투기 좋아하는

quarry (*for mining*) ch'aesŏktchang
채석장

quart yak 0.95lit'ŏ 약 0.95리터

quarter 1 *n* sabunŭi il 사분의 일; (*25
cents*) ishibossent'ŭ tongjŏn
이십오센트 동전; (*part of town*)
chiyŏk 지역; *a ~ of an hour*
shibobun 십오분; *a ~ of 5* tasŏtsshi
shibobun chŏn 다섯시 십오분 전; *~
after 5* tashŏtsshi shibobun 다섯시
십오분 **2** *v/t* saro nanuda 사로 나누[다]

quarterback SP k'wŏt'ŏbaek 쿼터백;
quarterfinal chunjun-gyŏlssŭng
준준결승; **quarterfinalist** chunjun-
gyŏlssŭng chinch'ultcha 준준결승
진출자

quarterly 1 *adj* kyeganŭi 계간의 **2** *ad[v]*
kyeganŭro 계간으로

quarter note MUS sabun ŭmp'yo 사[분]
음표

quarters MIL pyŏngnyŏng 병영

quartet MUS sajungju 사중주

quartz sŏgyŏng 석영

quaver 1 *n* (*in voice*) ttŏllinŭn sori
떨리는 소리 **2** *v/i* (*of voice*) ttŏllida
떨리다

queen yŏwang 여왕

queen bee yŏwangbŏl 여왕벌

queer (*peculiar*) kimyohan 기묘한

ench *thirst* kashige hada 가시게 다: *flames* kkŭda 끄다

ery 1 *n* ŭimun 의문 **2** *v/t* (*express doubt about*) ŭimunŭl chegihada 의문을 제기하다; (*check*) waginhada 확인하다; **~ X with Y** Yege Xe kwanhan ŭimunŭl chegihada Y에게 X에 관한 의문을 제기하다

estion 1 *n* chilmun 질문; (*matter*) nunje 문제; **in ~** (*being talked about*) munjeŭi 문제의; (*in doubt*) nunjeŭi 문제의; **it's a ~ of money / time** tonŭi / shiganŭi nunjeyeyo 돈의 / 시간의 문제예요; **out of the ~** chŏnhyŏ pulganŭnghan 전혀 불가능한 **2** *v/t person* hilmunhada 질문하다; LAW himmunhada 심문하다; (*doubt*) ishimhada 의심하다

estionable *honesty*, *figures* lishimsŭrŏun 의심스러운

estioning *look*, *tone* ŭishimtchŏgŏ nanŭn 의심쩍어 하는

estion mark murŭmp'yo 물음표

estionnaire chilmunsŏ 질문서

uick pparŭn 빠른; **be ~!** ppali hae! 빨리 해!; **let's have a ~ drink** ttak nan chanman mashija 딱 한 잔만 가시자; **can I have a ~ look?** chamkkan pwado toelkkayo? 잠깐 가도 될까요?; **that was ~!** ppalli naenneyo! 빨리 했네요!

uicksand yusa 유사; **quicksilver** suŭn 수은; **quickwitted** chaech'i nnŭn 재치 있는

uiet choyonghan 조용한; *life*, *town* koyohan 고요한; **keep ~ about** ...ŭl / rŭl pimillo haeduda ...을 / 를 비밀로 해두다; **~!** choyonghi hae! 조용히 해!

quieten down 1 *v/t children*, *class* choyonghage hada 조용하게 하다 **2** *v/i* (*of children*) choyonghaejida 조용해지다; (*of political situation*) chinjŏngdoeda 진정되다

uilt (*on bed*) nubi ibul 누비 이불

uinine k'inine 키니네

quip 1 *n* chaech'i innŭn mal 재치 있는 말 **2** *v/i* nollida 놀리다

quirky pyŏllan 별난

quit 1 *v/t job* kŭmanduda 그만두다; **~ doing sth** muŏt hanŭn kŏsŭl kŭmanduda 무엇 하는 것을 그만두다 **2** *v/i* (*leave job*) chiktchang-ŭl kŭmanduda 직장을 그만두다; COMPUT kkŭnnaeda 끝내다; **get one's notice to ~** (*from landlord*) chip piuranŭn t'ongjirŭl pat-tta 집 비우라는 통지를 받다

quite (*fairly*) kkwae 꽤; (*completely*) wanjŏnhi 완전히; **not ~ ready** chunbiga wanjŏnhi toeji anŭn 준비가 완전히 되지 않은; **I didn't ~ under-stand** ta ihaehal su ŏpssŏssŏyo 다 이해할 수 없었어요; **is that right? - not ~** majayo? – kŭŭi 맞아요? – 거의; **~!** chŏngmal! 정말!; **~ a lot** kkwae manŭn 꽤 많은; **it was ~ a surprise / change** kkwae nollaun iriŏssŏyo / kkwae k'ŭn pyŏnhwayŏssŏyo 꽤 놀라운 일이었어요 / 꽤 큰 변화였어요

quits: be ~ with ...wa / kwa p'ijangp'ajang-i toeda ...와 / 과 피장파장이 되다

quiver *v/i* hŭndŭllida 흔들리다

quiz 1 *n* k'wijŭ 퀴즈 **2** *v/t* murŏboda 물어보다

quiz program k'wijŭ p'ŭro 퀴즈 프로

quota mok 목

quotation (*from author*) inyong 인용; (*price*) kyŏnjŏk 견적

quotation marks inyong puho 인용 부호

quote 1 *n* (*from author*) inyongmun 인용문; (*price*) kyŏnjŏk 견적; (*quotation marks*) inyong puho 인용 부호; **give X a ~ for Y** Xege Yŭi piyong-ŭl kyŏnjŏk'ada X에게 Y의 비용을 견적하다 **2** *v/t text* inyonghada 인용하다; *price* kyŏnjŏk'ada 견적하다 **3** *v/i* inyonghada 인용하다; **~ from an author** chak-kkaŭi kŭrŭl inyonghada 작가의 글을 인용하다

R

rabbit t'okki 토끼
rabies kwanggyŏnpyŏng 광견병
raccoon miguk nŏguri 미국 너구리
race[1] n (of people) injong 인종
race[2] 1 n SP kyŏngju 경주; **the ~s**
(horse ~s) kyŏngma 경마 2 v/i (run
fast) chiltchuhada 질주하다; SP
kyŏngjuhada 경주하다; **he ~d
through his meal/work** kŭnŭn
kŭp'i shikssarŭl/irŭl haet-tta 그는
급히 식사를/일을 했다 3 v/t: **I'll ~
you** kyŏngjuhaja 경주하자
racecourse kyŏngju k'osŭ 경주 코스;
racehorse kyŏngjuma 경주마;
racetrack (for cars, athletics)
kyŏngjujang 경주장
racial injong-ŭi 인종의; **~ equality**
injong p'yŏngdŭng 인종 평등
racing kyŏngju 경주
racing car kyŏngjuch'a 경주차
racing driver kyŏngjuja 경주자
racism injong ch'abyŏltchuŭi 인종
차별주의
racist 1 n injong ch'abyŏltchuŭija
인종 차별의자 2 adj injong
ch'abyŏltchŏgin 인종 차별적인
rack 1 n (for parking cars)
chuch'adae 주차대; (for bags on
train) sŏnban 선반; (for CDs) kkoji
꽂이; (for coats) kŏri kŏri 걸이 2 v/t: **~
one's brains** mŏrirŭl tchada 머리를
짜다
racket[1] SP lak'et 라켓
racket[2] (noise) soŭm 소음; (criminal
activity) pujŏnghan tonppŏri 부정한
돈벌이
radar leida 레이다
radiant smile, appearance hwanhi
pinnanŭn 환히 빛나는
radiate v/i (of heat, light) pich'ŭl
parhada 빛을 발하다
radiation PHYS pangsasŏn 방사선
radiator (in room) nanbanggi 난방기;
(in car) ladiet'ŏ 라디에이터

radical 1 adj kŭnbonjŏgin 근본적인
POL views kŭptchinjŏgin 급진적인
2 n POL kŭptchinjuŭija 급진주의자
radicalism POL kŭptchinjuŭi 급진주
radically kŭnbonjŏgŭro 근본적으로
radio ladio 라디오; **on the ~**
ladioe(sŏ) 라디오에(서); **by ~**
mujŏnŭro 무전으로
radioactive pangsanŭng-i innŭn
방사능이 있는; **radioactivity**
pangsanŭng 방사능; **radio station**
ladio pangsongguk 라디오 방송국;
radiotherapy pangsanŭng yoppŏ
방사능 요법
radish mu 무
radius panjirŭm 반지름
raffle n chebi ppopkki 제비 뽑기
raft ttenmok 뗏목
rafter sŏkkarae 서까래
rag (for cleaning etc)
hŏnggŏptchogak 헝겊조각
rage 1 n kyŏngno 격노; **be in a ~**
kyŏngnohada 격노하다; **all the ~**
taeyuhaeng 대유행 2 v/i (of person)
kyŏngnohada 격노하다; (of storm)
sanapkke morach'ida 사납게
몰아치다
ragged edge tŭltchungnaltchuk'an
들쭉날쭉한; appearance namnuhar
남루한; clothes tchijŏjin 찢어진
raid 1 n (by troops, police) kŭpssŭp
급습; (by robbers) ch'imip 침입; FI
ilje maedo 일제 매도 2 v/t (of troo
police) kŭpssŭp'ada 급습하다; (of
robbers) ch'imip'ada 침입하다
raider (bank robber etc) ch'imiptch
침입자
rail (on track) ch'ŏlto 철도; (hand~)
nan-gan 난간; (for towel) sugŏn kŏ
수건 걸이; **by ~** kich'aro 기차로
railings (around park etc) ult'ari
울타리
railroad ch'ŏlto 철도
railroad station kich'ayŏk 기차역

ain 1 *n* pi 비; *in the ~* pitssoge(sŏ) 빗속에(서); *the ~s* changma 장마 2 *v/i* piga oda 비가 오다; *it's ~ing* piga onda 비가 온다

ainbow mujigae 무지개; raincheck: *can I take a ~ on that?* ŏnjen-ga taŭme hamyŏn andoelkkayo? 언젠가 다음에 하면 안될까요?; raincoat ubi 우비; raindrop pitppang-ul 빗방울; rainfall kang-u량; rain forest urim 우림; *tropical ~* yŏlttae urim 열대 우림; rainstorm p'okp'ung-u 폭풍우

ainy piga onŭn 비가 오는; *it's ~* piga onnŭn-gunnyo 비가 오는군요

ainy season changmach'ŏl 장마철

aise 1 *n* (*in salary*) insang 인상 2 *v/t shelf etc* ollida 올리다; *offer* nŏllida 늘리다; *children* k'iuda 키우다; *question* chegihada 제기하다; *money* moŭda 모으다

aisin kŏnp'odo 건포도

ake *n* (*for garden*) kalk'wi 갈퀴

ally *n* (*meeting, reunion*) taehoe 대회; MOT, (*in tennis*) laelli 랠리
rally around 1 *v/i* tourŏ moida 도우러 모이다 2 *v/t* ...ŭl/rŭl tourŏ tallyŏoda ...을/를 도우러 달려오다

RAM (= *random access memory*) laem 램

am 1 *n* sunnyang 숫양 2 *v/t ship, car* puditch'ida 부딪히다

amble 1 *n* (*walk*) sanch'aek 산책 2 *v/i* (*walk*) sanch'aek'ada 산책하다; (*when speaking, talk incoherently*) tusŏŏpsshi iyagihada 두서없이 이야기하다

ambler (*walker*) sanch'aek'anŭn saram 산책하는 사람

ambling 1 *n* (*walking*) sanch'aek 산책; (*in speech*) hoengsŏlsusŏl 횡설수설 2 *adj speech* tusŏŏmnŭn 두서없는

amp hanggonggiŭi t'ŭraep 항공기의 트랩; (*for raising vehicle*) raemp'ŭ 램프]

ampage 1 *v/i* nalttwimyŏ toradanida 날뛰며 돌아다니다 2 *n*: *go on the ~* nalttwimyŏ toradanida 날뛰며 돌아다니다

rampart sŏngbyŏk 성벽

ramshackle *building* kŭmbang-irado munŏjil tŭt'an 금방이라도 무너질 듯한; *car* kŭmbang-irado pusŏjil tŭt'an 금방이라도 부서질 듯한

ranch moktchang 목장

rancher moktchangju 목장주

rancid ssŏgŭn 썩은

rancor wŏnhan 원한

R & D (= *research and development*) yŏn-gu kaebal 연구 개발

random 1 *adj* mujagwiŭi 무작위의; *~ sample* mujagwi saemp'ŭl 무작위 샘플 2 *n*: *at ~* mujagwiro 무작위로

range 1 *n* (*of products*) pŏmwi 범위; (*of voice*) ŭmnyŏk 음역; (*of airplane*) hangssok kŏri 항속 거리; (*of gun, missile*) sajŏng kŏri 사정 거리; (*of mountains*) sanmaek 산맥 2 *v/i*: *from X to Y* Xesŏ Ykkaji irŭda X에서 Y까지 이르다

ranger (*forest ~*) sallim kyŏngbiwŏn 산림 경비원

rank 1 *n* MIL kyegŭp 계급; (*in society*) shinbun 신분; *the ~s* MIL ilban sabyŏng 일반 사병 2 *v/t* tŭnggŭbŭl maegida 등급을 매기다
♦ rank among ...(ŭ)ro p'yŏngkkahada ...(으)로 평가하다

ransack satssach'i twijida 샅샅이 뒤지다

ransom momkkap 몸값; *hold s.o. to ~* nugurŭl ŏngnyuhayŏ momkkapssŭl yoguhada 누구를 억류하여 몸값을 요구하다

rant: *~ and rave* koraegorae sorich'ida 고래고래 소리치다

rap 1 *n* (*at door etc*) t'okt'ok tudŭrigi 톡톡 두드리기; MUS laep 랩 2 *v/t table etc* t'okt'ok tudŭrida 톡톡 두드리다
♦ rap at *window etc* t'okt'ok tudŭrida 톡톡 두드리다

rape 1 *n* kanggan 강간 2 *v/t* kangganhada 강간하다

rape victim kanggan p'ihaeja 강간 피해자

rapid shinssok'an 신속한

rapidity shinssok 신속

rapids kŭmnyu 급류

rapist kangganbŏm 강간범

rapturous yŏlgwangtchŏgin 열광적인

rare tŭmun 드문; *antique, skills* chin-gihan 진기한; *steak* tŏl igŭn 덜 익은

rarely tŭmulge 드물게

rarity chinp'um 진품

rascal changnankkurŏgi 장난꾸러기

rash[1] MED paltchin 발진

rash[2] *action, behavior* sŏnggŭpp'an 성급한

raspberry namuttalgi 나무딸기

rat *n* chwi 쥐

rate 1 *n* (*of birth, death etc*) piyul 비율; (*of exchange*) hwannyul 환율; (*price*) yogŭm 요금; (*speed*) chindo 진도; *an hourly ~* (*of pay*) shigandang 시간당; *a weekly ~* (*of pay*) chudang 주당; *~ of interest* FIN ijayul 이자율; *at this ~* (*at this speed*) i chŏngdo sokttomyŏn 이 정도 속도면; (*carrying on like this*) kyesok irŏn sangt'aeramyŏn 계속 이런 상태라면 **2** *v/t* (*consider, rank*) p'yŏngkkahada 평가하다

rather (*somewhat*) taso 다소; (*preferably*) ohiryŏ 오히려; *I would ~ stay here* nanŭn ohiryŏ yŏgi innŭn p'yŏni natkkessŏyo 나는 오히려 여기 있는 편이 낫겠어요; *or would you ~ have coffee?* animyŏn ohiryŏ k'ŏp'iro hagessŏyo? 아니면 오히려 커피로 하겠어요?

ration 1 *n* paegŭmnyang 배급량 **2** *v/t supplies* paegŭp'ada 배급하다

rational hamnijŏgin 합리적인

rationality hamnisŏng 합리성

rationalization (*of production etc*) hyoyurhwa 효율화

rationalize 1 *v/t production* hyoyurhwahada 효율화하다; *actions etc* hamnihwahada 합리화하다 **2** *v/i* hamnihwahada 합리화하다

rat race kwada kyŏngjaeng sahoe 과다 경쟁 사회

rattle off *poem, list of names* kŏch'imŏpsshi chikkŏrida 거침없이 지껄이다

rattlesnake pang-ulbaem 방울뱀

ravage: *~d by war* chŏnjaeng-ŭro hwangp'yehaejin 전쟁으로 황폐해진

rave *v/i* (*talk deliriously*) hŏtssoriha 헛소리하다; (*talk wildly*) chŏngshinŏpsshi chikkŏrida 정신없이 지껄이다; *~ about sth* (*very enthusiastic*) yŏlgwanghada 무엇에 열광하다

raven kkamagwi 까마귀

ravenous *appetite* kegŏlssŭrŏun 게걸스러운

rave review kŭkch'anŭi p'yŏng 극찬의 평

ravine chobŭn koltchagi 좁은 골짜기

raving mad wanjŏnhi mich'in 완전히 미친

ravishing maehoktchŏgin 매혹적인

raw *meat, vegetables* nalkkŏsŭi 날것의; *sugar, iron* kagonghaji anŭn 가공하지 않은

raw fish hoe 회

raw materials wŏllyo 원료

ray pit 빛; *a ~ of hope* han kadak hŭimang ŭi 가닥 희망

razor myŏndok'al 면도칼

razor blade myŏndonal 면도날

re COM ...e kwanhayŏ ...에 관하여

reach 1 *n*: *within ~* (*close to hand*) soni tannŭn kose 손이 닿는 곳에; (*easily accessible*) kakkaun kose 가까운 곳에; *out of ~* soni tach'i annŭn kose 손이 닿지 않는 곳에 **2** *v/t city etc* toch'ak'ada 도착하다; (*go as far as*) ...e tat'a ...에 달다; *decision, agreement* ...e irŭda ...에 이르다

♦ **reach out** *v/i* sonŭl ppŏtch'ida 손을 뻗치다

react panjagyonghada 반작용하다; (*news etc*) panŭnghada 반응하다

reaction panjagyong 반작용; (*to news etc*) panŭng 반응

reactionary 1 *n* pandongjuŭija 반동주의자 **2** *adj* pandong-ŭi 반동의

reactor (*nuclear*) wŏnjaro 원자로

read 1 *v/t* iltta 읽다; *diskette* ...ŭi chŏngborŭl iltta ...의 정보를 읽다 **2** *v/i* iltta 읽다; *~ to s.o.* nuguege ilgŏ chuda 누구에게 읽어 주다

♦ **read out** *v/t* (*aloud*) k'ŭn soriro il 큰 소리로 읽다

ead up on ...ŭl/rŭl yŏn-guhada
.ŭl/rŭl yŏn-guhada

adable ilgŭl su innŭn 읽을 수 있는
ader (*person*) tokssŏga 독서가
adily *admit, agree* sŏntŭt 선뜻
adiness (*for action*) chunbiga toeŏ ssŭm 준비가 되어 있음;
(*willingness*) kikkŏi hanŭn maŭm 기꺼이 하는 마음
ading (*activity*) tokssŏ 독서; (*from meter etc*) ch'ŭktchŏng 측정
ading matter ilgŭl kŏri 읽을 거리
adjust 1 *v/t equipment, controls* chaejŏngnihada 재정리하다 **2** *v/i* (*to conditions*) chaejŏgŭnghada 재적응하다
ad-only file COMPUT p'andok chŏnyong p'ail 판독 전용 파일
ad-only memory COMPUT p'andok chŏnyong kiŏk changch'i 판독 전용 기억 장치
ady (*prepared*) chunbidoen 준비된; (*willing*) kikkŏi ...handa 기꺼이 ...하다; **he is always ~ to listen** kŭnŭn hangsang kikkŏi tŭnnŭnda 그는 항상 기꺼이 듣는다; **get** (*oneself*) **~** chunbihada 준비하다; **get ... ready** ...ŭl/rŭl chunbihada ...을/를 준비하다
ady-made *meal* miri mandŭrŏjyŏ innŭn 미리 만들어져 있는; *solution* chinbuhan 진부한
ady-to-wear kisŏngbok 기성복
al chintcha-ŭi 진짜의
al estate pudongsan 부동산
alism hyŏnshiltchuŭi 현실주의; (*in literature, art*) sashiltchuŭi 사실주의
alist hyŏnshiltchuŭija 현실주의자; (*in literature, art etc*) sashiltchuŭija 사실주의자
alistic hyŏnshiltchŏgin 현실적인
ality hyŏnshil 현실
alization (*of goal*) shirhyŏn 실현; (*understanding*) kkaedarŭm 깨달음
alize *v/t* kkaedat-tta 깨닫다; FIN ...ŭi iigŭl poda ...의 이익을 보다; **I ~ now that ...** nanŭn ijeya ...ranŭn kŏsŭl kkaedannŭnda 나는 이제야 ...라는 것을 깨닫는다
ally chŏngmallo 정말로; (*very*) taedanhi 대단히; **~?** chŏngmariyeyo?

정말이예요?; **not ~** (*not much*) pyŏlloyeyo 별로예요
real time COMPUT shilsshigan 실시간
real-time COMPUT shilsshiganŭi 실시간의
realtor pudongsan chunggaein 부동산 중개인
reap suhwak-ada 수확하다
reappear tashi nat'anada 다시 나타나다
rear 1 *n* paehu 배후 **2** *adj* twiŭi 뒤의; *lights* twittchogŭi 뒷쪽의
rearm 1 *v/t* chaemujangshik'ida 재무장시키다 **2** *v/i* chaemujanghada 재무장하다
rearmost maen twittchogŭi 맨 뒷쪽의
rearrange *flowers, chairs* chaebaeyŏrhada 재배열하다; *schedule* chaejŏngnihada 재정리하다
rear-view mirror paengmirŏ 백미러
reason 1 *n* (*faculty*) isŏng 이성; (*cause*) iyu 이유 **2** *v/t*: **~ with s.o.** nugurŭl sŏlttŭk'ae poda 누구를 설득해 보다
reasonable *person, behavior* punbyŏl innŭn 분별 있는; *price* chŏkttanghan 적당한; **a ~ number of people** sangdanghi manŭn saramdŭl 상당히 많은 사람들
reasonably *act, behave* ich'ie matkke 이치에 맞게; (*quite*) sangdanghi 상당히
reassure anshimshik'ida 안심시키다
reassuring anshimhage hanŭn 안심하게 하는
rebate (*money back*) hwanbul 환불
rebel *n* panyŏktcha 반역자; **~ troops** pallan-gun 반란군
rebellion pallan 반란
rebellious panhangjŏgin 반항적인
rebound *v/i* (*of ball etc*) toet'wida 되튀다
rebuff *n* kŏjŏl 거절
rebuild kaech'uk-ada 개축하다; *relationship* hoebok-ada 회복하다
rebuke *v/t* chilch'aek'ada 질책하다
recall *v/t ambassador* sohwanhada 소환하다; (*remember*) sanggihada 상기하다
recapture *v/t* MIL t'arhwan 탈환; *criminal* chaech'ep'ohada

재체포하다

receding *hair* pŏtkkyŏjinŭn 벗겨지는

receipt yŏngsujŭng 영수증; **acknowledge ~ of** …ŭl/rŭl padassŭmŭl injŏnghada …을/를 받았음을 인정하다; **~s** FIN suip 수입

receive pat-tta 받다

receiver (*of letter*) such'wiin 수취인; TELEC suhwagi 수화기; RAD sushingi 수신기

receivership: be in ~ chaesan kwalli sangt'aee noyŏ it-tta 재산 관리 상태에 놓여 있다

recent ch'oegŭnŭi 최근의

recently ch'oegŭne 최근에

reception (*in hotel, company*) p'ŭront'ŭ 프론트; (*formal party*) lisepsshyŏn p'at'i 리셉션 파티; (*welcome*) hwanyŏng 환영; RAD sushin 수신

reception desk annae tesŭk'ŭ 안내 데스크

receptionist chŏpssuwŏn 접수원

receptive: be ~ to …ŭl/rŭl chal padadŭrida …을/를 잘 받아들이다

recess (*in wall etc*) ump'uk tŭrŏgan kot 움푹 들어간 곳; EDU shwinŭn shigan 쉬는 시간; (*of legislature*) hyuhoe 휴회

recession pulgyŏnggi 불경기

recharge *battery* ch'ungjŏnhada 충전하다

recipe choribŏp 조리법

recipient (*of parcel etc*) such'wiin 수취인; (*of payment*) suryŏng-in 수령인

reciprocal sanghoganŭi 상호간의

recital MUS lisait'ŭl 리사이틀

recite *poem* nangsonghada 낭송하다; *details, facts* yŏlgŏhada 열거하다

reckless mumohan 무모한

reckon (*think, consider*) …rago saenggak'ada …라고 생각하다

♦ **reckon with: have s.o. / sth to ~** nugurŭl / muŏsŭl koryŏe nŏt'a 누구를 / 무엇을 고려에 넣다

reclaim *land from sea* kanch'ŏk'ada 간척하다

recline *v/i* kidaeda 기대다

recluse ŭndunja 은둔자

recognition (*of state, achievements*) injŏng 인정; (*of person*) arabom 알아봄; **change beyond ~** arabol ŏpssŭl chŏngdoro pyŏnhada 알아볼 수 없을 정도로 변하다

recognizable arabol su innŭn 알아 볼 수 있는

recognize *person, voice, tune* araboda 알아보다; (*distinguish*) puganhada 분간하다; POL *state* sŭnginhada 승인하다; **it can be ~d by** …(ŭ)ro pun-gandoel su it-tta …(으)로 분간될 수 있다

recollect hoesanghada 회상하다

recollection hoesang 회상

recommend ch'uch'ŏnhada 추천하다

recommendation ch'uch'ŏn 추천

reconcile *people* hwahaeshik'ida 화해시키다; *differences* chohwashik'ida 조화시키다; *facts* ilch'ishik'ida 일치시키다; **~ oneself to …** …ŭl/rŭl kamsuhada …을/를 감수하다; **be ~d** (*of two people*) hwahaehada 화해하다

reconciliation (*of people*) hwahae 화해; (*of differences*) chohwa 조화; (*of facts*) ilch'i 일치

recondition …ŭl/rŭl surihada …을/를 수리하다

reconnaissance MIL chŏngch'al 정찰

reconsider *v/t & v/i* chaegohada 재고하다

reconstruct *city* chaegŏnhada 재건하다; *one's life* tashi ch'usŭrida 다시 추스리다; *crime* chaehyŏnhada 재현하다

record 1 *n* MUS lek'odŭ 레코드; SP *etc* kyŏnggi kirok 경기 기록; (*written document etc*) kirok munsŏ 기록 문서; (*in database*) hanbŏrŭi teit'ŏ 한벌의 데이터; **~s** (*archives*) kirok munsŏ 기록 문서; **say sth off the** muŏsŭl pigongshigŭro marhada 무엇을 비공식으로 말하다; **have a criminal ~** chŏnkkwaga it-tta 전과가 있다; **have a good ~ for …** …i/ga chot'anŭn p'yŏngp'anŭl kajigo it-tta …이/가 좋다는 평판을 가지고 있다 **2** *v/t* (*on tape etc*) nogŭmhada 녹음하다

record-breaking kirogŭl kkaenŭn

기록을 깨는

ecorder MUS lik'odŏ 리코더

ecord holder kirok poyuja 기록
보유자

ecording nogŭm 녹음

ecording studio nogŭmshil 녹음실

ecord player nogŭmgi 녹음기

ecoup *losses* toech'at-tta 되찾다

ecover 1 *v/t* (*get back*) toech'at-tta
되찾다 **2** *v/i* (*from illness*)
hoebok'ada 회복하다

ecovery (*of sth lost, stolen money*)
toech'ajŭm 되찾음; (*from illness*)
hoebok 회복; **he has made a good
~** kŭŭi hoebogŭn sunjorowat-tta
그의 회복은 순조로왔다

ecreation orak 오락

ecruit 1 *n* MIL shinbyŏng 신병; (*to
company*) shinip sawŏn 신입 사원
2 *v/t new staff* mojip'ada 모집하다

ecruitment shin-gyu mojip 신규
모집

ecruitment drive shin-gyu mojip
k'aemp'ein 신규 모집 캠페인

ectangle chikssagak'yŏng 직사각형

ectangular chikssagak'yŏng-ŭi
직사각형의

ecuperate hoebok'ada 회복하다

ecur chaebarhada 재발하다

ecurrent chaebarhanŭn 재발하는

ecycle chaesaeng iyonghada 재생
이용하다

ecycling chaesaeng iyong 재생 이용

ed ppalgan saek 빨간 색; *hair* pulgŭn 붉은; *in
the ~* chŏktchaga nada 적자가 나다

Red Cross Chŏksshiptcha 적십자

redden *v/i* (*blush*) pulgŏjida 붉어지다

redecorate *v/t* sae tanjanghada 새
단장하다

redeem *debt* sanghwanhada 상환하다;
sinners kuwŏnhada 구원하다

redeeming: ~ *feature* kyŏltchŏmŭl
powanhae chunŭn changtchŏm
=결점을 보완해 주는 장점

redevelop *part of town*
chaegaebarhada 재개발하다

red-handed: catch ~
hyŏnhaengbŏmŭro chaptta
현행범으로 잡다; **redhead**
mŏrik'aragi pulgŭn saram
머리카락이 붉은 사람; **red-hot**

saeppalgak'e tan 새빨갛게 단; **red
light** ppalgan pul 빨간 불; **red light
district** hongdŭngga 홍등가; **red
meat** pulgŭn saegi tonŭn kogi 붉은
색이 도는 고기; **red tape**
kwallyojŏk hyŏngshiktchuŭi 관료적
형식주의

reduce churida 줄이다

reduction kamso 감소

redundant (*unnecessary*)
pulp'iryohan 불필요한

reed BOT kalttae 갈대

reef (*in sea*) amch'o 암초

reef knot ongmaedŭp 옭매듭

reek *v/i* naemsaega nada 냄새가 나다;
~ *of* ...ŭi naemsaega nada ...의
냄새가 나다

reel *n* (*of film*) lil 릴; (*of thread*)
shilp'ae 실꾸러미

refer *v/t*: ~ *a decision / problem to*
...ege kyŏltchŏng-ŭl / mun-jerŭl
nŏmgida ...에게 결정을 / 문제를
넘기다

♦ **refer to** (*allude to*) ...ŭl / rŭl ŏn-
gŭp'ada ...을 / 를 언급하다;
dictionary etc ...e chohoehada ...에
조회하다

referee SP shimp'an 심판; (*for job*)
shinwŏn pojŭng-in 신원 보증인

reference (*allusion*) ŏn-gŭp 언급;
(*for job*) ch'uch'ŏnsŏ 추천서; (~
number) chohoe 조회; **with ~ to** ...e
kwallyŏnhayŏ ...에 관련하여

reference book ch'amgo tosŏ 참고
도서

referendum kungmin t'up'yo 국민
투표

refill *v/t tank, glass* tashi ch'aeuda
다시 채우다

refine *oil, sugar* chŏngjehada
정제하다; *technique* chŏnggyohage
hada 정교하게 하다

refined *manners, language*
seryŏndoen 세련된

refinery chŏngjeso 정제소

reflation t'onghwa chaep'aengch'ang
통화 재팽창

reflect 1 *v/t light* pansahada 반사하다;
be ~ed in ... ...e pich'wŏjida ...에
비춰지다 **2** *v/i* (*think*) komgomhi
saenggak'ada 곰곰히 생각하다

reflection

reflection (*in water, glass etc*) pansadoen kŭrimja 반사된 그림자; (*consideration*) shimsasuk-kko 심사숙고

reflex (*in body*) pansa shin-gyŏng 반사 신경

reflex reaction pansa undong 반사 운동

reform 1 *n* kaehyŏk 개혁 **2** *v/t* kaehyŏk'ada 개혁하다

refrain[1] *v/i* samgahada 삼가하다; **please ~ from smoking** tambaerŭl samgahae chushigi paramnida 담배를 삼가해 주시기 바랍니다

refrain[2] *n* (*in song etc*) huryŏm 후렴

refresh *person* kiun ch'arige hada 기운 차리게 하다; **feel ~ed** sangk'waehage nŭkkida 상쾌하게 느끼다

refresher course chaegyoyuk kwajŏng 재교육 과정

refreshing *experience* ch'amshinhan 참신한; **~ drink** ch'ŏngnyang ŭmnyo 청량 음료

refreshments tagwa 다과

refrigerate naengjanghada 냉장하다

refrigerator naengjanggo 냉장고

refuel 1 *v/t airplane* yŏllyorŭl konggŭp'ada 연료를 공급하다 **2** *v/i* (*of airplane*) yŏllyorŭl pogŭp pat-tta 연료를 보급 받다

refuge p'inanch'ŏ 피난처; **take ~** (*from storm etc*) p'inanhada 피난하다

refugee nanmin 난민

refund 1 *n* hwanbul 환불 **2** *v/t* hwanburhada 환불하다

refusal kŏjŏl 거절

refuse kŏjŏrhada 거절하다; **~ to ...** ...hagirŭl kŏjŏrhada ...하기를 거절하다

regain *control, the lead* toech'at-tta 되찾다

regard 1 *n*: **have great ~ for** ...ŭl/rŭl chon-gyŏnghada ...을/를 존경하다; **in this ~** i chŏm kwanhaesŏnŭn 이 점 관해서는; **with ~ to** ...e kwanhaesŏ ...에 관해서; (*kind*) ~s anbu 안부; **give my ~s to Mina** Minaege anbu chŏnhaejuseyo 미나에게 안부

전해주세요; **with no ~ for** ...ŭl/rŭl koryŏhaji ank'o ...을/를 고려하지 않고 **2** *v/t*: **~ X as Y** Xŭl/rŭl Y(ŭ)ro kanjuhada X을/를 Y(으)로 간주하다 **as ~s** ...e kwanhaesŏnŭn ...에 관해서는

regarding ...e taehaesŏ ...에 대해서

regardless ŏtchaet-ttŭn 어쨌든; **~ of** ...e kaeŭich'i ank'o ...에 개의치 않고

regime (*government*) chŏngkkwŏn 정권

regiment *n* yŏndae 연대

region chibang 지방; **in the ~ of** yak... 약 ...; **in the ~ of $5,000** yak 5,000tallŏ 약 5,000달러

regional chiyŏgŭi 지역의

register 1 *n* tŭngnok 등록 **2** *v/t birth, death* shin-gohada 신고하다; *vehicle* tŭngnok'ada 등록하다; *letter* tŭngkkiro puch'ida 등기로 부치다; *emotion* nat'anaeda 나타내다; **send a letter ~ed** p'yŏnjirŭl tŭngkkiro ponaeda 편지를 등기로 보내다 **3** *v/i* (*at university*) ip'ak tŭngnogŭl hada 입학 등록을 하다; (*for a course*) tŭngnogŭl hada 등록을 하다; (*with police*) shin-gohada 신고하다

registered letter tŭngkki up'yŏn 등기 우편

registration (*at university*) ip'ak tŭngnok 입학 등록; (*for course*) tŭngnok'ada 등록하다

regret 1 *v/t* huhoehada 후회하다 **2** *n* yugam 유감

regrettable yugamsŭrŏun 유감스러운

regrettably yugamsŭrŏpkkedo 유감스럽게도

regular 1 *adj* kyuch'iktchŏgin 규칙적인; *pattern, shape* iltchŏnghan 일정한; (*normal*) pot'ong-ŭi 보통의 **2** *n* (*at bar etc*) tan-gol 단골

regulate kyujehada 규제하다

regulation (*rule*) kyuch'ik 규칙

rehabilitate *ex-criminal* sahoero pok-kkwishik'ida 사회로 복귀시키다

rehearsal lihŏsŏl 리허설

rehearse *v/t & v/i* lihŏsŏrhada 리허설하다

reign 1 *n* kullim 군림 **2** *v/i* kullimhada 군림하다

imburse …ŭi piyong-ŭl kapta …의 내용을 갚다

in koppi 고삐

incarnation hwansaeng 환생

inforce *structure* poganghada 보강하다; *beliefs* kanghwahada 강화하다

inforced concrete ch'ŏlgŭn k'onk'ŭrit'ŭ 철근 콘크리트

inforcements MIL chŭng-wŏn-gun 증원군

instate *person in office* poktchiksshik'ida 복직시키다; *paragraph in text* pogwŏnhada 복원하다

ject *v/t* kŏjŏrhada 거절하다

jection kŏjŏl 거절

lapse MED chaebal 재발; *have a ~* pyŏng-i chaebarhada 병이 재발하다

late 1 *v/t story* iyagihada 이야기하다; *~ X to Y* Xŭl/rŭl Yege yŏn-gyŏlshik'ida X을/를 Y에게 연결시키다 2 *v/i*: *~ to …* (*be connected with*) …wa/kwa kwallyŏni it-tta …와/과 관련이 있다; *he doesn't ~ to people* kŭnŭn saramdŭlgwa chal sŏk-kkijil mot'anda 그는 사람들과 잘 섞이질 못한다

lated (*by family*) ch'inch'ŏgi toenŭn 친척이 되는; *events, ideas etc* kwallyŏni innŭn 관련이 있는

lation (*in family*) ch'inch'ŏk 친척; (*connection*) kwan-gye 관계; *business / diplomatic ~s* saŏp / oegyo kwan-gye 사업 / 외교 관계

lationship kwan-gye 관계; (*sexual*) sŏnggwan-gye 성관계

lative 1 *n* ch'inch'ŏk 친척 2 *adj* sangdaejŏgin 상대적인; *X is ~ to Y* Xŭn/nŭn Ye piryehanda X은/는 Y에 비례한다

latively sandaejŏgŭro 상대적으로

lax 1 *v/i* p'yŏnhi shwida 편히 쉬다; *~!, don't get angry* maŭm p'yŏnhage saenggak'ae! hwanaeji mallagu 마음 편하게 생각 해! 화내지 말라구 2 *v/t muscle* himŭl ppaeda 힘을 빼다; *pace* nŭtch'uda 늦추다; *laws* wanhwashik'ida 완화시키다

reimburse …ŭi piyong-ŭl kapta …의 내용을 갚다

relaxation kinjang wanhwa 긴장 완화

relay 1 *v/t message* chŏnhada 전하다; *radio, TV signals* chunggyehada 중계하다 2 *n*: *~ (race)* kyeju kyŏnggi 계주 경기

release 1 *n* (*from prison*) sŏkppang 석방; (*of CD etc*) palmae 발매; (*of news, information*) palp'yo 발표 2 *v/t prisoner* sŏkppanghada 석방하다; *CD* palmaehada 발매하다; *parking brake* p'ulda 풀다; *information* konggaehada 발표하다

relent maŭmi nugŭrŏjida 마음이 누그러지다

relentless (*determined*) tanhohan 단호한; *rain etc* sajŏng-ŏmnŭn 사정없는

relevance kwallyŏnssŏng 관련성

relevant kwallyŏndoen 관련된

reliability shilloessŏng 신뢰성

reliable shilloehal su innŭn 신뢰할 수 있는

reliably hwaksshirhage 확실하게; *I am ~ informed that …* nanŭn …ranŭn kosŭl hwaksshirhage chŏnhae tŭrŏtta 나는 …라는 것을 확실하게 전해 들었다

reliance ŭijon 의존; *~ on s.o. / sth* nugue / muŏse taehan ŭijon 누구에 / 무엇에 대한 의존

relic yumul 유물

relief anshim 안심; *that's a ~* anshimi toemnida 안심이 됩니다

relieve *pressure, pain* churida 줄이다; (*take over from*) kyodaehada 교대하다; *be ~d* (*at news etc*) anshimi toeda 안심이 되다

religion chonggyo 종교

religious chonggyojŏgin 종교적인; *person* shinangshim-i kip'ŭn 신앙심이 깊은

religiously (*conscientiously*) yangshimjŏgŭro 양심적으로

relish 1 *n* (*sauce*) yangnyŏm 양념 2 *v/t idea, prospect* chŭlgida 즐기다

relive *the past* sanggihada 상기하다

relocate *v/i* (*of business*) ijŏnhada 이전하다; (*of employee*) chaebaech'ihada 재배치하다

reluctance naek'iji anŭm 내키지 않음

reluctant naek'iji annŭn 내키지 않는;

be ~ to do sth muǒsǔl hanǔn kǒshi naek'iji ant'a 무엇을 하는 것이 내키지 않다

reluctantly maji mot'ae 마지 못해

♦ **rely on** ǔijihada 의지하다; **~ s.o. to do sth** nuguege muǒt hanǔn kǒsǔl ǔijihada 누구에게 무엇 하는 것을 의지하다

remain (*be left*) namgyǒjida 남겨지다; (*stay*) kyesok … it-tta 계속 … 있다; **they ~ed silent** kǔdǔrǔn kyesok choyonghage issǒt-tta 그들은 계속 조용하게 있었다

remainder *also* MATH namǒji 나머지

remains (*of body*) yuhae 유해

remand 1 *v/t*: **~ s.o. in custody** nugurǔl kuryushik'ida 누구를 구류시키다 **2** *n*: **be on ~** kuryu chung-ida 구류 중이다

remark 1 *n* ǒn-gǔp 언급 **2** *v/t* ǒn-gǔp'ada 언급하다

remarkable chumok'al manhan 주목할 만한

remarkably taedanhi 대단히

remarry *v/i* chaehonhada 재혼하다

remedy *n* MED ch'iryo 치료; *fig* kujech'aek 구제책

remember 1 *v/t* kiǒk'ada 기억하다; **~ to lock the door** mun chamgǔnǔn kǒl, ittchi marayo 문 잠그는 걸, 잊지 말아요; **~ me to her** kǔnyǒege nae anburǔl chǒnhaejuseyo 그녀에게 내 안부를 전해주세요 **2** *v/i* kiǒk'ada 기억하다; **I don't ~** chǒnǔn kiǒki naji anayo 저는 기억이 나지 않아요

remind: **~ s.o. of sth** (*bring to their attention*) nuguege muǒsǔl ilkkaewǒjuda 누구에게 무엇을 일깨워주다; (*make remember*) nuguege muǒsǔl kiǒng nage hada 누구에게 무엇을 기억 나게 하다; **~ s.o. of s.o.** nugurǔl pomyǒn nugun-gaga saenggangnada 누구를 보면 누군가가 생각나다

reminder saegangnage hanǔn kǒt 생각나게 하는 것; COM tokch'oktchang 독촉장

reminisce hoesang 회상

reminiscent: **be ~ of sth** muǒsǔl yǒnsangshik'ida 무엇을 연상시키다

remnant yumul 유물

remorse chach'aek 자책

remorseless *person* mujabihan 무자비한; *demands* kkǔnimǒmnǔn 끊임없는; *pace* mǒmch'ul su ǒmnǔn 멈출 수 없는

remote *village* oettan 외딴; *possibility, connection* hǔibak'an 희박한; (*aloof*) ch'oyǒnhan 초연한 *ancestor* mǒn 먼

remote access COMPUT wǒnkkyǒ chǒpkkǔn 원격 접근

remote control wǒnkkyǒk chojon 원격 조종

remotely *connected* mǒlli 멀리; *just possible* kanǔngssǒng-i kǒǔi hǔibak'an 가능성이 거의 희박한

removal chegǒ 제거

remove ch'iuda 치우다; *top, lid* pǒtkkida 벗기다; *coat etc* pǒt-tta 벗다; *doubt, suspicion* ǒpssaeda 없애다

remuneration posu 보수

remunerative posuga ch'ungbunha 보수가 충분한

rename kaemyǒnghada 개명하다

render haenghada 행하다; **~ a service** pongsahada 봉사하다; **~ s.o. helpless / unconscious** nugurǔl mugiryǒk'age / ǔishigǔl ilk'e hada 누구를 무기력하게 / 의식을 잃게 하다

rendering (*of music*) yǒnju 연주

rendez-vous (*romantic*) langdebu 랑데부; MIL chipkkyǒltchi 집결지

renew *contract, license* kaengshinhada 갱신하다; *discussions* chaegaehada 재개하다

renewal (*of contract etc*) kaengshin 갱신; (*of discussions*) chaegae 재개

renounce *v/t title, rights* p'ogihada 포기하다

renovate *building* kaejohada 개조하다

renovation (*of building*) kaejo 개조

renown yumyǒng 유명

renowned yumyǒnghan 유명한

rent 1 *n* imdaeryo 임대료; **for ~** imdaeyong 임대용 **2** *v/t apartment, car* imdaehada 임대하다

rental (*money*) imdae kǔmaek 임대 금액

rental agreement imdae kyeyaksǒ

임대 계약서
●**ntal car** imdae chadongch'a 임대
자동차
●**nt-free** adv imdaeryoga ŏpsshi
임대료가 없이
●**open 1** v/t store chaegaejanghada
재개장하다; business, negotiations,
case chaegaehada 재개하다 **2** v/i (of
theater etc) chaegaejanghada
재개장하다
●**organization** chaep'yŏnsŏng
재편성
●**organize** chaep'yŏnsŏnghada
재편성하다
●**p** COM seiljŭ maen 세일즈 맨
●**paint** tashi ch'irhada 다시 칠하다
●**pair 1** v/t koch'ida 고치다 **2** n: **in a
good/bad state of ~** suriga chal
toen/chal toeji anŭn 수리가 잘
된/잘 되지 않은
●**pairman** surigong 수리공
●**patriate** songwanhada 송환하다
●**pay** money, person kaptta 갚다
●**payment** pyŏnje 변제
●**peal** v/t law p'yejihada 폐지하다
●**peat 1** v/t something said
panbok'ada 반복하다; performance,
experience toep'urihada 되풀이하다;
am I ~ing myself? chŏne marhaet-
ttŏn chŏgi innayo? 전에 말했던 적이
있나요? **I** v/t panbok'ada 반복하다; **I
~, do not touch it** tashi
marhanŭnde, kŭgŏsŭl manjiji
maseyo 다시 말하는데. 그것을
만지지 마세요 **3** n (TV program)
chaebangsong 재방송
●**peat business** COM chaegŏrae
재거래
●**peated** panboktoenŭn 반복되는
●**peat order** COM chaejumun
재주문
●**pel** v/t invaders, attack
kyŏkt'oehada 격퇴하다; insects
moranaeda 몰아내다; (disgust)
pulk'waegamŭl irŭk'ida 불쾌감을
일으키다
●**pellent 1** n (insect ~) pŏllee mulliji
ank'e hanŭn yak 벌레에 물리지 않게
하는 약 **2** adj pulk'waehan 불쾌한
●**pent** huhoehada 후회하다
●**percussions** p'agŭp hyokkwa 파급

효과
repetition (of word, event etc)
panbok 반복
repetitive toep'uridoenŭn 되풀이되는
replace (put back) toedollyŏnot'a
되돌려놓다; (take the place of)
taeshinhada 대신하다
replacement (person) huimja 후임자;
(thing) taech'ep'um 대체품
replacement part taech'ebup'um
대체부품
replay 1 n (recording) chaesaeng
재생; (match) chaeshihap 재시합
2 v/t match chaeshihap'ada
재시합하다
replica poktchep'um 복제품
reply 1 n taedap 대답 **2** v/t & v/i
taedap'ada 대답하다
report 1 n (account) pogosŏ 보고서;
(by journalist) podo 보도 **2** v/t
pogohada 보고하다; **~ one's find-
ings to s.o.** nuguege chosa
kyŏlgwarŭl pogohada 누구에게 조사
결과를 보고하다; **~ a person to the
police** saramŭl kyŏngch'are
kobarhada 사람을 경찰에 고발하다;
he is ~ed to be in Hong Kong
kŭnŭn hongk'onge innŭn kŏsŭro
pogodoeŏtta 그는 홍콩에 있는
것으로 보고되었다 **3** v/i (of
journalist) podohada 보도하다;
(present oneself) ch'ulttuhada
출두하다
♦**report to** (in business) …ege
pogohada …에게 보고하다
report card sŏngjŏkp'yo 성적표
reporter kija 기자
repossess COM miwanbuldoen
sangp'umŭl hoesuhada 미완불된
상품을 회수하다
reprehensible pinan padŭlmanhan
비난 받을만한
represent (act for) taerihada
대리하다; (stand for) taep'yohada
대표하다; (of images in painting etc)
myosahada 묘사하다
representative 1 n taeriin 대리인;
COM taep'yoja 대표자; POL taebyŏnja
대변자 **2** adj (typical)
chŏnhyŏngjŏgin 전형적인
repress revolt ŏgap'ada 억압하다;

feelings, natural urges ŏngnurŭda 억누르다; *laugh* ch'amtta 참다

repression POL chinap 진압

repressive POL ŏgaptchŏgin 억압적인

reprieve 1 *n* LAW chip'aeng yuye 집행 유예; *fig* ilshijŏk yŏn-gi 일시적 연기 **2** *v/t prisoner* chip'aeng-ŭl yuyehada 집행을 유예하다

reprimand *v/t* chilch'aek'ada 질책하다

reprint 1 *n* chaep'an 재판 **2** *v/t* chaep'anhada 재판하다

reprisal pokssu 복수; *take ~s* pokssuhada 복수하다

reproach 1 *n* pinan 비난; *be beyond ~* pinanŭi yŏjiga ŏptta 비난의 여지가 없다 **2** *v/t* pinanhada 비난하다

reproachful pinanhanŭn 비난하는

reproduce 1 *v/t atmosphere, mood* chaehyŏnhada 재현하다 **2** *v/i* BIO chaesaengshik'ada 재생식하다

reproduction BIO chaesaengshik 재생식; *(of sound, images)* chaesaeng 재생; *(piece of furniture)* poktche 복제

reproductive BIO chaesaengshik'anŭn 재생식하는

reptile p'ach'ungnyu 파충류

republic konghwaguk 공화국

Republic of Korea Taehanmin-guk 대한민국

republican 1 *n* konghwadangjuŭija 공화당주의자; *Republican* POL Konghwadang-wŏn 공화당원; *(supporter)* Konghwadang chijija 공화당 지지자 **2** *adj* Konghwadang-ŭl chijihanŭn 공화당을 지지하는

repudiate *(deny)* kŏjŏrhada 거절하다

repulsive mesŭkkŏun 메스꺼운

reputable p'yŏngp'ani chŏun 평판이 좋은

reputation p'yŏngp'an 평판; *have a good/bad ~* p'yŏngp'ani chot'a/nappŭda 평판이 좋다/나쁘다

request 1 *n* yoch'ŏng 요청; *on ~* yoch'ŏnge ttara 요청에 따라 **2** *v/t* ch'ŏnghada 청하다

require *(need)* p'iryohada 필요하다; *it ~s great care* seshimhan chuŭiga p'iryohamnida 세심한 주의가

필요합니다; *as ~d by law* pŏburo chŏnghaejyŏ it-ttŭshi 법으로 정해져 있듯이; *guests are ~d to ...* sonnimdŭrŭn ...ŭl/rŭl haeya hamnida 손님들은 ...을/를 해야 합니다

required *(necessary)* p'iryohan 필요

requirement *(need)* yogu 요구; *(condition)* chokkŏn 조건

reroute *airplane etc* k'osŭrŭl pyŏn-gyŏnghada 코스를 변경하다

rerun *tape* chaesangyŏnghada 재상영하다

rescue 1 *n* kujo 구조; *come to s.o. ~* nugurŭl kujoharŏ oda 누구를 구조하러 오다 **2** *v/t* kujohada 구조하다

rescue party kujodae 구조대

research *n* yŏn-gu 연구

♦ **research into** ...e taehan yŏn-gu ...에 대한 연구

research and development yŏn-gu kaebal 연구 개발

research assistant yŏn-gu pojowŏ 연구 보조원

researcher yŏn-guwŏn 연구원

research project yŏn-gu kyehoek 연구 계획

resemblance yusa 유사

resemble tamtta 닮다

resent ...e pun-gaehada ...에 분개하다

resentful pun-gaehan 분개한

resentment pun-gae 분개

reservation *(of room, table)* yeyak 예약; *(mental)* ŭigushim 의구심; *(special area)* t'ŭkpyŏl poryuji 특별 보류지; *I have a ~* nanŭn yeyagŭl haet-tta 나는 예약을 했다

reserve 1 *n* *(store)* pich'uk 비축; *(aloofness)* naengdam 냉담; SP hub sŏnsu 후보 선수; *~s* FIN poyugŭm 보유금; *keep sth in ~* muŏsŭl pich'uk'ada 무엇을 비축하다 **2** *v/t seat, table* yeyak'ada 예약하다; *judgment* poryuhada 보류하다

reserved *person, manner* malssuga chŏgŭm malsu가 적음; *table, seat* yeyaktoen 예약된

reservoir *(for water)* chŏsuji 저수지

reside kŏjuhada 거주하다

sidence (*house etc*) kŏjuji 거주지; (*stay*) ch'eryu 체류

sidence permit kŏju hŏga 거주 허가

sident 1 *n* kŏjuja 거주자 2 *adj* manager etc sangjuhanŭn 상주하는

sidential *district* chugŏŭi 주거의

sidue chanyŏmul 잔여물

sign 1 *v/t position* saimhada 사임하다; ~ oneself to h'enyŏmhago ...hagiro hada 체념하고 ...하기로 하다 2 *v/i* (*from job*) sagijk'ada 사직하다

signation (*from job*) sajik 사직; (*mental*) tannyŏm 단념

signed ch'enyŏmhanŭn 체념하는; we have become ~ to the fact that ... urinŭn ...ranŭn sashire annyŏmhage toeŏtta 우리는 ...라는 사실에 단념하게 되었다

silient *personality* k'waehwarhan 쾌활한; *material* naegussŏng-i kanghan 내구성이 강한

sin suji 수지

sist 1 *v/t enemy, s.o.'s advances* chŏhanghada 저항하다; *new measures* pandaehada 반대하다; *temptation* kyŏndida 견디다 2 *v/i* pŏt'ida 버티다

sistance chŏhang 저항

sistant *material* chŏhangnyŏgi innŭn 저항력이 있는

solute ŭijiga kudŭn 의지가 굳은

solution (*decision*) kyŏlssshim 결심; (*determination*) kyŏryŏnham 결연함

solution (*of problem*) haegyŏl 해결; (*of image*) sŏnmyŏngdo 선명도

solve *problem, mystery* haegyŏrhada 해결하다; ~ to do sth muŏsŭl hagi wihae kyŏlsshimhada 무엇을 하기 위해 결심하다

sort 1 *n* (*place*) hyuyangji 휴양지; as a last ~ majimak sudannŭro 마지막 수단으로

sounding *success* wanjŏnhan 완전한

source chawŏn 자원

sourceful kiryagi p'ungbuhan 기략이 풍부한

spect 1 *n* chon-gyŏng 존경; (*consideration*) paeryŏ 배려; show ~ to kyŏngŭirŭl p'yohada 경의를 표하다; with ~ to ...e taehayŏ ...에 대하여; in this / that ~ irŏhan / chŏrŏhan kwanchŏmesŏ 이러한 / 저러한 관점에서; in many ~s yŏrŏ myŏnesŏ 여러 면에서; pay one's last ~s to s.o. nuguege ch'oehuŭi kyŏng-ŭirŭl p'yohada 누구에게 최후의 경의를 표하다; ~ person, opinion chon-gyŏnghada 존경하다; law, privacy chonjunghada 존중하다

respectable hullyunghan 훌륭한

respectful chon-gyŏnghanŭn 존경하는

respectfully chŏngjunghage 정중하게

respective kak-kkagŭi 각각의

respectively kak-kki 각기

respiration hohŭp 호흡

respirator MED in-gong hohŭpkki 인공 호흡기

respite hyushik 휴식; without ~ shwim ŏpsshi 쉼 없이

respond (*answer*) taedap'ada 대답하다; (*react*) panŭnghada 반응하다

response (*answer*) taedap 대답; (*reaction*) panŭng 반응

responsibility ch'aegim 책임; (*duty*) ŭimu 의무; accept ~ for ch'aegimŭl chida 책임을 지다

responsible chaegimi innŭn 책임이 있는; (*trustworthy*) shilloehal su innŭn 신뢰할 수 있는; *job* ch'aegimi mugŏun 책임이 무거운

responsive *audience, brakes* panŭnghanŭn 반응하는

rest¹ 1 *n* hyushik 휴식 2 *v/i* shwida 쉬다; ~ on (*be based on*) ...e kich'ohada ...에 기초하다; (*lean against*) ...e kidaeda ...에 기대다; it all ~s with him modŭn kŏn kŭ saram sone tallyŏ issŭmnida 모든 건 그 사람 손에 달려 있습니다 3 *v/t* (*lean, balance etc*) kidaeda 기대다

rest²: the ~ namŏji 나머지

restaurant shikttang 식당

restaurant car RAIL shikttangch'a 식당차

rest cure anjŏng yoppŏp 안정 요법

rest home yoyangso 요양소

restless kamanit-tchi mot'anŭn

가만있지 못하는; **have a ~ night**
cham mot irunŭm pamŭl ponaeda 잠
못 이루는 밤을 보내다
restoration pok-kku 복구
restore *building etc* pok-kkuhada
복구하다
restrain *dog, troops* cheap'ada
제압하다; *emotions* ŏngnurŭda
억누르다; **~ oneself** chajehada
자제하다
restraint *(moderation)* ŏktche 억제
restrict chehanhada 제한하다; **I'll ~
myself to …** chŏnŭn …man
hagessŭmnida 저는 …만 하겠습니다
restricted *view* hanjŏngdoen 한정된
restricted area MIL chehan-guyŏk
제한구역
restriction chehan 제한
rest room hwajangshil 화장실
result *n* kyŏlgwa 결과; **as a ~ of this**
igŏsŭi kyŏlgwaro 이것의 결과로
♦ **result from** …e kiinhada …에
기인하다
♦ **result in** …(ŭ)ro kkŭnnada
…(으)로 끝나다
resume *v/t* chaegaehada 재개하다
résumé iryŏkssŏ 이력서
resurface 1 *v/t roads*
chaep'ojanghada 재포장하다 **2** *v/i
(reappear)* chaehyŏndoeda 재현되다
resurrection REL puhwal 부활
resuscitate sosaengshik'ida
소생시키다
retail 1 *adv* somaero 소매로 **2** *v/i:* **~ at
…** …e somaero p'alda …에 소매로
팔다
retailer somae sangin 소매 상인
retail price somae kagyŏk 소매 가격
retain kyesok yujihada 계속 유지하다;
lawyer koyonghada 고용하다
retainer FIN suimnyo 수임료
retaliate pokssuhada 복수하다
retaliation pokssu 복수
retarded *(mentally)* chŏnŭnghan
저능한
retire *v/i (from work)* ŭnt'oehada
은퇴하다
retired ŭnt'oehan 은퇴한
retirement ŭnt'oe 은퇴
retirement age chŏngnyŏn 정년
retiring naehyangjŏgin 내향적인

retort 1 *n* panbak 반박 **2** *v/i*
panbak'ada 반박하다
retrace *footsteps* toedoragada
되돌아가다
retract *v/t claws* omŭrida 오므리다;
undercarriage kkŭrŏdanggida
끌어당기다; *statement* ch'ŏlhoehada
철회하다
retreat 1 *v/i* MIL hut'oehada 후퇴하
(in discussion etc) mullŏsŏda
물러서다 **2** *n* MIL hut'oe 후퇴; *(pla*
p'inanch'ŏ 피난처
retrieve toech'at-tta 되찾다
retriever *(dog)* lit'ŭribŏ 리트리버
retroactive *law etc* sogŭp'anŭn
소급하는
retrograde *move* t'oebohada
퇴보하다; *decision* chŏrhoehada
철회하다
retrospect: in ~ hoegohae pomyŏn
회고해 보면
retrospective *(of movies)* hoegojŏn
회고전
return 1 *n (coming back, going back*
kwihwan 귀환; *(giving back)*
panhwan 반환; COMPUT shirhaeng
실행; *(in tennis)* pan-gyŏk 반격; **by
(of post)** pannŭn chŭksshiro 받는
즉시로; **~s** *(profit)* iik 이익; **many
happy ~s (of the day)** saeng-irŭl
ch'uk'ahamnida 생일을 축하합니다;
2 *v/t (give back)* tollyŏjuda 돌려주
(put back) tollyŏnot'a 돌려놓다;
favor, invitation podap'ada 보답하
3 *v/i (go back)* toedoragada
되돌아가다; *(come back)* toedorao
되돌아오다; *(of good times, doubts
etc)* chaehyŏnhada 재현하다
return flight wangbok pihaenggi 왕
비행기
return journey wangbok yŏhaeng
왕복 여행
reunification t'ong-il 통일
reunion chaehoe 재회
reunite *v/t country* chaet'onghap'ad
재통합하다; *old friends* chaehoehac
재회하다
reusable chaesayong-i kanŭnghan
재사용이 가능한
reuse chaesayonghada 재사용하다
rev *n* hoejŏn 회전; **~s per minute**

pun tang hoejŏn 분 당 회전

rev up *v/t engine* sokttorŭl ppparǔge hada 속도를 빠르게 하다

evaluation p'yŏngkkajŏlssang 평가절상

eveal (*make visible*) tŭrŏnaeda 드러내다; (*make known*) palk'ida 밝히다

evealing *remark* palk'yŏjunŭn 밝혀주는; *dress* noch'uldoen 노출된

evelation p'ongno 폭로

evenge *n* pobok 보복; ***take one's ~*** pobok'ada 보복하다

evenue seip 세입

everberate (*of sound*) ullyŏ p'ŏjida 울려 퍼지다

Reverend sŏngjiktcha 성직자

everent kyŏngŏnhan 경건한

everse 1 *adj sequence* kŏkkurodoen 거꾸로된 **2** *n* (*opposite*) pandae 반대; (*back*) twittchang 뒷장; (*of envelope*) twinmyŏn 뒷면; MOT hujin 후진 **3** *v/t sequence* kŏkkuro hada 거꾸로 하다; *vehicle* hujinhada 후진하다 **4** *v/i* MOT hujinhada 후진하다

eview 1 *n* (*of book, movie*) pip'yŏng 비평; (*of troops*) yŏlbyŏngshik 열병식; (*of situation etc*) chaegŏmt'o 재검토 **2** *v/t book, movie* nonp'yŏnghada 논평하다; *troops* sayŏrhada 사열하다; *situation etc* chaegŏmt'ohada 재검토하다; EDU pokssŭp'ada 복습하다

eviewer (*of movie etc*) p'yŏngnon-ga 평론가

evise *v/t opinion, text* sujŏnghada 수정하다

evision (*of opinion, text*) sujŏng 수정

evisionism POL sujŏngjuŭi 수정주의

evival (*of custom, old style etc*) puhwal 부활; (*of patient*) sosaeng 소생

evive 1 *v/t custom, old style etc* puhwarhada 부활하다; *patient* sosaengshik'ida 소생시키다 **2** *v/i* (*of business etc*) hoeboktoeda 회복되다

evoke *law, license* muhyoro hada 무효로 하다

evolt 1 *n* pallan 반란 **2** *v/i* pallanhada 반란하다

revolting (*disgusting*) hyŏmogamŭl nŭkkige hanǔn 혐오감을 느끼게 하는

revolution POL hyŏngmyŏng 혁명; (*turn*) hoejŏn 회전

revolutionary 1 *n* POL hyŏngmyŏngga 혁명가 **2** *adj spirit, forces* hyŏngmyŏng-ŭi 혁명의; *ideas* hyŏngmyŏngjŏgin 혁명적인

revolutionize hyŏngmyŏng-ŭl irŭk'ida 혁명을 일으키다

revolve *v/i* hoejŏnhada 회전하다

revolver kwŏnch'ong 권총

revolving door hoejŏnmun 회전문

revue THEA shisap'ungjagŭk 시사풍자극

revulsion kyŏkppyŏn 격변

reward 1 *n* posang 보상; (*financial*) posu 보수 **2** *v/t* (*financially*) posurŭl chuda 보수를 주다

rewarding porami innŭn 보람이 있는

rewind *v/t film, tape* tashi kamtta 다시 감다

rewrite *v/t* tashi ssŭda 다시 쓰다

rhetoric susa 수사

rheumatism lyumat'ijŭm 류마티즘

rhinoceros k'otppulsso 코뿔소

rhubarb changgunp'ul 장군풀

rhyme 1 *n* un 운 **2** *v/i* chakssihada 작시하다; ***~ with** *...wa/kwa uni mat-tta *...와 / 과 운이 맞다

rhythm lidŭm 리듬

rib *n* kalbippyŏ 갈비뼈

ribbon libon 리본

rice ssal 쌀; (*cooked*) pap 밥

rice bowl pap kŭrŭt 밥 그릇; **rice cake** ttŏk 떡; **rice cooker** chŏn-gi papssot 전기 밥솥; **ricefield, rice paddy** non 논; **rice planting** monaegi 모내기; **rice wine** mak-kkŏlli 막걸리

rich 1 *adj* puyuhan 부유한; *food* mashichinhan 맛이 진한 **2** *n*: **the ~** puja 부자

rid: ***get ~ of*** ŏpssaeda 없애다

riddle susukkekki 수수께끼

ride 1 *n* t'am 탐; (*journey*) yŏhaeng 여행; ***do you want a ~ into town?*** shinae t'aewŏ chulkkayo? 시내에 태워 줄까요? **2** *v/t horse, bike* t'ada 타다 **3** *v/i* (*on horse*) sŭngmahada

승마하다; (*on bike, in vehicle*) t'ada 타다

rider (*on horse*) kisu 기수; (*on bike*) chajŏn-gŏ t'anŭn saram 자전거 타는 사람

ridge (*raised strip*) ollagan t'ŏk 올라간 턱; (*of mountain*) santtŭngsŏng-i 산등성이; (*of roof*) chibung kkokttaegi 지붕 꼭대기

ridicule 1 *n* choso 조소 **2** *v/t* choronghada 조롱하다

ridiculous t'ŏmuniŏmnŭn 터무니없는

ridiculously t'ŏmuniŏpsshi 터무니없이

riding (*on horseback*) sŭngma 승마

rifle *n* soch'ong 소총

rift (*in earth*) tanch'ŭng 단층; (*in party etc*) kyunyŏl 균열

rig 1 *n* (*oil* –) kulch'ak changch'i 굴착 장치; (*truck*) t'ŭrŏk 트럭 **2** *v/t elections* chojak'ada 조작하다

right 1 *adj* (*correct*) mannŭn 맞는; (*proper, just*) olbarŭn 올바른; (*suitable*) chŏktchŏrhan 적절한; (*not left*) orŭntchogŭi 오른쪽의; **be** ~ (*of answer, person*) mat-tta 맞다; (*of clock*) chŏnghwak'ada 정확하다; **that's** ~! paro kŭgŏya! 바로 그거야!; **put things** ~ irŭl haegyŏrhada 일을 해결하다; **that's not** ~ (*not fair*) kŭgŏsŭn andoel irida 그것은 안될 일이다; → **alright 2** *adv* (*directly*) paro 바로; (*correctly*) olbarŭge 올바르게; (*completely*) wanjŏnhi 완전히; (*not left*) orŭntchogŭro 오른쪽으로; ~ **now** (*immediately*) tangjang 당장; (*at the moment*) chigŭm 지금 **3** *n* (*civil, legal etc*) kwŏlli 권리; (*not left*) orŭntchok 오른쪽; POL uik 우익; **on the** ~ orŭntchoge(sŏ) 오른쪽에(서); POL uige(sŏ) 우익에(서); **turn to the** ~, **take a** ~ orŭntchogŭro toshio 오른쪽으로 도시오; **be in the** ~ torie mat-tta 도리에 맞다; **know** ~ **from wrong** olk'o kŭrŭmŭl kubyŏrhada 옳고 그름을 구별하다

right-angle chik-kak 직각; **at** ~**s to** ...wa/kwa chik-kkagŭro ...와/과 직각으로

righteous army ŭibyŏng 의병

rightful *heir, owner etc* happ'ŏptchŏgin 합법적인

right-hand *adj* orŭntchogŭi 오른쪽의; **on the** ~ **side** orŭnp'yŏne 오른편에

right-hand drive MOT uch'ŭk haendul unjŏn 우측 핸들 운전;

right-handed orŭnsonjabiŭi 오른손잡이의; **right-hand man** shimbok 심복; **right of way** (*in traffic*) t'onghaeng usŏnkkwŏn 통행 우선권; (*across land*) t'onghaengkkwŏn 통행권; **right wing** n POL uik 우익; SP uch'ŭk konggyŏkssu 우측 공격수; **right-wing** *adj* POL uigŭi 우익의; **right-winger** POL uik chijija 우익 지지자; **right-wing extremism** POL kŭgup' 극우파

rigid *material* tandanhan 단단한; *principles* ŏmkkyŏk'an 엄격한; *attitude* wangohan 완고한

rigor (*of discipline*) ŏmkkyŏk 엄격; **the** ~**s of winter** kyŏurŭi hokttok'am 겨울의 혹독함

rigorous *discipline* ŏmkkyŏk'an 엄격한; *tests, analysis* myŏnmirhan 면밀한

rim (*of wheel*) t'eduri 테두리; (*of cup*) kajangjari 가장자리; (*of eyeglasses*) t'e 테

ring[1] (*circle*) wŏnhyŏng 원형; (*on finger*) panji 반지; (*in boxing, at circus*) ling 링

ring[2] **1** *n* (*of bell*) ullim 울림; (*of voice*) ullinŭn sori 울리는 소리 **2** *v/t bell* ullida 울리다 **3** *v/i* (*of bell*) ullida 울리다; **please** ~ **for attention** chong-ŭl ch'yŏsŏ pullŏjuseyo 종을 쳐서 불러주세요

ringleader chumoja 주모자

ring-pull chabadangginŭn kori 잡아당기는 고리

rink chang 장

rinse 1 *n* (*for hair color*) linssŭ 린스 **2** *v/t clothes, dishes* hengguda 헹구다 *hair* linssŭhada 린스하다

riot 1 *n* p'okttong 폭동 **2** *v/i* p'oktongŭl irŭk'ida 폭동을 일으키다

rioter p'okttongja 폭동자

riot police kyŏngch'al kidongdae 경찰 기동대

1 *n* (*in cloth etc*) tchijŏjin kot 찢어진 곳 **2** *v/t cloth etc* tchit-tta 찢다; **~ sth open** muŏsŭl tchijŏ ŏlda 무엇을 찢어 열다

ip off F (*cheat*) sogida 속이다; *customers* p'ongnirŭl ch'wihada 폭리를 취하다

e fruit igŭn 익은

en *v/i* (*of fruit*) iktta 익다

eness (*of fruit*) suksssŏng 숙성

o-off *n* F sagi 사기

ple *n* (*on water*) mulkkyŏl 물결

e 1 *v/i* (*from chair etc*) irŏnada 일어나다; (*of sun*) ttŏorŭda 떠오르다; (*of rocket*) sosaorŭda 솟아오르다; (*of price, temperature, water level*) orŭda 오르다 **2** *n* (*in price, salary*) insang 인상; (*in water level, temperature*) sangsŭng 상승

k 1 *n* wihŏm 위험; **take a ~** wihŏmŭl murŭpssŭda 위험을 우릅쓰다 **2** *v/t* wishŏme ppattŭrida 위험에 빠뜨리다; **let's ~ it** kamhaenghae popsshida 감행해 봅시다

sky wihŏmhan 위험한

ual 1 *n* ŭishik 의식 **2** *adj* ŭishigŭi 의식의

al 1 *n* kyŏngjaengja 경쟁자 **2** *v/t* ..wa/kwa kyŏngjaenghada ...와 / 과 경쟁하다; **I can't ~ that** i isang tŏ chal hal sunŭn ŏpssŏyo 이 이상 더 잘 할 수는 없어요

alry kyŏngjaeng 경쟁

er kang 강

erbed kangppadak 강바닥

erside kangbyŏn 강변

et 1 *n* taemot 대못 **2** *v/t* taemosŭro paktta 대못으로 박다

ad kil 길; **it's just down the ~** paro chŏtchoge issŏyo 바로 저쪽에 있어요 **adblock** parik'eidŭ 바리케이드; **oad hog** nanp'ok unjŏnja 난폭 운전자; **road holding** (*of vehicle*) chuhaeng anjŏngssŏng 주행 안정성; **oad map** toro chido 도로 지도; **oadside: at the ~** kilkkae 길가에; **oadsign** toro p'yojip'an 도로 표지판; **roadway** toro 도로; **road works** toro kongsa 도로 공사; **roadworthy** torochuhaeng-e almajŭn 도로 주행에 알맞은

roam toradtanida 돌아다니다

roar 1 *n* (*of traffic, engine*) urŭrŭnggŏrinŭn sori 우르릉거리는 소리; (*of lion*) p'ohyo 포효; (*of person*) koham 고함 **2** *v/i* (*of engine*) urŭrŭnggŏrida 우르릉거리다; (*of lion*) p'ohyohada 포효하다; (*of person*) kohamch'ida 고함치다; **~ with laughter** k'ŭge ut-tta 크게 웃다

roast 1 *n* (*of beef etc*) kuun ŭmshik 구운 음식 **2** *v/t* kuptta 굽다 **3** *v/t* (*of food*) kuwŏjida 구워지다; **we're ~ing** F tchidŭshi tŏptta 찌듯이 덥다

roast beef kuun soegogi 구운 쇠고기

roast pork kuun twaejigogi 구운 돼지고기

rob *person, bank* kangt'arhada 강탈하다; **I've been ~bed** kangdo tanghaessŏyo 강도 당했어요

robber kangdo 강도

robbery kangdojil 강도질

robe (*of judge*) pŏp-ppok 법복; (*of priest*) yebok 예복; (*bath~*) mogyok kkaun 목욕 가운

robin kaettong chippagwi sae 개똥 지빠귀 새

robot lobot 로봇

robust t'ŭnt'ŭnhan 튼튼한

rock 1 *n* tol 돌; MUS lak 락; **on the ~s** *drink* ŏrŭmŭl kyŏt-ttŭryŏ 얼음을 곁들여; *marriage* p'at'ane irŭrŏ 파탄에 이르러 **2** *v/t baby, cradle* choyonghi hŭndŭlda 조용히 흔들다; (*surprise*) nollage hada 놀라게 하다 **3** *v/i* (*on chair*) hŭndŭlgŏrida 흔들거리다; (*of boat*) chindonghada 진동하다

rock bottom: reach ~ mitppadagŭro ttŏrŏjida 밑바닥으로 떨어지다

rock-bottom *adj prices* ch'oejŏŭi 최저의

rocket 1 *n* (*space ~*) lok'et 로켓; (*firework*) ssoaollinŭn pulkkot 쏘아올리는 불꽃 **2** *v/i* (*of prices etc*) ch'isot-tta 치솟다

rocking chair hŭndŭl ŭija 흔들 의자

rock'n' roll lakk'ŭllol 락큰롤

rock star laksŭt'a 락스타

rocky *beach, path* pawiga manŭn

바위가 많은
rod makttae 막대; (*for fishing*) nakkshit-ttae 낚싯대
rodent sŏlch'iryu 설치류
rogue kŏndal 건달
ROK (= *Republic of Korea*) Taehanmin-guk 대한민국
role yŏk'al 역할
role model ponbogiga toenŭn saram 본보기가 되는 사람
roll 1 *n* (*bread*) lolppang 롤빵; (*of film*) lol 롤; (*of thunder*) ullim 울림; (*list, register*) mongnok 목록 2 *v/i* (*of ball etc*) kurŭda 구르다; (*of boat*) hŭndŭlgŏrida 흔들거리다 3 *v/t*: ~ *sth into a ball* muŏsŭl kongch'ŏrŏm kullida 무엇을 공처럼 굴리다
♦ **roll over** 1 *v/i* twinggulda 뒹굴다 2 *v/t person, object* kullyŏ nŏmŏttŭrida 굴려 넘어뜨리다; (*renew*) kiganŭl yŏnjangshik'ida 기간을 연장시키다; (*extend*) nŭllida 늘리다
♦ **roll up** 1 *v/t sleeves* kŏdŏollida 걷어올리다 2 *v/i* F (*arrive*) toch'ak'ada 도착하다
roll call chŏmho 점호
roller (*for hair*) mŏri manŭn lol 머리 마는 롤
roller blade *n* lollŏ pŭlleidŭ 롤러 블레이드; **roller coaster** lollŏ k'osŭt'ŏ 롤러 코스터; **roller skate** *n* lollŏ sŭk'eit'ŭ 롤러 스케이트
rolling pin panjugŭl minŭn pangmangi 반죽을 미는 방망이
ROM (= *read only memory*) lom 롬
Roman Catholic 1 *n* Loma K'at'ollik 로마 카톨릭 2 *adj* Loma K'at'ollik-kyoŭi 로마 카톨릭교의
Roman Catholicism Ch'ŏnjugyo 천주교
romance (*affair*) lomaensŭ 로맨스; (*novel, movie*) yŏnae 연애
romantic lomaent'ik'an 로맨틱한
roof chibung 지붕
roof rack MOT lup'ŭraek 루프랙
room pang 방; (*space*) changso 장소; **there's no ~ for ...** ...ŭl/rŭl wihan changsoga ŏptta ...을/를 위한 장소가 없다
room clerk kaekssil tamdangja 객실

담당자; **roommate** lum meit'ŭ 룸 메이트; **room service** lum ssŏbissŭ 룸 서비스
roomy *house etc* nŏlbŭn 넓은; *cloth* hŏllŏnghan 헐렁한
root ppuri 뿌리; (*of word*) kŭnwŏn 근원; ~s (*of person*) kohyang 고향
♦ **root out** (*get rid of*) chegŏhada 제거하다; (*find*) ch'at-tta 찾다
root directory COMPUT ŭddŭm tirekt'ori 으뜸 디렉토리
rope pattchul 밧줄
♦ **rope off** churŭl ch'ida 줄을 치다
rose BOT changmi 장미
Rose of Sharon Mugunghwa 무궁화
rostrum yŏndan 연단
rosy *cheeks* hongjorŭl ttin 홍조를 띤; *future* yumanghan 유망한
rot 1 *n* (*in wood, teeth*) ssŏgŭm 썩음 2 *v/i* (*of food, wood, teeth*) ssŏktta 썩다
rota tangbŏn 당번
rotate *v/i* hoejŏnhada 회전하다
rotation (*around the sun etc*) hoejŏn 회전; *do sth in ~* muŏsŭl kyodaero hada 무엇을 교대로 하다
rotten *food, wood etc* ssŏgŭn 썩은; *trick, thing to do* pup'aehan 부패한; *weather, luck* pulk'waehan 불쾌한
rough 1 *adj surface* ult'ungbult'unghan 울퉁불퉁한; *hands, skin, voice* kŏch'in 거친; (*violent*) nanp'ok'an 난폭한; *crossing, seas* sanaun 사나운; (*approximate*) taegang-ŭi 대강의; ~ *draft* ch'ogo 초고 2 *adv*: *sleep ~* nosuk'ada 노숙하다 3 *n* (*in golf*) lŏp'ŭ 러프 4 *v/t*: ~ *it* pulp'yŏnhan saenghwarŭl hada 불편한 생활을 하다
roughage (*in food*) sŏmnyujil 섬유질
roughly (*approximately*) taeryak 대략
roulette lullet 룰렛
round 1 *adj* tunggŭn 둥근; *in ~ figures* kkŭtchŭl charŭn sutcharo 끝자른 숫자로 2 *n* (*of mailman*) paedal kuyŏk 배달 구역; (*of toast*) tchok 쪽; (*of drinks*) ch'a 차; (*of competition*) hoe 회; (*in boxing match*) laundŭ 라운드 3 *v/t the corner* tolda 돌다 4 *adv, prep* → **around**

round off *edges* tunggŭlge hada 둥글게 하다; *meeting etc* mamurihada 마무리하다

round up *figure* kkŭtchŭl challa ollida 끝을 잘라 올리다; *suspects, criminals* kŏmgŏhada 검거하다

roundabout *adj route* uhoeŭi 우회의; *way of saying sth* kanjŏptchŏgin 간접적인; **round trip** wangbok 왕복; **round trip yŏhaeng** 왕복 여행; **round trip ticket** wangbok yŏhaengp'yo 왕복 여행표; **round-up** (*of cattle*) mori 몰이; (*of suspects, criminals*) kŏmgŏ 검거; (*of news*) yoyak 요약

rouse (*from sleep*) kkaeda 깨다; *interest, emotions* chagŭk'ada 자극하다

rousing *speech etc* kŭktchŏgin 극적인

route kil 길

routine 1 *adj* ilssangjŏgin 일상적인 **2** *n* ilgwa 일과; **as a matter of ~** ilssangjŏgŭro 일상적으로

row[1] (*line*) yŏl 열; **5 days in a ~** tatssae yŏniŏsŏ 닷새 연이어서

row[1] **1** *v/t boat* no chŏt-tta 노 젓다 **2** *v/i* chŏŏgada 저어가다

rowboat chŏnnŭn pae 젓는 배

rowdy nanp'ok'an 난폭한

row house yollip chut'aek 연립 주택

royal *adj* wang-ŭi 왕의

royalty (*royal persons*) wangjok 왕족; (*on book, recording*) loyŏlt'i 로열티

rub *v/t* munjirŭda 문지르다; (*to polish*) yun naeda 윤 내다

rub down (*clean*) ch'ŏngsohada 청소하다

rub off 1 *v/t dirt* munjillŏ ŏpssaeda 문질러 없애다; *paint etc* pŏtkkida 벗기다 **2** *v/i*: **it rubs off on you** tangshinege yŏnghyang-ŭl kkich'imnida 당신에게 영향을 끼칩니다

rub out (*with eraser*) chiuda 지우다

rubber 1 *n* (*material*) komu 고무 **2** *adj* komuŭi 고무의

rubble chapssŏk 잡석

ruby (*jewel*) lubi 루비

rucksack paenang 배낭

rudder paeŭi k'i 배의 키

ruddy *complexion* pulgŭn 붉은

rude muryehan 무례한; **it is ~ to ...**

...hanŭn kŏsŭn muryehada ...하는 것은 무례하다; **I didn't mean to be ~** muryehage haryŏgo haet-ttŏn ke aniyeyo 무례하게 하려고 했던 게 아니예요

rudeness murye 무례

rudimentary kich'oŭi 기초의

rudiments kich'o 기초

ruffian purhandang 불한당

ruffle 1 *n* (*on dress*) churŭm changshik 주름 장식 **2** *v/t hair* hŏngk'ŭrŏjige hada 헝클어지게 하다; *person* sŏngnage hada 성나게 하다; **get ~d** sŏng-i nada 성이 나다

rug kkalgae 깔개; (*blanket*) tamnyo 담요

rugged *scenery, cliffs* pawi t'usŏng-iŭi 바위 투성이의; *face* kŏch'in 거친; *resistance* wan-ganghan 완강한

ruin 1 *n* p'agoe 파괴; **~s** yujŏk 유적; **in ~s** (*of city, building*) p'agoedoen 파괴된; (*of plans, marriage*) p'amyŏrhan 파멸한 **2** *v/t party, birthday, vacation* mangch'ida 망치다; *plans* manggattŭrida 망가뜨리다; *reputation* p'agoehada 파괴하다; **be ~ed** (*financially*) p'asanhada 파산하다

rule 1 *n* (*of club, game*) kyuch'ik 규칙; (*of monarch*) chibae 지배; (*for measuring*) cha 자; **as a ~** taech'ero 대체로 **2** *v/t country* tasŭrida 다스리다; **the judge ~d that ...** p'ansanŭn ...rago p'an-gyŏrhaet-tta 판사는 ...라고 판결했다 **3** *v/i* (*of monarch*) t'ongch'ihada 통치하다

♦ **rule out** choeoehada 제외하다

ruler (*for measuring*) cha 자; (*of state*) t'ongch'ija 통치자

ruling 1 *n* p'an-gyŏl 판결 **2** *adj party* chibaehanŭn 지배하는

rum (*drink*) lŏm 럼

rumble *v/i* (*of stomach*) kkorŭrŭkkŏrida 꼬르륵거리다; (*of train in tunnel*) yoranhan sorirŭl naeda 요란한 소리를 내다

♦ **rummage around** twijyŏ ch'ajanaeda 뒤져 찾아내다

rummage sale chapttongsani p'anmae 잡동사니 판매

rumor 1 *n* somun 소문 **2** *v/t*: **it is ~ed**

that ... ...rago somuni nada ...라고 소문이 나다

rump (*of animal*) ŏngdŏngi 엉덩이

rumple *clothes, paper* kugida 구기다

rumpsteak lŏmp'ŭ sŭt'eik'ŭ 럼프 스테이크

run **1** *n* (*on foot*) talligi 달리기; (*in pantyhose*) orŭi p'ullim 올의 풀림; (*of play*) yŏnsok kong-yŏn 연속 공연; **go for a ~** choginghada 조깅하다; **make a ~ for it** tomangch'ida 도망치다; **a criminal on the ~** tomang chungin pŏmjoeja 도망 중인 범죄자; **in the short / long ~** tchalkke / kilge pomyŏn 짧게 / 길게 보면; **a ~ on the dollar** tallŏ kangse 달러 강세 **2** *v/i* (*of person, animal*) tallida 달리다; (*of river*) hŭrŭda 흐르다; (*of trains etc*) tallida 달리다; (*of paint, make-up*) pŏnjida 번지다; (*of nose, eyes*) hŭrŭda 흐르다; (*of faucet*) hŭrŭda 흐르다; (*of play*) yŏnsok kong-yŏndoeda 연속 공연된다; (*of engine, machine*) umjigida 움직이다; (*of software*) shirhaengtoeji ant'a 실행되지 않다; (*in election*) ch'ulmahada 출마하다; **~ for President** taet'ongnyŏnge ch'ulmahada 대통령에 출마하다 **3** *v/t race* kyŏngjuhada 경주하다; *3 miles etc* tallida 달리다; *business, hotel, project etc* unyŏnghada 운영하다; *software* shirhaenghada 실행하다; **he ran his eye down the page** kŭnŭn kŭ p'eijirŭl taegang hult'ŏ poat-tta 그는 그 페이지를 대강 훑어 보았다

♦ **run across** (*meet*) uyŏnhi mannada 우연히 만나다; (*find*) ch'at-tta 찾다

♦ **run away** taranada 달아나다

♦ **run down** **1** *v/t* (*knock down*) tŭribat-tta 들이받다; (*criticize*) hŏlttŭt-tta 헐뜯다; *stocks* kach'irŭl ttŏrŏttŭrida 가치를 떨어뜨리다 **2** *v/i* (*of battery*) taltta 닳다

♦ **run into** (*meet*) uyŏnhi mannada 우연히 만나다; *difficulties* ch'ŏhada 처하다; *car* tŭribat-tta 들이받다

♦ **run off** **1** *v/i* tomangch'ida 도망치다 **2** *v/t* (*print*) inswaehada 인쇄하다

♦ **run out** (*of contract*) man-giga

toeda 만기가 되다; (*of time*) ta had da hada 다 하다; (*of supplies*) ttŏrŏjida 떨어지다

♦ **run out of** *time, patience* ta ssŏbŏrida 다 써버리다; *supplies* ttŏrŏjida 떨어지다; **I ran out of gas** kassŭga ttŏrŏjyŏssŏyo 가스가 떨어졌어요

♦ **run over** **1** *v/t* (*knock down*) tŭribat-tta 들이받다; **can we ~ the details again?** tashi hanbŏn chasehan sahange taehae arabolkkayo? 다시 한번 자세한 사항에 대해 알아볼까요? **2** *v/i* (*of water etc*) nŏmch'ida 넘치다

♦ **run through** (*rehearse*) shiyŏnhad da 시연하다; (*go over, check*) kŏmt'ohada 검토하다

♦ **run up** *v/t debts* ssat'a 쌓다; *clothes* mandŭlda 만들다

run-down *person* chich'in 지친; *part of town, building* hŏrŭmhan 허름한

rung (*of ladder*) tan 단

runner (*athlete*) kyŏngjuja 경주자

runner-up ch'atchŏmja 차점자

running **1** *n* SP talligi 달리기; (*of business*) kyŏngyŏng kwalli 경영 관리 **2** *adj*: **for two days ~** yŏnido it'ŭl ttong-ane 연이어 이틀 동안에

running water (*supply*) yusu 유수

runny *liquid, nose* hŭrŭnŭn 흐르는

run-up SP toumdatkki 도움닫기; **in the ~ to** paro chiktchŏne 바로 직전에

runway hwaltchuro 활주로

rupture **1** *n* (*in pipe*), MED p'ayŏl 파열; (*in relations*) tanjŏl 단절 **2** *v/i* (*of pipe etc*) p'ayŏldoeda 파열되다

rural shigorŭl 시골의

rush **1** *n* mopsshi sŏdurŭm 몹시 서두름; **do sth in a ~** sodullŏ muŏsŭl hada 서둘러 무엇을 하다; **be in a ~** mopsshi sŏdurŭda 몹시 서두르다; **what's the big ~?** wae kŭrŏk'e kŭp'aeyo? 왜 그렇게 급해요? **2** *v/t person* sŏdurŭge hada 서두르게 하다; *meal* sŏdullŏ mŏktta 서둘러 먹다; **~ s.o. to the hospital** nugurŭl pyŏng-wŏnŭro kŭpssonghada 누구를 병원으로 급송하다 **3** *v/i* sŏdurŭda 서두르다

...sh hour ch'ult'oegŭn shigan 출퇴근
시간
...ussia Lŏshia 러시아
...ussian 1 adj Lŏshiaŭi 러시아의 2 n
...ŏshiain 러시아인; (language)
...ŏshiaŏ 러시아어
...st 1 n nok 녹 2 v/i nokssŭlda 녹슬다
...stle n (of silk, leaves) pasŭrak-
...kŏrinŭn sori 바스락거리는 소리
...rustle up F meal chaeppalli
...mandŭlda 재빨리 만들다
...st-proof adj nogi sŭlji annŭn 녹이
...슬지 않는

rust remover nok chegŏje 녹 제거제
rusty nogi sŭn 녹이 슨; *French, math
etc* sŏt'un 서툰; *I'm a little ~* chŏnŭn
yakkan sŏt'umnida 저는 약간
서툽니다
rut (*in road*) hom 홈; *be in a ~* p'ane
pak'in saenghwarŭl hada 판에 박힌
생활을 하다
ruthless kach'aŏmnŭn 가차없는
ruthlessness kach'aŏpssŭm
가차없음
rye homil 호밀
rye bread homil ppang 호밀 빵

S

sabbatical n (of academic) anshingnyŏn 안식년

sabotage 1 n kyehoektchŏgin p'agoe 계획적인 파괴 2 v/t kyehoektchŏgŭro p'agoehada 계획적으로 파괴하다

saccharin n sak'arin 사카린

sachet (of shampoo etc) pongji 봉지

sack 1 n (bag) p'odae 포대 2 v/t F haegohada 해고하다

sacred music chonggyojŏgin 종교적인; building, place shinsŏnghan 신성한

sacrifice 1 n chemul 제물; (act) hŭisaeng 희생; **make ~s** fig hŭisaenghada 희생하다 2 v/t pach'ida 바치다; one's freedom etc hŭisaenghada 희생하다

sad sŭlp'ŭn 슬픈

saddle n anjang 안장

sadism sadijŭm 사디즘

sadist sadisŭt'ŭ 사디스트

sadistic sadisŭt'ŭjŏgin 사디스트 적인

sadly say etc sŭlp'ŭge 슬프게; (regrettably) huhoesŭrŏpkkedo 후회스럽게도

sadness sŭlp'ŭm 슬픔

safe 1 adj anjŏnhan 안전한; investment, prediction anshimhal su innŭn 안심할 수 있는 2 n kŭmgo 금고

safeguard 1 n pohoch'aek 보호책; **as a ~ against** …e taehan pohoch'aegŭro …에 대한 보호책으로 2 v/t pohohada 보호하다

safekeeping: **give sth to s.o. for ~** anjŏnhage pogwanŭl wihae muŏsŭl nuguege chuda 안전한 보관을 위해 무엇을 누구에게 주다

safely arrive musahi 무사히; complete tests etc munjeŏpsshi 문제없이; drive anjŏnhage 안전하게; assume chalmot toel kŏktchŏng ŏpsshi 잘못 될 걱정 없이

safety anjŏn 안전; (of investment) anjŏnssŏng 안전성; **be in ~** musahada 무사하다

safety-conscious anjŏnŭl saenggak'anŭn 안전을 생각하는; **safety first** anjŏn usŏn 안전 우선; **safety pin** anjŏnp'in 안전핀

sag 1 n (in ceiling etc) nŭrŏjim 늘어 2 v/i (of ceiling, rope) ch'uk ch'ŏjida 축 처지다; (of output, tempo) chul⊘ 줄다

sage (herb) saelbiŏ 샐비어

sail 1 n tot 돛; (voyage) hanghae 항⊘ (in small boat) paennori 뱃놀이 2 ⊘ yacht ttŭiuda 띄우다 3 v/i hanghaehada 항해하다; (depart) ch'urhanghada 출항하다

sailboard 1 n windŭ sŏp'ing podŭ 윈드 서핑 보드 2 v/i windŭ sŏp'inghada 윈드 서핑하다

sailboarding windŭ sŏp'ing 윈드 서⊘

sailboat yot'ŭ 요트

sailing SP yot'ŭ kyŏnggi 요트 경기

sailing ship pŏmsŏn 범선

sailor (in the navy) subyŏng 수병; si⊘ yot'ŭ kyŏnggija 요트 경기자; **be a good/bad ~** paenmŏlmirŭl haji ant'a/hada 뱃멀미를 하지 않다/하⊘

saint sŏng-in 성인

sake: **for my/your ~** narŭl/nŏrŭl wihaesŏ 나를/너를 위해서; **for the of** …ŭl/rŭl wihayŏ …을/를 위하⊘

salad saellŏdŭ 샐러드

salad dressing sallŏdŭ tŭreshing 샐러드 드레싱

salary wŏlgŭp 월급

salary scale ponggŭp sujun 봉급 수준

sale p'anmae 판매; (reduced prices)⊘ harin p'anmae 할인 판매; **for ~** (sign) maemae 매매; **is this for ~?** igŏ p'anmŭmnikka? 이거 파는 겁니까?; **be on ~** p'anmae chung-i⊘ 판매 중이다; (at reduced prices) se⊘

chung-ida 세일 중이다

ales (*department*) p'anmaebusŏ 판매부서

ales clerk (*in store*) p'anmae chŏmwŏn 판매 점원; **sales figures** p'anmae kŭmaek 판매 금액; **salesman** seiljŭmaen 세일즈맨; **sales manager** p'anmae pujang 판매 부장; **sales meeting** p'anmae hoeŭi 판매 회의

aliva ch'im 침

almon yŏnŏ 연어

aloon (*bar*) sultchip 술집

alt sogŭm 소금

altcellar sogŭm kŭrŭt 소금 그릇

alty tchan 짠

alutary *experience* yuik'an 유익한

alute 1 *n* MIL kyŏngnye 경례; *take the ~* kyŏngnyerŭl pat-tta 경례를 받다 2 *v/t v/i* MIL kyŏngnyehada 경례하다

alvage *v/t* (*from wreck*) kujohada 구조하다

alvation REL kuwŏn 구원; *fig* kujo 구조

alvation Army Kusegun 구세군

ame 1 *adj* kat'ŭn 같은 2 *pron*: *the ~* kat'ŭn kŏt 같은 것; *Happy New Year – the ~ to you* saehae pok mani padŭseyo - saehae pok mani padŭseyo 새해 복 많이 받으세요 - 새해 복 많이 받으세요; *he's not the ~ any more* kŭ saram, yejŏn katchi anayo 그 사람, 예전 같지 않아요; *all the ~* kŭraedo 그래도; *men are all the ~* namjadŭrŭn ta ttokkat'ayo 남자들은 다 똑같아요; *it's all the ~ to me* chŏn, sanggwanŏpssŏyo 전, 상관없어요 3 *adv*: *smell/sound the ~* naemsaega / soriga ttok-kkat'ayo 냄새가 / 소리가 똑같아요

ample *n* (*for inspection*) kyŏnbon 견본; (*of behavior, work*) p'yobon 표본

anatorium yoyangso 요양소

anction 1 *n* (*approval*) hŏga 허가; (*penalty*) chejae 제재; *economic ~s* kyŏngje chejae 경제 제재 2 *v/t* (*approve*) hŏgahada 허가하다

anctity shinsŏng 신성

anctuary REL sŏngjŏn 성전; (*for*

(*animals*) poho kuyŏk 보호 구역

sand 1 *n* morae 모래 2 *v/t* (*with sandpaper*) sap'oro munjirŭda 사포로 문지르다

sandal saendŭl 샌들

sandbag morae chumŏni 모래 주머니

sand dune morae ŏndŏk 모래 언덕

sander (*tool*) sap'oro tangnŭn changch'i 사포로 닦는 장치

sandpaper 1 *n* sap'o 사포 2 *v/t* sap'oro taktta 사포로 닦다; **sandpit** moraep'an 모래판; **sandstone** saam 사암

sandwich 1 *n* saendŭwich'i 샌드위치 2 *v/t*: *be ~ed between two …* tu … saie kkida 두 … 사이에 끼이다

sandy *beach, soil* moraeŭi 모래의; *hair* moraesaegŭi 모래색의

sane chejŏngshinŭi 제정신의

sanitarium yoyangso 요양소

sanitary *conditions* wisaeng-ŭi 위생의; *installations* wisaengjŏgin 위생적인

sanitary napkin saengnidae 생리대

sanitation (*sanitary installations*) wisaengsŏlbi 위생설비; (*removal of waste*) wisaengch'ŏri 위생처리

sanitation department ch'ŏngsokkwa 청소과

sanity chejŏngshin 제정신

Santa Claus Sant'ak'ŭllosŭ 산타클로스

sap 1 *n* (*in tree*) suaek 수액 2 *v/t s.o.'s energy* yak'washik'ida 약화시키다

sapphire (*jewel*) sap'aiŏ 사파이어

sarcasm p'ungja 풍자

sarcastic pinjŏngdaenŭn 빈정대는

sardine chŏng-ŏri 정어리

sash (*on dress, uniform*) tti 띠; (*in window*) saesshi 새시

Satan Sat'an 사탄

satellite in-gong-wisŏng 인공위성

satellite dish in-gong-wisŏng chŏpsshi 인공위성 접시

satellite TV wisŏng t'ibŭi 위성 티브이

satin kongdan 공단

satire p'ungja 풍자

satirical p'ungjajŏgin 풍자적인

satirist p'ungjaga 풍자가

satisfaction manjok 만족; *get ~ out of sth* muŏesŏ manjogŭl nŭkkida

무엇에서 만족을 느끼다; *a feeling of* ~ manjok-kkam 만족감; *is that to your* ~? maŭme tŭshimnikka? 마음에 드십니까?

satisfactory manjok'an 만족한; (*just good enough*) kŭjŏ kŭrŏn 그저 그런; *this is not* ~ igŏsŭronŭn ch'ungbunch'i anayo 이것으로는 충분치 않아요

satisfy *customers* manjoksshik'ida 만족시키다; *hunger, sexual desires, conditions* ch'ungjokshik'ida 충족시키다; *I am satisfied* (*had enough to eat*) chŏnŭn ch'ungbunhi mŏgŏssŏyo 저는 충분히 먹었어요; *I am satisfied that …* (*convinced*) … ranŭn-gŏshi napttŭg kamnida …라는 것이 납득 갑니다; *I hope you're satisfied!* sogi shiwŏnhajiyo! 속이 시원하지요!

Saturday t'oyoil 토요일

sauce sossŭ 소스

saucepan naembi 냄비

saucer pach'im chŏpsshi 받침 접시

saucy *person* kŏnbangjin 건방진; *dress* mŏtchin 멋진

Saudi Arabia Saudi Arabia 사우디 아라비아

Saudi (Arabian) 1 *adj* Saudi Arabiaŭi 사우디 아라비아의 **2** *n* (*person*) Saudi Arabiain 사우디 아라비아인

sauna sauna 사우나

saunter *v/i* ŏsŭllŏnggŏrida 어슬렁거리다

sausage soshiji 소시지

savage *adj animal* yasaeng-ŭi 야생의; *attack* chaninhan 잔인한; *criticism* hokttok'an 혹독한

save 1 *v/t* (*rescue*) kuhada 구하다; (*put aside: money*) moanŭl 모아놓다; (*in bank*) chŏch'uk'ada 저축하다; *time, money* chŏryak'ada 절약하다; (*collect*) moŭda 모으다; COMPUT chŏjanghada 저장하다; *goal* chŏjihada 저지하다; *you could ~ yourself a lot of effort* tŏl himdŭrŏssŭl sudo issŏnnŭnde 덜 힘들었을 수도 있었는데 **2** *v/i* (*put money aside*) chŏgŭmhada 저금하다; SP maganaeda 막아내다 **3** *n* SP

tŭktchŏm maganaegi 득점 막아내기
♦ **save up for** …e taebihae moŭda …에 대비해 모으다

saving (*amount saved*) chŏryakpun 절약분; (*activity*) chŏryak 절약

savings yegŭm 예금

savings account pot'ong yegŭm 보통 예금

savings bank chŏch'uk ŭnhaeng 저축 은행

Savior REL Kuseju 구세주

savor *v/t* ŭmmihada 음미하다

savory *adj* (*not sweet*) tchaptcharhan 짭짤한

saw 1 *n* (*tool*) t'op 톱 **2** *v/t* t'obŭro charŭda 톱으로 자르다
♦ **saw off** t'obŭro k'yŏda 톱으로 켜다

sawdust t'op-ppap 톱밥

saxophone saekssŏp'on 색소폰

say 1 *v/t* marhada 말하다; *can I ~ something?* chega muŏl chom yaegihaedo toelkkayo? 제가 뭘 좀 얘기해도 될까요?; *that is to* ~ chŭk 즉; *what do you* ~ *to that?* kŭgŏse taehae ŏttŏk'e saenggak'anayo? 그것에 대해 어떻게 생각하나요? **2** *n have one's* ~ hago ship'ŭn marŭl hada 하고 싶은 말을 하다

saying sokttam 속담

scab (*on wound*) ttaktchi 딱지

scaffolding palp'an 발판

scald *v/t*: *be ~ed* teda 데다

scale[1] (*on fish*) pinŭl 비늘

scale[2] **1** *n* (*size*) kyumo 규모; (*on thermometer etc*) nunkkŭm 눈금; (*on map*) ch'ukch'ŏk 축척; MUS ŭmgye 음계; *on a larger / smaller* ~ chomdŏ k'ŭn / chagŭn kyumoro 좀더 큰 / 작은 규모로 **2** *v/t cliffs etc* orŭda 오르다

scale drawing ch'ukch'ŏk tomyŏn 축척 도면

scales (*for weighing*) chŏul 저울

scalp *n* mŏritkkajuk 머리가죽

scalpel oekkwayong mesŭ 외과용 메스

scalper amp'yosang 암표상

scam F sagi 사기

scan 1 *v/t horizon, page* chasehi salp'yŏboda 자세히 살펴보다; MED chŏngmil chosahada 정밀 조사하다;

ᴄOMPUT sŭk'aenhada 스캔하다 2 *n*
ᴍED ch'enae pangsanŭng punp'o
ᴀjin 체내 방사능 분포 사진
scan in ᴄOMPUT sŭk'aenhada
스캔하다
ᴀndal sŭk'aendŭl 스캔들
ᴀndalous *affair* such'isŭroun
ᴀ치스러 운; *prices* t'ŏmuniŏmnŭn
ᆏ무니없는
ᴀnner ᴍED, ᴄOMPUT sŭk'aenŏ
스캐너
ᴀntily *adv*: **~ clad** osŭl chedaero
ᴀᆾ춰 입지 않은 옷을 제대로
ᴀᆾ춰 입지 않은
ᴀnty *clothes* sonppadangmanhan
스ᄇ닥만한
ᴀpegoat hŭisaengnyang 희생양
ᴀr 1 *n* hyungt'ŏ 흉터 2 *v/t*
ᴀyungt'ŏrŭl namgida 흉터를 남기다
ᴀrce (*in short supply*) mojaranŭn
ᆯ자라는; **make oneself ~** sŭltchŏk
ᴀagada 슬쩍 나가다
ᴀrcely: **I had ~ begun to speak
when …** nanŭn …hajamaja marhagi
ᴀhijak'aet-tta 나는 …하자마자
ᆯ하기 시작했다; **I ~ know her** chŏn,
ᆨŭ yŏjarŭl kŏŭi mollayo 전, 그
ᆨ여자를 거의 몰라요; **~ any** kŏŭi
ᆩopta 거의 없다
ᴀrcity pujok 부족
ᴀre 1 *v/t* kŏptchuda 겁주다; **be ~d
ᴏf** musŏwŏhada 무서워하다 2 *n
panic, alarm*) puran 불안; **give s.o.
a ~** nuguege kŏptchuda 누구에게
ᆨ줍주다
scare away kŏptchuŏ 쫓아내다
ᴄhoch'anaeda 겁주어 쫓아내다
ᴀrecrow hŏsuabi 허수아비
ᴀremonger hŏtssomunŭl
ᆟttŭrinŭn saram 헛소문을 퍼뜨리는
ᴀ람
ᴀrf (*around neck*) mokttori 목도리;
over head) sŭk'ap'ŭ 스카프
ᴀrlet chuhongsaek 주홍색
ᴀrlet fever sŏnghongnyŏl 성홍열
ᴀry mushimushihan 무시무시한
ᴀthing t'ongnyŏrhan 통렬한
ᴀtter 1 *v/t leaflets, seeds* ppurida
ᆼ리다; **be ~ed all over the room**
ᴏang chŏnch'e-e ppuryŏjyŏ it-tta 방
ᄌᆫ체에 뿌려져 있다 2 *v/i* (*of crowd*

etc) hŭt'ŏjida 흩어지다
scatterbrained mŏriga sanmanhan
머리가 산만한
scattered *showers* sanbaltchŏgin
산발적인; *family, villages* hŭt'ŏjin
흩어진
scenario shinario 시나리오
scene THEA chang 장; (*view, sight*)
changmyŏn 장면; (*of accident, crime
etc*) hyŏnjang 현장; (*setting of novel,
in a movie*) paegyŏng 배경; (*part of
movie*) changmyŏn 장면; (*argument*)
soran 소란; **make a ~** soranŭl p'iuda
소란을 피우다; **~s** THEA mudae
paegyŏng 무대 배경; *jazz ~ / drugs
~* ᴊ chaejügye / mayak-kkye
재즈계 / 마약계; **behind the ~s** *fig*
nam morŭge 남 모르게
scenery p'unggyŏng 풍경; THEA
mudae paegyŏng 무대 배경
scent *n* (*smell*) hyanggi 향기;
(*perfume*) hyangsu 향수; (*of animal*)
naemsae 냄새
schedule 1 *n* (*of events*) yejŏng 예정;
(*of work*) iltchŏng 일정; (*for trains,
of lessons*) shiganp'yo 시간표; **be on
~** yejŏngdaeroida 예정대로이다; **be
behind ~** yejŏngboda nŭt-tta
예정보다 늦다 2 *v/t* (*put on ~*)
yejŏnghada 예정하다; **it's ~d for
completion next month** taŭmttare
kkŭnmach'igiro toeŏ issŏyo 다음달에
끝마치기로 되어 있어요
scheduled flight chŏngi
hanggongp'yŏn 정기 항공편
scheme 1 *n* (*plan*) kyehoek 계획;
(*wicked plot*) moŭi 모의 2 *v/i* (*plot*)
moŭihada 모의하다
scheming *adj* kyohwarhan 교활한
schizophrenia chŏngshin
punyŏltchŭng 정신 분열증
schizophrenic 1 *n* chŏngshin
punyŏltchŭng hwanja 정신 분열증
환자 2 *adj* chŏngshin punyŏltchŭng-
ŭi 정신 분열증의
scholar haktcha 학자
scholarship (*scholarly work*)
hangmun 학문; (*financial award*)
changhak-kkŭm 장학금
school hak-kkyo 학교; (*university*)
taehak 대학

schoolbag ch'aek-kkabang 책가방; **schoolboy** namhaksaeng 남학생; **schoolchildren** hakttong 학동; **school days** suŏbil 수업일; **schoolgirl** yŏhaksaeng 여학생; **schoolteacher** hak-kkyo sŏnsaengnim 학교 선생님

sciatica chwagol shin-gyŏng't'ong 좌골 신경통

science kwahak 과학

science fiction kongsang kwahak sosŏl 공상 과학 소설

scientific kwahaktchŏgin 과학적인

scientist kwahaktcha 과학자

scissors kawi 가위

scoff[1] v/t (eat fast) kegŏlsŭrŏpkke mŏkkta 게걸스럽게 먹다; (eat whole lot) ta mŏgŏ ch'iuda 다 먹어 치우다

scoff[2] v/i nollida 놀리다

♦ **scoff at** ...ŭl/rŭl piut-tta ...을/를 비웃다

scold v/t child, husband kkujit-tta 꾸짖다

scoop 1 n (for food) kuktcha 국자; (for mud, coal) sap 삽; (in journalism) t'ŭktchong 특종 **2** v/t p'uda 푸다; ice cream ttŭda 뜨다

♦ **scoop up** p'ŏ ollida 퍼 올리다; kids, books ana ollida 안아 올리다

scooter (with motor) sŭk'ut'ŏ 스쿠터; (child's) oe pal sŭk'eit'ŭ 외 발 스케이트

scope pŏmwi 범위; (opportunity) kihoe 기회; (latitude) yŏji 여지

scorch v/t kŭsŭllida 그슬리다

scorching hot tchinŭn tŭshi tŏun 찌는 듯이 더운

score 1 n sp tŭktchŏm 득점; (written music) akppo 악보; (of movie etc) ŭmak 음악; **what's the ~?** chŏmsuga ŏttaeyo? 점수가 어때요?; **have a ~ to settle with s.o.** nuguege ssain wŏnhanŭl p'ulda 누구에게 쌓인 원한을 풀다 **2** v/t goal, point chŏmsurŭl kirok'ada 점수를 기록하다; (cut: line) saegim nunŭl naeda 새김 눈을 내다 **3** v/i tŭktchŏmhada 득점하다; (keep the score) chŏmsurŭl kirok'ada 점수를 기록하다; **that's where he ~s** kŭge kŭ namjaŭi kangtchŏmiyeyo 그게 그

남자의 강점이예요

scorer (of goal, point) tŭktchŏmja 득점자; (score-keeper) chŏmsu kirogwŏn 점수 기록원

scorn 1 n kyŏngmyŏl 경멸; **pour ~ sth** muŏsŭl kyŏngmyŏrhada 무엇을 경멸하다 **2** v/t idea, suggestion kyŏngmyŏrhada 경멸하다

scornful kyŏngmyŏrhanŭn 경멸하는

Scot Sŭk'ot'ŭllaendŭin 스코틀랜드인

Scotch (whiskey) sŭk'ach'i 스카치

Scotland Sŭk'ot'ŭllaendŭ 스코틀랜드

Scottish Sŭk'ot'ŭllaendŭŭi 스코틀랜드의

scot-free: get off ~ pŏrŭl momyŏnhada 벌을 모면하다

scoundrel akttang 악당

scour[1] (search) ch'aja tanida 찾아 다니다

scour[2] pans munjillŏ takkta 문질러 닦다

scout n (boy ~) sŭk'aut'ŭ 스카우트

scowl 1 n tchinggŭrin ŏlgul 찡그린 얼굴 **2** v/i tchinggŭrida 찡그리다

scram F tomanggada 도망가다

scramble 1 n (rush) punmang 분망 **2** v/t message ilburŏ twisŏktta 일부러 뒤섞다 **3** v/i (climb) chaepparuge k orŭda 재빠르게 기어 오르다; **he ~ to his feet** kŭnŭn chaeppalli irŏna tta 그는 재빨리 일어났다

scrambled eggs sŭk'ŭraembŭrhan talgyal yori 스크램블한 달걀 요리

scrap 1 n (metal) p'yech'ŏl 폐철; (fight) ssaum 싸움; (little bit) chogŭm 조금 **2** v/t project etc p'yegishik'ida 폐기시키다; paragra etc chiuda 지우다

scrapbook sŭk'ŭraep puk 스크랩 북

scrape 1 n (on paintwork etc) kŭlk' chaguk 긁힌 자국 **2** v/t paintwork, one's arm etc kŭktta 긁다; vegetabl k'allo tadŭmtta 칼로 다듬다; **~ a living** irŏktchŏrŏk saenghwarhada 이럭저럭 생활하다

♦ **scrape through** (in exam) kanshinhi hapkkyŏk'ada 간신히 합격하다

scrap heap ssŭregi tŏmi 쓰레기 더; **good for the ~** amu tchagedo ssŭlmo ŏmnŭn 아무 짝에도 쓸모

없는

crap metal p'yech'ŏl 폐철

crappy *work* chirimyŏllŏrhan 지리멸렬한

cratch 1 *n* (*to stop itching*) kŭlkki 긁기; (*by cat etc*) halk'wigi 할퀴기; (*on paintwork*) kŭlk'in chaguk kŭlgin 자국; **have a ~** (*to stop itching*) kŭlkta 긁다; **start from ~** ch'ŏŭmbut'ŏ shijak'ada 처음부터 시작하다; **not up to ~** manjoksŭrŏptchi mot'an 만족스럽지 못한 **2** *v/t* (*to stop itching*) kŭkta 긁다; (*by cat etc*) halk'wida halk'wida 할퀴다 **3** *v/i* (*of cat, nails*) kŭkta 긁다

crawl 1 *n* hwigalgyŏ ssŭn kŭltcha 휘갈겨 쓴 글자 **2** *v/t* hwigalgyŏ ssŭda 휘갈겨 쓰다

cream 1 *n* oech'imsori 외침소리 **2** *v/i* sorich'ida 소리치다

creech 1 *n* (*of tires*) kkik'anŭn sori 끽하는 소리; (*scream*) pimyŏng sori 비명 소리 **2** *v/i* (*of tires*) kkik'anŭn soriga nada 끽하는 소리가 나다; (*scream*) pimyŏngŭl chirŭda 비명을 지르다

creen 1 *n* (*in room, hospital*) k'anmagi 칸막이; (*protective*) magi 막이; (*in movie theater*) sŭk'ŭrin 스크린; COMPUT hwamyŏn 화면; **on the ~** (*in movie*) ŭnmage 은막에; **on** (**the**) **~** COMPUT hwamyŏnsang-e 화면상에 **2** *v/t* (*protect, hide*) kamch'uda 감추다; *movie* sangyŏnghada 상영하다; (*for security reasons*) sŏnbyŏrhada 선별하다

creenplay kakppon 각본; **screen saver** COMPUT hwamyŏn pohogi 화면 보호기; **screen test** sŭk'ŭrin t'esŭt'ŭ 스크린 테스트

crew 1 *n* nasamot 나사못; V (*sex*) sŏnggyo 성교 **2** *v/t* V sŏnggyorŭl hada 성교를 하다; F (*cheat*) sogida 속이다; **~ sth to sth** muŏsŭl muŏse nasamosŭro kojŏngshik'ida 무엇을 무엇에 나사못으로 고정시키다

screw up 1 *v/t* *eyes* tchinggŭrida 찡그리다; *piece of paper* toldol mungch'ida 돌돌 뭉치다; F (*make a mess of*) mangch'ida 망치다 **2** *v/i* F (*make a bad mistake*) k'ŭn shilssuro

ŏngmang-i toege hada 큰 실수로 엉망이 되게 하다

screwdriver tŭraibŏ 드라이버

screwed up F (*psychologically*) pittŭrŏjin 비뚤어진

screw top (*on bottle*) pit'ŭrŏ yŏnŭn magae 비틀어 여는 마개

scribble 1 *n* kalgyŏ ssŭgi 갈겨 쓰기 **2** *v/t* (*write quickly*) kalgyŏ ssŭda 갈겨 쓰다 **3** *v/i* kalgyŏ ssŭda 갈겨 쓰다

script (*for play etc*) taebon 대본; (*form of writing*) kŭltchach'e 글자체

Scripture: the (**Holy**) **~s** Kyŏngjŏn 경전

scriptwriter chak-kka 작가

scroll *n* (*manuscript*) turumari 두루마리

♦ **scroll down** *v/i* COMPUT araero naerida 아래로 내리다

♦ **scroll up** *v/i* COMPUT wiro ollida 위로 올리다

scrounger kŏjŏ ŏnnŭn saram 거저 얻는 사람

scrub *v/t* *floors, hands* munjirŭda 문지르다

scrubbing brush sol 솔

scruffy chijŏbunhan 지저분한

♦ **scrunch up** *plastic cup etc* pusŏjida 부서지다

scruples todŏk kwannyŏm 도덕 관념; **have no ~ about doing sth** muŏsŭl hanŭn te issŏ todŏktchŏk chujŏhami ŏptta 무엇을 하는 데 있어 도덕적 주저함이 없다

scrupulous (*with moral principles*) todŏktchŏgin 도덕적인; (*thorough*) pint'ŭmŏmnŭn 빈틈없는; *attention to detail* kkomkkomhan 꼼꼼한

scrutinize chasehi chosahada 자세히 조사하다

scrutiny chosa 조사; **come under ~** semirhi chosadoeda 세밀히 조사되다

scuba diving sŭk'ubŏ taibing 스쿠버 다이빙

scuffle *n* nant'u 난투

sculptor chogak-kka 조각가

sculpture *n* (*art*) chogak 조각; (*sth sculpted*) chogak'p'um 조각품

scum (*on liquid*) tchikkŏgi 찌꺼기; *pej* ssŭregi 쓰레기

scythe n nat 낫

sea pada 바다; **by the ~** pada yŏp'e 바다 옆에

seafaring *nation* haeyang-ŭi 해양의; **seafood** haesanmul 해산물; **seafront** patattka 바닷가; **seagoing** *vessel* wŏnyang-ŭi 원양의; **seagull** kalmaegi 갈매기

seal[1] n (*animal*) mulkkae 물개

seal[2] 1 n (*on document*) pong-in 봉인; TECH milbong 밀봉 2 v/t *container* milbonghada 밀봉하다

♦ **seal off** *area* pongswaehada 봉쇄하다

sea level: **above / below ~** haesumyŏn wie / araee 해수면 위에 / 아래에

seam n (*on garment*) solgi 솔기; (*of ore*) kwangch'ŭng 광층

seaman sŏnwŏn 선원; **seaport** hanggudoshi 항구도시; **sea power** (*nation*) haegun-guk 해군국

search 1 n (*for missing person, object*) susaek 수색; (*for solution*) t'amsaek 탐색; COMPUT sŏch'i 서치; (*for happiness*) ch'ugu 추구 2 v/t *forest, room* ch'at-tta 찾다; COMPUT sŏch'ihada 서치하다

♦ **search for** *sth missing* ch'at-tta 찾다; *missing person* susaek'ada 수색하다; *solution* t'amsaek'ada 탐색하다; COMPUT sŏch'ihada 서치하다; *happiness* ch'uguhada 추구하다

searching *adj look* susaek'anŭn 수색하는; *question* nalk'aroun 날카로운

searchlight t'amjodŭng 탐조등; **search party** susaektttae 수색대; **search warrant** susaek yŏngtch'ang 수색 영장

seasick paemŏlmiga nan 배멀미가 난; **get ~** paemŏlmihada 배멀미하다; **seaside** haebyŏnkka 해변가; **at the ~** haebyŏne 해변에; **go to the ~** haebyŏnŭro kada 해변으로 가다; **seaside resort** haebyŏn lijot'ŭ 해변 리조트; **sea slug** haesam 해삼

season n (*winter etc*) kyejŏl 계절; (*for tourism etc*) ch'ŏl 철

seasoned *wood* chal kŏnjodoen 잘

건조된; *traveler etc* kyŏnghŏmŭl ssahŭn 경험을 쌓은

seasoning chomiryo 조미료

season ticket (*for transportation*) chŏnggi sŭngch'akkwŏn 정기 승차권; (*for stadium, opera*) chŏnggi iptchangkkwŏn 정기 입장권

seat 1 n chari 자리; (*of pants*) kungdung-i 궁둥이; **please take a ~** ch'akssŏk'ayŏ chushipsshio 착석하여 주십시오 2 v/t (*have seating for*) chwasŏgŭl kajigo it-tta 좌석을 가지고 있다; **please remain ~ed** ch'akssŏk'ayŏ kyeshigil paramnida 착석하여 계시길 바랍니다

seat belt chwasŏk pelt'ŭ 좌석 벨트

sea urchin sŏngge 성게

seaweed haech'o 해초; **edible ~** kim 김

secluded mŏlli ttŏrŏjyŏ hanjŏk'an 멀리 떨어져 한적한

seclusion mŏlli ttŏrŏjim 멀리 떨어짐

second 1 n (*of time*) ch'o 초; **just a ~** chamkkanmanyo 잠깐만요 2 *adj* tu pŏntchaeŭi 두 번째의; **~ biggest** tu pŏntchaero k'ŭn 두 번째로 큰 3 *adv come in* tu pŏntchaero 두 번째로 4 v/t *motion* ch'ansŏnghada 찬성하다

secondary pojojŏgin 보조적인; **of ~ importance** ich'ajŏgŭro chungyohan 이차적으로 중요한

secondary education chungdŭng kyoyuk 중등 교육

second-best *adj* tu pŏntchaero chal hanŭn 두 번째로 잘 하는; **second class** *adj ticket* idŭngsŏgŭi 이등석의; **second gear** MOT idan kiŏ 이단 기어; **second hand** (*on clock*) ch'och'im 초침; **secondhand** 1 *adj* chunggoŭi 중고의 2 *adv buy* chunggoro 중고로

secondly tultchaero 둘째로

second-rate iryuŭi 이류의

second thoughts: **I've had ~** chŏn, saenggagŭl pakkwŏssŏyo 전, 생각을 바꿨어요

secrecy kimil 기밀

secret 1 n pimil 비밀; **do sth in ~** muŏsŭl pimillie hada 무엇을 비밀리에 하다 2 *adj garden, passage* ⁱnmirhan 은밀한; *work, department* ⁱimirŭi 비밀의

•**cret agent** kanch'ŏp 간첩

•**cretarial** *tasks, job* pisŏŭi 비서의

•**cretary** pisŏ 비서; POL changgwan 장관

•**cretary of State** Kungmubu ·Changgwan 국무부 장관

•**crete** (*give off*) punbihada 룬비하다; (*hide*) sumgida 숨기다

•**cretion** (*of liquid*) punbiaek 룬비액; (*liquid secreted*) punbimul 룬비물; (*concealment*) ŭnnik 은닉

•**cretive** t'ŏ noch'i annŭn 터 놓지 낳는

•**cretly** ŭnmirhi 은밀히

•**cret police** pimil kyŏngch'al 비밀 령찰

•**cret service** pimil chŏngbo kigwan ·l밀 정보 기관

•**ct** punp'a 분파

•**ction** (*of book, text*) kwa 과; (*of ⁱpple*) chogak 조각; (*of building*) kuhoek 구획; (*of company*) pusŏ 쿠서

•**ctor** yŏngnyŏk 영역

•**cular** sesogŭi 세속의

•**cure 1** *adj shelf, job* anjŏnhan 난전한; *feeling* anshimhanŭn 난심하는 **2** *v/t shelf etc* anjŏnhage ·hada 안전하게 하다; *s.o.'s help, ⁱfunding* ŏt-tta 얻다

•**curity** (*in job*) anjŏnssŏng 안전성; ⁱ*for investment* pojang 보장; (*at ⁱairport etc*) poan 보안; (*department responsible for ~*) poankkwa 보안과; ⁱ*of beliefs etc*) hwaksshin 확신; **se-curities** FIN yukka chŭngkkwŏn ·유가 증권; **securities market** FIN yukka chŭngkkwŏn shijang 유가 증권 시장

•**curity alert** poan kyŏnggye 보안 령계; **security check** poan hwagin 보안 확인; **security-conscious** ·poanŭl chungshihanŭn 보안을 중시하는; **security forces** anjŏn-gun 안전군; **security guard** kyŏngbiwŏn 경비원; **security risk** (*person*) wihŏm inmul 위험 인물

•**edan** MOT ssallongch'a 쌀롱차

•**edative** *n* chinjŏngje 진정제

sediment ch'imjŏnmul 침전물

seduce (*sexually*) yuhok'ada 유혹하다

seduction (*sexual*) yuhok 유혹

seductive *dress* maeryŏktchŏgin 매력적인; *offer* yuhoktchŏgin 유혹적인

see poda 보다; (*understand*) alda 알다; *can I ~ the manager?* ch'aegimjarŭl mannal su issŭlkkayo? 책임자를 만날 수 있을까요?; *you should ~ a doctor* tangshinŭn ŭisahant'e kabwaya toemnida 당신은 의사한테 가봐야 됩니다; *~ s.o. home* nuga chibe musahi wannŭnjirŭl hwaginhada 누가 집에 무사히 왔는지를 확인하다; *I'll ~ you to the door* munkkaji paraeda chulkkeyo 문까지 바래다 줄께요; *~ you!* tto mannayo! 또 만나요!; *I ~ algessŏyo* 알겠어요

♦ **see about** (*look into*) salp'yŏboda 살펴보다

♦ **see off** (*at airport etc*) paeunghada 배웅하다; (*chase away*) tchoch'a ponaeda 쫓아 보내다

♦ **see to:** *~ sth* muŏshi chal ch'ŏri toeŏnnŭnji hwaginhada 무엇이 잘 처리 되었는지 확인하다; *~ it that sth gets done* muŏsŭl kkŭnnaenŭn kŏsŭl t'ŭllimŏpsshi hada 무엇을 끝내는 것을 틀림없이 하다

seed sshi 씨; (*in tennis*) sidŭ 시드; *go to ~* (*of person, district*) t'oerak'ada 퇴락하다

seedling (*of tree*) myomok 묘목; (*of plant*) myojong 묘종

seedy *bar, district* p'yŏngp'ani nappŭn 평판이 나쁜

seeing (**that**) ...(i)gi ttaemune ...(이)기 때문에

seeing-eye dog maengdogyŏn 맹도견

seek 1 *v/t employment* ch'at-tta 찾다; *truth* ch'uguhada 추구하다 **2** *v/i* t'amsaek'ada 탐색하다

seem ...kŏt kat-tta ...것 같다; *it ~s that* ...in kŏt kat'a poida ...인 것 같아 보이다

seemingly pogienŭn 보기에는

seep (*of liquid*) saeda 새다

♦ **seep out** (*of liquid*) saeŏnaoda 새어나오다

seesaw shiso 시소

see-through *dress, material* pich'inŭn 비치는

segment (*of chart, structure*) pubun 부분; (*of orange*) chogak 조각

segmented pubunchŏgin 부분적인

segregate pullihada 분리하다

segregation pulli 분리

seismology chijinhak 지진학

seize chaptta 잡다; *opportunity* p'och'ak'ada 포착하다; (*of customs, police etc*) amnyuhada 압류하다

♦ **seize up** (*of engine*) mŏmch'uda 멈추다

seizure MED paltchak 발작; (*of drugs etc*) amnyu 압류

seldom tŭmulge 드물게

select 1 *v/t* sŏnt'aek'ada 선택하다 **2** *adj* (*exclusive*) chŏngsŏnhan 정선한

selection (*choice*) sŏnt'aek 선택; (*that chosen*) sŏnt'aekttoen kŏt 선택된 것; (*people chosen*) sŏnt'aekttoen saram 선택된 사람; (*assortment*) kusaek 구색

selection process sŏnbal kwajŏng 선발 과정

selective anmogi nop'ŭn 안목이 높은

self chaa 자아

self-addressed envelope ponin chusorŭl chŏgŭn pongt'u 본인 주소를 적은 봉투; **self-assured** chashin innŭn 자신 있는; **self-catering** sŭsŭro ŭmshigŭl haemŏngnŭn 스스로 음식을 해먹는; **self-centered** chagi ponwiŭi 자기 본위의; **self-confessed** chainhanŭn 자인하는; **self-confidence** chashin 자신; **self-confident** chashin innŭn 자신 있는; **self-conscious** chaŭishigi kanghan 자의식이 강한; **self-contained** *apartment* tongnipshigŭi tongnipchŏgin 독립식의 독립적인; **self-control** chaje 자제; **self-defense** chagi pang-ŏ 자기 방어; **self-discipline** chagi suyang 자기 수양; **self-doubt** chagi pulshshin 자기 불신; **self-employed** chayŏng-ŭi 자영의; **self-evident** chamyŏnghan 자명한; **self-**

interest sarisayok 사리사욕

selfish igijŏgin 이기적인

selfless yokssimi ŏmnŭn 욕심이 없는

self-made man chasusŏnggahan saram 자수성가한 사람; **self-possessed** ch'imch'ak'an 침착한; **self-reliant** tongniptchŏgin 독립적인; **self-respect** chajonshim 자존심; **self-righteous** *pej* tokssŏnjŏgin 독선적인; **self-satisfied** *pej* chagi manjogŭi 자기 만족의; **self-service** *adj* selp'ŭssŏbisŭŭi 셀프서비스의; **self-service restaurant** selp'ŭssŏbisŭ shikttang 셀프서비스 식당

sell 1 *v/t* p'alda 팔다; **you have to ~ yourself** ne chashinŭl sŏnjŏnhaeya twaeyo 네 자신을 선전해야 돼요 **2** *v/i* (*of products*) p'anmaedoeda 판매되다

seller p'anmaeja 판매자

selling *n* COM p'anmae 판매

selling point COM p'anmae kangjŏchŏm 판매 강조점

semen chŏng-aek 정액

semester hak-kki 학기

semi (*truck*) t'ŭrŏk 트럭

semicircle panwŏn 반원; **semicircular** panwŏnhyŏngŭi 반원형의; **semiconductor** ELEC pandoch'e 반도체; **semifinal** chun-gyŏlsssŭng 준결승

seminar semina 세미나

semiskilled pan sungnyŏnŭi 반 숙련의

senate sang-wŏn 상원

senator sang-wŏnŭiwŏn 상원의원

send *v/t* ponaeda 보내다; **~ sth to s.o.** nuguege muŏsŭl ponaeda 누구에게 무엇을 보내다; **~ s.o. to s.o.** nugurŭl nuguege ponaeda 누구를 누구에게 보내다; **~ her my best wishes** kŭnyŏege anbu chŏnhae chuseyo 그녀에게 안부 전해 주세요

♦ **send back** *letter* pansonghada 반송하다; *person, food* tollyŏ ponaeda 돌려 보내다

♦ **send for** *doctor, help* purŭrŏ ponaeda 부르러 보내다

send in *troops* ponaeda 보내다; *next interviewee* tŭryŏ ponaeda 들여 보내다; *application form* chech'urhada 제출하다

send off *letter, fax etc* palssonghada 발송하다

send up (*mock*) nollida 놀리다

ender (*of letter*) palssong-in 발송인

enile nosoehan 노쇠한

enility nosoe 노쇠

enior (*older*) sonwiŭi 손위의; (*in rank*) sanggŭbŭi 상급의; **be ~ to X** (*in rank*) Xboda wittcharie innŭn X보다 윗자리에 있는

enior citizen ŏrŭshin 어르신

ensation (*feeling*) kamgak 감각; (*event*) sensseisyŏn 센세이션; (*person*) sŏnp'ungjŏgŭro inkki innŭn saram 선풍적으로 인기 있는 사람; (*thing*) sŏnp'ungjŏgŭro inkki innŭn kŏt 선풍적으로 인기 있는 것

ensational *news, discovery* sesangŭl ttŏdŭlssŏk'age hanŭn 세상을 떠들썩하게 하는; (*very good*) nŭkpushin 눈부신

ense 1 *n* (*meaning*) ttŭt 뜻; (*purpose, point*) ŭimi 의미; (*common ~*) sangshik 상식; (*of sight, smell etc*) kamgak 감각; (*feeling*) nŭtkkim 느낌; *in a ~* ŏttŏn ŭimiesŏnŭn 어떤 의미에서는; *talk ~, man!* ŏi, ich'ie mannŭn marŭl hae! 어이, 이치에 맞는 말을 해!; *it doesn't make ~* kŭgŏn mari andwaeyo 그건 말이 안돼요; *there's no ~ in waiting/trying* kidaril/shidohal iyuga ŏpssŏyo 기다릴/시도할 이유가 없어요 **2** *v/t s.o.'s presence* arach'aeda 알아채다

enseless (*pointless*) muŭimihan 무의미한

ensible *person, decision* punbyŏri innŭn 분별이 있는; *advice* hyŏnmyŏnghan 현명한

ensitive *skin* min-gamhan 민감한; *person* yeminhan 예민한

ensitivity min-gamham 민감함

ensual kwangnŭngtchŏgin 관능적인

ensuality kwangnŭng 관능

ensuous kamgaktchŏgin 감각적인

entence 1 *n* GRAM munjang 문장;

LAW p'an-gyŏl 판결 **2** *v/t* LAW p'an-gyŏrŭl naerida 판결을 내리다

sentiment (*emotion*) kamsang 감상; (*opinion*) sogam 소감

sentimental kamsangtchŏgin 감상적인

sentimentality kamsang 감상

sentry poch'o 보초

Seoul Sŏul 서울

separate 1 *adj* pyŏlgaeŭi 별개의; *keep X ~ from Y* Xwa/kwa Yŭl/rŭl pullihada X와/과 Y을/를 분리하다 **2** *v/t* pullihada 분리하다; *~ X from Y* Xŭl/rŭl Yesŏ pullihada X을/를 Y에서 분리하다 **3** *v/i* (*of couple*) pyŏlgŏhada 별거하다

separated *couple* pyŏlgŏhan 별거한

separately *pay, treat, deal with* ttaro 따로

separation pulli 분리; (*of couple*) pyŏlgŏ 별거

September kuwŏl 구월

septic pup'aessŏng-ŭi 부패성의; *go ~* komtta 곪다

sequel sokp'yŏn 속편

sequence *n* sunsŏ 순서; *in ~* sunsŏdaero 순서대로; *out of ~* sunsŏe mat-tchi ank'e 순서에 맞지 않게; *the ~ of events* sakkŏnŭi sunsŏ 사건의 순서

serene *person* ch'abunhan 차분한; *lake, smile* p'yŏng-onhan 평온한

sergeant chungsa 중사

serial *n* yŏnsongmul 연속물

serialize *novel on TV* yŏnsok pangyŏnghada 연속 방영하다

serial killer yŏnsok sarhaebŏm 연속 살해범; **serial number** (*of product*) illyŏnbŏnho 일련번호; **serial port** COMPUT sshiriŏl p'ot'ŭ 씨리얼 포트

series (*of numbers, events*) yŏnsok 연속

serious *illness, situation, damage* shimgak'an 심각한; (*person: earnest*) chinjihan 진지한; *company* shinmang innŭn 신망 있는; *I'm ~* chinshimiyeyo 진심이에요; *we'd better take a ~ look at it* uri kŭgŏse taehae chinjihage ponŭn ke choŭl kŏt kat'ayo 우리 그것에 대해 진지하게 보는 게 좋을 것 같아요

seriously *injured* shimhage 심하게; *understaffed* chinjŏnguro 진정으로; **~ intend to ...** chinjihage ...haryŏgo hada 진지하게 ...하려고 하다; **~?** chŏngmallo? 정말로?; **take s.o. ~** nugurŭl chinjihage saenggak'ada 누구를 진지하게 생각하다

sermon sŏlgyo 설교

servant koyongin 고용인

serve 1 *n* (*in tennis*) sŏbŭ 서브 **2** *v/t food, meal* naeda 내다; *person, guests* shijungdŭlda 시중들다; *customer in shop* moshida 모시다; *one's country, the people* pongsahada 봉사하다; **it ~s you / him right** nŏnŭn / kŭnŭn hapttanghan taeurŭl padat-tta 너는 / 그는 합당한 대우를 받았다 **3** *v/i* ch'arida 차리다; (*in post, job*) kŭnmuhada 근무하다; (*in tennis*) sŏbŭhada 서브하다

♦ **serve up** *meal* ch'aryŏnaeda 차려내다

server (*in tennis*) sŏbŭhanŭn saram 서브하는 사람; COMPUT sŏbŏ 서버

service 1 *n* sŏbissŭ 서비스; (*in tennis*) sŏbŭhanŭn kkŏt sŏbŭhanŭn kŏt 서브하는 것; **the ~s** kundae 군대 **2** *v/t vehicle, machine* sŏbissŭhada 서비스하다

service area hyugeso 휴게소; **service charge** (*in restaurant, club*) sŏbissŭryo 서비스료; **service industry** sŏbissŭ sanŏp 서비스 산업; **serviceman** MIL kunin 군인; **service provider** COMPUT sŏbissŭ chegonghoesa 서비스 제공회사; **service sector** sŏbissŭ sanŏp pubun 서비스 산업 부분; **service station** chuyuso 주유소

session (*of parliament*) kaejŏng chungim 개정 중임; (*with psychiatrist, consultant etc*) mit'ing 미팅

set 1 *n* (*of tools, books etc, in tennis, scenery*) set'ŭ 세트; (*group of people*) chipttan 집단; MATH chip'ap 집합; (*where a movie is made*) ch'waryŏngjangso 촬영장소; **television ~** t'ellebijŏn set'ŭ 텔레비전 세트 **2** *v/t* (*place*) not'a 놓다; *movie, novel etc* ...ŭi paegyŏng-ŭl

chŏnghada ...의 배경을 정하다; *date, time, limit* chŏnghada 정하다; *mechanism* chojŏnghada 조정하다; *alarm clock* match'uŏ not'a 맞추어 놓다; *broken limb* umjigiji ank'e kojŏnghada 움직이지 않게 고정하다; *jewel* paganot'a 박아붙이다; (*type~*) shiktchahada 식자하다; **~ the table** sang-ŭl ch'arida 상을 차리다; **~ a task for s.o.** nuguege ch'aegimŭl pugwahada 누구에게 책임을 부과하다 **3** *v/i* (*of sun*) chida 지다; (*of glue*) ŭnggohada 응고하다 **4** *adj views, ideas* hwak-kkohan 확고한; **be dead ~ on X** X hanŭn kŏsŭl hwakssirhi maŭm mŏktta X 하는 것을 확실히 마음 먹다; **be very ~ in one's ways** chagi pangshingmanŭl kojip'ada 자기 방식만을 고집하다; **~ book / reading** (*in course*) sojŏngŭi ch'aek / ilgŭlkkŏri 소정의 책 / 읽을거리; **~ meal** chŏngshik 정식

♦ **set apart**: **set X apart from Y** Xŭl / rŭl Ywa / kwa kubyŏrhada X을 / 를 Y와 / 과 구별하다

♦ **set aside** (*for future use*) ch'aenggyŏduda 챙겨두다

♦ **set back** (*in plans etc*) twich'yŏjige hada 뒤쳐지게 하다; **it set me back $400** nanŭn kŭgŏse 400tallŏrŭl ssŏt tta 나는 그것에 400달러를 썼다

♦ **set off 1** *v/i* (*on journey*) ch'ulbarhada 출발하다 **2** *v/t explosion* chŏmhwahada 점화하다; *chain reaction* shijak'age hada 시작하게 하다

♦ **set out 1** *v/i* (*on journey*) ch'ulbarhada 출발하다; **~ to do X** (*intend*) X hanŭn kŏsŭl chaktchŏnghada X 하는 것을 작정하다 **2** *v/t ideas, proposal* sŏlmyŏnghada 설명하다; *goods* naenot'a 내놓다

♦ **set to** (*start on a task*) shijak'ada 시작하다

♦ **set up 1** *v/t new company* sŏllip'ada 설립하다; *system* seuda 세우다; *equipment, machine* chorip'ada 조립하다; *market stall* set'inghada 세팅하다; F (*frame*) ummorŭl kkumida 음모를 꾸미다 **2** *v/i* (*in* *business*) kaeŏp'ada 개업하다

etback hut'oe 후퇴

tting (*of novel etc*) paegyŏng 배경;
of house) wich'i 위치

ttle 1 *v/i* (*of bird*) antta 앉다; (*of
liquid*) malgajida 맑아지다; (*of dust*)
karaantta 가라앉다; (*to live*)
chŏngch'ak'ada 정착하다 **2** *v/t
dispute, argument* hwahaeshik'ida
화해시키다; *uncertainty* haegyŏrhada
해결하다; *s.o.'s debts* ch'ŏngsanhada
청산하다; *check* chiburhada
지불하다; *that ~s it!* kŭgŏsŭro irŭn
kyŏltchŏngdwaessŏyo! 그것으로
일은 결정됐어요!

settle down (*stop being noisy*)
choyonghaejida 조용해지다; (*stop
wild living*) charijaptta 자리잡다; (*in
an area*) chŏngch'ak'ada 정착하다

settle for padadŭrida 받아들이다

ettlement (*of claim, debt*) ch'ŏngsan
청산; (*of dispute*) hwahae 화해;
(*payment*) chibul 지불; (*of building*)
ch'imha 침하

ettler (*in new country*) ijuja 이주자

et-up (*structure*) kujo 구조;
(*relationship*) kwan-gye 관계; F
(*frame-up*) kkumyŏjin il 꾸며진 일

even ilgop 일곱, ch'il 칠

eventeen yŏrilgop 열 일곱, shipch'il
십칠

eventeenth yŏrilgop pŏntchaeŭi 열
일곱 번째의

eventh ilgop pŏntchaeŭi 일곱 번째의

eventieth irhŭn pŏntchaeŭi 일흔
번째의

eventy irhŭn 일흔, ch'ilssip 칠십

ever *v/t arm, cable etc* chŏlttanhada
절단하다; *relations* chŏryŏnhada
절연하다

everal 1 *adj* myŏnmyŏch'ŭi 몇몇의
2 *pron* myŏt kae 몇 개

evere *illness, penalty* shimhan 심한;
teacher, face ŏmkkyŏk'an 엄격한;
winter, weather mojin 모진

everely shimhage 심하게; *speak,
stare* ŏmhage 엄하게

everity (*of illness*) shimham 심함; (*of
penalty*) kahok 가혹; (*of look*)
ŏmkkyŏk 엄격; (*of winter*) mojim
모짐

sew 1 *v/t* kkwemaeda 꿰매다 **2** *v/i*
panŭjirhada 바느질하다

♦ **sew on** *button* kkwemaeŏ talda
꿰매어 달다

sewage hasu 하수

sewage plant hasu ch'ŏrijang 하수
처리장

sewer hasugwan 하수관

sewing (*skill*) panŭjil 바느질; (*that
being sewn*) panŭjilkkŏri 바느질거리

sewing machine chaebongt'ŭl
재봉틀

sex (*act*) sŏnggyo 성교; (*gender*) sŏng
성; *have ~ with s.o.* nuguwa
sŏnggyohada 누구와 성교하다

sexual sŏngtchŏgin 성적인

sexual intercourse sŏnggyo 성교

sexually transmitted disease
sŏngppyŏng 성병

sexy ssekssihan 섹시한

shabby *coat etc* nalgŭn 낡은;
treatment piyŏrhan 비열한

shack odumakchip 오두막집

shade 1 *n* ŭngdal 응달; (*for lamp*)
karigae 가리개; (*of color*) saektcho
색조; (*on window*) pŭllaindŭ
블라인드; *in the ~* ŭngdare(sŏ)
응달에(서) **2** *v/t* (*from sun, light*)
karida 가리다

shadow *n* kŭrimja 그림자

shady *spot* kŭnŭljin 그늘진; *character,
dealings etc* ŭishimsŭrŏun
의심스러운

shaft (*of axle, hammer*) charu 자루;
(*of mine*) sugaeng 수갱

shaggy *hair, dog* tŏpssuruk'an
덥수룩한

shake 1 *n*: *give X a good ~* Xŭl/rŭl
toege hŭndŭlda X을/를 되게 흔들다
2 *v/t* hŭndŭlda 흔들다; *~ hands*
akssuhada 악수하다; *~ hands with
X* Xwa/kwa akssuhada X와/과
악수하다; *~ one's head* kogaerŭl
chŏt-tta 고개를 젓다 **3** *v/i* (*of hands,
voice*) ttŏlda 떨다; (*of building*)
hŭndŭllida 흔들리다

shaken (*emotionally*) hollansŭrŏun
혼란스러운

shake-up kujo chojŏng 구조 조정

shaky *table etc* hŭndŭlgŏrinŭn
흔들거리는; (*after illness, shock*)

pit'ŭlgorinŭn 비틀거리는; *grasp of sth, grammar etc* puranjŏnghan 불안정한

shall (*future*) ...hal kŏshida ...할 것이다; **I ~ do my best** nanŭn ch'oesŏnŭl tahal kŏshida 나는 최선을 다할 것이다 ◊ (*determined*) ...hagessŭmnida ...하겠습니다; **I shan't see them** nanŭn kŭdŭrŭl mannaji ank'essŭmnida 나는 그들을 만나지 않겠습니다 ◊ (*suggesting*): **~ we go now?** uri chigŭm kalkkayo? 우리 지금 갈까요?

shallow *water* yat'ŭn 얕은; *person* ch'ŏnbak'an 천박한

shaman mudang 무당

shaman rite kut 굿

shaman song muga 무가

Shamanism Musok Shinang 무속 신앙

shamanistic music muak 무악

shame 1 *n such'ishim* 수치심; **bring ~ on** ...e such'ishimŭl an-gyŏjuda ...에 수치심을 안겨주다; **what a ~!** chŏngmal andwaessŏyo? 정말 안됐어요!; **~ on you!** pukkŭrŏptchido anni! 부끄럽지도 않니! **2** *v/t* mangshinshik'ida 망신시키다; **~ X into doing Y** X(ŭ)ro hayŏgŭm pukkŭrŏwŏ Yhage hada X(으)로 하여금 부끄러워 Y하게 하다

shameful such'isŭrŏun 수치스러운

shameless p'aryŏmch'ihan 파렴치한

shampoo *n* shyamp'u 샴푸

shape 1 *n* moyang 모양 **2** *v/t clay* moyang-ŭl mandŭlda 모양을 만들다; *s.o.'s life, the future* sŏlgyehada 설계하다

shapeless *dress etc* polp'umŏmnŭn 볼품없는

shapely *figure* mommaega chŏun 몸매가 좋은

share 1 *n* mok 몫; FIN chushik 주식; **do one's ~ of the work** chagi mokssŭi irŭl hada 자기 몫의 일을 하다 **2** *v/t* punbaehada 분배하다; *room, bed* hamkke ssŭda 함께 쓰다; *s.o.'s feelings, opinions* hamkke hada 함께 하다 **3** *v/i* hamkke nanuda 함께 나누다

♦ **share out** kyundŭnghage nanuda 균등하게 나누다

shareholder chuju 주주

shark sangŏ 상어

sharp 1 *adj knife* nalk'aroun 날카로운; *mind* myŏngminhan 명민한; *pain* sarŭl enŭn tŭt'an sal에는 듯한; *taste* chagŭktchŏgin 자극적인; **~ tongue** tokssŏl 독설 **2** *adv* MUS panŭm nopkke 반음 높게; **at 3 o'clock** ~ seshi chŏnggage 세시 정각에

sharpen *knife* kalda 갈다; *skills* yŏnmahada 연마하다; *pencil* kkaktt 깎다

shatter 1 *v/t glass* pusuda 부수다; *illusions* kkaejida 깨지다 **2** *v/i* (*of glass*) pusŏjida 부서지다

shattered F (*exhausted*) chich'in 지친 (*very upset*) tandanhi ch'unggyŏgŭl padŭn 단단히 충격을 받은

shattering *news, experience* ch'imyŏngjŏgin 치명적인; *effect* ŏmch'ŏngnan 엄청난

shave 1 *v/t & v/i* myŏndohada 면도하다 **2** *n* myŏndo 면도; **have a ~** myŏndohada 면도하다; **that was a close** ~ kanshinhi myŏnhaet-tta 간신히 면했다

♦ **shave off** *beard* kkakkabŏrida 깎아버리다; *piece of wood* kkakkanaeda 깎아내다

shaven *head* sakpparhan 삭발한

shaver (*electric*) myŏndogi 면도기

shaving brush myŏndoyong sol 면도용 솔

shaving soap myŏndoyong pinu 면도용 비누

shawl shyol 숄

she kŭnyŏ 그녀, kŭ yŏja 그 여자; **~ is American** kŭnyŏnŭn Miguk saramiyeyo 그녀는 미국 사람이에요 ◊ (*omission of pronoun*): **who is ~?** - **~ is my teacher** nuguyeyo? – che sŏnsaengnimiyeyo 누구예요? – 제 선생님이에요

shears k'ŭn kawi 큰 가위

sheath *n* (*for knife*) k'alch'ip 칼집; (*contraceptive*) k'ondom 콘돔

shed¹ *v/t blood, tears* hŭllida 흘리다; *leaves* ttŏrŏttŭrida 떨어뜨리다; ~

light on fig haemyŏnghada 해명하다

hed n ch'anggo 창고

heep yang 양

heepdog yang chik'inŭn kae 양 지키는 개

heepish tanghwanghanŭn 당황하는

heepskin adj lining yanggajuk 양가죽

heer adj madness, luxury wanjŏnhan 완전한; drop kŏŭi sujigin 거의 수직인; cliffs kap'arŭn 가파른

heet (for bed) shit'ŭ 시트; (of paper) chang 장; (of metal, glass) p'an 판

helf sŏnban 선반; **shelves** yŏrŏgaeŭi sŏnban 여러개의 선반

hell 1 n (of mussel, egg etc) kkŏptchil 껍질; (of tortoise) tŭngttaktchi 등딱지; MIL yut'an 유탄; **come out of one's ~** fig maŭmŭl t'ŏnot'a 마음을 터놓다 2 v/t peas pŏtkkida 벗기다; MIL p'ogyŏk'ada 포격하다

hellfire p'ohwa 포화; **come under ~** p'ogyŏgŭl pat-tta 포격을 받다

hellfish kapkkangnyu 갑각류

helter 1 n (refuge) p'inanch'ŏ 피난처; (against air raids) taep'iho 대피호; (at bus stop) chŏngnyujang 정류장 2 v/i (from rain, bombing etc) p'ihada 피하다 3 v/t (protect) pohohada 보호하다

heltered place p'ihal su innŭn 피할 수 있는; **lead a ~ life** ŭndunsaenghwarŭl hada 은둔생활을 하다

hepherd n yangch'i-gi 양치기

herry seriju 셰리주

hield 1 n (in attitude, thinking) pangp'ae 방패; (sports trophy) usŭngp'ae 우승패; TECH magi 막이 2 v/t (protect) pohohada 보호하다

hift 1 n (in attitude, thinking) pyŏnhwa 변화; (switchover) pyŏngyŏng 변경; (in direction of wind etc) idong 이동; (period of work) kyodae 교대 2 v/t (move) omgida 옮기다; stains etc ŏpssaeda 없애다; ~ **the emphasis onto** ...(ŭ)ro kangjŏtchŏmŭl idonghada ...(으)로 강조점을 이동하다 3 v/i (move) omgida 옮기다; (of attitude, opinion) pyŏnhada 변하다; (of wind) idonghada 이동하다; **that's ~ing!** F kkwae pparŭgunyo! 꽤 빠르군요!

shift key COMPUT ship'ŭt'ŭ k'i 시프트 키

shift work kyodae kŭnmu 교대 근무

shifty pej kansahan 간사한

shifty-looking pej kansahae poinŭn 간사해 보이는

shimmer v/i arŭn-gŏrida 아른거리다

shin n chŏnggang-i 정강이

shine 1 v/i (of sun, moon) pinnada 빛나다; (of shoes) pantchagida 반짝이다; fig (of student etc) ttwiŏnada 뛰어나다 2 v/t flashlight etc pich'uda 비추다 3 n (on shoes etc) pantchak-kkŏrim 반짝거림

shingle (on beach) chagal 자갈

shingles MED taesangp'ojin 대상포진

shiny surface pantchak-kkŏrinŭn 반짝거리는

ship 1 n pae 배 2 v/t (send) ponaeda 보내다; (send by sea) sŏnjŏk'ada 선적하다

shipment (consignment) hwamul 화물

shipowner sŏnbak soyuja 선박 소유자

shipping (sea traffic) haesang kyot'ong 해상 교통; (sending) palssong 발송; (sending by sea) sŏnjŏk 선적

shipping company haeunhoesa 해운회사

shipshape adj chŏngdondoen 정돈된

shipwreck 1 n nanp'a 난파 2 v/t nanp'ashik'ida 난파시키다; **be ~ed** nanp'adoeda 난파되다; **shipyard** chosŏnso 조선소

shirk keŭllihada 게을리하다

shirt shyŏch'ŭ 셔츠

shirt sleeves: in his ~ usosŭl pŏtko 웃옷을 벗고

shit F 1 n ttong 똥; (bad quality goods, work) ssŭregi 쓰레기; **I need a ~** hwajangsire kayagessŏ 화장실에 가야겠어 2 v/i yongbyŏnboda 용변보다 3 interj: **~!** chegiral! 제기랄!

shitty F chinjŏlmŏri nanŭn 진절머리 나는

shiver v/i ttŏlda 떨다

shock 1 n ch'unggyŏk 충격; ELEC shyok'ŭ 쇼크; **be in ~** MED ch'unggyŏgesŏ pŏsŏnaji mot'ada 충격에서 벗어나지 못하다 2 v/t nollage hada 놀라게 하다; **be ~ed by** ch'unggyŏgŭl pat-tta 충격을 받다

shock absorber MOT wanch'unggi 완충기

shocking ch'unggyŏktchŏgin 충격적인; F (very bad) chidok'i choch'i anйn 지독히 좋지 않은

shoddy goods p'umjiri nappйn 품질이 나쁜; behavior such'isйroun 수치스러운

shoe shinbal 신발

shoelace shinbalkkйn 신발끈; **shoestore** shinbalkkage 신발가게; **shoestring; do X on a ~** Xйl/rйl aju chŏgйn yesanйro hada x을/를 아주 적은 예산으로 하다

♦ **shoo away** shwitsori naeŏ tchoch'abŏrida 쉿소리 내어 쫓아버리다

shoot 1 n BOT ŏrin-gaji 어린가지 2 v/t ssoda 쏘다; (and kill) ch'ongsarhada 총살하다; movie ch'waryŏnghada 촬영하다; **~ X in the leg** Xйi tarirйl ssoda X의 다리를 쏘다 3 v/i ch'ongйl ssoda 총을 쏘다

♦ **shoot down** airplane ssoa ttŏrŏttйrida 쏘아 떨어뜨리다; suggestion kŏjŏrhada 거절하다

♦ **shoot off** (rush off) taranada 달아나다

♦ **shoot up** (of prices) ch'isot-tta 치솟다; (of children) ssukssuk charada 쑥쑥 자라다; (of buildings etc) tanshigane chiŏjida 단시간에 지어지다; (of new suburbs) pulssuk saenggida 불쑥 생기다

shooting star yusŏng 유성

shop 1 n sangjŏm 상점; **talk ~** il iyagiman hada 일 이야기만 하다 2 v/i shijangboda 시장보다; **go ~ping** changborŏ kada 장보러 가다

shopkeeper somaesang-in 소매상인

shoplifter somaech'igi 소매치기

shopper shyop'inghanйn saram 쇼핑하는 사람

shopping (activity) shyop'ing 쇼핑;

(items) chang pon mulgŏn 장 본 물건; **do one's ~** changboda 장보다

shopping mall shyop'ingssent'ŏ 쇼핑센터

shop steward nodongjohabйi chiktchangwiwŏn 노동조합의 직장위원

shore mulkka 물가; **on ~** (not at sea) yukssang-e(sŏ) 육상에(서)

short 1 adj (in height) k'iga chagйn 키가 작은; road, distance tchalbйn 짧은; (in time) oraedoeji anйn 오래되지 않은; **be ~ of** mojarada 모자라다 2 adv: **cut a vacation/meeting ~** hyugarйl/hoeйirйl yejŏngboda ppalli kkйnnaeda 휴가를/회의를 예정보다 빨리 끝내다; **stop a person ~** sarami marhanйn kŏsйl kkйnŏborida 사람이 말하는 것을 끊어버리다; **go ~ of** chogйm mojarйge chinaeda 조금 모자르게 지내다; **in ~** yoyak'amyŏn 요약하면

shortage pujok 부족

short circuit n tallak 단락; **shortcoming** kyŏltchŏm 결점; **shortcut** chirйmkkil 지름길

shorten v/t dress, vacation, workday etc churida 줄이다; hair tchalkke hada 짧게 하다; **~ a movie** yŏnghwaйi pullyang-йl churida 영화의 분량을 줄이다

shortfall pujok 부족; **shorthand** n sok-kki 속기; **shortlist** n (of candidates) ch'oejong myŏngdan 최종 명단; **short-lived** tanmyŏnghan 단명한

shortly (soon) kot 곧; **~ before that** kй chŏne paro 그 전에 바로

shorts panbaji 반바지; (underwear) sogot 속옷

shortsighted kйnshiйi 근시의; fig kйnshianjŏgin 근시안적인; **shortsleeved** panp'arйi 반팔의; **shortstaffed** chigwŏni mojaranйn 직원이 모자라는; **short story** tanp'yŏnsosŏl 단편소설; **short-tempered** sŏnggйp'an 성급한; **short-term** tangigan 단기간; **short time: be on ~** (of workers) choŏp tanch'uk'ada 조업 단축하다; **short wave** tanp'a

...파

...ot (*from gun*) ch'ongssori 총소리;
(*photograph*) sajin 사진; (*injection*)
...husa 주사; **be a good/poor ~**
...h'ong-ŭl chal/mot ssonŭn saramida
총을 잘/못 쏘는 사람이다; **like a ~**
...ccept, run off ch'ong-algatchi
총알같이

...otgun yŏpch'ong 엽총
...ould haeya hada haeyŏ 하다; **what ~
do?** nanŭn musŭn irŭl haeya
...amnikka? 나는 무슨 일을 해야
...니까?; **you ~n't do that**
...angshinŭn kŭrŏk'e hamyŏn
...ndoemnida 당신은 그렇게 하면
...됩니다; **that ~ be enough** kŭgŏllo
...충분하겠죠; **you ~ have heard him!**
...ŏnŭn kŭga ttŏdŭnŭn kŏl turossŏya
...aessŏ! 너는 그가 떠드는 걸
...었어야 했어!
...oulder n ŏkkae 어깨
...oulder blade kyŏngapkkol 견갑골
...out 1 n pimyŏngsori 비명소리 2 v/i
...orich'ida 소리치다 3 v/t order
...nyŏngnyŏnghada 명령하다
...hout at ...e taego sorijirŭda ...에
...대고 소리지르다
...outing n sorijirŭm 소리지름
...ove 1 n ttemilgi 떼밀기 2 v/t
...mirŏnaeda 밀어내다 3 v/t milda 밀다
...hove in v/i (*in line-up*)
...aech'igihada 새치기하다
...hove off v/i F (*go away*) ka pŏrida
...가 버리다
...ovel n sap 삽
...ow 1 n THEA, TV shyo 쇼; (*display*)
...p'yohyŏn 표현; **on ~** (*at exhibition*)
...hŏnshi chung-in 전시 중인; **it's all
...done for ~** pej kŭgŏ shyohanŭn
...kŏeyo 그거 쇼하는 거에요 2 v/t
...passport, ticket poyŏjuda 보여주다;
...nterest, emotion nat'anaeda
...나타내다; (*at exhibition*)
...hŏnshihada 전시하다; *movie*
...sangyŏnghada 상영하다; **~ X to Y**
...Xrŭl Yege poyŏjuda X를 Y에게
...보여주다 3 v/i (*be visible*) poida
...보이다; (*of movie*) sangyŏngdoeda
...상영되다
show off 1 v/t *skills* parhwihada

발휘하다 2 v/i pej uttchuldaeda
우쭐대다
♦ **show up 1** v/t *shortcomings etc*
hwagyŏnhi poyŏjuda 확연히
보여주다; **don't show me up in
public** saramdŭl ap'esŏ narŭl
tanghwanghage haji maseyo 사람들
앞에서 나를 당황하게 하지 마세요
2 v/i (*arrive*) nat'anada 나타나다; (*be
visible*) poyŏjida 보여지다
show business shyo pijŭnisŭ 쇼
비즈니스
showdown han p'an taegyŏl 한 판
대결
shower 1 n (*of rain*) sonagi 소나기;
(*to wash*) shyawŏ 샤워; **take a ~**
shyawŏhada 샤워하다 2 v/i
shyawŏhada 샤워하다 3 v/t: **~ X with
compliments/praise** Xege
ch'ansarŭl/ch'ingch'anŭl p'ŏbut-tta
X에게 찬사를/칭찬을 퍼붓다
shower bath shyawŏ 샤워; **shower
cap** shyawŏ k'aep 샤워 캡; **shower
curtain** shyawŏ k'ŏt'ŭn 샤워 커튼;
showerproof pangsuŭi 방수의
show jumping chang-aemul
ttwiŏnŏmkki 장애물 뛰어넘기
show-off hŏp'ungjang-i 허풍장이
showroom shyo rum 쇼 룸; **in ~
condition** hanbŏndo sayongdoeji
anŭn 한번도 사용되지 않은
showy *jacket, behavior* nŏmu nune
ttŭinŭn 너무 눈에 띄는
shred 1 n (*of paper etc*) chogak 조각;
(*of evidence etc*) tanp'yŏn 단편 2 v/t
paper kalgari tchijŏbŏrida 갈가리
찢어버리다; (*in cooking*) chogak
naeda 조각 내다
shredder (*for documents*) sŏryu
chŏlttan-gi 서류 절단기
shrewd pint'ŭm ŏmnŭn 빈틈 없는
shriek 1 n pimyŏng 비명 2 v/i
pimyŏngŭl chirŭda 비명을 지르다
shrimp saeu 새우
shrine sŏnggorham 성골함
shrink v/i (*of material*) churŏdŭlda
줄어들다; (*of support etc*)
kamsohada 감소하다
shrink-wrap such'uk p'ojanghada
수축 포장하다
shrink-wrapping such'uk p'ojang

shrivel

584

수축 포장

shrivel tchugŭlgŏrige hada 쭈글거리게 하다

shrub, shrubbery kwanmok 관목

shrug 1 *n* ŏkkaerŭl ŭssŭk-kkŏrim 어깨를 으쓱거림 2 *v/i*: ~ (**one's shoulders**) ŏkkaerŭl ŭssŭk-kkŏrida 어깨를 으쓱거리다

shudder 1 *n* (*of fear, disgust*) momsŏrich'im 몸서리 침; (*of earth etc*) ttŏllim 떨림 2 *v/i* (*with fear, disgust*) momsŏrich'ida 몸서리치다; (*of earth, building*) ttŏllida 떨리다

shuffle 1 *v/t cards* twisŏkkta 뒤섞다 2 *v/i* (*in walking*) chiljil kkŭlmyŏ kada 질질 끌며 가다

shun *person* p'ihada 피하다; *drugs etc* kkŏrida 꺼리다

shut 1 *v/t* tat-tta 닫다 2 *v/i* tatch'ida 닫히다; **the shop was** ~ kagega munŭl tadat-tta 가게가 문을 닫았다

♦ **shut down** 1 *v/t business* p'yeŏp'ada 폐업하다; *computer* chongnyonaeda 종료시키다 2 *v/i* (*of business*) p'yeŏp'ada 폐업하다; (*of computer*) chongnyohada 종료하다

♦ **shut up** *v/i* (*be quiet*) choyonghi hada 조용히 하다; ~! choyonghi hae! 조용히 해!

shutter (*on window*) tŏnmun 덧문; PHOT shyŏt'ŏ 셔터

shuttle *v/i* wangbok'ada 왕복하다

shuttlebus (*at airport*) shyŏt'ŭlppŏsŭ 셔틀버스; **shuttlecock** SP paedŭmint'ŏn kong 배드민턴 공; **shuttle service** shyŏt'ŭl sŏbisŭ 셔틀 서비스

shy *person* sujubŏhanŭn 수줍어하는; *animal* sunhan 순한

shyness sujubŭm 수줍음; (*of animal*) sunham 순함

Siamese twins shyam ssangdung-i 샴 쌍둥이

sick ap'ŭn 아픈; *sense of humor* pulk'waehan 불쾌한; *society* kuyŏkchil nanŭn 구역질 나는; **I'm going to be** ~ (*vomit*) t'ohallaeyo 토할래요; **be** ~ **of** (*fed up with*) chigyŏpta 지겹다

sicken 1 *v/t* (*disgust*) yŏk-kkyŏwŏ hada 역겨워 하다 2 *v/i*: **be** ~**ing for**

chŭngsangŭl poida 증상을 보이다

sickening pulk'waehan 불쾌한

sickle wŏnhyŏng nat 원형 낫

sick leave pyŏngga 병가; **be on** ~ pyŏngga chung-ida 병가 중이다

sickly *person* pyŏngyak'an 병약한; *color* hyŏlssaegi nappŭn 혈색이 나[

sickness pyŏng 병

side *n* (*of box, house*) yŏmmyŏn 옆[(*of room, field*) ch'ungmyŏn 측면; (*of mountain*) kyŏngsa-myŏn 경사[(*of person*) yŏpkkuri 옆구리; SP t'ir 팀; **take** ~**s** (*favor one side*) p'yŏn tŭlda 편을 들다; **take** ~**s with** ...이 p'yŏnŭl tŭlda ...의 편을 들다; **I'm on your** ~ tangshin p'yŏniyeyo 당신 편이에요; ~ **by** ~ naranhi 나란히; **at the** ~ **of the road** kilkkae(sŏ) 길가에(서); **on the big** / **small** ~ k'ŭn / chagŭn p'yŏn 큰 / 작은 편

♦ **side with** chijihada 지지하다

sideboard ch'antchang 찬장; **side dish** panch'an 반찬; **side effect** pujagyong buc'ŏk-yong 부작용; **sidelight** MOT ch'ap'oktttŭng 차폭등; **sideline** 1 *n* puŏp 부업 2 *v/t*: **feel** ~**d** panggwanjach'ŏrŏm nŭkkida 방관자처럼 느끼다; **side street** kolmok-kkil 골목길; **sidetrack** *v/t* ...ŭi chuŭirŭl tollida ...의 주의를 돌리다; **he got** ~**ed into talking about politics again** kŭnŭn tto tashi yŏpkkilo ppajyŏ chŏngch'ie taehae iyagihaet-tta 그는 또 다시 옆길로 빠져 정치에 대해 이야기했다; **sidewalk** indo 인도; **sidewalk café** noch'ŏn k'ap'e 노천 카페; **sideways** *adv* yŏp'ŭro 옆으로; **siege** p'owi konggyŏk 포위 공격; **lay** ~ **to** p'owi konggyŏk'ada 포위 공격하다

sieve *n* ch'e 체

sift *v/t corn, ore* ch'ero ch'ida 체로 치다; *data* kŏllŏnaeda 걸러내다

♦ **sift through** *details, data* chosahay kŏllŏnaeda 조사하여 걸러내다

sigh 1 *n* hansum 한숨; **heave a** ~ **of relief** andoŭi hansumŭl shwida 안도의 한숨을 쉬다 2 *v/i* hansum chit-tta 한숨 짓다

sight *n* kwanggyŏng 광경; (*power of*

seeing) shiryŏk 시력; **~s** (*of city*) kyŏnggwan 경관; **catch ~ of** ...ŭl/rŭl ŏnttŭt poda ...을/를 언뜻 보다; **know by ~** ŏlgulloman alda 얼굴로만 알다; **within ~ of** ...i/ga poinŭn kose(sŏ) ...이/가 보이는 곳에(서); **out of ~** poiji annŭn 보이지 않는; **what a ~ you are!** ne kkori pol manhaguna! 네 꼴이 볼 만하구나!; **lose ~ of** main objective etc ...ŭl/rŭl ijŏbŏrida ...을/를 잊어버리다

◆**sightseeing** kwan-gwang 관광; **go ~** kwan-gwanghada 관광하다

sightseeing tour kwan-gwang yŏhaeng 관광 여행

sightseer kwan-gwanggaek 관광객

sign 1 *n* (*indication*) kimi 기미; (*road ~*) p'yojip'an 표지판; (*outside shop, on building*) kanp'an 간판; **it's a ~ of the times** yojŭm shidaega kŭrŏssŭmnida 요즘 시대가 그렇습니다 **2** *v/t & v/i* sŏmyŏnghada 서명하다

◆**sign up** (*join the army*) ipttaehada 입대하다

signal 1 *n* shinho 신호; **be sending out all the right/wrong ~s** wanjŏnhi parŭn/kŭrŭt-tten insang-ŭl chuda 완전히 바른/그릇된 인상을 주다 **2** *v/i* (*of driver*) shinhohada 신호하다

signatory sŏmyŏng-in 서명인

signature sŏmyŏng 서명

signature tune t'ema ŭmak 테마 음악

significance chungnyosŏng 중요성

significant *event etc* chungdaehan 중대한; (*quite large*) sangdanghan 상당한

signify ŭimihada 의미하다

sign language suhwa 수화

signpost kyot'ong p'yojip'an 교통 표지판

silence 1 *n* koyo 고요; (*of person*) ch'immuk 침묵; **in ~** *work, march* choyonghage 조용하게; **~!** choyonghi! 조용히! **2** *v/t* ch'immukshik'ida 침묵시키다

silencer (*on gun*) pang-ŭm changch'i 방음 장치

silent choyonghan 조용한; *forest* koyohan 고요한; *machine, suffering* sori ŏmnŭn 소리 없는; *movie* musŏng-ŭi 무성의; *stay ~* (*not comment*) ch'immugŭl chik'ida 침묵을 지키다

silent partner ingmyŏng tong-ŏptcha 익명 동업자

silhouette *n* shilluet 실루엣

silicon shillik'on 실리콘

silicon chip shillik'on ch'ip 실리콘 칩

silk 1 *n* pidan 비단 **2** *adj shirt etc* pidanŭi 비단의

Silla Silla 신라

silly ŏrisŏgŭn 어리석은

silver 1 *n* ŭn 은 **2** *adj ring* ŭnŭi 은의; *hair* ŭnppich'ŭi 은빛의

silver medal ŭnmedal 은메달

silver-plated ŭn togŭmhan 은 도금한

similar pisŭt'an 비슷한

similarity yusa 유사

simmer *v/i* (*in cooking*) sŏsŏhi kkŭltta 서서히 끓다; (*with rage*) pugŭlbugŭl hwaga kkŭlt'a 부글부글 화가 끓다

◆**simmer down** ch'imch'ak'aejida 침착해지다

simple (*easy*) shwiun 쉬운; (*not very bright*) tansunhan 단순한

simplicity kanttanham 간단함

simplify tansunhwahada 단순화하다

simplistic chinach'ige tansunhwadoen 지나치게 단순화된

simply (*absolutely*) chŏngmal 정말; (*in a simple way*) kanttanhage 간단하게; **it is ~ the best** tumal hal kŏt ŏpsshi ch'oegoimnida 두말 할 것 없이 최고입니다

simulate hyungnaenaeda 흉내내다

simultaneous tongshiŭi 동시의

simultaneously tongshie 동시에

sin 1 *n* choe 죄 **2** *v/i* choe chit-tta 죄 짓다

since 1 *prep* ihuro 이후로; **~ last week** chinan chu ihuro 지난 주 이후로 **2** *adv* iraero 이래로; **I haven't seen him ~** iraero kŭrŭl pon chŏgi ŏptta 이래로 그를 본 적이 없다 **3** *conj* (*expressions of time*) ...han hue ...한 후에; (*seeing that*) ...hagi ttaemune ...하기 때문에; **~**

you left nega ttŏnan hue 네가 떠난 후에; **~ you don't like it** nega kŭgŏsŭl sirŏhagi ttaemune 네가 그것을 싫어하기 때문에

sincere sŏngshirhan 성실한

sincerely chinshimŭro 진심으로; **hope** chinshillo 진실로

sincerity sŏngshil 성실

sinful choega innŭn 죄가 있는

sing v/t & v/i noraehada 노래하다

Singapore Shinggap'orŭ 싱가포르

Singaporean 1 adj Shinggap'orŭŭi 싱가포르의 **2** n (person) Shinggap'orŭin 싱가포르인

singe v/t kŭllida 그을리다

singer kasu 가수

single 1 adj (sole) hana 하나; (not double) han kyŏp 한 겹; (not married) toksshinja 독신자; **there wasn't a ~ ...** tan hanaŭi ...to ŏpssŏt-tta 단 하나의 ...도 없었다; **in ~ file** chul chiŏ chul chiŏ 줄 지어 **2** n MUS singgŭlp'an 싱글판; **~s** (in tennis) tanshik tanshik 단식

♦ **single out** (choose) sŏnbarhada 선발하다; (distinguish) kubyŏrhada 구별하다

single-breasted oejul tanch'uŭi 외줄 단추의; **single-handed 1** adj tandogŭi tandogŭi 단독의 **2** adv honjasŏ 혼자서; **single-minded** chŏnnyŏmhanŭn 전념하는; **single mother** p'yŏnmo 편모; **single parent family** p'yŏnbumo sŭrhaŭi kajŏng 편부모 슬하의 가정

singular GRAM **1** adj tansuŭi 단수의 **2** n tansu 단수; **in the ~** tansuro 단수로

sinister sky, look etc pulgirhae poinŭn 불길해 보이는; person saak'an 사악한

sink 1 n shingk'ŭ 싱크 **2** v/i (of ship, object) karaantta 가라앉다; (of sun) chida 지다; (of interest rates etc) churŏdŭlda 줄어들다; **he sank onto the bed** kŭnŭn ch'imdaee p'ulssŏk tŭrŏnuwŏt-tta 그는 침대에 풀썩 드러누웠다 **3** v/t ship karaanch'ida 가라앉히다; funds t'ujahada 투자하다

♦ **sink in** (of liquid) ppajida 빠지다; **it still hasn't really sunk in** yŏjŏnhi

hyŏnshillo padadŭryŏjiji anayo 여전히 현실로 받아들여지지 않아요

sinner choein 죄인

sinusitis MED ch'ungnongtchŭng 축농증

sip 1 n holtchak-kkŏrim 홀짝거림 **2** v/i holtchak-kkŏrida 홀짝거리다

sir sŏnsaengnim 선생님; **excuse me, ~** shillyehamnida실례합니다

siren sairen 사이렌

sirloin soŭi hŏri witbubun kogi 소의 허리 윗부분 고기

sister yŏja hyŏngje 여자 형제

sister-in-law (elder brother's wife) hyŏngsu 형수; (wife's younger sister) ch'ŏje 처제; (husband's younger/elder sister) shinui 시누이; (younger/elder brother's wife) olk'e 올케

sit 1 v/i antta 앉다 **2** v/t exam ch'irŭda 치르다

♦ **sit down** antta 앉다

♦ **sit up** (in bed) irŏna antta 일어나 앉다; (straighten back) ttokpparo antta 똑바로 앉다; (wait up at night) chaji ank'o kkaeŏ it-tta 자지 않고 깨어 있다

sitcom shit'ŭk'om 시트콤

site 1 n changso 장소 **2** v/t new offices etc ...ŭi wich'irŭl chŏnghada ...의 위치를 정하다

sitting (of committee, court) kaejŏng 개정; (for artist) moderi toegi 모델이 되기; (for meals) shikssa shigan 식사 시간

sitting room kŏshil 거실

situated: be ~ wich'ihada 위치하다

situation sanghwang 상황; (of building etc) wich'i 위치

six yŏsŏt 여섯, yuk 육

sixteen yŏlyŏsŏt 열 여섯, shimyuk 십육

sixteenth yŏlyŏsŏt pŏntchaeŭi 열 여섯 번째의

sixtieth yesun pŏntchaeŭi 예순 번째의; **~ birthday** hwan-gap 환갑

sixth yŏsŏt pŏntchaeŭi 여섯 번째의

sixty yesun 예순, yukssship 육십

size (of room, car, company) k'ŭgi 크기; (of loan, project) kyumo 규모; (of jacket, shoes) ch'issu 치수

size up p'yŏngkkahada 평가하다

‌‌**zeable** *house* sangdanghi k'ŭn 상당히 큰; *meal, order* kkwae manŭn 꽤 많은

zzle chigŭlgŏrida 지글거리다

‌ate 1 *n* sŭk'eit'ŭ 스케이트 **2** *v/i* sŭk'eit'ŭ t'ada 스케이트 타다

‌ateboard *n* sŭk'eit'ŭbodŭ 스케이트보드

‌ater sŭk'eit'ŭ t'anŭn saram 스케이트 타는 사람

‌ating sŭk'eit'ŭ t'agi 스케이트 타기

‌eleton haegol 해골

‌eleton key kyŏtssoe 곁쇠

‌eptic hoeŭironja 회의론자

‌eptical hoeŭijŏgin 회의적인

‌epticism hoeŭiron 회의론

‌etch 1 *n* sŭk'ech'i 스케치; THEA ch'ŏngŭk 촌극 **2** *v/t* sŭk'ech'ihada 스케치하다

‌etchbook sŭk'ech'ibuk 스케치북

‌etchy *knowledge etc* tanp'yŏntchŏgin 단편적인

‌i 1 *n* sŭk'i 스키 **2** *v/i* sŭk'i t'ada 스키 타다

‌id 1 *n* mikkŭrŏm 미끄럼 **2** *v/i* mikkŭrŏjida 미끄러지다

‌ier sŭk'i t'anŭn saram 스키 타는 사람

‌iing sŭk'i t'agi 스키 타기

‌i lift sŭk'i lip'ŭt'ŭ 스키 리프트

‌ill kisul 기술

‌illed sungnyŏndoen 숙련된

‌illed worker sungnyŏn-gong 숙련공

‌illful nŭngsuk'an 능숙한

‌im *surface* sŭch'idŭt chinagada 스치듯 지나가다

skim off *the best* sŏnch'wihada 선취하다

skim through *text* taech'ung hult'ŏboda 대충 훑어보다

‌immed milk t'alchi uyu 탈지 우유

‌impy *account etc* pinyak'an 빈약한; *little dress* kkwak choenŭn 꽉 죄는

‌in 1 *n* (*of person*) p'ibu 피부; (*of animal*) kajuk 가죽; (*of fish*) kkŏptchil 껍질 **2** *v/t* …ŭi kkŏptchirŭl pŏtkkida …의 껍질을 벗기다

‌in diving sŭk'in taibing 스킨 다이빙

‌inny kkangmarŭn 깡마른

skin-tight mome kkok mannŭn 몸에 꼭 맞는

skip 1 *n* (*little jump*) ttwiŏ orŭm 뛰어 오름 **2** *v/i* kkangch'unggŏrimyŏ ttwiŏdanida 깡충거리며 뛰어다니다 **3** *v/t* (*omit*) ppattŭrida 빠뜨리다

ski pole sŭk'i chip'ang-i 스키 지팡이

skipper NAUT sŏnjang 선장; (*of team*) chujang 주장

skirt *n* ch'ima 치마

ski run sŭk'i hwaltchuro 스키 활주로

ski tow sŭk'it'o 스키토

skull tugaegol 두개골

sky hanŭl 하늘

skylight ch'aegwangch'ang 채광창; **skyline** sŭk'airain 스카이라인; **skyscraper** mach'ŏllu 마천루

slab (*of stone*) sŏkp'an 석판; (*of cake etc*) tut'umhage k'ŭn chogak 두툼하게 큰 조각

slack *discipline, rope* nŭsŭnhan 느슨한; *person, work* pujuŭihan 부주의한; *period* pulgyŏnggiŭi 불경기의

slacken *v/t rope* nŭsŭnhage hada 느슨하게 하다; *pace* nŭtch'uda 늦추다

♦ **slacken off** *v/i* (*of trading*) yak'wadoeda 약화되다; (*of pace*) nŭtch'uŏjida 늦추어지다

slacks paji 바지

slam 1 *v/t door* k'wang tat-tta 쾅 닫다 **2** *v/i* (*of door etc*) k'wang tach'ida 쾅 닫히다

♦ **slam down** t'ŏlssŏk naeryŏnot'a 털썩 내려놓다

slander 1 *n* chungsang 중상 **2** *v/t* chungsanghada 중상하다

slang sogŏ 속어; (*of a specific group*) ŭnŏ 은어

slant *v/i* kiulda 기울다 **2** *n* kyŏngsa 경사; (*given to a story*) kwantchŏm 관점

slanting *roof* pisŭdŭmhan 비스듬한; *eyes* ch'ik'yŏ ollagan 치켜 올라간

slap 1 *n* (*blow*) ch'igi 치기 **2** *v/t* ch'alssak ttaerida 찰싹 때리다

slash 1 *n* (*cut*) pegi 베기 2 *v/t skin etc* naeribeda 내리베다; *prices, costs* sak-kkamhada 삭감하다; ~

one's wrists tongmaegŭl peda 동맥을 베다

slate *n* sŭlleit'ŭ 슬레이트

slaughter 1 *n* (*of animals*) tosal 도살; (*of people, troops*) haksal 학살 **2** *v/t animals* tosarhada 도살하다; *people, troops* haksarhada 학살하다

slave *n* noye 노예

slay sarhaehada 살해하다

slaying (*murder*) sarhae 살해

sleazy *bar, character* t'arak'an 타락한

sled(ge) *n* ssŏlmae 썰매

sledge hammer taehyŏng mangch'i 대형 망치

sleep 1 *n* cham 잠; **go to ~** chami tŭlda 잠이 들다; **I need a good ~** ch'ungbunhage chaya haeyo 충분히 자야 해요; **I couldn't get to ~** chal suga ŏpssŏssŏyo 잘 수가 없었어요 **2** *v/i* chada 자다

♦ **sleep on** *v/t proposal, decision* ch'ungbunhi saenggak'ada 충분히 생각하다

♦ **sleep with** (*have sex with*) …wa/kwa kach'i chada …와/과 같이 자다

sleeping bag sŭllip'ing paek 슬리핑 백; **sleeping car** ch'imdaech'a 침대차; **sleeping pill** sumyŏnje 수면제

sleepless *night* cham mot irunŭn jam 못 이루는 잠

sleepwalker mongnyuppyŏngja 몽유병자

sleepy *yawn* chollin 졸린; *town* choyonghan 조용한; **I'm ~** chollyŏyo 졸려요

sleet *n* ssaragi nun 싸라기 눈

sleeve (*of jacket etc*) somae 소매

sleeveless somaega ŏmnŭn 소매가 없는

sleight of hand kamtchok-kkat'ŭn sonnollim 감쪽같은 손놀림

slender *figure, arms* kanyalp'ŭn 가냘픈; *chance* hŭibak'an 희박한; *income, margin* ŏlma andoenŭn 얼마 안되는

slice 1 *n* (*of bread, tart*) chogak 조각; (*of profits etc*) pubun 부분 **2** *v/t loaf etc* yalke charŭda 얇게 자르다

sliced bread challanoŭn ppang 잘라놓은 빵

slick 1 *adj performance* nŭngsuk'an 능숙한; *pej* (*cunning*) kyomyohan 교묘한 **2** *n* (*of oil*) mak 막

slide 1 *n* (*for kids*) mikkurŏmt'ŭl 미끄럼틀; PHOT sŭllaidŭ 슬라이드 **2** *v/i* mikkŭrojida 미끄러지다; (*of exchange rate etc*) ttŏrŏjida 떨어지다 **3** *v/t* mirŏnŏt'a 밀어넣다

sliding door midaji mun 미닫이 문

slight 1 *adj person, figure* kanyalp'ŭ 가냘픈; *difference etc* yakkanŭi 약간의; **no, not in the ~est** anio, chogŭmdo animnida 아니오. 조금도 아닙니다 **2** *n* (*insult*) moyok 모욕

slightly yakkan 약간

slim 1 *adj* nalsshinhan 날씬한; *chanc* hŭibak'an 희박한 **2** *v/i* sal ppaeda 살 빼다

slime kkŭnjŏk-kkŭnjŏk'an kŏt 끈적끈적한 것

slimy *liquid* chilch'ŏk'an 질척한; *person* allanggŏrinŭn 알랑거리는

sling 1 *n* (*for arm*) samgak-kkŏn 삼각건 **2** *v/t* (*throw*) tŏnjida 던지다

slip 1 *n* (*on ice etc*) mikkŭrŏjim 미끄러짐; (*mistake*) shilssu 실수; *a* **of paper** chagŭn chong-i 작은 종이 *a* ~ **of the tongue** shirŏn 실언; **give s.o. the ~** nugurŭl ttadollida 누구를 따돌리다 **2** *v/i* (*on ice etc*) mikkŭrŏjida 미끄러지다; (*of quality etc*) chŏhadoeda 저하되다; **he ~ped out of the room** kŭnŭn saltchak pangŭl nagat-tta 그는 살짝 방을 나갔다 **3** *v/t* (*put*) saltchak not'a 살짝 놓다; **he ~ped it into his briefcas** kŭnŭn sŏryugabang-e kŭgŏsŭl salmyŏshi nŏŏt-tta 그는 서류가방에 그것을 살며시 넣었다

♦ **slip away** (*of time*) sunshik-kkane chinagada 순식간에 지나가다; (*of opportunity*) kŭnyang sarajida 그냥 사라지다; (*die quietly*) choyonghi sesang-ŭl ttŭda 조용히 세상을 뜨다

♦ **slip off** *v/t jacket etc* pŏt-tta 벗다

♦ **slip out** *v/i* (*go out*) ppajyŏ nagada 빠져 나가다

♦ **slip up** *v/i* (*make mistake*) shilssuhada 실수하다

slipped disc ch'uganp'an 추간판

lipper süllip'ŏ 슬리퍼

lippery mikkŏroun 미끄러운

lipshod kkomkkomhaji anün 꼼꼼하지 않은

lit 1 *n* (*tear*) tchijŏjin kot 찢어진 곳; (*hole*) kumŏng 구멍; (*in skirt*) kilge t'ŭn kot 길게 튼 곳 **2** *v/t* tchijŏ yŏlda 찢어 열다; *throat* peda 베다

lither *v/i* mikkŭrŏjida 미끄러지다

lobber *v/i* kunch'im hüllida 군침 흘리다

logan süllogŏn 슬로건

lop *v/t* ppurida 뿌리다

lope 1 *n* (*of roof*) kyŏngsa 경사; (*of handwriting*) kiulgi 기울기; (*of mountain*) kisŭk 기슭; **built on a ~** kisŭlge sewŏjin 기슭에 세워진 **2** *v/i* kyŏngsajida 경사지다; **the road ~s down to the sea** kiri padatchogŭro kyŏngsajyŏ it-tta 길이 바다쪽으로 경사져 있다

loppy *work* pujuŭihan 부주의한; (*in dress*) tangjŏngch'i mot'an 단정치 못한; (*too sentimental*) chinach'ige kamsangjŏgin 지나치게 감상적인

loshed F (*drunk*) sul ch'wihan 술 취한

lot *n* t'ŭmsae 틈새; (*in schedule*) tcham 짬, piŏinnŭn shigan 비어있는 시간

♦ **slot in 1** *v/t* kkiuda 끼우다 **2** *v/i* kkiwŏjida 끼워지다

slot machine (*for vending*) chap'an-gi 자판기; (*for gambling*) süllot mŏshin 슬롯 머신

slouch *v/i* momŭl kuburida 몸을 구부리다

slovenly tanjŏngch'i mot'an 단정치 못한

slow nürin 느린; *be ~* (*of clock*) nürida 느리다

♦ **slow down 1** *v/t* nürige hada 느리게 하다 **2** *v/i* nüryŏjida 느려지다

slowdown (*in production*) t'aeŏp 태업

slow motion: in ~ nürin tongjagŭro 느린 동작으로

slug *n* (*animal*) mindalp'aeng-i 민달팽이

sluggish *pace* nürin 느린; *river* wanmanhan 완만한; *start* hwalbarhaji mot'an 활발하지 못한

slum *n* pinmin-ga 빈민가

slump 1 *n* (*in trade*) pulgyŏnggi 불경기 **2** *v/i* (*of economy*) soet'oehada 쇠퇴하다; (*collapse: of person*) ssürŏjida 쓰러지다

slur 1 *n* (*on s.o.'s character*) pibang 비방 **2** *v/t* *words* punmyŏnghaji ank'e marhada 분명하지 않게 말하다

slurred *speech* parŭmi punmyŏngch'i anŭn 발음이 분명치 않은

slush nok-kki shijak'an nun 녹기 시작한 눈; *pej* (*sentimental stuff*) nunmul tchage hanŭn kŏt 눈물 짜게 하는 것

slush fund pijagŭm 비자금

slut p'umhaeng-i nappŭn yŏja 품행이 나쁜 여자

sly kyohwarhan 교활한; *on the ~* nam mollae saltchak 남 몰래 살짝

smack 1 *n* sonppadagŭro han tae ttaerigi 손바닥으로 한 대 때리기 **2** *v/t* *child, bottom* sonppadagŭro ch'alssak ttaerida 손바닥으로 찰싹 때리다

small 1 *adj* (*in size*) chagŭn 작은; (*in amount*) chŏgŭn 적은 **2** *n:* **the ~ of the back** hŏri tüngtchogŭi chilluk'an pubun 허리 등쪽의 질룩한 부분

small change chandon 잔돈; **small hours** shimnya 심야; **smallpox** ch'ŏnyŏndu 천연두; **small print** (*on a contract*) sebu chohang 세부 조항; **small talk** chapttam 잡담

smart 1 *adj* (*elegant*) mŏtchin 멋진; (*intelligent*) ttokttok'an 똑똑한; *pace* sangdanghi pparün 상당히 빠른; *get ~ with* (*fresh*) …ege kŏnbangjige kulda …에게 건방지게 굴다 **2** *v/i* (*hurt*) ssushida 쑤시다

smart card chŏnja k'adŭ 전자 카드

♦ **smarten up** *v/t* malssuk'age hada 말쑥하게 하다

smash 1 *n* (*noise*) pusŏjinŭn sori 부서지는 소리; (*car crash*) ch'ungdol 충돌; (*in tennis*) sŭmaeshi 스매시 **2** *v/t* (*break*) pusuda 부수다; (*hit hard*) kangt'ahada 강타하다; *~ X to pieces* Xül / rül sansanjogak naeda

X을/를 산산조각 내다 **3** *v/i* (*break*)
pusŏjida 부서지다; *the driver ~ed
into ...* unjŏnjanŭn ...e
ch'ungdorhaet-tta 운전자는 ...에
충돌했다

smash hit F taehit'ŭ 대히트

smashing F kkŭnnaejunŭn 끝내주는

smattering (*of a language*) ŏsŏlp'ŭn
shillyŏk 어설픈 실력

smear 1 *n* (*of ink etc*) ŏlluk 얼룩; MED
tomal p'yobon kŏmsa 도말 표본
검사; (*on character*) otchŏm 오점
2 *v/t paint etc* parŭda 바르다;
character tŏrŏp'ida 더럽히다

smear campaign chungsang moryak
중상 모략

smell 1 *n* naemsae 냄새; *sense of ~*
hugak 후각 **2** *v/t* ...ŭi naemsaerŭl
mat-tta ...의 냄새를 맡다 **3** *v/i*
(*unpleasantly*) naemsaega nada
냄새가 나다; (*sniff*) naemsaerŭl mat-
tta 냄새를 맡다; *what does it ~ of?*
ŏttŏn naemsaega nanŭndeyo? 어떤
냄새가 나는데요? *you ~ of beer*
tangshinhant'esŏ maektchu
naemsaega nayo 당신한테서 맥주
냄새가 나요

smelly naemsae nanŭn 냄새 나는

smile 1 *n* miso 미소 **2** *v/i* misojit-tta
미소짓다

♦ **smile at** ...ege misojit-tta ...에게
미소짓다

smirk 1 *n* nŭnggŭlmajŭn usŭm
능글맞은 웃음 **2** *v/i* nŭnggŭlmatkke
ut-tta 능글맞게 웃다

smog sŭmogŭ 스모그

smoke 1 *n* yŏn-gi 연기; *have a ~*
tambaerŭl p'iuda 담배를 피우다 **2** *v/t*
cigarettes p'iuda 피우다; *bacon*
hunjehada 훈제하다 **3** *v/i* yŏn-giga
nada 연기가 나다; *I don't ~* chŏn,
tambaerŭl p'iuji anayo 전, 담배를
피우지 않아요

smoker (*person*) hŭbyŏnja 흡연자

smoking hŭbyŏn 흡연; *no ~* kŭmyŏn
금연

smoky *air* yŏn-giga chauk'an 연기가
자욱한

smolder (*of fire*) yŏn-giman p'iuda
연기만 피우다; (*with anger*) sogŭro
ssaida 속으로 쌓이다; (*with desire*)

tŭlkkŭlt'a 들끓다

smooth 1 *adj surface, skin, sea*
maekkŭrŏun 매끄러운; *ride*
pudŭroun 부드러운; *transition*
sunjoroun 순조로운; *pej: person*
chinach'ige yejŏl parŭn 지나치게
예절 바른 **2** *v/t hair* ssŭdadŭmda
쓰다듬다

♦ **smooth down** (*with sandpaper etc*)
pudŭrŏpkke mandŭlda 부드럽게
만들다

♦ **smooth out** *paper, cloth* p'yŏda
펴다

♦ **smooth over**: *smooth things over*
wŏnmanhage haegyŏrhada 원만하게
해결하다

smother *flames* tŏp'ŏ kkŭda 덮어
끄다; *person* chilsshik shik'ida 질식
시키다; *~ X with kisses* Xege
k'isŭrŭl p'obut-tta X에게 키스를
퍼붓다

smudge 1 *n* ŏlluk 얼룩 **2** *v/t* tŏrŏp'ida
더럽히다

smug chal nan ch'ehanŭn 잘 난
체하는

smuggle *v/t* milssuhada 밀수하다

smuggler milssuŏptcha 밀수업자

smuggling milssu 밀수

smutty *joke* ŭmnanhan 음란한

snack *n* kanshik 간식

snack bar kani shikttang 간이 식당

snag (*problem*) ttŭt'aji anŭn chang-
ae 뜻하지 않은 장애

snail talp'aeng-i 달팽이

snake *n* paem 뱀

snap 1 *n* ttak'anŭn sori 딱하는 소리;
PHOT sŭnaep sajin 스냅 사진 **2** *v/t*
(*break*) purŏttŭrida 부러뜨리다; (*say
sharply*) ttakttak-kkŏrida 딱딱거리다
3 *v/i* (*break*) purŏjida 부러지다 **4** *adj
decision, judgment* sunshik-kkanŭi
순식간의

♦ **snap up** *bargain* ŏllŭn sada 얼른
사다

snappy *person, mood* sŏngkkŭp'an
성급한; *decision, response*
minch'ŏp'an 민첩한; (*elegant*) uahan
우아한

snapshot sŭnaep sajin 스냅 사진

snarl 1 *n* (*of dog*) ŭrŭrŏnggŏrim
으르렁거림 **2** *v/i* ŭrŭrŏnggŏrida

으르렁거리다

atch 1 v/t chabach'aeda 잡아채다;
(steal) humch'ida 훔치다; (kidnap)
yugoehada 유괴하다 2 v/i
habach'aeda 잡아채다

azzy seryŏdoen 세련된

eak 1 v/t (remove, steal) sŭltchŏk
kajyŏgada 슬쩍 가져가다; ~ **a**
glance at kyŏnnunjirhada
곁눈질하다 2 v/i: ~ **into the**
room/out of the room sŭlgŭmŏni
pang-ŭro tŭrŏgada / pang-esŏ nagada
슬그머니 방으로 들어가다 / 방에서
나가다

eakers undonghwa 운동화

eaking: have a ~ suspicion that
... ...ranŭn ŭishimŭl ŭn-gŭnhi kajida
...라는 의심을 은근히 가지다

eaky F (crafty) kyomyohan 교묘한

eer 1 n piusŭm 비웃음 2 v/i piut-tta
비웃다

eeze 1 n chaech'aegi 재채기 2 v/i
chaech'aegihada 재채기하다

iff 1 v/i (to clear nose) k'orŭl
hultchŏk-kkŏrida 코를 훌쩍거리다;
(to catch scent) k'orŭl
k'ŭngk'ŭnggŏrida 코를 킁킁거리다
2 v/t (smell) k'oro tŭrishwida 코로
들이쉬다

iper chŏgyŏkppyŏng 저격병

itch F 1 n (telltale) kojajiltchaeng-i
고자질쟁이 2 v/i kojajirhada
고자질하다

ob songmul 속물

obbish songmurŭi 속물의

ooker tanggu 당구

snoop around kiutkkŏrimyŏ
toradanida 기웃거리며 돌아다니다

ooty kŏmanhan 거만한

ooze 1 n cholgi 졸기; **have a ~**
cholda 졸다 2 v/i cholda 졸다

ore v/i k'o kolda 코 골다

noring n k'o kolgi 코 골기

norkel sŭnok'ŭl 스노클

nort v/i (of animal) k'otkkimŭl
naeppumtta 콧김을 내뿜다; (of
person: disdainfully) k'otppanggwi
kkwida 콧방귀 뀌다

nout (of pig) chudung-i 주둥이

now 1 n nun 눈 2 v/i nuni naerida
눈이 내리다

♦ **snow under: be snowed under**
with ... ...(ŭ)ro apttodanghada
...(으)로 압도당하다

snowball n nunttŏng-i 눈덩이; **snow-**
bound nune katch'in 눈에 갇힌;
snow chains MOT sŭnou ch'ein
스노우 체인; **snowdrift** ssain
nundŏmi 쌓인 눈더미; **snowdrop**
anemone 아네모네; **snowflake**
nunsong-i 눈송이; **snowman**
nunssaram 눈사람; **snowplow**
chesŏlgi 제설기; **snowstorm**
nunbora 눈보라

snowy weather nuni onŭn 눈이 오는;
roads, hills nuni ssain 눈이 쌓인

snub 1 n naengdae 냉대 2 v/t
naengdaehada 냉대하다

snub-nosed chumŏk k'oŭi 주먹코의

snug anŭk'an 아늑한; (tight-fitting)
kkok mannŭn 꼭 맞는

♦ **snuggle down** p'ogŭnhage momŭl
mut-tta 포근하게 몸을 묻다

♦ **snuggle up to** ...ŭl/rŭl kkŭrŏ antta
...을/를 끌어 안다

so 1 adv nŏmu 너무; ~ **hot/cold**
nŏmu tŏun/ch'uun 너무 더운/추운;
not ~ much nŏmu manch'i ank'e
너무 많지 않게; ~ **much bet-**
ter/easier hwŏlsshin tŏ
choŭn/shwiun 훨씬 더 좋은/쉬운;
eat/drink ~ much nŏmu mani
mŏktta/mashida 너무 많이
먹다/마시다; **I miss you ~** nega
koengjanghi pogo shiptta 네가
굉장히 보고 싶다; ~ **am I/do I** nado
kŭraeyo/kŭrŏk'e haeyo 나도
그래요/그렇게 해요; ~ **is she/does**
she kŭ yŏjado kŭraeyo/kŭrŏk'e
haeyo 그 여자도 그래요/그렇게
해요; **and ~ on** kŭ it'a tŭngdŭng 기타
등등; ~ **what?** kŭraesŏ ŏtchaet-
ttanŭn kŏya? 그래서 어쨌다는 거야?
2 pron: **I hope ~/think ~** kŭrŏk'e
toegil paramnida/kŭrŏk'e
saenggak'amnida 그렇게 되길
바랍니다/그렇게 생각합니다; **you**
didn't tell me - I did = nahant'e
marhaji anassŏ - ani, marhaessŏ
나한테 말하지 않았어 - 아니,
말했어; **50 or ~** oship chŏngdo 오십
정도 3 conj (for that reason)

kŭgŏsŭro inhaesŏ 그것으로 인해서; (*in order that*) kŭraesŏ 그래서; **and ~ I missed the train** kŭraesŏ nanŭn kich'arŭl notch'ŏt-tta 그래서 나는 기차를 놓쳤다; **~ (*that*) I could come too** kŭrŏk'e haesŏ na yŏkssi ol su itssŏtta 그렇게 해서 나 역시 올 수 있었다

soak v/t (*steep*) tamgŭda 담그다; (*of water, rain*) chŏksshida 적시다

◆ **soak up** *liquid* pparadŭrida 빨아들이다

soaked hŭmppŏk chŏjŭn 흠뻑 젖은

so-and-so F (*unknown person*) amugae 아무개; (*annoying person*) shirŭn nom 싫은 놈

soap n (*for washing*) pinu 비누

soap (opera) yŏnsok tŭrama 연속 드라마

soapy *water* pinuŭi 비누의

soar (*of rocket etc*) sosa orŭda 솟아 오르다; (*of prices*) ch'isot-tta 치솟다

sob 1 n hŭnŭkkim 흐느낌 **2** v/i hŭnŭkkyŏ ulda 흐느껴 울다

sober (*not drunk*) ch'wihaji anŭn 취하지 않은; (*serious*) chinjihan 진지한

◆ **sober up** suri kkaeda 술이 깨다

so-called (*referred to as*) lago hanŭn kŏsŭn 라고 하는 것은; *pej* sowi 소위

soccer ch'uk-kku 축구

sociable sagyojŏgin 사교적인

social *adj* sahoeŭi 사회의; (*recreational*) ch'inmogŭi 친목의

socialism sahoejuŭi 사회주의

socialist 1 *adj* sahoejuŭijŏgin 사회주의적인 **2** n sahoejuŭija 사회주의자

socialize saramgwa sagwida 사람과 사귀다

social work sahoe saŏp 사회 사업

social worker sahoe saŏpkka 사회 사업가

society sahoe 사회; (*organization*) tanch'e 단체

sociology sahoehak 사회학

sock[1] (*for wearing*) yangmal 양말

sock[2] n (*punch*) kangt'a 강타 **2** v/t (*punch*) sege ch'ida 세게 치다

socket ELEC sok'et 소켓; (*of eye*) angu 안구; (*of arm*) kwanjŏl 관절

soda (*~ water*) t'ansansu 탄산수; (*ice cream ~*) k'ŭrimsoda 크림소다; (*soft drink*) ch'ŏngnyang ŭmnyo 청량 음료

sofa sop'a 소파

sofa bed sop'ashik ch'imdae 소파식 침대

soft *pillow, chair* p'uksshinhan 푹신한 *voice, music, skin, color* pudŭrŏun 부드러운; *light* onhwahan 온화한; (*lenient*) kwandaehan 관대한; **have a ~ spot for** …ŭl/rŭl koengjanghi choahada …을/를 굉장히 좋아하다

soft drink ch'ŏngnyang ŭmnyo 청량 음료

soften 1 v/t pudŭrŏpkke hada 부드럽게 하다, wanhwahada 완화하다 **2** v/i (*of butter, ice cream*) pudŭrŏwŏjida 부드러워지다

softly pudŭrŏpkke 부드럽게

software sop'ŭt'ŭwŏ 소프트웨어

soggy chŏjŭn 젖은; *pastry* sŏlguwŏjin 설구워진

soil 1 n (*earth*) hŭk 흙 **2** v/t tŏrŏp'ida 더럽히다

solar energy t'aeyang enŏji 태양 에너지

solar panel t'aeyang chŏnjip'an 태양 전지판

soldier kunin 군인

sole[1] n (*of foot, shoe*) padak 바닥

sole[2] *adj* tan hanaŭi 단 하나의

solely ojik 오직

solemn (*serious*) ŏmssuk'an 엄숙한

solid *adj* (*hard*) tandanhan 단단한; (*without holes*) kyŏn-gohan 견고한; *gold, silver* sun 순; (*sturdy*) t'ŭnt'ŭnhan 튼튼한; *evidence* hwakkkohan 확고한; *support* kangnyŏk'an 강력한

solidarity tan-gyŏl 단결

solidify v/i kudŏjida 굳어지다

solitaire (*card game*) sollit'erŭ 솔리테르

solitary *life, activity* kodok'an 고독한 (*single*) tan hanaŭi 단 하나의

solitude kodok 고독

solo 1 n MUS (*of vocalist*) tokch'ang 독창; (*of instrumentalist*) toktchu 독주 **2** *adj* honjaŭi 혼자의

soloist (*vocalist*) tokch'angja 독창자

(*instrumentalist*) toktchuja 독주자

oluble *substance* kayongssŏng-ŭi 가용성의; *problem* haegyŏrhal su innŭn 해결할 수 있는

solution haedap 해답; (*mixture*) honhap 혼합

solve p'ulda 풀다

solvent *adj* (*financially*) chibul nŭngnyŏgi innŭn 지불 능력이 있는

somber (*dark*) kŏmusŭrŭmhan 거무스름한; (*serious*) ch'imurhan 침울한

some 1 *adj* ŏttŏn 어떤, ŏlmaganŭi 얼마간의; *people say that ...* ŏttŏn saramdŭrŭn ... rago malhanda 어떤 사람들은 ...라고 말한다; *would you like ~ water / cookies?* mul / kwaja chom tŭshigessŏyo? 물/과자 좀 드시겠어요? **2** *pron* (*people*) ŏttŏn saramdŭl 어떤 사람들; (*things*) ŏttŏn kŏt 어떤 것; *~ of the group* kŭrubŭi ŏttŏn idŭl 그룹의 어떤 이들; *would you like ~?* chom hashigessŏyo? 좀 하시겠어요? *give me ~* chogŭm chuseyo 조금 주세요 **3** *adv* (*a bit*) chogŭm 조금; *we'll have to wait ~* urin chogŭm kidaryŏya hae 우린 조금 기다려야 해

somebody nugun-ga 누군가

someday ŏnjen-ga 언젠가

somehow (*by one means or another*) ŏttŏk'edŭnji 어떻게든지; (*for some unknown reason*) ŏtchŏnji 어쩐지

someone → **somebody**

someplace → **somewhere**

somersault 1 *n* chaeju nŏmkki 재주 넘기 **2** *v/i* chaeju nŏmtta 재주 넘다

something muŏshin-ga 무엇인가; *would you like ~ to drink / eat?* mashil / ŏgŭl kŏt chom hashigessŏyo? 마실/먹을 것 좀 하시겠어요?; *is ~ wrong?* muŏshi chalmot toeŏssŭmnikka? 무엇이 잘못 되었습니까?

sometime ŏnjen-ga 언젠가; *~ last year* changnyŏn ŏnjen-ga 작년 언젠가

sometimes ttaettaero 때때로

somewhat *adv* ŏdin-gae 어딘가에

somewhere 1 *adv* ŏdin-ga 어딘가에 **2** *pron*: *let's go ~ quiet* ŏdi choyonghan kosŭro kapsshida 어디

조용한 곳으로 갑시다; *is there ~ to park?* ŏdie chuch'ahal koshi issŏyo? 어디 주차할 곳이 있어요?

son adŭl 아들

song norae 노래

songwriter chakssa chak-kkok-kka 작사 작곡가

son-in-law sawi 사위

son of a bitch F kaesaekki 개새끼

soon kot jŏt; *as ~ as ...* haja maja ...하자 마자; *as ~ as possible* kanŭnghan han ppalli 가능한 한 빨리; *~er or later* choman-gan 조만간; *the ~er the better* pparŭmyŏn pparŭlssurok choayo 빠르면 빠를수록 좋아요

soot kŭrŭm 그을음

soothe chinjŏngshik'ida 진정시키다

sophisticated *person*, *tastes* seryŏndoen 세련된; *machine* chŏnggyohan 정교한

sophomore ihangnyŏn 이학년

soprano *n* sop'ŭrano 소프라노

sordid *affair*, *business* tŏrŏun 더러운

sore 1 *adj* (*painful*) ap'ŭn 아픈; F (*angry*) hwaga nan 화가 난; *is it ~?* ap'ayo? 아파요? **2** *n* sangch'ŏ 상처

sorrow *n* sulp'ŭm 슬픔

sorry (*sad*) *day* sŭlp'ŭn 슬픈; *sight* pulssanghan 불쌍한; (*I'm*) ~ (*apologizing*) mianhae 미안해; (*polite*) mianhamnida 미안합니다; (*I'm*) ~ *but I can't help* (*regretting*) mianhajiman, chega toul suga ŏmneyo 미안하지만, 제가 도울 수가 없네요; *I will be ~ to leave Seoul* Sŏurŭl ttŏnani yugamimnida 서울을 떠나니 유감입니다; *I won't be ~ to go home* chŏnŭn chibe kanŭn ke natkkessŏyo 저는 집에 가는 게 낫겠어요; *I feel ~ for her* kŭ yŏjaga andwaetkkunyo 그 여자가 안됐군요

sort 1 *n* chongnyu 종류; *~ of ...* F taso ...다소 ...; *is it finished? ~ ~ of* F kkŭnnassŏyo? - kŭrŏndaeroyo 끝났어요? - 그런대로요 **2** *v/t* pullyuhada 분류하다; COMPUT kubunhada 구분하다

♦ **sort out** *papers* karyŏnaeda 가려내다; *problem* haegyŏrhada 해결하다

so-so adv kŭjŏ kŭrŏn 그저 그런
soul REL yŏnghon 영혼; fig (of a nation etc) chŏngshin 정신; (character) t'ŭkssŏng 특성; (person) saram 사람
sound[1] adj (sensible) punbyŏl innŭn 분별 있는; (healthy) kŏn-ganghan 건강한; **~ sleep** sungmyŏn 숙면
sound[1] 1 n sori 소리 2 v/t (pronounce) parŭmhada 발음하다; MED ch'ŏngjinhada 청진하다; **~ one's horn** kyŏngjŏgŭl ullida 경적을 울리다 3 v/i: **that ~s interesting** chaemiissŭl kŏt kat'ayo 재미있을 것 같아요; **that ~s like a good idea** choŭn saenggak kat'ayo 좋은 생각 같아요; **she ~ed unhappy** kŭ yŏjanŭn purhaenghage tŭllyŏtta 그 여자는 불행하게 들렸다
sound card COMPUT saundŭ k'adŭ 사운드 카드
soundly sleep kip'i 깊이; beaten wanbyŏk'age 완벽하게
soundproof adj pang-ŭmŭi 방음의
soundtrack paegyŏng ŭmak 배경 음악
soup (western) sup'ŭ 수프; (Korean) kuk 국
soup bowl (western) sup'ŭ chŏpsshi 수프 접시; (Korean) kuk kŭrŭt 국 그릇
sour adj apple shin 신; milk sanghan 상한; comment shimsulgujŭn 심술궂은
source n wŏnch'ŏn 원천; (of river) suwŏnji 수원지; (person) chŏngbo chegongja 정보 제공자
south 1 adj namtchogŭi 남쪽의 2 n namtchok 남쪽; (of country) namtchok chibang 남쪽 지방; **to the ~ of** …ŭi namtchoge …의 남쪽에 3 adv namtchogŭro 남쪽으로
South Africa Namap'ŭrik'a 남아프리카; **South African** 1 adj Namap'ŭrik'aŭi 남아프리카의 2 n Namap'ŭrik'ain 남아프리카인; **South America** Nammi 남미; **South American** 1 adj Nammiŭi 남미의 2 n Nammiin 남미인; **southeast** 1 n namdongtchok 남동쪽 2 adj namdongtchogŭi 남동쪽의 3 adv

namdongtchogŭro 남동쪽으로; **it's ~ of** …ŭi namdongtchoge it-tta …의 남동쪽에 있다; **Southeast Asia** Tongnam Ashia 동남 아시아; **Southeast Asian** adj Tongnam Ashiaŭi 동남 아시아의; **southeastern** namdongtchogŭi 남동쪽의
southerly adj namhyang-ŭi 남향의
southern nambuŭi 남부의
South Korea Namhan 남한
South Korean 1 adj Namhanŭi 남한의 2 n (person) Namhanin 남한인
southward adv namtchogŭro 남쪽으로
southwest 1 n namsŏtchok 남서쪽 2 adj namsŏtchogŭi 남서쪽의 3 adv namsŏtchogŭro 남서쪽으로; **it's ~ o** …ŭi namsŏtchoge it-tta …의 남서쪽에 있다
southwestern namsŏtchogŭi 남서쪽의
souvenir n kinyŏmp'um 기념품
sovereign adj state tongnibŭi 독립의
sovereignty (of state) tongnipkkuk 독립국
Soviet Union Soryŏn 소련
sow[1] n (female pig) amt'waeji 암돼지
sow[2] v/t seeds ppurida 뿌리다
soy bean k'ong 콩; **soy milk** tuyu 두유; **soy sauce** kanjang 간장
spa onch'ŏn 온천
space n (atmosphere) uju 우주; (area pin k'an 빈 칸; (room) konggan 공간
♦ **space out** iltchŏnghan kan-gyŏgŭl tuda 일정한 간격을 두다
spacebar COMPUT sŭp'eisŭ pa 스페이스 바; **spacecraft**, **spaceship** ujusŏn 우주선; **space shuttle** uju wangbokssŏn 우주 왕복선; **space station** uju chŏnggŏjang 우주 정거장; **spacesuit** ujubok 우주복
spacious tŭnŏlbŭn 드넓은
spade n sap 삽; **~s** (in card game) sŭp'eidŭ 스페이드
Spain Sŭp'ein 스페인
span v/t (in time, of bridge) kŏlch'ida 걸치다
Spaniard Sŭp'ein saram 스페인 사람
Spanish 1 adj Sŭp'einŭi 스페인의 2 n (language) Sŭp'einŏ 스페인어

spank sonppadaguro ttaerida 손바닥으로 때리다

spare 1 v/t money pillida 빌리다; *time* naeda 내다; (*do without*) ŏpsshi chinaeda 없이 지내다; *can you ~ the time?* shiganŭl nael su issŏyo? 시간을 낼 수 있어요?; *there were 5 to ~* 5kaega nama issŏssŏyo 5개가 남아 있었어요 **2** adj yebiŭi 예비의 **3** n (*part*) yebip'um 예비품 **spare ribs** kalbi 갈비; **spare room** yebi pang 예비 방; **spare time** namnŭn shigan 남는 시간; **spare tire** MOT yebi t'aiŏ 예비 타이어; **spare wheel** yebi pak'wi 예비 바퀴

spark n pulkkot 불꽃

sparkle v/i pinnada 빛나다

sparkling wine shyamp'ein 샴페인

spark plug chŏmhwajŏn 점화전

sparrow ch'amsae 참새

sparse vegetation sanjaehanŭn 산재하는

sparsely: *~ populated* in-guga hŭibak'an 인구가 희박한

spatter v/t mud, paint t'wigida 튀기다

speak 1 v/i marhada 말하다; (*make a speech*) yŏnsŏlhada 연설하다; *we're not ~ing (to each other)* urinŭn sŏro maldo anhaeyo 우리는 서로 말도 안해요; *~ing* TELEC chŏndeyo 전데요 **2** v/t foreign language marhada 말하다; *~ one's mind* songmaŭmŭl t'ŏnot'a 속마음을 터놓다

speak for ...ŭl/rŭl taep'yohada ...을/를 대표하다

♦ **speak out** kŏrikkimŏpsshi marhada 거리낌없이 말하다

♦ **speak up** (*speak louder*) k'ŭn soriro marhada 큰 소리로 말하다

speaker (*at conference*) yŏnsŏltcha 연설자; (*orator*) ungbyŏn-ga 웅변가; (*of sound system*) sŭp'ik'ŏ 스피커

spearmint sŭp'iamint'ŭ 스피아민트

special t'ŭkpyŏrhan 특별한; (*particular*) t'ŭktchŏnghan 특정한

specialist chŏnmun-ga 전문가

specialize (*of company*) chŏnmunŭnro hada 전문으로 하다; (*of student*) chŏn-gonghada 전공하다; *~ in* (*of company*)

...ŭl/rŭl chŏnmunŭnro hada ...을/를 전문으로 하다; (*of student*) ...ŭl/rŭl chŏn-gonghada ...을/를 전공하다

specially → especially

specialty chŏnmun 전문

species chong 종

specific t'ŭktchŏnghan 특정한

specifically t'ŭk'i 특히

specifications (*of machine etc*) myŏngsesŏ 명세서

specify myŏnggihada 명기하다

specimen (*of work*) kyŏnbon 견본; MED p'yobon 표본

speck (*of dust, soot*) chagŭn ŏlluk 작은 얼룩

spectacle (*impressive sight*) changgwan 장관

spectacular adj nunbushin 눈부신 *profit* kwalmok'al manhan 괄목할 만한

spectator kwan-gaek 관객

spectrum fig pŏmwi 범위

speculate v/i ch'uch'ŭk'ada 추측하다; FIN t'ugihada 투기하다

speculation ch'uch'ŭk 추측; FIN t'ugi 투기

speculator FIN t'ŭgiŏptcha 투기업자

speech (*address*) yŏnsŏl 연설; (*in play*) taesa 대사; (*ability to speak*) marhanŭn nŭngnyŏk 말하는 능력; (*way of speaking*) malt'u 말투

speechless hal marŭl irŭn 할 말을 잃은

speech defect ŏnŏ chang-ae 언어 장애; **speech therapist** ŏnŏ ch'iryo chŏnmun-ga 언어 치료 전문가; **speech writer** yŏnsŏlmun chakssŏngja 연설문 작성자

speed 1 n soktto 속도; *at a ~ of 150 mph* shisok 150mairŭi sokttoro 시속 150마일의 속도로 **2** v/i ppalli kada 빨리 가다; (*drive too quickly*) kwasok'ada 과속하다

♦ **speed by** ppalli chinagada 빨리 지나가다

♦ **speed up 1** v/i ppalli hada 빨리 하다 **2** v/t ppalli hage hada 빨리 하게 하다

speedboat k'waesoktchŏng 쾌속정

speedily pparŭge 빠르게

speeding n (*when driving*) kwasok 과속

speeding fine kwasok pŏlgŭm 과속 벌금

speed limit soktto chehan 속도 제한

speedometer sokttogye 속도계

speedy pparŭn 빠른

spell[1] v/t & v/i ch'ŏltchahada 철자하다

spell[2] n (period of time) kigan 기간

spellbound mabŏbe kŏllin 마법에 걸린; **spellcheck** COMPUT ch'ŏltcha hwagin 철자 확인; **do a ~ on** …ŭi ch'ŏltcharŭl hwaginhada …의 철자를 확인하다; **spellchecker** COMPUT ch'ŏltcha hwagin togu 철자 확인 도구

spelling ch'ŏltcha 철자

spend money ssŭda 쓰다; time ponaeda 보내다

spendthrift adj nangbibyŏgi shimhan 낭비벽이 심한

sperm chŏngja 정자; (semen) chŏngaek 정액

sperm bank chŏngja ŭnhaeng 정자 은행

sphere ku 구; fig punya 분야; **~ of influence** seryok-kkwŏn 세력권

spice n (seasoning) yangnyŏm 양념

spicy food maeun 매운

spider kŏmi 거미

spiderweb kŏmijul 거미줄

spike n ppyojuk'an kkŭt 뾰죽한 끝; (on railings) taemot 대못

spill 1 v/t ŏptchirŭda 엎지르다 **2** v/i ŏptchillŏjida 엎질러지다

spin[1] n (turn) hoejŏn 회전 **2** v/t hoejŏnshik'ida 회전시키다 **3** v/i (of wheel) hoejŏnhada 회전하다; **my head is ~ning** moriga tol chigyŏng-iyeyo 머리가 돌 지경이예요

spin[2] v/t wool, cotton pangjŏk'ada 방적하다; web tchada 짜다

♦ **spin around** (of person, car) chaepparŭge tolda 재빠르게 돌다

♦ **spin out** kkŭlda 끌다

spinach shigŭmch'i 시금치

spinal ch'ŏkch'uŭi 척추의; problem, defect chungch'ujŏgin 중추적인

spinal column ch'ŏkch'u 척추

spin doctor taebyŏnin 대변인; **spin-dry** v/t t'alssuhada 탈수하다; **spin-dryer** t'alssugi 탈수기

spine ch'ŏkch'u 척추; (of book) tŭng 등; (on plant, hedgehog) kashi 가시

spineless (cowardly) kŏbi manŭn 겁이 많은

spin-off pusanmul 부산물

spiral 1 n nasŏnhyŏng-ŭi 나선형의 **2** v/i (rise quickly) kŭpssok'i orŭda 급속히 오르다

spiral staircase nasŏnhyŏng-ŭi ch'ŭnggye 나선형의 층계

spire ppyojokt'ap 뾰족탑

spirit n (attitude) chŏngshin 정신; (soul) yŏnghon 영혼; (energy) hwal-gi 활기; (courage) yonggi 용기

spirited performance hwalbarhan 활발한

spirit level kip'o sujun-gi 기포 수준기

spirits[1] (alcohol) chŭngnyuhayŏ mandŭn sul 증류하여 만든 술

spirits[2] (morale) sagi 사기; **be in good/poor ~** kibuni chot'a/p'uri chugŏit-tta 기분이 좋다/풀이 죽어있다

spiritual adj chŏngshinchŏgin 정신적인

spiritualism shimnyŏngjuŭi 심령주의

spiritualist n shimnyŏngjuŭija 심령주의자

spit v/i (of person) ch'imŭl paet-tta 침을 뱉다; **it's ~ting with rain** posŭlbiga ogo it-tta 보슬비가 오고 있다

♦ **spit out** food, liquid naebaet-tta 내뱉다

spite n agŭi 악의; **in ~ of** pulguhago 불구하고

spiteful agŭi innŭn 악의 있는

spitting image: be the ~ of s.o. nuguwa ttok-kkat-tta 누구와 똑같다

splash 1 n (noise) mul t'winŭn sori 물 튀는 소리; (small amount of liquid) soryang 소량; a ~ of red/blue ppalgan/p'aran taejo saekssang 빨간/파란 대조 색상 **2** v/t t'wigida 튀기다 **3** v/i murŭl t'wigida 물을 튀기다; (of water) t'wida 튀다

♦ **splash down** (of spacecraft) susan ch'angnyuk'ada 수상 착륙하다

♦ **splash out 1** v/t money ssŭda 쓰다 **2** v/i: **I splashed out on a round the world trip** nanŭn segye ilchu hanŭnde tonŭl mani ssŏssŏyo 나는

세계 일주 하는데 돈을 많이 썼어요
splendid mŏtchin 멋진
splendor hwaryŏham 화려함
splint n MED pumok 부목
splinter 1 n kashi 가시 **2** v/i
chogangnada 조각나다
splinter group punp'a 분파
split 1 n (in wood) tchogaejim 쪼개짐;
(in leather) tchijŏjim 찢어짐;
(disagreement) purhwa 불화;
(division, share) mok 몫 **2** v/t logs
tchogaeda 쪼개다; leather tchit-tta
찢다; (cause disagreement in)
punyŏlshik'ida 분열시키다; (divide)
nanuda 나누다 **3** v/i (of wood)
tchogaejida 쪼개지다; (of leather)
tchijŏjida 찢어지다; (disagree)
punyŏldoeda 분열되다
♦ **split up** v/i (of couple) heŏjida
헤어지다
split personality PSYCH ijung
inkkyŏk 이중 인격
splitting: ~ *headache* ppagaejinŭn
tŭt'an tut'ong 빠개지는 듯한 두통
spoil v/t mangch'ida 망치다; child
pŏrŭdŏpsshi mandŭlda 버릇없이
만들다
spoilsport F punwigi kkaenŭn saram
분위기 깨는 사람
spoilt adj child pŏrŭtŏmnŭn 버릇없는;
be ~ for choice nŏmu manasŏ
korŭl suga ŏptta 너무 많아서 고를
수가 없다
spoke (of wheel) sal 살
**spokesman, spokesperson,
spokeswoman** taebyŏnin 대변인
sponge n sŭp'onji 스펀지
♦ **sponge off** F pilbut'ŏ salda 빌붙어
살다
sponger F pilbut'ŏ sanŭn saram
빌붙어 사는 사람
sponsor 1 n (for membership etc)
pojŭngin 보증인; (for sports, cultural
event) huwŏnja 후원자 **2** v/t (for
membership etc) pojŭnghada
보증하다; (for sports, cultural event)
huwŏnhada 후원하다
sponsorship huwŏn 후원
spontaneous chabaltchŏgin 자발적인
spooky F mushimushihan 무시무시한
spool n (for film) ril 릴; (for thread)

shilp'ae 실패
spoon n sutkkarak 숟가락; ~ *and
chopsticks* sujŏ 수저
spoonfeed fig chinach'ige pohohada
지나치게 보호하다
spoonful han sutkkarak han 숟가락
sporadic sanbaltchŏgin 산발적인
sport n sŭp'och'ŭ 스포츠
sporting event undong-ŭi 운동의;
(fair, generous) kwandaehan 관대한
sportscar sŭp'och'ŭ k'a 스포츠 카:
sportscoat undong-yong chaek'it
운동용 재킷; **sports journalist**
sŭp'och'ŭ kija 스포츠 기자; **sportsman** namja undongga 남자 운동가;
sports news sŭp'och'ŭ nyusŭ
스포츠 뉴스; **sports page**
sŭp'och'ŭran 스포츠란; **sportswoman** yŏja undongga 여자 운동가
sporty person sŭp'och'ŭrŭl
choahanŭn 스포츠를 좋아하는;
clothes sŭp'ot'ihan 스포티한
spot[1] (pimple) yŏdŭrŭm 여드름;
(from measles etc) panjŏm 반점;
(part of pattern) mulppang-ul munŭi
물방울 무늬
spot[2] (place) changso 장소; *on the ~*
(in the place in question) hyŏnjang-
esŏ 현장에서; (immediately) chŭksshi
즉시; *put s.o. on the ~* nugurŭl
kollanhan ch'ŏjie not'a 누구를
곤란한 처지에 놓다
spot[3] v/t (notice) arach'aeda 알아채다;
(identify) shikppyŏrhada 식별하다
spot check mujagwi ch'uch'ul kŏmsa
무작위 추출 검사; *carry out spot
checks* mujagwiro kŏmsahada
무작위로 검사하다
spotless mŏnji han chŏm ŏmnŭn
먼지 한 점 없는
spotlight n sŭp'otŭrait'ŭ
스포트라이트
spotted fabric mulppang-ul munŭiŭi
물방울 무늬의
spotty (with pimples) yŏdŭrŭmi nan
여드름이 난
spouse fml paeuja 배우자
spout 1 n chudung-i 주둥이 **2** v/i (of
liquid) punch'uldoeda 분출되다
sprain 1 n ppim 삠 **2** v/t ppida 삐다
sprawl v/i k'ŭn taetcharo ppŏt-tta 큰

대자로 뻗다; (*of city*) sabang-ŭro ppŏt-tta 사방으로 뻗다; **send s.o. ~ing** nugurŭl ttaeryŏ nup'ida 누구를 때려 눕히다

sprawling *city, suburbs* ppŏdŏnagago innŭn 뻗어나가고 있는

spray 1 *n* (*of sea water, from fountain*) mulbora 물보라; (*paint, for hair*) sŭp'ŭrei 스프레이 **2** *v/t* ppurida 뿌리다; **~ X with Y** Xe Yŭl/rŭl ppurida X에 Y을/를 뿌리다

spraygun punmugi 분무기

spread 1 *n* (*of disease, etc*) manyŏn 만연; (*of religion*) pogŭp 보급; F (*big meal*) chanch'itssang 잔칫상 **2** *v/t* (*lay*) p'yŏlch'ida 펼치다; *butter, jam* parŭda 바르다; *news, rumor, disease* p'ŏttŭrida 퍼뜨리다; *arms, legs* pŏllida 벌리다 **3** *v/i* p'ŏjida 퍼지다; (*of butter*) pallajida 발라지다

spreadsheet COMPUT sŭp'ŭredŭshit'ŭ 스프레드시트

spree: **go on a ~** F shinnage surŭl mashimyŏ nolda 신나게 술을 마시며 놀다; **go on a shopping ~** hŭngch'ŏngmangch'ŏng shyop'ing-ŭl hada 흥청망청 쇼핑을 하다

sprightly wŏn-giwangsŏnghan 원기왕성한

spring[1] *n* (*season*) pom 봄

spring[2] *n* (*device*) yongsuch'ŏl 용수철

spring[3] **1** *n* (*jump*) ttwigi 뛰기; (*stream*) saem 샘 **2** *v/i* irŏsŏda 일어서다; **~ from** ...esŏ pirot-ttoeda ...에서 비롯되다

springboard taibing tae 다이빙 대; **spring chicken: she's no ~** (*hum*) kŭnyŏnŭn kŭrŏk'e chŏmtchi anayo 그녀는 그렇게 젊지 않아요; **spring-cleaning** pommaji taech'ŏngso 봄맞이 대청소; **springtime** pomch'ŏl 봄철

springy *ground* t'ansŏng-i innŭn 탄성이 있는; *walk, mattress* t'allyŏgi innŭn 탄력이 있는

sprinkle *v/t* ppurida 뿌리다; **~ X with Y** Xe Yŭl/rŭl ppurida X에 Y을/를 뿌리다

sprinkler (*for garden*) salssugi 살수기; (*in ceiling*) chadong sohwa changch'i 자동 소화 장치

sprint 1 *n* SP tan-gŏri yukssang kyŏnggi 단거리 육상 경기; (*for the bus etc*) chiltchu 질주 **2** *v/i* chiltchuhada 질주하다

sprinter SP tan-gŏri yukssang sŏnsu 단거리 육상 선수

sprout 1 *v/i* (*of seed*) t'ŭda 트다 **2** *n:* (**Brussels**) ~**s** ssagyangbaech'u 싹양배추

spruce *adj* maepsshi innŭn 맵시 있는

spur *n fig* chagŭk 자극; **on the ~ of the moment** ch'ungdongtchŏgŭro 충동적으로

♦ **spur on** (*encourage*) chagŭk'ada 자극하다

spurt 1 *n* (*in race*) punbal 분발; **put on a ~** soktto naeda 속도 내다 **2** *v/i* (*of liquid*) ppumŏjyŏ naoda 뿜어져 나오다

spy 1 *n* kanch'ŏp 간첩 **2** *v/i* kanch'ŏp norŭsŭl hada 간첩 노릇을 하다 **3** *v/t* yŏtppoda 엿보다

♦ **spy on** kamshihada 감시하다

squabble 1 *n* maldat'um 말다툼 **2** *v/i* maldat'umhada 말다툼하다

squalid chijŏbunhan 지저분한

squalor nuch'uham 누추함

squander *money* nangbihada 낭비하다

square 1 *adj* (*in shape*) sagak'yŏng-ŭi 사각형의; **~ mile/yard** p'yŏngbang mail/yadŭ 평방 마일/야드 **2** *n* (*shape*) sagak'yŏng 사각형; (*in town*) kwangjang 광장; (*in board game*) k'an 칸; MATH chegop 제곱; **we're back to ~ one** urinŭn wŏntchŏmŭr torawat-tta 우리는 원점으로 돌아왔다

square root chegopkkŭn 제곱근

squash[1] *n* (*vegetable*) hobak 호박

squash[2] *n* (*game*) sŭk'wŏshi 스쿼시

squash[3] *v/t* (*crush*) nullŏ tchigŭrŏttŭrida 눌러 찌그러뜨리다

squat 1 *adj* (*in shape*) ttangttalmak'an 땅딸막한 **2** *v/i* (*sit*) ungk'urigo antta 웅크리고 앉다; (*illegally*) mudan kŏjuhada 무단 거주하다

squatter mudan kŏjuja 무단 거주자

squeak 1 *n* (*of mouse*) tchiktchkkkŏrinŭn sori 찍찍거리는 소리; (*of*

..inge) ppigŏk-kkŏrinŭn sori
삐걱거리는 소리 **2** *v/i* (*of mouse*)
chiktchk-kkŏrida 찍찍거리다; (*of ..inge, shoes*) ppigŏk-kkŏrida
삐걱거리다

...ueal **1** *n* kkaek-kkaek-kkŏrinŭn
...ori 꽥꽥거리는 소리 **2** *v/i* kkaek-
...kkaek-kkŏrida 꽥꽥거리다

...ueamish mŏlmiga chal nanŭn
걸미가 잘 나는

...ueeze **1** *n* (*of hand, shoulder*)
...kkwak chwim 꽉 쥠 **2** *v/t* (*press*)
...kkwak chwida 꽉 쥐다; (*remove ..uice from*) tchada 짜다

...squeeze in **1** *v/i* (*to a car etc*)
...kkwak kkiida 꽉 끼이다 **2** *v/t* kkiŏ
...nŏt'a 끼어 넣다

...squeeze up *v/i* (*to make space*)
...mirŏ puch'ida 밀어 붙이다

...quid ojing-ŏ 오징어

...quint *n* sap'alnun 사팔눈

...quirm (*wriggle*) pŏdunggŏrida
...버둥거리다; (*in embarrassment*) pibi
...kkoda 비비 꼬다

...quirrel *n* taramjwi 다람쥐

...quirt **1** *v/t* ppumŏnaeda 뿜어내다 **2** *n*
...pej F p'unnaegi 풋내기

...ab **1** *n* F shido 시도 **2** *v/t person*
...tchirŭda 찌르다

...tability anjŏngssŏng 안정성

...tabilize **1** *v/t prices, currency*
...anjŏngshik'ida 안정시키다; *boat*
...kojŏngshik'ida 고정시키다 **2** *v/i* (*of ..prices etc*) anjŏngdoeda 안정되다

...able¹ *n* (*for horses*) magutkkan
...마구간

...able² *adj* anjŏngdoen 안정된

...tack **1** *n* (*pile*) tŏmi 더미; (*smoke~*)
...kulttuk 굴뚝 **2** *v/t* ssaoollida
...쌓아올리다

...tadium kyŏnggijang 경기장

...taff *n* (*employees*) chigwŏn 직원;
...(*teachers*) kyosa 교사

...taffroom (*in school*) kyomushil
...교무실

...tage (*in life, project etc*) tan-gye
...단계; (*of journey*) yŏjŏng 여정

...tage² **1** *n* THEA mudae 무대; *go on the ~* paegua toeda 배우가 되다 **2** *v/t play* kong-yŏnhada 공연하다; *demonstration, strike* pŏrida 벌이다

stage door punjangshil ipku 분장실
입구

stagger 1 *v/i* hwich'ŏnggŏrida
휘청거리다 **2** *v/t* (*amaze*) kkamtchak
nollage hada 깜짝 놀라게 하다;
coffee breaks etc sŏro ŏtkkallige
hada 서로 엇갈리게 하다

staggering kiga mak'inŭn 기가
막히는

stagnant *water* koeŏ innŭn 괴어
있는; *economy* ch'imch'ehan 침체한

stagnate (*of person, mind*)
ch'imch'ehada 침체하다

stag party ch'onggak p'at'i 총각 파티

stain 1 *n* (*dirty mark*) ŏlluk 얼룩; (*for wood*) ch'akssaek 착색 **2** *v/t* (*dirty*)
tŏrŏp'ida 더럽히다; *wood*
ch'aksaek'ada 착색하다 **3** *v/i* (*of wine etc*) ŏllugi saenggida 얼룩이
생기다; (*of fabric*) tŏrŏwŏjida
더러워지다

stained glass sŭt'eindŭ kŭllasŭ
스테인드 글라스

stainless steel 1 *n* sŭt'einlesŭ
스테인레스 **2** *adj* sŭt'einlesŭŭi
스테인레스의

stain remover ŏlluk chegŏje 얼룩
제거제

stair kyedan 계단; *the ~s* ch'ŭnggye
층계

staircase ch'ŭnggye 층계

stake 1 *n* (*of wood*) malttuk 말뚝;
(*when gambling*) p'antton 판돈;
(*investment*) t'uja 투자; *be at ~*
wigie ch'ŏhada 위기에 처하다 **2** *v/t tree* malttugŭro chijihada 말뚝으로
지지하다; *money* kŏlda 걸다; *person*
kyŏngjejŏgŭro wŏnjohada
경제적으로 원조하다

stale *bread* shinsŏnhaji anŭn 신선하지
않은; *air* k'wik'wihan 퀴퀴한; *news*
chinbuhan 진부한

stalemate (*in chess*) suga modu
mak'im 수가 모두 막힘; *fig*
chint'oeyangnan 진퇴양난

stalk¹ *n* (*of fruit, plant*) chulgi 줄기

stalk² *v/t animal* ch'ujŏk'ada
추적하다; *person* twirŭl paltta 뒤를
밟다

stalker (*of person*) sŭt'ok'ŏ 스토커

stall¹ *n* (*at market*) chinyŏltttae 진열대;

(for cow, horse) han k'an 한 칸

stall² 1 *v/i (of vehicle, plane, engine)* mŏmch'uda 멈추다; *(play for time)* kyomyohage shiganŭl kkŭlda 교묘하게 시간을 끌다 2 *v/t engine* kkŭda 끄다; *people* chiyŏnshik'ida 지연시키다

stallion chongma 종마

stalwart *adj* tŭndŭnhan 든든한

stamina ch'eryŏk 체력

stammer 1 *n* maldŏdŭm 말더듬 2 *v/i* marŭl tŏdŭmtta 말을 더듬다

stamp¹ 1 *n (for letter)* up'yo 우표; *(device)* tojang 도장; *(mark made with device)* tojang chaguk 도장 자국 2 *v/t letter* up'yo puch'ida 우표 붙이다; *document, passport* tojang tchiktta 도장 찍다

stamp² *v/t:* ~ *one's feet* parŭl kurŭda 발을 구르다

♦ **stamp out** *(eradicate)* kŭnjŏrhada 근절하다

stampede *n (of cattle etc)* ururu taranam 우루루 달아남; *(of people)* swaedo 쇄도

stance *(position)* iptchang 입장

stand 1 *n (at exhibition)* kwallamsŏk 관람석; *(witness ~)* chŭng-insŏk 증인석; *(support, base)* patch'imttae 받침대; *take the* ~ LAW chŭnggŏrŭl chech'urhada 증거를 제출하다 2 *v/i (be situated: of person)* sŏda 서다; *(of object, building)* wich'ihada 위치하다; *(as opposed to sit)* sŏda 서다; *(rise)* irŏsŏda 일어서다; ~ *still* umjigiji ank'o sŏ it-tta 움직이지 않고 서 있다; *where do I ~ with you?* urinŭn ŏttŏn kwan-gyein-gayo? 우리는 어떤 관계인가요? 3 *v/t (tolerate)* ch'amtta 참다; *(put)* not'a 놓다; *you don't ~ a chance* tangshinhant'enŭn kamang ŏpssŏyo 당신한테는 가망 없어요; ~ *one's ground* mullŏsŏji ant'a 물러서지 않다

♦ **stand back** mullŏna it-tta 물러나 있다

♦ **stand by** 1 *v/i (not take action)* panggwanhada 방관하다; *(be ready)* taegihada 대기하다 2 *v/t person* chijihada 지지하다; *decision*

kojip'ada 고집하다

♦ **stand down** *(withdraw)* mullŏna mullŏna it-tta 물러나다

♦ **stand for** *(tolerate)* ch'amtta 참다; *(represent)* p'yoshihada 표시하다

♦ **stand in for** taeshinhada 대신하다

♦ **stand out** nune ttŭida 눈에 띄다

♦ **stand up 1** *v/i* irŏsŏda 일어서다 2 F param mach'ida 바람 맞히다

♦ **stand up for** pang-ŏhada 방어하다

♦ **stand up to** matssŏda 맞서다

standard 1 *adj (usual)* pot'ong-ŭi 보통의 2 *n (level of excellence)* kijun 기준; *(expectation)* kidae 기대; TEC p'yojun 표준; *be up to* ~ p'yojune tarhada 표준에 달하다; *not be up ~* p'yojune midarhada 표준에 미달하다

standardize *v/t* kyugyŏk'wahada 규격화하다

standard of living saenghwal sujun 생활 수준

standby: *on* ~ *(for flight)* taegihago innŭn 대기하고 있는

standby passenger t'apssŭng taeg 탑승 대기자

standing *n (in society etc)* chiwi 지위 *(repute)* myŏngsŏng 명성; *a musician of some* ~ p'yŏngp'ani choŭ ŭmak-kka 평판이 좋은 음악가

standing room ipssŏk 입석

standoffish ssalssarhan 쌀쌀한;

standpoint kwanchŏm 관점;

standstill: *be at a* ~ mŏmch'un mŏmchŏ 멈춘; *bring to a* ~ mŏmch'uge ha 멈추게 하다

staple¹ *n (foodstuff)* chuyo shikp'u 주요 식품

staple² 1 *n (fastener)* hoch'ik'isŭ al 호치키스 알 2 *v/t* hoch'ik'isŭro tchiktta 호치키스로 찍다

staple diet chuyoshikttan 주요식당

staple gun sŭt'eip'ŭl kŏn 스테이플

stapler hoch'ik'isŭ 호치키스

star 1 *n* pyŏl 별; *fig* sŭt'a 스타 2 *v/t (movie)* chuyŏnŭro hada 주연으로 하다 3 *v/i (in movie)* chuyŏnhada 주연하다

starboard *adj* uch'ŭgŭi 우측의

stare 1 *n* ppanhi ch'yŏdabom 빤히 쳐다봄 2 *v/i* ppanhi ch'yŏdaboda

601

빤히 쳐다본다; **~ at** ...을 / 를 빤히 쳐다보다
ch'yŏdaboda ...을 / 를 빤히 쳐다보다

starfish pulgasari 불가사리

stark 1 *adj landscape* sangmak'an 삭막한; *reminder, contrast etc* chŏngnarahan 적나라한 **2** *adv*: **~ naked** holttak pŏsŭn 홀딱 벗은

starling tchirŭregi 찌르레기

Stars and Stripes sŏngjogi 성조기

start 1 *n* shijak 시작; **get off to a good / bad ~** (*in race*) choŭn / nappŭn ch'ulbarŭl hada 좋은 / 나쁜 출발을 하다; (*in marriage, career*) choŭn / nappŭn shijagŭl hada 좋은 / 나쁜 시작을 하다; **from the ~** ch'ŏŭmbut'ŏ 처음부터; **well, it's a ~!** kŭraedo shijagŭn han semijiyo! 그래도 시작은 한 셈이지요! **2** *v/i* shijakdoeda 시작되다; (*set off*) ch'ulbarhada 출발하다; (*of engine, car*) shidongdoeda 시동되다; **~ing from tomorrow** naeirbut'ŏ shijak'aesŏ 내일부터 시작해서 **3** *v/t* shijak'ada 시작하다; *engine, car* shidongshik'ida 시동시키다; *business* seuda 세우다; **~ to do X** Xhagi shijak'ada X하기 시작하다

starter (*part of meal*) ep'it'aijyŏ 에피타이저; (*of car*) shidongjangch'i 시동장치

starting point (*for walk*) ch'ulbaltchŏm 출발점; (*for discussion, thesis*) kitchŏm 기점

starting salary ch'ŏtwŏlgŭp 첫 월급

startle kkamtchak nollage hada 깜짝 놀라게 하다

startling kkamtchak nollage hanŭn 깜짝 놀라게 하는

starvation kia 기아

starve *v/i* kumjurida 굶주리다; **~ to death** kulmŏchuktta 굶어 죽다; **I'm starving** F pae kop'a chukkessŏyo 배 고파 죽겠어요

state¹ 1 *n* (*of car, house etc*) sangt'ae 상태; (*part of country*) chu 주; (*country*) kuk-kka 국가; **the States** Miguk 미국 **2** *adj capital etc* chu(rib)ŭi 주(립)의; *banquet etc* kongshiktchŏgin 공식적인

state² *v/t* kongshiktchŏguro

parŏnhada 공식적으로 발언하다

State Department (Mi)Kungmusŏng (미)국무성

statement (*to police*) chinsul 진술; (*announcement*) palp'yo 발표; (*bank ~*) (ŭnhaeng) t'ongjang (은행) 통장

state of emergency pisangsat'ae 비상사태

state-of-the-art *adj* ch'oech'ŏmdanŭi 최첨단의

statesman chŏngch'iga 정치가

state trooper churib kyŏngch'al 주립 경찰

state visit kongsshik pangmun 공식 방문

static (*electricity*) chŏngjŏn-gi 정전기

station 1 *n* RAIL yŏk 역; RAD, TV pangsongguk 방송국 **2** *v/t guard etc* paech'ihada 배치하다; **be ~ed at** (*of soldier*) ...e paech'idoeda ...에 배치되다

stationary chŏngjihan 정지한

stationer munbanggu 문방구

stationery store munbanggujŏm 문방구점

station wagon waegŏn 왜건

statistical t'onggyeŭi 통계의

statistically t'onggyejŏguro 통계적으로

statistics (*science*) t'onggyehak 통계학; (*figures*) t'onggye 통계

statue sang 상

Statue of Liberty chayuŭi yŏshinsang 자유의 여신상

status chiwi 지위

status symbol shinbunŭi sangjing 신분의 상징

statute pŏmnyŏng 법령

staunch *adj* ch'ungshirhan 충실한

stay 1 *n* ch'eryu 체류 **2** *v/i* (*in a place*) mŏmurŭda 머무르다; (*in a condition*) yujihada 유지하다; **~ in a hotel** hot'ere muktta 호텔에 묵다; **~ right there!** kŏgisŏ kkomtchak hajima! 거기서 꼼짝도 하지마!; **~ put** ŏdiro ka pŏriji ant'a 어디로 가 버리지 않다
♦ **stay away** ttŏrŏjyŏ it-tta 떨어져 있다
♦ **stay away from** ...put'ŏ ttŏrŏjyŏ it-

stay 602

tta …부터 떨어져 있다
♦ **stay behind** twie namtta 뒤에 남다
♦ **stay up** (*not go to bed*) (chaji
ank'o) irŏna it-tta (자지 않고)
일어나 있다

steadily *improve etc* chŏmch'ajŏguro
점차적으로
steady 1 *adj* (*not shaking*) ttŏlliji
annŭn 떨리지 않는; (*regular*)
iltchŏnghan 일정한; (*continuous*)
kkŭnimŏmnŭn 끊임없는 **2** *adv*: *be
going* ~ iltchŏnghage sagwida
일정하게 사귀다; ~ *on!*
ch'imch'ak'age hae! 침착하게 해!
3 *v/t* anjŏngshik'ida 안정시키다
steak sŭt'eik'ŭ 스테이크
steal 1 *v/t money etc* humch'ida
훔치다 **2** *v/i* (*be a thief*)
toduktchirhada 도둑질하다; ~
into/out of (*move quietly*)
salgŭmŏni tŭrŏgada/ppajyŏnagada
살그머니 들어가다/빠져나가다
stealthy mollae hanŭn 몰래 하는
steam 1 *n* kim 김 **2** *v/t food* tchida
찌다
♦ **steam up 1** *v/i* (*of window*) kimi
sŏrida 김이 서리다 **2** *v/t*: *be
steamed up* F yŏl pat-tta 열 받다
steamer (*for cooking*) tchimt'ong
찜통
steam iron sŭt'im tarimi 스팀 다리미
steel 1 *n* kangch'ŏl 강철 **2** *adj*
kangch'ŏllo mandŭn 강철로 만든
steep¹ *adj hill etc* kap'arŭn 가파른; F
prices pissan 비싼
steep² *v/t* (*soak*) tamgŭda 담그다
steeplechase (*in athletics*) chang-
aemul kyŏnggi 장애물 경기
steer¹ *n* (*animal*) kŏsehan hwangso
거세한 황소
steer² *v/t car, boat* chojonghada
조종하다; *person, conversation*
ikkŭlda 이끌다
steering (*of motor vehicle*) sŭt'ŏring
스티어링
steering wheel haendŭl 핸들
stem¹ *n* (*of plant*) chulgi 줄기; (*of
glass*) sonjabi 손잡이; (*of pipe*) tae
대; (*of word*) ŏgan 어간
♦ **stem from** …esŏ yuraehada …에서
유래하다

stem² *v/t* (*block*) ŏktchehada
억제하다
stemware sultchan 술잔
stench akch'wi 악취
step 1 *n* (*pace*) kŏrŭm 걸음; (*stair*)
kyedan 계단; (*measure*) choch'i 조치
~ *by* ~ ch'arye ch'aryero 차례
차례로 **2** *v/i* han-gŏrŭm naedidida
한걸음 내디디다; *don't* ~ *on it*
paltchi mara 밟지 마라
♦ **step down** (*from post etc*)
mullŏnada 물러나다
♦ **step out** *v/i* (*go out for a short time*)
chamkkan nagada 잠깐 나가다
♦ **step up** *v/t* (*increase*)
chŭnggashik'ida 증가시키다
stepbrother ŭibut'yŏngje 의붓형제;
stepdaughter ŭibut-ttal 의붓딸;
stepfather kyebu 계부; **stepladder**
palp'an tallin sadari 발판 달린
사다리; **stepmother** kyemo 계모
stepping stone tidimttol 디딤돌; *fig*
palp'an 발판
stepsister ŭibut-chamae 의붓자매
stepson ŭibudadŭl 의붓아들
stereo *n* (*sound system*) sŭt'ereo
스테레오
stereotype *n* chŏnhyŏng 전형
sterile *woman, man* purimŭi 불임의;
equipment salgyundoen 살균된
sterilize *woman* purimk'ehada 불임케
하다; *equipment* sodok'ada 소독하다
sterling *n* FIN p'aundŭ 파운드
stern *adj* ŏmkkyŏk'an 엄격한
steroids sŭt'eroidŭ 스테로이드
stethoscope ch'ŏngjin-gi 청진기
Stetson® k'auboi moja 카우보이
모자
stevedore pudu nodongja 부두
노동자
stew *n* sŭt'yu 스튜
steward (*on plane, ship*) samujang
사무장
stewardess (*on plane, ship*)
sŭt'yuŏdisŭ 스튜어디스
stick¹ *n* (*wood*) makttaegi 막대기; (*of
policeman*) konbong 곤봉; (*walking
~*) chip'ang-i 지팡이; *the ~s* F
tumesankkol 두메산골
stick¹ *v/t* (*with adhesive*) puch'ida
붙이다; F (*put*) nŏt'a 넣다 **2** *v/i* (*jam*

603

stir

tallabut-tta 달라붙다; (*adhere*) put-tta 붙다

- **stick around** F mŏmullŏ it-tta 머물러 있다
- **stick by** F …ege ch'ungshirhada …에게 충실하다
- **stick out** *v/i* (*protrude*) pulssuk naoda 불쑥 나오다; (*be noticeable*) nune ttŭida 눈에 띄다
- **stick to** (*adhere to*) …e tallabut-tta …에 달라붙다; *plan etc* …e ch'ungshirhada …에 충실하다; *path* chal ttaragada 잘 따라가다; *story* kosuhada 고수하다; F (*follow*) ttarŭda 따르다
- **stick together** F kach'i put'ŏit-tta 같이 붙어있다
- **stick up** *poster* puch'ida 붙이다
- **stick up for** onghohada 옹호하다
- **ticker** sŭt'ik'ŏ 스티커
- **ticking plaster** panch'anggo 반창고
- **tick-in-the-mud** kut'ae-ŭiyŏnhan saram 구태의연한 사람
- **sticky** *hands, surface* kkŭnjŏk-kkŏrinŭn 끈적거리는; *label* punnŭn 붙는
- **sticky rice** ch'apssal 찹쌀
- **tiff 1** *adj brush, leather* ppŏtppŏt'an 뻣뻣한; *muscle, body* ppŏgŭnhan 뻐근한; *mixture, paste* toen 된; (*in manner*) ttakttak'an 딱딱한; *drink* tok'an 독한; *competition* shimhan 심한; *penalty* kwajunghan 과중한 **2** *adv*: **be scared** ~ F koengjanghi kŏbe chillida 굉장히 겁에 질리다; **be bored** ~ F koengjanghi chiruhaejida 굉장히 지루해지다
- **tiffen** *v/i* ttattak'aejida 딱딱해지다
- **stiffen up** (*of muscle*) ppŏtppŏt'age hada 뻣뻣하게 하다
- **stifle** *v/t yawn, laugh* kkuk ch'amtta 꾹 참다; *criticism, debate* ŏktchehada 억제하다
- **stifling** tapttap'an 답답한
- **stigma** omyŏng 오명
- **still**¹ **1** *adj* koyohan 고요한 **2** *adv* kamanhi 가만히; **keep ~!** kamanhi issŏ! 가만히 있어!; **stand ~!** kamanhi sŏ issŏ! 가만히 서 있어!
- **still**² *adv* (*yet*) ajikkto 아직도;

(*nevertheless*) kŭraedo 그래도; **do you ~ want it?** ajikto kŭgŏsŭl kajigo ship'ŏyo? 아직도 그것을 가지고 싶어요?; **she ~ hasn't finished** kŭnyŏnŭn ajikkto kkŭnnaeji anassŏyo 그녀는 아직도 끝내지 않았어요; **she might ~ come** kŭnyŏnŭn kŭraedo oltchi morŭmnida 그녀는 그래도 올지 모릅니다; **they are ~ my parents** kŭdŭrŭn kŭraedo na-ŭi pumonimimnida 그들은 그래도 나의 부모님입니다; **~ more** tŏ-uk tŏ 더욱 더

- **stillborn: be ~** sasandoeda 사산되다
- **stilted** ttakttak'an 딱딱한
- **stilts** (*under house*) kidung 기둥
- **stimulant** chakŭktche 자극제
- **stimulate** *person, growth, demand* chagŭk'ada 자극하다
- **stimulating** chagŭktchŏgin 자극적인
- **stimulation** hŭngbun 흥분
- **stimulus** (*incentive*) chagŭk 자극
- **sting 1** *n* (*from bee, jellyfish*) ssoin sangch'ŏ 쏘인 상처 **2** *v/t* (*of bee, jellyfish*) ssoda 쏘다 **3** *v/i* (*of eyes, scratch*) ttakkŭmgŏrida 따끔거리다
- **stinging** *remark, criticism* shillarhan 신랄한
- **stingy** insaek'an 인색한
- **stink 1** *n* akch'wi 악취; F (*fuss*) malssŏng 말썽; **make a ~** F malssŏng-ŭl purida 말썽을 부리다 **2** *v/i* koyak'an naemsaega nada 고약한 냄새가 나다; F (*be very bad*) hyŏngp'yŏnŏpsshi nappŭda 형편없이 나쁘다
- **stint** *n* (*period*) iltchŏng kigan 일정 기간
- **stint on** …ŭl/rŭl akkida …을/를 아끼다
- **stipulate** kyujŏnghada 규정하다
- **stipulation** kyujŏng 규정
- **stir 1** *n*: **give the soup a ~** kugŭl hwijŏt-tta 국을 휘젓다; **cause a ~** *fig* sodong-ŭl irŭk'ida 소동을 일으키다 **2** *v/t* hwijŏt-tta 휘젓다 **3** *v/i* (*of sleeping person*) twich'ŏgida 뒤척이다
- **stir up** *crowd* sŏndonghada 선동하다; *bad memories* irŭk'ida

일으키다

stir-crazy: be ~ F mŏriga saltchakton mŏriga sal tchak ton 머리가 살짝 돈

stir-fry v/t poktta 볶다

stirring *music, speech* changk'waehan 장쾌한

stitch 1 n (*in sewing*) panŭltttam 바늘땀; (*in knitting*) k'o 코; **~es** panŭl 바늘; **take the ~es out** MED shirŭl ppoptta 실을 뽑다; **have a ~** ssushida 쑤시다 **2** v/t *sew* kkwemaeda 꿰매다
♦ **stitch up** *wound* kkwemaeda 꿰매다

stitching (*stitches*) panŭjil 바느질

stock 1 n (*reserves*) chŏjang 저장; (COM: *of store*) chaego 재고; (*animals*) kach'uk 가축; FIN chushik 주식; (*ingredient*) sup'ŭ chaeryo 수프 재료; **in ~** maejang-e innŭn maejang-e in nŭn 매장에 있는; **out of ~** (*of products*) maejindoen 매진된; **we are out of ~** ta p'allyŏnnŭndeyo 다 팔렸는데요; **take ~** kŏmt'ohada 검토하다 **2** v/t COM katch'uda 갖추다
♦ **stock up on** tŭryŏnot'a 들여놓다

stockbroker chushik chungmae-in 주식 중매인; **stock exchange** chŭngkkwŏn kŏraeso 증권 거래소; **stockholder** chuju 주주

stocking sŭt'ak'ing 스타킹

stock market chŭngkkwŏn shijang 증권 시장; **stockmarket crash** chŭngkkwŏn shijang punggoe 증권 시장 붕괴; **stockpile 1** n (*of food, weapons*) pich'uk 비축 **2** v/t pich'uk'ada 비축하다; **stockroom** ch'anggo 창고; **stock-still: stand ~** kkomtchagank'o innŭn 꼼짝않고 있는; **stocktaking** chaego josa 재고 조사

stocky ttangttalmak'an 땅딸막한

stodgy *food* sohwaga chal andoenŭn 소화가 잘 안되는

stomach 1 n (*organ*) wi 위; (*abdomen*) pae 배 **2** v/t (*tolerate*) ch'amtta 참다

stomach-ache pokt'ong 복통

stone n (*material*) sŏktcho 석조; (*pebble*) tol 돌; **precious ~** posŏk 보석

stoned F (*on drugs*) ch'wihan 취한

stone-deaf aju kwiga mŏgŭn 아주 귀가 먹은

stonewall v/i F ŏlbŏmurida 얼버무리다

stony *ground, path* tori manŭn 돌이 많은

stool (*seat*) (tŭng-i ŏmnŭn) kŏlssang (등이 없는) 걸상

stoop¹ 1 n: **he has a ~** kŭnŭn tŭng-kuburŏjyŏssŏyo 그는 등이 구부러졌어요 **2** v/i (*bend down*) ungk'ŭrida 웅크리다; (*have bent back*) tŭng-i kuptta 등이 굽다

stoop² n (*porch*) hyŏn-gwan ipkku-ch'ŭngch'ŭngdae 현관 입구의 층층대

stop 1 n (*for train*) yŏk 역; (*for bus*) chŏngnyujang 정류장; **come to a ~** mŏmch'uda 멈추다; **put a ~ to** ...ŭl/rŭl mŏmch'uda ...을/를 멈추 **2** v/t (*put an end to*) mŏmch'uda 멈추다; (*prevent*) mot'age hada 못하게 하다; (*cease*) kŭmanduda 그만두다; *person in street* seuda 세우다; *car, bus, train, etc: of driver* mŏmch'uge hada 멈추게 하다; **~ talking immediately!** yaegirŭl chŭksshi kŭmanduseyo! 얘기를 즉시 그만두세요!; **I ~ped her from leaving** nanŭn kŭnyŏrŭl mot-ttŏnage haet-tta 나는 그녀를 못떠나게 했다; **it has ~ped raining** piga kŭch'yŏt-tta 비가 그쳤다; **~ a check** chiburŭl chŏngjishik'ida 지불을 정지시키다 **3** v/i (*come to a halt*) mŏmch'uda 멈추다; (*of snow, rain*) kŭch'ida 그치다; (*in a particular place: of bus, train*) sŏda 서다
♦ **stop by** (*visit*) tŭllŭda 들리다
♦ **stop off** tojung-e tŭllŭda 도중에 들리다
♦ **stop over** chamshi mŏmurŭda 잠시 머무르다
♦ **stop up** *sink* maktta 막다

stopgap imshi pyŏnt'ong 임시 변통; **stoplight** (*traffic light*) ppalgan pul 빨간 불; (*brake light*) sŭt'op lait'ŭ 스톱 라이트; **stopover** chamshi mŏmum 잠시 머뭄

stopper (*for bath, basin*) kumŏng magae 구멍 마개; (*for bottle*) pyŏn

magae 병 마개

stopping: no ~ (*sign*) mŏmch'um ch'ŏngji 멈춤 정지

stop sign mŏmch'um shinho 멈춤 신호

stopwatch sŭt'op wŏch'i 스톱 위치

storage pogwan 보관; **put in ~** …ŭl/rŭl ch'anggo-e nŏ-ŏ pogwanhada …을/를 창고에 넣어 보관하다; **be in ~** pogwan chung-ida 보관 중이다

storage capacity COMPUT kiŏk yongnyang 기억 용량; **storage jar** hang-ari 항아리; **storage space** pogwan changso 보관 장소

store 1 *n* kage 가게; (*stock*) chŏjang 저장; (*storehouse*) ch'anggo 창고 2 *v/t* chŏjanghada 저장하다; COMPUT kiŏk'ada 기억하다

storefront sangjŏmŭi chŏngmyŏn 상점의 정면; **storehouse** ch'anggo 창고; **storekeeper** kage chuin 가게 주인; **storeroom** ch'anggo 창고; **store window** shyowindo 쇼윈도

storm *n* p'okp'ung 폭풍; (*with rain*) p'okp'ung-u 폭풍우

storm drain paesuro 배수로; **storm window** tŏt-ch'angmun 덧창문

storm warning p'okp'ungju-ŭibo 폭풍주의보

stormy *weather* p'okp'ung-u-ga ch'inŭn 폭풍우가 치는; *relationship* kyŏngnyŏrhan 격렬한

story[1] (*tale, account*) iyagi 이야기; (*newspaper article*) kisa 기사; F (*lie*) chiŏnaen iyagi 지어낸 이야기

story[2] (*of building*) ch'ŭng 층

stout *adj* person ttungttunghan 뚱뚱한; *boots* chilgin 질긴

stove (*for cooking*) yoriyong konno 요리용 곤로; (*for heating*) sŭt'obŭ 스토브

stow chibŏnŏt'a 집어넣다

♦ **stow away** *v/i* mirhanghada 밀항하다

stowaway mirhangja 밀항자

straight 1 *adj* line, hair kodŭn 곧은; back kkotkkot'an 꼿꼿한; (*honest, direct*) soltchik'an 솔직한; (*not criminal*) chŏnkkwaga ŏmnŭn 전과가 없는; *whiskey etc* sŭt'ŭreit'ŭ

스트레이트; (*tidy*) chŏngdondoen 정돈된; (*conservative*) kojishik'an 고지식한; (*not homosexual*) tongsŏng-yŏnaejaga anin 동성연애자가 아닌; **be a ~ A student** sŏngjŏgi maeu usuhan hakssaeng 성적이 매우 우수한 학생 2 *adv* (*in a straight line*) ttokpparo 똑바로; (*directly, immediately*) kot-tchang 곧장; **stand up ~!** paro sŏ! 바로 서!; **look … in the eye** …ŭi nunŭl ttokpparo ch'ŏdaboda …의 눈을 똑바로 쳐다보다; **go ~** F (*of criminal*) ch'akssirhan saenghwarŭl hada 착실한 생활을 하다; **give it to me ~** F naege ttokpparo yaegihaejuseyo! 내게 똑바로 얘기해주세요!; **~ ahead** *be situated* paro ap'e 바로 앞에; *walk, drive* ttokpparo 똑바로; *look* ttokpparŭn 똑바른; **carry ~ on** (*of driver etc*) ttokpparo kada 똑바로 가다; **~away, ~ off** chŭksshi 즉시; **~ out** soltchik'age 솔직하게; **~ up** (*without ice*) sŭt'ŭreit'ŭ 스트레이트

straighten *v/t* ttokpparŭge hada 똑바르게 하다

♦ **straighten out 1** *v/t* situation haegyŏrhada 해결하다 **2** *v/i* (*of road*) pallajida 발라지다

♦ **straighten up** hŏrirŭl p'yŏda 허리를 펴다

straightforward (*honest, direct*) soltchik'an 솔직한; (*simple*) kanttanhan 간단한

strain[1] 1 *n* (*on rope*) p'aengp'aengham 팽팽함; (*on engine, heart*) muri 무리; (*on person*) kinjang 긴장 2 *v/t* (*injure*) murirŭl hada 무리를 하다; *finances, budget* pudamŭl chuda 부담을 주다

strain[2] *v/t* vegetables murŭl kŏrŭda 물을 거르다; *oil, fat etc* kŏllŏnaeda 걸러내다

strainer (*for vegetables etc*) ch'e 체

strait haehyŏp 해협

straitlaced ŏmkkyŏk'an 엄격한

strand[1] *n* (*of hair, wool, thread*) kadak 가닥

strand[2] *v/t* odogado mot'age hada 오도가도 못하게 하다; **be ~ed**

odogado mot'ada 오도가도 못하다

strange (*odd, curious*) isanghan 이상한; (*unknown, foreign*) morŭnŭn 모르는

strangely (*oddly*) isanghage 이상하게; **~ enough** isanghagedo 이상하게도

stranger (*person you don't know*) natssŏn saram 낯선 사람; *I'm a ~ here myself* yŏginŭn nado chal morŭnŭn koshimnida 여기는 나도 잘 모르는 곳입니다

strangle *person* kyosarhada 교살하다

strap *n* (*of purse*) kajuk-kkŭn 가죽끈; (*of bra, dress, shoe*) kkŭn 끈; (*of watch*) chul 줄

♦ **strap in** kojŏngshik'ida 고정시키다

strapless ŏkkaekkŭni ŏmnŭn 어깨끈이 없는

strategic chŏllyaktchŏgin 전략적인

strategy MIL chŏllyak 전략; (*plan*) kyehoek 계획

straw[1] miltchip 밀짚; *that's the last ~!* innaeŭi han-gyerŭl nŏmkke hanŭn kŏshida! 인내의 한계를 넘게 하는 것이다!

straw[2] (*for drink*) sŭt'ŭro 스트로

strawberry ttalgi 딸기

stray 1 *adj animal* chuin ŏmnŭn 주인 없는; *bullet* pinnagan 빗나간 **2** *n* (*dog, cat*) ttŏdori chimsŭng 떠돌이 짐승 **3** *v/i* (*of animal*) kirŭl ilt'a 길을 잃다; (*of child*) yŏp killo pinnagada 옆 길로 빗나가다; (*of eyes, thoughts*) hemaeda 헤매다

streak *n* (*of dirt, paint*) chulmunŭi ŏlluk 줄무늬 얼룩; (*of nastiness etc*) kimi 기미 **2** *v/i* (*move quickly*) pŏn-gaech'ŏrŏm tallida 번개처럼 달리다 **3** *v/t: be ~ed with* …(ŭ)ro churi chida …(으)로 줄이 지다

stream 1 *n* kaeul 개울; (*of people*) mulkkyŏl 물결; *come on ~* saengsanŭl kadonghada 생산을 가동하다 **2** *v/i* hŭrŭda 흐르다; *~ out of* …esŏ nŏmch'yŏ hŭrŭda …에서 넘쳐 흐르다; *sunlight ~ed into the room* haetppich'i pang-anŭro nŏmch'yŏ tŭrŏwatt-tta 햇빛이 방안으로 넘쳐 들어왔다

streamer ch'uktcheyong chong-i

t'eip'ŭ 축제용 종이 테이프

streamline *v/t fig* nŭngnyultchŏgŭro hada 능률적으로 하다

streamlined *car, plane* yusŏnhyŏng-ŭi 유선형의; *fig: organization* nŭngnyultchŏgin 능률적인

street kŏri 거리

streetcar chŏnch'a 전차; **streetlight** karodŭng 가로등; **streetpeople** purangja 부랑자; **streetwalker** ch'angnyŏ 창녀; **streetwise** *adj* sesang multchŏng-e palgŭn 세상 물정에 밝은

strength him 힘; *fig* (*strong point*) changtchŏm 장점; (*of wind, current*) kangdo 강도; (*of emotion, friendship etc*) kangham 강함; (*of currency*) kangse 강세

strengthen 1 *v/t* kanghage hada 강하게 하다 **2** *v/i* kanghaejida 강해지다

strenuous himdŭn 힘든

stress 1 *n* (*emphasis*) akssent'ŭ 악센트; (*tension*) sŭt'ŭresŭ 스트레스; *be under ~* sŭt'ŭresŭrŭl pat-tta 스트레스를 받다 **2** *v/t syllable* akssent'ŭrŭl chuda 악센트를 주다; *importance etc* kangjohada 강조하다; *I must ~ that …* nanŭn …ranŭn kŏsŭl kangjohaeyagesssŭmnida 나는 …라는 것을 강조해야겠습니다

stressed out F sŭt'ŭresŭrŭl shimhage pannŭn 스트레스를 심하게 받는

stressful sŭt'ŭresŭga shimhan 스트레스가 심한

stretch 1 *n* (*of land, water, road*) p'yŏlch'yŏjim 펼쳐짐; *at a ~* (*non-stop*) tansume 단숨에 **2** *adj fabric* shinch'uksssŏng innŭn 신축성 있는 **3** *v/t material* nŭrida 늘이다; *small income* akkyŏ ssŭda 아껴 쓰다; F *rules* hwakttae chŏgyonghada 확대 적용하다; *he ~ed out his hand* kŭnŭn sonŭl naemirŏt-tta 그는 손을 내밀었다; *a job that ~es me* nae nŭngnyŏgŭl hankkŏt parhwihage hanŭn chigŏp 내 능력을 한껏 발휘하게 하는 직업 **4** *v/i* (*to relax muscles*) tchuk ppŏt-tta 쭉 뻗다; (*to reach sth*) naemilda 내밀다; (*extend*) ppŏtch'ida 뻗치다; (*of fabric: give*)

nŭrŏnada 늘어나다; (*of fabric: sag*) **nŭrŏjida** 늘어지다; **~ *from X to Y*** (*extend*) Xesŏ Ykkaji ppŏdŏ it-tta X에서 Y까지 뻗어 있다

retcher tŭlkkŏt 들것

rict *person* ŏmhan 엄한; *instructions, rules* ŏmkkyŏk'an 엄격한

rictly ŏmkkyŏk'age 엄격하게; *it is ~* **forbidden** kŭgŏsŭn ŏmkkyŏk'age kŭmjidoeŏ it-tta 그것은 엄격하게 금지되어 있다

ride 1 *n* k'ŭn kŏrŭm 큰 걸음; *lengthen one's ~* songnyŏgŭl naeda 속력을 내다; *take sth in one's ~* muŏsŭl shwipkke ttwiŏnŏmtta 무엇을 쉽게 뛰어넘다 2 *v/i* sŏngk'ŭmsŏngk'ŭm kŏt-tta 성큼성큼 걷다

rident kwie kŏsŭllinŭn 귀에 거슬리는; *demands* soranhan 소란한

rike 1 *n* (*of workers*) p'aŏp 파업; (*in baseball*) sŭt'ŭraik'ŭ 스트라이크; (*of oil*) palgyŏn 발견; *be on ~* tongmaeng p'aŏp chung-ida 동맹 파업 중이다; *go on ~* tongmaeng p'aŏbŭl kyŏrhaenghada tongmaeng 파업을 결행하다 2 *v/i* (*of workers*) tongmaeng p'aŏbada 동맹 파업하다; (*attack*) konggyŏk'ada 공격하다; (*of disaster*) ttŏrŏjida 떨어지다; (*of clock*) ch'ida 치다 3 *v/t person* ttaerida 때리다; *object* pudich'ida 부딪히다; *fig* (*of disaster, illness*) kaptchagi tŏpch'ida 갑자기 덮치다; *match* kŭt-tta 긋다; (*of idea, thought*) ttŏ-orŭda 떠오르다; *oil* palgyŏnhada 발견하다; *she struck me as being ...* kŭnyŏnŭn naege ...(ŭ)ro poyŏt-tta 그녀는 내게 ...(으)로 보였다

strike out *v/t* (*delete*) saktchehada 삭제하다

trikebreaker p'aŏp panghaeja 파업 방해자

triker (*person on strike*) p'aŏptcha 파업자

triking (*marked*) tudŭrŏjinŭn 두드러지는; (*eye-catching*) insangjŏgin 인상적인

tring *n* (*cord*) kkŭn 끈; (*of violin, tennis racket etc*) chul 줄; *~s*

(*musicians*) hyŏnak-kki yŏnjuja 현악기 연주자; *pull ~s* paehu-esŏ chojonghada 배후에 조종하다; *a ~ of* (*series*) illyŏnŭi 일련의

♦ **string along** 1 *v/i* ttaragada 따라가다 2 *v/t*: *string X along* (*deceive*) Xŭl / rŭl sogida X을 / 를 속이다

♦ **string up** F kyosuhyŏng-e ch'ŏhada 교수형에 처하다

stringed instrument hyŏnak-kki 현악기

stringent ŏmjunghan 엄중한

string player hyŏnak-kki yŏnjuja 현악기 연주자

strip 1 *n* kanŭlgo kin chogak 가늘고 긴 조각; (*comic ~*) manhwaran 만화란 2 *v/t* (*remove*) pŏtkkida 벗기다; *leaves from tree* ttŏrŏttŭrida 떨어뜨리다; (*undress*) osŭl pŏtkkida 옷을 벗기다; *~ X of Y* Xegesŏ Yŭl / rŭl ppaeat-tta X에게서 Y을 / 를 빼앗다 3 *v/i* (*undress*) osŭl pŏt-tta 옷을 벗다; (*of stripper*) sŭt'ŭripsshorŭl hada 스트립쇼를 하다

strip club sŭt'ŭripsshorŭl hanŭn kot 스트립쇼를 하는 곳

stripe chulmunŭi 줄무늬; (*indicating rank*) kyegŭp 계급

striped chulmunŭi-ŭi 줄무늬의

stripper sŭt'ŭrip'ŏ 스트리퍼

strip show sŭt'ŭripssho 스트립쇼

striptease sŭt'ŭripssho ch'ŭrip쇼

strive 1 *v/t*: *~ to do ...* ...ŭl / rŭl haryŏgo noryŏk'ada ...을 / 를 하려고 노력하다 2 *v/i*: *~ for ...* ...ŭl / rŭl ŏdŭryŏgo noryŏk'ada ...을 / 를 얻으려고 노력하다

stroke 1 *n* MED noejol 뇌졸; (*in writing, painting*) hoek 획; (*style of swimming*) suyŏngppŏp 수영법; *~ of luck* ttŭtppakkŭi haeng-un 뜻밖의 행운; *she never does a ~* (*of work*) kŭnyŏnŭn sonkkaraktto kkadak'aji annŭnda 그녀는 손가락도 까닥하지 않는다 2 *v/t* ssŭdadŭmtta 쓰다듬다

stroll 1 *n* sanch'aek 산책 2 *v/i* sanch'aek'ada 산책하다; *she ~ed over to the radio* kŭnyŏnŭn ladio

innŭn tchogŭro ŏsullŏnggŏrimyŏ
kŏrŏgat-tta 그녀는 라디오 있는
쪽으로 어슬렁거리며 걸어갔다
stroller (*for baby*) yumoch'a 유모차
strong *person* himssen 힘센; *feeling*
kanghan 강한; *structure* kyŏn-gohan
견고한; *candidate* yuryŏk'an 유력한;
support, supporter kangnyŏk'an
강력한; *wind* ssen 센; *tea, coffee*
chinhan 진한; *alcoholic drink* tok'an
독한; *taste, perfume* kangnyŏrhan
강렬한; *smell* chidok'an 지독한;
views, objections kanggyŏnghan
강경한; *currency* kangseŭi 강세의
stronghold *fig* kŭn-gŏji 근거지
strongly *object, feel* kanghage 강하게
strong-minded shimjiga kujŭn
심지가 굳은
strong-willed ŭijiga kanghan 의지가
강한
structural kujosang-ŭi 구조상의
structure 1 *n* (*sth built*)
kŏnch'ungmul 건축물; (*mode of
construction*) kujo 구조 **2** *v/t* tchada
짜다
struggle 1 *n* (*fight*) ssa-um 싸움; (*for
power*) t'ujaeng 투쟁; (*hard time*)
aktchŏn kot'u 악전 고투 **2** *v/i* (*with a
person*) momburimch'ida
몸부림치다; (*have a hard time*)
aktchŏn kot'uhada 악전 고투하다;
(*mentally*) aessŭda 애쓰다 **3** *v/t*: **~ to
do** ...ŭl/rŭl haryŏgo
momburimch'ida ...을/를 하려고
몸부림치다; *she was struggling to
understand* kŭnyŏnŭn ihaeharyŏgo
aessŏt-tta 그녀는 이해하려고 애썼다
strum kabyŏpkke ch'ida 가볍게 치다
strut *v/i* kŏdŭlmŏk-kkŏrimyŏ kŏt-tta
거들먹거리며 걷다
stub 1 *n* (*of cigarette*) kkongch'o 꽁초;
(*of check, ticket*) tteŏjugo namŭn
tchok 떼어주고 남은 쪽 **2** *v/t*: **~
one's toe** palkkŭch'ŭl ch'ae-ida
발끝을 채이다
♦ **stub out** pibyŏ kkŭda 비벼 끄다
stubble (*on man's face*)
kkach'irhaejin suyŏm 까칠해진 수염
stubborn kojibi ssen 고집이 센;
refusal, defense wan-ganghan 완강한
stubby mungttuk'an 뭉뚝한

stuck: **be ~ on ...** F (*romantically*)
...ege panhae it-tta ...에게 반해
있다
stuck-up F kŏmanhan 거만한
student hakssaeng 학생
student movement hakssaeng
undong 학생 운동; **student nurse**
kanho shilssŭpssaeng 간호 실습생;
student teacher kyoyuk
shilssŭpssaeng 교육 실습생,
kyosaeng 교생
studio (*of artist, sculptor*) chagŏpss
작업실; (*recording ~*) nogŭmshil
녹음실; (*film ~*) yŏnghwa
ch'waryŏngso 영화 촬영소; (*TV ~*)
pangsongshil 방송실
studious yŏlsshimhi kongbuhanŭn
열심히 공부하는
study 1 *n* (*room*) sŏjae 서재;
(*learning*) kongbu 공부; (*research*)
yŏn-gu 연구 **2** *v/t* (*at school,
university*) kongbuhada 공부하다;
(*examine*) chal salp'yŏboda 잘
살펴보다 **3** *v/i* kongbuhada 공부하다
stuff 1 *n* (*things*) mulgŏn 물건;
(*belongings*) chim 짐 **2** *v/t turkey*
sogŭl ch'ae-uda 속을 채우다; **~ X
into Y** Xŭl/rŭl Ye ch'aewŏ nŏt'a
x을/를 Y에 채워 넣다
stuffed toy inhyŏng 인형
stuffing (*for turkey*) sok 속; (*in cha*
teddy bear) sogŭl ch'aenŭn chaer
속을 채우는 재료
stuffy *room* t'ongp'ung-i chal
andoenŭn 통풍이 잘 안되는; *perso*
ttattak'an 딱딱한
stumble hŏt-ttidida 헛디디다
♦ **stumble across** uyŏnhi majuch'i
우연히 마주치다
♦ **stumble over** ...e kŏllyŏ nŏmŏjid
...에 걸려 넘어지다; *words* tŏdŭmt
더듬다
stumbling block chang-aemul 장애
stump 1 *n* (*of tree*) kŭrut'ŏgi 그루터
2 *v/t* (*of question, questioner*)
nanch'ŏhage hada 난처하게 하다
♦ **stump up** F tonŭl naeda 돈을 내다
stun (*with a blow*) kijŏlsshik'ida
기절시키다; (*by news*)
ŏribŏngbŏnghage hada 어리벙벙하게
하다

stunning (*amazing*) koengjanghan 굉장한; (*very beautiful*) maeu mŏshinnŭn 매우 멋있는

stunt n (*for publicity*) imogŭl kkŭlgi wihan haengdong 이목을 끌기 위한 행동; (*in movie*) wihŏmhan changmyŏn 위험한 장면

stuntman sŭt'ŏnt'ŭmaen 스턴트맨

stupefy mŏnghage hada 멍하게 하다

stupendous koengjanghan 굉장한; (*very large*) ŏmch'ŏngnan 엄청난

stupid ŏrisŏgŭn 어리석은; *book, movie* shishihan 시시한

stupidity ŏrisŏgŭm 어리석음

stupor (*drunken*) insa pulssŏng 인사 불성

sturdy ŏksen 억센; *object* t'ŭnt'ŭnhan 튼튼한

stutter v/i marŭl tŏdŭmtta 말을 더듬다

style n (*method, manner*) pangbŏp 방법; (*of writing*) munch'e 문체; (*of architecture*) yangshik 양식; (*fashion*) yuhaeng 유행; (*elegance*) p'umkkyŏk 품격; **go out of ~** yuhaeng-i chinada 유행이 지나다

stylish mŏshinnŭn 멋있는

stylist (*hair ~*) sŭt'aillisŭt'ŭ 스타일리스트

subcommittee punkkwa wiwŏnhoe 분과 위원회

subcompact (*car*) sohyŏng chadongch'a 소형 자동차

subconscious: *the ~* (*mind*) muŭishik 무의식

subcontract v/t hach'ŏnghada 하청하다

subcontractor hach'ŏng-ŏptcha 하청업자

subdirectory COMPUT ttallin tirekt'ori 딸린 디렉토리

subdivide v/t sebunhada 세분하다

subdued kara-anjŭn 가라앉은; *lighting* natch'un 낮춘

subheading chagŭn chemok 작은 제목

subject 1 n (*of country*) kungmin 국민; (*topic*) chuje 주제; (*branch of learning*) kwamok 과목; GRAM chuŏ 주어; **change the ~** hwajerŭl pakkuda 화제를 바꾸다 2 *adj*: **be ~**

to …hagi shwiun …하기 쉬운; **~ to availability** yŏbuni nama innŭn hando naeesŏ 여분이 남아 있는 한도 내에서 3 v/t: **~ s.o. to** nuguege …ŭl/rŭl kyŏk-kke hada 누구에게 …을/를 겪게 하다

subjective chugwanjŏgin 주관적인

sublet v/t chŏndaehada 전대하다

submachine gun kigwan tanch'ong 기관 단총

submarine chamsuham 잠수함

submerge 1 v/t chamgige hada 잠기게 하다 2 v/i (*of submarine*) chamsuhada 잠수하다

submission (*surrender*) hangbok 항복; (*to committee etc*) chech'uran 제출안

submissive sunjongjŏgin 순종적인

submit v/t plan, proposal chech'urhada 제출하다

subordinate 1 *adj* arae-ŭi 아래의 2 n araet saram 아랫 사람

subpoena 1 n sohwantchang 소환장 2 v/t person sohwanhada 소환하다

♦ **subscribe to** magazine etc chŏnggi kudok'ada 정기 구독하다; *theory* …e tong-ŭihada …에 동의하다

subscriber (*to magazine*) chŏnggi kudoktcha 정기 구독자

subscription chŏnggi kudok 정기 구독

subsequent ttarasŏ irŏnan 따라서 일어난

subsequently kŭ hu-e 그 후에

subside (*of flood waters*) ppajida 빠지다; (*of winds, fears*) karaantta 가라앉다; (*of building*) naeryŏantta 내려앉다

subsidiary n chahoesa 자회사

subsidize pojogŭmŭl chigŭp'ada 보조금을 지급하다

subsidy pojogŭm 보조금

♦ **subsist on** … (ŭ)ro sara nagada … (으)로 살아 나가다

subsistence farmer chagumnong 자급농

subsistence level ch'oejŏ saenghwal sujun 최저 생활 수준

substance (*matter*) multchil 물질

substandard p'yojun midarŭi 표준 미달의

substantial sangdanghan 상당한

substantially (*considerably*) sangdanghage 상당하게; (*in essence*) shiltchiltchŏguro 실질적으로

substantiate chŭnggŏrŭl taeda 증거를 대다

substantive *adj* shiltchiltchŏgin 실질적인

substitute 1 *n* (*for person*) taeriin 대리인; (*for commodity*) taeyongp'um 대용품; SP pogyŏl sŏnsu 보결 선수 **2** *v/t* taeshinŭro ssŭda 대신으로 쓰다; ~ **X for Y** X(ŭ)ro Yŭl/rŭl taeshinhada X(으)로 Y을/를 대신하다 **3** *v/i*: ~ **for s.o.** nugurŭl taeshinhada 누구를 대신하다

substitution (*act*) taeyong 대용; **make a ~** SP taeshin kiyonghada 대신 기용하다

subtitle 1 *n* chamak 자막 **2** *v/t movie* chamagŭl talda 자막을 달다

subtle mimyohan 미묘한

subtract *v/t number* ppaeda 빼다; ~ **X from Y** Yesŏ Xŭl/rŭl ppaeda Y에서 X을/를 빼다

suburb kyo-oe 교외; **the ~s** kŭn-gyo 근교

suburban kŭn-gyo-ŭi 근교의

subversive 1 *adj* chŏnbokshik'inŭn 전복시키는 **2** *n* chŏnbok 전복

subway chihach'ŏl 지하철

subzero *adj* yŏnghaŭi 영하의

succeed 1 *v/i* (*be successful*) sŏnggonghada 성공하다; (*to the throne*) kyesŭnghada 계승하다; (*in office*) in-gyehada 인계하다; ~ **in doing** …ŭl/rŭl hanŭn te sŏnggonghada …을/를 하는 데 성공하다 **2** *v/t* (*come after*) huimjaga toeda 후임자가 되다; *monarch* kyesŭnghada 계승하다

succeeding twiiŭn 뒤이은

success sŏnggong 성공; **be a ~** taesŏnggong-ida 대성공이다

successful sŏnggongtchŏgin 성공적인

successfully sŏnggongtchŏguro 성공적으로

succession (*sequence*) yŏnsok 연속; (*to the throne*) kyesŭng 계승; (*to office*) in-gye 인계; **in ~** kyesok'aesŏ 계속해서

successive it-ttarŭn 잇따른

successor huimja 후임자

succinct kan-gyŏrhan 간결한

succulent *meat, fruit* chŭbi manŭn 즙이 많은

succumb (*give in*) kulbok'ada 굴복하다; ~ **to temptation** yuhoge kulbok'ada 유혹에 굴복하다

such 1 *adj* (*of that kind*) kŭrŏn 그런; ~ **a** (*to that extent*) kŭ chŏngdo-ŭi 그 정도의; ~ **as** …wa/kwa kat'ŭn …와/과 같은; **there is no ~ word as …** …wa/kwa kat'ŭn marŭn ŏptta …와/과 같은 말은 없다 **2** *adv* kŭrŏk'e 그렇게; **as ~** kŭrŏsŏ 그로서; **it was ~ a hot day** kŭrŏk'e tŏun nariŏssŏyo 그렇게 더운 나라이었어요

suck *candy* ppara mŏktta 빨아 먹다; ~ **one's thumb** sonkkaragŭl ppalda 손가락을 빨다; ~ **X from Y** Yesŏ Xŭl/rŭl ppalda Y에서 X을/를 빨다

♦ **suck up 1** *v/t* pparadŭrida 빨아들이다 **2** *v/i*: ~ **to s.o.** nuguege ach'ŏmhada 누구에게 아첨하다

sucker F (*person*) chal songnŭn saram 잘 속는 사람; (*lollipop*) makttaegi sat'ang 막대기 사탕

sucking pig chŏnmŏgi twaeji 젖먹이 돼지

suction hŭbip 흡입

sudden kaptchakssŭrŏn 갑작스런; **all of a ~** kaptchagi 갑자기

suddenly kaptchagi 갑자기

suds (*soap ~*) kŏp'um 거품

sue *v/t* kosohada 고소하다

suede *n* sŭweidŭ 스웨이드

suffer 1 *v/i* (*be in pain*) kosaenghada 고생하다; (*deteriorate*) nappajida 나빠지다; (*of school work etc*) chijang-ŭl pat-tta 지장을 받다; **be ~ing from** …ranŭn pyŏng-ŭl kajigo it-tta …라는 병을 가지고 있다 **2** *v/t*: ~ **a loss** sonhaerŭl iptta 손해를 입다; ~ **a setback** panghaerŭl pat-tta 방해를 받다

suffering *n* kot'ong 고통

sufficient ch'ungbunhan 충분한

sufficiently ch'ungbunhage 충분하게

suffocate 1 *v/i* chilsshiksssahada 질식사하다 **2** *v/t* chilsshiksshik'ida 질식시키다

suffocation chilsshik 질식

sugar 1 *n* sŏlt'ang 설탕 **2** *v/t* sŏlt'angŭl nŏt'a 설탕을 넣다

sugar bowl sŏlt'ang-t'ong 설탕통

sugar cane sat'ang susu 사탕 수수

suggest *v/t* cheanhada 제안하다; *I ~ that we stop now* nanŭn uriga chigŭm kŭmandul kŏsŭl cheanhamnida 나는 우리가 지금 그만둘 것을 제안합니다

suggestion chean 제안

suicide chasal 자살; *commit ~* chasarhada 자살하다

suit 1 *n* yangbok han pŏl 양복 한 벌; *(in cards)* tchakp'ae han pŏl 짝패 한 벌 **2** *v/t* *(of clothes, color)* ŏullida 어울리다; *~ yourself!* maŭmdaero haseyo! 마음대로 하세요!; *be ~ed for* ...e chŏk'ap'ada ...에 적합하다

suitable ŏullinŭn 어울리는; *choice of words, time* chŏkttanghan 적당한

suitcase yŏhaeng kabang 여행 가방

suite *(of rooms)* sŭwit'ŭ 스위트; *(furniture)* sop'a sett'ŭ 소파 셋트; MUS chogok 조곡

sulfur yuhwang 유황

sulk *v/i* purut'unghaejida 부루퉁해지다

sulky purut'unghan 부루퉁한

sullen ch'imurhan 침울한

sultry *climate* hut'ŏptchigŭnhan 후텁지근한; *(sexually)* kwannŭngjŏgin 관능적인

sum *(total)* ch'onggye 총계; *(amount)* kŭmaek 금액; *(in arithmetic)* kyesan 계산; *a large ~ of money* manŭn ton 많은 돈; *the ~ insured* hwaktchŏng kŭmaek 확정 금액; *the ~ total of his efforts* kŭŭi noryŏgŭi ch'ongch'e 그의 노력의 총체

♦ **sum up 1** *v/t (summarize)* yoyak'ada 요약하다; *(assess)* p'yŏngkkahada 평가하다 **2** *v/i* LAW p'ansaga kaegwarhayŏ marhada 판사가 개괄하여 말하다

summarize *v/t* yoyak'ada 요약하다

summary *n* yoyak 요약

summer yŏrŭm 여름

summit *(of mountain)* chŏngsang 정상; *fig* chŏltchŏng 절정; POL sunoe hoedam 수뇌 회담

summon sojip'ada 소집하다

♦ **summon up** *strength* pullŏ irŭk'ida 불러 일으키다

summons LAW sohwantchang 소환장

sump *(for oil)* kirŭmt'ong 기름통

sun t'aeyang 태양; *in the ~* haetppyŏch'e(sŏ) 햇볕에(서); *out of the ~* kŭnŭre(sŏ) 그늘에(서); *he has had too much ~* kŭnŭn haetppyŏch'ŭl nŏmu tchoe-ŏt-tta 그는 햇볕을 너무 쬐었다

sunbathe ilgwangnyogŭl hada 일광욕을 하다; **sunblock** haetppyŏt ch'adannyong k'ŭrim 햇볕 차단용 크림; **sunburn** haetppyŏch'e t'am 햇볕에 탐; **sunburnt** haetppyŏch'e t'an 햇볕에 탄

Sunday iryoil 일요일

sundial haeshigye 해시계

sundries chap-ppi 잡비

sunglasses saegan-gyŏng 색안경

sunken *cheeks* holtchuk'an 홀쪽한

sunny *day* hwach'anghan 화창한; *disposition* myŏngnanghan 명랑한; *it's ~* hwach'anghan narimnida 화창한 날압니다

sunrise ilch'ul 일출; **sunset** ilmol 일몰; **sunshade** p'arasol 파라솔; **sunshine** haetppit 햇빛; **sunstroke** ilssappyŏng 일사병; **suntan** haetppyŏch'e t'am 햇볕에 탐; *get a ~* haetppyŏch'e t'aeuda 햇볕에 태우다

super 1 *adj* F ch'oegoŭi 최고의 **2** *n (of apartment block)* kwalliin 관리인

superb koengjanghi ttwiŏnan 굉장히 뛰어난

superficial *analysis* p'yomyŏnjŏgin 표면적인; *person* ch'ŏnbak'an 천박한; *wounds* yat'ŭn 얕은

superfluous *pulp* iryohan 불필요한

superhuman *efforts* ch'oinjŏgin 초인적인

superintendent *(of apartment block)* kwalliin 관리인

superior 1 *adj (better)* poda ttwiŏnan 보다 뛰어난; *pej: attitude* kŏmanhan

거만한 2 n (in organization, society) witssaram 윗사람

supermarket sup'ŏmak'et 수퍼마켓; **supernatural 1** adj powers ch'ojayŏnjŏgin 초자연적인 2 n: **the ~** ch'ojayŏnjŏgin hyŏnsang 초자연적인 현상; **superpower** POL ch'ogangdaeguk 초강대국; **supersonic** ch'oŭmsogŭi 초음속의

superstition mishin 미신

superstitious person mishinŭl minnŭn 미신을 믿는

supervise kamdok'ada 감독하다

supervisor (at work) kamdoktcha 감독자

supper chŏnyŏk shiksa 저녁 식사

supple yuyŏnhan 유연한

supplement (extra payment) ch'ugaaek 추가액

supplier COM konggŭbwŏn 공급원

supply 1 n konggŭp 공급; **~ and demand** konggŭpkkwa suyo 공급과 수요; **supplies** konggŭpp'um 공급품 2 v/t goods konggŭp'ada 공급하다; **X with Y** Xege Yŭl/rŭl konggŭp'ada X에게 Y을/를 공급하다; **be supplied with** …i/ga naejangdoeŏ it-tta …이/가 내장되어 있다

support 1 n (structural) t'odae 토대; (backing) chiji 지지 2 v/t building, structure chit'aenghada 지탱하다; (financially) puyanghada 부양하다; (back) chijihada 지지하다

supporter chijija 지지자; (of football team etc) huwŏnja 후원자

supportive chal towajunŭn 잘 도와주는

suppose (imagine) kajŏnghada 가정하다; **I ~ so** ama kŭrŏk'etchi 아마 그렇겠지; **be ~d to** … (be meant to) …hagiro toeŏit-tta …하기로 되어있다; (be said to be) …(ŭ)ro allyŏjyŏ it-tta …(으)로 알려져 있다; **you are not ~d to** … (not allowed to) …haji ank'iro toeŏit-tta …하지 않기로 되어있다

suppository MED chwayak 좌약

suppress rebellion etc chinap'ada 진압하다

suppression chinap 진압

supremacy chudokkwŏn 주도권

supreme being, commander ch'oegowŭi 최고의의; effort, courage, delight kŭkttoŭi 극도의

Supreme Court Kodŭng Pŏbwŏn 고등 법원

surcharge n puga yogŭm 부가 요금

sure 1 adj hwaksshinhanŭn 확신하는 I'm **~** hwaksshinhamnida 확신합니다; I'm not **~** kŭlsseyo 글쎄요; be **~ about** …e taehae hwaksshinhada …에 대해 확신하다 make **~ that** …ranŭn kŏsŭl hwaksshirhage hada …라는 것을 확실하게 하다 2 adv: **~ enough** chŏngmallo 정말로; it **~ is hot today** F onŭrŭn hwaksshirhi tŏpkkunnyo 오늘은 확실히 덥군요; **~!** mullon! 물론!

surely (certainly) pandŭshi 반드시; (gladly) kikkŏi 기꺼이; (slight doubt) sŏlma 설마; (strong doubt) kyŏlk'o 결코; **~ you don't mean that** sŏlma chinjŏngŭro kŭrŏk'e marhanŭn kŏ anigetchiyo 설마 진정으로 그렇게 말하는 건 아니겠지요; **~ that can't be right** kyŏlk'o majŭl li ŏpssŏyo 결코 맞을 리 없어요

surf 1 n (on sea) millyŏdŭnŭn p'ado 밀려드는 파도 2 v/t: **~ the Net** int'ŏnesŭl tullŏboda 인터넷을 둘러보다

surface 1 n (of table, object) p'yomyŏn 표면; (of water) sumyŏn 수면; **on the ~** fig kŏt'ŭronŭn 겉으로는 2 v/i (of swimmer, submarine) ttŏorŭda 떠오르다; (appear) nat'anada 나타나다

surface mail yukssang up'yŏnmul 육상 우편물

surfboard sŏp'ing podŭ 서핑 보드

surfer (on sea) sŏp'inghanŭn saram 서핑하는 사람

surfing sŏp'ing 서핑; **go ~** sŏp'ingharŏ kada 서핑하러 가다

surge n ELEC chŏllyuŭi tongnyo 전류의 동요; (in demand etc) kŭppssangssŭng 급상승

♦ **surge forward** (of crowd) millyŏnagada 밀려나가다

surgeon oekkwa ŭisa 외과 의사

surgery susul 수술; **undergo ~** susurŭl pat-tta 수술을 받다

surgical susurŭi 수술의

surly muttukttuk'an 무뚝뚝한

surmount *difficulties* kŭkppok'ada 극복하다

surname sŏng 성

surpass nŭnggahada 능가하다

surplus 1 *n* ing-yŏ 잉여 **2** *adj* namŏjiŭi 나머지의

surprise 1 *n* nollaum 놀라움; *it'll come as no ~* nollaptchi anŭn iri toel kŏshida 놀랍지 않은 일이 될 것이다 **2** *v/t* nollage hada 놀라게 하다; *be / look ~d* nollada / nolla poida 놀라다 / 놀라 보이다

surprising nollaun 놀라운

surprisingly nollapkke 놀랍게

surrender 1 *v/i* MIL hangbok'ada 항복하다 **2** *v/t* (*hand in: weapons etc*) nŏmgyŏjuda 넘겨주다 **3** *n* hangbok 항복; (*handing in*) indo 인도

surrogate mother taerimo 대리모

surround *v/t* tullŏ ssada 둘러 싸다; *be ~ed by* …(ŭ)ro tullŏssaida …(으)로 둘러싸이다

surrounding *adj* chuwiŭi 주위의

surroundings hwan-gyŏng 환경

survey 1 *n* (*of modern literature etc*) kaekwan 개관; (*of building*) chosa 조사 **2** *v/t* (*look at*) tullŏboda 둘러보다; *building* chosahada 조사하다

surveyor kŏnmul chosawŏn 건물 조사원

survival saranamŭm 살아남음; *struggle for ~* saengjon kyŏngjaeng 생존 경쟁; *~ of the fittest* chŏktcha saengjon 적자 생존

survive 1 *v/i* (*of species, patient*) saranamtta 살아남다; *how are you? – surviving* ŏttŏseyo? – kŭjŏ kŭraeyo 어떠세요? – 그저 그래요; *his two surviving daughters* kŭga namgin tu ttal 그가 남긴 두 딸 **2** *v/t* *accident, operation* saranamtta 살아남다; (*outlive*) poda orae salda 보다 오래 살다

survivor saengjonja 생존자; *he's a ~ fig* kŭnŭn saengjonnyŏgi kanghada 그는 생존력이 강하다

susceptible (*emotionally*) kamsusŏng-i kanghan 감수성이 강한; *be ~ to the cold / heat* ch'uwie / yŏre min-gamhada 추위에 / 열에 민감하다

suspect 1 *n* hyŏmŭija 혐의자 **2** *v/t* *person* ŭishimhada 의심하다; (*suppose*) chimjak'ada 짐작하다

suspected *murderer* hyŏmŭirŭl pannŭn 혐의를 받는; *cause, heart attack etc* chimjakttoenŭn 짐작되는

suspend (*hang*) maedalda 매달다; (*from office, duties*) chŏngjishik'ida 정지시키다

suspenders (*for pants*) melppang 멜빵

suspense sŏsŭp'ensŭ 서스펜스

suspension (*in vehicle*) sŏsŭp'enshyŏn 서스펜션; (*from duty*) chŏngji 정지

suspension bridge hyŏnsugyo 현수교

suspicion ŭishim 의심

suspicious (*causing suspicion*) susanghan 수상한; (*feeling suspicion*) ŭishimsŭrŏun 의심스러운; *be ~ of* …ŭl / rŭl ŭishimhada …을 / 를 의심하다

sustain *pressure etc* chit'aenghada 지탱하다; *injuries* pat-tta 받다

swab *v/t* kŏllejirhada 걸레질하다

swagger *n* ppomnaenŭn kŏrŭm 뽐내는 걸음

swallow[1] *v/t & v/i* samk'ida 삼키다

swallow[2] *n* (*bird*) chebi 제비

swamp 1 *n* nŭp 늪 **2** *v/t*: *be ~ed with* …(ŭ)ro mirŏdakch'yŏ it-tta …(으)로 밀어닥쳐 있다

swampy *ground* nŭp kat'ŭn 늪 같은

swan paektcho 백조

swap 1 *v/t*: *~ X for Y* Xŭl / rŭl Ywa / kwa pakkuda X을 / 를 Y와 / 과 바꾸다 **2** *v/i* pakkuda 바꾸다

swarm 1 *n* (*of bees*) tte 떼 **2** *v/i* (*of ants, tourists etc*) tterŭl chit-tta 떼를 짓다; *the town was ~ing with tourists* toshinŭn kwan-gwanggaegŭro ttejŏ issŏt-tta 도시는 관광객으로 떼지어 있었다

swarthy kŏmusŭrehan 거무스레한

swat *v/t* *insect, fly* ch'alssak ch'ida

찰싹 치다

sway 1 n (influence, power) seryŏk 세력 **2** v/i hŭndŭlgŏrida 흔들리다

swear v/i (use swearword) yogŭl hada 욕을 하다; (promise) maengsehada 맹세하다; LAW sŏnsŏhada 선서하다; **~ at** ...ege yogŭl hada ...에게 욕을 하다

♦ **swear in: ~ as a witness** chŭnginŭro sŏnsŏhada 증인으로 선서하다

swearword yok kok 욕

sweat 1 n ttam 땀; **covered in ~** ttamt'usŏng-iin 땀투성이인 **2** v/i ttamŭl hŭllida 땀을 흘리다

sweater sŭwet'ŏ 스웨터

sweatshirt sŭwet'ŭ shyŏch'ŭ 스웨트 셔츠

sweaty hands ttami paen 땀이 밴; smell ttamnae nanŭn 땀내 나는

Swede Sŭweden saram 스웨덴 사람

Sweden Sŭweden 스웨덴

Swedish 1 adj Sŭwedenŭi 스웨덴의 **2** n Sŭweden mal 스웨덴 말

sweep 1 v/t floor, leaves ssŭlda 쓸다 **2** n (long curve) man-gok 만곡

♦ **sweep up** v/t mess, crumbs ssurŏ moŭda 쓸어 모으다

sweeping adj generalization, statement taegang-ŭi 대강의; changes chŏnmyŏngjŏgin 전면적인

sweet adj taste, tea tan 단; F (kind) ch'injŏrhan 친절한; F (cute) kwiyŏun 귀여운

sweet and sour adj saek'omdalk'omhan 새콤달콤한

sweetcorn okssusu 옥수수

sweeten v/t drink, food talgehada 달게 하다

sweetener (for drink) kammiryo 감미료

sweetheart aein 애인

swell 1 v/i (of limb) put-tta 붓다 **2** adj F (good) mŏtchin 멋진 **3** n (of the sea) kubich'im 굽이침

swelling n MED pugi 부기

sweltering chinun tŭt'an 찌는 듯한

swerve v/i (of driver, car) pinnagada 빗나가다

swift adj pparŭn 빠른

swim 1 v/i suyŏnghada 수영하다; **go ~ming** suyŏngharŏ kada 수영하러

가다; **my head is ~ming** hyŏn-gijŭng-i nanda 현기증이 난다 **2** n suyŏng 수영; **go for a ~** suyŏngharŏ kada 수영하러 가다

swimmer suyŏnghanŭn saram 수영하는 사람

swimming suyŏng 수영

swimming pool suyŏngjang 수영장

swimsuit suyŏngbok 수영복

swindle 1 n sagi 사기 **2** v/t sagirŭl ch'ida 사기를 치다; **~ X out of Y** Xegesŏ Yŭl/rŭl sach'wihada X에게서 Y를/을 사취하다

swine F (person) saekki 새끼

swing 1 n (of pendulum) hŭndŭllim 흔들림; (for child) kŭne 그네; **there has been a ~ to the Democrats** yŏroni Minjudang tchoguro kiulgo it-tta 여론이 민주당 쪽으로 기울고 있다 **2** v/t hŭndŭlda 흔들다 **3** v/i hŭndŭlgŏrida 흔들거리다; (turn) hoejŏnshik'ida 회전시키다; (of public opinion etc) kiulda 기울다

swing-door hoejŏnmu 회전문

Swiss adj Sŭwisŭŭi 스위스의

switch 1 n (for light) sŭwich'i 스위치; (change) chŏnhwan 전환 **2** v/t (change) pakkuda 바꾸다 **3** v/i (change) pakkwida 바뀌다

♦ **switch off** v/t lights, engine, PC kkŭda 끄다

♦ **switch on** v/t lights, engine, PC k'yŏda 켜다

switchboard paejŏnban 배전반

switchover (to new system) chŏnhwan 전환

Switzerland Sŭwisŭ 스위스

swivel v/i hoejŏnhada 회전하다

swollen puŭn 부은

swoop v/i (of bird) naeri tŏpch'ida 내리 덮치다

♦ **swoop down on** prey ...ŭl/rŭl hyanghae naeri tŏpch'ida ...을/를 향해 내리 덮치다

♦ **swoop on** (of police etc) tŏpch'ida 덮치다

sword kŏm 검

sycamore k'ŭn tanp'ungnamu 큰 단풍나무

syllable ŭmjŏl 음절

syllabus kaeyo 개요
symbol (*character*) kiho 기호; (*in poetry etc*) sangjing 상징
symbolic sangjingjŏgin 상징적인
symbolism sangjingjuŭi 상징주의
symbolize sangjinghada 상징하다
symmetric(al) taech'ingjŏgin 대칭적인
symmetry taech'ing 대칭
sympathetic (*showing pity*) tongjŏnghanŭn 동정하는; (*understanding*) chal arajunŭn 잘 알아주는; **be ~ toward a person / an idea** nugurŭl / saenggagŭl chal ihaehada 누구를 / 생각을 잘 이해하다
sympathize with *person, views* chal ihaehada 잘 이해하다
sympathizer POL tongjoja 동조자
sympathy (*pity*) tongjŏngshim 동정심; (*understanding*) ihae 이해; **don't expect any ~ from me!** naege ihaebadŭl saenggagŭn ilch'e haji mara 내게 이해받을 생각은 일체 하지 마라
symphony kyohyanggok 교향곡
symptom MED, *fig* chŭnghu 증후

symptomatic: *be ~ of* ...ŭi chŭnghurŭl poida ...의 증후를 보이다
synchronize shiganŭl match'uda 시간을 맞추다
synonym tong-ŭiŏ 동의어
syntax munjangnon 문장론
synthetic hapssŏng-ŭi 합성의
syphilis maedok 매독
syringe chusagi 주사기
syrup shirŏp 시럽
system ch'egye 체계; (*structure: political etc*) chojik 조직; (*method*) pangshik 방식; (*orderliness*) sunsŏ 순서; (*computer*) shisŭt'em 시스템; **the braking / fuel injection ~** pŭreik'ŭ changch'i / yŏllyo konggŭp changch'i 브레이크 장치 / 연료 공급 장치; **digestive ~** sohwa kyet'ong 소화 계통
systematic *approach* chojiktchŏgin 조직적인
systematically *study* ch'egejŏgŭro 체계적으로; *destroy* kyehoektchŏgŭro 계획적으로
systems analyst COMPUT shisŭt'em punsŏk-kka 시스템 분석가

T

tab *n* ttagae 따개; (*in text*) t'aep 탭;
pick up the ~ hant'ŏk naeda 한턱
내다
table *n* sang 상; (*of figures*) p'yo 표
tablecloth shikt'akppo 식탁보
tablespoon k'ŭn sutkkarak 큰 숟가락
tablet MED allyak 알약, chŏngje 정제
table tennis t'ak-kku 탁구
tabloid *n* (*newspaper*) t'abŭlloidŭp'an
shinmun 타블로이드판 신문
taboo *adj* kŭmgiŭi 금기의
tacit muŏnŭi 무언의
tack 1 *n* (*nail*) aptchŏng 압정 **2** *v/t*
(*sew*) shich'imjirhada 시침질하다
3 *v/i* (*of yacht*) kaltchitchahyŏng-ŭro
naagada 갈짓자형으로 나아가다
tackle 1 *n* (*gear*) togu 도구; SP t'aek'ŭl
태클 **2** *v/t* SP t'aek'ŭrhada 태클하다;
problem ...wa/kwa sshirŭmhada
...와/과 씨름하다; *intruder* ...e
tallyŏdŭlda ...에 달려들다
tacky *paint, glue* kkŭnjŏk-kkŭnjŏk'an
끈적끈적한; (*cheap, poor quality*)
polp'um ŏmnŭn 볼품 없는; *behavior*
ch'ŏnbak'an 천박한
tact chaech'i 재치
tactful chaech'i innŭn 재치 있는
tactical chŏnsultchŏgin 전술적인
tactics chŏnsul 전술
tactless chaech'i ŏmnŭn 재치 없는
tadpole olch'aeng-i 올챙이
Taedong River Taedonggang 대동강
T'aekwondo T'aekkwŏndo 태권도
tag (*label*) kkorip'yo 꼬리표
tail *n* kkori 꼬리
tail light midŭng 미등
tailor chaebongsa 재봉사
tailor-made *suit* match'umŭi 맞춤의;
solution ansŏng match'umŭi 안성
맞춤의
tail wind sunp'ung 순풍
tainted *food* ssŏgŭn 썩은; *reputation,
atmosphere* tŏrŏp'yŏjin 더럽혀진
Taiwan Taeman 대만

Taiwanese 1 *adj* Taemanŭi 대만의
2 *n* Taemanin 대만인; (*dialect*)
Taemanŏ 대만어
take *v/t* (*remove*) kajigo kada 가지고
가다; (*steal*) humch'ida 훔치다;
(*transport*) t'aewŏ chuda 태워 주다;
(*accompany*) terigo kada 데리고
가다; (*accept: money, gift, credit
cards*) pat-tta 받다; (*study: math,
French*) suganghada 수강하다; *exam*
ch'ida 치다; *degree* ch'widŭk'ada
취득하다; *s.o.'s temperature* chaeda
재다; (*endure*) ch'amtta 참다;
(*require*) p'iryoro hada 필요로 하다;
this bus will ~ you to the center
pŏsŭrŭl t'amyŏn sent'ŏkkaji kal su
issŭmnida 이 버스를 타면 센터까지
갈 수 있습니다; ***a photograph o***
s.o. nuguŭi sajinŭl tchikta 누구의
사진을 찍다; ***a photocopy***
pokssahada 복사하다; ***a stroll***
sanch'aek'ada 산책하다; *it ~s 2
hours* 2shigani kŏllida 2시간이
걸리다; *how long does it ~?*
ŏlmana kŏllimnikka? 얼마나
걸립니까?; *I'll ~ it* (*when shopping*)
igŏsŭro hagessŭmnida 이것으로
하겠습니다
♦ **take after** ...wa/kwa tamtta
...와/과 닮다
♦ **take away** *pain* ŏpssaeda 없애다;
object kajigo kada 가지고 가다;
MATH ppaeda 빼다; ***take sth away
from s.o.*** (*by force*) nugurobut'ŏ
muŏsŭl ppaeasakada 누구로부터
무엇을 빼앗아가다
♦ **take back** (*return: object*)
toedollyŏjuda 되돌려주다; *person*
teryŏdajuda 데려다주다; (*accept
back: husband etc*) tashi padadŭrid
다시 받아들이다; *that takes me
back* yennal saenggagi nage handa
옛날 생각이 나게 한다
♦ **take down** (*from shelf*) naerida

내리다; *scaffolding* haech'ehada 해체하다; *pants* pŏt-tta 벗다; (*lengthen*) nŭrida 늘이다; (*write down*) pada chŏktta 받아 적다

♦ **take in** (*take indoors*) chibanŭro tŭrida 집안으로 들이다; (*give accommodation*) mukke hada 묵게 하다; (*make narrower*) churida 줄이다; (*deceive*) sogida 속이다; (*include*) p'ohamhada 포함하다

♦ **take off 1** *v/t clothes, hat* pŏt-tta 벗다; *10% etc* kkaktta 깎다; (*mimic*) hyungnaenaeda 흉내내다; **can you take a bit off here?** (*to barber*) yŏgirŭl chogŭmman challa chushigessŭmnikka? 여기를 조금만 잘라 주시겠습니까?; **take a day/week off** harurŭl/iltchuirŭl shwida 하루를/일주일을 쉬다 **2** *v/i* (*of airplane*) iryuk'ada 이륙하다; (*become popular*) inkkirŭl ŏt-tta 인기를 얻다

♦ **take on** *job* mat-tta 맡다; *staff* koyonghada 고용하다

♦ **take out** (*from bag, pocket*) kkŏnaeda 꺼내다; *stain* chiuda 지우다; *appendix, tooth* ppoptta 뽑다; *word from text* ppaenaeda 빼내다; *money from bank* inch'urhada 인출하다; (*to dinner etc*) terigo nagada 데리고 나가다; *insurance policy* ...e tŭlda ...에 들다; **take it out on s.o.** nuguege hwap'urihada 누구에게 화풀이하다

♦ **take over 1** *v/t company etc* insuhada 인수하다; **tourists ~ the town** kwan-gwanggaekttŭri toshirŭl kadŭk ch'aeuda 관광객들이 도시를 가득 채우다 **2** *v/i* (*of new management etc*) chang-ak'ada 장악하다; (*do sth in s.o.'s place*) taeshinhada 대신하다

♦ **take to** (*like*) choahage toeda 좋아하게 되다; (*form habit of*) ...hanŭn sŭpkkani tŭlda ...하는 습관이 들다

♦ **take up** *carpet etc* turŏ ollida 들어 올리다; (*carry up*) wiro unbanhada 위로 운반하다; (*shorten*) churida 줄이다; *hobby, new job* shijak'ada 시작하다; *judo, new language* paeugi

shijak'ada 배우기 시작하다; *offer* surak'ada 수락하다; *space, time* ch'ajihada 차지하다; **I'll take you up on your offer** tangshinŭi cheŭirŭl padadŭrigessŭmnida 당신의 제의를 받아드리겠습니다

take-home pay shilssuip 실수입; **takeoff** (*of airplane*) iryuk 이륙; (*impersonation*) hyungnae 흉내; **takeover** COM insu 인수; **takeover bid** konggae maeip 공개 매입

takings maesanggo 매상고

talcum powder ttamtti karu 땀띠 가루

tale iyagi 이야기

talent chaenŭng 재능

talented chaenŭng-i innŭn 재능이 있는

talk 1 *v/i* marhada 말하다; **can I ~ to ...?** ...wa/kwa marhal su issŭmnikka? ...와/과 말할 수 있습니까?; **I'll ~ to him about it** chega kŭege kŭgŏse kwanhae iyagi hagessŏyo 제가 그에게 그것에 관해 이야기 하겠어요 **2** *v/t English* marhada 말하다; *business* ŭinonhada 의논하다; **~ s.o. into sth** nugurŭl sŏlttŭk'ayŏ muŏshŭl shik'ida 누구를 설득하여 무엇을 시키다 **3** *n* (*conversation*) taehwa 대화; (*lecture*) kangnyŏn 강연; **he's all ~** kŭnŭn hŏp'ungjang-iyeyo 그는 허풍장이에요

♦ **talk over** ŭinonhada 의논하다

talkative mari manŭn 말이 많은

talk show chwadamhoe 좌담회

tall k'iga k'ŭn 키가 큰

tall order murihan yogu 무리한 요구

tall story hŏp'ung 허풍

tame *adj animal* kildŭryŏjin 길들여진; *joke etc* shishinan 시시한

♦ **tamper with** manjijak-kkŏrida 만지작거리다; (*deliberately interfere with*) hamburo manjida 함부로 만지다

tampon t'amp'on 탐폰

tan 1 *n* (*from sun*) ssŏnt'en 썬텐; (*color*) hwanggalssaek 황갈색 **2** *v/i* (*in sun*) haetppyŏch'e t'ada 햇볕에 타다 **3** *v/t leather* mudujirhada 무두질하다

tandem (*bike*) 2인승 chajŏn-gŏ 2인승 자전거

tangerine milgam 밀감, kyul 귤

tangle n ŏngk'im 엉킴
♦ **tangle up**: *get tangled up* (*of string etc*) ŏngk'ida 엉키다

tango n t'aenggo 탱고

tank chŏjang t'aengk'ŭ 저장 탱크; MOT, MIL, (*for skin diver*) t'aengk'ŭ 탱크

tanker (*ship*) yujosŏn 유조선; (*truck*) yujoch'a 유조차

tanned (*sun~~*) haetppyŏch'e t'an 햇볕에 탄

tantalizing kamjilnage hanŭn 감질나게 하는

tantamount: *be ~ to* ...wa/kwa tongdŭnghada ...와/과 동등하다

tantrum tchatchŭng 짜증

Taoism Togyo 도교

tap 1 n kkoktchi 꼭지 **2** v/t (*knock*) kabyŏpkke tudŭrida 가볍게 두드리다; *phone* toch'ŏnghada 도청하다
♦ **tap into** *resources* iyonghagi shijak'ada 이용하기 시작하다

tap dance n t'aepttaensŭ 탭댄스

tape 1 n (*for recording, sticky*) t'eip'ŭ 테이프 **2** v/t *conversation etc* nogŭmhada 녹음하다; (*video*) nok'wahada 녹화하다; (*with sticky tape*) t'eip'ŭro puch'ida 테이프로 붙이다

tape deck k'aset'ŭ p'ŭlleiŏ 카셋트 플레이어; **tape drive** COMPUT paegŏp tŭraibŭ 백업 드라이브; **tape measure** chulja 줄자

taper v/i chŏmjŏm kanŭrŏjida 점점 가늘어지다
♦ **taper off** (*of production, figures*) chŏmjŏm churŏdŭlda 점점 줄어들다

tape recorder nogŭmgi 녹음기

tape recording t'eip'ŭ nogŭm 테이프 녹음

tapestry t'aep'isŭt'ŭri 태피스트리

tar n t'arŭ 타르

tardy nŭjŭn 늦은

target 1 n (*in shooting*) kwanyŏk 과녁, p'yojŏk 표적; (*for sales, production*) mokp'yo 목표 **2** v/t *market* mokp'yoro hada 목표로 하다

target date mokp'yo magamil 목표 마감일; **target group** COM mokp'yo kŭrup 목표 그룹; **target market** p'yojŏk shijang 표적 시장

tariff (*price*) yogŭmp'yo 요금표; (*tax*) kwanse 관세

tarmac (*at airport*) hwaltchuro 활주로

tarnish v/t *metal* pyŏnsaeksshik'ida 변색시키다; *reputation* sonsangshik'ida 손상시키다

tarpaulin pangsup'o 방수포

tart n kwail p'ai 과일 파이

task immu 임무

task force t'ŭkppyŏl chosadan 특별 조사단; MIL t'ŭksu kidongdae 특수 기동대

tassel sul 술

taste 1 n (*sense*) migak 미각; (*of food etc*) mat 맛; (*in clothes, art etc*) ch'wihyang 취향; *he has no ~ in clothes* kŭnŭn amurŏn p'aeshyŏn kamgagi ŏptta 그는 아무런 패션 감각이 없다 **2** v/t *also fig* matppoda 맛보다

tasteful kamgaginnŭn 감각있는

tasteless *food* ammu mat ŏmnŭn 아무 맛 없는; *remark, person* mŏdŏmnŭn 멋없는

tasty mashinnŭn 맛있는

tattered *clothes, book* tchijŏjin 찢어진

tatters: *in ~ also fig* nudŏgiga toeŏ 누더기가 되어

tattoo munshin 문신

taunt 1 n chorong 조롱 **2** v/t choronghada 조롱하다

taut p'aengp'aenghan 팽팽한

tax 1 n segŭm 세금; *before/after ~* segŭmŭl p'ohaman/kongjehan 세금을 포함한/공제한 **2** v/t *people* ...ege segŭmŭl pugwahada ...에게 세금을 부과하다; *product* ...e segŭmŭl pugwahada ...에 세금을 부과하다

taxation kwase 과세; (*collection of taxes*) chingse 징세

tax code segŭm kiho 세금 기호; **tax-deductible** segŭm kongjega kanŭnghan 세금 공제가 가능한; **tax evasion** t'alsse 탈세; **tax-free** myŏnseŭi 면세의

taxi t'aeksshi 택시

axidriver t'aeksshi unjŏnsa 택시 운전사

ax inspector semu chosagwan 세무 조사관

ax rank t'aeksshi sŭngch'ajang 택시 승차장

ax payer napsseja 납세자

ax return (*form*) napsse shin-gosŏ 납세 신고서

ea (*drink*) ch'a 차; (*meal*) tagwa 다과; **green ~** nokch'a 녹차; **black ~** hongch'a 홍차

eabag ch'a pongji 차 봉지

each 1 *v/t person, subject* karŭch'ida 가르치다; **~ s.o. to do sth** nuguege muŏt hanŭn kŏsŭl karŭch'ida 누구에게 무엇 하는 것을 가르치다 **2** *v/i* karŭch'ida 가르치다

eacher sŏnsaeng 선생; (*form of address*) sŏnsaengnim 선생님; (*describing profession*) kyosa 교사

eachers' Day Sŭsŭng-ŭi nal 스승의 날

eacher training kyosa hullyŏn 교사 훈련

eaching (*profession*) kyojik 교직

eaching aid pojo kyojae 보조 교재

eaching assistant kangsa 강사

ea cloth marŭn haengju 마른 행주; **teacup** ch'atchan 찻잔; **tea drinker** ch'a aehoga 차 애호가

eak t'ik'ŭ namu 티크 나무

ea leaves ch'annip 찻잎

eam t'im 팀

eam spirit tanch'e chŏngshin 단체 정신

eamster t'ŭrŏk unjŏnsa 트럭 운전사

eamwork hyŏpttong chagŏp 협동 작업

eapot chattchujŏnja 찻주전자

tear[1] **1** *n* (*in cloth etc*) tchijŏjin t'ŭm 찢어진 틈 **2** *v/t paper, cloth* tchit-tta 찢다; **be torn between two alternatives** tu taean saiesŏ mangsŏrida 두 대안 사이에서 망설이다 **3** *v/i* (*go fast*) chiltchuhada 질주하다

♦ **tear up** *paper* kalgigalgi tchit-tta 갈기갈기 찢다; *agreement* ch'wisohada 취소하다

tear[2] (*in eye*) nunmul 눈물; **burst into ~s** urŭmŭl t'ŏttŭrida 울음을

터뜨리다; **be in ~s** nunmurŭl hŭllida 눈물을 흘리다

teardrop nunmul pang-ŭl 눈물 방울

tearful nunmul ŏrin 눈물 어린

tear gas ch'oerugasŭ 최루가스

tearoom chattchip 찻집

tease *v/t* (*maliciously*) koerop'ida 괴롭히다; (*for fun*) nollida 놀리다

tea service, tea set ch'attchan set'ŭ 찻잔 세트; **teaspoon** ch'atssutkkarak 찻숟가락

teat chŏttkkoktchi 젖꼭지

technical kisultchŏgin 기술적인; (*relating to particular field*) chŏnmunŭi 전문의

technicality (*technical nature*) chŏnmunsŏng 전문성; LAW sasohan sahang 사소한 사항; **that's just a ~** kŭgŏsŭn kŭnyang sasohan iril ppunida 그것은 그냥 사소한 일일 뿐이다

technically kisultchŏgŭro 기술적으로; (*strictly speaking*) ŏmmirhi marhamyŏn 엄밀히 말하면

technician kisultcha 기술자

technique kisul 기술; (*of performer*) kigyo 기교

technological kwahak kisulsang-ŭi 과학 기술상의

technology kwahak kisul 과학 기술

technophobia kwahak kisul kongp'otchŭng 과학 기술 공포증

tedious chiruhan 지루한

tee *n* (*in golf*) t'i 티

teem: be ~ing with rain p'oguga ssodajigo it-tta 폭우가 쏟아지고 있다; **be ~ing with tourists / ants** kwan-gwanggaekttŭllo / kaemidŭllo nŏmch'ida 관광객들로 / 개미들로 넘치다

teenage *fashions* ship taeŭi 십 대의

teenager t'ineijŏ 틴에이저

teens: be in one's ~ ship taeida 십 대이다; **reach one's ~** ship taega toeda 십 대가 되다

telecommunications t'ongshin 통신

telegram chŏnbo 전보

telegraph pole chŏnshinju 전신주

telepathic chŏngshin kamŭng-ŭi 정신 감응의; **you must be ~!** maŭmi t'onghaetkkunyo! 마음이 통했군요!

telepathy chŏngshin kamŭng 정신 감응

telephone 1 n chŏnhwa 전화; **be on the ~** (be speaking) t'onghwa chung-ida 통화 중이다; (possess a phone) chŏnhwaga it-tta 전화가 있다 **2** v/t person ...ege chŏnhwarŭl kŏlda ...에게 전화를 걸다 **3** v/i chŏnhwahada 전화하다

telephone booth kongjung chŏnhwa pakssŭ 공중 전화 박스; **telephone call** chŏnhwa 전화; **telephone directory** chŏnhwa pŏnhobu 전화 번호부; **telephone exchange** chŏnhwa kyohwan-guk 전화 교환국; **telephone number** chŏnhwa pŏnho 전화 번호

telephoto lens mang-wŏn lenjŭ 망원 렌즈

telesales chŏnhwa p'anmae 전화 판매

telescope mang-wŏn-gyŏng 망원경

televise pang-yŏnghada 방영하다

television t'ellebijŏn 텔레비전; (set) t'ellebijŏn susanggi 텔레비전 수상기; **on ~** t'ellebijŏne(sŏ) 텔레비전에(서); **watch ~** t'ellebijŏnŭl poda 텔레비전을 보다

television program t'ellebijŏn p'ŭrogŭraem 텔레비전 프로그램; **television set** t'ellebijŏn susanggi 텔레비전 수상기; **television studio** t'ellebijŏn nok'washil 텔레비전 녹화실

tell 1 v/t story marhada 말하다; lie kŏjinmarhada 거짓말하다; the difference kubyŏrhada 구별하다; **~ s.o. sth** nuguege muŏsŭl marhada 누구에게 무엇을 말하다; **don't ~ Mom** ŏmmahant'e marhajima 엄마한테 말하지마; **could you ~ me the way to ...?** ...(ŭ)ro kanŭn kirŭl karŭch'yŏ chushigessŏyo? ...(으)로 가는 길을 가르쳐 주시겠어요?; **~ s.o. to do sth** nuguege muŏsŭl harago marhada 누구에게 무엇을 하라고 말하다; **you're ~ing me!** chŏngmal kŭraeyo! 정말 그래요! **2** v/i (have effect) yŏnghyang-ŭl mich'ida 영향을 미치다; the heat is **~ing on him** kŭnŭn tŏwirŭl mŏk-

kko it-tta 그는 더위를 먹고 있다; **time will ~** shigani chinamyŏn kkaedatkke toel kŏshida 시간이 지나면 깨닫게 될 것이다

♦ **tell off** (reprimand) kkujit-tta 꾸짖다

teller ŭnhaeng ch'ullabwŏn 은행 출납원

telltale 1 adj signs sashirŭl tŭrŏnaenŭn 사실을 드러내는 **2** n kojajiljaeng-i 고자질쟁이

temp 1 n (employee) imshi chigwŏn 임시 직원 **2** v/i imshijigŭro irhada 임시직으로 일하다

temper (bad ~) sŏngjil 성질, kibun 기분; **be in a ~** hwarŭl naego it-tta 화를 내고 있다; **keep one's ~** hwarŭl ch'amtta 화를 참다; **lose one's ~** hwarŭl naeda 화를 내다

temperament kijil 기질

temperamental (moody) pyŏndŏkssŭrŏun 변덕스러운

temperature ondo 온도; (fever) yŏl 열; **have a ~** yŏri it-tta 열이 있다

temple¹ REL sawŏn 사원

temple² ANAT kwanjanori 관자놀이

tempo MUS paktcha 박자; (of work) sokto 속도

temporarily ilsshijŏgŭro 일시적으로

temporary ilsshijŏgin 일시적인

tempt yuhok'ada 유혹하다

temptation yuhok 유혹

tempting yuhoktchŏgin 유혹적인

ten yŏl 열, ship 십

tenacious wan-ganghan 완강한

tenant ch'ayongja 차용자

tend¹ v/t (look after) tolboda 돌보다

tend²: **~ to do sth** muŏt hanŭn p'yŏnida 무엇 하는 편이다; **~ toward sth** muŏsŭi kyŏnghyang-i it-tta 무엇의 경향이 있다

tendency kyŏnghyang 경향

tender¹ adj (sore) manjimyŏn ap'ŭn 만지면 아픈; (affectionate) tajŏnghan 다정한; steak yŏnhan 연한

tender² n COM ipch'al 입찰

tenderness (soreness) manjimyŏn ap'ŭm 만지면 아픔; (of kiss etc) tajŏngham 다정함; (of steak) yŏnham 연함

tendon himtchul 힘줄

tennis t'enissŭ 테니스
tennis ball t'enissŭ kong 테니스 공;
tennis court t'enissŭ chang 테니스
장; **tennis player** t'enissŭ sŏnsu
테니스 선수; **tennis racket** t'enissŭ
lak'et 테니스 라켓
tenor *n* MUS t'enŏ 테너
tense[1] *n* GRAM shije 시제
tense[2] *adj muscle* kinjangdoen
긴장된; *voice, person* kinjanghan
긴장한; *moment* kinjangdoenŭn
긴장되는
♦ **tense up** kinjangdoeda 긴장되다
tension (*of rope*) p'aengp'aengham
팽팽함; (*in atmosphere, voice*)
kinjang 긴장; (*in movie, novel*)
kinbak-kkam 긴박감
tent ch'ŏnmak 천막
tentacle ch'okssu 촉수
tentative chujŏhanŭn 주저하는
tenterhooks: be on ~
chobashimhada 조바심하다
tenth yŏl pŏntchaeŭi 열 번째의
tepid *water, reaction* mijigŭnhan
미지근한
term (*period of time*) kigan 기간;
(*condition*) kiil 기일; (*word*) yong-ŏ
용어; **be on good / bad ~ with s.o.**
nuguwa choŭn / nappŭn kwan-
gyeida 누구와 좋은 / 나쁜 관계이다;
in the long / short ~
changgijŏgŭro / tan-gijŏgŭro
장기적으로 / 단기적으로; **come to ~s
with sth** muŏsŭl padadŭrida 무엇을
받아들이다
terminal 1 *n* (*at airport, for buses*)
t'ŏminŏl 터미널; (*for containers*)
chip'atchang 집하장; ELEC tanja
단자; COMPUT tanmal changch'i 단말
장치 **2** *adj illness* pulch'iŭi 불치의
terminally *adv:* **~ ill** pulch'ippyŏng-ŭi
불치병의
terminate 1 *v/t contract* wanjŏnhi
kkŭnnaeda 완전히 끝내다; **~ a
pregnancy** nakt'aeshik'ida
낙태시키다 **2** *v/i* kkŭnnada
끝나다
termination (*of contract*) man-gi
만기; (*of pregnancy*) nakt'ae 낙태
terminology chŏnmun yong-ŏ 전문
용어

terminus (*for buses, trains*)
chongtchŏm 종점
terrace (*on hillside*) kyedanshik pat
계단식 밭; (*patio*) t'erasŭ 테라스
terra cotta t'erak'ot'a 테라코타
terrain chihyŏng 지형
terrestrial 1 *n* chiguin 지구인 **2** *adj
television* chisang-ŭi 지상의
terrible kkŭmtchik'an 끔찍한
terribly (*very*) mopssi 몹시
terrific koengjanghan 굉장한
terrifically (*very*) koengjanghage
굉장하게
terrify kŏmnage hada 겁나게 하다; *be
terrified* kŏbe chillida 겁에 질리다
terrifying kŏmnage hanŭn 겁나게
하는
territorial yŏngt'oŭi 영토의
territorial waters yŏnghae 영해
territory yŏngt'o 영토; *fig* kuyŏk 구역
terror kongp'o 공포
terrorism t'erŏrijŭm 테러리즘
terrorist t'erŏbŏm 테러범
terrorist organization t'erŏ chojik
테러 조직
terrorize wihyŏp'ada 위협하다
test 1 *n* shihŏm 시험 **2** *v/t* shihŏmhada
시험하다; *new product, drug etc*
shirhŏmhada 실험하다
testament (*to a person, life etc*)
kinyŏmmul 기념물; *Old / New Testament* REL Kuyak / Shinyak Sŏngsŏ
구약 / 신약 성서
testicle kohwan 고환
testify *v/i* LAW chŭng-ŏnhada
증언하다
testimonial ch'uch'ŏntchang 추천장
test tube shihŏmgwan 시험관
test-tube baby shihŏmgwan agi
시험관 아기
testy sŏngmi kŭp'an 성미 급한
tetanus p'asangp'ung 파상풍
tether 1 *v/t horse* maeda 매다 **2** *n:* **be
at the end of one's ~** han-gyee
irŭda 한계에 이르다
text ponmun 본문
textbook kyokkwasŏ 교과서
text file COMPUT t'eksŭt'ŭ p'ail 텍스트
파일
textile chingmul 직물
texture (*of skin, material*) kyŏl 결; (*of

food) sship'inŭn nŭkkim 씹히는
느낌

Thai 1 *adj* T'aegugŭi 태국의 **2** *n*
(*person*) T'aegugin 태국인;
(*language*) T'aegugŏ 태국어

Thailand T'aiguk 태국

than ...poda ...보다; *bigger / faster*
me naboda tŏ k'ŭn / pparŭn 나보다
더 큰/빠른

thank *v/t* kamsahada 감사하다; *~ you*
(*polite*) kamsahamnida 감사합니다,
komapssŭmnida 고맙습니다; F
komawŏ 고마워; *no ~ you*
komaptchiman, kwaench'ansŭmnida
고맙지만, 괜찮습니다

thanks kamsa 감사, komaum 고마움;
~! komapssŭmnida! 고맙습니다!; (*to
friend, to younger people*) komawŏ!
고마워!; *~ to* ...tŏkt'aege ...덕택에

thankful kamsahanŭn 감사하는

thankfully kamsahagedo 감사하게도,
komapkkedo 고맙게도; (*luckily*)
tahaenghido 다행히도

thankless *task* poram ŏmnŭn 보람
없는

Thanksgiving (Day) Ch'usu
Kamsajŏl 추수 감사절

that 1 *adj* chŏ 저; *~ one* (*thing*)
chŏgŏt 저것; (*person*) chŏ saram 저
사람 **2** *pron* (*thing*) chŏgŏt 저것;
(*person*) chŏ saram 저 사람; *what is ~?* chŏgŏsŭn muŏshimnikka? 저것은 무엇입니까?;
who is ~? chŏ saramŭn
nuguimnikka? 저 사람은
누구입니까?; *~'s mine* kŭgŏsŭn che
kŏshimnida 그것은 제 것입니다; *~ tea* kŭgŏsŭn ch'aimnida 그것은
차입니다; *~'s very kind* kŭgŏsŭn
chŏngmal ch'injŏrhan irimnida
그것은 정말 친절한 일입니다 ◊
(*relative*) ...hanŭn ...하는; *the person / car ~ you see* tangshini pogo
innŭn saram / ch'a 당신이 보고 있는
사람 / 차 **3** *conj*: *I think ~ ...* jŏnŭn
...rago saenggak'amnida 저는 ...라고
생각합니다 **4** *adv* (*so*) kŭrŏk'e
그렇게; *~ big* kŭrŏk'e k'ŭn 그렇게 큰

thaw *v/i* (*of snow, frozen food*)
nokta 녹다

the ◊ (*no equivalent in Korean*): *~ border* kuk-kkyŏng 국경 ◊

(*identifying or with previous
reference*) kŭ 그; *~ doctor who
treated me* narŭl ch'iryohan kŭ
ŭisa 나를 치료한 그 의사; *is that ~ ring he gave you?* igŏshi kŭga
tangshinege chun kŭŭi panjiyeyo?
이것이 그가 당신에게 준 그
반지예요?; *~ blue bag is mine* kŭ
p'aran kabang-i che kŏshiyeyo 그
파란 가방이 제 것이에요 ◊: *~ sooner ~ better* pparŭmyŏn
pparŭlsurok chot'a 빠르면 빠를수록
좋다

theater yŏn-gŭk 연극; (*building*)
kŭktchang 극장

theatrical yŏn-gŭgŭi 연극의;
(*overdone*) kwajangdwen 과장된

theft toduktchil 도둑질

their kŭdŭrŭi 그들의; (*his or her*):
somebody has left ~ coat behind
nugun-ga k'ot'ŭrŭl nwadugo
kassŏyo 누군가 코트를 놔두고
갔어요

theirs kŭdŭrŭi kŏt 그들의 것; *a
friend of ~* kŭdŭrŭi ch'in-gu 그들의
친구

them kŭdŭl 그들; *that's for ~* kŭdŭrŭi kŏshimnida 그들의
것입니다; *who's that? - it's ~ again* nuguyeyo? - tto kŭdŭriyeyo
누구예요? - 또 그들이에요 ◊ (*him or
her*): *nobody had a car with ~* amudo ch'arŭl kajigo oji anassŏyo
아무도 차를 가지고 오지 않았어요

theme t'ema 테마

theme park t'ema kong-wŏn 테마
공원

theme song chujega 주제가

themselves kŭdŭl chashin 그들 자신;
by ~ (*alone*) kŭdŭl sŭsŭro 그들
스스로

then (*at that time*) kŭ ttae 그 때;
(*after that*) kŭrigo nasŏ 그리고 나서;
(*deducing*) kŭrŏt'amyŏn 그렇다면;
by ~ kŭ ttaeenŭn 그 때에는

theology shinhak 신학

theoretical ironŭi 이론의; *~ physics*
iron mullihak 이론 물리학

theory iron 이론; *in ~* ironsang-ŭro
이론상으로

therapeutic ch'iryoŭi 치료의

herapist ch'iryo chŏnmun-ga 치료 전문가

herapy ch'iryo 치료

here kŭ kose 그 곳에; **over ~/down ~** chŏ wie/araee 저 위에/아래에; **~ is** ...i it-tta ...이 있다; **~ are** ...tŭri it-tta ...들이 있다; **is/are ~...?** ...i/tŭri issŭmnikka? ...이/들이 있습니까?; **isn't/aren't ~...?** ...i/tŭri ŏpssŭmnikka? ...이/들이 없습니까?; **~ you are** (giving sth) yŏgi issŭmnida 여기 있습니다; (finding sth) yŏgi issŏkkunyo 여기 있었군요; (completing sth) twaessŭmnida 됐습니다; **$50 ~ and back** wangbok 50tallŏimnida 왕복 50달러입니다; **~ he is!** kŭga chŏgi itkkunyo 그가 저기 있군요!; **~, ~!** cha, cha! 자, 자!

hereabouts kŭ chŏngdo 그 정도

herefore ttarasŏ 따라서, kŭrŏmŭro 그러므로

hermometer ondogye 온도계

hermos flask poonbyŏng 보온병

hermostat chadong ondo chojŏl changch'i 자동 온도 조절 장치

hese 1 adj igŏttŭrŭi 이것들의, i ...dŭl 이 ...들 **2** pron igŏttŭl 이것들

hesis nonmun 논문

hey kŭdŭl 그들; (things) kŭgŏttŭl 그것들 ◊ (he or she): **if anyone knows ~ should say so** manyak nugurado andamyŏn, kŭrŏk'e yegihaeya hamnida 만약 누구라도 안다면, 그렇게 얘기해야 합니다 ◊ (impersonal): **~ say that ...** kŭdŭri ...rago marhada 그들이 ...라고 말하다; **~ are going to change the law** kŭdŭrŭn pŏbŭl pakkul kŏshida 그들은 법을 바꿀 것이다

hick tukkŏun 두꺼운; F (stupid) tunhan 둔한; fog chit'ŭn 짙은; soup kŏltchuk'an 걸쭉한; **~ hair** such'i manŭn mŏri 술이 많은 머리

hicken sauce kŏltchuk'age hada 걸쭉하게 하다

hickset ttangttalmak'an 땅딸막한

hickskinned fig ppŏnppŏnsŭrŏun 뻔뻔스러운

hief totuk 도둑

high nŏptchŏkttari 넓적다리

himble kolmu 골무

thin material yalbŭn 얇은; hair, line kanŭn 가는; person marŭn 마른; soup mulgŭn 묽은

thing samul 사물; **~s** (belongings) soyumul 소유물; **how are ~s?** ŏttŏk'e chinaeseyo? 어떻게 지내세요?; **good ~ you told me** naege marŭl chal haet-tta 내게 말을 잘 했다; **what a ~ to do/say!** musŭn chishiya/mariya! 무슨 짓이야/말이야!

thingumajig F kŭ mwŏrago hanŭn kŏt 그 뭐라고 하는 것; (person) kŭ mwŏrago hanŭn saram 그 뭐라고 하는 사람

think saenggak'ada 생각하다; **I ~ so** kŭrŏn kŏt kat'ayo 그런 것 같아요; **I don't ~ so** kŭroch'i anŭn kŏt kat'ayo 그렇지 않은 것 같아요; **I ~ so too** chŏdo kŭrŏk'e saenggakhaeyo 저도 그렇게 생각해요; **what do you ~?** ŏttŏk'e saenggak'aseyo? 어떻게 생각하세요?; **what do you ~ of it?** kŭgŏsŭl ŏttŏk'e saenggak'aeyo? 그것을 어떻게 생각해요?; **I can't ~ of anything more** kŭ isang-ŭn saenggangnaji anayo 그 이상은 생각나지 않아요; **~ hard!** chal saenggak'ae pwa! 잘 생각해 봐!; **I'm ~ing about emigrating** nanŭn imin-ganŭn kŏsŭl saenggak chung-ida 나는 이민가는 것을 생각 중이다

♦ **think over** suk-kohada 숙고하다

♦ **think through** yomojomo saenggak'ae poda 요모조모 생각해 보다

♦ **think up** plan saenggak'aenaeda 생각해내다

third 1 adj chesamŭi 제3의, se pŏntchaeŭi 세 번째의 **2** n (in sequence) chesam 제3, se pŏntchae 세 번째; (fraction) sambunŭi il 삼분의 일

thirdly se pŏntchaerŏnŭn 세 번째로는

third-party insurance ch'aegim pohŏm 책임 보험; **third-rate** samnyuŭi 삼류의; **Third World** Chesam Segye 제3 세계

thirst kaltchŭng 갈증

thirsty mongmarŭn 목마른; **be ~**

mongmarŭda 목마르다

thirteen yŏlsset 열 셋, shipssam 십삼

thirteenth yŏlsse pŏntchaeŭi 열 세 번째의

thirtieth sŏrŭn pŏntchaeŭi 서른 번째의

thirty sŏrŭn 서른, samship 삼십

Thirty-Eighth Parallel Samp'alssŏn 삼팔선

this 1 adj i 이; ~ **one** igŏt 이것 **2** pron igŏt 이것; ~ **is good** igŏsŭn chota 이것은 좋다; ~ **is** (introducing) i saramŭn ...imnida 이 사람은 ...입니다; TELEC chŏnŭn ...imnida 저는 ...입니다 **3** adv: ~ **big / high** i chŏngdoro k'ŭda / noptta 이 정도로 크다 / 높다

thorn kashi 가시

thorough search, person ch'ŏltchŏhan 철저한; knowledge wanjŏnhan 완전한

thoroughbred sunjong 순종

those 1 adj people kŭdŭrŭi 그들의; things, animals kŭgŏttŭrŭi 그것들의; **in ~ days** kŭ tangshienŭn 그 당시에는 **2** pron (people) kŭdŭl 그들; (things, animals) kŭgŏttŭl 그것들

though 1 conj (although) ...ijiman ...이지만; **even ~ ...** ...handa hadŏrado ...한다 하더라도; ~ **it might fail** shilp'aehagetchiman 실패하겠지만; **as ~** mach'i ...ch'ŏrŏm 마치 ...처럼 **2** adv kŭrŏt'ŏrado 그럴더라도; **it's not finished** ~ kŭrŏt'arado ajik kkŭnnan kŏsŭn anida 그렇더라도 아직 끝난 것은 아니다

thought (single) sago 사고, saenggak 생각; (collective) sasang 사상

thoughtful saenggagi kip'ŭn 생각이 깊은; book shimssasuk-kkohan 심사숙고한; (considerate) saryŏ kip'ŭn 사려 깊은

thoughtless namŭl koryŏhaji annŭn 남을 고려하지 않는

thousand ch'ŏn 천; ~**s of** su ch'ŏnŭi 수 천의; **ten ~** man 만; **hundred ~** shim man 십만

thousandth adj ch'ŏn pŏntchaeŭi 천 번째의

thrash v/t magu ttaerida 마구 때리다;

SP ch'amp'aeshik'ida 참패시키다

♦ **thrash around** (with arms etc) momburimch'ida 몸부림치다

♦ **thrash out** solution nonŭihaesŏ haegyŏrhada 논의해서 해결하다

thrashing ch'aetchiktchil 채찍질; SP ch'amp'ae 참패

thread 1 n shil 실; (of screw) nasasar 나사산 **2** v/t needle, beads ...e shirŭl kkwaeda ...에 실을 꿰다

threadbare tarŭn 닳은

threat wihyŏp 위협

threaten wihyŏp'ada 위협하다

threatening gesture, tone wihyŏp'anŭn 위협하는; sky tchip'urin 찌푸린; **a ~ letter** hyŏppak p'yŏnji 협박 편지

three set 셋, sam 삼

Three Han Samhan 삼한; **Three Kingdoms** Samguk 삼국; **three-quarters** n sabunŭi sam 사분의 삼

thresh v/t corn t'algok'ada 탈곡하다

threshold (of house) muntchibang 문지방; (of new age) ch'ulbaltchŏm 출발점; **on the ~ of ...** ...ŭi ch'ulbaltchŏme ...의 출발점에

thrift chŏryak 절약

thrifty chŏryak'anŭn 절약하는

thrill 1 n chŏnyul 전율 **2** v/t: **be ~ed** kamgyŏk'ada 감격하다

thriller sŭrillŏmul 스릴러물

thrilling kamgyŏk'age hanŭn 감격하게 하는

thrive (of plant) ulch'anghage charada 울창하게 자라다; (of economy) pŏnch'anghada 번창하다

throat mokkumŏng 목구멍

throat lozenges mok sat'ang 목 사탕

throb 1 n (of heart) maekppak 맥박; (of music) ttŏllimŭm 떨림음 **2** v/i (of heart) ttwida 뛰다; (of music) ttŏllida 떨리다

thrombosis hyŏltchŏntchŭng 혈전증

throne wangjwa 왕좌

throttle 1 n (on motorbike, boat) sokto chojŏl changch'i 속도 조절 장치 **2** v/t (strangle) moktchorŭda 목조르다

♦ **throttle back** v/i kamsok'ada 감속하다

through 1 prep ◊ (across) ...ŭl

t'onghayŏ ...을 통하여; **go ~ the
city** toshirŭl chinagada 도시를
지나가다 ◊ (*during*) ...ŭi tong-an
naenae ...의 동안 내내; **~ the win-
ter／summer** kyŏul／yŏrŭm tong-an
naenae 겨울／여름 동안 내내; **Monday – Friday** wŏryoilbut'ŏ
kŭmnyoil tong-an naenae
월요일부터 금요일 동안 내내 ◊
(*thanks to*) ...tŏkppune ... 덕분에;
arranged ~ him kŭ tŏkppune 그
덕분에 2 adv: **wet ~** mongttang
chŏjŏt-tta 몽땅 젖었다; **watch a
movie ~** yŏnghwarŭl kkŭtkkaji
poda 영화를 끝까지 보다; **read a
book ~** ch'aegŭl kkŭtkkaji iltta 책을
끝까지 읽다 3 adj: **be ~** (*of couple*)
kwan-gyega kkŭnnada 관계가
끝나다; (*have arrived: of news etc*)
toch'ak'ada 도착하다; **you're ~**
TELEC yŏn-gyŏldwaessŭmnida
연결됐습니다; **I'm ~ with** person
nanŭn ...wa／kwa kwan-gyerŭl
kkŭnnaet-tta 나는 ...와／과의 관계를
끝냈다; (*no longer need*) nanŭn
...ŭl／rŭl ta ssŏt-tta 나는 ...을／를 다
썼다

through flight chik'aeng pihaenggi
직행 비행기

throughout 1 prep journey, night
...tong-an naenae ...동안 내내;
novel ...ŭi toch'ŏe ...의 도처에
2 adv (*in all parts*) chŏnch'ejŏguro
전체적으로

through train chik'aeng yŏlch'a 직행
열차

throw 1 v/t tŏnjida 던지다; (*of horse*)
naep'aenggaech'ida 내팽개치다;
(*disconcert*) tanghwanghage hada
당황하게 하다; party yŏlda 열다 2 n
tŏnjigi 던지기

◆ **throw away** pŏrida 버리다

◆ **throw out** old things naebŏrida
내버리다; person naetchot-tta 내쫓다;
plan pugyŏrhada 부결하다

◆ **throw up** v/t ball wiro tŏnjida
위로 던지다; **~ one's hands** tu son
tŭlda 두 손 들다 2 v/i (*vomit*)
t'ohada 토하다

throw-away remark amurŏch'i ank'e
han 아무렇지 않게 한; (*disposable*)

irhoeyong 일회용

throw-in SP sŭroin 스로인

thru → through

thrush (*bird*) kaettongjippagwi
개똥지빠귀

thrust v/t (*push hard*) sege tchirŭda
세게 찌르다; **~ sth into s.o.'s
hands** muŏsŭl nuguŭi sone ŏktchiro
ttŏmatkkida 무엇을 누구의 손에
억지로 떠맡기다; **~ one's way
through the crowd** kunjung sogŭl
hech'igo naagada 군중 속을 헤치고
나아가다

thud n k'unghanŭn sori 쿵하는 소리

thug hyung-akppŏm 흉악범

thumb 1 n ŏmji sonkkarak 엄지
손가락 2 v/t: **~ a ride**
p'yŏnsŭnghada 편승하다

thumbtack app'in 압핀

thump 1 n (*blow*) chumŏktchil
주먹질; (*noise*) k'unghanŭn sori
쿵하는 소리 2 v/t person ch'ida 치다;
~ one's fist on the table t'eibŭrŭl
chumŏgŭro tudŭrida 테이블을
주먹으로 두드리다 3 v/i (*of heart*)
tugŭndugŭn ttwida 두근두근 뛰다; **~
on the door** mune k'unghago
puditch'ida 문에 쿵하고 부딪치다

thunder n ch'ŏndung 천둥

thunderstorm noeu 뇌우

thundery weather ch'ŏndung-i
morach'il tŭt'an 천둥이 몰아칠 듯한

Thursday mogyoil 목요일

thus ttarasŏ 따라서

thwart person, plans panghaehada
방해하다

thyroid (*gland*) kapssangsŏn 갑상선

Tibet Tibet'ŭ 티베트

Tibetan 1 adj Tibet'ŭŭi 티베트의 2 n
(*person*) Tibet'ŭin 티베트인;
(*language*) Tibet'ŭŏ 티베트어

tick 1 n (*of clock*) ttokttak sori 똑딱
소리; (*checkmark*) chŏmgŏm p'yoshi
점검 표시 2 v/i (*of clock*) ttokttak-
kkŏrida 똑딱거리다

◆ **tick off** (*reprimand*) chuŭi chuda
주의 주다

ticket p'yo 표

ticket collector kaech'arwŏn 개찰원;
ticket inspector p'yo kŏmsawŏn 표
검사원; **ticket machine** p'yo

chadong p'anmaegi 표 자동 판매기;
ticket office (*at station*) maep'yoso
매표소

tickle 1 *v/t person* kanjirŏp'ida
간지럽히다 2 *v/i* (*of material*)
kanjilkanjirhada 간질간질하다; (*of
person*) kanjirida 간질이다

ticklish *person* kanjirŏumŭl chal
t'anŭn 간지러움을 잘 타는

tidal wave chosŏkp'a 조석파

tide chosu 조수; *high ~* manjo 만조;
low ~ kanjo 간조; *the ~ is in / out*
milmurida / ssŏlmurida
밀물이다 / 썰물이다

tidy *person, habits* tanjŏnghan 단정한;
room, house chŏngdondoen 정돈된

♦ **tidy up** 1 *v/t room, shelves*
chŏngdonhada 정돈하다; *tidy oneself up* tanjŏnghi hada 단정히 하다
2 *v/i* chŏngdonhada 정돈하다

tie 1 *n* (*necktie*) nekt'ai 넥타이; (SP:
even result) tongtchŏm 동점; *he
doesn't have any ~s* kŭnŭn amu
yŏn-gojado ŏptta 그는 아무
연고자도 없다 2 *v/t knot* choida
조이다; *hands* muktta 묶다; *two
ropes together* tu kaeŭi kkŭnŭl
hamkke muktta 두 개의 끈을 함께
묶다 3 *v/i* SP tongtchŏmi toeda
동점이 되다

♦ **tie down** (*with rope*) mukkŏ not'a
묶어 놓다; (*restrict*) kusok'ada
구속하다

♦ **tie up** muktta 묶다; *boat* maeda
매다; *I'm tied up tomorrow* nanŭn
naeil yaksogi it-tta 나는 내일
약속이 있다

tier ch'ŭng 층

tiger horang-i 호랑이

tight 1 *adj clothes* kkok kkinŭn 꼭
끼는; *security* tandanhan 단단한;
(*hard to move*) kkok kkiin 꼭 끼인;
(*properly shut*) kkok tach'in 꼭
닫힌; (*not leaving much time*)
ch'okppak'an 촉박한; F (*drunk*)
ch'wihan 취한 2 *adv hold* tandanhi
단단히; *shut* kkok 꼭

tighten *screw* tandanhi choida 단단히
조이다; *control, security*
kanghwahada 강화하다; *~ one's
grip on sth* muŏsŭl chang-ak'ada

무엇을 장악하다

♦ **tighten up** *v/i* (*in discipline,
security*) ŏmhage hada 엄하게 하다

tight-fisted insaek'an 인색한

tightrope p'aengp'aenghan chul
팽팽한 줄

tile t'ail 타일

till[1] → *until*

till[2] (*cash register*) ton sŏrap 돈 서랍

till[3] *v/t soil* kyŏngjak'ada 경작하다

tilt 1 *v/t* kiurida 기울이다 2 *v/i* kiulda
기울다

timber moktchae 목재

time shigan 시간; (*occasion*) pŏn 번; *~
is up* ije shigani ta twaet-tta 이제
시간이 다 됐다; *for the ~ being*
tangbun-gan 당분간; *have a good ~*
choŭn shiganŭl ponaeda 좋은 시간을
보내다; *have a good ~!* choŭn
shiganŭl ponaeseyo! 좋은 시간을
보내세요; *what's the ~?* myŏt
shiimnikka? 몇 시입니까?; *the first
~* ch'ŏŭmŭro 처음으로; *four ~s* ne
pŏn 네 번; *~ and again* myŏt
pŏnina kyesok 몇 번이나 계속; *all
the ~* nŭl 늘; *three at a ~* han pŏne
set 한 번에 셋; *at the same ~*
speak, reply etc tongshie 동시에;
(*however*) kŭrŏmyŏnsŏdo
그러면서도; *in ~* shiganŭl match'uŏ
시간을 맞추어; *on ~* chŏnggage
정각에; *in no ~* kot 곧

time bomb shihan p'okt'an 시한
폭탄; **time clock** (*in factory*)
ch'ult'oegŭn shigan kirok-kkye
출퇴근 시간 기록계; **time-
consuming** manŭn shigani kŏllinŭn
많은 시간이 걸리는; **time lag** shich'a
시차; **time limit** chehan shigan 제한
시간

timely chŏksshiŭi 적시의

time out SP t'aim aut 타임 아웃

timer t'aimŏ 타이머

timesaving *n* shigan chŏryak 시간
절약; **timescale** (*of project*) shigi
시기; **time switch** t'aim sŭwich'i
타임 스위치; **timetable** shiganp'yo
시간표; **timewarp** waegokttoen
shigandae 왜곡된 시간대; **time zone**
p'yojun shiganttae 표준 시간대

timid *person, animal* kŏmmanŭn

-ming (*choosing a time*) shigirŭl match'ugi 시기를 맞추기; (*of actor, dancer*) t'aiming 타이밍

-n (*metal*) chusŏk 주석

-nfoil ŭnjong-i 은종이

-nge (*of color*) yŏt'ŭn saektcho 엷은 색조; (*of sadness*) kisaek 기색

-ngle v/i ttakkŭmgŏrida 따끔거리다

♦ **tinker with** manjijak-kkŏrida 만지작거리다

-nkle n (*of bell*) ttallangttallang 딸랑딸랑

-nsel pantchak-kkŏrinŭn kŭmsok changshik 반짝거리는 금속 장식

-nt 1 n (*of color*) yŏnhan saektcho 연한 색조; (*in hair*) yŏmsaek 염색 2 v/t hair yŏmsaek'ada 염색하다

-nted glasses saek-kkal innŭn 색깔 있는

-ny chogŭmahan 조그마한

-p n (*of stick, finger*) kkŭt 끝; (*of mountain*) chŏngsang 정상; (*of cigarette*) p'ilt'ŏ 필터

-p² 1 n (*piece of advice*) pigyŏl 비결; (*money*) t'ip 팁 2 v/t waiter etc ...ege t'ibŭl chuda ...에게 팁을 주다

♦ **tip off** pimil chŏngborŭl chuda 비밀 정보를 주다

♦ **tip over** jug, liquid twiŏptta 뒤엎다; he tipped water all over me kŭnŭn na-ege murŭl ont'ong twijibŏ ssŭiwŏt-tta 그는 나에게 물을 온통 뒤집어 씌웠다

-pped cigarettes p'ilt'ŏ innŭn tambae 필터 있는 담배

-ppy-toe: on ~ palkkŭt'ŭro 발끝으로

-psy ŏlk'ŭnhage ch'wihan 얼큰하게 취한

-ire¹ n t'aiŏ 타이어

-ire² 1 v/t chich'ige hada 지치게 하다 2 v/i chich'ida 지치다; he never ~s of it kŭnŭn kŭgŏsŭl kyŏlk'o shiltchŭng naeji annŭnda 그는 그것을 결코 싫증 내지 않는다

-ired p'igonhan 피곤한; be ~ of s.o. / sth nugue / muŏse shiltchŭng nada 누구에 / 무엇에 싫증 나다

-ireless efforts chich'il chul morŭnŭn 지칠 줄 모르는

-iresome kwich'anŭn 귀찮은,

sŏnggashin 성가신

tiring chich'ige hanŭn 지치게 하는

tissue ANAT chojik 조직; (*handkerchief*) hwajangji 화장지

tissue paper p'ojangji 포장지

tit¹ (*bird*) pakssae 박새

tit²: **- for tat** matppadach'igi 맞받아치기

tit³ ∨ (*breast*) chŏtkkasŭm 젖가슴

title (*of novel etc*) chemok 제목; (*of person*) chik'am 직함; LAW kwŏlli 권리

titter v/i k'ik'ik-kkŏrida 킥킥거리다

to 1 prep ...(ŭ)ro ...(으)로; ~ Korea Han-gugŭro 한국으로; ~ Chicago Shik'agoro 시카고로; go ~ my place uri chibŭro kada 우리 집으로 가다; walk ~ the station yŏgŭro kŏrŏgada 역으로 걸어가다; ~ the north / south of ...ŭi puktchogŭro / namtchogŭro ...의 북쪽으로 / 남쪽으로; give sth ~ s.o. muŏsŭl nuguege chuda 무엇을 누구에게 주다; from Monday ~ Wednesday wŏryoilbut'ŏ suyoilkkaji 월요일부터 수요일까지; from 10 ~ 15 people 15myŏng-ŭi saramdŭl 10명에서 15명의 사람들 2 (*with verbs*) ...hagi wihae ...하기 위해; ...hanŭn kŏt ...하는 것; ~ speak marhanŭn kŏt 말하는 것; learn ~ drive unjŏnhanŭn kŏsŭl paeuda 운전하는 것을 배우다; nice ~ eat mŏk-kkie choŭn 먹기에 좋은; too heavy ~ carry unbanhagie nŏmu mugŏun 운반하기에 너무 무거운; be honest with you nŏhant'e soltchik'i marhajamyŏn 너한테 솔직히 말하자면 3 adv: ~ and fro apttwiro 앞뒤로

toad tukkŏbi 두꺼비

toadstool tokppŏsŏt 독버섯

toast 1 n t'osŭt'ŭ 토스트; (*when drinking*) kŏnbae 건배; propose a ~ to s.o. nugurŭl wihae kŏnbaehajago hada 누구를 위해 건배하자고 하다 2 v/t person kŏnbaehada 건배하다

tobacco tambae 담배

toboggan n ssŏlmae 썰매

today onŭl 오늘

toddle (*of child*) ajang-ajang kŏt-tta
아장아장 걷다

toddler ajang-ajang kŏnnŭn ai
아장아장 걷는 아이

toe 1 *n* palkkarak 발가락; (*of shoe*)
palkkŭt pubun 발끝 부분 **2** *v/t:* ~
the line kyuch'igŭl ttarŭda 규칙을
따르다

toffee t'op'i 토피

tofu tubu 두부

together hamkke 함께; (*at the same time*) tongshie 동시에

toil *n* nogo 노고

toilet hwajangshil 화장실; **go to the ~** hwajangshire kada 화장실에 가다

toilet paper hwajangji 화장지, hyuji
휴지

toiletries semyŏn yongp'um 세면
용품

Tok Island Toktto 독도

token (*sign*) p'yoshi 표시; (*gift ~*)
sangp'umkkwŏn 상품권; (*for slot machine*) t'ok'ŭn 토큰

Tokyo Tonggyŏng 동경

tolerable *pain etc* ch'amŭl su innŭn
참을 수 있는; (*quite good*) kkwae
kwaench'anŭn 꽤 괜찮은

tolerance kwanyong 관용

tolerant kwanyong innŭn 관용 있는

tolerate *noise, person* ch'amtta 참다; **I won't ~ it!** igŏsŭn ch'amŭl suga
ŏpssŏyo! 이것은 참을 수가 없어요!

toll[1] *v/i* (*of bell*) ch'ŏnch'ŏnhi
kyesok'aesŏ ullida 천천히 계속해서
울리다

toll[2] (*deaths*) hŭisaeng 희생

toll[3] (*for bridge, road*) t'onghaengnyo
통행료; TELEC t'onghwaryo 통화료

toll booth yogŭm chingsuso 요금
징수소; **toll-free** TELEC muryo
t'onghwa 무료 통화; **toll road** yuryo
toro 유료 도로

tomato t'omat'o 토마토

tomato ketchup t'omat'o k'ech'ap
토마토 케챂

tomb mudŏm 무덤

tomboy malgwallyang-i 말괄량이

tombstone pisŏk 비석

tomcat suk'oyang-i 수코양이

tomorrow naeil 내일; **the day after ~** more 모레; **~ morning** naeil
ach'im 내일 아침

ton t'on 톤

tone (*of color*) saektcho 색조; (*musical instrument*) ŭmsaek 음색; (*of conversation etc*) ŏjo 어조; (*of neighborhood*) punwigi 분위기; **~ of voice** moksssori 목소리

♦ **tone down** *demands, criticism*
pudŭrŏpkke hada 부드럽게 하다

toner ch'onŏ 토너

tongs chipkke 집게; (*for hair*) mŏri
indu 머리 인두

tongue *n* hyŏ 혀

tonic MED kangjangje 강장제

tonic (*water*) t'onik wŏt'ŏ 토닉 워터

tonight onŭl pam 오늘 밤

tonsillitis p'yŏndosŏnnyŏm 편도선염

tonsils p'yŏndosŏn 편도선

too (*also*) ttohan 또한, to 도; (*excessively*) nŏmu 너무; **me ~** chŏdoyo 저도요; **~ big / hot** nŏmu
k'ŭn / ttŭgŏun 너무 큰 / 뜨거운; **~ much food** nŏmu manŭn ŭmshik
너무 많은 음식; **eat ~ much**
nŏmuna mani mŏktta 너무 많이
먹다

tool togu 도구

tooth i 이

toothache ch'it'ong 치통; **toothbrush** ch'itssol 칫솔; **toothless** iga
ŏmnŭn 이가 없는; **toothpaste**
ch'iyak 치약; **toothpick** issushigae
이쑤시개

top 1 *n* (*upper part*) witppubun 윗부분; (*of mountain, tree*)
kkoktttaegi 꼭대기; (*lid: of bottle etc, pen*) ttukkŏng 뚜껑; (*of class, league*)
sangnyu 상류; (*clothing*) sang-ŭi
상의; (MOT: *gear*) t'opkkiŏ 톱기어;
on ~ of ...ŭi wie ...의 위에; **at the ~ of** ...ŭi witchoge ...의 위쪽에; **get to the ~** (*of company etc*) chŏngsang-e
orŭda 정상에 오르다; **be over the ~**
(*exaggerated*) kwangjangdoeda
과장되다 **2** *adj branches* kkoktttaegiŭi
꼭대기의; *floor* maenwiŭi 맨위의;
management, official sangbuŭi
상부의; *player* ch'oesang-ŭi 최상의;
speed, note ch'oegoŭi 최고의 **3** *v/t:*
~ped with cream k'ŭrimŭro tŏp'in
크림으로 덮힌

◆ **top up** *glass, tank* kaдük ch'aeuda 가득 채우다

op hat chungsanmo 중산모

opheavy puranjŏnghan 불안정한

opic hwaje 화제

opical hwajeŭi 화제의

opless, *t'op'ŭllisŭ* tŭrŏnaen 가슴을 드러낸, t'op'ŭllisŭ 토플리스

opmost *branches, floor* ch'oesang-ŭi 최상의

opping *(on pizza)* t'op'ing 토핑

opple 1 *v/i* ssŭrŏjida 쓰러지다 2 *v/t* *government* ssŭrŏttŭrida 쓰러뜨리다

op secret kŭkppi 극비

opsy-turvy *adj (in disorder)* twijukppaktchugin 뒤죽박죽인; *world* hollansŭrŏun 혼란스러운

orch *(with flame)* hwaetppul 횃불

orment 1 *n* kot'ong 고통 2 *v/t* *person, animal* koerop'ida 괴롭히다; *~ed by doubt* ŭishimŭro koerowahanŭn 의심으로 괴로와하는

ornado hoeori param 회오리 바람

orrent kŭmnyu 급류; *(of lava)* punch'ul 분출; *(of abuse, words)* yŏnbal 연발

orrential *rain* ŏksssugat'ŭn 억수같은

ortoise kŏbuk 거북

orture 1 *n* komun 고문 2 *v/t* komunhada 고문하다

oss 1 *v/t ball* kabyŏpkke tŏnjida 가볍게 던지다; *rider* ttŏrŏttŭrida 떨어뜨리다; *salad* pŏmurida 버무리다; ~ *a coin* tongjŏnŭl tŏnjyŏ chŏnghada 동전을 던져 정하다 2 *v/i*: ~ *and turn* twich'ŏk-kkŏrida 뒤척거리다

otal 1 *n* hapkkye 합계 2 *adj sum, amount* chŏnch'eŭi 전체의; *disaster, idiot, stranger* wanjŏnhan 완전한; ~ *amount of money* ch'ong-aek 총액 3 *v/t* F *(car)* wanjŏnhi pusuda 완전히 부수다

otalitarian chŏnch'ejuŭiŭi 전체주의의

otally wanjŏnhi 완전히

ote bag taehyŏng haendŭbaek 대형 핸드백

otter *(of person)* pit'ŭlgŏrida 비틀거리다

ouch 1 *n (act of touching)* chŏpch'ok 접촉; *(sense)* ch'ok-kkam 촉감; *(little bit)* yakkan 약간; SP t'ŏch'i 터치; *lose ~ with s.o.* nuguwa yŏllagi kkŭnkkida 누구와 연락이 끊기다; *keep in ~ with s.o.* nuguwa kyesok yŏllak'ada 누구와 계속 연락하다; *be out of ~* chopch'ok'aji ank'o chinaeda 접촉하지 않고 지내다 2 *v/t* manjida 만지다; *(emotionally)* kamdongshik'ida 감동시키다 3 *v/i* manjida 만지다; *(of two lines etc)* chŏpch'ok'ada 접촉하다

◆ **touch down** *(of airplane)* ch'angnyuk'ada 착륙하다; SP tŭktchŏmhada 득점하다

◆ **touch on** *(mention)* kandanhi ŏn-gŭp'ada 간단히 언급하다

◆ **touch up** *photo* sonjirhada 손질하다

touchdown *(of airplane)* ch'angnyuk 착륙; SP t'ŏch'idaun 터치다운

touching *adj* kamdongshik'inŭn 감동시키는

touchline SP t'ŏch'irain 터치라인

touchy *person* chinach'ige yeminhan 지나치게 예민한

tough *person* ŏkssen 억센; *meat* chilgin 질긴; *question, exam* ŏryŏun 어려운; *material* kŏch'in 거친; *punishment* ŏmhan 엄한

tough guy ŏkssen sanai 억센 사나이

tour 1 *n* kwan-gwang 관광 2 *v/t area* kwan-gwanghada 관광하다

tourism kwan-gwang-ŏp 관광업

tourist kwan-gwanggaek 관광객

tourist (information) office kwan-gwang annaeso 관광 안내소

tournament shihap 시합

tour operator kwan-gwang-ŏptcha 관광업자

tousled *hair* hŏngk'ŭrŏjin 헝클어진

tow 1 *v/t car, boat* kkŭlda 끌다 2 *n* kkŭlgi 끌기; *give s.o. a ~* nugurŭl kkŭrŏjuda 누구를 끌어주다

◆ **tow away** *car* kyŏninhada 견인하다

toward *prep* ...ŭl/rŭl hyanghayŏ ...을/를 향하여; *(in behavior, attitude)* ...ege ...에게

towel sugŏn 수건

tower *n* t'ap 탑

town toshi 도시

town council shi ŭihoe 시 의회

town hall shich'ŏng 시청

township myŏn 면

towrope kyŏninnyong patchul 견인용 밧줄

toxic tokssŏng-ŭi 독성의

toy changnankkam 장난감

♦ **toy with** *object* kajigo nolda 가지고 놀다; *idea* halkkamalkka saenggak'ada 할까말까 생각하다

trace 1 *n* (*of substance*) hŭnjŏk 흔적 2 *v/t* (*find*) susaek'ada 수색하다; (*follow: footsteps*) ch'ujŏk'ada 추적하다; (*draw*) kŭrida 그리다

track *n* (*path*) kil 길; (*on race course*) t'ŭraek 트랙; (*race course*) k'osŭ 코스; RAIL ch'ŏltto 철도; ~ **10** RAIL 10ppŏn sŏllo 10번 선로; **keep ~ of sth** muŏshi kirogŭl namgida 무엇의 기록을 남기다

♦ **track down** twitchoch'a ch'ajanaeda 뒤쫓아 찾아내다

tracksuit poon undongbok 보온 운동복

tractor t'ŭraekt'ŏ 트랙터

trade 1 *n* (*commerce*) sang-ŏp 상업; (*between countries*) muyŏk 무역; (*profession, craft*) chigŏp 직업 2 *v/i* (*do business*) changsahada 장사하다; ~ **in sth** musŭn changsarŭl hada 무슨 장사를 하다 3 *v/t* (*exchange*) kyohwanhada 교환하다; ~ **sth for sth** muŏtkkwa muŏsŭl kyohwanhada 무엇과 무엇을 교환하다

♦ **trade in** *v/t* (*when buying*) uttonŭl naego shinp'umgwa kyohwanhada 웃돈을 내고 신품과 교환하다

trade fair muyŏk chŏnshihoe 무역 전시회; **trademark** tŭngnok sangp'yo 등록 상표; **trade mission** muyŏk-kkwan 무역관

trader sang-in 상인

trade secret kiŏp pimil 기업 비밀

tradesman (*plumber etc*) surigong 수리공; (*deliveryman etc*) paedarwŏn 배달원

trade(s) union nodong chohap 노동 조합

tradition chŏnt'ong 전통

traditional chŏnt'ongjŏgin 전통적인

traditionally chŏnt'ongjŏgŭro 전통적으로

traffic *n* kyot'ong 교통; (*in drugs*) milssu 밀수

♦ **traffic in** *drugs* milssuhada 밀수하다

traffic circle lot'ŏri 로터리; **traffic cop** F kyot'ong sun-gyŏng 교통 순경; **traffic jam** kyot'ong ch'ejŭng 교통 체증; **traffic light** shinhodŭng 신호등; **traffic police** kyot'ong sun-gyŏng 교통 순경; **traffic sign** kyot'ong shinho 교통 신호; **traffic violation** kyot'ong wiban 교통 위반

tragedy pigŭk 비극

tragic pigŭktchŏgin 비극적인

trail 1 *n* (*path*) kil 길; (*of blood*) hŭnjŏk 흔적 2 *v/t* (*follow*) ttaragada 따라가다; (*tow*) kkŭlda 끌다 3 *v/i* (*lag behind*) kkŭllida 끌리다

trailer (*pulled by vehicle*) t'ŭreillŏ 트레일러; (*mobile home*) idong chut'aek 이동 주택; (*of movie*) yegop'yŏn 예고편

train¹ *n* kich'a 기차; **go by** ~ kich'aro kada 기차로 가다

train² 1 *v/t team, athlete, dog* hullyŏnshik'ida 훈련시키다; *employee* kyoyukshik'ida 교육시키다 2 *v/i* (*of team, athlete*) yŏnssŭp'ada 연습하다; (*of teacher etc*) kyoyukpatta 교육받다

trainee kyŏnsŭpssaeng 견습생

trainer SP k'och'i 코치; (*of dog*) hullyŏnsa 훈련사

trainers (*Br shoes*) undonghwa 운동화

training (*of new staff*) kyoyuk 교육; SP hullyŏn 훈련; **be in** ~ SP hullyŏn chung-ida 훈련 중이다; **be out of** ~ SP hullyŏn chung-i anida 훈련 중이 아니다

training course kyŏnsŭp kwajŏng 견습 과정

training scheme hullyŏn kyehoek 훈련 계획

train station kich'ayŏk 기차역

trait t'ŭksssŏng 특성

traitor paebanja 배반자

tramp 1 *n pej* (*woman*) kŏlle 걸레; *Br* (*hobo*) ttŏdori 떠돌이 2 *v/i* k'ungk'ung kŏt-tta 쿵쿵 걷다

trample v/t: **be ~d to death** palp'yŏ chuktta 밟혀 죽다; **be ~d underfoot** magu chitppalp'ida 마구 짓밟히다

◆ trample on person, object palba munggaeda 밟아 뭉개다

trampoline t'ŭraemp'ollin 트램폴린

trance honsu sangt'ae 혼수 상태; **go into a ~** honsu sangt'aee ppajida 혼수 상태에 빠지다

tranquil p'yŏngon-han 평온한

tranquility p'yŏng-on 평온

tranquilizer chinjŏngje 진정제

transact deal, business ch'ŏrihada 처리하다

transaction kŏrae 거래

transatlantic Taesŏyang hoengdanŭi 대서양 횡단의

transcendental ch'owŏltchŏgin 초월적인

transcript (of meeting, trial) sabon 사본

transfer 1 v/t omgida 옮기다; money songgŭmhada 송금하다; player ijŏk'ada 이적하다 2 v/i (switch) pakkuda 바꾸다 (when traveling) omgyŏt'ada 옮겨타다 3 n idong 이동; (in travel) karat'agi 갈아타기; (of money) songgŭmhwan 송금환

transferable ticket yangdohal su innŭn 양도할 수 있는

transform v/t pyŏnhyŏngshik'ida 변형시키다

transformation pyŏnhyŏng 변형

transformer ELEC pyŏnapkki 변압기

transfusion chuip 주입

transistor t'ŭraenjisŭt'ŏ 트랜지스터; (radio) t'ŭraenjisŭt'ŏ ladio 트랜지스터 라디오

transit: in ~ goods susong chung-in 수송 중인; ~ passenger t'onggwa yŏgaek 통과 여객

transition pyŏnhwa 변화

transitional kwadojŏgin 과도적인; ~ period kwadogi 과도기

transit lounge (at airport) t'onggwa yŏgaek taehapsshil 통과 여객 대합실

translate pŏnyŏk'ada 번역하다

translation pŏnyŏk 번역

translator pŏnyŏkka 번역가

transliterate ŭmnyŏk'ada 음역하다

transmission (of news, program) pangsong 방송; (of disease) chŏnyŏm 전염; MOT pyŏnsokki 변속기

transmit program pangsonghada 방송하다; disease chŏnyŏmshik'ida 전염시키다

transmitter RAD, TV songshin-gi 송신기

transpacific T'aep'yŏngyang hoengdanŭi 태평양 횡단의

transparency PHOT sŭllaidŭ 슬라이드

transparent t'umyŏnghan 투명한; blouse sogi pich'inŭn 속이 비치는; (obvious) myŏngbaek'an 명백한

transplant MED 1 v/t ishik'ada 이식하다 2 n ishik susul 이식 수술

transport 1 v/t goods, people susonghada 수송하다 2 n (of goods, people) susong 수송

transportation (of goods, people) susong 수송; means of ~ kyot'ong sudan 교통 수단; public ~ taejung kyot'ong 대중 교통; Department of Transportation Kyot'ongbu 교통부

transvestite isŏng-ŭi osŭl ipki choahanŭn saram 이성의 옷을 입기 좋아하는 사람

trap 1 n (for animal) tŏt 덫; (question, set-up etc) hamjŏng 함정; set a ~ for s.o. nugurŭl hamjŏng-e ppattŭrida 누구를 함정에 빠뜨리다 2 v/t animal tŏch'ŭro chaptta 덫으로 잡다; person hamjŏng-e ppattŭrida 함정에 빠뜨리다; be ~ped hamjŏng-e ppajida 함정에 빠지다; (in marriage, bad job etc) tŏch'e kŏllida 덫에 걸리다

trapdoor tŭlch'angmun 들창문

trapeze kogyeyong kŭne 곡예용 그네

trappings (of power) pugamul 부가물

trash (garbage) ssŭregi 쓰레기; (poor product) pullyangp'um 불량품; (book, movie etc) choltchak 졸작; (despicable person) in-gan ssŭregi 인간 쓰레기

trashcan ssŭregi t'ong 쓰레기 통

trashy goods, novel ssŭlmoŏmnŭn 쓸모없는

traumatic chŏngshinjŏgŭro k'ŭn ch'unggyŏgŭl chunŭn 정신적으로 큰 충격을 주는

travel 1 *n* yŏhaeng 여행; **~s** yŏhaeng 여행 **2** *v/i* yŏhaenghada 여행하다 **3** *v/t miles* yŏhaenghayŏ chinagada 여행하여 지나가다

travel agency yŏhaengsa 여행사

travel bag yŏhaeng kabang 여행 가방

traveler yŏhaenggaek 여행객

traveler's check yŏhaengja sup'yo 여행자 수표; **travel expenses** yŏhaeng piyong 여행 비용; **travel insurance** yŏhaeng pohŏm 여행 보험

trawler t'ŭrol ŏsŏn 트롤 어선

tray (*for food etc*) chaengban 쟁반; (*to go in oven*) p'an 판; (*in printer, copier*) holdŏ 홀더

treacherous paebanhanŭn 배반하는; *currents, roads* wihŏmhan 위험한

treachery paeban 배반

tread 1 *n* palkkŏrŭm 발걸음; (*of staircase*) tidimp'an 디딤판; (*of tire*) t'ŭredŭ 트레드 **2** *v/i* paltta 밟다
♦ **tread on** paltta 밟다

treason panyŏk 반역

treasure 1 *n* pomul 보물; (*person*) sojunghan saram 소중한 사람 **2** *v/t gift etc* sojunghi hada 소중히 하다

treasurer hoegye tamdangja 회계 담당자

Treasury Department Chaemusŏng 재무성

treat 1 *n* (*pleasure*) k'ŭn kippŭm 큰 기쁨; *it was a real* **~** chŏngmal kippŏssŏ 정말 기뻤어; *I have a ~ for you* tangshinŭl nollage hae tŭril iri issŭmnida 당신을 놀라게 해 드릴 일이 있습니다; *it's my ~* (*I'm paying*) chega hant'ŏk naegessŭmnida 제가 한턱 내겠습니다 **2** *v/t materials* taruda 다루다; *illness* ch'iryohada 치료하다; (*behave toward*) taeuhada 대우하다; **~ s.o. to sth** nuguege muŏsŭl taejŏp'ada 누구에게 무엇을 대접하다

treatment (*of materials*) ch'wigŭp 취급; (*of illness*) ch'iryo 치료; (*of people*) taeu 대우

treaty choyak 조약

treble[1] MUS ch'oegoŭmbuŭi 최고음부의

treble[2] **1** *adv*: **~ the price** sebaero ttwin kagyŏk 세배로 뛴 가격 **2** *v/i* sebaero chŭnggahada 세배로 증가하다

tree namu 나무

tremble (*of person*) ttŏlda 떨다; (*of hand, voice*) ttŏllida 떨리다; (*of building*) hŭndŭllida 흔들리다

tremendous (*very good*) koengjanghan 굉장한; (*enormous*) aju kŏdaehan 아주 거대한

tremendously (*very*) koengjanghi 굉장히; (*a lot*) maeu 매우

tremor (*of earth*) yaktchin 약진

trench ch'amho 참호

trend kyŏnghyang 경향; (*fashion*) yuhaeng-ŭi kyŏnghyang 유행의 경향

trendy ch'oeshin yuhaeng-ŭi 최신 유행의; *person* yuhaeng-ŭl ttarŭnŭn 유행을 따르는

trespass ch'imip'ada 침입하다; **no -ing** ch'urip kŭmji 출입 금지
♦ **trespass on** *land* …e ch'imip'ada …에 침입하다; *privacy* …ŭl/rŭl ch'imhaehada …을/를 침해하다; *s.o.'s time* …ŭl/rŭl ppaeat-tta …을/를 빼앗다

trespasser pulpŏp ch'imiptcha 불법 침입자

trial LAW kongp'an 공판; (*of equipment*) shihŏm 시험; **on ~** LAW kongp'an chung 공판 중; **have sth on ~** *equipment* muŏsŭl shihŏmhae poda 무엇을 시험해 보다

trial period (*for employee*) kyŏnsŭp kigan 견습 기간; (*for equipment*) shihŏm kigan 시험 기간

triangle samgak'yŏng 삼각형; MUS t'ŭraiaenggŭl 트라이앵글

triangular samgak'yŏng-ŭi 삼각형의

tribe pujok 부족

tribunal shimp'an wiwŏnhoe 심판 위원회

tributary (*river*) chiryu 지류

trick 1 *n* (*to deceive*) sogimsu 속임수; (*knack*) kigyo 기교; *play a ~ on s.o.* nuguege changnanjirŭl hada 누구에게 장난질을 하다 **2** *v/t* sogida 속이다; **~ s.o. into doing sth** nugurŭl sogyŏsŏ muŏsŭl shik'ida 누구를 속여서 무엇을 시키다

trickery sagi 사기

trickle v/i ttokttok ttŏrŏjida 뚝뚝 떨어지다

trickster sagikkun 사기꾼

tricky (difficult) tarugi himdŭn 다루기 힘든; person kyohwarhan 교활한

tricycle sebal chajŏn-gŏ 세발 자전거

trifle (triviality) hach'anŭn kŏt 하찮은 것

trifling hach'anŭn 하찮은

trigger n pang-asoe 방아쇠; (on camcorder) shijak pŏt'ŭn 시작 버튼; (cause) yubal yoin 유발 요인
♦ **trigger off** yubarhada 유발하다

trim 1 adj (neat) malkkŭmhan 말끔한; figure nŭlsshinhan 늘씬한 **2** v/t hair, hedge sonjirhada 손질하다; budget, costs sak-kkamhada 삭감하다; (decorate: dress) changshik'ada 장식하다 **3** n (cut) saltchak charŭm 살짝 자름; just a ~, please (to hairdresser) kŭnyang saltchak tadŭmŏ chuseyo 그냥 살짝 다듬어 주세요; in good ~ car, machine, boxer chal chŏngbidoen 잘 정비된; house chal kakkuŏjin 잘 가꾸어진

trimming (on clothes) tŏtppuch'in changshik 덧붙인 장식; with all the ~s modŭn pugaŭi kŏttŭlgwa 모든 부가의 것들과

trinket chajilgurehan changshin-gu 자질구레한 장신구

trio MUS samjungju 삼중주

trip 1 n (journey) yŏhaeng 여행 **2** v/i (stumble) kŏllyŏ nŏmŏjida 걸려 넘어지다 **3** v/t person kŏllyŏ nŏmŏttŭrida 걸려 넘어뜨리다
♦ **trip up 1** v/t (cause to fall) kŏrŏ nŏmŏttŭrida 걸어 넘어뜨리다; (cause to go wrong) shilp'aehage hada 실패하게 하다 **2** v/i (fall) nŏmŏjida 넘어지다; (make a mistake) shilssuhada 실수하다

tripe (food) yang 양

Tripitaka Koreana REL P'almandaejanggyŏng 팔만대장경

triple → **treble[2]**

triplets se ssangdung-i 세 쌍둥이

tripod PHOT samgakttae 삼각대

trite chinbuhan 진부한

triumph n sŭngni 승리

trivial sasohan 사소한

triviality sasohan kŏt 사소한 것

trombone t'ŭrombon 트럼본

troops kundae 군대

trophy usŭngk'ŏp 우승컵

tropic hoegwisŏn 회귀선

tropical yŏlttaeŭi 열대의

tropics yŏlttae chibang 열대 지방

trot v/i ch'ongch'ong kŏrŭmŭro kada 총총 걸음으로 가다

trouble 1 n (difficulties) munje 문제; (inconvenience) pulp'yŏn 불편; (disturbance) malssŏng 말썽; go to a lot of ~ to do sth muŏsŭl hagi wihae manŭn sugorŭl hada 무엇을 하기 위해 많은 수고를 하다; no ~ munje ŏpssŭmnida 문제 없습니다; get into ~ malssŏng-i nada 말썽이 나다 **2** v/t (worry) kŏktchŏngshik'ida 걱정시키다; (bother, disturb) kwich'ank'e hada 귀찮게 하다; (of back, liver etc) koerop'ida 괴롭히다

trouble-free kojang-i ŏmnŭn 고장이 없는; **troublemaker** malssŏngkkun 말썽꾼; **troubleshooter** (problem solver) munje haegyŏlssa 문제 해결사; (mediator) punjaeng chojŏngja 분쟁 조정자; **trouble-shooting** (problem solving) munje haegyŏl 문제 해결; (for faulty equipment) kojang suri 고장 수리

troublesome kolch'i ap'ŭn 골치 아픈

trousers Br paji 바지

trout song-ŏ 송어

truce hyujŏn 휴전

truck hwamulch'a 화물차

truck driver t'ŭrŏk unjŏnsa 트럭 운전사; **truck farm** ship'anyong nongsanmul chaebae nongga 시판용 농산물 재배 농가; **truck farmer** ship'anyong nongsanmul chaebae nongbu 시판용 농산물 재배 농부; **truck stop** t'ŭrŏk unjŏnsa shikttang 트럭 운전사 식당

trudge 1 v/i mŏlgo ŏryŏpkke kada 멀고 어렵게 가다 **2** n mŏlgo ŏryŏun kil 멀고 어려운 길

true chŏngmarŭi 정말의; friend, American chintchaŭi 진짜의; come ~ (of hopes, dream) shirhyŏndoeda 실현되다

truly chŏngmallo 정말로; *Yours ~* ...ollim ...올림

trumpet n t'ŭrŏmp'et 트럼펫

trunk (*of tree*) chulgi 줄기; (*of body*) momttung-i 몸뚱이; (*of elephant*) k'o 코; (*container, of car*) t'ŭrŏngk'ŭ 트렁크

trust 1 n (*in person, car etc*) shilloe 신뢰; (*in an organization*) shinyong 신용; FIN witak 위탁 **2** v/t shilloehada 신뢰하다; *I ~ you* tangshinŭl shilloehamnida 당신을 신뢰합니다

trusted shilloehal su innŭn 신뢰할 수 있는

trustee p'ishint'agin 피신탁인

trustful, trusting shilloehanŭn 신뢰하는

trustworthy shilloehal su innŭn 신뢰할 수 있는

truth chinshil 진실; (*fact*) sashil 사실

truthful chinshirhan 진실한; *account* chintchaŭi 진짜의

try 1 v/t noryŏk'ada 노력하다; *food* mŏgŏboda 먹어보다; *plan, route* shidohada 시도하다; LAW chaep'anhada 재판하다; *~ to do sth* muŏsŭl haryŏgo hada 무엇을 하려고 하다; *I ~ haebeoda* 해보다; *you must ~ harder* tangshinŭn tŏ yŏlshimhi noryŏk'aeya hamnida 당신은 더 열심히 노력해야 합니다 **3** n shido 시도; *can I have a ~?* hanbŏn matppwado toelkkayo? 한번 맛봐도 될까요?; (*at doing sth*) hanbŏn haebwado toelkkayo? 한번 해봐도 될까요?

♦**try on** *clothes* ibŏboda 입어보다

♦**try out** *machine, method* shihŏmhae poda 시험해 보다

trying (*annoying*) tchajŭngnanŭn 짜증나는

T-shirt t'ishyŏch'ŭ 티셔츠

tub (*bath*) yoktcho 욕조; (*of liquid*) t'ong 통; (*for yoghurt, ice cream*) kwak 곽

tubby adj t'ongt'onghan 통통한

tube (*pipe*) kwan 관; (*of toothpaste, ointment*) t'yubŭ 튜브

tubeless *tire* t'yubŭga ŏmnŭn 튜브가 없는

tuberculosis kyŏrhaek 결핵

tuck 1 n (*in dress*) tan 단 **2** v/t (*put*) kkiwŏ nŏt'a 끼워 넣다

♦**tuck away** (*put away*) ch'iuda 치우다; (*eat quickly*) sunshik-kkane mŏgŏch'iuda 순식간에 먹어치우다

♦**tuck in 1** v/t *children* ibultŭl tŏp'ŏjuda 이불을 덮어주다; *sheets* ...ŭi kkŭch'ŭl chŏbŏ nŏt'a ...의 끝을 접어 넣다 **2** v/i (*start eating*) mŏkki shijak'ada 먹기 시작하다

♦**tuck up** *sleeves etc* kŏdŏ ollida 걷어 올리다; *tuck s.o. up in bed* nugurŭl ch'imdaee nŏk'o iburŭl tŏp'ŏjuda 누구를 침대에 넣고 이불을 덮어주다

Tuesday hwayoil 화요일

tuft sul 술; (*of grass*) sup'ul 수풀

tug 1 n (*pull*) chaba tanggim 잡아 당김; NAUT yeinsŏn 예인선 **2** v/t (*pull*) chaba tangida 잡아 당기다

tuition suŏp 수업; *private ~* kaein kyosŭp 개인 교습

tulip t'yullip 튤립

tumble v/i kullŏ ttŏrŏjida 굴러 떨어지다; (*of wall*) munŏjida 무너지다

tumbledown munŏjilttut'an 무너질 듯한

tumbler (*for drink*) chan 잔; (*in circus*) kogyesa 곡예사

Tumen River Tuman-gang 두만강

tummy pae 배

tummy ache pokt'ong 복통

tumor chongnyang 종양

tumult soran 소란

tumultuous soransŭrŏun 소란스러운

tuna ch'amch'i 참치

tune 1 n koktcho 곡조; *in ~* ŭmjŏng-i mannŭn 음정이 맞는; *out of ~* ŭmjŏng-i t'ŭllin 음정이 틀린 **2** v/t *instrument* choyurhada 조율하다

♦**tune in** v/i RAD, TV ch'aenŏrŭl match'uda 채널을 맞추다

♦**tune in to** (*on radio*) ch'ŏngch'wihada 청취하다; (*on TV*) shich'ŏnghada 시청하다

♦**tune up 1** v/i (*of orchestra, players*) ak-kkiŭi ŭmŭl match'uda 악기의 음을 맞추다 **2** v/t *engine* chojŏrhada 조절하다

tuneful arŭmdaun sŏnyurŭi 아름다운 선율의

uner (*hi-fi*) t'yunŏ 튜너

unic EDU kyobok sang-ŭi 교복 상의

unnel *n* t'ŏnŏl 터널

urbine t'ŏbin 터빈

urbot kajami 가자미

urbulence (*in air travel*) nan-giryu 난기류

urbulent *love affair* kyŏngnyŏrhan 격렬한; *meeting, life* tongnyoranŭn 동요하는; *weather* kŏch'in 거친

urf chandibat 잔디밭; (*piece*) chandi 잔디

Turk T'ŏk'iin 터키인

Turkey T'ŏk'i 터키

turkey ch'ilmyŏnjo 칠면조

Turkish 1 *adj* T'ŏk'iŭi 터키의 **2** *n* (*language*) T'ŏk'iŏ 터키어

turmoil hollan 혼란

urn 1 *n* (*rotation*) hoejŏn 회전; (*in road*) mot'ung-i 모퉁이; (*in vaudeville*) ch'arye 차례; **take ~s doing sth** muŏsŭl kyodaero hada 무엇을 교대로 하다; **it's my ~** che ch'aryeimnida 제 차례입니다; **it's not your ~ yet** ajik tangsin sunsŏga animnida 아직 당신 순서가 아닙니다; **take a ~ at the wheel** ch'arŭl kyodaero unjŏnhada 차를 교대로 운전하다; **do s.o. a good ~** nuguege ch'injŏrhage hada 누구에게 친절하게 하다 **2** *v/t key, screw etc* tollida 돌리다; *wheel* hoejŏnshik'ida 회전시키다; *corner* tolda 돌다; *food, sheets* twijipta 뒤집다; *pages of book* nŏmgida 넘기다; **~ one's back on s.o.** nuguege tŭng-ŭl tollida 누구에게 등을 돌리다 **3** *v/i* (*of driver, car*) tolda 돌다; (*of wheel*) hoejŏndoeda 회전되다; **~ right/left here** yŏgisŏ orŭntchoguro/oentchoguro toseyo 여기서 오른쪽으로/왼쪽으로 도세요; **it has ~ed cold** shiŏjyŏt-tta/ch'uwŏjyŏt-tta 시어졌다/추워졌다; **he has ~ed 40** kŭnŭn sashibi nŏmŏt-tta 그는 40이 넘었다

♦ **turn around 1** *v/t object* tollida 돌리다; *company* hojŏnshik'ida 호전시키다; (COM: *deal with*) chumune match'uda 주문에 맞추다 **2** *v/i* (*of person, driver*) tolda 돌다

♦ **turn away 1** *v/t* (*send away*) tchoch'abŏrida 쫓아버리다 **2** *v/i* (*walk away*) chinach'yŏ kada 지나쳐 가다; (*look away*) oemyŏnhada 외면하다

♦ **turn back 1** *v/t edges, sheets* twijipta 뒤집다 **2** *v/i* (*of walkers etc*) toedoragada 되돌아가다; (*in course of action*) mullŏsŏda 물러서다

♦ **turn down** *v/t offer, invitation* kŏjŏrhada 거절하다; *volume, TV, heating* churida 줄이다; *edge, collar* chŏptta 접다

♦ **turn in 1** *v/i* (*go to bed*) chamjarie tŭlda 잠자리에 들다 **2** *v/t* (*to police*) shin-gohada 신고하다

♦ **turn off 1** *v/t TV, heater, engine* kkŭda 끄다; *water* chamgŭda 잠그다; F (*sexually*) sŏngtchŏk hŭngmirŭl ilk'e hada 성적 흥미를 잃게 하다 **2** *v/i* (*in driving etc*) tarŭn killo tŭrŏsŏda 다른 길로 들어서다; (*of machine*) kkŏjida 꺼지다

♦ **turn on 1** *v/t TV, heater, engine* k'yŏda 켜다; *water* t'ŭlda 틀다; F (*sexually*) sŏngtchŏguro hŭngbunshik'ida 성적으로 흥분시키다 **2** *v/i* (*of machine*) k'yŏjida 켜지다

♦ **turn out 1** *v/t lights* kkŭda 끄다 **2** *v/i*: *as it turned out* kyŏlguk 결국

♦ **turn over 1** *v/i* (*in bed*) twich'ŏk-kkŏrida 뒤척거리다; (*of vehicle*) twijibŏjida 뒤집어지다 **2** *v/t* (*put upside down*) twijipta 뒤집다; *page* nŏmgida 넘기다; FIN ...ŭi maesang-ŭl ollida ...의 매상을 올리다

♦ **turn up 1** *v/t collar* seuda 세우다; *volume, heating* nop'ida 높이다 **2** *v/i* (*arrive*) nat'anada 나타나다

turning mot'ung-i 모퉁이

turning point chŏnhwanjŏm 전환점

turnip sunmu 순무

turnout (*people*) ch'amsŏktcha 참석자; **turnover** FIN maesanggo 매상고; **turnpike** yuryo kosokttoro 유료 고속도로; **turnstile** shiptchahyŏng hoejŏnshik mun 십자형 회전식 문; **turntable** (*of record player*) t'ŏnt'eibŭl 턴테이블

turquoise *adj* ch'ŏngnokssaegŭi

청록색의
turret (*of castle*) t'ap 탑; (*of tank*)
p'ot'ap 포탑
turtle kŏbuk 거북
turtleneck (**sweater**) t'ŏt'ŭllek
sŭwet'ŏ 터틀넥 스웨터
turtle ship kŏbuksŏn 거북선
tusk ŏmni 엄니
tutor: (**private**) ~ kaein kyosa 개인
교사
tutorial n kaebyŏl chido shigan 개별
지도 시간
tuxedo t'ŏksshido 턱시도
TV t'ibi 티비, t'ellebi 텔레비; **on ~**
t'ibie 티비에
TV program t'ibi p'ŭrogŭraem 티비
프로그램
twang 1 n (*in voice*) k'otssori 콧소리
2 v/t guitar string t'winggida 튕기다
tweezers choktchipkke 족집게
twelfth adj yŏldu pŏntchaeŭi 열 두
번째의
twelve yŏldul 열 둘, shibi 십이
twentieth adj sŭmu pŏntchaeŭi 스무
번째의
twenty sŭmul 스물, iship 이십
twice tu pŏn 두 번; ~ **as much** tu
paeŭi yang-ŭro 두 배의 양으로
twiddle manjijak-kkŏrida
만지작거리다; ~ **one's thumbs**
pindunggŏrida 빈둥거리다
twig n kaji 가지
twilight noŭl 노을
twin han ssang-ŭi hantchok 한 쌍의
한쪽; ~**s** ssangdung-i 쌍둥이
twin beds t'ŭwin pedŭ 트윈 베드
twinge (*of pain*) ssushinŭn tŭt'an
ap'ŭm 쑤시는 듯한 아픔
twinkle v/i (*of stars*) pantchagida
반짝이다; (*of eyes*) pinnada 빛나다
twin town chamae toshi 자매 도시
twirl 1 v/t pingbing tollida 빙빙 돌리다
2 n (*of cream etc*) soyongdori kkorŭi
changshik 소용돌이 꼴의 장식
twist 1 v/t kkoda 꼬다; ~ **one's ankle**

palmogŭl ppida 발목을 삐다 2 v/i (*o
road, river*) kuburŏjida 구부러지다
3 n (*in rope*) kkoim 꼬임; (*in road*)
kulgok 굴곡; (*in plant, story*) ttŭt
pakkŭi chŏn-gae 뜻 밖의 전개
twisty road kkubulkkuburhan
꾸불꾸불한
twit F pabo 바보
twitch 1 n (*nervous*) kyŏngnyŏn 경련
2 v/i (*jerk*) kyŏngnyŏni ilda 경련이
일다
twitter v/i (*of birds*) chijŏgwida
지저귀다
two tul 둘, i 이; **the ~ of them** kŭdŭl
tul 그들 둘
two-faced ijung in-gyŏgŭi 이중
인격의; **two-stroke** adj engine
ihaengjŏng ssaik'ŭrŭi 이행정
싸이클의; **two-way traffic**
yangbanghyang t'onghaengno
양방향 통행로
tycoon kŏmul 거물
type 1 n (*sort*) yuhyŏng 유형; **what ~
of …?** ŏttŏn yuhyŏng-ŭi …? 어떤
유형의 …? 2 v/i (*use a keyboard*)
t'aja ch'ida 타자 치다 3 v/t (*with a
typewriter*) t'ajagiro ch'ida 타자기로
치다
typewriter t'ajagi 타자기
typhoid (**fever**) changt'ip'usŭ
장티푸스
typhoon t'aep'ung 태풍
typhus paltchint'ip'usŭ 발진티푸스
typical chŏnhyŏngjŏgin 전형적인;
that's ~ of him! kŭnŭn hangsang
kŭrŏch'anayo! 그는 항상
그렇잖아요!
typically ilbanjŏgŭro 일반적으로; ~
American chŏnhyŏngjŏgin Miguin
전형적인 미국인
typist t'aip'isŭt'ŭ 타이피스트
tyrannical p'okkunjŏgin 폭군적인
tyrannize aptchehada 압제하다
tyranny chŏnje chŏngch'i 전제 정치
tyrant p'ok-kkun 폭군

U

ugly hyunghan 흉한; *situation* kkŭmtchik'an 끔찍한

UK (= *United Kingdom*) Yŏngguk 영국

ulcer kweyang 궤양

Ullung Island Ullŭngdo 울릉도

ultimate (*best, definitive*) ch'oesang-ŭi 최상의; (*final*) kunggŭktchŏgin 궁극적인; (*fundamental*) kibonjŏgin 기본적인

ultimately (*in the end*) kyŏlguk 결국

ultimatum ch'oehu t'ongch'ŏp 최후 통첩

ultrasound MED ch'oŭmp'a 초음파

ultraviolet *adj* chaoeŭi 자외의; **~ rays** chaoesŏn 자외선

umbilical cord t'aetchul 탯줄

umbrella usan 우산

umpire *n* shimp'an 심판

umpteen F musuhan 무수한

UN (= *United Nations*) Kuktche Yŏnhap 국제 연합

unable: *be ~ to do X* (*not know how to*) Xŭl/rŭl hal churŭl morŭnda X을/를 할 줄을 모른다; (*not be in a position to*) Xŭl/rŭl hal su ŏptta X을/를 할 수 없다

unacceptable padadŭril su ŏmnŭn 받아들일 수 없는; *poverty* issŭl su ŏmnŭn 있을 수 없는; *it is ~ that...* ...ranŭn kŏsŭn padadŭril su ŏptta ...라는 것은 받아들일 수 없다

unaccountable sŏlmyŏnghal su ŏmnŭn 설명할 수 없는

unaccustomed: *be ~ to X* Xe ikssuk'aji ant'a X에 익숙하지 않다

unadulterated *fig* (*absolute*) sunjŏnhan 순전한

un-American panmiguktchŏgin 반미국적인

unanimous *verdict* manjang-ilch'iŭi 만장일치의; *be ~ on* ...e manjang-ilch'ihada ...에 만장일치하다

unanimously *vote, decide* manjang-ilch'iro 만장일치로

unapproachable *person* kkakkaihagi ŏryŏun 가까이하기 어려운

unarmed *person* pimujang-ŭi 비무장의; **~ combat** yukt'anjŏn 육탄전

unassuming kyŏmsonhan 겸손한

unattached (*without a partner*) toksshinin 독신인

unattended naebŏryŏdun 내버려둔; *leave X ~* Xŭl/rŭl naebŏryŏduda X을/를 내버려두다

unauthorized muhŏgaŭi 무허가의

unavoidable p'ihal su ŏmnŭn 피할 수 없는

unavoidably: *be ~ detained* pulgap'ihage nŭjŏjida 불가피하게 늦어지다

unaware: *be ~ of* ...ŭl/rŭl kkaedatchi mot'ada ...을/를 깨닫지 못하다

unawares: *catch X ~* Xŭl/rŭl pulsshie sŭpkkyŏk'ada X을/를 불시에 습격하다

unbalanced kyunhyŏng-ŭl irŭn 균형을 잃은; PSYCH puranjŏnghan 불안정한

unbearable kyŏndil su ŏmnŭn 견딜 수 없는; *he's ~* kŭnŭn kyŏndil su ŏmnŭn saramieyo 그는 견딜 수 없는 사람이에요

unbeatable *team, quality* amudo ttaraol su ŏmnŭn 아무도 따라올 수 없는

unbeaten *team* ch'ŏnhamujŏgŭi 천하무적의

unbeknown(st): **~ to his parents** kŭŭi pumonim mollae 그의 부모님 몰래

unbelievable midŭl su ŏmnŭn 믿을 수 없는; F (*heat, value*) ŏmch'ŏngnan 엄청난; *he's ~* F (*very good / bad*) kŭnŭn koengjanghi choŭn / mot-ttoen saramimnida 그는

굉장히 좋은/못된 사람입니다
unbias(s)ed p'yŏn-gyŏnŏmnŭn
편견없는
unblock *pipe* ttult'a 뚫다
unborn ajik t'aeŏnaji anŭn 아직
태어나지 않은; *an ~ baby* t'aea 태아
unbreakable *plate, world's record*
kkaejiji annŭn 깨지지 않는
unbutton p'ulda 풀다
uncalled-for chujenŏmŭn 주제넘은
uncanny *skill, feeling* myohan 묘한;
have an ~ resemblance to
…ŭl/rŭl myohage tamtta …을/를
묘하게 닮다
unceasing kkŭnimŏmnŭn 끊임없는
uncertain *future, weather*
purhwaksshirhan 불확실한; *origins*
pulmyŏnghwak'an 불명확한; *be ~
about X* Xŭl/rŭl hwaksshinhaji
mot'ada X을/를 확신하지 못하다;
it's ~ hwaksshirhaji anssŭmnida
확실하지 않습니다
uncertainty (*of the future*)
purhwaksshilssŏng 불확실성; *there
is still ~ about* …ŭn/nŭn ajik
purhwaksshirhamnida …은/는 아직
불확실합니다
unchecked *go ~* chŏjidoeji ant'a
저지되지 않다
uncle (*in general*) ajŏsshi 아저씨;
(*father's brother, single*) samch'on
삼촌; (*mother's brother, single*)
oesamch'on 외삼촌; (*father's sister's
husband*) komobu 고모부; (*mother's
sister's husband*) imobu 이모부
uncomfortable pulp'yŏnhan 불편한;
feel ~ about X (*about decision etc*)
Xi/ga kkŏrimch'ik'ada X이/가
꺼림칙하다; *I feel ~ with him* nanŭn
kŭga pulp'yŏnhada 나는 그가
불편하다
uncommon hŭnhaji anŭn 흔하지
않은; *it's not ~* kŭgŏsŭn hŭnhaji
anŭn irida 그것은 흔하지 않은
일이다
uncompromising t'ahyŏp'aji annŭn
타협하지 않는
unconcerned shin-gyŏngssŭji annŭn
신경쓰지 않는; *be ~ about X* Xe
shin-gyŏngssŭji annŭnda X에
신경 쓰지 않는다

unconditional mujokkŏnŭi 무조건의
unconscious MED muŭishik
sangt'aeŭi 무의식 상태의; PSYCH
muŭishiktchŏgin 무의식적인; *knock
~ ch'yŏsŏ kijŏlshik'ida 쳐서
기절시키다; *be ~ of X* (*not aware*)
Xŭl/rŭl kkaedatchi mot'ada X을/를
깨닫지 못하다
uncontrollable *anger, desire* chajehal
su ŏmnŭn 자제할 수 없는; *children*
kamdanghal su ŏmnŭn 감당할 수
없는
unconventional pigwansŭptchŏgin
비관습적인
uncooperative pihyŏptchojŏgin
비협조적인
uncork *bottle* magaerŭl ppoptta
마개를 뽑다
uncover (*remove covering from*)
tŏpkkaerŭl pŏtkkida 덮개를 벗기다;
(*discover*) palgurhada 발굴하다; *plot*
palk'yŏnaeda 밝혀내다
undamaged sonsangdoeji anŭn
손상되지 않은
undaunted: *carry on ~* kurhaji ank'o
haenaeda 굴하지 않고 해내다
undecided *matter* chŏnghaji anŭn
정하지 않은; *be ~ about X* Xŭl/rŭl
kyŏltchŏnghaji mot'ada X을/를
결정하지 못하다
undelete COMPUT twesalligi 되살리기
undeniable pujŏnghal su ŏmnŭn
부정할 수 없는
undeniably pujŏnghal su ŏpsshi
부정할 수 없이
under 1 *prep* (*beneath*) …ŭi arae …의
아래에; (*less than*) … miman … 미만;
~ $500 500tallŏ miman 500달러
미만; *~ the water* mul mit'e 물
밑에; *it is ~ review/investigation*
kŭgŏsŭn kŏmt'o/chosa chung-ida
그것은 검토/조사 중이다
(*anesthetized*): *the patient is still ~*
hwanjanŭn ajik mach'iesŏ kkaeŏnaji
anassŭmnida 환자는 아직 마취에서
깨어나지 않았습니다
underage *drinking etc* misŏngnyŏnŭi
미성년의; *be ~* misŏngnyŏnjaida
미성년자이다
underarm *adv throw* mit'ŭro tŏnjyŏ
밑으로 던져

undercarriage ch'angnyuk changch'i 착륙 장치

undercover *adj* agent pimillie sumgyŏjin 비밀리에 숨겨진

undercut *v/t* COM poda tŏ kkakka chegonghada 보다 더 깎아 제공하다

underdog yaktcha 약자

underdone *meat* tŏl ik'in 덜 익힌; *I prefer my steak* ~ chŏnŭn tŏl ik'in sŭt'eik'ŭga chossŭmnida 저는 덜 익힌 스테이크가 좋습니다

underestimate *v/t* person, skills, task kwasop'yŏngkkahada 과소평가하다

underexposed PHOT noch'uri pujok'an 노출이 부족한

underfed yŏngnyangbujogŭi 영양부족의

undergo *surgery, treatment* pat-tta 받다; *experiences* kyŏkta 겪다

underground 1 *adj* passages etc chihaŭi 지하의; POL resistance, newpaper etc pimirŭi 비밀의; ~ *activities* POL chiha undong 지하 운동 **2** *adv* work chiha-esŏ 지하에서; *go* ~ POL chiharo ŭnnik'ada 지하로 은닉하다

undergrowth tŏmbul 덤불

underhand *adj* (devious) ŭmhŏmhan 음험한

underlie *v/t* …ŭi kŭn-gŏga toeda …의 근거가 되다

underline *v/t* text mitchul kŭt-tta 밑줄 긋다

underlying *causes, problems* kŭnwŏnjŏgin 근원적인

undermine *v/t* s.o.'s position mollae hwesonhada 몰래 훼손하다; *theory* hŭndŭlda 흔들다

underneath 1 *prep* …ŭi mit'e …의 밑에 **2** *adv* mit'e 밑에

underpants p'aench'ŭ 팬츠

underpass (for pedestrians) chihado 지하도

underprivileged hyet'aekpat-tchi mot'an 혜택받지 못한

underrate *v/t* kwasop'yŏngkkahada 과소평가하다

undershirt rŏning shyŏch'ŭ 러닝 셔츠

undersized pot'ongboda chagŭn 보통보다 작은

underskirt sokch'ima 속치마

understaffed chŏgŭn suŭi chigwŏnŭl kajin 적은 수의 직원을 가진

understand *v/t* ihaehada 이해하다; *I* ~ *that you* … naega algienŭn tangshini … 내가 알기에는 당신이 …; *they are understood to be in Canada* kŭdŭrŭn K'aenadae innŭn kŏsŭro allyŏjyŏit-tta 그들은 캐나다에 있는 것으로 알려져있다 **2** *v/i* ihaehada 이해하다

understandable ihaehal su innŭn 이해할 수 있는

understandably ihaehal su itkke 이해할 수 있게

understanding 1 *adj* person ihaeshiminnŭn 이해심있는 **2** *n* (of problem, situation) ihae 이해; (agreement) tong-ŭi 동의; *on the ~ that* …ranŭn chokkŏn ha-e …라는 조건 하에

understatement ŏktchedoen p'yohyŏn 억제된 표현

undertake task surak'ada 수락하다; ~ *to do X* (agree to) Xŭl/rŭl hal kŏsŭl surak'ada X을/를 할 것을 수락하다

undertaking (enterprise) saŏp 사업; (promise) yakssok 약속

undervalue *v/t* kwaso p'yŏngkkahada 과소 평가하다

underwear sogot 속옷, naeŭi 내의

underweight *adj* person ch'ejung midarŭi 체중 미달의

underworld (criminal) amhŭk-kka 암흑가; (in mythology) chŏsŭng 저승

underwrite *v/t* FIN pojŭnghada 보증하다

undeserved padŭl kach'iga ŏmnŭn 받을 가치가 없는

undesirable features, changes paramjik'aji annŭn 바람직하지 않은; person pulk'waehan saram 불쾌한 사람; ~ *element* nune kashi 눈에 가시

undisputed champion, leader amudo nŏmboji mot'al 아무도 넘보지 못할

undo parcel, wrapping, buttons p'ulda 풀다; s.o. else's work soyong-ŏpkke hada 소용없게 하다

undoubtedly ŭishimhal yŏji ŏpsshi 의심할 여지 없이

undreamt-of riches kkumdo mot kkul chŏngdoŭi 꿈도 못 꿀 정도의

undress 1 *v/t* pŏtkkida 벗기다; *get ~ed* osŭl pŏt-tta 옷을 벗다 **2** *v/i* ot pŏtkkida 옷 벗기다

undue (*excessive*) chinach'in 지나친

unduly chinach'ige 지나치게

unearth *ancient remains* palgurhada 발굴하다; *fig* (*find*) palgyŏnhada 발견하다; *secret* p'ahech'ida 파헤치다

unearthly: *at this ~ hour* ŏngttunghan shigane 엉뚱한 시간에

uneasy *relationship, peace* puranhan 불안한; *feel ~ about* …ŭl/rŭl puranhae hada …을/를 불안해 하다

uneatable mŏgŭl su ŏmnŭn 먹을 수 없는

uneconomic iigi andoenŭn 이익이 안되는

uneducated kyoyukppat-tchi mot'an 교육받지 못한

unemployed shiltchik'an 실직한; *the ~* shirŏptcha 실업자

unemployment shirŏp 실업

unending kkŭdŏmnŭn 끝없는

unequal ttokkatchi anŭn 똑같지 않은; *pay* pulgongp'yŏnghan 불공평한; *be ~ to the task* kŭ irŭl hal nŭngnyŏgi ŏptta 그 일을 할 능력이 없다

unerring *judgment, instinct* t'ŭllimŏmnŭn 틀림없는

uneven *quality* kyunirhaji anŭn 균일하지 않은; *surface, ground* korŭji anŭn 고르지 않은

unevenly *distributed, applied* korŭji ank'e 고르지 않게; *~ matched* sangdaega andoenŭn 상대가 안되는

uneventful *day, journey* pyŏril ŏmnŭn 별일 없는

unexpected yesanghaji mot'an 예상하지 못한

unexpectedly yesang pakke 예상 밖에

unfair pulgongjŏnghan 불공정한

unfaithful *husband, wife* pujŏnghan 부정한; *be ~ to X* X morŭge paramŭl p'iuda X 모르게 바람을 피우다

unfamiliar ikssŭk'aji anŭn 익숙하지 않은; *be ~ with X* Xe ikssŭk'aji ant'a X에 익숙하지 않다

unfasten *belt* p'ulda 풀다

unfavorable *weather conditions*

hogami an-ganŭn 호감이 안가는; *report, review* hoŭijŏgi anin 호의적이 아닌

unfeeling *person* mujŏnghan 무정한

unfinished kkŭnnaeji anŭn 끝내지 않은; *leave X ~* Xŭl/rŭl kkŭnnaeji anŭn ch'aero tuda X을/를 끝내지 않은 채로 두다

unfit (*physically*) undong pujogin 운동 부족인; (*not morally suited*) pujŏkkyŏgin 부적격인; *be ~ to eat/drink* mŏk-kkie/mashigie pujŏkttanghada 먹기에/마시기에 부적당하다

unfix *part* pullihada 분리하다; *screw* ppaenaeda 빼내다

unflappable ch'imch'ak'an 침착한

unfold 1 *v/t sheets, letter, one's arms* p'yŏda 펴다 **2** *v/i* (*of story, view etc*) p'yŏlch'ŏjida 펼쳐지다

unforeseen yesanghaji mot'an 예상하지 못한

unforgettable ijŭl su ŏmnŭn 잊을 수 없는

unforgivable yongsŏhal su ŏmnŭn 용서할 수 없는; *that was ~ of you* kŭgŏsŭn yongsŏpat-tchi mot'al irida 그것은 용서받지 못할 일이다

unfortunate *people* un ŏmnŭn 운 없는; *choice of words, event* chalmot-ttoen 잘못된; *that's ~ for you* kŭgŏt chŏngmal andwaetkkunyo 그것 정말 안됐군요

unfortunately purhaenghi 불행히

unfounded kŭn-gŏŏmnŭn 근거없는

unfriendly pulch'injŏrhan 불친절한; *software* tarugi ŏryŏun 다루기 어려운

unfurnished kaguga ŏmnŭn 가구가 없는

ungodly: *at this ~ hour* ŏngttunghan shigane 엉뚱한 시간에

ungrateful kamsahal chul morŭnŭn 감사할 줄 모르는

unhappiness purhaeng 불행

unhappy purhaenghan 불행한; (*not satisfied*) pulmansŭrŏun 불만스러운; *be ~ with the service* sŏbissŭe pulmanida 서비스에 불만이다

unharmed musahan 무사한

unhealthy *person* kŏn-ganghaji

mot'an 건강하지 못한; *conditions* choch'i anŭn 좋지 않은; *food, atmosphere* kŏn-gang-e choch'i anŭn 건강에 좋지 않은; *economy, balance sheet* choch'i mot'an 좋지 못한

unheard-of chŏllye ŏmnŭn 전례 없는

unhurt tach'iji anŭn 다치지 않은

unhygienic piwisaengjŏgin 비위생적인

unification t'ong-il 통일

uniform 1 *n* MIL chebok 제복; (*of school pupil*) kyobok 교복; (*of sportsman, air hostess*) yunip'om 유니폼 **2** *adj* iltchŏnghan 일정한

unify t'ong-irhada 통일하다

unilateral ilbangjŏgin 일방적인

unimaginable sangsanghal su ŏmnŭn 상상할 수 없는

unimaginative sangsangnyŏgi ŏmnŭn 상상력이 없는

unimportant chungnyohaji anŭn 중요하지 않은

uninhabitable sal su ŏmnŭn 살 수 없는

uninhabited sarami salji annŭn 사람이 살지 않는

uninjured sangch'ŏ ŏmnŭn 상처 없는

unintelligible ihaehal su ŏmnŭn 이해할 수 없는

unintentional koŭiga anin 고의가 아닌

unintentionally ŭidoch'i ank'e 의도치 않게

uninteresting chaemi ŏmnŭn 재미 없는

uninterrupted *sleep, two hours' work* kkŭnimŏmnŭn 끊임없는

union POL yŏnhap 연합; (*labor ~*) nojo 노조

unique tokt'ŭk'an 독특한; ***with his own ~ humor / style*** kŭ t'ŭgyuŭi yumŏro / sŭt'aillo 그 특유의 유머로 / 스타일로

unit (*of measurement*) tanwi 단위; (*section: of machine, structure*) pup'um 부품; (*department*) pusŏ 부서; MIL pudae 부대

unit cost COM tanwi wŏnkka 단위 원가

unite 1 *v/t* kyŏrhap'ada 결합하다; *company* hap-ppyŏnghada 합병하다

2 *v/i* hanaga toeda 하나가 되다

united hanaga toen 하나가 된; *group, organization, country* yŏnhapttoen 연합된

United Kingdom Yŏngguk 영국

United Nations Kuktche Yŏnhap 국제 연합; ***~ troops*** Yuen-gun 유엔군

United People's Party T'ong-il Kungmindang 국민당

United States (of America) Miguk 미국, Mihaptchungguk 미국미합중국 *fml*

unity t'ong-il 통일; (*of all being*) tanilssŏng 단일성

universal (*general*) pop'yŏnjŏgin 보편적인; *language* kongt'ong-ŭi 공통의

universally pop'yŏnjŏgŭro 보편적으로

universe uju 우주

university taehak-kkyo 대학교; ***he is at ~*** kŭnŭn taehaksaeng-ida 그는 대학생이다

unjust pulgongjŏnghan 불공정한

unkempt tanjŏnghaji mot'an 단정하지 못한

unkind pulch'injŏrhan 불친절한

unknown 1 *adj* allyŏjiji anŭn 알려지지 않은 **2** *n*: ***a journey into the ~*** mijiroŭi yŏhaeng 미지로의 여행

unleaded (gasoline) muyŏn hwibaryu 무연 휘발유

unless ...haji anŭmyŏn ...하지 않으면; ***~ he pays us tomorrow*** kŭga naeilkkaji tonŭl chuji anŭmyŏn 그가 내일까지 돈을 주지 않으면

unlike *prep* kach'i anŭn 같지 않은; ***it's ~ him to drink so much*** kŭrŏk'e mani mashidani kŭdaptchi ant'a 그렇게 많이 마시다니 그답지 않다; ***the photograph was completely ~ her*** kŭ sajinŭn kŭnyŏgach'i anboinda 그 사진은 그녀같이 안보인다

unlikely issŭl kŏt kach'i anŭn 있을 것 같지 않은; ***he is ~ to win*** kŭnŭn igil kŏt kach'i ant'a 그는 이길 것 같지 않다; ***it is ~ that*** ...hal kŏt kach'i ant'a ...할 것 같지 않다

unlimited hanŏmnŭn 한없는

unload (*baggage etc*) naerida 내리다

unlock chamulsoerŭl yŏlda 자물쇠를 열다

unluckily unŏpkke 운없게

unlucky *day, choice, person* unŏmnŭn 운없는; *that was so ~ for you!* chŏngmal uni ŏpssŏtkkunyo! 정말 운이 없었군요!

unmade-up *face* hwajanghaji anŭn 화장하지 않은

unmanned *spacecraft* muinŭi 무인의

unmarried mihonŭi 미혼의

unmistakable t'ŭllimŏmnŭn 틀림없는

unmoved (*emotionally*) tongnyo ŏmnŭn 동요 없는

unmusical *person* ŭmaktchŏk sojiri ŏmnŭn 음악적 소질이 없는; *sounds* kwie kŏsŭllinŭn 귀에 거슬리는

unnatural pujayŏnsŭrŏun 부자연스러운; *it's not ~ to be annoyed* hwananŭn kŏt-tto tangnyŏnhamnida 화내는 것도 당연합니다

unnecessary pulp'iryohan 불필요한

unnerving kŏmnage hanŭn 겁나게 하는

unnoticed: *it went ~* nune ttŭiji anassŏyo 눈에 띄지 않았어요

unobtainable *goods* ŏdŭl su ŏmnŭn 얻을 수 없는; TELEC yŏn-gyŏri andoenŭn 연결이 안되는

unobtrusive nune ttŭiji annŭn 눈에 띄지 않는

unoccupied *building, house, post* piŏinnŭn 비어있는; *room* amudo ŏmnŭn 아무도 없는; *person* hal il ŏmnŭn 할 일 없는

unofficial pigongshiktchŏgin 비공식적인

unofficially pigongshiktchŏguro 비공식적으로

unpack *v/t & v/i* p'ulda 풀다

unpaid *work* mugŭbŭi 무급의

unpleasant pulk'waehan 불쾌한; *he was very ~ to her* kŭnŭn kŭnyŏŭi kibunŭl sanghage haet-tta 그는 그녀의 기분을 상하게 했다

unplug *v/t* TV, *computer* ...ŭi p'ŭllŏgŭrŭl ppoptta ...의 플러그를 뽑다

unpopular *person* inkkiŏmnŭn 인기없는; *decision* chijipat-tchi mot'anŭn 지지받지 못하는

unprecedented chŏllye ŏmnŭn 전례 없는; *it was ~ for a woman to ...* yojaga ...hanŭn kŏsŭn ijŏnenŭn ŏptton iriŏt-tta 여자가 ...하는 것은 이전에는 없던 일이었다

unpredictable *person, weather* yech'ŭk'al su ŏmnŭn 예측할 수 없는

unprincipled *pej* pidodŏktchŏgin 비도덕적인

unpretentious hŏshigŏmnŭn 허식없는

unproductive *meeting, discussion* pisaengsanjŏgin 비생산적인

unprofessional *person, behavior* chŏnmunindaptchi anŭn 전문인답지 않은; *workmanship* pip'ŭrojŏgin 비프로적인

unprofitable iigi ŏmnŭn 이익이 없는

unpronounceable parŭmhal su ŏmnŭn, parŭmi pulganŭnghan 발음할 수 없는, 발음이 불가능한

unprotected *borders* mubangbiŭi 무방비의; *machine* pohodoeji anŭn 보호되지 않은; *~ sex* k'ondomŭl sayonghaji ank'o hanŭn sŏnggyo 콘돔을 사용하지 않고 하는 성교

unprovoked *attack* tobaldoeji anŭn 도발되지 않은

unqualified *worker, doctor etc* chagyŏgi ŏmnŭn 자격이 없는

unquestionably (*without doubt*) murŏ pol p'iryodo ŏpsshi 물어 볼 필요도 없이

unquestioning ŭishimŏmnŭn 의심없는

unravel *v/t string, mystery* p'ulda 풀다

unreadable *book* ilkki ŏryŏun 읽기 어려운

unreal *creature* shiltchaehaji annŭn 실재하지 않는; (*unrealistic*) pihyŏnsshiltchŏgin 비현실적인; *this is ~!* F midŭl su ŏpssŏyo! 믿을 수 없어요!

unrealistic pihyŏnsshiltchŏgin 비현실적인

unreasonable pihamnijŏgin 비합리적인

unrelated kwan-gyeŏmnŭn 관계없는

unrelenting kkujunhan 꾸준한
unreliable midŭl su ŏmnŭn 믿을 수
없는
unrest puran 불안
unrestrained *emotions* ŏktchedoeji
anŭn 억제되지 않은
unroadworthy wihŏmhal chŏngdoro
kojangna innŭn 위험할 정도로
고장나 있는
unroll *v/t carpet, scroll* p'ida 피다
unruly tarugi himdŭn 다루기 힘든
unsafe anjŏnhaji anŭn 안전하지 않은;
~ to drink / eat mashigie / mŏk-kkie
anjŏnhaji anŭn 마시기에 / 먹기에
안전하지 않은
unsanitary piwisaengjŏgin 비위생적인
unsatisfactory manjokssŭrŏptchi
mot'an 만족스럽지 못한
unsavory *person, reputation*
pulk'waehan 불쾌한; *district*
hŏmak'an 험악한
unscathed tach'in te ŏmnŭn 다친 데
없는; *(not damaged)*
hŭmtchibŏmnŭn 흠집없는
unscrew nasarŭl p'ulda 나사를 풀다;
top magaerŭl yŏlda 마개를 열다
unscrupulous pudodŏk'an 부도덕한
unselfish it'ajŏgin 이타적인
unsettled *issue* kyŏltchŏngdoeji anŭn
결정되지 않은; *weather, stock market*
pyŏnhagi shwiun 변하기 쉬운;
lifestyle iltchŏngch'i anŭn 일정치
않은; *bills* migyŏltcheŭi 미결제의; *of
stomach* paet'allan 배탈난
unshaven myŏndohaji anŭn 면도하지
않은
unsightly pogi hyunghan 보기 흉한
unskilled misuk'an 미숙한; **~ labor**
misungnyŏn nodongja 미숙련 노동자
unsociable pisagyojŏgin 비사교적인
unsophisticated tansunhan 단순한
unstable *person, structure*
puranjŏnghan 불안정한; *area,
economy* puranhan 불안한
unsteady *(on one's feet)*
pit'ŭlgŏrinŭn 비틀거리는; *ladder*
hŭndŭlgŏrinŭn 흔들거리는
unstinting: be ~ in one's efforts
noryŏgŭl akkiji ant'a 노력을 아끼지
않다
unstuck: come ~ *(of notice etc)*

ttŏrŏjida 떨어지다; *(of plan etc)*
manghada 망하다
unsuccessful *writer, party etc*
shilp'aehan 실패한; *candidate*
nakssŏndoen 낙선된; *attempt*
sŏnggonghaji mot'an 성공하지 못한;
he tried but was ~ kŭnŭn
noryŏk'aet-tchiman shilp'aehaet-tta
그는 노력했지만 실패했다
unsuccessfully *try, apply*
sŏnggongjŏgiji mot'age 성공적이지
못하게
unsuitable pujokttanghan 부적당한
unsuspecting ŭichimhaji annŭn
의심하지 않는
unswerving *loyalty, devotion*
hwakkobudonghan 확고부동한
unthinkable saenggak'al su choch'a
ŏmnŭn 생각할 수 조차 없는
untidy chijŏbunhan 지저분한
untie *knot, laces* p'ulda 풀다; *prisoner*
p'urŏjuda 풀어주다
until 1 *prep* kkaji 까지; **from Monday
~ Friday** wŏryoilbut'ŏ
kŭmnyoilkkaji 월요일부터
금요일까지; **I can wait ~ tomorrow**
naeilkkaji kidaril su issŭmnida
내일까지 기다릴 수 있습니다; **not ~
Friday** kŭmnyoil chŏnenŭn malgo
금요일 전에는 말고; **it won't be
finished ~ July** ch'irwŏlkkajinŭn
mot kkŭnnael kŏt kassŭmnida
칠월까지는 못 끝낼 것 같습니다
2 *conj* hal ttaekkaji 할 때까지; **can
you wait ~ I'm ready?** chega
chunbidoel ttaekkaji kidaril su
itkkessŭmnikka? 제가 준비될 때까지
기다릴 수 있겠습니까?; **they won't
do anything ~ you say so**
tangshini kŭrŏrago hal ttaekkaji
kŭdŭrŭn amu kŏtto haji anŭl
kŏshimnida 당신이 그러라고 할
때까지 그들은 아무 것도 하지 않을
것입니다
untimely *death* ttae anin 때 아닌
untiring *efforts* chich'iji annŭn 지치지
않는
untold *riches, suffering* makttaehan
막대한; *story* palk'yŏjiji anŭn
밝혀지지 않은
untranslatable pŏnyŏk'al su ŏmnŭn

번역할 수 없는

untrue sashiri anin 사실이 아닌

unused *goods* sayonghaji anŭn 사용하지 않은

unused²: **be ~ to sth** muŏse ikssuk'aji ant'a 무엇에 익숙하지 않다; **be ~ to doing sth** muŏsŭl hanŭn kŏshi ikssuk'aji ant'a 무엇을 하는 것이 익숙하지 않다

unusual tŭmun 드문

unusually tŭmulge 드물게

unveil *memorial, statue etc* pŏtkkida 벗기다; *plans* konggaehada 공개하다

unwell (*physically*) momi choch'i anŭn 몸이 좋지 않은; (*mentally*) kibuni choch'i anŭn 기분이 좋지 않은

unwilling: **be ~ to do sth** muŏsŭl hanŭn kŏsŭl naek'yŏhaji ant'a 무엇을 하는 것을 내켜하지 않다

unwind *v/t tape* p'ulda 풀다 **2** *v/i* (*of tape, story*) p'ullida 풀리다; (*relax*) kinjang-ŭl p'ulda 긴장을 풀다

unwise hyŏnmyŏnghaji mot'an 현명하지 못한

unwrap *gift* p'urŏ poda 풀어 보다

unwritten *rule* kwansŭptchŏgin 관습적인; *~ law* kkŭnnasda 관습법

up 1 *adv* wie 위에; **~ in the sky / on the roof** hanŭl / chibung wie 하늘 / 지붕 위에; **~ here / there** yŏgi / chŏgi wie 여기 / 저기 위에; **be ~** (*out of bed*) irŏna it-tta 일어나 있다; (*of sun*) ttŏolla it-tta 떠올라 있다; (*be built*) sewŏjyŏ it-tta 세워져 있다; (*of shelves*) sŏlch'idoeŏ it-tta 설치되어 있다; (*of prices, temperature*) olla it-tta 올라 있다; (*have expired*) kkŭnnasda 끝나다; **what's ~?** musŭn il issŭmnikka? 무슨 일 있습니까?; **~ to the year 1989** 1989nyŏnkkaji 1989년까지; **he came ~ to me** kŭnŭn na-ege tagawat-tta 그는 나에게 다가왔다; **what are you ~ to these days?** yojŭm musŭn irŭl hamyŏ chinaeshimnikka? 요즘 무슨 일을 하며 지내십니까?; **what are those**

kids ~ to? aidŭri musŭn chisŭl hago it-tchi? 아이들이 무슨 짓을 하고 있지?; **be ~ to something** (*bad*) mot-ttoen chisŭl hago it-tta 못된 짓을 하고 있다; **I don't feel ~ to it** nanŭn kŭrŏl kibuni tŭlji ansssŭmnida 나는 그럴 기분이 들지 않습니다; **it's ~ to you** tangshinhant'e tallyŏssŏyo 당신한테 달렸어요; **it's ~ to them to solve it** kŭdŭri haegyoerhaeyajiyo 그들이 해결해야지요; **be ~ and about** (*after illness*) hoebok'ayŏ toradanida 회복하여 돌아다니다 **2** *prep*: **further ~ the mountain** sanŭi tŏ nop'ŭn tchoge sdanŭi tŏ nop'ŭn tchoge 산의 더 높은 쪽에; **he climbed ~ a tree** kŭnŭn namurŭl t'ago ŏllagat-tta 그는 나무를 타고 올라갔다; **they ran ~ the street** kŭdŭrŭn kirŭl ttara tallyŏt-tta 그들은 길을 따라 달렸다; **the water goes ~ this pipe** murŭl i kwanŭl ttara hŭrŭmnida 물은 이 관을 따라 흐릅니다; **we traveled ~ to Kang-wondo** urinŭn Kangwŏndokkaji yŏhaenghae ollagat-tta 우리는 강원도까지 여행해 올라갔다 **3** *n*: **~s and downs** kibok 기복

upbringing kajŏng kyoyuk 가정 교육

upcoming *adj* tagaonŭn 다가오는

update 1 *v/t file, records* ch'oeshinŭi kŏsŭro pakkuda 최신의 것으로 바꾸다; **~ s.o. on sth** nuguege muŏse kwanhan ch'oeshin chŏngborŭl chuda 누구에게 무엇에 관한 최신 정보를 주다 **2** *n* (*of files, records*) ch'oeshin kŏsŭroŭi pasch'e 최신 것으로의 교체; **can you give me an ~ on the situation?** kajang ch'oegŭnŭi sanghwang-ŭl allyŏjushigessŭmnikka? 가장 최근의 상황을 알려주시겠습니까?

upgrade 1 *v/t computers, ticket etc* ŏpkkŭreidŭhada 업그레이드하다; (*replace with new version*) saeroun kŏsŭro kyoch'ehada 새로운 것으로 교체하다; *product* hyangsangshik'ida 향상시키다 **2** *n* (*software version*) ŏpkkŭreidŭ 업그레이드

upheaval (*emotional, physical*) k'ŭn pyŏnhwa 변화; (*political, social*) kyŏkppyŏn 격변

uphill 1 *adv walk* ŏndŏk wiro 언덕 위로; *the road goes* ~ orŭmak kirida 오르막 길이다 **2** *adj struggle* himdŭnŭn 힘드는

uphold *traditions, rights* yujihada 유지하다; (*vindicate*) hwaginhada 확인하다

upholstery (*fabric*) kagu changshik 가구 장식; (*padding*) kaguŭi sok 가구의 속

upkeep *n* (*of buildings, parks etc*) yuji 유지

upload *v/t* COMPUT ŏprodŭhada 업로드하다

upmarket *adj restaurant, hotel* kop'umkkyŏgŭi 고품격의

upon → *on*

upper *part of sth* wi tchogŭi 위 쪽의; *stretches of a river* sangnyuŭi 상류의; *atmosphere* wiŭi 위의; ~ *deck* sanggapp'an 상갑판

upper-class sangnyuch'ŭng-ŭi 상류층의

upper classes sangnyuch'ŭng 상류층

UPP (= *United People's Party*) T'ongil Kungmindang 통일국민당

upright 1 *adj citizen* parŭn 바른 **2** *adv sit* ttokpparo 똑바로

upright (*piano*) ŏmnit'ŭ p'iano 업라이트 피아노

uprising p'okttong 폭동

uproar (*loud noise*) soran 소란; (*protest*) hang-ŭi 항의

upset 1 *v/t drink, glass* twijiptta 뒤집다; (*emotionally*) kibun sanghagehada 기분 상하게하다 **2** *adj* (*emotionally*) kibun sanghan 기분 상한; *get* ~ *about sth* muŏse kibun sanghada 무엇에 기분 상하다; *have an* ~ *stomach* paet'allada 배탈나다

upsetting sokssanghan 속상한

upshot (*result, outcome*) kyŏlgwa 결과

upside down *adv* kŏkkuro 거꾸로; *turn* ~ *box etc* muŏsŭl kŏkkuro twijiptta 무엇을 거꾸로 뒤집다

upstairs 1 *adv* wich'ŭng-e 위층에 **2** *adj room* wich'ŭng-ŭi 위층의

upstart pyŏrak ch'ulssehan nom 벼락 출세한 놈

upstream *adv* sangnyuro 상류로

uptight F (*nervous*) anjŏlbujŏl mot'anŭn 안절부절 못하는; (*inhibited*) kinjang-ŭro ttaktttak'aejin 긴장으로 딱딱해진

up-to-date *fashions, data* ch'oeshinŭi 최신의

upturn (*in economy*) hojŏn 호전

upward *adv fly, move* wiro 위로; ~ *of 10,000* man isang-ŭro 만 이상으로

uranium uranyum 우라늄

urban toshiŭi 도시의

urbanization toshihwa 도시화

urchin kkoma 꼬마

urge 1 *n* ch'ungdong 충동; *I felt an* ~ *to hit him* nanŭn kŭrŭl ttaerigo ship'ŭn ch'ungdong-ŭl nŭkkyŏt-tta 나는 그를 때리고 싶은 충동을 느꼈다 **2** *v/t*: ~ *X to do Y* Xege Y(ŭ)rago puch'ugida X에게 Y(으)라고 부추기다

♦ **urge on** kyŏngnyŏhada 격려하다

urgency (*of situation*) kin-gŭp 긴급

urgent *job, letter* kŭp'an 급한; *be in* ~ *need of* …i/ga kŭp'age p'iryohada …이/가 급하게 필요하다; *is it* ~? kŭp'an kŏshimnikka? 급한 것입니까?

urinate sobyŏnŭl poda 소변을 보다

urine sobyŏn 소변

urn tanji 단지

us uri 우리; *that's for* ~ uri kŏshimnida 우리 것입니다; *who's that? - it's* ~ nuguseyo? - uriyeyo 누구세요? - 우리예요

US(A) (= *United States* (*of America*)) Miguk 미국, Mihaptchungguk 미합중국 *fml*

usable ssŭl su innŭn 쓸 수 있는

usage (*linguistic*) ŏppŏp 어법

use 1 *v/t* ssŭda 쓰다, sayonghada 사용하다; *pej: person* iyonghada 이용하다; *I could* ~ *a drink* F mwŏ chom mashyŏyagessŏyo 뭐 좀 마셔야겠어요 **2** *n* sayong 사용, ssŭgi 쓰기, iyong 이용; *be of great* ~ *to s.o.* nuguege k'ŭge ssŭlmo it-tta 누구에게 크게 쓸모 있다; *be of no* ~ *to s.o.* nuguege ssŭlmo ŏptta 누구에게 쓸모 없다; *is that of any* ~? ssŭlmo issŭmnikka? 쓸모

있습니까?; *it's no* ~ soyong ŏmnŭn irimnida 소용 없는 일입니다; *it's no* ~ *trying* / *waiting* haebwaya / kidaryŏbwaya soyong ŏpssŭmnida 해봐야 / 기다려봐야 소용 없습니다
♦ **use up** ta ssŏbŏrida 다 써버리다
used[1] *car etc* ch'unggo 중고
used[2]: *be ~ to s.o. / sth* nugue / muŏse ikssuk'aejyŏ it-tta 누구에 / 무엇에 익숙해져 있다; *get ~ to s.o. / sth* nugue / muŏse ikssuk'aejida 누구에 / 무엇에 익숙해지다; *be ~ to doing sth* muŏsŭl hanŭn kŏse ikssuk'aejyŏ it-tta 무엇을 하는 것에 익숙해져 있다; *get ~ to doing sth* muŏsŭl hanŭn kŏse ikssuk'aejida 무엇을 하는 것에 익숙해지다
used[3]: *I ~ to like / know him* hanttae nanŭn kŭrŭl choahaessŏt-tta / arassŏt-tta 한때 나는 그를 좋아했었다 / 알았었다; *I don't work there now, but I ~ to* chigŭmŭn anijiman, yejŏnenŭn kŭ gosesŏ irhaessŏssŏyo 지금은 아니지만, 예전에는 그 곳에서 일했었어요; *I ~ to work with him* nanŭn kŭwa kach'i irhaessŏssŭmnida 나는 그와 같이 일했었습니다
useful ssŭlmoinnŭn 쓸모있는
usefulness ssŭlmo 쓸모
useless ssŭlmoŏmnŭn 쓸모없는; F

person mojaran 모자란; *it's ~ trying* noryŏk'aebwattcha ssŭlmoŏmnŭn chishida 노력해봤자 쓸모없는 짓이다
user (*of product*) sayongja 사용자
user-friendly sayonghagi shwiun 사용하기 쉬운
usher *n* (*at wedding*) annaeja 안내자
♦ **usher in** *new era* ...(ŭ)ro indohada ...(으)로 인도하다
usual pot'ong-ŭi 보통의; *as ~* pot'ong ttaech'ŏrŏm 보통 때처럼; *the ~, please* nŭl hanŭn kŏsŭro chushipsshio 늘 하는 것으로 주십시오
usually pot'ong 보통
utensil yonggu 용구
uterus chagung 자궁
utility (*usefulness*) yuyongssŏng 유용성; (*software*) yut'illit'i 유틸리티; *public utilities* kong-ik saŏp 공익 사업
utilize yuyonghage hada 유용하게 하다
utmost 1 *adj* ch'oedaehanŭi 최대한의 **2** *n*: *do one's ~* ch'oesŏnŭl tahada 최선을 다하다
utter 1 *adj* wanjŏnhan 완전한 **2** *v/t sound* parhada 발하다
utterly wanjŏnhi 완전히
U-turn yut'ŏn U턴; *fig* (*in policy*) wanjŏnhan t'albakkum 완전한 탈바꿈

V

vacant *building* piŏ innŭn 비어 있는; *position* kongsŏgin 공석인; *look* mŏnghan 멍한

vacate *room* piuda 비우다

vacation *n* hyuga 휴가; **be on ~** hyuga chung-ida 휴가 중이다; **go to ... on ~** hyugaro ...e kada 휴가로 ...에 가다; **take a ~** hyugarŭl katta 휴가를 갖다

vacationer hyuga yŏhaenggaek 휴가 여행객

vaccinate yebang chŏptchonghada 예방 접종하다; **be ~d against ...** yebang chŏptchong chusarŭl mat-tta ... 예방 접종 주사를 맞다

vaccination yebang chŏptchong 예방 접종

vaccine paekshin 백신

vacuum 1 *n* PHYS chin-gong 진공; *fig* (*in one's life*) konghŏ 공허 **2** *v/t* *floors* chin-gong ch'ŏngsogiro ch'ŏngsohada 진공 청소기로 청소하다

vacuum cleaner chin-gong ch'ŏngsogi 진공 청소기; **vacuum flask** chin-gonggwan 진공관; **vacuum-packed** chin-gongp'ojangŭi 진공포장의

vagina chil 질

vaginal chirŭi 질의

vague mohohan 모호한; *feeling* ŏryŏmp'ut'an 어렴풋한; *taste of sth, resemblance* hŭirit'an 흐릿한; **he was very ~ about it** kŭnŭn kŭ il ttaehae mohohan t'aedorŭl ch'wihaet-tta 그는 그 일에 대해 모호한 태도를 취했다

vaguely *answer* mohohage 모호하게; (*slightly*) yakkan 약간

vain 1 *adj person* hŏyŏngshimi manŭn 허영심이 많은; *hope* hŏt-ttoen 헛된 **2** *n*: **in ~** hŏt-ttoege 헛되게; *their efforts were in ~* kŭdŭrŭi noryŏgŭn hŏtssugoro torakat-tta 그들의

노력은 헛수고로 돌아갔다

valet (*person*) shijung tŭnŭn saram 시중 드는 사람

valet service (*for clothes*) set'ak sŏbissŭ 세탁 서비스; (*for cars*) sech'a sŏbissŭ 세차 서비스

valiant yonggamhan 용감한

valid *passport, document* yuhyohan 유효한; *reason, argument* t'adanghan 타당한

validate (*with official stamp*) yuhyohage hada 유효하게 하다; (*back up*) chŭngmyŏnghada 증명하다

validity t'adangsŏng 타당성

valley koltchagi 골짜기

valuable 1 *adj* kwijunghan 귀중한 **2** *n*: **~s** kwijungp'um 귀중품

valuation kamjŏng 감정; **at his ~** kŭga kamjŏnghan paronŭn 그가 감정한 바로는

value 1 *n* kach'i 가치; **be good ~** kŭmanhan kach'iga it-tta 그만한 가치가 있다; **get ~ for money** ton mank'ŭmŭi kach'irŭl ŏt-tta 돈 만큼의 가치를 얻다; **rise/fall in ~** kach'iga orŭda/ttŏrŏjida 가치가 오르다/떨어지다 **2** *v/t s.o.'s friendship, one's freedom* sojunghi yŏgida 소중히 여기다; **I ~ your advice** tangshinŭi ch'unggorŭl sojunghi saenggak'aeyo 당신의 충고를 소중히 생각해요; **have an object ~d** ŏttŏn mulgŏnŭi kapssŭl p'yŏngkkabat-tta 어떤 물건의 값을 평가받다

valve paelbŭ 밸브

van ponggoch'a 봉고차

vandal koŭijŏgŭro konggongmurŭl pusunŭn saram 고의적으로 공공물을 부수는 사람

vandalism koŭijŏk p'agoe 고의적 파괴

vandalize koŭijŏgŭro p'agoehada 고의적으로 파괴하다

vanilla 1 *n* panilla 바닐라 **2** *adj*
panillaŭi 바닐라의
vanish sarajida 사라지다
vanity chamanshim 자만심; (*of hopes*)
konghŏham 공허함
vanity case hwajangp'um kabang
화장품 가방
vantage point (*on hill etc*)
chŏnmang-i chohŭn chijŏm 전망이
좋은 지점
vapor chŭnggi 증기
vaporize *v/t* (*of bomb*)
chŭngbalshik'ida 증발시키다
vapor trail pihaeng-un 비행운
variable 1 *adj amount* kabyŏnŭi
가변의; *moods, weather*
pyŏndŏkssŭrŏun 변덕스러운 **2** *n*
MATH, COMPUT pyŏnssu 변수
variation pyŏndong 변동
varicose vein nojang chŏngmaek
노장 정맥
varied *range, diet* tayanghan 다양한
variety pyŏnhwa 변화; (*type*)
tayangssŏng 다양성; *a ~ of things
to do* yŏrŏ kaji hal il yŏrŏ kaji hal
일 여러 가지 할
various (*several*) yŏrŏ 여러;
(*different*) kaji kakssaegŭi 가지
각색의
varnish 1 *n* nisŭ 니스 **2** *v/t* nisŭrŭl
ch'irhada 니스를 칠하다
vary 1 *v/i* pakkwida 바뀌다; *it varies*
ch'ŏnch'amanbyŏrijiyo
천차만별이지요 **2** *v/t* pakkuda 바꾸다
vase kkotppyŏng 꽃병
vast *desert, city* kwanghwarhan
광활한; *collection, knowledge*
pangdaehan 방대한
vaudeville shyo 쇼
vault¹ *n* (*in roof*) tunggŭn ch'ŏnjang
둥근 천장; *~s* (*cellar*) chiha ch'anggo
지하 창고
vault² *n* SP toyak 도약 **2** *v/t beam etc*
ttwiŏnŏmtta 뛰어넘다
VCR (= *video cassette recorder*)
pŭi ssi al 브이 시이 알
veal songaji kogi 송아지 고기
vegan 1 *n* ch'ŏltchŏhan
ch'aeshiktchuŭija 철저한 채식주의자
2 *adj* ch'ŏltchŏhan ch'aeshigŭi
철저한 채식의

vegetable yach'ae 야채
vegetarian 1 *n* ch'aeshiktchuŭija
채식주의자 **2** *adj* ch'aeshigŭi 채식의
vehicle unban sudan 운반 수단; (*for
information etc*) chŏndal sudan 전달
수단
veil *n* peil 베일 **2** *v/t* karida 가리다
vein (*in leg etc*) chŏngmaek 정맥
Velcro® *n* tchiktchigi 찍찍이
velocity soktto 속도
velvet pelbet 벨벳
vending machine chadong
p'anmaegi 자동 판매기
vendor LAW maegagin 매각인
veneer (*on wood*) peniŏ happ'an
베니어 합판; (*of politeness etc*)
hŏshik 허식
venereal disease sŏngppyŏng 성병
venetian blind penishyŏn pŭllaidŭ
베니션 블라인드
vengeance pokssu 복수; *with a ~*
kyŏngnyŏrhage 격렬하게
venison sasŭm kogi 사슴 고기
venom (*of snake*) tok 독
vent *n* (*for air*) t'onggi kumŏng 통기
구멍; *give ~ to feelings* t'ŏttŭrida
터뜨리다
ventilate *room* hwan-gihada 환기하다
ventilation t'onggi 통기
ventilation shaft hwan-gigaeng
환기갱
ventilator hwan-gi changch'i 환기
장치
ventriloquist pok'wasulssa 복화술사
venture 1 *n* (*undertaking*) mohŏm
모험; COM t'ugijŏk saŏp 투기적 사업
2 *v/i* kwagamhi haeboda 과감히
해보다
venue (*for meeting etc*) changso 장소
veranda peranda 베란다
verb tongsa 동사
verdict LAW p'yŏnggyŏl 평결;
(*opinion, judgment*) p'andan 판단
verge *n* (*of road*) kajangjari 가장자리;
kyŏnggye 경계; *be on the ~ of ruin,
collapse, tears* ... ilbo chiktchŏne it-
tta ... 일보 직전에 있다
♦ **verge on** kŏŭi kat-tta 거의 같다
verification iptchŭng 입증;
(*confirmation*) hwagin 확인
verify (*check out*) chŭngmyŏnghada

증명하다; (*confirm*) hwaginhada 확인하다

vermicelli perŭmich'elli 베르미첼리

vermin haech'ung 해충

vermouth perŭmut'ŭju 베르무트주

vernacular *n* ilssang-yong-ŏ 일상용어

versatile *person* tajaedanŭnghan 다재다능한; *equipment, mind* mannŭng-ŭi 만능의

versatility (*of person*) tajaedanŭng 다재다능; (*of equipment, mind*) mannŭng 만능

verse (*poetry*) shi 시; (*part of poem, song*) chŏl 절

versed: *be well ~ in a subject* han chujee chŏngt'onghada 한 주제에 정통하다

version (*of song, book*) p'an 판; *what is your ~ of what happened?* kŭ sakkŏne taehae ŏttŏk'e saenggak'aeyo? 그 사건에 대해 어떻게 생각해요?

versus SP, LAW tae 대

vertebra ch'ŏkch'ugol 척추골

vertebrate *n* ch'ŏkch'udongmul 척추동물

vertical sujigŭi 수직의

vertigo hyŏn-gitch'ŭng 현기증

very 1 *adv* taedanhi 대단히; *was it cold? – not ~* ch'uwŏssŏyo? – maninŭn aniŏssŏyo 추웠어요? – 많이는 아니었어요; *the ~ best* kajang choŭn 가장 좋은
2 *adj* paro 바로; *in the ~ act* hyŏnhaengbŏmŭro 현행범으로; *that's the ~ thing I need* chŏgŏshi paro naega p'iryoro hanŭn kŭ mulgŏniyeyo 저것이 바로 내가 필요로 하는 그 물건이에요; *the ~ thought* paro kŭ saenggak 바로 그 생각; *right at the ~ top / bottom* kkoktaegi / padag-ŭi paro kŏgie 꼭대기/바닥의 바로 거기에

vessel NAUT pae 배

vest chokki 조끼

vestige (*of previous civilization etc*) yujŏk 유적; (*of truth*) hŭnjŏk 흔적

vet¹ *n* (*for animals*) suŭisa 수의사

vet² *v/t applicants etc* chŏmgŏmhada 점검하다

vet³ *n* MIL koch'ambyŏng

veteran 1 *n* pet'erang 베테랑 **2** *adj* (*old*) orae sayonghan 오래 사용한; (*experienced*) pet'erang-ŭi 베테랑의

veterinarian suŭisa 수의사

veto 1 *n* kŏbukkwŏn 거부권 **2** *v/t* kŏbuhada 거부하다

vexed (*worried*) komindoenŭn 고민되는; *the ~ question of ...* nollanŭi yŏjiga manŭn ... munje 논란의 여지가 많은 ... 문제

via kyŏngnyuhayŏ 경유하여

viable *life form, company* saengjonhal su innŭn 생존할 수 있는; *alternative, plan* hyoryŏgi innŭn 효력이 있는

vibrate *v/i* hŭndŭllida 흔들리다

vibration chindong 진동

vice ak 악; *the problem of ~* sahoeagŭi munje 사회악의 문제

vice president (*of company*) pusajang 부사장; (*of state*) put'ongnyŏng 부통령

vice squad p'unggi sabŏm tansokppan 풍기 사범 단속반

vice versa pandaero 반대로

vicinity kŭnch'ŏ 근처; *in the ~ of ...* ŭi kŭnch'ŏe(sŏ) ...의 근처에(서); (*with figures*) taeryak ... 대략 ...

vicious *dog* sŏngjiri koyak'an 성질이 고약한; *attack, temper, criticism* chidok'an 지독한

victim hŭisaeng 희생

victimize hŭisaengshikida 희생시키다

victor sŭngnija 승리자

victorious sŭngnihan 승리한

victory sŭngni 승리; *win a ~ over ...* e taehae sŭngnihada ...에 대해 승리하다

video 1 *n* pidio 비디오; *have X on ~* Xŭl / rŭl pidioe tamtta X을 / 를 비디오에 담다 **2** *v/t* pidioro ch'waryŏnghada 비디오로 촬영하다

video camera pidio k'amera 비디오 카메라; **video cassette** pidio k'aset'ŭ 비디오 카세트; **video cassete recorder** pidio k'aset'ŭ nok'wagi 비디오 카세트 녹화기; **video conference** TELEC hwasang hoeŭi 화상 회의; **video game** chŏnja orak 전자 오락; **videophone** pidio chŏnhwa 비디오 전화; **video**

recorder pidio nok'wagi 비디오 녹화기; **video recording** pidio nok'wa 비디오 녹화; **videotape** pidio t'eip'ǔ 비디오 테이프

Vietnam Pet'ǔnam 베트남, Wǒlnam 월남

Vietnamese 1 *adj* Pet'ǔnamǔi 베트남의, Wǒlnamǔi 월남의 **2** *n* Pet'ǔnamin 베트남인, Wǒlnamin 월남인; (*language*) Pet'ǔnamǒ 베트남어, Wǒlnamǒ 월남어

view 1 *n* kyǒngch'i 경치; (*of situation*) kyǒnhae 견해; **in ~ of** ...ǔl/rǔl salp'yǒbomyǒn ...을/를 살펴보면; **be on ~** (*of paintings*) chǒnshi chung-ida 전시 중이다; **with a ~ to** ...hal moktchǒgǔro ...할 목적으로 **2** *v/t events, situation* paraboda 바라보다; *TV program* shich'ǒnghada 시청하다; *house for sale* tullǒboda 둘러보다 **3** *v/i* (*watch TV*) shich'ǒnghada 시청하다

viewer TV shich'ǒngja 시청자

viewfinder PHOT p'aindǒ 파인더

viewpoint kwantchǒm 관점

vigor (*energy*) hwalgi 활기

vigorous *person* hwalbarhan 활발한; *shake* kyǒksshimhan 격심한; *denial* kangnyǒk'an 강력한

vile *smell* mopsshi yǒk-kkyǒun 몹시 역겨운; *thing to do* piyǒrhan 비열한

village maǔl 마을

villager maǔl saram 마을 사람

villain akttang 악당

vindicate ...ǔi chinshirǔlip-tchǔnghada ...의 진실을 입증하다; **I feel ~d** kyǒlbaek'aejin nǔkkimiyeyo 결백해진 느낌이에요

vindictive poboktchǒgin 보복적인

vine p'odonamu 포도나무

vinegar shikch'o 식초

vineyard p'odowǒn 포도원

vintage 1 *n* (*of wine*) ch'oegogǔp p'odoju 최고급 포도주 **2** *adj* (*classic*) oraedoeǒ kabǒch'iga innǔn 오래되어 값어치가 있는

violate *rules, treaty* wibanhada 위반하다; *sanctity of place* modok'ada 모독하다

violation (*of rules, treaty, traffic*) wiban 위반; (*of sanctity*) modok 모독

violence (*of person, movie*) p'ongnyŏk 폭력; (*of emotion, reaction*) kyŏngnyŏrham 격렬함; (*of gale*) kangnyŏrham 강렬함; **outbreak of ~** p'ongnyŏk sat'aeǔi palssaeng 폭력 사태의 발생

violent *person, movie* nanp'ok'han 난폭한; *emotion, reaction* kyŏngnyŏrhan 격렬한; *gale* kangnyŏrhan 강렬한; **have a ~ temper** sŏngkkyŏgi nanp'ok'ada 성격이 난폭하다

violently *react* nanp'ok'age 난폭하게; *object* kangnyŏk'age 강력하게; **fall ~ in love with s.o.** nuguwa kyŏktchŏngjŏgŭro sarange ppajida 누구와 격정적으로 사랑에 빠지다

violet (*color*) poratppit 보라빛; (*plant*) chebikkot 제비꽃

violin paiollin 바이올린

violinist paiollin yŏnjuja 바이올린 연주자

VIP pǔi ai p'i 브이 아이 피이

viral *infection* pairŏsǔǔi 바이러스의

virgin (*female*) ch'ŏnyŏ 처녀; (*male*) sutch'onggak 숫총각

virginity tongjŏng 동정; **lose one's ~** sun-gyŏrŭl ilt'a 순결을 잃다

virile *man* namjadaun 남자다운; *prose* kanggŏnhan 강건한

virility namsŏngdaum 남성다움; (*sexual*) saengshik nŭngnyŏk 생식 능력

virtual sashilssang-ŭi 사실상의

virtual reality kasang hyŏnshil 가상 현실

virtually kŏŭi 거의

virtue tŏk 덕; **in ~ of** ttaemune 때문에

virtuoso MUS kŏjang 거장

virtuous kogyŏrhan 고결한

virulent *disease* yudok'an 유독한

virus MED, COMPUT pairŏsǔ 바이러스

visa pija 비자

visibility nune poim 눈에 보임; (*range of vision*) shiya 시야

visible *object* poinŭn 보이는; *difference* nune ttŭinŭn 눈에 띄는; *anger* myŏngbaek'an 명백한; **not ~ to the naked eye** yuganŭronŭn poiji annŭn 육안으로는 보이지 않는

visibly *different* nune ttŭige 눈에

띄게; *he was ~ moved* kŭnŭn kamdong padŭn kŏshi yŏngnyŏk'aet-tta 그는 감동 받은 것이 역력했다

vision (*eyesight*) shiryŏk 시력; REL *etc* hwanyŏng 환영

visit 1 *n* pangmun 방문; *pay a ~ to the doctor/dentist* ŭisa/ch'ikkwaŭisarŭl ch'ajagada 의사/치과의사를 찾아가다; *pay s.o. a ~* nugurŭl pangmunhada 누구를 방문하다 **2** *v/t* pangmunhada 방문하다

visiting card myŏngham 명함

visiting hours (*at hospital*) myŏnhoe shigan 면회 시간

visitor (*guest*) sonnim 손님; (*to museum etc*) kwallamgaek 관람객; (*tourist*) kwan-gwanggaek 관광객

visor ch'aeng 챙

visual shigaktchŏgin 시각적인

visual aid shigak kyojae 시각 교재

visual display unit yŏngsang p'yoshi changch'i 영상 표시 장치

visualize maŭm soge ttŏollida 마음 속에 떠올리다; (*foresee*) yegyŏnhada 예견하다

visually shigaktchŏguro 시각적으로

visually impaired shigaktchŏguro sonsangdoen 시각적으로 손상된

vital (*essential*) p'ilssujŏgin 필수적인; *it is ~ that* ...ranŭn kŏsŭn kŭk'i chungdaehamnida ...라는 것은 극히 중대합니다

vitality (*of person, city etc*) hwallyŏk 활력

vitally: ~ important kŭk'i chungdaehan 극히 중대한

vital organs chungyo shinch'e kigwan 중요 신체 기관

vital statistics (*of woman*) mommae ch'itssu 몸매 치수

vitamin pit'amin 비타민

vitamin pill pit'amin chŏngje 비타민 정제

vivacious k'waehwarhan 쾌활한

vivacity k'waehwal 쾌활

vivid *color* kangnyŏrhan 강렬한; *memory* sŏnmyŏnghan 선명한; *imagination* saengsaenghan 생생한

V-neck Vchahyŏng mokssŏn V자형

목선

vocabulary ŏhwi 어휘

vocal mokssoriŭi 목소리의; (*expressing opinions*) sori nop'yŏ chujanghanŭn 소리 높여 주장하는

vocal cords sŏngdae 성대

vocal group MUS pok'ŏl kŭrup 보컬 그룹

vocalist MUS pok'ŏllisŭt'ŭ 보컬리스트

vocation (*calling*) samyŏng 사명; (*profession*) chigŏp 직업

vocational *guidance* chigŏpssang-ŭi 직업상의

vodka podŭk'a 보드카

vogue yuhaeng 유행; *be in ~* yuhaeng chung-ida 유행 중이다

voice 1 *n* mokssori 목소리 **2** *v/t* *opinions* p'yomyŏnghada 표명하다

voicemail ŭmsŏng up'yŏn 음성 우편

void 1 *n* pin konggan 빈 공간 **2** *adj: ~ of* ...i/ga ŏmnŭn ...이/가 없는

volatile *personality, moods* pyŏndŏkssŭrŏun 변덕스러운

volcano hwasan 화산

volley *n* (*of shots*) iltchesagyŏk 일제사격; (*in tennis*) palli 발리

volleyball paegu 배구

volt polt'ŭ 볼트

voltage chŏnap 전압

volume (*of container*) ip-ppang yongjŏk 입방 용적; (*of work, business, liquid etc*) yang 양; (*of book*) han kwŏn 한 권; (*of radio etc*) ŭmnyang 음량

volume control ŭmnyang chojŏlgi 음량 조절기

voluntary *adj* chabaltchŏgin 자발적인

volunteer 1 *n* chawŏnja 자원자 **2** *v/i* chajinhaesŏ hada 자진해서 하다

voluptuous yuk-kkamjŏgin 육감적인

vomit 1 *n* kut'o 구토 **2** *v/i* t'ohada 토하다

♦ **vomit up** t'ohada 토하다

vomiting t'oham 토함

voracious *appetite* wangsŏnghan 왕성한

vote 1 *n* t'up'yo 투표; *have the ~* t'up'yokkwŏnŭl kajida 투표권을 가지다 **2** *v/i* POL t'up'yohada 투표하다; *~ for/against* ...e ch'ansŏng/pandae t'up'yohada ...에

찬성/반대 투표하다 3 *v/t*: ***they ~d him President*** kŭdŭrŭn kŭrŭl taet'ongnyŏng-ŭro t'up'yohaet-tta 그들은 그를 대통령으로 투표했다; ***they ~d to stay behind*** kŭdŭrŭn twiro mullŏsŏ itkkirŭl t'up'yohaet-tta 그들은 뒤로 물러서 있기를 투표했다

♦ **vote in** *new member* sŏnch'urhada 선출하다

♦ **vote on** *issue* p'yogyŏrhada 표결하다

♦ **vote out** (*of office*) t'up'yoe ŭihae ch'ubanghada 투표에 의해 추방하다

voter yukkwŏnja 유권자

voting t'up'yo 투표

voting booth kip'yoso 기표소

vouch for *person, truth* pojŭnghada 보증하다

voucher harinkkwŏn 할인권

vow 1 *n* sŏyak 서약 **2** *v/t*: ~ ***to do sth*** muŏt hal kŏsŭl maengsehada 무엇 할 것을 맹세하다

vowel moŭm 모음

voyage (*by sea*) hanghae 항해; (*in space*) ujuyŏhaeng 우주여행

vulgar *person, language* chŏsok'an 저속한

vulnerable (*to attack*) konggyŏk tanghagi shwiun 공격 당하기 쉬운; (*to criticism etc*) sangch'ŏ patkki shwiun 상처 받기 쉬운

vulture tokssuri 독수리

W

wad n (of paper) tabal 다발; (of absorbent cotton etc) mungch'i 뭉치; **a ~ of $100 bills** paek talla chip'ye han tabal 백 달러 지폐 한 다발

waddle v/i twittunggŏrimyŏ kŏt-tta 뒤뚱거리며 걷다

wade kŏrŏsŏ kŏnnŏda 걸어서 건너다
♦ **wade through** book, documents himdŭlge haenagada 힘들게 해나가다

wafer (cookie) weip'ŏ 웨이퍼; REL chebyŏng 제병

waffle[1] n (to eat) wap'ŭl 와플

waffle[2] v/i pujirŏmnŭn marŭl hada 부질없는 말을 하다

wag 1 v/t tail, finger hŭndŭlda 흔들다 2 v/i (of tail) hŭndŭlgŏrida 흔들거리다

wage[1] v/t war ch'irŭda 치르다

wage[2] n wŏlgŭp 월급

wage earner kajang 가장

wage freeze imgŭm tonggyŏl 임금 동결

wage packet wŏlgŭp pong'u 월급 봉투

wager n naegi 내기

waggle v/t hips, ears hŭndŭlda 흔들다; loose screw, tooth etc hŭndŭlgŏrida 흔들거리다

wagon: **be on the ~** F surŭl kkŭnt'a 술을 끊다

wail 1 n (of person, baby) ulbujijŭm 울부짖음; (of siren) kusŭlp'ŭn sori 구슬픈 소리 2 v/i (of person, baby) ulbujit-tta 울부짖다; (of siren) kusŭlp'ŭn sorirŭl naeda 구슬픈 소리를 내다

waist hŏri 허리

waistline hŏrisŏn 허리선

wait 1 n kidarim 기다림 2 v/i kidarida 기다리다; **we'll ~ until he's ready** urinŭn kŭga chunbidoel ttaekkaji kidaril kŏshimnida 우리는 그가 준비될 때까지 기다릴 것입니다 2 v/t

meal miruda 미루다; **~ table** shikttang kŭppsa norŭsŭl hada 식당 급사 노릇을 하다
♦ **wait for** …ŭl/rŭl kidarida …을/를 기다리다; **~ me!** narŭl kidaryŏ chuseyo! 나를 기다려 주세요!
♦ **wait on** person …ŭi shijung-ŭl tŭlda …의 시중을 들다
♦ **wait up** chaji ank'o kidarida 자지 않고 기다리다

waiter weit'ŏ 웨이터; **~!** weit'ŏ! 웨이터!

waiting n kidarinŭn kŏt 기다리는 것; **no ~ sign** kidariji mashio 기다리지 마시오

waiting list taegija myŏngdan 대기자 명단

waiting room taegishil 대기실

waitress weit'ŭrisŭ 웨이트리스

waive (relinquish) p'ogihada 포기하다; (dispense with) ch'ŏlhoehada 철회하다

wake[1] (of ship) paega chinagan chari 배가 지나간 자리; **in the ~ of** fig …ŭl/rŭl it-ttara …을/를 잇따라; **follow in the ~ of** …ŭl/rŭl it-ttarŭda …을/를 잇따르다
♦ **wake up** 1 v/i chami kkaeda 잠이 깨다 2 v/t kkaeuda 깨우다

wake-up call moning k'ol 모닝 콜

Wales Weiljŭ 웨일즈

walk 1 n kŏtkki 걷기; (in front of house) toroesŏ chipkkajiŭi kil 도로에서 집까지의 길; **it's a five-minute ~ from the station** yŏgesŏ kŏrŏ o pun kŏriida 역에서 걸어 오 분 거리이다; **it's a long / short ~ to the office** samushilkkajinŭn kŏrŏsŏ mŏn / kakkaun kŏriida 사무실까지는 걸어서 먼 / 가까운 거리이다; **go for a ~** sanch'aekhada 산책하다 2 v/i kŏt-tta 걷다; (as opposed to taking the car / bus etc) kŏrŏsŏ kada 걸어서 가다; (hike) tobo yŏhaenghada 도보

여행하다; **~ up to** tagagada 다가가다
3 v/t dog sanch'aekshik'ida
산책시키다; **~ the streets** (walk
around) kŏriŭl toradanida 거리를
돌아다니다

♦ **walk out** (on spouse, of room etc)
kaptchagi ttŏnada 갑자기 떠나다;
(go on strike) tongmaeng p'aŏp'ada
동맹 파업하다

♦ **walk out on** spouse, family
…ŭl/rŭl pŏrida …을/를 버리다

walker (hiker) pohaengja 보행자; (for
baby, old person) pohaenggi 보행기;
be a slow/fast ~ kŏrŭmi nŭrida/
pparŭda 걸음이 느리다/빠르다

walkie-talkie mujŏn-gi 무전기

walk-in closet taehyŏng ot-tchang
대형 옷장

walking (as opposed to driving)
kŏnnŭn kŏt 걷는 것; (hiking) tobo
yŏhaeng 도보 여행; **be within ~
distance** kŏrŏsŏ kal su innŭn
kŏriida 걸어서 갈 수 있는 거리이다

walking stick chip'ang-i 지팡이

walking tour tobo yŏhaeng 도보 여행

Walkman® wŏk'ŭmaen 워크맨

walkout (strike) tongmaeng p'aŏp
동맹 파업; **walkover** n (easy win)
naksssŭng 낙승; **walk-up** n
ellibeit'ŏga ŏmnŭn ap'at'ŭ
엘리베이터가 없는 아파트

wall (of room, house) pyŏk 벽;
(around garden) tam 담; fig (of
silence etc) pyŏk 벽; **go to the ~** (of
company) p'asanhada 파산하다;
drive ... up the ~ F …ŭl/rŭl
mich'ige hada …을/를 미치게
하다

wallet chigap 지갑

wallop F 1 n (to ball) kangt'a 강타;
get a ~ shimhage mat-tta 심하게
맞다 2 v/t ttaerida 때리다; ball ch'ida
치다; (defeat) ch'amp'aeshik'ida
참패시키다

wallpaper 1 n pyŏktchi 벽지 2 v/t
pyŏktchirŭl parŭda 벽지를 바르다

Wall Street Wŏl Sŭt'ŭrit'ŭ (Miguk
kŭmyunggye) 월 스트리트 (미국
금융계)

wall-to-wall carpet match'um
k'ap'et 맞춤 카펫

walnut hodu 호두

waltz n walch'ŭ 왈츠

wan face ch'angbaek'an 창백한

wander v/i (roam) ttŏdoradanida
떠돌아다니다; (of tourist) toradanida
돌아다니다; (stray) hemaeda 헤매다;
(of attention) sanmanhaejida
산만해지다

♦ **wander around** yŏgijŏgi
toradanida 여기저기 돌아다니다

wane (of interest, enthusiasm)
chŏmjŏm churŏdŭlda 점점 줄어들다

wangle v/t F yong-k'e kuhada 용케
구하다

want 1 n: **for ~ of** …i/ga ŏpssŏsŏ
…이/가 없어서 2 v/t (desire)
wŏnhada 원하다; (need) p'iryohada
필요하다; **~ to do sth** muŏsŭl hago
shiptta 무엇을 하고 싶다; **I ~ to stay
here** nanŭn yŏgi mŏmulgo
shipssŭmnida 나는 여기 머물고
싶습니다; **do you ~ to go too? - no,
I don't ~ to** tangshindo kago
ship'ŏyo?- aniyo, nanŭn kago
shiptchi anayo 당신도 가고 싶어요?
- 아니요, 나는 가고 싶지 않아요;
you can have whatever you ~
tangshini wŏnhanŭn kŏsŭn
muŏshidŭn kajil su issŏyo 당신이
원하는 것은 무엇이든 가질 수
있어요; **it's not what I ~ed** kŭgŏn
naega wŏnhaet-ttŏn kŏshi aniyeyo
그건 내가 원했던 것이 아니에요;
she ~s you to go back kŭnyŏnŭn
tangshini toragagil wŏnhaeyo 그녀는
당신이 돌아가길 원해요; **he ~s a
haircut** kŭnŭn mŏrirŭl
challayagessŏyo 그는 머리를
잘라야겠어요 3 v/i: **~ for nothing**
pujok'ami ŏptta 부족함이 없다

want ad saenghwal kwanggo 생활
광고

wanted adj (by police) chimyŏng
subaedoen 지명 수배된

wanting: be ~ in …i/ga mojarada
…이/가 모자라다

wanton adj chemŏt-ttaeroin
제멋대로인

war n chŏnjaeng 전쟁; **be at ~**
kyojŏn chung-ida 교전 중이다

warble v/i (of bird) chijŏgwida

지저귀다

ward (*in hospital*) pyŏngdong 병동; (*child*) p'ihugyŏnin 피후견인

♦ **ward off** *blow, attacker* p'ihada 피하다; *cold, illness* yebanghada 예방하다

warden (*of prison*) kyodosojang 교도소장

wardrobe (*for clothes*) ot-tchang 옷장; (*clothes*) otkkaji 옷가지

warehouse ch'anggo 창고

warfare chŏnjaeng 전쟁

warhead t'andu 탄두

warily choshimhaesŏ 조심해서

warm *adj welcome, smile etc* ttattŭt'an 따뜻한; *summer* tŏun 더운

♦ **warm up 1** *v/t person, room* ttattŭt'age hada 따뜻하게 하다; *soup, plates* teuda 데우다 **2** *v/i* (*of person, room*) ttattŭt'aejida 따뜻해지다; (*of soup*) tewŏjida 데워지다; (*of athlete etc*) chunbi undong-ŭl hada 준비 운동을 하다

warmhearted ch'injŏrhan 친절한

warmly *dressed, welcome, smile* ttattŭt'age 따뜻하게

warmth on-gi 온기; (*of welcome, smile*) onjŏng 온정

warn kyŏnggohada 경고하다

warning *n* kyŏnggo 경고; *without ~* kaptchagi 갑자기

warp 1 *v/t wood* hwigehada 휘게 하다; *character* pitturŏjige hada 비뚤어지게 하다 **2** *v/i* (*of wood*) hwida 휘다

warped *fig* pitturŏjin 비뚤어진

warplane kunyonggi 군용기

warrant *n* yŏngtchang 영장 **2** *v/t* (*deserve, call for*) chŏngdanghwahada 정당화하다

warranty pojŭng 보증; *be under ~* pojŭng kigan chung-ida 보증 기간 중이다

warrior chŏnsa 전사

warship kunham 군함

wart samagwi 사마귀

wartime chŏnshi 전시

wary *look, response* shinjunghan 신중한; *keep a ~ eye on ...* ŭl/rŭl seshimhage poda ...을/를 세심하게 보다; *be ~ of ...* ŭl/rŭl ŭishimhada

...을/를 의심하다

wash 1 *n: have a ~* sshit-tta 씻다; *that jacket/shirt needs a ~* chŏ chaek'isŭn/shyŏch'ŭnŭn pparaya handa 저 재킷은/셔츠는 빨아야 한다 **2** *v/t clothes* ppalda 빨다; *dishes* taktta 닦다; *one's hands* sshit-tta 씻다 **3** *v/i* sshit-tta 씻다

♦ **wash up** (*wash one's hands and face*) sshit-tta 씻다

washable ppal su innŭn 빨 수 있는

washbasin, washbowl semyŏn-gi 세면기

washcloth sugŏn 수건

washed out kiuni ŏmnŭn 기운이 없는

washer (*for faucet etc*) washyŏ 와셔; → **washing machine**

washing ppallae 빨래; *do the ~* ppallaerŭl hada 빨래를 하다

washing machine set'ak-kki 세탁기

Washington (*city*) Wŏshingt'ŏn 워싱턴

washroom hwajangshil 화장실

wasp (*insect*) malbŏl 말벌

waste 1 *n* nabngi 낭비; (*from industrial process*) p'yegimul 폐기물; *it's a ~ of time/money* kŭgŏsŭn shiganŭi/tonŭi nangbiyeyo 그것은 시간의/돈의 낭비예요 **2** *adj* ssŭlmoŏmnŭn 쓸모없는 **3** *v/t* nangbihada 낭비하다

♦ **waste away** yawida 야위다

wasteful nangbiga shimhan 낭비가 심한

wasteland hwangp'ye chiyŏk 황폐 지역; **wastepaper** hyuji 휴지; **wastepaper basket** hyujit'ong 휴지통; **waste pipe** (*for water*) paesugwan 배수관; **waste product** p'yegimul 폐기물

watch 1 *n* (*timepiece*) shigye 시계; *keep ~* mangboda 망보다 **2** *v/t movie, TV* poda 보다; (*observe*) chal poda 잘 보다; (*spy on*) kamshihada 감시하다; (*look after*) tolbwajuda 돌봐주다 **3** *v/i* chik'yŏboda 지켜보다

♦ **watch for: he is watching for his father** kŭnŭn abŏjiga onŭnji chik'yŏbogo it-tta 그는 아버지가 오는지 지켜보고 있다

◆ **watch out** choshimhada 조심하다; *~!* choshimhae! 조심해!

◆ **watch out for** (*be careful of*) ...ŭl/rŭl choshimhada ...을/를 조심하다

watchful chu-ŭigip'ŭn 주의깊은

watchmaker shigye chejoin 시계 제조인

water 1 *n* mul 물; *~s* NAUT yŏnghae 영해 **2** *v/t plant* murŭl chuda 물을 주다 **3** *v/i* (*of eyes*) nunmuri nada 눈물이 나다; *my mouth is ~ing* ch'imŭl hŭllida 침을 흘리다

◆ **water down** *drink* murŭl t'ada 물을 타다

watercolor (*paint*) such'aehwa mulkkam 수채화 물감; (*painting*) such'aehwa 수채화; **watercress** mulnaeng-i 물냉이; **waterfall** p'okp'o 폭포

watering can mulppurigae 물뿌리개

watering hole (*hum*) sultchip 술집

water level suwi 수위; **water lily** suryŏn 수련; **waterline** (*at shore*) hae-ansŏn 해안선; (*of ship*) hollssusŏn 홀수선; **waterlogged** mure chamgin 물에 잠긴; **watermark** chip'yeŭi naebich'inŭn munŭi 지폐의 내비치는 무늬; **watermelon** subak 수박; **water polo** sugu 수구; **waterproof** *adj* pangsudoenŭn 방수되는; **watershed** punsuryŏng 분수령; **waterside** *n* mulkka 물가; *at the ~* mulkkae(sŏ) 물가에(서); **waterskiing** susangsŭk'i 수상스키; **watertight** *compartment* pangsuŭi 방수의; **waterway** suro 수로; **waterwings** suyong yŏnsŭmnyong t'yubŭ 수영 연습용 튜브

watery mulgŭn 묽은

watt wat'ŭ 와트

wave[1] *n* (*in sea*) p'ado 파도

wave[2] **1** *n* (*of hand*) sonŭl hŭndŭnŭn shinho 손을 흔드는 신호 **2** *v/i* (*with hand*) sonŭl hŭndŭlda 손을 흔들다; (*of flag*) p'ŏllŏgida 펄럭이다; *~ to s.o.* nuguege sonŭl hŭndŭlda 누구에게 손을 흔들다 **3** *v/t flag etc* hŭndŭlda 흔들다

wavelength RAD p'ajang 파장; *be on the same ~* *fig* chal t'onghada 잘

통하다

waver chujŏhada 주저하다

wavy *hair, line* kupssŭlgŏrinŭn 곱슬거리는

wax *n* (*for floor, furniture*) wakssŭ 왁스; (*in ear*) kwiji 귀지

way 1 *n* (*method*) pangbŏp 방법; (*~ of doing sth*) pangshik 방식; (*route*) kil 길; *this* (*like this*) irŏk'e 이렇게; (*in this direction*) itchogŭro 이쪽으로; *by the ~* (*incidentally*) kŭrŏnde 그런데; *by ~ of* (*via*) ...ŭl/rŭl kŏch'yŏsŏ ...을/를 거쳐서; (*in the form of*) ...ŭl/rŭl hal semŭro ...을/를 할 셈으로; *in a ~* (*in certain respects*) ŏttŏn myŏnesŏnŭn 어떤 면에서는; *be under ~* chinhaeng chung-ida 진행 중이다; *give ~* MOT yangbohada 양보하다; (*collapse*) munŏjida 무너지다; *give ~ to* (*be replaced by*) ...(ŭ)ro pakkwida ...(으)로 바뀌다; *have one's* (*own*) *~* chagi maŭmdaero hada 자기 마음대로 하다; *OK, we'll do it your ~* choayo, tangshin pangshigŭro hagessŏyo 좋아요, 당신 방식으로 하겠어요; *lead the ~* (*go first*) apssŏ kada 앞서 가다; (*be the leader, pioneer*) solssŏnhada 솔선하다; *lose one's ~* kirŭl ilt'a 길을 잃다; *make ~* kirŭl pik'yŏjuda 길을 비켜주다; *be in the ~* panghaega toeda 방해가 되다; *it's on the ~ to the station* yŏgŭro kanŭn kire issŏyo 역으로 가는 길에 있어요; *I was on my ~ to the station* nanŭn yŏgŭro kanŭn chung-iŏssŏyo 나는 역으로 가는 중이었어요; *no ~!* ŏrimdo ŏpssŏ! 어림도 없어!; *there's no ~ he can do it* kŭnŭn kŭgŏsŭl kyŏlk'o hal su ŏpssŏyo 그는 그것을 결코 할 수 없어요 **2** *adv* F (*far*) nŏmu 너무; *it's ~ too soon to decide* kyŏltchŏnghagienŭn nŏmu illŏyo 결정하기에는 너무 일러요; *they are ~ behind with their work* kŭdŭrŭn iri nŏmu millyŏ issŏyo 그들은 일이 너무 밀려 있어요

way back yejŏne 예전에; **way in** ippku 입구; **way of life** saenghwal pangshik 생활 방식; **way out**

ch'ulgu 출구; *fig (from situation)* haegyŏlch'aek 해결책

we uri 우리; ~ *are American* Miguk saramiyeyo 우리는 미국 사람이에요

weak yak'an 약한; *tea, coffee* yŏnhan 연한

weaken 1 *v/t* yak'agehada 약하게 하다 **2** *v/i* yak'aejida 약해지다

weakling yaktcha 약자

weakness yaktchŏm 약점; *have a ~ for (liking)* …ege yak'ada …에게 약하다

wealth pu 부; *a ~ of* p'ungbuhan 풍부한

wealthy puyuhan 부유한

wean *v/t* chŏjul tteda 젖을 떼다

weapon mugi 무기

wear 1 *n*: ~ *(and tear)* tarŭm 닳음; *clothes for everyday ~ / evening ~* ilssangbok / p'at'ibok 일상복 / 파티복 **2** *v/t (have on)* iptta 입다; *(damage)* talk'e hada 닳게 하다 **3** *v/i (of carpet, fabric: ~ out)* tarhajida 닳아지다; *(last)* kyŏndida 견디다

♦ **wear away 1** *v/i* tarhajida 닳아지다 **2** *v/t* talk'e hada 닳게 하다

♦ **wear off** *(of effect, feeling)* chŏmjŏm ŏpssŏjida 점점 없어지다

♦ **wear out 1** *v/t (tire)* chich'ige hada 지치게 하다; *shoes* tara ttŏrŏjige hada 닳아 떨어지게 하다 **2** *v/i (of shoes, carpet)* tara ttŏrŏjida 닳아 떨어지다

wearily chich'yŏsŏ 지쳐서

wearing *(tiring)* chich'ige hanŭn 지치게 하는

weary chich'in 지친

weasel choktchebi 족제비

weather 1 *n* nalsshi 날씨; *be feeling under the ~* momi tchibudŭdŭhada 몸이 찌부드드하다 **2** *v/t crisis* ttulk'o nagada 뚫고 나가다

weather-beaten pibarame shidallin 비바람에 시달린; **weather chart** ilgido 일기도; **weather forecast** ilgi yebo 일기 예보; **weatherman** kisang yebowŏn 기상 예보원

weave 1 *v/t* tchada 짜다 **2** *v/i (move)* nubida 누비다

web tchasŏ mandŭn kŏt 짜서 만든 것;

spider's ~ kŏmijip 거미집; *the Web* Wep 웹

webbed feet mulgalk'wiga tallin pal 물갈퀴가 달린 발

web browser wep pŭraujŏ 웹 브라우저; **web page** wep p'eiji 웹 페이지; **website** wep sa-it'ŭ 웹 사이트

wedding kyŏrhonshik 결혼식

wedding anniversary kyŏrhon kinyŏmil 결혼 기념일; **wedding cake** weding k'eik'ŭ 웨딩 케이크; **wedding day** kyŏrhonshingnal 결혼식날; **wedding dress** weding tŭresŭ 웨딩 드레스; **wedding hall** yeshiktchang 예식장; **wedding ring** kyŏrhon panji 결혼 반지

wedge *n (to hold sth in place)* sswaegi 쐐기; *(of cheese etc)* sswaegi moyang 쐐기 모양

Wednesday suyoil 수요일

weed 1 *n* chapch'o 잡초 **2** *v/t* chapch'orŭl ppoptta 잡초를 뽑다

♦ **weed out** ch'uryŏnaeda 추려내다

weedkiller chech'oje 제초제

week chu 주; *a ~ tomorrow* p'aril twie 팔일 뒤에

weekday p'yŏng-il 평일

weekend chumal 주말; *on the ~* chumare 주말에

weekly 1 *adj* maeju-ŭi 매주의; ~ *payment* chugŭp 주급 **2** *n (magazine)* chugan 주간 **3** *adv* maejumada 매주마다

weep ulda 울다

weeping willow suyang pŏdŭl 수양 버들

weigh 1 *v/t* mugerŭl talda 무게를 달다; ~ *anchor* tach'ŭl ollida 닻을 올리다 **2** *v/i* mugega nagada 무게가 나가다

♦ **weigh down**: *be weighed down with* …ŭi mugero nullyŏjida …의 무게로 눌려지다; *with worries* kibuni karaantta 기분이 가라앉다

♦ **weigh up** *(assess)* p'yŏngkkahada 평가하다

weight *(of person, object)* muge 무게

weightless mujungnyŏgŭi 무중력의

weightlessness mujungnyŏk 무중력

weightlifter yŏktto sŏnsu 역도 선수

weightlifting yŏktto 역도
weir tuk 둑
weird isanghan 이상한
weirdo n 「isanghan saram 이상한 사람
welcome 1 adj hwanyŏng pannŭn 환영 받는; **you're ~** ch'ŏnmaneyo 천만에요; **you're ~ to try some** ŏlmadŭnji haseyo 얼마든지 하세요 **2** n (for guests etc) hwanyŏng 환영; (to news, proposal) kikkŏi padadŭrim 기꺼이 받아들임 **3** v/t guests etc hwanyŏnghada 환영하다; decision etc kikkŏi padadŭrida 기꺼이 받아들이다
weld v/t yongjŏp'ada 용접하다
welder yongjŏpkkong 용접공
welfare poktchi 복지; (financial assistance) saenghwal pojo 생활 보조; **be on ~** saenghwal pojorŭl pat-tta 생활 보조를 받다
welfare check saenghwal pojogŭm 생활 보조금; **welfare state** poktchi kuk-kka 복지 국가; **welfare work** poktchi saŏp 복지 사업; **welfare worker** poktchi saŏpkka 복지 사업가
well[1] n (for water) umul 우물; **oil ~** yujŏn 유전
well[2] adv chal 잘; **as ~** (too) …do …도; **as ~ as** (in addition to) …ppunmananira …do …뿐아니라 …도; **he came as ~** kŭdo wat-tta 그도 왔다; **he has a motorbike as ~ as a car** kŭnŭn ch'apunman anira ot'obaido kajigo it-tta 그는 차뿐만 아니라 오토바이도 가지고 있다; **I can't swim as ~ as you** nanŭn tangshinmank'ŭm suyŏng-ŭl chal hal su ŏpssŏyo 나는 당신만큼 수영을 잘 할 수 없어요; **it's just as ~ you told me** naege yaegihaesŏ mach'im chal toeŏssŭmnida 당신이 내게 얘기해서 마침 잘 되었습니다; **very ~** (acknowledging an order) chal algessŭmnida 잘 알겠습니다; (reluctant agreement) ŏtchaet-ttŭn chossŭmnida 어쨌든 좋습니다; **~, ~!** (surprise) irŏn, irŏn! 이런, 이런!; **~ …** (uncertainty, thinking) kŭlsse …

글쎄 … **2** adj: **be ~** chal it-tta 잘 있다; **feel ~** momi chot'a 몸이 좋다; **get ~ soon!** ppalli na-ŭseyo! 빨리 나으세요!
well-balanced person, meal, diet kyunhyŏng chap'in 균형 잡힌; **well-behaved** p'umhaeng-i tanjŏnghan 품행이 단정한; **well-being** pongni 복리; (feeling) haengbok 행복; **well-done** meat chal igŭn 잘 익은; **well-dressed** choŭn osŭl ibŭn 좋은 옷을 입은; **well-earned** che himŭro ŏdŭn 제 힘으로 얻은; **well-heeled** puyuhan 부유한; **well-known** allyŏjin 잘 알려진; **well-made** chal mandŭrŏjin 잘 만들어진; **well-mannered** yeŭi parŭn 예의 바른; **well-meaning** sŏnŭiŭi 선의의; **well-off** puyuhan 부유한; **well-read** pakssik'an 박식한; **well-timed** ttaerŭl chal match'un ttae 때를 잘 맞춘; **well-to-do** puyuhan 부유한; **well-worn** tarappjin 닳아빠진
west 1 n sŏtchok 서쪽; (western part of a country) sŏbu 서부; **the West** (western nations) Sŏyang 서양 **2** adj sŏ 서; **~ wind** sŏp'ung 서풍 **3** adv sŏtchogŭro 서쪽으로; **~ of** …ŭi sŏtchoge …의 서쪽에
West Coast (of USA) (Miguŭi) T'aep'yŏng-yang Yŏnan (미국의) 태평양 연안
westerly direction sŏtchogŭi 서쪽의; wind sŏtchogesŏ punŭn 서쪽에서 부는
western 1 adj sŏtchogŭi 서쪽의; **Western** Sŏyang-ŭi 서양의 **2** n (movie) sŏbugŭk 서부극
Westerner Sŏyang saram 서양 사람
westernized sŏyanghwadoen 서양화된
westward sŏtchogŭro 서쪽으로
wet adj chŏjŭn 젖은; (rainy) piga onŭn 비가 오는; **"~ paint"** ch'il chuŭi 칠 주의; **be ~ through** hamppak chŏt-tta 함빡 젖다
whack 「1 n (blow) ch'ŏlssŏk ttaerim 철썩 때림 **2** v/t ch'ŏlssŏk ttaerida 철썩 때리다
whale korae 고래
whaling koraejabi 고래잡이

wharf *n* pudu 부두

what 1 *pron* ◊ muŏt 무엇; **~ *is that?*** chŏgŏsŭn muŏshimnikka? 저것은 무엇입니까?; **~ *is it?*** (*what do you want?*) wae? 왜?; (*what did you say?*) mwŏrago? 뭐라고?; (*astonishment*) musŭn soriya? 무슨 소리야? **~ *about some dinner?*** chŏnyŏgŭl mŏnganŭn kŏshi ŏttŏk'essŏyo? 저녁을 먹는 것이 어떻겠어요? **~ *about heading home?*** chibŭro kanŭn kŏshi ŏttŏk'essŏyo? 집으로 가는 것이 어떻겠어요?; **~ *for?*** (*why?*) wae? 왜?; **so ~?** kŭraesŏ? 그래서? ◊ (*relative*) ...hanŭn kŏt ...하는 것; *that's not ~ I meant* kŭgŏn naega ŭiimihanŭn kŏshi aniyeyo 그건 내가 의미하는 것이 아니에요; *that's ~ I like* kŭgŏshi chega choahanŭn kŏshiyeyo 그것이 제가 좋아하는 것이에요 **2** *adj* ◊ (*what kind of*) ŏttŏn 어떤; **~ *color is the car?*** kŭ ch'anŭn ŏttŏn saek-kkarimnikka? 그 차는 어떤 색깔입니까? ◊ (*which*) ŏnŭ 어느; **~ *university are you at?*** tangshinŭn ŏnŭ taehage tanigo issŭmnikka? 당신은 어느 대학에 다니고 있습니까? **3** *adv*: **~ *a lovely day!*** ŏlmana nalsshiga choŭn narinjiyŏ! 얼마나 날씨가 좋은 날이지요!

whatever 1 *pron* ...hanŭn kŏsŭn muŏshidŭnji ...하는 것은 무엇이든지; (*regardless of*) ...i / ga ...hal chirado ...이 / 가 ...할 지라도; **~ *people say,* I believe her** saramdŭri musŭn marŭl hal chirado, nanŭn kŭnyŏrŭl minnŭnda 사람들이 무슨 말을 할 지라도, 나는 그녀를 믿는다 **2** *adj* ŏttŏn ...(i)rado ŏttŏn 어떤 ...(이)라도; *you have no reason ~ to worry* tangshinŭn hanado kŏktchŏnghal iyuga ŏpssŏyo 당신은 하나도 걱정할 이유가 없어요

wheat mil 밀

wheedle: **~ *X out of Y*** Yŭl / rŭl kkoshyŏsŏ Xŭl / rŭl ŏdŏnaeda Y을 / 를 꼬셔서 X을 / 를 얻어내다

wheel 1 *n* pak'wi 바퀴; (*steering ~*) haendŭl 핸들 **2** *v/t* *bicycle* mirŏ

umjigida 밀어 움직이다 **3** *v/i* (*of birds*) pingbing tolda 빙빙 돌다

♦ **wheel around** panghyang-ŭl hwik pakkuda 방향을 휙 바꾸다

wheelbarrow illyunch'a 일륜차; **wheelchair** hwilch'eŏ 휠체어; **wheel clamp** *n* ch'aryang chomsoe 차량 좀쇠

wheeze *v/i* sshigŭn-gŏrida 씨근거리다

when 1 *adv* ŏnje 언제; **~ *is the baby due?*** ainŭn ŏnje t'aeŏnal yejŏng-ingayo? 아이는 언제 태어날 예정인가요? **2** *conj* ...hal ttae ...할 때; **~ *I was a child*** naega ŏryŏssŭl ttae 내가 어렸을 때

whenever (*each time*) ...hal ttaemada ...할 때마다; (*regardless of when*) ...hal ttaenŭn ŏnjedŭnji ...할 때는 언제든지; *call me ~ you like* hago ship'ŭl ttaenŭn ŏnjedŭnji naege chŏnhwahaseyo 하고 싶을 때는 언제든지 내게 전화하세요

where 1 *adv* ŏdi 어디; **~ *were you born?*** kohyang-i ŏdiimnikka? 고향이 어디입니까?; **~ *from?*** ŏdiesŏ wassŭmnikka? 어디에서 왔습니까?; **~ *to?*** ŏdiro kamnikka? 어디로 갑니까? **2** *conj* ...hanŭn kot ...하는 곳; *this is ~ I used to live* yŏgiga naega sarat-ttŏn koshimnida 여기가 내가 살았던 곳입니다

whereabouts *adv* ŏditchŭme(sŏ) 어디쯤에(서)

wherever 1 *conj* (*anywhere*) ...hanŭn kosŭn ŏdidŭnji ...하는 곳은 어디든지; (*regardless of where*) ŏdirŭl ...(ha)dŏrado ŏdi ...(하)더라도; **~ *you go, don't forget it*** ŏdirŭl kadŏrado kŭgŏsŭl ittchi maseyo 어디를 가더라도 그것을 잊지 마세요 **2** *adv* taech'e ŏdi-e 대체 어디에

whet *appetite* shigyogŭl totkkudŭnŭn kŏt 식욕을 돋구는 것

whether ...inji ...인지; *he asked ~ I knew you* kŭnŭn naega tangshinŭl anŭnji murŏbwassŏyo 그는 내가 당신을 아는지 물어봤어요; **~ *or not*** ...inji aninji ...인지 아닌지; *I don't know ~ to tell him or not* kŭege marŭl haeya haltchi anhaeya haltchi morǔgessǒyo 그에게 말을 해야 할지 안해야 할지 모르겠어요; **~ ... or ... ...inji ...inji ...인지 ...인지; I don't know ~ he is a student or a teacher** kǔga hakssaenginji sǒnsaengniminji morǔgessǒyo 그가 학생인지 선생님인지 모르겠어요; **~ ... or not** (*regardless*) ...inji anidǔnji kane ...인지 아니든지 간에

which 1 *adj* ǒnǔ 어느; **~ one is yours?** ǒnǔ kǒshi tangshin kǒshimnikka? 어느 것이 당신 것입니까? 2 *pron* (*interrogative*) ǒnǔ kǒt 어느 것; (*relative*) ...hanǔn ...하는; **the subject ~ I'm studying** naega kongbuhanǔn kwamok 내가 공부하는 과목; **take one, it doesn't matter ~** ǒnǔ kǒsǔl kajyǒdo sanggwanǒpssǔmnida 어느 것을 가져도 상관없습니다

whichever 1 *adj* ǒnǔ ...irado 어느 ...이라도 2 *pron* ...hanǔn kǒsǔn ǒnǔ kǒshidǔn ...하는 것은 어느 것이든

whiff (*smell*) huk p'unggim 훅 풍김

while 1 *conj* ...hanǔn tong-an ...하는 동안; (*although*) ...hal chirado ...할 지라도 2 *n*: **a long ~** orae tong-an 오래 동안; **for a ~** chamshi tong-an 잠시 동안; **I'll wait a ~ longer** nanǔn chomdǒ kidarigessǔmnida 나는 좀더 기다리겠습니다
♦ **while away** pindungbindung chinaeda 빈둥빈둥 지내다

whim pyǒndǒk 변덕; **on a ~** kǔnyang kaptchagi 그냥 갑자기

whimper *v/i* hultchǒk-kkǒrida 훌쩍거리다; (*of animal*) kkingkking-gǒrida 낑낑거리다

whine *v/i* (*of dog*) kkingkking-gǒrida 낑낑거리다; F (*complain*) ch'ingǒlgǒrida 칭얼거리다

whip 1 *n* ch'aetchiktchil 채찍질 2 *v/t* (*beat*) ch'aetchiktchirhada 채찍질하다; cream hwijǒǒ kǒp'umǔl naeda 휘저어 거품을 내다; F (*defeat*) kyǒkp'ahada 격파하다
♦ **whip out** F (*take out*) hwik kkǔijǒbǒnaeda 휙 끄집어내다
♦ **whip up** (*arouse*) tobalshik'ida 도발시키다

whipped cream saeng k'ǔrim 생 크림

whipping (*beating*) ch'aektchiktchil 채찍질; F (*defeat*) p'aebae 패배

whirl 1 *n*: **my mind is in a ~** nae maǔmi kalp'irǔl mot-tchamnǔnda 내 마음이 갈피를 못잡는다 2 *v/i* p'ing tolda 핑 돌다

whirlpool (*in river*) soyongdori 소용돌이; (*for relaxation*) chak'uji 자쿠지

whirlwind hoe-oribaram 회오리바람

whir(r) *v/i* wingwing tolda 윙윙 돌다

whisk 1 *n* (*kitchen utensil*) hwijǒnnǔn kigu 휘젓는 기구 2 *v/t* eggs hwijǒt-tta 휘젓다
♦ **whisk away** ssak kajyǒgabǒrida 싹 가져가버리다

whiskers (*of man*) kurenarut 구레나룻; (*of animal*) suyǒm 수염

whiskey wisǔk'i 위스키

whisper 1 *n* sokssagim 속삭임 2 *v/t* & *v/i* sokssagida 속삭이다

whistle 1 *n* (*sound*) hwip'aram 휘파람; (*device*) hogak 호각 2 *v/i* hwip'aramǔl pulda 휘파람을 불다; (*of wind*) sshing pulda 씽 불다 3 *v/t* hwip'aramǔro noraehada 휘파람으로 노래하다

white 1 *n* (*color*) hayan saek 하얀 색; (*of egg*) hǔinja 흰자; (*person*) paegin 백인 2 *adj* hayan 하얀; person paegin 백인

white-collar worker samujik sawǒn 사무직 사원; **White House** Paegakkwan 백악관; **white lie** agǔi-ǒmnǔn kǒjinmal 악의없는 거짓말; **white meat** hǔin kogi 흰 고기; **whiteout** (*for text*) sujǒng-aek 수정액; **whitewash** 1 *n* paekssaek toryo 백색 도료; *fig* tullǒdaenǔn kǒjinmal 둘러대는 거짓말 2 *v/t* paekssaek toryoǔl ch'irhada 백색 도료를 칠하다; *fig* hodohada 호도하다; **white wine** paekp'odoju 백포도주

whittle wood kkakka tadǔmtta 깎아 다듬다
♦ **whittle down** churida 줄이다

whizz *n*: **be a ~ at** F koengjanghi chal hada 굉장히 잘 하다
♦ **whizz by** (*of time, car*) sshing chinagada 씽 지나가다

whizzkid F shindong 신동

who (*interrogative*) nugu 누구; (*relative*) ...hanŭn ...하는; *is that over there?* chŏ sarami nuguimnikka? 저 사람이 누구입니까?; *the woman ~ saved the boy* kŭsonyŏnŭl kuhan yŏja 그소년을 구한 여자

whodun(n)it ch'urimul 추리물

whoever ...hanŭn nugudŭnji ...하는 누구든지

whole 1 *adj* modŭn 모든; *a ~ chicken* t'ongdak han mari 통닭 한 마리; *two ~ hours* kkobak tu shigan 꼬박 두 시간; *the ~ town / country* ma-ŭl / kuk-kka chŏnch'e 마을 / 국가 전체; *it's a ~ lot easier / better* kŭgŏsŭn hwolsshin shwiptta / nat-tta 그것은 훨씬 쉽다 / 낫다 **2** *n* chŏnch'e 전체; *the ~ of the United States* Miguk chŏnch'e 미국 전체; *on the ~* taech'ero 대체로

whole food chayŏn shikp'um 자연 식품; **whole-hearted** chinshimŭi 진심의; **wholemeal bread** t'ongmilppang 통밀빵; **wholesale 1** *adj* tomae-ŭi 도매의; *fig* taeryang-ŭi 대량의 **2** *adv* tomaekkapssŭro 도매값으로; **wholesaler** tomae-ŏptcha 도매업자; **wholesome** (*healthy*) kŏn-gang-e choŭn 건강에 좋은; *attitude etc* kŏnjŏnhan 건전한

wholly wanjŏnhi 완전히

wholly owned subsidiary chahoesa 자회사

whom *fml* nugurŭl 누구를

whooping cough paegirhae 백일해

whore *n* ch'angnyŏ 창녀

whose 1 *pron* (*interrogative*) nuguŭi kŏt 누구의 것; (*relative*) ...hanŭn ...하는; *~ is this?* igŏsŭn nuguŭi kŏshimnikka? 이것은 누구의 것입니까?; *a country ~ economy is booming* kyŏngje-ŭi pumi irŏnago innŭn nara 경제의 붐이 일어나고 있는 나라 **2** *adj* nuguŭi 누구의; *~ bike is that?* chŏgŏsŭn nuguŭi chajŏn-gŏ-imnikka? 저것은 누구의 자전거입니까?

why (*interrogative*) wae 왜; (*relative*) wae ...hanŭnji 왜 ...하는지; *that's ~* kŭraesŏ-ida 그래서이다; *~ not?* wae andwae? 왜 안돼?; (*agreeing to suggestion*) wae kŭrŏjo 그러죠; *I don't know ~ he left* kŭga wae ttŏnannŭnji mollayo 그가 왜 떠났는지 몰라요

wick shimji 심지

wicked saak'an 사악한

wicker pŏdŭlgaji 버들가지

wicker chair pŏdŭllo mandŭn ŭija 버들로 만든 의자

wicket (*in station, bank etc*) ch'anggu 창구

wide *adj* nŏlbŭn 넓은; *experience* p'ong-nŏlbŭn 폭넓은; *range* kwangbŏmwihan 광범위한; *be 12 foot ~* p'ogi shibip'it'ŭ-ida 폭이 12피트이다

wide-awake wanjŏnhi chami kkaen 완전히 잠이 깬

widely *used, known* nŏlke 넓게

widen 1 *v/t* nŏlp'ida 넓히다 **2** *v/i* nŏlbŏjida 넓어지다

wide-open *window* nŏlke yŏllin 넓게 열린; *eyes* k'ŭge ttŭn 크게 뜬

widespread manyŏndoen 만연된

widow kwabu 과부

widower horabi 홀아비

width p'ok 폭

wield *weapon, power* hwidurŭda 휘두르다

wife anae 아내

wig kabal 가발

wiggle *v/t hips, loose screw* hŭndŭlda 흔들다

wild 1 *adj animal, flowers* yasaeng 야생; *teenager, party* kŏch'in 거친; *scheme* mich'in tŭt'an 미친 듯한; *applause* yŏlgwangtchŏgin 열광적인; *be ~ about* (*enthusiastic*) ...e yŏltchunghada ...에 열중하다; *go ~* (*become angry*) mopsshi hŭngbunhada 몹시 흥분하다; *run ~* (*of children*) chemot-ttaero nolda 제멋대로 놀다; (*of plants*) magu charada 마구 자라다 **2** *n: the ~s* migaeji 미개지

wildcard character COMPUT amugaemunja 아무개문자

wilderness hwangmuji 황무지

wildfire: spread like ~ sapsshigane

p'ŏjida 삽시간에 퍼지다; **wildgoose chase** ttŭn-gurŭm chapkki 뜬구름 잡기; **wildlife** yasaeng tongmul 야생 동물

will¹ *n* LAW yusŏ 유서

will² *n* (*willpower*) ŭiji 의지

will³: *I - let you know tomorrow* naeil allyŏdŭrigessŭmnida 내일 알려드리겠습니다; *~ you be there?* kŏgi issŭl kkŏyeyo? 거기 있을 꺼예요?; *I won't be back until late* nanŭn nŭtkkekkaji toraoji anŭl kkŏyeyo 나는 늦게까지 돌아오지 않을 꺼예요; *you ~ call me, won't you?* chege chŏnhwahashilkkŏjyo? 제게 전화하실꺼죠?; *I'll pay for this - no you won't* chega naegessŭmnida - ani, kŭrŏji maseyo 제가 내겠습니다 - 아니, 그러지 마세요; *the car won't start* ch'a-e shidong-i an-gŏllyo 차에 시동이 안걸려; *~ you tell her that ...?* tangshini kŭnyŏege ...rago marhae chushigessŭmnikka? 당신이 그녀에게 ...라고 말해 주시겠습니까?; *~ you have some more tea?* ch'arŭl tŏ tŭshigessŏyo? 차를 더 드시겠어요?; *~ you stop that!* kŭmandwŏ! 그만둬!

willful *person* kojibi sen 고집이 센; *action* ilburŏ-ŭi 일부러의

willing: *be ~ to do ...* kikkŏi ...hada 기꺼이 ...하다

willingly kikkŏi 기꺼이

willingness kikkŏi hanŭn maŭm 기꺼이 하는 마음

willow pŏdŭnamu 버드나무

willpower ŭijiryŏk 의지력

willy-nilly (*at random*) mujagwiro 무작위로

wilt (*of plant*) shidŭlda 시들다

wily kkoega manŭn 꾀가 많은

wimp F mugiryŏk'an saram 무기력한 사람

win 1 *n* sŭng-ni 승리 **2** *v/t* igida 이기다; *lottery* tangch'ŏmdoeda 당첨되다; *money* ttada 따다; *~ a prize* susanghada 수상하다 **3** *v/i* igida 이기다

wince *v/i* ŏlgurŭl tchip'urida 얼굴을 찌푸리다

winch *n* kwŏnyanggi 권양기

wind¹ 1 *n* param 바람; (*flatulence*) hŏtppae purŭm 헛배 부름; *get - of ...* ...ŭi somunŭl tŭt-tta ...의 소문을 듣다 **2** *v/t:* *be ~ed* hŏlttŏgida 헐떡이다

wind² 1 *v/i* kubijida 굽이지다 **2** *v/t* kamtta 감다

◆ **wind down 1** *v/i* (*of party etc*) sŏsŏhi kkŭnnada 서서히 끝나다 **2** *v/t* car window naerida 내리다; *business* p'ye-ŏp'aryŏgo hada 폐업하려고 하다

◆ **wind up 1** *v/t* clock kamtta 감다; *car window* ollida 올리다; *speech, presentation* kkŭch'ŭl maet-tta 끝을 맺다; *affairs* kyŏlmarŭl chit-tta 결말을 짓다; *company* p'ye-ŏp'ada 폐업하다 **2** *v/i* (*finish*) kkŭnnada 끝나다; *~ in the hospital* kyŏlguk pyŏng-wŏn shinserŭl chida 결국 병원 신세를 지다

windfall hoengjae 횡재

winding *adj* kkubulkkuburhan 꾸불꾸불한

wind instrument kwanak-kki 관악기

windmill p'ungch'a 풍차

window ch'angmun 창문; COMPUT windou 윈도우; *in the ~* (*of store*) chinyŏldoen 진열된

windowpane ch'ang-yuri 창유리; **window-shop:** *go ~ping* aishyop'inghada 아이쇼핑하다; **windowsill** ch'angt'ŏk 창턱

windpipe sumt'ong 숨통; **windshield** (chadongch'a) amnyuri (자동차) 앞유리; **windshield wiper** waip'ŏ 와이퍼

windsurfer (*person*) windŭsŏp'inghanŭn saram 윈드서핑하는 사람; (*board*) windŭsŏp'ing podŭ 윈드서핑 보드

windsurfing windŭsŏp'ing 윈드서핑

windy *weather, day* param punŭn 바람 부는; *it's getting ~* parami pulgi shijak'anda 바람이 불기 시작한다

wine p'odoju 포도주

wine list p'odoju menyu 포도주 메뉴

wing *n* nalgae 날개; *right ~ / left ~* SP, *politics* uik / chwaik 우익 / 좌익

wink 1 *n* wingk'ŭ 윙크 **2** *v/i* (*of person*) wingk'ŭhada 윙크하다; **~ at** …ege wingk'ŭhada …에게 윙크하다

winner usŭngja 우승자; (*in election*) tangsŏnja 당선자; (*in lottery*) tangch'ŏmja 당첨자; (*of prize*) susangja 수상자

winning *adj* igin 이긴; *lottery ticket* tangch'ŏmdoen 당첨된

winning post kyŏlsŭngjŏm 결승점

winnings sanggŭm 상금

winter *n* kyŏul 겨울

winter sports kyŏul sŭp'och'ŭ 겨울 스포츠

wintry kyŏul kat'ŭn 겨울같은

wipe *v/t* taktta 닦다; *tape* chiuda 지우다

♦ **wipe off** *dirty mark* takkanaeda 닦아내다; (*from tape*) chiuda 지우다

♦ **wipe out** (*kill, destroy*) chŏnmyŏlshik'ida 전멸시키다; *debt* wanje 완제

wire ch'ŏlssa 철사; ELEC chŏngit-tchul 전깃줄

wireless musŏnŭi 무선의

wire netting ch'ŏlmang 철망

wiring ELEC paesŏn 배선

wiry *person* tandanhan 단단한

wisdom chihye 지혜

wisdom tooth sarang-ni 사랑니

wise hyŏnmyŏng-han 현명한

wisecrack *n* ppyŏga innŭn nongdam 뼈가 있는 농담

wise guy *pej* anŭn ch'ŏk'anŭn nom 아는 척하는 놈

wisely *act* hyŏnmyŏng-hage 현명하게

wish 1 *n* sowŏn 소원; *best ~es* modŭn iri chal toegirŭl paramnida 모든 일이 잘 되기를 바랍니다 **2** *v/t* …igirŭl parada …이기를 바라다; *I ~ that …* nanŭn …hagirŭl paramnida 나는 …하기를 바랍니다; *~ s.o. well* nuga chal toegirŭl parada 누가 잘 되기를 바라다; *I ~ed him good luck* nanŭn kŭŭi haeng-unŭl pirŏt-tta 나는 그의 행운을 빌었다

♦ **wish for** parada 바라다

wishful thinking anihage nak-kkwanjŏgin saenggak 안이하게 낙관적인 생각

wishy-washy *person* shishihan

wistful tamnaenŭn tŭt'an 탐내는 듯한

wisp (*of hair*) tabal 다발; (*of smoke*) chulgi 줄기

wistful tamnaenŭn tŭt'an 탐내는 듯한

wit (*humor*) chaech'i 재치; (*person*) chaech'i-innŭn saram 재치있는 사람; *be at one's ~'s end* mŏrŭda 어찌할 바를 모르다; *keep one's ~s about one* ch'imch'ak'age it-tta 침착하게 있다

witch manyŏ 마녀

witchcraft mabŏp 마법

with ◊ (*accompanied by, proximity*) …wa/kwa hamkke …와/과 함께; *I live ~ my aunt* nanŭn nae ajumŏniwa hamkke samnida 나는 내 아주머니와 함께 삽니다; *compare X ~ Y* Xŭl/rŭl Ywa/gwa pigyohada X을/를 Y와/과 비교하다; *be connected ~* …wa/kwa kwallyŏndoeda …와/과 관련되다; *are you ~ me?* (*do you understand?*) che marŭl aradŭrŭl su issŭmnikka? 제 말을 알아들을 수 있겠습니까?; *~ no money* ton ŏpssi 돈 없이 ◊ (*instrument*) …(ŭ)ro …(으)로; *stabbed ~ a knife* k'allo tchillin 칼로 찔린 ◊ (*cause*) …(ŭ)ro …(으)로; *shivering ~ fear* turyŏumŭro ttŏnŭn 두려움으로 떠는 ◊ (*possession*) …i/ga innŭn …이/가 있는; *the house ~ the red door* ppalgan muni innŭn kŭ chip 빨간 문이 있는 그 집 ◊: *~ a smile* / *~ a wave* usŭmyŏnsŏ/sonchit'amyŏnsŏ 웃으면서/손짓하면서 ◊: *be angry ~ s.o.* nuguege hwaga nada 누구에게 화가 나다; *be satisfied ~ sth* musŏse manjok'ada 무엇에 만족하다

withdraw 1 *v/t* *complaint, application* ch'wisohada 취소하다; *money from bank* ppaenaeda 빼내다; *troops* ch'ŏlssushik'ida 철수시키다 **2** *v/i* (*of competitor*) mullŏnada 물러나다; (*of troops*) ch'ŏlssuhada 철수하다

withdrawal (*of complaint, application*) ch'wiso 취소; (*of money*) inch'ul 인출; (*of troops*) ch'ŏlssu 철수; (*from drugs*) kkŭnŭm 끊음

withdrawal symptoms kŭmdan hyŏnsang 금단 현상

withdrawn adj person naesŏngjŏgin 내성적인
wither shidŭlda 시들다
withhold poryuhada 보류하다
within prep (inside) …ane(sŏ) …안에(서); (time) …inae-e …이내에; (distance) …ane …안에; *is it a walking distance?* kŏrŏsŏ kal su innŭn kŏri-imnikka? 걸어서 갈 수 있는 거리입니까?; *we kept ~ the budget* urinŭn yesanŭl nŏmtchi anat-tta 우리는 예산을 넘지 않았다; *~ my power / my capabilities* nae him/nŭngnyŏgŭro hal su innŭn ŭi 내 힘/능력으로 할 수 있는; *~ reach* kakkaun kose 가까운 곳에
without …ŏpsshi …없이; *~ look-ing/~ asking* poji ank'o/murŏboji ank'o 보지 않고/물어보지 않고
withstand kyŏndiŏnaeda 견디어내다
witness 1 n (at trial) chŭng-in 증인; (of accident, crime) mok-kkyŏktcha 목격자; (to signature) chŭng-inŭro sŏmyŏngham 증인으로 서명함 **2** v/t accident, crime mok-kkyŏk'ada 목격하다; signature chŭng-inŭro sŏmyŏnghada 증인으로 서명하다
witness stand chŭng-insŏk 증인석
witticism chaech'i 재치
witty chaech'i-innŭn 재치있는
wobble v/i hŭndŭlgŏrida 흔들거리다
wobbly hŭndŭlgŏrinŭn 흔들거리는; voice ttŏllinŭn 떨리는
wolf 1 n (animal) nŭkttae 늑대; fig (womanizer) paramdung-i 바람둥이 **2** v/t: *~ (down)* kyegŏlssŭre mŏktta 게걸스레 먹다
wolf whistle n maeryŏktchŏgin yŏjarŭl pogo punŭn hwip'aram 매력적인 여자를 보고 부는 휘파람
woman yŏja 여자
woman doctor yŏŭisa 여의사
womanizer paramdung-i 바람둥이
womanly yŏjadaun 여자다운
woman priest yŏja moksa 여자 목사
womb chagung 자궁
women's lib yŏsŏng haebang undong 여성 해방 운동
women's libber yŏsŏng haebang undongga 여성 해방 운동가
won FIN wŏn 원

wonder 1 n (amazement) nollaum 놀라움; *no ~!* tang-yŏnhae! 당연해!; *it's a ~ that* …ranŭn kŏsŭn nollaun irida …라는 것은 놀라운 일이다 **2** v/i ŭi-ahage yŏgida 의아하게 여기다 **3** v/t kunggŭmhada 궁금하다; *I ~ if you could help* tangshini towajul su innŭnji kung-gŭmhamnida 당신이 도와줄 수 있는지 궁금합니다
wonderful nollaun 놀라운
wood namu 나무; (forest) sup 숲
wooded namuga ugŏjin 나무가 우거진
wooden namuro toen 나무로 된
woodpecker ttakttaguri 딱따구리
woodwind MUS mok-kkwanak-kki 목관악기
woodwork (wooden parts) moktcho pubun 목조 부분; (activity) mok-kkong tagi 목공
wool yangmo 양모
woolen 1 adj mojik 모직 **2** n mojingmul 모직물
word 1 n tanŏ 단어; (in Bible) pogŭm 복음; (news) soshik 소식; (promise) yakssok 약속; *I couldn't under-stand a ~ of what he said* kŭga hanŭn marŭn hanado ihaehal su ŏpssŏssŏyo 그가 하는 말은 하나도 이해할 수 없었어요; *is there any ~ from …?* …(ŭ)robut'ŏ soshigi issŏyo? …(으)로부터 소식이 있어요?; *you have my ~* naega yakssok'agessŭmnida 내가 약속하겠습니다; *~s* (of song) kasa 가사; *have ~s* (argue) maldat'umhada 말다툼하다; *have a ~ with* …wa/kwa handu madi marhada …와/과 한두 마디 말하다 **2** v/t article, letter marŭl kollasŏ ssŭda 말을 골라서 쓰다
wording p'yohyŏn 표현
word processing wŏdŭ p'ŭrosesŭrŭl sayong 워드 프로세스를 사용
word processor (software) wŏdŭ p'ŭrosesŏ 워드 프로세서
work 1 n il 일; *out of ~* shiltchik'an 실직한; *be at ~* irhago it-tta 일하고 있다; (at office) chiktchang-e it-tta 직장에 있다; *I go to ~ by bus* nanŭn

pŏsŭro ch'ulgŭnhamnida 나는 버스로 출근합니다 **2** *v/i (of person)* irhada 일하다; *(of student)* kongbuhada 공부하다; *(of machine)* umjigida 움직이다; *(succeed)* chal toeda 잘 되다; *how does it ~?* *(of device)* ŏttŏk'e sayonghamnikka 어떻게 사용합니까? **3** *v/t employee* irŭl shik'ida 일을 시키다; *machine* sayonghada 사용하다

♦ **work off** *bad mood, anger* ttan irŭl haesŏ ijŏbŏrige hada 딴 일을 해서 잊어버리게 하다; *flab* undong-ŭro sarŭl ppaeda 운동으로 살을 빼다

♦ **work out 1** *v/t problem* p'ulda 풀다; *solution* haegyŏrhada 해결하다 **2** *v/i* *(at gym)* undonghada 운동하다; *(of relationship etc)* chal toeda 잘 되다

♦ **work out to** *(add up to)* naoda 나오다

♦ **work up** *enthusiasm* pullŏ irŭk'ida 불러 일으키다; *appetite* totkkuda 돋구다; *get worked up (angry)* hwaga nada 화가 나다; *(nervous)* puranhaejida 불안해지다

workable *solution* shirhaeng kanŭnghan 실행 가능한

workaholic n ilppŏlle 일벌레

workday *(hours of work)* kŭnmu shigan 근무 시간; *(not a holiday)* p'yŏng-il 평일

worker nodongja 노동자; *she's a good ~ (of student)* kŭnyŏnŭn kongburŭl yŏlsshimi handa 그녀는 공부를 열심히 한다

workforce *(of company)* chŏn chong-ŏbwŏn 전 종업원; *(of country)* nodong in-gu 노동 인구

work hours kŭnmu shigan 근무 시간

working class nodongja kyegŭp 노동자 계급; **working-class** nodongja kyegŭbŭi 노동자 계급의; **working knowledge** kibonjŏgin chishik 기본적인 지식

workload ŏmmuryang 업무량; **workman** chagŏp inbu 작업 인부; **workmanlike** somsshi innŭn 솜씨 있는; **workmanship** somsshi 솜씨; **work of art** yesul-p'um 예술품; **workout** yŏnsŭp 연습; **work permit** nodong hŏga 노동 허가; **workshop**

chagŏptchang 작업장; *(seminar)* wŏk'ŭshyop 워크숍; **work station** tongnip chagŏp konggan 독립 작업 공간

world segye 세계; *(social)* sesang 세상; *the ~ of computers / the ~ of the theater* k'ŏmpyut'ŏgye / yŏngŭk-kye 컴퓨터계 / 연극계; *out of this ~* F tŏ hal nawiŏmnŭn 더 할 나위없는

worldly sesoktchŏgin 세속적인; *person* sesang multchŏng-e palgŭn 세상 물정에 밝은; *~ goods* chaemul 재물

world power segyejŏk kangdaeguk 세계적 강대국; **world war** segye taejŏn 세계 대전; **worldwide 1** *adj* segyejŏgin 세계적인 **2** *adv* segyejŏgŭro 세계적으로

worm n pŏlle 벌레

worn-out *shoes, carpet, part* tarhappajin 닳아빠진; *person* chich'in 지친

worried kŏktchŏngsŭrŏn 걱정스런

worry 1 n kŏktchŏng 걱정 **2** *v/t* kŏktchŏngshik'ida 걱정시키다; *(upset)* puranhage hada 불안하게 하다 **3** *v/i* kŏktchŏnghada 걱정하다; *it will be alright, don't ~!* kwaench'anŭl kŏshimnida, kŏktchonghaji maseyo! 괜찮을 것입니다, 걱정하지 마세요!

worrying kŏktchŏngdoenŭn 걱정되는

worse 1 *adj* tŏ nappŭn 더 나쁜 **2** *adv* tŏ nappŭge 더 나쁘게

worsen *v/i* tŏ nappajida 더 나빠지다

worship 1 n sungbae 숭배 **2** *v/t* sungbaehada 숭배하다; *fig* maeu saranghada 매우 사랑하다

worst 1 *adj* kajang nappŭn 가장 나쁜 **2** *adv* kajang nappŭge 가장 나쁘게 **3** n: *the ~* ch'oe-ak 최악; *if the ~ comes to ~* ch'oe-agŭi sangt'ae-enŭn 최악의 상태에는

worth *adj*: *$20 ~ of gas* iship tallŏ ŏch'iŭi kasŭ 이십 달러 어치의 가스; *be ~ …ŭi kach'iga it-tta …의 가치가 있다; *how much is it ~?* kŭgŏsŭn ŏlmaimnikka? 그것은 얼마입니까?; *be ~ reading / seeing* ilgŭl / pol manhada 읽을 / 볼 만하다; *be ~ it* hal manhada 할 만하다

worthless *object* kach'iga ŏmnŭn 가치가 없는; *person* ssŭlmo ŏmnŭn 쓸모없는

worthwhile *cause* porami innŭn 보람이 있는; *be ~ (beneficial, useful)* ssŭlmoit-tta 쓸모있다; *(worth the effort)* hal manhada 할 만하다

worthy *chon-gyŏnghal manhan 존경할 만한; *cause* chijihal manhan 지지할 만한; *be ~ of (deserve)* …ŭl/rŭl padŭl manhan …을/를 받을 만한

would: *I ~ help if I could* towadŭril su issŭmyŏn towadŭrigettchiyo 도와드릴 수 있으면 도와드리겠지요; *I said that I ~ go* nanŭn kaget-ttago maraessŭmnida 나는 가겠다고 말했습니다; *I told him I ~ not leave unless ...* nanŭn kŭege ...haji annŭn han ttŏnaji ank'et-ttago maraessŭmnida 나는 그에게 ...하지 않는 한 떠나지 않겠다고 말했습니다; *~ you like to go to the movies?* yŏnghwa porŏ kalkkayo? 영화 보러 갈까요?; *~ you mind if I smoked?* tambaerŭl p'iwŏdo kwaench'anayo? 담배를 피워도 괜찮아요?; *~ you tell her that ...?* kŭnyŏege ...rago marhaejushigessŭmnikka? 그녀에게 ...라고 말해주시겠습니까?; *~ you close the door?* munŭl tadajushigessŭmnikka? 문을 닫아주시겠습니까?; *I ~ have told you but ...* tangshinege yaegihaessŏya haetchiman... 당신에게 얘기했어야 했지만...; *I ~ not have been so angry if ...* ...myŏn nanŭn kŭrŏk'e hwarŭl naeji anassŭl kŏshimnida ...면 나는 그렇게 화를 내지 않았을 것입니다

wound 1 *n* sangch'ŏ 상처; *(in war)* pusang 부상 2 *v/t (with weapon)* sangch'ŏrŭl ip'ida 상처를 입히다; *(with remark)* sanghage hada 상하게 하다

wow *interj* wa 와

wrap *v/t parcel, gift* ssada 싸다; *(cover, wind)* kamtta 감다

♦ **wrap up** *v/i (against the cold)* ttattŭt'age iptta 따뜻하게 입다

wrapper *(for product, candy)* p'ojangji 포장지

wrapping p'ojang chaeryo 포장 재료

wrapping paper p'ojangji 포장지

wrath punno 분노

wreath hwahwan 화환

wreck 1 *n* chanhae 잔해; *be a nervous ~* shin-gyŏng soeyagida 신경 쇠약이다 2 *v/t* ŏngmang-ŭro p'agoehada 엉망으로 파괴하다; *plans, career, marriage* ŏngmang-ŭro mandŭlda 엉망으로 만들다

wreckage *(of car, plane)* chanhae 잔해; *~ of marriage / career* mangch'yŏjin kyŏrhon / kyŏngnyŏk 망쳐진 결혼 / 경력

wrecker kujoch'a 구조차

wrecking company ch'aryang kujo hoesa 차량 구조 회사

wrench 1 *n (tool)* lench'i 렌치; *(injury)* pp'im 삠 2 *v/t (injure)* pit'ŭlda 비틀다; *(pull)* ŏktchiro ppaeda 억지로 빼다

wrestle sshirŭmhada 씨름하다

♦ **wrestle with** *problems* ...wa / kwa sshirŭmhada ...와 / 과 씨름하다

wrestler *(Korean)* sshirŭm sŏnsu 씨름 선수; *(western)* lesŭlling sŏnsu 레슬링 선수

wrestling *(Korean)* sshirŭm 씨름; *(western)* lesŭlling 레슬링

wrestling contest *(Korean)* sshirŭm kyŏnggi 씨름 경기; *(western)* lesŭlling kyŏnggi 레슬링 경기

wriggle *v/i (squirm)* momburimch'ida 몸부림치다; *(along the ground)* kkumt'ŭlgŏrimyŏ naagada 꿈틀거리며 나아가다

♦ **wriggle out of** hech'yŏnagada 헤쳐나가다

♦ **wring out** *cloth* tchada 짜다

wrinkle 1 *n* churŭm 주름 2 *v/t clothes* churŭmjige hada 주름지게 하다 3 *v/i (of clothes)* churŭmjida 주름지다

wrist sonmok 손목

wristwatch sonmok shigye 손목 시계

writ LAW yŏngtchang 영장

write 1 *v/t* ssŭda 쓰다; *music* chak-kkok'ada 작곡하다 2 *v/i* ssŭda 쓰다; *(of author)* kŭrŭl ssŭda 글을 쓰다; *(send a letter)* p'yŏnjirŭl ssŭda

편지를 쓰다
♦ **write down** padajŏktta 받아적다
♦ **write off** *debt* ch'ŏngsanhada
청산하다; *car* pakssallaeda 박살내다
writer chak-kka 작가; (*of song*) chak-
kkok-kka 작곡가
write-up p'yŏngnon 평론
writhe momburimch'ida 몸부림치다
writing (*as career*) kŭl ssŭgi 글 쓰기;
(*hand-~*) kŭlsshi 글씨; (*words*) ssŭgi
쓰기; (*script*) kirok 기록; *in ~*
sŏmyŏnŭro 서면으로
writing desk ch'aekssang 책상
writing paper p'ilgi yongji 필기 용지
wrong 1 *adj* t'ŭllin 틀린; *decision,
choice* chalmot-ttoen 잘못된; *be ~*

(*of person*) t'ŭllida 틀리다; (*morally*)
nappŭda 나쁘다; *what's ~?* musŭn
iriyeyo? 무슨 일이예요?; *there is
something ~ with the car* ch'a-e
muŏshin-ga isang-i it-tta 차에
무엇인가 이상이 있다 **2** *adv* chalmot
잘못; *go ~* (*of person*) t'ŭllida
틀리다; (*of marriage, plan etc*)
chalmot-ttoeda 잘못되다 **3** *n* chalmot
잘못; *be in the ~* chalmoshida 잘못이다
wrongful pudanghan 부당한
wrongly pudanghage 부당하게
wrong number chalmot kŏllin
chŏnhwa 잘못 걸린 전화
wry pikkonŭn 비꼬는

XY

xenophobia oegugin hyŏmo 외국인 혐오

X-ray 1 *n* Xsŏn X선 **2** *v/t* Xsŏn ch'waryŏng-ŭl hada X선 촬영을 하다

yacht yot'ŭ 요트

yachting yot'ŭ t'agi 요트 타기

yachtsman yot'ŭ chojongja 요트 조종자

Yalu River Amnok-kkang 압록강

Yank *n* F Miguk saram 미국 사람

yank *v/t* hwaek tanggida 확 당기다

yap *v/i* (*of dog*) k'aengk'aeng chit-tta 캥캥 짖다; F (*talk a lot*) chaejalgŏrida 재잘거리다

yard¹ (*of prison, institution etc*) kunae 구내; (*behind house*) twinmadang 뒷마당; (*for storage*) mulgŏn tunŭn kot 물건 두는 곳

yard² (*measurement*) yadŭ 야드

yardstick *fig* ch'ŏkto 척도

yarn *n* (*thread*) shil sal 실; F (*story*) kkumyŏnaen iyagi 꾸며낸 이야기

yawn 1 *n* hap'um 하품 **2** *v/i* hap'umhada 하품하다

year nyŏn 년; **for ~s** F yŏrŏ hae tong-an 여러 해 동안

yearly 1 *adj* maenyŏnŭi 매년의 **2** *adv* maenyŏn 매년

yearn *v/i* kalmanghada 갈망하다

♦ **yearn for** …ŭl/rŭl mopsshi parada …을/를 몹시 바라다

yearning *n* kalmang 갈망

yeast hyomo 효모

yell 1 *n* koham 고함 **2** *v/i* koham chirŭda 고함 지르다 **3** *v/t* kohamch'yŏ purŭda 고함쳐 부르다

yellow 1 *n* norang 노랑 **2** *adj* noran 노란

yellow pages ŏptchongbyŏl chŏnhwa pŏnhobu 업종별 전화 번호부

Yellow Sea Hwanghae 황해, Sŏhae 서해

yelp 1 *n* kkaengkkaenggŏrinŭn sori

kkaengkkaenggŏrida 깽깽거리다

yen FIN en 엔

yes ye 예 ◊ (*using 'no', i.e no, that is not right*): **you don't know the answer, do you? - oh ~, I do** tabŭl morŭjyo? - aniyo, arayo 답을 모르죠? - 아니요, 알아요

yesman *pej* ach'ŏmkkun 아첨꾼

yesterday ŏje 어제; **the day before ~** kŭjŏkke 그저께

yet 1 *adv* ajik 아직; (*so far*) chigŭmkkaji 지금까지; **as ~** ajik-kkaji 아직까지; **have you finished ~?** inje ta kkŭnnaessŏyo? 인제 다 끝냈어요?; **he hasn't arrived ~** kŭnŭn ajik toch'ak'aji anat-tta 그는 아직 도착하지 않았다; **is he here? - not ~** kŭnŭn yŏgi wassŏyo? - ajik anwassŏyo 그는 여기 왔어요? - 아직 안왔어요; **~ bigger / longer** tŏuk tŏ k'ŭn / kin 더욱 더 큰 / 긴 **2** *conj* (*all the same, still*) yŏjŏnhi 여전히; **~ I'm not sure** yŏjŏnhi hwaksshinhal su ŏpssŏyo 여전히 확신할 수 없어요

yield 1 *n* (*from fields etc*) sanch'ul 산출; (*from investment*) iik 이익 **2** *v/t* fruit, good harvest sanch'urhada 산출하다; *interest* iigŭl naeda 이익을 내다 **3** *v/i* (*give way*) yangbohada 양보하다

yin and yang ŭmyang 음양

YMCA (= **Young Men's Christian Association**) Kidok-kkyo Ch'ŏngnyŏnhoe 기독교 청년회

yoghurt yogurŭt'ŭ 요구르트

yolk norŭnja 노른자

you ◊ nŏ 너; (*polite*) tangshin 당신; (*plural*) nŏhŭidŭl 너희들; (*plural polite*) yŏrŏbundŭl 여러분들; **he knows ~** kŭnŭn tangshinŭl arayo 그는 당신을 알아요; **that's for ~** naŭi kŏshida 나의 것이다 ◊ (*omission of pronoun*): **when are**

~ coming back? ŏnje toraol kŏmnikka? 언제 돌아올 겁니까? ◊: **~ never know** kyŏlk'o al su ŏmnŭn iriyeyo 결코 알 수 없는 일이예요; **~ can't trust him** kŭnŭn midŭl su ŏpssŏyo 그는 믿을 수 없어요

young chŏlmŭn 젊은; *wine* sukssŏngdoeji anŭn 숙성되지 않은

youngster chŏlmŭni 젊은이

your nŏŭi 너의; (*polite*) tangshinŭi 당신의

yours nŏŭi kŏt 너의 것; (*polite*) tangshinŭi kŏt 당신의 것; *a friend of* ~ nŏŭi/tangshinŭi ch'in-gu 너의/당신의 친구; **Yours ...** (*at end of letter*) ...ollim ...올림

yourself ne chashin 네 자신; (*polite*) tangshin chashin 당신 자신; *by* ~ honjasŏ 혼자서

yourselves nŏhŭidŭl chashin 너희들 자신; (*polite*) tangshindŭl chashin 당신들 자신; *by* ~ nŏhŭidŭl sŭsŭro 너희들 스스로

youth (*age*) ch'ŏngch'un-gi 청춘기; (*young man*) chŏlmŭni 젊은이; (*young people*) chŏlmŭn saram 젊은 사람

youthful chŏlmŭn 젊은

youth hostel yusŭ hosŭt'el 유스 호스텔

Z

zap *v/t* (*delete*) saktchehada 삭제하다;
F (*kill*) haech'iuda 해치우다; F (*hit*)
ch'ida 치다
◆**zap along** F (*move fast*) chaepssage
umjigida 잽싸게 움직이다
zapped F (*exhausted*) chich'in 지친
zappy F *car, pace* pparŭn 빠른; (*lively,
energetic*) wŏn-giwangsŏnghan
원기왕성한
zeal yŏlsshim 열심
zebra ŏllungmal 얼룩말
Zen sŏn 선
Zen Buddhism sŏnbulgyo 선불교
zero kong 공, yŏng 영; *10 below ~*
yŏngha 10to 영하 10도
◆**zero in on** (*identify*) aranaeda
알아내다
zero growth chero sŏngjang 제로
성장
zest yŏltchŏng 열정
zigzag 1 *n* chigŭjaegŭhyŏng
지그재그형 **2** *v/i* chigŭjaegŭro
umjigida 지그재그로 움직이다
zilch F amu kŏt-tto opssŭm 아무 것도
없음

zinc ayŏn 아연
◆**zip up** *v/t* chip'ŏrŭl chamgŭda
지퍼를 잠그다; COMPUT apch'uk'ada
하다
zip code up'yŏn pŏnho 우편 번호
zipper chip'ŏ 지퍼
zither (*with seven strings*) ajaeng
아쟁; (*plucked*) kŏmun-go 거문고
zodiac hwangdodae 황도대; *signs of
the ~* hwangdodaeŭi shibi kung
황도대의 십이 궁
zombie F (*barely human person*)
nŏng nagan saram 넋 나간 사람;
feel like a ~ (*exhausted*)
kijinmaektchinhan 기진맥진한
zone chidae 지대
zoo tongmurwŏn 동물원
zoological tongmurhakssang-ŭi
동물학상의
zoology tongmurhak 동물학
zoom F (*move fast*) kŭp'i kada 급히
가다
◆**zoom in on** PHOT chumnenjŭro
match'uda 줌렌즈로 맞추다
zoom lens chumnenjŭ 줌렌즈

Numbers

	Korean			Sino-Korean	
0	kong	공		yŏng	영
1	hana	하나		il	일
2	tul	둘		i	이
3	set	셋		sam	삼
4	net	넷		sa	사
5	tasŏt	다섯		o	오
6	yŏsŏt	여섯		yuk	육
7	ilgop	일곱		ch'il	칠
8	yŏdŏl	여덟		p'al	팔
9	ahop	아홉		ku	구
10	yŏl	열		ship	십
11	yŏrhana	열 하나		shibil	십일
12	yŏldul	열 둘		shibi	십이
13	yŏlsset	열 셋		shipssam	십삼
14	yŏllet	열 넷		shipssa	십사
15	yŏldasŏt	열 다섯		shibo	십오
16	yŏlyŏsŏt	열 여섯		shimyuk	십육
17	yŏrilgop	열 일곱		shipch'il	십칠
18	yŏlyŏdŏl	열 여덟		shipp'al	십팔
19	yŏrahop	열 아홉		shipkku	십구
20	sŭmul	스물		iship	이십
21	sŭmul hana	스물 하나		ishibil	이십일
30	sŏrŭn	서른		samship	삼십
35	sŏrŭn tasŏt	서른 다섯		samshibo	삼십오
40	mahŭn	마흔		saship	사십
50	shwin	쉰		oship	오십
60	yesun	예순		yukssship	육십
70	irhŭn	일흔		ch'ilsship	칠십
80	yŏdŭn	여든		p'alssship	팔십
90	ahŭn	아흔		kuship	구십
100	*no native Korean*			paek	백
101	*numbers above 99*			paegil	백일
200				ibaek	이백
1,000				ch'ŏn	천
2,000				ich'ŏn	이천
10,000				man	만
20,000				iman	이만
100,000				shimman	십만
1,000,000				paengman	백만
2,000,000				ibaengman	이백만
10,000,000				ch'ŏnman	천만
100,000,000				ŏk	억
1,000,000,000				ship ŏk	십억
8,655				p'alch'ŏnyuk- paegoshibo	팔천육백오십오

	Korean	Sino-Korean
1st	ch'ŏt pŏntchaeŭi 첫 번째의	che irŭi 제 1의
2nd	tu pŏntchaeŭi 두 번째의	che iŭi 제 2의
3rd	se pŏntchaeŭi 세 번째의	che samŭi 제 3의
4th	ne pŏntchaeŭi 네 번째의	che saŭi 제 4의
5th	tasŏt pŏntchaeŭi 다섯 번째의	che oŭi 제 5의
6th	yŏsŏt pŏntchaeŭi 여섯 번째의	che yugŭi 제 6의
7th	ilgop pŏntchaeŭi 일곱 번째의	che ch'irŭi 제 7의
8th	yŏdŏl pŏntchaeŭi 여덟 번째의	che p'arŭi 제 8의
9th	ahop pŏntchaeŭi 아홉 번째의	che kuŭi 제 9의
10th	yŏl pŏntchaeŭi 열 번째의	che shipŭi 제 10의
11th	yŏrhan pŏntchaeŭi 열 한 번째의	che shibirŭi 제 11의
12th	yŏldu pŏntchaeŭi 열 두 번째의	che shibiŭi 제 12의
13th	yŏlsse pŏntchaeŭi 열 세 번째의	che shipsamŭi 제 13의
14th	yŏlne pŏntchaeŭi 열 네 번째의	che shipsaŭi 제 14의
15th	yŏldasŏt pŏntchaeŭi 열 다섯 번째의	che shiboŭi 제 15의
16th	yŏl yŏsŏt pŏntchaeŭi 열 여섯 번째의	che shimyugŭi 제 16의
17th	yŏrilgop pŏntchaeŭi 열 일곱 번째의	che shipch'irŭi 제 17의
18th	yŏlyŏdŏl pŏntchaeŭi 열 여덟 번째의	che shipp'arŭi 제 18의
19th	yŏrahop pŏntchaeŭi 열 아홉 번째의	che shipguŭi 제 19의
20th	sŭmu pŏntchaeŭi 스무 번째의	che ishibŭi 제 20의
21st	sŭmul han pŏntchaeŭi 스물 한 번째의	che ishibirŭi 제 21의
30th	sŏrŭn pŏntchaeŭi 서른 번째의	che samshibŭi 제 30의
40th	mahŭn pŏntchaeŭi 마흔 번째의	che sashibŭi 제 40의
50th	shwin pŏntchaeŭi 쉰 번째의	che oshibŭi 제 50의
60th	yesun pŏntchaeŭi 예순 번째의	che yuksshibŭi 제 60의
70th	irhŭn pŏntchaeŭi 일흔 번째의	che ch'ilsshibŭi 제 70의
80th	yŏdŭn pŏntchaeŭi 여든 번째의	che p'alsshibŭi 제 80의
90th	ahŭn pŏntchaeŭi 아흔 번째의	che kushibŭi 제 90의
100th	paek pŏntchaeŭi 백 번째의	che paekŭi 제 100의

Korean numbers are usually used with countwords such as **chan** 잔 (cup), **myŏng** 명 (person), **k'yŏlle** 켤레 (pair), **pŏn** 번 (time). When used in this way **hana**, **tul**, **set**, and **net** contract to **han**, **tu**, **se**, **ne**:

k'ŏp'i han chan
커피 한 잔
a cup of coffee

kyosu se myŏng
교수 세 명
three professors

Sino-Korean cardinal numbers are used with (amongst other things) dates, money and foreign loanwords. To tell the time, Korean numbers are used for hours and Sino-Korean for minutes and seconds:

ich'ŏnillyŏn irwŏl iril
이천일년 일월 일일
1st January 2001

samship k'illomit'ŏ
삼십 킬로미터
30 kilometers

ohu seshi samship-ppun
오후 세시 삼십분
3.30pm

han shigan shippun och'o
한 시간 십분 오초
1 hour, 10 minutes and 5 seconds